Critical Acclaim
C̶h̶e̶ G̶u̶e̶v̶a̶r̶a̶: A̶ R̶e̶v̶o̶l̶...

'An admirably balanced account of the Argentine adventu... real achievements and his Robin Hood appeal ... an excellent guide to the myth behind the martyr'
Ian Thomson, *Independent*

'Thoroughly researched ... A masterly and absorbing account of Latin America's famous guerrilla leader ... Anderson's book, easily the best so far on Guevara, is a worthy monument to a flawed but heroic Utopian dreamer'
Frank McLynn, *Sunday Times*

'[Anderson] has researched diligently and has had access to much unpublished documentation ... [This biography is] absorbing and convincing because of its wealth of new information and willingness to let Guevara himself speak, in quotations from unpublished letters and diaries ... [Anderson] has written an indispensable work of contemporary history and conveyed much of his subject's awkward grandeur'
Robin Blackburn, *Guardian*

'*Che Guevara: A Revolutionary Life* is exhaustive and contains much that is new ... [Anderson] never mislays a key to understanding him'
Nicholas Shakespeare, *Daily Telegraph*

'[Che's] ideal, that curious mixture of resoluteness and recklessness ... is brilliantly evoked in Jon Lee Anderson's massive biography which traces, with exacting precision, the avatars of Che's epic life in a voice happily devoid of hagiographical rhetoric and with a healthy curiosity about seemingly irrelevant details. Anderson has deftly tapped unique sources, many for the first time ... The portrait is now as complete as it will ever be'
Alberto Manguel, *Times Literary Supplement*

'A sweeping biography of a revolutionary icon'
Financial Times

'Excellent'
The Times

'Mr Anderson has done his homework ... He found new sources, including Guevara's unpublished 1957–59 war diary ... [He] also spoke at length with top government officials as well as to survivors who fought with him ... Ernesto Guevara was 39 when he died, but, as Mr Anderson tells it, Che lives'
Economist Review

www.booksattransworld.co.uk

'This biography is rich in new material, including first-hand information from the CIA agent who was with him when he was shot ... Anderson's book is rich in Latin American and military history, and he exposes Che as a tough demanding leader'
Mary Banotti, *Irish Independent*

'Anderson [is] a thorough researcher ... This huge biography will add to [Guevara's] iconic status ... it is also the only one to carry interviews with Che's widow, Aleida'
Publishers Weekly

'[An] exceptional and exciting biography of the life and death of the larger-than-life revolutionary Ernesto 'Che' Guevara ... [Anderson's] formidable research [fills] this ample history of Che, which is, as well, a significant history of the turbulent post-World War II world of Latin America ... Anderson's up-close look, with beauty marks and tragic flaw so effortlessly rendered, brings the reader face-to-face with a man whose "unshakable faith in his beliefs was made more powerful by his unusual combination of romantic passion and coldly analytical mind" ... [This book] will be an invaluable addition to the literature of American revolutionaries'
Booklist

'A sweeping biography of the Latino revolutionary and pop-culture hero ... Drawing on a vast range of interviews and secondary sources ... Anderson paints a portrait of Guevara as both hero and fanatic ... Students of Che's life and deeds need look no further than Anderson's volume'
Kirkus Reviews

'Groundbreaking ... Anderson's book is an epic end run around the guardians of the Che legend'
New Yorker

'A skillful interviewer, Anderson elicited information from dozens of participants in Guevara's life ... Combining contradictory sources and an immense amount of detail, Anderson produces a multifaceted view of Guevara as a person, seething with ambiguities and complexities. This is an achievement that makes *Che Guevara* essential for anyone seriously interested in Guevara or the Cuban revolution'
The Nation

'A revealing portrait of the many Ches: the quixotic, freewheeling youth rambling around South and Central America in search of the good fight; the willful, asthmatic 'Jacobin of the Cuban Revolution'; and finally ... the holy martyr of armed rebellion at age 39 ... Che lives on as a paradox of his own time and ours'
Time Out New York

Che Guevara

A REVOLUTIONARY LIFE

Jon Lee Anderson

BANTAM BOOKS
LONDON • NEW YORK • TORONTO • SYDNEY • AUCKLAND

for Erica

and in memory of my mother,
Barbara Joy Anderson,
1928–1994

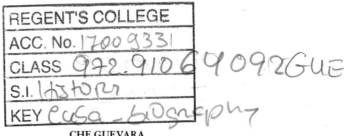

CHE GUEVARA
A BANTAM BOOK : 978 0 553 40664 1

Originally published in Great Britain by Bantam Press,
a division of Transworld Publishers

PRINTING HISTORY
Bantam Press edition published 1997
Bantam edition published 1997

20

Copyright © 1997 by Jon Lee Anderson

Design by Laura Hammond Hough

Bantam Books are published by Transworld Publishers,
61–63 Uxbridge Road, London W5 5SA,
a division of The Random House Group Ltd,
in Australia by Random House Australia (Pty) Ltd,
20 Alfred Street, Milsons Point, Sydney, NSW 2061, Australia,
in New Zealand by Random House New Zealand Ltd,
18 Poland Road, Glenfield, Auckland 10, New Zealand
and in South Africa by Random House (Pty) Ltd,
Endulini, 5a Jubilee Road, Parktown, 2193, South Africa.

Printed and bound in the United Kingdom by
Mackays of Chatham plc, Chatham, Kent

Contents

Acknowledgments

A biography is written by one person, but it is achieved only through the collaboration of others. With a project such as this, which has spanned five years, there are a great many people to thank. Some of them may not approve of the final result. To them, I can say only what I have always said: My sole loyalty in this book is to Che Guevara himself; to write what I perceive to be his truth, not anyone else's. But, for the peace of mind of everyone, I should say here that "the author is solely responsible for the content of this book."

In Cuba, where the bulk of my time was spent and research done, I owe a special debt of gratitude to Che Guevara's widow, Aleida March, who dared to emerge from three decades of hibernation to open up to an impertinent, prying "Yanqui." I know that it wasn't easy for her, and that there were many who advised her against it. I appreciate her bravery and her trust in allowing me to draw my own conclusions about what I learned from her. To María del Carmen Ariet, Aleida's brilliant aide-de-camp and confidante, and probably the world's foremost Che Guevara expert, I owe a great deal. Many thanks, María, from *"el gringo feo."* Orlando Borrego, Che's protégé and close friend, opened up his vast knowledge to me and treated me as a friend, and for that I am forever grateful. Manuel Piñeiro Losada, alias "Red Beard," Cuba's spymaster and the keeper of its secrets for the past thirty-five years, came out of the shadows to help clear up some of the mysteries surrounding Che's clandestine activities, an unprecedented privilege for which I am very appreciative. Also many thanks to Aleida Piedra, my assistant and faithful friend, who practically became one of the family.

To Denís Guzmán, the Cuban Communist Party Central Committee official who channeled my initial request to work in Cuba and who tried to smooth over the early glitches of our stay; María Flores, Roberto de Armas, the late Jorge Enrique Mendoza—my original official "host"—who sadly committed suicide shortly after my arrival; Julie Martin and her father Lionel Martin, a wonderful man and good friend who shared his thoughts, years of experience, and personal archives on Che with me; Manuel, Alejandro, Katia *y toda la Familia Gato*; Lorna Burdsall, Pascal and Isis Fletcher, Lisette, Ron Ridenour, Veronica Spasskaya, Roberto Salas, Encarna, Fernando, and Laly Barral, Leo and Michi Acosta, Micaela and Fernando, Miguel and Tanja, Julio and Olivia, Marta and Carmen, Isaac and Ana, Dinos and Maribel Philippos, Ángel Arcos Vergnes, Juan Gravalosa, Tirso Saenz, Harry Villegas, Cristina Campuzano, Alberto Castellanos, Alberto Granado; Osvaldo de Cárdenas, Ana María Erra, María Elena Duarte, Estela and Ernesto Bravo, Mariano, Gustavo Sánchez, Jesús del Valle, Paco Usallan, Marta Vitorte, Cari and Margarita *"la profe."* At Cuba's Council of State, Pedro Álvarez Tabío allowed me into the coveted "Che" archives, where I was helped greatly by Efraín González; also, Heberto Norman Acosta. Historian Andrés Castillo Bernal provided me with a copy of his own extensively researched manuscript on the Cuban revolutionary war and other documents.

In Argentina, I must thank Calica Ferrer, Carlos Figueroa, Chicho and Mario Salduna, Pepe and Chuchi Tissera, Roberto and Celia Guevara, Julia Constenla, Rogelio García Lupo, Reynaldo Sietecase, Hector Jouve, Alberto Korn, Héctor "Toto" Schmucler, Oscar del Barco, Benjamín and Elsa Elkin, Nelly Benbibre de Castro, Emilizano Acosta, Tatiana and Jaime Roca, and everyone in the Equipo Argentino de Antropología Forense—Anahi, Patricia, Darío, and Mako—and especially Alejandro Inchaurregui, whom I have come to consider a good friend. Also, Roberto Baschetti, Julio Villalonga, María Laura Avignolo, and Claudia Korol.

In Bolivia, special thanks to Loyola Guzmán and Humberto Vázquez-Viaña. Also, to Rosa and Natalí Alcoba, Martín and Matilde; Ana Urquieta, Juan Ignacio Siles, Chato Peredo, Rene Rocabado, Carlos Soria, Clovis Díaz, Miguel Ángel Quintanilla, and Tania at the Hotel Copacabana. My cheers of success for the Equipo de Baloncesto Anderson in Vallegrande. Retired General Reque Terán generously shared his time, documents, and collection of captured photographs.

In Paraguay, Socorro Selich and her daughters, especially Zorka, took me in on trust, unveiling the secrets of the late Colonel Andrés Selich, a key figure in the final hours of Che Guevara's life. I thank them for their confidence and their warm hospitality, and also Tilín for his help in making copies of thirty-year-old tapes and photographs.

In Mexico, all my research was either coordinated or conducted by Phil Gunson, an excellent journalist, veteran Latin America hand, and good friend. To him I owe a special debt of gratitude, for his forbearance and tireless help in ferreting out people and archives in Mexico, Guatemala, Nicaragua, and Panama.

In the United Kingdom: Richard Gott and John Rettie gave their encouragement, information, and contacts, which were invaluable. Also thanks to Duncan Green and Raquel at LAB, Pedro Sarduy and Jean Stubbs; Noll Scott, Landon Temple, Muhammad and Helena Poldervaart, Carlos Carrasco, Ashok Prasad, and Peter Molloy.

In Moscow: Irina Kalinina, Anatoli, Esperanza, Volodya, Mario Monje, and Alexandr Alexiev. In Spain, Henry Lerner, Carmen González-Aguilar, and her late brother, Pepe, who gave me time although he was already on his deathbed. In Sweden, Ciro Bustos, who opened up his home and heart in our long talks. In Cairo, Carol Berger, who went out of her way to track people down for me. In Germany, Peter Müller helped with the Stasi files and showed his support in other ways as well. The Swiss filmmaker Richard Dindo generously gave me contacts and tips for Bolivia and also provided some of the photographs for the book.

In Washington, Peter Kornbluh at the National Security Archive, Scott Armstrong, David Corn, Sergo Mikoyan, and Phil Brenner. In Miami, many thanks to my friends and repeat hosts—all of whom took an active and kind interest in this book and my travails—Rex and Gabriela Henderson, David and Inés Adams, and José and Gina de Córdoba.

These and other friends and relatives, spread around the world, have made this long endeavor a much warmer experience. They include Vanadia Sandon-Humphries, Doris Coonrad, David Humphries, Jonathon Glancey, Michelle, Tina, Meim, Nohad Al-Turki, Nick Richards, Christopher and Monique Maxwell-Libby, Colin Pease, David Ridd, Simon Tucker, Ros Bain, Laurie Johnston, Cathy Booth, Tim Golden, Jeff Russell, Chuck and Bex, Michele Labrut, Bertha Thayer, Mike and Joan Carabini-Parker, Janet and Terry Parker, Maria Elena, Matilde Stone, Martin and Eva Barrat, Ingrid Vavere, Colin Lizieri, and Jos and Kien Schreurs-Timmermans.

These past five years have seen the deaths of a number of people close to me. To them, this is a farewell acknowledgment. My mother, Barbara Joy Anderson, who was my first mentor and dear friend, passed away suddenly while I was in Cuba. Sofía Gato, who helped raise Che's children and also did the same for us, quickly became our greatest friend. She died last year, and we all miss her very, very much.

It seems uniquely fitting that this book is being published by Grove Press, which first introduced many of Che Guevara's writings to the United States. The Grove offices were bombed in the sixties after its "radical" magazine, *Evergreen,* was published bearing the same painting of Che on its cover that now graces the jacket of this book. My publisher, Morgan Entrekin, has stood by me throughout the years. Although he has never said so, I am sure that at times it was against his better judgment, and I am grateful he never shared such thoughts with me. The same goes for my agent, Deborah Schneider. To Carla Lalli and Elisabeth Schmitz, for their many efforts on my behalf, Anton Mueller, Kenn Russell, Muriel Jorgensen, Miwa, Judy, and everyone else at Grove Press who helped make me feel at home: Joan, Eric, Jim, Scott, Lauren, Lissa, Amy, Kirsten, Tom, Lea, and Ben—many thanks. Also, to Patty O'Connell, who sorted out my tangled syntax and lapses into Spanglish. And for their backing and endurance, my publishers at Transworld, Emecé, Baldini & Castoldi, List, and Objetiva.

Few writers are fortunate enough to have a brother and a close friend, who also happen to be authors, as their editors, and yet I was uniquely privileged to have Scott Anderson and Francisco Goldman as the slashers of my once overwhelmingly ponderous tome. If this book is now readable, they are due most of the credit.

My wife, Erica, has been my unflagging companion and bolster throughout the entire "Che" odyssey. With true British aplomb, she accepted our move from Oxford to Havana and proceeded to set up a home there, even as that society seemed to crumble around us. She withstood my many foreign trips, most of them lasting several months, without complaint, and has given me a healthy and boisterous family to return to each time. For our children, Bella, Rosie, and Máximo, this book has become an inextricable part of their lives. For all of them, Che Guevara was the first personality they could identify outside of our immediate family. Rosie and Máximo's first language was Spanish, while Bella began her morning classes with the hymn "Seremos como el Che": We will be like Che.

Introduction

The revelation slipped out almost casually during a long morning's conversation over coffee in November 1995. Sitting in the garden of his private walled compound on the outskirts of the Bolivian city of Santa Cruz, retired General Mario Vargas Salinas divulged to me his role in the secret burial of the man he had helped hunt down twenty-eight years earlier: the Argentine-born revolutionary Ernesto "Che" Guevara.

The general's confession broke silence on one of Latin America's most enduring mysteries. After his capture and murder by the Bolivian military and in the presence of a CIA agent in October 1967, the body of Fidel Castro's right-hand man had vanished. In his Santa Cruz garden, Vargas Salinas disclosed that he had been part of a nocturnal burial detail, that Che's body—minus his hands, which had been amputated—and those of several of his comrades were buried in a mass grave near the dirt airstrip outside the little mountain town of Vallegrande in central Bolivia. The officers who had defeated the world's most charismatic guerrilla fighter sought to deny him a burial place that could become a place of public homage. With his disappearance, they hoped, the myth of Che Guevara would end.

Instead, the Che myth grew and spiraled beyond anyone's control. Millions mourned his passing. Poets and philosophers wrote impassioned eulogies to him, musicians composed tributes, and painters rendered his portrait in a myriad of heroic poses. Marxist guerrillas in Asia, Africa, and Latin America anxious to "revolutionize" their societies held his banner aloft as they went into battle. And, as the youth in the United States and Western Europe rose up against the established order over the Vietnam War, racial prejudice, and social orthodoxy, Che's defiant visage became the ultimate icon of their fervent if largely futile revolt. Che's body might have vanished, but his spirit lived on; Che was nowhere and everywhere at once.

Who was this man who, at the age of thirty-six, had left his wife and five children, as well as given up his honorary citizenship, ministerial position, and commander's rank in revolutionary Cuba, in hopes of sparking a "continental revolution"? What had compelled this son of an aristocratic Argentine family, a medical school graduate, to try to change the world?

These were questions I had been trying to answer for some time. I first became interested in Che in the late 1980s while researching a book I was writing about modern-day guerrillas. In the battlegrounds of Burma, El Salvador, the Western Sahara, and even in Muslim Afghanistan, I found that Che remained a figure of veneration for guerrillas of all kinds. His writings on guerrilla warfare, but, even more, the revolutionary principles he seemed to exemplify—self-sacrifice, honesty, and dedication to the cause—had transcended time and ideology to nurture and inspire new generations of fighters and dreamers.

Fascinated, I searched for books on Che Guevara. I found few still in print, and no enduring biographies to speak of; most were either official Cuban hagiographies or equally tiresome demonizations written by his ideological foes. I soon realized Che's life had yet to be written because much of it was still cloaked in secrecy. The gaps in his life posed fascinating riddles, and it seemed clear that if one could unravel the mysteries of Che's life story, one might also shed light one some of the most relevant, but least known aspects of the Cold War era: the Cuban revolution's support for guerrilla movements, and the spawning of proxy wars in the Third World by both East and West.

The answers to most of these questions, it seemed to me, lay in Cuba, and I went there in hope of finding them out. It was 1992, a confusing time in Cuba, for the USSR had just collapsed, and with it had ended its thirty-year patronage of Fidel Castro. Castro was shaken but not bowed; he stood firmly on his Caribbean island, still daring to hold the socialist banner aloft even as the Cuban ship of state seemed to sink beneath him.

On a second visit, that same year, I met Che's widow, Aleida March, and she told me she would "cooperate" with my project to write a biography of her late husband. This was fortunate because the revolutionary apparatchik who had first "approved" me and who was to be my official minder soon committed suicide by shooting himself twice in the chest. In early 1993, I moved to Havana with my family, for a stay that stretched into nearly three years. There, with his widow's help—and with additional research in Argentina, Paraguay, Bolivia, Mexico, Russia, Sweden, Spain, and the United States—I tried to find out who Che Guevara was and what had taken place in his life. Above all I tried to gain an understanding of the man behind the mythic public image. This book is the result of that five-year effort.

Curiously, Che's myth is still potent enough to both enthrall and engender debate, as well as to cause political turmoil. The posthumous details about him shared with me by General Vargas Salinas have proven to be a catalyst for a deluge of new information, not only about Che Guevara's death, but about his life as well. These details have also had a tumultuous effect on the nation of Bolivia.

Besieged by the press, Bolivia's civilian president signed a decree ordering the military to find and exhume the body of Che Guevara, and those of his two dozen guerrilla comrades similarly "disappeared." The ensuing public spectacle of former guerrillas, soldiers, and forensic experts digging holes on the outskirts of Vallegrande as gawking crowds gathered and newsmen prowled for quotes reopened many old wounds in the country, threatening to reveal the murkier details of an episode long regarded as a state secret. The Bolivian armed forces complied with the president's order but were angry at Vargas Salinas' for his "betrayal," and they pressured him to guard his tongue. After appearing in Vallegrande to declare he could not remember "exactly" where Che was buried, he returned home, where he was placed under temporary house arrest. Afterwards, he took an extended trip abroad, and thereafter maintained a low profile. The search effort in Vallegrande continued, but without a precise location to work in, the search effort was exceedingly difficult. Nevertheless, after several weeks' digging, four guerrilla corpses were uncovered, but then the trail went cold again. By early 1997, the searchers had still not found the ultimate objective of their quest: the grave containing the skeleton of a man with no hands.

Part One

Unquiet Youth

I

A Mate Plantation in Misiones

I

The horoscope was confounding. If the famous guerrilla revolutionary Ernesto "Che" Guevara was born on June 14, 1928, as stated on his birth certificate, then he was a Gemini—and a lackluster one at that. The astrologer, a friend of Che's mother, did her calculations again to find a mistake, but the results she came up with were the same. The Che that emerged was a grey, dependent personality who had lived an uneventful life. There were only two possibilities: Either she was right about Che, or she was worthless as an astrologer.

When shown the dismal horoscope, Che's mother laughed. She then confided a secret she had guarded closely for over three decades. Her famous son had actually been born one month earlier, on May 14. He was no Gemini, but a headstrong and decisive Taurus.

The deception had been necessary, she explained, because she was three months pregnant on the day she married Che's father. Immediately after their wedding, the couple had left Buenos Aires for the remote jungle backwater of Misiones. There, as her husband set himself up as an enterprising *yerba mate* planter, she went through her pregnancy away from the prying eyes of Buenos Aires society. When she was near term, they traveled down the Paraná River to the city of Rosario. She gave birth there, and a doctor friend falsified the date on her baby's birth certificate, moving it forward by one month to help shield them from scandal.

When their baby son was a month old, the couple notified their families. Their story was that they had tried to reach Buenos Aires, but at Rosario Celia Guevara had gone into labor prematurely. A baby born at seven months, after all, is not an out-of-the-question occurrence. If there were any doubts, the couple's story and their child's official birth date were quietly accepted by their families and friends, and remained unchallenged for years.

If that child had not grown up to become the renowned revolutionary Che, his parents' secret might well have gone with them to their graves. He must be one of the rare public figures of modern times whose birth and death certificates are both falsified. Yet it seems uniquely fitting that Guevara, who spent most of his adult life engaged in clandestine activities and who died as the result of a secret conspiracy, should have also begun life with a subterfuge.

II

When, in 1927, Ernesto Guevara Lynch first met Celia de la Serna, she had just graduated from the exclusive Buenos Aires Catholic girls' school, Sacré Coeur. She was a dramatic-looking girl of twenty with an aquiline nose, wavy dark hair, and brown eyes. Celia was well read but unworldly, devout but questioning. Ripe, in other words, for a romantic adventure.

Celia de la Serna was a true Argentine blue blood of undiluted Spanish noble lineage. One ancestor had been the Spanish royal viceroy of colonial Peru; another a famous Argentine military general. Her paternal grandfather had been a wealthy landowner, and Celia's own father had been a renowned law professor, congressman, and ambassador. Both he and his wife died while Celia was still a child, leaving her and her six brothers and sisters to be raised by a religious guardian aunt. But despite her parents' untimely deaths, the family had conserved its revenue-producing estates, and Celia was due a comfortable inheritance when she reached the legal age of twenty-one.

At twenty-seven, Ernesto Guevara Lynch was both moderately tall and handsome, with a strong chin and jaw. The glasses he wore for astigmatism gave him a deceptively clerkish appearance, for he had an ebullient, gregarious personality, a hot temper, and an outsized imagination. He also possessed Argentine surnames of good vintage: He was the great-grandson of one of South America's richest men, and his ancestors included both Spanish and Irish nobility. But over the years, his family had lost most of its fortune.

During the nineteenth century Rosas tyranny, the male heirs of the wealthy Guevara and Lynch clans had fled Argentina to join the California gold rush. After returning from exile, their American-born offspring, Roberto Guevara Castro and Ana Isabel Lynch, had married. Ernesto was the sixth of their eleven children. They lived well, but they were no longer landed gentry. While her husband worked as a geographical surveyor, Ana

Isabel raised the children in Buenos Aires. They summered at a rustic country house on her inherited slice of the old family seat. To prepare his son for a working life, Roberto Guevara had sent him to a state-run school, telling him: "The only aristocracy I believe in is the aristocracy of talent."

But Ernesto still belonged by birthright to Argentine society. He had grown up on his mother's stories of California frontier life, and listening to his father's own terrifying tales of Indian attacks and sudden death in the high Andes. His family's illustrious and adventurous past was a legacy too powerful to overcome. He was nineteen when his father died, and although he went to college, studying architecture and engineering, he dropped out before graduation. He wanted to have his own adventures and make his own fortune, and he used his father's modest inheritance to pursue the goal.

By the time he met Celia, Ernesto had invested most of his money with a wealthy relative in a yacht-building company, the Astillero San Isidro. He worked there for a time as an overseer, but it was not enough to hold his interest. Soon he was enthused about a new project: A friend had convinced him he could make his fortune by growing *yerba mate,* the stimulating native tea ritually drunk by millions of Argentines.

Land was cheap in the *yerba*-growing province of Misiones, twelve hundred miles up the Paraná River from Buenos Aires on Argentina's northern border with Paraguay and Brazil. Originally settled by Jesuit missionaries and their Guaraní Indian converts in the sixteenth century, annexed only fifty years earlier by Argentina, Misiones was just then opening up to settlement. Land speculators, well-heeled adventurers, and poor European migrants were flocking in. Guevara Lynch went to see it for himself, and caught *"yerba mate* fever." His own money was tied up in the *astillero,* but, with Celia's inheritance, they would be able to buy enough land for a *yerba mate* plantation, and, he hoped, become rich from the lucrative "green gold."

Unsurprisingly, Celia's family closed ranks in opposition to her dilettante suitor. Celia was not yet twenty-one, and under Argentine law she needed her family's approval to marry or receive her inheritance. She asked for it, but they refused. Desperate, for by now she was pregnant, she and Ernesto staged an elopement to force her family's consent. She ran away to an older sister's house. The show of force worked. The marriage was approved, but Celia still had to go to court to win her inheritance. By order of the judge, she was granted a portion of her inheritance, including title to a cattle and grain-producing *estancia* in central Córdoba province, and some cash bonds from her trust fund—enough to buy a mate plantation in Misiones.

On November 10, 1927, she and Ernesto were wed in a private ceremony at the home of a married older sister, Edelmira Moore de la Serna.

La Prensa of Buenos Aires gave the news in its "Día Social" column. Immediately afterward, they fled Buenos Aires for the wilderness of Misiones bearing their mutual secret. "Together we decided what to do with our lives," wrote Guevara Lynch in a memoir published years later. "Behind lay the penitences, the prudery and the tight circle of relatives and friends who wanted to impede our marriage."

III

In 1832, British naturalist Charles Darwin had witnessed the atrocities waged against Argentina's native Indians by gaucho warlord Juan Manuel de Rosas, and predicted: "The country will be in the hands of white Gaucho savages instead of copper-coloured Indians. The former being a little superior in education, as they are inferior in every moral virtue."

But even as the blood flowed, Argentina had spawned its own pantheon of civic-minded historical heroes, from General José de San Martín, the country's liberator in the independence struggle with Spain, to Domingo Sarmiento, the crusading journalist, educator, and president who had finally wrested Argentina into the modern age as a unified republic. Sarmiento's 1845 book, *Facundo* (Civilization and Barbarity), had been a clarion call to his compatriots to choose the path of civilized man over the brutality of the archetypal Argentine frontiersman, the gaucho.

Yet even Sarmiento had wielded a dictator's authority to lead the country, and with his death the Argentine cult of the strongman, or caudillo, had not disappeared. Caudillismo would remain a feature of politics well into the next century as government swung back and forth between caudillos and democrats in a bewildering, cyclical dance. Indeed, as if reflecting the sharp contrasts of the great land they had conquered, there was an unreconciled duality in the Argentine temperament, seemingly balanced in a state of perpetual tension between savagery and enlightenment. At once passionate, volatile, and racist, Argentines were also expansive, humorous, and hospitable. The paradox had produced a flourishing culture and found expression in classic works of literature such as Ricardo Güiraldes's *Don Segundo Sombra* and the gaucho epic poem *Martín Fierro* by José Hernández.

Since the 1870s, the country had become more stable. And, when the conquest of the southern pampas was finally secured after an officially sponsored campaign to exterminate the native Indian population, vast new lands had opened up for colonization. The pampas were fenced in as grazing and farming lands; new towns and industries sprang up; railroads, ports, and roads were built. By the turn of the century, its population had tripled, swollen by the influx of over a million immigrants from Italy, Spain, Germany, Britain, Russia, and the Middle East who had poured into the rich southern land of opportunity—and still they came.

A dismal colonial garrison on the vast Río de la Plata estuary only a century before, the city of Buenos Aires now had a melting pot's combustive quality, epitomized by the sensuous new culture of tango, its dark-eyed crooner Carlos Gardel giving redolent voice to a burgeoning national pride. Its population spoke their own creole street dialect called *lunfardo,* an Argentine cockney rich in double entendres, cribbed from Quechua, Italian, and local gaucho Spanish.

The city's docks were bustling: Ships carried Argentina's meat, grains, and hides off to Europe while others docked bringing American Studebakers, gramophones, and the latest Paris fashions. The city boasted an opera house, a stock exchange, and a fine university; rows of imposing neoclassical public buildings and private mansions; landscaped green parks with shade trees and polo fields, as well as ample boulevards graced with heroic statues and sparkling fountains. Electric streetcars rattled and zinged along cobbled streets past elegant, bronzed-doored *confiterías* and *wiskerías* with gold lettering on etched glass windows. In their mirrored and marble interiors, haughty white-jacketed waiters with slicked-down hair posed and swooped like vigilant, gleaming eagles.

But while Buenos Aires's *porteños,* as they called themselves, looked to Europe for their cultural comparisons, much of the interior still languished in nineteenth-century neglect. In the north, despotic provincial caudillos held sway over vast expanses of cotton- and sugar-growing lands. Among their workers, diseases such as leprosy, malaria, and even bubonic plague were still common. In the Andean provinces, the indigenous Quechua- and Aymara-speaking Indians known as *coyas* lived in conditions of extreme poverty. Women would not be given the vote for another two decades, and legal divorce would take even longer. Vigilante justice and indentured servitude were features of life in much of the hinterland.

Argentina's political system had not kept pace with its changing society and had stagnated. For decades, two parties, the Radical and the Conservative, had ruled the country's destiny. The current Radical president, Hipólito Yrigoyen, was aging and eccentric, a sphinxlike figure who rarely spoke or appeared in public. Workers had few rights, and strikes were often suppressed by gunfire and police batons. Criminals were transported by ship to serve terms of imprisonment in the cold southern wastes of Patagonia. But, with immigration and the twentieth century, new political ideas had also arrived. Feminists, socialists, anarchists, and now Fascists began making their voices heard. In the Argentina of 1927, political and social change was inevitable, but had not yet come.

IV

With Celia's money, Guevara Lynch bought two hundred hectares (about five hundred acres) of jungle along the banks of the Río Paraná. On a bluff overlooking the coffee-colored water and the dense green forest of the Paraguayan shore, they erected a roomy wooden house on stilts, with an outdoor kitchen and outhouse. They were a long way from the comforts of Buenos Aires, but Guevara Lynch was enraptured. With an entrepreneur's eager eye, he looked into the jungle around him, and he saw the future.

Perhaps he believed he could, as his grandfathers had done before him, "restore" the family fortunes by intrepidly striking out into new and unexplored lands. Whether or not he was consciously emulating his forefathers' experiences, it is clear that for Guevara Lynch, Misiones was his own "Wild West" adventure. To him, it was not just another backward Argentine province, but a thrilling place full of "ferocious beasts, dangerous work, robbery and murders, jungle cyclones, interminable rains and tropical diseases."

He wrote: "There, in mysterious Misiones . . . everything attracts and entraps. It attracts like all that is dangerous, and entraps like all that is passionate. There, nothing was familiar, not its soil, its climate, its vegetation, nor its jungle full of wild animals, and even less its inhabitants. . . . From the moment one stepped on its shores, one felt that the safety of one's life lay in the machete or revolver. . . ."

Their homestead was in a place named Puerto Caraguataí, named in Guaraní after a beautiful native red flower, but its *puerto* was just a small wooden jetty. Caraguataí was reached by a two-day river journey up from the old trading port of Posadas on the *Ibera,* a venerable Victorian paddlewheel steamer that had done prior service carrying British colonials up the Nile. The nearest outpost was the small German settlers' community of Montecarlo, five miles away, but the Guevaras found they had a friendly neighbor who lived a few minutes' walk through the forest. Charles Benson was a retired English railway engineer and an avid angler, and just above the river he had built himself a white, rambling bungalow with its own internal "water closet" imported from England.

For a few months, the Guevaras spent an enjoyable time settling in and exploring the area. They sportfished, boated, and rode horses with Benson, or else drove into Montecarlo on their mule-drawn buggy. To eight-year-old Gertrudis Kraft, whose parents ran a little hostel on the Montecarlo road, the Guevaras were admirable, "rich and elegant people," whose rustic home by the river was "a mansion."

The Guevaras' honeymoon idyll, such as it was, did not last long. Within a few short months, Celia's pregnancy was well advanced, and it was time to return to civilization, where she could give birth in greater comfort and security. The couple set out downriver and ended their journey in

Rosario, an important Paraná port city of three hundred thousand inhabitants. There, Celia went into labor, and their son Ernesto Guevara de la Serna was born.

His doctored birth certificate, drawn up at the civil registrar's office on June 15, was witnessed by a cousin of Guevara Lynch's who lived in Rosario and a Brazilian taxi driver evidently drafted at the last minute. The document says the baby was delivered at 3:05 A.M. on the morning of June 14, in his parent's "domicile" on Calle Entre Ríos 480.

The Guevaras remained in Rosario while Celia recovered from the delivery of "Ernestito." They rented a spacious, three-bedroom apartment with servant's quarters in an exclusive new residential building near the city center, at the address given on the birth certificate. Their stay was prolonged when, shortly after his birth, the baby contracted bronchial pneumonia. Ernesto's mother, Ana Isabel Lynch, and his spinster sister Ercilia came to help out.

If the couple's families suspected anything, they kept quiet about it. Che's younger brother Roberto says that his mother told *him* that "Ernesto was born in a clinic in Rosario on the 14 of June 1928. The address that appears on the birth register is where he lived the first days, but not where he was born. Possibly it was the house of a friend, or that of the taxi driver who was a witness. . . ."

Of course, the truth, as Celia later told Julia Constenla de Giussani (who had arranged for Che's astral chart to be drawn up by their mutual astrologer friend), was that she had actually given birth in May, on the same day, and at the same hour as a striking dockworker nicknamed "Diente de Oro" (Gold Tooth) died of gunshot wounds.

The yellowing archives of Rosario's daily newspaper *La Capital* confirm the story. In May 1928, a strike by Rosario's dockworkers had escalated into violence. Almost every day, stabbings and shootings had taken place, most of them carried out by strikebreaking armed scabs working for the stevedores' hiring agency, the Sociedad Patronal. At 5:30 P.M. on Tuesday, May 13, 1928, a twenty-eight-year-old stevedore named Ramón Romero, alias "Diente de Oro," was shot in the head during a fracas at the Puerto San Martín. At dawn the next day, May 14, he died in the Granaderos a Caballo Hospital in San Lorenzo, about twenty kilometers north of Rosario.

V

After a whirlwind round of visits with their families in Buenos Aires to show off their infant son, the Guevaras returned to their homestead in Misiones.

Guevara Lynch now made a serious attempt to get his plantation off the ground. He hired a Paraguayan foreman, or *capataz,* named Curtido, to oversee the clearing of his land and the planting of his first crop of *yerba mate*. But when it came to hiring laborers, he had to confront the system of labor bondage, still practiced widely in the untamed region.

In Misiones, loggers and owners of *yerbatales* usually hired itinerant Guaraní Indian laborers called *mensu,* who were given binding contracts and cash advances against future work. Paid low wages according to how much they produced, *mensu* received not cash but private bonds, valid only to purchase basic essentials at the overpriced plantation stores. The system virtually ensured that they could never redeem their original debts. Armed plantation guards called *capangas* kept vigilant watch over the work crews to prevent escapes, and violent deaths by gunshot and machete were frequent occurrences. Fugitive *mensu* who escaped the *capangas* but fell into the hands of police were inevitably returned to their *patrones*. Guevara Lynch hired *mensu* himself, but he was no *yerba* baron, and, horrified at the stories he heard, he paid his workers in cash. It made him a popular *patrón,* and many years later, he was still remembered by local workers as "a good man."

As Guevara Lynch worked his plantation, his young son was learning how to walk. To help train him, his father used to send him to the kitchen with a little pot of *yerba mate* to give the cook for boiling. Invariably stumbling along the way, Ernestito would angrily pick himself up and carry on. Another routine developed as a consequence of the pernicious insects that infested Caraguataí. Every night, while his son lay sleeping in his crib, Guevara Lynch and Curtido crept quietly into his room. While his *patron* trained a flashlight on his son, Curtido carefully used the burning tip of his cigarette to dislodge the day's harvest of chiggers burrowed into the baby's flesh.

In March 1929, Celia became pregnant again. She hired a young Galician-born nanny to look after Ernestito, who was not yet a year old. Carmen Arias proved to be a welcome new addition to the family; she would live with the Guevaras until her own marriage eight years later, and remain a lifelong family friend. Freed from child-minding, Celia began taking daily swims in the Paraná. She was a good swimmer, but one day when she was six month's pregnant, the river's current caught her. She would probably have drowned if two of her husband's axmen clearing the forest nearby hadn't seen her and thrown out liana vines to pull her to safety.

Guevara Lynch reprovingly recalled many such near-drowning episodes involving Celia in the early years of their marriage. Already, Celia and Ernesto's very different personalities had begun to collide. She was aloof, a loner, and seemingly immune to fear, while he was an emotionally needy man who liked having people around him, a chronic worrier whose vivid imagination magnified the risks he saw lurking everywhere.

But while the early signs of their future marital discord were already in evidence, they had not yet pulled apart. The Guevaras took family excursions together, either horse rides on the forest trails, with Ernestito riding on the saddle mount in front of his father, or river excursions aboard the *Kid,* a wooden launch with a four-berth cabin that Guevara Lynch had built at the Astillero San Isidro. Once, they traveled upriver to the famous Iguazu falls, where the Argentine and Brazilian borders meet, and watched the clouds of vapor rise from the brown cascades that roar down from the virgin jungle cliffs.

In late 1929, the family packed up once more for the long trip downriver to Buenos Aires. Their land was cleared and their *yerbatal* had just been planted, but Celia was about to give birth to their second child, and Guevara Lynch's presence was urgently needed at the Astillero San Isidro. During his absence, business had gone badly, and now one of its investors had withdrawn. They planned to be away only a few months, but they would never return as a family to Puerto Caraguataí. It was the end of what Ernesto Guevara Lynch recalled as "difficult but very happy years."

VI

Back in Buenos Aires, Guevara Lynch rented a bungalow for his family on the grounds of a large colonial residence owned by his sister María Luisa and her husband, located conveniently near his troubled boatbuilding firm in the residential suburb of San Isidro.

They had not been there long when Celia gave birth, in December, to their second child, a little girl they named Celia. For a time, while Guevara Lynch went to work at the *astillero,* family life revolved around outings to the San Isidro Yacht Club, near the spot where the Paraná and Uruguay Rivers join to form the Río de la Plata estuary.

Guevara Lynch found the shipyard on the edge of bankruptcy, purportedly due to the lack of business sense of his second cousin and business partner, Germán Frers. For Frers, independently wealthy and a sailing regatta champion, the *astillero* was a labor of love. Such was his enthusiasm to create nautical works of art that he had poured money into fine craftsmanship and expensive imported materials, which often cost the company more than the agreed-to selling prices of the boats it produced. Guevara Lynch's investment was in serious risk of evaporating. Then, soon after his return, a fire destroyed the shipyard. Boats, timber, and paint all went up in flames.

If the shipyard had been covered by insurance, the fire might have seemed a fortuitous event. But Frers had forgotten to pay the insurance premium, and Guevara Lynch lost his inheritance overnight. All he had left from his investment was the launch *Kid*. As partial compensation, Frers gave Guevara Lynch the *Alá,* a twelve-meter motor yacht.

All was not lost. The *Alá* was worth something, and they still had their Misiones plantation, which Guevara Lynch had placed in the hands of a family friend to administer in his absence. Hopefully, they would soon see annual revenues from its harvests. In the meantime, they had the annual income from Celia's Córdoba estate. Between them, they had plenty of family and friends; they weren't going to starve.

In early 1930, Guevara Lynch certainly didn't seem unduly worried about the future. For some months he lived the sporting life, spending weekends cruising with friends aboard the *Alá,* picnicking on the myriad islands of the delta further upriver. In the hot Argentine summer (November to March), the family spent the days on the beach of the San Isidro Yacht Club, or visited rich cousins and in-laws on their country *estancias.*

One day in May 1930, Celia took her two-year-old son for a swim at the yacht club, but it was already the onset of the Argentine winter, cold and windy. That night, the little boy developed a coughing fit. The doctor who attended him diagnosed him as suffering from asthmatic bronchitis and prescribed the normal remedies, but instead of subsiding, the attack lasted for several days. As the family soon realized, young Ernesto had developed a chronic asthma condition that would afflict him for the rest of his life and irrevocably change the course of their own.

Before long, the attacks returned and became worse. Ernesto's asphyxiating bouts of wheezing left his parents in a state of anguish. They desperately sought medical advice and futilely tried out every known treatment available. The atmosphere in their home was soured. Guevara Lynch recriminated with Celia for her imprudence that day at the beach and blamed her for provoking their son's affliction.

In fact, Guevara Lynch was being less than fair. Celia was a highly allergic person and suffered from asthma herself. In all likelihood, she had passed the same propensity to Ernesto genetically. Later, a couple of his brothers and sisters also developed allergies and asthma, although none were to suffer from it as severely as he would. Ernesto's exposure to the cold air and water had probably only activated symptoms that were already latent in him.

Whatever its cause, Ernesto's asthma ruled out a return to the damp climate of Puerto Caraguataí. It was also evident that even San Isidro, so close to the Río de la Plata, was too humid for their son. In 1931, the Guevaras moved again, this time into Buenos Aires itself, to a fifth-floor rented apartment near Palermo Park. They were close to Ana Isabel, Guevara Lynch's mother, and his spinster sister Beatriz, who lived with her. Both women showered affection on the sickly boy.

Celia gave birth for the third time in May 1932, to another boy. They named him Roberto after his California-born paternal grandfather. Little Celia was now a year and a half old, taking her first steps, and four-year-old Ernesto was learning how to pedal a bicycle in Palermo's gardens.

But the move didn't cure him of his asthma. For Guevara Lynch, his son's illness was a kind of curse: "Ernesto's asthma had begun to affect our decisions. Each day imposed new restrictions on our freedom of movement and each day we found ourselves more at the mercy of that damned sickness."

On the advice of doctors recommending a dry climate to stabilize Ernesto's asthma, the Guevaras traveled to the central highlands of Córdoba province. For several months, they made trips back and forth between Córdoba and Buenos Aires, living briefly in hotels and temporarily rented houses, as Ernesto's attacks calmed, then worsened again, without any apparent pattern. Unable to attend to his affairs or get a new business scheme going, Guevara Lynch became increasingly frustrated. He felt "unstable, in the air, unable to do anything."

Their doctor now urged them to stay in Córdoba for at least four months to ensure Ernesto's recovery. A family friend suggested they try Alta Gracia, a small spa town in the foothills of the Sierras Chicas, a small mountain range near Córdoba, with a fine, dry climate that had made it a popular retreat for people suffering from tuberculosis and other respiratory ailments. They took his advice. Thinking of a short stay, the family moved to Alta Gracia, little imagining it would become their home for the next eleven years.

2

The Dry Climate of Alta Gracia

I

In the early thirties, Alta Gracia was an appealing little hill resort of several thousand people, surrounded by farms and unspoiled countryside. The air carried a mountain scent that was fresh, pure, and invigorating.

Ernesto's asthma condition improved in Alta Gracia, but he still had his attacks. At first, the family stayed in the Hotel de La Gruta, a German-run sanatorium on Alta Gracia's hilly outskirts. Most of its clients suffered from lung ailments, and it took its name from a nearby chapel and grotto built to venerate the Virgin of Lourdes, a popular pilgrimage site for miracle-seekers.

It was a bucolic setting, and for Celia and the children life was an extended holiday. She took them on hikes to swimming holes or on mule rides, and began meeting the locals. But Guevara Lynch didn't go with them. As their funds began to dwindle, his sense of frustration at being unable to work now deepened to despair. He felt isolated, hemmed in by the surrounding hills, and suffered from insomnia. Spending long nights awake in the hotel, he grew increasingly depressed.

Just as it had brought them to Alta Gracia in the first place, the Guevaras' concern for Ernesto's health would continue to chart their future path as a family, dominating their lives to an extraordinary degree. Before long, they had decided to stay on in Alta Gracia indefinitely, for after a few months in the Hotel de La Gruta they could see an improvement in Ernesto. The dry mountain climate had indeed "stabilized" his asthma. Here, his attacks had become intermittent, rather than the chronic affliction they had been in Buenos Aires. In spite of his asthma, he was now a lively, willful five-year-old, joining in the *barras,* the gangs of local children who played games of trench warfare, cops and robbers, and rode their bicycles pell-mell down Alta Gracia's hilly streets.

Guevara Lynch found an unoccupied villa to rent, on Calle Avellaneda in the neighborhood of Villa Carlos Pellegrini only five minutes' walk from the opulent Sierras Hotel, an imitation of a landmark Raj hotel in Calcutta and Alta Gracia's social hub. Villa Chichita was a Gothic two-story chalet that he likened to a lighthouse. Virtually surrounded by overgrown fields, it looked out to the sierras on one side, and the open yellow plains spreading toward Córdoba on the other.

In January 1934, Celia gave birth to her fourth child, a girl they named Ana María after her paternal grandmother. While he fought frequently with Celia and Roberto, young Ernesto became especially solicitous of his youngest sister, taking her for walks when she was still a toddler and telling her stories. When his wheezing fatigued him, he rested his weight on her shoulder.

Family photographs show Ernesto Guevara as a full-faced, stocky five-year-old with pale skin and unruly dark hair. He was dressed invariably in short pants and sandal-shoes with socks, wearing a variety of hats to shield him from the mountain sun; his expressions were private and intense, his moods clearly not easy to capture on camera. In photos taken two years later, he had thinned out, but his face was sallow and drawn, no doubt the result of a prolonged bout of asthma.

When Ernesto was seven, the Guevaras moved from Villa Chichita into a new, more comfortable home directly across the lane. Villa Nydia was a one-story chalet shielded by a tall pine tree, with three bedrooms, a study, and servant's quarters set in almost a hectare of land. The rent, though not as "insignificant" as Villa Chichita, was still low, at only seventy pesos a month, the equivalent of about twenty dollars, and their new landlord was "El Gaucho" Lozada, the owner of Alta Gracia's church and mission house.

During their years in Alta Gracia, they would move again, living in several different seasonally rented villas. But Villa Nydia was where the Guevaras lived the longest, and it was the place they most considered home. As cheap as it was, however, Guevara Lynch, who was broke much of the time, frequently found himself unable to meet the rent.

Guevara Lynch was in a real bind. He couldn't return to Buenos Aires because of Ernesto's health, but neither had he been able to find any work locally. His main hope for an income had been the Misiones plantation, but the market prices for *yerba mate* had plummeted, and the revenues from Celia's *estancia* in southern Córdoba had dropped due to a prolonged drought. In Alta Gracia, at least, life was relatively cheap, and the children were healthy.

Over the coming years, the Guevaras continued to depend upon the revenues from their farms, but, affected both by climate and market condi-

tions that fluctuated yearly, the incomes they produced were erratic and
generally small. According to both family and friends, it was Celia's money,
presumably what remained of her cash bonds, that carried the family
through the 1930s. "They were really bad times for us," admitted Guevara
Lynch. ". . . So full of economic difficulties. The children were getting bigger; Ernesto still had his asthma. We spent a lot on doctors and remedies;
we had to pay for domestic help, because Celia couldn't manage alone with
[the] kids. There was school, rent, clothes, food, trips. It was all outgoing
costs, with little coming in."

But at least some of their economic woes were due to the fact that
neither he nor Celia was practical with money, and insisted on maintaining
a lifestyle that was far beyond their means. They gave dinner parties, owned
a riding trap and an automobile, took summer holidays, and employed three
servants. Each summer, depending on their pocketbook, they summered
either at Mar del Plata, the exclusive Atlantic seaside resort favored by
Argentina's wealthy, or at grandmother Ana Isabel's country *estancia* at
Santa Ana de Irineo Portela.

The Guevara parents became fixtures of the social scene at the Sierras
Hotel. They may not have had money, but they belonged to the right social
class, with the right bearing and surnames. All those who knew them agreed
that the Guevaras had "style." They seemed blessed by that innate confidence
of those born into affluence that things would turn out all right in the end—
and they usually did. When they didn't, friends and family bailed them out.

A telling anecdote is recalled by Carlos "Calica" Ferrer. The fun-loving
son of a well-to-do Alta Gracia lung physician who treated Ernesto's asthma,
Calica and Ernesto had become close friends, and he joined the Guevaras
for some of their summer holidays. On one of their trips, the family set off
on the train to Buenos Aires, but when Ernesto's father realized he had
brought no money with him, he asked Calica to loan him the pocket money
his parents had given him for the vacation.

It was some time before Guevara Lynch made good on his newfound
social connections in Alta Gracia and obtained paying work. In 1941, using
his brother Federico's credentials as an architect and his own as a "master
of works and general contractor," he won a contract to expand and improve
the Sierras Golf Course. While the job lasted, there was money coming in,
but apart from this enterprise there is no record of Guevara Lynch working during the family's long stay in Alta Gracia.

II

Because of his asthma, Ernesto didn't go to school regularly until he was
nearly nine years old, so Celia patiently tutored him at home, teaching him

to read and write. This period undoubtedly consolidated the special relationship that had already formed between them.

The symbiosis between mother and son was to acquire dramatic resonance in the years ahead as they sustained their relationship through a rich flow of soul-baring correspondence that lasted until Celia's death in 1965. Indeed, by the age of five, Ernesto had begun to reveal a personality that echoed his mother's in many ways. Both enjoyed courting danger, were naturally rebellious, decisive, and opinionated, and developed strong intuitive loyalties with other people. Already, Ernesto had his "favorite" parent, and he had favorite relatives as well—his spinster aunt Beatriz and paternal grandmother, Ana Isabel.

The childless Beatriz was especially fond of Ernesto, and she spoiled him by sending him gifts. One of Ernesto's first letters, in which he tells his aunt Beatriz that his asthma has improved, dates from 1933. Obviously penned by one of his parents, it was signed laboriously in a five-year-old's scrawl, "Teté." It was Beatriz's pet name for Ernesto, and had been adopted by the family as his nickname.

Ernesto's asthma continued to be a source of anxiety for his parents. Desperate to isolate the causes of his ailment, they took the extreme measure of noting down all of Ernesto's daily activities, monitoring everything from the humidity and the type of clothing he wore to the foods he ate. In his father's notebook for one of ten-year-old Ernesto's "good days" in November 1938, the entry reads: "Wednesday 15: Semi-cloudy morning—dry atmosphere—he awoke very well. Slept with the window open. Doesn't go to the swimming pool. Eats with a good appetite, the same as previous days. He is fine until five in the afternoon."

They changed his bedclothes, as well as the stuffing of his pillows and mattress, removed carpets and curtains from his bedroom, dusted the walls, and banished all pets from the house and garden. All in vain. At one point his father resorted to quackery. Someone told him that placing a live cat in bed with the boy at night would prevent the attacks from happening. Guevara Lynch found a cat and put it Ernesto's bed, but in the morning, his asthma was unabated and the cat dead, apparently asphyxiated underneath the sleeping child during the night.

In the end, the Guevaras realized that there was no rigid pattern to Ernesto's asthma. The most they could do was to find ways to contain it. Having seen that his asthma seemed to diminish after he swam, for instance, they joined the Sierras Hotel swimming pool club. They also placed restrictions on him: He was banned from eating certain foods that gave him asthma—such as fish—permanently, and was placed on strict diets during his attacks. These enforced fasts soon gave rise to behavior that would last his whole life. Even as a child, he showed an unusually strong self-discipline by adhering to his asthma diets, but once his attacks had subsided, he gorged himself, and became known for his ability to consume huge quantities of food at a single sitting.

Often unable even to walk, and confined to bed for days at a time, Ernesto spent long solitary hours reading books or learning to play chess with his father. These pursuits also remained with him for life, and he later credited his periods of childhood quarantine with helping to bring about his love of reading.

During his asthma-free spells, however, Ernesto was understandably impatient to test his physical boundaries. It was here, in the physical realm, where he first felt the need to compete. He threw himself into sports, playing soccer, table tennis, and golf. He learned to ride horseback, went shooting at the local target range, swam at the Sierras Hotel or in the dammed-up pools of local streams, hiked in the hills, and took part in organized rock fights between the warring juvenile *barras*.

Over her husband's opposition, Celia encouraged these outdoor activities, insisting that their son be allowed to grow up as normally as possible. But the consequences were sometimes disastrous, with Ernesto being carried home prostrate and wheezing by his friends. Such episodes didn't deter the boy from doing exactly the same thing again, however, and this too became a routine over which Guevara Lynch eventually lost all control.

Guevara Lynch was never able to discipline his eldest son, and Celia never tried. The result was that Ernesto became increasingly wild and disobedient. To escape punishment for a transgression, Ernesto would run off into the brushy countryside, returning only when his parents' fears for his safety had long since overcome their anger. But to Carlos Figueroa, another friend whose family had a summer villa just down the street, Ernesto's "escapes to the bush" were his way of escaping his parents' arguments, which he remembered as "terrible."

Whether the emotional upset caused by these arguments helped provoke Ernesto's asthma isn't clear, but both family and friends agree that Celia and Ernesto Guevara began to have regular shouting matches in Alta Gracia. Both had extremely hot tempers, and the stories of their domestic disputes there are legion.

No doubt their perennial economic woes were partly to blame, a vicious cycle aggravated by Ernesto's asthma and Guevara Lynch's inability to find work, which, in his mind, led directly back to Celia's "imprudence" and the swimming incident at San Isidro. But the real source of the rift, according to Celia's closest friends, was Guevara Lynch's affairs with other women—activity that, in a small place such as Alta Gracia, must have been impossible to conceal. With divorce still not legal in Argentina, or perhaps for the children's sake, the Guevaras stuck it out.

Ernesto's own Huckleberry Finn days of running free were finally curbed when Alta Gracia's education authorities visited his parents and ordered them to send him to school. Ernesto was now nearly nine years old, and Celia had little choice but to relinquish him. Because of her tutoring, he already knew to read and write, so he was able to skip the first and "upper first" grades of Argentina's primary school system. In March 1937, nearly a year older than most of his peers, Ernesto entered the second-grade class at the Escuela San Martín.

Ernesto's grades for the 1938 third-grade school year are summed up as "satisfactory" in his report card, revealing high marks in history, a "steady improvement" in natural sciences, reading, writing, geography, geometry, morals, and civics, while in drawing, organized athletics, music and dance, he showed little interest. His conduct, termed "good" throughout the year, was "deficient" in the third semester. This change in behavior coincides with an abrupt change in his attendance. After missing only about four days in the first two semesters, his record for this one shows he missed school for twenty-one days, a lapse probably caused by a prolonged attack of asthma.

Elba Rossi de Oviedo Zelaya, the school's headmistress and his teacher for the third grade, remembered him as a "mischievous, bright boy, undistinguished in class, but who exhibited leadership qualities on the playground." Recalling his early school days, Ernesto "Che" Guevara later told his second wife, Aleida, that Elba Rossi had been a strict disciplinarian and was forever spanking him. One day, facing his customary punishment, he had gotten even with her by placing a brick in his shorts. When she hit him, she hurt her hand instead.

Ernesto was an incorrigible "show-off" during his primary school years. Whether by inclination or to compensate for his perceived sickliness, the stigma young asthmatics tend to suffer from, he developed a fiercely competitive personality, engaging in attention-getting high jinks that confounded adults and awed his peers. Always willing to provide an audience, his old classmates recall a legion of exploits: He drank ink out of a bottle, ate chalk during class, and climbed the trees in the schoolyard; hung by his hands from a railroad trestle spanning a chasm; explored a dangerous abandoned mine shaft; and played *torero* with an irascible ram.

Another time, he and his *barra* cohorts went around Alta Gracia shooting out the streetlights with their slingshots. Once, he and his friend Juan Míguez settled a score with a member of a rival gang by defecating onto the ivory keys of his parents' grand piano. And then there was the glorious occasion when he shot burning firecrackers through an open window into a neighbor's formal dinner party, scattering the guests.

Ernesto's antics earned the Guevaras some local notoriety, but they also stood out in other ways. "Bohemian" is the term most often used to describe their buoyant, disorderly household. They observed few social conventions in their home: Neighborhood youngsters who arrived at teatime or supper were invited to stay and eat, and there were always extra mouths to feed at the dinner table. The Guevara children made friends indiscriminately, and played with the sons of golf caddies and others whose homes were in "lower" Alta Gracia.

It was Celia *madre,* however, who made the greatest impression as a free-thinking individual. Headmistress Elba Rossi recalled Celia setting the record for many "firsts" for women in the socially stratified community with such activities as driving a car herself and wearing trousers. Others cited Celia's smoking of cigarettes as a direct challenge to social norms of the day.

Celia got away with these radical-seeming gestures because of her social standing and displays of generosity. She regularly drove her own children and their friends to and from school in the family car they had dubbed "La Catramina" (The Heap), a massive old 1925 Maxwell convertible with a jump seat in back. She inaugurated the school's daily "cup of milk" by paying for it herself, a custom later adopted by the local school board to ensure that poorer children had some nutrition during the school day.

Unlike most of their neighbors, Ernesto's parents espoused anticlerical views. Guevara Lynch's mother was an atheist and had given him a secular upbringing. The religiously schooled Celia's views were less certain, and throughout her life she retained a penchant for the spiritual side of life. When they first arrived in Alta Gracia, Celia had attended Sunday Mass, taking the children with her, but according to her husband she did so for "the spectacle" more than out of any residual religious faith.

Yet, for all their libertarian views, the Guevaras shared with many other lapsed Catholics a contradiction between belief and practice, never entirely forsaking the traditional rituals that ensured social acceptance in their conservative society. While they no longer attended church, the Guevaras still had their children baptized according to Catholic rites. Ernestito's godfather was the wealthy Pedro León Echagüe, through whom Celia and Guevara Lynch had met, and who had convinced Guevara Lynch to seek his fortune in Misiones.

By the time Ernesto entered school, however, Celia had stopped going to Mass, and the Guevaras asked for their children to be excused from religion classes. Roberto recalled playing after-school soccer games formed by opposing teams of children: those who believed in God and

those who didn't. Those who "didn't" invariably lost because they were so few in number.

Although he was rarely seen studying, Ernesto's classmates in Alta Gracia unanimously noted his quickness in class. But he didn't show a competitive urge for grades, which were usually mediocre. It was a phenomenon that mystified his father. This theme was a constant refrain during Ernesto's formative years. His father never seems to have understood what made his eldest son tick, just as he never completely understood his wife, Celia. To him, Celia was "imprudent from birth" and "attracted to danger," and she was at fault for passing these traits on to their eldest son. Guevara Lynch, meanwhile, who admitted to being "overly cautious," was fretful, and forever worrying about the dangers and risks in life. In some ways, he was the more maternal of the two parents, while Celia was her son's confidante and coconspirator. Guevara Lynch was also a man with an "Irish" temper, and friends from Alta Gracia all had memories of his tantrums, especially when he considered something an affront to a member of his family. Exaggerated or not, Guevara Lynch's famous temper was something he passed on to his eldest son. Ernestito became "uncontrollable with rage" if he felt he had been unjustly reprimanded or punished as a child, Guevara Lynch wrote, and he got into frequent fistfights with his *barra* rivals. His temper never left him, but by the time he reached college he had learned to bring it under control, usually substituting a notoriously razor-sharp tongue for the threat of physical violence. But on rare occasions he sometimes struck out physically.

Although an intelligent man, Guevara Lynch nonetheless looked across a perceptual divide to his wife and Ernesto, who were far more intellectually akin. While he read books of adventure and history, and passed on his love for these works to Ernesto, he had little scholarly patience or discipline. Celia, on the other hand, was an avid reader of fiction, philosophy, and poetry, and it was she who eventually opened their son's mind to these interests.

They would evolve and mature in the coming years, but the character traits that later acquired legendary dimension in the adult Ernesto Guevara were already present in the boy. His physical fearlessness, inclination to lead others, stubbornness, competitive spirit, and self-discipline—all were clearly manifest in the young "Guevarita" of Alta Gracia.

III

Between 1932 and 1935, Paraguay and Bolivia fought an intermittent, bloody conflict over control of the parched *chaco* wilderness shared by the two countries.

Ernesto Guevara Lynch followed the "Chaco War" closely in the newspapers, and because of his time spent among Paraguayans in Misiones, he sided with their country. At one point, he declared he was "willing to take up arms" to help defend Paraguay. Caught up in his father's enthusiasm, the eldest son began following the war's progress. Before long, noted Guevara Lynch, the conflict had found its way into the local children's games of war, with one side playing at being Paraguayans, their opponents as Bolivians.

Guevara Lynch later sought to portray his son's interest in this war as influential in shaping his political consciousness. This seems unlikely, since Ernesto was only seven years old when the war ended. But the adult Che did recall his father's passion for the conflict and, in tones that were both affectionate and sarcastic, told Argentine friends about his father's bombastic threats "to join" the fighting. For the son, it summed up one of the bittersweet truths about his father, a well-intentioned man who spent his life coming up with schemes, but who rarely managed to achieve anything concrete.

The Spanish Civil War, lasting from 1936 to 1939, was probably the first political event to impinge significantly on Ernesto Guevara's consciousness. Indeed, its effect was inescapable. Beginning in 1938, as the war in Spain turned in favor of Franco's Fascists, a number of Spanish Republican refugees began arriving in Alta Gracia.

Among them were the four González-Aguilar children, who showed up with their mother. Their father, Juan González Aguilar, the republic's naval health chief, had remained behind at his post, but joined them after the fall of Barcelona in January 1939. With their own and the Guevaras' children roughly the same ages, attending the same school and sitting out religion classes together, the two families soon became close friends.

And for a time the Guevaras shared their home with Celia's eldest sister, Carmen, and her two children while their father, the Communist poet and journalist Cayetano "Policho" Córdova Iturburu, was off in Spain covering the war for the Buenos Aires newspaper *Critica*. When Policho's letters and dispatches arrived in the post, Carmen read them aloud to the gathered clan, bringing the raw impact of the war home in a way no newspaper article could do.

Soon, the Guevaras too found themselves caught up in the emotional campaign to support the embattled republic. In the early thirties, there had been little in Argentina's domestic politics to enthuse the liberal Guevaras. Argentina had been ruled by a succession of conservative military regimes in on-off coalitions with factions of the traditional "liberal" party, the Unión Cívica Radical, which had splintered and foundered in ineffectual opposition since President Hipólito Yrigoyen's overthrow in 1930. The war for the Spanish Republic, however, symbolizing a dramatic stand against the growing threat of international Fascism, was something one could become passionate about.

Guevara Lynch helped found Alta Gracia's own little Comité de Ayuda a la Republica, part of a national solidarity network with Republican Spain. He befriended the exiled Spanish newcomers. One whom he particularly admired was General Jurado, a military hero who had defeated Franco's troops and their Italian Fascist allies in the battle for Guadalajara, and who now had to support himself by selling life insurance policies. Guevara Lynch hosted him for meals in his home and, together with his family, listened enthralled to his war stories.

Surrounded by people so emotionally involved with the Spanish Republican cause, ten-year-old Ernesto developed a keen interest in the conflict himself. According to family lore, he named his family's pet dog, a schnauzer-pinscher, Negrina—both because she was black and in honor of the republic's prime minister, Juan Negrín. While the war lasted, he followed its developments by marking the Republican and Fascist armies' positions on a map with little flags.

No sooner had the Spanish Republic been defeated than the European war began in earnest. Following his annexation of Austria, his move into Czechoslovakia secured with the signing of the Munich Pact, Adolf Hitler invaded Poland in September 1939. Great Britain and France entered the war against the Axis powers, and World War II had begun. In Alta Gracia, as elsewhere, people began to choose sides.

Guevara Lynch now threw his energies into Acción Argentina, a pro-Allied solidarity group, and he established a local branch in Alta Gracia. From the Lozada family, he rented a little office built into the exterior stone wall of their Jesuit mission overlooking the willow-rimmed Tajamar lake. Now eleven, Ernesto joined the "youth wing" of Acción Argentina and possessed his own membership card, which, according to his father, he "exhibited with pride."

Guevara Lynch traveled around the province, speaking in public meetings and following up tips about possible "Nazi infiltration." His group feared an eventual Nazi invasion of Argentina and monitored all suspicious activities in Córdoba's sizeable German community. As for young Ernesto, said his father: "All the free time he had outside his playtime and studies, he spent collaborating with us."

In Córdoba, one of the chief targets of concern was the German settlement in the Calamuchita valley near Alta Gracia. In late 1939, after inflicting damage on British warships in the Atlantic, the crippled German battleship *Admiral Graf Spee* was chased into the Río de la Plata, where its captain scuttled it in the waters off Montevideo. The response of the Argentine authorities was to "intern" the ship's officers and crew in Córdoba.

Suspicious of the German naval internees, Guevara Lynch's outfit spied on them and, according to his memoirs, observed them conducting military training exercises with dummy wooden rifles. Another time, they supposedly detected trucks loaded with arms from Bolivia, headed for the valley. They suspected a German-owned hotel in another town of providing cover for a Nazi spy ring, complete with a clandestine radio transmitter that communicated directly to Berlin, but were thwarted from obtaining precise intelligence because of its heavy security.

In Guevara Lynch's rendition of these missions, there is an inescapable sense of the Walter Mitty in him. He desperately wished to live a life of adventure and daring, but he was destined to live his life, for the most part, at the periphery of the large events of his time. He had trumpeted his willingness to fight for Paraguay, but he had not gone. The Spanish Civil War and World War II gave him new issues to champion, and later he would take up others, but as always he did so from the sidelines. In the end, it was not these activities he would be remembered for, but his role as the father of Ernesto "Che" Guevara.

Meanwhile, alarmed at what they believed to be evidence of a flourishing Nazi underground network in Córdoba, Guevara Lynch and his colleagues sent a detailed report to the headquarters of Acción Argentina in Buenos Aires, expecting prompt action to be taken by the pro-Allied administration of President Roberto Ortiz. But in 1940, with his health seriously ailing, Ortiz was effectively replaced in his duties by Ramón Castillo, his wily and corrupt vice president. Castillo's government displayed strongly pro-Axis inclinations, and, according to Guevara Lynch, no substantive measures were taken by his regime against the Nazi network.

Argentina's ambiguous position throughout the war—it remained officially neutral until the eve of Germany's defeat in 1945—owed as much to its economic concerns as to the considerable pro-Axis sentiments within its political and military establishment. Traditionally dependent on Europe, particularly Great Britain, as an export market for its beef, grain, and other agricultural products, Argentina was devastated by the Allied blockade of Europe. In return for supporting the Allies, the Ortiz administration sought guarantees for its surplus exports from the emerging American superpower, which supplied most of Argentina's manufactured goods. But Ortiz's inability to get a "fair deal" helped usher in the pro-Axis Castillo regime, during which Argentina's ultranationalists looked to ascendant Germany as a potential new market for Argentine exports and as a military supplier for its armed forces.

IV

As World War II raged abroad and Argentina's own politics grew increasingly volatile, Ernesto Guevara became a teenager. Although his physical development was slow—he remained short for his years and didn't experience a growth spurt until he was sixteen—he was intellectually curious, questioning, and prone to answering back to his elders. His favorite books, however, were still mostly "boy's own adventure" classics: the adventure stories of Emilio Salgari, Jules Verne, and Alexandre Dumas.

In March 1942, just before his fourteenth birthday, Ernesto began high school, or *bachillerato*. Since Alta Gracia's schools offered only primary school education, he began traveling by bus each day to Córdoba, twenty-three miles away, to attend the Colegio Nacional Dean Funes, a state-run school considered one of the city's best outside the private sector.

One morning that year, someone took a photograph of Ernesto posed with the other passengers of the Alta Gracia–Córdoba morning bus. Impishly grinning into the camera, wearing a blazer and tie but still in shorts and crumpled kneesocks, he sat on the front fender of the bus, surrounded by older students attired in button-down collars, suits, ties, and trousers.

During the summer holidays in early 1943, the Guevaras moved to Córdoba, Guevara Lynch having finally found a partner in the city to launch a building firm. With Ernesto already commuting to school, and his sister Celia about to enter a girl's high school in Córdoba, the move from Alta Gracia seemed a practical choice.

3

The Boy of Many Names

I

The Guevaras' move to Córdoba was buoyed by a brief upswing in their economic fortunes, but it was also the beginning of the end of their days as a united family. An attempted reconciliation resulted in the birth of their fifth and last child, Juan Martín, in May 1943, but the strains between Celia and Ernesto deepened, and by the time they left for Buenos Aires four years later, their marriage was finished.

As before, according to family friends, the problem was Guevara Lynch's chronic womanizing. "The father had pretensions of being a play-boy," recalled Tatiana Quiroga, a friend of the Guevara children. "But he was a disorderly playboy, because when he worked and earned money, he spent it all . . . on going out with 'young ladies,' on clothes, on stupidities, nothing concrete . . . and the family would get nothing."

If the family lived somewhat better in Córdoba, the reason was that Guevara Lynch finally made some money. His business partner was an eccentric architect who was known as the "Marqués de Arias" because of his extreme height and aloof, aristocratic air. The Marqués came up with the building contracts, usually houses, and Guevara Lynch oversaw their construction as "master of works."

"We lived divinely, and all the money just went; they never thought in terms of investments," said Ernesto's sister Celia. But before the crunch came, Ernesto Guevara Lynch bought a country chalet in the hills outside Córdoba at Villa Allende and joined Córdoba's exclusive Lawn Tennis Club, where his children swam and learned to play tennis. The Guevaras settled into their new, two-story rented home at Calle Chile 288 near the end of the street, where it met with Avenida Chacabuco, a boulevard lined with bulbous shade trees known as *palos borrachos*. Across the avenue lay the clipped green expanse and woods of Parque Sarmiento, the city zoo, the Lawn Tennis Club, and beyond, the University of Córdoba.

The Guevara home at Calle Chile retained the free, open atmosphere their friends had so enjoyed in Alta Gracia. Dolores Moyano, a new friend from one of Córdoba's richest families, found it all very exotic. In the Guevara house, where the furniture could barely be seen because of the books and magazines piled everywhere, there were no fixed mealtimes that she could discern—one just ate when one felt hungry. The children were allowed to ride their bicycles from the street, through the living room, into the backyard.

But Dolores soon discovered that the Guevaras exacted a price for their open-house policy. Once they sensed any pomposity, pedantry, or pretense in visitors, they would tease them mercilessly. Ernesto, whom she clearly found intimidating, led these attacks, and more than once Dolores found herself a target. Ernesto's mother was just as provocative and could be exceedingly stubborn. Ernesto Sr., on the other hand, was immensely likeable, a man who exuded warmth and vitality. "He spoke in a booming voice, and was rather absentminded. Occasionally, he sent the children on errands which he had forgotten by the time they returned."

II

The move to Córdoba also coincided with the onset of Ernesto's adolescence. He began increasingly to assert himself, questioning his bickering parents' values and forming the first glimmerings of his own worldview.

In his first year at Córdoba's Colegio Nacional Dean Funes, Ernesto made new friends. The closest of these was Tomás Granado, the youngest of three sons of a Spanish emigré who worked as a railway conductor. At fourteen, Ernesto was still short for his years, but he was now slim instead of stocky. The bigger, huskier Tomás wore his hair stylishly slicked back, but Ernesto had an unfashionable buzz-cut. It also earned him the nickname "El Pelao" (Baldy), one of several he acquired during his adolescence.

Before long, Tomás's older brother Alberto had entered their circle as well. A first-year student of biochemistry and pharmacology at the University of Córdoba, the twenty-year-old Alberto, or "Petiso" (Shorty), was barely five feet tall and had a huge beaked nose, but he sported a barrel chest and a footballer's sturdy bowed legs; he also possessed a good sense of humor and a taste for wine, girls, literature, and rugby. He and Ernesto were separated by age, but in time their friendship became stronger than that between Ernesto and Tomás.

Alberto Granado was the coach of the local rugby team, Estudiantes, and Ernesto wanted desperately to try out for the team. Alberto looked upon the boy with a critical eye. "The first impression wasn't very favorable . . . also he wasn't very robust, with very thin arms."

But Alberto decided to give "Pelao" a try, and accepted him for training. Soon the wheezing lad was practicing with Estudiantes two evenings a week at a local playing field. El Pelao earned a reputation as a fearless attacker on the pitch, which he accomplished by running headlong at the player with the ball yelling: "Look out, here comes 'El Furibundo' [Furious] Serna!"* This war cry of his soon led Alberto to give him a new nickname, "Fuser," while Alberto became affectionately "Mial" (for "mi Alberto").

Impressed by the younger lad's dauntless disposition, Alberto Granado took a special interest in Ernesto. Often, while waiting for another team to finish playing before Estudiantes could begin its practice, Granado observed him reading books, usually seated on the ground, his back supported by the playing field's lightposts. One day, he found out that Fuser was already reading Freud, enjoyed the poetry of Baudelaire, and had read Dumas, Verlaine, and Mallarmé "in their original tongue" as well as most of the books by Émile Zola, Argentine classics such as Sarmiento's epic *Facundo*, and the latest American literature by William Faulkner and John Steinbeck.

A zealous reader himself, Granado was intrigued. He couldn't comprehend how such a "little kid" could have read so much. Ernesto explained that he had begun reading for something to occupy himself during his asthma attacks, when his parents made him stay at home, treating himself with the "inhalations" they prescribed. As for his reading in French, this was the result of Celia's influence, who had continued tutoring him throughout his primary school years during his asthma-enforced absences.

For all their new friends and comforts in Córdoba, Alta Gracia remained dear to the Guevaras, and the family often returned there, sometimes renting cottages during the holidays, and Ernesto was able to keep up his friendships with Calica Ferrer, Carlos Figueroa, and other members of his old *barra*. Their friends the González-Aguilars had followed them to Córdoba, installing themselves in a home not far from theirs, and they remained close. When Juan Martín, the Guevara's fifth child, named for Celia's father, was born, the González-Aguilars were his godparents at his baptism ceremony.

Their new family home on Calle Chile turned out to have some disadvantages that had been overlooked by Guevara Lynch in his initial enthusiasm over its close proximity to Parque Sarmiento and the Lawn Tennis Club. Their neighborhood of Nueva Córdoba, built on a hill rising up from

*His abbreviated maternal surname.

the city center, was still in the process of being urbanized. The result was a hodgepodge of residential homes surrounded by a welter of undeveloped vacant lots called *baldíos*. On these lots, and in the dry creeks that ran through the zone, poor people had built shanties.

One of these shantytowns lay directly across from the Guevaras' new home. It was inhabited by colorful personalities who were a source of fascination to the Guevaras and their friends, especially the man with no legs who rode around on a little wooden cart on wheels, pulled by a team of six mongrel dogs he urged on with a long, cracking whip.

As a close friend of Ernesto's youngest sister, Ana María, Dolores Moyano was now a constant visitor. As she recalled, one of their pastimes was to sit on the curb of the "safe side" of the street and watch the goings-on among the slum dwellers of the *baldío*. One of them was a woman in black who nursed her baby under a *paraíso* tree and spit phlegm over his head, and the dwarfish twelve-year-old called Quico who had no eyebrows or eyelashes. They bribed him with sweets to show them his strange white tongue, after which he would dart back into his "*baldío* hole."

Although they were much better off than their poor neighbors in their hovels of cardboard and tin, the Guevaras soon discovered that their own home was built on shaky foundations. Before long, huge cracks began appearing in the walls, and from his bed at night, Guevara Lynch could see the stars through the crack in his ceiling. Yet, for a builder, he was remarkably casual about the dangers. In the children's room, where another crack appeared, he remedied the situation by moving their beds away from the wall in case it collapsed. "We found the house comfortable and we didn't want to move, so we decided to stay as long as we could," he commented.

The sharp contrasts of urban life may have been new to the Guevaras but were becoming increasingly typical in Argentina and throughout Latin America. Since the late nineteenth century, changing economics, immigration, and industrialization had brought about a radical rural-to-urban population shift, as poor farmworkers migrated from the countryside to the cities in search of jobs and a better way of life. Many of them ended up in the shantytowns, or *villas miserias,* that sprang up in Córdoba and Argentina's other large cities.

In a span of only fifty years, Argentina's demographics had reversed completely, from an urban population of 37 percent in 1895 to 63 percent in 1947. During the same period, Argentina's population had quadrupled from four million to sixteen million people.

Despite this ongoing social transformation, Argentina's second-largest city of Córdoba retained a placid, provincial air in the 1940s. Surrounded by the limitless yellow pampa, its horizons broken only by the blue

ranges of the sierras, Córdoba was still mostly untouched by the industrialization and construction boom that was rapidly turning Buenos Aires into
a modern metropolis. As the site of the country's first university, founded
by the Jesuits, and with many old churches and colonial buildings, Córdoba
had earned a reputation as a center of learning, and *cordobeses* were proud
of their cultural heritage.

The city's leading role in education had been secured in 1918 when
Radical party students and teachers at the University of Córdoba spearheaded the "University Reform" that guaranteed university autonomy, a
movement that had spread beyond Córdoba to Argentina's other universities and throughout much of Latin America. Dolores Moyano recalled the
Córdoba of her youth as "a city of bookstores, religious processions, student
demonstrations, and military parades; a city gentle, dull, almost torpid on
the surface but simmering with tensions."

Those tensions burst out shortly after the Guevaras' move to the city.
On June 4, 1943, in Buenos Aires, a secret cabal of military officers banded
together and overthrew President Castillo, who had named as his successor
a wealthy provincial strongman with ties to British corporate monopolies.
Early reaction to the coup was guardedly positive, among both liberal Argentines who regarded Castillo's pro-German administration with suspicion and nationalists fearing further encroachment by foreign economic
interests.

Within forty-eight hours a leader had emerged: war minister General
Pedro Ramírez, representing the military's ultranationalist faction. Very
quickly, he took repressive measures to silence all domestic opposition.
Declaring a state of siege, his regime postponed elections indefinitely, dissolved congress, gagged the press, intervened in the country's universities
and fired protesting faculty members. In a second wave of edicts at year's
end, all political parties were dissolved, compulsory religious instruction in
schools decreed, and even stricter press controls established. In Córdoba,
teachers and students took to the streets in protest. Arrests followed, and in
November 1943 Alberto Granado was imprisoned along with other students
in Córdoba's central jail, behind the colonnades of the old whitewashed
cabildo on the city's Plaza San Martín. There, his brothers and El Pelao visited him, bringing him food and news of the outside world.

The weeks dragged by, with no sign that the students were to be
charged or released anytime soon. The detainees' underground "prisoners'
committee" asked for Córdoba's secondary school students to march in the
streets demanding their liberty. Alberto asked the fifteen-year-old Ernesto
if he would join, but surprisingly he refused. He would do so, he said, only
if given a revolver. He told Alberto the planned march was a futile gesture

that would accomplish little, and the students would "get the shit beaten out of them with truncheons."

In early 1944, after a couple of months in detention, Alberto Granado was released from police custody. Despite Ernesto's refusal to demonstrate on his behalf, their friendship remained intact. In light of his penchant for risky daredevil stunts, Ernesto's unwillingness to help his friend is striking. And, given his extreme youth and apparent unconcern with Argentine politics, his "principled" stance seems dubious. Yet this paradoxical behavior of expressing radical-sounding declamations while displaying a complete apathy about political activism was to become a consistent pattern during Ernesto's growing-up years.

III

As yet unknown to most of the public, the éminence grise behind the political changes taking place in Argentina was an obscure army colonel with a fleshy face and Roman nose whose name—Juan Domingo Perón—would soon be very familiar. After returning from a military posting in Mussolini's Italy, where he became a fervent admirer of Il Duce, Perón had briefly been a troop instructor in the province of Mendoza before going to work at military headquarters in Buenos Aires. There, he had made his move as the driving force behind the shadowy military group calling itself the Grupo de Oficiales Unidos, or GOU, which had launched the June 1943 coup.

Over the next three years, Perón maneuvered his way to the top. After the coup he became undersecretary for war, serving under his mentor, General Edelmiro Farrell. When Farrell assumed the vice presidency in October 1943, Perón asked for and was given the presidency of the National Labor Department. It quickly became his power base. Within a month, he had transformed his obscure-seeming job into a ministry renamed the Department of Labor and Welfare, and was answerable only to the president.

A sweeping series of reformist labor decrees began to flow from Perón's office. His measures were aimed at appealing to disenfranchised workers at the same time as he broke up organized labor groups linked to the traditional political parties. Before long, Perón had brought the country's workforce to heel under his own centralized authority. The phenomenon that would be known as *"peronismo"* had begun, one that, very soon, would radically alter Argentina's political landscape.

By late 1943, with the United States in the war, Nazi Germany was on the defensive throughout Europe and North Africa, and Mussolini had been overthrown in Italy. Suspecting the Argentine regime, and Perón in particular, of serving as thinly disguised representatives for the Third Reich in Latin America, the United States stepped up its pressure on Argentina to abandon its official neutrality in the war. Many Argentines shared the Americans' suspicions. Perón's populist appeals to the social "underclass" in rhetoric reeking of Fascism had alienated Argentina's liberal middle classes. They were joined by the traditional oligarchy, which saw the existing status quo in danger, and most people of the Guevaras' social class had become virulent *antiperonistas*. But their opposition did not stop Perón from becoming even more powerful.

In March 1944, Farrell assumed the presidency. Perón became war minister, and by July he was vice president as well. Of the three high-level positions he now held, however, the most important was still his post as secretary of labor and welfare. Perón was now known to everyone in Argentina.

Meanwhile, Guevara Lynch remained active in Acción Argentina, and he and Celia also joined Córdoba's Comité Pro–De Gaulle, a solidarity network aimed at helping the French Resistance in Nazi-occupied France. And, unknown to them, Ernesto resumed the old Nazi-hunting activities his father had left unfinished.

With a school friend, Osvaldo Bidinost Payer, Ernesto stealthily returned to the small sierra community of La Cumbre, a favorite retreat for Córdoba's landed aristocracy, where his father's group had earlier surveilled a heavily guarded hotel suspected of being the headquarters for Nazi operations in Argentina's interior, complete with a clandestine radio transmitter used to communicate with Berlin. Guevara Lynch had called off the surveillance and warned Ernesto against sniffing around, telling him that of the two government investigators sent to investigate, only one had returned, the other presumably having been murdered.

Motivated by a desire for adventure and risk, the boys went anyway. They approached the hotel at night. Through an open window, said Bidinost, they caught a glimpse of a couple of men busy at "a long table with lots of metal boxes and things." But before they could see more, their presence was detected. "They heard us, someone came out with lanterns, and they fired two shots at us. We left and never returned."

In spite of such escapades, Ernesto's commitment to political causes fell far short of any active militancy during his high school years. He and his friends, who included children of Spanish Republican refugees such as the González-Aguilars, were, like their parents, politically "anti-Fascist," and given to arguing precociously over what had "really happened" in Spain. But they had much less notion, or even interest, in the events taking place in Argentina at the time. When Ernesto did espouse a political opinion, it was usually provocative, designed to shock his parents or peers. For instance, on an occasion when Córdoba's *peronista* militants were rumored to be preparing a stoning attack against the local Jockey Club, a symbol of the conservative landed oligarchy, Ernesto declared his willingness to join them. "I wouldn't mind throwing some stones at the Jockey Club myself," some of his friends heard him say. They assumed this was a sign of his *properonista* sentiments, but it was just as likely he was being a bloody-minded teenager, trying to unsettle them and get them talking.

When Argentina's government finally broke off diplomatic relations with the Axis powers, Ernesto's parents were overjoyed. But his younger friend Pepe González Aguilar had never seen Ernestito so angry as the moment when he confronted his celebrating parents. "I couldn't understand how he, who had always been anti-Nazi, didn't share our happiness." Later, Pepe surmised that Ernesto's anger was due to the fact that the decision had been made not on principle, but because of U.S. pressure, and he shared Argentine nationalists' sense of shame that their country had buckled under to the Americans.

But when the Allied forces liberated Paris in September 1944, Ernesto joined the celebrating crowd in Córdoba's Plaza San Martín accompanied by several of his Dean Funes friends, their pockets stuffed with metal ball bearings, ready to hurl at the hooves of the horses of the mounted police called in to keep order.

(In recognition of his own efforts, Guevara Lynch received a certificate signed by de Gaulle himself, thanking him for the support he had given to the "people of France" in their hour of need. For the rest of his life, Guevara Lynch kept it with him as one of his proudest possessions.)

Despite some retrospective attempts to see the early hint of socialist ideals in the teenaged Ernesto Guevara, virtually all his Córdoba schoolmates recalled him as politically disinterested. To his friend José María Roque, Ernesto didn't have "a defined political ideal" at the time. "We all loved to argue politics, but I never saw Guevara [get involved] in any sense."

Nor did Ernesto let his "anti-Fascism" get in the way of friendship. One of his classmates was Domingo Rigatusso, a poor Italian immigrant's son who worked after school selling sweets to the moviegoers in the local cinemas. As an Italian, Rigatusso steadfastly supported Mussolini in the war, as did his father, and Guevara referred to him affectionately as a *"tano fascio,"* slang for "Italian Fascist."

But Raúl Melivosky, a year younger than Ernesto and the son of a Jewish university professor, recalled briefly belonging to an FES "cell" with Ernesto in 1943, at a time when the militant youth wing of the pro-Nazi Alianza Libertadora Nacionalista was intimidating students sympathetic to the Allies. Just beginning his first year at Dean Funes, Melivosky knew about Guevara before they were introduced. He was pointed out as the only student in school who had stood up in class to a notoriously pro-Nazi history professor over a factual inaccuracy. This act alone merited Guevara great respect in Melivosky's eyes.

Then the FES decided to form three-man "cells" as a defensive measure against the right-wing students of the Alianza Libertadora Nacionalista. Melivosky and another first-year student were both assigned an older boy to be their cell "leader," who turned out to be Ernesto Guevara. "We were cells in name only," he recalled. "We didn't meet, and practically the only thing we did was to call ourselves cells."

But, one afternoon, when he and some other students were blocked from leaving the school grounds by some Alianza bullies who were brandishing penknives embossed with their group's condor insignia, Melivosky witnessed Guevara hurl himself at the throng, whirling his school satchel around and around his head like a dervish. To the grateful Melivosky, Guevara seemed "more than brave . . . He was absolutely fearless."

The only other time their "cell" was activated was the day when, making use of his authority as leader, Ernesto ordered Melivosky and the other boy under his tutelage to "skip" school the following day. It was an exploit that could cost them their expulsion, and Melivosky knew it. "He didn't order us only to skip school, but to go to a movie that was prohibited to minors. We were thirteen and fourteen, and you had to be eighteen, so we weren't going to be able to fool anybody. None of us was very tall or robust. But he ordered us to each come wearing a hat, with a cigarette, and with the money we needed for the tickets."

Such were Ernesto's earliest incursions into "politics." Twenty years later, in a letter to a sycophantic editor intending to publish a hagiography about him, Guevara wrote bluntly: "I had no social preoccupations in my adolescence and had no participation in the political or student struggles in Argentina."

Searching, noncomformist, and with a yearning for adventure—this was Ernesto Guevara at the end of World War II, just before his seventeenth birthday.

IV

Ernesto was now a full-fledged teenager, and along with his voracity for books he had developed a strong curiosity about the opposite sex. He managed to satisfy both interests when he discovered and read the unabridged and highly erotic original edition of *A Thousand and One Nights* at a friend's home.

Beyond such titillation, though, actual sexual fulfillment remained an abstract ideal to most boys of Ernesto's generation. In the provincial Argentina of the mid-1940s, prevailing values concerning sex and marriage were still very much those of a traditional Catholic society: Women didn't have the right to divorce, and "good" girls were expected to retain their virginity until marriage.

"We were little angels," recalled Tatiana Quiroga, who went out with Ernesto and other friends on "double dates." "We went to dance, to converse, to drink a coffee, and at twelve-thirty you had to be back, or they would kill you; that was the period when you could barely go out. How could we little girls go to some boy's house, all alone? Never! The most we ever did was to escape the parties and go drink some mate."

For sex, boys of Ernesto's social milieu either visited brothels or looked for conquests among girls of the lower class, where their social and economic differences gave them advantages. For many, the first sexual experience was with the family *mucama,* or servant girl, usually an Indian or poor mestiza from one of Argentina's northern provinces.

It was Calica Ferrer who had provided Ernesto with his first introduction to sex, when he was fourteen or fifteen, in a liaison with his family *mucama,* a woman called "La Negra" Cabrera. Rodolfo Ruarte was present at Ernestito's initiation ceremony and, with several other youths, spied on him and La Negra through the keyhole of the bedroom door. They observed that, while he conducted himself admirably on top of the pliant maid, he periodically interrupted his lovemaking to suck on his asthma inhaler. The spectacle soon had them in stitches and remained a source of amusement for years afterward. But Ernesto was unperturbed, and his sessions with La Negra continued as a regular pastime.

Along with his discovery of sex, Ernesto nurtured a new love of poetry, and he enjoyed reciting passages he had memorized. With the aid of the seventeenth-century Spanish poet Francisco de Quevedo's *Picaresque Sonnets and Romances,* he began displaying a sense of the ribald. One day, he employed it to effect on a blushing Dolores Moyano. He had overheard her pedantically discussing the poetry of the Spanish-Arab mystics, and when he challenged her knowledge of the topic, she found herself gullibly explaining: "The lover and the mystic in St. John's poetry have this double vision. The inner eye and the outward eye, the lover-mystic sees both ways. . . ." At that point, she recalled, Ernesto interrupted her, and affecting an exaggerated Cordoban accent, he recited a profane couplet about a one-eyed nun and a cross-eyed saint.

The incident highlights the schism that existed between male and female adolescents of Guevara's social class and generation. The girls, virginal and innocent, steeped themselves in romantic poetry, saving themselves for true love and marriage, while boys like Ernesto, hormones bursting, sought out the real world of sex as best they could in bawdy poems and brothels, or by bedding the hapless family *mucamas.*

During the summer holidays of 1945 and 1946, Ernesto's pretty cousin Carmen Córdova Iturburu de la Serna, "La Negrita," reappeared, and she developed a crush on the iconoclastic cousin three years her senior. Her father, the poet Cayetano Córdova Iturburu, always brought a trunkful of newly published books from Buenos Aires with him, and she used to rummage through it for books of poetry. It was her passion, one she found that she shared with Ernesto, and he recited to her from Pablo Neruda's *Twenty Poems of Love and a Desperate Song,* which he had recently discovered.

"In the full bloom of adolescence, Ernestito and I were a little more than friends," she recalled years later. "One day we were playing on a terrace of my house. . . . Ernesto asked me if I was now a woman. . . ." A lover's tryst ensued between them, and later on, when the Guevaras moved to Buenos Aires, Ernesto and La Negrita continued to see one another. She often stayed in the Guevaras' home, where she recalled romantic interludes with Ernesto on the stairwell, talking "of literature . . . and of love because, as often happens between cousins, we too had our idyll. Ernesto was so handsome!"

And he was. By the age of seventeen, Ernesto had developed into an extremely attractive young man: slim and wide-shouldered, with dark-brown hair, intense brown eyes, clear white skin, and a self-contained, easy confidence that made him alluring to girls. "The truth is, we were all a little in love with Ernesto," confessed Miriam Urrutia, another well-born Córdoba girl.

At an age when boys tend to try hard to impress girls, Ernesto's insouciance regarding appearances was especially compelling. One evening, Ernesto showed up with an elegantly attired society girl at the Cine Opera, where his *fascio* friend Rigatusso sold sweets. Ernesto had come dressed, as usual, in an old, oversized trench coat, its pockets stuffed with food and a mate thermos, and when he spotted Rigatusso, he pointedly left his date standing on her own while he chatted to his "socially inferior" friend.

Ernesto was quickly evolving the social persona that was to leave a lasting memory with his Córdoba peers. His devil-may-care attitude, contempt for formality, and combative intellect were all now visible traits of his personality, and would become accentuated in coming years. Even his sense of humor was confrontational, challenging social decorum, although it was often expressed in a self-mocking guise.

His friend Alberto Granado became very familiar with Ernesto's penchant for shocking people. "He had several nicknames. They also called him 'El Loco' [Crazy] Guevara. He liked to be a little bit of a terrible lad. . . . He boasted about how seldom he bathed, for example. They also called him 'Chancho' [The Pig]. He used to say, for instance: 'It's been twenty-five weeks since I washed this rugby shirt.'"

One day Ernesto stopped wearing short pants to school and arrived dressed in trousers. No doubt to forestall the ribbing he was bound to receive from the older boys about suddenly growing up, Ernesto announced that the reason he now wore trousers was because his shorts were so dirty, he'd had to throw them away.

Throughout his five years at the Colegio Nacional Dean Funes, Ernesto cultivated the image of himself as an irrepressible rascal. He delighted in doing things to shock his teachers and classmates, such as wordlessly lighting up his pungent "Dr. Andreu" anti-asthma cigarettes in the middle of class; debating openly with his mathematics and literature teachers about inaccuracies he'd caught them in; organizing weekend outings with his "gang" to the outlying sierras or back to Alta Gracia, where he engaged in the same kinds of daredevil stunts that had so horrified his parents when he was a child: "tightrope-walking" pipelines over steep chasms, leaping from high rocks into rivers, and bicycling along train tracks.

His behavior was duly noted by the school authorities. On the first of June 1945, his fourth year at Dean Funes, he received "ten admonishments [twenty-five meant expulsion] by rectoral order, for acts of indiscipline and for having entered and left the establishment outside of hours, without the corresponding permission."

His grades, on the whole, were "good." As always, however, they reflected his proclivity for subjects such as mathematics, natural history, geography, and history, although with each year he also showed a gradual improvement in French, Spanish, writing, and music.

His extracurricular book-reading continued unabated. His friend Pepe Aguilar noticed, as had Alberto Granado, that Ernesto's tastes were eclectic and often advanced for his years. "He read with anxiety, devouring the library of his parents . . . from Freud to Jack London, mixed with Neruda, Horacio Quiroga, and Anatole France, even an abbreviated edition of *Das Kapital* in which he made observations in tiny letters."

However, Ernesto found the dense Marxist tome incomprehensible, and years later, as Comandante Ernesto "Che" Guevara, he confessed to his wife in Cuba that he "hadn't understood a thing" in his early readings of Marx and Engels.

V

In the 1945 school year, a more serious side to Ernesto began to emerge. That year, he took his first course in philosophy. It engaged his interest, as his "very good" and "outstanding" grades reveal. He also began writing his own "philosophical dictionary."

His first handwritten notebook, 165 pages in length, was ordered alphabetically, and carefully indexed by page number, topic, and author. Consisting of pocket biographies of noted thinkers and a wide range of quoted definitions, its entries include such concepts as love, immortality, hysteria, sexual morality, faith, justice, death, God, the devil, fantasy, reason, neurosis, narcissism, and morality.

Clearly, he made use of every source available to him. His quotations on Marxism were culled from *Mein Kampf* and featured passages revealing Hitler's obsession with a Jewish-Marxist conspiracy. For his sketches of Buddha and Aristotle, he used H. G. Wells's *Brief History of the World,* while Bertrand Russell's *Old and New Sexual Morality* was his source on love, patriotism, and sexual morality. But Sigmund Freud's theories also obviously fascinated him, and Ernesto quoted his *General Theory of Memory* on everything from dreams and libido to narcissism and the Oedipus complex. Other attributions came from Jack London on society and Nietzsche on death; and, for revisionism and reformism, he drew definitions from a book written by his uncle Cayetano Córdova Iturburu.

This notebook was only the first in a series of seven that he continued to work on over the next ten years. He would add new entries and replace older ones as his studies deepened and his interests became more focused. Future notebooks reflected his reading of Jawaharlal Nehru and also his intensified reading on Marxism, quoting not Hitler but Marx, Engels, and Lenin themselves.

His choice of fictional reading material now began to shift to books with more of a social content. Indeed, in the opinion of his friend Osvaldo Bidinost Payer, "everything began with literature" for Ernesto Guevara. Around this time, he and Ernesto were reading the same novels by authors such as Faulkner, Kafka, Camus, and Sartre. In poetry, Ernesto was reading the Spanish Republican poets García Lorca, Machado, and Alberti, and the Spanish translations of Walt Whitman and Robert Frost—while his overall favorite remained Pablo Neruda.

But Bidinost soon discovered that Ernesto had also delved into Latin American literature by authors such as Ciro Alegría, Jorge Icaza, Rubén Darío, and Miguel Ángel Asturias. Their novels and poetry often dealt unprecedentedly with Latin American themes—including the unequal lives of marginalized Indians and mestizos—ignored in fashionable literature and virtually unknown to Ernesto's social group. Bidinost believes that such literature gave Ernesto an inkling of the society he inhabited but did not know firsthand. "It was a kind of advance glimpse of what he wanted to experience, and what was around him was objectively Latin America and *not* Europe or Wyoming."

The other major influence in Ernesto's social formation was his mother Celia. As Ernesto's friends in Alta Gracia had been, Bidinost was bewitched by the Guevara household's egalitarian informality and by Celia *madre*. To him, it was a home that sheltered a cult of creativity, and of what he called "the discovery of the world through the service entrance," as Celia collected all kinds of colorful people, irrespective of their social status, and brought them home. At her house he met itinerant painters who worked as bootblacks, wandering Ecuadorean poets, and university professors, who sometimes stayed a week or a month, depending on their level of hunger. "It was a fascinating human zoo."

While Celia presided over her all-hours salon, Ernesto's father came and went on an old motorbike he had named "La Pedorra" (The Farter), for the sputtering noise it issued from its exhaust. He and Celia slept in the same house but were estranged, and lived increasingly separate lives.

Another Córdoba youth who found himself caught up in the Guevara magic was Roberto "Beto" Ahumada, a school friend of Ernesto's brother Roberto. Ahumada recalled many occasions when, invited back to the Guevaras' for dinner by Roberto, the family unblinkingly divided up the prepared meal into smaller portions so that he could join them. "Nobody was worried about eating a little less because one of the kids had brought friends. They brought who they wanted and nobody cared!"

Not surprisingly, in this rollicking home replete with children, itinerant guests, and conversation, Ernesto found it difficult to read or study undisturbed, and he acquired the habit of reading for hours on end in the bathroom, a habit he kept for the rest of his life.

One day, an old childhood *barra* mate named Enrique Martín unexpectedly bumped into Ernesto in Alta Gracia. Enrique was surprised to see him there: it was a weekday, and the school year was not over. Swearing him to secrecy, Ernesto told him he had rented a small back room in the Cecil Hotel, near the bus station, a place where nobody knew him. "I'm here to isolate myself from everybody," he said.

Exactly what Ernesto wanted isolation for, Enrique Martín didn't think to ask, but he loyally guarded his friend's secret for many years. Whether Ernesto wanted a place to think and study, or to rendezvous with one of Alta Gracia's promiscuous *mucamas,* remains unknown, but this was clearly not the same extroverted madcap Loco, Chancho, or Pelao known to his friends in class and on the rugby pitch, but a distinctly private youth who craved isolation.

VI

By the beginning of 1946 Perón had attained power. He had survived a brief ouster from office by rival military officers, a brief exile on Martín García island in the Rio de La Plata estuary, then, after a huge popular demonstration demanding his release, had made a triumphant comeback to win the presidency in the general elections of February.

And he was no longer on his own. Months earlier he had married his mistress, a young, blond radio actress named Eva Duarte. Nobody knew it yet, but "Evita" was to leave an imprint on Argentina's popular consciousness that rivaled her husband's.

Nineteen forty-six was also Ernesto's final year of high school. He celebrated his eighteenth birthday in June, just ten days after the Peróns assumed office. While continuing with his studies, he also began a paying job for the first time in his life, in the laboratory of Córdoba's Dirección Provincial de Vialidad, a public works office that oversaw road construction in the province.

His friend Tomás Granado was with him. The two youths, similarly adept in subjects such as math and science, were already discussing plans to study engineering at the university the following year. They had obtained their jobs, offering useful practical experience for future engineers, after Ernesto's father had asked a friend to allow them into a special course given for field analysts at Vialidad. They successfully passed the course, and now they were "soils specialists," examining the quality of materials used by the private companies contracted to build roads. In the lab, where they worked part-time, Ernesto made everyone fruit shakes in the blender used for mixing soils.

When they graduated from Dean Funes, they began working full-time and were assigned to jobs in different parts of the province. Ernesto was sent to inspect the materials going into roadworks at Villa María, 150 kilometers to the north. His contract came with a modest salary, the use of a company truck, and free lodging.

In March 1947, with Ernesto still in Villa María, his family moved back to Buenos Aires after an absence of fifteen years. But it was not a triumphant return: his parents had decided to split up, and they were once again in very bad shape economically. Guevara Lynch's building business had floundered, and he had been forced to sell the summer house in Villa Allende. Soon he would have to sell the Misiones plantation as well. There was little money coming in from it, and for the last couple of years he had fallen behind in paying the annual property taxes.

In Buenos Aires, the family moved into the fifth-floor apartment owned by Guevara Lynch's aged mother, Ana Isabel, at the corner of Calles

Arenales and Uriburu. In early May, however, the ninety-six-year-old Ana Isabel fell ill, and the Guevaras sent a telegram to Ernesto to advise him of her delicate state.

On May 18, he worriedly wrote back, asking them to send another telegram with more details of her condition, and saying that if she worsened, he was prepared to resign his job and come immediately to Buenos Aires.

Within days, the bad news came: His grandmother had suffered a stroke and was gravely ill. Ernesto quit his job and raced to Buenos Aires. He made it in time for the deathwatch. She lasted for seventeen days, during which he was constantly at her bedside. "We could all see that her illness was fatal," wrote Guevara Lynch. "Ernesto, desperate at seeing that his grandmother didn't eat, tried with incredible patience to get her to eat food, entertaining her, and without leaving her side. And he remained there until my mother left this world."

When his grandmother died, Ernesto was disconsolate. His sister Celia had never seen her self-contained older brother so grief-stricken. "He was *very* sad; it must have been one of the great sadnesses of his life."

4

His Own Man

I

Immediately after his grandmother's death, Ernesto informed his parents that he had decided to study medicine instead of engineering. That same month, he applied for admission to the Faculty of Medicine at the University of Buenos Aires.

La Facultad de Medicina is an early modern monolith: unremittingly grey, all straight lines and small box windows. A chilly monument to medical science, it thrusts fifteen stories bleakly into the sky over an otherwise elegant district of tall, fin de siècle townhouses with vaulted ceilings, ornately grilled balconies, and French windows. It overlooks an open square, dominated by the gentle handworked dome of an old Catholic chapel. Here and there, bronze bas-reliefs on stone tablets depict surgeons operating on patients.

Guevara himself never spelled out his exact reasons for having chosen a medical career, except to say, years later, that he had been motivated by a desire for a "personal triumph": "I dreamed of becoming a famous investigator . . . of working indefatigably to find something that could be definitively placed at the disposition of humanity."

He had shown himself to be adept at sciences, and a career in engineering had been an easy choice, but he wasn't passionately interested in the field. In medicine, at least, he could do something that was worthwhile. His family thought his decision was due to his frustration at the incapacity of modern medicine to lessen the agonies of his dying grandmother, and his resolution to do something himself to alleviate human suffering. The shock of her death, despite her advanced age, may have helped spur Ernesto's decision to switch careers, but as his choice of specialties soon revealed, he was also obsessed with finding a cure for his own asthma condition.

Along with his studies, Ernesto held down a number of part-time jobs, but of all of them, the work he did at the Clínica Pisani, an allergy-treatment clinic, was the most absorbing as well as the longest-lasting. Beginning first as one of Dr. Salvador Pisani's patients for treatment of his own asthma condition, Ernesto showed a quick intelligence and curiosity in the field that soon led to Pisani offering him a post as an unpaid research assistant. For a young medical student, it was a privileged opportunity to be involved in a new field of medical research.

Pisani had pioneered a system for treating allergies through vaccinations concocted from semidigested food substances, and he had treated Ernesto's asthma using these methods with some success. Ernesto became so enthused with the positive results and his own laboratory work that he decided to specialize in allergies for his medical career.

The family-run clinic became a kind of surrogate home. Dr. Pisani, his sister Mafalda, and their mother all lived together in a spacious home next door, and they quickly developed a strong affection for Ernesto. The women fed him special treats of carrot juice, corn bread, and oat cakes for his antiasthma diet, and put him to bed when he suffered attacks. Ernesto responded favorably to the mothering they gave him, and Dr. Pisani began looking upon him as a special protégé who might follow in his footsteps and go far one day in allergy research.

To his father, meanwhile, Ernesto became a fleeting figure, always in a hurry, with never enough time. "Active and diligent, he ran from one place to the other to fulfill his obligations. And how could he not be in a hurry? He had to work to support himself, because I helped him little, and also because he didn't want me to give him a cent. He took care of things as best he could."

But Ernesto's industrious outward appearance concealed an inner world of turmoil. Months earlier, back in Villa María, he had confronted his crowded feelings on four pages of small notepaper. Written as a free-verse poem, it provides a rare look into the unsettled emotions of Ernesto Guevara at a crucial moment in his life. The following is an extract from the passage he wrote on January 17, 1947.

> *I know it! I know it!*
> *If I get out of here the river swallows me. . . .*
> *It is my destiny: Today I must die!*
> *But no, willpower can overcome everything*
> *There are the obstacles, I admit it*
> *I don't want to come out.*
> *If I have to die, it will be in this cave.*

The bullets, what can the bullets do to me if
my destiny is to die by drowning. But I am
going to overcome destiny. Destiny can be
achieved by willpower.

Die, yes, but riddled with
bullets, destroyed by the bayonets, if not, no. Drowned, no . . .
a memory more lasting than my name
Is to fight, to die fighting.

Ernesto's evident personal upheaval transcended any anxieties he felt about his family's problems or about which college he should choose, but dealt with the questions of inner strength, destiny, and whether to take a "safe" or "risky" road in life: "Die, yes, but riddled with bullets, destroyed by bayonets, if not, no. Drowned, no . . ."

At the same time, his references to drowning, "the deep well," may have been symbolic allusions to his asthma, which had imposed limitations on his life and must have seemed to pose a predetermined route to death. It was, he seemed to be saying, a condition he had to fight to overcome through willpower. But, without Ernesto Guevara's own explanation, it is probably best to accept this piece of writing for what it certainly was: a melodramatic outpouring by a confused and self-absorbed eighteen-year-old.

These had been traumatic months for Ernesto. His parent's marital and economic collapse, the forced move to Buenos Aires, and now the death of his beloved grandmother had brought his sense of family security crashing down around him. As the eldest son, he felt the burden of needing to "help out," and his future must have suddenly felt mortgaged. Even before the news about his grandmother had brought him to Buenos Aires, he had begun assuming a new sense of family duty. Just before leaving Villa María, he had written to his mother: "Tell me how you have sorted out the question of housing, and if the kids have schools to go to."

Now they were all in Buenos Aires, but because they had no money the question of a home remained a problem. For the time being they were stuck, and for the next year, the entire family continued living in the late Ana Isabel's apartment. Then Guevara Lynch sold the Misiones plantation and gave Celia the money it brought in to buy a home.

The house she found was an old, ugly house at 2180 Calle Araoz and came with unwelcome elderly tenants who occupied the ground floor, but it was well situated, at the edge of the select Palermo district with its parklands and playing fields. They had their own home again, but things were different. The older children had to find paying jobs, and their parents, though still legally married, were now "separated." Ernesto Guevara Lynch no longer shared Celia's bed; he slept on a sofa in the living room.

The altered family circumstances also brought about a fundamental shift in the relationship between Ernesto and his father. "We joked with one another as if we were the same age," wrote Guevara Lynch. "He teased me continuously. As soon as we found ourselves at the table in our house, he would goad me with arguments of a political character. . . . Ernesto, who at the time was twenty years old, surpassed me in this area, and we argued constantly. Those who overheard us might have thought we were fighting. Not at all. Deep down there existed a true camaraderie between us."

II

During his first year at the university, Ernesto was called up by Argentina's military draft. In the physical checkup, his asthma was detected, and he was rejected on grounds of "diminished physical abilities." The decision saved him from spending a year away from his studies in some army barracks, and he was overjoyed, telling friends he "thanked his shitty lungs for doing something useful for a change."

At the Facultad, meanwhile, he had the usual classes in anatomy and physiology. One of the first friends he made was a young woman, Berta Gilda Infante, or "Tita." The daughter of a deceased Córdoba lawyer and politician whose family had recently moved to the capital, Tita felt immediately attracted to Ernesto, who struck her as "a beautiful and uninhibited young boy."

A rather gruesome photograph from the 1948 class year shows Ernesto and Tita, one of only two girls, standing among a group of white-coated medical students arrayed behind the naked cadaver of a man lying on a slab in the foreground. His shaved and openmouthed head is lolling over the edge of the slab, and his chest cavity is gaping open like a gutted chicken. The tableau must have appealed to Ernesto's sense of the incongruous: In the photograph most of the students are serious, affecting the humorless mien of their intended profession; a few are smiling; but Ernesto is the only one present beaming toothily straight at the camera.

Their anatomy class encounter sparked off a deep, platonic friendship between Ernesto and Tita. For Ernesto, she was someone he could trust and confide in at an emotionally unstable time in his life. It was a role she was glad to fulfill. Every Wednesday, they met in the Museum of Natural Sciences for a class on the nervous system, cutting up fish under the guidance of an elderly German professor. They met in cafés and at her home to talk about their classes or personal problems; they swapped books and discussed them, and recited favorite stanzas of poetry to one another.

Ernesto and Tita's relationship seems to have been based upon their mutual need for a close, uncompromised friendship. Both were lonely and hungry for affection, both came from broken homes—Tita's father had died three years earlier—and were relative newcomers to the sprawling capital city of five million people. Their relationship was long-lasting; after Ernesto left Argentina, the two maintained contact through a stream of letters almost rivaling the correspondences that he carried on with his mother and his spinster aunt Beatriz.

Escaping his own home, which was constantly full of people, Ernesto spent a great deal of time at his aunt Beatriz's apartment. Throughout his childhood, Beatriz had mothered Ernesto in ways Celia never did, sending him books and gifts, new asthma remedies, encouraging him at his studies and worrying about him. Now, as before, Beatriz was there for him.

He came regularly to the Arenales apartment where Beatriz still lived, twenty blocks from Calle Araoz, to eat his meals and study at night. She prepared food and clucked over him to make sure he was feeling well, eating right, and had his supply of asthma medicine. Guevara Lynch recalled: "My sister didn't sleep while Ernesto studied; she always had his mate ready to prepare for him and accompanied him when he took a break, and she did all this with the greatest affection."

Ernesto's special relationship with Beatriz was witnessed firsthand by Mario Saravia, a cousin seven years younger than Ernesto. In 1951, he came from Bahía Blanca in southern Argentina, where his family lived, to attend a school in the capital, and he lived with the Guevaras for the next two years, sharing Ernesto and Roberto's bedroom. As Beatriz's other pet nephew, Mario often joined Ernesto for his meals at her house.

Beatriz was so straitlaced that she wore gloves to handle money, and if she shook hands with a stranger, she washed them afterward, said Saravia. Distrustful of the morals of the lower classes, Beatriz would put pincers on the locked service door when the *mucama* who cooked for her went to bed at night, so the doorknob couldn't be turned. Ernesto loved to shock Beatriz, and at one dinner he announced his plans to go out with a certain girl. "But what is her *surname*?" asked Beatriz. When Ernesto blithely replied that he didn't know, his mortified aunt became extremely upset.

With this woman who loved him so unconditionally, Ernesto never got into an acrimonious confrontation. Instead he humored her and, meanwhile, did what he liked, frequently teasing her to scandalize her imagination with hints of the unsavory activities he might secretly be up to.

According to Saravia, some of those activities would have made Beatriz "drop dead on the spot from a heart attack" if she knew about them, for they included seducing the maid she so carefully locked into her bedroom at night.

At one lunch, between servings, Mario Saravia watched in astonishment from his place at the dining table through the open doors leading to the kitchen as Ernesto had quick sex with the *mucama* on the kitchen table, directly behind their unsuspecting aunt's back. When he was done, Ernesto returned to the table and continued eating, his aunt none the wiser. "He was like a rooster," observed Saravia. "He mated and then continued with his other functions."

III

Not surprisingly, Ernesto was an elusive figure to his classmates on campus. He gave the impression of being a young man in a great hurry. And he was, whether working at one of his jobs, studying, or indulging his growing passion for travel. In some respects, Buenos Aires was merely a base for the progressive expansion of his geographical horizons as he set out hitchhiking, first on weekend or holiday jaunts back to Córdoba and to his late grandmother's *estancia* at Santa Ana de Irineo Portela, but gradually extending his radius farther afield and for longer periods.

In spite of the changes that had occurred in Ernesto's life, some things had remained constant. He still had his asthma, he continued playing chess— now one of his favorite hobbies—and rugby; he read assiduously and worked on his philosophical notebooks. He also wrote poetry. One of his earliest surviving poems, scribbled on the back inside cover of his fifth philosophical notebook, dates from this period.

A short, unpolished ode, it appears to be an evocation of a gravesite. As with most of the other poems he wrote in his twenties, it is both awkward and pretentious, but reveals the unfurling of a strong romantic imagination and, in his love of words, the early stirrings of his growing desire to write.

> *Inconclusive tombstone of abstract garden,*
> *With your archaic architecture,*
> *You strike at the cubic morality of man.*
> *Horrible figurines dye your verse with blood*
> *and panegyric facades stain your front with light,*
> *Portentous whims sully your dark name*
> *Dressing you like all the rest.*

His private world of study and reflection began to dominate more and more of his time. His brother Roberto was astounded to find Ernesto systematically reading through the entire twenty-five-volume collection of their father's *Contemporary History of the Modern World;* his philosophical notebooks are full of references to these tomes.

With the same methodical approach, he began writing an index of the literature he read. In a black, clothbound book with alphabetically ordered pages, he wrote entries for authors, their nationalities, the book titles, and genres. The selection of titles is lengthy and eclectic, including popular modern novels, European, American, and Argentine classics, medical texts, poetry, biographies, and philosophy. Interesting anomalies are scattered throughout the index, such as *My Best Chess Games* by the Russian Alexandr Aleksei, the *1937 Socialist Yearbook,* and *The Manufacture and Use of Celluloid, Bakelite, Etc.* by R. Bunke. But he still loved adventure classics, especially Jules Verne. He had read the entire collected works, and the vintage three-volume leatherbound set he owned was one of his most prized possessions. A decade later, as a revolutionary *comandante* in Cuba, he had it brought to him from Argentina.

Ernesto also continued to read extensively on sexuality and social behavior in books by Freud and Bertrand Russell, and displayed a growing interest in social philosophy: he was now reading everyone from the ancient Greeks to Aldous Huxley. Given the tightening focus of his interests, there is a great deal of crosshatching between his literary index and his philosophical notebooks.

His exploration into the concepts and origins of socialist thought was gathering momentum. He consulted Benito Mussolini on Fascism, Josef Stalin on Marxism, Alfredo Palacios, the flamboyant Argentine Socialist party founder, on justice, Zola for a highly critical definition of Christianity, and Jack London for a Marxist description of social class. He had read a French biography of Lenin; *The Communist Manifesto,* some speeches by Lenin; and had dipped again into *Das Kapital.* In his third journal, he began to show a special interest in Karl Marx, filling dozens of pages with a thumbnail biography of the German philosopher's life and works, culled from R. P. Ducatillon's *Communism and Christianity.* (The figure of Marx became an enduring fascination: In 1965, while living clandestinely in Africa, he found the time to sketch an outline for a biography of Marx, fully intending to write it himself.)

He also copied out a portrait of Lenin from Ducatillon's book that describes him as a singular historical personality who "lived, breathed and slept" socialist revolution, subjugating all else in his life to its cause. The passage is remarkable, for it presages to an uncanny degree the descriptions made of Ernesto "Che" Guevara by his future revolutionary comrades.

Yet for all his curiosity about socialism, now, as before, Ernesto showed no inclination to become formally affiliated with the left. In fact, throughout his university years, he remained on the political sidelines—observing, listening, and sometimes debating, but studiously avoiding any active participation himself.

By 1950, Perón's mandate had evolved into the populist-nationalist movement officially known as *peronismo*. With Perón as "Conductor" and his bejeweled young wife, Evita, as its messianic avenging angel, the movement now possessed its own quasi-spiritual social philosophy officially defined as *justicialismo,* with an "organized community" of man living in harmony as its ultimate goal.

Against this backdrop of high-minded rhetoric, however, Perón had stepped up the repression of his opponents. Political adversaries were silenced by intimidation or with jail terms under toughened laws for *desacato,* or disrespect of public officials. The officially lionized *descamisados* (shirtless ones), or working masses, were won over by the shower of gifts and public works projects sponsored by Evita, now recast in a regal public image and president of her own Eva Perón Foundation.

Perón defined the international posture of this new Argentina as the "Third Position," an opportunistic and intentionally ambiguous balancing act between the capitalist West and Communist East. In Perón's words, "It is an ideological position which is in the center, left, or the right according to circumstances. We obey the circumstances."

Perón's cynicism was all too transparent, yet it was clear his policy was motivated by a desire to reinvent Argentina as a sovereign state beholden to no foreign power, and, exhibiting a kind of grudging respect, Ernesto had dubbed him *"el capo."* Aside from such ambiguous remarks, Ernesto shied away from expressing his sympathies, for either Perón or his opponents. In the ranks of the political opposition, there was little that was attractive. Argentina's established parties displayed little social vision and had shown a woeful inability to counter Perón's momentum. The Argentine Communist party was still a legal political organization, but its power base in the unions and the Central General de Trabajadores (CGT) workers' confederation had been weakened by Perón's creation of new structures to co-opt Argentina's workers. The party's response was to ally itself with the centrist Radical party and a grouping of smaller left-of-center parties in strategic opposition to Perón. It was doctrinaire, bogged down in theoretical wranglings; it lacked charismatic leadership or a popular base of support, and by allying itself with the status quo ante as a tactic for survival, its appeal to Ernesto as an alternative force for social change must have been weak indeed.

At the university, the Federación Juvenil Comunista, or Communist Youth, was active, and Ernesto knew some of its militants. One of them was Ricardo Campos, who recalled their talks on politics as "brusque and difficult." Once, he convinced Ernesto to attend a "Fede" meeting, but, shocking the other participants, Ernesto stalked out while it was still in progress. "He had very clear ideas about certain things. Above all from an ethical perspective. More than a political person, I saw him at that time as someone with an ethical posture."

To Tita Infante's brother Carlos, another Communist, Ernesto was a "progressive liberal" whose main interests seemed to be medicine and literature. They discussed the works of the Argentine Marxist writer Aníbal Ponce, but when it came to the Argentine Communist party, Ernesto was very critical of its sectarianism and skeptical about its role in Argentine politics.

Ernesto was putting his reading to the test, employing concepts he found appealing in discussions with those around him. At the funeral of an uncle in 1951, he argued with his cousin Juan Martín Moore de la Serna over philosophy and politics, pitting his own interpretations of Marx and Engels against Moore's defense of French Catholic philosophers. And, on a visit back to Córdoba, he mortified Dolores Moyano with a Nietzschean putdown of Jesus Christ. The Korean conflict also sparked strong arguments between Ernesto and his father, with Ernesto opposing the Americans' role—accusing them of imperial designs—and his father supporting them.

It was in such personal encounters, rather than any militancy in Argentina's politics, that Ernesto's emerging worldview began to reveal itself. But none of his friends or relatives thought of Ernesto as a Marxist; and indeed, neither did *he,* at the time. They attributed his outspoken espousal of unfashionable positions to his "bohemian" upbringing and his iconoclastic personality, in keeping with his informal dress and gypsy penchant for travel. Many of them probably assumed he would grow out of it in time.

His uncompromising posture found analogous bolsters in the complex Argentine political environment. Perón's Machiavellian exercise of power illuminated a formula for effecting radical political change *in spite of* the powerful opposition of a conservative oligarchy, the Catholic clergy, and sectors of the armed forces. Observing Perón, Ernesto could see at work a political master who more often than not showed he could manipulate the magic keys to political success: knowing the mood of the people, knowing who his real friends and enemies were—and knowing when to act. The lesson was clear: What was required to make political headway in a place such as Argentina was strong leadership and a willingness to use force to meet one's goals.

Given his own nationalistic viewpoints, Perón's attempt to strengthen Argentina's political and economic sovereignty must have held some appeal for Ernesto. In this sense, his passion for Nehru's 1946 book *The Discovery of India* seems especially instructive. He read Nehru's book with great interest, underlining and scribbling comments about passages he found thought-provoking, and talked about the book admiringly to his friends.

Perón and Nehru may seem strange bedfellows, for their leadership styles were very different, but some close parallels existed between Nehru's effort to "decolonize" India and Perón's program to make Argentina economically self-sufficient. Their concerns as national leaders also highlighted a dependency syndrome common to underdeveloped nations, whether among the European colonial dominions in Asia and Africa, or in the neocolonial American domination of certain Latin American nations. In the formation of Ernesto's worldview, Perón and Nehru were impressive figures. Although his own ideology would acquire radical new dimensions, their influence undoubtedly helped inform his future calls for the "Third World" to liberate itself from capitalist imperialism, to undergo industrialization quickly, and for strong and charismatic leaders to oversee the revolutionary processes of change.

Both Perón and Nehru promoted the rapid industrialization of their overwhelmingly agrarian nations as an essential step in gaining fuller independence from the powerful countries—principally Great Britain and the United States—upon whom their economic fortunes rose and fell. Both India and Argentina were hugely reliant on foreign imports, particularly manufactured goods, and faced capricious export markets for their raw materials. Neither had well-developed industrial bases of their own.

Nehru had written: "In the context of the modern world, no country can be politically and economically independent, even within the framework of international interdependence, unless it is highly industrialized and has developed its power resources to the utmost."

This same concept was echoed in Perón's platform of "social justice, economic independence and political sovereignty" for Argentina at a time when foreign interests—in particular British, but increasingly American as well—still held significant monopolies in the country's utilities, transportation, and railroad sectors, and supplied most of its manufactured goods. In his first year in office, Perón had embarked on an ambitious "import-substitution" program of industrial expansion. And in 1947, when he moved to nationalize foreign-owned utilities and railroads and to pay off the country's foreign debt, it was Argentina's "economic independence" that was at stake.

Perón had a fertile field to sow. In Argentina, there was widespread distrust of foreign capital interests, arising from the economic hardships caused by repeated price-drops for Argentine agricultural exports during the global Depression of the late 1920s and early '30s, during both world wars, and caused by the proven inadequacy of local industries to compensate in the face of rising prices of industrial imports. The ignominious 1933 Roca-Runciman Pact, renewed in 1936, had forced Argentina to buy British goods and grant concessions to British investors in return for Britain's continuing purchase of Argentine wheat, wool, and beef. Foreign capital investment had become increasingly symbolic of foreign interference and was a rallying point for Argentine nationalist sentiments.

"Yankee" interference had reached onerous heights in the period leading up to the 1946 general election in which Spruille Braden, briefly the American ambassador to Buenos Aires, and then assistant secretary of state for Latin America, openly campaigned against Perón. With characteristic panache, Perón had turned the American's interference around to his favor, appealing to nationalist sentiments with counterslogans suggesting that the election was not between Argentines at all, but a case of "Braden or Perón."

Many Argentines took a caustic attitude when the Truman administration began lobbying for a hemispheric "mutual defense treaty" between the United States and its Latin American neighbors. Nevertheless, such a treaty, adhering to the recently announced "Truman Doctrine" outlining Washington's adoption of a hard-line global commitment to contain Soviet Communism, was signed by the hemisphere's governments at Rio de Janeiro in 1948 amid speeches extolling the new fraternal concept of pan-Americanism. Latin American Communists denounced the new U.S.-sponsored "brotherhood" as a warmed-over update of the old Monroe Doctrine, handing Latin America over to the colonialist interests of "Wall Street and the 'capitalist monopolies.'" In effect, the Rio Treaty gave Washington the right to intervene militarily in neighboring states "to support free peoples who are resisting attempted subjugation by armed minorities or by outside pressures." Ernesto took note of the Rio conference and also wrote an entry for *"panamericanismo"* in his notebooks, quoting a pious, God-invoking definition given by one of the conference delegates.

During the early 1950s, Ernesto's strongest political emotion was a deep-seated hostility toward the United States, according to Dolores Moyano. "In his eyes, the twin evils in Latin America were the native oligarchies and the United States. The only things he liked about this country were its poets and novelists; I never heard him say one good thing about anything else. He would disconcert both nationalists and Communists by being anti-American without subscribing to either of their points of view. With much bad luck, since my mother was American, I would often rally to the defense of the United States. I was never able to convince him that United States foreign policy was, more often than not, the bumbling creature of ignorance and error rather than the well-designed strategy of a sinister cabal. He was convinced of the dark princes of evil who directed every United States move abroad."

In the Latin America of the postwar years, there was plenty of available evidence to nurture such perceptions. Ernesto was coming of age at a time when the United States was at an imperial apogee, aggressively pursuing its own combined economic and strategic interests in the region with little regard to local social or political reform. In the anti-Communist atmosphere of the Cold War, U.S. support of right-wing military dictatorships—Anastasio Somoza in Nicaragua, Rafael Trujillo in the Dominican Republic, Manuel Odría in Peru, and Marcos Pérez Jiménez in Venezuela—at the expense of outspoken nationalists or left-wing regimes, was rationalized in the name of national security.

While Soviet expansion in postwar Europe was the central focus of alarm in Washington, by late 1950, the new Central Intelligence Agency (CIA) felt sufficient concern about the hemispheric threat posed by Communism to elaborate a secret assessment entitled *Soviet Capabilities and Intentions in Latin America*. "With respect to Latin America," the report reads, "the objective of the USSR must be presumed to be to reduce support of the US as greatly as possible until the sovietization of the area becomes possible and its resources become available directly to augment Soviet strength."

The CIA was especially concerned about the potential for coordination between pro-Soviet Latin Communist parties and Moscow to conduct sabotage and civil unrest in the event of a war breaking out between the two superpowers. It noted the potential for Communist exploitation of existing anti-American sentiments, commenting that already in Argentina "the Communists, playing upon Argentine isolationism, found a ready response among non-Communists to their incitement against the sending of Argentine troops to Korea," while in Cuba, a recent incident in which American servicemen urinated on a statue of the Cuban nationalist hero José Martí had been "magnified" by local Communists, "thereby seriously, if temporarily, lowering popular esteem of the US." The CIA also warned that the Communists could exploit "liberal democratic aversion to dictatorial rulers" in some nations, straining relations between their countries and dictatorships friendly to Washington.

Ernesto was in his fourth year of medical school when, citing his own Communist threat, Perón began cracking down on the left. During the purge, a Córdoba acquaintance his own age, Fernando Barral, was arrested for "Communist agitation" and held in police custody for seven months. Barral was a Spanish Republican exile whose father, a famous sculptor, had been killed while defending Madrid. As a foreign national, he was to be deported back to an uncertain fate in Franco's Spain, but after the Argentine Communist party secured Hungary's offer to receive him as a political exile, he was allowed to go there instead.

Except for random encounters, Barral and Ernesto had not had much contact since the Guevaras' move to Buenos Aires. Barral had meanwhile fallen in love with Ernesto's cousin, La Negrita Córdova Iturburu. Although his romantic feelings were unrequited, Barral and La Negrita were close friends. Perhaps Ernesto viewed Barral as a rival for his cousin's affections; perhaps he simply disliked Barral's "dogmatism," a speculation later made by Barral himself. Whatever the case, throughout Barral's imprisonment, Ernesto remained unmoved. He neither visited him in prison nor (in a repeat performance of his behavior during Alberto Granado's detention) joined the efforts to secure his release.

One friend recalled Ernesto advising his maids to vote for Perón because his policies favored their "social class." He also used the Peronist system to his own advantage when it behooved him. According to his cousin Mario Saravia, Ernesto joined a Peronist youth organization on campus in order to use its extensive library facilities and check out books otherwise unavailable to him. Another time, on the suggestion, half in jest, of Tatiana Quiroga, prior to an ambitious trip through Latin America he was planning, he drafted a letter to Perón's gift-giving wife, Evita, asking her for "a jeep." Tatiana helped him write it, and remembers that they had fun doing it, but no reply ever came from Argentina's flamboyant First Lady.

IV

By his early twenties, Ernesto stood out socially as an attractive oddball whom others found difficult to categorize. Indeed, he defied definition. Eccentric in his appearance, he was nonethless oblivious to ridicule. At a time when youths of his social class dressed impeccably in ties, blazers, pressed slacks, and polished shoes to avoid the dreaded stigma of being misidentified as a working-class immigrant's son, he wore grimy windbreakers and odd-fitting, old-fashioned shoes that he bought at remainder sales.

By his early twenties, Ernesto had perfected this untended image. As Dolores Moyano recalled, Ernesto's sloppiness was a favorite topic of conversation among her friends.

"One has to know the mentality of the provincial oligarchy to appreciate the remarkable effect of Ernesto's appearance. Terribly clothes-conscious, all the boys we knew put a great deal of effort and money into obtaining the latest fads: cowboy boots, blue jeans, Italian shirts, British pullovers, etc., back then in the early fifties. Ernesto's favorite piece of clothing in those days was a nylon shirt, originally white but gray from use, which he constantly wore and called La Semanera, claiming he washed it once a week. His trousers would be wide, floppy, and once, I recall, held up by a piece of clothesline. With Ernesto's appearance into a party, all conversation would cease, while everyone tried to look nonchalant and unimpressed. Ernesto, enjoying himself hugely and perfectly aware of the sensation he was creating, would be in complete command."

Ernesto was hopelessly tone-deaf and learned to dance only when his friends taught him the steps and pacing of the beat. At the beginning of each dance, he would ask which dance-tune it was, whether a tango, waltz, or mambo. Once informed, he asked girls out to dance, and, mentally counting out the tune's supposed beat to keep pace, clumsily guided them around the dance floor.

"Dancing didn't interest him in the slightest," recalled his close friend Carlitos Figueroa, explaining that in those days Ernesto was a "shameless *caradura,*" an extroverted and relentless seducer of girls, and the only reason he danced was to get close to his prey. He had few inhibitions about trying to seduce an available-seeming woman, and was unconcerned by appearances or age differences.

Only a few of his closest male friends and relatives were privy to these dalliances. According to his cousin Mario Saravia, Ernesto "would do *anything* for a plate of food." As an example, he cited Ernesto's liaison with his family maid, a Bolivian Indian woman in her late thirties named Sabina Portugal, with whom Ernesto slept regularly in Buenos Aires. "She was the ugliest woman I have ever seen," said Saravia. "But when she invited him, he would go to her room."

Ernesto was informal with his parents, calling them affectionately "vieja" and "viejo," but was equally self-deprecating when it came to himself. His new nickname, "El Chancho" (The Pig), was a particular source of enjoyment because of the outraged reaction it elicited from his socially sensitive father. When Guevara Lynch discovered that Carlos Figueroa had been its originator, he stormed at him, furious over what he perceived as a slight to the family honor.

In spite of or possibly because of his father's displeasure, Ernesto kept up the nickname and, in the rugby magazine *Tackle* he founded and edited for the eleven issues it survived, signed his articles "Chang-Cho." Written in a quickly paced sportswriter's jargon, peppered with rugby Anglicizations, Ernesto's reviews mercilessly analyzed the games played.

While Ernesto's relationship with his father was combative, with his mother he had become even more solicitous, due to her ill health. In 1946 she had been diagnosed as having breast cancer and undergone a mastectomy, and he remained concerned about a resurgence of the disease. Their "special relationship" was noticed by family friends. To some, their union was so special that it excluded the other children, and several friends spoke sympathetically about the effect it had on Roberto in particular. Physically fitter and two years younger than Ernesto, Roberto eventually excelled at rugby, but within the family his own triumphs were overshadowed by his older brother's, who was always seen as "conquering" his asthma. According to family relatives, it took Roberto many years to overcome the resentment he had felt toward Ernesto since childhood.

Everyone in the family simply ignored the fact that Guevara Lynch and Celia were not sleeping together. In time, the family's friends became used to seeing Guevara Lynch come in late and, oblivious to whatever else was going on around him, flop himself down on the sofa and go to sleep. Guevara Lynch's other eccentricities made this behavior seem natural.

In Buenos Aires, his penchant for phobias and superstitions became accentuated. He could not leave the house without intentionally forgetting something, like his keys, in order to come back. It was "bad luck" if he didn't. This became an obsessive ritual. If anyone said "snake" around the family table, he would immediately say "wild boar," the "countervenom" to the bad luck ushered in by the uttered word.

Celia, meanwhile, continued to run her house like a salon. The dinner table was her throne. Here she sat for endless hours playing solitaire, which—like the cigarettes she habitually smoked—she had become addicted to, but she was always ready to receive some young person for conversation or to dispense advice.

As for the practicalities of everyday life, Celia was above the fray. She was clueless about what went on inside the kitchen and, on her cook's days off, threw together meals with whatever happened to be in the refrigerator, with no notion of measurements or recipes. With true aplomb, she was unperturbed when she found nothing there.

Visitors invariably noted the absence of furniture, adornments, or paintings in the house, but were struck by the plethora of books, shelved and stacked everywhere. There were other peculiarities: The kitchen stove had a perennial short-circuit, and the walls were "live," giving off electrical shocks to incautious newcomers who leaned against them.

Just as Ernesto found the space and quiet he needed to study at Beatriz's apartment or in the university library, his father soon found some refuge in a rented studio on nearby Calle Paraguay. He had found a new business partner, and together they set up a combination real estate agency and building-contracting firm called "Guevara Lynch y Verbruch." Before long, they had found some business around the city, but, as always with Guevara Lynch, it was touch-and-go.*

Although the studio had a bedroom, Guevara Lynch had outfitted it with desks and architect's drawing tables, and so he continued sleeping on the living room sofa at Calle Araoz or else at his sister Beatriz's apartment.

Inevitably, however, with Calle Araoz so crowded, his studio also became a spillover study for the Guevara youngsters and their friends. "El Viejo" Guevara had extra keys made, and his children and their friends came and went as they pleased. Ernesto used it to cram for his medical school exams, as did Roberto, who went into law school. Celia, Ana Maria, and her boyfriend Carlos Lino, who all studied architecture, regularly worked on their projects there, and for a time it also served as the editorial offices of the short-lived rugby review, *Tackle*.

For money, which was always short, Ernesto embarked on a series of commercial schemes that were as impractical as they were inventive. These enterprises usually involved his old friend Carlitos Figueroa, who was now studying law in Buenos Aires and, like him, forever in search of cash to fill his pockets. Their first venture was Ernesto's inspiration. He had decided that the locust insecticide Gamexane would make a good domestic roach-killer. After testing it in the neighborhood with good results, he decided to go into industrial production. And so, together with Figueroa and a patient of Dr. Pisani's, he began packaging boxes of the stuff, mixed with talcum powder, in the garage of his home.

He wanted to give it a registered trademark and came up with "Al Capone," but was advised he needed authorization by the Capone family to use the name. His next choice was "Atila," for Attila the Hun, the idea being that it would "kill everything in its path," but there was already a product with this name. In the end, he decided on "Vendaval," which in Spanish

---

*Guevara Lynch seemed especially damned when it came to choosing partners, for once their business was up and running, Verbruch abandoned him after going through a personal tragedy and succumbing to a deep, lasting depression. Afterward, Guevara Lynch found another partner, Rossi, to work with. Their company survived, with ups and downs, until the right-wing military coup in 1976 forced Guevara Lynch to flee the country.

means a strong southerly gale, and he acquired a patent for it. Enthused by his son's progress, Guevara Lynch offered to introduce him to potential investors, but Ernesto, who by now had a jaundiced view of his father's business partners, declined, telling him: "Old man, do you really believe I'd allow myself to be swallowed up by your friends?"

His family put up with Ernesto's Vendaval factory as long as they could, but it gave off a horrible and pervasive stench. "A nauseous smell expanded throughout the house," said his father. "Everything we ate tasted to us like Gamexane; but Ernesto, imperturbable, continued his work." The end came soon enough, however, when first his helpers and then Ernesto himself began feeling sick, and the business was abandoned.

The next business scheme was "El Gordo" Figueroa's brainstorm. It involved buying a lot of shoes cheaply at a wholesale auction, then selling them door-to-door at higher prices. It seemed like a good idea, but after successfully bidding for a lot of shoes—sight unseen—they discovered they had bought a great pile of remaindered odd and ends, many of them mismatched. After sorting them out, they managed to find enough matching pairs to sell. When they had sold these, they then went out selling the shoes that merely *resembled* each other.

Finally, they were left with a series of right- and left-footed shoes with no pairs at all and sold one shoe to a one-legged man who lived down the street. This gave rise to the joking suggestion by family and friends that they should track down as many one-legged people as they could find and sell off the rest. Memories of the episode endured because for some time afterward Ernesto himself—no doubt relishing the stares his appearance provoked—wore a pair of the unsold shoes, each one a different color.

Apart from his money-making enterprises, Ernesto began conducting medical research experiments at home. For a time, he kept on his bedroom balcony caged rabbits and guinea pigs, which he injected with cancer-causing agents. He also practiced, although with less lethal ingredients, on his friends. Carlos Figueroa innocently allowed himself to be experimentally injected by Ernesto one day, and when he swelled up in reaction to the shot, Ernesto happily exclaimed, "That was the reaction I was expecting!," then gave him another injection to alleviate the symptoms.

A medical school classmate of Ernesto's recalled a trip he and Ernesto made in the Buenos Aires underground train carrying an amputated human foot. They had cadged it from assistants at the anatomy theater in order to "practice" on it at home, then wrapped it in newspaper for the metro journey. Soon, they were receiving terrified looks from commuters who had noticed what the two were trying to conceal in their poorly wrapped package. Ernesto relished the spectacle of the other passengers' mortified reactions, and by the time they arrived home he was convulsed with laughter.

In such ways, the high jinks of Ernesto's childhood found a new focus in the opportunities provided by his medical studies and sports activities, and on his hitchhiking trips. For a while, his new sport of gliding, which he took up on weekends at an airfield on Buenos Aires's outskirts with his free-spirited uncle, Jorge de la Serna, also fulfilled some of his urge to test the unknown.*

It was on Ernesto's travels away from home, however, that he experienced the most freedom. On many of his jaunts by thumb, usually back to Córdoba, his frequent companion was Carlitos Figueroa. The normally ten-hour car journey would take them seventy-two, usually on the backs of trucks, and they sometimes had to earn their way by unloading truck cargos.

These trips afforded real pleasure to Ernesto, and he longed to extend his horizons farther. The open road beckoned. On January 1, 1950, at the end of his third year in medical school, he took off on a bicycle outfitted with a small Italian Cucchiolo engine, heading into Argentina's interior, on his first real trip alone.

Before leaving, he hammed it up for a photograph. It shows him seated on his bike, legs poised on the ground and hands gripping the handlebars as if at the starting line of a race, wearing a cap, sunglasses, and a leather bomber's jacket. A spare bicycle tire is looped over his neck and shoulder like a *pistolero*'s bandolier.

He headed toward Córdoba. From there, he planned to go to San Francisco del Chañar, 150 kilometers (about 95 miles) farther north, where Alberto Granado was now working at a leprosarium and running a pharmacy on the side.

He set off from home in the evening, first using his little motor to get himself quickly out of the city, and then he began pedaling. Before long, a bicyclist caught up with him, and they cycled together until morning. Passing through Pilar, a town outside Buenos Aires that he had set as his first goal, and which some "well-intentioned tongues" at home had predicted would mark the end of his adventure, he "felt the first happiness of one who triumphs." He was on his way.

*Jorge was Celia's younger brother and a colorful personality, given to wandering around the country as a kind of solitary adventurer. He was much loved by the family—and a favorite of Ernesto's—but quite mad, and had to be institutionalized at least once in a psychiatric hospital, from which he eventually emerged with a shaven head and dressed entirely in leather.

V

Ernesto's journey broke new ground for him in two activities that were to become lifelong rituals: traveling and writing a diary. For the first time in his life he felt inspired to keep a running account of his day-to-day life.* He was twenty-two years old.

On the second night he reached his birthplace of Rosario, and by the next evening, "forty-one hours and seventeen minutes" after setting out, he reached the Granado family's home in Córdoba. Along the way, he had adventures. First, after allowing himself to be pulled along by a car at sixty kilometers an hour, his rear tire burst and he ended up in a roadside heap, awakening a *linyera,* or hobo, who happened to be sleeping there. They struck up a conversation, and the hobo companionably prepared an infusion of mate "with enough sugar in it to sweeten up a spinster." (Ernesto preferred his mate bitter.)

Ernesto spent several days in Córdoba visiting friends, and then took off with Alberto's brothers, Tomás and Gregorio, to camp at a waterfall north of the city, where they had another string of boyish adventures: rock-climbing, diving from great heights into shallow pools of water, and nearly getting swept away by a flash flood.

Gregorio and Tomás returned to Córdoba, and Ernesto went on to join Alberto at the José J. Puente leprosarium, on the outskirts of San Francisco del Chañar. With Alberto investigating the immunological susceptibilities of lepers, and Ernesto involved in allergy research at the Clínica Pisani, the two now had more in common than rugby and books. To Granado, the world of medical research "was a kind of conductive thread for us both, in what seemed at the time would be our future."

Greatly interested in Alberto's work, Ernesto escorted him on his rounds with his leprosy patients. But they soon had a confrontation. It arose over Alberto's treatment of a leprosy patient, a pretty young girl named Yolanda who so far exhibited the dreaded leprosy symptoms—large spots with deadened flesh—only on her back. Granado knew that every time a new doctor arrived, unaware of the seriousness of her case, the girl tried to convince him of the injustice that was being committed by having her interned. "Ernesto was no exception to this rule, and visibly impressed by the beauty of the girl and the pathetic presentation of her case, he came to see me. Soon an argument erupted between the two of us."

---

*After Che's death, this diary was discovered by his father, who transcribed it and included it in his memoir, *Mi Hijo el Che* (My Son Che). Except for some illegible sections, he said, the published version was entirely faithful to the original.

Ernesto argued that more care should be taken in the decisions leading to the internment and isolation of the sick. Alberto tried to explain that
the girl's case was a desperate one, and highly contagious. He proved his
point by jabbing a long hypodermic needle into the dead flesh of the unsuspecting girl's back. The girl didn't feel it. "I looked triumphantly at Ernesto,
but the look he gave me froze the smile. The future 'Che' ordered me
brusquely: 'Mía!, tell her to go!' And when the patient had left [the room],
I saw a contained rage reflected in the face of my friend. . . . Until that
moment I had never seen him like this and I had to withstand a storm of
reproaches. 'Petiso,' he told me, 'I never thought you could lose your sensi-
tivity to such an extent. You have fooled that young girl just to show off
your knowledge!'" Finally, after more explanations by Granado, the two
friends made up, and the incident was over, if never forgotten.

After several days at the leprosarium, Ernesto was anxious to be off
again. By now, he had decided to extend his journey even farther, "with the
pretentious intention" of reaching Argentina's remote and little-traveled
northern and westernmost provinces, and he convinced Alberto, who owned
a motorcycle, to accompany him on the first leg of the trip.

The two friends made their departure, Petiso pulling Pelao behind his
own motorcycle by a rope. The rope kept breaking, and after some distance
they agreed it was better if Ernesto continued on alone. Alberto turned back
to San Francisco del Chañar, and Ernesto wrote: "We gave each other a not
very effusive hug, as between two *machitos,* and I watched him disappear
like a knight on his bike, saying good-bye with his hand."

Crossing the "silver-dyed land" of the Salinas Grandes, the Argentine
Sahara, without problems, Ernesto arrived in Loreto, a small town where
the local police put him up for the night. Discovering he was a medical
student, they urged him to stay on and become the town's only doctor. Nothing could have been further from his mind at that moment, and the next
day he hit the road again.

In Santiago del Estero, the provincial capital, a local correspondent for
a Tucumán daily interviewed him—"The first article about me in my life,"
Ernesto wrote exultantly—then he headed toward Tucumán, the next city
north. On the way, while repairing his umpteenth tire puncture, he met
another itinerant *linyera,* and they fell into conversation.

"This man was coming from the cotton harvest in the Chaco and, after
vagabonding awhile, thought to go to the grape harvest in San Juan. Discovering my plan to travel through several provinces and after realizing that
my feat was purely recreational, he grabbed his head with a desperate air:
'Mama mía, all that effort for nothing?'"

Ernesto could not have adequately explained to the hobo what he hoped to gain from his travels, apart from repeating that he wanted to see more of his own country. But the man's remark made him more reflective. In his journal, until now a rendition of facts and glib description laced with anecdotes, he began examining himself and his feelings more deeply.

Finding himself in a forested region north of Tucumán on the road to Salta, he halted and got off his bike to walk into the dense foliage, and he experienced a kind of rapture at the natural world surrounding him. Afterward he wrote: "I realize that something that was growing inside of me for some time . . . has matured: and it is the hate of civilization, the absurd image of people moving like *locos* to the rhythm of that tremendous noise that seems to me like the hateful antithesis of peace."

Later that same day, he met a motorcyclist riding a brand-new Harley-Davidson, who offered to pull him on a rope. Remembering his recent mishaps, he declined, but he and the motorcyclist shared some coffee before going on their separate ways. A few hours later, arriving in the next town, he saw a truck unloading the same Harley-Davidson and was informed that its driver had been killed. The incident, and his own close escape from the same fate, provoked a new bout of introspection.

"The death of this motorcyclist doesn't have the impact to touch the nerve endings of the multitudes, but the knowledge that a man goes look- ing for danger without even the vaguest of heroic intentions that bring about a public deed, and can die at a bend in the road without witnesses, makes this unknown adventurer seem possessed of a vague suicidal 'fervor.'"

At Salta, Ernesto presented himself at the hospital as a medical student and asked for a place to sleep. Allotted the seat of a truck, he "slept like a king" until being roused by the driver early the next morning. After waiting out a torrential rain, he headed off through a beautiful green land- scape of dripping wet foliage towards Jujuy, Argentina's northernmost city.

In Jujuy, "anxious to know the value of the province's hospitality," he made his way to the local hospital, where he once again made use of his medical "credentials" to obtain a bed. He was granted one, but only after paying his way by picking a complaining little Indian boy's head clean of lice.

It was as far north as he would go on this trip. He had wanted to go all the way to the rugged frontier with Bolivia, but as he wrote his father, "several flooding rivers and an active volcano are fucking up travel [in the area]." Also, his fourth term of medical school was due to begin in a few weeks' time.

Turning back to Salta, he reappeared at the hospital and was asked by the staff what he had seen on his journey. The query provoked him to thoughtful reflection. "[I]n truth, what *do* I see? At least I am not nourished in the same ways as the tourists, and I find it strange to find, on the tourist brochures of Jujuy, for example, the Altar of the Fatherland, the cathedral where the national ensign was blessed, the jewel of the pulpit and the miraculous little virgin of Río Blanco and Pompeii. . . . No, one doesn't come to know a country or find an interpretation of life in this way. That is a luxurious facade, while its [true] soul is reflected in the sick of the hospitals, the detainees in the police stations or the anxious passersby one gets to know, as the Río Grande shows the turbulence of its swollen level from underneath."

For the first time in his adult life, Ernesto had witnessed the harsh duality of his country by crossing the divide from its transported European culture, which was also *his,* and plunging into its ignored, backward, *indigenous* heartland. For Ernesto, the iconography of modern Argentine nationhood was merely a superficial veneer, "a luxurious facade" under which the country's true "soul" lay; and that soul was rotten and diseased.

The injustice of the lives of the socially marginalized people he had befriended along his journey—lepers, hobos, detainees, hospital patients— bore witness to the submerged "turbulence" of the region that lay "underneath" the "Río Grande." This enigmatic reference to the Río Grande—not among the rivers he crossed on his journey—may be significant, for it appears to refer to the river that has long been a politically symbolic dividing line between the rich North and poor South along the U.S.-Mexican border. If so, this is an early glimmering of an idea that would come to obsess him: that the United States, as an expression of neocolonial exploitation, was ultimately to blame for perpetuating the sorry state of affairs he saw around him.

In Argentina's northern provinces, the vast uninhabited land gave way to a few old cities, still run by a handful of oligarchic landowning families of immense wealth and privilege. For centuries they and the colonial structures their forefathers erected had coexisted alongside a faceless "alien" indigenous majority over which they held power. It was the region of strongmen such as Catamarca's Senator Robustiano Patrón Costas, the despotic sugar mill owner who, as the handpicked successor of President Castillo, had been prevented from taking office by the Perón-backed army coup of 1943.

Justifying that coup years later, Perón accused Patrón Costas of being an "exploiter" who ran his sugar mill like a "feudal estate," the representative of an "inconceivable" system that had to be done away with if Argentina was to take its place in the modern age. Describing Patrón Costas, one of Perón's biographers echoed him, writing: "His mills flourished on something akin to slave labour that was fortunate if it did not succumb to the leprosy, the malaria, the trachoma, the tuberculosis and the mange that were endemic in the senator's primitive home base."

It was from such areas that the Argentine Indians, commonly referred to as *coyas,* and the mixed-blood *cabezitas negras* (little black heads) fled in steadily increasing numbers, pouring into the cities in search of work and setting up shantytowns like the one in front of the Guevaras' home in Córdoba. From their ranks came domestic servants such as "La Negra" Cabrera and Sabina Portugal, and the cheap labor force for Argentina's new industries and public works projects. Theirs was the despised social class Perón had appealed to when he called upon the nation to incorporate the *descamisados,* whose rude presence and noisome clamor so irritated the white elites in their once-exclusive metropolitan idylls. For the first time, these people were not servants or symbols to Ernesto; he had traveled in their midst.

Ernesto returned to Buenos Aires in time for the start of the school term. In his six weeks on the road, he had traveled through twelve provinces and covered over four thousand kilometers. He took his little bicycle engine back to the Amerimex company, where he had bought it, for an overhaul. When they learned the distance he had covered on the engine, the delighted management proposed he do an advertisement; in exchange they would fix his engine free of charge.

As agreed, he wrote a letter outlining his recent odyssey and lauding the company's Cucchiolo engine that had carried him, saying: "It has functioned perfectly during my extensive tour, and I have noted only that toward the end it lost compression, the reason for which I send it to you for repair."

VI

That year, his fourth at medical school, Ernesto passed five more exams toward his degree and continued his work at the Clínica Pisani. He also kept up his rugby-playing and his gliding lessons with his uncle Jorge.

But the hunger to explore the world had awakened in him, and following the success of his Argentine "raid," as he called it, he began concocting new travel plans. Then, in October, just before the end of the term, something new happened to him. For the first time in his life, he fell in love.

Carmen, one of the Gónzalez Aguilar daughters, was to be married, and the entire Guevara clan traveled to Córdoba to attend the wedding. At the party, he met sixteen-year-old María del Carmen "Chichina" Ferreyra, the beautiful daughter of one of Córdoba's oldest and wealthiest families. Although they had previously known one another, Chichina had been only a little girl when Ernesto had lived in Córdoba. She was still only sixteen but had suddenly blossomed into a highly desirable young woman, a brunette with soft white skin and full lips, and the impression she made on Ernesto was, according to the eyewitness Pepe Aguilar, "like a lighting bolt."

In Chichina's own words, the attraction was mutual. She was fascinated by what she called "his obstinate physique" and his playful, unsolemn character. "His messiness in his dress made us laugh and was a little embarrassing at the same time. . . . We were so sophisticated that Ernesto seemed an opprobrium. He accepted our jokes immutably."

For Ernesto, at least, the ensuing romance was serious. By all accounts, although Chichina was very young, she was not all feminine frippery but was extremely bright and imaginative, and Ernesto apparently became convinced she was the woman of his life.

It was almost a fairy-tale romance. While Ernesto was from a family of pauperized aristocrats, Chichina was blue-blooded Argentine gentry, heiress to the Ferreyra family empire, the Malagueño lime quarry and factory complex, one of the Córdoba region's few industries at the time. In town, the Ferreyras owned an imposing, French-built château, the Palacio Ferreyra, on enclosed parklike grounds at the foot of Avenida Chacabuco. Built at the turn of the century, it was the family seat where Chichina's grandmother, matriarch of the Ferreyra clan, lived. Chichina and her parents lived in another large residence nearby, only two blocks from the Guevaras' old home. Just outside Córdoba, they owned a huge *estancia* called Malagueño, where the family summered.

Malagueño's two-thousand-hectare spread, wrote Dolores Moyano, "included two polo fields, Arabian stallions, and a feudal village of workers for the family's limestone quarries. The family visited the village church every Sunday for Mass, worshipping in a separate alcove to the right of the altar with its own separate entrance and private communion rail, away from the mass of workers. In many ways, Malagueño exemplified everything Ernesto despised. Yet, unpredictable as always, Ernesto had fallen madly in love with the princess of this little empire, my cousin Chichina Ferreyra, an extraordinarily beautiful and charming girl, who, to the dismay of her parents, was equally fascinated by Ernesto."

Their two families were already loosely acquainted during the Guevara family's Córdoba years through Guevara Lynch's professional contacts and his children's friendships.* Whatever they felt about Ernesto's suitability for their daughter, Chichina's parents didn't reject him from the outset. At first, they found him endearingly eccentric and precocious. Pepe Aguilar, who witnessed their courtship, remembered the Ferreyras' amusement at Ernesto's sloppy appearance and his informality, but noticed that when he talked of literature, history, or philosophy, or told anecdotes from his travels, they listened attentively.

If the Ferreyras were unperturbed by Ernesto's originality and his wanderlust, the reason was that they themselves were a colorful bunch. Pepe Aguilar described them as a unique and compelling family whose members were cultured, worldly, and sensitive, and who stuck out notably in a conservative, provincial society that idolized them as much as it envied them. Chichina's adventurous father had traveled through the Amazon on a journey that even today would be dangerous. They had participated in car races when there were almost no roads and piloted the first planes under the watchful recommendation of the grandmother who, according to the family anecdote, urged them to "fly low." During the Second World War, as he was on his way to join up in the ranks of General de Gaulle, one of Chichina's uncles had died on board a ship sunk by the Germans.

For Ernesto, the "Ferreyra atmosphere" must have been extremely stimulating—and challenging. He was soon making regular trips back to Córdoba to see Chichina. During 1951, he became a frequent visitor to the Ferreyras' home in the city and to Malagueño, joining Chichina and her large group of friends who assembled there.

Of all her relatives, it was Chichina's eccentric uncle Martín who, according to her friends, "most liked" Ernesto. *Tío* Martín was an elderly recluse who lived at Malagueño, where he bred Arabian stud horses, and who never left the *estancia* grounds. He also stood out for having steadfastly supported Nazi Germany during the Second World War, while the rest of the clan were staunch supporters of the Allied forces. He was a night owl, an accomplished classical pianist, and he played for Ernesto, Chichina, and their friends as they talked and danced, often until dawn.

But, altogether too soon, Ernesto was trying to convince Chichina to marry him and, for their honeymoon, travel with him throughout South

*Chichina and Dolores Moyano were first cousins, and Dolores's architect father knew Guevara Lynch through his building work. The Ferreyras were also intermarried with the illustrious Roca family, whose son Gustavo was a friend of Ernesto's. His father, one of the University Reform's founders, was another eminent Córdoba architect of Guevara Lynch's acquaintance. And Tatiana Quiroga, a childhood friend of both the Ferreyras and Guevaras, was dating Chichina's first cousin Jaime "Jimmy" Roca, whom she would later marry.

America in a *"casa rodante,"* a motor caravan. "This was when the conflicts arose," said Pepe Aguilar. "Chichina was only sixteen years old and she was undecided; nor did her parents view this project with kindly eyes."

After he proposed, Ernesto's presence began to take on a subversive quality among the Ferreyra clan. "Family opposition to him was fierce," recalled Dolores Moyano. "At any social gathering, the directness, the candor, the mocking quality of his opinions made his presence dangerous. When Ernesto came to dinner at my family's, we would wait for the worst to happen with a mixture of dread and delight."

Tatiana Quiroga portrayed Ernesto as a "hippyish and sickly" figure who appeared to seat himself at formal Ferreyra family dinners—"with his asthma and his permanent inhaler . . . and wearing his horrifying dirty nylon shirt"—while his hosts watched in appalled silence. In her opinion, Ernesto was all too aware of the disapproval his appearance elicited, which provoked him to say outrageous things "so as not to feel so diminished."

The tensions reached a head one night at Malagueño during a dinner conversation about Winston Churchill, for which Dolores and Pepe Aguilar were both present. The Ferreyras were supremely Anglophilic, and in their home Churchill's name was invoked with reverence. As each elderly member of the family contributed his favorite anecdote of the man, recalled Dolores, Ernesto listened with undisguised amusement.

Finally, unable to contain himself, Ernesto leapt in, bluntly dismissing the venerated figure as just another "ratpack politician." Pepe Aguilar remembered the uncomfortable moment. "Horacio, Chichina's father, said: 'I can't put up with this,' and left the table. I looked at Ernesto thinking to myself that if anyone had to leave, it was us, but he merely smiled like a naughty child and began eating a lemon in bites, peel and all."

Chichina continued to see Ernesto, but secretly. Once, when she and her family traveled to Rosario to watch her father play in a polo match, Chichina arranged for Ernesto to join her there, concealed in another car with her girlfriends. While her father played, the two met clandestinely.

Chichina's devoutly religious mother, Lola, was aware of her daughter's feelings and had become so alarmed at the prospect of having Ernesto Guevara as her son-in-law that, according to Tatiana Quiroga, she made a vow to Argentina's patron saint, the Virgin of Catamarca. If Chichina broke the romance off, she would make a personal pilgrimage to the Virgin's distant shrine. (In the end, Lola did make her pilgrimage, but it turned into such an ordeal, with a prolonged breakdown in the hot desert, albeit in a chauffeur-driven car, that the journey itself became part of the enduring Ferreyra family folklore.)

At the end of school term in December 1950, Ernesto did not come to Córdoba to be close to Chichina as one might have expected. Instead, he obtained a male nurse's credential from the Ministry of Public Health and applied for work as a ship's "doctor" with the shipping line of the state petroleum company, Yacimientos Petrolíferos Fiscales, YPF.

On the surface, Ernesto's wanderlust would seem to have won out over the pull of Chichina's enchantments, but more likely his shipping out was a way of earning even more "manly credit" in her eyes, perhaps an attempt to compete with the dashing exploits of her revered father and uncles.

He left for Brazil on February 9, 1951, aboard the tanker *Anna G,* spending six weeks at sea. From then until June, his fourth and last voyage, he spent more time at sea than on dry land, traveling as far south as the Argentine port of Comodoro Rivadavia in Patagonia, and up South America's Atlantic coast to the British colony of Trinidad and Tobago, visiting Curaçao, British Guiana, Venezuela, and Brazilian ports along the way.

Chichina was never far from his mind. As soon as he was back in port he would call his sister Celia to ask if there were any letters from her. "He asked me to go running to the docks, and I ran and ran like he asked and I took him the letters," she remembered years later. "Once he asked me to run very fast because the ship was about to sail, and I ran very hard with the letter in my hand, but when I arrived the ship was pulling away from the shore, and he was there watching . . . until he saw me with the letter in my hand waving good-bye to him."

Meanwhile, to his friends and siblings, Ernesto nurtured the impression that he was living a romantic life, bringing them back exotic little souvenirs from his port calls and spinning tales of life on the high seas. And he did have some adventures. He told Carlos Figueroa about a fight he had in a Brazilian port with an American sailor—his sister Celia recalled it as having been with an Englishman, in Trinidad—an incident that seemed to confirm his latent animosity toward Anglo-Saxons. And he told Osvaldo Bidinost of conducting an appendectomy on a sailor at sea with a kitchen knife because the ship's only scalpel had already been used in a knife fight and embargoed as court evidence.

But in spite of his efforts to evoke its romance, the sailor's life did not live up to his expectations. He was frustrated that the petrol tankers on which he served spent too little time in port, giving him little time to see anything. In May, at the same time as classes began for his fifth term at the university, he made his last voyage and, when he returned in mid-June, put out to sea no more.

Ernesto obviously did a great deal of reading and thinking while at sea because when he returned to Buenos Aires, he gave his father a curious present. It was a notebook containing an autobiographical essay he had written and dedicated to him, entitled "Angustia (Eso Es Cierto)"—"Anguish (That's Right)." Laced with quotations from philosophers, it was headed with a quotation from Ibsen: "Education is the capacity to confront the situations posed by life."

Written in a enigmatic cloak of dense metaphors, "Anguish" is an introspective and existentialist sojourn into the causes and nature of a depression Ernesto experienced, and overcame, while at sea. The narrative is built around Ernesto's shore leave with some shipmates, in the tropical Caribbean port of Trinidad. As melodramatic as it is, it was Ernesto's first known attempt to write a short story. Although he prefaced it by stating that he had overcome his depression and could once again "smile optimistically and breathe in the air around him," in the story, he expresses deep loneliness and seems to be anguished over his relationship with Chichina, chafing against and wanting to free himself from the constraints of society.

"I fall on my knees, trying to find a solution, a truth, a motive. To think that I was born to love, that I wasn't born to sit permanently in front of a desk asking myself whether man is good, because I know man is good, since I have rubbed elbows with him in the country, in the factory, in the logging camp, in the mill, in the city. To think that he is physically healthy, that he has a spirit of cooperation, that he is young and vigorous like a billy goat but he sees himself excluded from the panorama: that is anguish. . . . To make a sterile sacrifice that does nothing to raise up a new life: that is anguish."

VII

By late June, Ernesto was back in school. He was now twenty-three and still had two years to go before obtaining his medical degree, but he no longer found the routine of classes and exams stimulating. A malaise had set in: he was lovelorn and restless. His wanderlust had been whetted by his motorbike journey and recent months at sea, but his hopes of marrying Chichina and carrying her off had stagnated.

Barely seventeen, Chichina was still very much her family's girl. The weighty combination of her parent's intractable opposition and her own youthful indecision had placed her relationship with Ernesto into an uneasy and unresolved holding pattern. This dilemma wasn't helped by the fact that they were apart.

Rescue came in the form of Alberto Granado, who had lately begun weaving grandiose plans to spend a year traveling the length of the South American continent. He had been talking about such a trip for years but done nothing about it, and his family had long since written "Alberto's trip" off as a harmless fantasy. But now, nearly thirty years old, Alberto realized that if he didn't do it now, he never would. He decided he needed a companion. Who else but El Pelao would throw everything up for a chance at an adventure like this? When Alberto asked him, Ernesto, "fed up with the Faculty of Medicine, with hospitals and exams," accepted on the spot.

During his October break from classes, Ernesto traveled to Córdoba to see Alberto and plot their trip. As he later lyrically evoked it, they sat under the grape arbor of Alberto's house, drank sweet mate, and fantasized about where they would go. "Along the roads of daydreams we reached remote countries, navigated on tropical seas and visited all of Asia. And suddenly . . . the question arose: And if we go to North America? To North America? How? With La Poderosa, man. And this was how the trip was decided, which forever after would be pursued along the same general lines it was planned: Improvisation."

La Poderosa was the motorcycle with which Alberto had unsuccessfully tried to pull Ernesto on his recent visit to San Francisco del Chañar. A vintage 500 cc Norton motorcycle, Alberto had nostalgically named it La Poderosa II (The Powerful II) in honor of an old bicycle of his youth, the Poderosa I.

On January 4, 1952, they set out on the road to the Atlantic coast and headed for the beach resort of Miramar, where Chichina was on holiday with a chaperone aunt and some friends. Ernesto wanted to say good-bye, and, as he rode on the back of the motorcycle, he carried a gift in his arms. It was a young, wriggly puppy, and he had given it an English name: "Come-back."

5

Escape to the North

I

Miramar, where Chichina was staying, was the final hurdle between them and the open road, for Ernesto was still in love and nagged by doubts about leaving her. Was he doing the right thing? Would she wait for him? He hoped to receive her assurances and had decided that if she accepted the puppy Come-back, it would be "a symbol of the ties" demanding his return.

At his side, Alberto was worried, too, lest his friend end their journey before it had even begun. Ernesto knew this, and wrote in his journal:* "Alberto saw the danger and imagined himself alone on the roads of America but didn't raise his voice. The struggle was between she and I."

Their planned two-day stay "stretched like rubber into eight," as Ernesto tried to extract Chichina's promise to wait for him. Holding hands with Chichina "in the enormous womb of a Buick," Ernesto asked her for the gold bracelet she wore on her wrist, as a talisman and keepsake on his journey. She refused. "Poor thing! Despite what they say, I know it wasn't the gold that weighed on her: her fingers tried to feel the love that led me to ask for the requested carats."

In the end, Ernesto decided to go. He had received neither the symbolic keepsake he demanded nor Chichina's benediction for his journey, but she had accepted Come-back over her girlfriends' sneers that the dog wasn't, as Ernesto claimed, a purebred German shepherd at all, but was an "ugly little mongrel." And she gave him fifteen American dollars to

---

*Notas de Viaje was the account Ernesto wrote following his journey, using extracts from his journal. It was transcribed and published posthumously by Che's Cuban widow, Aleida March. It is supposedly an authentic and unabridged version of the original. It was first published in English in 1995 as The Motorcycle Diaries.

buy her a scarf when he reached the United States. As a symbolic exchange of undying affection and loyalty on her part, it wasn't much, and it must have been with a sense of foreboding that Ernesto climbed back on La Poderosa on January 14.

II

The road was clear to begin their great trek, and the two gypsies sped off. It took them four more weeks, however, to leave Argentina. Before they were halfway across the settled pampa west of Bahía Blanca, Ernesto succumbed to fever and had to be hospitalized for several days; then they returned to the dust and pound of the trail.

By the time they reached the picturesque Lake District in the forested eastern slopes of the Andean cordillera, bordering Chile, their meager revenues had dwindled, and the two were becoming expert freeloaders, or *"mangueros motorizados"* (motorized scroungers), as Ernesto wryly defined it, throwing themselves on the mercy of unsuspecting roadside families in search of food and hospitality. It became a contest between Ernesto and Alberto to see who could outdo the other in the art of grubbing for survival.

Sometimes, rejected by their prospective hosts, they were forced to pitch their tent. But more often than not, they were successful, finding floor space for their cots in garages, kitchens, barns, and frequently police stations, where they shared cells and meals with an interesting variety of criminals. In the ski resort of Bariloche, a detained merchant marine deserter regaled them with his tall tales of the time he "bought" a fourteen-year-old Japanese girl, took her on the high seas with him, then gave her away when he tired of her.

Staying for a night in the barn of an Austrian family, Ernesto awoke to hear scratching and growling at the barn door, and saw a pair of glowing eyes peering in. Having been warned about the fierce local "Chilean pumas," he aimed the Smith & Wesson that Guevara Lynch had given him to take on the journey and fired a single shot. The noises stopped, and he went back to sleep. But in the morning he and Alberto awoke to discover that Ernesto had bagged not a puma, but their hosts' beloved Alsatian dog, Bobby. The two escaped, pushing La Poderosa downhill—for she wouldn't start— followed by their hosts' wails, imprecations, and insults.

In the Lake District, they hiked around lakes, climbed a peak—scaring themselves by nearly falling to their deaths—and used Guevara Lynch's revolver to poach a wild duck. At one particularly scenic lakeside spot they fantasized about returning together to set up a medical research center. Back in Bariloche's jailhouse after their jaunt, Ernesto opened a letter he had just received from Chichina informing him that she had decided *not* to wait for him. Outside, a storm raged. "I read and reread the incredible letter. Just like that, all [my] dreams . . . came crashing down. . . . I began to feel afraid for myself and began to write a weepy letter, but I couldn't, it was useless to try."

Their romance was over. In this chapter of *Notas de Viaje,* which he called "Breaking the Last Tie," Ernesto didn't divulge Chichina's reasons for breaking off their relationship, but evidently she had begun seeing someone else. Struggling to conjure up Chichina in his mind, he tried to give the impression that the breakup had not devastated him. "In the twilight that surrounded us phatasmagoric figures swirled around and around, but 'she' didn't want to come. . . . I should fight for her, she was mine, she was mine, she was m . . . I slept."

Forever afterward, Alberto wondered if he bore some responsibility for the breakup. He'd "picked up" one of the Ferreyras' *mucamas,* dressed in a bathing costume belonging to Chichina's own aunt, and taken her with him to the beach, *into* the tent he had pitched there. He did so in full view of Chichina and her friends, defying the unwritten but unanimously understood social convention prohibiting intimacy with the servant class. "Chichina didn't like that very much," recalled Granado. "And I think she resented me as the person who was taking Ernesto away from her."

Meanwhile, outwardly reconciling himself to his loss, Ernesto was determined to enjoy the rest of the journey. Writing about their crossing of the Andes to Chile, Ernesto invoked the lines of a poem that began: "And now I feel my great root floating naked and free . . ."

Entering Chile, they obtained free passage on a ferry across Lake Esmeralda by manning the bilge pumps of the leaky cargo barge it pulled in its wake. Aboard, they met some Chilean doctors, to whom Ernesto and Alberto introduced themselves as "leprologists." The gullible Chileans told them of the Pacific territory of Easter Island, Rapa Nui, where Chile's only leper colony existed alongside hordes of sensuous, pliant women. Hearing this, Ernesto and Alberto immediately extracted a letter of recommendation from their new friends for the "Society of Friends of Easter Island," in Valparaiso, where they might secure free ship passages to the island. By the time they reached dry land, they had resolved to add this exotic new destination to their ambitious itinerary.

They climbed back on La Poderosa. They took little note of the scenery, though: Easter Island beckoned, and they were in a hurry to get there.

Their next stop was the Pacific port of Valdivia, where they paid a visit to the local newspaper, the *Correo de Valdivia,* and came away with a glowing profile of themselves, published under the headline "Two Dedicated

Argentine Travelers on Motorcycle on Their Way through Valdivia." Not
ones to miss a good opportunity, Ernesto and Alberto had solemnly rein-
vented themselves as "leprosy experts," with "previous research in neighboring countries"—and the unsuspecting *Correo* reprinted their claims. In
addition to leprology, Ernesto and Alberto must have given free rein to their
judgments on a wide variety of topics, for the *Correo* went on to laud them
for having, "during their very short stay in our country, penetrated its social, economic and sanitary problems." But there was more. In a final gesture of magnanimity, they announced in the *Correo*'s editorial offices that
they would dedicate their journey to the city of Valdivia, then celebrating
its four hundredth anniversary.

They moved on to Temuco, where again they got themselves interviewed. The article published in *El Austral de Temuco* on February 19, 1952,
appeared under the even more affirmative headline "Two Argentine Experts in Leprology Travel South America on Motorcycle." An accompanying photograph shows the coconspirators striking a heroic pose. Ernesto is
serious and staring straight at the camera. With his thumbs locked casually
in his belt, he looks more like a dashing film heartthrob than a medical student, while at his side the shorter Alberto, leaning toward him deferentially,
wears a rather impish expression.

Press clippings in hand, which Ernesto proudly called "the condensa-
tion of our audacity," they were off again. A day later, La Poderosa took a
fall, smashing her gear box and snapping a steering column. As they repaired
her in a workshop in the whistlestop of Lautaro, they became instant celebrities as the locals gathered around to watch. They managed to scrounge a
few free meals and, after La Poderosa had been patched up, were invited to
drink some wine with their new friends. Ernesto found the Chilean wine
delicious, so much so that by the time he and Alberto arrived at a village
dance, he felt "capable of great feats." There, having drunk even more, he
invited a married woman to dance and began to lead her outside while her
husband watched. The woman tried to resist, Ernesto continued "dragging
her," and she fell to the floor. After that, Ernesto and Alberto were chased
from the hall by infuriated dancers.

With Ernesto at the helm of La Poderosa, they left town, "fleeing places
that were no longer so hospitable to us," but only a few kilometers out of
town, at a tight bend in the road, Poderosa's rear brake failed, and then, as
she picked up speed downhill, her hand brake failed as well. Ernesto
swerved to avoid a herd of wandering cows that suddenly loomed in front
of him, and they crashed into the road bank. Miraculously, Poderosa was
apparently undamaged, and, finding her rear brake once again mysteriously
working, they continued their trek. But the day was not yet over.

"Backed up as always by our 'press' letter of recommendation, we were put up by some Germans who treated us in a very cordial manner," wrote Ernesto. "During the night I got a colic which I didn't know how to stop; I was ashamed to leave a souvenir in the chamberpot, so I climbed onto the window, and gave up all of my pain to the night and the blackness. . . . The next morning I looked out to see the effect and I saw that two meters below lay a great sheet of zinc where they were sun-drying their peaches: the added spectacle was impressive. We beat it from there."

Leaving a lengthening trail of irate hosts behind them, the two continued their escape to the north, but their faithful steed began to fail them. Every time they reached a hill, Poderosa balked, and on their second day's journey she gave up completely at the first steep hill. It was their last day as "motorized scroungers."

A truck deposited them and the crippled Poderosa in the next town, Los Angeles. They found lodging in the local firehouse after chatting up the three daughters of its fire chief. Later, Ernesto paid coy homage to the uninhibited girls as "exponents of the grace of the Chilean women who, whether pretty or ugly, have a certain something of spontaneity, of freshness, that captivates immediately."

Alberto was more explicit. "After dinner we went out with the girls. Once again I noticed the different attitudes toward freedom between Chilean women and our own. . . . We returned to the firehouse lax and silent, each one ruminating on his experience. . . . Fuser made his bed, really agitated, I don't know if from the asthma or the girl."

The next day they left on a truck headed for Santiago, lugging the carcass of La Poderosa with them like the body of a fallen comrade. The Chilean capital made little impression on them, and after finding a garage where they could leave the motorcycle, they were off again, on their own. As intent as ever on reaching Easter Island, they planned to wangle free passage aboard a ship from the nearby port of Valparaíso.

III

Camped out at a bar, La Gioconda, whose generous owner fed and housed them for free, the two prowled the port of Valparaíso. They returned disappointed, having been told that the next ship to Easter Island didn't leave for six months. But they didn't lose hope, for they had yet to call upon the Society of Friends of Easter Island.

Meanwhile, their imaginations took flight with the stories they heard. Quoting some of them, Ernesto wrote: "Easter Island! . . . 'There, to have a white boyfriend is a honour for the females.' 'There—what a wish—the women do all the work. One eats, sleeps, and keeps them content. . . .' What would it matter to stay a year there, who cares about work, studies, family, etc. . . ."

In between meals at La Gioconda, they climbed up and down the serpentine steps of the city, amid houses built of colorfully painted zinc overlooking the "leaden blue of the bay." To Ernesto, it had an "insane asylum's beauty."

After making abundant use of his alleged doctor's "degree," Ernesto was asked to look in on one of La Gioconda's clients, who turned out to be an elderly servant woman, prostrate with chronic asthma and a failing heart. He found her room, where he breathed in an odor "of concentrated sweat and dirty feet." She was surrounded by "the ill-concealed acrimony" of her family, who seemed to suffer her presence badly. She was dying, and there was little Ernesto could do for her. After giving her a prescription for her diet, what remained of his own supply of Dramamine tablets, and a few other medicines, he left, "followed by the praising words of the old lady and the indifferent stares of her relatives."

The encounter affected him deeply and led him to think about the heartlessness of poverty. "There, in the final moments of people whose farthest horizon is always tomorrow, one sees the tragedy that enfolds the lives of the proletariat throughout the whole world; in those dying eyes there is a submissive apology and also, frequently, a desperate plea for consolation that is lost in the void, just as their body will soon be lost in the magnitude of misery surrounding us. How long this order of things based on an absurd sense of caste will continue is not within my means to answer, but it is time that those who govern dedicate less time to propagandizing the compassion of their regimes and more money, much more money, sponsoring works of social utility."

A few days later, after the Society of Friends confirmed that no ships would be sailing to Easter Island for many months, Ernesto and Alberto reluctantly resigned themselves to their original itinerary. After a fruitless round of the wharves asking for work on board ships, they stowed away on board the *San Antonio,* a cargo ship headed to the port of Antofagasta in northern Chile. Slipping aboard at dawn with the collusion of a friendly sailor, they crept into a latrine, where they hid. Once the ship started moving, Alberto began vomiting. The stench in the latrine was terrible, but they remained where they were until they could bear it no longer. "At five in the afternoon, dead of hunger and with the coast no longer in sight, we presented ourselves to the captain."

The captain turned out to be a good sport and, after giving them a thundering scolding in front of his junior officers, ordered them to be fed and given chores to do to help pay their way. Ernesto recalled: "We devoured our rations contentedly; [but] when I found out that I was in charge of cleaning the famous latrine, the food backed up in my throat, and when I went down protesting under my breath, followed by the joking stare of Alberto, in charge of peeling the potatoes, I confess I felt tempted to forget everything written about the rules of comradeship and request a change of jobs. It's just not fair! He adds his good portion to the shit that's accumulated there and I have to clean it up!"

Once they had finished their chores, the captain treated them as honored guests, and the three of them played canasta and drank together long into the night. The next day, as the long Chilean coastline slipped by, Alberto again did kitchen duty while Ernesto cleaned the decks with kerosene under the watchful eye of an irascible steward. That night, after another "tiring round of canasta," the two friends stood together at the ship's rail to look out at the sea and sky, with the lights of Antofagasta just beginning to appear in the distance.

In Antofagasta, a second attempt at stowing away on a ship heading farther north failed when the two, already hidden on board, were discovered before the ship set sail. It was their own fault. Hidden under a tarpaulin with a load of tasty melons, they had been devouring the fruit and heedlessly hurling the rinds overboard. The ever-growing procession of waterborne melon rinds eventually drew the captain to their hiding place. "A long line of melons, perfectly peeled, floated in Indian file upon the tranquil sea. The rest was ignominious."

After their fantasy of continuing at sea had been so rudely truncated, they hitchhiked inland. Peru was their next destination, but first they wanted to see the Chuquicamata copper mine, the world's largest open pit mine and the primary source of Chile's wealth.

As he approached the huge U.S.-run copper mine, Ernesto's antipathies were already aroused. Chuquicamata was the subject of an acrid debate within Chile as the ultimate symbol of "foreign domination" of its economy. As with Chile's other copper mines, "Chuqui" was run by American mining monopolies such as Anaconda and Kennecott. What's more, Kennecott's Chilean subsidiary was the Braden Copper Company, once owned by the family of the American proconsul Spruille Braden, whose meddling in Argentina's politics during Perón's rise to power had raised so many nationalist hackles there.

While these companies reaped huge profits, Chile's economy was hugely dependent on the revenues it received from them, which varied from year to year depending on the fluctuating copper market. Resentful over the terms of this unequal partnership, many Chileans, particularly on the left, were lobbying for a nationalization of the mines. In response, the United States had actively pressured Chile's recent governments to break up the mining unions and outlaw the Communist party.

Stuck waiting for vehicles in the arid desert mountains halfway to the mine, Ernesto and Alberto met a marooned couple. As the hours drew on, and the Andean night fell in all its harsh coldness, they talked. He was a miner, just released from prison, where he had been held for striking. He was lucky, he told them: Other comrades had disappeared after their arrests and had presumably been murdered. But as a member of the outlawed Chilean Communist party, he was unable to find work and so, with his wife, who had left their children with a charitable neighbor, was headed for a sulphur mine deep in the mountains. There, he explained, working conditions were so bad that no questions about political allegiances were asked.

Afterward, Ernesto wrote at length about this encounter. "By the light of the single candle which illuminated us . . . the contracted features of the worker gave off a mysterious and tragic air. . . . The couple, frozen stiff in the desert night, hugging one another, were a live representation of the proletariat of any part of the world. They didn't even have a miserable blanket to cover themselves, so we gave them one of ours, and with the other, Alberto and I covered ourselves as best we could. It was one of the times when I felt the most cold, but it was also the time when I felt a little more in fraternity with this, for me, strange human species."

Here were the shivering flesh-and-blood victims of capitalist exploitation. Ernesto and Alberto had momentarily shared their lives—equally cold and hungry, equally tired and stranded. Yet he and Alberto were traveling for their own pleasure, while this couple were on the road because they had been persecuted for their beliefs.

The next morning, a truck heading for Chuqui came by. Leaving the couple behind to their uncertain future, Ernesto and Alberto climbed on board. With their image still fresh in his mind, the visit to the Chuquicamata copper mine became a wholly political experience for Ernesto. He wrote disdainfully of the American mine administrators as "blonde, efficient and impertinent masters" who grudgingly let them see the mine quickly on the condition they left as soon as possible because Chuqui wasn't a "tourist attraction."

Their appointed guide, a Chilean, but a "faithful dog of the yankee masters," nonetheless excoriated his bosses as he led them around. Telling them that a miners' strike was brewing, he said: "Imbecile gringos, they lose millions of pesos a day in a strike in order to deny a few centavos more to a poor worker."

Ernesto opined: "We'll see if one day, a miner somewhere will willingly take up a pickaxe and go to poison his lungs with conscious happiness. They say that *there,* from where the red flame comes that dazzles the world, it is so, that is what they say. I don't know."

Ernesto dedicated a special chapter in his journal to the mine, carefully detailing its production process and political importance to Chile. In his depiction, the ore-rich mountains surrounding Chuquicamata are "exploited proletariat," too.

"The hills show their grey backs prematurely aged in the struggle against the elements, with elderly wrinkles that don't correspond to their geological age. How many of these escorts of their famous brother [Chuquicamata] enclose in their heavy wombs similar riches to his, as they await the arid arms of the mechanical shovels that devour their entrails, with their obligatory condiment of human lives?"

Chile was in a heated presidential campaign. Ernesto and Alberto found most of the working-class people they questioned supportive of the right-wing candidate, the former dictator General Carlos Ibañez del Campo, a man with aspirations to a populist caudillismo similar to those of Argentina's Perón.

In his *Notas de Viaje,* Ernesto called the political scene "confusing," but ventured some guesses. Disqualifying the leftist candidate, Salvador Allende, from any chance at the polls due to the legal prohibition on Communist voters, Ernesto predicted Ibañez's electoral victory on an anti-American nationalistic platform that would include a mines-nationalization policy and large-scale public works projects.* He concluded with a recommendation and a prescient caveat for this "potentially rich" Latin American country. "The biggest effort it should make is to shake the uncomfortable Yankee friends from its back and that task is, at least for the moment, Cyclopean, given the quantity of dollars invested and the ease with which they can exercise efficient economic pressure the moment their interests seem threatened."

---

*As he predicted, in the subsequent elections, Ibañez was elected president, while Salvador Allende came in last. The mines, however, would not be nationalized under Ibañez, who soon had to go begging to the International Monetary Fund to cover a major balance-of-payments deficit.

The IMF's harsh anti-inflationary terms caused widespread unrest, further polarizing the country's politics. The preponderant American role in Chile's economy continued until 1970, when Salvador Allende became the hemisphere's first popularly elected socialist president; one of his first acts was to nationalize the mines. American influence in Chile did not lessen, however. Within three years Allende's government was violently overthrown in a U.S.-backed military coup.

After Chuquicamata, the two friends set out for Peru, crossing the border a few days later. Riding on the backs of trucks loaded with taciturn Aymara Indians, they headed inland climbing toward Lake Titicaca, five thousand meters above sea level. As the land unfolded, revealing ancient Incan canals sparkling with cascading water cut into the steep mountain slopes, and higher up the snowcapped Andean peaks poking through clouds, Ernesto became jubilant. "There we were in a legendary valley, detained in its evolution for centuries and which is still there today for us, happy mortals, to see."

IV

Ernesto's euphoria didn't last long. Stopping in the Indian town of Tarata, he looked around him for visible effects of the Spanish conquest, and he found them: "[A] beaten race that watches us pass through the streets of the town. Their stares are tame, almost fearful, and completely indifferent to the outside world. Some give the impression that they live because it is a habit they can't shake."

As they wandered through the Andes over the next several weeks, the sustained contact with the "beaten race" of his continent had an impact on Ernesto. The harsh historical realities of four centuries of white domination were all too evident. If the indigenous people in his own country were almost completely eradicated, devoured in the melting pot of modern Argentina with its millions of European migrants, here in Peru's highlands they were still a visible majority, their culture largely intact but pathetically subjugated.

In the crowded trucks they traveled on, carrying produce and human cargo alike in squalid heaps, he and Alberto were usually invited to ride up front with the drivers. It was *cholos*, or Indians, with their filthy ponchos, their lice and unwashed stench, who sat in the exposed open backs of the trucks. For all their lack of money and need to "scrounge" their way, theirs was a privileged journey, and they knew it. As whites, professionals, and Argentines, they were the "social superiors" of those around them and, as such, were able to obtain favors and concessions beyond the imagining of Peru's indigenous citizens.

For accommodation and the occasional meal, they threw themselves at the mercy of Peru's Guardia Civil, the national police force with posts in every town. They were almost never refused. In one town, the police chief reacted to their plight by exclaiming: "What? Two Argentine doctors are going to sleep uncomfortably for lack of money? It can't be . . . ," and insisted on paying for them to stay in a hotel.

In Juliaca, they were having drinks in a bar as guests of a drunken Guardia Civil sergeant who, to show off his prowess as a marksman, fired his revolver into the wall. When the bar's owner, an Indian woman, ran for help and returned with a superior officer, Ernesto and Alberto went along with their host's story that no gunshot had been fired. Alberto, they said, had set off a "firecracker." After an admonishment, they were free to go. As they exited the bar, the Indian woman screamed in futile protest behind their retreating backs: "These Argentines, they think they are the owners of everything." They were white, she was Indian. They had power, she didn't.

They were repeatedly asked questions by Peruvian Indians eager to hear about the "marvellous land of Perón, where the poor have the same rights as the rich." Ernesto and Alberto knew it wasn't so, but like doctors lying to terminally ill patients, they found themselves telling their listeners what they wanted to hear.

The spectacular colonial city of Cuzco, built on the ruins of the Incan capital, with its outlying temples and fortresses, drove Ernesto to fill his journal with lyrical and studious descriptions of the area's architecture and history. He and Alberto spent hours in the city's museum and library to gain a clearer understanding of the mysterious Incan archeology and the culture that had created it.

Their luck as expert scroungers held out in Cuzco. Alberto went to see a doctor he had once met at a medical conference. The doctor graciously put a Land-Rover and driver at their disposal to visit the Valley of the Incas, and obtained free tickets for their train journey to the temple ruins of Machu Picchu.

They spent hours prowling the stone ruins built upon sheer jungle peaks. After joining in a rural soccer game and showing off what Ernesto called their "relatively stupendous skills" at the sport, they were invited to stay on by the manager of the local tourist inn. After two days and nights, though, they were asked to leave, to make way for a busload of paying American tourists.

Returning to Cuzco on the stop-and-start, narrow-gauge train through the mountains, Ernesto saw the filthy third-class wagon reserved for Indian passengers and compared it to the kind used to transport cattle in Argentina. Evidently still smarting over being forced to leave Machu Picchu for *their* convenience, he vented his spleen at "American tourists." "Naturally the tourists who travel in their comfortable buses would know nothing of the condition of these Indians. . . . The majority of the Americans . . . fly directly from Lima to Cuzco, visit the ruins and then return, without giving any importance to anything else."

By now, he found it hard to contain his antipathy. He went out of his way in his journal to take jabs at the "blonde, camera-toting, sportshirted correspondents from another world" whose presence he found irritating and intrusive. In a chapter called "The Land of the Inca," he derided Americans as "ignorant of the moral distance separating them from the living remnants of the fallen [Incan] people, because only the semiindigenous spirit of the South American can appreciate these subtle differences."

New thoughts were gelling in Ernesto's mind, associations coming together. He felt a fraternity with the indigenous "conquered races," through whose lands he now traveled, whose ruins he now visited, whose ancestors his own forebears had helped put to the knife. Their two races, the Indian and the European, had initially met in a vast bloodletting, and centuries of intolerance and injustice still held them apart, but it was also what joined them together, for it was from this unholy union that a new race, the mestizo, had been born. As the progeny of their shared history, the mestizo was perhaps the truest Latin American of all. But together, all of them—European-blooded Creoles, mestizos, and Indians—were closer to one another than these Anglo-Saxons from the north, strolling around Cuzco and Machu Picchu's ruins like so many "aliens." They had a common language, a common history and culture, and faced common problems.

Like the medical researcher he was on his way to becoming, Ernesto immediately searched for a cause when he saw a symptom. And, having found what he thought was the cause, he searched for its antidote. Thus, in Ernesto's mind, the dying old lady in Valparaíso and the persecuted miner couple on the road to Chuqui had become "living examples of the proletariat in the whole world," who lived in misery because of an unjust social order, and whose lives would not improve until future enlightened governments changed the state of things. Symptom and cause were wrapped up into one ugly package. Standing behind the local regimes holding sway and perpetuating the injustice were the Americans and their overwhelming economic power. Ernesto's antidote in the case of Chile was to "get the uncomfortable American friend off its back," but he warned in the same breath of the dangers and difficulties of expropriation. Ernesto didn't have the cure for all these ills, but he was searching. Perhaps the "red flame dazzling the world" was the answer, but he wasn't yet sure.

V

After a fortnight in the domain of the Inca, Ernesto and Alberto traveled on to the Andean town of Abancay. Having made so much out of themselves as "leprosy experts," they were trying to live up to the name, and they had secured a letter from their Cuzco doctor friend recommending them to the authorities at the remote Huambo leprosarium.

They were still broke, and their modus operandi for travel by cajoling and begging their way aboard trucks was unchanging. In Abancay, they requested, and received, free room and board at the hospital. In return, they gave some "lectures" on leprosy and asthma, and flirted with the nurses. There, Ernesto came down with an attack of asthma, which had hardly bothered him since leaving Argentina; it was serious, and Alberto had to inject him with adrenaline three times.

They continued their journey toward Huambo. At the village of Huancarama, with the leper colony still several miles away over the forested hills, and with Ernesto's asthma so bad he could barely stand up, they asked the "lieutenant governor" for help in obtaining horses. A little while later, a Quechua-speaking guide appeared before them with two skinny horses.

After traveling for several hours, Ernesto and Alberto saw they were being pursued on foot by an Indian woman and boy. When the pair finally caught up, they learned that the horses they were riding were their property; the Huancarama governor had simply seized them to fulfill his promise to help "the Argentine doctors." After many apologies, Ernesto and Alberto returned their horses and continued on foot.

The Huambo leprosarium was a rudimentary compound of thatched huts with dirt floors built in a mosquito-infested jungle clearing, where a small but dedicated medical staff worked on a minuscule budget. From the doctor in charge they learned that its founder, Dr. Hugo Pesce, director of Peru's leper-treatment program, was also a prominent Communist, and resolved to look him up when they reached Lima.

They were lodged and fed at the nearby home of a wealthy local hacendado, who told them the system he used to settle his immense wilderness landholding. He invited poor *colonos,* or settlers, onto his land to clear a patch of forest and plant their crops, then, after their first harvests came in, had them dislodged, moving them gradually to higher and less hospitable terrain. In this fashion, he confided, his land was cleared for free.

They spent a couple of days in Huambo but, after the onset of heavy rains and a worsening of Ernesto's asthma, decided he should get proper hospital treatment. For the trek out, the hacendado sent one of his Indian servants with them. As they rode on the horses he had provided, the *cholo,* on foot, carried their bags. Ernesto observed: "In the mentality of the rich people of the zone it's completely natural that the servant, although travelling on foot, should carry all the weight and discomfort." Once out of sight of the rancher, he and Alberto relieved the Indian of their bags. But if they expected gratitude, it eluded them, for the *cholo*'s face "revealed nothing" about what he thought of their gesture.

In the town of Andahuaylas they found medicines, and Ernesto went into the hospital for two days until his asthma subsided. From there they moved into the Guardia Civil barracks to wait for a truck leaving for Lima. These were hungry days: They had little to eat except potatoes, corncobs, and yucca, and to cook them they shared the stove of the prisoners held in the barracks, which doubled as the local jail. Most of them, they found, were not criminals, but Indians who had deserted from the military during their three years of obligatory service.

Ernesto and Alberto were welcome in the barracks until the day Alberto witnessed one of the guards lewdly fondling the Indian women bringing food to their detained husbands. Alberto protested, and afterward, the atmosphere in the barracks cooled considerably. Fortunately, a cattle truck was leaving Andahuaylas, and Ernesto and Alberto were able to depart before they were kicked out.

For another ten uncomfortable and hungry days, they followed an uncertain route through the Andes toward Lima on Peru's desert Pacific coast. As Ernesto put it, "Our trip continued in the same fashion, eating once in a while, whenever some charitable soul took pity on our indigence." Without a doubt, these were the most miserable days of their entire journey, and their strategies for obtaining hospitality now verged on the desperate, with results ranging from the embarrassing to the sublime.

By now they had perfected a formula for obtaining a free meal. As Ernesto told it, their ruse consisted of provoking the curiosity of their "candidates" by speaking in exaggerated Argentine accents. That generally broke the ice and initiated conversation. Next, either Ernesto or Alberto would begin "softly mentioning their difficulties, with the gaze lost in the distance," while the other remarked on the "coincidence" that today was the first anniversary of their year on the road. Then, "Alberto, much more *caradura* [brazen] than myself, would launch a terrible sigh and say (as in a confidence to me): 'What a shame to be in this condition, since we can't celebrate it.'"

At this point their "candidate" invariably offered to stand them a round of drinks, over Ernesto's and Alberto's protests that they couldn't possibly accept, since they couldn't reciprocate, until finally they "gave in." This was followed by Ernesto's coup de grâce. "After the first drink I categorically refuse to accept more booze and Alberto makes fun of me. The buyer becomes angry and insists, I refuse without giving reasons. The man insists and then I, with a great deal of shame, confess that in Argentina the custom is to drink while *eating*."

VI

On May 1, "penniless but content" after four months on the road, they arrived in Lima, at the foothills of the Andes. Once the acclaimed colonial "city of the Viceroys," founded by conquistador Francisco Pizarro in 1535, Lima was still a beautiful, but socially stratified capital city in 1952. To Ernesto, the city represented "a Peru which has not left the feudal state of the colonial era: it still awaits the blood of a true emancipating revolution."

After a morning spent wandering from one police barracks to another until they were finally given some rice to eat, they called upon the leprologist Dr. Hugo Pesce. Pesce received them warmly and arranged for them to stay in the Hospital de Guía for lepers. There his warmhearted female assistant, Zoraida Boluarte, took them in hand. Before long, Ernesto and Alberto had won her over entirely, and they were soon eating their meals and having their laundry done at the Boluarte home.

For the next three weeks they ate, rested, caught up on correspondence, and explored the city. Most importantly, they received some money from their families. They also attended some of Pesce's hospital lectures and were his frequent dinner guests, after which they talked for hours about everything from leprosy and physiology to politics and philosophy.

Alberto became conscious of a special affinity growing between Ernesto and the man he called respectfully *"el maestro."* For both young men, Pesce was someone worthy of their admiration. After graduating from medical school in Italy, Pesce had returned home, met the Peruvian Marxist philosopher José Carlos Mariátegui, and become a disciple. Mariátegui's pioneering 1928 work, *Seven Interpretative Essays on Peruvian Reality,* outlined the revolutionary potential of Latin America's disenfranchised Indians and peasantry as a new path forward for socialism in countries such as Peru.

Since Mariátegui's death in 1930, Pesce had remained a prominent member of the Peruvian Communist party while continuing his career in medicine. In addition to earning renown as a leprologist, he was a university lecturer and a researcher in tropical diseases, with several discoveries to his credit in the field of malaria. Due to his politics, President Odría had exiled him for a period in the Andes but eventually allowed him to return to his university teaching post in Lima. He had published a book called *Latitudes del Silencio* (Latitudes of Silence) based on his exile experience.

Pesce was the first man of medicine Ernesto had met who was consciously dedicating his life to the "common good." He must have seemed a Peruvian Schweitzer or Gandhi, a man applying his skills to Latin America's own endemic problems, pursuing the kind of highly principled life Ernesto hoped to lead himself. Coming at the right moment in his own quest for a guiding social philosophy, Pesce's beliefs and personal example offered a potential structure to emulate.

From then on, the idea that he should find something similar for himself began forming in Ernesto's mind. As for Marxism-Leninism, he was interested, but he still had to acquire more knowledge before committing himself to a particular ideology. First he needed to finish the journey with Alberto, return to Argentina and finish his exams to get his degree, and explore the world some more. . . .

Pesce seems to have sensed the younger man's anxiety to find his place in the world and responded by giving him a great deal of time and encouragement. A decade later, Ernesto Guevara acknowledged Pesce's formative influence when he sent him a copy of his first book, *Guerrilla Warfare*. It was inscribed with the following dedication: "To Doctor Hugo Pesce: who, without knowing it perhaps, provoked a great change in my attitude toward life and society, with the same adventurous spirit as always, but channeled toward goals more harmonious with the needs of America."

But not all their time in Lima was spent on philosophical enlightenment. They found time to play soccer with local youths near the Guía Hospital, told jokes to the lepers, and met the Boluarte youngsters' student friends. One Sunday, they went to a bullfight. It was Ernesto's first *corrida de toros,* and he recorded his impressions in laconic style. "In the third *(corrida)* there was a certain degree of excitement when the bull flamboyantly hooked the *torero* and sent him flying into the air, but there was no more than that. The party ended with the death of the sixth animal, without shame or glory. I don't see art in it; bravery, after a fashion; skill, very little; excitement, relative. In summary, it all depends on what there is to do on a Sunday."

With Ernesto recovered from his asthma, and modestly back in funds, they resolved to continue their journey. They had given up their original hope of getting to the United States but planned to reach Venezuela. First, they would travel to the San Pablo leper colony, the largest of Pesce's three treatment centers located in Peru's Amazonia region.

Before they left, Dr. Pesce gave them some clothes to replace their soiled and patched garments. Ernesto inherited a tropical white suit of the doctor's that was far too small for him, but he wore it with pride anyway. Zoraida Boluarte gave them a jar of marmalade, and the hospital patients and staff took up a collection and presented them with one hundred Peruvian soles, the national currency, and a portable Primus stove.

A week later, after another muddy, stop-and-start bus crossing of the Andes, they were on the Río Ucayali, installed as first-class passengers on the river launch *La Cenepa.* It was bound for Iquitos, the old rubber-boom capital of Peru's Amazonia. Among their fellow passengers who strung their hammocks on *La Cenepa*'s gangways were rubber-tappers, lumber merchants, a few adventurers, a couple of tourists, some nuns, and a seductive-looking young prostitute. The third-class passengers traveled on a barge being towed behind and loaded with a cargo of pigs and lumber.

The journey took seven days, which they spent in conversation with the passengers and crew, playing cards, fighting off mosquitoes, and gazing out at the muddy current and passing jungle. They flirted with the prostitute, whose loose behavior scandalized the nuns and wreaked havoc among the men on board.

"Fuser and I are no exception to the rule," confessed Alberto after several days on board. "Especially me, who has a very sensitive heart for tropical beauties." In spite of a recurrence of his asthma, Ernesto was also drawn by the prospect of a shipboard romp. Describing their second day on the river, he wrote, "The day passed without novelties, except for making friends with a girl who seemed really loose and who must have thought we might have a few pesos, despite the tears we wept every time she talked of money."

Not ones to be defeated by talk of money, the two young Argentines found a way around it. Wrote Alberto of their joint effort: "She is enthused with our accounts of the things seen and the marvels still to see; she has resolved to become a traveller. As a result, without interfering, Fuser and I are trying to give her the necessary tutorials. Of course, the honorariums are (paid) in advance and in kind." A couple of days later, he added: "The rhythm of the days is the same as before. The girl divides her charms amongst good talkers like ourselves, and good payers like the man in charge of the card games."

For Ernesto, his sexual encounter brought on a nostalgic mood. "A careless caress from the little whore who sympathized with my physical condition, penetrated like a spike into the dormant memories of my pre-adventure life. During the night, unable to sleep for the mosquitoes, I thought of Chichina, now converted into a distant dream, a dream which was very pleasant and whose ending . . . leaves more melted honey than ice in the memory. I sent her a soft and unhurried kiss that she might take as from an old friend who knows and understands her; and memory took the road back to Malagueño, in the great hall of so many long nights where she must have been at that moment pronouncing some of her strange and composed phrases to her new heartthrob."

Looking into the star-filled night sky, Ernesto once again asked himself if it was worth it to lose Chichina for *this,* and something in the nocturnal void told him that it was.

Arriving on June 1 in Iquitos—a decaying rubber boomtown surrounded by jungle and tinged red from the laterite mud of its streets—Ernesto and Alberto made for the regional health service authorities with their recommendations from Dr. Pesce. Pending the embarkation of a boat headed down the Amazon to the San Pablo leprosarium, they bunked in the headquarters for the regional anti–yellow fever campaign and ate meals at the Iquitos general hospital.

But Ernesto's asthma was crippling him, and he spent the six days they were in Iquitos prostrate, giving himself injections of adrenaline, and writing letters home. With his aunt Beatriz, he was at his jocular best. Referring to an earlier letter telling her of their proposed route through the Amazon, he wrote:

"By the way, I have to make a confession. What I wrote you about the head-hunters, etc. . . . was a lie. Unfortunately it seems that the Amazon is as safe as the [Argentine] Paraná." He requested only for her to send him a new asthma inhaler and ampules of Yanal antiasthma medicine to the Colombian capital of Bogotá, taking care to reassure her, falsely, that he was well, underlining *"I don't have asthma";* he only wished to be prepared for any eventuality.

On June 6 Ernesto and Alberto set out for the two-day journey to San Pablo aboard the river launch *El Cisne.* Located on the banks of the Amazon near Peru's jungle frontiers with Colombia and Brazil, the leprosarium had six hundred patients who lived in their own village, isolated from the facility's administrators and medical staff. This was where Ernesto and Alberto stayed for the next fortnight.

Here, as at the Hospital de Guía, the two of them made quite an impression on everyone by enthusiastically joining the doctors on their patient visits, playing soccer, and making friends with the lepers. At other times, while Alberto spent hours looking through microscopes in the laboratory, Ernesto read poetry, played chess, or went fishing with San Pablo's doctors. The daredevil in him also reared its head, and one afternoon Ernesto impulsively swam across the wide Amazon, taking two hours to do so and greatly unnerving the doctors, who watched him from the shore.

On June 14, Ernesto's twenty-fourth birthday, the staff threw him a party that was well lubricated by *pisco,* the Peruvian national liquor, and he stood up to make a speech of thanks, which he recorded in his diary under the heading "Saint Guevara's Day." After grandiloquently expressing his profound gratitude to his hosts, he finished up with a heartfelt "Latin Americanist" soliloquy.

". . . We believe, and after this trip even more firmly than before, that [Latin] America's division into illusory and uncertain nationalities is completely fictitious. We constitute a single *mestizo* race, which from Mexico to the Straits of Magellan presents notable ethnographic similarities. For this, in an attempt to rid myself of the weight of any meagre provincialism, I raise a toast for Peru and for a United America."

The party went on until three in the morning in a house on stilts where a band played Peruvian waltzes, Brazilian *shoras,* Argentine tangos, and the popular Cuban mambo. By prior arrangement, Alberto gave the tone-deaf Ernesto a poke every time a tango was played. Once, when the band struck up an agitated *shora* number that had been a favorite of Chichina's, Alberto nudged Ernesto, saying: "Do you remember?"

But Ernesto, with his eye on a nurse across the room, believed Alberto's nudge to be a "tango signal," and took to the floor, doggedly dancing a slow and passionate tango while everyone around them jiggled to the *shora.* Realizing something was wrong, Ernesto came over to ask Alberto for advice, but Alberto was too convulsed with laughter at the spectacle to issue any instructions.

When they felt ready to push on, the lepers and staff built them a raft, calling it the *Mambo-Tango,* and gave them presents of clothes, pineapples, fishing hooks, and two live chickens. The evening before they embarked, a lepers' orchestra came by canoe to the staff compound dock and gave them a musical serenade. In a letter to his mother, Ernesto described the scene. "In reality it was one of the most interesting spectacles we've seen until now: the singer was blind and the accordionist had no fingers on the right hand and had replaced them with some sticks tied to his wrist." The other musicians were similarly deformed, and appeared as "monstrous figures" in the lights of the lanterns and torches reflected on the river.

The serenade was followed by good-bye speeches, ending with shouts of "three hurrahs for the doctors." In return, Alberto thanked them with outstretched arms and a display of demagogic rhetoric so purple, wrote Ernesto, that he seemed like "Perón's successor."

The next day, Ernesto and Alberto pushed their raft into the Amazon's current. Feeling a little more like explorers, they steered the *Mambo-Tango* downriver, entertaining the notion of traveling all the way to the city of Manaus, far downriver in Brazil. From there, they had been told, they could reach Venezuela through its back door, along the Amazon's tributaries.

Three days later, however, having been swept downriver past the tiny Colombian port of Leticia, and after losing their fishing hooks and their remaining chicken, they decided to give up their ambitious intentions. After convincing a riverside *colono* to row them back upriver in exchange for their raft and provisions, they made for Leticia, where a twice-monthly plane flew to the Colombian capital of Bogotá.

Scroungers again, they secured themselves free room and board with the police, as well as the promise of a 50 percent discount on the next airplane out, and were hired as soccer coaches by Leticia's Independiente Sporting team. Argentina's reputation for having Latin America's best soccer players served them well. The local team was facing an upcoming series of playoff matches, and it needed their "expertise" to help them win. By teaching them some of the latest Buenos Aires footwork, Ernesto and Alberto *were* able to improve the team's performance. Although it didn't win the tournament, their team came in a respectable second, and everyone was pleased.

On July 2, settled in comfortably with a cargo of virgin rubber, military uniforms, and mailbags, they took off from Leticia in an ancient twin-engined Catalina hydroplane that Ernesto said "shook like a cocktail tray." The airplane ride marked another euphoric first for Alberto, who had never flown before, and his excitement led him to wax poetic for their fellow passengers about his vast flying experience.

VII

On its high green mountain plateau, the city of Bogotá was a tense island of rigidly enforced law and order as a vicious civil war swirled around it in the countryside. Ernesto and Alberto found the atmosphere unfriendly and unsettling. They were given lodging at a hospital, thanks to another letter from Dr. Pesce, and were able to eat their meals at the university, where they made friends among the students, but to his mother, Ernesto wrote:

"Of all the countries we have traveled through, this is the one in which individual guarantees are the most suppressed; the police patrol the streets with their rifles on their shoulders and constantly demand one's passport. . . . It is a tense calm that indicates an uprising before long. The plains are in open revolt and the army is impotent to repress it; the conservatives fight among themselves and can't agree on anything; and the memory of the 9th of April 1948 weighs like lead over everyone's spirit. . . . In summary, an asphyxiating climate, which the Colombians can stand if they want, but we're beating it as soon as we can."

Ernesto was referring to the April 1948 assassination of the popular Liberal party leader, Jorge Eliécer Gaitán, which had led to the violent breakdown of Colombia's political system. Suspecting the incumbent Conservative government of having ordered his death, Gaitán's supporters had taken to the streets of the capital in three days of bloody rioting that became known as "El Bogotazo."

The riots occurred during a summit meeting of hemispheric foreign ministers who, under U.S. auspices, had gathered to sign the charter of the Organization of American States (OAS). At the same time, an "anti-imperialist" Latin American students' conference had been convened to protest the summit, and student leaders from all over the region had come for the event.

Among them had been a twenty-one-year-old Cuban law student named Fidel Castro Ruz. He took up arms in the uprising that followed Gaitán's killing, but avoided arrest after escaping to the Cuban embassy. He had returned to Cuba, became increasingly active in politics, and was now secretly plotting an armed uprising against the recently installed regime of Fulgencio Batista.

Meanwhile, in Colombia, the violence spawned by the Bogotazo had polarized the political climate. After the late Gaitán's Liberal party had refused to participate in the 1949 presidential elections, the ruling Conservative party's military-supported candidate Laureano Gómez was elected unopposed. Many Liberals had found allies among Colombia's fledgling Communist guerrilla groups based in the countryside. As the anarchy spread, the army and groups of armed peasant vigilantes led by Conservative political bosses took reprisals, and massacres had become commonplace. The bloodshed was called simply "La Violencia," the euphemism for what had become a national plague, and in 1952 there was still no end in sight.

Before they could "beat it," Ernesto and Alberto found themselves in trouble with the police. One day, on their way to the Argentine consulate to pick up letters from home, they were stopped, questioned, and searched by a suspicious police agent. The agent confiscated a knife Ernesto had in his possession, a silver replica gaucho's dagger that had been a going-away gift from his brother Roberto. Then, when the policeman discovered his asthma medicine, Ernesto tactlessly taunted: "Be careful, it's a very dangerous poison." Promptly arrested, they were hauled to several police stations and finally, before a judge, accused of "making fun" of the authorities. The incident was defused after they showed proof of their identities.

But for Ernesto, the matter hadn't ended. It was a question of honor for him to recuperate his knife, which the arresting police agent had kept for himelf. After repeated visits to police precincts, the knife was finally returned to him, but in the process he had raised the policemen's hackles. Ernesto's student friends urged him and Alberto to leave Colombia immediately, warning them that the police were bound to seek revenge. They even took up a collection of money to help them depart.

Without regrets, they left Bogotá by bus, heading to the Venezuelan border. Ernesto's asthma had not bothered him since Iquitos, but as they descended into the tropical lowlands, it returned. Alberto had to give Ernesto so many adrenaline injections that he began worrying about its effects on his friend's heart.

At a pit stop a day's journey from Caracas, they discussed their prospects. Both were enthusiastic about forging on to Central America and Mexico. On the other hand, they had no money to continue traveling. They reached an agreement. If the Caracas-based partner of Ernesto's horse-breeding uncle Marcelo would let him on the plane they used to transport their horses, he would return to Buenos Aires to finish his medical studies. Alberto would try to stay on in Venezuela, working either at a leprosarium or for one of the universities to which he carried letters of recommendation. If neither of these plans worked out, they would somehow try to continue as far as Mexico.

The next day, July 17, they reached the bustling city of Caracas, rich from the country's oil boom, swollen with migrants. New flat-roofed skyscrapers rose to overtake the skyline of colonial red tiled roofs. Squalid workers' slums spread like a rash up the surrounding hillsides.

Except for his shore leaves in places such as Brazil and Trinidad, Ernesto had rarely been around black people. They were a rarity in his native Argentina, but common on South America's Caribbean coast, and after meandering through a black Caracas barrio, he made observations hardly reflective of a "common-man" champion, but rather stereotypical of white, especially Argentine, arrogance and condescension.

"The blacks, those magnificent examples of the African race who have conserved their racial purity by a lack of affinity with washing, have seen their patch invaded by a different kind of slave: the Portuguese. The two races now share a common experience, fraught with bickering and squabbling. Discrimination and poverty unite them in a daily battle for survival but their different attitudes to life separate them completely: the black is indolent and fanciful, he spends his money on frivolity and drink; the European comes from a tradition of working and saving which follows him to this corner of America and drives him to get ahead, even independently, of his own individual aspirations."

They had first installed themselves in a shabby pension, but after they contacted Margarita Calvento, the aunt of a friend of Ernesto's, their lives improved. She fed them and found them lodging at a Catholic Youth hostel, and from there they set out on their respective missions: Ernesto to look for his uncle's partner, and Alberto for a job.

With a letter of recommendation from Dr. Pesce, Alberto was offered, and accepted, a well-paying job at a leprosarium near Caracas, and Ernesto was granted a seat on the next plane transporting his uncle's racehorses from Buenos Aires to Miami. When it stopped for refueling in Caracas, Ernesto would board it, and after unloading its cargo in Miami he would fly home.

The two friends' last days in Caracas together were weighed down by sadness over their impending separation. Both tried to hide their feelings by discussing their immediate futures. Ernesto would get his degree and rejoin Alberto in a year's time. If all went well, he could also get work at the leprosarium, and after saving some money they would go off on new adventures together.

On July 26, Ernesto boarded the Douglas plane with its equine cargo and flew to Miami. Upon landing, however, the pilot discovered an engine fault. They would have to lay over until it was repaired. Expecting a delay of a few days, Ernesto went to stay with Chichina's cousin Jaime "Jimmy" Roca, who was in Miami finishing up architecture school. Roca was as broke as Ernesto, but he had made a deal to eat his meals on credit at a Spanish restaurant until he sold his car. Ernesto's meals were now added to his bill.

As the repairs on Ernesto's plane dragged on, and the days turned into weeks, the two youths devoted themselves to having as good a time as possible without cash, going to the beach every day and roaming the city. A friendly Argentine waiter at the Spanish restaurant gave them extra food, and at a bar another friend of Roca's slipped them free beers and french fries. When Roca learned that Ernesto was still carrying the fifteen dollars Chichina had given him to buy her a scarf, he tried to convince him to spend it. Ernesto refused. Chichina might have broken up with him, but he was determined to keep his promise, and despite Roca's entreaties he went out and bought her scarf.*

Finally, Roca arranged for Ernesto to earn some pocket money cleaning the apartment of a Cuban airline stewardess he knew. But it was a disaster; Ernesto didn't have a clue how to go about his task, and after his one attempt the stewardess told Roca not to send him anymore. Instead of cleaning it, she said, Ernesto had somehow managed to leave her place dirtier than it was before. In spite of this, she had taken a liking to Ernesto and helped get him a temporary job washing dishes at a restaurant.

Ernesto was finally in the United States, that "country to the north" whose exploitative presence in Latin America had rankled him so during

---

*According to Pepe Aguilar, Ernesto did not try to see Chichina again when he returned home, but he did send her the scarf.

his journey. What he saw there evidently confirmed his negative preconceptions, for he later told friends in Buenos Aires that he had witnessed incidents of white racism against blacks and had been questioned by American policemen about his political affiliations. But Roca would recall only that Ernesto had once spoken to him about "the need" for low-income housing for Latin America's poor. They didn't talk politics, he said, but had just tried to enjoy themselves.

6

"I Am Not the Same I Was Before"

I

Ernesto returned to an Argentina that had altered in his absence. Five days before his arrival in Buenos Aires, Evita Perón had succumbed to cancer at the age of thirty-three.

Her funeral had been the occasion of an unprecedented public display of grief, and her body was to lie in state for two weeks before being taken away for permanent embalming. A monument larger than the Statue of Liberty was being planned for its future display, fitting for a woman whose acolytes expected the pope to grant her official sainthood. Her grieving husband, Juan Domingo Perón, carried on with his presidential duties while his courtiers whispered confidences and his enemies conspired. It was politics as usual in Argentina, but to those around him Perón seemed adrift, less whole, since his young wife's death.

In the meantime, Ernesto had his own dramas to attend to. In those days, a doctor's degree was achieved after passing examinations in thirty subjects; he had sixteen under his belt before taking off with Granado, but if he wanted his diploma in the coming school year, he needed to pass fourteen more by May.

He had little time to waste, for the first round of exams was scheduled for November. He began studying furiously, barricading himself behind his books at his aunt Beatriz's apartment and sometimes at his father's studio on Calle Paraguay, coming home only for the occasional meal. Despite the pressure, he also put in time at the allergy clinic, where Dr. Pisani was glad to have him back.

He also began to take stock of his just-completed journey by writing up *Notas de Viaje* from his travel diary. He decided that the journey had changed him. "The person who wrote these notes died upon stepping once again onto Argentine soil, he who edits and polishes them, 'I,' am not I; at least I am not the same I was before. That vagabonding through our 'America' has changed me more than I thought."

At home things were much the same. His father continued to struggle with his construction and property-rental business. His mother, the abstracted queen bee of Calle Araoz, played solitaire and looked after Juan Martín, now nine and still in grade school. Roberto had finished high school and was doing his compulsory military service, while Celia and Ana María were both studying architecture at Buenos Aires University. Celia *madre*'s salon had grown; some new personalities had attached themselves to the Guevara clan. Ana María had formed a study-circle of student friends from the Faculty of Architecture. Among them were Fernando Chávez and Carlos Lino, both of whom were vying for her attentions. For now, she was dating Lino but would eventually marry Chávez. The Guevaras were pleased that Ernesto was home, hoping he had rid himself of his wanderlust and that he would settle down in Buenos Aires as a doctor or allergy researcher.

In November 1952, Ernesto was scheduled to sit for his first round of exams. In the midst of them, he fell seriously ill, not from his asthma this time, but from a fever contracted by exposing himself to diseased human viscera. Pisani had acquired a special machine designed to grind human viscera for research purposes, and, impatient to use it, Ernesto had obtained some infected human remains from the Medical Faculty and began grinding them up without using a protective shield. Afterward he felt ill and took to his bed with a very high fever. His father found him there. Alarmed, and seeing him appear to worsen by the minute, Guevara Lynch offered to call Dr. Pisani. Ernesto refused. Some time passed; Guevara Lynch waited by his side, watching his son closely. "All of a sudden he made me a sign and, when I drew near, he told me to call a hospital to bring him a cardiac stimulant immediately, and to call Dr. Pisani."

Guevara Lynch realized it was serious and made the phone calls. Within minutes, a hospital nurse and Pisani had arrived, and Pisani took charge of the situation, staying alone for several hours with Ernesto. When he left, he told the family to buy certain medicines and ordered complete rest for Ernesto. Anguished, the family stayed up the whole night, only one of many such episodes they suffered over the years due to what his father called Ernesto's "imprudence."

"At about six in the morning," recalled his father, "Ernesto had improved a great deal, and, to our great surprise, we saw that he began to get dressed. I didn't say anything. I knew he was very stubborn, but in the end, seeing he was dressing to go outside, I asked him: 'What are you going to do?' 'I've got an exam, the examiners arrive at eight in the morning.' 'But don't be an animal,' I replied. 'Don't you see you can't do that?' All the objections I made to him at that moment were in vain. He had decided to take his exam that day and he had to do it. And that is what he did."

Despite his bout with illness, Ernesto passed three exams in November and ten more the next month. It left him with only one remaining examination to pass in April before he qualified for his medical degree and could return to Venezuela. In the meantime, he spent as much time as possible on his research at the Pisani Clinic. He was finding it exciting, for he could not only apply himself to the cases of actual patients afflicted by allergies, but also attempt to isolate their causes and find antidotes in the laboratory.

Pisani encouraged him as much as possible and began giving him credit in some published findings. One, published in the scientific quarterly *Alergia* for the period November 1951–February 1952, listed Ernesto's name along with Dr. Pisani's and several others as coauthors of a research paper entitled "Sensibilization of Guinea Pigs to Pollens through Injections of Orange Extract."

On April 11, 1953, Ernesto sat for his final exam. His father remembered the occasion: "I was in my studio when the telephone rang. I picked it up and instantly recognized his voice, which said: 'Dr. Ernesto Guevara de la Serna speaking.' And he put emphasis on the word Doctor."

"My happiness was great," wrote his father. "But it lasted only a short time. Almost at the same time we found out he'd graduated as a doctor, he announced his new journey: this time his companion would be his old childhood friend, Carlos "Calica" Ferrer."

Ever since Ernesto had promised to take him on his next trip, Calica, who had dropped out of medical school, had been anxiously awaiting his return. Now the trip was really on and they immediately began their preparations for the journey. "We began putting together all our connections," remembered Calica. "We decided we were going to go through Bolivia because Ernesto wanted to visit the Incan ruins there, which he had studied and knew a lot about, and then our next target was Machu Picchu."

As for their longer-range plans, Ernesto spoke of going to India, while Calica, more interested in the good life, saw himself in Paris, well dressed at cocktail parties, with pretty women on his arm. "Our goal, as I recall it," said Calica, "was to get to Venezuela, work a little, as little as possible, and then go to Europe."

Watching all the activity, wrote Guevara Lynch: "Our illusions collapsed like a deck of cards; we knew what awaited him, and we knew it well: he would walk leagues and leagues and go hanging onto any car or truck. . . . He didn't even remotely consider his asthma or his state of health. . . .

As for us, his parents and siblings, we couldn't do anything about it. . . . He was no longer the child or the youth, but Dr. Ernesto Guevara de la Serna, who did whatever he wanted."

When Ernesto informed Dr. Pisani he was leaving, the doctor tried to convince him to stay. He offered him a paying job, an apartment at the clinic, and a future at his side in allergy research. Ernesto refused. His mind was made up; he didn't want to "stagnate" like Pisani.

In June, Ernesto obtained a copy of his doctor's degree, and a few days later he celebrated his twenty-fifth birthday. With his title in hand and duly legalized, he was now a bona fide doctor. All that remained was for him and Calica to obtain their visas and sufficient funds for the trip, and once again it was a matter of scrounging. He and Calica developed a plan of attack. As Calica recalled: "First, we asked our aunts. All our aunts, grandmothers . . . , whoever we could ask for a loan. And as we went along, Ernesto and I made our calculations. 'Did you hit up so-and-so?' 'Yes, I asked her for so much.' 'My grandmother's going to give me some, and Mama is also going to give me money.'"

Soon, Ernesto and Calica had collected the equivalent of three hundred American dollars each and all the visas they needed, except for Venezuela. But, with its oil-boom economy, Venezuela had become a magnet for thousands of foreign job-seekers and had clamped down on visas. When they presented themselves at the Venezuelan consulate, they were refused visas because they didn't have return airplane tickets.

They left the Venezuelan consulate empty-handed, but Ernesto told Calica not to worry, they would get the visas in another country along the way. Meanwhile, he turned the incident into a humorous anecdote for his friends. With Tita Infante, he said it had all been a simple misunderstanding: The consul had mistaken one of his asthma attacks, which contorted his features, for anger and became frightened for his own safety.

It was July 1953. Calica had been designated the "economist" of the trip—that is, he would carry the money. His mother sewed him a money belt for him to wear inside his underwear, and when Ernesto saw it he immediately dubbed it "the chastity belt." They bought second-class tickets for the July 7 train to Bolivia leaving from Belgrano station. They were ready to go.

A large crowd of family and friends gathered at the station to see them off. Ernesto was dressed in military fatigues, a gift from his brother Roberto. They dragged in all their baggage, far too much, as usual, with Ernesto having packed more books than clothes for the journey.

They sat down on the wooden benches in their second-class compartment crowded with Indians and their bundles. Both young men were suddenly painfully aware of the contrast between their humble fellow passengers and their own well-dressed relatives and friends. At the last minute, a plethora of gifts and packages of goodies were pressed into their hands: cakes from Calica's mother, sweets from someone else.

Watching from the platform, Celia Guevara de la Serna suddenly clutched the hand of Roberto's fiancée, Matilde, and said forlornly: "My son is leaving, I won't see him again." The conductor whistled and the train began to move out of the station. Everyone shouted their good-byes and waved.

As the train pulled slowly away, a lone figure separated itself from the throng to run alongside the compartment where Ernesto and Calica sat. It was Ernesto's mother, Celia, who waved and waved a handerchief in the air. She said nothing, but tears ran down her face. She ran alongside the train until the station platform ended and she could run no more, and then the train had gone.

7

"Without Knowing
Which Way Is North"

I

Ernesto Guevara, medical doctor and veteran road gypsy, was off again. "This time," he wrote in a new journal he entitled "Otra Vez" (Once Again),* "the name of the sidekick has changed, now Alberto is called Calica, but the journey is the same: two disperse wills extending themselves through America without knowing precisely what they seek or which way is north."

Ernesto's train had not been long gone when his cousin Mario Saravia made a surprising discovery. Returning to the Guevara home, where he was staying, Saravia noticed that his three new silk shirts were missing. He suspected Ernesto of taking them, and told Celia *madre*. Shocked, she replied: "No, how could he have?" Saravia wrote Ernesto to ask him if he had taken his shirts. When it came, Ernesto's reply was affirmative. Not to worry, he told Saravia, his shirts had been put to good use. He had sold them and, with the money, been able to "eat and sleep for fifteen days." In revenge, Saravia wrote him back to inform him, falsely, that he'd sold the prized microscope Ernesto had left with him for safekeeping, and used the money to go "on holiday."

After languishing in the dusty border post of La Quiaca for three days, recovered, the two friends continued their journey into Bolivia by train. But at Calica's insistence, they now traveled in a first-class sleeping compartment.

---

*This unpublished journal, spanning the next three years of Guevara's life, was found and transcribed by his widow Aleida March after his death. Except for a few rare extracts, it has never previously been made public, but she made the entire text available to the author. It is apparently largely unabridged, except for several sexually graphic passages that she acknowledges having deleted in the interests of preserving the "propriety" of her late husband's image.

Two days later, they descended from the freezing brown altiplano and into the great natural crater where the city of La Paz huddled in its sunstruck and treeless exposure like some kind of experimental lunar colony.

The setting was impressive: At the city's far edges the clean lines of the crater hemming it in broke up into an eroded badlands of fantastic geology, an entire valleyful of giant white stalagmites jutting upward like stone daggers. Above, the land climbed into a swooping rise of alpine rock and glacial ice to form the blue and white volcano of Mt. Illimani.

Ernesto was enthralled. "La Paz is the Shanghai of the Americas," he wrote enthusiastically in his journal. "A rich gamut of adventurers of all the nationalities vegetate and flourish in the polychromatic and mestizo city."

They wasted no time in getting to know the city. After checking into a dingy hotel, the "City," they set out to explore its steep cobblestoned streets thronged with colorfully costumed Indians and groups of armed vigilantes. Here they were in revolutionary Bolivia, Latin America's most Indian of nations and also one of its poorest, with a notorious history of exploitation. The majority indigenous population had languished as virtual serfs for centuries while a ruling handful of families were made extremely wealthy from their tightfisted control of the tin mines, Bolivia's prime source of income, and its productive agricultural land.

Now that state of affairs appeared to have been overturned. Since seizing power in a popular revolt a year earlier, the Movimiento Nacionalista Revolucionario (MNR) had disbanded the army and nationalized the mines. A hotly debated agrarian reform law was due to come into effect in a few weeks' time. But Bolivia remained unsettled, with many political forces still at odds and threatening the regime's stability. In the countryside, impatient peasants were forcing the land-reform issue by attacking private haciendas, while miners led by the newly created independent trade union federation, the Central Obrera Boliviana (COB), marched in displays of force to extract further concessions from the government.

Armed people's militias roamed the streets, and rumors flew of countercoups by disgruntled elements of the disbanded army. One conspiracy had already been quelled in January. At the same time, right- and left-wing branches within the ruling MNR coalition pursued opposing agendas, with the Communists calling for a total handover of power to the workers, while its center-right wing, including President Víctor Paz Estenssoro, sought to follow a middle road that isolated both the Communists and the local oligarchs, called *rosqueros*.

Prowling around town, they bumped into a young Argentine they had met on their train ride. He was visiting his father, Isaías Nogues, a prominent politician and sugar-mill owner from the province of Tucumán, now exiled as an opponent of Perón. After introductions, it emerged that Nogues was acquainted with both their families, and he invited Calica and Ernesto to his home for dinner.

At Nogues's house they attended an elaborate Argentine *asado* and met other members of La Paz's expatriate Argentine community. To Ernesto, their host was a hidalgo, a nobleman whose demeanor reminded him of Mt. Illimani's "august serenity." "Exiled from Argentina, he is the center of the [expatriate] colony, which sees in him a leader and a friend. His political ideas have been outdated in the world for some time now, but he maintains them independently of the proletarian hurricane that has been let loose on our bellicose sphere. He extends a friendly hand to any Argentine without asking who he is or why he has come, and his august serenity throws over us miserable mortals his eternal, patriarchal protection."

They also met Nogues's visiting playboy brother "Gobo," just back from the good life in Europe. A social high roller with an open wallet and a great many contacts, Gobo showed them an invitation card to the wedding of his "friend," the Greek shipping tycoon Aristotle Onassis. Gobo took a liking to the young travelers and showed them around the city's bars and restaurants. With him they discovered the Gallo de Oro (Golden Rooster), an Argentine-owned cabaret where politicians, exiles, and adventurers mingled with La Paz's fast set over drinks, and it soon became one of their regular hangouts. Here they were able to see a different Bolivia than the one pullulating on the streets outside. Once, suffering from diarrhea, Ernesto made a dash to the Gallo's men's washroom, returning a few minutes later to tell Calica in a shocked tone that he had just observed two men inside snorting cocaine.

Another hangout was the terrace of the Hotel La Paz, where Argentine exiles dallied over drinks and coffee while discussing the politics of home and the Bolivian revolution. It was a good aerie from which to observe the activity of the nation: Daily processions of Indians marched by on their way to the presidential palace, clamoring for one or another demand from the government.

For Ernesto and Calica it proved a boon for other reasons as well. One day, looking out at the sidewalk crowds, Calica spotted a pair of pretty girls and ventured down to see if he could pick one of them up. The girls were accompanied by an older man who turned out to be a Venezuelan general named Ramírez, serving in "gilded exile" as his country's military attaché. Showing good grace in spite of Calica's blatant intentions, the general invited him for a drink, and before long Calica had extracted Ramírez's promise to grant his and Ernesto's previously denied Venezuelan visas.

Ernesto's own longing for female companionship strayed over into his diarized prose. "La Paz, ingenuous, candid like a provincial girl, shows proudly her constructed marvels." A few days later, however, he met a flesh-and-blood female who seemed promising, and he wrote matter-of-factly: "Something undulating and with a maw has crossed my path, we'll see . . ."

That "something undulating" turned out to be Marta Pinilla, the rich daughter of an aristocratic landowning family whose lands extended for miles outside the capital. He met her during an evening out with General Ramírez, who by now had not only secured him and Calica their visas, but invited them out on the town. Calica was also accompanied, having paired off with one of the girls he'd met with Ramírez on their first encounter. On July 22, buoyed by the upturn in their fortunes, Calica wrote his mother a spirited letter. Things were looking up. Thanks to Nogues, they had been able to move out of their dingy hotel and were now being well looked after as paying guests in the home of an affluent Argentine family. They were living "an intense social life."

"The best people of La Paz invite us to lunch . . . they drive us around the city and have invited us to a party. . . . We went to a boîte, the Gallo de Oro, owned by an Argentine. They haven't let us pay for any of this. All the Argentines here are very united, they have behaved fantastically with us. All the time it's tea, meals in the Sucre and the Hotel La Paz, the two best ones. . . . This afternoon we're having tea with a couple of rich girls, and tonight we're going to a dance."

Their life was schizophrenic as they shuttled back and forth constantly between the city's low-life and "high-life." Ernesto wanted to get to know the Bolivian revolution better, though his and Calica's social contacts gave them entrées into a La Paz elite that was the natural enemy of the changes taking place. Calica recalled, for instance, that Marta's wealthy family was about to have its lands expropriated in the upcoming agrarian reform bill.

Little incidents occurred as they traversed the fragile social fabric of revolutionary Bolivia. One night, as they returned to the city from the Gallo de Oro, their car was stopped at gunpoint by one of the ubiquitous Indian patrols roaming the city. Recalled Calica: "They made us get out, asked us for documents, and Gobo, a bit drunk, said to one of them, '*Indio,* put away that shotgun, use it to shoot partridges.'"

While Calica echoed the racist attitudes of their rich white friends uncritically, Ernesto ruminated reflectively about what he was seeing. "The so-called *good* people, the cultured people, are astonished at the events [taking place] and curse the importance given to the Indian and the *cholo,* but in everyone I seem to sense a spark of nationalist enthusiasm with some of the government's actions. . . . Nobody denies the need to finish off the state of things symbolized by the power of the three tin-mine hierarchies, and the young people believe it has been a step forward in the struggle toward a greater equality in people and fortunes."

Ernesto's "one-week stay" was beginning to stretch out, and so were his and Calica's available funds. "I am a little disillusioned about not being able to stay here," Ernesto wrote his father on July 22, "because this is a very interesting country and it is living through a particularly effervescent moment. On the second of August the agrarian reform goes through, and fracases and fights are expected throughout the country. We have seen incredible processions of armed people with Mausers and 'piripipí' [tommy guns], which they shoot off for the hell of it. Every day shots can be heard and there are wounded and dead from firearms."

"The government shows a near-total inability to restrain or lead the peasant masses and miners, but these respond to a certain degree and there is no doubt that in the event of an armed revolt by the Falange, the opposing party, they will be at the side of the MNR. Human life has little importance here and it is given and taken without any great to-do. All of this makes this a profoundly interesting situation to the neutral observer."

Having given the impression he was leaving, Ernesto was actually planning to stay and see what happened on August 2. He wanted to be a witness to a historic and possibly tumultuous event. Meanwhile, he and Calica took advantage of every invitation from Nogues to dinner to fill their bellies. Calica wrote his mother: "Ernesto eats as if he hasn't eaten in a week, he's famous in the group." Delighting in his display of appetite, Gobo placed bets on how much Ernesto could eat in one sitting, and promised that if they met up in Lima, where they were all headed next, he would take Ernesto and Calica to a restaurant where the food was free if the clients ate enough. It would give him great pleasure, he declared, "to show off these proud examples of the Argentine race."

It was during one of these evenings at the Nogueses' that they met the Argentine lawyer Ricardo Rojo. A tall, beefy man with a balding pate and a mustache, Rojo was already a seasoned political veteran of twenty-nine. An *antiperonista* of the opposition Unión Cívica Radical, Rojo had recently escaped from police custody in Buenos Aires, where he had been detained on suspicion of terrorism.

After taking refuge in the Guatemalan embassy he had been flown out to Chile with travel documents from the leftist Guatemalan government of President Jacobo Arbenz. He had made his way to La Paz and, like Guevara and every other Argentine passing through, had beat a path to the home of Isaías Nogues. Proud of his recent exploit, he carried a clipping from *Life* magazine with an account of his escape and flight to safety. From Bolivia he planned to go to Peru, then to Guatemala, and eventually to the United States.

At the Nogues home, Rojo also took notice of Guevara's "savage" eating habits and was surprised to find out he was a doctor, since he talked mostly about archeology. "The first time I saw him, Guevara didn't particularly impress me. He spoke little, preferring to listen to the conversation of others. But then, suddenly, he would cut the speaker down with a disarming smile and a razor-sharp comment."

It was a trait they shared. Rojo too had a mordant wit and sharp tongue, and he enjoyed debating as much as Guevara. That first night, they walked back together to Ernesto's hostel, talking. According to Rojo, they "became friends, although the only thing we really had in common at the time was that we were both young university students pressed for money. I wasn't interested in archeology, nor he in politics, at least not in the sense that politics had meaning for me then and would later have for him."

Following this encounter the two arranged to meet again; in fact, Rojo was to become an ubiquitous figure, someone who kept popping in and out of Guevara's life over the next decade.*

Despite his keenness to be present in La Paz for the second of August, with its rumored threat of a counterrevolutionary uprising, Ernesto was also anxious to see the conditions in the notorious Bolivian mines for himself, and so, although it meant being away on that momentous day, he and Calica arranged a visit to the Bolsa Negra wolframite mine, near La Paz. At an altitude of over seventeen thousand feet, the mine sat overshadowed by the scree and ice of Mt. Illimani. The mine's engineers showed their visitors the place where, during a strike before the revolution, the company's guards had placed a machine gun and fired it against the miners and their families; now the miners had triumphed and the mine belonged to the state. Here, as at Chuquicamata, Ernesto was moved by what he saw. "The silence of the mine assails even those like us who don't know its language."

Ernesto and Calica spent a night at the mine, and, as they prepared to depart for La Paz, met up with truckloads of miners returning from La Paz, where they had gone in a show of strength to support the agrarian reform law. They were armed and shooting off their guns into the sky. To Ernesto, with their "stony faces and red plastic helmets" they appeared to be "warriors from other worlds." In the end, they learned, the day had passed without major unrest in the capital.

For Ernesto, the mine visit had been worthwhile. Once again he had seen for himself stark evidence of Latin America's dependency on the United

*See the appendix for elaboration.

States. He wrote of Bolsa Negra's ore: "Today it is the only thing that keeps Bolivia going; it is a mineral the Americans buy and for this reason the government has ordered production increased." Here was proof positive of his prediction already extended to Chile in its own mines-nationalization dilemma. As long as the Americans controlled the export market for the minerals, true independence was impossible.

Bolivia's revolutionary government was well aware of the fact and had already come under strong pressure from the new Eisenhower administration to proceed cautiously with its reforms. And it had heeded the advice; the triumphant MNR revolution had confiscated only the mines of the three biggest tin barons. What's more, Bolivia was still dependent on the United States, both as a buyer for its minerals and for the prices they brought. During World War II, the United States had bought up at low prices huge tin stocks, which it held as buffer reserves, and it was now in a position to dictate the world price of the mineral by selling off those stocks.

Economic pressure was not the only risk Bolivia's revolution faced. Since Eisenhower had assumed office, the United States had embarked on an aggressive policy to contain "Soviet-Communist expansionism" abroad. Bolivia's President Paz Estenssoro had only to look around in the summer of 1953 to see what difficulties his government might encounter should he incur Washington's wrath.

Accused of tilting toward Communism, Guatemala's left-leaning government was coming under mounting attack from Washington for its own 1952 agrarian reform bill, which had nationalized the powerful United Fruit Company interests there. United Fruit wanted revenge and was already showing it had influential friends in high places, particularly in the Eisenhower administration.

The world was arriving at a new threshold. In the Soviet Union, Josef Stalin had died in March. With the West, however, the Cold War would continue unabated. In a bid to achieve strategic-arms parity with the United States, the USSR was also putting the finishing touches on the world's first hydrogen bomb, which it would explode on August 12.

Amid prisoner-of-war exchanges by both sides in Korea, Chinese and United Nations troops clashed in a final round of bloodletting, but that three-year conflict, which had cost the lives of over three million Korean civilians, now ended in an armistice. Signed on July 27, the truce left the peninsula divided and in ruins. Now East and West faced each other across another hostile border, adding a tense new flash point to an increasingly divided world.

In Cuba, a country considered "safe" by Washington, events were taking place that would soon take on a profound significance in Guevara's life.

On July 26, a group of young armed rebels hoping to spark off a national rebellion against the military dictator Fulgencio Batista attacked and temporarily overran the Moncada army barracks in the eastern city of Santiago. Only eight had died in the actual Moncada fighting, while nineteen government soldiers had been killed, but their action was routed and turned into a bloodbath. Despite attempts by Batista to link the rebellion to "Communists," Cuba's Communist party decried the uprising as a "bourgeois putsch" and denied any involvement. Sixty-nine of the young rebels were summarily executed or tortured to death after capture. After church intervention, the remaining survivors, including the revolt's twenty-six-year-old student leader, Fidel Castro, and his younger brother, Raúl, were rounded up and taken into custody.

II

Back in revolutionary La Paz, Ernesto and Calica visited the newly created Ministry of Peasant Affairs and met with its head, Ñuflo Chávez, whose job it was to implement the announced agrarian reform bill. Ernesto found his ministry "a strange place, full of Indians of different groups of the altiplano waiting their turns to be received in audience. Each group had its typical costume and was led by a caudillo or indoctrinator who addressed them in their own native tongue. The employees dusted them upon entering with DDT."

The spectacle made Ernesto indignant, for it pointed to the cultural divide that still existed between the revolution's leaders and the common people they were supposed to represent. To Calica, the DDT spraying seemed reasonable enough, since the Indians "were filthy and crawling with lice, and the ministry's carpets and curtains had to be protected from such vermin." Afterward, whenever they saw an Indian in the street with his hair dusted white, he and Ernesto would look at one another and remark, "Look, he's been with Ñuflo Chávez."

By now Ernesto and Calica had been in La Paz nearly a month. They had spent half of their available capital and they had their visas for Venezuela. It was time to get back on the road, but both of them were finding it difficult to pull up roots. Finally, they agreed to leave, and Ernesto wrote: "Each one of us had his amorous reference to leave behind. My good-bye was more in the intellectual plane, without sweetness, but I believe there is something between us, her and me." Calica, meanwhile, believed he was in love, and he had made promises to return to La Paz for his new sweetheart after he had found his feet in Caracas.

After a brief sojourn to Lake Titicaca, Ernesto and Calica reached the Peruvian border. At the customs post in the border town of Puno, Ernesto's books provoked an incident. As he told it, "they confiscated two books: *Man in the Soviet Union* and a publication of the Ministry of Peasant Affairs, which was described as Red, Red, Red in exclamatory and recriminating tones." After a "juicy chat," however, the police chief let them go, telling Ernesto his books would be sent to Lima, where he'd asked for them to be returned.

They traveled from Puno to Cuzco. Ernesto was delighted to be back, but Calica was singularly unimpressed by the historic place. He wrote his mother that it was an interesting city, but "the dirtiest you can possibly imagine," so filthy that it "obliged one to bathe." However, he told her jokingly, in the eight days they were there, "El Chancho bathed once and by mutual agreement, for health purposes only."

After a few days, Calica's complaints about the dirt and discomfort had begun to wear on Ernesto. Writing to Celia on August 22, he vented his frustrations. "Alberto threw himself on the grass to marry Incan princesses, to recuperate [lost] empires. Calica curses the filth and every time he steps into one of the innumerable turds that litter the streets, instead of looking at the sky and a cathedral framed in space, he looks at his dirty shoes. He doesn't smell the evocative mystery of Cuzco, but instead the odor of stew and dung; a question of temperaments. We've decided to leave this city rapidly in view of how little he likes it."

As for his future, he told her, he was uncertain because he "didn't know how things were" in Venezuela. As for the more distant future, he said he hadn't budged on his hopes to somehow earn "$10,000 U.S.," apparently the sum of money he planned to save there. Then, "with Alberto, maybe we'll take a new trip, but in a North-South direction, and maybe by helicopter. After Europe and after that, darkness." In other words, anything was possible.

After a detour to Machu Picchu, which, although still crawling with American tourists, continued to entrance Ernesto, they set out on a grueling three-day bus trip to Lima. Some comic relief came at a rest-stop where he and Calica climbed down the hillside for a swim in the cold waters of the Rio Abancay. Stark naked, Ernesto took a special delight in leaping up and down to wave to the shocked female passengers back up on the road. Arriving exhausted in Lima, they found a hotel and slept "like dormice."

On September 4 Ernesto wrote his father, complaining that he had expected to discover "a ton of letters" from Buenos Aires, but had found only one, from him. "I'm glad to hear the economic difficulties aren't so many that some little help from me is urgently needed. I am happy for all of you . . . but don't forget to tell me *'si las papas queman'* [if things get bad], to hurry up a bit."

Clearly, he felt under pressure to find paying work with which to help out his family, and his father's reassurances that things were all right had eased his conscience for the time being. In the same letter, he sent a barbed reproof to pass on to his mother for not writing him. He suggested she try writing him each time she sat down to play solitaire as a "cure" for her addiction to the game.

In Lima, Calica was finally in his element. "I like it a lot, it's modern, clean, with all the comforts, a great city," he wrote his mother on September 8. They were well taken care of, having met up with Ernesto's friends at the Guía leprosarium and with Dr. Pesce, who had helped them find a clean pension with hot water and a university cafeteria in which to eat their meals. And they had met up again with Gobo Nogues. "Gobo has introduced us to the social life, we've eaten twice in the Country Club, really good, super-expensive, naturally they didn't let us put our hand in our pockets and we've been a lot to the Gran Hotel Bolívar [Lima's most expensive hotel]," he gushed.

Ernesto, by contrast, was viewing Lima with the critical eye of a detached ascetic. "Her churches full of magnificence inside don't achieve externally—my opinion—the display of august sobriety of Cuzco's temples. . . . The cathedral . . . seems to have been built in a period of transition when the warrior fury of Spain entered into decadence to give way to a love of luxury, of comforts." In his journal, there is a dismal mention about attending a party in which "I wasn't able to drink because I had asthma, but it allowed Calica to get totally smashed." As for their visit to a cinema to see a "revolutionary" new "3-D" film for the first time, he was unimpressed. "It doesn't seem to be a revolution in anything and the films are still the same."

Ernesto saw Dr. Pesce a couple of times and once again enjoyed "a long and amenable discussion on a wide range of topics." But afterward he and Calica were detained, interrogated, and their hostel room turned upside down by Peruvian detectives, apparently mistaking them for a pair of "wanted kidnappers." The incident was cleared up, but afterward, Ernesto decided to avoid further contact with Pesce in case the police still had them under scrutiny. He didn't want to cause the doctor, or themselves, any more problems.

Ernesto wasn't entirely convinced that their brush with the police was simply a matter of mistaken identity. There had been the fuss over his "Red" literature confiscated at the frontier with Bolivia, and his and Calica's names were probably on file as suspicious characters. With Peru's dictator Manuel Odría still in power and undoubtedly worried about Bolivia's left-wing revolution "contaminating his chicken coop," as Ernesto put it to Calica, he didn't want the Peruvian authorities to draw any undue links between them and the Communist Dr. Pesce. He also gave up his hopes of retrieving his confiscated books, deciding that it could only complicate their stay in Lima.

On September 17, Ernesto received a letter from his mother, who informed him that she had arranged for them to be "put up" by the president of Ecuador when they arrived in his country. The next day, an excited Calica wrote his mother to give her this wonderful news, crowing jubilantly that he and Ernesto could now look ahead to "a beautiful panorama in terms of room and board."

They also bumped into their exiled Argentine friend, Ricardo Rojo, again. He was on his way to Guayaquil, where he hoped to board a boat for Panama. Since this was also their next port of call, Rojo gave them the name of a Guayaquil pension where they could find him.

III

With Ernesto suffering again from asthma, they traveled by bus up the Peruvian coast. After entering Ecuador on September 28 and waiting for transport in the border town of Huaquillas, Ernesto complained of "losing a day's traveling, which Calica took advantage of by drinking beer." Another day and night of boat travel down a river, into the Gulf of Guayaquil, and across its swampy delta brought them to the seamy tropical port city of Guayaquil. They were met at the pier by Ricardo Rojo and three law student friends from Argentina's Universidad de La Plata, who led them back to the pension where they were staying. Rojo's companions were Eduardo "Gualo" García, Oscar "Valdo" Valdovinos, and Andro "Petiso" Herrero. Like Rojo, they were heading next to Guatemala, and trying to have a bit of an adventure along the way.

Their pension was a crumbling old colonial mansion with a canoe dock on the muddy banks of the Río Guayas in a run-down quarter called the Quinta Pareja. Its large rooms were in the process of being subdivided into tiny cubicles fashioned from wooden automobile shipping crates. When Ernesto and Calica arrived, they joined the four others in a cavernous room as the house's internal dimensions gradually shrunk around them.

The pension's hard-pressed owner was a good-hearted woman named María Luisa. Life in her rustic establishment was like being part of a large, chaotic family going through hard times. María Luisa ran the place with her mother, Agrippina—an ancient crone who spent her days swinging in a hammock in the foyer, endlessly smoking cigarettes—and her husband,

Alexander. He too had been a guest, so the story went, but his debts had grown so high, he had been forced to marry María Luisa.

In the end, they didn't have to go to Quito to call upon President Velasco Ibarra. Learning that the chief of state was visiting Guayaquil, Ernesto and Calica got dressed up and went to throw themselves on the mercy of his private secretary. On October 21, Ernesto wrote his mother to tell her mockingly how his interview had gone. "He told me that I couldn't see Velasco Ibarra, that the disastrous [personal] economic situation I had painted for him was one of life's low points, adding in a philosophical tone: 'For life has highs and lows, you are in a low one, have spirit, have spirit.'" Ernesto and Calica were back where they had been, virtually broke, and so were their companions. Meanwhile, their debts with María Luisa were mounting. They pooled their funds and instituted a strict economic regimen that Ernesto enforced. Calica may have started out the trip as the wearer of the "chastity belt," but their time on the road had made it all too clear who was the better economizer. Ernesto established a slogan of "absolute thrift" which he himself broke only to buy the occasional banana, practically all he was eating at the time.

In mid-October, Ricardo Rojo and Oscar Valdovinos shipped out to Panama on a boat belonging to the United Fruit Company; the others would have to follow on the next available ship. For now, Ernesto and Calica remained camped out with Gualo García and Andro Herrero. While they pondered their next move, enjoying the camaraderie of their group and unwilling quite yet to depart for Venezuela, Ernesto explored Guayaquil. In the pension he played chess and conversed with his new friends. They were all a little homesick for Argentina, and they talked of their families, their pasts, and their future hopes. Ernesto asked the others to call him "Chancho," and his asthma improved.

8

Finding North

I

There was nothing compelling holding Ernesto in Guayaquil, a city he dismissed as "a pretend city almost without its own life, which revolves around the daily event of ships coming and going."

But he didn't leave. He hung around, counting his pennies and sharing the poverty of his marooned new friends. He confessed to Andro Herrero that he had never previously enjoyed this experience of unconditional comradeship, where everyone shared what they had without misgivings and faced common problems together, while discussing everything under the sun. The closest he had come to it before was in rugby; his fellow players were good "mates," they were fine to go out for a drink with, but none of them were really close, and off the pitch their kinship had ended. His closest friend, he said, was Alberto, and Calica was "a good guy" whom he had known since childhood, but the truth was they had little in common.

True camaraderie, he told Andro, had eluded him. It was something he had always craved but felt lacking in his own family, as fragmented and overrun with adopted outsiders as it was. He spoke a lot about his mother, and it was obvious to Andro that Ernesto felt a special tug there, but he also blurted out that his mother had surrounded herself with poets and frivolous literary types, women who were "probably lesbians." A few years older than Ernesto, Andro understood his remarks as expressing his feelings of emotional exclusion, and felt instinctively that he was a lonely young man in great need of affection.

"Guevara was a very particular guy," recalled Andro. "At times he seemed inexpressive, with a demeanor that was almost disagreeable. But it was because of his asthma, the effort to breathe caused him to contract, and he could appear *hard*. But afterward, he would relax and his eyes smiled; the sides of his eyes wrinkled."

The severity of Ernesto's asthma attacks had come as a shock to his new companions, and they reacted by helping him as much as they could. "I remember waking up in the night with Guevara trying to reach his Asmapul [medicine]," recalled Andro, "but not having the strength to reach it, and one of us having to get it for him."

While he reveled in this newfound fraternal atmosphere, Ernesto was torn by conflicting feelings about what to do next. He had a path that was already laid out for him; before he had left Buenos Aires, Alberto Granado had written to say a job awaited him at his leprosarium. If he needed money to get there, not to worry, Alberto would lend it to him. Ernesto had some emotionally powerful motives for going, as well. He told Andro that he wanted to earn enough money to send his mother to Paris for specialized medical treatment. He feared she still had cancer, and wanted her treated by the best doctors available.

One day, his dilemma was resolved when Gualo García threw out a casual invitation to come along with him and Andro to Guatemala. They were going off to Guatemala to see something new, a leftist revolution that had challenged America's might and was now struggling for its survival in a drama whose outcome might determine the future of Latin America. And just like that, Ernesto accepted, abandoning his former plans and throwing all his promises out the window.

It was one thing to have decided to go to Guatemala, another to actually get there. For Ernesto and his friends, leaving Guayaquil was the first hurdle they faced. They would need visas for Panama, which also required having an onward passage.

Since they were broke and this was impossible, they would need to convince friendly ship captains to vouch for them with the Panamanian authorities while agreeing to take them for free. It was a tall order, and they knew it, but they doggedly began making the rounds of the docks. Their first attempts met with failure, and the days wore on in a penny-pinching tedium.

Ernesto made friends with the crew of an Argentine scrap vessel making a port call. It brought him back fond memories of the *Anna G.,* one of the ships he had worked on in 1951, and after he went on board to eat and drink red wine a few times, he returned to the pension loaded down with American cigarettes and *yerba mate.* An Argentine diplomat on the ship who knew his family gave Ernesto unexpected news from home, informing him "almost in passing" of the recent death of his aunt Edelmira Moore de la Serna. With an almost cruel bluntness that was beginning to characterize his correspondence with his family, he wrote a condolence letter to his uncle and cousins, saying: "It is very hard to send words of hope in circumstances like these and it is even more so for me, who for reasons emanating from my position toward life, cannot even insinuate the religious consolation that so helped Edelmira in her final years."

The days passed. By now, Calica was impatient to make a move, and he decided to proceed alone as far as Ecuador's inland capital, Quito. Ernesto would give it a few more days, and if the situation didn't improve, he would telegram Calica in Quito to wait for him, and they would go on to Caracas together. Then, a few days after Calica's departure, the *Guayos* captain gave them a false letter vouching for their onward passage from Panama, and they obtained their visas. But no sooner had Ernesto telegrammed Calica telling him *not* to wait for him than the *Guayos*'s sailing date was postponed "indefinitely."

Ernesto succumbed to asthma, made worse by medicine that caused nausea and diarrhea. He and his friends also had a huge unpaid bill at María Luisa's pension, and every day their debt grew larger. They discussed dodging out without paying but abandoned this plan after realizing it would impossible to get past the indomitable Agrippina in the foyer. They began to sell their possessions.

On October 22, Ernesto wrote his mother to announce his "new position as a 100% adventurer." Breaking the news that he was going to Guatemala, he told her he had sold the new suit she had given him as a farewell gift. "The pearl of your dreams died heroically in a pawnshop, and the same fate befell all the unnecessary things of my luggage." He had even decided to sell his treasured camera, but "the bourgeois remnants of my proprietorial hunger" made him balk when a buyer appeared. A few days later, Ernesto noted in his diary with desperation: "There's practically nothing left to sell, and so our situation is really precarious: we don't have a peso on us and our debt is 500 [Ecuadorean sucres], possibly 1000, that's the thing."

It was Andro who came up with a solution. He would stay behind as guarantor for their debts, and the others would try to send him funds so he could leave and join them. Ernesto argued against this plan, saying that after all *he* was the newcomer, and if anyone should stay behind, it was himself. But Andro was firm about it, and the matter was settled when a friend of his, a food-buyer for the elegant Hotel Humboldt, agreed to pay off most of their debts if Andro stayed behind and worked for him.

(In the end, Andro was never able to rejoin his comrades but languished for months in Ecuador working at a variety of odd jobs, including one as a "human cannonball" in a circus. Calica reached Caracas, contacted Alberto, and found a job. He lived in Venezuela for almost ten years before returning home. Neither he nor Andro would ever see Ernesto again.)

Now there were two of them. After further delays, the *Guayos* was ready to sail. Ernesto traded his seaman's duffel bag with its collapsible internal wood frame to Andro for a bigger suitcase in which to lug all his books. On October 31, Andro saw Ernesto and Gualo off on a wharf that was piled with coconuts. Ernesto's account of their leave-taking was detached: "The instant of the farewells as usual cold, always inferior to one's hopes, finding oneself in that moment incapable of showing deep feelings."

But Andro's memory of the moment is distinct; he remembers the normally reserved Ernesto "crying like a child," telling him how much he valued his friendship. Andro was touched by this display of feeling and, overcome with emotion himself, turned away and left the dock before the *Guayos* sailed.

II

As he sailed north to Central America, Ernesto knew he was about to enter a region "where the countries were not true nations, but private *estancias*," belonging to the dictators of turn. A few years before, his favorite poet, Pablo Neruda, had written a poem called "The United Fruit Co.," damning the company for its exploitation and for creating a slew of subservient "banana republics" ruled by loyal local despots. "The Tyrannical Reign of the Flies," Neruda called it. "Trujillo the fly, and Tacho the fly, the flies called Carías, Martínez, Ubico . . . the bloody domain of the flies."

Indeed, in 1953, with the sole exception of Guatemala, the clutch of backward agrarian nations on the Central American isthmus were all U.S.-dominated "banana republics." On the slender neck of land joining the North and South American continents, Panama was barely a sovereign state fifty years after its creation by Teddy Roosevelt to ensure American control over the newly built Panama Canal. Despite mounting nationalist sentiment, the United States retained jurisdiction over the Canal Zone bisecting the country, complete with its own military bases, and exercised a preponderant role in Panama's economy and political life.

Nicaragua had been ruled by the corrupt General Anastasio "Tacho" Somoza García since the 1930s. Somoza's rule had been secured by treachery, after he ordered the assassination of nationalist guerrilla leader Augusto César Sandino during talks to end years of civil war and repeated incursions to "restore order" by American marines. Staunchly anti-Communist, Somoza had a lot of friends in Washington, and it had been on his urging that the CIA had first initiated hostilities against Guatemala's reformist revolution.

Similarly, tiny El Salvador was firmly in the hands of its coffee-growing oligarchy. A succession of military rulers had run the country ever since a Communist-inspired peasant rebellion had been quelled twenty years earlier at the cost of thirty thousand lives, and life for the peasant majority there remained feudal. Neighboring Honduras was almost roadless, undeveloped and underpopulated, and its governments of turn were woefully subservient to the United Fruit Company, which had extensive plantations there and owned the country's ports and railroads.

Costa Rica was an exception to the rule. It also played host to the Fruit Company, but since its own 1948 reformist revolution led by José "Pepe" Figueres, Costa Rica had extracted better trade terms for itself while managing to stay on Washington's good side by abstaining from expropriating foreign interests. Touted as the "Switzerland of Central America," Costa Rica exuded an atmosphere of political tolerance and moderation.

The neighboring Caribbean islands, with their plantation economies and poor black populations descended from African slaves, were a soup of imperial dominions ruled by white governors appointed from London, Paris, or the Hague. These same European powers still had colonies on the mainland as well: tiny British Honduras on the Yucatán peninsula, and the remote Guyanas on South America's northern cape remained in Dutch, French, and British hands. The United States had joined this imperial crowd with its virtual annexation of Puerto Rico. After seizing it from Spain a half century earlier, Puerto Rico had been made the first U.S. "commonwealth" only the year before. Only Haiti, the Dominican Republic, and Cuba were independent republics, and all languished under rule that was unstable, corrupt, or both. The egomaniacal and sinister General Rafael Trujillo had ruled and robbed the Dominican Republic since 1930. As for black Haiti, politically shaky since a 1950 coup, it would soon succumb to the terrifying rule of Dr. François "Papa Doc" Duvalier. And, since the year before, Cuba was under the freewheeling grip of General Fulgencio Batista, who had come to power in a military coup.

III

When the *Guayos* docked in Panama, Ernesto and Gualo made their way to a cheap pension where they were allowed to sleep in the hallway for a dollar a day each. At the Argentine consulate, they discovered that Rojo and Valdovinos had already gone on to Guatemala but had left a letter for them. It contained the names of some contacts at the Panama university students' federation, and the surprising news that Valdovinos had gotten married after a whirlwind romance to twenty-three-year-old Luzmila Oller, the daughter of a Panamanian congressman.

They met Luzmila, who had stayed behind, and learned that her sudden marriage with Valdo had caused a "revolution" in the Oller family: Her father had moved out of their home; Luzmila's mother had refused to meet Valdo; and it had all been a real scandal, complete with accusations by the Ollers that Valdo was a rascal and a gold digger. In his journal, Ernesto disparaged Valdo for taking off to Guatemala without having "gotten a screw or, it seems, even a serious feel" with his bride. As for the new Mrs. Valdovinos, she was *"muy simpática,* seems really intelligent but is far too Catholic for my tastes."

Ernesto and Gualo began to hustle. The Argentine consul was helpful, and so were their university contacts. They quickly made friends among the students and fell in with an interesting crowd of poets, artists, and political activists who hung out at two cafés, the Iberia and the Coca-Cola. Their new friends helped them pay their pension bill and steered Ernesto toward magazine editors, to see if he could publish some travel articles, and to the university medical faculty, where it was arranged for him to give a talk on allergy.

He was paid twenty dollars for an article he wrote about his raft adventure with Alberto Granado, published in *Panama-America;* but in his journal he remarked that the one on Machu Picchu was "being fought over" with the editors of *Siete* because of its pronounced anti-American slant. In "Machu Picchu, Enigma de Piedra en America," eventually published on December 12, 1953, Ernesto fired both cannons at the Yankee looters of Peru's archeological patrimony. After describing the history of the Incan Empire and Hiram Bingham's discovery of Machu Picchu, he wrote: "Here comes the sad part. All the ruins were cleared of overgrowth, perfectly studied and described and . . . totally robbed of every object that fell into the hands of the researchers, who triumphantly took back to their country more than two hundred boxes containing priceless archeological treasures. . . . [W]here can one go to admire or study the treasures of the indigenous city? The answer is obvious: in the museums of North America." It isn't surprising that he had trouble with his editors: these were provocative words to be printed in American-dominated Panama, with its U.S.-run Canal Zone and military bases. And his conclusion revealed his emerging political viewpoint. "Let's be content then, with giving the [Incan] city its two possible significances: for the fighter who . . . with a voice of stone shouts with continental reach: 'Citizen of Indoamerica, reconquer the past'; for others . . . a valid phrase can be found in the visitor's book of the hotel, left imprinted there by an English subject with all the bitterness of his imperial nostalgia: 'I am lucky to find a place without a Coca-Cola advertisement.'"

To Ernesto, it must have seemed to him an appropriate place to initiate hostilities against the country he had come to see as a mortal enemy. Meanwhile, in his journal, Ernesto began listing and describing the people he met, evaluating them according to their human qualities and, increasingly, for their political "soundness" as well.

At Panama University he mentioned meeting a "Dr. Carlos Moreno, who impressed me as an intelligent demagogue, very knowledgeable of the psychology of the masses but not so much in the dialectics of history. He is very simpatico and cordial and treated us with deference. He gives the impression of knowing what he does and where he is going but he wouldn't take a revolution further than the strictly indispensable to contain the masses."

Dr. Moreno's knowledge of Marxist ideology and his potential value as a *revolutionary* were what mattered to Ernesto. One cannot help but feel that in these portraits he was consigning people to his notes for their potential future use as players in a revolution that transcended national boundaries, as if the early glimmerings of his future program were already seeping into his consciousness.

While Ernesto honed his sword in tropical Panama, back in Buenos Aires Guevara Lynch was fussing over his vagabond son. He had fumed ever since Ernesto's letter from Guayaquil in which he told of having pawned his suit. Determined that his son, "El Doctor Guevara," should be properly attired, Guevara Lynch decided to have a new wardrobe tailored and sent to Ernesto.

When Ernesto received the new suit, blazer, and ties, he sent a letter to his father that said: "What little value Argentine clothes have—for the whole lot I got only one hundred dollars!"

By late November, Ernesto and Gualo's economic situation was getting desperate again. A ship they had hoped to get to Guatemala had been delayed. They resolved to continue overland but faced new visa problems again. "Our situation is bad," he wrote in his diary. "The Costa Rican consul is a dickhead and won't give us the visa. . . . the struggle becomes hard . . ."

By now, Luzmila was ready to leave and join Valdo in Guatemala. Things had been smoothed over with her family, and she was hoping for a possible diplomatic post at the Panamanian embassy in Guatemala. Before she took off, she came to Ernesto and Gualo's rescue, lending them forty-five dollars. They had finally obtained their Costa Rican visas and were ready to go. With five dollars remaining in their pockets after paying debts, they were off. But they didn't get very far before things started going wrong.

Somewhere in the middle of northern Panama the truck they were riding in broke down, then later drove off the road. After two more days cadging rides on rural trains and hiking on foot, they crossed into Costa Rica and reached the pretty Pacific port of Golfito, a United Fruit Company banana port, built for its "10,000 employees." Ernesto took note of the "city's division into well-defined zones with guards who impede entry, and, of course, the best zone is that of the gringos. It looks something like Miami but, naturally, without poor people there, and [the gringos] are trapped behind the four walls of their homes and the narrow [social] group they make up."

He visited the company hospital and observed critically: "The hospital is a comfortable house where correct medical attention can be given but the benefits vary according to the category of person working in the company. As always, the class spirit of the gringos can be seen."

They embarked the next day aboard a United Fruit Company ship Ernesto nicknamed "the famous *Pachuca* (which transports *pachucos,* bums)." The ship's real name was the *Río Grande,* and it made the run to the Pacific coast port of Puntarenas, in Costa Rica. The trip started well enough, but within a few hours the seas got rough and "*La Pachuca* began to fly."

Wrote Ernesto: "Almost all the passengers including Gualo started to vomit. I stayed outside with a *negrita,* Socorro, whom I'd picked up, more whorish than a hen with sixteen years on her back." Seasoned mariner that he was, Ernesto was unaffected by seasickness, and spent the next two days at sea romping with the pliant Socorro. After docking at Puntarenas, he said good-bye to her, and he and Gualo headed inland for the Costa Rican capital of San José.

A tiny city of red-tiled and tin roofs nestled under clear blue skies and perched on gently rolling green hills, San José was the new headquarters for the Caribbean Legion. A regional prodemocracy political alliance, previously based in Havana, where it had enjoyed the patronage of Cuba's former president, Carlos Prío Socarrás, the legion had moved to San José following Batista's coup. Now, under the guiding hand of President Figueres, exiled political leaders from the dictatorships in Venezuela, the Dominican Republic, and Nicaragua met in San José to plot and conspire.

Pepe Figueres was that rarity, a Latin American politician whose opinion was respected in Washington by both conservative and liberal policymakers. The diminutive Costa Rican had achieved this feat by treading a cautious middle ground in his political reforms: He had abolished Costa Rica's army, nationalized the banks, extended state control over the economy, but left foreign interests untouched. He had further endeared himself by banning Costa Rica's Communist party, while lobbying Washington to move away from its traditional reliance on dictatorships in the region and support democratic reform.

At the time, in addition to Figueres, Latin America's leading "democratic alternatives" were Victor Raúl Haya de la Torre's Alianza Popular Revolucionaria Americana, or APRA, movement in Peru, and Venezuela's Acción Democrática, led by Rómulo Betancourt, who had presided over a liberal coalition government until it was toppled by the military in favor of Marcos Pérez Jiménez. The policies they espoused were moderately "social democratic," yet firmly anti-Communist, while promoting social reform and foreign investment at the same time. The Dominican Partido Democrático Revolucionario, led by mulatto storyteller and politician Juan Bosch, represented the most left-wing of the exile parties, though it too fell short of an overtly Marxist platform.

While Haya de la Torre was in his fifth year of political asylum as a guest of the Colombian embassy in Lima, both Bosch and Betancourt were in Costa Rica, and Ernesto very much wished to hear their ideas on social and political reform. He was especially interested in their positions regarding the United States, a topic that had become his weather vane for determining political legitimacy. But he and Gualo also needed to survive, and so a new round of scrounging began as they pursued their double agenda.

They spent a day chatting with Juan Bosch and Costa Rican Communist leader Manuel Mora Valverde. A few days later, Ernesto finally met Romulo Betancourt. Of the three, it was the Communist Mora Valverde, "a calm man . . . with a series of movements like tics that indicate a great internal restlessness," who most impressed Ernesto. He took careful notes of Mora's analysis of Costa Rica's recent history and of Figueres's pro-American policies. Summing up, Ernesto wrote: "When Figueres is disabused of his faith in the compassion of the Department of State comes the *incognita:* Will he fight or submit? There is the dilemma and we will see what happens."

Ernesto described Juan Bosch as "a literary man of clear ideas and of leftist tendency. We didn't speak of literature, simply of politics. He described Batista as a gangster surrounded by gangsters." In his appraisal of Rómulo Betancourt, Ernesto was scathing. "He gives me the impresson of being a politician with some firm social ideas in his head but the rest are fluttery and twistable in the direction of the best advantages. In principle he's on the side of the United States. He went along with the [1948] Rio [Inter-American Defense] Pact and dedicated himself to speaking horrors of the Communists."

Soon afterward, Ernesto and Gualo set out hitchhiking for the land he called the *"estancia* of Tacho [Somoza]"—Nicaragua. Across the border, during a torrential downpour, Ricardo Rojo suddenly reappeared. He was traveling with two Argentine brothers, the Beverragis, who were driving their own car to South America. Feeling at loose ends after a few weeks in Guatemala, Rojo had come along for the ride. Seeing that the road into Costa Rica was impassable, Rojo and his companions went to the coast to see about a ferry south, while Ernesto and Gualo went by bus to the Nicaraguan capital of Managua.

For Ernesto, the parched, hot lakeside city of Managua held little interest, and he spent his time in "a pilgrimage to consulates with its entourage of imbecilities," hunting for visas. But in the Honduran consulate, Rojo and his companions reappeared. They had been unable to get a ferry. On the spot, the group decided to split ranks: Rojo and Walter Beverragi would fly to San José; Ernesto and Gualo would drive with Domingo back to Guatemala, where Domingo would sell the car.

That night, they had a long discussion about Argentina and its politics, and, as Ernesto recorded it, they concluded the following about one another's political positions. "Rojo, Gualo and Domingo were *radicales intransigentes* [a liberal wing of the Argentine Unión Cívica Radical, led by Dr. Arturo Frondizi, Rojo's mentor]; Walter was a *laborista* [of the leftist Partido Laborista] and I am a *sniper* according to 'El Gordo' [Rojo]."

Walter Beverragi had been imprisoned and tortured for his part in a 1948 plot to overthrow Perón. Beverragi had escaped but been stripped of his citizenship while in exile in the United States.* It was a reminder of how far Perón would go to punish his opponents, and Rojo was nervous for himself because he and Valdovinos had given a press conference in Guatemala City airing their own charges against Perón. Ernesto himself was mostly aloof from this Argentine polemic, but he *was* interested and listened intently, occasionally launching one of the barbed commentaries that had earned him the Sniper nickname.

Ernesto drove on with Gualo and Domingo Beverragi to the Honduran border. They had only twenty dollars among them. Stopping only to change punctured tires, they continued their journey across an arid stretch of rural Honduras, crossed little El Salvador's volcano-dominated landscape in a day, and pushed on to the green highlands of Guatemala. They paid the border tolls in kind, with coffee upon exiting El Salvador, and a lantern upon entering Guatemala. On the morning of December 24, they arrived in Guatemala City with a total of three dollars left.

*In later years, Walter Beverragi became a prominent ultranationalist, espousing anti-Semitic views and, in his book *El Dogma Nacionalista,* attacked "democracy" and "liberalism" as twin evils of modern, decadent society.

IV

In the 1950s, Guatemala City was a small, conservative provincial city, a privileged white and mestizo urban enclave in an overwhelmingly rural and Indian country of astonishing natural beauty. The surrounding highlands of forested volcanos, lakes, and coffee plantations—dotted with the villages of indigenous peasants—drop away to the tropical Pacific coastal lowlands with their sugar plantations and farms.

But the picture-postcard image presented by successive Guatemalan governments to outsiders, one of colorfully clad natives working happily in harmonious communion with their habitat, was deceptive. Guatemala was a place where the Spanish conquest seemed fresh despite the passage of time, a place where a white and mixed-blood Creole minority had ruled for centuries over a native majority who existed by laboring on the vast private plantations of the oligarchy, or those of the United Fruit Company.

This state of affairs was a fact of life until the reformist "revolution" of Juan José Arévalo had overturned the ruthlessly authoritarian Ubico dictatorship in the 1940s and called for democratic change. Arévalo had been unable to implement all the reforms he promoted, but he was succeeded by a left-leaning Guatemalan colonel, Jacobo Arbenz, who pushed on with them. The most inflammatory of these was the land-reform decree Arbenz had signed into law in 1952, ending the oligarchic *latifundia* system and nationalizing the properties of United Fruit.

The action had earned Arbenz the undying enmity of Guatemala's conservative elite and of the powerful United Fruit Company, which enjoyed extraordinarily close contacts with the Eisenhower administration. Among them were the Dulles brothers—the secretary of state and CIA director respectively. Both had been associated with United Fruit through their work with the Sullivan and Cromwell law firm, and its client the J. Henry Schroder Banking Corporation, in turn the financial advisor to the International Railways of Central America, IRCA. IRCA had owned most of Guatemala's railways before selling out to United Fruit in a deal handled by John Foster Dulles. His brother, Allen Dulles, had been a director of the Schroder Bank, which the CIA also used to launder its funds for covert operations.

The relationships between the Eisenhower administration and United Fruit were downright cozy, and the list went on. Among others, Assistant Secretary for Inter-American Affairs John Moors Cabot's family owned interests in United Fruit, and Eisenhower's personal secretary was also the wife of the company's public relations director. With such friends, the United Fruit Company could afford to throw its weight around. To ratchet up the pressure, it hired the tenacious Spruille Braden, Truman's former top Latin emissary, as a consultant. In March 1953, Braden gave a fiery speech at Dartmouth College, urging the Eisenhower administration to intervene militarily against the "Communists" in Guatemala. Immediately afterward, in a hint of how far it was prepared to go, United Fruit had organized an armed uprising in the provincial capital of Salamá. In the subsequent trials of some of the captured raiders, United Fruit's involvement in the rebellion was unmasked, but what *wasn't* known publicly yet was that the CIA was also involved, and was discussing further plans with United Fruit to overthrow Guatemala's government.

By the end of 1953, the battle lines were clearly drawn between Guatemala and Washington; Guatemala's Central American neighbors, especially dictators such as Somoza, were vociferous about their concerns of a spillover effect to their countries. Meanwhile, either as political exiles, or, like Ernesto, merely eager to see Guatemala's "socialist" experiment firsthand, hundreds of Latin American leftists had arrived in Guatemala, and their presence had lent a combustive element to Guatemala's hothouse atmosphere as the war of words between the Arbenz government and Eisenhower administration escalated daily.

Although it remained mostly concealed beneath his politically aloof exterior, by the time he arrived in Guatemala, Ernesto seems to have undergone a political conversion—or at least he was trying to talk himself into one. Although he wouldn't act on his new beliefs for a while, they do help explain what drew him to Guatemala. Part of the evidence for this lies in an enigmatic passage he had written in Buenos Aires while writing up his *Notas de Viaje*. Appropriately, he called it "Note on the Margin," for it didn't mesh with the rest of his travel narrative at all.

Without mentioning where the "revelation" had taken place, Ernesto had situated himself in "a mountain village under a cold star-filled night sky." A great blackness surrounded him, and a man was there with him, lost in the darkness, visible only by the whiteness of his four front teeth. "I don't know if it was the personality of the individual or the atmosphere that prepared me to receive the revelation, but I know that I had heard the arguments many times by different people and they had never impressed me. In reality, our speaker was an interesting guy; when he was young he had fled some European country to escape the dogmatizing knife; he knew the taste of fear (one of the experiences that makes you value life), and afterwards, after rolling from country to country and compiling thousands of adventures, he had come to rest his bones in this remote region where he patiently awaited the coming of the great event.

"After the trivial phrases and the common places with which each put forth his positions, the conversation languished, and we were about to part ways. Then, with the same rascally boy's smile which always accompanied him, accentuating the disparity of his four front incisors, he let slip: 'The future belongs to the people, and little by little or in one fell swoop they will seize power, here and in the whole world. The bad thing is that they have to become civilized, and this can't happen before, but only after taking power. They will become civilized only by learning at the cost of their own errors, which will be serious ones, and which will cost many innocent lives. Or perhaps not, perhaps they won't be innocent, because they will have committed the enormous sin *contra natura* signified by lacking the capacity to adapt.

"'All of them, all the unadaptable ones, you and I, for example, will die cursing the power we, with enormous sacrifice, helped to create. . . . In its impersonal form, the revolution will take our lives, and even utilize the memory of that which for them remains exemplary, as a domesticating instrument for the youth who will come after. My sin is greater, because I, more subtle and with more experience, call it what you wish, will die knowing that my sacrifice is due only to an obstinacy which symbolizes the rotten civilization that is crumbling. . . .'"

This mystery speaker, by inference a Marxist refugee from Stalin's pogroms whose conscious sin was his "inability to adapt" to the new power wielded by the uncivilized masses, now turned his premonitory attention to Ernesto.

"'You will die with the fist clenched and jaw tense, in perfect demonstration of hate and of combat, because you are not a symbol (something inanimate taken as an example), you are an authentic member of a society which is crumbling: the spirit of the beehive speaks through your mouth and moves in your actions; you are as useful as I, but you don't know the usefulness of the help you give to the society which sacrifices you.'"

And now, duly warned of the consequences of the revolutionary path, came Ernesto's own "revelation." "I saw his teeth and the picaresque expression with which he took a jump on history, I felt the squeeze of his hands and, like a distant murmur, the protocolar salute of farewell. . . . In spite of his words, I now knew . . . I will be with the people, and I know it because I see it etched in the night that I, the eclectic dissector of doctrines and psychoanalyst of dogmas, howling like one possessed, will assault the barricades or trenches, will bathe my weapon in blood and, mad with fury, will slit the throat of any enemy who falls into my hands.

"And I see, as if an enormous tiredness shoots down my recent exaltation, how I die as a sacrifice to the true standardizing revolution of wills, pronouncing the exemplary *mea culpa*. And I feel my nostrils dilated, tasting the acrid smell of gunpowder and of blood, of dead enemy; now my body contorts, ready for the fight, and I prepare my being as if it were a sacred

place so that in it the bestial howling of the triumphant proletariat can reso-
nate with new vibrations and new hopes."

This passage reveals the extraordinarily passionate—and melodramatic—impulses at work inside Ernesto Guevara at the age of twenty-
five. Powerful and violent, uncannily precognitive of Ernesto Guevara's own
future death and the posthumous exploitation of his legacy by many so-called
revolutionaries, "Note on the Margin" must be seen as a decisive personal
testimonial, for the sentiments it contained would soon emerge from the
penumbra of his submerged thoughts to find expression in his future
actions.*

V

After looking up Valdo and his bride, Luzmila, Ernesto and his cohorts went
and found a pension where, as Ernesto put it, "we could get stuck in and
begin owing money."

Rojo arrived back in Guatemala and soon introduced Ernesto to a
woman who would become an important addition to his life. She was Hilda
Gadea, a short, plump woman in her late twenties with Chinese-Indian
features. She was an exiled leader of the youth wing of Peru's APRA, now
working with the Arbenz government.

She later wrote of that encounter: "On our first meeting, Guevara made
a negative impression on me. He seemed too superficial to be an intelligent
man, egotistical and conceited."

Despite her initial negative impression, which she admitted had been
componded by her innate "distrust" of Argentines, who are renowned
among their neighbors for their snobbery and conceit, Hilda soon became
infatuated with Ernesto. For the time being, however, Ernesto's mind was
elsewhere: He was busy meeting people to see about getting a job, and took
little notice of Hilda beyond briefly mentioning her in his journal as the
person who had introduced him to the Marxist American professor Harold
White.

"I met a strange gringo who writes stupidities about Marxism and
translates it to Spanish. The intermediary is Hilda Gadea, and Luzmila and
I are the ones who do the work. Until now we've charged 25 dollars, [and]
I give classes of English-Spanish to the gringo." But this activity was just a
time-filler. What Ernesto was hoping for was an interview with Guatemala's
minister of public health, but all his attempts to meet with the man he began
calling "the grey *capo*" failed.

*See the appendix for elabortion.

Wrote Ernesto in a letter to Andro Herrero, still stuck in Guayaquil: "My perspectives for work aren't quick but in the end everything will work out, and we'll find some dough from somewhere to send you, and you'll get to see this; my personal opinion is that it [Guatemala] is interesting, although, like all revolutions, it loses something with intimacy."

"Revolutionary" Guatemala may not have fulfilled all of Ernesto's expectations, but then he had yet to venture into the countryside, where the land reform had taken place. The capital remained largely unchanged: Its small commercial center was noisy with street vendors, cluttered with neon signs, and the wealthy residents in the outlying residential districts continued living tranquilly behind their bougainvillea-shrouded walled compounds.

Yet in spite of its outwardly quotidian demeanor, Guatemala City was still a compelling place to be in early 1954. Every day, Ernesto met new people among the eclectic community of Latin American political exiles gathered there. There were *apristas* from Peru, Nicaraguan Communists, Argentine *antiperonistas,* Venezuelan social democrats, and Cuban *antibatistianos.*

After a meeting with a Honduran exile, Elena Leiva de Holst, he wrote enthusiastically: "She's close on some points to the Communists and she gave me the impression of being a very good person. In the evening I had a discussion with [Nicanor] Mujíca [an exiled Peruvian *aprista*] and Hilda, and I had a little adventure with a dirty female teacher. From now on I will try to write in my diary every day and try to get closer to the political reality of Guatemala."

Try as he did to find gainful employment in Guatemala's health ministry, Ernesto had not come this far just for a job. He was on a personal political quest, and if his family had been previously unaware of the fact, his letters now dispelled any other notions they may have harbored. Revelation by revelation, he began to let them see what was truly impelling him.

On December 10, while still in San José, he had sent an update of his journey to Aunt Beatriz. For the first time, his ideological convictions made a marked appearance in his personal correspondence. "My life has been a sea of found resolutions until I bravely abandoned my baggage and, backpack on my shoulder, set out with *el compañero* García on the sinuous trail that has brought us here. Along the way, I had the opportunity to pass through the dominions of the United Fruit, convincing me once again of just how terrible these capitalist octopuses are. I have sworn before a picture of the old and mourned comrade Stalin that I won't rest until I see these capitalist octopuses annihilated. In Guatemala I will perfect myself and achieve what I need to be an authentic revolutionary."

After this declamation, which must have been quite mystifying to Beatriz, Ernesto signed off with hugs and love and kisses "from your nephew of the iron constitution, the empty stomach and the shining faith in the socialist future. Chau, Chancho."

In Managua, Ernesto had checked the Argentine consulate for mail from home and found a "stupid" telegram from his father, who was anxious for news of him and had offered to wire him money if he needed it. It had infuriated Ernesto, and in his first letter from Guatemala, on December 28, he was as harsh as he could be. "I guess you now realize that even if I'm dying I'm not going to ask you for dough, and if a letter from me doesn't arrive when expected you'll just have to be patient and wait, sometimes I don't even have stamps but I am getting along perfectly and I always manage to survive. If you ever are worried about anything, take the money that you're going to spend in a telegram, and go and drink with it or something like that, but I'm not going to answer any telegram of that type from now on."

His harsh tone seemed to be Ernesto's way of throwing up a defensive line between himself and his family. From a safe distance away, in a place where he couldn't be stopped or sidetracked by their persuasions, he was saying: "This is me, the real me, like it or not; you can't do anything about it, so you'd better get used to the idea."

9

"Days without Shame or Glory"

I

For the first time in his life, Ernesto openly identified with a political cause.
For better or worse, he had chosen Guatemala's leftist revolution. Despite
its many flaws and defects, he told his family, this was the country in which
one could breath the "most democratic air" in Latin America. The skeptic,
the analytical "sniper," the "eclectic dissector of doctrines and psychoanalyst
of dogmas" had taken the plunge.

Finding something useful to do was the next hurdle he faced. Paradoxically, he never would. His time in Guatemala was to be invaluable as a
practical immersion course in politics, but, as he chased unsuccessfully after
jobs in which he could be of some service to the revolution, the next six
months became a frustrating succession of "days without shame or glory, a
refrain that," he wrote, "has the characteristics of repeating itself to an alarming degree."

Meanwhile, however, he was meeting people. To help him in his quest
to obtain a medical post, the well-connected Hilda Gadea introduced him
to some high-level government contacts of hers. They included the aristocratic minister of economy, Alfonso Bauer Paiz, and President Arbenz's secretary, Jaime Díaz Rozzoto. He began having meetings with these men,
grilling them about Guatemala's revolution while also expressing his desire to find a medical post. In these early days, he entertained hopes of working in leprosy treatment in Guatemala's remote Petén jungle, coincidentally
also the site of the Mayan temple complex of Tikal, the country's richest archeological site.

Hilda also introduced Ernesto to Profesor Edelberto Torres, a Nicaraguan political exile and a scholar of the late poet Rubén Darío. Torres's
pretty young daughter, Myrna, had just returned from a year in California

studying English, and worked with Gadea in the Instituto de Fomento a la Producción, a farm credit agency set up by the Arbenz government. Myrna's brother Edelberto Jr., who was secretary general of Guatemala's Communist Youth organization, the Juventud Democrática, had just come back from a trip to China. The congenial Torres household was a gathering point for Hilda and other exiles, and Ernesto and Gualo were welcomed into this circle as well. On his first day at the Torreses', Ernesto met some Cuban exiles who had already been in town for several months. The Cubans were Antonio "Ñico" López, an extremely tall and thin man; Armando Arencibia, Antonio "Bigotes" Darío López, and Mario Dalmau. Ebullient, outspoken, and informal, the Cubans were a breath of fresh air to the other members of Guatemala's exile community.

The Cubans stood out from the other political expatriates. They alone were veterans of an armed uprising against a dictatorship, and although their effort had failed, they had shown determination and bravery, and earned widespread admiration and even more publicity for their campaign against Batista. After participating in the attacks led by the young lawyer Fidel Castro Ruz against the Moncada and Bayamo army barracks six months earlier, Ñico and his comrades had eluded capture by taking refuge in the Guatemalan embassy in Havana. Granted asylum by the Arbenz regime, the *moncadistas,* as they were called, were cooling their heels in Guatemala as guests of the government until they received further orders from their organization. Meanwhile, they were celebrities, de rigueur dinner guests at dinner parties and picnics given by members of the exile colony.

At that moment, things did not look good for the Cubans. Their leader, Fidel Castro, had just been tried in a Cuban courtroom and sentenced to fifteen years' imprisonment, and was now serving his sentence in a solitary cell in a prison on the Isle of Pines. But despite the adverse circumstances, the Cubans in Guatemala, and particularly Ñico, spoke with passionate conviction about the future of their struggle.

"Ñico was sure that his stay in Guatemala would be a short one," wrote Hilda, "and that soon he would be leaving for another country to join Fidel and work for the revolution. His faith was so great that whoever listened to him was forced to believe him."

Ernesto too was impressed and quickly developed a strong liking for the warm and extroverted Ñico. They continued to see one another socially and became friends. To earn some pocket money, Ñico and his comrades teamed up with Ernesto selling products on commission. From Ñico, who nicknamed him "El Che Argentino"—for his friend's stereotypical Argentine habit of using the Guaraní word *Che* to mean "Hey you"—Ernesto also began learning about the incipient Cuban struggle and its leader, Fidel Castro.

When another Cuban exile, José Manuel "Che-Che" Vega Suárez, who lived in their hostel, fell ill with sharp stomach pains, Ñico and Dalmau called for Ernesto's help. Ernesto examined Vega, called an ambulance, and accompanied him to the hospital, where he was treated and improved within a few days. After that experience, said Dalmau, the Cubans saw Guevara almost every day, either in the Central Park or in the pension.

Right now, however, it was Guatemala, not Cuba, that took priority for Ernesto.

He struck out in his efforts with the minister of public health, having been informed he needed to go back to medical school for a year in order for his Argentine medical degree to be revalidated for use in Guatemala. Calling the Guatemalan medical profession "a tight and oligarchic circle" against which he was going to "break his spears," he rejected this option and now followed up other leads.

He made light of his economic woes to his family, quipping in a letter on January 15: "I am selling a precious image of the Lord of Esquipulas, a black Christ who makes amazing miracles. . . . I have a rich list of anecdotes of the Christ's miracles and I am constantly making up new ones to see if they will sell."

In case his family thought he was joking, they were wrong. He had fallen in with Ñico López on an entrepreneurial scheme to cash in on the widespread devotion incited by Guatemala's black Christ. Ñico had come up with what he thought was a lucrative gimmick: placing little portraits of the idol behind glass frames and rigging up an electrical light bulb at the base to illuminate them. Ñico made them, and Ernesto helped sell them.

Meanwhile, for all Ernesto's banter, his family worried, and especially his aunt Beatriz. She sent him some money in a letter that never arrived, and then another asking if he'd received it. His reply to her second letter, on February 12, was doggedly tongue-in-cheek. He told Beatriz he could only presume that a "democratic post office employee made a just distribution of the riches. Don't send me any more money, as you can't afford it and here I find dollars lying around on the ground. I should tell you that at first I got lumbago from so much bending to pick them up."

II

As Ernesto and Gualo continued their struggle for survival, Myrna Torres and some of her girlfriends had begun to entertain romantic notions about the two Argentines. One night, she and a friend, Blanca Mendez, the daughter of Guatemala's director of petroleum reserves, tossed a coin to see which of them would "get" Ernesto. "Blanca won," wrote Myrna later. "Ernesto of course, never knew anything about it."

But soon enough, Myrna became aware that it was the older, plainer Hilda who most attracted Ernesto. "Little by little, my friends too, came to realize that the Argentines, especially Ernesto, preferred to talk with Hilda because she could discuss politics. It became evident that Hilda wasn't inviting us to some of the gatherings. This bothered me some at first, but then I understood that they really wanted to know about the Guatemalan Revolution and were after Hilda to introduce them to the revolutionary leaders. They would come to our little parties, but they didn't dance; they preferred to converse with my father and my brother."

On January 11, Myrna noted in her diary: "These Argentine boys are the strangest persons: today they came through my office on their way to Hilda's, and all they said was, '*Buenos días,*' and when they came back, just '*Adiós, Myrna. . . .*' It seemed odd to me because I'm so used to that effusiveness of the Cubans. Actually they were sociable enough; but they just preferred political connections."

Hilda was well read, politically oriented, and generous with her time, her contacts, and her money, and she appeared in Ernesto's life when he was in need of all these things. Hilda later claimed to have introduced Ernesto to Mao and Walt Whitman, while he widened her knowledge of Sartre, Freud, Adler, and Jung, about whom they disagreed. Hilda rejected what she saw as the narrowness of Sartre's existentialist philosophy and Freud's sexual interpretation of life, while Ernesto had been influenced by these concepts. Over time, she said, Ernesto's adherence to these points of view softened as his interpretations gradually became more and more Marxist.

Meanwhile, Hilda's own philosophy had some Marxist influences but remained couched within a social democratic outlook. It was one of their main bones of contention. Ernesto pointed out the contradiction that while Hilda "thought" like a Marxist, she was a member of the APRA party, whose constituency was primarily the urban middle class. In conversations with other *apristas,* Ernesto had discerned that at the core of APRA's ideology lay a fundamental anti-Communism. He viewed the party and its leader, Víctor Raúl Haya de la Torre, with disdain, accusing him of abandoning his original anti-imperialist platform that had called for struggle against the Yankees and the nationalization of the Panama Canal. Hilda countered that the party's guiding philosophy was still anti-imperialist and anti-oligarchist, that any abandonment of APRA's original principles was purely tactical, and that once power was attained, a "true social transformation'" would be carried out.

Ernesto argued back that given present circumstances in Latin America, no party that participated in elections could remain revolutionary. They inevitably would be forced to compromise with the right and then seek an accommodation with the United States. For a revolution to succeed, a head-on confrontation with "Yankee imperialism" was unavoidable. At the same time, he was critical of the Communist parties, who he felt had moved away from the "working masses" by engaging in tactical alliances with the right in order to gain a quota of power.

Others joined in these debates. Frequently, they included Ricardo Rojo and the Honduran exile Elena Leiva de Holst, with whom Ernesto had quickly developed a close rapport. She was politically active, versed in Marxism, and had traveled to the USSR and China. Ernesto's political differences with Rojo, however, were becoming sharper, and the two argued incessantly.

"Whenever Rojo joined our discussions," wrote Hilda, "they ended in near-fights. . . . Guevara would tell about his great sympathy for the achievements of the revolution in the Soviet Union, while Rojo and I frequently interposed objections. . . . But I admired the [Soviet] revolution, while Rojo deprecated it with superficial arguments. Once after one of these discussions, while they were taking me home, the discussion started again and promptly became bitter. The subject was always the same. The only way, said Ernesto, was a violent revolution; the struggle had to be against Yankee imperialism and any other solutions, such as those offered by APRA, Acción Democrática, MNR (National Revolutionary Movement, of Bolivia), were betrayals. Rojo argued strongly that the electoral process did offer a solution. The discussion became more heated with each argument offered."

Ernesto grew furious and shouted her down when Hilda tried to quiet him, and later, when they were alone, he apologized and told her: "Forgive me. I get carried away with the discussion and I do not realize what I say. . . . It's just that this fat fellow with his arguments for surrendering makes me lose my mind. He will end up as an agent for imperialism."

While Ernesto and his friends debated political theory, the Central Intelligence Agency was well along in its plans to bury Guatemala's brief experiment with social revolution. By January 1954 the covert program even had a code name: "Operation Success." Throughout the region, friendly dictators such as Trujillo, Somoza, Pérez Jiménez, and the presidents of neighboring Honduras and El Salvador were brought in on the CIA's planning. A Guatemalan figurehead had been handpicked to lead the anti-Arbenz "Liberation Army," an ex–army colonel and furniture salesman named Castillo Armas. His paramilitary force was now being armed and trained in Nicaragua.

To better coordinate the operation, loyal CIA men had replaced American envoys in Costa Rica, Nicaragua, and Honduras. John Puerifoy, the flamboyant new ambassador to Guatemala, had taken up his post only two months earlier. He had been selected for the specific purpose of coordinating Operation Success and its hoped-for result, the transition of power in Guatemala.

At the end of January, the covert campaign was unmasked when correspondence between Castillo Armas, Trujillo, and Somoza detailing their machinations in alliance with a "government to the North" was leaked. The Arbenz government promptly made the news public and demanded an explanation from the "Government of the North" (the United States). In a February 2 letter to his father, Ernesto wrote: "Politically, things aren't going so well because at any moment a coup is suspected under the patronage of your friend Ike."

The State Department denied any knowledge of the plots being hatched and refused any further comment. Meanwhile, the CIA calmly continued with its preparations. Its agents circulated throughout Guatemala and the neighboring countries with an openness that would seem buffoonish today, but their blatancy also had a purpose: The CIA's program counted on creating a climate of tension and uncertainty to prompt divisions in the armed forces, weaken Arbenz's resolve, and, hopefully, provoke a coup d'etat.

In this unsettled atmosphere, Ernesto's habitual suspicions about Americans were sharpened. When Rojo introduced him to Robert Alexander, a Rutgers University professor who was gathering material for a book about the Guatemalan revolution, Ernesto wondered aloud if Alexander was an FBI agent. Neither Hilda nor Rojo shared Ernesto's suspicions, but they found it difficult to convince him and had to admit that he might be right.

At the same time, among the exiles, he found few whose philosophies seemed rigid enough to stand up against imperialism in their own countries, and even fewer who appeared willing to fight in defense of Guatemala's threatened revolution. Here was a chance to fight for political freedom, just as internationalists had fought to defend the Spanish Republic in the 1930s, and yet nothing was happening.

His criticisms extended to the Arbenz government, which he saw as too complacent in view of the mounting threats against it. The Darío scholar Edelberto Torres recalled Ernesto expressing his worries about the rivalries and lack of real unity between the government's coalition partners. Alfonso Bauer Paiz, the minister of economy, remembered the young Argentine stressing the same points. Ernesto emphasized the real danger of an armed invasion organized by the United States and doubted Guatemala's readiness to defend itself. "He believed it was necessary to organize a *defensa popular* [an armed people's militia] and be prepared for the worst."

Interestingly, in the wake of his own recent attempt at writing slanted journalism, one of Ernesto's chief targets of scorn was the unbridled freedom of Guatemala's press. In a January 5 letter to Aunt Beatriz, Ernesto wrote: "This is a country where one can expand one's lungs and fill them with democracy. There are dailies here run by United Fruit, and if I were Arbenz I'd close them down in five minutes, because they're shameful and yet they say whatever they want and help contribute to creating the atmosphere that North America wants, showing this as a den of thieves, communists, traitors, etc."

In a letter to his family, he predicted: "In the [upcoming OAS] conferences of Caracas, the Yankees will set all their traps to impose sanctions on Guatemala. It is certainly true that the governments bow to them, and their battle horses are Pérez Jiménez, Odría, Trujillo, Batista, Somoza. That is to say, among the reactionary governments, the ones that are most fascist and anti-popular. Bolivia was an interesting country, but Guatemala is much more so, because it has set itself against whatever comes, without having even an iota of economic independence and withstanding armed attempts of all sorts . . . yet without even going against the freedom of expression."

With the storm clouds gathering menacingly on the horizon, many of the political exiles now began leaving town. These included most of the Venezuelans and Hilda's *aprista* comrades. In early February, Oscar Valdovinos and Luzmila took off. Valdo was homesick, and Luzmila had wangled herself a diplomatic post in Argentina. Now, Rojo and Gualo announced their intention to leave as well.

In contrast, Ernesto declared his intention to stay for the time being, come what may. Responding to a letter from Beatriz that carried an invitation from his aunt Ercilia to come and stay with her in New York, where she was living, he told Beatriz that "in principle" his answer was "no."

"The U.S. doesn't interest me much beyond giving it a little look, so as to complete my record of countries visited in America. At any rate I'll stay here six months at least, since I have a job that allows me to eat and the possibility of two good posts as a doctor. Anyway . . . Guatemala right now is the most interesting country in America and must be defended with all possible means."

III

As his job quest continued, Ernesto read up on medical topics that interested him, occasionally treated patients, such as the Cuban Che-Che Vega, and helped out in the lab of Dr. Peñalver, a Venezuelan malaria specialist.

Now he began work on something that wedded his two chief interests, medicine and politics, in a single project. He informed Beatriz in his February 15 letter: "In the field of social medicine, and built on my small personal experience, I am preparing a very pretentious book that I think will take me two years of work. Its title is *The Role of the Doctor in Latin America* and [so far] I only have the general outline and the two first chapters written. But I think that with patience and method I can say something good."

Once he had done a bit of work on the book, he showed what he had written to Hilda. "It was an analysis of the lack of state protection and the scarcity of resources that the medical profession had to face, and of the tremendous problem of sanitation prevailing in our countries," she recalled. "He asked me to help him collect health statistics for each Latin American country, and I promised to do so, as I believed it a very worthwhile work. Moreover, it showed me that this was the work of a restless mind, sensitive to social problems."

Indeed, according to Cuban historian María del Carmen Ariet, the only outsider allowed by Guevara's widow to study and paraphrase the surviving document in family archives, the proposed work was a manual for the role of the doctor in a revolutionary society, and in it he outlined a social function not only for doctors throughout Latin America but also for himself. There seems little coincidence in the fact that he planned to take two years to finish the book, the same length of time he hoped to serve as a doctor in the Guatemalan backwoods. Right now, he was coming to his threshold as a political revolutionary through the prism of what he called "social medicine." As yet he had no military training; medicine was the only skill he possessed with which to apply himself.

Ernesto sketched out a book outline, charting the history of medicine in Latin America from the colonial period to the present day, the range of clinical problems, and their geographic and economic contributing factors. He then embarked on an broad analysis for treatment. In his judgment, only a preventive program of social medicine could adequately deal with the ills caused by underdevelopment, and as a consequence a socialist form of government was the correct political course to follow.

In his chapter sketch for "The Doctor and the Environment," Ernesto set forth his thesis for a future scenario in which the doctor would play a direct role in helping to bring about a revolutionary transformation to socialism. First, he defined the contemporary political reality in Latin America as colonialism, made up of the following components: domination by large landowners, unpopular and bullying authorities, domination by the clergy, the absence of effective laws, and economic predominance by foreign corporate monopolies.

Playing his part in the struggle against those components, the revolutionary doctor would have to confront openly the established authorities in order to obtain adequate medical attention for the people and wipe out pillage and profit. This stage of transition between "armed neutrality" and "open war" he saw as one of preparation, a period in which the doctor should acquaint himself intimately with the people under his care and their health conditions, and help raise their class consciousness and their awareness of the importance of good health in daily life. Finally, it was the duty of the *médico revolucionario* to fight against all the blights—social or otherwise—adversely affecting the people, who were the "only sovereigns" he should serve.

Undoubtedly, Ernesto's thesis was based largely on his analysis of present conditions in revolutionary Guatemala. At that moment, Guatemala's internal situation could be described as one of "armed neutrality," while "open war" was threatened by the U.S.-backed Liberation Army of Castillo Armas. This perhaps explains his belief in the need for the "revolutionary doctor" in the field during the period of armed neutrality that preceded open war. Ernesto still hoped that when the crisis came, the PGT's [Communist party] militants would be armed by the government to help in its defense. If this were to happen and the "people" were successful in repelling the invasion, a socialist revolution could be unequivocally established in Guatemala.

His work on the book led him to take his knowledge of Marxism further, and he deepened his readings of Marx, Lenin, Engels, and the Peruvian José Carlos Mariátegui. Hilda joined in this reading marathon, and they spent many hours discussing the works and the points they raised. Hilda had a copy of Mao Tse-tung's *New China,* and she lent it to Ernesto.

"It was the first work he had read on the great revolution. When he had read it and we talked about the book, he expressed great admiration for the long struggle of the Chinese people to take power, with the help of the Soviet Union. He also understood that their road toward socialism was somewhat different from the one followed by the Soviets and that the Chinese reality was closer to that of our Indians and peasants. Since I also admired the Chinese Revolution, we often talked about it and about all that was being done there." Ernesto also talked about China with Elena Leiva de Holst and Edelberto Torres, who had both been there. Enthused with what he heard, he now added China to his list of future countries to visit.

Somewhat ironically, given his antipathy for and suspicion of Americans, one of the key figures in Ernesto's political education during this time was Harold White. Ernesto's initial reserve about the older man had softened, and before long he told Hilda: "This is a good gringo. He is tired of capitalism and wants to lead a new life."

He, Hilda, and White now spent a lot of time together, just the three of them, and most weekends they organized a picnic in the countryside. With Ernesto's rudimentary English and White's rough Spanish, smoothed by Hilda's frequent translation, they discussed everything from current events "to Marxism, Lenin, Engels, Stalin, Freud, science in the Soviet Union, and Pavlov's conditioned reflexes."

IV

By late February Gualo García and Ricardo Rojo had left. Ernesto was now on his own; his closest remaining friend was Hilda. Already, their mutual acquaintances teased them about what they saw as a budding romance, but in fact nothing had yet happened between them.

Besides their intellectual affinities and her physical attraction to him, Hilda's infatuation with Ernesto appears to have been spurred on at least partly by maternal instincts. Soon after they met, Ernesto had told her "about his illness," recalled Hilda. "Thereafter, I always felt a special concern for him because of his [asthma] condition." For his part, Ernesto, all too aware of the effect he had on Hilda, seems to have exploited her feelings while trying to avoid committing himself to a serious relationship.

A few days after Gualo and Rojo's departure, she called upon Ernesto at his boardinghouse. She found him waiting for her in the downstairs lobby, in the grips of an asthma attack. "It was the first time I had seen him or anyone else suffering from an acute attack of asthma, and I was shocked by the tremendous difficulty with which he breathed and by the deep wheeze that came from his chest. I hid my concern by insisting that he lie down; he agreed that it would be better, but he couldn't climb the stairs and refused to accept my help. He told me where his room was and asked me to go up and bring him a syringe that was ready to use. . . . I did as he said and watched him as he applied an injection of adrenaline.

"He rested a bit and began to breathe more easily. We went slowly up the stairs; we reached his room and he lay down. He told me that since the age of ten he had been able to give himself injections. It was at that moment that I came to a full realization of what his illness meant. I could not help admiring his strength of character and his self-discipline. His dinner was brought up—boiled rice and fruit. . . . Trying to conceal how much I had been touched by all this, I conversed about everything and anything, all the while thinking what a shame it was that a man of such value who could do so much for society, so intelligent and so generous, had to suffer such an affliction; if I were in his place I would shoot myself. I decided right there to stick by him without, of course, getting involved emotionally."

Perhaps Hilda still harbored reservations about getting involved with Ernesto, but within a few weeks she evidently began coming on strongly to him. Although in her pubished memoir, she portrayed Ernesto as the one who chased her, Ernesto's journal describes *her* as the hunter. In late February, he wrote: "I haven't budged due to the asthma, although it seemed to reach a climax with vomiting last night. . . . Hilda Gadea continues worrying a great deal about me and constantly comes by to see me and brings me things."

Meanwhile, the main contender for Ernesto's attentions in February and March of 1954 was a nurse named Julia Mejía. She had arranged a house at Lake Amatítlan where Ernesto could go and spend the weekends; she helped him in his job search as well. Soon, they were having a casual affair.

Unaware of Ernesto's secret fling, Hilda continued using her contacts to help him find a job. She spoke to a man who worked in her office, Herbert Zeissig, a member of the youth wing of the Partido Guatemalteco de los Trabajadores (PGT), the Guatemalan Communist party. Zeissig found Ernesto a job but told Hilda he would first have to join the party. Ernesto's reaction was angry: He told Hilda to tell Zeissig that when he joined the party he would "do so on his own initiative," but refused on ethical grounds to do so for the purpose of getting a job. This principled stance made Hilda admire Ernesto even more.

Meanwhile, Ernesto's money situation remained critical. Ricardo Rojo had paid Gualo's half of their pensión bill before leaving, but he was still seriously in arrears and the occasional paying work he found was simply not enough.

On February 28, he wrote his parents and asked them for the address of Ulíses Petit de Murat, an actor friend of his father's who made films in Mexico: "Just in case I beat it to there." Meanwhile, he told them, he had an offer to work in a sign-painting factory but was not inclined to take it, since it would rob him of time to look for work in the health field. He had offered his services as a doctor to a peasant cooperative and a banana plantation, but both jobs had slipped from his grasp because he didn't belong to the "shitty" Guatemalan doctors' union.

He heard from home that his aunt Sara de la Serna, his mother's sister, was gravely ill with cancer, and betraying his self-absorption with an almost casual brutality he wrote Celia *madre:* "I can offer you no type of consolation, not even that of my presence which is impossible due to the economic reasons you're aware of. Just a strong embrace and look to the future, distance yourself a little from the present is my only advice. Chau."

In March, Ernesto's situation changed very little. Hilda paid off part of his pension bill, and Julia Mejía got him a job interview for a medical post in the eastern Petén jungle, which briefly lifted his spirits. "I Am Optimistic," he wrote in his diary. The Petén was precisely the place he wanted to go. He wrote his mother and father that the Petén was "a splendid place because that is where the Mayan civilization flourished . . . and because there are more illnesses there than shit, one can really learn in style (if one wants to, of course)!"

The Petén job, however, was tied to the approval of the doctors' union, and Ernesto decided to go and see its president. His summation of the interview was caustic. "A man with hopes of conserving his job, anticommunist, an intriguer it seems to me, but he appears disposed to helping me. I wasn't sufficiently cautious but I didn't take too many risks either."

When Hilda heard of the Petén job possibility, she kicked up a fuss, apparently demanding some kind of commitment from him in their relationship. A few days later, Ernesto wrote: "Hilda told me of a dream she had in which I was the protagonist and which clearly betrayed her sexual ambitions. Though I hadn't dreamt, I had an asthma attack. Up to what point asthma is an escape is something I would like to know. The funny thing is that a self-analysis leads me honorably—as far as one can take it—to the conclusion that I don't have anything to run from. And yet . . . Hilda and I are slaves of the same boss and both of us deny it with our actions. Maybe I am more consistent but deep down it's the same."

Here, Ernesto seems to be trying to say something important about himself. Despite the allusiveness of his language, it's clear that he translated the tentativeness he recognized in his personality into the political arena as well, for he added: "When I heard the Cubans make grandiloquent affirmations with absolute serenity I felt small. I can make a speech ten times more objectively. . . . I can read it better and convince an audience that I am saying something that is right but I don't convince myself, and the Cubans do. Nico left his soul in the microphone, and for that reason he enthused even a skeptic such as myself. The Petén puts me face to face with my asthma problem and myself, and I believe I need it. I have to triumph without help and I believe I can do it, but it also seems to me that the triumph will be more the work of my natural aptitudes—which are greater than my subconscious beliefs—than the faith I put in them."

Ernesto seemed to be saying that both he and Hilda were revolutionaries at heart, but neither had taken the plunge of total commitment to the cause. Mere identification with Guatemala's revolution wasn't enough, and Ernesto knew it. Hilda was still affiliated with APRA, and at the crucial moment Ernesto himself had abstained from joining the PGT. However principled his motives for doing so, the fact was that he was *still* hanging back, still the skeptical outsider; the same dispassionate "sniper" as before. In contrast, he now had the example of Ñico López, who spoke with such faith in his struggle, a faith he couldn't yet share, for he was not yet a true participant in a political struggle. He also wondered if his asthma was his way of evading such commitments.

Now he had a job offer in the Petén, a humid jungle region that would undoubtedly be terrible for his affliction, yet it was also the right setting for him to implement his plan to be a "revolutionary doctor," and it was something he felt he had to do to prove to himself he could be true to his beliefs and overcome his asthma at the same time. His asthma had come to symbolize the malignant shackle of heredity that he was in the process of rejecting. He wished to form a new identity, to reforge himself as a revolutionary, to vanquish once and for all the limitations he had been born with.

Ernesto's bout of self-analysis helped clear his mind a little, but his asthma endured relentlessly. A few days later, prostrate in his pension bed, he wrote that "not much and a lot has happened." The job was looking likely, the union president had told him. "Hilda declared her love in epistolary and practical form. I was with a lot of asthma, if not I might have fucked her. I warned her that all I could offer her was a casual contact, nothing definitive. She seemed very embarrassed. The little letter she left me upon leaving is very good, too bad she is so ugly. She is twenty-seven."

By now Ernesto was telling everyone he was going to the Petén, even though he didn't have the slightest assurance that he really was. "I'm about to prepare a list of necessary things to take," he wrote in March. "I burn to go. Hilda has me feeling nervous, on top of the anxiety I have about becoming ever more trapped in this country."

At the same time, the political pressure on Guatemala was ratcheting up. In March, at the Tenth Inter-American Conference of the Organization of American States (OAS) held in Caracas, John Foster Dulles had twisted enough arms to obtain the majority resolution signed on March 26, effectively justifying armed intervention in any member state that was "dominated by Communism" and which therefore constituted a "hemispheric threat." Only Mexico and Argentina withheld their votes, and Guatemala, the target of the resolution, was the only state to vote against it.

The game was rolling. Having secured this diplomatic victory in its campaign, the Eisenhower administration now pressed its advantage. The CIA's military training of Guatemalan exiles was well along on one of

Somoza's ranches in Nicaragua. It had also hired a crew of mercenary pilots and smuggled a couple of dozen planes into Nicaragua, Honduras, and the Panama Canal Zone for use in the coming attack. Meanwhile, its psychological warfare operatives were busy preparing taped recordings for propaganda and disinformation broadcasts, printing leaflets to be dropped from the skies over Guatemala, and buying up Soviet-issue weapons to be planted in Guatemala at the right moment as "evidence" of Soviet involvement with Arbenz.

Myrna Torres left Guatemala, flying off to Canada, where she had a fiancé. In Ernesto's words, she left behind her "a balance of broken hearts and without knowing what she wants, but the worst of it is I don't know if I'm leaving. Always the same uncertainty . . ." A few days later, his uncertainty had deepened, after the medical union president seemed cool and evasive when he saw him about his Petén post. He consoled himself in his journal, "Only Julia responds to me. And she's good. . . ."

But Julia aside, Ernesto's mood was bitter. He now referred to the union president as an *"hijo de puta,"* a son of a whore. He expected "nothing" from their next meeting and complained he had had to stop writing letters because of all his running around. "Enthusiasm depends on health and circumstances. Both are failing me. The post in the Petén seems farther away all the time. . . . Everything is getting fucked up. I don't know what the shit to do. Hilda is being a pain in the neck. I feel like flying the fuck away. Maybe Venezuela."

But he couldn't leave, since he had no money. And his Pilgrim's Progress continued. To do something productive with his time, he persisted in his studies of parasitic diseases at Peñalver's lab; it turned out that the banana plantation job, at a place called Tequisate, was still a possibility after all. With some jewelry Hilda gave him for the purpose, he paid off part of his pension bill, but he still owed several months. Now his landlady extracted his promise to pay off a month within a few days. The agreed day of reckoning came.

"Things got ugly in the pension when I couldn't pay even five centavos. I pawned my watch, a gold chain and a ring stone of Hilda's, and promised a gold ring—also Hilda's. After pawning my jewelry I went to Tequisate and on the road my asthma unleashed itself, as a vision of what things will be like if I go there."

He heard from home that his aunt Sara had died. Taking a break from his own travails, he mulled over his feelings. "I didn't love her but her death affected me. She was a healthy person and very active and a death of this kind seemed the most unlikely, which nonetheless is a solution, since the conditions in which the illness would have left her would have been hor-

rible for her." With a peppy brevity that was unfeeling under the circumstances but increasingly characteristic of his letters home, he wrote his
mother. "Have spirit, what happened to Sara is now over and Paris awaits."

It was now April, and his chief remaining obstacle for securing the
Tequisate job was obtaining his Guatemalan residency. He was becoming
fatalistic. "The days keep passing but I could care less. Maybe one of these
days I'll go stay at Elena de Holst's, maybe not, but I know one way or another matters have to fix themselves so I'm not going to overheat my brains
anymore."

One weekend, returning from the countryside, Ernesto, Hilda, and
Harold White witnessed a candlelit Easter procession of hooded men car-
rying an effigy of Christ, which gave him the chills. "There was a moment
I didn't like at all, when those with the lances passing by gave us ugly looks."

On April 9, Guatemala's Catholic Church issued a pastoral letter denouncing the presence of Communism in the country and calling on all
Guatemalans to rise up against it. The euphemistic language was lost on no
one. What wasn't known to the public was that the pastoral letter had been
the direct result of a CIA approach to Guatemalan Archbishop Mariano
Rossell Arellano. As priests read the letter aloud in churches across Guatemala, the CIA's fliers dropped thousands of leaflets bearing the message all
over rural Guatemala.

Ernesto wrote his mother a long letter. In their recent correspondence
she had been enthusiastic about the prospect of their meeting in Paris. He had
warned her it might be the only chance they would have to see one another
in the next ten years, the period of time he planned to be exploring the world.

She had evidently inquired if he was interested in becoming an an-
thropologist, given his interests in archeology and the condition of Latin
America's Indians, but he shot that down, writing: "It seems a little paradoxical to make as the goal of my life the investigation of that which is irre-
mediably dead." He was sure of "two things," he told her. First, that he
would reach his "authentically creative stage at around thirty-five years of
age," would work in "nuclear physics, genetics or some field like that"; and
second, that "America will be the theater of my adventures and of a much
more important character than I had thought; I truly believe I have come to
understand her and I feel [Latin] American in the sense that we possess a
distinctive nature compared to any other of the world's peoples."

In the final days of April Ernesto shook himself awake from his
somnolence. He had made a "heroic and unbreakable" decision. He
would leave Guatemala within fifteen days if his residency had not been
approved. He informed his pension's owners of his decision and began arranging places to leave his possessions. The news of his impending depar-

ture worried Hilda. "Hilda persists and is offering me *el oro y el moro* [the gold and the Moor] so that I don't leave. A kilo of adrenaline arrived, sent by Alberto from Venezuela, and a letter in which he asks me to go, or rather invites me to go. I don't really want to."

As Ernesto prepared to leave, Washington was taking the next step in activating its destabilization plan. With a great deal of intentional publicity, Ambassador Puerifoy had been recalled to Washington for consultations. Well-placed news leaks indicated that the purpose of his visit was to discuss U.S. measures against Arbenz in view of the recent Caracas resolution against Communist involvement in the hemisphere. On April 26, Eisenhower used warlike language in a speech to Congress, warning that "the Reds" were already in control of Guatemala and now sought to spread their "tentacles" to El Salvador and other neighbors.

Ernesto was called to go and present himself to the police, a step prior to obtaining his Guatemalan residency. This was a breakthrough, he noted wryly, comparing his efforts at Guatemala's Foreign Ministry to the recent siege by Ho Chi Minh's Vietnamese fighters against Dien Bien Phu, the French military garrison.

By May 15, Ernesto's decision about where to go was made for him when he was told officially that he would have to leave the country to renew his visa. Just before leaving, he wrote to his brothers, whose birthdays were coming up, and his letter was a madcap version of the letters to his parents. Once he got his doctor's job, he told them, he would lead a serious life "until my friend Mao calls me." On Central America's politics, he wrote:

"Central America is *rechulo* [cute], as they say around here, no year passes without some rumpus in favor or against something or other. . . . Right now Honduras is in the midst of a fantastic strike where almost 25% of the country's workers are stopped and Foster Dulles, who is the lawyer of the fruit company in these parts, says that Guatemala has meddled in it. There's a clandestine radio that calls for revolt and the opposition dailies also do it so it wouldn't be strange that with the help of the U.F. [United Fruit] they send a little revolution here so as not to lose the habit. . . . I believe if the United States doesn't intervene directly (which isn't probable yet) Guatemala can withstand any attempt of this type well, and it also has its back covered, because there's a lot of people in Mexico who sympathize with the movement."

Despite Ernesto's optimistic prognosis, an incident occurred on that same day that irrevocably doomed the Arbenz regime. The Swedish freighter *Alfhem,* which had left a Polish port a month earlier secretly loaded with Czechoslovakian arms, docked in Guatemala's Atlantic seaport of Puerto Barrios. Tipped off in Poland about the mysterious voyage and suspicious about its cargo and final destination, the CIA had monitored the ship as it crossed the Atlantic and altered its course several times. When it reached Puerto Barrios, Washington was quickly apprised of the true nature of *Alfhem*'s cargo—over two tons of war materiel for the Arbenz regime— and went into action.

The *Alfhem* provided Washington with the evidence of Soviet-bloc involvement in Guatemala that it so badly needed. CIA Director Allen Dulles immediately convened his executive intelligence advisory board and the National Security Council, and got their backing to set the Guatemalan invasion date for the next month. On May 17, the State Department issued a statement denouncing the arms delivery, and Eisenhower followed up with a public warning that the Czech arms could allow the consolidation of a "Communist dictatorship" in Central America.

Guatemala was in an unenviable position. Having arranged for the shipment secretly and being discovered in flagrante, Arbenz suddenly looked like a man with something to hide. In succeeding days, Eisenhower and Secretary Dulles told the press that the arms shipment was larger than Guatemala's military needs, and hinted that Guatemala's real intention might be to invade its neighbors to impose Communist rule and, possibly, to launch an attack on the U.S.-controlled Panama Canal. With Washington's propaganda machine in full swing, few journalists remembered the fact that the United States had thwarted the Arbenz regime's efforts to upgrade its army's equipment, repeatedly rejecting direct appeals for American military assistance and blocking moves by other Western countries to sell Guatemala the arms it requested.

Less than a week after the *Alfhem* docked, Secretary Dulles signed a "mutual security treaty" with Honduras. It followed a similar treaty signed with Nicaragua's dictator, Somoza, only weeks earlier. This move came in the wake of U.S. and Honduran accusations that Guatemalan government agents had instigated the Honduran general strike then taking place. Now Honduras would be defended by the United States in the event of a "Guatemalan invasion." To drive the point home, U.S. military cargo planes were ostentatiously flown to the two countries, ostensibly carrying weaponry for their defense needs. In fact, the shipments were to be handed over to Castillo Armas's Liberation Army, awaiting its marching orders to move to the Guatemalan border.

On May 20, in a move authorized by Allen Dulles to stop the delivery of the *Alfhem*'s weapons to Guatemala City, a band of CIA saboteurs set explosives on the railroad tracks outside Puerto Barrios. The explosives did little damage, and so the CIA men opened fire as the military train passed. One Guatemalan army soldier was killed and several were wounded, but the train and its cargo reached its destination without further problems.

Against this backdrop of escalating political drama, Ernesto left his pension. He still owed about three months' rent, but the proprietors let him go in return for an IOU. With Hilda, he went to spend the night in the village of San Juan Sacatepéquez. It was their first night alone together. A few days later, Ernesto left for El Salvador with twenty borrowed dollars in his pocket.

V

For a declared partisan in the confrontation, he was behaving in a remarkably carefree fashion, once again absenting himself at a climactic moment in the crisis. At the same time, amid the continuing furor over the *Alfhem,* Ernesto couldn't have picked a worse time to be visiting Guatemala's neighbors. He had some "questionable literature" confiscated by police at the Salvadoran border, but was allowed to enter after paying a bribe.

After obtaining a new Guatemalan visa in the provincial city of Santa Ana, he continued on to the capital, San Salvador. There, he applied for a Honduran visa, thinking he might visit the Mayan ruins of Copán and also "check out" the ongoing workers' strike. Over the weekend, he took off for the nearby Pacific coast and camped out on the beach.

There, he made friends with some young Salvadoran men. Writing to his mother later, he told her that when they were all a bit drunk, he engaged in a little "Guatemalanesque propaganda and recited some verses of profoundly red color. The result was that we all appeared in a police station, but they let us go right away, after a *comandante* . . . advised me to sing about roses in the afternoon and other beauties instead. I would have preferred making a sonnet with smoke [gunfire]."

Returning to San Salvador, he found his Honduran visa had been denied and believed it was because he had come from Guatemala, almost a criminal offense in the current political climate. With Honduras no longer an option, he headed to Chalchuapa in western El Salvador to see the pre-Columbian Pipil Indian pyramid of Tazumal.

He explored the ruins, making studious observations in his journal. That night, he slept by the roadside outside Santa Ana, and in the morning, hitchhiked back across the Guatemalan border, heading for the ancient Indian ruins of Quiriguá in southern Guatemala. The next day he reached Jalapa, then got a train to the town of Progreso, where a woman took pity on him and gave him twenty-five cents. He set out on foot along the nearly completed new road to the now infamous port of Puerto Barrios. He reached the ruins of Quiriguá, where he noted similarities in the stone constructions to those of the Incas in Peru. But he was especially struck by the carvings' Asian features and thought that one figure carved onto a stela looked "reminiscent of Buddha," while another resembled "Ho Chi Minh."

The next day he hit the road again, deciding to strike out *"a lo macho"* for Puerto Barrios. He spent his last money on the train trip. It was a gamble, but it worked out. Right away, he found a night job unloading barrels of tar on a road construction crew. "The work is twelve hours straight, from six in the evening to six in the morning and is really a killer, even for guys with more *training* than me. At 5:30 we were automatons or *'bolos,'* as they call drunks here." He worked a second night—"with a lot less desire than the first"—but he proudly completed his shift, despite "the mosquitoes that are a real bother and the lack of gloves . . ."

The next morning, promised a train ticket back to Guatemala City from Puerto Barrios by one of the foremen, Ernesto relaxed at an abandoned shack at the sea's edge, exulting in his feeling of achievement. It was the first sustained stint of physical labor he had ever done. "I have turned into a perfect *chancho,* full of dust and asphalt from the head down, but really content. I got the ticket, the old woman where I ate on credit told me to pay a dollar to her son in Guatemala [City], and I demonstrated that I am capable of standing whatever comes, and if it weren't for the asthma, even more than that."

VI

"I paid back the dollar," Ernesto wrote proudly after his return to Guatemala City. Hilda was surprised and pleased to see him back, for she had feared he wouldn't return. As invasion jitters mounted, more people were leaving the country. A government official she knew had urged her to seek asylum, and Harold White had already advised her to do the same.

In the paranoid climate of the capital, rumors abounded, and one of the first Ernesto heard had to do with himself. He learned from a Paraguayan acquaintance that he was widely believed to be a Perónist agent. Apparently, he quashed the rumor. He didn't return to the pension, evidently because he couldn't repay his debt, but ate his meals at Elena de Holst's and shared a room with Ñico López and another Cuban who sang tangos. He was sneaked in and out of the room clandestinely, and since there were only two single beds, they pushed them together and slept sideways. Ñico was preparing to leave for Mexico on the orders of his organization, and spent his days "shitting with laughter but doing little else."

Despite his expectations, his life settled back into the same routine as before. The medical post beckoned like a mirage. He was told to come back for a meeting, then to wait, and, finally, to give it another week. He was in the doldrums again. There were few letters from home. Ñico left, and Ernesto moved into another room with a Guatemalan named Coca. Elena

Leiva de Holst was also preparing to leave but promised to fix him up for meals at another woman's house and to talk one last time for him with the minister of public health. To top everything off, his asthma returned.

Ernesto's days of tedium were about to end, however, because of increased activity in the U.S.-Guatemala standoff. American warships had begun inspecting all suspicious shipping in the Caribbean, and Secretary Dulles was noisily preparing a document calling for sanctions against Guatemala to be ratified in the next OAS conference, slated for July. CIA man Howard Hunt (of future Watergate fame), the propaganda chief of Operation Success, was the organizer of a recent Congress Against Soviet Intervention in Latin America in Mexico City held to focus attention on Guatemala.

All over Latin America, the CIA was placing newspaper articles and propaganda films and handing out booklets that warned of the growing Communist threat in Guatemala. Arbenz sent his foreign minister to speak to Ambassador Puerifoy, offering conciliatory measures to begin negotiations with Washington and ward off the invasion. The overture went nowhere.

The CIA's psychological warfare campaign was paying off. On June 2, a plot against Arbenz was foiled, and some arrests made. The next day, a group of military officers asked Arbenz to dismiss all Communists from government posts. He brushed away their fears, telling them he had the Communists under control. But many officers remained unsettled, and on June 5 a retired air force chief defected, soon making his voice heard on the CIA's radio broadcasts.

Under the direction of CIA agent David Atlee Phillips, the radio station, calling itself "La Voz de Liberación" exhorted Guatemalans to help the Liberation Army, giving the impression it had thousands of fighters. It also played on military fears by accusing Arbenz of planning to disband the armed forces and turn weapons over to Communist-controlled unions to form "peasant militias." On June 6, invoking the invasion threat, Arbenz suspended constitutional guarantees for thirty days.

On June 14, Ernesto celebrated his twenty-sixth birthday. The next day, President Eisenhower called a high-level meeting to put the final touches on Operation Success. Two days later American mercenaries began flying bombing missions over Guatemala. On June 18, at the head of his paltry Liberation Army of some four hundred fighters, Castillo Armas drove across the Honduran border into Guatemala. The invasion had begun, and with it so did Ernesto Guevara's future.*

*See the appendix for elaboration.

IO

"A Terrible Shower of Cold Water"

I

When the first aerial attacks came in Guatemala City, Ernesto thrilled at being under fire for the first time. In a letter to Celia, he confessed to "feeling a little ashamed for having as much fun as a monkey. . . . The magic sensation of invulnerability" he felt watching people run in the streets during the bombardments made him "lick his lips with pleasure."

Ernesto was awed by the violence. "Even the light bombings have their grandeur. I watched one go against a target relatively close to where I was and one could see the plane get bigger by the moment while from the wings intermittent little tongues of fire came out and you could hear the sound of its machine gun and the light machine guns that fired back at it. All of a sudden it stayed suspended in the air, horizontal, and then made a rapid dive, and you could feel the shaking of the earth from the bomb."

A few days later, in a more sober frame of mind, Ernesto wrote in his journal: "The latest developments belong to history. It is a quality that I believe appears for the first time in my notes. A few days ago, planes coming from Honduras crossed the frontier with Guatemala and passed over the city, machine-gunning people and military targets in the full light of day. I signed up with the health brigades to collaborate in the medical area and in the youth brigades [of the Communist Alianza Democrática] that patrol the city at night."

A nocturnal blackout had been imposed, and one of Ernesto's patrol duties was to ensure that nobody showed any lights for fear of providing bombing targets. Hilda also did her bit, attaching her name to a public communiqué signed by political exiles in support of Guatemala's revolution and assembling a woman's brigade at her office to take food to the men on patrol duty.

On June 20, Ernesto sent a birthday letter to his mother. "I imagine you've been a little worried about me," he wrote. "I'll tell you that if right now there is nothing to fear, the same can't be said for the future, although personally I have the sensation of being inviolable (inviolable isn't the word but maybe the subconscious gave me a bad turn)."

Despite the provocations posed by the aerial attacks and Castillo Armas's ground incursion, he told her, the Arbenz government had proceeded cautiously, allowing the mercenaries to get far enough into Guatemala so as to avoid any border incidents that would allow the United States and Honduras to claim Guatemalan aggression and invoke their mutual security treaty. So far, Guatemala had limited itself to a diplomatic protest against Honduras, and to a presentation of its case to the United Nations Security Council for a special hearing. "The incident has served to join all the Guatemalans together under their government, and those like myself, who came attracted to Guatemala." To end, he offered a judgment that would soon prove woefully wrong. "Without a doubt Colonel Arbenz is a guy with guts, and he is ready to die in his post if necessary."

Initially, the news from the battlefronts was encouraging. The government forces were fighting back, with some success. Castillo Armas had managed to enter the town of Esquipulas, home of the holy pilgrimage site of Guatemala's black Christ, but elsewhere his troops had bogged down in their pushes against their main objectives, the towns of Zacapa and Puerto Barrios. Despite the early panic they had caused, the CIA's mercenary planes had so far done relatively little damage, frequently missing their targets. Several of them had been hit by ground fire and been put out of action. A Honduran ship, the *Siesta de Trujillo,* had been seized at Puerto Barrios as it tried to offload a cargo of arms and munitions to the invaders. Finally, as the victim of an attack coming from outside its borders, Guatemala had a good case for requesting UN intervention on its behalf.

On the same day Ernesto wrote those words, June 20, the American overseers of Operation Success were becoming alarmed at the likelihood that their Liberation Army was about to be routed. Then, at Allen Dulles's request, Eisenhower authorized the dispatch of two more fighter-bombers to the field. By June 23 the new planes were in action and remained there for the next three days, strafing and bombing important targets in key Guatemalan towns, including the capital.

Simultaneously, the United States was engaged in a blocking maneuver to thwart Guatemala's request for a special session of the UN Security Council to discuss the crisis. The acting council president for June was U.S. Ambassador Henry Cabot Lodge, who went to battle with UN Secretary General Dag Hammarskjöld over the affair. Lodge finally agreed to convene a session on June 25, by which time the new bombers had wreaked their havoc, allowing Castillo Armas's forces to regroup and launch new assaults.

On June 24 the invaders seized the small town of Chiquimula, and Castillo Armas proclaimed it as the headquarters of his "provisional government." La Voz de Liberación beat the war drums, giving listeners the impression the Liberation Army forces were an unstoppable military juggernaut, scoring successes left and right as government defenses crumbled before it.

The confidence of Arbenz and some of his top military men began to crack. Meanwhile, Ambassador Lodge was busily lobbying other council members to vote against Guatemala's request for a UN investigative team to be sent to Guatemala. Particular pressure was put on Britain and France, with Eisenhower and John Foster Dulles leaning on visiting British Prime Minister Winston Churchill in Washington. Their message was that if London and Paris didn't go along with the Americans on Guatemala, U.S. help would not be forthcoming in dealing with their own problems in Cyprus, Indochina, and the Suez. When the Security Council vote was taken on June 25, the United States scored a narrow victory, a 5–4 vote against a UN inquiry, with Britain and France abstaining. Guatemala was on her own.

II

By July 3, Operation Success had earned its name. That day, The "Liberator" Castillo Armas flew into Guatemala City with U.S. Ambassador John Puerifoy at his side. His ascension to power, brokered by the Americans, followed a confusing week of power struggles between Guatemalan military leaders after they forced Arbenz's resignation on June 27.

"A terrible shower of cold water has fallen over the Guatemalan people," observed Ernesto a few days later. He wrote Celia again, rueful over the heroic rhetoric of his last letter, explaining that he had written it "full of glorious dreams, just before going to the front I would never reach, to die if it were necessary . . .

"It's all happened like a wonderful dream which one clings to after awakening. Reality is knocking on many doors, and now the sound of gunfire can be heard, the rewards for the more ardent adherents to the *ancien régime*. Treason continues to be the patrimony of the army, and once more proves the aphorism that calls for the liquidation of the army as the true principle of democracy (if the aphorism doesn't exist I create it)."

In Ernesto's mind, the other culpable sectors were the "reactionary" press and the Catholic Church, which had aided and abetted Arbenz's downfall, and he mentally earmarked them as problem sectors needing special attention if socialist revolutions were to succeed elsewhere in the future.

Ernesto went on to castigate Arbenz—who had immediately sought asylum in the Mexican embassy*—for buckling under to the military officers who, egged on by Puerifoy, had demanded and won his resignation, especially for his reluctance to "arm the people" to defend the country.

Ernesto was in an understandably bitter mood. In the final days of June, he had joined an armed militia organized by the Communist Youth, hoping to reaching the war front. A Nicaraguan volunteer, Rodolfo Romero, was the "military chief" for the "Augusto César Sandino Brigade" at a house in northern Guatemala City. Ernesto was accepted into the brigade and remained with them several days, anxiously awaiting his chance to go to the front and do some fighting, but the public health minister appeared and transferred him to a hospital to await further orders. At this point, Romero and Ernesto lost sight of one another. (They would meet again four and a half years later, when Romero, in search of support for an anti-Somoza guerrilla war, flew into the newly liberated Cuban capital of Havana at the invitation of Comandante Ernesto "Che" Guevara.)

At the hospital, Ernesto had once again offered to go to the front, but, as he noted in frustration, "They haven't paid me any mind." He waited for another visit by the health minister, but on Saturday, June 26, the day before Arbenz's resignation, he lost his last chance when the minister came and left while he was out visiting Hilda.

During the tense buildup to Arbenz's downfall, Hilda recalled Ernesto desperately seeking to forestall the collapse, speaking to anyone he could to get the message to Arbenz that he should turn his back on his military advisors and arm the people, leading them into the mountains to fight a guerrilla war. (In fact, two days before his ouster, Arbenz had tried to distribute arms to the militias like the one Ernesto had joined, but the army had refused.) Now, from his post in the hospital, Ernesto watched the events unfold with increasing anxiety and frustration, as one capitulation after another led to the consolidation of Castillo Armas's triumph and the ignominious demise of the Guatemalan "revolution." The repression began even before Castillo Armas's arrival: With the declaration of martial law and a decree banning the PGT (Communist party), the embassies began filling with fearful asylum-seekers. Ernesto predicted his own expulsion from the

---

*In August, Castillo Armas finally allowed Arbenz to leave for Mexico, but reserved a special humiliation for him at the airport, where he was jeered by Castillo Armas supporters and then, at customs, forced publicly to strip off his clothing.

hospital, since he was seen as a "Red," while Hilda took precautions by moving into new lodgings.

On the day of Castillo Armas's entry to the city, Ernesto observed that "the people really applauded him." His swaggering army of straw-hatted, submachine-gun-toting paramilitary followers roamed the city, savoring their status as the country's "liberators," and looking for trouble. Edelberto Torres Jr. was arrested, accused of being a Communist, and Ernesto worried openly about the fate of his father, the Rubén Darío scholar. His own situation was tenuous, and, after being kicked "shitting" out of the hospital, as he had predicted he would be, Ernesto found refuge in the home of two Salvadoran women who had already sought asylum.

Amid all the political upheaval, he and Hilda continued their cat-and-mouse romance. She sent him some verses she'd written in which she spoke "stupidities," as he called them. "What is happening to her," he wrote in his diary, "is a mixture of calculation to win me over, fictive imagination, and the sense of honor of a free woman affronted by my indifference. I sent her a little animaloid verse:

> Surrender yourself like the birds do,
> I'll take you like the bears do,
> and, maybe, I'll kiss you slowly
> So I can feel like a man, I who am a dove.

". . . I gave her a new ultimatum, but the abundance of these meant that it didn't have much effect. What *did* affect her was that I confessed about the fuck with the nurse. She still has hopes of marrying me."

By mid-July, the new regime's witch-hunt had begun in earnest. Everyone connected with the Arbenz regime or suspected of Communism was being arrested, and that now included Ernesto. Those people who had not already fled Guatemala were attempting to do so. Elena Leiva de Holst took off, and his refuge at the Salvadorans' home ended, too, with the arrival of a daughter who had come to help her sisters leave the country. The house was to be closed, and Ernesto needed to find a new hiding place.

Taken in at the home of Elena Leiva de Holst's aunt, he spent his days going to and coming from the Argentine embassy, but did not yet seek asylum himself. According to Hilda, he took advantage of his access to the embassy and the confusion in Guatemala City "to carry out errands for those in asylum at the embassy, to collect some arms, and to arrange asylum for those in difficult positions or those who wished to leave the country."

Ernesto continued his activities unscathed for a few more days, but then Hilda was arrested and hauled away to a prison cell. Ernesto learned from the women at her house that before Hilda was taken away, the police had questioned her about him. It was a warning Ernesto couldn't ignore, and he too now requested and was granted asylum at the Argentine embassy. But just before he went, he reflected on his future plans in his journal.

"My plans are very fluid, although most probably I'll go to Mexico. . . . Far or near, I don't know why but I'm in one of those moments in which a slight pressure from one side could twist my destiny around completely."

III

Ernesto joined a large and "heterogeneous group of people" already installed inside the walled compound of the Argentine embassy, but once there he quickly became restless and began to fret. "One can't call asylum boring but sterile, yes, because one can't do what one wants, because of all the people there."

His asthma had worsened. Hilda had been released after several days in custody, as he learned from the newspapers, when she had gone on a hunger strike to obtain her freedom. He didn't understand why she hadn't come to see him yet, and wondered whether it was "ignorance about where I am or whether she doesn't know she can visit me."

For the first time, Ernesto now seemed intent upon a particular destination to head toward. Mexico City was the place where Arbenz and most of his allies who had escaped arrest—as well as many of the Latin American political exiles in Guatemala—were heading. Since its own "anti-imperialist" revolution only four decades earlier, the politically tolerant and culturally dynamic Mexican capital had become a sanctuary for thousands of left-wing political exiles from around the world, including significant numbers of European Jews and Spanish Republicans fleeing Fascism in the 1930s and '40s. Obviously, Ernesto had decided that Mexico was also the next best place for him.

For now, Ernesto stayed put. To pass the time, he began recording his impressions of his fellow asylum-seekers. The first to catch his interest was the renowned Communist peasant leader Carlos Manuel Pellecer. Ernesto concluded that Pellecer was "an intelligent man and, it seems, brave. He seems to have a great ascendancy over the other asylum-seekers, an ascendancy that emanates I'm not sure whether from his own personality or because of the fact that he is the maximum leader of the party. . . . [But] he is somewhat effeminate in his gestures, and he wrote a book of verse in earlier years, a sickness very common in these parts. His Marxist formation doesn't have the solidity of other figures I have known and he hides [its lack] behind a certain petulance. The impression he gives me is of an individual who is sincere but overexcited, one of those ambitious persons who at a wrong footing will renounce their faith violently, but are yet capable of carrying out the highest sacrifices at a determined moment."*

Of his Cuban acquaintance José Manuel "Che-Che" Vega Suárez, he wrote: "He is as dumb as a piece of rubble and lies like an Andalusian. Of his previous life in Cuba there is nothing certain except for indications that he was what is called a *"jodedor"* [carouser] to whom Batista's police gave a royal beating. . . . His behavior before taking asylum was cowardly. Here he is entertaining with his unmalicious exaggerations. He is a big boy, selfish and spoiled who believe that everyone else should put up with his caprices. He eats like a pig."

Suffering from asthma and now "deeply bored," Che watched more days slip by. Once, having run out of asthma medicine, he slipped out to retrieve some he had left at Elena Holst's. In the embassy, his days were spent in "meaningless arguments and every other possible way of wasting time."

On August 2, there was a revolt by army cadets, ashamed by their degradation at the hands of Castillo Armas's undisciplined Liberation Army, and, from inside the embassy, Ernesto could hear the gunfire. The revolt ended after Ambassador Puerifoy sent word that the United States expected the Guatemalan military to stand solidly behind Castillo Armas. Ernesto noted that the CIA appointee's power base was "now totally consolidated."

Meanwhile, the people packed into the embassies awaited word as to whether Castillo Armas would grant them safe-conduct passes to leave the country. The safety of hundreds of people depended on his decision. Ernesto was not concerned for himself, since, as an Argentine citizen, his name did not appear on the asylee list of Guatemalans and other nationalities; he was merely biding his time until he felt it was safe to reemerge and travel to Mexico.

In fact, the asylees' situation was much more tenuous than they ever realized. Anxious to consolidate its victory over "Communism" in this first important Cold War skirmish in Washington's backyard with a propaganda campaign, the CIA had dispatched teams of agents to Guatemala to collect and, in some cases, to "plant" evidence of the "true pro-Soviet" nature of Arbenz's former government. The Dulles brothers were also demanding that Castillo Armas arrest all suspected Communists and their suspected sympathizers remaining in the country.

Castillo Armas was a willing partner in this campaign, and had already carried out the first of a series of repressive measures to shore up his own

---

*Ernesto's appraisal was prescient: The patrician Pellecer later found asylum in Mexico. There he repudiated his earlier beliefs and wrote anti-Communist pamphlets under CIA sponsorship.

power while rolling back all of the revolution's reforms. On July 19, "El Libertador" had created a "National Committee for Defense against Communism," followed up by a "Preventive Penal Law against Communism," which imposed the death penalty for a wide range of crimes, including so-called "political sabotage." The committee had broad powers to arrest and detain anyone suspected of Communism, and illiterate voters were banned by decree from voting, a measure that instantly disenfranchised the vast majority of Guatemala's population. The agrarian reform laws were overturned, and all political parties, labor unions, and peasant organizations outlawed. Books considered "subversive" were confiscated and burned; the blacklist included novels by Victor Hugo and Dostoevsky, and those by Guatemala's noted (and future Nobel prize–winning) writer Miguel Angel Asturias, who would even be stripped of his citizenship.*

Yet Secretary of State Dulles was still not satisfied. He insisted that Castillo Armas go after the estimated seven hundred asylum-seekers holed up in the capital's foreign embassies. "Dulles feared that they might 'recirculate' throughout the hemisphere if they were allowed to leave Guatemala," wrote the authors of *Bitter Fruit,* the authoritative account of the Arbenz overthrow. "His fear soon became an obsession. All through the summer he bombarded Puerifoy with telegrams insisting that Castillo Armas be ordered to arrest the 'asylees.' Early in July, he told Puerifoy to instruct the new regime to bring 'criminal charges' against 'Communist' refugees as a way of preventing them from leaving the country."

Secretary Dulles went so far as to propose a plan in which Castillo Armas would grant safe-conduct to Communists on the condition they be sent directly to Moscow, but the new Guatemalan dictator resisted, apparently feeling that such a breach of international norms would be going too far, even for him, and in early August he began approving safe-conduct visas to most of the embassy refugees. When the good news reached the Argentine embassy, there was great jubilation.

By mid-August, the first few safe-conduct passes had arrived, but for Ernesto life was unchanging. He spent his time playing chess, sending notes out to Hilda, and writing his psycho-political profiles of his fellow asylees. He now turned his attention to the Guatemalans, using their revolutionary aptitudes as his measure of them.

Roberto Castañeda, a photographer and dancer, had traveled "behind the Iron Curtain and is a sincere admirer of all of that but won't enter the

---

*Asturias's son was in future years to become a top guerrilla leader under his nom de guerre of Gaspar Ilom, adopted from an Indian character in one of his father's novels.

party. He lacks theoretical knowledge of Marxism, and maybe he wouldn't be a good militant for what we could call these bourgeois defects, but it is sure that in the moment of action he would be up to the task. . . . He doesn't have practically any of the effeminate mannerisms of a dancer." And of another, Arana, he wrote: "He is weak and without an ideological base but he is loyal to the party. Of medium intelligence, he is [nonetheless] sufficiently intelligent to realize that the only ideal path for the working class is communism."

Hilda twice visited the embassy, now under heavy guard, but was prevented from entering. Ernesto's asthma continued to plague him. He resolved to fast for a day and see if it would help "purge" his system. Hilda sent him a bottle of honey and a letter.

The days dragged on, and his diary entries, dominated now by his asylee profiles, describe an order of monotony. He helped out in the embassy kitchen, but complained that the effort tired him out, and the weariness of his muscles showed how out of shape he was. His profiles had become more caustic, and he was especially critical of the large number of young Guatemalan leftists who also claimed to be poets. The verse of eighteen-year-old student Marco Antonio Sandoval, for instance, was "plagued with meditations upon death," while Sandoval was an "energetic admirer of himself." When the poet Hugo Blanco escaped from the embassy by leaping over the fence, Ernesto wrote: "A bad poet. I don't even think he is an intelligent person. The inclination that seems to accompany them all is compassion. The good boy's smile accompanies the poet."

Safe-conduct passes continued to trickle in, and news came that Perón had agreed to grant asylum in Argentina to those in the embassy, along with their families. For those he respected, Ernesto issued some informal *salvoconductos* of his own, in the form of notes addressed to his family and friends.

Then, one night, the fugitive Communist leader Víctor Manuel Gutiérrez sneaked into the embassy by climbing over a wall. With Gutiérrez high on Castillo Armas's wanted list, the incident caused an uproar between the Argentine ambassador and Guatemalan officials, but Gutiérrez was granted asylum and placed in a room with his comrade Pellecer.

Soon afterward, Ernesto was confined in the embassy garage along with twelve others viewed as troublesome "Communists." They became known as "The Group of Thirteen." According to Ernesto's less than explicit notes, the extreme measure was taken after Humberto Pineda, Myrna Torres's boyfriend, began some sort of uproar. They were threatened with force if they did not go along with the measure, and prohibited from talking with the other asylees.

In the Group of Thirteen's first night in detention, however, Humberto Pineda and his brother both escaped from the embassy. They were planning to participate in some kind of antigovernment resistance. In her book, Hilda said they took their action at Ernesto's urgings. In his diary, Ernesto simply lauded the two as having "a lot of balls."

He now focused on his immediate comrades in the garage. "Ricardo Ramírez," he wrote, "is perhaps one of the most capable leaders of the [Communist] youth. . . . His general level of culture is high and his manner of facing problems is much less dogmatic than that of other comrades."*

August was now coming to an end, with everyone's patience wearing thin in the prolonged confinement. Finally, two more men escaped from the embassy, and the men in the garage were placed under even stricter confinement after Che-Che Vega "raised a ruckus with a whore who is a *mucama,* a cleaning girl." Tensions eased somewhat when 118 of the Argentine embassy asylees—including Pellecer and Gutiérrez—were evacuated on five planes sent from Buenos Aires.

Ernesto had also been offered passage home to Argentina, but, adamant about going to Mexico, had rejected the offer. Since the ambassador could not force him to seek repatriation, he reluctantly allowed Ernesto to leave the embassy grounds.

Ernesto was back in funds since a friend of Gualo García's had come in on one of the evacuation flights, bringing 150 dollars sent by his family, as well as "two suits, 4 kilos of *yerba* and a mountain of stupid little things." To his family, he wrote of his plans to forge on to Mexico. He thanked them for their gifts but warned he might not take along the clothes they sent. "My slogan is little baggage, strong legs and a fakir's stomach."

IV

When, in late August, Ernesto left the embassy that had been his home for the past month, the first thing he did was to go find Hilda.

Since her own release from prison on July 26, she had been living in a lonely and frightened limbo, having been refused a passport at the Peruvian embassy and now awaiting clearance from Lima. In a bizarre audience

---

*Then only twenty-three years old, Ricardo Ramírez would go on to become "Rolando Morán," leader of the Ejército Guerrillero de los Pobres (EGP), the strongest of several Marxist guerrilla forces that emerged in the early 1960s to fight successive Guatemala governments for the next nearly four decades. As of January 1997, the EGP and its allies in the URNG guerrilla coalition prepared to demobilize after long negotiations finally culminated in a peace agreement signed in December 1996, which ended thirty-six years of civil war.

with Castillo Armas at the Presidential Palace, to which she had been summoned at his request, Hilda had been assured she would not be rearrested while she awaited the uncertain outcome of her passport petition. Since then she had lived quietly in a rented apartment in the center of town and waited anxiously for Ernesto to leave his embassy refuge.

They met in a restaurant where she usually took her meals. Recalling the moment he showed up, Hilda wrote: "He appeared there one day while I was having lunch. Everyone in the restaurant studiously ignored him, except for my good friend the proprietress, who invited him to come and eat anything he wished. And when we walked through the downtown streets after lunch, everyone who knew us looked at us in surprise and were afraid to speak with us; they wouldn't even wave. They doubtless thought we were being watched by the police."

Deciding that there was nothing concrete that could be held against him, Ernesto turned his passport in to the immigration police for his exit permit, the first step toward getting his Mexican visa. While he waited, he went to Lake Atitlán and the Guatemalan highlands. Within a few days, he returned to Guatemala City, picked up his passport, and finally obtained his Mexican visa.

His relationship with Hilda had reached a *via crucis*. Ernesto was ready to hit the road again, on his own, for a new adventure in Mexico, while Hilda expected to head home to Peru. According to Hilda, Ernesto seemed unconcerned about their separation and made cavalier assurances that they would eventually meet up in Mexico and marry, while she sadly contemplated the prospect of losing him forever. The air was thick between them. They took a good-bye excursion together to their old picnic haunt of San Juan Sacatepéquez and had what Ernesto described as "a profusion of fondles and a superficial screw."

In fact, marriage with Hilda was the furthest thing from Ernesto's mind. On the same day as their final tryst, he wrote: "I believe I'll take advantage of the fact that she can't leave yet to split definitively. Tomorrow I will spend saying good-bye to all the people I want to and on Tuesday morning I'll begin the great adventure to Mexico."

In mid-September, Ernesto crossed the Guatemalan border and headed for Mexico City. While he had some small doubts about his safety, the journey passed uneventfully.*

---

*In fact, Ernesto had been in a position more potentially exposed than he realized, since the CIA had already begun a file on him. As Peter Grose, the author of a courteous biography of the CIA director Allen Dulles (*Gentleman Spy: The Life of Allen Dulles,* Houghton Mifflin, 1994) wrote: "Sorting through the files of the fallen Arbenz regime in Guatemala a few

In the end, John Foster Dulles's instincts about the political exiles would prove correct. Besides Ernesto "Che" Guevara, a host of future revolutionaries had escaped his grasp in Guatemala. In Mexico and elsewhere, they *would* regroup and, from the ashes of the Arbenz debacle, eventually reemerge—often with Guevara's help—as the Marxist guerrillas who would haunt American policy-makers for the next forty years.

---

weeks after the coup, David Atlee Phillips came across a single sheet of paper about a twenty-five-year-old Argentine physician who had arrived in town the previous January to study medical care amid social revolution. 'Should we start a file on this one?' his assistant asked. The young doctor, it seemed, had tried to organize a last-ditch resistance by Arbenz loyalists; then he had sought refuge in the Argentine Embassy, eventually moving on to Mexico. 'I guess we'd better have a file on him,' Phillips replied. Over the coming years the file for Ernesto Guevara, known as 'Che,' became one of the thickest in the CIA's global records."

11

"My Proletarian Life"

I

In the early fifties, Mexico City still retained some of the political and artistic effervescence that had peaked in the thirties and forties. The influx of thousands of exiles fleeing Fascism in Europe had given it a cosmopolitan sophistication and helped spark a Mexican cultural renaissance. It was the time when artists such as Diego Rivera, Orozco, Siqueiros, Frida Kahlo, and Tina Modotti were doing the work that made them famous. Writers, artists, and political figures mingled at night in the thriving cabaret scene featuring the great stars of the Mexican bolero; a booming movie industry was spawning cinema legends such as the director Emilio "El Indio" Fernández, the comic actor Cantinflas, and the screen idols Dolores del Río and María Félix. From the French writers Antonin Artaud and André Breton to the contemporary Beat poets and writers Jack Kerouac and William S. Burroughs, numerous foreigners had flocked to seek nourishment in Mexico's creative ambience.

Since the postrevolutionary consolidation of power by the ruling Partido Revolucionario Institucional (PRI)* Mexico had earned itself a widespread popularity amongst anti-imperialist Latin nationalists, and a grudging respect from Washington. In the 1930s, President Lázaro Cárdenas nationalized Mexico's oilfields, and had pushed through a sweeping agrarian reform program. Espousing a foreign policy fiercely independent of Washington, Mexico was also a highly politicized environment, full of intrigue, where both the United States and the USSR had important embassies and intelligence operations, and where exiles, spies, and wanderers mingled and conspired. Mexico

---

*After several name changes, following its creation in 1929, Mexico's ruling party adopted its present name in 1946.

City had hosted some infamous assassinations—those of the Cuban Communist leader Julio Antonio Mella in 1929 and of Leon Trotsky in 1940.

These two worlds, the political and the creative, had always intermingled and become suffused with one another. Modotti had been the lover of the assassinated Mella; Kahlo had had an affair with Trotsky; the muralist Siqueiros had led a machine-gunning attack against Trotsky's home, before the Stalinist agent Ramón Mercader achieved grisly success with an icepick.

Mexico City in the 1950s was far from the smog-shrouded megalopolis it has become: you could still see the snowcapped volcanoes Popocatepl and Ixtaccihuatl towering on the horizon. Apart from its historic labyrinthine downtown—the old Spanish colonial city built on the ruins of the Aztec capital—it was a city of serene, village-like neighborhoods and tree-lined boulevards. Even in the fifties, it was not uncommon to see men dressed as *charros*—Mexico's cowboy-dandies—promenading on horseback down the Paseo de la Reforma on Sunday afternoons.

There is no single defining moment for the eclipse of Mexico's so-called "romantic era," but few events are more emblematic of its passage than the last public appearance made by the ailing Frida Kahlo, on July 2, 1954. That cold, damp day, the pneumonia-stricken artist left her bed to join a mass protest against the CIA's overthrow of Arbenz. Kahlo's husband, Diego Rivera, pushed her wheelchair through the streets to the rally, held outside the white-domed pantheon of Mexican culture, the Palacio de Bellas Artes. There, for four long hours, Kahlo joined in the crowd's cries of *"Gringos Asesinos, fuera!"* and held aloft her glittering, ring-festooned hands. In her left, she held up a banner depicting a dove of peace, while she raised her right in a clenched fist of defiance. Afterward, the forty-seven-year-old artist's condition deteriorated rapidly, and eleven days later, on July 13, she died.

II

The first letter Ernesto wrote home from Mexico, on September 30, was to Aunt Beatriz. "Mexico, the city, or better said the country, of the *mordidas* [bribes], has received me with all the indifference of a big animal, neither caressing me or showing me its teeth."

His immediate plans were to find work and make enough money to survive, then travel around Mexico and "ask for a visa from the Titan of the North [the United States]." If successful, he would visit Aunt Ercilia in New York, "and if not, to Paris." Guessing that his money would hold out at most two months, he immediately began looking up contacts. One was

Ulíses Petit de Murat, a friend of his father's who now worked as a screen-writer for the Mexican film world. Before leaving Guatemala, he had told Hilda of Petit and mentioned that there might be an opportunity for him in Mexico to work as a film extra, trying out his "unrealized artistic ambi-tions of becoming an actor." Hilda called this a frivolous scheme and begged him not to waste his talents, but to pursue his medical career instead. Ac-cording to Hilda, a somewhat chastened Ernesto had defended the idea, saying that he had merely thought of it as a means of making ends meet, but finally agreed with her and promised not to be sidetracked.

But now he needed work, and Petit de Murat was one of the few con-tacts Ernesto had in Mexico. Their meeting went well enough. "He took me out to show me around and we argued about politics," reported Ernesto in his diary. "He has a nice daughter, but she comes from a typical clericaloid bourgeois education." Petit and his daughter Marta took Ernesto to see the Aztec pyramids of Teotihuacan on the city's outskirts. Using Marta as a model, he tried out a new toy he had bought himself with half of his re-maining funds—a 35 mm Zeiss camera.

Petit invited him to stay at his house and offered to help him get some kind of study grant, but Ernesto declined the offer. In a letter to his father on September 30, Ernesto said, without apparent irony, that he had "decided to maintain a certain degree of independence as long as the pesos you sent hold out." Certainly, he and Petit were not a good match politically. "We locked horns over the same argument you and I always had about liberty, etc., and he is as blind as you are, with the aggravating element that it's easy to see that deep down what has happened in Guatemala makes him happy."

Several "zero days" followed, in which Ernesto explored the city, vis-ited museums, and looked up friends. He tracked down Elena Leiva de Holst, who had left Guatemala for exile in Mexico as well. Afterward he wrote in his diary that there seemed to be "something weird" going on be-tween her and Hilda, as she had spoken of Hilda in a "very disparaging manner." Whatever Elena told him must have been convincing, for he wrote in his diary: "I believe I must cut off this unsustainable situation with Hilda."

From home, he heard that most of the "Guatemalan lefties" who had been evacuated to Argentina had been imprisoned. An October letter to his mother was full of recriminations about why his family hadn't done more for the comrades he had sent their way.

In an aside to his spleen-venting, he shared with Celia his frustration over what had occurred in Guatemala, and confessed to feeling torn once again about what to do with himself. In light of events, he declared himself "completely convinced that [political] halfway measures can mean nothing other than the antechamber to treason. The bad thing is that at the same time I haven't taken the decisive attitude that I should have taken a long time ago, because deep down (and on the surface) I am a complete bum and I don't feel like having my career interrupted by an iron discipline."

Ernesto was still digesting his Guatemalan experience, and in his letters he carried on a kind of extended postmortem. He wanted everyone to understand what he thought was the "truth" about what had happened there. To his friend Tita Infante, whose last letter to him in Guatemala he thought had betrayed a concern that went beyond the platonic, he wrote: "Today, with the distance—material and spiritual—that separates me from Guatemala, I reread your last letter and it seemed strange. I found in it a special warmth, in your desperation over not being able to do anything, that really moves me." Like the Spanish Republic, he said, Guatemala had been betrayed "inside and out," but had not fallen without the same nobility. What sickened him most of all was the false revisionism taking place about the Arbenz government. "Falsehoods" were being printed in newspapers all over the Americas. For one thing, he told her, "there were no murders or anything like it. There *should* have been a few firing squads early on, which is different; if those shootings had taken place the government would have retained the possibility of fighting back."

Ernesto was convinced that the American intervention in Guatemala was merely the first skirmish in what would be a global confrontation between the United States and Communism, and he brought up this terrifying prospect rather inopportunely in a letter to his sister Celia. He had learned she was engaged to marry the young architect and Guevara family friend Luis Rodríguez Argañaraz. She had evidently inquired about job prospects in Mexico, for he wrote: "Stay there without thinking nonsense about other countries, because the storm is coming, and although it might not be atomic it'll be the other, that of hunger, and Argentina will be one of the less affected because it depends less on the friend of the north [United States]."

Ernesto also repeated these dire predictions to his father. A world war was inevitable, he announced in a letter sent a few months later. The risks had grown "gigantically" in the wake of the ongoing shake-up in the Kremlin since Stalin's death. "Argentina is the oasis of America, and we have to give Perón all possible support to avoid entering into a war that promises to be terrible—whether you like it or not, that's the way it is. [U.S. Vice President Richard] Nixon is traveling through all these countries, apparently to set the quotas of men and cheap primary resources (paid with expensive and old machinery) with which each of the poor states of America will contribute to the new Koreas."

When he wasn't doomsaying in his correspondence home, Ernesto continued looking for work. He was trying to get interviews for hospital jobs but making little headway. For the time being, he used his new camera to earn money, taking people's portraits in the city's parks and plazas. Over the coming months, which he described as "a routine chain of hopes and deceptions that characterize my proletarian life," he would hold down various other jobs: as a night watchman, a photo correspondent for the Argentine news agency, Agencia Latina, and an allergist and researcher at both the General Hospital and the Pediatric Hospital.

While he was thus engaged, Hilda Gadea reentered his life. Just after Ernesto's departure from Guatemala, Hilda had been rearrested, jailed overnight, and sent under escort to the Mexican border. After a few days, she had been smuggled across the river border by her own guards, for a fee. After being stranded in the border town of Tapachula for eight days, waiting to be granted political asylum by the Mexican government, she made her way to Mexico City and to Ernesto. But Ernesto's thoughts and actions since their parting had not been those of a concerned lover. Even after hearing that she was marooned at the border, he did nothing to help her but commented idly in his diary: "Hilda is in Mexico in Tapachula and it isn't known in what condition."

As usual, Ernesto and Hilda's accounts about their on-off relationship don't dovetail in regard to events in Mexico City. Following their first meeting, Ernesto wrote: "With Hilda it seems we've reached a status quo, we'll see." Hilda's rendition, meanwhile, reasserted her characteristic position. "Again Ernesto spoke of the possibility of getting married. I said we should wait. . . . I had the feeling that my ambiguous response had created a certain tenseness, because he then said that we would just be friends. I was a little surprised: I was only asking him to wait. But I accepted his decision. I had just arrived and here we were already quarreling."

While they continued to see one another, occasionally going out for a meal together or to the cinema, Hilda soon moved into a boardinghouse in the affluent Condesa neighborhood, together with an exiled Venezuelan poet, Lucila Velásquez, and like Ernesto she too began making the rounds of contacts to look for work.

A happier development was Ernesto's accidental reunion with the Cubans he had met in Guatemala, notably his friend Ñico López. One day, while Ernesto was on duty as a volunteer at the General Hospital, Ñico showed up seeking treatment for a comrade who was suffering from allergies. As Hilda told it, Ernesto and Ñico immediately rekindled their friendship. Ñico was buoyant about the future, telling Ernesto confidently that he expected *moncadista* leader Fidel Castro, his brother Raúl, and his other imprisoned comrades to be released from prison before too long.

The exiled Cuban followers of Fidel Castro had been trickling into Mexico City from around the hemisphere since early 1954, when the order had gone out for them to assemble there. They had established an informal headquarters at the apartment of María Antonia González, a Cuban woman married to a professional Mexican wrestler named "Dick" Medrano.

Back in Cuba, where Castro had become a nationwide cause célèbre, Batista had called for elections to legitimize his de facto rule, and now there was mounting public pressure on him to release Castro and the other imprisoned *moncadistas* in an amnesty. Once he was free, Ñico told Ernesto, Mexico was to be the base for Fidel Castro's grand scheme, to organize and train an armed insurrectionary movement that would return to the island and fight a guerrilla war to topple Batista. For Ernesto, however, such grandiose plans must have seemed a very distant promise—and did nothing to alleviate his perennial financial problems.

Ernesto wrote his mother again. He responded to a letter in which she had criticized the behavior of the Guatemalan Communist exiles he had sent to their house. "The communists don't have the same sense of friendship that you have, but among themselves they possess it equally, or better than your own. I saw it clearly in the hecatomb that Guatemala became after the fall, where everyone thought only of saving themselves, [but] the communists maintained their faith and comradeship intact, and were the only group which continued to work there. . . . I believe they are worthy of respect and that sooner or later I will join the Party; more than anything else what impedes me from doing it now is that I still have a fantastic urge to travel through Europe, and I couldn't do that submitted to an iron discipline."

A month later, in December, he wrote his mother again, apparently in response to a letter in which she had expressed her alarm over his declaration of intent to eventually join the Communist party. He told her: "That which you so fear is reached by two roads: positively, by being directly convinced, or negatively, after a deception with everything. I reached it by the second route only to immediately become convinced that one has to follow the first. The way in which the gringos . . . treat America had been provoking a growing indignation in me, but at the same time I studied the theory behind the reasons for their actions and I found it scientific. Afterward came Guatemala."

What he had seen in Guatemala had merely added weight to his convictions, he wrote, and at some moment he had begun to *believe*. "At which moment I left the path of reason and took on something akin to faith I can't tell you even approximately because the path was very long and with a lot of backward steps." There it was. If his family hadn't had enough prior warning, Ernesto had now declared himself and described his conversion. He was a Communist.

III

Nineteen fifty-five began with little change for Ernesto. For the moment, his reality remained that of a young Argentine vagabond—who just happened to have a medical degree—scrabbling for work in a foreign country. His and Hilda's "status quo" had had its ups and downs, but reached a comfortable plateau in the new year. This appears to have had less to do with any reconciliation over their basic differences than the fact that Ernesto now needed Hilda again for the occasional loan and, as he had written in his diary, to satisfy his "urgent need for a woman who will fuck." By now, he knew her well enough to realize she was always available for both.

To make up for his absence at New Year's, he brought her a late present: a miniature copy of the Argentine classic *Martín Fierro* by José Hernández, bound in green leather. It was one of Ernesto's all-time favorite books. In it, he wrote what must for Hilda have seemed a maddeningly ambivalent message, but she nonetheless took it as proof of his feelings for her. "To Hilda, so that on the day of our parting, you retain a sense of my ambitions for new horizons and my militant fatalism. Ernesto 20-1-55."

Hilda was still jobless but sustained by funds from home, and she had found ways to keep herself busy. In January, she had signed up for a two-month course on the Mexican revolution at the Autonomous University. She discussed what she was learning with Ernesto, and they read books related to the topic, including John Reed's *Insurgent Mexico* and Pancho Villa's memoirs.

By now, there were a dozen or so Cuban *moncadistas* in Mexico City. Several were installed in a rooming house on Calle Gutenberg, while Ñico López and Calixto García were decamped separately in the downtown Hotel Galveston. They kept in close contact with the movement's unofficial coordinator, María Antonia González, at her apartment in an ugly modern pink building at 49 Calle Emparán in the city center. Since his chance encounter with Ñico López at the hospital, Ernesto had stayed in intermittent contact with him and his comrades, gradually meeting more of the new arrivals. He hired two of them, Severino "El Guajiro" Rossell and Fernando Margolles, to develop photos he took for Agencia Latina, covering the Second Pan American Games held in March. Another, José Ángel Sánchez Pérez, a *moncadista* just in from Costa Rica, came to live in Ernesto's pension on Calle

Tígres. A couple of months earlier, Sánchez Pérez had joined in the fighting in Costa Rica to defend President Figueres from a Somoza-backed invasion bid against him.

Just before the games began, Sánchez Pérez took Ernesto to introduce him to María Antonia. According to Heberto Norman Acosta, a Cuban Council of State researcher and the son-in-law of one of Castro's rebel expeditionaries—who has spent fifteen years researching the "exile" period prior to the Cuban revolution—Ernesto was taken in as a trusted friend by María Antonia on the basis of his contacts with Ñico López, Calixto García, and the other Cubans. He also hit it off right away with María's husband, the wrestler "Dick" Medrano, and began stopping by regularly.

Meanwhile, Hilda was anxious to renew her affair with Ernesto, which he had interrupted after a recent argument. "I decided that, since I missed Ernesto and wanted to make up," she wrote, "I should take the initiative." Hilda's opportunity came with the arrival back from Canada of Myrna Torres; she had decided to marry her boyfriend Humberto Pineda, who was now in Mexico after months on the run in Guatemala. "Taking advantage of her friendship, I asked her to accompany me to visit the house of the Cubans; I knew that Ernesto was frequently there developing pictures." The visit gave Hilda the opening she wanted. Ernesto agreed to come and see her and, as she hoped, resumed their affair.

At the end of the Pan American Games came the unhappy news that Agencia Latina was folding. Perón's bid to create an Argentine international news agency had not paid off, and with its demise went Ernesto's main source of income. He calculated that the agency owed him five thousand pesos. "It's an amount that I could really use," he wrote. "With it, I could pay off some debts, travel around Mexico, and beat it to hell." Ernesto waited anxiously for the money, but just in case, he made off with one of the agency's cameras.

On the "scientific" side of things, he was starting to make some headway. He had turned down a tempting offer to go and work in Nuevo Laredo, on the Mexican border with the United States, unwilling to commit himself to a two-year contract. In an April 9 letter, he also self-righteously rejected his aunt Beatriz's offer to use her contacts to get him a job in a pharmaceutical laboratory.

"In spite of my vagabonding, my repeated informality and other defects, I have deep and well-defined convictions. These convictions prevent me from taking a job of the type you describe, because these places are dens of thieves of the worst type, who traffic with human health that is supposed to be under my qualified custody . . . I am poor but honest." In case poor Beatriz harbored any doubts about where he was coming from, he signed the letter "Stalin II."

In April, Ernesto traveled to León in Guanajuato state, to attend an allergy conference. There he presented his paper: "Cutaneous Investigations with Semidigested Food Antigens." It received what he described as a "discreet reception" but was commented upon favorably by Dr. Mario Salazar Mallén, his boss at Mexico City's General Hospital, and was due to be published in the next issue of the journal *Alergia*. Afterward, Salazar Mallén, "the *capo* of Mexican allergy," as Ernesto called him, offered him an internship at the General Hospital and a small sinecure to carry out new allergy research.

In May, Salazar Mallén made good on his offer, and Ernesto began his internship at the General Hospital. He was on a minuscule salary of 150 pesos a month, with free lodging, board, and laundry. For now, at least, the job covered his basic needs. In a letter to his mother he wrote: "If it weren't for the charity of friends I would have gone on the police blotter as a death by starvation." As for wages, he was indifferent: "Money is an interesting luxury but nothing more."

Hilda offered to marry and maintain him. "I said no," he wrote in his diary. ". . . That [instead] we should stay as little lovers until I beat it to hell, and I don't know when that'll be." But when, soon afterward, Hilda invited Ernesto to move into the apartment she shared with Lucila Velásquez, he accepted. The two women had recently moved into a new apartment on Calle Rhin, and Hilda had also found herself a temporary job at the UN's Economic Commission for Latin America and the Caribbean (ECLAC).

For Ernesto, living with Hilda not only solved the question of food—and offered a more comfortable lodging than the hospital bed he had been granted—but also enriched his circle of contacts. Hilda knew a great many people among Mexico's flourishing exile community, enhanced by the recent exodus from Guatemala. They included the prominent Cuban exile Raúl Roa, an editor of the magazine *Humanismo,* and his coeditor, the Puerto Rican exile Juan Juarbe y Juarbe. Others were the young Peruvian lawyer Luis de la Puente Uceda,* leader of a leftist youth wing of APRA, and Laura Meneses, the Peruvian wife of Pedro Albizu Campos, the Puerto Rican independence fighter imprisoned in the United States for leading a 1950 attack on the Governor's Palace in San Juan.

Ernesto hit it off especially well with the Puerto Ricans, and began stopping by with Hilda to see them and discuss Latin American politics, particularly the issue of Puerto Rican independence, a cause he had come to sympathize with strongly.

---

*Ernesto and Luis de la Puente Uceda did not meet this time, for Uceda had already left for Peru by the time Hilda and Ernesto had patched things up. Despite their missed opportunity, he and Ernesto would meet a few years later, in Cuba, while Uceda was organizing a Peruvian guerrilla movement.

Ernesto's life with Hilda slipped into an unexciting, but not unhappy routine of work, study, and domesticity. They met with friends, went to the occasional movie, and cooked dinners at home. Many nights, Lucila came home to find the two of them deeply absorbed in study, usually of books on economy. On such occasions she didn't speak, but tiptoed past them to her bedroom and retired for the night.

In the middle of May, he and Hilda consecrated their union with a weekend tryst at the popular retreat of Cuernavaca near Mexico City and began exploring other sites within easy reach of the capital. His life, as he told his mother in a letter sent in mid-June, had acquired a "monotonous Sunday-style rhythm."

But in Cuba, the pace of political events had begun to quicken. Standing unopposed, Batista had won Cuba's presidential elections, held the previous November, and in January his mandate had received the Eisenhower administration's blessing in a congratulatory visit by Vice President Richard Nixon. Then, in April, over the Easter weekend, CIA Director Allen Dulles had visited Havana and met with Fulgencio Batista. Concerned about Communist encroachment in the hemisphere, Dulles successfully urged Batista to open a special police intelligence bureau to deal with the threat. The result, largely funded and advised by the CIA, was BRAC, the "Buro de Represión a las Actividades Comunistas." Soon enough, its own activities were to earn it a sinister reputation.

Ironically, neither Dulles nor Havana's CIA station chief had Fidel Castro in mind when they proposed BRAC's creation, and in May Fidel Castro, his brother Raúl, and the eighteen other *moncadistas* incarcerated with them on the Isle of Pines were granted their freedom in an amnesty bill. Batista described his ill-advised act of leniency as a goodwill gesture in honor of "Mother's Day."

IV

Batista was not the worst of Latin America's dictators at the time. In the neighboring Dominican Republic, Rafael Leonidas Trujillo had ruled over his poor nation as absolute dictator since the thirties thanks to the ruthless efficiency of his secret police, while imposing an official cult of personality that was unparalleled in the Western Hemisphere. The capital, Santo Domingo, had been renamed Ciudad Trujillo. Orwellian-sounding signs bearing messages like "God Is in Heaven—Trujillo Is on Earth" and "We Live in Happiness Thanks to Trujillo" were ubiquitous.

Compared with the flamboyant despotism of his Dominican colleague, Batista was a political choirboy. A mulatto army officer, he had left the barracks to be Cuba's president once before, in the forties. That time, he had won office through elections generally considered fair, ruling afterward over a coalition government with Cuba's Communist Partido Socialista Popular. Then, Cuba had languished through the uninspired, graft-ridden presidencies of Grau San Martín and Carlos Prío Socarrás. With his 1952 coup Batista had put an end to Carlos Prío Socarrás's presidency, and although he may have legitimized his rule in Washington's eyes—with his elections and by turning on his old Communist allies—to Cuba's disenfranchised political parties, the students, and the urban middle-class intelligentsia, he was a dictator who had usurped power and sabotaged their hopes for a constitutional reform to bring about social change and a genuine Cuban democracy.

Since the Moncada assault, Batista had shown that he was not averse to resolving challenges to his rule through police death-squad tactics, and official graft and bribery flourished as never before. By the mid-fifties, Cuba was earning a sleazy reputation as "the whorehouse of the Caribbean," where weekending Americans came to gamble, drink, and carouse with Havana's many prostitutes. A notorious character named Schwartzmann ran a theater featuring hard-core "blue" films and live-sex performances, and the American crime syndicates were moving in, as well, opening nightclubs and gambling casinos.

Perceiving him to be a half-caste gangster, Cuba's aristocracy despised Batista vehemently, and it put him in his place when as president he applied for membership in one of Havana's most exclusive whites-only country clubs and was summarily rejected. To Cuba's new generation of nationalist idealists, exemplified by Fidel Castro, Batista was little more than a pimp, selling off their country to degenerate foreigners, compounding the resentment they already felt over such issues as the continued U.S. naval presence at Guantánamo Bay, a legacy of the ignominious days earlier in the twentieth century when (after the United States had won the Spanish-American War and ousted the Spaniards from Cuba) Washington had governed Cuba like a vassal state.

Fidel Castro wanted to change his country, and his time in prison had only toughened his resolve. When he emerged from the gates of the Modelo prison on May 15, he was in an ungrateful, scrappy mood. Amid the media fanfare that greeted him, he was unapologetic, vowing to continue the struggle against Batista's "despotism."

At this point, his movement had a fairly hard inner core of mostly middle-class, reform-minded Cuban professionals who were united by their hatred of Batista. Except for a handful, the *moncadistas* were not Communists but activists from the youth wing of the Ortodoxo opposition party.

Fidel Castro himself had emerged as the most charismatic leader in the vacuum left by the 1951 suicide of the party's leader, Eduardo Chibás.

The audacious Castro was a leader to rally around, a Young Turk who, since Moncada, had shown he was not just full of bombast. More than anything else, Castro's followers were nationalists, imbued with the romantic rhetoric of José Martí, the diminutive "apostle" of Cuban independence who in 1895 was shot off his horse during a reckless charge against Spanish colonial troops.

Thrown into this group were a few tactfully undeclared Marxists such as Ñico López, Calixto García, and Fidel Castro's younger brother, Raúl. Castro's own ideology was publicly anti-Communist, but he was already showing signs of the wily political opportunism he was to become famous for, gathering useful people from all political stripes to help implement his goals. The reckonings would come later. For now there was an uphill battle that needed to be waged, and he needed all the help he could get. The movement's actual philosophy could be ironed out over time; what held them all together for now was their attraction to Fidel Castro.

Castro's organization had acquired a name—the July 26 Movement— but so far, it remained a secret known only to his closest followers. Publicly, Castro denied any intentions of forming his own political party and strenuously reavowed his loyalty to the Ortodoxo party. Actually, Castro's plan was to use his freedom in Cuba to build up his base of support before going to Mexico and preparing for the next phase of the struggle, the guerrilla war that would oust Batista and bring his own party to power.

Taking advantage of Batista's amnesty, Ñico López and Calixto García returned to Havana to meet with their leader and help him coordinate strategy. Two days before they left Mexico, on May 27, Ernesto wrote an intriguing letter to his father. Opening with a description of his allergy research, he began to ramble on about his future travel plans, enigmatically letting slip the possibility that he "might go to Cuba."

He was involved in two separate "collaborations," he wrote. One involving allergy research, and the other—in an allusion that must have mystified his father—with a "good chemist" in Mexico "about a problem of which I only have an intuition, but I believe something very important is going to come out. . . . I hope for a recommendation to the places where the dawn is ripening, as they say. . . . Havana in particular attracts me as a place to fill my heart with landscape, well mixed with quotes from Lenin."

Yet, when he heard of a ship sailing for Spain in early July, he was prepared to abandon all his plans to jump at the opportunity. He was also told he could attend the upcoming Communist Youth Congress in China if he could pay for part of his travel costs, but as tempting as it was to see "the land of Mao," the pull of Europe was stronger, "almost a biological necessity," as he wrote his mother a few days later. In the end, he remained where he was, immersed in "a succession of ward, laboratory and library, made enjoyable with some English translations."

V

Anxious for some new excitement, Ernesto joined an "improvised" attempt to scale the snowcapped 5,400-meter-high Mt. Popocatépetl, one of two majestic volcanos towering over Mexico City. Although he and his companions reached only the lower lip of the summit's crater, he did get to "peer into the entrails of Pacha Mama [Mother Earth]."

Meanwhile, he followed the news from Argentina with mounting anxiety. On June 16, taking advantage of a spiraling dispute between Perón and the Catholic Church, the Argentine navy launched a bloody assault to topple Perón, and hundreds of civilians died in its messy aerial bombardment of the Presidential Palace. The attempt failed, but Perón was shaken after the upheaval, and an atmosphere of tense uncertainty lingered as his regime teetered on the brink of collapse.

Ernesto wrote his mother, asking for news because he didn't trust the reports being published in Mexico: "I hope the thing isn't as bad as they paint it, and that there's none of ours stuck in a dispute where there's nothing to be gained." Aware of his family's strong *antiperonista* sentiments, Ernesto was concerned that some of them, especially his brother Roberto, who worked for the navy, might be at risk. Moving on to his own news, Ernesto told Celia he was now spending much of his free time imparting the "doctrine of San Carlos," his euphemism for Karl Marx, to "a bunch of sixth-year kids."

Simultaneously with the chaos taking place in Argentina, the political climate in Havana had deteriorated rapidly. Since his release, Castro had been busy recruiting new members to his organization and unceasing in his denunciations of Batista to the press. On the night of June 12, in a secret meeting in colonial Old Havana, the Movimiento 26 de Julio was formally founded with an eleven-member National Directorate, headed by Fidel Castro. Political violence committed by the police, students, and Castro's party militants resumed with a vengeance. A returned exile was murdered; a wave of bombs ripped through Havana. Castro accused the government of unleashing the violence, while the authorities accused Raúl Castro of placing one of the bombs and issued an arrest warrant for him. Fidel publicly accused the regime of plotting to kill him and his brother. On June 16, having already banned him from making radio broadcasts, the police closed down his chief remaining media outlet, the tabloid daily *La Calle*.

Realizing he had little time left with which to act, Fidel ordered Raúl to flee to Mexico and prepare the way for his own arrival. After seeking asylum in the Mexican embassy in Cuba and spending a week holed up there, Raúl flew to Mexico City on June 24. He went straight to María Antonia's house. Among those waiting to meet him was Ernesto Guevara.

By all accounts, the two hit it off immediately. First of all, they shared an ideological affinity. Raúl, Fidel's younger brother by five years, was a Marxist; he had joined the Cuban Communist party's youth wing at Havana university, helped edit its publication *Saeta*, and in May 1953 attended the World (Communist) Youth Festival held in Sofia, Bulgaria. No doubt Raúl had already heard about Ernesto from Ñico López, who had stayed with him and Fidel after returning to Havana.

Soon after Raúl's arrival, Ernesto invited him over to Hilda and Lucila's apartment for dinner. Although Ernesto didn't mention the event in his diary, in her own memoirs, Hilda said she had liked him immediately. "In spite of his youth," Hilda recalled, "twenty-three or twenty-four years, and his even younger appearance, blond and beardless and looking like a university student, his ideas were very clear as to how the revolution was to be made and, more important, for what purpose and for whom."

Raúl spoke of his faith in his older brother and of his personal belief, echoing Ernesto's views, that in Cuba and the rest of the region power could be gained not through elections, but only through war. With popular support, one could gain power and then transform society from capitalism to socialism. Wrote Hilda: "He promised to bring Fidel to our house as soon as the latter arrived in Mexico. From then on he came to our house at least once a week, and Ernesto saw him almost every day."

A mystery that has endured over the years is the question of *when* the Soviets became involved with the Cuban revolution. Although "involvement" is probably too strong a term to use, the earliest contacts between Fidel Castro's revolutionaries and Soviet officials took place in Mexico City during the summer of 1955.

By a curious coincidence, a twenty-seven-year-old Soviet Foreign Ministry official whom Raúl had met two years earlier was also in Mexico City. His name was Nikolai Leonov, and on the month-long voyage that brought Raúl back from the European youth festival in 1953, they had become friends. The last they had seen of one another was when Raúl had disembarked in Havana. Within a few weeks, Raúl had joined in the Moncada assault and gone to prison, while Leonov had traveled on to Mexico, to take up his junior post at the Soviet embassy and attend a Spanish-language course at the Autonomous University. Now chance had brought Nikolai Leonov and Raúl Castro together again.

According to Leonov (who retired from the KGB in 1992 as deputy chief of its First Chief Directorate, covering the United States and Latin America), he happened to bump into Raúl Castro while shopping in the street one day. Delighted to see him again, Raúl gave Leonov the address of María Antonia's house and invited him to drop by. Prohibited from initiating any social contacts without the prior knowledge of the embassy, Leonov nonetheless violated this rule and made his way to 49 Calle Emparán. There, he met Ernesto Guevara.

"He was acting as a doctor, treating Raúl, who was suffering from flu," said Leonov. "My first impression was of a happy man, a joker; practically all he did to treat Raúl was to cheer him up, telling him anecdotes, jokes . . ."

After the introductions were made, Ernesto and Leonov began to talk. Leonov says Guevara was full of questions about Soviet life and pumped him about everything from Soviet literature to "the concept of Soviet man"— "'How do they think? How do they live?'" Instead of answering all his queries, Leonov offered to give him some Soviet literature to read; if he still had questions afterward, they could talk some more. Ernesto agreed, and requested three books: *Chanaev,* about the Soviet civil war; *Thus Steel Is Forged,* by the Communist writer Ostrovksy; and *A Man Complete,* about a World War II Soviet aviation hero. A few days later, Guevara showed up at the embassy to pick up the books, and, as Leonov put it, they talked again, "but this time, as friends." They agreed to keep in touch, and Leonov gave him his embassy card. That, says Leonov, was the last they saw of one another in Mexico.

12

"God and His New Right Hand"

I

That summer, Ernesto wrote in his diary: "A political occurrence is having met Fidel Castro, the Cuban revolutionary, a young man, intelligent, very sure of himself and of extraordinary audacity; I think there is a mutual sympathy between us."

Their encounter had actually taken place several weeks before, a few days after Castro's arrival in Mexico on July 7. As he had with Raúl, Ernesto met Fidel at 49 Calle Emparán. After talking for a while, Ernesto, Fidel, and Raúl had left María Antonia's to have dinner together at a restaurant down the block. After several hours more, Fidel Castro had invited Ernesto to join his guerrilla movement. Ernesto had accepted on the spot.

Che, as the Cubans had begun calling him, was to be their doctor. It was the early days—Fidel was a long way from putting together his ambitious scheme—but it was the cause Ernesto had been searching for.

II

Ernesto Guevara and Fidel Castro were natural opposites. At twenty-eight, Castro was a consummate political animal, overflowing in self-confidence, one of nine children from a landowning family in eastern Cuba's Mayarí province. His father, Ángel Castro, had been an illiterate Galician immigrant who had arrived in Cuba penniless and made himself a modest fortune in land, sugar, lumber, and cattle. Presiding over his large *finca,* Manacas, with its own store, slaughterhouse, and bakery, Castro was a rural patriarch who ruled the destinies of three hundred workers and their families.

Ángel Castro bought his bright, rebellious third son (the offspring of his second marriage, to Lina Ruz, the family's cook) the best education money could buy: the Marist-run Dolores primary school in Santiago, as a boarder at Havana's exclusive Jesuit Colegio Belén high school, and law school at Havana University. Intensely competitive and hot-tempered, Fidel acquired a reputation as a gun-toting rabble-rouser on the volatile Havana University campus. Even before Moncada he had been linked to two shootings—one of a policeman—but had successfully avoided arrest in both cases.

Coming of age during the Grau San Martín and Prío Socarrás presidencies, marked by high-level corruption, gangsterism, and police brutality, Castro immersed himself in student politics, invoking the purist rhetoric of Cuba's national hero, José Martí, in his calls for clean government, students' rights, and social equality. When the vociferous Senator "Eddy" Chibás formed his own Ortodoxo party to run for president against Grau San Martín in 1947, Castro joined the new party's youth wing; before long, Castro was seen by many as Chibás's successor. While he had friends in the Communist party and sided with them on certain issues, this did not prevent him from campaigning with Catholic factions against them in student elections.

Fidel was also strongly anti-imperialist and joined several student associations propounding such views, including one promoting independence for the U.S. territory of Puerto Rico. He was all too aware of Cuba's own recent status as a neocolony of the United States after the Spanish-American War and subsequent U.S. military occupation.

Cuba's putative "independence" had been won at the cost of the ignominious 1901 Platt Amendment, granting Washington the right to intervene in Cuba's "defense" at will and ceding Guantánamo Bay to the United States as a naval base on open-ended terms. By the time Fidel was in high school, the Platt Amendment had been abrogated, but the Americans retained Guantánamo Bay, had large stakes in Cuba's sugar-based economy, and took a proconsular role in its political life. In 1949, after the incident in which American sailors urinated on the hallowed statue of José Martí in Old Havana's Parque Central, Fidel had helped organize a protest in front of the U.S. embassy, and was beaten by Cuban police. In 1951, both he and his brother Raúl (echoing Ernesto Guevara's own stance in distant Argentina) had vocally opposed the Prío government's intention of sending Cuban troops to fight in the "American war" in Korea.

Fidel Castro felt a deep antipathy toward the "Yankees" who had turned independent Cuba into a "pseudo-republic" and allowed venal dictatorships to take root there. His native Mayarí province was a virtual vassal state of the United Fruit Company, where it owned gigantic tracts of land and most of the sugar *ingenios* [mills]. As in its Central American dominions, the American and privileged Cuban employees enjoyed an exclusive life on the company's housing estates, complete with shops, hospitals, sports facilities, and private schools. Fidel's own father depended on "the Company" as well. Having leased much of his land from it, he was required to sell his sugarcane to United Fruit's mills.

Not surprisingly, Fidel saw the United States as responsible for perpetuating Cuba's export-dependent plantation economy, creating a wealthy class of land barons while consigning the workers to lives of endemic poverty. When Washington legitimized Batista's seizure of power by recognizing his regime, it had only compounded Castro's personal determination to bring an end to American influence in Cuba.

Fidel Castro had probably always thought of himself as Cuba's future leader. At school, if he joined in any activity, he fought to become the undisputed leader of his peers, whether it was coming in first in a poetry competition in grade school, becoming captain of the basketball team in Colegio Belén, or winning recognition in student politics at Havana University.

At the age of twelve, he had sent a precocious letter to Franklin Delano Roosevelt to congratulate him on his third inauguration as president and to ask him for "a dollar." Later on, while José Martí remained his lifelong inspiration, he came to admire powerful historical figures such as Julius Caesar, Robespierre, and Napoleon. He seemed to possess an innate knack for the horse-trading and cunning that make for success in politics, and knew how to dissemble artfully.

These traits pointed up a major distinction between him and the man who would later stand at his right-hand side, Ernesto Guevara. For Guevara, politics were a mechanism for social change, and it was social change, not power itself, that impelled him. If he had insecurities, they were not social ones. He lacked the chip on his shoulder that Castro evidently possessed and had converted into a source of strength. His own family were blue bloods, however bankrupt, and he had grown up with the social confidence and sense of privilege that come from knowing one's heritage. The Guevaras may have been black sheep within Argentine society, but they were still *society*. However much Ernesto sought to reject his birthright and to sever his family links, he was indelibly imprinted by them.

While Ernesto Guevara certainly had a robust ego, even he did not possess it to the awesome degree of Fidel Castro. In large groups, where Guevara tended to hang back, to observe and listen, Fidel Castro was compelled to take over and be recognized as the authority on whichever topic was under discussion, from history and politics to animal husbandry.

Because of his asthma, Guevara was all too aware of his physical shortcomings, whereas the burly Castro recognized none in himself. Castro was not a natural athlete but felt he could excel in anything if he set his mind to it, and as a result very often did. Above all, he had the urge to *win*. For Ernesto, it had been an achievement just to be able to *play* rugby and the other sports of his youth, to be accepted as a team member. It was camaraderie, not leadership, that he craved.

Taller than average, with Brylcreemed hair and a small mustache that didn't suit him, Fidel had the well-fed look of a city man used to pampering himself. And he was. He loved food and liked to cook it. In prison he wrote letters to friends describing in detail the meals he had whipped up with the relish of a sensualist. Ernesto, two years younger, was both shorter and slighter, with the pallor and dark dramatic eyes associated with a stage actor or poet. In many ways, their physiques reflected their personality differences: Fidel, unconsciously self-indulgent; Ernesto, a creature of the self-discipline imposed upon him by asthma.

Despite their many differences, Ernesto and Fidel shared some traits. Both were favored boys from large families and extremely spoiled; careless about their appearance; sexually voracious, but men to whom relationships came in second to their personal goals. Both were imbued with Latin machismo: believers in the innate weakness of women, contemptuous of homosexuals, and admirers of brave men of action. Both were possessed of an iron will and imbued with a larger-than-life sense of purpose. And finally, both wanted to carry out revolutions. By the time they met, each had already tried to play direct roles in historic events of their time, only to be thwarted, and they identified a common nemesis—the United States.

In 1947, while still at the university, Fidel had joined a group of Cubans and Dominicans undergoing military training on a remote Cuban key with the intention of invading the Dominican Republic to overthrow General Trujillo. But the expedition was aborted at the last minute by Cuban troops, after President Grau San Martín had been alerted by Washington. Next, as a delegate to the 1948 Bogotá "anti-imperialist" youth congress organized by Perón, Fidel had joined in the rioting of El Bogotazo after the Liberal party opposition leader Eliécer Gaitán's assassination and tried to organize a popular resistance against the Conservative government. Afterward had come Batista's coup, Moncada, and prison.

From prison, Fidel had followed the events in Guatemala with interest and had sympathized with the beleaguered Arbenz government's battle against that familiar specter, the United Fruit Company. The fall of Arbenz was also highly instructive: It taught Fidel that if he were to be successful in his planned revolution for Cuba, he would have to proceed cautiously, to acquire a strong foothold in power before antagonizing the powerful American interests. To rule Cuba with a free hand, however, it was just as obvious that foreign companies such as United Fruit would have to be national-ized. The trick, Fidel knew, was to proceed with tact and guile.

It was obvious to Ernesto, as it was to most people who met him, that Fidel Castro possessed that rare personality, enhanced by the utter convic-tion that he would ultimately succeed. And if Fidel was politically not yet as convinced as Ernesto that socialism was the correct course to follow, he exhibited sympathy for the same goals. The potential was there. It would be up to those close to him, including Ernesto Guevara, to ensure that Fidel Castro's revolution followed a socialist course.

As he told Hilda not long after meeting Fidel, "Ñico was right in Guatemala when he told us that if Cuba had produced anything good since Martí it was Fidel Castro. He will make the revolution. We are in com-plete accord. . . . It's only someone like him I could go all out for." He ad-mitted that Fidel's scheme of landing a boatful of guerrillas on Cuba's well-defended coasts was a "crazy idea," but he felt compelled to support him anyway.

On July 20, Ernesto wrote Aunt Beatriz, enigmatically telling her: "Time has provoked a sifting out of the torrent of projects I was doing and now . . . I can be certain of finishing only one, which . . . will be ex-ported to the next country I visit, the name of which no one knows but God and his new right hand."

In honor of his new friend and comrade, Ernesto asked Hilda and Lucila to prepare a dinner for Fidel, and to invite Laura Albizu Campos and Juan Juarbe as well. That night, Castro displayed three of the traits he was to become famous for: keeping others waiting interminably, his tremen-dous personal charisma, and his ability to pontificate for hours on end. While Lucila took offense at the long delay and went to her room, Hilda waited patiently and was suitably impressed:

"He was young, only thirty [sic], light of complexion, and tall, about six feet two inches, and solidly built. . . . He could very well have been a handsome bourgeois tourist. When he talked, however, his eyes shone with passion and revolutionary zeal, and one could see why he could command the attention of listeners. He had the charm and personality of a great leader, and at the same time an admirable simplicity and naturalness."

After dinner, Hilda finally overcame her awe and asked Castro why he was in Mexico if his struggle lay in Cuba. "He answered: 'Very good question. I'll explain.' Fidel's answer lasted four hours, explaining the situ-ation in Cuba and outlining his plans for an armed revolution.

A few days later, Ernesto told Hilda his intention of joining the rebel invasion of Cuba. Soon afterward, Hilda informed him she was pregnant.

III

On July 26, to commemorate the second anniversary of the Moncada assault, Fidel organized a ceremony, complete with speeches given by himself and other Latin American exiles in Chapultepec park. Afterward, they all gathered at a home where Fidel prepared one of his favorite dishes, *spaghetti alle vongole*.

At dinner, Ernesto sat quietly without saying much. Noticing his reserve, Fidel called out: "Hey Che! You're very quiet. Is it because your controller's here now?" It was a reference to Hilda. She wrote: "Obviously Fidel knew we were planning to get married; hence the joke. I then realized that they did a great deal of talking together. I knew very well that when Ernesto felt at ease he was talkative; he loved discussions. But when there were many people around he would remain withdrawn."

Hilda interpreted Ernesto's silence as a meditation on the momentousness of the enterprise he was involved in, but this has the unmistakable ring of after-the-fact mythification. It seems much more likely he was pondering the dilemma he faced with her. He had decided to marry her—it was, after all, the honorable thing to do—but, as he wrote in his journal: "For another guy it would be transcendental; for me it is an uncomfortable episode. I am going to have a child and I will marry Hilda in a few days. The thing had dramatic moments for her and heavy ones for me. In the end, she gets her way—the way I see it, for a short while, although she hopes it will be lifelong."

Certainly, for a man who had always resisted any domesticity, and who had just found a cause and a leader to follow, the prospect could not have come at a worse moment. Nonetheless, Ernesto went through with it, and on August 18, he and Hilda were married, at the civil registrar's office in the little town of Tepozotlán on the capital's outskirts. Their legal witnesses were Lucila Velásquez; Jesús Montané Oropesa, a short, flap-eared public accountant (and a member of the movement's freshly formed National Directorate) who had just arrived from Havana as Fidel's treasurer; and two of Ernesto's colleagues from the General Hospital. Raúl Castro went along for the occasion but, on Fidel's orders to keep a low profile, didn't sign the ledger. Fidel, suspecting his actions were being monitored by Batista's secret police and the American FBI, did not attend for security reasons, but showed up at the party Ernesto and Hilda gave afterward, at which Ernesto prepared an *asado*, Argentine-style.

After the wedding, Ernesto and Hilda moved out of the apartment with Lucila into their own flat, in a five-story Deco apartment building on Calle Nápoles in Colonia Juárez. Then they broke their news to their respective parents. Wrote Hilda: "My parents sent back a letter scolding us for not telling them in advance, so they could come for the wedding. They also sent us a bank draft for five hundred dollars as a present, asked us to send photographs, and Mother asked for a church wedding and said we should send her the exact date so she could have the announcements made for our friends back home."

Ernesto wrote back to his new in-laws, employing a mixture of unswerving candor and light ribaldry that must have raised some eyebrows in the middle-class Gadea household. "Dear Parents: I can imagine your surprise at receiving our bombshell of news, and can understand the flood of questions it must have provoked. You're of course correct in scolding us for not having informed you of our marriage. We thought it wiser to do it this way, in view of the numerous difficulties that we encountered, not foreseeing that we would have a child so soon. . . . We are very grateful for the expressions of affection you've given us, I know they're sincere: I've known Hilda long enough to feel that I know her family. I shall try to show that I deserve her at all times. I am also grateful for the 'small gift': You've done more than enough. Don't worry about us. It is true that we're not wealthy, but Hilda and I earn enough to keep up a home properly. . . .

"I believe this adequately answers your affectionate letter, but I should add something about our future plans. First we wait for 'Don Ernesto.' (If it's not a boy, there's going to be trouble.) Then we'll consider a couple of firm propositions I have, one in Cuba, the other a fellowship in France, depending on Hilda's ability to move around. Our wandering life isn't over yet and before we definitely settle in Peru, a country that I admire in many ways, or in Argentina, we want to see a bit of Europe and two fascinating countries, India and China. I am particularly interested in New China because it accords with my own political ideals. I hope that soon, or if not soon someday, after knowing these and other really democratic countries, Hilda will think like me.

"Our married life probably won't be like yours. Hilda works eight hours a day and I, somewhat irregularly, around twelve. I'm in research, the toughest branch (and poorest paid). But we've fitted our routines together harmoniously and have turned our home into a free association between two equals. (Of course, Sra. Gadea, Hilda's kitchen is the worst aspect of the house—in order, cleanliness, or food. . . .) I can only say that this is the way I've lived all my life, my mother having the same weakness. So a sloppy house, mediocre food and a salty mate, if she's a true companion, is all I want from life.

"I hope to be received into the family as a brother who has long been traveling the same path toward an equal destiny, or at least that my peculiarities of character (which are many) will be overlooked in view of the unqualified affection of Hilda for me, the same as I have for her. With an *abrazo* for the family from this new son and brother—Ernesto."

To his own family, Ernesto downplayed the news of his marriage and impending fatherhood, placing it at the end of a letter sent September 24 to his mother. The letter dwelt overwhelmingly with his reaction to the military coup d'état that had finally toppled Perón four days earlier. "I will confess with all sincerity that the fall of Perón deeply embittered me, not for him, but for what it means for all of America, because as much as you hate to admit it, and in spite of the enforced renunciation of recent times,* Argentina was the Paladin of all those who think the enemy is in the North."

After predicting further social divisions and political violence for his homeland, he got around to his own news, writing: "Who knows in the meantime what will come of your wandering son. Maybe he will have decided to return and settle his bones in the homeland . . . or begin a period of real struggle. . . . Maybe a bullet of those so profuse in the Caribbean will end my existence (this isn't a boast or a concrete possibility, it's just that the bullets really do wander around a lot in this latitude) . . . or I'll just simply carry on vagabonding for as long as necessary to finish off a solid training and to satisfy the desires I reserved for myself within my life's program, before dedicating myself seriously to the pursuit of my ideal. Things are moving with tremendous speed and no one can know or predict where or for what reason one will be next year."

Almost as a postscript, he added: "I don't know if you've received the protocolar news of my marriage and of the coming of the heir. . . . If not, I communicate the news officially, so that you share it out among the people; I married Hilda Gadea and we shall have a child within some time. . . ."

Around this same time, the health of María, an elderly asthma patient Ernesto had been treating over the past year, suddenly deteriorated. Despite all his efforts, she died, asphyxiated by her asthma. He was at her bedside when she took her last gasp. The experience drove him to write a poem in which he poured out his anger over the social neglect he felt had driven her to death.

In "Old María, You're Going to Die," the dying woman personifies all the wasted, poor lives of Latin America. To Ernesto, she had become the old lady in Valparaíso, the fugitive couple in Chuquicamata, and the browbeaten Indians of Peru.

---

*A reference to Perón's recent rapprochement with American financial interests, and his controversial attempt to push through a bill allowing Standard Oil to undertake explorations in the Patagonian oilfields.

Poor old María . . .
don't pray to the inclement god that denied your hopes
your whole life
don't ask for clemency from death,
your life was horribly dressed with hunger,
and ends dressed by asthma.
But I want to announce to you,
in a low voice virile with hopes,
the most red and virile of vengeances
I want to swear it on the exact
dimension of my ideals.
Take this hand of a man which seems like a boy's
between yours polished by yellow soap,
Scrub the hard calluses and the pure knots
in the smooth vengeance of my doctor's hands.
Rest in peace, old María,
rest in peace, old fighter,
your grandchildren will all live to see the dawn.

IV

For now, the world of "red vengeance" was forced to boil away in Ernesto's imagination. The only places he had to channel his indignation were in his prose, the occasional political discussion, and his growing hopes for Fidel Castro's revolutionary project.

And that project was moving slowly forward. Fidel, who had turned twenty-nine in August, was keeping in regular contact with members of his movement still in Cuba through couriers, and was busy planning, plotting, reading, writing, issuing orders, and, above all, talking, always talking.

As he had done in Cuba, Fidel took over the lives of whoever in Mexico proved susceptible to his varied charms and powers of persuasion. Arzacio Vanegas Arroyo, a short, Indian-faced printer and wrestler ("Kid Vanegas"), a friend of María Antonia and her husband, was drafted to print up two thousand copies of Fidel's "Manifesto No. 1 to the Cuban People." Fidel then had another friend smuggle copies back to Cuba, with orders to distribute them at Chibás's gravesite on August 16, the fourth anniversary of his late mentor's death. The manifesto revealed the formation of the July 26 Movement as a revolutionary organization seeking the restoration of democracy and justice in Cuba. Point by point, it outlined Fidel's call for reforms: elimination of the feudal landowning oligarchy, or *latifundia,* and distribution of the lands to peasants; the nationalization of public services; a mandatory rent decrease, an ambitious housing, education, industrialization, and rural electrification program; and so on, encompassing virtually every aspect of Cuban life. In essence, it was a call for the imposition of radical measures to turn Cuba into a modern, more humane society.

Fidel's plans had also progressed beyond pamphleteering and veered into military strategy. He had decided to land his future invasion force along an isolated stretch of Cuba's southeastern coast that juts out in a cape, and where, inland, the land rises up to form the Sierra Maestra mountain range. It was there, in the mountains of Oriente, where Fidel would launch his guerrilla war. Oriente was not only Fidel's home region, but also the region where Cuba's nineteenth-century patriots, including José Martí, had launched their invasions to fight against the Spanish.

Beyond symbolism, there was a sound strategic reason: the sierra's close proximity to Cuba's second-largest city of Santiago. Here, Fidel counted upon the able offices of his underground coordinator, a twenty-year-old student named Frank País. Once his men had landed and were in the mountains, Santiago would provide a nearby pool of funds, intelligence, weapons, and recruits to fuel the war.

Celia Sánchez, a plantation doctor's daughter and a recent convert to the movement, had procured the coastal charts Fidel needed and handed them over to Pedro Miret. Miret, an old university friend, was responsible for coordinating the invasion plans, and he had gone over the area personally to pick possible landing sites; in September he came to Mexico to give the charts to Fidel and discuss strategy. Meanwhile, the movement's cells were screening their memberships for future fighters, and it was also Miret's job to get the chosen ones to Mexico to undergo military training.

For someone to train his future force, Fidel had already approached a man with experience: the one-eyed, Cuban-born Spanish Civil War veteran and military adventurer General Alberto Bayo. Now retired from the military, working as a university lecturer and running a furniture factory in Mexico, Bayo had been a career officer in the Spanish army, fighting in the colonial campaign against the Moroccan guerrilla leader Abd-El-Krim, then with the republican forces against Franco. Later, he had advised and trained men for several wars around the Caribbean and Central America, and had penned a book, *Storm in the Caribbean,* on these experiences. Bayo seemed to be just the man Fidel needed.

Fidel next began preparing for a speaking and fund-raising tour among the Cuban emigré communities of Florida, New York, Philadelphia, and New Jersey. For this effort he was to be joined by his friend Juan Manuel Márquez, an Ortodoxo party leader with good contacts in the United States. In the meantime, he kept up a continuous stream of messages to his National Directorate in Cuba, instructing them to raise funds there as well, and outlining new rules governing the duties and obligations of movement members.

By now, his Cuban comrades were getting to know the man they called Che well enough to recognize his idiosyncrasies, and one of the personality traits that rubbed plenty of them wrong at first was his self-righteousness. When Jesús Montané's newlywed wife, the Moncada veteran Melba Hernández, arrived from Havana, he took her to meet "El Che" at the General Hospital. Guevara took one look at Melba, just off the plane, and still dressed up and bejeweled, and told her bluntly that she couldn't possibly be a revolutionary with so much jewelry on. "Real revolutionaries adorn themselves on the inside, not on the surface," he declared. Stung by this greeting, Hernández's first impression of Che was understandably negative. This changed when she got to know him better. She realized, as others did, that while he was judgmental and even rude to others, he was equally tough on himself. Eventually, Hernández has said, she mulled over Che's remark, decided he was right, and thereafter wore less jewelry.

Meanwhile, Ernesto continued with his physical conditioning, and in the second week of October he scaled Popocatépetl again. And on this, his third try, he finally reached the volcano's true summit after six and a half hours, placing an Argentine flag on it for the occasion of National Flag Day.

Lately, he had begun experimenting with cats for his allergy research, and Raúl Castro sometimes went along to assist him in the laboratory. Raúl has jokingly said that after seeing Ernesto give a few injections to the hapless cats, he lost all faith in his Argentine friend's medical abilities and thereafter refused to let him ever give him an injection. Ernesto also continued visiting the library at the Instituto de Intercambio Cultural Ruso-Mexicano, often accompanied by Raúl, Jesús Montané, and his wife, Melba.

In a mordant October letter to Beatriz, Ernesto joshed her about the name he planned for his son ("Vladimiro Ernesto") and about the "new Argentina" since Perón's ouster. "Now the people of class can put the common scum back in their proper place, the Americans will invest great and beneficent quantities of capital in the country, in sum, [it will be] a paradise." With mock morbidity, he lamented the rejection of his offer of services to the Mexican government in the wake of the "aptly named" Hurricane Hilda, denying him the opportunity of seeing the catastrophe up close. "Part of the city was flooded and the people were left in the street but it doesn't matter because no people of class live there, they're all pure Indians." Characteristically, he signed off by begging her to send him more *yerba mate*.

In mid-November, Ernesto and a visibly swelling Hilda took off for Chiapas and the Yucatán peninsula to see the Mayan ruins. The high point of their five-day stay in Veracruz was finding in port an Argentine ship, from which Ernesto managed to cadge a few kilos of *yerba*. "One can imagine Ernesto's joy," wrote Hilda. "Mate of course was an inveterate habit with him; he was never without his equipment, the *bombilla, boquilla,* and a two-liter thermos for hot water. Studying, conversing, he always drank mate; it was the first thing he did when he got up and the last thing he did before going to sleep."

As they traveled south to the Mayan temples at Palenque in the tropical swelter of Chiapas, Ernesto's asthma—all but vanquished in the high altitude of Mexico City—suddenly returned. When she offered to give him an injection, it brought on what Hilda called the "first spat" of their trip. "He violently refused. I realized that it was that he did not want to feel protected, to be helped when he was sick. I kept quiet in the face of his brusqueness, but I was hurt."

He was entranced with Palenque's temple pyramids and their carved bas-reliefs, calling them "magnificent." He scribbled page after page in his journal on Palenque and the Mayan sites of Chichén Itzá and Uxmal, combining elaborately detailed physical descriptions of the ruins with histories of the ancient civilizations that had built them. He ran around the ruins excitedly, dragging a weary Hilda along behind him. "Ernesto joyfully wanted to climb every temple," she wrote. "I gave out on the last one, the tallest. I stopped halfway up, partly because I was very tired, and partly because I was worrying about my pregnancy. He kept urging me not to play coy and join him."

Finally, feeling "tired, impatient and thoroughly cross," Hilda refused to budge another step. Undeterred, Ernesto asked someone to snap their picture posed in front of the ancient stones. In the photograph, a dowdy-looking Hilda glares angrily out from under a Mexican sombrero. At her side, wearing a dark short-sleeved shirt and a Panama hat, Ernesto looks slim, youthful, and thoroughly preoccupied.

After visiting Uxmal, they sailed back to Veracruz on a small coastal freighter, the *Ana Graciela*. Hilda was reluctant to go to sea, but Ernesto was teasingly reassuring, telling her that at least they'd "die together." The voyage began peacefully enough, but on their second day out a strong northerly blew, and Ernesto wrote gleefully that it gave them "a good dance." Hilda's own rendition was more sour. "Almost all of the passengers were seasick. I didn't exactly feel great either. But Ernesto was like a boy. Wearing swimming shorts, he was all over the decks, jumping from one side to the other, calculating the roll of the boat to keep his balance, taking pictures and laughing at the discomfiture of the others."

Hilda's implication was obvious: Ernesto had been inconsiderate and irresponsible, and she didn't appreciate it one bit. Pleading the safety of her unborn child, Hilda's took to her bunk for the rest of the trip, plied by a rueful Ernesto with mugs of hot tea and lemon. But afterward, Hilda romanticized their recent experience. "They had been fifteen days of unforgettable travel, with the immense satisfaction of being in one another's company at all times, alone in the midst of all that beauty." By contrast, in his own written account of their trip, Ernesto never once mentioned Hilda.

Before Christmas, Fidel returned to Mexico. His fund-raising and organizing trip to the United States had been a great success. He had traveled up and down the East Coast for two months speaking, convincing, and promising. He had invoked Chibás and Martí and made grandiose vows such as: "In 1956 we shall be free or we will be martyrs"; in return, he had been applauded and given money, enough to begin organizing his rebel army. July 26 Movement chapters and "Patriotic Clubs" had been opened in several of the cities he had visited. His media profile had grown even larger, and in Cuba his widely publicized intention to launch a "revolution" had spurred a mood of mounting expectation. Back in Mexico, Fidel Castro was invigorated, on a roll, ready for war.

On Christmas Eve he cooked a traditional Cuban dinner of roast pork, beans, rice, and yucca. Che and Hilda were there, and Fidel expounded on his plans for Cuba's future with "such certainty," said Hilda, that she imagined for a moment that the war had already been fought and won.

V

On his own word, 1956 was to be the decisive year for Fidel Castro's revolution. To be in shape, Ernesto had kept up his mountain-climbing, but he now threw himself at Ixtaccihuatl, the smaller but more difficult volcano next to Popocatépetl, making several abortive attempts to reach the summit.

During January and February, Fidel's future fighters began arriving in Mexico City from Cuba, and a half-dozen safe houses, called "casa-campamentos," were rented around the city to house them. By mid-February, there were twenty or so future expeditionaries in place. With strict codes of discipline and secrecy imposed on them, their training began. At first, it consisted of marathon walks around the city. Then, led by the Mexican wrestler-printer Arzacio Vanegas, the men went on conditioning and endurance hikes on hills around the capital's outskirts. He made them climb backward and sideways to strengthen their legs and teach them balance. On one outing, Vanegas found Che gasping for breath and struggling with his asthma inhaler. Later, when Che had recovered, he asked Vanegas not to tell anyone, even Fidel, what he had seen. He was clearly worried about being dropped from the force because of his asthma affliction and was under the illusion that his comrades didn't know about it.

At the Calle Bucarelli gymnasium, owned by some of his friends, Vanegas also gave the men exercise and "personal defense" classes. "I was very brusque with them," says Vanegas. "I told them they were not señoritas, and had to become tough if they wanted to make war." He showed Che and the others "how to hit people to cause maximum pain, to kick them in the balls, to grab their clothes and throw them on the ground."

Alberto Bayo started giving classes in guerrilla warfare theory to the men in the safe houses, and in February a select group including Ernesto Guevara began going to a firing range, Los Gamitos, to practice their shooting skills. By an arrangement between Fidel and its owner, Los Gamitos was closed down on certain days so his men could shoot in privacy, with live turkeys sometimes provided so they could practice on moving targets.

VI

Ernesto and Hilda spent St. Valentine's Day, February 14, moving into a larger apartment on a different floor of the same building on Calle Nápoles. That very night, Hilda went into labor, and gave birth the next day.

"A lot of time has passed and many new developments have declared themselves," Ernesto noted soon afterward. "I'll only note the most important: as of the 15th of February 1956 I am a father; Hilda Beatriz is the first-born. . . . My projects for the future are nebulous but I hope to finish a couple of research projects. This year could be important for my future. I have left the hospitals. I will write with more details."

But he never did. These were the last lines Ernesto wrote in the journal he had begun nearly three years before, after passing his medical exams and taking to the road with Calica Ferrer. He had set out intending to rejoin his friend Alberto Granado at his leprosarium in Venezuela. Instead, he had veered off in an altogether different direction, on the road to revolution.

13

"The Sacred Flame within Me"

I

Like a marooned sailor who has finally seen the hope of rescue on the horizon, a reinvigorated Ernesto threw his energies into the Cuban revolutionary enterprise. To keep down his weight, he cut out his traditional steak for breakfast and went on a diet consisting of meat, salad, and fruit for supper. In the afternoons, he went straight to the gymnasium.

The physical training wasn't enough for Ernesto, however; already looking ahead to the day when the revolution triumphed, he wanted to have a firm grasp of political and economic theory. Intensifying his study of economics, he embarked on a cram course of books by Adam Smith, Keynes, and other economists, boned up on Mao and Soviet texts borrowed from the Instituto Cultural Ruso-Mexicano, and discreetly sat in on meetings of the Mexican Communist party. Most evenings, he joined the Cubans at the safe houses for discussions on the situation in Cuba and other Latin American countries.

His knowledge of Marxism was maturing. Using his old philosophical notebooks as a base, he streamlined them into a single volume. Totaling over three hundred typewritten pages, this final *cuaderno filosófico* reflects the narrowing of his interests and shows a deepening study of the works of Marx, Engels, and Lenin. The last entry in the index, on the concept of "I," is attributed to Freud, citing Dschelaladin Rumi in "Clinical Histories," and reads: "There, where love awakens, dies the I, dark despot."

He had begun to live a double life, withdrawing from contact with everyone not of complete trust. He repeatedly warned Hilda to be cautious with her friends, so as not to disclose his involvement with Fidel's rebel movement. Finally, he asked her to stop meeting her Peruvian *aprista* acquaintances—whom he especially distrusted—altogether. Apart from the Cubans, he saw very few people now.

Ernesto spent his spare moments with the baby. He was delighted with her, and on February 25 he wrote his mother to announce the birth. "Little grandmother: The two of us are a little older, or if you consider fruit, a little more mature. The offspring is really ugly, and one doesn't have to do more than look at her to realize she is no different than all the other children of her age, she cries when she is hungry, pees with frequency . . . the light bothers her and she sleeps all the time; even so, there is one thing that differentiates her immediately from any other baby: her papa is named Ernesto Guevara."

Meanwhile, in his other identity—as Che the apprentice guerrilla—he was turning out to be a very good marksman. On March 17, Miguel "El Coreano" Sánchez—a U.S. Army Korean War veteran enlisted by Fidel in Miami to become his force's shooting instructor—summed up Guevara's performance on the firing range. "Ernesto Guevara attended 20 regular shooting lessons, an excellent shooter with approximately 650 bullets [fired]. Excellent discipline, excellent leadership abilities, physical endurance excellent. Some disciplinary press-ups for small errors at interpreting orders and faint smiles."

Already, Che stood out from the crowd. His strong personality, closeness to Fidel and Raúl, and rapid rise to preeminence within the group doubtless aggravated the early resentment felt by some of the Cuban trainees toward this "foreigner" in their midst. Most of them called him impersonally "El Argentino," while "Che" was used only by those who knew him best.

Fidel later recalled "a small, disagreeable incident" that took place after he appointed Che—"because of his seriousness, his intelligence, and his character"—as leader of one of the Mexico City safe houses. "There were about twenty or thirty Cubans there in all," said Fidel, "and some of them . . . challenged Che's leadership because he was an Argentine, because he was not a Cuban. We of course criticized this attitude . . . this ingratitude toward someone who, although not born in our land, was ready to shed his blood for it. And I remember the incident hurt me a great deal. I think it hurt him as well."

In fact, Guevara was not the only foreigner in the group. Another was Guillén Zelaya, a young Mexican whom he had briefly met months earlier through Elena Leiva de Holst at a meeting of Honduran exiles. Only nineteen, Zelaya had run away from home to join up with Fidel and been accepted. In time there would be others, including a Dominican exile and an Italian merchant marine, but that was where Fidel drew the line, explaining he didn't want a "mosaic of nationalities."

In his letters home, the revolutionary dominance in Ernesto's life now became more manifest, even in his wit. Writing about his infant daughter, Ernesto lent a new twist to father's pride in an April 13 letter to Celia. "My communist soul expands plethorically: she has come out exactly like Mao Tse-tung. Even now, the incipient bald spot in the middle of the head can be noted, the compassionate eyes of the boss and his protuberant jowls; for now she weighs less than the leader, five kilos, but with time this will even out."

At the same time, his irritation with Hilda, held in abeyance during her pregnancy, also grew more evident. Returning to the familiar theme of Argentina in his correspondence, he badgered his mother about the capitulation of Argentina's new regime to U.S. corporate interests, and then went out of his way to take a swipe at Hilda.

"It consoles me to think that the aid of our great neighbors isn't confined only to this region and that my land too can benefit from it . . . [and] . . . it now seems that it has lent its help to APRA and soon everyone will be [back] in Peru and Hilda can go there in tranquility. Big pity that her intemperate marriage to [this] fervent slave of the red plague will rob her of the enjoyment of a well-remunerated salary as deputy in the next parliament . . ."

As Ernesto told Hilda, the revolution was a cause for which they both had to make sacrifices, the first of which would be their prolonged separation. Although she claimed to feel both pain and pride at the idea of his going off to war, Hilda was most likely deeply unhappy about the turn of events. Having espoused a certain revolutionary commitment herself, however, she could not very well hold him back; if she tried, he would have cited it as proof that she was petite bourgeoisie and hopelessly tied to her middle-of-the-road *aprista* political philosophy.

Meanwhile, Fidel was searching for a place outside Mexico City where his men could complete their field training in greater secrecy. Money had begun to trickle in from his supporters in the United States and Cuba. He now had some guns and was acquiring more through Antonio del Conde, a Mexican arms trafficker he nicknamed "El Cuate" (The Pal), whom he sent on an arms-buying trip to the United States and asked to look for a suitable boat for his "army" to sail to Cuba on when the time came.

Fidel was evidently hoping to time his invasion to coincide with the third anniversary of Moncada, on July 26. Not only had he made a public vow to launch his revolution in 1956, but recent events had shown him that if he wanted to maintain the revolutionary trump card, he needed to act soon. He was facing increasingly serious competition from several quarters.

Among his potential rivals was former president Carlos Prío Socarrás. After first testing the insurrectionary waters by assisting the recently formed Directorio Revolucionario, a militant underground student group, in an abortive plan to assassinate Batista, Prío had taken advantage of the general amnesty that had freed Fidel, and returned to Cuba. Publicly renouncing the use of violence, he was trying to extend his base of support by declaring his intention of opposing Batista through legal, democratic means.

The autumn of 1955 had been fractious in Cuba, with civic unrest countered by police brutality, and some armed attacks against police by the Directorio. At year's end, a broad spectrum of opposition groups, including Fidel's July 26 Movement, backed a sugar workers' strike, and more street riots ensued. While an atmosphere of rebellion was spreading, there was still little organization or unity in opposition circles, and for now Batista retained the upper hand.

When that balance shifted, Fidel planned to be at the fore. In March 1956, he publicly broke with the Ortodoxo party, accusing its leadership of not supporting the "revolutionary will" of its rank and file. This was a clever move, for it left him a free hand to proceed with his revolution without feigning loyalty to a political party he hoped to supersede. Now everyone in Cuba's various *antibatistiano* camps would have to choose a side, and Fidel would be able to see more clearly who his friends and enemies were.

But he was vigilant about the danger of betrayal and had already taken precautionary measures, creating a cell structure for his men in Mexico. They had been separated into groups, met up only during training sessions, and were forbidden to inquire about one another. Only Fidel and Bayo knew the location of each of the safe houses. Finally, Fidel had drawn up a list of punishments for infractions. The movement now lived according to the rules of war, and the punishment for the crime of betrayal was death.

Fidel had good reason to be security conscious, for he knew that if Batista wanted to have him killed, he had the ways and means to do it, even in Mexico. Fidel didn't have to wait long to confirm that he was indeed an assassination target. In early 1956, Batista's Servicio de Inteligencia Militar (SIM) denounced Castro's conspiracy and conducted a wave of arrests of his followers in Cuba. Shortly after the SIM investigations chief arrived in Mexico, Fidel got wind of a SIM-sponsored plan to assassinate him. When Fidel let it be known he was aware of the plot, the scheme was aborted, but Cuban government agents and Mexicans on their payroll remained active, tracking his movements and reporting back to Batista.

The political climate within Cuba continued to heat up. In April, police uncovered a plot by army officers to overthrow Batista. A Directorio squad tried unsuccessfully to take over a Havana radio station, and in the effort one of its members was gunned down. Days later, in an emulation of Castro's Moncada assault, a militant group of Prío's *auténticos* attacked some provincial army barracks in a bid to force their leader out of his public posture of peaceful opposition. They were massacred for their efforts. Afterward the regime unleashed a massive crackdown on Prío's party, and he fled back into exile in Miami.

In Mexico, the number of Cubans with Fidel had grown to about forty. Ernesto's tireless distinction in the training exercises had become obvious to Fidel, and one day he used the Argentine as an example to the others as a reproof of their own flagging efforts. In May, the trainees were asked to evaluate the performances of their comrades, and Ernesto was unanimously judged by his mates to be qualified for a "leadership or chief of staff position." For Ernesto, it was an important threshold; he had won the respect he so craved from his new peers.

II

In May, Ernesto finally fulfilled his old urge to try out his acting skills, although it was not as a film extra. Bayo and Ciro Redondo, one of Fidel's right-hand men, had found a ranch for sale at Chalco, about thirty-five miles east of the city. The Rancho San Miguel was huge. Encompassing both range land and rough hills, it was perfect terrain for guerrilla training. The main house itself was not large, but its grounds were surrounded by a fortress-like high stone wall, complete with crenellated sentry's turrets at the corners. There was one problem: Its price tag was almost a quarter of a million dollars. The ranch's owner, Erasmo Rivera, had a colorful personal history, having fought alongside Pancho Villa in his youth, but being a revolutionary veteran had apparently not made him impervious to greed.

In his negotiations with Rivera, Bayo claimed to be the front man for a wealthy "Salvadoran colonel" interested in the purchase of a large ranch outside his native country. Excited by the prospect of the large sale, Rivera fell for the story, whereupon Bayo introduced the foreign-sounding Guevara as "the Colonel." Rivera either couldn't tell the difference between the Salvadoran and Argentine accents, or else decided against asking any questions that might offend his rich client. The con job worked. Rivera agreed to a token rent of eight dollars per month while certain necessary "repairs" to the main house were made to bring the place up to "the Colonel's" specifications, and after that the sale would go through. The repairs meanwhile would be undertaken by several dozen "Salvadoran laborers" to be brought in especially for the purpose.

As soon as the deal was struck, Fidel ordered Bayo to select a first group of fighters to go to the ranch. Bayo thought highly of Ernesto and, in recognition of his Argentine pupil's skills—he later called Guevara "the best guerrilla of them all"—named him his "chief of personnel." In late May, they departed for the ranch with a first group of trainees. Ernesto said goodbye to Hilda, telling her he might not be back. (Fidel had located a military-surplus American PT boat for sale in Delaware and hoped to buy it and have it brought to Mexico in time to sail for Cuba in July. If everything worked out, they would finish their training at the ranch and go directly from there to the boat, and on to Cuba.)

Out at Chalco, the training was tough. Their headquarters was the walled compound at Rancho San Miguel, but the men spent most of their time on forays out from two rudimentary camps in the adjacent parched, brushy hills meant to prepare them for the rigors they could face in Cuba. Food and water were in short supply, and Bayo and Che led them on endurance hikes and night marches lasting from dusk to dawn. When they weren't slogging through the bush, they engaged in simulated combat and stood guard.

This was the first time Che had shared life on a sustained daily basis with the Cubans. Some men still resented his presence, regarding him as an interloping foreigner, and now they had him as their direct jefe. They found him to be a rigid disciplinarian, but one who also joined in the marches and exercises, on top of his doctor's duties.

It must have been a shock to the Cubans to find that this well-educated, well-born Argentine doctor was also something of a slob. From their time spent in the city, he was already seen as an oddball because of his perennially worn shabby brown suit, which clearly didn't jibe with the Cubans' image of how a "professional" should look. They may have been revolutionaries, but they were still image-conscious, and in the socially stratified Latin America of the 1950s, being well kempt and formally attired was the norm for any self-respecting urban male. Now, out in the field, they discovered that he didn't like to wash either. According to Hilda, "Ernesto used to be amused at the Cubans' mania for cleanliness. When the daily work was done, they all took baths and changed their clothes. 'That's fine,' he said, 'but what will they do in the hills? I doubt we'll ever be able to take a bath or change clothes.'"

Alluding to Che's rigidity, one of the Cuban rebels, the mulatto songwriter Juan Almeida, wrote about an episode in which one of the men refused to go any farther, protesting about the long marches, the excessive discipline, and the lack of food. Almeida wrote that the infractor "sat down on the trail in frank protest against the Spanish [Bayo] and Argentine [Guevara] leadership."

At this act of defiance, Che ordered the men back to camp. Insubordination was a severe breach of discipline, one that called for the death sentence. Fidel and Raúl were immediately notified of the incident and came quickly from Mexico City to hold a court-martial. In keeping with the Cuban revolution's tradition of glossing over such unpleasant episodes, Almeida omitted the name of the rebellious trainee, but in his memoirs Alberto Bayo recounted the dramatic trial of the man whom he identified as Calixto Morales. In Bayo's account, the Castro brothers called for the death sentence to be applied, comparing Morales with a "contagious disease" that had to be "exterminated" before he infected his comrades. Despite a plea by Bayo to spare his life, Morales was sentenced to death, but Fidel later pardoned him, and Morales went on to win back favor during the guerrilla war. Despite the fact that it was Che who had called for Morales's court-martial, says Cuban historian María del Carmen Ariet, he argued against his execution.

Universo Sánchez, Fidel's aide responsible for counterintelligence at the time, was to have been Morale's executioner. In an interview with Tad Szulc, author of the most complete biography of Fidel Castro, Sanchez also divulged that other trials took place and that at least one of them, of an unmasked spy in their midst, ended in execution. Wrote Szulc: "The man, whose identity is unknown, was sentenced by a safe house court-martial and executed on Universo's instructions by one of the rebels. 'He was shot and buried there in a field,' he says."

Today, locals living in the vicinity of Rancho San Miguel speak of three bodies lying buried within the compound's sturdy walls; but for Universo Sánchez's admission, such rumors could be dismissed easily as folklore. In Cuba, any mention of these events is taboo, and they remain officially unclarified and ignored.

By early June, Almeida's group had returned to the city, and a second group arrived at the ranch for training. On the fourteenth, Che celebrated his twenty-eighth birthday. Everything seemed to be progressing nicely when, on June 20, armed Mexican police agents arrested Fidel and two companions on a downtown Mexico City street. Within days, virtually all the movement's members in the city had been rounded up. Safe houses were raided, documents and arms caches seized. Alerted, Bayo and Raúl went into hiding, while Che remained in command of the ranch. Before she too was arrested, Hilda— whose address was used by Fidel as a secret letter-drop—managed to hide Fidel's correspondence and Ernesto's more inflammatory political writings. Interrogated repeatedly about the activities of Ernesto and Fidel, she spent a night in custody with the baby before being released.

Fidel and his comrades were accused of plotting Batista's assassination in collusion with Cuban and Mexican Communists, and Havana had demanded their extradition. Then, on June 22, Fidel was allowed to issue a carefully worded public denial of his alleged Communist affiliations, pointing out his signal relationship with the late anti-Communist Ortodoxo leader Eduardo Chibás. Meanwhile, still at large, Raúl and other comrades scrambled to assemble his legal defense team.

Out at the ranch, Che prepared for the inevitable police raid. After moving most of the weaponry to new hiding places, he and twelve comrades were waiting for the police when they arrived on June 24. Anxious to avoid a confrontation, Fidel went along to instruct Che to surrender himself and his men. Che obeyed and was taken away to join his comrades in the Interior Ministry's prison on Calle Miguel Schultz.

III

The Mexican police mug shots of Ernesto show a determined-looking young man, clean-shaven but with unkempt hair. In the frontal shot, he stares straight into the camera. In the profile shot, his prominent forehead is plainly visible, his mouth is set, and his expression is decidedly thoughtful.

The rap sheet beneath the photograph gives his name, date and place of birth, local address, and physical characteristics; and the offense he was officially charged with—overstaying his visa. Beneath, a one-line declaration informs: "He says he is a tourist."

On June 26, two days after the mug shot was taken, Ernesto elaborated in his first police statements but admitted only as much as the police already knew about him. Explaining the circumstances of his arrival from Guatemala, he admitted having been an Arbenz sympathizer and having served his administration. Once in Mexico, someone whose name he couldn't remember had introduced him to María Antonia González. Later, he became aware that her house was a hub for Cubans "discontented" with their country's political regime. Eventually he had met Fidel Castro Ruz, their leader. When, about a month and a half before, he learned that the Cubans were undergoing training to direct a revolutionary movement against Batista, he had offered his services as a doctor and was accepted. At Castro's request, he had also served as his intermediary for the lease of the Chalco ranch. He dissembled on the quantity of men and guns at the ranch, saying they had only two rifles, which they had used for target practice and small-game hunting, as well as a .38 revolver for "personal defense."

That same day, Mexico's broadsheet pro-government daily *Excelsior* ran the story of the arrests across its front page in a banner headline: "Mexico Breaks Up the Revolt against Cuba and Arrests 20 Ringleaders."

The next day, a follow-up story quoting Mexican federal police sources revealed "More Apprehensions of Cuban Plotters Who It Is Said Had Help of Communists."

The chief culprit, according to Dirección Federal de Seguridad (DFS) sources, was none other than "the Argentine doctor Ernesto Guevara Serna . . . the principal link between the Cuban plotters and certain communist organizations of an international nature. . . . Doctor Guevara, who has also figured in other political movements of an international nature in the Dominican Republic and Panama—was identified by the DFS as an 'active member of the Instituto Intercambio Cultural Mexicano-Ruso.'" In the caption to a group photograph taken of the detained rebels, he was signaled prominently alongside Fidel as the man whose "intimate links with communism have led to suspicions that the movement against Fulgencio Batista was cosponsored by Red organizations."

While the media flurry continued, Fidel's people worked hard to free him. His lawyer friend Juan Manuel Márquez flew in from the United States and hired two defense attorneys. A sympathetic judge issued Fidel's release order on July 2, but Mexico's Interior Ministry blocked it. Despite this setback, the judge managed to stay the deportation order. Trying other routes, Fidel reportedly authorized Universo Sánchez to try to bribe a high-level government official to win their freedom, but this bid failed. The men went on hunger strike, and on July 9 twenty-one of the Cubans were released, with several more freed a few days later. Fidel, Che, and Calixto García, however, remained behind bars.

Che wrote his parents on July 6, informing them of his predicament and finally coming clean on his activities. "Some time ago, quite a while now, a young Cuban leader invited me to join his movement, a movement for the armed liberation of his country, and I, of course, accepted."

As for the future, he told them, "My future is linked with that of the Cuban Revolution. I either triumph with it or die there. . . . If for any reason that I can't foresee, I can't write anymore, and later it is my luck to lose, regard these lines as a farewell, not very grandiloquent but sincere. Throughout life I have looked for my truth by trial and error, and now, on the right road, and with a daughter who will survive me, I have closed the cycle. From now on I wouldn't consider my death a frustration, only, like Hikmet [the Turkish poet]: 'I will take to the grave only the sorrow of an unfinished song.'"

Despite all the police leaks and sensational headlines regarding their revolutionary conspiracy, they were still officially detained only on charges of violating Mexico's immigration laws. Meanwhile, a behind-the-scenes wrangle between Mexican and Cuban officials was taking place over what should be done with them.

At the same time, the police were trying to find out more about Ernesto Guevara. In the first week of July, he was interrogated at least twice more. Inexplicably, he now spoke freely and at length. These police declarations have never been made public, but classified copies were obtained by Heberto Norman Acosta, the Cuban Council of State historian. A perusal of these carefully guarded papers reveals that Ernesto Guevara now openly admitted his Communism and declared his belief in the need for armed revolutionary struggle, not only in Cuba but throughout Latin America.

Over the years since, Fidel has occasionally alluded to Che's Mexican police declarations in a tone of fond admonishment, citing them as an example of how his late comrade was "honest to a fault." At the time, however, Fidel was understandably furious. While Che prattled on about his Marxist convictions, here *he* was, billing himself as a patriotic reformer in the best Western nationalistic and *democratic* tradition. Since the one thing certain to mobilize increased support for Batista's regime from the Eisenhower administration was a Communist threat, any evidence that Fidel or his followers contemplated turning Cuba into a Communist state would doom his revolution before it began. In this context, Che's remarks were extraordinarily reckless, for they provided Castro's enemies with just the kind of ammunition they needed.

In a second public statement on July 15, Castro accused the American embassy of pressuring the Mexican authorities to thwart his release. Where he got his information is unclear, but he was right: The Americans *had* asked the Mexicans to hold up his release. But Washington's move had less to do with any disquiet felt about Fidel Castro than it did with placating Batista for its own interests. The Cuban leader had threatened to boycott the July 22 summit of American presidents held in Panama if Castro was freed; the Americans wanted to make sure everyone attended.

Nonetheless, Fidel was taking no chances, and this time he went even further than before in distancing himself from Communism. Calling such allegations "absurd," he pointed out Batista's own past alliance with Cuba's Partido Socialista Popular and named "Captain Gutiérrez Barrios" of Mexico's Dirección Federal de Seguridad (DFS), the number three man in Mexico's secret police hierarchy, as a witness to his being cleared of any links to "communist organizations."

Fidel's mention of Fernando Gutiérrez Barrios was revealing. By now Fidel had struck some kind of a deal with the Mexican police official who, at twenty-seven, was two years his junior. Although neither Gutiérrez Barrios nor Fidel has ever given details of their pact, the Mexican's help was obviously a key factor in Castro's eventual liberation.

Why did Gutiérrez Barrios help Fidel? At the very least, he seems to have been, like so many others, won over by Castro's larger-than-life personality. In an interview years later, he admitted to having "sympathized" with Castro from the outset. "First, because we were of the same generation, and second, for his ideals and his sense of conviction. He has always been a charismatic leader. And at that time it was obvious that there were no alternatives for him other than to triumph in his revolutionary movement or die. . . . These reasons explain why there was a cordial relationship from the beginning. . . . I never considered him to be a criminal, but a man with ideals who sought to overthrow a dictatorship and whose crime was to violate the [immigration] laws of my country."

With little love felt by Mexican nationalists (whose own revolution had occurred only four decades before) for their ever-meddling American neighbors, a certain "stick-it-in-your-eye" attitude very likely played a part in Gutiérrez Barrios's gesture as well. Indeed, later on, in his long career as Mexico's secret police chief for over thirty years, Gutiérrez Barrios granted protection to many other Latin American revolutionary exiles, including several on Washington's wanted list.

On the same day as Fidel's second public statement, July 15, Ernesto responded defiantly to a remonstrative letter from Celia. Judging from his tone, she had questioned his motives for being involved with Fidel Castro in the first place, and wondered pointedly why he hadn't being freed along with the others after their hunger strike. He told her he would probably remain in prison even after Fidel's release, like Calixto, because they were the only two without their immigration papers in order. As soon as he was freed, he would leave Mexico for a nearby country and await Fidel's orders, to be "at the ready whenever my services are necessary."

"I am not Christ or a philanthropist, old lady, I am all the contrary of a Christ. . . . I fight for the things I believe in, with all the weapons at my disposal and try to leave the other man *dead* so that I don't get nailed to a cross or any other place. . . . What really terrifies me is your lack of comprehension of all this and your advice about moderation, egoism, etc. . . . that is to say, all of the most execrable qualities an individual can have. Not only am I not moderate, I shall try not ever to be, and when I recognize that the sacred flame within me has given way to a timid votive light, the least I could do is to vomit over my own shit. Insofar as your call to moderate self-interest; that is to say, to rampant and fearful individualism . . . I must tell you I have done a lot to eliminate these. . . .

"In these days of prison and the previous ones of training I identified totally with my comrades of the cause. . . . The concept of 'I' disappeared

totally to give place to the concept 'us.' It was a communist morale and naturally it may seem a doctrinaire exaggeration, but really it was (and is) beautiful to be able to feel that removal of I." Breaking the severity, he wisecracked:
"The stains [on the stationery] aren't bloodstains, but tomato juice. . . ." Then
he went on: "It is a profound error on your part to believe that it is out of
'moderation' or 'moderate self-interest' that great inventions or artful
masterpieces come about. For all great tasks, passion is needed, and for the
revolution, passion and audacity are needed in large doses, things we have
as a human group."

Soul-searching out loud, he ended with a soliloquy on their changed
personal relationship: "Above all, it seems to me that that pain, pain of a
mother who is growing old and who wants her son alive, is respectable,
which I have an obligation to attend to, and which I also *want* to attend to,
and I would like to see you not only to console you, but to console myself
for my sporadic and unconfessable pinings." He signed the letter with his
new identity: "Your son, El Che."

What Che didn't tell his mother was that he was mostly responsible
for his own prolonged detention. In the end, he cared less about this than
the future of the Cuban revolutionary enterprise, and the most important
thing at the moment was for Fidel to be freed so that the struggle could go
forward.

Fidel was not released on July 16, however, but held through the
Panama summit. Mollified, Batista attended the meeting, and on July 22 the
convened presidents signed a joint declaration committing the hemisphere
to a pro-Western course of political and economic development. While
Eisenhower was rubbing shoulders with military dictators, Fidel's lawyers
went to see Lázaro Cárdenas, Mexico's former president and the architect
of its land reform. Cárdenas was receptive and agreed to use his influence
with President Adolfo Ruíz Cortines on Fidel's behalf. It worked, and Fidel
was finally released on July 24, on the condition he leave the country within
two weeks.

Now, as predicted, only Che and Calixto García were left in prison,
for the official reason that their immigration status was more "complicated."
But in Che's case, his Communist affiliations undoubtedly had a lot to do
with it. García was apparently held over because he had stayed illegally in
Mexico for the longest period, since March of 1954. Meanwhile, even as the
threat of extradition continued to hang over both their heads, Che refused
offers made by his Guatemalan friend Alfonso Bauer Paiz and Ulíses Petit
de Murat to pull diplomatic strings on his behalf. An uncle of Che's happened to be the Argentine ambassador to Havana, and Hilda was pushing
the idea of using him to secure Che's release. Wrote Hilda: "Fidel approved,

but when we explained the idea to Ernesto, he said: By no means! I want the same treatment as the Cubans."

While Che balked, Fidel was under pressure to get moving. Mexico was no longer a safe place; he was vulnerable to both Mexican police and Batista's agents. As a precaution, he had dispersed his men, sending most of them to await developments in remote areas far from Mexico City. Aware of Fidel's need for urgency, Che told him to proceed without him, but Fidel swore he would "not abandon" him. It was a magnanimous gesture that Che never forgot, and he later wrote: "Precious time and money had to be diverted to get us out of the Mexican jail. That personal attitude of Fidel's toward people whom he holds in esteem is the key to the fanatical loyalty he inspires."

Around this time he penned an ode that he called "Canto a Fidel." He showed it to Hilda and told her he planned to give it to Castro when they were at sea, on their way to Cuba. Though sophomoric and purple, the poem reveals the depth of Ernesto's feelings toward Castro at the time.

> *Let's go, ardent prophet of the dawn,*
> *along remote and unmarked paths*
> *to liberate the green caiman you so love . . .**
> *When the first shot sounds*
> *and in virginal surprise the entire jungle awakens,*
> *there, at your side, serene combatants*
> *you'll have us.*
> *When your voice pours out to the four winds*
> *agrarian reform, justice, bread and liberty,*
> *there, at your side, with identical accent,*
> *you'll have us.*
> *And when the end of the battle for*
> *the cleansing operation against the tyrant comes,*
> *there, at your side, ready for the last battle,*
> *you'll have us . . .*
> *And if our path is blocked by iron,*
> *we ask for a shroud of Cuban tears*
> *to cover the guerrilla bones*
> *in transit to American history.*
> *Nothing more.*

---

*"Green caiman" was a metaphor for the reptilian-shaped island of Cuba coined by Cuba's Communist poet Nicolás Guillén.

IV

In mid-August, after fifty-seven days of incarceration, Che and Calixto García were freed, their freedom apparently won through a bribe paid by Fidel. Che hinted as much to Hilda, and he later wrote that Fidel had done "some things for the sake of friendship which, we could almost say, compromised his revolutionary attitude . . ."

As with their comrades before them, Che and Calixto were freed on condition they leave Mexico within a few days. And, like the others, they too went underground. First, Che went home to sort out his affairs and to see the baby. During those three days, Hilda found him frequently sitting by Hildita's crib, reciting poetry aloud to her or simply watching her in silence. Then he was gone again.

On Fidel's orders, he and Calixto went to the weekend retreat of Ixtapan de la Sal, outside the capital. They registered in a hotel there under false names.

During this underground period, lasting three months, Ernesto returned discreetly to the city a couple of times, but mostly Hilda traveled to see him on weekends. She found him once in a hotel in Cautla registered under the name "Ernesto González." But Ernesto's absorption with the twin topics of Marxism and revolution now dominated his life. Even when home on visits, he was unrelenting, either delivering sermons to Hilda on "revolutionary discipline" or burying himself behind dense books on political economy. He was even ideological with the baby: One of the poems he always recited to Hildita was the Spanish Civil War poem by Antonio Machado in honor of General Lister, and he regularly referred to her as "my little Mao."

Once, Hilda observed as Ernesto picked up their daughter and told her in a serious voice: "My dear little daughter, my little Mao, you don't know what a difficult world you're going to have to live in. When you grow up this whole continent, and maybe the whole world, will be fighting against the great enemy, Yankee imperialism. You too will have to fight. I may not be here anymore, but the struggle will inflame the continent."

In early September, after suffering a resumption of his asthma, Ernesto and Calixto moved from Ixtapan de la Sal to Toluca, where the climate was drier. Then Fidel called for them to join some of the other expeditionaries for a meeting in Veracruz. There, Che met up with many comrades he hadn't seen for months.

From Veracruz, Che and Calixto returned to the capital, where they moved into one of the new *casas-campamentos*. For several weeks they lived in the Casa de Cuco, near the Catholic holy shrine to the Virgin of Guadalupe in the northern suburb of Linda Vista. By now, the men knew the time for their departure was drawing near; Fidel was desperately trying to get things ready, and the men were asked to provide "next-of-kin" information in the event of their deaths. Che recalled it later as a transcendental moment for him and his comrades, as the reality of what they proposed to do struck home, and they realized that they might soon die.

Since his release, Fidel had kept up a frenetic pace. It was a full load, involving problems of politics, security, fund-raising, and logistics. Besides having to move his men around to avoid surveillance in Mexico, he sought to shore up a political alliance with the increasingly competitive Directorio Revolucionario. Its leader, José Antonio Echeverría, had flown into Mexico to meet him at the end of August. After a marathon two-day meeting, they had signed a document called the "Carta de Mexico," voicing their two organizations' mutual commitment to the struggle against Batista. It fell short of an actual partnership, but the two groups agreed to advise one another ahead of any actions taken, and to coordinate their efforts once Castro and his rebels landed in Cuba.

A few weeks later, forty new recruits for the war arrived from Cuba and the United States. With the loss of the Rancho San Miguel, they had to be trained at far-flung bases—one in Tamaulipas just south of the U.S.-Mexican border and another at Veracruz. By now, most of Fidel's general staff, or *estado mayor,* had joined him in Mexico City, leaving regional chiefs behind to coordinate activities on the island. But his coffers were nearly dry, and he still had no vessel to carry his men to Cuba. The hoped-for purchase of the PT boat had fallen through, as did a short-lived scheme to buy a vintage Catalina flying boat.

In September, Fidel made a secret trip across the U.S. border to Texas, where he met with his erstwhile enemy and a former president, Carlos Prío Socarrás. Since his ouster, Prío had been linked to several anti-Batista conspiracies, and the latest reports had him plotting an invasion of Cuba together with the Dominican dictator, Trujillo, but now he agreed to bankroll Fidel. Perhaps he believed that by backing Castro he would be able to have the young upstart do the heavy lifting of war, then sweep back into power, or perhaps he simply saw Fidel as a useful diversion in his campaign against Batista. Whatever Prío's motivations were, Castro came away from the meeting with at least fifty thousand dollars—and with more handed over later—according to those involved in arranging the encounter.

Fidel took a political risk by accepting money from the man he had so vociferously accused of corruption while president, but right now he had little choice. According to Yuri Paporov, the KGB official who bankrolled the Instituto Cultural Ruso-Mexicano at the time, the money Fidel received was not Prío's at all, but the CIA's. He did not specify his sources for that assertion, but if true, it would lend weight to reports that the American

intelligence agency had tried early to win over Castro, just in case he succeeded in his war against the increasingly embattled Batista. According to
Castro's biographer Tad Szulc, the CIA *did* funnel money to his July 26
Movement, but later on, during a period in 1957 and 1958, via an agent attached to the American consul's office in Santiago, Cuba.

Whatever the provenance of Fidel's money, he continued to act as
his own man. He may have made a pact with the devil in the form of Prío,
but no evidence has emerged that he ever delivered his end of the deal—
if indeed there were strings attached. In the end, any funding he received
from Prío—or, unwittingly, from the CIA—must be seen as a calculated
maneuver by Castro that certainly had no negative repercussions on his
quest for power.

Now back in funds, Fidel still needed to find a boat, and in late September he found one. It was the *Granma,* a battered thirty-eight-foot motor
yacht owned by Robert Erickson. Erickson, an American expatriate, was
willing to sell the yacht as long as Fidel also bought his riverside house in
the Gulf port town of Tuxpan, and the two came together as a forty-thou-
sand-dollar package. The boat was neither seaworthy nor nearly large
enough for his needs, but Fidel was desperate and agreed to Erickson's terms.
After making a partial down payment, he assigned several men to live in
the house and oversee the *Granma*'s overhaul.

In late October, Che and Calixto moved to a more centrally located
safe house in Colonia Roma. Che continued seeing Hilda on the weekends,
but each time he left she knew he might not return. This uncertainty and
the stress of his impending departure wore down her nerves, and she became increasingly anxious. To lift her spirits, Che told her he would try to
take her to Acapulco for a short holiday.

"I had begun to be hopeful about the Acapulco trip, if only for a weekend," wrote Hilda. "Then came the news . . . that the police had broken into
the house of a Cuban woman in Lomas de Chapultepec, where Pedro Miret
was staying, and that they had confiscated some weapons and arrested him.
On Saturday, when Ernesto came, I told him about it. He reacted very
calmly, saying only that [the group's previous] precautions had to be doubled
because the police might be watching. Early Sunday, Guajiro came. I knew
right away he was nervous from the way in which he asked: 'Where's Che?'
I told him that Ernesto was taking a bath, whereupon he marched right into
the bathroom. When Ernesto came out, still combing his hair, he said calmly:
'It seems that the police are on the hunt, so we have to be cautious. We're
going to the interior and I probably won't be back next weekend. Sorry, but
we'll have to leave our Acapulco trip until later.'"

Hilda became upset, and she suspected that "something was up." She asked Ernesto if there was anything imminent about to happen. "'No, just precautions . . . ,' he answered, gathering his things and not looking at me. When he finished, as he was always accustomed to doing before leaving, he went to the crib and caressed Hildita, then he turned, held me, and kissed me. Without knowing why, I trembled and drew closer to him. . . . He left that weekend and did not come back."

The discovery of Miret's safe house alarmed Fidel, for it meant that his organization had a traitor in its ranks. Suspicions focused on Rafael Del Pino, one of Castro's closest friends and confidants. Of late, Del Pino had been entrusted with helping El Cuate to procure and smuggle arms. But he had recently vanished and was the only person unaccounted for who had known where Miret was staying. (Subsequent Cuban investigations unearthed evidence that Del Pino had actually been an FBI informant for several years. If he didn't do more damage, it was possibly because he had been holding out on his American handlers in exchange for more money.)

Taking no chances, Fidel ordered the men in Mexico City into new safe houses and ordered the repairs on the *Granma* to be sped up. Che and Calixto hid themselves away in a little servant's room in the apartment where Alfonso "Poncho" Bauer Paiz lived with his family. The first night they spent there, however, they came dangerously close to being rearrested when a robbery in a neighbor's apartment led to a door-to-door police search. Alerted beforehand, Che hid Calixto (who was black and therefore attracted attention in Mexico) underneath the mattress of the bed in their room. When the police arrived, he went out to stall them. The tactic worked, and the police left the flat without searching his room. They were safe for the moment, but the next day Calixto went off to a new hiding place, leaving Ernesto alone at Bauer Paiz's house. He was to stay there until it was time to leave.

Fidel, meanwhile, was dealing with a number of last-minute hurdles. In recent weeks, both friends and rivals had tried convincing him to postpone his invasion. His Oriente coordinator, Frank País, came twice to see him—in August and October. He was in charge of sparking off armed uprisings throughout eastern Cuba to coincide with the *Granma*'s landing, but argued with Fidel that his people weren't yet ready to undertake such a grandiose plan. Fidel was insistent, however, and País agreed to try to do what he could. Fidel told him he would send a coded message with his expedition's landing time just before leaving Mexico.

In October, the Cuban Communist party (PSP) sent emissaries to meet with Fidel. Their urgent message from the party was that conditions weren't right for an armed struggle in Cuba, and they tried to win Fidel's agree-

ment to join forces in a gradual campaign of civil dissent leading up to an
armed insurrection—in which the PSP would also participate. He refused
and told them he would go ahead with his plans, but hoped the party and
its militants would support him nonetheless by carrying out uprisings upon
his rebel army's arrival in Cuba.

At this point, Fidel's relations with the Cuban Communists were cordial but strained. Despite his public repudiation of any such links, he still
had some close friends in the PSP, and he had allowed Marxists such as Raúl
and Che into his inner circle. He discreetly maintained open lines of communication with the Cuban PSP but kept a critical distance—not only to
avoid negative publicity but to avoid any political compromises until he was
in a position of strength.

Meanwhile, there was discomfiture at the Soviet embassy resulting
from the unwelcome publicity over the links between members of Castro's
group with the Instituto Cultural Ruso-Mexicano. In early November,
Nikolai Leonov was recalled to Moscow, he says, as "punishment" for initiating contact with the Cuban revolutionaries without prior approval.

The Communists were not alone in trying to find a place at Cuba's
insurrectionary table. As Fidel prepared to leave Mexico, a game of
brinksmanship ensued as the Directorio jostled to hold the revolutionary
trump card. In spite of the fraternal document signed by José Antonio
Echeverría in August, the Directorio had persisted in carrying out violent
actions on its own. Shortly after a second meeting between Fidel and
Echeverría in October, Directorio gunmen had murdered Colonel Manuel
Blanco Rico, the man in charge of Batista's Military Intelligence Service,
SIM. Remarkably, for a man about to launch an invasion, Fidel publicly
condemned the killing as "unwarranted and arbitrary." His insinuation to
Cuba's opposition-minded citizens was obvious: *He* was the responsible
revolutionary, while Echeverría was a loose cannon, a terrorist whose activities could reap only more violence. Within days, Fidel's words acquired a
retrospective halo of prescience when police hunting for the colonel's assassins murdered ten hapless young asylum seekers inside the Haitian embassy.

On November 23, the moment for which Che had prepared for so long
had finally come. Fidel had decided it was time to go and had ordered the
rebels in Mexico City, Veracruz, and Tamaulipas to converge the next day
in Pozo Rico, an oil town just south of Tuxpan. Without any notice, Che
had been picked up by the Cubans and driven to the Gulf coast. That night,
the twenty-fourth, they would load up the yacht and depart.

The irony to all this cloak-and-dagger activity was that Fidel Castro's
planned invasion of Cuba had become public knowledge. Everyone in Cuba
knew he was going to do it; the only question was exactly where and when

he planned to land his rebel force. Indeed, a few days earlier, Batista's chief of staff had held a press conference in Havana to discuss—and deride—the revolutionary leader's possibilities of success, while beefing up military land and sea patrols along the island's Caribbean coast.

For success, therefore, Fidel was gambling on the support of the July 26 Movement in Oriente under Frank País, and on keeping the exact date and place of the *Granma*'s landing secret until the last minute. Fidel had estimated their voyage would take five days, and so, just before leaving Mexico City, he dispatched a coded message to País that the *Granma* would arrive November 30 at a deserted beach in Oriente called Playa las Coloradas.

In the predawn darkness of November 25, Che was among the throng of men scrambling to board the *Granma*. The final hours of Fidel Castro's rebel army on Mexican soil were jittery and confusing. Not everyone had arrived, while others who had come were left behind at the last minute for lack of space. Now, for better or worse, they were off. Crammed with eighty-two men and a heap of guns and equipment, the overloaded *Granma* pushed off from the Tuxpan riverbank and slipped downriver toward the Gulf of Mexico and Cuba.

Before leaving, Ernesto left behind a letter to be forwarded to his mother. In that letter, he wrote that, "to avoid premortem patheticisms," it would not be sent until "the potatoes are really on the fire and then you will know that your son, in a sunstruck American country, will be cursing himself for not having studied more of surgery to attend to a wounded man. . . .

"And now comes the tough part, old lady; that from which I have never run away and which I have always liked. The skies have not turned black, the constellations have not come out of their orbits nor have there been floods or overly insolent hurricanes; the signs are good. They signal victory. But if they are mistaken, and in the end even the gods make mistakes, then I believe I can say like a poet whom you don't know: 'I will only take to my grave / the nightmare of an unfinished song.' I kiss you again, with all the love of a good-bye that resists being total. Your son."

Part Two
Becoming Che

14

A Disastrous Beginning

I

For all the melodrama of his last letter home, Ernesto's words were as prescient about the dangers he faced as they were mistaken about his own reactions to them. As it turned out, when the "potatoes burned," in the form
of an army ambush that caught the rebels by surprise a few days after the
Granma landed, the last thing on Ernesto's mind was his inexperience with
field surgery.

In the panicked melee that followed, as men were shot down and others
fled in all directions, Ernesto faced a split-second decision over whether to
rescue a first-aid kit or a box of ammunition. He chose the latter. If there
was ever a decisive moment in Ernesto Guevara's life, that was it. He may
have possessed a medical degree, but his true instincts were those of a fighter.

Moments later, hit by a ricochet bullet in the neck and believing himself to be mortally wounded, he went into shock. After firing his rifle once
into the bushes, he lay still and in a reverie began pondering "the best way
to die." The image that came to him was from Jack London's story "To Build
a Fire," about a man in Alaska who, unable to light a fire, sits against a tree
to freeze to death with dignity.

Ernesto had envisioned himself fighting back tenaciously to the shout
of *"victoria o muerte,"* but in the shock of ambush and his own wounding,
he momentarily gave up hope. In contrast to many of his comrades—who
either lost their nerve completely or responded as soldiers, firing back at the
enemy while moving toward cover—Ernesto lay back, cooly meditating on
the prospect of his imminent death.

If his reaching for ammunition rather than a medical kit in his first
taste of combat revealed something fundamental about Ernesto Guevara,
so did his wounding: a fatalism about death. Over the next two years of war,

this trait became manifest as he developed into a combat-seasoned guerrilla with a distinctive taste for battle and a notorious disregard for his own safety. In war, Celia's errant son finally found his true metier.

II

The voyage of the *Granma* had been an unmitigated disaster. Instead of the expected five days, the journey took seven. Then, weakened from seasickness crossing the choppy Gulf of Mexico, the rebels landed at the wrong spot on Cuba's Caribbean coast. Their arrival was to have coincided with the rebel uprising in Santiago led by Frank País, and a reception party awaited them at the Cabo Cruz lighthouse with trucks and a hundred men. The joined forces were to have attacked the nearby town of Niquero, then hit the city of Manzanillo before escaping into the Sierra Maestra. But the revolt in Santiago had gone off without them, and any element of surprise Fidel had hoped for was irrevocably gone. The army, already quelling the fighting in Santiago, was on the alert; Batista had rushed troop reinforcements to Oriente province, and dispatched naval and air force patrols to intercept Fidel's landing party.

Before dawn on the morning of December 2, the *Granma* approached Cuba's southeastern coast. As the men on board anxiously strained to spot the Cabo Cruz lighthouse, the navigator fell overboard. Rapidly using up the precious remaining minutes of darkness, the boat circled until his cries were heard, and he was rescued. Then, after Fidel ordered the pilot to aim for the nearest point of land, the *Granma* struck a sandbar, turning their arrival in Cuba into more of a shipwreck than a landing. Leaving most of their ammunition, food, and medicines behind, the rebels waded ashore in the broad daylight of midmorning.

They didn't know it yet, but they had been spotted by a Cuban coast guard cutter, which in turn had alerted the armed forces. They had also landed more than a mile short of their intended rendezvous point, and between them and dry land lay a mangrove swamp. Their reception party, after waiting in vain for two days, had withdrawn the night before. They were on their own.

Split into two groups after reaching dry land, the exhausted rebels floundered on through the bush, jettisoning more equipment as they went. As Che depicted them later, they were "disoriented and walking in circles, an army of shadows, of phantoms walking as if moved by some obscure psychic mechanism." As they did, government planes flew continuously overhead looking for them, machine-gunning the bush for good measure. Two days went by before the two groups found one another and, with the guidance of a local peasant, trekked inland, moving eastward toward the Sierra Maestra mountain range.

Just after midnight on the morning of December 5, the column halted to rest in a sugarcane field where they devoured stalks of cane—carelessly leaving traces of their presence—before marching on until daybreak to a place called Alegría de Pío. Their guide now left them, making tracks to report their presence to the nearest detachment of soldiers. The rebels passed the day bivouacked in a glade at the edge of the cane field, totally unaware of what awaited them.

At four-thirty that afternoon, the army attacked. Caught by surprise, the rebels panicked and milled around as volleys of bullets flew into their midst. Fidel and his closest companions ran from the cane field into the forest, ordering the others to follow. In their effort to do so, men abandoned their equipment and ran off in headlong flight. Others, paralyzed by shock or terror, stayed where they were. That was when Che tried to rescue the box of bullets: as he did, a burst of gunfire hit a man next to him in the chest, and Che in the neck. "The bullet hit the box first and threw me on the ground," Che recorded cryptically in his field diary. "I lost hope for a couple of minutes."*

Surrounded by wounded and frightened men screaming for surrender and believing himself to be dying, Che slipped into his languor, but Juan Almeida snapped him out of it, telling him to get up and run. Joining him and three other men, Che ran into the jungle with the sound of the cane field roaring with flames behind them.

Che had been lucky—his neck wound was only superficial. Although some of his comrades escaped with their lives, over the coming days Batista's troops summarily executed many of the men they captured, including the wounded and even some of those who surrendered. For the dispersed survivors, their urgent priority was to seek refuge in the mountains and, somehow, find one another. Of the eighty-two men who came ashore from the *Granma,* only twenty-two ultimately regrouped in the sierra.**

*Che's *Diario de un Combatiente* (A Fighter's Diary), was the source for his book *Pasajes de la Guerra Revolucionaria* (Episodes of the Cuban Revolutionary War), first published in Havana in 1963. A carefully censored version of the first three months of the diary has been published by the Cuban government, but the original text, obtained by the author from Che's widow, Aleida March, has never before been made public, and provides raw and revealing glimpses of Guevara's life during the guerrilla war. (See also the appendix.)

**The exact figure of *Granma* survivors has remained imprecise. Official accounts have always referred to the number who survived and regrouped to form the core of the rebel army as twelve. This figure, with its unabashed apostolic symbolism, was consecrated by the revolutionary Cuban journalist and official historian Carlos Franqui in his book *Los Doce* (The Twelve). Like many other early supporters, Franqui later went into exile as an opponent of Castro.

Che and his comrades stumbled on through the night. At dawn the next day, they found a cave and took refuge in it, making a portentous pledge to fight to the death if they were encircled. For them at least, there was no going back, but their actual situation could not have been worse. In his diary, Che wrote: "We had a tin of milk and approximately one liter of water. We heard the noise of combat nearby. The planes machine-gunned. We came out at night, guiding ourselves with the moon and North Star until they disappeared and [then] we slept."

They knew they had to keep heading east to reach the sierra, and the "North Star" was Che's discovery, but his recollection of astronomy was less complete than he thought. It was only much later that he realized they had actually followed a different star, and it had been sheer luck that they had marched in the right direction.

Desperate from thirst, the five fugitives hiked through the forest. They had no water, and their only tin of milk had been accidentally spilled. They ate no food that day. The next day, December 8, they came within sight of the coast and spotted a pond of what appeared to be fresh water below. But dense forest and fifty-meter cliffs lay between them and it, and before they could find a way down, airplanes appeared overhead and once again they had to take cover, waiting out the daylight hours with only a liter of water between them. By nightfall, desperate from hunger and thirst, they gorged themselves on the only thing they could find, prickly pears. Moving through the night, they came across a hut where they found three more comrades from the *Granma*. Now they were eight, but they had no idea who else had survived. All they knew was their best chance of finding any others was by heading east, into the Sierra Maestra.

The next days were an ordeal of survival as the little band hunted for food and water, dodging army airplanes and enemy foot patrols. Once, from a cave overlooking a coastal bay, they watched as a naval landing party disembarked on the beach to join the hunt for rebel stragglers. That day, unable to move, Che and his friends shared water, drinking from the eyepiece of their binoculars. "The situation was not good," wrote Che afterward. "If we were discovered, not the slightest chance of escape; we would have no alternative but to fight it out on the spot to the end." After dark they moved off again, determined to escape a place where they felt like "rats in a trap."

On December 12, they found a peasant's hut. Hearing music playing, they were about to enter it when they overheard a voice inside make a toast: "To my comrades in arms." Assuming the voice to be a soldier's, they ran off. Finding a stream bed, they marched along it until midnight when, reeling from exhaustion, they could go no farther.

After another day spent hiding without food or water, they took up the march again, but morale was low among the weary men, and many of them balked, saying they no longer wanted to continue. The mood changed late that night when they reached a farmer's home, and despite Che's wariness they knocked at the door and were received warmly. Their host turned out to be a Seventh-Day Adventist pastor and a member of the fledgling July 26 peasant network in the region.

"They received us very well and gave us food," Che wrote in his field diary. "The people got sick from eating so much." But when recalling this experience later, in *Pasajes,* Che rendered the experience with dark humor: "The little house that sheltered us turned into an inferno. Almeida was the first to be overcome by diarrhea; and, in a flash, eight unappreciative intestines gave evidence of the blackest ingratitude."

They spent the next day recovering from their gluttony and receiving an endless succession of curious Adventists from the surrounding community. The rebel landing was big news, and, thanks to a flourishing bush telegraph, the locals were surprisingly well informed about what had taken place. Che and his companions learned that sixteen of the *Granma*'s men were known to be dead, murdered immediately after surrendering. Five more were believed to have been taken prisoner alive, while an unknown number had, like themselves, managed to escape into the mountains. It wasn't yet known whether Fidel had survived.

For their own security, they decided to spread themselves out, staying in different homes in the area. They took other precautions as well, shedding their uniforms and dressing up as *guajiros,* Oriente peasants, and hiding their weapons and ammunition in a peasant's home. Only Che and Almeida, acting jointly as the unofficial leaders of the group, each kept a pistol. Too sick to move, one of the men was also left behind. But as they moved out, they learned that the news of their presence had reached the army's ears. Earlier that day, only hours after they had left it, soldiers had raided the house where they had been, found their weapons cache, and taken their sick comrade away as a prisoner. Obviously, there had been a *chivatazo*—someone had squealed to the army—and now the soldiers were hot on their trail.

Fortunately, help arrived quickly. Alerted to their presence, Guillermo García, a key member of the July 26 peasant network, came to guide them out of harm's way. From him they learned that Fidel, or "Alejandro,"* as he was known by his nom de guerre, was still alive; with two companions,

*Castro's full name is Fidel Alejandro Castro Ruz.

he had made contact with the rebel movement's collaborators and sent García out to look for survivors.

Several days of marching still lay between them and Fidel's refuge deeper in the mountains, but thanks to García, Che and his comrades were aided by friendly peasants along the way. Finally, at dawn on December 21, they reached the coffee *finca* where Fidel awaited them. There they found that Raúl Castro too had survived, arriving separately with four companions after his own grueling odyssey.

Despite the catastrophic setback to his plans, Fidel was already organizing things. Peasants had been enlisted to help find any of the *Granma*'s survivors still on the run, while a courier had been dispatched to Santiago and Manzanillo to seek help from Frank País and Celia Sánchez, the woman who had set up the July 26 *guajiro* network in the sierra. Still, the outlook was grim. Out of the eighty-two men who had come ashore from the *Granma,* only fifteen had reassembled, with only nine weapons left between them. Almost three weeks had passed, and the possibility of finding new stragglers grew slimmer by the day. With Che's arrival came word of Jesús Montané's capture and the death of Fidel's friend Juan Manuel Márquez and two others. By now, Che also knew that his friend Ñico López had been killed. Over the coming days, five more expeditionaries would trickle in, including Che's old prison mate Calixto García, but Fidel's rebel army was a mere shell; from now on, it would have to rely upon local peasants to rebuild its strength.

What's more, their reunion with Fidel was not a happy one for Che and his companions, because Fidel was furious with them for having lost their arms. "You have not paid for the error you committed," Fidel told them. "Because the price to pay for the abandonment of your weapons under such circumstances is your life. The one and only hope of survival that you would have had, in the event of a head-on encounter with the army, was your guns. To abandon them was both criminal and stupid." That night, Che suffered an asthma attack, very possibly caused by the emotional upset of Fidel's disapproval. Several years later, Che admitted that Fidel's "bitter reproach" had remained "engraved on his mind for the duration of the campaign, and even today."

Fidel certainly had a valid point, but his tirade was somewhat gratuitous, for by then his courier had returned from Manzanillo with Celia Sánchez's promise of new weapons. Indeed, the day after Che arrived, so did the new guns, which included some carbines and four submachine guns. Che's asthma vanished, but the arms delivery didn't cheer him up much, for there was important symbolism in the way Fidel distributed the weapons. Taking away Che's pistol—a symbol of his status—Fidel gave it to the leader of his peasant network, a wily *guajiro* strongman named Crescencio Pérez. In its place, Che was given what he sourly called "a bad rifle."

It was a firsthand lesson in Fidel's masterful ability to manipulate the feelings of those around him, by bestowing or withdrawing his favors at a moment's notice. For his part, Che was extremely sensitive to Fidel's approval and anxious to retain his status as a member of his inner circle; it had been only a few months since he had penned his "Ode to Fidel," swearing his undying loyalty and describing him as an "ardent prophet of the dawn," and to have fallen in his idol's approval must have been a very hard blow indeed.

But the next day, perhaps aware of Che's wounded feelings, Fidel gave him a chance to redeem himself. Deciding suddenly to carry out a surprise test of combat readiness among the men, he selected Che to pass on his orders to prepare for battle. Che responded with alacrity. In his diary, he wrote: "I came running to give the news. The people responded well with a good fighting spirit."

That day Celia's couriers arrived from Manzanillo with more arms, bringing three hundred rifle bullets, forty-five more for their Thompson submachine gun, and nine sticks of dynamite. Che was overjoyed when the expedition's only other doctor, Faustino Pérez, dispatched to Havana to assume duties there as Fidel's point man, gave him his own brand-new rifle with a telescopic scope—"a jewel"—gushed Che elatedly in his diary.

Things had righted themselves again. Fidel's ire had abated as he turned his mind to the exigencies of organizing for war, and Che probably felt he had been resurrected. Even so, Fidel's upbraiding must have been galling. Fidel may have hung onto *his* weapon in flight, but his judgments had led them into catastrophe in the first place, beginning with the *Granma*'s grounding offshore. And after the ambush at Alegría de Pío, in the absence of any contingency plans, it had been a matter of *"sálvase quien puede"*— "every man for himself"—and Che's group had done the best it could and survived.

If Che harbored any resentment, he didn't dwell on it, but over the next several days a certain impatience with Fidel's style of command began to creep into his diary. On December 22, Che observed that it had been "a day of almost total inactivity." The next day, they were "still in the same place." And on Christmas Eve, in "a wait that seems useless to me," they remained rooted in spot awaiting more arms and ammunition.

He described Christmas Day with fine irony: "At last, after a sumptuous feast of pork we began the march toward Los Negros. The march began very slowly, breaking fences with which [our] visiting card was left. We carried out an exercise of assaulting a house, and as we did the owner,

Hermes, appeared. We [then] lost two hours between coffee and conversation. At last we resolved to take to the road and advanced some more but
the noise [we made] betrayed our presence to any hut along the way, and
they abound. At dawn we reached our destination."

Che wanted to see more organization, discipline, and action. He
wanted the war to begin. One item that did cheer him up a bit during this
period was a report in a Cuban newspaper about a loathsome personality in
Fidel's expeditionary force, "an Argentine communist with terrible ante-
cedents, expelled from his country." Wrote Che: "The surname, of course:
Guevara."

III

In Mexico, as elsewhere, the news of the rebels' debacle at Alegría de Pío
had made front-page news. The American UPI correspondent in Havana
had fallen for the Batista government's claims of a total victory and sent it
out on the wires as a news-scoop, and many papers had picked it up. Along
with Fidel and Raúl Castro, Ernesto Guevara was listed among the dead.

Hilda heard the news at her office. "When I arrived at work I found
everyone with solemn looks: there was an embarrassed silence, and I wondered what was happening. Then I became conscious that everyone was
looking at me. A fellow coworker handed me a newspaper and said: 'We
are very sorry—about the news.'"

Devastated, Hilda was given leave to go home. Over the following days,
her friends rallied around her, including Myrna Torres, Laura de Albizu
Campos, and General Bayo. Trying to comfort her, Bayo reminded her that
the report had not yet been confirmed and insisted that he for one didn't
believe it. She anxiously waited for more news, but little appeared in the
press to confirm or deny the initial reports.

The Guevara family was equally distraught by the news reports. The
first to hear, Ernesto Sr. rushed to the newsroom of *La Prensa* to ask for
confirmation, but was told all he could do was wait. Celia called the Associated Press, and received the same reply.

As Christmas approached, the Guevara household remained plunged
in gloom. Many days had gone by, and there was still no word. Then one
day, a letter with a Mexican postmark arrived. It was the letter Ernesto had
left with Hilda to be mailed after his departure on the *Granma,* in which he
talked to his mother of death and glory. She had sent it on, and now, with
incredibly bad timing, it had reached its destination. "For our family it was
simply horrifying," recalled Che's father. "My wife read it aloud to all of us
without shedding a tear. I gritted my teeth and could not understand why

Ernesto had to get involved in a revolution that had nothing to do with his homeland."

Some days later, Ernesto Sr. was summoned to the Argentine Foreign Ministry, where a cable had just come in from his cousin, the ambassador in Havana. According to his inquiries, Ernesto was not among the dead and wounded rebels, nor among the prisoners held by the Batista regime. It was good enough for Che's father, who ran home excitedly to give the news. "That afternoon everything changed there," he wrote. "A little halo of optimism enveloped us all, and my house once again became a noisy and happy place."

Ernesto's father telephoned Hilda and told her the promising news. Afterward, Hilda heard other rumors that renewed her hopes that Ernesto was still alive. "I lived on that hope," she recalled years later. Meanwhile, she went ahead with her plans to go home to Peru and spend Christmas with her family. But as she prepared to leave, Hilda was still very distraught. "The last few days in Mexico I was so upset and worried by the lack of news clarifying Ernesto's situation that I was unable to take care of our belongings. I gave away most things or just abandoned them."* On December 17, she and ten-month-old Hilda Beatriz left Mexico for Lima.

While they still awaited proof that Ernesto was alive, the Guevaras hung their faith on the promising report from the Argentine embassy in Havana. Christmas came and went. Then, at around 10 P.M. on December 31, the family was preparing to celebrate New Year's when an airmail letter was pushed under the front door. It was addressed to Celia *madre* and had postmarks on it from Manzanillo, Cuba.

Inside, on a single sheet of notepaper, in Ernesto's unmistakable hand, was written the following message: "Dear old folks: I am perfectly, I spent two and I have five left. I am still doing the same work, news is sporadic and will continue to be, but have faith that God is an Argentine. A big hug to you all, Teté."

They understood his oblique message immediately: Using his pet toddler's name of Teté, Ernesto was letting them know he was fine, and, like a cat, had only used up two of his seven lives.** The Guevaras were overjoyed: the champagne was uncorked and the toasts began. Then, just before midnight struck, another envelope was pushed under the door. This too was addressed to Celia. Inside was a card with a red rose printed on it, and a note that said: "Happy New Year. TT is perfectly well."

---

*Presumably, when Hilda lost many of Ernesto's letters, poems, and other writings he had left in her care

**Che apparently believed cats had seven, not nine, lives.

"This surpassed all our expectations," recalled Ernesto Sr. "The bells of the New Year rang out and all the people who had come to my house began to show their happiness. Ernesto was safe, at least for now."

IV

Spreading along most of Cuba's anvil-shaped southeastern tip for a hundred miles, the Sierra Maestra mountain range rises sharply from the Caribbean coastal shelf, forming a rugged natural barrier between it and the fertile lowlands that spread from its opposite flanks, thirty miles inland. Dominated by Cuba's highest mountain, the 7,300-foot Pico Turquino, the sierra was also home to one of the island's few remaining wildernesses in the late 1950s, where indigenous rain forest, too inaccessible to cut down, still survived.

With only a few small towns and villages, the sierra was sparsely inhabited by sixty thousand or so of the hardscrabble farmers called *guajiros:* the poor, illiterate black, white, and mulatto peasants whose beaten-up straw hats, gnarled bare feet, and unintelligible, devoweled, rapid-fire Spanish vernacular had made them the favored butt of derisory jokes among Cuba's urban middle class. To be called a *"guajiro"* was to be called stupid, a half-witted hillbilly. Some of the *guajiros* were tenant farmers, but many were also illegal squatters, or *precaristas,* who had built their own dirt-floored huts, cleared a patch of land, and eked out a living as subsistence farmers, honey collectors, or charcoal burners. For cash, like the rest of Cuba's rural peasantry, the *guajiros* descended to the llano to work as sugarcane cutters during the *zafra,* or harvest season, or as cowboys on the cattle ranches. To supply the demand in Cuba's cities, some enterprising souls grew marijuana illegally, and used a series of smuggling trails to evade the *guardia* and get it to market. A few logging companies had concessions to extract timber from the forests, and there were some coffee plantations, but for the most part the sierra had little gainful employment, virtually no roads or schools, and practically no modern amenities. News of the outside world traveled by transistor radio or more commonly through the flourishing "bush telegraph" system known as "Radio Bemba."

The starkness of the lives of the Sierra Maestra's *guajiros* contrasted sharply with those of its landowners and, for that matter, with most of the people living in Oriente province's towns and cities: Santiago, Manzanillo, Bayamo, and Holguín. The best land in the sierra, and that of the llano below, was privately owned, often by absentee landlords living in Cuba's cities and administered by armed foremen called *mayorales,* whose job it was to chase off the persistent *precaristas.* These freewheeling, sometimes brutal men carried real weight in the area, and acted as a virtual second police force to the ill-trained, underpaid *guardia rural* units based in outposts and garrisons throughout the region. Because of its remoteness and ruggedness, the Sierra Maestra was also a traditional redoubt for criminals escaping the law, and in lieu of an effective governmental writ, blood feuds and acts of vengeance were settled in the hills by machete and revolver. Exploiting the *guajiros'* poverty and fear of authority, the *guardia* used *chivatos,* or informers, to keep abreast of occurrences and to investigate crimes. In the hunt for Fidel and his men in the days immediately after the *Granma* landing, they had already deployed their *chivato* network to devastating success.

Between the *precaristas* and *mayorales,* not surprisingly, there was frequent violence. "The *mayoristas* might burn down the *precaristas'* house who in turn might respond by murder," wrote historian Hugh Thomas. "Each side had its known leaders and gangs of followers." One was Crescencio Pérez, who worked as a truck driver for sugar tycoon Julio Lobo but was also a *precarista* boss rumored to have killed several men and to have fathered "eighty children" throughout the sierra. As a result, Pérez had a huge extended family, numerous contacts, and quite a few men at his beck and call. It was to him that Celia Sánchez had gone to prepare for a civilian rebel support network in the sierra. With no love lost for the authorities, Pérez had placed himself, his family and relatives such as Guillermo García—his nephew—as well as some of his workers at Fidel's disposal.

If Fidel had any qualms about working with such a man, he didn't show it. Restructuring his "general staff" the day after Christmas 1956, he promoted Crescencio Pérez and one of his sons to a new five-man *estado mayor,* presided over by himself as *comandante;* his bodyguard, Universo Sánchez; and Che. His brother Raúl and Juan Almeida, having shown their mettle by leading their groups out of Alegría de Pío, were made platoon leaders—commanding five men each. As advance scouts, he named Ramiro Valdés, a Moncada veteran and one of Fidel's early adherents; the newly resurrected Calixto Morales; and another man, Armando Rodríguez.

Given his recent debacle and the actual size of his force—not to mention his dubious prospects for success—Fidel's grandiloquent handout of officer's rank to seven of the fifteen men with him might seem almost comic, but it was also born of Fidel's unique irrepressibility and seemingly boundless faith in himself. He was not the kind of man who discouraged easily. He had lost over two-thirds of his force and practically all his armaments and supplies, but he had reached the sierra, renewed his lifelines to the July 26 underground in the cities, and he now had Crescencio Pérez at his side to help familiarize him with the new terrain and to rebuild his army. In return, he had conferred a special status on his *guajiro* ally, a status that he

could—and would—take away, as befitted his needs. He placed his new
guajiro officer in charge of all peasant recruits, with his nephew Guillermo
García as his deputy.

Indeed, Fidel was already behaving as if he were Cuba's commander
in chief. By carrying out his "restructuring," he had quickly established a
rigid hierarchy for the army he intended to lead to power, with himself situated firmly at the top. The autocratic nature he would become famous for
was already visible as he fired off messages to the llano, demanding weapons and supplies from the hard-pressed urban underground while simultaneously turning his attention to bringing the sierra and its inhabitants under
his domain.

For all the post-triumph revolutionary lyricism about the "noble peasantry" of the Sierra Maestra, it is clear that in these early times Fidel and his
men were very much on alien ground. They neither knew nor understood
the hearts and minds of the locals, but relied on Crescencio and his men to
negotiate for them—and often with disastrous results. Perhaps the truest
measure of how tenuous was Fidel's familiarity with the terrain he had
chosen was the fact that, in many of his early contacts with the area's peasants, he frequently passed himself off as an army officer, gingerly feeling
out where their true sympathies might lie.

Over the next few days, anxious about the danger of being trapped
by the army if they remained too long in one spot, Che bristled at Fidel's
decision to linger. As they waited for some volunteers being sent by Celia
Sánchez, he wrote in his journal: "It doesn't seem wise to me but Fidel
insists on it." Couriers came and went from Manzanillo, bringing hand
grenades, dynamite, and machine-gun ammo, along with three books Che
had requested: "Algebra, and a basic history of Cuba, and a basic Cuba
geography."

While the promised volunteers didn't appear, a half-dozen new *guajiro*
recruits did trickle into camp; after its near-decimation and less than a month
after its arrival in Cuba, the rebel army had begun to grow. Most importantly, it was *locals* who were volunteering, so this was indeed an early triumph. Finally, on December 30, Fidel decided to wait no longer and to head
deeper into the mountains toward new sanctuary.

Che's enthusiasm with the positive trend was palpable in his diary
entries, which now acquired a more reassured, secure tone. Late on New
Year's Eve, a courier brought the news that an army battalion was preparing to come into the sierra after them. Che wrote: "The last day of the year
was spent in instruction of the new recruits, reading some, and doing the
small things of war."

V

New Year's Day brought rain and new details of the enemy's plans. Four hundred soldiers were on their way into the mountains, and all the local garrisons had been reinforced. Guided by a local *guajiro,* the rebels continued their exhausting trek. The night of January 2 was an ordeal recorded by Che as "a slow and fatiguing march, through muddy trails, with many of the men suffering from diarrhea," but the next day his diary bore a note of grim satisfaction: "The good news was received that Nene Jérez was badly wounded and is dying. Nene Jérez was the one who guided the soldiers to the place we were [ambushed] in la Alegría [de Pío]." By January 5 they could see the thirteen-hundred-meter high Pico Caracas, the first of the series of jungle-covered mountains crowning the Sierra Maestra's central spine. Pleased, Che observed: "The perspectives are good, because from here to La Plata is all steep and forested, ideal for defense."

Two days later, camped in the Mulato valley on the flanks of Mt. Caracas, their numbers had been bolstered by nine of the promised Manzanillo volunteers, but before pushing ahead blindly they awaited updates on the army's movements. Contradictory reports were coming in from their *guajiro* couriers: One said there were no soldiers in the vicinity, while another gave the alarming news that a *chivato* had gone to report their presence to a nearby coastal garrison.

On January 9, the rebels decided to move off again and, by the next afternoon, from a new bivouac with a good vantage point, saw that the report about the *chivatazo* had been accurate: Eighteen naval marines appeared walking along the road leading from the Macías garrison, apparently heedless to any danger. But the rebels didn't attack. They were waiting for Guillermo García—returning from a fruitless final mission to look for *Granma* survivors—and a food delivery, and Fidel wanted to be well prepared before engaging the enemy in battle. But even so, Che rued the lost opportunity, writing in his journal: "It would have been an easy target."

Their first day of combat was approaching. To counter government claims of their defeat and build up civilian confidence in their fighting capabilities—as well as to boost their own morale—the rebels needed to prove they were a force to be reckoned with. This meant launching an attack, preferably against a remote and ill-defended garrison where they retained the element of surprise, and La Plata, some small coastal barracks with reportedly few *guardias,* seemed to offer the perfect opportunity to Fidel. Che had different ideas, and wrote in his diary on January 10: "Fidel's plan is to carry out an ambush and escape to the forests with enough food for several days. It doesn't seem bad to me but it's a lot of weight [to carry]. My plan was to form a [central] camp with abundant food and [from there] send out assault troops."

Che was also concerned about the men who could be counted on in the event of combat. "Together with the temporary casualty of Ramiro [Valdés, who had hurt his knee in a fall], there are one or two definitive casualties among the *manzanilleros.*" One had already been told he could leave after announcing—"suspiciously," it seemed to Che—that he had tuberculosis, and a couple of the others seemed indecisive. He was also worried about the menace posed by *chivatos,* and in his journal he vowed to deal with this threat: "A lesson must be given." He didn't know it yet, but a traitor had already infiltrated their ranks, and very soon Che would have his opportunity to give a lesson.

The next day, as Che had predicted, five of the *manzanilleros* opted to leave the field, but Fidel decided to press on: their presence in the area had become too well known for them to stay put. A first goal was to kill three local *mayorales,* or plantation foremen, who, Che wrote, "were the terror of the peasants." The three overseers referred to worked for the Nuñez-Beattie timber and sugar company and had earned notoriety among the *guajiros* for their brutality. To strike a blow against these despots would win popularity for Fidel's rebels among the locals.

After leaving the incapacitated Ramiro at the home of a friendly peasant, with a pistol to defend himself, they headed off for La Plata. Guillermo García had shown up with some new peasant recruits—the rebel "army" had now swelled to thirty-two men—but they were still short of arms, with only twenty-three weapons and a few sticks of dynamite and hand grenades between them. They hiked into the night, their path laid out for them by a collaborator who had cut marks into the trees with a machete, and escorted by Eutimio Guerra, a well-known local *precarista* leader who had volunteered himself and a neighbor to be their guides.

On January 15, with a hostage in tow—a local teenager they had found collecting honey and decided to keep with them in case he was tempted to spread the alarm—the rebels reached a point overlooking the mouth of the Río de La Plata, a mere kilometer away from the army encampment. Using their telescopic sights, they could see their target, a half-built barracks sitting in the middle of a clearing between the riverbank and the beach, and observed a group of half-uniformed men doing domestic chores. Just beyond lay the home of one of the *mayorales* they had vowed to execute. They kept up their scrutiny and at dusk watched as a coast guard patrol boat loaded with soldiers appeared and apparently signaled to the men on shore. Uncertain what this activity meant, the rebels decided to stay hidden and delay their attack until the following day.

At dawn they posted lookouts to observe the barracks. The patrol boat had vanished and no soldiers could be seen, which unnerved them, but by midafternoon they decided to make their approach. The whole group forded the river and took up positions alongside the trail leading to the barracks. A few minutes later two men and two boys appeared on the trail, and the rebels seized them. One was a suspected *chivato*. To extract information, he was "squeezed a little," as Che worded it euphemistically in his diary. The man told them that there were ten soldiers in the barracks and that Chicho Osorio, considered the worst of the three *mayorales* on their hit list, was headed in their direction and could be expected any minute.

A few minutes later, Osorio duly appeared, mounted on a mule and escorted on foot by a young black boy. The rebels decided to trick him, and shouted out: *"Halt, the rural guard!"* Osorio immediately shouted back *"Mosquito!"* the soldiers' code word, and then his name. The rebels moved in, confiscating Osorio's revolver and a knife found on the boy before leading them over to where Fidel waited.

What happened next has become Cuban revolutionary folklore. As Che told it later in his published account of the episode, "[Fidel] made him think he was a colonel of the *guardia rural* who was investigating some irregularities. Osorio, who was drunk, then gave an account of all the enemies of the regime who in his own words 'should have their balls cut off.' There was the confirmation of who were our friends and who weren't."

If the situation hadn't been so deadly serious, this ludicrous encounter might be recalled with humor; as it was, with each word he spoke, the unsuspecting Osorio dug his own grave a little deeper. "Colonel" Fidel asked him what he knew about Eutimio Guerra, their guide, and Osorio replied that it was known that Guerra had hidden Fidel Castro. In fact, Osorio said he had been looking for Guerra, and if he found him, he would kill him. Giving the inebriated *mayoral* even more rope, Fidel opined that if "Fidel" were found, he should also be killed. Osorio agreed enthusiastically and added that Crescencio Pérez too should die. Really into his stride now, Osorio went on to brag about men he had killed and mistreated and, as evidence of his prowess, pointed to his own feet. "'Look,' he said," wrote Che afterward, "pointing to the Mexican-made boots he wore (and which we wore also), 'I got them off one of those sons . . . [of whores] we killed.' There, without knowing it, Chicho Osorio had signed his own death sentence."

Then, either so drunk or naive as to believe that Fidel was indeed a *guardia* officer, and anxious to win his favor, Osorio offered to guide them to the barracks to point out the weakness in its security defenses, and even allowed himself to be tied up as a pretend prisoner to play his role in "the inspector's" charade. As they advanced on the barracks, Osorio explained where the sentry stood watch and where the guards slept. One of the rebels was sent ahead to check and returned to report that Osorio's information was accurate. The rebels finally made ready for the attack, leaving Osorio behind in the custody of two men. "Their orders were to kill him the minute the shooting started," Che wrote matter-of-factly, "something they obeyed with strictness."

It was 2:40 A.M. The rebels fanned out into three groups. Their targets were the zinc-roofed barracks and the rustic house next to it, owned by the second of their targeted *mayorales*. When they were about forty meters (130 feet) away, Fidel fired two bursts from his machine gun, then everyone opened fire. They shouted for the soldiers to surrender but were answered with gunfire. Che and a *Granma* comrade, Luis Crespo, threw their grenades, but neither exploded. Raúl threw a burning stick of dynamite, but nothing happened then either. Fidel ordered them to set fire to the overseer's house. Two initial attempts were repelled by gunfire, but a third try by Che and Crespo was successful, except that it wasn't the overseer's house but a storehouse next to it, full of coconuts.

That was enough: The soldiers inside the barracks, evidently fearing they were going to be burned alive, began fleeing. One practically ran into Crespo, who shot him in the chest; Che fired at another man and, although it was dark, believed he had hit him. For a few minutes, bullets flew back and forth, and then the firefight abated. The soldiers in the barracks surrendered, and an inspection of the overseer's house showed it to be full of wounded men. The fight was over, and Che took a tally in his diary: "The result of the combat was 8 Springfields, one machine gun and about a thousand rounds [captured]. We had spent approximately 500 [rounds]. Also [we got] cartridge belts, helmets, canned food, knives, clothes and even rum."

The *guardia* had been hit badly, their barracks so riddled with bullets it looked like "a sieve." Two soldiers lay dead and five were wounded, three mortally. Three others were taken prisoner. There were no rebel casualties. Before they withdrew, they set the buildings on fire. Che personally set fire to the house of "the wretched" overseer who, along with the barracks' commander, a sergeant, had managed to escape.

Back in the hills, the rebels freed their prisoners and their civilian hostages, after issuing a warning to the suspected *chivato*. Overriding Che's opposition, Fidel gave all their medicine to the released soldiers to treat their wounded men who remained in the ravaged clearing below. A sour note came when the rebels realized that their first hostage, the teenaged boy, had run away during the fracas, along with a scout. Worse, they had taken with them two weapons—a shotgun and the late Chicho Osorio's confiscated revolver.

It was still only 4:30 A.M. Taking advantage of the remaining darkness, they fled east toward Palma Mocha, a farming community named for
the river entering the sea about three kilometers away. They arrived in time
to witness what Che described as "a pitiful spectacle"—civilian families fleeing with their belongings after being warned that the air force was going to
bomb the area. "The maneuver was obvious," wrote Che accusingly in his
diary. "To evict all the peasants and later the [Nuñez-Beattie] company
would take over the abandoned lands."

Having seen firsthand the fallout from their action, the rebels moved
on, looking for a place to ambush the soldiers they knew would be coming in after them. The men were keyed up and tired when, at a pit stop in
the march, Fidel ordered a review of their ammunition. Each man was
supposed to have forty rounds. When Sergio Acuña, one of the new *guajiro*
recruits, was found with a hundred rounds, Fidel asked him to give up
the excess, but he refused. Fidel ordered him arrested, but Acuña cocked
his rifle threateningly. The incident was defused when Raúl and Crescencio
convinced Acuña to hand over his weapon and ammunition, telling him
that his infraction would be ignored if he made a "formal request" to stay
with the rebels. Che was displeased with this solution but wrote in his
journal that "Fidel agreed, creating a really negative antecedent that would
later rear its head, because Acuña was seen to have gotten away with imposing his will."

With the minimutiny over for now, the rebels marched on and reached
a peasant's home in a clearing, surrounded by a forested rise of land on three
sides, and near a creek that Che christened the "Arroyo del Infierno" (Hell's
Creek). The site offered both water and an escape route, and was a perfect
place to lay an ambush. As they arrived, the owner was preparing to join
the exodus to the coast, leaving the place to the rebels, and over the next few
days they organized themselves, setting out an ambush position in the forest
with good views of the house and the dirt track leading into the clearing.

The men were jumpy, though, and one morning as he and Fidel inspected the fighters' position, Che was almost shot when one of the fighters
saw him coming from a distance and fired off a round at him. It was partly
Che's own fault: he was wearing an army corporal's cap he had taken as a
trophy at La Plata. Even more alarming was the reaction of the other rebels,
who, instead of scrambling into defensive positions at the sound of the gunshot, immediately ran off into the bush. In his later published account, Che
told of being shot at but omitted any mention of the men running away.
Instead, he used the anecdote as a parable to exalt the condition of men at
war. "This incident was symptomatic of the state of high tensions that prevailed as we waited for the relief the battle would bring. At such times, even

those with nerves of steel feel a certain trembling in the knees and each man longs for the arrival of that luminous moment of battle."

All remained quiet for a few more days. Fidel ordered provisions from some of the few peasants who had remained in the area, and he repaid a farmer who showed up looking for a lost pig, one that Fidel had shot for food on their first day in camp. They began hearing rumors of army reprisals being inflicted on local peasants for the La Plata attack. Their new guide Eutimio Guerra took off for his home, carrying some messages for Fidel and orders to find out about the army's movements. The rebels anxiously listened to their radio, but no news of army activity was broadcast.

Before dawn on January 22, distant gunshots alerted them that the army was approaching. The rebels readied themselves for battle, but the morning dragged by and no soldiers appeared. Then, at noon, a lone figure appeared in the clearing. Calixto García, seated next to Che, spotted him first. They looked through their telescopic sights: It was a soldier. As they watched, a total of nine figures came into view and gathered around the huts in the clearing. Then the shooting began. As Che recorded in his field diary: "Fidel opened fire and the man fell immediately shouting *"Ay mi madre"*; his two companions fell immediately [as well]. All of a sudden I realized there was a soldier hidden in the second house barely twenty meters from my position; I could only see his feet so I fired in his direction. At the second shot he fell. Luis [Crespo] brought me a grenade sent by Fidel because they had told him there were more people in the house. Luis covered me and I entered but fortunately there was nothing else."

Che recovered the rifle and cartridge belt of the soldier he had hit, then inspected the body. "He had a bullet under the heart with exit on the right side, he was dead." To his certain knowledge, Che had killed his first man.

VI

At the same time as Che was proving himself in combat, Hilda and the baby were visiting with the Guevara family in Argentina. At New Year's, Ernesto Sr. had called her with the news of Ernesto's "Teté" message and sent her a ticket to fly to Buenos Aires. It was the first real proof Hilda had that Ernesto had survived the ambush at Alegría de Pío, and she was overjoyed. On January 6, after three weeks at home with her own family in Lima, she and the baby flew to Buenos Aires, to meet her in-laws for the first time.

The Guevaras were delighted with the baby and welcoming to Hilda, but soon began bombarding her with questions. Why had their Ernesto gone into harm's way for a foreign cause? Who was Fidel Castro anyway? It was quickly apparent to Hilda that Ernesto, or "Ernestito" as his aunts still called him, was the family's favorite son. "Because of their deep affection for Ernesto," wrote Hilda, "his parents found it hard to adjust to the idea of his being in danger. They kept coming back to the feeling that it would be better if he were in Argentina." She did her best to explain what she knew of Ernesto's process of political evolution, but she was merely repeating things he had already told them in his letters, which they had obvious difficulty in accepting.

But it was Celia who most needed her reassurances. "I told Dona Celia, my mother-in-law, of the deep tenderness that Ernesto felt for her. This was not exaggeration for the sake of comforting her: I knew what she meant to him. She suffered continually, with the agonizing question apparent in all she did: 'Where is my son?'"

Hilda and the baby stayed a month with the Guevaras. It was the height of the hot *porteño* summer, and so they all went to stay at the family *estancia* at Irineo Portela. One day, Hilda was able to see firsthand her father-in-law's trademark bombast. A letter arrived from a Guevara relative in the United States in which they heard for the first time of Che's wounding at Alegría de Pío. In an ebullient mood, Ernesto Sr. "declared emotionally that, if Ernesto were captured in Cuba, he would go there in a boat and rescue him!"

When Hilda returned to Lima she found a letter from Ernesto waiting for her. It was dated January 28, 1957. "*Querida vieja:* Here in the Cuban jungle, alive and thirsting for blood, I'm writing these inflamed, Martí-inspired lines. As if I really were a soldier (I'm dirty and ragged at least), I am writing this letter over a tin plate with a gun at my side and something new, a cigar in my mouth."

In the same boasting, hearty tone, he breezily recapped everything that had happened since the "now famous" *Granma* landing, emphasizing the dangers faced and hardships overcome: "Our misfortunes continued. . . . [W]e were surprised in the also now famous Alegría, and scattered like pigeons. . . . I was wounded in the neck, and I'm still alive only due to my cat's lives. . . . [F]or a few days I walked through those hills thinking I was seriously wounded . . . we got reorganized and rearmed and attacked a troop barracks, killing five soldiers. . . . [They] sent select troops after us. We fought these off and this time it cost them three dead and two wounded. . . . Soon after we captured three guards and took their guns.

"Add to all this the fact that we had no losses and that the mountains are ours and you'll get an idea of the demoralization of the enemy. We slip through their hands like soap just when they think they have us trapped. Naturally the fight isn't all won, there'll be many more battles. But so far it's going our way, and each time will do so more."

Signing the letter "Chancho," he sent a *"gran abrazo"* to her, hugs and kisses for the baby, and told her that in his rush to leave he had left behind the snapshots he had of them in Mexico City. Could she send them? He gave her the address of a mail drop in Mexico where letters would be forwarded to him eventually.

Hilda couldn't have been very pleased by the letter, which she reproduced without comment in her memoirs. While she, the despondent wife and mother, had done little else but worry about him, he had made it abundantly clear he was having a rousing adventure, thoroughly enjoying life as an unwashed, cigar-smoking, and "bloodthirsty" guerrilla. When he had finally written, he hadn't even inquired or expressed concern for her own possible travails.

VII

Over the next three weeks, the rebels roamed across the Sierra Maestra, picking up a few new volunteers, but also dogged by desertions and *chivatazos*. On January 30, the air force bombed the place they had chosen for a base camp, on the slopes of Mt. Caracas; while the raid caused no casualties, it sent the rebels on a panicked exodus through the forest. Meanwhile, their army pursuers, led by the notoriously brutal officer—Major Joaquín Casillas—who was said to possess a private collection of human ears shorn from previous victims—sent out spies disguised as civilians to follow them. His soldiers left a trail of burnt huts and murdered peasants, accused of collaborating with the rebels, in their passage.

Che was now emerging as an audacious, even reckless guerrilla fighter. Evidently eager to prove himself and to make up for his sorely felt error of losing his rifle en route from Alegría de Pío, he routinely volunteered for the most dangerous tasks. During the aerial bombardment on Mt. Caracas, when everyone—including Fidel—ran away, Che stayed behind to pick up stragglers and retrieve abandoned belongings, including weapons and Fidel's *comandante* cap.

Other strong traits were emerging: He had begun to show a prosecutorial severity with guerrilla newcomers, especially anyone from the city, usually distrusting their personal valor, fortitude, and commitment to the struggle. No less mistrustful of the peasants they met, he often described them in his diary as "charlatans, fast talkers," or "nervous." He was also developing a deep hatred of cowards, an obsession that was soon to be one of his most renowned and feared wartime traits. He disliked one member of the band in particular, "El Gallego" José Morán, a *Granma* veteran whom he suspected of cowardice and viewed as a potential deserter.

By now acutely aware of the dangers posed by spies and *chivatos,* Che sought an opportunity to mete out punishment as an example to others. When three army spies were detained by the rebels and confessed their true identities, Che was among those who called for their deaths. Instead, Fidel chose to show mercy by sending them back to their barracks with a warning and carrying a personal letter from him to their commander. Keen to see the guerrillas tempered into a tough, disciplined fighting force and worried about Fidel's toleration of malingerers and insubordinates, Che was gratified when Fidel finally laid down the law at the end of January. From that moment on, Fidel told his men, three crimes would be punishable by death: "desertion, insubordination, and defeatism." When one deserter, Sergio Acuña, met a grisly end at the hands of army captors—Acuña was tortured, shot four times, then hung by the neck—Che termed the incident "sad but instructive."

By the end of January, there were growing signs that Fidel's little band was having an effect throughout Cuba. Word arrived from Havana that Faustino Pérez, Fidel's man there, had raised thirty thousand dollars for the rebels, that the July 26 urban cells were carrying out sabotage in the cities, and that there was simmering discontent in army ranks over the embarrassing rebel attacks. While rumored to be planning to fire his army chief of staff, Batista and his generals still persisted in their claims that the rebels had been virtually exterminated, were on the run, and posed no threat to the army. This propaganda campaign greatly irked Fidel, and he ordered Faustino Pérez to arrange an interview for him with a credible journalist who could come to the sierra and verify his existence to the world at large. He also wanted to hold a meeting with his National Directorate to coordinate national strategy, and sent word to Frank País and Celia Sánchez to organize a conference.

In early February the rebels spent a few days resting up, enduring torrential rains and aimless daily bombing runs by the air force; in the comparative lull, Che even began giving French language lessons to Raúl. These were interrupted when they set out again, and Che was weakened by diarrhea, and a crippling but short-lived bout of malaria. In an army ambush on a hill called Los Altos de Espinosa, Julio Zenon Acosta—an illiterate black *guajiro* whom Che had recently begun teaching the alphabet—was killed, the rebels' first combat death since the *Granma*'s landing. Later, Che would exalt Zenon Acosta, whom he called "my first pupil," as the kind of "noble peasant" who made up the heart and soul of the revolution.

As time had worn on, Che and Fidel had begun to suspect their peasant guide Eutimio Guerra—who repeatedly came and went, and whose absences always coincided with the army's attacks—as a traitor in their midst. After the ambush on Los Altos de Espinosa, they learned from knowledgeable peasants that their suspicions were correct: On one of his outings, Guerra had been captured by the army and promised a reward if he betrayed Fidel, and both the aerial bombardment on Mt. Caracas and the latest ambush had been carried out with his collusion. Even with this knowledge, the rebels could do little about it because Guerra had vanished—and immediately afterward, so had El Gallego Morán.

By mid-February a number of men were sick and demoralized, and Fidel decided to conduct a purge, giving them guarded "convalescent leave" at a *guajiro*'s farm under Crescencio Pérez's care. At the same time, couriers brought word that the July 26 National Directorate was on its way, and that Herbert Matthews, a prominent *New York Times* journalist, was arriving to interview Fidel. They were to meet on February 17 at a farmhouse on the sierra's northern flanks.

Anxious about Eutimio Guerra's whereabouts and another army ambush, Fidel's dwindling band moved off cautiously across the mountains toward the rendezvous point. It was to be a fateful meeting, for, in the span of just three days, several events would occur to alter the course of the war, one of which would reveal a new side to the emerging personality of Ernesto "Che" Guevara.

15

Days of "Water and Bombs"

I

Ernesto Guevara was now at *war*, trying to create a revolution, the result of a conscious leap of faith. He had crossed a boundary that was invisible to outsiders and had entered a domain where lives could be taken for an ideal and where the end *did* justify the means.

To Ernesto, people were no longer just people; each person represented a place within the overall scheme of things, a framework for which had lodged itself convincingly in his mind. Just as his worldview had first expanded by leaving home, it had then contracted when his quest to decide what he believed in found a home within a Marxist perception.

To him, reality was now a matter of black and white, but at the same time he believed the faith he had chosen had limitless boundaries. His conviction that what he was doing had a historic imperative allowed him to be a judge and he now viewed people, for the most part, as either friends or enemies. Anyone in between was distrusted, as they had to be, for his goal was to make war and take power, and he awoke each day with the prospect of killing and dying for this cause.

II

On the second day of their trek to the farmhouse where the National Directorate meeting would be held, as the rebels sat down to eat a goat stew cooked for them by a friendly black family, El Gallego Morán suddenly reappeared. He told an unconvincing tale to explain his disappearance: He had gone out hunting for food and spotted the traitor Eutimio Guerra. When he lost him, he was unable to find his way back to camp. Che remarked in his diary: "The truth of El Gallego's behavior is very difficult to know, but to me it is simply a matter of a frustrated desertion. . . . I advised killing him there and then, but Fidel blew off the matter."

Heading on, they reached a rural store owned by a friend of Eutimio Guerra's. Finding him gone, they broke down the door and found "a true paradise of canned goods," which they proceeded to devour. After laying a false trail to throw off pursuers, they marched through the night and, at dawn on February 16 reached the farm of the peasant collaborator named Epifanio Díaz where their meetings were to take place.

The members of the National Directorate had begun arriving. Frank País and Celia Sánchez were already there; next came Faustino Pérez and Vílma Espín, a new female movement activist from Santiago; then Haydée Santamaría and her fiancé, Armando Hart. This was the active inner core of the July 26 steering group that Fidel had assembled in the summer of 1955 after his release from prison on the Isle of Pines.

At twenty-three, Frank País was the youngest of the Directorate's members, but he had already chalked up an impressive career as a political activist in Oriente, where he was vice president of the student federation. Since the creation of the July 26 Movement, he had thrown in his lot with Fidel as coordinator of rebel activities in Oriente. Celia Sánchez, thirty-seven, had been active in the campaign to free the Moncada prisoners and, from her home base in Manzanillo, had collaborated with Fidel since the movement's founding. It was she who had recruited Crescencio Pérez and organized the reception party that had awaited the *Granma*'s arrival. Like Fidel, the thirty-seven-year-old doctor Faustino Pérez, unrelated to Crescencio, had come out of Havana University and been a student leader in opposition to Batista after his 1952 coup. Joining forces with Fidel, he had gone to Mexico and been aboard the *Granma*. Law student Armando Hart, the twenty-seven-year-old son of a prominent judge, had come out of the Ortodoxo Youth movement, joined Faustino Pérez in organizing student opposition to Batista, and helped found Fidel's movement. His twenty-five-year-old fiancée, Haydée Santamaría, had joined the Moncada assault and been jailed for seven months afterward; she too was a July 26 founder and had joined in the November 1956 uprising in Oriente led by Frank País. Her family had already paid dearly for their involvement with Fidel. Her brother Abel, an Ortodoxo Youth militant, had been Fidel's deputy until his death by torture at Moncada, and her brother Aldo was in prison for movement activities. The newest face, Vílma Espín, was the twenty-seven-year-old, MIT-educated daughter of an affluent Santiago family, a member of Frank País's student group, which had fused with the July 26 Movement, and had participated in the November 1956 uprising. Among them, these young, mostly upper-middle-class urbanites were in charge of the movement's entire national underground structure, responsible for everything including recruiting new members, obtaining and smuggling arms and volunteers into the sierra, raising cash and supplies, disseminating propaganda, foreign relations, urban sabotage, and the ongoing effort to come up with a political platform.

For all, it was a historic day. Fidel was meeting Celia Sánchez—soon to become his closest confidante, and lover—for the first time. And that same day, Raúl met the woman who would become his future wife: Vílma Espín. For Che, it was his first look at the men and women who formed the elite backbone of Fidel's revolutionary movement, and he wanted to take their measure.

In general, Che already viewed Fidel's July 26 colleagues as hopelessly bound by their middle-class upbringings and privileged educations to timid notions of what their struggle should achieve, and he was correct in thinking they held views very divergent from his own. Lacking his Marxist conception of a radical social transformation, most saw themselves as fighting to oust a corrupt dictatorship and to replace it with a conventional Western democracy. Che's initial reaction to the urban leaders reinforced his negative presentiments. "Through isolated conversations," he wrote in his diary, "I discovered the evident anticommunist inclinations of most of them, above all Hart." By the next day, however, his analyses had modified slightly. "Of the women, Haydée seems the best oriented politically, Vílma the most interesting, Celia Sánchez is very active but politically strangled. [And] Armando Hart [is] permeable to the new ideas."*

As the urban leaders met with Fidel over the next couple of days, however, one thing became clear: Fidel wanted to make his rebel army the absolute priority of the movement. They had come with their own ideas about what the movement's national strategy should be, but Fidel told his visitors that all their efforts should be directed toward sustaining and strengthening his guerrillas as a matter of urgent priority. He sidestepped Faustino's proposal to open a "second front" nearer Havana in the Escambray mountains of Villa Clara province, and Frank País's argument that he leave the sierra to give speeches and raise funds abroad. In the end, the others were overwhelmed by Fidel's persuasions and agreed to begin organizing a national "civic resistance" support network; Frank País promised to send him a contingent of new fighters from Santiago within a fortnight. Epifanio Díaz's farm, which in the future would serve as their secret gateway to the sierra, was to be the meeting place.

*See the appendix for elaboration.

Che was not a member of the National Directorate and, careful not to overstep his authority at this early stage, did not attend these meetings. But he was privy to all that transpired in them, and, as his diary reveals, the early signs of the future rift that would develop between the armed fighters in the sierra and their urban counterparts in the llano were already in evidence. For now, Fidel was able to plead his case for the sierra's priority as an undeniable issue of survival. But over the future months, as the war expanded, this rift would break into the open as an ideological dispute between left and right, and as a struggle for power between the llano leaders and Fidel over control of the rebel movement. In the end, and with Che's invaluable assistance, Fidel would emerge triumphant.

The senior *New York Times* correspondent Herbert Matthews, a press veteran of the Spanish Civil War, Mussolini's Abyssinian campaign, and World War II, arrived in camp early on the morning of February 17. Che wasn't present for Matthews' three-hour interview with Fidel, but Fidel briefed him afterward, and in his diary Che noted the points of most significance to him: Fidel had complained about the military aid lent to Batista by the United States, and, when Matthews had asked if he were anti-imperialist, Fidel had responded carefully that he was if this meant a desire to rid his country of its economic chains. This did not imply, Fidel hastened to add, that he felt hatred for the United States or its people. "The gringo," Fidel told Che, "had shown friendliness and didn't ask any trick questions."

Fidel had engaged in a little trickery of his own, however, by prearranging with a fighter to sweatily burst in, bearing "a message from the Second Column." Fidel hoped to make Matthews believe he had a sizeable number of fighters, when in fact his rebel army at this point numbered less than twenty armed men. When the interview was over, Matthews was driven back to Manzanillo, where he would go on to Santiago, fly to Havana, and board another plane for New York; he knew he had a major scoop on his hands and wanted to publish it as quickly as possible.

"The gringo left early," wrote Che in his diary. "And I was on guard when they came to tell me to redouble the vigilance because Eutimio was at Epifanio's house." Juan Almeida led a rebel patrol to seize the traitor, who, unaware his treason had been discovered, was taken prisoner, disarmed, and brought before Fidel. By now, an army safe-conduct pass bearing Eutimio's name and proving his colloboration with the enemy had fallen into the rebels' hands, and Fidel showed it to him.

"Eutimio got down on his knees asking that he be shot to have it over with," Che wrote. "Fidel tried to trick him, making him believe he would pardon his life, but Eutimio remembered the scene with Chicho Osorio and didn't allow himself to be deceived. Then Fidel announced he would be executed and Ciro Frías inflicted a heartfelt sermon on him in the tone of an old friend. The man awaited death in silence and a certain dignity. A tremendous downpour began and everything turned black."

Precisely what happened next has remained a carefully guarded Cuban state secret for four decades. None of the eyewitnesses to Eutimio Guerra's execution—the first traitor executed by the Cuban rebels—has ever said publicly who fired the fatal shot. It is easy to see why. The answer is to be found in Che's private diary.

"The situation was uncomfortable for the people and for [Eutimio], so I ended the problem giving him a shot with a .32 [-caliber] pistol in the right side of the brain, with exit orifice in the right temporal [lobe]. He gasped a little while and was dead. Upon proceeding to remove his belongings I couldn't get off the watch tied by a chain to his belt, and then he told me in a steady voice farther away than fear: 'Yank it off, boy, what does it matter. . . . ' I did so and his possessions were now mine. We slept badly, wet and I with something of asthma."

Che's narrative is as chilling as it is revealing about his personality. His matter-of-factness in describing the execution, his scientific notations on his bullet's entry and exit wounds, suggest a remarkable detachment from violence. To Che, the decision to execute Eutimio himself was, in his own words, a way to "end an uncomfortable situation." As for his recollection of Eutimo's posthumous "last words," it is simply inexplicable and lends a surreal dimension to the grim scene.

It is also in stark contrast to Che's published account of the event. In an article entitled "Death of a Traitor," he rendered the scene with literary aplomb and turned it into a dark revolutionary parable about redemption through sacrifice. Describing the moment when Eutimio fell on his knees in front of Fidel, he wrote: "At that moment he seemed to have aged; on his temple were a good many grey hairs we had never noticed before."

Of Ciro's "lecture," in which he upbraided Eutimio for causing the deaths and suffering of many of their mutual friends and neighbors, Che wrote: "It was a long and moving speech, which Eutimio listened to in silence, his head bent. We asked him if he wanted anything and he answered yes, that he wanted the Revolution, or rather us, to take care of his children." The revolution had kept its promise to Eutimio, wrote Che, but his name had "already been forgotten, perhaps even by his children," who bore new names and were attending Cuba's state schools, receiving the same treatment as the other children and preparing themselves for a better life.

"But one day," he added, "they will have to know that their father was executed by the revolutionary power because of his treachery. It is also just that they be told how their father—a peasant who had allowed himself to be tempted by corruption and had tried to commit a grave crime, moved by the desire for glory and wealth—had nevertheless recognized his error, and had not even hinted at a desire for clemency, which he knew he did not deserve. Finally, they should also know that in his last moments he remembered his children and asked that they be treated well."

Che completed his parable with a description of the final moment of Eutimio's life heavily imbued with religious symbolism. "Just then a heavy storm broke and the sky darkened; in the midst of a deluge, the sky crossed by lightning and the noise of thunder, as one of these strokes of lightning burst and was closely followed by a thunderbolt, Eutimio Guerra's life was ended and even those comrades standing near him did not hear the shot."

This incident was seminal in the growth of Che's mystique among the guerrillas and peasants of the Sierra Maestra. From then on he acquired a reputation for a cold-blooded willingness to take direct action against transgressors of the revolutionary norms. In fact, according to Cuban sources who prefer anonymity, Che stepped forward to kill Eutimio when it had become clear that nobody else wanted to take the initiative. Presumably, this included Fidel, who, having given the order for Eutimio's death without selecting someone to carry it out, simply moved away to shelter himself from the rain.

One of the *guajiros* wanted to place a wooden cross on Eutimio's grave, but Che forbade it on the grounds that it could compromise the family on whose land they were camped. Instead, a cross was carved into a nearby tree.

If Che was bothered by the act of executing Eutimio, there seemed little sign of it by the next day. In his journal, commenting on the arrival of a pretty July 26 activist at the farm, he wrote: "[She is a] great admirer of the Movement who seems to me to want to fuck more than anything else."

III

By the morning of February 18, the July 26 summit was over. Fidel spent the morning writing a "manifesto" for his urban comrades to disseminate throughout the island. Fidel's "Appeal to the Cuban People" contained combative language close to Che's heart, and he applauded it in his diary as "really revolutionary."

The manifesto led with a brief resume of the war, delivered in rhetoric that was suitably overblown for the occasion. Far from being an exterminated force, he argued, the rebels had "bravely resisted" the modern weapons and vastly superior forces of the enemy in eighty days of fighting, and their ranks had been "steadily reinforced by the peasants of the Sierra Maestra."

He ended with a six-point "guideline to the country," calling for stepped-up economic sabotage against the sugar harvest, public utilities, transportation and communications systems; and for "the summary and immediate executions of the henchmen who torture and kill revolutionaries, the regime's politicians whose stubbornness and inflexibility have brought the country to this situation, and all those who stand in the way of the Movement's success." He also called for the organization of a "civic resistance" throughout Cuba; an increase in money-raising efforts "to cover the rising costs of the Movement," and a "general revolutionary strike" to bring the struggle against Batista to a climax.

Defending his decree to burn sugarcane, Fidel wrote: "To those who invoke the workers' livelihoods to combat this measure, we ask: Why don't they defend the workers when . . . they suck dry their salaries, when they swindle their retirement pensions, when they pay them in bonds and they kill them from hunger during eight months?* Why are we spilling our blood if not for the poor of Cuba? What does a little hunger today matter if we can win the bread and liberty of tomorrow?"

Fidel's "Appeal" was based on more than a little deception, however. Just as he had tricked Herbert Matthews into believing he had many more troops than he did, he now declared that his army's ranks were "steadily increasing" because of his "peasant support." That support was largely fictitious at this point and arose from a beginning that was less than spontaneous, having been "purchased" by Fidel after obtaining Crescencio's loyalties. Since then, the rebel band had nearly been annihilated through the betrayal of a peasant, Eutimio Guerra, while many more had heeded the army's advice and fled the sierra after their attack on La Plata. While there were some notable exceptions, many of the peasants they relied upon had self-interest at heart, either as paid smugglers or as providers of food and other supplies. Certainly Fidel's continuing habit of passing himself off as a *guardia* with unfamiliar peasants showed that he was well aware of the precarious nature of his hold on the peasants' loyalties.

Heading back into the mountains from the Díaz farm, Fidel confronted a detained peasant, and told him he and his men were *guardias rurales,* looking for information about "the revolutionaries." The frightened man denied all knowledge of them, but when Fidel insisted he promised in the future to go to the nearest garrison to report if he saw anyone strange.

---

*Most Cuban sugarcane workers were hired only for the four months of *zafra,* or harvest season. Most survived the *tiempo muerto,* or "dead time," by wandering the country as itinerant laborers or as pickers of other crops, such as coffee and tobacco.

As Che rendered it in his diary, "Fidel [finally] told him we were revolutionaries and that we defended the poor man's cause, but since he had shown willingness to help the *guardia* he would be hung. The reaction of the man, Pedro Ponce, was extraordinary, he arose sweating and trembling. 'No, how can it be, come to my house to eat chicken with rice.' After a phillipic from Fidel complaining about the lack of help from the peasants we took him up on his offer of food."

This episode was left out of Che's published accounts of the war, no doubt because it showed that Fidel sometimes took his penchant for deception a little too far. While this time, he got what he wanted in the end, he had resorted to a death threat to extract Pedro Ponce's cooperation, and he could never know the petrified man's true feelings.

Still, Fidel was probably wise to take such precautions. Some *guajiros* proved sympathetic without prodding, but to many more the rebels were a nettlesome presence who had brought death and destruction with them to the Sierra Maestra, while offering little incentive or security in return for their allegiance. The army was still the preponderant force. It controlled the towns and roads, and it could win over individuals, as it had done with Eutimio Guerra, through a combination of material incentives and terror. If Fidel wanted to win over the peasants in the sierra, he would have to become the dominant military force. Until then, he had to use every means available to him to gain a foothold, and, in addition to the positive blandishments made possible through his peasant volunteer network, this included the use of trickery, bribery, and selective terror to neutralize potential traitors or spies.

As the rebels moved back into the mountains in late February, they found that the army's violent reprisals against civilians were working. It was now common knowledge among the *guajiros* that whoever helped the rebels would likely suffer for it. They heard that their main food supplier had been murdered by Major Casillas's troops, and, when they arrived at his parents' house a few days later, the old man and woman locked themselves inside, refusing to come out, and yelled at them to go away.

The civilians were caught in a vicious trap between the army's rampaging brutality on the one hand and the guerrillas' reprisals against informers on the other. For there to be a war, this was the way it had to be, however, and by executing Eutimio Guerra, Che had come to the fore in spearheading the rebel army's new policy of "swift revolutionary justice," simultaneously launching his reputation for fierceness and implacability.

A new incident had underscored that on February 18. Just as the members of the Directorate were preparing to leave the Díaz farm, a pistol shot rang out nearby and everyone grabbed weapons. But it was a false alarm, for, as Che recorded: "Right away we heard a shout of 'It's nothing, it's nothing,' and El Gallego Morán appeared, wounded by a .45 bullet in one leg. . . . I gave him emergency treatment, dosing him with penicillin, and left the leg stretched out with a splint. . . . Fidel and Raúl accused him of doing it on purpose. I'm not sure of one thing or the other." Once again, firm evidence of Morán's true motivations eluded them, but the timing of his "accident," coming only a day after Eutimio's execution and just prior to the departure of their last visitors—permitting him to be evacuated from the field—made it look suspicious.

Morán must have suffered from an abiding fear of Che Guevara. He knew that "desertion, insubordination, and defeatism" were capital offenses, and he was openly suspected of wanting to desert. Che was his particular nemesis, observing him constantly, and just days earlier had argued for his execution—and with Eutimio's death Che had shown he was perfectly capable of carrying out such sentences personally. Morán must have thought his days were numbered, and he was probably right.

Later on, Che wrote a epitaph for El Gallego, who defected to the Batista regime. "Morán's subsequent history, his treachery and his death at the hands of revolutionaries in Guantánamo, seems to establish that he [*had*] shot himself intentionally." This brief conclusion to his narrative about Morán resembles many of his portraits of men who took part in the war; conscious of his role as an architect of Cuba's new official history, Che gave each individual totemistic significance as a representative of the values to be cherished or vilified in the "new" Cuba. Eutimio Guerra was a peasant whose soul had been corrupted, whose name had become synonymous with treachery, and whose errors should never be repeated. By contrast, the *guajiro* Julio Zenon Acosta became in his prose a revolutionary martyr, an exemplary archetype for workers and peasants to imitate. El Gallego Morán was a deserter, and then a traitor, and that he eventually paid the ultimate price for his treachery was a fate Che emphatically endorsed for enemies of the revolution. Its formal enemies were the army troops and the secret police, to be sure, but as great a danger was posed by the enemy *within*.

Buried in the hearts and souls of his comrades lay the keys to their true allegiances and with them the destiny of "The Revolution," and few men were immune to Che's distrusting eye. There was a Calvinistic zeal evident in Che's persecution of those who had strayed from the "right path." He had wholeheartedly embraced *"la revolución"* as the ultimate embodiment of history's lessons and the correct path to the future. Now, convinced he was right, he looked around with an inquisitor's eye for those who might endanger its survival.

IV

As they moved off into the hills, having decided to stay in the vicinity to await the promised March 5 arrival of Frank País's volunteers, Che's asthma returned with a vengeance, bringing on what Che later called "for me personally the most bitter days of the war."

Although this attack eventually abated, for the duration of the war, Che would periodically succumb to debilitating bouts of his chronic condition, leading sturdier comrades to marvel at his willpower as he struggled to keep up on their marathon marches. But many would also have to help Che, at times to physically carry him, when his asthma left him incapacitated. It was ironic that a severe asthmatic such as Che should have ended up in humid, subtropical Cuba, a country with a disproportionately high per capita asthma rate, possibly the highest of any country in the Western Hemisphere.

It is hard to escape the sense that Che's deeply felt desire to rid himself of his "I" and to become part of a group derived from the inherent isolation imposed by his asthma. Happily for him, he had found that fraternity he sought, and although he had not—and never would—overcome his affliction, he no longer had to endure it alone. Indeed, in the Sierra Maestra, there were times when he was completely helpless, and his dependency on the support of his comrades became quite literally a matter of life or death. And yet, in this communal life of guerrilla war, no one suffered alone; the interdependency wrought by the need to survive was mutual. One day, it was Che who needed help; it would be another man's turn the next. Quite possibly, it was this sense of sharing, more than any other factor, that gave rise to his intense personal reverence for the ethos of guerrilla life.

On February 25—"a day of water and bombs," as he termed it—Che and his comrades awoke to the sound of mortar blasts and machine-gun and rifle fire that gradually drew nearer to them. Suspecting that the army was combing the area, they moved camp after dark, but they were in bad shape: Their food was practically finished and they were surviving on chocolate and condensed milk. What's more, Che had felt the stirrings of a "dangerous asthma attack" for several days and it now struck him with full force, worsening to the point where sleep was impossible. Then, after a peasant collaborator fed them pork, which made most of them ill, Che was weakened still further by two days of vomiting. Following a rain-sodden march, Che's wheezing became constant. They were in a zone where the peasants wanted nothing to do with them, they were out of food, and their latest guide had abruptly disappeared. Fearing a new Eutimio-style *chivatazo,* Fidel ordered his men to withdraw into the hills, but by now Che was so weak, he could no longer walk. As the others waited, he injected one of the last two adrenaline ampules he had with him, giving him just enough strength to get back on his feet.

Reaching the crest of a hill, they spotted a column of enemy troops climbing up to occupy the ridge, and they broke into a run to get there first. When the first mortar shell exploded, the rebels realized the soldiers were onto them; as Che later acknowledged, he almost didn't make it. "I couldn't keep up the pace of the march, and I was constantly lagging behind. . . ." Fortunately, his faithful sidekick Luis Crespo was at his side, and helped Che by alternately carrying him and his backpack, and threatening to hit him with his rifle butt, calling him an "Argentine son of a whore."

They escaped the troops, but, hiking on, Che was drenched in another heavy rain and, barely able to breath, had to be carried the final part of their trek. They found sanctuary in a place appropriately called Purgatorio, where Fidel reached a decision. With Che clearly unable to continue farther without medicine, Fidel paid a peasant to make a quick trip to Manzanillo for asthma medicine and, after leaving Che with a *guajiro* escort, he and the others went on. The new plan was that as soon as Che was better, he should return to the Díaz farm in time to meet the new rebel volunteers, then lead them into the sierra and rejoin Fidel.

The man delegated to remain behind with Che was called *"el Maestro"* (the Teacher), a recent volunteer who claimed falsely to be a Moncada veteran, but whom they had accepted into their ranks anyway. As Che described him later, he was "a man of doubtful repute but great strength." After Fidel's departure, he and the Teacher concealed themselves in the forest to await the return of the peasant with the medicine. One night, unable to sleep, Che caught up on his diary. "It was one of those days that are imprinted on the memory as examples of discomfort, like a viscous thing. Sitting 100 meters from the house . . . I spent 12 hours, with my asthma rising and abating but without going away. Later I walked 10 steps, and [now] spend the whole night on an uncomfortable hillside with the asthma clinging to my throat, without being able to sleep until dawn and knowing that I must irremissibly wait until tomorrow at three, if the man goes through with his mission. At night, three earth tremors put a different note to the passage of the nocturnal hours full of gasps. During the day, the rattle of the machine guns and mortars in the same bit of bush where we spent our last day, showed that the troops must have some news of our appearance in the place, and maybe tomorrow they will comb the bush where we are now. The Teacher, my companion, spends the time very nervously, continually trying to hide himself deeper in the jungle."

After two days of "hope and fear," Che's courier arrived with the asthma medicine. "True, only one bottle," noted Che, "but he brought it, as well as some milk, chocolate, and some biscuits." But the medicine only partially relieved his symptoms; that night Che still couldn't walk. On March 3, Che made a supreme effort to get moving, wanting at all costs to be at the Díaz farm on the appointed date. But that day's results were frustrating in the extreme: He spent five hours struggling to climb a hill that normally should have taken one, and that night he wrote that it had been a "day marked by a spiritual victory and a corporal defeat."

Despite all his efforts, it took him a week to reach the Díaz farm— five days late. Che had little help from the Teacher and, at one point suspecting him of planning to desert, challenged him to do so if he wanted. The Teacher refused, and Che remarked: "His behavior isn't clear but *le tiré los cojones* [literally, 'I yanked his balls']." He received little help from the peasants either, finding a normally friendly peasant farmer so nervous upon seeing him that Che wrote witheringly: "His fear is such that it looks like it might break *shitometers*."

On March 10, with his asthma gradually improving, Che finally reached his destination only to discover that the new troops had not yet arrived. Epifanio Díaz had news for him, but it wasn't good. A few days earlier, after a new *chivatazo,* Fidel's column had been surprised by enemy troops at a place called Los Altos de Merino and split into two groups. No word had yet come of Fidel's fate.

V

In one of the many ironies that would mark the Cuban revolution, the most desperate days of the rebel band in the Sierra Maestra coincided with one of the most devastating blows to the Batista regime.

In late February, the news of Fidel's defiant interview with Herbert Matthews had hit Cuba like a bombshell, causing a political uproar and a media frenzy. As Che noted euphorically: "The interview of Matthews with Fidel has surpassed all expectations." Batista's defense minister swiftly denounced the interview as a hoax cooked up by Matthews and challenged him to produce a photograph of himself with Fidel, but the general's bluster was only one of a rapid-fire series of embarrassing blunders that came to haunt Batista. They began when he lifted press censorship on February 25, a day after the first of Matthews's three-part series was published in the *New York Times.*

Immediately translated and reprinted in newspapers, sparking comments and debate on the airwaves throughout Cuba, Matthews's interview not only proved Fidel was still alive and well, despite the government's claims to the contrary, but also gave Fidel a major international publicity debut through its publication in the most powerful American newspaper. Not least of all, the articles were favorable; the fifty-seven-year-old correspondent had obviously been won over by Fidel and sympathized with his cause.

"Fidel Castro, the rebel leader of Cuba's youth," wrote Matthews, "is alive and fighting hard and successfully in the rugged, almost impenetrable vastness of the Sierra Maestra, at the southern tip of the island. . . . [T]housands of men and women are heart and soul with Fidel Castro and the new deal for which they think he stands. . . . Hundreds of highly respected citizens are helping Señor Castro . . . [and] a fierce Government counterterrorism [policy] has aroused the people even more against General Batista. . . . From the look of things, General Batista cannot possibly hope to suppress the Castro revolt."

In his portrait of Fidel, Matthews evoked an admirable and virile image, and showed he had been taken in by Fidel's deceptions as to the real size of his force: "This was quite a man—a powerful six-footer, olive-skinned, full-faced, with a straggly beard. He was dressed in an olive-grey fatigue uniform and carried a rifle with a telescopic sight, of which he was very proud. It seems his men have something more than fifty of these and he said the soldiers feared them. 'We can pick them off at a thousand yards with these guns,' he said. . . . The personality of the man is overpowering. It was easy to see that his men adored him and also to see why he has caught the imagination of the youth of Cuba all over the island. Here was an educated, dedicated fanatic, a man of ideals, of courage and of remarkable qualities of leadership."

Defining the "Rebel Army's" political slant in almost the terms of an FDR liberal, Matthews wrote: "It is a revolutionary movement that calls itself socialistic. It is also nationalistic, which generally in Latin America means anti-Yankee. The program is vague and couched in generalities, but it amounts to a new deal for Cuba, radical, democratic and therefore anti-Communist. The real core of its strength is that it is fighting against the military dictatorship of President Batista. . . . [Castro] has strong ideas of liberty, democracy, social justice, the need to restore the Constitution, to hold elections."

The media battle continued to rage over the next few days, followed with relish by the rebels on their radio. It reached a head on February 28 when the *New York Times* published a photo of Matthews together with Fidel, dramatically crushing the regime's incautious claims that the journalist had dreamed up the entire encounter. Further boasts by the Oriente military commander that "the zone where the imaginary interview took place is physically impossible to enter" merely lent weight to Fidel's claims of being invincible and impossible to catch.

On the heels of Fidel's media splash came the bad news that Frank País and Armando Hart had been arrested. Then, on March 13, as Che awaited the new rebel volunteers at the Díaz farm, radio reports began broadcasting the first details of an attempt on Batista's life in Havana. Armed groups belonging to the Directorio Revolucíonario led by José Antonio Echeverría, together with some of Carlos Prio's *auténticos,* had launched an audacious daylight assault on the Presidential Palace and temporarily seized the twenty-four-hour Radio Reloj station in Havana. But the assaults failed, and in the shoot-outs that ensued, over forty people had died. The dead included Echeverría and more than thirty of his followers, five palace guards, and an American tourist who happened to be in the wrong place at the wrong time. Batista himself, who was ironically reading a book about Lincoln's assassination when the attack came, survived unscathed.

In his private notes Che routinely referred to the Directorio as *"el grupo terrorista,"* indicating his feelings toward this militant university-based group. Fidel and Echeverría may have signed a paper pact in Mexico City, but in reality the two leaders were bitter rivals. The failed assassination attempt left little doubt that Echeverría had hoped to deliver a fait accompli in Havana, displacing Fidel and his movement in the struggle for power. With the death of its leader, the Directorio had suffered a heavy blow, but, as events would prove, it was not yet eliminated from the scene; it would continue to pose challenges to Fidel's hegemony, right up to the end. For now, the July 26 cells in Havana came to the rescue, helping to tend the wounded and hide men in its own safe houses, and opportunistically taking possession of an unused Directorio weapons cache.

For Batista, the attempt on his life brought some short-term positive results, with the conservative business community rallying around him to condemn "the terrorist act." Just as important, he came out of the affair looking strong and in control, a *caudillo* who offered the last line of defense between traditional Cuban society and anarchy. In the succeeding days his police carried out numerous arrests and gunned down several fugitive survivors of the assault. Suspected of links to the attempt, Pelayo Cuervo Navarro, a prominent former senator and the acting Ortodoxo party leader, was murdered by police.

In spite of a few mishaps, fifty recruits from Santiago and a handful of new weapons arrived at the Díaz farm on March 17. After hiding the newcomers in the bush, Che's biggest problem was to find sufficient food to feed so many men, and then to move them through the hills to rejoin Fidel at their previously arranged rendezvous, a spot not far from Los Altos de Espinosa. As they marched out, Che observed that the new troops from Santiago possessed all of the same flaws as the *Granma* men had at the beginning—little sense of military discipline, and less physical endurance. They complained about the food they were given, and some could barely make it up the first hill they climbed.

Once they had scaled it, Che let them rest for an entire day to recuperate from what for them, as he ironically put it in his diary, "had been the greatest achievement of the revolution so far."

Sending for some *guajiros* to come and help, Che began slowly moving the new men into the sierra, and after eight days of slow and painful hiking they met up with Fidel and the others—who had, after all, survived their recent ambush. For the moment they were safe; Che had accomplished his mission, and the Ejército Rebelde was no longer only eighteen men, but now seventy.

16

Lean Cows and Horsemeat

I

After a weeklong climb into the Sierra Maestra with his army of blistered and complaining greenhorns, Che rejoined Fidel at the remote hillside community of La Derecha. Once again Che was scolded by Fidel, this time for not having sufficiently imposed his authority over Jorge Sotús, leader of the new volunteers. The newcomer's arrogance had irritated Che and brought angry protests from many of his men en route, but Che had limited himself to giving the man a sermon about the need for "discipline," evidently preferring to let Fidel deal with Sotús.

As Fidel saw it, Che had not "taken command," and his displeasure was reflected in his general staff reorganization, undertaken as soon as Che arrived. He handed out some new officers' promotions and divided the troops into three expanded platoons, led by Raúl, Juan Almeida, and Jorge Sotús, while Che was reconfirmed in his humble capacity as general staff doctor. In his diary, Che noted: "Raúl tried to argue that I be made political commissar as well, but Fidel was opposed."

This tidbit went unmentioned in Che's published accounts about the war, but it is noteworthy for revealing not only Raúl's regard for Che, but Fidel's political acumen. Batista was already accusing Fidel of being a Communist, a charge Fidel was vigorously denying, and to appoint an unabashed Marxist such as Che his political commissar would only play into Batista's hands and alienate many of the July 26 rank and file, who were overwhelmingly anti-Communist.

Fidel then held a conclave with his top eight men, including Che, to decide their immediate war plans. Che urged an immediate return to battle, arguing that they should engage the army to give the new men their first test of fire, but Fidel and most of the others were opposed, preferring to break them in gradually. "[It was] resolved," wrote Che in his diary, "that we would walk through the bush toward [Mt.] Turquino, trying to avoid battle."

Then, on March 25, a courier brought a message smuggled out of Frank País's Santiago jail cell, imparting some alarming intelligence about Crescencio Pérez. According to his sources, País wrote, Crescencio had struck a deal with Major Joaquín Casillas to betray their location to the army at a time when all the rebels were in one place together and could be wiped out. In his diary, Che seemed to give credence to País's information, for he already had reasons to doubt Crescencio's loyalties. The *guajiro* leader had been away for some time, entrusted with the mission of recruiting peasant fighters, and he had recently sent a message claiming to have enlisted 140 armed men. En route from the Díaz farm, however, Che had stopped in to see him and found only four men with him—the remnants of the convalescing fighters—and no new recruits. He had also found Crescencio confused and upset over Fidel's decree to burn sugarcane. This disagreement underscored the gulf of incomprehension existing between the rebel leadership and its foremost peasant ally over revolutionary strategy at a crucial moment. Whether this had escalated to treason, the leadership could not be sure, but they could not take any chances. Fidel summoned his small group of most trusted men and told them they would mobilize that same night.

But their very first trek as the revamped Rebel Army was more like a scene out of *Keystone Kops*. Climbing up the first large hill, one of their most exotic new volunteers—one of three teenaged American runaways from the U.S. naval base at Guantánamo Bay—fainted from exhaustion. On the descent, two men from the advance squad became lost, promptly followed by the entire second platoon. Then Sotús's platoon and the rearguard unit got lost as well. "Fidel threw a terrible tantrum," wrote Che. "But in the end, we all reached the agreed-upon house."

After a day spent resting and devouring yucca and plaintains raided from a farmer's field, they made what Che called "another pathetic ascent" up Los Altos de Espinosa, the hill where they had been ambushed. At the spot where Jorge Zenon Acosta was buried, they honored him in a brief ceremony. Caught in the bramble nearby, Che found the blanket he had lost, a reminder of his "speedy strategic retreat," and he vowed to himself that he would never again lose any equipment in that manner. A new man—"a mulatto named Paulino"—was named to the general staff to help carry Che's heavy load of medicine, for the strain of carrying it had already begun to give him asthma.

This was to be the pattern of the rebels' existence for the next few weeks. Fidel had intended to use their break from combat to build up reserves of food, arms, and ammunition, and to expand his peasant support network, but first they had to find enough food just to get them from one day to the next. As they moved around the sierra, he made deals with peasants to reserve a portion of their future harvests for his men's needs, but for now things remained extremely tight—and with the rebels numbering over eighty men, they could no longer arrive en masse at a peasant's home and expect to be fed. Meat had become a rarity, and their diet often consisted of plantains, yucca, and *malanga,* the starchy, purple colored tuber that is a staple of Cuba's peasants. For Fidel, who enjoyed a good meal, this period of *"vacas flacas,"* or "lean cows," was particularly disagreeable and sank him into a bad mood. On April 8, Che saw Fidel's temper flare after he left camp on a short mission and missed his evening meal. "[Fidel] returned late, pissed off because we had eaten rice and because things hadn't worked out the way he had hoped."

The lack of food soon led them to carry out more desperate actions as well, including some that bordered on simple banditry. One night men were sent to plunder a general store, while another group was dispatched to give a reputed *chivato* named Popa a scare and confiscate one of his cows. When the second squad returned, Che noted: "They struck a good blow and took a horse from Popa, but have come away with the impression that he isn't a *chivato* [after all]. He wasn't paid for the horse, but was promised he would be if he behaved himself." The horse went into the cooking pot, but at first the *guajiros,* outraged that a useful working animal had been killed for food, refused to eat it. Leftovers were then salted to be made into *tasajo,* a kind of jerky. Meanwhile, its slow preparation prompted Fidel to delay his plans to move camp. As Che observed dryly, "The consideration for the *tasajo* made Fidel change his mind."

Outside the Sierra Maestra, the political climate had become volatile. In the face of increasing violence, the political parties were demanding that Batista schedule new elections. A few politicians called for "talks with the insurrectionary groups," suggesting the rebels were being taken more seriously, but then Batista declared such talks were unnecessary because "no rebels even existed." The hollowness of his posturing became obvious shortly afterward, however, with the news that Major Barrera Pérez, the "pacifier" of Santiago's November uprising, was being promoted to colonel, and given fifteen hundred soldiers to clean up the Sierra Maestra.

As the political maneuvering continued in Cuba's cities, the rebels roamed the Sierra Maestra's hills. Fidel finally received a garbled message from Crescencio Pérez, in which the *guajiro* leader admitted that he didn't have the number of men he had previously claimed—nor were they armed—but that he had now gathered some volunteers together, and asked if Fidel could come and pick them up; he couldn't bring them himself, he said, because he had a "bad leg." Che's notes were cryptic: "Fidel answered him that he accepted all offers that were serious, and that he should come later with [the] armed men." Plainly, Fidel had decided to be cagey, avoiding any situation that might be a trap in case the *guajiro* was playing a double cross.

By necessity, the rebels began making a stronger effort to establish their own relationships with the sierra's inhabitants. Che even began holding open-air medical *consultorias*. "It was monotonous," Che recalled afterward. "I had few medicines to offer and the clinical cases in the sierra were all more or less the same: prematurely aged and toothless women, children with distended bellies, parasitism, rickets, general vitamin deficiency . . ." Blaming their symptoms on overwork and meager diets, Che wrote: "There, during those consultations, we began to feel in our flesh and blood the need for a definitive change in the life of the people. The idea of agrarian reform became clear, and oneness with the people ceased being theory and was converted into a fundamental part of our being." Perhaps without consciously realizing it, Che had evolved into the "revolutionary doctor" he had once dreamed of becoming. His ideas about revolutionary policies such as agrarian reform were already present, of course, but the experience of living among the campesinos helped crystallize those concepts in his own mind.

II

While the rebels adapted to life in the sierra, the movement leaders in the llano were working hard to build them a lifeline through the "Resistencia Cívica" underground support network. Frank País had recruited Raúl Chibás, president of the Ortodoxo party and brother of the late senator Eddy Chibás, to head its Havana branch. Following the cue of his son, Javier Pazos—who had helped arrange the Herbert Matthews interview—economist Felipe Pazos, the former Cuban National Bank president, joined in as well. In Santiago, the network was headed up by a well-known physician, Dr. Angel Santos Buch.

But coordination efforts had been dealt a blow with the recent captures of key members of the National Directorate. Under suspicion of links to the palace assault, Faustino Pérez and journalist Carlos Franqui, the July 26 Movement's underground propagandist, had both been arrested. They joined Armando Hart in Havana's El Príncipe prison, while Frank País remained in custody in Santiago. Even in prison, however, their covert activities persisted, and they maintained contact with one another, and with Fidel, via smuggled letters. Virtually alone among the movement leadership, Celia Sánchez remained at large, and she had become Fidel's principal contact with the outside world. He constantly sent her letters, alternately cajoling and irate, demanding more funds and supplies for his growing army.

By April 15 the rebels were back in Arroyo del Infierno, where Che had killed his first man. Rebel squads were sent out to find food and collect intelligence from the locals, and, from one, they learned of the nearby presence of a *chivato* named Filiberto Mora. While Guillermo García, one of the new squad leaders, went off to capture the suspect, Fidel fretted: The news of the *chivato* had coincided with the overflight of a government plane, and he was anxious to move camp again. As they prepared to head out, Guillermo García showed up with the alleged squealer. Following Fidel's method, García had impersonated an army officer to trick the suspect into coming with him, and the *chivato*'s dismay at reaching the rebel camp was instantaneous. "The man, Filiberto, had been deceived," wrote Che in his journal, "but the minute he saw Fidel he realized what was happening and started to apologize." Terrified, Filiberto confessed all his past crimes, including his role in guiding the troops to the Arroyo del Infierno ambush. Even more alarming, it emerged that one of Mora's cohorts had gone off to inform the army of the rebels' present location. Che's notes concluded: "The *chivato* was executed; ten minutes after giving him the shot in the head I declared him dead."

As they decamped, a runner arrived with a letter from Celia and five hundred dollars. She told Fidel that more money would be coming soon and, responding to his petition for more journalists, promised to find some and bring them into the sierra herself. A letter also came from Armando Hart, smuggled out from his jail cell. Che was displeased and suspicious with whatever Hart wrote, for he remarked in his journal: "In it he shows himself to be positively anticommunist and he even insinuates a certain kind of deal with the Yankee embassy."*

By the end of April, more peasants had joined up, and the rebels' supply system had begun to work more effectively. Men and mules now arrived daily with foodstuffs. Word arrived that two gringos, Robert Taber and Wendell Hoffman from the American CBS network, would be arriving to meet with Fidel, accompanied by Celia Sánchez and Haydée Santamaría. It certainly hadn't taken Celia long to find journalists who wanted to go to

---

*This particular letter has disappeared from the official record of Cuba's revolutionary history, as have any on-the-record admissions about the secret contacts made during the guerrilla campaign between the July 26 underground and the U.S. government, but such contacts evidently did take place. Previous accounts have speculated that the contacts began in the summer of 1957. Che's remark suggests that the U.S. government officials were making overtures to Fidel's underground comrades as early as March.

the sierra, for Herbert Matthews's *New York Times* articles on Fidel and the rebellion in Cuba had sparked widespread interest in the American press. Taber was to file for CBS radio, and he and his cameraman also planned to make a television documentary about the rebels. For their arrival, Fidel moved his *estado mayor* above the main rebel camp onto the summit of a hill, both for increased protection and, as Che noted, "to impress the journalists."

The journalists were suitably impressed and began working right away, spending their first day interviewing the three American runaways, who had become *causes célèbres* in the United States since joining up with the rebels. For his own interview, Fidel had another spectacular media coup in mind: He wanted to climb Cuba's highest peak, Mt. Turquino, and give a press conference at its summit. On April 28, almost everyone made the climb to the top—1,850 meters, (or about 7,300 feet) according to Fidel's handy altimeter. There, at Cuba's highest point, Fidel gave his filmed interview to Taber and Hoffman, and everyone dramatically fired off their weapons. Wheezing from asthma, Che was the last man up but felt immensely pleased with himself for having made it.

After descending from Mt. Turquino, Che observed with relief that his asthma had begun to clear, but, even so, Fidel assigned him to the rear guard to assist Victor Buehlman, one of the three American runaways, who was weak, complaining of stomachache, and unable to carry his backpack. Che helped him grudgingly and grumbled into his journal that he suspected the young American of suffering more from "homesickness" than anything else.

Their Turquino ascension coincided with the influx of a new type of volunteer the rebels had not seen before, youths romantically attracted to the cause due to the rebels' spreading publicity. One who showed up said he had been trying to track them for two months. Two other adolescents, from central Cuba's Camagüey province, Che dismissed initially as "a couple of adventurers," but the Ejercito Rebelde could not afford to be too choosy, and so accepted them. As Che noted later, one of these striplings, Roberto Rodríguez, eventually became one of the "most likeable and best-loved figures of our revolutionary war, 'Vaquerito' [Little Cowboy]," whose fearless exploits would earn him a hallowed place in Cuba's revolutionary pantheon of heroes.

In addition to his doctor's role, Che had begun exercising an important new responsibility. Despite Fidel's earlier refusal to name him political commissar, the job of interrogating newcomers and giving them some rudimentary political orientation had become Che's informal duty. When Vaquerito showed up, Che questioned him, but, as he later wrote: "Vaquerito did not have a political idea in his head, nor did he seem to be anything other than a happy, healthy boy, who saw all of this as a marvelous adventure. He came barefoot and Celia lent him an extra pair of shoes, which were made of leather and were the type worn in Mexico; this was the only pair that fit him, since his feet were so small. With the new shoes and a great palm leaf hat, Vaquerito looked like a Mexican cowboy, or vaquero, which is how he got his name."

Another new volunteer was a *guajiro* named Julio Guerrero, one of the late Eutimio Guerra's neighbors in the valley of El Mulato. Under suspicion of having rebel links, his home had been burned down, and he was now on the run from the army. Guerrero revealed that the army had offered him a bounty to kill Fidel, but a much more modest one than the reputed ten thousand dollars that Eutimio had been promised: a mere three hundred dollars, and a pregnant cow.

Just as the rebels could not afford to turn away prospective fighters whose political mettle was unproven, neither could it be overly selective about its civilian allies. When a July 26 man brought news that the weapons rescued from the Directorio's failed palace assault had been smuggled to Santiago, Fidel asked for an assortment of weapons from the cache and sent him back with a local guide who, as Che noted in his journal, knew the entire sierra well, "thanks to his profession of marijuana distributor."

To Che's disagreeable surprise, a well-known face also reappeared— El Gallego Morán. Still limping from his wounded leg, Morán was positively brimming over with excitement about a "supersecret plan" he wished to propose. Fidel listened to Morán's "plan," and afterward Che was chagrined to learn that Fidel had accepted the proposal, writing in his diary: "[Fidel told me] he would send El Gallego to Mexico to bring another expedition with the men who were left behind, then go to the United States to raise funds and carry out propaganda. Everything I said to him about how dangerous it was to send a man like El Gallego, a confessed deserter, with low morals, a charlatan, an intriguer and liar to the maximum . . . was useless. He argues that it is better to send El Gallego to do something, and not let him go to the U.S. feeling resentful." Still not convinced, Che added: "All the Gallego wants is to go to the U.S. and abandon this."

(In the end, his suspicions proved well founded because soon afterward Morán defected to Batista's military intelligence corps, actively collaborating in its pursuit of rebel suspects.)

As Morán went off to carry out his missions, word arrived that another American reporter was on his way to meet Fidel. Taber's cameraman had already left, with the film smuggled out separately, but Taber was staying on to do a story for *Life* magazine. When he heard about the new reporter, Taber asked Fidel to hold him up until he had finished, so he could be sure of having an exclusive. Fidel agreed and ordered the other reporter detained en route for several days.

Their *marijuanero* guide returned, bringing supplies, money, and the news that a rendezvous point for the arrival of the new weapons had been arranged in an area several days' march northeast of Mt. Turquino. As they prepared to move out, Che carried the message from Fidel to where most of the rebels were camped, but it was after dark and he became lost. He spent the next three days on his own, alternately hiding and wandering around the bush until he found his way back to his comrades. Reaching the rebels' rearguard camp, where the new journalist, a Hungarian-American free-lancer named Andrew St. George, was still being detained, his comrades welcomed him with spontaneous applause. Obviously touched, Che wrote: "The reception from everyone was affectionate," but he was disquieted to learn that on their own, these fighters had held a "people's trial." "They told me that they had liquidated a *chivato* named Napoles and freed two others who weren't so guilty. The men are doing whatever they please."

In Che's absence, Bob Taber had left, taking with him two of the three American boys, who had decided to return to their homes.* All together again, the rebels marched toward their weapons delivery-point near the sawmill community of Pino del Agua, but when no one came to the rendezvous, they withdrew uncertainly back into the hills, where they met up with Crescencio Pérez. The *guajiro* had finally arrived with his long-promised band of peasant volunteeers, a group of twenty-four poorly armed men. They had stumbled onto an army patrol, attacked it, and escaped, but a young rebel had been taken prisoner, shot, and bayoneted to death, his body dumped in the road. Seeking vengeance, most of the rebels, including Che, demanded the execution of an army corporal they had just taken prisoner, but Fidel, still seeking to win over members of the armed forces, insisted on releasing him unharmed. (Any lingering doubts over Crescencio's loyalties either had been forgotten or were ironed out in secrecy, for Che never mentioned them again in his diary, nor has the episode in which he was under suspicion ever been referred to in other published accounts of the war.)

As the rebels awaited word about the new time and place for the weapons drop, the radio carried news that their cause had won an important symbolic victory. The Santiago trial of a large number of their July 26 comrades, including survivors from the *Granma,* had ended. As expected, they were sentenced to prison terms, but over the dissenting votes of the prosecutor and the tribunal president, Manuel Urrutia, who had bravely declared

---

*The third youth, Charles Ryan, stayed on for a few months more until, weary of guerrilla life, he too decided to leave.

that because of the "abnormal situation" in the country, the defendants were within their constitutional rights to take up arms. An added bonus was the release of Frank País from custody, indicating that the authorities were still unaware of his true status in the rebel movement. These positive developments were followed by a quick visit of two July 26 men, who came to arrange the new weapons-drop and revealed that they now had even more arms to deliver—"a total of about fifty irons," Che noted gleefully.

But these positive developments were not enough to cheer up Fidel, who had been in a foul mood ever since the failed weapons delivery. He had pointedly ignored the new journalist, Andrew St. George, who impatiently challenged Che to find out if Fidel was intending to give him an interview or not. After spending two weeks already with the rebels, he was anxious to complete his assignment. He was planning a radio interview and had already submitted a questionnaire that Che had translated into Spanish. Since no one present spoke English, and both he and St. George spoke French, Che had become his escort and interpreter, but Che was finding his role as intermediary with Fidel increasingly embarrassing. "I invented any number of things to excuse [Fidel]," he confided in his journal, "but the truth is that his behavior is really rude; during the photo session he didn't move from his hammock, where he lay reading *Bohemia* with an air of offended majesty, and finally he threw out all the members of the general staff. The radio interview is translated and all that is needed is the taping session. [But] during the night, Fidel's bad humor continued, he didn't want to do the taping, leaving it for the next day, and he refused to eat with us, alleging that the food was bad."

Before the interview could take place the next day, word came of an enemy mobilization, and the rebels had to move camp quickly, marching out under a heavy rain. St. George was furious, wrote Che: "The man got into a foul temper and bitterly complained to me about the falsehoods used as reasons to postpone the interview; I didn't know how to excuse myself." Reaching an arroyo where they camped for the night, Fidel postponed the interview once again on the grounds that the stream made "too much noise."

That same night the rebels faced a mass defection that began when one of the youngest recruits, a boy of fifteen, asked permission to leave on health grounds. Immediately, another man asked to go with him; then a sixteen-year-old joined in, and finally another man, claiming "weakness." According to Che's journal, Fidel ordered the older men in the group detained but let the youths go, out of "consideration for their ages." Noting the need for the detentions, Che observed that seven previously cashiered rebels had been captured, they told everything they knew, and "in this case the situation is particularly dangerous because the troops [would] know where the arms will arrive."

For St. George, matters finally improved when Fidel deigned to grant him the long-awaited interview. On May 18, however, the radio reported that the next day Taber's film, *The Story of Cuba's Jungle Fighters,* was to be broadcast throughout the United States, as was his radio interview with Fidel. Evidently upset by this news, St. George left without saying good-bye.

The next day, word came that the weapons had arrived at their agreed point of contact, and twenty-five men were sent to collect them. They returned the next morning at dawn carrying what Che called their "precious cargo": three machine-gun tripods, three Madsen machine guns, nine M-1 carbines, ten Johnson repeaters, and six thousand bullets. "For us it was the most marvelous spectacle in the world," Che wrote afterward. "The instruments of death were on exhibit before the covetous eyes of all the combatants."

Including his own. When Fidel distributed the new guns, Che was ecstatic to learn that one of the Madsens would go to the *estado mayor,* and he was to be the man in charge of it. "In this way," he wrote later, "I made my debut as a full-time combatant, for until then I had been a part-time combatant and my main responsibility had been as the troop's doctor. I had entered a new stage."

III

With their new weapons, the rebels were ready to attack. The "new" troops were no longer new—after two months of steady hiking and foraging in the Sierra Maestra, they were tougher and leaner—but they were still not combat-tested, and it was time for their baptism of fire.

The area they were in, Pino del Agua, was a timber extraction zone, dotted with sawmills and crisscrossed by roads frequently patrolled by the army. Che was eager to ambush some army troop trucks, but Fidel claimed he had a better plan: to attack the coastal army garrison at El Uvero. It was farther to the east than they had ever operated, and, with sixty soldiers, would be the biggest target they had yet attacked; success would have a tremendous moral and political impact.

To carry out his plan, Fidel was able to count on the help of an old childhood friend, Enrique López, who worked near El Uvero as the manager of a sawmill owned by the Lebanese-Cuban Babún brothers. The Babúns themselves—cement manufacturers, shipbuilders, and landowners with extensive lumber interests in Oriente—had already lent their secret cooperation to the rebels, helping to transport their latest cache of weapons on one of their company's boats from Santiago, and then allowing their land to be used as the weapons drop. Enrique López, meanwhile, had already begun buying food and other supplies for the rebels, disguised within the purchases he made for his own employees.

As they got ready to mobilize, Fidel made some adjustments in the troops. Che was assigned a new squad of four youths to help carry and operate his Madsen machine gun. They were two brothers, Pepe and Pestan Beatón, another named Oñate—soon changed to "Cantinflas," after the Mexican comic actor—and a new fifteen-year-old boy named Joel Iglesias. Like El Vaquerito, Joel would go on to become one of Che's devoted tag alongs.*

Finally, on the eve of battle, Fidel decided to "clean the air" by giving anyone who wanted to leave their final opportunity to do so. A large number of men raised their hands. "After Fidel treated them harshly, some of them tried to change their minds but they were not permitted to," Che wrote. "In the end, a total of nine left leaving the total number of men at 127; almost all are now armed."

The rebels moved off, heading deeper into the hills. They were camped in the mountains when they heard a startling report on the radio: An armed rebel expeditionary force had landed on the northern Oriente coast at Mayarí and run into an army patrol; of the twenty-seven on board, five had reportedly been captured. The Fidelistas didn't know it yet, but this was the *Corynthia,* a boat that had left Miami days before under the command of an *auténtico* man and U.S. army veteran named Calixto Sánchez. The expedition, made up of *auténticos* and some Directorio men, was armed and paid for by Carlos Prío, the ever-scheming former president, evidently anxious to field a force of his own to compete with Fidel's Ejercito Rebelde. (The initial reports were misleading: Twenty-three of the *Corynthia*'s men, including Sánchez, were captured, and then executed after a few days. A few months later, one of the three survivors reached the sierra and joined Fidel's forces.)

El Uvero sawmill manager Enrique López, meanwhile, had sent word that three *guardias* in civilian clothes were sniffing around his installation, and Fidel ordered some men to go and capture them. They returned with two of the spies, one having already fled by the time they got there. Che observed in his journal that the two, a black man and a white man—who was "crying his heart out"—confessed to being spies for Major Joaquín Casillas, adding: "They inspired not pity, but repugnance for their cowardice."

---

*After the war, the Beatón brothers became outlaws, murdering a revolutionary commander and taking up arms against the revolution before they were caught and executed. Joel Iglesias became an army commander and leader of the Juventud Rebelde (Rebel Youth) organization. After the war, Cantinflas remained in the army with the rank of lieutenant.

For now, the two were kept as prisoners, but the next morning Fidel gathered his officers together and ordered them to have all their men and arms ready, for there would be combat within forty-eight hours. As the last order of business, the two army spies were shot. "The pit was dug for the two *chivato* guards and the marching orders were given," noted Che in his diary. "The rear guard executed them."

They marched all night to reach El Uvero. Near the sawmill, they met up with Gilberto Cardero, another friendly Babún Company employee. Cardero had been sent ahead to warn the sawmill administrator to evacuate his wife and children, but the family had refused to leave so as not to bring suspicion upon themselves later. Fidel said they would take precautions to avoid harming the civilians, but the attack would take place anyway, at dawn.

Daybreak on the morning of May 28 revealed a "disagreeable reality," for the rebels couldn't see the garrison clearly from their positions occupied during the night. While Che himself had a clear view, it was about five hundred meters (1,625 feet) from the target. It was too late for changes, however, and the attack began.

"As soon as the firing order was given, with the shot from Fidel, the machine guns began to rattle. The garrison returned fire with a great deal of effectiveness, as I realized later. Almeida's people advanced in the open impelled by his fearless example. I could see Camilo advancing with his cap adorned with the July 26 armband. I advanced along the left with two helpers carrying clips and Beatón with the short machine gun."

Che's group was joined by several more men. They were within sixty meters (195 feet) of the enemy position now and continued to advance behind tree cover. Reaching open ground, they began to crawl, but a man at Che's side, Mario Leal, was shot. After giving Leal mouth-to-mouth resuscitation, Che covered the wound with the only bandage he could find, a piece of paper, then left him in the care of young Joel as he went back to his Madsen, firing at the garrison. Moments later another man, Manuel Acuña, fell wounded, hit in the right hand and arm. Then, just as the rebels were mustering their courage for a frontal assault, the garrison surrendered.

The Fidelistas had their victory, but it came at a high cost. In all, they had lost six men, among them one of their original *guajiro* guides, Eligio Mendoza. He had flung himself into battle with abandon, claiming he had a "saint" who protected him, but within minutes he had been shot down. Also dead was Julito Díaz, a *Granma* veteran, hit in the head at Fidel's side soon after the fighting began. Mario Leal, shot in the head, and another man, Silleros, with a lung wound, were in critical condition. Seven others were wounded as well, including Juan Almeida, hit in the right shoulder and leg.

In turn, they had killed fourteen soldiers, wounded nineteen more, and taken fourteen prisoners; only six had escaped. Remarkably, given the intense gunfire, none of the civilians in the area, including the administrator's family, had been casualties.

Before they withdrew, the many wounded had to be tended to—soldiers as well as rebels—and Che felt overwhelmed by the task at hand. "My knowledge of medicine had never been very extensive; the number of wounded was enormous and my vocation at the moment was not centered on health care." He asked the garrison doctor for help, but despite his advanced age the latter claimed he had little experience. "Once more I had to change from soldier to doctor, which in fact involved little more than washing my hands." Che saw to as many men as he could.

"My return to the medical profession had a few poignant moments," he recalled in a published account. "My first patient was Comrade Silleros. . . . His condition was critical, and I was able only to give him a sedative and bind his chest tightly so he could breathe more easily. We tried to save him in the only way possible at that time. We took the fourteen prisoners with us and left our two [most] wounded men, Leal and Silleros, with the enemy, having received the doctor's word of honor that they would be cared for. When I told this to Silleros, mouthing the usual words of comfort, he answered me with a sad smile that said more than any words could have, expressing his conviction that it was all over for him."

(In fact, the Cuban army treated the two wounded rebels with decency, but Silleros died before he reached a hospital. Mario Leal miraculously survived his head wound and spent the rest of the war in the Isle of Pines prison.)

Using the Babúns' trucks, the rebels withdrew from El Uvero, carrying their dead and lesser-wounded men and as much equipment as they could plunder from the garrison. Che tried to take as many medical supplies as he could find and was the last to leave. That evening he treated the wounded and was present for the burial of his six dead comrades at a bend in the road. Realizing the army would soon be coming after them, they agreed that Che would stay behind with the wounded men, while the main column made its escape. Fidel's friend Enrique López would be Che's liaison, helping him with guides and transportation, a hiding place, and contacts for a regular supply of medicine to treat the men.

The next morning, the army reconnaissance planes began circling overhead, and the rebels knew it was time to leave. Staying behind with Che were the seven wounded men, a guide, and Che's two faithful assistants, Joel and Cantinflas. Also remaining behind to help his wounded uncle, Manuel Acuña, was Juan Vitalio "Vilo" Acuña, another of the sierra war veterans whose fate would forever be linked to Che's own. (Before the end of the war, Vilo Acuña would attain the rank of *comandante* in the rebel army, and in 1967, as "Joaquín," be one of Che's guerrillas in Bolivia.)

After the war, Che credited the bloody action at El Uvero as a turning point for the rebel army. "If one considers that we had about 80 men and they had 53, for a total of 133 men, of whom 38—that is to say more than a quarter—were put out of action in a little over two and a half hours of fighting, one can see what kind of battle it was. It was an assault by men who had advanced bare-chested against an enemy protected by very poor defenses. Great courage was shown on both sides. For us this was the victory that marked our coming of age. From this battle on, our morale grew tremendously; our decisiveness and our hopes for triumph increased also."

El Uvero had indeed caught the Batista regime off guard, for during the long period of inactivity by Fidel's rebels, the dictator and his officers had returned to their trumpetings of victory. Colonel Barrera Pérez, who in March had taken over antiguerrilla operations in the sierra, had stayed only a short while. After launching a "psy-ops" campaign to win over the sierra peasants with free food and medical services, he had returned to Havana claiming to have isolated the rebels from their civilian pool of support. The army's embarrassing defeat at Uvero showed the failure of Barrera Pérez's mission, however, and he was now ordered back into the field.

The colonel set up a new command center at the Estrada Palma sugar mill, just north of the sierra foothills, but his "hearts and minds" campaign was shelved in favor of a tough new antiguerrilla strategy. His boss, Oriente commander Díaz Tamayo, was replaced by a new officer, Pedro Rodríguez Ávila, with orders from Batista's armed forces chief of staff, General Francisco Tabernilla, to crush the rebels by any means necessary. The new policy called for the forced evacuation of civilians from rebel areas, to create free-fire zones where the air force could conduct a campaign of massive aerial bombardment. Most significantly, the action at El Uvero showed the army that it couldn't defend its small garrisons located in remote areas, and the army soon began abandoning them, leaving the territory open to the rebels.

After Fidel's departure, Che confronted the nightmare prospect of moving his wounded charges to safety in the face of an imminent army incursion. He was additionally burdened with the weapons captured from the garrison, too many for the escaping fighters to carry. For *his* escape, he was dependent on Enrique López; when López didn't show up with a promised truck, Che had no choice but to conceal most of the arms temporarily and move out on foot. Most of the men were able to walk, but one man was lung-shot, and the three bullet wounds of another were infected; making improvised stretchers from hammocks to carry them, the band moved slowly into the forest.

Over the coming days, as they moved from one farm to another in search of food, rest, and sanctuary, Che had to make all major decisions. With his captain's rank, Juan Almeida was theoretically Che's senior in the field, but he was in no shape to take charge. One of Che's biggest headaches was in finding men to carry the wounded. On their third day out, they came across some disarmed soldiers wandering through the bush—the same prisoners from Uvero whom Fidel had set free. After letting them go on their way, Che gleefully congratulated himself in his diary for giving the soldiers the false impression that the rebels "controlled" the countryside, but he also worried they would soon relay word of his group's presence in the area.

On the trek, Che was introduced to a man who would soon prove extremely helpful. He was David Gómez, the *mayoral* on the Peladero estate belonging to a Havana lawyer. Che's first impression was not good, but it was tempered by his group's desperate situation. "D. is an individual of the old *auténtico* type, Catholic and racist, with a servile loyalty toward the *patron* who only believes in electoral ends and in saving for his master all his ill-gotten lands in this region; I also suspect him of having participated in the dispossession of the peasants. But, leaving that aside, he is a good informant and he is ready to help."

In fact, Gómez was already helping: The cows they had been eating were his bosses' property, killed with his connivance. And Gómez offered to do more. As an initial test, Che gave Gómez a list of purchases to make in Santiago and, craving information from the outside world, included a special request for the latest editions of *Bohemia*. Che's relationship with the overseer showed that he was becoming more like his jefe. Fidel had always understood that one of the keys to success in a struggle for power was to make short-term, tactical alliances, even with one's ideological foes. Now, as the leader of a group of hunted men in alien territory, Che found he had needs that only Gómez could satisfy, and he was able to swallow his distaste and be pragmatic.

Indeed, his time in Cuba had already shown Che that the revolution was not going to be won by an idealized fraternity of high-minded souls. Among the rebel ranks were any number of scoundrels: former rustlers, fugitive murderers, juvenile delinquents, and marijuana traffickers. The corrupt Carlos Prío himself had helped pay for the *Granma,* and the battle of El Uvero had been a success in large measure thanks to the aid of the wealthy and duplicitous Babún brothers who, though friends of Batista, probably hoped to protect their interests in Oriente by helping the rebels.

When David Gómez arrived back from Santiago with the promised supplies, a more trusting Che sent him on a new mission, this time with messages for the National Directorate. By now, three weeks after the El

Uvero battle, most of the men had recovered from their wounds, and all of them could walk. Thirteen new volunteers had shown up, although only one with a weapon—a .22-caliber automatic pistol. On June 21, Che took stock of his growing force. "The army ascends to: 5 recovered wounded, 5 healthies who accompany the wounded, 10 men from Bayamo, 2 more just joined up and 4 men of the area, total 26 but deficient in armaments."

A few days later, after beginning their slow march into the mountains, Che observed that his army now consisted of "36 terrible soldiers." The next day, he gave all those who wanted to leave their chance. Three took up his offer, including one who had joined the previous day. In the succeeding days, more men joined and others left, either deserting or sent packing by Che. But as "terrible" as most of them were, they were the core of a new guerrilla force growing spontaneously under his direction. By the end of June, Che's small army was functioning autonomously, with its own system of couriers, informants, suppliers, and scouts.

July 1 was a bad day for Che personally—he awoke with asthma and spent the day lying in his hammock—but an interesting one in terms of news, for the radio reported news of rebel actions taking place all over Cuba. "In Camagüey they are patrolling in the streets," Che noted in his diary. "In Guantánamo, some tobacco deposits were burned, and they tried burning the sugar warehouses of a strong American company. In Santiago itself they killed two soldiers and wounded a corporal. Our casualties were 4 men, among them, a brother of Frank País called Josué."

July 2 marked the seven-month anniversary of the *Granma* landing, but Che spent it leading his weary men up a 1,550-meter mountain called La Botella. During the day two men deserted, and by the time they pitched camp that evening, three more asked permission to leave. Their case provided Che with a funny anecdote to relate later. "Chicho [was the] spokesman for a small group, who swore they would all follow us until death, in a tone of extraordinary conviction and determination. Imagine our surprise when . . . camping in a small valley for the night, this same group expressed to us its desire to leave the guerrillas. We agreed to this, and jokingly baptized the place 'the Valley of Death,' for Chicho's tremendous determination had lasted only up to that point."

To forestall any more desertions, Che again gave anyone who wanted to leave another chance to do so, telling them it was "their last opportunity." Two men accepted the offer, but by that afternoon three new men had arrived, each with a weapon. Two were ex-army sergeants from Havana, and Che didn't trust them. "According to them they are instructors," he wrote in his diary that night, "but to me they're a couple of shiteaters who are trying to accommodate themselves." Despite his suspicions, he let them stay.

The next adherent to Che's band was none other than Fidel's Babún Company friend, Enrique López, who had decided to join the armed struggle himself. Another man showed up telling Che he had a "fantastic plan" to attack a guard post where he said there were forty soldiers without a commanding officer. He also asked for two men to go and "skin a *chivato*." Che turned him down: "I told him to stop fucking around . . . to kill the *chivato* with his own people and then send them here."

In order to meet up with Fidel, who had returned to their old haunts around Palma Mocha and El Infierno, Che was moving his force westward across the sierra toward Mt. Turquino. Che's runners brought word of a large troop presence in the direction they were heading and of heavy combat near the army base at Estrada Palma, and a report that Raúl Castro had been wounded—a rumor that later proved unfounded—but Che decided to forge on anyway, taking a tougher route over the mountains to avoid the enemy.

On July 12 Che's guide, Sinecio Torres, and another rebel, René Cuervo, deserted with their weapons. After a fruitless chase, Che learned new details about the two: Both, it was now revealed, were *bandoleros,* fugitive outlaws, and they had probably gone off to raid the marijuana plantation owned by two other newcomers to his force, Israel Pardo and Teodoro Bandera. Suspecting the two *marijuaneros* would desert next to defend their interests, Che decided to get rid of them by ordering them to go in pursuit of the deserters; he didn't expect them back. The next day brought a new problem, when Che learned of a mass-desertion plot being hatched among a small group of men. Their alleged plan was to escape with their weapons, rob and kill a *chivato* they knew, then form an outlaw gang to carry out more assaults and robberies. Che spoke with several of the men implicated in the plot, each of whom denied their roles and blamed a man called "El Mexicano" instead. When El Mexicano realized his plan had been discovered, he came voluntarily before Che to profess his innocence. Che found his explanations wanting, but wrote: "We let it pass as if it were the truth so as to avoid more complications."*

During their trek, Che also made his debut as a dentist. Without anesthesia to give his hapless patients, he used what he called "psychological

*Israel Pardo and Teodoro Bandera returned without finding René Cuervo or Sinecio Torres, but Cuervo was later caught and executed by a revolutionary firing squad. Sinecio Torres's fate is unknown. Bandera later died in battle. Pardo survived and remained in the revolutionary army after the war, attaining the rank of captain. El Mexicano rose to captain's rank in the rebel army, but when one of the men who had informed on him was killed during a battle, there was suspicion that El Mexicano may have murdered him. As of 1962, according to Che, he was living in Miami, "a traitor to the Revolution."

anesthesia," which consisted of cursing at his patients if they complained too much. He proved successful with Israel Pardo, but when it came to Joel Iglesias, he found it impossible, writing later that he would have needed a stick of dynamite to extract the rotten molar. The stubborn tooth remained in Joel's mouth, broken in several places, until the end of the war, and Joel claimed the experience gave him a lifelong terror of dentists. Although Che suffered from toothache himself during this trip, he wisely left his own teeth alone.

By July 16, they were back in familiar terrain on the western flanks of Mt. Turquino, and reached Fidel's camp the next day. Che immediately saw that the rebel army had matured in the past month and a half, now numbering some two hundred men who seemed well disciplined and confident. There were new weapons as well. Most important of all, since repelling a recent army incursion by tenacious Captain Ángel Sánchez Mosquera—one of several officers leading troops against them—the rebels now possessed their own "liberated territory."

But Che's reunion was dampened by his discovery that Fidel had just signed a pact with two representatives of the bourgeois political opposition— Raúl Chibás and Felipe Pazos—both of whom were staying in Fidel's camp at that moment. Their pact, entitled "The Manifesto of the Sierra Maestra," was dated July 12 and had already been sent out for publication in *Bohemia*. The manifesto came at an opportune time, as months of political wrangling between Batista and his mainstream opposition climaxed with the congressional passage of a reform bill scheduling presidential elections for June 1, 1958. Despite Batista's avowal not to stand as a candidate himself, widespread skepticism persisted as to his true intentions; most observers suspected him of intending to manipulate the elections on his behalf or that of a handpicked successor. The election initiative was repudiated by Carlos Prío's Auténtico party and Chibás's Ortodoxo party, but breakaway factions from both formed a coalition with a grouping of smaller parties and announced their intention to run.

The "Sierra Pact" represented Fidel's own cleverly timed repudiation of Batista's schemes. By allying himself with Chibás and Pazos, two respected Ortodoxos, Fidel hoped to obtain a moral high ground and secure a broader base of support among Cuban moderates with nowhere else to turn. Writing in his diary on July 17, Che was circumspect, but it clearly didn't please him to find Pazos and Chibás wielding influence over Fidel. As he saw it, the manifesto bore the indelible imprint of these "middle-of-the-road" politicians, precisely the species Che mistrusted and despised most. "Fidel was telling me projects and realities; a text has already been sent out that calls for Batista's immediate resignation, rejects the Military Junta, and proposes a member of the civic institutions as a candidate for the transition, which should last no more than one year, and elections [should be] called within that time. It also includes a miminal program in which the foundations of the Agrarian Reform are outlined." Then he added: "Fidel didn't say so but it seems to me that Pazos and Chibás have polished his declarations a great deal."

The truth, of course, was more complex. Fidel had *sought* the support of Chibás and Pazos, and if he signed a manifesto less radical than his true aspirations, it could only *help* him in the short term. This pact, like so many others Fidel was to sign in his life, was merely one more tactical alliance— to be broken at the first opportunity. As Che admitted later: "We were not satisfied with the agreement, but it was necessary; at the time it was progressive. It could not last beyond the moment when it would represent a brake on the revolution's development. . . . We knew that this was a minimum program, a program that limited our efforts, but we also had to recognize that it was impossible to impose our will from the Sierra Maestra."

If he thought any more about the Sierra Pact at the time, Che didn't make note of it in his diary. Instead, his chief concern was his new command, which Fidel had bestowed upon him on July 17, the same day Che arrived in camp. Che recorded the news in his diary with no trace of the excitement he surely felt. "[Fidel] told me that poor Universo [Sánchez] had been removed from his coveted position. . . .* There are [also] new promotions such as Ramirito [Valdés] to Captain, Ciro [Redondo] to Lieutenant, *el Guajiro* [Luis Crespo] to Universo's post, Almeida to Second Commander and myself to Captain and head of a column that should hunt down Sánchez Mosquera in Palma Mocha."

For troops, Che was to have a total of seventy-five men. In addition to the men he had arrived with, he was to take command of the platoons led by *Granma* comrades Ramiro Valdés and Ciro Redondo, and another led by Lalo Sardiñas, a sierra merchant who had recently joined up after killing a stranger at his house. Lalo Sardiñas was also to be his deputy.

Che's new position represented Fidel's ultimate seal of approval. Che had fought hard to obtain recognition for his abilities, and the process had matured him. He had been given a difficult mission to accomplish on his own—bringing the wounded men to safety—and he had succeeded. He had fulfilled his doctor's duties by returning the men to health while managing

---

*Universo Sánchez had been Fidel's bodyguard since Mexico, but in his last handout of promotions, in March, Fidel had promoted his companion to the general staff as the troop squadron commander, and named one of Crescencio Pérez's *guajiros*—the former butcher Manuel Fajardo—as his new bodyguard.

to avoid battle and the risk of new casualties, had added to the strength of the rebel army by building up a new column, and had made invaluable contacts among the civilian population at the same time. He had shown himself to be a strict taskmaster, harsh with slackers and cheats, and to be scrupulously honest himself. Above all, Che had shown he could be a leader of men, and now he had been rewarded with his first military command.*

Che went to work immediately, leaving the next morning with his men to take up an ambush position on the Maestra, a hill between two rivers, the Palma Mocha and La Plata. Che's position happened to be the same place where the executed *chivato* Filiberto Mora was buried, and he named it after him: "the summit of Filiberto." The next three days were spent preparing ambushes and sending scouts out to look for soldiers. On the morning of July 22, a rebel accidentally fired his gun and was brought before Fidel, who was in a newly hardened, unforgiving mood, and he summarily ordered the man to be shot. "Lalo, Crescencio and I had to intercede with him to reduce the sanction," wrote Che, "because the unfortunate didn't deserve such a punishment as drastic as that."

Later that morning, all the rebel officers signed a letter to Frank País being sent by Fidel on behalf of the rebels, expressing their condolences for the recent death of his brother. Without any advance notice, Fidel chose the same moment to give Che an unexpected *new* promotion. Che later explained that when his turn came to sign the letter, Fidel told him to put down *"comandante"* as his rank. "Thus, in a most informal manner, almost in passing, I was promoted to commander of the second column of the guerrilla army, which would later become known as Column No. 4."**

---

*Instituting a hierarchy, Che dubbed the novices in his column "Los Descamisados"—"The Shirtless Ones," Peron's famous eulogism for his working-class supporters. Everyone began as a lowly *descamisado*, doing "grunt work" before earning recognition as a *combatiente*.

**Che's command was called "the Fourth Column" in order to disinform the enemy as to it's real troop strength.

Cuban historians often cite Che's promotion as evidence of the high regard Fidel felt for him, pointing out that he had been favored over Fidel's brother, without offering any explanation as to why Raúl hadn't earned the honor. But Che's laconic diary entry for that fateful day may hold part of the answer. "There were several promotions. I [now] had the rank of *comandante*. The *guajiro* Luis [Crespo] was given the rank of lieutenant, Ciro [Redondo] captain and Raúl Castro, who had been stripped of rank for an insubordination of his entire platoon, was named lieutenant."

Exactly *what* transpired between Raúl and his men was left out of Che's later public writings and all official histories of the Cuban revolution. Today, Cuba's historians would have a hard time dredging up such details of the past: Raúl Castro is the powerful head of Cuba's Revolutionary Armed Forces and the designated heir to his incumbent brother.

With his promotion, Che was also given the adornments of his new office. "My insignia, a small star, was given to me by Celia. The award was accompanied by a gift: one of the wristwatches ordered from Manzanillo." It was a great honor. *Comandante,* equivalent to major, was the highest rank in the rebel army, one so far possessed only by Fidel, and the next man to receive it had not been a Cuban but Che, *"El Argentino."*

"There is a bit of vanity hiding somewhere within every one of us," wrote Che afterward. "It made me feel like the proudest man on earth that day." In fact, he remained proud of the title, and from that moment on, to all but his closest friends, he was Comandante Che Guevara.

17

Enemies of All Kinds

I

With his new command came new responsibilities, and Che was itching to show he was up to the task. His orders were to pursue Sánchez Mosquera, but no sooner had his column departed from Fidel's than he found out that his prey had already left the mountains.

As he pondered his options, Che set about imposing his fiat over his unruly and heterogeneous fighters, many of whom were still *"descamisados."* Almost immediately, he was plagued by new desertions, and he responded with new severity. Sending fighters to track down one fugitive, he gave them orders to "kill him if they found him." At the same time, his wariness about guerrilla newcomers increased after receiving a message from his overseer ally David Gómez warning of army plans to infiltrate *chivato* assassins among the rebels.

To debut his new command, Che devised a plan to strike at the army on the other side of Mt. Turquino to distract attention from Fidel's column, and he and his men started moving in that direction. On July 28, Baldo, one of the two men in the execution squad Che had sent after the deserter, returned on his own, telling a story that Che recorded as "simple and pathetic."

According to Baldo, his companion, Ibrahim, had tried to desert, and Baldo had "killed him with three shots. The body has remained unburied on la Maestra." Che decided to use Ibrahim's fate as a lesson for his men, especially for some new volunteers whose arrival had coincided with the incident. As he later recounted, "I gathered the troop together on the hill facing the spot where this grim event had taken place. I explained to our guerrillas what they were going to see and what it meant. I explained once again why desertion was punishable by death and why anyone who betrayed the revolution must be condemned. We passed silently, in single file, before the body of the man who had tried to abandon his post. Many of the men had never seen death before and were perhaps moved more by personal feelings for the dead man and by political weakness natural at that period than by any disloyalty to the revolution. These were difficult times, and we used this man as an example."

But in his diary, Che told of his own misgivings: "I am not very convinced of the legality of the death, although I used it as an example. . . . The body was on its stomach, showing at a glance that it had a bullet hole in the left lung and had its hands together and the fingers folded as if they were tied."

They marched on. Che now decided to hit the army garrison of Bueycito, a day's march away. The attack took place on the night of July 31, but, as he admitted afterward, it did not go according to his "simple but pretentious" plan. When some of his units didn't show up on time, Che began the attack on his own, walking straight up to the barracks and coming face-to-face with the sentry. Che aimed his Thompson submachine gun and shouted "Halt!" but the sentry moved; Che decided not to wait any longer and pulled his trigger, aiming at the soldier's chest. Nothing happened. The young rebel who was with Che then tried to shoot the sentry, but his rifle didn't fire, either. At that point, Che's survival instincts took over, and he ran away under a hail of bullets from the sentry's own rifle. "I ran with a speed I have never matched since," he wrote afterward, "and in full flight turned the corner and landed in the cross street."

The sentry's shots brought down a hail of bullets from the hidden rebels, but Che saw little more of the action; by the time he repaired his tommy gun, the garrison had surrendered. Ramiro's men had broken in from the rear and taken the twelve soldiers inside prisoner. Six soldiers were wounded, two fatally, while the rebels had lost one man. After looting the garrison, they set it afire and left Bueycito in trucks, taking as prisoners the sergeant in charge of the post and a *chivato* named Orán.

Their escape was laced with cold beer—provided gratis by a *bodeguero* along the way—and an explosion, as they stopped to dynamite a small wooden bridge. They entered the village of Las Minas to the "vivas" of the civilians, and here Che indulged in some street theater with an Arab merchant. "A Moor *who is one of ours* improvised a speech asking that we set free the two prisoners. I explained to him that we had taken them to prevent [the army] taking reprisals against the people but if that was the will of the inhabitants, I had nothing more to say." After freeing the prisoners, the rebels went on their way, stopping only to bury their dead man in the local cemetery.

II

Back in the rebel haunt of La Maestra, they heard the news that Frank País, the movement coordinator for Oriente, had been murdered by police in Santiago. The movement had stepped up its antigovernment actions in Santiago to commemorate July 26, and police repression had escalated, as well. Under police chief Colonel José Salas Cañizares and his thugs, arrests and killings of rebel suspects had become commonplace; tortured bodies were found hanging from trees or dumped at the roadsides. The twenty-three-year-old País had been in hiding since his release from jail, moving from one safe house to the other, but in his last letters to Fidel he had expressed doubts about how much longer he could avoid detection. On July 30, País's luck ran out when his refuge was discovered, and in broad daylight he and a companion were summarily executed on the street.

Frank País's killing caused a huge outcry, and his funeral sparked noisy antigovernment demonstrations, with strikes spreading across the entire island. In response to the unrest, Batista reimposed the state of siege and media censorship. Unfortunately for the dictator, the events in Santiago coincided with a visit by the new American ambassador, Earl Smith, who had just arrived in Cuba's second-largest city for a get-acquainted tour.

By mid-1957, few officials in the State Department retained any illusions about Fulgencio Batista. His increasingly repressive and corrupt regime was becoming an embarrassment. There had still been no official policy change regarding the dictator; U.S. envoy Smith had merely been instructed to appear evenhanded in his new post to offset the widespread impression in Cuba that Washington was committed to keeping Batista in office.

In general, U.S. policy toward Cuba was aimed at protecting the sizeable American interests there. Unrest was not good for business, and the prevailing opinion in Washington held that the best method of defusing the violence was to encourage Batista to "democratize" Cuba by holding elections, after which, hopefully, one of the "safe" traditional parties would assume office. But Fidel's persistence had thrown a wild card into the equation, and the State Department, CIA, and Department of Defense were divided over how best to deal with him, with the result that throughout 1957 and into 1958, various U.S. government agencies pursued their own, not always compatible, Cuban agendas.

Taking soundings in Washington before assuming his post, Smith had come away with the definite impression that the State Department wanted to see Batista out, and that it was actively, if covertly, supporting Castro's bid for power. Roy Rubottom, assistant secretary for Latin American affairs, and the newly appointed head of State's Caribbean desk, William Wieland, both opposed Batista, as did the CIA's Cuban specialist, J. C. King. When he got to Cuba, Smith found the CIA men there to be anti-Batista, as well. The officers in the American military mission, on the other hand, continued to enjoy a close relationship with their Cuban counterparts. The anti-Communist police bureau, BRAC, functioned with American support, and more controversially Batista's military was using American war materiel assigned to Cuba for "hemispheric defene" in its antiguerrilla campaign.

Opinion was similarly divided as to Castro's political orientation, but few policymakers credited Batista's repeated denunciations of him as a Communist. At his first press conference, Smith had trod a careful line by praising Cuba's efforts in the common struggle against Communism, while saying he did not believe Castro was pro-Communist. But in Santiago, after witnessing the police turn their batons and water hoses on a crowd of demonstrating women, Smith had publicly deplored the rough police tactics and, before leaving, laid a wreath at País's tomb. This gesture gave Cubans hopes of a policy shift in Washington, for it stood out in sharp contrast to the pro-Batista attitudes of Smith's predecessor, Arthur Gardner. The unpopular Gardner had never said anything publicly to criticize Batista's excesses and privately had gone so far as to suggest the dictator send an assassin into the sierra to kill Fidel.

After Smith's indelicate remarks about police brutality in Santiago, the debate over Castro began to heat up, with Batista officials and American ultra-conservatives accusing Washington of going soft on Communism. In August, the ubiquitous Spruille Braden, who had served as U.S. ambassador during Batista's first *elected* term as president during World War II, threw down the gauntlet, denouncing Castro as a Communist "fellow traveler."

And in truth, the CIA was already pursuing contacts with Fidel's rebel movement through its officials stationed in Santiago and Havana. The first inkling of such contacts is revealed by Che's scathing reference to Armando Hart's letter "suggesting a deal with the Yankee embassy" in April 1957. The next reference is in a July 5 letter sent by Frank País to Fidel. Informing Fidel that he had managed to get an American visa for Lester "El Gordito" Rodríguez, a July 26 official who was to help coordinate U.S. fund-raising and arms purchases for the rebels, País explained: "The very meritorious and valuable American embassy came to us and offered any kind of help in exchange for our ceasing to loot arms from their [Guantánamo] base.* We promised this in exchange for a two-year visa for El Gordito and for them

---

*The July 26 Movement had a flourishing underground operating among the Cuban employees at the Guantánamo base, and had been stealing weapons and ammunition from its stores since before the *Granma* expedition. As with most of the wartime rebel correspondence quoted by the author, this comes from Carlos Franqui's *Diary of the Cuban Revolution*, New York, Viking Press, 1980.

Ernesto "Che" Guevara, 1960. *Salas*

The Guevara family in the Hotel Sierras swiming pool, Alta Gracia, Argentina, 1936. From left, the eight-year-old Ernesto; his father, Ernesto Guevara Lynch; sister Celia; mother, Celia Guevara de la Serna; sister Ana María; and brother Roberto. *Cuban Council of State Office of Historical Affairs*

The extended family in Alta Gracia, 1939. From left, grandmother Ana Isabel Guevara Lynch with Ana María, Ernesto Guevara Lynch, the eleven-year-old "Che" with his beloved Aunt Beatriz. *Cuban Council of State Office of Historical Affairs*

Ernesto and his *barra* (childhood gang) mates in Alta Gracia, 1939 or 1940. Ernesto is second from right, wearing a woolen vest. At far right, his younger brother Roberto. At far left, their younger sister, Ana María. *Cuban Council of State Office of Historical Affairs*

Celia Guevara de la Serna and Ernesto Guevara Lynch with their sickly firstborn son, Ernesto, Alta Gracia, 1935. After contracting asthma at the age of two, Ernesto would be afflicted by the condition throughout his life. *Cuban Council of State Office of Historical Affairs*

Celia Guevara with her children in Alta Gracia, 1937. From left: Celia, Celia Guevara de la Serna, Roberto (dressed as a cowboy), Ernesto, wearing the Indian headdress, and Ana María. *Cuban Council of State Office of Historical Affairs*

The young Che was a daredevil throughout his youth. This picture, taken when he was about twenty-two, shows him walking along a pipeline suspended over a gorge. *Cuban Council of State Office of Historical Affairs*

In 1942, the fourteen-year-old Ernesto began attending high school in Córdoba, traveling by bus every day from Alta Gracia in the company of older students. He is perched on the front fender of the bus, third from left. *Courtesy of Carlos Barceló*

The Argentine first couple Juan and Evita Perón, waving to the crowds, 1951. As Ernesto Guevara came of age in the late forties and early fifties, the Peróns radically altered Argentine politics, making a sharp impact on Ernesto's generation. *Corbis-Bettmann*

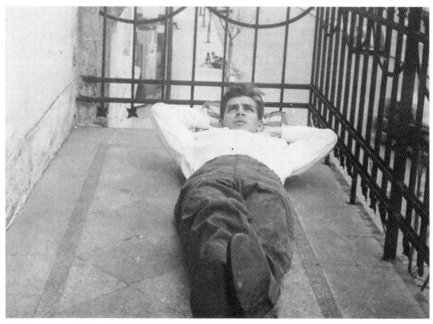

Ernesto Guevara, now a medical student, lying contemplatively on the balcony of his family's new home on Calle Araoz in Buenos Aires, 1948 or 1949. *Cuban Council of State Office of Historical Affairs*

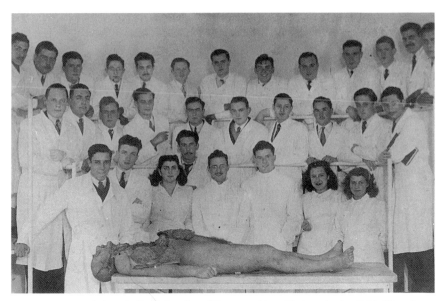

Guevara entered the Medical Faculty of Buenos Aires University in 1947. Here he is, a year later, with fellow students in the anatomy theater (grinning incongruously, sixth from right, top row). The girl standing second from the right (front row) is Berta Gilda "Tita" Infante, with whom he became close friends. *Cuban Council of State Office of Historical Affairs*

In his early twenties, Ernesto Guevara was a handsome extrovert. Here, in 1952 or 1953, he poses with a carload of girls. *Cuban Council of State Office of Historical Affairs*

In 1950, Ernesto fell in love with María del Carmen "Chichina" Ferreyra, the sixteen-year-old daughter of one of Córdoba's wealthiest families. He wanted to marry her, but her family was opposed. In 1952, she broke off their romance. *Cuban Council of State Office of Historical Affairs*

Hitchhiking, 1948. While he was in college, Ernesto yearned to extend his horizons. He began taking weekend hitchhiking trips into the countryside. Soon, he began to travel farther afield. *Cuban Council of State Office of Historical Affairs*

Hamming it up with his friends the Granado brothers. From left: Ernesto, Gregorio, and Alberto Granado. This 1950 picture was taken during a pit stop in Ernesto's first long solo trip, to northern Argentina. *Cuban Council of State Office of Historical Affairs*

Ernesto setting out on his solo motorbike trip, 1950. This photo was later used as an advertisement by the company that sold him his engine. *Cuban Council of State Office of Historical Affairs*

During his university years, Ernesto took up gliding with Jorge de la Serna, an oddball uncle whom he particularly liked. *Cuban Council of State Office of Historical Affairs*

A swimming break while on the road in Central America, 1953. Ernesto is seated in the foreground. Standing behind him, from left, traveling companions Eduardo "Gualo" García and Ricardo Rojo. *Courtesy of Carlos "Calica" Ferrer*

Guatemala, 1954. Ernesto standing next to his future first wife, Hilda Gadea, a Peruvian political exile. Before long, they would become lovers. From right: Ricardo Rojo, Hilda, Ernesto (wearing white suit). Gualo García is squatting in the foreground. *Courtesy of Carlos "Calica" Ferrer*

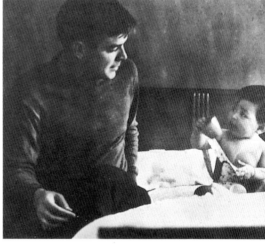

Yucatán honeymoon, 1955. After the CIA's overthrow of Guatemalan president Jacobo Arbenz, Ernesto and Hilda fled to Mexico. Hilda became pregnant, and in August 1955 they were married. In the Yucatán, Ernesto dragged an unwilling Hilda along with him to see Mayan temples. *Cuban Council of State Office of Historical Affairs*

In February 1956, Hilda gave birth to a baby girl they named Hilda Beatriz, after her mother and in honor of Ernesto's favorite aunt, but Ernesto called her "my little Mao." *Cuban Council of State Office of Historical Affairs*

Deposed Guatemalan president Jacobo Arbenz (left) arriving in Mexico in September 1954, following his forced resignation. Arbenz's incapacity to "arm the people" to defend his leftist regime was a watershed in the political evolution of Ernesto Guevara. *AP/ Wide World Photos*

Guatemala's so-called Liberator, Colonel Carlos Castillo Armas. A dedicated anti-Communist, Castillo Armas was handpicked to lead the CIA's 1954 "Operation Success" against the leftist government of Jacobo Arbenz. *AP/ Wide World Photos*

Cuba's dictator General Fulgencio Batista drinking *mojitos* with visiting American vice president Richard Nixon and his wife, Pat, in Havana, 1955. Nixon's visit gave Batista, who had seized power in a 1952 coup, the Eisenhower administration's seal of approval, but popular discontent with Batista's rule soon led to civil war. *UPI/Corbis-Bettmann*

A beardless Fidel Castro, May 1955, leaving the Cuban prison where he had spent nearly two years after leading a failed attack against the Moncada army garrison in July 1953. From left front: Raúl Castro, Juan Almeida, Fidel Castro, and Ciro Redondo. *Cuban Council of State Office of Historical Affairs*

This is the first known picture of Ernesto "Che" Guevara and Fidel Castro together. After joining Castro's force in Mexico and undergoing military training, Guevara became one of Castro's officers. In June 1956, Castro and most of his men were arrested by Mexican police; this photo was taken in the cell Guevara and Castro shared in prison. *Cuban Council of State Office of Historical Affairs*

Ernesto Guevara, already being called "Che" by his Cuban comrades, went mountain climbing regularly in Mexico to condition his body for the rigors of the impending Cuban guerrilla war. Here, in 1956, he is seen climbing the 17,887-foot Mt. Popocatepetl. *Cuban Council of State Office of Historical Affairs*

Ernesto Guevara's Mexican police mug shot, summer 1956. *Cuban Council of State Office of Historical Affairs*

After sailing from Mexico aboard an overcrowded yacht and landing in a swamp in eastern Cuba in December 1956, Castro's rebels were ambushed by Batista's army and dispersed. Fewer than twenty reassembled in the nearby Sierra Maestra mountains. This picture, taken in early 1957, shows Che Guevara seated (foreground) with several Cuban comrades. *Cuban Council of State Office of Historical Affairs*

Che, lighting up a Cuban cigar, with Fidel Castro, in the early days of the Cuban guerrilla war. Very quickly, Fidel realized that Che was much more than a doctor, and in July 1957, he honored his fighting prowess by promoting him to *comandante*. *Cuban Council of State Office of Historical Affairs*

Che and Raúl Castro, the two "radicals" of Fidel Castro's rebel army. *Cuban Council of State Office of Historical Affairs*

After less than a year in the mountains, Che Guevara had established a "liberated territory" in a Sierra Maestra valley. Proud of his achievement, he had his men design this flag proclaiming, "Happy 1958." *Cuban Council of State Office of Historical Affairs*

In 1958, Argentine journalist Jorge Ricardo Masetti (right) made his way into the Sierra Maestra, and Che Guevara's voice was broadcast to the world for the first time. Later, Masetti became one of Che's protégés, leading a guerrilla mission to Argentina. In 1964 he died, somewhere in the northern Argentine jungle. *Cuban Council of State Office of Historical Affairs*

Che and Camilo Cienfuegos (right), a swashbuckling, good-natured Cuban rebel officer. Cienfuegos became one of Che's closest friends and a hero of the revolution. *Cuban Council of State Office of Historical Affairs*

In the final push to victory in late 1958, Guevara launched a series of attacks against army garrisons in Cuba's central Las Villas province. As one town after the other fell under his control, Che prepared to attack the city of Santa Clara, the last remaining government bastion before Havana. Here, he speaks to civilians in the town of Cabaiguán. *Cuban Council of State Office of Historical Affairs*

In the midst of the fighting in Las Villas, Che talks to some of his young *escoltas*, or teenaged bodyguards, with fellow rebel commander Víctor Bordón (back turned). At the far left is Hermes Peña: Five years later, he would die in Argentina fighting in a guerrilla war that Guevara intended to join. *Cuban Council of State Office of Historical Affairs*

On December 29, 1958, Che's fighters derailed an armored government train bringing weapons and troop reinforcements to the besieged army in Santa Clara. It was the death knell for Batista's regime. Two days later, in the predawn darkness of January 1, 1959, Batista fled into exile, and the Cuban army quickly surrendered to Fidel Castro's rebel forces. *Cuban Council of State Office of Historical Affairs*

In November 1958, as Che waged war from his base in the Escambray mountains, he met Aleida March, a twenty-four-year-old rebel fighter. Weeks later, during the battle of Santa Clara, Che realized he had fallen in love with her. In another six months, she would become his second wife. *Cuban Council of State Office of Historical Affairs*

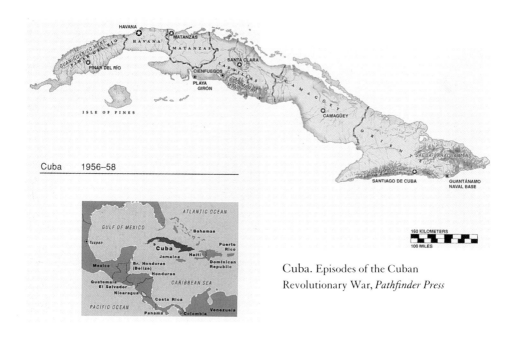

Cuba. Episodes of the Cuban
Revolutionary War, *Pathfinder Press*

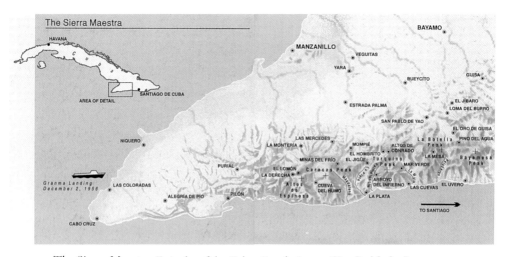

The Sierra Maestra. Episodes of the Cuban Revolutionary War, *Pathfinder Press*

to get him out of the country. Today they fulfilled their promise: the consul took him out personally, and the papers, letters and the maps that he needed were taken out in the diplomatic pouch. Good service . . ."

On July 11, País had written to Fidel again to tell him: "María A. told me very urgently at noon today that the American vice-consul wanted to talk with you, in the presence of some other man, but she didn't know who. . . . I'm sick and tired of so much backing and forthing and conversations from the embassy, and I think it would be to our advantage to close ranks a bit more, without losing contact with them, but not giving them as much importance as we now do; I see that they are maneuvering but I can't see clearly what their real goals are."

In his biography of Fidel Castro, Tad Szulc wrote that between the autumn of 1957 and mid-1958 the CIA paid out at least fifty thousand dollars to various July 26 agents, and named Wiecha as the man who disbursed the funds.

Fidel agreed to the meeting. In an undated reply to Frank País, he wrote: "I don't see why we should raise the slightest objection to the U.S. diplomat's visit. We can receive any U.S. diplomat here, just as we would any Mexican diplomat or a diplomat from any country." He then continued with the kind of bombast that seems to indicate he expected the letter to be passed on to the Americans. "If they wish to have closer ties of friendship with the triumphant democracy of Cuba? Magnificent! This is a sign they acknowledge the final outcome of this battle. If they propose friendly mediation? We'll tell them no honorable mediation, no patriotic mediation—no mediation is possible in this battle. . . ."

Despite Fidel's approval, the meeting between him and the CIA men apparently never came about. Possibly it was postponed because of País's death and then dropped when the CIA's policy shifted. But the agency's contacts with the National Directorate's llano officials continued for some time, and evidently paid off in funding and possibly other forms of aid to the movement. It is worth noting that the CIA overtures coincided with País's meetings with representatives of a group of reformist officers at Cuba's Cienfuegos naval base who were plotting an uprising against Batista; the officers also had secret U.S. support for their plan.

William Williamson, the CIA number two man in Havana, had told the naval conspirators that if they were successful, they could count on U.S. recognition. By July, the group had made contact with Faustino Pérez in Havana and Frank País in Santiago to propose an alliance of forces. After hearing them out, País had strongly endorsed the plan and passed it along to Fidel.

It was a tempting proposition: The officers were planning not a mere barracks coup but a full-scale uprising to oust Batista, assisted by dissident

factions within the air force and army, with simultaneous uprisings in Cienfuegos, Santiago, and Havana. Despite his public opposition to any kind of
post-Batista military junta that could preempt his own bid for power, Fidel
was not one to miss an opportunity and had little to lose by supporting the
Cienfuegos plotters. First, it would be the movement's llano people, not his
men from the sierra, who would take part, giving him some deniability if
the plot were discovered. Second, if he opposed the plan and the conspirators were successful, he would have alienated them and would still be trapped
in the mountains. Of course, if he *did* help, there was the risk he could be
outmaneuvered, but he could then continue to fight from the hills, as he
had promised in the manifesto. For the time being, Fidel's position was good.
The Americans and, now, Cuban military mutineers were coming to *him*.
He had become a power broker, and he could afford to remain circumspect
about the deals on offer while continuing to fight his war in the sierra.

In the meantime, he faced other problems. País's murder had come at
a time of mounting tensions between himself and his National Directorate
in the llano over the control and direction of the July 26 Movement. Ever
since their meeting at Epifanio Díaz's farm in February, País and Faustino
Pérez had lobbied Fidel to permit the establishment of a "Second Front."

They had a double agenda: A second guerrilla front would not only
ease matters for Fidel's rebels by helping to divert the attention of the
enemy, but also offset Fidel's maneuverings to exercise total control of
the armed struggle. Fidel was just as adamant that the movement make
the support of *his* fighters in the sierra its priority; until his forces were
secure, he argued, no arms should be diverted elsewhere. His view had
won out in February, and the "Second Front" plan had been temporarily
shelved, but not forgotten.

That had been only the beginning of the rift between the sierra and
the llano. During their time in prison together, Carlos Franqui, Faustino
Pérez, and Armando Hart had talked at length with jailed representatives
of most of the other Cuban opposition parties. They had concluded that
insurmountable differences of ideology prevented a July 26 alliance of
forces with the Partido Socialista Popular, Cuba's Communist party, which
remained critical of Fidel's "putschist" strategy for taking power. They saw
genuine possibilities of a pact with the Directorio, however, but so far a
working alliance had been thwarted primarily due to Directorio fears about
Fidel's perceived *caudillismo,* or strongman tendencies. Fidel had long been
criticized for this trait, one that the movement men also recognized; the llano
officials themselves had begun to resent Fidel's autocratic demands and
ceaseless complaints about their efforts on his behalf. His letters show that
he regarded them as little more than his suppliers, rather than equal part-

ners in a common struggle involving both rural and urban guerrilla warfare, and he seemed to ignore the precarious existence they led in the cities, exposed to the constant dangers of arrest, torture, and execution.

In addition to their efforts to broaden the movement's links with other groups, the llano people oversaw the campaign of urban bombings, sabotage, and assassination as well as counterintelligence operations within the armed forces; they also operated clandestine safe houses, clinics, and arms-smuggling rings. They now had the added duties of implementing the campaign of rural and industrial sabotage as decreed by Fidel in his February "Appeal": the formation of a national worker's front group to compete with the Batista-controlled labor union movement, organizing a general strike, and, last but not least, the unceasing program to supply Fidel with money and weapons through the Resistencia Cívica network.

The prospect of opening new guerrilla fronts became viable only after the movement seized the weapons left over from the Directorio's assault on the Presidential Palace. Some of these had been sent to Fidel just before Uvero, but with the remainder Frank País had formed a new rebel group led by a former law student, René Ramos Latour, aka "Daniel." Daniel's group had based itself in Oriente's small but strategic Sierra Cristal mountain range—east of the Sierra Maestra, with Santiago on one side and Guantánamo on the other—but its first action in June against an army garrison had failed and resulted in the loss of many arms and several men. Frank País had rescued some weapons and hidden Daniel and twenty of his men in Santiago safe houses. País had then come up with an audacious new plan: to explode a time bomb at a pro-Batista rally being held by political gangster Rolando Masferrer, the leader of his own armed paramilitary force called "Los Tigres" (The Tigers). The bomb had failed to go off, however, and, soon after, the final blow to País's bid to assert himself had come when his own brother, Josué, and two comrades were killed.

Following these failures, País had begun lobbying Fidel to widen his political appeal by forging links with mainstream political figures, including encouraging the sierra visit of Raúl Chibás and Felipe Pazos. He also had outlined a plan with Armando Hart—who coincidentally had just escaped police custody—to revamp the entire structure of the movement by putting decision making in the hands of a new executive body, while six provincial leaders would form the new National Directorate. The plan clearly implied a major vast curtailment of Fidel's powers by reducing him to one of the six provincial leaders representing his rebels in the sierra. "If you have any suggestions or tasks to be done," País wrote Fidel, "tell me so. In any case, when the draft of the program is complete, I will send it for you to look over and give your opinion."

Fidel's response came in the form of his Sierra Maestra Manifesto, effectively quashing País's curtailment efforts. Writing to him afterward, Fidel deftly avoided mentioning País's proposal, saying ambiguously: "I'm very happy—and I congratulate you—that you so clearly saw the necessity of formulating working plans on a national and systematic scale. We'll keep fighting here as long as it is necessary. And we'll finish this battle with either the death or triumph of the *real* Revolution. . . ."

A couple of weeks later, Frank País was dead, and Fidel made haste to fill the breach. The day after his death, on July 31, Fidel wrote to Celia Sánchez expressing his sorrow and outrage over the loss, and asked her to assume "a good portion of Frank's work." Meanwhile, to replace País on the National Directorate, he proposed Faustino Pérez, and urged her to bring him up to date on País's duties. On this matter, however, the National Directorate won a rare victory over Fidel, choosing not Pérez but Daniel— René Ramos Latour—as País's replacement.

Lately, to implement his wishes, Fidel had begun to rely more and more heavily on Celia Sánchez, whom he regularly bombarded with letters, telling her she was indispensable to his survival and all the while complaining bitterly about his lack of support from the llano. Indeed, ever since their first meeting in February, Celia had become Fidel's primary confidante in the llano, and now her authority increased. The other July 26 officials quickly comprehended Celia's new status, and began dealing with her as their principal intermediary with Fidel.

As Daniel tried to carry on País's effort to assert more control over Fidel and his rebels, he singled out Che in particular as someone who needed to be reined in, complaining to Fidel that Che had not even contacted him since he had replaced País, and was causing problems by making his own supply arrangements with people not authorized by the Directorate. Fidel's response was to ignore Daniel while sending increasingly bitter letters to Celia about the llano's "abandonment" of the sierra. The dispute continued to boil away, unresolved, and in the meantime the war continued.

III

As Che prepared for another attack against the forces of Major Joaquín Casillas, he found himself dealing with the usual problems of green recruits, deserters, and *chivatos*. A group of new volunteers from Las Minas joined him, among them his first female volunteer, a seventeen-year-old girl named Oniria Gutiérrez. In the usual pattern, though, he let several of them go a few days later when they began showing signs of *"cofard,"* the French word he used to describe cowardice.

He learned of the fate that had befallen David Gómez, his overseer collaborator, who had been arrested, tortured, and apparently murdered. The army had then occupied the Peladero estate where he worked, where they had pressured one of the workers into telling them everything he knew about the rebels' local ties. Incensed, Che wrote in his diary: "The result was that they killed 10 people, including two of David's muleteers, took all the merchandise, burned down all the houses in the area, and beat several of the neighbors badly, some of whom later died and others, like Israel's father, who suffered broken bones. According to the reports, there were three *chivatos,* and I asked for volunteers to kill them. Several offered themselves but I chose Israel, his brother Samuel, Manolito and Rodolfo. They left early with some little signs that read: *Executed for being a traitor to the people M-26-7.*"

The execution team returned a week later, having tracked down and killed one of the *chivatos.* (The reports of David's death turned out to be inaccurate; he later came personally to tell Che that although he had been arrested and brutally tortured, he had not opened his mouth.) Soon afterward, moving his column back through the same territory he had traversed after the El Uvero battle, Che was contacted by a deserter from that odyssey, René Cuervo, who sent him a letter asking his forgiveness and telling him, as if to win back favor, that he had killed a *chivato.* In La Mesa, Che heard from one of his suppliers that Cuervo was loitering in his village, and the supplier asked what should be done about him. Che's response to the man was blunt: "I told him to kill him if he bothers them too much."*

By late August, Che's column was camped in the valley of El Hombrito. Despite his efforts to seek out the enemy, his men had seen no combat since Bueycito nearly a month before. On August 29, a peasant warned Che of a large column of enemy soldiers approaching, then led him to where the soldiers were camped. Che decided to attack immediately, before the enemy advanced farther. That night he positioned his fighters along both sides of a trail leading from the soldiers' bivouac, and up which they would march the following day. His plan was to allow the first ten or twelve soldiers to pass, then ambush the middle of the column, dividing the soldiers into two groups that could be easily surrounded and picked off.

---

*The first section of Guevara's campaign diary obtained by the author begins on December 2, 1956, and ends on August 12, 1957. The middle section (August 13, 1957, to April 17, 1958) is missing; the second section in the author's possession runs from April 18, 1958, through December 3, 1959, one month before the war's end. For information on the missing months, the author relied upon personal interviews and other published material, including Guevara's own writings dealing with the relevant periods. See *Episodes of the Cuban Revolutionary War* in "Selected Bibliography."

At first light, they saw the soldiers rousing themselves and putting on helmets, ready to march out. As the soldiers began climbing the hill toward them, Che felt restless, anxious with the tension of coming battle, and eager to test his new Browning for the first time. As the soldiers drew near, Che began counting. But when he got to the sixth man, one of them shouted, and Che reacted reflexively, opening fire and shooting the sixth man in line. At his second shot, and before his own men had reacted, the other five soldiers visible vanished from sight. Che ordered his units to attack; as they did, the enemy column recovered from its surprise and opened fire with bazookas. As Che ordered a retreat to a fallback position, he learned that Hermes Leyva, Joel Iglesias's cousin, had been killed. From their new vantage point, a kilometer away (a little over half a mile), they watched as the soldiers advanced, stopped, and then, in full view of them, desecrated Leyva's body by burning it. "In our impotent rage," recalled Che, "we were limited to long-range firing, which they answered with bazookas."

They exchanged fire all day, and by nightfall the enemy column had retreated. To Che, the action constituted "a great triumph," despite the fact that he had lost a valuable man and captured only one enemy weapon. With their handful of arms, his men had fought off an entire army company of 140 soldiers armed with bazookas, halting their advance. But a few days later, Che learned that the army company had murdered several peasants and burned down their homes in reprisal for their suspected complicity with his forces, a chastening reminder of the price paid by unprotected civilians after rebel attacks in their areas. Che resolved to evacuate civilians in advance of attacks to prevent more such atrocities in the future.

After the battle Che met up again with Fidel, who had just attacked an army encampment near Las Cuevas; he had lost four men, but inflicted casualties and forced the army to retreat. Deciding to press their advantage, Fidel and Che planned a coordinated attack on Pino del Agua, where there was a small army garrison. If they found troops, they would attack; if not, they would advertise their presence to draw the army into the hills. Fidel's column would be the bait, while Che would lay an ambush. With the plan worked out, the two columns headed toward the target area.

But in Che's column, things were not going well. There were several more desertions, and then a young rebel, disarmed after being insubordinate with his lieutenant, borrowed a revolver and shot himself in the head before his shocked comrades. When he was buried, a disagreement ensued between Che and some of his men over whether or not the dead youth should be given military honors. Che was opposed. "I argued that committing suicide under such conditions should be repudiated, whatever good qualities the man may have possessed. After a few stirrings of insubordination by some of the men, we wound up holding a wake, without rendering him honors."

The discontent among his men spurred Che to take strict new measures, and he named a boy to head up a new disciplinary commission. Enrique Acevedo, a fifteen-year-old runaway who had recently joined the column as a *descamisado* with his older brother, Rogelio, recalled it as a decision that caused bad blood among the fighters. "It was like a small military police," said Acevedo. "Among other things, it was to make sure that nobody talked in loud voices, didn't light fires before nightfall, ensure that there were buckets of water next to fires in case the aviation appeared . . . , to check up on those doing guard duty, and prevent anyone from keeping a diary. Finally, it made sure that we felt the rigor of the new disciplinary measures. And the candidate enjoyed his job so much that it became a nightmare for all of us. . . ."

Che's penchant for strict discipline was notorious among the rebels, and there were those who asked to be transferred out of his column. Young Acevedo, who had reluctantly been allowed to stay on despite Che's initial rejection—*"What do you think this is, an orphanage or a crèche?"*—continued to observe Che with great caution. In his own "illegal" diary, he wrote: "Everyone treats him with great respect. He is hard, dry and at times ironic with some men. His manners are smooth. When he gives an order you can see he really commands respect. It is obeyed at once."

A few days later, the brothers witnessed an example of Che's summary justice. Enrique Acevedo recorded the moment vividly: "At dawn they bring in a big man dressed in green, head shaved like the military, with big mustaches: it's [René] Cuervo, who is stirring up trouble in the zone of San Pablo de Yao and Vega la Yua. He has committed abuses under the flag of the July 26. . . . Che receives him in his hammock. The prisoner tries to give him his hand, but doesn't find a response. What is said doesn't reach our ears, even though their words are strong. It seems to be a summary trial. At the end [Che] sends him away with a contemptuous gesture of his hand. They take him to a ravine and they execute him with a .22 rifle, because of which they have to give him three shots. [Finally] Che jumps out of his hammock and shouts: 'Enough!'" Afterward, said Acevedo, the place became known as the "Hoyo del Cuervo [The Crow's Hole]."

Later on, Che was unapologetic about his decision to kill Cuervo. "Using the pretext of fighting for the revolutionary cause and executing spies, he simply victimized an entire section of the population of the sierra, perhaps in collusion with the army. In view of his status as a deserter, the trial was speedy, then proceeding to his physical elimination. The execution of antisocial individuals who took advantage of the prevailing atmosphere in the area to commit crimes was, unfortunately, not infrequent in the Sierra Maestra."

But a few weeks later, at a new brief battle, another, more merciful side of Che was revealed, showing that if he was implacable toward traitors, spies, and cowards, he respected his enemies who were brave enough to confront death in battle. After ambushing a truckload of soldiers near Pino del Agua, Che approached to inspect the damage. As he told it: "In capturing the first truck, we found two dead and one wounded soldier, who was still going through the motions of fighting as he lay dying. One of our fighters finished the man off without giving the man an opportunity to surrender—which he was unable to do, being only half-conscious. The combatant responsible for this barbaric act had seen his family wiped out by Batista's army. I reproached him violently, unaware that my remarks were overheard by another wounded soldier, concealed and motionless under some tarpaulins on the truck bed. Emboldened by my words and by the apology of our comrade, the enemy soldier made his presence known and begged us not to kill him. He had a fractured leg and remained at the side of the road while the battle went on elsewhere. Every time a fighter passed near him he would shout, 'Don't kill me! Don't kill me! Che says not to kill prisoners!' When the battle was over we transported him to the sawmill and gave him first aid."

IV

As they made their way through the hills during that first week of September, the rebels heard that the national uprising had finally taken place. On September 5, rebels had attacked and seized the naval base and police headquarters in the city of Cienfuegos. Along with the naval mutineers and a smattering of men from other groups, including the *auténticos,* a large number of July 26 fighters had participated. But things hadn't gone as planned: At the last minute, the rebel's co-conspirators in Havana and Santiago had stalled, and the Cienfuegos uprising had gone off alone.

The rebels held the city that morning, but by afternoon the regime had sent in tanks from the large Santa Clara garrison and dispatched American-made B-26 bombers to hit them from the air. The rebels committed the fatal mistake of making a stand in the city instead of escaping to the nearby Escambray mountains, and they were slaughtered. The three July 26 officials involved—Javier Pazos, acting head of the Havana underground; Julio Camacho, action chief for Las Villas province; and Emilio Aragonés, the July 26 leader for Cienfuegos—managed to flee, but as many as three

hundred of the estimated four hundred men involved from various organizations were killed, many of them shot after surrendering. The revenge
taken against the rebels was barbaric: Reports emerged of wounded men
being buried alive, while the captured ringleader, the former naval lieutenant Dionisio San Román, was tortured for months before being killed.

It had been the biggest and bloodiest action so far in the Cuban conflict, and there was plenty of fallout. Fidel was accused of treachery by Justo
Carrillo, a former Prío cabinet minister and leader of his own "Montecristi"
anti-Batista group, who had been in league with one of the military factions
involved in the conspiracy. Previously, Carrillo had also provided money
to the July 26 Movement; he flirted with—but declined—Fidel's invitation
for an alliance at the time of the Sierra Pact. Now, Carrillo accused Fidel of
perfidy for allegedly giving his go-ahead to the Cienfuegos revolt, knowing it would fail and result in the deaths of the military men whom he saw
as rivals for power. Indirectly answering this charge later, Che wrote: "The
July 26 Movement, participating as an unarmed ally, could not have changed
the course of events, even if its leaders had seen the outcome clearly, which
they did not. The lesson for the future is: he who has the strength dictates
the strategy."

But Batista would also face repercussions from Cienfuegos. To the
State Department, his use of U.S.-supplied firepower in quelling the revolt
was a blatant breach of U.S. defense treaties with Cuba; the tanks and B-26
bombers had been supplied for Cuba's hemispheric defense, not to suppress internal uprisings. The Americans asked for explanations from Cuba's
armed forces and, when these weren't forthcoming, began considering the
suspension of future arms shipments to the regime.

Meanwhile, in the Sierra Maestra, Che and Fidel had drawn close to
their next military target. On September 10, the two columns reached Pino
del Agua. Fidel made sure the locals knew where he was headed, expecting
someone to leak it to the army, then marched his column off. That night
Che surreptitiously set up his ambushes along the roads and trails where
the enemy forces were expected to arrive. If their plan worked, they hoped
to hit a motorized army convoy and capture several trucks. After a week of
waiting in a forest on a cliff overlooking one of the main roads, Che and his
units finally heard the sounds of truck engines approaching. The enemy had
seized the bait.

As battles went, it was a decidedly small-scale affair. Once the ambush
began, two truckloads of soldiers were able to escape, but the rebels captured
the three remaining trucks—which they burned—and captured some valuable new weapons and ammunition. They had also killed three soldiers and
taken one prisoner, a corporal who ended up joining them and becoming

their cook. But to their great sadness, they had lost "Crucito," a *guajiro* poet who had entertained the fighters in poetic dueling sessions with the other rebel lyricist, Calixto Morales. Crucito had nicknamed himself "the nightingale of the Maestra" and dubbed his rival "the buzzard of the plains."

V

Che moved his men toward Peladero, where Fidel's column had headed. Along the way, he confiscated a mule owned by a merchant. Although the man, Juan Balansa, had not been hostile to the rebels, he was believed to be pro-Batista and friendly with the large landowners. That was enough for Che, who had an additional incentive. As Che wrote afterward, "Juan Balansa had a mule, celebrated in the vicinity for its staying power, and as a kind of war tax, we made off with it." The mule might well have been slaughtered for its meat, but it showed itself to be surefooted and agile, and Che pardoned it, feeling it had "won its right to live." Eventually, Che took over the mule as his own personal mount and kept it until it was "recaptured" by Captain Angel Sánchez Mosquera, the officer who was becoming his personal nemesis, later in the war.

The time had come for the rebels to assert their authority over the sierra's inhabitants and establish a semblance of law and order in the region. The Sierra Maestra was now crawling with armed men, and a kind of anarchy reigned as deserters, freelance outlaw groups and some of the rebels themselves committed abuses, using their weapons and the absence of government control to rob, rape, and commit murder. The new rigid code of conduct for rebel behavior, meanwhile, was causing resentments, particularly in Che's column, where tensions were running high over the zeal displayed by his newly appointed "disciplinary commission." Those tensions now reached a bloody climax.

A couple of days after his column had arrived at Peladero, Che went off to meet Fidel, camped nearby. Not long after he and Fidel had begun talking, Ramiro Valdés came to interrupt them. It was urgent; something very bad had happened. "Lalo Sardiñas, in an impulsive act of punishment toward an undisciplined comrade, had held his pistol to the man's head as if to shoot him," wrote Che later. "The gun went off unintentionally and the man was killed on the spot. There were stirrings of a riot among the troops."

Arriving back in his camp, Che found himself facing a full-scale mutiny over Lalo's action, with many of the men demanding a summary trial and execution. He began to take evidence from the men, some of whom said Lalo had carried out an act of premeditated murder, with others saying it was an accident. Fidel arrived, and a trial was held to determine Lalo's fate. Lalo was not only an officer but a good and brave fighter, and both Che and Fidel wished to spare his life. But the fighters also had to be consulted, and their speeches made it obvious most of them wanted the death penalty. Che finally spoke out: "I tried to explain that the comrade's death had to be ascribed to the conditions of the struggle," he recounted later, "to the very fact that we were at war, and that it was after all the dictator Batista who was guilty. My words, however, were not convincing to this hostile audience."

Fidel's turn came next. According to Che's account, he spoke at length in Lalo's defense. "He explained that, in the end, this reprehensible act had been committed in defense of the concept of discipline and that we should keep that fact in mind." Many of the men were swayed by what Che termed Fidel's "enormous powers of persuasion," but many still disagreed. Finally, it was agreed that a vote would be held to put the matter to rest: Lalo would be either shot to death, or demoted. The majority would decide. Che tallied up the votes in a notebook. In the end, out of the 146 fighters, 70 voted for death, 76 for demotion.

Lalo's life was spared. He was stripped of rank and ordered to win his rehabilitation by fighting as a common soldier. But the matter hadn't ended. A large group of fighters remained unhappy over the decision, and the next day they threw down their weapons and demanded to leave. Curiously, among them was the head of Che's disciplinary commission and several of its members. As was his custom, when writing about this incident later on, Che made sure to point out that among those who left, some went on to betray the revolution. "These men, who had not respected the majority and abandoned the struggle, subsequently put themselves at the service of the enemy, and it was as traitors that they returned to fight on our soil."

In spite of Che's best efforts at ascribing treasonous motivations to the men who left, the incident is less convincing as a moral tale of revolution than as a glimpse into his hardened personality at the time. Che's trail through the Sierra Maestra was littered with the bodies of *chivatos,* deserters, and delinquents, men whose deaths *he* had ordered and in some cases carried out himself. The code of discipline he had imposed *within* and *without* his growing family of fighters had created an atmosphere in which acts such as Lalo's could easily occur. The leader sets the example, and Che's underlings were merely emulating his behavior in their own crude way.

After the mutiny, Fidel transferred some fighters to Che's command to replace those who had left, and named a substitute for Lalo: Camilo Cienfuegos. The handsome, blond, and extroverted former baseball player now became the captain of Che's vanguard platoon. It was a good move, for Camilo's devil-may-care personality helped offset Che's strictness. The two men shared a great mutual respect, and Che allowed Camilo a degree of intimacy that he permitted no one else, their dialogues a ribald banter laced with friendly put-downs and goads.

It was time to move out again. Fidel gave Che new orders. "Our mission was to neutralize a group of bandits who, cloaking themselves under the banner of our revolution, were committing their crimes in the region where we had begun our struggle, as well as in the region close to Caracas and El Lomón. Camilo's first mission in our column was to advance rapidly and capture all those elements, who would then be put on trial."

While Camilo went off in pursuit of the "bandits," Che returned to the area that was becoming his own headquarters—the valley of El Hombrito. Since his ambush there in August the army had not returned, and Che had begun to establish the rudiments of a permanent base; he had left a *guajiro* named Aristidio in charge of a halfway house for new volunteers in the valley and had even built an oven for baking bread. But despite the present calm, an army incursion was greatly feared by local peasants. Sánchez Mosquera had established a base in Minas de Bueycito and was expected to launch a raid into the mountains soon. Aristidio was evidently not immune to the general sense of alarm, for in Che's absence he had sold his revolver and imprudently told people he planned to make contact with the army *before* it arrived. Che was soon notified, and he took immediate action. "These were difficult moments for the revolution," he recalled. "In my capacity as chief of the sector, we conducted a very summary investigation, and Aristidio was executed."

The adolescent Enrique Acevedo watched as Aristidio was brought in. "By our side passes a barefoot prisoner, they have him tied. It's Aristidio. Nothing remains of his chieftain's facade. Later a shot can be heard. When we get to the place they are throwing the dirt on top of him. At dawn, after an exhausting day, he [Che] explains to us that Aristidio was executed for misusing the funds and resources of the guerrillas."

But later Che sounded almost apologetic about Aristidio's fate. "Aristidio was a typical example of a peasant who joined the ranks of the revolution without having any clear understanding of its significance. . . . Today we may ask ourselves whether he was really guilty enough to deserve death, and if it might not have been possible to save a life that could have been put to use by the revolution in its constructive phase. War is harsh, and at a time when the enemy was intensifying its aggressiveness, one could not tolerate even the suspicion of treason. It might have been possible to spare him months earlier, when the guerrilla movement was much weaker, or months later, when we were far stronger."

After executing Aristidio, Che moved off toward Mt. Caracas on another purging mission, this time to help Camilo hunt down an armed gang led by "Chino Chang," a Chinese-Cuban bandit. Although loosely allied with the rebels, Chang had robbed and killed peasants in the vicinity. Camilo had already captured some of the culprits and was holding them pending their trial before a revolutionary tribunal; for the first time, the rebels had a real lawyer on hand to implement their system of justice: Humberto Sorí Marín, a well-known lawyer and July 26 man from Havana.

When Chino Chang was caught, the trials began. Most of the gang were acquitted, but Chang and a peasant who had raped a girl were sentenced to death. As usual, Che observed their last moments with a keen eye, noting whether they displayed courage or cowardice as they met their deaths. "First we executed Chino Chang and the peasant rapist. They were tied to a tree in the forest, both of them calm. The peasant died without a blindfold, his eyes facing the guns, shouting 'Long live the revolution!' Chang met death with absolute serenity but asked for the last rites to be administered by Father Sardiñas, who was at that minute far from the camp.* Since we were unable to grant this request, Chang said he wanted it known he had asked for a priest, as if this public testimony would serve as an extenuating circumstance in the hereafter."

For three of the youths in Chang's gang, the rebels decided to teach them a lesson by conducting a mock execution. The boys went through the experience of being sentenced to death and, after witnessing Chang's and the rapist's executions, awaited their own. As Che explained: "They had been deeply involved in Chang's outrages, but Fidel felt they should be given another chance. We blindfolded them and subjected them to the anguish of a simulated firing squad. After shots were fired in the air, the boys realized they were still very much alive. One of them threw himself on me, and, in a spontaneous gesture of joy and gratitude, gave me a big noisy kiss, as if I were his father." As Che told it later, the decision to spare their lives proved worthwhile; the three stayed in the rebel army, one of them in Che's column, and earned their redemption by becoming "good fighters for the revolution."

The journalist Andrew St. George had reappeared and was present for the executions—both simulated and real—and took photographs of the drama as it unfolded. His photographs and accompanying article were published in *Look* magazine, and he also apparently filed reports to American intelligence. (St. George has never refuted reports that he used his visits to gather information on Fidel and his rebel movement for the U.S. government.)

*Father Guillermo Sardiñas, a priest from Santiago, had joined the rebels in June.

A few days later, more transgressors were caught. Among them was Dionisio Oliva, a peasant who had been instrumental in unmasking Eutimio Guerra; in the intervening months he and his brother-in-law had stolen provisions intended for the rebels and become cattle rustlers. Dionisio had also commandeered private homes in which he maintained two mistresses. Captured along with them were several others, including a youth named Echeverría. Several of Echeverría's brothers were rebels, and one had even been aboard the *Granma,* but this boy had joined a freelance armed gang instead. Still, as Che admitted, his case was "poignant." Echeverría begged to be allowed to die in battle—he did not want to disgrace his family by dying in front of a revolutionary firing squad—but the tribunal's decision was firm. Before he was shot, said Che, Echeverría wrote a letter to his mother, "explaining the justice of his punishment and asking her to remain faithful to the revolution."

The last man to die was none other than the Teacher, Che's skittish companion during his asthma-plagued trek to meet the new volunteers from Santiago. Claiming illness, the Teacher had since left the guerrillas and "dedicated himself to a life of immoralities." His real crime was to have passed himself off as Che "the doctor," then attempting to rape a peasant girl who came to him as a patient.

After the revolutionary triumph Fidel talked about these executions with the July 26 journalist, Carlos Franqui. He was dishonest in his accounting of the number of executions he had authorized during the war but became downright voluble on the case of the Teacher. "We lined up very few people before firing squads, very few indeed. During the entire war we did not shoot more than 10 guys in twenty-five months." As for the Teacher, Fidel said: "He was an orangutan; he grew a huge beard. He was also a born clown and carried loads as though he were Hercules, but he was a bad soldier. . . . [And] he liked being a doctor more than being a teacher! What stupidity to pretend he was Che, in that area, where we had spent a long time, where everyone knew all of us. . . . And now, with the new beard, the Teacher was passing himself off as Che: *'Bring me women. I'm going to examine them all!'* Did you ever hear of anything so outrageous? We shot him."

VI

After the wave of executions, Che and his men headed back to El Hombrito. It was now late October 1957, and Che wanted to begin building an "industrial" infrastructure to sustain a permanent guerrilla presence there. His ambitious intentions were given a boost by the arrival of a couple of former Havana university students, who were put to work on building a dam to produce hydroelectric energy from the Río Hombrito. Their other task was to help start a guerrilla newspaper, *El Cubano Libre* (The Free Cuban). By early November, they had printed their first issue, run off on a vintage 1903 mimeograph machine brought into the mountains especially for the purpose.

Che took up the pen again, writing the first of a series of columns under his old handle of "El Francotirador" (The Sniper). In his first article, entitled "The Beginning of the End," he took precise aim at the issue of American military aid to Batista, deftly pegging it to the recent protests by animal lovers outside the UN building in New York over the Soviet decision to send a dog named Laika into space aboard its *Sputnik II* satellite. (The month before, the Soviets had launched *Sputnik I*, the world's first satellite, into orbit around the earth.)

"Compassion fills our soul at the thought of the poor animal that will die gloriously to further a cause that it doesn't understand. But we haven't heard of any philanthropic American society parading in front of the noble edifice asking clemency for our *guajiros,* and they die in good numbers, machine-gunned by the P-47 and B-26 airplanes . . . or riddled by the troops' competent M-1s. Or is it that within the context of political convenience a Siberian dog is worth more than a thousand Cuban *guajiros?*"

The newspaper was only the beginning. Che had visions of a proper social infrastructure for El Hombrito, and he built a rudimentary hospital, with plans for still another. Soon, in addition to his bread oven, there was an embryonic pig and poultry farm as well as a shoemaking and saddler's workshop, and his "armory" was going full tilt. Work had begun to produce some primitive land mines and rifle-launched grenades, dubbed "Sputniks" in honor of the new Soviet satellites, and once they had obtained the right materials, the next project was to make mortars. To symbolically crown these achievements, Che commissioned the sewing of a huge July 26 flag emblazoned with *"Feliz Año 1958!"* to be placed at the summit of El Hombrito mountain. As he oversaw all this activity, Che felt proud that he was establishing "a real authority" in the area but, mindful of the marauding troops of Captain Sánchez Mosquera, had his men construct antiaircraft shelters and defensive fortifications along the routes leading into their little fiefdom. "We intend to stand fast here," he wrote Fidel on November 24, "and not give this place up for anything."

But even as Che wrote, reports came in that Sánchez Mosquera's troops were on the march up the adjacent valley of Mar Verde, burning peasants' homes as they went. Che dispatched Camilo Cienfuegos ahead of him to ambush the troops, then he followed, intending to hit the enemy column from behind.

As the soldiers advanced up the Mar Verde valley, Che and his men stuck to the flanking forested hills, trying to catch up with them without being seen. They tried to speed up their pace but discovered that their new mascot, a puppy, had stubbornly trailed them. Che ordered the fighter who was looking after the puppy, a man named Félix, to make it go back, but the little dog continued trotting loyally behind. They reached an arroyo where they rested, and the puppy inexplicably began howling; the men tried to hush it with comforting words, but the little dog didn't stop. Che ordered it killed. "Félix looked at me with eyes that said nothing," Che wrote later. "Very slowly he took out a rope, wrapped it around the animal's neck, and began to tighten it. The cute little movements of the dog's tail suddenly became convulsive, before gradually dying out, accompanied by a steady moan that escaped from its throat, despite the firm grasp. I don't know how long it took for the end to come, but to all of us it seemed like forever. With one last nervous twitch, the puppy stopped moving. There it lay, sprawled out, its little head spread over the twigs."

The band of men moved on without speaking. The enemy had now moved well beyond them. Hearing distant gunshots, they knew Camilo's ambushes had struck, but when Che sent scouts ahead to check, they found nothing except a freshly dug grave. Che ordered it dug up, and inside they found the body of an enemy soldier; whatever clash had taken place was over, and both the enemy troops and Camilo's squad were gone. Disappointed at having missed the action, they walked back down the valley, reaching the hamlet of Mar Verde after nightfall. All its inhabitants had fled, leaving their possessions behind. The rebels cooked a pig and some yucca, and one of the men began singing along to a guitar.

"I don't know whether it was the sentimental tune, or the darkness of night, or just plain exhaustion," wrote Che. "What happened though, is that Félix, while eating seated on the floor, dropped a bone, and a house dog came out meekly and grabbed it up. Félix patted its head, and the dog looked at him. Félix returned the glance, and then he and I exchanged a guilty look. Suddenly everyone fell silent. An imperceptible stirring came over us, as the dog's meek yet roguish gaze seemed to contain a hint of reproach. There in our presence, although observing us through the eyes of another dog, was the murdered puppy."

They were still in Mar Verde the next day when scouts brought word that Sánchez Mosquera's troops were camped less than two kilometers away. Camilo's force had taken up a position near the enemy and was waiting for Che's column before attacking. Che quickly moved his men to the spot. By dawn the next morning, November 29, the rebels were in ambush positions along the Río Turquino, covering all of Sánchez Mosquera's possible escape routes. For himself and his own unit, Che chose a particularly vulnerable spot; if the soldiers came their way, they would have to fire on them at point-blank range.

Che and two or three others were concealed behind trees when a small group of soldiers passed directly before them. Armed with only a Luger pistol, Che nervously rushed his first shot and missed. The firefight began, and in the confusion the soldiers escaped into the bush. Simultaneously the other units opened up on the farmhouse where most of the enemy soldiers were positioned. Then, during a lull in the firing, Joel Iglesias was hit by six bullets as he searched for the escaped soldiers. Che found him covered with blood but still alive. After evacuating the boy to his field hospital at El Hombrito, Che rejoined the fray, but Sánchez Mosquera's troops were well entrenched and kept up a heavy return fire, making any rush on their position extremely dangerous. When army reinforcements began arriving, Che sent patrols to stop them while he kept Sánchez Mosquera pinned down. Then, in an attempt to move in closer, Che's friend Ciro Redondo, a fellow *Granma* veteran, was killed by a bullet in the head.

By midafternoon it was over. The enemy reinforcements had fought their way past Che's ambushes, and he had finally ordered his men to retreat. It had been a bloody day. In addition to Ciro, they had lost another man when he was taken prisoner and then murdered; five more, including Joel, had been wounded. Expecting an army pursuit, they rushed back to Hombrito to prepare themselves for the next showdown.

After a few feverish days preparing their defenses, the alert sounded: Sánchez Mosquera's troops were on their way. Che had evacuated his wounded fighters and reserve stocks to his new fallback position at La Mesa. To stop the enemy advance into El Hombrito, Che invested high hopes in his armory's new land mines, which were placed along the approach road. When the soldiers did come, however, the mines didn't explode, and Che's forward ambush units had to retreat quickly; the enemy now had a clear path into El Hombrito. With little time to lose, Che and his men withdrew from the valley along a road leading up a hill dubbed "Los Altos de Conrado" for a Communist peasant who lived there and had helped them. It was a steep climb up to his abandoned house, the spot Che thought best to lie in wait for the enemy, and they found an ambush site behind a boulder overlooking the road. They were to wait there for the next three days.

This time, Che's plan was modest but risky. Hidden behind a large tree next to the track, Camilo Cienfuegos would try to kill the first soldier who appeared, shooting at point-blank range. Sharpshooters flanking the road would then open fire while others began shooting from the front. Che and a couple of men were situated in a reserve position twenty meters away, but Che was only partially concealed behind a tree, and the men near him were in similarly exposed positions. He had ordered that no one was to peer out—they would know the soldiers had arrived only upon hearing the first shot—but Che broke his own rule to sneak a look.

"I could at that moment sense the tension prior to combat," he wrote later. "I saw the first soldier appear. He looked around suspiciously and advanced slowly. . . . I hid my head, waiting for the battle to begin. There was the crack of gunfire and then shooting became generalized." The forest filled with the roar of combat as the two sides blasted away at each other at close quarters. The army hastily fired mortars, but they landed well beyond the rebels, and then Che was hit. "Suddenly I felt a disagreeable sensation, similar to a burn or the tingling of numbness. I had been shot in the left foot, which had not been protected by the tree trunk."

Che heard some men moving through the brush in his direction and realized he was now defenseless. He had emptied his rifle clip and hadn't had time to reload; his pistol had fallen on the ground and now lay beneath him, but he couldn't lift himself up to get it for fear of showing himself to the enemy. Desperately he rolled over and managed to grab the pistol just as he saw one of his own men, Cantinflas, coming toward him. Cantínflas had come to tell him his own gun was jammed and that he was retreating. Che snatched the gun, adjusted the clip, and sent the youth off with an insult. In a display of courage, Cantinflas left the tree cover to fire upon the enemy only to be hit himself by a bullet that entered his left arm and exited through his shoulder blade.

Both Che and Cantinflas were now wounded, with no idea as to where their comrades were. To escape the line of fire, they began crawling until they found help. Fleeing, they set off for a peasant collaborator's house a couple of kilometers away. Cantinflas was in a hammock-stretcher, but Che, his adrenaline still pumping, did the first part of the trip on his own two feet before the pain from his wound overcame him and he had to be lifted onto a horse.

Fearing the army might advance farther, Che again organized ambush positions at La Mesa and urgently sent a letter to Fidel informing him of the latest developments: "Rapid help with 30-06s and .45 automatics would be most timely." Telling Fidel that he had exacted vengeance for the loss of El Hombrito by killing "at least three enemy soldiers," he then broke the bad news: They had lost a rifle, recovered none from the enemy, and he was wounded. "I'm terribly sorry not to have heeded your advice, but the morale of the men was quite low . . . and I considered my presence on the front lines absolutely necessary. For the most part, I took good enough care of myself, and the wound was accidental."

After writing his letter, Che found that their situation wasn't as bad as he had feared. Rather than press their advantage, the enemy troops had completely withdrawn from the area. There was other good news. Young Joel Iglesias had been operated on and would recover. In their new refuge, one of the doctors who had joined the rebels in recent months also "operated" on Che, using a razor blade to extract the M-1 bullet from his foot, and Che was able to start walking again.

When he returned to El Hombrito, however, he found devastation. "Our oven had been painstakingly destroyed; in the midst of the smoking ruins we found nothing but some cats and a pig; they had escaped the destructive fury of the invading army only to wind up in our mouths." They would have to start all over again, but not in El Hombrito. As his first year of war came to an end, and 1958 began, Che set about erecting a new base at La Mesa.

VII

In his December 9 letter to Fidel, Che also addressed a problem that went far beyond his immediate military dilemma. It concerned his growing dispute with the July 26 National Directorate in the llano. Che had never liked the llano people—nor they, evidently, him—but now the relationship had reached the point of open acrimony.

The problem was formally over supply arrangements. Since becoming a *comandante,* Che had disregarded Frank País's successor, Daniel, as the rebel army's Oriente coordinator and made independent deals with suppliers unauthorized by the Directorate. But that was only the surface problem. Che was now known within the National Directorate as a "radical" Marxist. To the growing alarm of Armando Hart and Daniel, both manifestly anti-Communist, the Argentine commander headed his own column with almost total autonomy and clearly enjoyed influence over Fidel, while their own rapport with him had weakened. Che's refusal to even contact Daniel or use his organization in Santiago was undercutting the llano's authority, and they wished to assert control over him by forcing him to use "correct channels."

To resolve the growing rift, Daniel and Celia Sánchez journeyed into the Sierra Maestra to see Fidel in late October. The visit coincided with new political developments taking place outside the sierra. Armando Hart, as chief of the July 26 "general organization" in the llano, reported potentially positive moves made by the opposition parties to form a revolutionary government in exile, in which the July 26 Movement and Prío's *auténticos* would predominate. At the same time, he wrote Fidel in October, "cordial relations with certain diplomatic circles" were continuing, and he had learned that people "close to the [U.S.] embassy" had been talking with the ambassador on their behalf. "I think this is the best policy," Hart concluded, "since we are kept up to date on everything happening there and of all the possible U.S. plans, and at the same time the Movement does not officially commit itself."

In the wake of the failed Cienfuegos uprising, endorsed covertly by the CIA, the Americans were probably hedging their bets, fishing around for an alternative means to see Batista out of office. A broad-based coalition of Cuba's *acceptable* political groups—including a reined-in July 26 Movement—must have appeared an ideal solution. The Cuban conflict was getting out of hand, the army had proved itself utterly incapable of dealing the rebels a decisive blow, and Batista's solution had been to unleash his dogs. Murders of rebel suspects by his police were now routine, while periodic massacres of peasants by the army in Oriente exacerbated the atmosphere of growing anarchy. Army Colonel Alberto del Río Chaviano, notorious for his role in the torture-murders of the Moncada rebels, had been promoted to take over the antiguerrilla campaign in the Sierra Maestra, and a hundred-thousand-dollar reward had been placed on Castro's head.

Batista's enemies were also stepping up their violence. In October and November, the July 26 Movement went after spies and traitors in the cities, finally putting an end to the life of the traitor El Gallego Morán, who had caused havoc after going to work for Batista's military intelligence service. The brutal army commander of Holguín, Colonel Fermín Cowley, responsible for the massacre of the *Corynthia* men and numerous other murders, was assassinated by a July 26 action group. The rebels also stepped up their economic sabotage, sending units out from the sierra to burn cane fields on a much larger scale than before. To break the war out of its isolation in the Sierra Maestra and turn it into a national campaign, Fidel was planning to expand the attack on the economy; to show he meant business, he promised to burn his family's own sizeable cane fields in Birán.

Paradoxically, Cuba's economy was booming in spite of the conflict, thanks to improved sugar prices and increased foreign investment, most of it from the United States. The American-owned nickel concerns in Oriente had recently announced expansion plans, and in Havana port facilities were being expanded to cope with the increasing maritime trade. Tourists continued to flood into Havana, and new luxury hotels were being built to cope with the influx. The latest sugar harvest had been one of Cuba's best, reaping several hundred million dollars in extra revenues for the state.

But, uncertain about Batista's ability to hold things together, Washington continued to give off mixed signals to his regime. Despite increased dissatisfaction with Batista at State and in the CIA, the U.S. military were strongly supportive of the Cuban dictator. In a November ceremony Batista's air force chief, Colonel Carlos Tabernilla, had been awarded the U.S. Legion of Merit, and Batista himself was toasted as "a great general and a great president" in a speech by U.S. Marine Corps General Lemuel Sheperd. After a few months in his new post, Ambassador Earl Smith had heard more about the rebels' "Communist influences" and was increasingly skeptical of Fidel Castro, even cabling CIA Director Allen Dulles to suggest sending a spy into the Sierra Maestra to determine the "extent of Communist control" in his movement.

All the while, Fidel was walking a delicate tightrope in his quest to emerge as the de facto leader of Cuba's political opposition. To be successful, he had to acquire military muscle by expanding the war, but he also needed more political and economic support to pursue that objective. To obtain it, he had to present a suitably moderate, nonthreatening front.

After receiving Armando Hart's letter telling of the impending unity pact, Fidel shot off a letter to his U.S. representative, urging him to lead a delegation to the planned November 1 meeting, and gave him a list of his own nominees for key posts in the proposed alliance. No doubt confident that his wishes would be met, Fidel went back to the business of directing his guerrilla war. After their meetings, an evidently chastened Daniel returned to Santiago, and was soon working hard to get Fidel the ammunition and other supplies he said he needed. But Celia Sánchez remained behind. Fidel had told her he wanted her "feminine presence" at his side for some time, and she had assented. She would stay with him until the end of the war.

On November 1, in Miami, a "Cuban Liberation Junta" was formed, with representatives signing on behalf of most of Cuba's main opposition groups. The Communists had been excluded, but the July 26 Movement dominated the new junta's national committee. Without Fidel's consent, Felipe Pazos had acted as the official July 26 representative, which Fidel saw as a bid to upstage him. And apart from the standard calls for Batista's resignation, fair elections, and a return to constitutionality, the pact had pandered openly to Washington. There was no statement opposing foreign intervention or the idea of a military junta succeeding Batista—something Fidel greatly feared—and it called for the "postvictory" incorporation of Fidel's guerrillas into the Cuban armed forces, thereby ensuring the rebel army's future dissolution. The issue of economic injustice was similarly passed over with a tepid clause promising only to create more jobs and raise living standards. In sum, it was a political manifesto designed to warm Washington's heart.

The news began to filter through to the sierra in notes from Daniel and Armando Hart, who claimed to be upset with the terms of the pact, but intimated that they could "live with it." Raúl was openly livid, accusing Felipe Pazos of outright treachery, and wildly proposed that he be shot. Fidel let it be known he was unhappy but had yet to pronounce himself publicly, and as the llano officials scrambled to clarify their positions he kept an enigmatic silence. Immersed in the war, Che kept quiet but anxiously awaited Fidel's speaking his mind. On December 1, after the battle of Mar Verde, Che had diplomatically urged Fidel to issue a statement he could print in *El Cubano Libre*. Then came Che's retreat from El Hombrito and his injury at Altos de Conrado. It was in his December 9 letter from La Mesa that Che finally threw down the gauntlet to Fidel. Invoking his suspicions of the National Directorate and accusing it of intentionally "sabotaging" him, he demanded he be allowed to take unspecified "stern measures" to remedy the situation, or else resign. However diplomatically couched, it was an ultimatum to the jefe.* Not only Che's future relationship with Fidel Castro hinged on the reply but, in fact, the political course of Cuba's revolutionary struggle.

In four days, Che received his reply. The contents of the letter have never been revealed, but whatever they were, Che experienced a reaffirmation of faith. On December 15, he wrote Fidel: "At this very moment, a messenger arrived with your note of the thirteenth. I confess that it . . . filled me with peace and happiness. Not for any personal reason, but rather for what this step means for the Revolution. You know well that I didn't trust the people on the National Directorate at all—neither as leaders nor as revolutionaries. But I didn't think they'd go to the extreme of betraying you so openly."

Che went on to tell Fidel that his continued silence was "inadvisable"; the Americans were obviously "pulling the wires behind the scenes," and it was time to take the gloves off. "We unfortunately have to face Uncle Sam before the time is ripe." He again urged Fidel to sign a written document denouncing the Miami Pact; he would run off ten thousand copies and distribute them all over Oriente and Havana—the whole island if he could. "Later, if it becomes more complicated, with Celia's help, we can fire the entire National Directorate."

---

*Che acknowledged his period of doubt—in which this episode was an important milestone— in his farewell letter to Fidel, written as he left for the Congo in 1965. "Reviewing my past life, I believe I have worked with sufficient integrity and dedication to consolidate the revolutionary triumph. My only serious failing was not having had more confidence in you from the first moments in the Sierra Maestra, and not having understood quickly enough your qualities as a leader and a revolutionary."

Fidel *did* break his silence. On the day of his letter to Che, he issued a statement condemning the Miami Pact and sent it to Che, to the National Directorate, and to each of the pact signatories, accusing them of showing "lukewarm patriotism and cowardice." "The leadership of the struggle against the tyranny is, and will continue to be, in Cuba and in the hands of revolutionary fighters." As for the postvictory future of his guerrilla forces, he intoned: "The July 26 Movement claims for itself the role of maintaining public order and reorganizing the armed forces of the republic." Finally, to sabotage what he perceived to be Felipe Pazos's attempt to secure for himself the presidency of a future transition government, Fidel designated his own candidate: elderly Santiago jurist Manuel Urrutia. Fidel completed his tour de force by declaring: "These are our conditions. . . . If they are rejected, then we will continue the struggle on our own. . . . To die with dignity does not require company."

It was a powerful indictment, and it had its desired effect, effectively destroying the newly created junta. The Ortodoxos withdrew from the pact; Pazos resigned from the July 26 Movement; and Faure Chomón, the new leader of the Directorio, bitterly attacking Fidel's stance, began planning his own invasion of Cuba. Fidel still faced a showdown with his llano Directorate; that would come in a few months' time. Meanwhile, Che and Daniel crossed swords in a bitter exchange of letters. Defiantly proclaiming his Marxist beliefs and his restored faith in Fidel "as an authentic leader of the leftist bourgeoisie," Che castigated Daniel and the Directorate's "rightists" for having shamefully allowing the rebel movement's "ass to be buggered" in Miami. Daniel vigorously denied Che's charges and accused him of thinking Cuba would be better off under future "Soviet domination." He and his llano comrades also had their reservations about the Miami Pact, Daniel insisted, but believed that before breaking with it, the July 26 Movement should decide, "once and for all," what it stood for and where it was headed.*

More than any other documents, those of the epistolary war between Daniel and Che reveal the depth of the ideological divisions within the Cuban rebel movement at the time. Daniel wrote his rebuttal letter to Che before knowing of Fidel's break with the Miami Pact, but the die had already been cast—Cuba's other opposition groups were being informed they could have a role in the Cuban revolution only after acknowledging Fidel as its paramount leader, and on his conditions. And soon, the news of Fidel's rupture was all over Cuba. As promised, Che ran Fidel's letter off on his mimeograph machine, and on February 2, *Bohemia* reproduced it in

---

*See the appendix for elaboration.

a special press run of half a million copies. On January 6, as he was having it printed, Che wrote Fidel to praise him for the "historic" document. "Lenin already said it, the policy of principle is the best policy. The end result will be magnificent. . . . Now you are on the great path as one of the two or three [leaders] of America who will get to power by a multitudinous armed struggle."

At the time, only a few people besides Che were aware of the momentous step Fidel had actually taken, one that would eventually affect the lives of millions of people in Cuba and beyond. His public break with the Miami Pact was only the visible tip of a much greater political decision that, for now, was to still remain a carefully guarded secret.

VIII

Fidel had always known that one day he was going to have to confront the Americans, but he had hoped to avoid doing so until *after* he seized power. Their tentacles in his homeland went too deep for half-measures, and if he was ever to govern as he saw fit and achieve a genuine national liberation for Cuba, he was going to have to sever them completely. As Che understood it, this meant carrying out a socialist revolution, although Fidel had carefully refrained from ever mentioning the dreaded word in public.

Until now, Fidel had carefully kept the Communist party of Cuba, the Partido Socialista Popular, at arm's length. To gain ground, he had temporized his political message to appeal to a broad-based political alliance and to avoid antagonizing the Americans. But the unmistakable signs of U.S. influence in the Miami Pact and over some of the July 26 people in the llano had shown Fidel that the days of temporizing were over.

Enter the Communists. On the eve of the *Granma*'s sailing, the PSP had made clear to Fidel that it supported his goal of ousting Batista but disagreed over his tactics.

As time went on, the PSP was forced to consider increasing its involvement in the armed struggle. Despite its continued discomfort with Fidel's war strategy, it made sense for the Communist party to come to terms with him in some sort of alliance if it wanted a say in the country's political future. It also had little to lose. Under U.S. pressure, Batista had begun to persecute party members ruthlessly, using them as scapegoats for the political violence, while the war directly affected the lives of many party constituents. In view of Che Guevara's known political affinities and his close relationship with Fidel, he was the obvious rebel leader for the party to approach as they pursued the goal of closer links with Castro. These overtures came early in the struggle. On party orders to assist him, a young Communist traveled from Havana to join Che in the summer of 1957.

Pablo Ribalta, a black Cuban, had studied at Prague's International Union of Students and graduated from the Communist party's elite school for political cadres. At the time of his trip, Ribalta was a member of the National Secretariat of the Communist Youth. Ribalta has confirmed that he was selected by the party in mid-1957 to join Che in the sierra for the specific mission of carrying out political indoctrination among the rebel troops. "Che had asked for a person with my characteristics: a teacher, with a good level of political education and some experience in political work."

Ribalta entered the sierra from Bayamo and arrived at La Mesa at a time when Che was on the move. In his absence, Ribalta organized the incorporation of local Communists into the guerrilla forces and set up a political indoctrination school. When Che finally returned, he sat Ribalta down and questioned him on his knowledge. Apparently satisfied, Che ordered Ribalta to undergo a period of guerrilla training. A few months later, Che sent him to Minas del Frío, where he had established a permanent rearguard base with a school for recruits, a prison, and other facilities. Ribalta was to be an instructor, and his task was to produce 'integrally educated' fighters. "I had precise instructions not to say that I was a member of the PSP," Ribalta said, "although a group of leaders, including Fidel, knew it; but at that moment it could [have] created divisions, and I complied to the letter of the law. . . ."

The party had also maintained discreet contacts with Fidel and other Directorate officials, culminating in an October 1957 meeting between Fidel and Ursino Rojas, a PSP official and former leader of the Sugar Workers' Union. According to Rojas, they discussed the possibility of forging a coalition between their organizations and also explored the main obstacles to such a plan—the rampant anti-Communism of some of the movement's llano leaders, and within the new July 26 labor front group, the FON (Frente Obrero Nacional). For Fidel, some sort of an alliance with the PSP made good practical sense. Whatever his differences were with the party, the PSP had the best organized political group in the country, with deep long-standing ties to organized labor, making its active participation in the upcoming general strike vital. Until Fidel was able to impose his leadership over the entire July 26 Movement, however, any closer links with the PSP would have to be both gradual and discreet.

Feeling more secure about the political direction of the revolution, and with the renewal of his faith in Fidel, Che became more open about his Marxist convictions. He even indulged in some discreet proselytizing among his fighters, most of whom were not only politically ignorant but viscerally anti-Communist, much like their American neighbors in the Cold War. Communism was widely perceived as the "Red threat," a kind of insidious foreign infection to be both feared and resisted. How Che dealt with this mentality among his own men is interesting.

Enrique Acevedo, the fifteen-year-old runaway who had joined up with his older brother and been assigned to Che's "Descamisados," recalled an incident involving some of the men were arguing over whether their jefe was a Communist, in Che's absence. One of them who insisted Che was a *ñangaro*—a "Red"—challenged the others. "Haven't you noticed that in the commander's squad there is a great mystery surrounding his books, and they read them at night in a closed circle? That's how he works: first he recruits those closest to him, and later they go filtering it throughout the troops."

Acevedo was too much in awe of Che to approach him personally on the topic, but gradually he and the other fighters in Che's column came to realize that their *comandante* believed in socialism. The first to know it were the rebels attached to his general staff. One of them was Ramón "Guile" Pardo, a teenager who had joined the column in August 1957, following in his older brother Israel's footsteps. Over the course of several months, the younger Pardo became one of Che's group of devoted mascots, mostly teen-aged boys who served as his couriers and personal bodyguards.

"When we were in El Hombrito," recalled Pardo, "I heard it said that there were some peasants who belonged to the Popular Socialist party. . . . On our trips, Che visited them and I noticed that he had an affinity with them. He also argued politics a lot with Father [Guillermo] Sardiñas, who stayed awhile in our column. Che had a blue book, which was one of the selected works of Lenin, and he studied it frequently. I was curious and wanted to know who Lenin was and I asked him. He explained: 'You know of José Martí, Antonio Maceo and Máximo Gómez.* Lenin was like them. He fought for his people.' It was the first time someone spoke to me of Lenin."

The young fighters were clean slates upon whom Che made a lasting imprint. He personally taught Israel Pardo and Joel Iglesias, who were illiterate, how to read and write. And for Guile and some of the others, who had more learning, he initiated daily study circles. The study material gradually evolved from Cuban history and military doctrine to politics and Marxism. When Joel had finally learned to read, Che gave him a biography of Lenin to study.

Just as he was circumspect about his own political role during the war, Che made only oblique references to the early PSP–July 26 links in his later published writings. He sought to depict the revolution as evolving *naturally*

---

*Cuba's late-nineteenth-century national independence war heroes toward socialism, an organic result of the rebel army's life among the neglected peasants of the Sierra Maestra.

"The guerrillas and the peasantry began to merge into a single mass, without our being able to say at what precise moment on the long revolutionary road this happened, or at which moment the words became profoundly real and we became a part of the peasantry."

Writing of the peasantry's own gradual acceptance of the revolution, Che employed religious symbolism, rendering their travails as a kind of Pilgrim's Progress in which individuals found redemption through sacrifice, attaining final enlightenment by learning to live for the Common Good. "It is a new miracle of the revolution that—under the imperative of war—the staunchest individualist, who zealously protected the boundaries of his property and his own rights, joined the great common effort of the struggle. But there is an even greater miracle: the rediscovery by the Cuban peasant of his own happiness, within the liberated zones. Whoever witnessed the apprehensive murmurs with which our forces were formerly received in each peasant household notes with pride the carefree clamor, the happy, hearty laughter of the new Sierra inhabitant. That is a reflection of the self-confidence that the awareness of his own strength gave to the inhabitant of our liberated area."

Che wrote this article, called "War and the Peasantry," only seven months after the war had ended. However consciously he had idealized life in the sierra for public consumption, his evocation of a pastoral Utopia wrought through armed struggle was a vision he sought afterward to replicate on an international scale. Most important of all, he identified revolution as the ideal circumstance in which to achieve a socialist consciousness. In essence, socialism was the natural order of mankind, and guerrilla war the chrysalis from which it would come about.

18

Extending the War

I

By December 1957 Fidel wanted to bring the war down from the Sierra Maestra. Rebel squads began trickling down into the llano to launch harassment attacks, firing on garrisoned soldiers as far away as Manzanillo, and burning cane trucks and passenger buses on the highway. While serving the obvious goal of expanding the war, the strategy also had the effect of diverting attention from the Sierra Maestra, where the rebels had moved quickly to consolidate their control over the terrain. The uneasy standoff persisted into the new year, with the army mounting no new incursions and the rebels likewise refraining from large-scale assaults.

In the relative calm, no one, perhaps, was more active than Che Guevara. At his new base of operations at La Mesa, facilities were built to replace those destroyed at El Hombrito, among them a butcher shop, a leather workshop, and even a cigar factory. By now, Che had become addicted to Cuban tobacco, and, like Fidel, smoked cigars whenever they were available.

The leather workshop was to provide the troops with shoes, knapsacks, and cartridge belts. When the first army cap was produced, Che proudly presented it to Fidel. Instead of compliments, however, he was greeted with raucous laughter; unwittingly, he had produced a cap almost identical to those worn by Cuban bus drivers. Recalled Che: "The only one showing me any mercy was a municipal councillor from Manzanillo who was visiting . . . and who took it back with him as a souvenir."

To break through the government-imposed censorship and army disinformation, he gave top priority to the rebel army's media projects. *El Cubano Libre* was now being printed on a new mimeograph machine, while one of the most ambitious projects was the installation of a small radio transmitter. By February, Radio Rebelde was transmitting its first broadcasts.

Che also put great effort into improving the quality and output of war materiel from his reestablished armory, and was especially enthusiastic about the new M-26 bombs, or "Sputniks." The first Sputniks were small bombs catapulted from the elastic bands of underwater spearguns. They were later perfected and became rifle-launched, but these first models were little more than explosive slingshots—a bit of gunpowder packed into condensed milk tins. They made a huge and frightening noise but inflicted little damage, and before long the enemy learned to put up "anti-Sputnik" nets of wire mesh around their camps. In early 1958 they had not yet been tested in battle, and Che had high hopes for their performance.

Meanwhile, Fidel made a curious overture to Batista. If the army was withdrawn from Oriente, Fidel told a go-between, he would agree to internationally supervised elections. His proposal coincided with an upsurge in public concern over rebel sabotage and police atrocities in the cities, and Fidel apparently wanted to give the impression that he too wanted peace. The would-be mediator duly carried the proposal to Havana, where the offer was so vehemently rejected by the Batista regime that the messenger fled into exile.

At the same time, the international press was beating a path to Fidel's door. Cuba had become a big story, scrutinized in regular editorials by the *New York Times,* and covered by the *Chicago Tribune*'s Latin American correspondent, Jules Dubois. In January and February, a veritable flood of reporters climbed into the sierra for interviews, including correspondents from the *New York Times, Paris Match,* and various Latin American dailies. Andrew St. George came back, and Fidel made suitably placatory declarations to him for his American audience. He even wrote an article for publication in *Coronet,* one of St. George's media outlets, where it appeared in February. In it, Fidel avowed he was in favor of free enterprise and foreign investment, and against nationalization. The provisional government he envisioned as replacing Batista would be composed of Rotary Club members and other solidly middle-class professionals.

In January, the movement suffered a potentially disastrous setback when Armando Hart and two other July 26 men were arrested after visiting Fidel. By all accounts, their captors were planning to execute them, but the American vice-consul (and CIA agent) in Santiago, Robert Wiecha, came to their rescue by getting Ambassador Smith to inquire about their fates.

Unfortunately, when captured, Hart had been carrying a rather incriminating document, a critical salvo he had written to Che in response to Che's fiery missive to Daniel, addressing the issue of Che's and Raúl's Marxism as well as the llano-sierra dispute. Fidel had seen the letter and ordered Hart not to send it, fearing that if the epistolary war continued, a letter would

eventually fall into enemy hands and give Batista a new propaganda weapon
to use against him. These fears had now been realized. Within days of Hart's
arrest, Rafael Díaz-Balart, Fidel's former brother-in-law—who despised
him passionately—went on a radio broadcast to cite the letter as evidence
of Communist influence in Fidel's rebel organization.

The propaganda campaign was quickly squandered, however. Only
days after Hart's capture, the army took twenty-three rebel suspects from
the prison in Santiago to the sierra foothills and massacred them, then reported that the twenty-three had been killed in battle, with no army casualties. Writing as the Sniper in his *Cubano Libre* column, "Wild Shot," Che
delivered a scathing attack. After listing a number of other revolutionary
wars occurring around the world, Che noted:

> All of them have common characteristics: A) The govern-
> ing power "has inflicted numerous casualties on the rebels." B)
> There are no prisoners. C) "Nothing new" [to report] by the gov-
> erning power. D) All the revolutionaries, whatever the name of
> the country or region, are receiving "surreptitious help from the
> communists."
>
> How Cuban the world seems to us! Everything is the same.
> A group of patriots are murdered, whether or not they have arms,
> whether or not they are rebels, always after "a fierce fight" . . . ,
> they kill all the witnesses, that is why there are no prisoners. The
> government never suffers a casualty, which at times is true, because
> killing defenseless human beings is not very dangerous, but at
> times it is also a great lie; the Sierra Maestra is our unimpeachable
> witness.
>
> And, finally, the same handy accusation as always: "commu-
> nists." Communists are always those who pick up their arms tired
> of so much misery, wherever in the world the action takes place;
> democrats those who kill the indignant people, whether they be
> men, women or children. How Cuban the world is! But every-
> where, as in Cuba, the people will have the last word, that of vic-
> tory, against brute force and injustice."

But if the slaughter of the Santiago prisoners deflected Cuban public
attention from Batista's propaganda offensive about Communist influence
in Fidel's group, it did not divert the Americans. For Ambassador Earl
Smith, the revelations contained in Hart's captured letter lent further credence to his mounting suspicions of "Red" infiltration of the July 26 Movement, fueling his growing acceptance of Batista. In January, Smith made a

trip to Washington to lobby for the dictator at the State Department, based on Batista's promise to restore constitutional guarantees and go through with the June elections if the United States kept up its arms deliveries to him. As for Castro, Smith told reporters, he did not trust him, and did not think the U.S. government able to "do business" with him.

By early February, Che's armory raced to put the finishing touches on the "Sputniks" in preparation for the rebel army's first major military action of the year. Fidel had decided to attack again the sawmill community of Pino del Agua, where an army company had established a permanent presence. Batista had just lifted censorship in all of Cuba except Oriente, and Fidel wanted to "strike a resounding blow" to earn some headlines.

II

The attack began at dawn on February 16. Fidel's plan was to surround and attack the army camp, destroy its guard posts, and then ambush the enemy reinforcements when they came. Che's men brought along six Sputniks, to be fired at the beginning of the attack. Another of his armory's creations, a land mine made from unexploded airplane bombs, was also given its first test, placed in a road that the army was expected to use. The result was disappointing. The Sputniks fired successfully but did litttle damage, while the land mines produced what Che called "a lamentable result": Their first victim was a civilian truck driver who happened along at just the wrong moment.

The attack started well enough. The first-wave fighters overran the guard posts, killing a half-dozen sentries and taking three prisoners, but the main body of soldiers had quickly rallied, effectively stopping the rebels' advance. Within minutes, four rebels were killed, two more mortally wounded; Camilo Cienfuegos was wounded twice trying to rescue an abandoned machine gun.

The rebels had better luck against the army reinforcements who rushed to the battle. The first patrol walked directly into a rebel ambush and was wiped out. But Che still wanted to inflict a total defeat and begged Fidel to attack the entrenched enemy camp again, to completely overrun it this time. At his insistence, Fidel sent a couple of platoons to give it another try, but they too were repulsed under heavy fire. Che then asked Fidel to be given command of a new assault force; he would try to rout the soldiers by torching their camp. Grudgingly, Fidel let him go but warned him to take great care.

Just as he was preparing the advance, however, Che received a note from Fidel. "February 16, 1958. CHE: If everything depends on the attack from this side, without support from Camilo and Guillermo [García], I do not think anything suicidal should be done, because there is a risk of many casualties and failure to achieve the objective. I seriously urge you to be careful. You yourself are not to take part in the fighting. That is a strict order. Take charge of leading the men well; that is the most important thing right now. Fidel."

Fidel knew Che would probably not go forward with his plan if he couldn't take part in the fighting himself—and he was right. As Che wrote later: "With all this responsibility weighing on my shoulders, it was too much, and crestfallen, I took the same path as my predecessor." He ordered his men to withdraw.

It was merely the latest time Fidel held Che back for his own safety. Later, speaking of Che's reckless tenacity in battle, Fidel said: "In a way, he even violated the rules of combat—that is, the ideal norms, the most perfect methods—risking his life in battle because of that character, tenacity, and spirit of his. . . . Therefore, we had to lay down certain rules and guidelines for him to follow."

The next morning, with government planes buzzing overhead, the rebels retreated back into the hills, taking five prisoners and forty new weapons with them. After they withdrew, the army apparently murdered thirteen peasants found hiding near the rebel positions. Denouncing this atrocity in *El Cubano Libre,* Che calculated the enemy losses at eighteen to twenty-two dead, while the army produced different statistics. An official dispatch claimed that "sixteen insurgents and five soldiers" had died in the battle but could not confirm reports that "the well-known Argentine communist Che Guevara was wounded." Pointing up Che's status as a favorite new bugbear for the *antifidelísta* press, another Havana paper reported that the attack had been led by "the international communist agent known as 'Che' Guevara."

The weeks following the battle at Pino del Agua saw increased rebel sabotage attacks throughout the country. Then, on February 23, in one of the most spectacular publicity coups carried out by the movement so far, a July 26 action unit kidnapped Juan Manuel Fangio, a world-famous Argentine race-car driver who was in Havana to compete in an international championship. Later released unharmed, Fangio declared that his kidnapping had been "friendly," his treatment "warm and cordial."

The Directorio, virtually crippled after its disastrous palace attack in March 1957, was now becoming more active as well. A tiny Directorio breakaway group had already been operating in the central Escambray mountains near Cienfuegos for several months. It was led by Eloy Gutiérrez Menoyo, whose brother had died leading the palace assault, and was aided by an American military veteran named William Morgan. In February, their effort was bolstered with the arrival of a fifteen-man armed Directorio expeditionary force from Miami led by Faure Chomón. Temporarily joining ranks, they carried out a few hit-and-run attacks, then issued a somewhat grandiose proclamation calling for a Cuba with ample employment and educational opportunities, and appealing for the formation of a Bolivarian-style "confederation of American republics." Hearing the news, Fidel played the magnanimous elder statesman, sending a note to welcome the Directorio's guerrillas to the "common struggle" and offering them his assistance.

Fidel took new steps to extend his own theater of operations. On February 27, he named his three principal lieutenants—his brother Raúl, Juan Almeida, and Camilo Cienfuegos—as *comandantes* of their own columns. In keeping with his custom of exaggerating his force's size, Fidel numbered Raúl's "Frank País" unit Column Six, and Almeida's "Santiago de Cuba" unit Column Three. Raúl was to open up a "Second Eastern Front" in the Sierra Cristal in northeastern Oriente, adjacent to the American naval base at Guantánamo Bay, while Almeida was to start up the "Third Eastern Front," covering the area from the eastern Sierra Maestra to the city of Santiago. (Camilo's theater of operations would be determined once he recovered from his wounds suffered at Pino del Agua.)

Fidel also set about consolidating his power within the *"territorio libre"* of the Sierra Maestra. The former *auténtico* lawyer Humberto Sorí-Marín, who had assisted at the "bandit trials" of October, now drafted judicial legislation to impose revolutionary authority over the inhabitants of rebel-held territory. Sorí-Marín then drafted an agrarian reform law, a measure to give "legal" backing to a practice Fidel had already begun: the wholesale rustling of cattle herds from landowners, and their distribution among his fighters and the peasants of the region.* In March, impetus was given to another pending project, the creation of a training school for recruits and officers at Minas del Frío. It was to be run under Che's direction, with day-to-day administration handled by a new convert named Evelio Lafferte.

It was a remarkable partnership, for just a month earlier Lafferte had been a twenty-six-year-old army lieutenant fighting against the rebels at Pino del Agua, and, of all the rebel leaders, the one he most feared was Che Guevara. "The [army] propaganda against him was massive. It said that he

---

*By the end of the war, an estimated ten thousand cattle had been "liberated" in this fashion by the rebels in Oriente. By making many peasants the owners of livestock for the first time in their lives, it was one of the rebel army's most popular measures and won it the support of numerous *guajiros*.

was a murderer for hire, a pathological criminal . . . a mercenary, who lent his services to international communism, that he used terrorist methods and that he *socialized* [brainwashed] the women and took away their sons. . . . [It was said] any soldiers he took prisoner he tied to a tree and opened up their guts with a bayonet."

Lafferte's anxiety only increased when, immediately after the ambush in which he was captured and so many of his fellow soldiers killed, he was led before the feared Argentine. "He told me: 'So you are one of the little officers who come to finish off the Rebel Army, huh?' He repeated that 'little officer' and this angered me. It was in an ironic tone and it seemed to me a hint of worse to come." Still convinced the rebels meant to kill him, Lafferte was taken to an improvised prison at Che's La Mesa camp, but, given deferential treatment, he gradually began losing his fear.

The rebels realized they had a potentially valuable man on their hands: Lafferte not only was a bright and distinguished young officer, the best of his class at Cuba's military academy, but was beset by doubts over the army's brutal conduct of the war. Fidel personally urged him to join his side. After a month in detention, Lafferte accepted the offer; immediately made a captain by Fidel, he was dispatched to run Che's recruit training school in Minas del Frío.

Che was careful in his dealings with Lafferte, bringing him around to new points of view with tact and discretion. He spent time with the young officer, talking about his family, and about literature and poetry, a love they shared. Lafferte showed him some poems he had written, and Che gave him a copy of Pablo Neruda's "Canto General." He listened to Lafferte's suggestions for running the school and accepted those he found convincing. One he did not accept was Lafferte's idea that recruits should "swear by God" in their oath of allegiance.

"When the comrades come to the Sierra," Che told him, "we don't take into account whether they believe in God or not, so we can't oblige them to swear by God. For example, I don't believe, and I am a fighter of the Rebel Army. . . . Do you think it's right to force me to swear an oath to something I don't believe in?"

Lafferte felt discomfited but was swayed by Che's argument: "I didn't like that, because I was Catholic, but I understood the correctness of what he was proposing, and I took God out of the oath."

Once the school was up and running, Che brought over Pablo Ribalta, the Communist Youth leader, to take direct charge of the ideological orientation of the recruits. Using the pseudonym "Moisés Pérez," Ribalta successfully concealed his true identity from his fellow rebels. So as not to scare off his pupils with Marxist texts, he used the experiences of the sierra war, Cuban history, the writings and speeches of Fidel "and other guerrilla leaders" to drive his points home. One of the "other guerrilla leaders" was none other than Mao Tse-tung.

That is what Harry Villegas Tamayo, then a sixteen-year-old youth from the Oriente town of Yara, remembers from his time at Minas del Frío. "For Che, the guerrilla war wasn't just a military proving-ground, but also a cultural and educational one. He was concerned with forming the future cadres of the Revolution."

Che's forward thinking paid off. Like some of the other youths hand-picked by Che to receive his special attention, Villegas went on to become a loyal cadre of the revolution, first as a member of Che's personal team of bodyguards, then remaining at his side through the guerrilla struggles in the Congo and Bolivia, later becoming one of Cuba's top generals. Today, still only in his mid-fifties, Villegas is one of few living Cubans honored with the official distinction of "Hero of the Revolution."

III

The unusual degree of devotion Che inspired in his men was evident to the reporters who met him in the Sierra Maestra, and some of them came away as his unswerving admirers and disciples. One of those was the Uruguayan Carlos María Gutiérrez, who first met Che immediately after the battle of Pino del Agua.

Sipping his cherished *yerba mate,* Che walked over to Gutiérrez and immediately began pumping him with questions about his photographic equipment. What light meters did he use? How long did he expose his film? And, a question he was to repeat to every visitor from the Cono Sur, had he brought some *yerba mate* with him? Over the next few days, Che showed Gutiérrez the base hospital and his "shoe factory," and all the while the Uruguayan kept up his observations, taking special note of an unusual warmth and camaraderie among Che's men.

"There were no orders [given], nor permissions [granted], nor military protocol, the guerrillas of La Mesa reflected a discipline that was more intimate, derived from the men's confidence in their leaders. Fidel, Che and the others lived in the same places, ate the same, and at the hour of combat fired from the same line as they did. Guevara didn't have to abandon his *porteño*'s brusqueness to show that he loved them, and they paid him back with the same virile reticence, with an adherence that went deeper than mere obedience."

Another visitor to the sierra in the spring of 1958 was the young Argentine journalist Jorge Ricardo Masetti. Like some of his predecessors,* Masetti, a handsome but otherwise undistinguished journalist, with a background in an ultraright Perónist youth group, would find his life irrevocably changed by the experience, and his infatuation with the revolution was to have dramatic consequences.

By coincidence, Masetti came with a letter of introduction from none other than Ernesto Guevara's old acquaintance, Ricardo Rojo, the lawyer, who had returned to Argentina in 1955 after the right-wing military coup that toppled Perón.** In late 1957, Masetti tracked down Rojo at the Café La Paz, a literary and theater hangout in central Buenos Aires, and asked for help in meeting the Sierra Maestra rebels. Rojo penned a quick note to Guevara.

"Dear Chancho: The bearer is a newspaperman and friend who wants to do a news program for El Mundo radio station in Buenos Aires. Please take good care of him, he's a good man." Rojo signed it, "The Sniper," the nickname he and Guevara had traded back and forth in their Central American days, little knowing that his young friend had once again appropriated it for himself.

In March, Masetti made it into the Sierra Maestra. He was the first Argentine visitor to the mountains, and some of the young rebels excitedly asked if he was Che's "brother." Masetti seemed determined not to feel impressed at their first meeting: "From his chin sprouted a few hairs that wanted to be a beard. . . . The famous Che Guevara seemed to me to be a typical middle class Argentine boy."

Over a shared breakfast, Masetti prodded Che on why he was fighting in a land that was not his own. Che puffed on a pipe as he spoke, and

*Bob Taber, the CBS journalist, would eventually cross the line altogether by becoming an activist, helping to found the Fair Play for Cuba Committee and lobbying in the United States on behalf of the Castro government. Herbert Matthews's early romantic boosterism of Fidel Castro undermined his journalistic credibility and ultimately damaged his career at the *New York Times*. The young Ecuadorean journalist Carlos Bastidas, who came up to the sierra in early 1958, left determined to take up the movement's cause with the Organization of American States in Washington. Before he could leave the country, however, Bastidas was murdered by Batista's intelligence police.

**Rojo had gone to work for his political mentor, Arturo Frondízi, who in 1956 had formed the liberal Radical party breakaway, the Union Cívica Radical Intransigente. When General Aramburu acceded to elections, Rojo was instrumental in setting up talks between Frondízi's party and Perón—still powerful in exile—for the purpose of winning Frondízi the crucial *peronísta* vote. The bid was successful: Frondízi won the presidential elections held in February 1958, and Rojo was repaid for his efforts with a diplomatic post in Bonn.

Masetti thought his accent sounded no longer Argentine but a mixture of "Cuban and Mexican." "In the first place," he told Masetti, "I consider my fatherland to be not only Argentina, but all of America. I have predecessors as glorious as Martí and it is precisely in his land where I am adhering to his doctrine. What is more, I cannot conceive that it can be called interference to give myself personally, to give myself completely, to offer my blood for a cause I consider just and popular, to help a people liberate themselves from tyranny.... No country until now has denounced the American interference in Cuban affairs nor has a single daily newspaper accused the Yankees of helping Batista massacre his people. But many are concerned about me. I am the meddling foreigner who helps the rebels with his flesh and blood. Those who provide the arms for a civil war aren't meddlers. I am."

As Che spoke, it struck Masetti that he spoke in a completely impersonal fashion, although a smile seemed constantly to play on his lips. Masetti next asked about Fidel Castro's Communism. At this, Che smiled broadly but answered with the same detachment as before. "Fidel isn't a communist. If he was, we would have at least more arms. But this revolution is exclusively Cuban. Or better said, Latin American. Politically Fidel and his movement can be said to be 'revolutionary nationalist.' Of course it is anti-Yankee, in the measure that the Yankees are antirevolutionaries. But in reality we don't put preach anti-Yankism. We are against the United States because the United States is against our peoples. The person most attacked with the label of communism is myself."

As for his own reasons in joining the Cuban force in Mexico, Che saw a strong connection to his years of travel. "The truth is that after the experiences of my wanderings across all of Latin America and, to top it off, in Guatemala, it didn't take much to incite me to join any revolution against a tyrant, but Fidel impressed me as an extraordinary man. He faced and overcame the most impossible things. He had an exceptional faith in that once he left for Cuba, he would arrive. And that once he arrived, he would fight. And that fighting, he would win. I shared his optimism.... [It was time to] stop crying and fight."

Masetti returned to Argentina with his scoop: He had interviewed Fidel, and Che—who had spoken for the first time to an international broadcast audience. He also returned with a recorded greeting from Che to the Guevara family. Masetti's visit was an exciting moment for the Guevara clan, for during the past year letters from their "Ernesto" had been rare. More often than not, they learned about him through magazines and newspapers. The family had glowed with pride over a photograph published with Herbert Matthews's famous interview in the *New York Times,* in which Ernesto appeared holding a gun and sporting a scraggly beard. Matthews's articles had also calmed the Guevaras' anxieties about their son's adopted cause. "Now we knew," his father wrote, "that Ernesto was fighting for a cause recognized as just." In the spring of 1958, Che's father saw an article written by Bob Taber about Che entitled: "Will Che Be Able to Change the Destiny of America?" To the elder Guevara, it proved his son was *someone*. "I confess that what Taber wrote impressed the whole family. Ernesto was now not just another guerrilla, but was mentioned as a future leader of countries."

Other news came from Dolores Moyano, Ernesto's childhood friend who now lived in New York, and who sent the Guevaras clippings from the Miami-based Spanish-language *Diario de las Americas,* and from the July 26 committee in New York, which sent them copies of rebel army communiqués. And soon Guevara Lynch was getting regular briefings from the *Chicago Tribune*'s Latin American correspondent, Jules Dubois. Dubois had looked up Che's father on a visit to Buenos Aires, and ever since they had made a habit of meeting for a chat over whisky whenever Dubois was in town.

The meetings were eagerly looked forward to by both men. Dubois visited Cuba frequently, and, in exchange for all the details on Che's latest exploits, he pumped the elder Guevara to find out whatever he could on the young Che. Guevara Lynch finally became suspicious when Dubois asked him to write down a summary of what he knew about Fidel Castro. Later, claimed Guevara Lynch, his suspicions were confirmed by "a very good source" that Dubois was actually a CIA official. (True or not, this charge had become official dogma in Cuba, where the elder Guevara was living when he wrote his memoir.)

When the Uruguayan journalist Carlos María Gutiérrez returned home from Cuba, he too looked up Che's family in Buenos Aires, brimming with admiration for the revolution and for Che. "When he talked to us about Ernesto," recalled Guevara Lynch, "his words didn't entirely convince us, because he spoke of a romantic and bohemian hero." Also a very busy one; according to Gutiérrez, Che "had laid the bases for agrarian reform in the Sierra; built an arms factory; invented a bazooka rifle; inaugurated the first bread factory in the mountains; built and equipped a hospital . . . created the first school and . . . installed a radio transmitter called Radio Rebelde . . . and he still had time left to found a small newspaper to inform the rebel troops."

Masetti's visit crowned the Guevara family's feeling of vicarious celebrity. They listened to the recording their son's latest admirer had brought them, and the radio broadcasts of his interviews on Radio El Mundo. After their first visits, Masetti and Gutiérrez became frequent visitors and family friends, and, infected by their enthusiasm, Guevara Lynch soon took to the Cuban revolution with fervor. "The defense of the Cuban Revolution entrapped us all," he wrote. "My house on Calle Araoz turned into a revolutionary center." He rented another studio near his office and turned it into a branch of the local July 26 support committee, and, in a move reminiscent of his work during the Spanish Civil War and World War II, founded a "Comité de Ayuda a Cuba," which held dances and sold bonds to raise funds. His son's cause had now become his.

In Lima, Hilda had also taken up support activities for the July 26 Movement, becoming its official representative in Peru. By then, July 26 chapters had been set up throughout Latin America and the United States, raising funds, advertising its aims, and disseminating information to the press. "I worked, complying with instructions sent me by the committee, on propaganda and money collection," wrote Hilda. With some members from the leftist wing of APRA, which she had rejoined, she founded a support group to help Cuban exiles seeking refuge in Peru.

Yet, for all her political activity, Hilda's reminiscence of the period betrays a certain scolding quality. "Letters came from time to time from Ernesto. Only a few of mine managed to reach him, however, although I followed his instructions. . . . When Hildita was two years old, February 15, 1958, I wrote Ernesto and asked him to authorize my coming to the mountains of Cuba, to be with him and help; the child was then old enough to be cared for either by my family or his. His reply took about four or five months to arrive. He said I couldn't come yet; the fight was at a dangerous stage, and an offensive would begin in which he himself would not remain in any one place."

But there was another reason why Hilda's presence in the Sierra Maestra would not be opportune. In the spring of 1958, Che had taken a lover, a young *guajira* named Zoila Rodríguez. Che's adolescent protégé, Joel Iglesias, observed the lightning courtship. "In Las Vegas de Jibacoa, Che met a black girl, or better said a *mulata,* with a really beautiful body, called Zoila, and he liked her a lot. A lot of women went crazy over him, but he was always very strict and respectful in that sense . . . but he liked *that* girl. They hooked up and were together for a time."

Zoila was a single mother of eighteen and still living on her father's farm when she met Che. "It was about four in the afternoon of a date I can't remember," she reminisced years later. "I was coralling some cows when he came. He came mounted on a mule. . . . He was dressed in a strange green uniform, with a black beret." He had come looking for her father, a rebel collaborator, to see if he could shoe his mule; with her father away, Zoila offered to do it for him. "As I shoed the mule, I looked at him sideways and

I realized he was observing me, but he was looking at me in the way boys look at girls and I got really nervous. When I went to the box of irons to choose a rasp, he asked me what I was going to do and I explained that I had cut the hooves and now I had to level them off to mount the shoes. Guevera said was it really necessary to make them so beautiful. I said that's the way it had to be. He kept looking at me in that way . . . a stare a little bit naughty, like he wanted to scold me for something I hadn't done."

When Zoila had finished shoeing the mule she offered Che coffee. As he drank it he asked Zoila about herself. Where had she learned how to shoe mules? Was she married or single? If Che had been wooing her, it worked. "He impressed me a lot, the truth is that and I can't deny it, as a woman I liked him very much, above all his stare, he had such beautiful eyes, a smile so calm that it would move any heart, it could move any woman."

When Zoila's father returned home, he explained to her in admiring tones who Guevara was, an extraordinary man who had come to lift them from their misery and disgrace. Soon afterward, Zoila began to carry out small errands for the rebels, meeting Che occasionally, until one day he finally asked her to stay on permanently at Minas del Frío. She helped out in the kitchen and in the hospital, and she worked hard.

"He told me he admired me for that and he admired the peasants for the difficult work we had to do," Zoila recalled. "He asked me many things about the Sierra Maestra, how the plants were called, what were they good for, especially the medicinal one. . . . He wanted to know all about the animals and the birds of the bush. A great and beautiful love arose in me and I committed myself to him, not just as a fighter but as a woman."

For the next several months, Zoila stayed by Che's side. Interestingly, he doesn't appear to have tried to educate her politically. Zoila remembered one day when she saw one of his books and was amazed at the sight of its golden letters. "I asked him if they were made of gold. He thought the question was funny. He laughed, and he said: 'That book is about Communism.' I was too shy to ask him what Communism meant, because I had never heard that word before."

IV

In March 1958, Fidel Castro faced a new potential roadblock in his path to power: a peace initiative. Calling for an end to rebel violence and the creation of a national-unity government, the Catholic Church named a "harmony commission" made up of conservative politicians, businessmen, and a priest to mediate. While Batista himself made appropriately receptive sounds, Fidel rejected the commission as overly pro-Batista. It was a risky gamble, however, for there was growing public support for a negotiated settlement, and Fidel ran the risk of being viewed as the impediment. At the crucial moment, Batista gave him a way out.

The catalyst was provided when a Havana judge indicted two of Batista's most notorious henchmen for murder; the dictator responded by again suspending constitutional guarantees and throwing out the indictment, causing the offending judge to flee the country. In response, the United States suspended all arms shipments to Cuba. In the face of Washington's disapproval, increased rebel sabotage, and mounting calls for his resignation by Cuban civic institutions, Batista compounded his problems by postponing the scheduled June elections until November. Then, his firepower reinforced by a planeload of weapons, flown directly on a C-47 transport from Costa Rica to a rendezvous point near Estrada Palma, Fidel met with his National Directorate (less Armando Hart, who was imprisoned on the Isle of Pines and would remain there until the rebel victory).* On March 12, they signed a joint manifesto calling for preparations to begin for the long-planned general strike and for "total war" against the regime.

The goal was nothing less than a complete paralysis of the nation: As of April 1 no taxes were to be paid; by April 5 anyone remaining in the executive branch of government would be considered a traitor, while those joining the armed forces were to be considered criminals, judges should resign their offices. When the strike call was announced over the radio, the rebels would launch armed attacks in Havana and throughout the country. While Faustino Pérez, recently released from prison, would organize the strikes in Havana, Fidel prepared his army for what he hoped would be a full-scale insurrection.

Eager to be involved, the Communist party of Cuba, the PSP, ordered its own militants to heed the call and to begin organizing for action, but once again the conservative llano leaders of the National Directorate blocked their involvement. Even after the PSP had sent an emissary to Fidel to plead its case, and Fidel responded by ordering the movement to allow "all Cuban

---

*With the arms shipment came Pedro Miret, who had been in prison in Mexico at the time of the *Granma* sailing; he now rejoined Fidel as a member of his general staff. Accompanying him was Huber Matos, a Manzanillo schoolteacher and rice grower who had gone into exile after helping transport the first rebel reinforcements to the sierra the year before. Fidel made Matos an officer, and he would later become *comandante* of Column No. 9. The pilot of the plane—which the rebels burned after unloading its cargo—was Pedro Luis Díaz Lanz, a defector from Batista's air force. Before the war was over, Díaz Lanz would make a number of arms deliveries to the rebels and be named the revolution's air force chief; later, he would become one of the Castro regime's most dangerous enemies.

workers, no matter what their political or revolutionary affiliations," to participate in the strike committees, the llano leaders studiously excluded the Communists.

The strike call came on April 9, and it was a catastrophe. The Batista-controlled Confederación de Trabajadores Cubanos (CTC) and the disenfranchised PSP disregarded the strike order. In Havana, most shops and factories remained open, and the key sectors of electricity and transport were unaffected. In Santiago, the strike fizzled as well, and by the end of the day as many as thirty more people lay dead at the hands of police and Rolando Masferrer's death squads. As for the other decrees for resignations and non-payment of taxes, they were scarcely heeded. Nonethless, Fidel put a brave face on things, and in a broadcast on April 10 thundered: "All Cuba burns and erupts in an explosion of anger against the assassins, the bandits and gangsters, the informers and strikebreakers, the thugs and military still loyal to Batista."

But for all of Fidel's face-saving rhetoric, the strike failure had been a severe blow to the rebel cause, and what Fidel avoided admitting publicly he poured out in a letter to Celia on April 16. "The strike experience involved a great moral rout for the Movement, but I hope that we'll be able to regain the people's faith in us. The Revolution is once again in danger and its salvation rests in our hands." If Fidel's pride had been hurt, his ego was essentially undamaged. "We cannot continue to disappoint the nation. There are many things we must do, do them well and on a grand scale; and I will do them. Time will justify me one day."

The recriminations followed. Fidel blamed the llano leadership, while the Communists blamed the July 26 Movement generally for "adventurism." For Batista, the April 9 fiasco was a boon. Given five planeloads of war materiel by his old enemy, dictator Rafael Trujillo of the Dominican Republic, and with a notable drop-off in rebel activity after the strike, he began drawing up ambitious plans to launch a summer offensive for liquidating Fidel's insurgency once and for all.

The strike also brought the movement under uncomfortable new scrutiny from outsiders, for Fidel's ill-disguised appeal for "workers' unity" was fresh evidence that the Communists and Castro were getting cozy. Indeed, for all the past secrecy of its discussions with Fidel, the PSP had suddenly become rather public in its support for the rebel movement. In February, the National Committee of the PSP had issued a document stating that "in spite of the radical discrepancies it has with the tactics of the '26 de Julio' in the rest of the territory of the country, [the party] justifies and comprehends the guerrilla action in the Sierra Maestra." This was clearly intended as an endorsement of the rebel leadership in the sierra, while stressing the party's deep reservations over the movement's right-wing llano leaders. Then, on March 12, in its weekly bulletin, *Carta Semanal,* it had published an article entitled "Why Our Party Supports the Sierra Maestra."

"We don't only limit ourselves to view with sympathy the activity of the forces in arms commanded by Fidel Castro, 'Che' Guevara and others. We adopt the position of supporting actively, in all of the guerrilla zone, the troops who fight against the [Batista] tyranny. . . . In addition to trying to aid the activities of the patriotic forces that operate in the Sierra Maestra, we are trying to push forward the links between the guerrilla action and the class struggle in all the neighboring zone."

Even today, most surviving former Soviet officials of the period adhere to the official dogma that Soviet leaders were largely ignorant of events in Cuba and that the rebel victory in January 1959 caught them by surprise, but such claims fly in the face of an abundance of contrary evidence. For a start, the Soviets had already had direct contacts with Che and Raúl Castro in Mexico, where the USSR maintained an important embassy, and where its officials kept in touch with leaders of the region's Communist parties, including the Cuban PSP. And while old Latin American Communists bristle at the notion that they were minions of Moscow, the fact was that most of the regional Communist parties of the day depended on Moscow for subsidies as well as policy directives. It would appear unlikely almost to the point of absurdity that the Soviets remained unaware of the Cuban party's moves toward an alliance with Fidel Castro's revolution in the spring of 1958. What *is* certain is that by early 1958, more Communists had begun joining the rebel army, in particular Che's and Raúl's columns.

Meanwhile, Fidel was preparing to deal a master stroke against the movement in the llano. The failure of the general strike had painfully borne out the leadership's weaknesses, and it gave Fidel a new position of strength from which to assert direct control over the entire movement. As he told Celia Sánchez at the time, "no one will ever be able to make me trust the organization again. . . . I am the supposed leader of this Movement, and in the eyes of history I must take the responsibility for the stupidity of others. . . . With the excuse of fighting *caudillismo,* each one attempts to do more and more what he feels like doing. I am not such a fool that I don't realize this, nor am I a man given to seeing visions and phantoms."

On April 16, after Camilo Cienfuego's column had returned to the sierra from a brief foray onto the plains, Fidel named him military chief of the triangle of land between Bayamo, Manzanillo, and Las Tunas, with orders to coordinate all guerrilla activities in the region. He was to take over command of sabotage and supply in those cities from the llano's action squads, to carry out agrarian reform, and "to modify the civil code"—

extending Fidel's revolutionary writ from the Sierra Maestra to the llano. With this grab of authority, Fidel's rebels could now theoretically strike anywhere in Oriente, but before he could give real teeth to his new plan, Fidel realized he was going to have to dig in and defend the Sierra Maestra; it was now clear Batista planned to launch a major army offensive.

In mid-April Fidel and Che moved from their bases at La Plata and La Mesa to the northeast foothills, Fidel setting up his command headquarters at El Jíbaro, while Che's unit was a day's march away, near the village of Minas de Bueycito, where Sánchez Mosquera had quartered his troops. Che's mission was to hold the rebel front line against army penetration, and he based himself in a commandeered landowner's house in a place called La Otilia, located just two kilometers from the enemy base. Neither side seemed eager to risk a decisive battle. At night the rebels fired their M-26 bombs and their patrols routinely skirmished with the army, but Sánchez Mosquera's main activity took the form of reprisals against civilians in the area, burning and looting homes and killing suspected rebel collaborators. For some reason, La Otilia was not attacked.

"I have never been able to find out why Sánchez Mosquera allowed us to be comfortably settled in a house," Che wrote later, "in a relatively flat area with little vegetation, without calling the enemy air forces to attack us. Our guess was that he was not interested in fighting and that he did not want to let the air force see how close his troops were, because he would then have to explain why he did not attack."

La Otilia may have remained unscathed, but its approaches were a dangerous free-fire zone. One night, returning to base from a visit with Fidel, Che and his guide came upon a chilling scene. "In this last leg of the trip, already near the house, a strange spectacle presented itself by the light of a full moon that clearly illuminated the surroundings: in one of those rolling fields, with scattered palm trees, there appeared a row of dead mules, some with their harnesses on. When we got down from our horses to examine the first mule and saw the bullet holes, the guide's expression as he looked at me was an image out of a cowboy movie. The hero of the film arrives with his partner and sees a horse killed by an arrow. He says something like, 'The Sioux,' and makes a special face for the occasion. That's what the man's face was like and perhaps my own as well, although I did not bother to look at myself. A few meters further on was the second, then the third, then the fourth or fifth dead mule. It had been a convoy of supplies for us, captured by one of Sánchez Mosquera's expeditions. I seem to recall that a civilian was also murdered. The guide refused to follow me. He claimed he did not know the terrain and simply got on his mount. We separated amicably."

Within a few weeks of setting up camp at La Otilia, Che received new orders. In preparation for the army invasion, which appeared more imminent by the day, Fidel wanted Che to take direct charge of the recruit training school at Minas del Frío; a large number of new volunteers had assembled there, and they were to provide the backbone of a new command that was to undertake a risky crossing of the island as soon as they were ready and conditions were right. Taking charge of Che's column in the line against Sánchez Mosquera would be his deputy, Ramiro Valdés.

As a safeguard, Fidel also wanted to consolidate the rebel army's infrastructure. Radio Rebelde and *El Cubano Libre* were moved from La Mesa to his command base at La Plata. With its hospitals, electric generators, and munition stores, La Plata was a vital nerve center the rebels could not afford to lose, and it was to be the last line of defense. Food and medicine had to be brought and stockpiled for what could be a long siege.

Feeling fretful, Che set off to assume his new duties accompanied by a small handpicked group of fighters. His diary reflected his dampened mood: "We left at dawn, me with the spirits low, for having to abandon a zone that I had under my control for nearly a year, and in really critical moments, because Sánchez Mosquera's troops are coming up with more enthusiasm."

Fidel's new orders had also dashed Che's hopes of joining Camilo Cienfuegos on the expanded war front of the llano. When Camilo learned of Che's reassignment, he wrote a note to console him.

"Che. Soul brother: I see Fidel has put you in charge of the Military School, which makes me very happy because now we can count on having first-class soldiers in the future. . . . You've played a very principal role in this showdown and if we need you in this insurrectional stage, Cuba needs you even more when the war ends, so the Giant [Fidel] does a good thing in looking after you. I would like to be always at your side, you were my chief for a long time and you will always continue to be. Thanks to you I now have the opportunity to be more useful, I'll do the unspeakable to not make you look bad. Your eternal *chicharrón,* Camilo."

V

For the rest of April, Che was constantly on the move. Together with some pilots now working for the rebels, he searched for a good site to build an airstrip and found one near La Plata; he left men in charge of clearing the brush and digging a tunnel in which to hide the supply planes from view. He inspected the work under way at the still-unfinished recruits' school at Minas del Frío and met every few days with Fidel.

   In Cuba and abroad, the maneuverings of the opposition groups to
Batista's regime continued unbated. The palpable weakening of Batista's
grip, however, emboldened the opposition not to unity, but rather to increased internal jockeying. Given the prominence and moral authority of
Fidel Castro and his rebel band, a succession of other groups engaged in
a byzantine game, trying to curry his favor in the form of alliances while
simultaneously trying to undermine his position and divert his support.
Justo Carrillo, the exiled leader of a failed 1956 military uprising who still
had deep connections in the Cuban army, offered Fidel military support
in return for a manifesto "eulogizing" the armed forces. While Fidel was
interested in winning over sectors of the armed forces, he also saw the
danger of being outfoxed. A military-backed coup organized by Carrillo,
together with his still-imprisoned co-conspirator, Colonel Ramón Barquín,
would probably appeal to the Cuban business community, traditional
political parties, and Washington. Carrillo could then simply turn against
Fidel.
   Perhaps the greatest threat to his power, however, was to be found
within his own July 26 Movement, and on May 1 he summoned the National
Directorate leaders to Altos de Mompié. With the embarrassing failure of
the general strike, Fidel now had the final ammunition he needed to move
against the llano leaders, and he did so swiftly. Che played a principal role
in the dramatic May 3 showdown.
   "I made a small analysis of the situation," Che wrote in his diary, "setting forth the reality of two antagonistic policies, that of the Sierra and that
of the Llano, the validity of the Sierra's policies and our correctness in fearing for the success of the strike." He also blamed the llano leaders' "sectarianism" in blocking the PSP's involvement, which had doomed the strike
before it even started. "I gave my opinion that the greatest responsibility fell
upon the chief of the workers, on the top leader of the [llano militia] brigades and on the chief for Havana, that is to say Mario [David Salvador],
Daniel, and Faustino. So they should resign."
   After heated debate that lasted into the evening, Fidel put Che's proposals to a vote, and the measures passed. The result was a total revamping
of the llano leadership, with Faustino, Daniel, and David Salvador dismissed
from their posts and transferred to the Sierra Maestra. The most important
change of all was that the National Directorate would be moved to the Sierra
Maestra. Fidel was now the "General Secretary," with sole authority over
foreign affairs and arms supply, as well as "commander in chief" of the
movement's nationwide network of underground militias. A five-member
secretariat would serve under him, dealing with finances, political affairs,
and workers' issues, while the July 26 office in Santiago, once the Oriente

headquarters, would now be a mere outpost, a "delegation" answerable to the general secretary.

In "A Decisive Meeting," which Che wrote for the armed forces magazine *Verde Olivo* in late 1964, he summed up the achievements of that fateful day in Fidel Castro's career: "At this meeting decisions were taken that confirmed Fidel's moral authority, his indisputable stature, and the conviction among the majority of revolutionaries present that errors of judgment had been committed. . . . But most important, the meeting discussed and passed judgment on two conceptions that had clashed with one another throughout the whole previous stage of directing the war. The guerrilla conception would emerge triumphant from that meeting. Fidel's standing and authority were consolidated. . . . There now arose only one authoritative leadership, the Sierra, and concretely one single leader, one commander in chief, Fidel Castro."*

If others had been concerned about Fidel's *caudillismo*, it was now a moot point. It had never been a problem for Che. He had always thought ahead to the day when the *true* revolution would be built, and believed only a strongman could do it. From now on, the road forward was clear.

Che had little time to savor the victory. Already, the army had begun to make moves in its summer offensive, positioning troops along the flanks of the mountains and reinforcing the garrisons along the coast. Ambush positions had to be selected, trenches dug, supply and fallback routes worked out, all within a coordinated plan of action. To the west, in the hills around Mt. Caracas, Crescencio Pérez would have to hold the line with his "small and poorly armed groups," while Ramiro Valdés was to hold the land around La Botella and La Mesa to the east. A huge responsibility was resting on Che's shoulders, and he kept up a frenetic pace of activity to meet it. "This small territory had to be defended, with not much more than two hundred functioning rifles, when a few days later Batista's army began its 'encirclement and annihilation' offensive."

VI

Along with the rainy season, which had broken open with full force, an air of crisis now pervaded the sierra, including daily reports and rumors of enemy troops closing in. On May 6, the army occupied two rice farms at the edge of the sierra and took a rebel prisoner. On May 8, more troops disembarked at two points along the coast. On May 10, La Plata was bombed from the air and from the sea. Che rushed from one place to the other, moving or reinforcing the rebel positions according to the latest intelligence.

*See the appendix for elaboration.

Along with inspecting the front lines, Che pursued other missions, pushing forward with the agrarian reform and the collection of taxes from Oriente landowners and planters. Fidel wanted to get in as much money as he could to help sustain the rebel army during the offensive, but Che found the plantation owners recalcitrant. "Later," he wrote in his diary, "when our strength was solid, we got even."

Drawing recruits from the school at Minas del Frío, now up and running with the Communist Pablo Ribalta as its political commissar, Che formed a new column, Number Eight, named in honor of his late comrade Ciro Redondo. To add to the colorful hybrid of personalities, the school also had a new volunteer weapons instructor, an American Korean War veteran named Herman Marks.

Fidel, meanwhile, was quite clearly alarmed about the ability of his forces to withstand the invasion, and had begun hatching schemes that verged on the apocalyptic. On April 26, he had told Celia: "I need *cyanide*. Do you know any way to obtain it in some quantity? But we also need *strychnine*—as much of it as possible. We must get these very circumspectly, for if word leaks out, it will be of no use. I have some surprises in store for the time the offensive hits us." Whether or not Fidel obtained the poisons, or what he planned to do with them, is unknown. Presumably he planned to poison the water supplies in his camps if they were overrun. In the grips of this bunker mentality, he sent an urgent note to Che, inspecting the frontline defenses, and ordered him back to headquarters.

Answering the summons, Che took with him a newcomer, Oscar "Oscarito" Fernández Mell, a twenty-five-year-old doctor who had just left Havana to join up. With Che at the helm of a jeep, they drove back at breakneck speeds along a narrow dirt road that skirted steep precipices. Noticing Oscarito's nervousness at his driving, Che told him not to worry but added, "When we get to where we're going, I want to tell you something." When they arrived, Che informed Oscarito that it was the first time he had ever driven—which was true. With his old sidekick, Alberto Granado, Che had learned to drive a motorbike, but he had never sat at the wheel of a car before.

As Che waited at headquarters for Fidel to return from an inspection of the coastal front, he saw off his female courier, Lidia, on a mission to make contact with "friends" in Havana, Camagüey, and Manzanillo. Already in her mid-forties, Lidia had left her bakery in San Pedro de Yao to accompany the rebel force after her only son had joined up. Over the past year, she had become Che's special messenger, carrying the "most compromising" rebel communiqués and documents in and out of the Sierra Maestra to Havana and Santiago. These were highly dangerous assignments that involved repeatedly crossing enemy lines, and would have meant her torture and almost certain death if she were caught. On this mission, she would have to exit the sierra at a place where there was a *guardia* presence.

Lidia was to become one of Che's most revered revolutionary personalities, a woman he exalted for exemplifying the virtues of self-sacrifice, loyalty, honesty, and bravery. "When I think of Lidia," he later wrote, "I feel something more than just affectionate appreciation for this unblemished revolutionary, for she showed a special devotion for me and preferred working under my orders, regardless of the front to which I might be assigned."

In addition to entrusting her with his most confidential missions, Che had repaid Lidia's loyalty by leaving her in command of an auxiliary front-line camp situated close to enemy lines. The camp became increasingly dangerous and several times Che had tried to pull her out, but Lidia refused to leave, defending it with a suicidal zeal that frightened her male comrades. Only when *he* was transferred did she agree to leave it in order to follow him. But the position's riskiness was not the only reason he wanted her out of there.

Betraying a certain complicit glee, Che wrote that Lidia had led the camp "with spirit and a touch of high-handedness, causing a certain resentment among the Cuban men under her command, who were not accustomed to taking orders from a woman." Finally, in an uncanny echo of the terms used by his guerrilla comrades to describe him, Che extolled Lidia's "unlimited boldness" and "her contempt for death."

Between May 15 and 18, as Che awaited Fidel's return from his reconnaissance trip, he hosted a number of visits from political representatives. His journal entries are vague but indicate he was fielding overtures from political groups, including the Communist party, which were seeking alliances with the July 26 Movement. The most significant was from someone he described only as "Rafael, an old acquaintance," and a PSP man named Lino, who carried a proposal for a united front of revolutionary forces but expressed the party's enduring doubts over the "negative attitude" of the National Directorate. By May 19, the other visitors had left, but the PSP men had stayed on to meet with Fidel. Then the journalist José Ricardo Masetti unexpectedly reappeared in camp, having returned to the sierra for another interview with Fidel. His arrival meant a further delay in Fidel's meeting with the Communists, for, as Che noted in his diary, "it isn't convenient that he [Masetti] hears anything."

On May 22, with Masetti finally gone, the PSP-Fidel summit got under way. "We talked with Rafael and Lino," Che wrote, "who propose the need for a union of all the revolutionary forces. Fidel accepts in principle, but he put up some reservations about the forms without ending the discussion."

Right then the paramount item on Fidel's agenda was to beat back the unfolding enemy offensive, and while unity of forces on the llano was desirable, it was not essential at the moment. He hoped to avoid a protracted and bloody showdown with the armed forces, and the way to do that was by breaking their morale in the sierra; then he would sweep down onto the llano, and political alliances would be his for the asking. And, as always, Fidel's fear of American intervention on Batista's behalf dictated that he continue his go-slow policy with the Communist party.

There were certainly signs this fear was not misplaced. In spite of the State Department's suspension of arms shipments to Batista, the U.S. Defense Department had just delivered three hundred rockets to the Cuban air force from its stocks at the American base at Guantánamo. Fueling Fidel's suspicions that Trujillo and Somoza were working as U.S. proxies to provide Batista with war materiel, a ship from Nicaragua had arrived with thirty tanks in early May.

If anything, American concern about Fidel's true political sentiments had grown over the past few months. In May, Jules Dubois, the *Chicago Tribune* correspondent, used Radio Rebelde's newly boosted transmitter links with the outside world to conduct an interview with Fidel from Caracas; his foremost line of inquiry centered on charges linking the rebel leader to Communism. Once again denying the charge, Fidel accused Batista of spreading the rumor in order to obtain U.S. arms, and denied any intention of nationalizing industry or the private business sector. While he had no presidential aspirations of his own, Fidel explained, the July 26 Movement would become a political party after the revolution, to "fight with the arms of the Constitution and of the law."

But there was a growing gulf between Fidel's public reassurances and his private thoughts, as revealed in a June 5 note he wrote to Celia, shortly after the first American-supplied rockets were used by Batista's air force in the Sierra Maestra, hitting a civilian's home. "When I saw the rockets that they fired on Mario's house, I swore that the Americans are going to pay dearly for what they're doing. When this war is over, I'll start a much longer and bigger war of my own: the war I'm going to fight against them. I realize that will be my true destiny."

As for the short term, Fidel waged a campaign to win over key military officers—penning a flattering note to General Eulogio Cantillo, the commander of the Havana military headquarters—while through the media waging a simultaneous psychological war against the troops massed in the sierra.

"The armed forces are now facing a very difficult task," he claimed in a statement to the Venezuelan press. "Every entrance to the Sierra Maestra is like the pass at Thermopylae, and every narrow passage becomes a death trap. The Cuban army has lately begun to realize that it has been led into a real war, an absurd war, a meaningless war, which can cost it thousands of lives, a war that is not theirs, because after all, we are not at war against the armed forces but against the dictatorship. These circumstances always have led inevitably to a military rebellion."

Fidel's day-to-day existence had become increasingly administrative and sedentary. The exigencies of his role as "supreme commander" of rebel forces demanded that he stay close to headquarters and his new communications link, and he kept up an all-consuming pace of activity. In letters and telephone conversations to his new appointees abroad, he cajoled and coordinated new planeloads of weapons. He kept track of the munitions disbursed to his field commanders, repeatedly warning them not to waste it, giving them precise instructions on how it should be used. He wrote letters to wealthy Cubans soliciting contributions and had received promising signals that they were willing *if* he could vanquish the army offensive. All the same, he complained bitterly to Celia about having to assume so much control himself.

"I'm tired of the role of overseer and going back and forth without a minute's rest, to have to attend to the most insignificant details, just because someone forgot this or overlooked that. I miss those early days when I was really a soldier, and I felt much happier than I do now. This struggle becomes a miserable, petty bureaucratic task for me."

For all his complaints, it was Fidel's nature to take control, and at the same time that he plotted the overall strategy of his war, he obsessed over the tiniest and most mundane details. In between orders for blasting caps and rifle grease, he hounded Celia to provide him with personal comforts he missed. "I need a fountain pen," he wrote one day. "I hate being without one." On May 8, he carped: "I'm eating hideously. No care is paid to preparing my food. . . . I'm in a terrible mood." By May 17, the list of complaints had expanded. "I have no tobacco, I have no wine, I have nothing. A bottle of rosé wine, sweet and Spanish, was left in Bismarck's house, in the refrigerator. Where is it?"

While Fidel lacked faith in the judgment and decision-making of virtually all of his subordinates, this doubt did not extend to Che, who had become his chief confidant as well as his de facto military chief of staff. When they were apart, he kept up a constant stream of notes to Che, confiding military plans, financial matters, political machinations, and, like an enthusiastic youth, recounting experiments with new weapons from the armory.

"It's been too many days since we've talked," he wrote Che on May 19, "and that's a matter of necessity between us. I miss the old comrades here. Yesterday I carried out an experiment with a tin grenade that produced terrific results. I hung it from a tree branch about 6 feet from the ground and set it off. It showered lethal fragments in all directions. It sends fragments downward and on all sides, as if it were a sprinkler. I think that in open terrain it could kill you at 50 yards."

During the third week of May, the government troops began their initial probes of rebel territory. General Cantillo had a total of fourteen battalions in hand for his assault on the sierra, in addition to the support of the air force, and artillery and tank regiments. Cantillo's plan was to drive into the sierra from several points, gradually surrounding the rebels and reducing their territory until he could attack and destroy Fidel at his La Plata *comandancia* on the central ridge of the Sierra Maestra.

To the south, the coastal garrisons had been reinforced, and naval frigates stood ready to provide artillery support and seal off escape in that direction. To the north, flanking the western and eastern limits of rebel territory, Cantillo had deployed two army units composed of two battalions each. A few miles north of Las Mercedes, held by Crescencio's column, an army company led by Major Raúl Corzo Izaguirre had assembled at the sugar *central* of Estrada Palma. To the east, at Bueycito, a company under Sánchez Mosquera, now a lieutenant colonel, was prepared to enter the hills held by Che's old column, led by Ramiro Valdés. If Cantillo had one weakness, it was the readiness of his men: of ten thousand troops, only a third were experienced soldiers, the rest conscripts recently called up for the occasion. But if all went according to plan, the rebels would simply be squeezed into an ever-tightening circle.

That circle was never that wide to begin with. The entire rebel stronghold, with its precious installations at La Plata, Las Vegas de Jibacoa, Mompié, and Minas del Frío, was actually only a tiny area of a few square miles. The distance between Fidel's *comandancia* and the northern frontline village of Las Mercedes was twelve kilometers, and the recruits' school at Minas del Frío sat halfway between them. To the south, less than eight kilometers (5 miles) from rebel headquarters, lay the coast. And to defend his mountain fastness, Fidel counted on about 280 armed fighters, with approximately fifty bullets apiece.

On May 19, after an aerial barrage to soften up the rebel defenses, Corzo Izaguirre's troops tried to march on Las Mercedes, but Crescencio's units held the line just beyond its outskirts. The battle lines were drawn, with both sides facing off from one another at a distance of about four hundred meters, or just under a quarter mile. But even as his communiqués trumpeted the "stout resistance" displayed by his fighters and a brief quiet settled on the battlefront, Fidel was privately worried about Crescencio's abilities as a leader; a few days later, he asked Che to go and assume command personally.

In an almost surreal gesture, before leaving for Las Mercedes Che attended an assembly called by Humberto Sorí-Marín with the area's peasants to discuss how to carry out the coffee harvest; a surprising 350 farmers showed up. Although it passed completely unnoticed by the outside world, it was an important moment; as the first consultation between Cuban civilians and the guerrillas who now ruled their destinies, it symbolized the first practical step in the agrarian reform process undertaken by the Cuban revolution. Che watched the proceedings with keen interest.

"It was proposed by the steering committee which included Fidel to adopt the following measures: to create a type of Sierra currency to pay the workers, to bring the straw and sacking for the packing, to create a work and consumer cooperative, to create a commission to supervise the work and provide troops to help in the coffee picking. Everything was approved, but when Fidel was going to close the ceremony with his speech the planes started to machine-gun in the zone of Las Mercedes and the people lost interest." It was May 25, and, it seemed, the enemy offensive had finally begun in earnest.

Che rushed to Las Mercedes. From this moment on for the next three months, he was rarely still as he rallied rebel defenses to resist the overwhelming firepower and troop strength of Batista's invading army. Back from her mission, his courier Lidia caught up with him. She informed him that Faustino Pérez, who was in Havana with orders to hand over his post, was balking. "The thing looks worse all the time," observed Che in his diary, obviously concerned about an open split with the disgruntled llano faction of the movement.

With the beginning of the army offensive, Che did not have time to do more than register Lidia's news. Then it was back to the war. Along with distributing new weapons trickling in from outside, he selected volunteers from among the students at Minas del Frío to go to the front, while selecting others—"the bad ones"—to dig fortifications at Las Mercedes. And, as always, there were disciplinary problems with recruits trying to escape the tightening army net.

When Fidel was visiting, a recruit who had escaped was captured and brought in. "Fidel wanted to shoot him immediately," wrote Che in his journal, "but I opposed it and in the end the thesis of condemning him to indefinite reclusion at [the rebel prison of] Puerto Malanga triumphed. There was another student punished by me to go ten days without eating who asked Fidel for clemency, and he gave him the option of choosing between lifting his fast and going to Puerto Malanga or staying as he was. He didn't decide for either and so it was decided to send him to Puerto Malanga for a month." A few days later, showing the often arbitrary nature of Fidel's application of revolutionary justice, he reacted to another desertion by "absolving" the captured culprit. And for all of Fidel's rhetoric about turning the mountain passes into death traps for the army, Che's diary revealed just how undermanned the rebels really were, and how tenuous their morale.

"Fidel left early for his part of the camp," Che wrote on June 4, "and within an hour two fighter-bombers paid us a visit with rocket charges, firing 6 of them and machine-gunning a little. The reaction among the students was negative, 10 of whom asked to be licensed [cashiered]." Later that same day, two of Che's volunteer grenade-throwers backed out, and he had to scramble for substitutes. Returning to the school the next day, he found the enemy planes had made another bombing run, which had "provoked the flight of eight more [students]."*

With enemy troops disembarking on the coast, Fidel took charge of the defense of Las Vegas and sent Che to put order into Crescencio Pérez's command, where one of the officers was reportedly acting abusively toward his men. Before leaving, Che held a summary trial for a rebel officer accused of murder, and sentenced him to death. Che spent his thirtieth birthday sitting in judgment of Crescencio's officer, whom he decided to strip of his command.

Returning to the front, he found it in disarray, with army troops advancing on all fronts. Fidel had moved on to Mompié; Las Vegas had been overrun. Minas del Frío was now threatened, and Che spent several days shoring up Fidel's front with his own men, building new defensive lines, stripping another officer of his command, and disarming others who had been insubordinate.

On June 26, he met up with Fidel again at Mompié, and Fidel ordered him to stay with him for the moment. The outlook was grim; the rebels were ceding ground everywhere. Fidel had ordered Camilo and Almeida to bring their columns back to the sierra to help out, but a defeatist attitude had begun to permeate the rebel ranks.

---

*On June 8, amid the general chaos, a strange American visitor apparently showed up at the rebel camp. Che wrote that he was "a suspicious *gringo* with messages from people in Miami and some eccentric plans." The man wanted to see Fidel, but he was kept where he was. The next morning, after an intense aerial bombardment in the eastern part of the front around the village of Santo Domingo, Che found Fidel and told him about his visitor. "Fidel had received word that the *gringo* was either FBI or hired to kill him." According to Pedro Álvarez Tabío, the director of the Cuban government's historical archives, the visitor was probably Frank Fiorini, a gunrunner. Later, under the alias "Frank Sturgis," Fiorini want to work for the CIA in its anti-Castro operations, and in the 70s, earned notoriety as one of the Watergate "burglars."

"In the night there were three escapes," Che wrote the next day. "One of them was double; Rosabal, condemned to death for being a *chivato,* Pedro Guerra from Sori's squad and two military prisoners. Pedro Guerra was captured; he had stolen a revolver for the escape. He was executed immediately."

By the end of June, the rebels had their first clear victory—an army company under Sánchez Mosquera had been repulsed, with the rebels capturing twenty-two soldiers and fifty or sixty weapons—but elsewhere the army was on the move, with reports flowing in of enemy advances on La Maestra and other hills in the area. The second wave of the offensive had clearly begun. Hearing of soldiers advancing to take the heights of Altos de Merino, Che rushed over there on the morning of July 3.

"Upon arriving I found that the guards were already advancing. A little combat broke out in which we retreated very quickly. The position was bad and they were encircling us, but we put up little resistance. Personally I noted something I had never felt before: the need to live. That had better be corrected in the next opportunity."

It is hard to imagine many other men in the same situation making this sort of critical self-judgment, but this was how Ernesto Guevara, in his new identity as Che, now confronted life. It was one of the facets of his character that set him apart from the vast majority of his guerrilla comrades, who even as they fought, still hoped to survive the experience.

Indeed, most of the problems he encountered on a daily basis with his men pointed up this fundamental difference between them. Their nervousness, lack of "combativity," the desertions, not being where they should on the front line—all the complaints and observations that peppered his daily journal came down to the same complaint: They felt *"the need to live."*

VII

Amid the army offensive, Che received a letter from his mother in Buenos Aires. On the eve of battle, he had used the new radio-communication links from the Sierra Maestra to call her, and she had now written back to wish him a happy thirtieth birthday.

Dear Teté:

I was so overcome to hear your voice after so much time. I didn't recognize it—you seemed to be another person. Maybe the line was bad or maybe you have changed. Only when you said "old lady" did it seem like the voice of old. What wonderful news you gave me. What a pity the communication was cut before I could give you mine. And there is a lot to tell. Ana [María, Che's youngest sister] was married on the 2 of April to Petít [Fernando Chávez] and they went to Vienna. . . . What a thing all of my children leaving! She left behind a very big emptiness in the house. . . . Roberto has two beautiful blond daughters who will be two and one on the first of July, and the [male] heir is expected in August. He is working hard and well to maintain his numerous family. . . .

Celia has just won an important [architectural] prize together with Luis [Argañaraz, her fiancée] and Petít. Between the three of them they get 2 and ½ million pesos. I am so proud of having such capable children that I don't fit in my clothes. Juan Martín, of course, [now] fits into your clothes. It isn't that he's tall. He's as puny as his brothers and sisters were and he is still an enchanting child. Life is not going to knock this one around.

María Luisa [Che's aunt] is the same as before. Physically and emotional incapacitated and very sad. It seems a characteristic of her illness. She always asks about you. . . . I too am the same. With a few years more and a sadness that is no longer so sharp. It has turned into a chronic sadness, blended once in a while with great satisfactions. The prize won by Celia was one of them, the return of the Little One will be another, hearing your voice was a very big one. I have become very solitary. I don't know how to write you, or even what to say to you: I have lost the measure.

The housework tires me out a lot. For a long time now I have been my own cook and you know how I detest the chores of the home. The kitchen is my headquarters and there I spend most of my time. With the old man [Che's father] there was a big blow-up and he no longer comes around. My companions are Celia, Luis and Juan Martín. So many things I wanted to say, my dear. I am afraid to let them out. I leave them to your imagination.

A hug and a long kiss of years, with all my love, Celia.

One might wonder how Che reacted to this poignant letter, whether he read it with emotional detachment or if he suffered pangs of nostalgic yearning for the normal life that continued in his absence: brothers and sisters growing up, getting married, leaving home and having children; his parents growing older. And what of his own family, his wife, Hilda, and their daughter, Hildita?

But more than Teté's voice had changed. Hand in hand with his commitment to the revolution was his conscious choice to divorce himself from his "outside" life. He seldom wrote to Hilda or his parents, although he had opportunities to do so. In late April, Fidel had told him that someone in Peru, presumably Hilda, had tried to call him on the radio; evidently Che did not phone back, for Hilda made no mention of it in her memoirs. Indeed, one of the most remarkable aspects of his diary of the time is the almost total lack of personal details or introspection, especially when compared to the self-absorption of the vagabond Ernesto just a few short years before.

VIII

For all the Cuban army's grand plans of trapping the rebels inside a steadily tightening noose, it appeared they didn't fully take into account the topography of their battlefield. In the Sierra Maestra's thick forests and deep ravines, attacking army units quickly bogged down or lost contact with one another. For the rebels, it meant giving ground when necessary while carrying out their own encirclements of isolated units. Quite quickly, it seemed, it was the rebels who were on the offensive.

To press their advantage, Che and Fidel decided to split forces again, Fidel setting off to attack the army troops at Jigüe, while Che stayed to defend Mompié and command the resistance at Minas del Frío. As Che arrived in Mompié on July 11, the Cuban air force launched a ferocious aerial bombardment of the place, this time dropping napalm as well as bombs. Then came unsettling news. Fidel's brother Raúl, leading rebel forces in the Sierra Cristal, had just taken forty-nine Americans hostage. Now, Che noted, Raúl had "written a manifesto made out to the entire world and signed by him. It was too strong and together with the arrest of the 49 Americans it seemed a note of dangerous 'extremism.'"

In the four months since his move to the Sierra Cristal, Raúl had rapidly built up his fighting strength and made his presence felt throughout eastern Oriente. By July, he had over two hundred men under arms and had built up a guerrilla infrastructure complete with an armory, hospitals and schools, a road-building unit, an intelligence service, and a revolutionary judicial system. But all of that was now under threat from the army offensive. Although he was not facing the same kind of full-scale ground assault as his brother in the Sierra Maestra, Raúl's forces were being pounded by Batista's planes. In late June, with his forces dangerously low on ammunition, he decided to take drastic action by ordering the seizure of all Americans found within his territory.

On June 26 his fighters attacked the American-owned Moa Bay Mining Company and made off with twelve American and Canadian employees;
another dozen were grabbed at the Nicaro nickel mine and the United Fruit
Company's sugar mill at Guaro. Twenty-four American sailors and marines
were then abducted from a bus on the outskirts of the Guantánamo naval base.
In a public statement sent to the press, Raúl claimed he had taken the action
to protest the U.S. delivery of rockets and napalm to Batista, and the secret
refueling and loading of bombs onto Cuban warplanes at Guantánamo base.
The action immediately sparked outrage in Washington, with several sena-
tors demanding American military intervention. Park Wollam, the American consul in Santiago, journeyed to meet with Raúl, and negotiations began.

Alerted to the crisis through news reports, Fidel had reacted by immediately ordering Raúl to release the hostages in a Radio Rebelde broadcast.
He carefully balanced his public statements by declaring that hostage-taking
was not movement policy, but that such actions were comprehensible in light
of the U.S. delivery of rockets to Batista. Then he sent Raúl a private follow-
up note, in which he appeared to be warning his brother not to take any
drastic steps with the hostages that might endanger the rebels' image in the
United States.*

Raúl's dramatic show of force brought him some immediate dividends,
however. Proving the extent of American influence over Batista after all,
the air attacks against his forces in the Sierra Cristal suddenly ceased. Ac-
cordingly, Raúl didn't release all the hostages immediately, but drew the
process out and used the lull to resupply his forces. It was July 18 before he
freed his last hostages, after which the attacks resumed, but by then his Second Front was resupplied, able to defend itself, and ready for action.

The hostage crisis highlighted a facet of Raúl's character that was
worrying to some of his comrades; as Che put it quite aptly, his "extremism." Without strict controls, Raúl was something of a loose cannon, and in
the future other widely publicized excesses would earn Raúl a reputation
as a violent man who would stop at nothing to ensure revolutionary security.

In the meantime, deaths of comrades were beginning to occur on a daily
basis in the Sierra Maestra. Geonel Rodríguez, who had helped Che found *El
Cubano Libre* back in the days when El Hombrito was the first "free territory"
of the Sierra Maestra, was mortally wounded in a mortar blast. In his journal,
Che eulogized him with the highest praise. "He was one of our most loved
collaborators, a true revolutionary." That night, word came of the death of
Carlitos Más, whom Che described as a "old-young fighter who died from the
burns and breaks he suffered together with Geonel." Perhaps most frustrat-

*See the appendix for elaboration.

ing of all, these deaths could not be translated into advances on the battlefield, at least not in Che's sector. He continued to hold the line at Minas del Frío, but a stalemate had settled in, with the enemy soldiers digging trenches instead of advancing or falling back. The aerial bombardments continued. On July 17, the planes hit the hospital at Mompié, and Che oversaw the evacuation of its patients to a new place. The next day, he wrote: "Nothing new in the zone. The only pastime of the guards is killing the pigs we left around."

As Che tried to rally his perimeter defenses around Minas del Frío, Fidel was beginning to wear down the enemy troops in his siege at Jigüe. In two days in early July, he took nineteen prisoners and captured eighteen weapons, including bazooka grenades, and he thought the enemy force, now without food supplies, would surrender within forty-eight hours.

Discovering that the enemy commander, Major José Quevedo, was an old law school classmate of his, Fidel wrote the officer a curious note on July 10. "I have often remembered that group of young officers who attracted my attention and awakened my sympathies because of their great longing for culture and the efforts they made to pursue their studies. . . . What a surprise to know that you are around here! And however difficult the circumstances, I am always happy to hear from one of you, and I write these lines on the spur of the moment, without telling you or asking you for anything, only to greet you and to wish you, very sincerely, good luck."

If Fidel had hoped to weaken Quevedo's resolve with such tactics, it didn't work. He then used loudspeakers to barrage the besieged force with broadcasts of "well-prepared talks and careful slogans," hoping to wear down its morale. On July 15 he wrote again to Quevedo, this time directly appealing to him to surrender. "It will not be a surrender to an enemy of the fatherland but to a sincere revolutionary, to a fighter who struggles for the good of all Cubans."

Still Quevedo held out. Fidel then had one of his men, masquerading as an army communications man, radio the air force that the rebels had taken the camp. The trick brought the desired results: Planes attacked Quevedo's force, spreading panic among his troops. By July 18, Fidel had 42 prisoners, a booty of 66 weapons and 18,000 rounds of ammunition, and he told Che: "The encircled troops are on the verge of collapse."

The fall of Jigüe finally came on the evening of July 20: Quevedo walked out of the camp in surrender, 146 soldiers following behind. For the rebels it was a watershed victory; the army's offensive had been effectively routed, and now it would be their turn to press their advantage.*

---

*Fidel convinced Quevedo to join the rebel army, one of several army officers to do so in the course of the war.

The same day as Quevedo's surrender, the "Caracas Pact" was announced over Radio Rebelde. Previously signed by Fidel on behalf of the July 26 Movement, it brought together eight opposition groups, including Carlos Prío's Auténticos, the Directorio Revolucionario, the so-called "Barquínista" military faction, and Justo Carrillo's Montecristi movement, committing them to a common strategy of overthrowing Batista through armed insurrection, and the formation of a brief provisional government. Most important, the "Unity Manifesto of the Sierra Maestra" acknowledged Fidel Castro's authority as "commander-in-chief of revolutionary forces." As in all the previous pacts, the most notable Cuban opposition group not invited to sign was the PSP, and Che, who evidently thought it would be, remarked in his journal: "The unity seems to be going well on the outside but in the announcement the Partido Socialista [PSP] is not included, which seems strange to me." (It would appear that on the issue of PSP–July 26 links, Fidel was momentarily keeping his own counsel from Che, and that in spite of their ongoing high-level talks, the two organizations had evidently decided to keep their dialogue secret and avoid a premature public merger, which could only provoke controversy.)

Through the Red Cross, a two-day truce was finally arranged, and on July 23 and 24 a total of 253 famished and exhausted army prisoners were handed over, including 57 wounded. They left behind a total of 161 weapons in rebel hands, including two mortars, a bazooka, and two heavy machine guns. Two hours before the cease-fire ended, Che mobilized his men; some of the men were to hold the pass at La Maestra, while all the others would go and lay siege to the troops in Las Vegas.

Within a day, they had the camp encircled, and, following Fidel's example in Jigüe, Che urged the soldiers there to surrender. On the morning of July 28, Che met with two emissaries from the army captain in charge at a farmhouse between the lines. The enemy officers had come with an offer: If Che let them withdraw, they would leave all their food behind but take their arms with them. Che told them this was impossible, and returned to his own lines. Soon afterward, a sentinel warned him that the enemy company was beating a retreat in vehicles, flying a white flag and a Red Cross flag; the meeting had obviously been a diversionary tactic. Che ordered his men to open fire while he led units in pursuit.

"A desolate spectacle could be seen," he wrote. "Backpacks and helmets thrown around along the road, bags with bullets and all kinds of belongings, even a jeep and a tank that was still intact . . . Later the first prisoners started falling, among them the company doctor." As Che's units pressed the advance, however, they increasingly came under "friendly fire" from rebels hidden in the surrounding hills; one of Che's prisoners was killed and a rebel officer badly wounded. "I had the uncomfortable situation of being besieged by our forces who opened fire every time they saw a helmet. I sent a soldier to stop the fire with his hands up and in one place it gave results but in the other they continued firing for a while, wounding two more soldiers."

When the situation was finally normalized and the scores of captured *guardias* were being led back to Las Vegas, an urgent message from Fidel reached Che just as he was inspecting the captured tank. Apparently, the army's second retreat that day, from the sector of Santo Domingo, had been a ruse, for as the rebels had chased after the retreating troops, Sánchez Mosquera's company had taken the Arroyones hilltop near Las Mercedes and outflanked them. One of the two rebel captains commanding the fighters there had been killed, while the other—Che's former llano rival René Ramos Latour (Daniel) —had survived and was fighting back, but the battle was fierce. By the afternoon of the following day, however, Daniel was dead from a mortar wound in the stomach. "Profound ideological discrepancies separated me from René Ramos," Che wrote in his journal that evening, "and we were politicial enemies, but he knew how to die fulfilling his duty, on the front line. Whoever dies like that does so because he feels an interior impulse [the existence of] which I had denied him and which I rectify at this time."

Over the next chaotic week of combat, there developed a new, almost comical focus to the fighting—the army tank Che had captured at Las Mercedes. Indicative of just how small-scale the Cuban revolution really was, the single tank was a grand prize Fidel wanted to preserve at all costs, and the enemy just as desperately sought its destruction. Enemy planes were repeatedly sent on sorties to bomb it, while Fidel and his forces tried to extract it from where it sat, stuck fast in the mud of a road.

All the exertions of both sides proved fruitless; the tank remained resolutely unscathed. On August 5, Fidel commissioned a peasant with a team of oxen to drag it free, but in the process its steering wheel was broken, and there was little hope of repairing it. "Hopes dashed," Fidel wrote Che that night. "It has been a long time since I've had such great pipe dreams."

Two days later, shielded by a withering cover-fire, the army began to move out en masse from its last besieged position in the Sierra Maestra. Batista's vaunted offensive was over—but not the dying. On August 9, Beto Pesant, a veteran of the first group of volunteers from Manzanillo, was killed when an antiaircraft shell he was handling exploded. Che's lover Zoila Rodríguez was at the scene.

"Comandante Guevara, other rebels and myself were carrying out a mission when Beto Pesant died. When I heard an explosion, I saw that Guevara's mule, called Armando, was injured and had thrown him [Che] into the air, I ran to his side but he was already getting up. I looked over at Pesant and saw that he was missing an arm, his head was destroyed and his

chest was open. . . . I began to scream: 'Beto, don't die, don't die.' They attended to him quickly. The *comandante* told me: 'Zoila, he's dead.'" Che
ordered the dead man's wife in Manzanillo to be contacted, and when she
arrived, Zoila recalled: "She began to weep at his tomb, and we all cried and
when I looked at Guevara he had tears in his eyes."

In the wake of the army's withdrawal, Fidel held another 160 soldiers,
including wounded, and he was eager to be rid of them. After much back-
and-forth negotiating, a meeting was arranged among him, Che, the army
commanders, and Red Cross representatives on the morning of August 11.
They met and talked amenably over coffee. Over the next two days, a truce
held in the Sierra Maestra as the wounded men and their able-bodied comrades were released. At one point, Che and Fidel even went on a short helicopter ride with their enemy counterparts. The truce also allowed the rebels
to pause for judicial proceedings. As Che recorded: "An army deserter who
had tried to rape a girl was executed."

In the lull, a high-level army emissary who the rebels believed to be
Batista's personal representative urged Fidel to enter into negotiations with
the regime. "He indirectly proposed his [Batista's] replacement with
a magistrate of the Supreme [Court] (the oldest one) and a peaceful solution," observed Che. "[But] nothing concrete was reached." Fidel was noncommittal to the overture. He saw no reason to rush into negotiations, for
he was planning to extend the war across the island and still had hopes of
wooing General Cantillo, whose offensive he had just defeated. As Che
concluded later: "Batista's army came out of that last offensive in the Sierra
Maestra with its spine broken, but it had not yet been defeated. The struggle
would go on." Indeed, on August 14, after a rare act of civility in which the
army airlifted some blood plasma to the rebels, the air force's bombing and
strafing attacks resumed.

Meanwhile, unnoticed by either the enemy or Fidel's putative allies in
the Caracas Pact, an important visitor to the Sierra Maestra took his leave
from rebel territory. Communist Party Central Committee official Carlos
Rafael Rodríguez had held secret talks with Fidel, after first visiting Raúl's
Second Front in the Sierra Cristal. Che recorded Rodríguez's visit circumspectly, mentioning it in his journal only upon the PSP official's departure.
"Carlos Rafael left for the free zone. His impression is positive despite all
the internal and external intrigues."*

---

*Rodríguez himself has never said much about this trip, except to say that in Raúl's zone he
had found "nothing but understanding for the Communists, but when I got to Fidel in the
Sierra Maestra, the understanding had turned to suspicion." Rodríguez was undoubtedly
referring to the antagonism his presence had provoked in Carlos Franqui, Faustino Pérez,

Despite the enduring secrecy surrounding Rodríguez's visit, he evidently received Fidel's go-ahead to pursue a PSP–July 26 merger in a reconstituted labor front. Another cooperative signal was Fidel's authorization for the party to send a permanent representative to the sierra. Only three weeks after Rodríguez left, Luis Más Martín, a veteran PSP official and an old Castro friend, arrived, and in September Rodríguez himself returned, staying with Fidel until the end of the war.

In the Sierra Cristal, meanwhile, Fidel's brother Raúl and the PSP had forged much more than an "understanding." In fact, serious organizational links had begun as soon as Raúl had arrived in his new zone in early March. Around the same time as Raúl left the Sierra Maestra to open his new front, José "Pepe" Ramírez, chief of the PSP-controlled National Association of Small Farmers (ANAP), was ordered by the party to make his way to the Sierra Cristal and "report to Raúl." When Ramírez arrived, Raúl gave him the job of organizing the peasants living within his territory and preparing a "Peasant Congress" to be held in the autumn. That work was now well under way, Ramírez conducting a series of meetings with the help of the local PSP network, as was the formation of a Communist-run troop instructors' school, complete with Marxist political orientation.

Curiously, in addition to the support of the Communists, Raúl also enjoyed the support of a considerable number of militant Catholics from the city of Santiago. And here too, could be found an American volunteer, named Evans Russell, who worked in Raúl's bomb factory. But it was the Communist influence that was the salient characteristic of Raúl's Second Front. Indeed, Raúl's front was the spawning ground for many of Cuba's future Communist party officials. Although he was not formally a party member since his ouster from the Socialist Youth after his role in Fidel's "putschist" adventure at Moncada, Raúl had remained faithful and, with a wink and a nod from Fidel, now proceeded to cement his ties.

These developments could not have been very comforting to the Americans, but for now there was little they could do to assuage their growing fears about the true goals of the increasingly powerful Cuban rebel army. Right now, those goals called for an ambitious expansion of the war. Che and Camilo Cienfuegos were to leave the Sierra Maestra and take the war to central and western Cuba. Che's "Ciro Redondo" column

---

and other llano men who were now in the sierra. Che seemed to have been alluding to this when he noted, a few days after Rodríguez's departure, "the formation of an opposition directed by Faustino and composed also of Franqui and Aldo Santamaría [brother of Haydée and the late Abel Santamaría] in the Sierra Maestra."

was to assume revolutionary authority in the Escambray mountains of central Las Villas province, "strike relentlessly at the enemy," and cut the island in half. Meanwhile, Camilo was to emulate the feat of his column's illustrious nineteenth-century namesake, Cuban independence war hero Antonio Maceo, by marching all the way to Cuba's westernmost province of Pinar del Río.

Che was anxious to get going, but on August 15 he complained: "I haven't been able to organize the column yet because of a cumulus of contradictory orders as to its composition." It was a matter of finding the men to go with him, and so far only a disappointingly tiny trickle of volunteers had filtered in from different squads. Che himself didn't help matters by telling the fighters that probably only half of those who came with him would survive the mission, and that they should be prepared to do battle continuously and go hungry most of the time. Clearly, Che's mission was not for everybody. Fidel summoned him to Mompié. He had organized one squad for him, led by El Vaquerito, and told Che to recruit any other men he needed from the platoons on hand. Che's political commissar at Minas del Frío, Pablo Ribalta, began selecting men from the school using a dossier he had compiled on Che's orders.

Over the next fortnight, under incessant aerial bombardments, Che painstakingly pieced his expeditionary force together: a column of 148 men, and a half-dozen jeeps and pickup trucks. Camilo's smaller force of 82 men was also assembled and ready to go. Then, on the night of August 29—as he prepared for a dawn departure by loading some jeeps with ammunition just flown in from Miami—the army captured two of his pickups loaded with merchandise, and all his gasoline for the journey. His remaining vehicles now useless, he resolved to set out on foot.

On August 31, as he finally prepared to leave, Zoila asked to accompany him. Che refused her. They said farewell in the village of El Jíbaro, the last time they would be together as lovers. "He left me in charge of his mule Armando," Zoila recalled. "I cared for him as if he were a real Christian."

19

The Final Push

I

For the next six weeks, through the unceasing downpours of the Cuban rainy season, Che and Camilo's columns waded through the rice fields and swamps of the llano, forded swollen rivers, dodged the army, and came under frequent aerial attacks. The "exhausting marches," through "stinking swamps" and along "devilish trails," Che wrote, became "truly horrible." They had been detected by the enemy early on, and after sustaining firefights on September 9 and 14 the army had tracked their movements closely.

"Hunger, thirst, weariness, the feeling of impotence against the enemy forces that were increasingly closing in on us, and above all, the terrible foot disease that the peasant call *mazamorra*—which turned each step our soldiers took into an intolerable torment—had made us an army of shadows. It was difficult to advance, very difficult. Our troop's physical condition worsened day by day, and the meals—today yes, tomorrow no, the next day maybe—in no way helped to alleviate the level of misery we were suffering."

Several men were killed in firefights, others deserted, and Che allowed a few more demoralized or frightened men to leave. As always, *chivatos* were a problem. Che reported to Fidel that "the social consciousness of the Camagüeyan peasantry is minimal, and we had to face the consequences of numerous informers."

Meanwhile, the government's propaganda about Che's Communism had intensified. On September 20, following the engagements with his forces on the llano, Batista's chief of staff, General Francisco Tabernilla, reported that army troops had "destroyed" a hundred-man column led by "Che Guevara," and had captured evidence that his rebels were "being trained through communist methods."

Which was, in fact, the truth. "What happened," Che explained to Fidel later, "was that in one of the knapsacks [left behind after a firefight] they found a notebook that listed the name, address, weapon, and ammunition of the entire column, member by member. In addition, one member of this column, who is also a member of the PSP [Pablo Ribalta] left his knapsack containing documents from that organization."

Combined with its public propaganda blitz, the army was exploiting its new "Communist evidence" to instill fear and hatred of the rebels among its troops. In a September 21 cable sent to the army units stationed along Che's route, Lieutenant Colonel Suárez Suquet exhorted his officers to use all available resources and "muster courage" to stop the "guerrilla enemy" that was "murdering men no matter what their beliefs are," and pointed out that "the recent capture of communist documentation from the foreigner known as 'Che Guevara' and his henchmen, who have always lived beyond the law . . . , [shows they are] all paid by the Kremlin. . . . Onward Cuban Soldier: we will not permit these rats who have penetrated surreptitiously in this province to leave again."

As if having the army on his tail wasn't bad enough, as Che approached the Escambray, he knew he was heading into a hornet's nest of rivalries and intrigues. Various armed groups were operating in the area, virtually all of them were competing for influence and territorial control, and some were little more than rustling marauders, or *"comevacas"* (cow-eaters). On October 7, while still en route, he had been visited by a rebel delegation from the Escambray, who gave him "a rosary of complaints" about Eloy Gutiérrez Menoyo, who had broken away from Chomón's Directorio and created his own "Second National Front of the Escambray." There was open hostility between the two factions, and each had carved out a territory. Most recently, Gutiérrez Menoyo had briefly seized Víctor Bordón Machado, leader of the July 26 guerrilla force operating in Las Villas, and their two forces were now on the verge of an armed confrontation. Che sent word that Bordón should come and see him, and wrote in his diary: "From here I get the impression there are a lot of dirty rags to wash on all sides."

In addition to taking the war to central Cuba, Fidel had ordered him to "unify" the various factions and bring them under his control, but he wasn't counting on much help from the July 26 Movement. Instead, his experience on the llano so far had shown him who his natural allies were: the PSP.

Che's arrival provided the PSP with a golden opportunity to acquire a central role in the armed struggle, something the other factions in the area had consistently denied them. In rural Yaguajay, in northern Las Villas, the PSP now had its own rebel front, the "Máximo Gómez," with sixty-five armed men led by party official Félix Torres, but Torres had been refused links by both the local July 26 Movement chapter and Gutiérrez Menoyo's "Segundo Frente."

With Che's approach to the region, the party quickly sent emissaries to greet him in early October. They offered him guides and money, and promised a radio transmitter and mimeograph machine for his propaganda efforts once he was installed in the Escambray. A grateful Che accepted and asked for a direct connection with the PSP leadership in Las Villas.

It was another miserable week of slogging through mud and swamp, as well as periodic harassment by warplanes, before Che and his men reached a farm in the foothills of the Escambray. They were hungry, sick, and exhausted, but they had crossed more than half the length of Cuba, a distance of over six hundred kilometers (about 370 miles), mostly on foot. And here, as he had requested, a Communist party official met them.

At twenty-six, Ovidio Díaz Rodríguez was secretary of the Juventud Socialista for Las Villas province. The party had dispatched him to await Che's arrival, and he had set out on horseback to intercept him. It was a miserable day when they met—it had been raining, and everything was wet and dripping—but Díaz was euphoric. The government's incessant propaganda about the "Argentine Communist" had fueled his awe of Guevara, and, as he neared the rendezvous, Díaz felt overwhelmed with emotion. "I wanted to hug him when I met him," he recalled, but when Che extended his hand in greeting, Díaz shyly abandoned his plan. "I saw he was very thin and I imagined all the penuries he had surely gone through since leaving the Sierra Maestra. I was struck by his personality and the respect everyone showed him. The admiration I felt increased."

Then, with his characteristic bluntness, Che chastised Díaz for incautiously approaching his camp head-on. "You should have followed my tracks," he said, before inviting Díaz to sit down and talk. "He asked me to summarize everything I knew about the situation of the Escambray, of the armed groups that existed, the situation of the Party in the Province and in the mountains, the support it had, whether the socialist bases were strong in the zone. He spoke to me with respect and in an affable way."

Che noted in his diary on October 15 that he had met with "a representative of the PSP," who told him that the party was "at his disposition" if he could forge a unity deal with the various armed groups. It was a good start.

By now, Camilo had also made contact with the PSP. His column had veered north, to Yaguajay, where Félix Torres's column was located, and on October 8 the two men had met in the field. Torres had happily placed himself and his men under Camilo's orders, and, just as happily, Camilo had accepted. Thereafter, the two maintained separate camps but coordinated actions with one another. Fidel was so pleased with the arrangement that he ordered Camilo to stay on in Las Villas and act as a bolster to Che's operations, instead of pushing on to Pinar del Río.

Over the next couple of days, as Che and his men moved on into the Escambray proper, Díaz revisited him to coordinate matters. Each time, he came away that much more impressed with Che's leadership abilities. "He knew his men perfectly well: who had come from the different revolutionary organizations, who had risen up as workers or peasants, who were anticommunists due to a lack of culture. He measured his men for their fighting spirit but he knew how to distinguish perfectly between those of left or right."

It was, as usual, a heterogeneous group. In addition to the relatively inexperienced graduates of Minas del Frío, Che had brought along his protégés. Apart from the Communists Ribalta and Acosta, there was Ramiro Valdés, his trusted deputy. Ramirito now sported a sinister-looking goatee, which Che liked to say made him resemble Feliks Dzerzhinsky, the KGB founder. The young doctor, Oscarito Fernández Mell, whose company Che enjoyed, and whom he liked to tease as a "petit bourgeoie," had also come along.

Next came the loyal youngsters such as Joel Iglesias, Guile Pardo, El Vaquerito, who led his own daredevil "Suicide Squad," and the Acevedo brothers. And there were exotic characters such as "El Negro" Lázaro, a huge, brave black man with a equally grand sense of humor who dragged a horse saddle with him throughout the invasion, saying he wanted it for the day when he found a horse to ride, which, of course, he never did.

Finally, there was a group of youths whose destinies were to become permanently linked to Che's, many of whom stayed with him after the war as his personal bodyguards, and joined him on his future guerrilla adventures. To most of them, with few political notions but eager for adventure, Che was their key to glorious future lives, in which they too would become modern-day "liberation heroes."*

What was it about Che that so magnetized them? He could not have been more different from most of them. He was a foreigner, an intellectual, a professional, and he read books they did not understand. As their leader, he was demanding, strict, and notoriously severe in his punishments—especially with those he had selected to become "true revolutionaries." When young Harry Villegas and a few other youths went on a hunger strike at Minas del Frío over the bad quality of the food, Che had at first threatened to shoot them. In the end, after conferring with

*See the appendix for elaboration.

Fidel, he had softened the sanction, making them go without food for five days, "so they could know what real hunger was." Nor had this punishment been an isolated incident; there were many more times when they suffered Che's severity for mistakes that other commanders might have passed over or even committed themselves.

But Che was different, and they knew it. He demanded more of himself, so he demanded more of them, too. Each sanction he meted out came with an explanation, a sermon about the importance of self-sacrifice, personal example, and social conscience. He wanted them to know why they were being punished, and how they could redeem themselves. Naturally, Che's unit was not for everyone. Many fell by the wayside, unable to take the hardship and his rigorous demands, but for those who stuck it out, being "with Che" became a special source of pride. And because he lived as they did, refusing extra luxuries due to his rank, taking the same risks as they did in battle, he earned their respect and devotion. For these youths, about half of them black, many from poor farming families, Che was their guide and teacher, a role model to emulate and live up to, and in time they wanted to believe whatever he believed in.*

Meanwhile, although he was careful to conceal it, Che was paying a personal price for the austere revolutionary image he had constructed for himself. His relationship with Zoila, his attachment to his mules, his habit of keeping pets, all could be taken as signs that he craved tenderness and solace to ease the harsh life he had adopted.

When he arrived in the Escambray, he was expecting his personal messenger, Lidia, to join him. She was to be his courier for communication with Fidel and Havana, and she had also promised to bring him a puppy to replace "Hombrito," a little dog named after the valley he'd fought over, which he'd had to leave behind in the Sierra Maestra. But Lidia never made it. She and her companion, a woman called Clodomira, were betrayed, captured, and then "disappeared" by Batista's agents.

---

*Che had many good men with him on his long march to the Escambray, but some began to suffer from what he called *"apendijîtis,"* or "yellowitis." "In an attempt to clean out the scum of the column," he told Fidel, he had cashiered seven men on October 7. The next night, the American volunteer Herman Marks, who had a captain's rank, left as well. Although the gringo, a Korean War veteran, had been an excellent instructor of Che's fighters in recent months, and proven himself repeatedly in battle, Che wasn't sorry to see him go, and in his journal he wrote: "He was wounded and ill, but fundamentally, he didn't fit into the troop." Enrique Acevedo explained in more detail. The American was "brave and crazy in combat, tyrannical and arbitrary in the peace of camp." In particular, according to Enrique Acevedo, he had displayed a disquieting predilection for executing condemned men, often volunteering for the task with an enthusiasm that was unseemly.

Che felt her loss deeply. As he wrote a few months after her murder, "[For] me personally—Lidia occupies a special place. That is why I offer today these reminiscences in homage to her—a modest flower laid on the mass grave that this once happy island became."

Crossing Camagüey, Che lost the military cap that had once belonged to Ciro Redondo, and which he had worn ever since Ciro's death. He replaced it with the black beret that would eventually become his personal trademark, but at that moment he had lost something that could not be replaced. Oscarito Fernández Mell had rarely seen Che as upset as on that day. "That cap was a disaster," recalled Oscarito. "The visor was fallen down, it was dirty and shitty, but because it had belonged to that man, it was what he wanted to wear . . . a bit like the continuation of his friendship with Ciro. Che was a man who was both hard and extraordinarily sentimental."

II

As Che sized up the feuding rebel groups in the Escambray, he knew he would have to act quickly to impose his authority and organize an effective fighting front. His first mission was to attack the local military detachments and interrupt all traffic in Las Villas, as part of the rebel strategy to sabotage the "farcical" presidential elections scheduled for November 3, only two weeks away.

The limited field of candidates did indeed seem a study in out-of-touch politics. Standing against Batista's successor candidate, Prime Minister Andrés Rivero Agüero, were the Ortodoxo splinter politician Carlos Márquez Sterling and Ramón Grau San Martín, the discredited former president now heading his own Auténtico faction. Not surprisingly, there was little enthusiasm among the citizens, and voter turnout was expected to be minimal.

The rebels, by contrast, were moving from strength to strength. To a growing segment of the public, they, the *barbudos*—as the bearded, long-haired guerrillas were now popularly known—held the keys to Cuba's political future, not the dapper *políticos* in Havana. To capitalize on this growing popularity, Fidel wanted to use the election to launch an island-wide offensive, and this time he expected the public to show its solidarity. In addition to a traffic ban, Fidel decreed a consumer boycott of the lottery, and a halt to purchases of newspapers and attendance at parties or festivities of any kind; the citizens should buy only the barest essentials so as to deny the regime revenue. In case anyone harbored doubts about his opposition to the elections, Fidel also threatened all candidates with prison or death.

To enforce his decrees, Fidel sent out new columns to operate on the llano of Oriente and Camagüey, and gave Juan Almeida orders to begin encircling the city of Santiago. He also took the urban action groups off their tether, and in September they carried out some spectacular assaults in Havana, destroying the transmitting facilities of two government radio stations and setting fire to Rancho Boyeros, the country's main airport.

At the same time, political repression by the regime continued unabated. Several gruesome police murders of civilians, including those of two young sisters in Havana, had outraged and sickened the public. The tortures of political suspects detained by the CIA-funded Buró de Represión a las Actividades Comunistas (BRAC) had become so notorious that the CIA's own inspector general complained. In September, one of Che's columns in Camagüey fell into an ambush. Eighteen rebels were killed, and the eleven captured survivors, including wounded men, were summarily executed.

The revolution in Cuba was also drawing in players far from its shore. With the American State Department still blocking new arms shipments to the Cuban regime, Batista had begun turning to alternative arms suppliers. When the sale of fifteen British Sea Fury warplanes to Cuba was reported, Fidel's intermediaries appealed to Prime Minister Harold Macmillan to halt the sale, only to be snubbed. Fidel responded by decreeing the confiscation of all British-owned property in Cuba, and called for a public boycott of British goods.

In a dress rehearsal for their future showdown, Fidel and Washington had begun a war of words. The White House rebuffed a rebel appeal to withdraw the U.S. military mission to Cuba, while a more hostile State Department hinted it might "take action" after rebels briefly seized two American Texaco employees in an ambush. In late October, Batista withdrew his soldiers guarding the American nickel mine of Nicaro. When Raúl's forces moved in to occupy the mine, the U.S. Navy sent a transport ship, backed up by an aircraft carrier, to evacuate the fifty-five American civilians there. The State Department issued a veiled threat of retaliatory action if American hostages were again taken.

Fidel quickly fired back his own warning, that if the State Department made the error of "leading its country into an act of aggression against our sovereignty, be certain that we will know how to defend it honorably."

Meanwhile, ever since the army's failed military offensive, there were increasing reports of discontent brewing within the armed forces. Keen to exploit this trend, Fidel used every opportunity to broadcast his praise for the men of the Cuban armed forces, while urging that they reconsider their service at the hands of "the tyranny" rather than to "the fatherland," which *he* represented. Any officers or soldiers who chose the latter were welcome in the rebel's "Free Territory" as long as they brought their weapons with them; their current salaries would continue to be paid, and they were prom-

ised free room and board through the end of the war. He wrote again to
General Cantillo, urging him to lead a military revolt against Batista, but
the army commander remained noncommittal; their game of cat and mouse
would go on, right through to the end. At the same time, one of Fidel's agents
was trying to convince some dissident officers to defect and form a rebel
army column of their own. Such a move would be a major propaganda coup
for Fidel and would accelerate the disintegration of the armed forces.

As Fidel plotted and schemed, a stream of visitors and emissaries came
and went from the Sierra Maestra, some, such as PSP official Carlos Rafael
Rodríguez, staying on as permanent guests. Life there had certainly improved. Thanks to a new cook brought up especially from a restaurant on
the llano, Fidel was eating well again and had even gained weight. He had
his own jeep and permanent electric power from a generator. He had time
to read books and listen to classical records on his phonograph machine. He
could speak by telephone to the outside world when he wanted to. Celia,
the proverbial lion at his door, was also sharing his double bed. Life was good.

Fidel was confident, but not complacent, about the future. In Oriente,
the rebel army now numbered over eight hundred men. Arms and ammunition were no longer in short supply, thanks to the materiel captured in
the summer offensive and to continuing arms-supply flights from abroad.
He was also successfully filling his war chest. He had imposed a fifteen cent
tax on each 250-pound bag of sugar harvested, and the sugar mills of Oriente,
including U.S.-owned ones, were paying up. He even had his own modest
rebel air force under the command of Pedro Luis Díaz Lanz.

At the same time, he announced his long-planned agrarian reform bill,
called "Law 1 of the Sierra Maestra." In the decree, he promised to distribute
state land and any lands owned by Batista to landless peasants, guaranteed
the continued ownership of lands not exceeding 150 acres, and promised compensation to those with large "idle" landholdings, if confiscated. Most significantly, at least in terms of future world events, Fidel was also edging ever closer
to an overt alliance with the Communist party. By late October, the formation of a new labor front—FONU (Frente Obrera Nacional de Unidad)—
that included the PSP was announced.

As usual, Fidel was operating on several levels. At the same time as he
pacified his anti-Communist allies with a middle-of-the-road agrarian reform bill, he was shoring up a working alliance with the Communists that
went far beyond the labor unity deal. The practical groundwork was already
being carried out by Che, Raúl, and Camilo.

In Raúl's Second Front, a political-military alliance between the PSP
and July 26 was up and running. The "Peasant Congress" that Pepe Ramírez
had organized was held in September, presided over by Raúl. Similarly,

immediately after arriving in Las Villas, Camilo set in motion plans for a "National Conference of Sugar Workers." Although it wasn't held until the eve of the rebel victory in December, Camilo's initiative, like those Che was about to set in motion elsewhere, was one of the first steps in the gradual July 26–PSP merger that eventually culminated in the creation of a new Cuban Communist party, headed by Fidel.

Che marched through Oriente and Camagüey with agrarian reform in mind, but had been too busy trying to survive to do very much about it. A week after setting out, in the rice-growing region of eastern Camagüey, he had urged workers at a large private farm to form a rice growers' union, and had gotten an enthusiastic reaction. "One person with a social consciousness could work wonders in this area," he told Fidel later, "and there is plenty of vegetation to hide in. . . . An armed guerrilla unit of 30 men could work wonders in this zone, and revolutionize it."

Three weeks later, in western Camagüey, finding himself on a large rice farm owned by an associate of Batista, Che stopped to talk with its American manager. As he noted in his journal: "I spoke to the administrator to explain the essence of our economic concepts and our assurances for the protection of the rice industry so that he could transmit it to his boss." Joel Iglesias recalled the encounter in more detail.

"When we left there, [Che] asked me: 'What did you think of him?' I replied that I didn't like those guys. He told me: 'Me neither, [and] in the end we'll have to fight against them,' and added: 'I would die with a smile on my lips, on the crest of a hill, behind a rock, fighting against these people.'"

But before he fought the Yankees, Che had to confront a different kind of enemy. After entering the Escambray proper on October 16, Che found himself engulfed by the intrigue there. Gutiérrez Menoyo's Directorio faction, the "Segundo Frente," not only had acted with hostility toward July 26 commander Víctor Bordón, but was also at odds with the official Directorio Revolucionario armed group, led by Faure Chomón. And there were disputes within the July 26 itself.

A delegation representing the Las Villas July 26 directorate came to complain about Bordón, who they said had become "aggressive" and was acting on his own. Hoping to settle things, Che called for a council to be held at the Directorio's base camp in a few days' time. Meanwhile, he tried to convince the July 26 men of the need for a local unity agreement, and proposed a strategy for joint urban uprisings and guerrilla attacks in Las Villas's cities during the elections. "I didn't find much enthusiasm on the idea," he noted.

Che had just established a provisional camp at a place called Los Gavilanes when he was approached by an officer of Gutiérrez Menoyo's

Second Front. Despite the front's anti-Communist ethos and its reputation for banditry, Che was anxious to see if some form of anti-Batista coalition could be forged. In mid-October, he and his men set out for the camp of one of the most notorious Second Front warlords, Comandante Jesús Carreras. When they reached the camp after a two-day hike, they found Carreras gone, but he had left behind a threatening notice. As Che recounted in his diary, the notice warned that "no troops could pass through this territory, that they would be warned the first time but the second, expelled or exterminated."

When Carreras returned, Che saw that "he had already drunk half a bottle of liquor, which was approximately half his daily quota." When Che boldly announced he could not "permit" Carreras's use of the word "warning," the front commander quickly backed down, explaining that the threat had been intended only for marauding fighters from the Directorio faction. Che left believing he had handled things diplomatically, but he also knew that Carreras was "an enemy."*

Moving on to the Directorio headquarters at Los Arroyos, Che met with its leaders, Faure Chomón and Rolando Cubela. They were open to the idea of cooperation with the July 26 Movement but rejected any talks with the Second Front or the Communists, and stressed their unwillingness to cede their independent status in a unity pact with Che. As an alternative, Che proposed they work out "measures to partition territory and zones of influence where the forces of other organizations could operate freely." Setting aside the fine points, he suggested launching a joint attack against Güinía de Miranda, a town with an army garrison at the base of the Escambray, after which the Directorio force and his would split any weapons captured. "They accepted in principle but without enthusiasm," he noted in his diary.

It was not much, but at least Che was getting *somewhere*. At the same time, he was grappling with the July 26 Movement, whose new Las Villas coordinator, Enrique Oltuski, aka "Sierra," had come to see him.

It was a pitch-black night when Oltuski arrived in Che's camp, and the guerrillas were milling around a bonfire. Oltuski approached, trying to make out faces. "I had in my mind the image of Che that I had seen published in the newspapers. None of these faces was that face. But there was a man, of regular build, who was wearing a beret over very long hair. The beard was not very thick. He was dressed in a black cape with his shirt open.

---

*After the revolution, Carreras returned to the Escambray with other disgruntled former revolutionary fighters and took up arms in a guerrilla war against the revolution. He was captured and executed in 1961.

The flames of the bonfire and the mustache, which fell over either side of the mouth, gave him a Chinese aspect. I thought of Genghis Khan."

Their first meeting did not go well. The Havana-born son of Polish emigrants, Oltuski was trained as an engineer but had put aside his career for the revolution. He had helped to organize the Civic Resistance, and was a member of the July 26 National Directorate. He was also an anti-Communist.

He and Che immediately locked horns, their first clash coming over Che's proposal to carry out bank robberies in Las Villas to acquire funds. Oltuski and his llano comrades were vehemently opposed. As Che wrote contemptuously in his diary:

"When I told him to give us a report of all the banks in the towns, to attack them and take their money, they threw themselves on the ground in anguish. [And] with their silence they opposed the free distribution of land and demonstrated their subordination to the great capital interests, most of all Sierra [Oltuski]."

In his memoir, Oltuski reconstructed his own version of their argument over land reform, which reads as follows:

Guevara: When we have broadened and consolidated our territory we will implement an agrarian reform. We will divide the land among those who work it. What do you think of the agrarian reform?

Oltuski: It is indispensable. [*Che's eyes lit up*] Without agrarian reform economic progress is not possible.

Guevara: Or social progress.

Oltuski: Yes social progress, of course. I have written an agrarian thesis for the Movement.

Guevara: Really? What did it say?

Oltuski: That all idle land should be given to the peasants and that large landowners should be pressured to let them purchase the land with their own money. Then the land would be sold to the peasants at cost, with payment terms and credits to produce.

Guevara: That is a reactionary thesis! [*Che boiled over with indignation*] How are we going to charge those who work the land? You're just like all the other Llano people.

Oltuski: [*I saw red*] Damnit, and what do you think we should do?! Just give it to them? So they can destroy it as in Mexico? A man should feel that what he owns has cost him effort.

Guevara: Goddamnit, listen to what you're saying! [*Che shouted and the veins on his neck bulged*]

Oltuski: In addition, one must disguise things. Don't think that the Americans are going to sit idly by and watch us do things so openly. It is necessary to be more discreet.

Guevara: So you're one of those who believes we can make a revolution behind the backs of the Americans. What a shiteater you are! The revolution must be carried out in a life-and-death struggle against imperialism from the very first moment. A true revolution cannot be disguised.

On October 22, with the issues between Che and his local July 26 colleagues unresolved, a new problem arose with the Second Front when he was visited by Commander Peña, "famous in the region for rustling the peasants' cattle." In his diary, Che wrote: "He began by being very friendly but later showed his true colors. We parted cordially, but as declared enemies."

Pena had warned Che not to attack Güinía de Miranda, which lay within *his* territory—"naturally," wrote Che, "we paid no attention"—but before he could go ahead with the attack, his men, whose boots were rotting on their feet after their long trek, needed new footwear. He was enraged to learn that a shipment of forty boots sent by the July 26 Movement for his men had been "appropriated" by the Second Front. For Che, it was nearly the last straw. Between his and the Second Front forces, "a storm was brewing."

Amid this crisis, "Diego," the July 26 action chief for Las Villas, arrived, bringing five thousand pesos and an old letter from Fidel, both forwarded by Oltuski. Che gave Diego his orders for the upcoming offensive, "to burn the voting centers in two–three important cities on the llano and to give Camilo the order to attack Caibarién, Remedios, Yaguajay and Zulueta [towns in northern Las Villas]." Che had yet to work out exactly what his own plan of attack would be. Everything depended on the cooperation he got from the other rebel forces.

On October 25, Víctor Bordón, the local July 26 guerrilla chief, finally came to see Che and was immediately humbled. Among other things, Che found Bordón guilty of overstepping his authority and of having lied about a supposed meeting with Fidel which had never taken place. He degraded him to captain's rank, and ordered Bordón's two hundred–odd men to bring their weapons and place themselves under *his* command; those not in agreement were told to leave the mountains.

That very night, the Directorio leaders came to tell Che they were "not in a condition" to join his attack against Güinía de Miranda, planned for the next day. Che had suspected as much and told them he would go ahead without them. The following night, he and his men hiked down to Güinía de Miranda and opened fire on the barracks with a bazooka. Its first shot missed the target, however, and the soldiers returned fire. A fierce firefight ensued, punctuated by three more wild shots from the bazooka. Rebels began to drop. In desperation, Che grabbed the weapon himself and hit the barracks on his first shot. The fourteen soldiers inside surrendered immediately.

Despite the surrender, Che was far from pleased with the results. "We captured very few bullets and [only] eight rifles, our loss, because of the amount of ammunition wasted and grenades used." In addition, two rebels had died and seven were injured. By dawn they were safely back in the hills, but before returning to camp, Che pointedly left a jeep he had stolen as "a gift" for the Directorio near their camp, a memento from the battle in which they had not participated.

With or without help from the other factions, Che decided to keep up the pressure on the army. The next night he set off to attack the Jíquima garrison, defended by fifty soldiers. More cautious this time, he suspended the attack just before daylight when Fonso, his bazooka-man, told him he couldn't find a good firing position. Back in the sierra on October 30, Che received visits from the July 26 action chiefs from Sancti Spíritus, Cabaiguán, Fomento, and Placetas; all endorsed his plans to attack their towns during the coming days. "They were also in agreement with the bank robberies," Che noted, "and promised their help."

After a few more days of skirmishing, Che set about organizing his men for the series of attacks that would be carried out on November 3, Election Day, in concert with the urban action groups. On the eve of battle, however, he was visited by the very anxious action chief for Sancti Spíritus. The city coordinator for Sancti Spíritus had learned of the bank robbery scheme, the action chief explained, and had refused all help, had even made threats if the plan went ahead. A short time later, Che received a threatening letter from Sierra/Oltuski, the July 26 coordinator for Las Villas, ordering him to abort the robbery plan. Che immediately fired back a withering letter:

> You say that not even Fidel himself did this when he had nothing to eat. That is true. But when he had nothing to eat he was also not strong enough to carry out an action of this type. . . . According to the person who brought me the letter, the local leaderships in the towns are threatening to resign. I agree that they should do so. Even more, I demand it now, since it is impermissible to have a deliberate boycott of a measure that would be so beneficial to the interests of the revolution.
>
> I find myself faced with the sad necessity of reminding you that I have been named commander-in-chief, precisely to provide the

Movement with unity of command and to improve things. . . . Whether
they resign or don't resign, I intend to sweep away, with the authority vested in me, all the weaklings from the villages surrounding the
mountains. I never imagined things would come to a boycott by my
own comrades.

Now I realize that the old antagonism we thought had been overcome is resurrected with the word *Llano*. You have leaders divorced
from the masses stating what they think the people believe. I could ask
you: Why is it that no peasant disagrees with our thesis that the land
belongs to those who work it, while the landlords do?

Is this unrelated to the fact that the mass of combatants are in favor
of the assault on the banks when they are all penniless? Have you never
considered the economic reasons for this respect toward the most arbitrary of financial institutions? Those who make their money loaning
out other people's money and speculating with it have no right to special consideration. . . . Meanwhile, the suffering people are shedding
their blood in the mountains and on the plains, and suffering on a daily
basis from betrayal by their false leaders.

You warn me that I bear total responsibility for the destruction of
the organization. I accept this responsibility, and I am prepared to
render an account of my behavior before any revolutionary tribunal,
at any moment decided by the National Directorate of the Movement.
I will give an accounting of every last cent provided to the combatants
of the Sierra, however it was obtained. But I will also ask for an accounting of each of the fifty thousand pesos you mention.*

You asked me for a signed receipt, something I am not accustomed
to doing among comrades. . . . My word is worth more than all the
signatures in the world. . . . I will end by sending you revolutionary
greetings, and I await your arrival together with Diego.**

Once again, Che's plans had been fouled by the llano. On the very day
they were supposed to be waging war together against the regime, his city-
based comrades had done nothing, choosing to attack him instead.

*Oltuski had said this amount had been collected by the llano, and that part of it would be
given to Che to show him they had enough support to make robbing banks unnecessary.

**Víctor Paneque, aka "Diego," was action chief for Las Villas; Oltuski had told Che that
Diego also opposed the bank robberies. Later, in his memoir of the episode, Oltuski wrote
that Diego had reacted with shock when he heard of Che's plans, and said it was "craziness,"
that it would alienate July 26 supporters, and that he was "sure" that Fidel wouldn't approve
such actions.

Still determined to do something, Che ordered a three-pronged attack on the town of Cabaiguán, and, once again it was to begin with a bazooka blast. At around four in the morning, however, his captain, Angel Frías, reported that he couldn't fire "because there were too many guards." Furious, Che wrote in his diary: "The indecision of this captain has cost us much prestige, because everyone knew we were going to attack Cabaiguán and we had to retreat without firing a shot."

Arriving back in the Escambray the next morning, Che ordered a new attack on Jíquima that night, but this too was aborted when Angel Frías couldn't find "a good firing position." Che's disappointments over these poor showings were offset by good news coming in from around the province.

The combination of his actions and Camilo's attacks in the north had brought most traffic in Las Villas to a standstill on Election Day, with voter abstention very high. In the rest of the country, the results were similar, while in Oriente the rebels had compounded the paralysis by launching multiple attacks. Nationwide, the rebel strategy had been a tremendous success, with perhaps less than 30 percent of the eligible voters showing up at the polls. As expected, Rivero Agüero had won, thanks to massive voting fraud carried out with the assistance of the armed forces, and he was to assume the presidency in less than four months' time. The rebels were determined to see that his February 24 inauguration never took place.

For a few days, Che stayed in the hills to oversee the construction work at the Cabellete de Casas base. It was to be his permanent rearguard base, to be defended at all costs against an enemy offensive. He supervised the work being put into trenches and fortifications, and deposits for food and ammunition reserves. The work was proceeding well, and several adobe houses were already finished, but to accelerate things Che organized the nearly two hundred men he had assembled into work crews. He set up a recruits' school, modeled on Minas del Frío, which he named the "Ñico López" in honor of his late comrade, and, once again, the Communist party official Pablo Ribalta was made its political commissar. Within a few days, his new communications personnel arrived and began installing his field radio system, courtesy of the PSP. His promised mimeograph machine also arrived, and by mid-November he had founded a newspaper called *El Miliciano* (The Militiaman). Soon, there would be an electrical plant, a hospital, a tobacco factory, leather and metals workshops, and an armory.

Several people who were to become closely linked to Che now joined him in the Escambray. The movement in Santa Clara sent Che a smart, serious young accountancy student from Holguin named Orlando Borrego, who wanted to join up. In time they would become best friends, but at their first meeting Che greeted him imperiously.

"I didn't have a very friendly reception," recalled Borrego. "He was very rough, very cold, and was contemptuous of students." Borrego was one of seven children raised on a hardscrabble farm in Holguín, Oriente. His father was a farm foreman turned taxi driver, and his mother was a rural schoolteacher. Money had always been a struggle, and Orlando had gone to work at fourteen to help his family. Since then, he had learned what he knew from night classes, and now he had run away to join the rebels, but *this* was the welcome he got. One of Che's bodyguards, Orlando "Olo" Pantoja, diplomatically intervened, suggesting that Che take Borrego on to help him manage his funds. Che agreed to let Borrego stay on as his treasurer, but ordered him to first undergo a military training course at Caballete de Casas.

At the training camp, Borrego made friends with a lively young July 26 guerrilla of twenty-two named Jesús Suárez Gayol, aka "El Rubio," for his fair hair. A former student leader from Camagüey, he had abandoned his architectural studies to join a July 26 expedition that had landed in Pinar del Río in April. Bright, with a fun-loving personality, Suárez Gayol had taken his personality into the war with him. In his latest exploit, from which he was still recovering, Suárez Gayol had rushed into a radio station in Pinar del Río in broad daylight, carrying a stick of fused dynamite in one hand and a pistol in the other. After removing the fuse, he somehow caught himself on fire. Stripped to his underpants, with severe burns on his legs, he rushed out into the street—just as the building blew—to come face-to-face with a policeman. Luckily for him, the shocked policeman ran away. Then, still waving his pistol, Suárez Gayol ran down the street and leapt into an old woman's house. Fortunately the woman was a rebel sympathizer, and she hid him and treated his wounds until he could be smuggled out of the province and up into the Escambray. When the war was over, Suárez Gayol and Borrego remained close friends and became two of Che's most trusted disciples.

A young lawyer from a patrician Havana family also arrived at the Escambray camp in early November. Miguel Ángel Duque de Estrada had joined July 26 to participate in a struggle for social justice. Although not a Marxist, he admired Che, had closely followed the reports of his march across Cuba, and had asked to be sent to Che's Escambray unit. Che needed to find someone qualified to enforce the guerrilla legal code in rebel territory, and the young lawyer fit the bill; he made Duque de Estrada his *auditor revolucionario,* or judge.

"He had a clear political strategy worked out in his mind," said Duque de Estrada. "He told me prisoners were to be kept alive, there were to be no firing squads. This would change later, but for now he didn't want executions to put off men who might surrender to his forces." Like Borrego and

Suárez Gayol, Duque de Estrada would become one of Che's select cadres after the war.

Indeed, even as he pursued the war, Che was looking ahead to the future. Just as he had already assembled many of his guerrilla cadres for future revolutionary struggles, he was recruiting a brain trust of aides and advisors to help in the coming postwar battle: the political and economic revolution that would be necessary to build socialism in Cuba and free it from U.S. domination through its single export-crop economy, "King Sugar."

In Che's selection of candidates, political ideology was not the essential factor; he believed that if they had progressive outlooks, he could eventually make them believe in socialism. It appears he was right. As with most of his guerrilla protégés, professionals such as Borrego, Duque de Estrada, and Suárez Gayol were not Marxists at first but ended up *formally* adopting Che's ideology as their own.

In fact, by the time he reached the Escambray, Che was actively planning a central role for himself in the postwar revolutionary transformation of Cuba's economy. Whether this was the result of an understanding worked out with Fidel and the PSP is a point that has been left intentionally unclarified in Cuba, but there is strong evidence to suggest this was the case. Che had been studying political economy ever since his days in Mexico. At Fidel's behest, he had helped set the agrarian reform process in motion in the Sierra Maestra, had been a key participant in the delicate talks with the PSP, and was now empowered to carry out land reform in Las Villas.

But it was not a one-man show. For both his present and future projects, Che was now relying on the PSP for its full collaboration—and besides the Communists already working with him in the Escambray, there was a small, well-placed group of party militants at his service in Havana. One of them was thirty-seven-year-old Alfredo Menéndez, a sugar expert employed at the Instituto Cubano de Estabilización del Azúcar (Cuban Institute for the Stabilization of Sugar), the sugar-industry syndicate headquarters in Havana. A veteran Communist, Menéndez had for years used his strategic position to feed economic intelligence to the PSP Politburo, and he now did the same for Che.

With the aid of a colleague, Juan Borroto, and two July 26 men at the sugar institute, Menéndez sent Che sugar industry reports and other economic intelligence. Their efforts would not go unrewarded; although none would meet Che until the war was over, he would send for his four "moles" within a few days of his arrival in Havana and ask for their help in establishing the vehicle for Cuba's future revolutionary government, the Instituto Nacional de Reforma Agraria, or INRA.

But if Che was now depending on the PSP for help, he still wanted to avoid any appearance that he was in their pocket. Ovidio Díaz Rodríguez, the Socialist Youth leader who helped coordinate Che's agrarian reform efforts in Las Villas, was present when a party man came to a meeting carrying a present for Che. "It was a tin of Argentine mate and in front of everyone he said: 'Look Commander, this is a gift from the Party Directorate.' He accepted it without saying anything, but afterward he told me: 'Tell the Party not to send me such indiscreet comrades.'"

III

Che may have entertained ambitious plans for Cuba's revolutionary future, but the war for power had yet to be won. In Las Villas, a strategic cornerstone in rebel strategy for the final push to victory, Che had finally begun making headway. By simple virtue of launching attacks in the zone—something few of the other groups had done despite their months in the Escambray—he had become the de facto authority in the zone, and people began arriving to pay him their respects.

On November 8, two dairy company inspectors visited to ask if they could continue to collect milk in the area; their dairy business was almost paralyzed because of the rebel activities. "I told them yes, but that we would charge an extraordinary war tax, with which they agreed." A transport union leader from Santa Clara came proposing joint actions in the city. Che told him he was willing if the man could organize a union meeting and if all the leaders requested it. A delegation from Placetas brought him diagrams of the town and offered him their support if he attacked it.

Clearly put out by Che's seizure of the limelight in "their" zone of influence, the Second Front's warlords were making increasingly bellicose noises. Che received notes from William Morgan, the American military veteran helping Gutiérrez Menoyo, ordering him to return the weapons that Bordón had brought over when he joined Che. Entirely ignoring Morgan, Che wrote a strongly worded letter to Gutiérrez Menoyo and meanwhile ordered his men "not to hand over a single weapon and to repel any attack" from the rival group. If the Second Front persisted in its hostile behavior, he was ready to take armed action.

Che also wrote to Directorio leader Faure Chomón to inform him of the "delicate situation" with the Second Front. The situation was of "crisis proportions," he said, "making it impossible to reach an agreement with this organization." He also urged Chomón to consider including the PSP in their proposed alliance. "In official talks with members of the Popular Socialist Party, they have openly expressed a pro-unity stance and have placed their organization in the towns and their guerrillas on the Yaguajay front at the disposal of this unity."

Next, Che heard that soldiers loyal to Second Front commander Peña were extorting money from local civilians, and he sent out men to detain the culprits. Within a few days, two complete Second Front columns were brought in. Che warned them that they could no longer operate in the zone, much less use their arms to extort from the people. At this show of authority, one of the columns asked to join his force, and Che accepted. Before letting the rest go, he confiscated the "war taxes" they had extorted—a total of three thousand pesos—and sent a note to Peña. In this "Military Order No. 1," Che's first decree as "commander in chief of the Las Villas region for the July 26 Movement," he made it clear that life in the area was about to change. After first outlining the terms for agrarian reform, he turned in oblique fashion to his Second Front competitors.

"Any member of a revolutionary organization other than the July 26 Movement may pass through, live and operate military in this territory. The only requirement shall be to abide by the military orders that have been or will be promulgated.

"No one who is not the member of a revolutionary organization has the right to bear arms in this territory. No member of any revolutionary body is permitted to drink alcoholic beverages in public establishments. . . . Any shedding of blood due to violation of this order will fall under the Penal Code of the revolutionary army. . . .

"All military or civil crimes committed within the borders of the administrative territory encompassed by this order will fall under the jurisdiction of our appropriate regulations."

Perhaps intimidated by this display of force, the Directorio faction now accepted unification with Che's group, agreeing to impose a single tax in the area and to divide the proceeds equally between their two organizations. As a practical first step for their new alliance, they planned to begin launching joint attacks. The one area of disagreement that remained was Chomón's refusal to widen the alliance to include the PSP. Che let the matter rest, for the refusal didn't prevent him from working with the Communists; on December 3, less than three weeks after the Directorio–July 26 unity agreement, he and PSP leader Rolando Cubela signed the "Pedrero Pact," declaring their alliance in the struggle as "brothers."

The quarrels within the July 26 Movement continued, however. Enrique Oltuski, together with Marcelo Fernández, the new July 26 Havana chief, and three officials from the Las Villas directorate, called on Che in late

November for another round of talks. Che found Fernández "full of airs
about himself," and he prepared for battle. "We argued all night. . . . We
accused each other mutually, they [accused me of being a] communist and
I [accused them of being] imperialists. I told them the facts on which I based
myself to give such an opinion and they did the same to me. When the argument ended we were more apart than when we began."

As Oltuski recalled, Che was away when they arrived, and they were
received by one of his young bodyguards, Olo Pantoja. As an act of courtesy, Pantoja offered them some goat meat, which they noticed was already
green with rot. So as not to offend, they each tried a bite, a decision Oltuski
immediately regretted: overcome by nausea, he discreetly went outside and
spat out his mouthful. When Che returned at midnight and settled before
the meal, Oltuski watched with horrified fascination.

"As he spoke," Oltuski wrote, "he took the pieces of meat with dirty
fingers. Judging from the relish with which he ate, it tasted gloriously to
him. He finished eating and we went outside. . . . Che handed out cigars.
They were rough, no doubt made in the zone by some *guajiro*. I inhaled the
bitter and strong smoke: I felt a warmth in my body and a light dizziness.
To my side, Che smoked and coughed, a damp cough, as if he was all wet
inside. He smelled bad. He stank of decomposed sweat. It was a penetrating odor and I fought it with the tobacco smoke. . . . Che and Marcelo had
some verbal wrangles. Among other things, they argued over the program
of the 26 of July. . . .

"When we were on our way back, Marcelo asked me: 'What do you
think?'

"'In spite of everything, one can't help admiring him. He knows what
he wants better than we do. And he lives entirely for it.'"

IV

It was not love at first sight. Comandante Che Guevara may have been one
of the most talked-about men in Cuba and a guerrilla leader of legendary
courage, but viewed up close by Aleida March, he didn't seem much of a
romantic prospect. Her first impression of him was that he looked "old,"
not to mention "skinny and dirty." Neither of them realized it yet, but their
lives were about to collide.

It was late November, and Aleida had traveled to Che's base from
Santa Clara on a special mission for "Diego," her boss in the Las Villas rebel
underground. Until now, she had managed to elude Batista's secret police,
who had been hunting for the woman identified in their dossiers only as
"Cara Cortada" (Scarface) and "Teta Manchada" (Stained Tit). They knew

she was Diego's *lugarteniente,* his right hand, and the person whom he entrusted with his most delicate missions.

Aleida's unlovely nicknames had been coined from the descriptions of *chivatos,* who told police about the small scar on her right cheek, from a childhood dog-bite, and the large pink birthmark that spread from her left breast to above her collarbone. But the police intelligence sheets were misleading, for, in spite of her scars, Aleida March was a pretty blond woman of twenty-four.

The youngest of six children, Aleida had been raised on a fifty-acre tenant farm in the hilly agricultural country south of Santa Clara. Her mother was tiny, barely five feet, while her father was tall, with blond hair and blue eyes, "a decent man of some culture," as she would later describe him. Both were from once-affluent Spanish emigré families who had lost their wealth, but Aleida liked to say that her family was "middle class" because their home had a concrete floor; their neighbor's homes and the one-room grammar school she attended until the sixth grade had dirt floors.

Except for its concrete floors, however, their two-bedroom house was much like everyone else's, with a palm-thatched roof and whitewashed mud walls, a family room with a kitchen, and a "front room" for receiving visitors. The ceiling was yellow from all the rice bags Aleida's father stored in the attic. A vertical wood strut rising from the floor between the living room and the kitchen held up the roof, and in the evenings her father sat down and leaned his back against it to read her stories. At night, Aleida could hear her mother singing to her father in their bedroom next to her's. A river ran across their land; this was where her mother washed their clothes, and where Aleida and her sisters bathed.

Their part of Las Villas was populated by people much like themselves—poor white farmers, the descendants of immigrants from impoverished parts of Spain—Galicians, Andalusians, and *"isleños"* (Canary Islanders). In the pecking order of socially and racially stratified Villa Clara, as in much of Cuba, such families languished at the bottom rung of white society, but they were still head and shoulders above the mulattos and blacks. Only three generations out of slavery, *"los negros"* were the dirt-poor laborers, the despised effluvia of Cuban society. In 1958, Santa Clara's central park was still off-limits to blacks; there was a fence around it, and blacks could congregate around its edges, but not go inside.

Like many poor whites, Aleida's mother was both a racist and a snob. She liked to brag about the illustrious lineage of Aleida's father, whose Castilian ancestors had supposedly been noblemen. When she was small, mimicking her mother, Aleida used to tell people she was related to the "Dukes of Castile." Whether her father was of direct noble lineage or an illegitimate offspring, Aleida never knew, but it *was* true that both her parents' families had once possessed land and money. Her father's family had owned a sugar plantation but had lost their land years before, and the land her father now sharecropped had belonged to Aleida's maternal grandparents, before they too lost it in the hard times of the twenties. When her parents married, they had rented back her mother's old family farm and settled in as tenant farmers. The last remaining legacy of their comfortable past, an antique crystal *bonbonnière,* stood prominently displayed on an old wood bureau in the front room, where guests were received.

The family's "high" status was further bolstered by the fact that the local schoolteacher lodged with them throughout Aleida's childhood, theirs being the only home in the area "decent" enough for the teacher. But the Marches also had their blemishes. Her mother, a devout church-going Presbyterian, had caused a local scandal by giving birth to Aleida at the ripe age of forty-two, well past "appropriate" childbearing years. This was a source of perpetual mortification for Aleida's sisters—the next closest in age was fifteen years older—and they used to tell people that Aleida was not their sister at all, but the daughter of the much-younger schoolteacher.

The nearest community was Seibabo, just a hamlet with a few houses in it, but once a month her father saddled up his horse and rode into the city of Santa Clara to buy provisions on credit from the Chinese bodegas. He had fruit orchards, grew vegetables, and owned a couple of dairy cows, but he still had to go into debt to feed his family. When the crops didn't give him enough to pay off the landlord, he had to sell things. One year, disaster struck, and he had to part with a prized calf to meet his rent.

When Aleida reached the sixth grade, she went to live with a married sister in Santa Clara and attended high school there. Her world began to open up. She decided to become a teacher and, when she finished high school, went on to Santa Clara University to earn a degree in education. While she was there, Fidel carried out his Moncada assault. The event and its violent aftermath awakened her politically, as it did many other young Cubans of her generation. By the time the *Granma* landed, she had graduated from college and was an active member of the local July 26 underground.

Until she reached her early twenties, Santa Clara was the biggest city Aleida had ever seen. She made her first trip to the capital, Havana, on a mission for the July 26 Movement, and it was the first time she had seen four-lane roads. Gino Donne, an Italian merchant marine, first mentioned "Che Guevara" to her.

Donne had been on the *Granma,* become separated from his comrades at Alegría del Pío, and eventually, after many misadventures, made it to Santa Clara. Covered in blisters, famished from hunger, and with a pounding toothache, Donne was given refuge at the house of María Dolores "Lolita" Rossell, a pretty, dark-haired mother of four and a kindergarten teacher. Lolita's brother Allan Rossell was the July 26 coordinator for Las Villas, and her house functioned as a way station on the rebels' underground railroad.

It was because of Donne's arrival that Lolita and Aleida met for the first time, and they soon became close friends. By then, Aleida was chief liaison for the July 26 action chief in Villa Clara and was earning a reputation as extremely audacious, smuggling weapons and bombs around the province under her full-length fifties skirts. "She wasn't afraid of anything," Lolita recalled. "She was totally dedicated, very serious, [had stayed] single, and wasn't one for parties and that kind of thing."

Aleida came to Lolita's house to plan sabotage attacks with Donne, and for a time the two carried out missions around the city. But Donne didn't stay long; disillusioned by the festive mood he saw in Santa Clara that first Christmas—which he perceived as revealing a lack of insurrectionary spirit —he found a ship leaving Cuba and went with it.

Aleida herself stayed active, participating personally in the September 1957 uprising in Cienfuegos, and in armed actions during the April 1958 general strike in Las Villas. During the security crackdown that followed the strike, the Las Villas Directorate organized a guerrilla force to operate in the rural areas of the province. Aleida helped: sneaking hunted fugitives out into the countryside; smuggling food, weapons and ammunition, and messages to them. After Che's arrival, Aleida made repeated trips to and from the sierra, taking visitors and carrying correspondence and money to the controversial guerrilla commander in chief. By November, an effective, if not acrimony-free partnership between the llano and sierra July 26 factions had been secured in the Escambray, and Aleida, as the principal courier, was becoming a familiar face at Che's encampment. One day, Che told her he had decided to impose a war tax on sugar-mill owners, and asked her help in collecting it. It was after returning from such a mission in late November that Aleida found out her cover had been blown and that the police had raided her home. Returning to Santa Clara was now out of the question, but when she went to ask Che's permission to remain in the guerrilla zone, he was not pleased; as a rule, women were not permitted to live in the guerrilla camps. Given Aleida's dilemma, however, the *comandante* relented.

Like most of her llano comrades, Aleida had a poor opinion of the Cuban Communist party. Her own antipathy stemmed from her university days, when she had a Communist professor who was vociferously opposed to any insurrectional activity. Now, however, the war was at a critical stage, and Che's unifying efforts had helped to defuse the sectarian rivalries and galvanized Las Villas's opposition groups into action. And if she initially distrusted *"El comunista Che,"* she put her feelings aside, for very soon she found herself falling in love with him. (Eventually, because of Che, Aleida would alter her negative opinion of "socialists," but she would never lose her distrust of the "old Communists" of the PSP.)

By late November, the air force was pounding Che's front with daily bombardments, and the army had begun moving several companies of heavily armed troops and tanks toward Pedrero in a three-pronged offensive. Camilo came with some of his units to help out, and for six days the two sides battled. By December 4, the army's offensive was shattered. The guerrillas had stopped the advance on all fronts, then chased the soldiers all the way to Fomento in the west and to the village of Santa Lucia in the east. They also captured a healthy supply of war materiel, including a tank equipped with a 37 mm cannon. One of Che's squads destroyed two strategic bridges, isolating the army garrisons in Cabaiguán, Sancti Spíritus, and Trinidad, and opening up a large new swath of territory to the rebel forces. Now, it was Che's turn to go on the offensive.

Before Camilo Cienfuegos returned to his main forces at Yaguajay, he and Che mapped out a joint strategy for a province-wide offensive. Like an enthusiastic surgeon especially deft at amputations, Che set about systematically severing road and railway bridges, isolating the province's towns and garrisons and cutting them off from reinforcements. On December 16, his men blew the principal Central Highway bridge and railway link leading east from Santa Clara, effectively separating Havana and Santa Clara from central and eastern Cuba, and cutting the nation in half. These actions, together with the offensive taking place in Oriente, where llano garrisons had begun falling like dominoes to the guerrillas, made it clear the Batista regime had little time left.

For the last two weeks of December 1958, Che's life was a blur of battle as he moved around the province attacking and capturing one garrison after the other. First, he laid siege to the strategic town of Fomento, with its key military garrison, and, despite a sustained enemy air assault, secured its surrender after two days of fighting. He immediately moved on to the towns of Guayos and Cabaiguán. Guayos surrendered on December 21, Cabaiguán two days later. In Cabaiguán, Che fell off a wall and fractured his right elbow. Dr. Fernández Mell made him a splint and cast, and he carried on. His next target was Placetas, where his troops fought together with the Directorio for the first time. After a single day's fighting, Placetas surrendered on December 23. That same day, Sancti Spíritus surrendered to Captain Armando Acosta. Meanwhile, the Second Front had finally moved into action, joining Directorio forces in a siege of Trinidad and other garrisons in the south. To the north, Camilo's forces were closing in on the main garrison town of Yaguajay.

At some point amid the chaos and euphoria of battle, Che and Aleida became lovers. Perhaps the first to take note of the romance was Oscarito Fernández Mell, although even he could not remember when or where in the headlong rush of events. "Suddenly, Aleida was with Che wherever he went, in the combat, everywhere. . . . They went around in the jeep together; she carried his papers for him, she washed his clothes . . ."

A less observant Minas del Frío graduate, Alberto Castellanos, nearly put his foot in it, however. A cocksure twenty-four-year-old, Alberto had already been sanctioned by Che for prankish behavior, but had nonetheless endeared himself to the jefe, who made him a general staff orderly. Alberto considered himself quite a lad with the ladies, and when Aleida showed up she caught his eye as "a good looker." Deciding to try his luck, he walked up to her and delivered a saucy *"piropo,"* or come-on line. Che was watching, however, and as soon as Castellanos had uttered the words, he realized Aleida was definitely *not* available. "From the way Che looked at me, I said to myself: 'Beat it, Alberto, there's nothing for you here.'"

Aleida herself recalled how it all began. One night, unable to sleep, she left her room and went outside to sit by the road. It was three or four in the morning, and the offensive was in full swing. Suddenly a jeep raced up the dark road and came to a halt next to her. Che was at the wheel. "What are you doing here?" he asked her. "I couldn't sleep," she replied. "I'm going to attack Cabaiguán," he said. "Do you want to come along?" "Sure," she replied, and hopped in the jeep next to him. "And from that moment on," recalled Aleida with a playful smile, "I never left his side—*or* let him out of my sight."

V

Given their divergent beliefs, Che and Aleida made an unlikely couple. Aleida came from the faction within the Cuban revolution most despised by Che. She was from the llano, she was anti-Communist, and what is more, she still possessed many of the social prejudices she had been brought up with. Although it wasn't a factor in these early days, things such as dress were important to her, and she shared her mother's racial disdains. By contrast, Che was a radical Communist, the arch-nemesis of most of her colleagues. He was also famously careless about his appearance and personal hygiene, and had surrounded himself with *negros* and uneducated *guajiros*.

But, when it came to women, especially attractive women, Che tended to put his political philosophies on hold—and Aleida March was very attractive. She was also worthy of respect, for she was undeniably brave, having proved repeatedly that she knew how to face death. She also had a paradoxical personality that clearly appealed to Che, very shy, but with an acute and earthy sense of humor. When she did speak out, she was tactlessly sincere, much like Che himself.

Whatever it was that had brought them together, it was a new fact of life their comrades quickly noticed and accepted. To his orderlies, Aleida was a welcome addition to their daily lives, for she helped temper Che's disciplinary streak. And from then on, they all went everywhere together.

After fracturing his arm, Che had made Castellanos his driver and, with him at the wheel, Che and Aleida roared around the province in his jeep with his young bodyguards—Harry Villegas, Jesús Parra, or "Parrita," José Argudín, and Hermes Peña. Soon, a rumor spread that Che was traveling with "three women: a blonde, a black, and a *jabao*"—a Cuban term for a white mulatto. Aleida was obviously the blonde, but sixteen-year-old Villegas, who was black and beardless, and fellow stripling Parrita, a white, with wild blond hair, were mortified to realize they had been misidentified as girls. The erroneous gossip aside, what Che had created was not a harem but his own little guerrilla family. Che and Aleida played the roles of the parents, and the young guerrillas were their wayward "children."

"Che knew us like parents know their children," recalled Villegas. "He knew when we had done something naughty, when we hid something from him, when we did something wrong by accident or through mischief. [And] he had strict norms, which at the beginning we didn't fully understand. For example . . . he didn't want anyone to have special privileges. If he saw I had extra food he would call me to find out where I had gotten it from or where it came from—why I had accepted it—and he called Aleida over and made her responsible to see that it didn't happen again. And Aleida helped us a lot, you could say she was like our godmother, because we were mischievous, and Che [was strict], and she was the intermediary on many occasions when she evaluated the situation differently from him, and made him see he was being too severe with us."

All the while, the offensive against the Batista regime continued in full swing. Following the surrender of Placetas, Che moved north and, on Christmas Day, attacked Remedios and the port of Caibarién; both fell the next day. Villa Clara had become a chaos of defeated army troops, cheering civilians, and long-haired guerrillas racing around, while in the skies, government planes kept up their strafing and bombing. By December 27 only one garrison, in the town of Camajuaní, remained between Che's forces and the Las Villas capital; when its troops fled without a fight, the way was clear for the assault on Santa Clara, the fourth-largest city of Cuba.

The fighters were euphoric. They knew now that they were on the verge of winning the war, but Che ordered his men not to celebrate victory prematurely; maintaining troop discipline and establishing a semblance of law and order in the province were among his top priorities. To prevent anarchy, Che had named provisional revolutionary authorities in each town he liberated, and set down rules of behavior for his men. Bars and bordellos were strictly off-limits, but for many of his young guerrillas, suddenly finding themselves in towns and cities as conquering heroes after months of abstinence in the bush, the temptation to indulge themselves was too much. For the most part, they were remarkably well behaved, but invariably some succumbed to the delights on offer. On the day Remedios fell, platoon leader Enrique Acevedo almost lost control of his men when a bordello owner delivered a free truckload of prostitutes and a case of rum as an expression of his "admiration."

"I watched our ambush disintegrate as furtive couples began heading to the bushes. Without thinking I yelled at the guy: 'If you've done this to affect our ambush you'll pay for it. Pick up the wagonload of whores you've dumped here immediately!'" Afterward Acevedo took stock and realized he had reacted just in time. "Not everyone had sinned, the majority hadn't abandoned the ambush. But in any case maintaining order in the face of such temptation was a titanic effort."

As Che plotted his next move, Fidel wrote him a letter by flashlight from outside the entrenched army garrison of Maffo, which his forces had been besieging for six days: "The war is won, the enemy is collapsing with a resounding crash, we have ten thousand soldiers bottled up in Oriente. Those in Camagüey have no way of escaping. All this is the result of one thing: our determined effort . . . It's essential for you to realize that the political aspect of the battle at Las Villas [province] is fundamental.

"For the moment, it is supremely important that the advance toward Matanzas and Havana be carried out exclusively by the 26th of July forces. Camilo's column should be in the lead, the vanguard, to take over Havana when the dictatorship falls, if we don't want the weapons from Camp Columbia [military headquarters] to be distributed among all the various groups, which would present a very serious problem in the future."

On the eve of inflicting a battlefield defeat on the Cuban armed forces, Fidel was determined to prevent rivals from snatching the political spoils at the last moment. His anxieties were the opposite of those being voiced in Washington. Past differences between State and the CIA had been put aside, and there was now a broad consensus that Castro was too slippery to be allowed to take power. With the events of recent weeks, however, any hopes entertained by the Eisenhower administration that the November 3 elections might somehow ameliorate the Cuban crisis had vanished.

In addition to Che and Camilo's offensive in Las Villas, new rebel columns were roaming throughout Oriente and Camagüey. Numerous garrisons had surrendered to Raúl's forces, Holguín's water and electricity supply had been blown up, and Santiago itself was under mounting pressure as rebel units probed its outskirts. At the end of November, after a bloody siege, Fidel's forces had taken the major garrison of Guisa, and he too had moved his forces from the mountains onto the llano. Ambassador Smith had dutifully shuttled to Washington to seek support for President-elect Rivero Agüero, but in vain; it was clear to all that the military situation was deteriorating rapidly, and fears were growing that Batista might not even last until the scheduled February handover of power.

Smith was instructed to tell Batista that a Rivero Agüero government could not expect Washington's support and that he should resign immediately in favor of a civilian-military junta acceptable to the United States. Batista refused, evidently still believing he could somehow hold things together. In early December, he had rebuffed a similar petition by the CIA's station chief in Havana and by William Pawley, a former ambassador to Cuba and founder of the national airlines, Cubana de Aviación.

Shortly after, the port of Nicaro fell to Raúl, and then the La Maya barracks in Guantánamo after a rebel pilot had dropped a napalm bomb on the compound. Raúl had also captured vast quantities of weapons and was holding over five hundred prisoners. As Fidel lay siege to Maffo in mid-December, his forces controlled most of the Central Highway through Oriente and had the army pinned down seemingly everywhere.

As the rebels pushed on, the CIA had begun exploring the possibility of backing a preemptive military coup, and its agents were fishing around for suitable junta candidates. Once again, Justo Carrillo proposed Colonel Barquín, still imprisoned on the Isle of Pines. Barquín enjoyed strong loyalties within the armed forces and was on most people's lists as a candidate to assume military control once Batista was gone. This time, the CIA gave its go-ahead, and gave Carrillo money to bribe prison officials to spring Barquín.

Simultaneously, sensing an opening for themselves, Batista's coterie of top officers began hatching coup plots. General Francisco Tabernilla, army chief of staff, told General Cantillo, commander of Oriente province, to open negotiations with Fidel by proposing a military-rebel alliance for the final push against Batista, and the installation of a joint military-rebel junta. It would include Cantillo himself, another officer to be decided upon, president-in-waiting Manuel Urrutia, and two civilians selected by Fidel.

The unofficial slogan of all these last-ditch efforts was, of course, "Stop Castro," and Fidel saw little reason to accommodate them. He rejected the putschists' proposal and sent word to Cantillo that he wanted a face-to-face meeting to give *his* proposals.

All the while, Batista's army kept crumbling. Across the country, towns and cities were being occupied by the rebels, greeted by enthusiastic civilians, many of whom—genuine supporters or not—wore the red and black July 26 armband. By Christmas, Che's and Camilo's forces had taken most of the major towns and cities in Las Villas except for Santa Clara, Cienfuegos, Trinidad, and Yaguajay. Víctor Bordón had taken a string of towns to the west, cutting off Santa Clara from potential reinforcement from Cienfuegos or Havana. In Oriente, meanwhile, the major garrisons at Caimanera and Sagua de Támano fell, and a naval vessel, the *Máximo Gómez,* stood off Santiago awaiting rebel orders to defect. After a quick Christmas visit with his mother in Birán, Fidel prepared for his meeting with Cantillo. He still had plenty of worries, but on the night of December 26 he felt confident enough to give Che the orders all in the rebel movement had dreamed of for a very long time: preparations for the assault on Havana itself.

Fidel had been correct in his end-game analysis that the battle for Las Villas was crucial, for the city of Santa Clara had become the last cornerstone in Batista's defensive strategy. As the major transport and communications hub of central Cuba, with a population of 150,000, it was the one remaining obstacle to a rebel assault on the capital; if Santa Clara fell, only the port of Matanzas lay between the rebels and Havana. Batista now placed all his hopes in holding Santa Clara, beefing up its garrison with over 2,000 new soldiers to bring its troop strength to 3,500, and sending his ablest soldier, Joaquín Casillas, now a colonel, to take over its defense. To support Casillas, he had dispatched an armored train, loaded with weapons, ammunition, and communications equipment; it was to serve as a reserve arsenal and mobile communications link with military headquarters at Camp Columbia.

Even as he reinforced Santa Clara, however, Batista knew he had little time left. He already knew of Tabernilla's scheming against him and had chosen to side with General Cantillo, telling the Oriente commander he would hand over power to a junta headed by him in late January. At the same time, Batista wasn't taking any chances; over Christmas he arranged for several airplanes to stand ready to evacuate himself and a short list of handpicked officers and friends with their families from the country. A few days later, he sent his children to the United States for safety.

Meanwhile, Che was getting ready to attack Santa Clara. On December 27, he was joined in newly liberated Placetas by Antonio Nuñez Jiménez, a young geography professor from Santa Clara University, who brought maps and diagrams to help plan Che's approach to the city. With Ramiro

Valdés, they plotted a route over back roads leading to the university, on the northeastern outskirts of the city. They set out that night, with a disparity in numbers similar to those that had marked nearly every engagement between the rebels and the Cuban army; with eight of his own platoons, and a 100-man Directorio column led by Rolando Cubela, Che had 340 fighters to tackle an enemy force ten times larger and supported by tanks and aviation.

Che's convoy arrived at the university at dawn the next day, and Aleida's friend Lolita Rossell was on hand to meet them. She was shocked by how "dirty and messed-up" the guerrillas looked. Standing next to her, her father muttered, incredulously: "*These* are planning to take Santa Clara?" Then Lolita spotted Che, and she was struck both by how young he looked and by his unmistakable air of authority. This impression was bolstered when one of his men, his face a battle-weary mask, asked her how many soldiers were in the city. When she told him "about five thousand," he nodded and said: "Good, with our jefe that's no problem."

After setting up a provisional *comandancia* at the university in Aleida's old stamping ground, the Pedagogical Faculty, Che and his men set out for the city itself, walking in the irrigation ditches along the way. Stopping at the CMQ radio station, he went on the air to address the city and appeal for civilian support. Shortly after, B-26 bombers and new British-made Sea Furies strafed and bombed the outskirts of town, looking for his fighters.

The enemy had occupied a series of well-fortified positions around the city, but Che's first priority was the armored train, stationed at the entrance to the Camajuaní road leading to the university. At the eastern edge of the city, the army had occupied the strategic Capiro Hills that overlooked both the university road and the road and rail line leading out to Placetas. Over a thousand soldiers were holed up in the Leoncio Vidal garrison in the northwestern suburbs, and nearby was police headquarters, with four hundred defenders. In the city center, the courthouse, provincial government building, and jail had all been made redoubts, and to the south, the "No. 31" and Los Caballitos garrisons guarded the road to Manicaragua. With most of the province now in rebel hands, Che's chief concern was to prevent enemy reinforcements from the western Havana-Matanzas road, but Víctor Bordón's force had cut the highway at several points and seized the key town of Santo Domingo.

Over that night and into the morning of December 29, Che moved his forces from the university into the city, targeting all the enemy positions but concentrating on the armored train. He moved his *comandancia* to a public-works building a kilometer from town and had a section of rail track pulled up with tractors; then his men attacked, going against the police station, the Capiro Hills, and the armored train. At the same time, Cubela's

Directorio column, which had entered from the south the day before, laid siege to the No. 31 and Caballitos garrisons. The battle was on.

Over the next three days, Santa Clara became a bloody battleground as rebels slowly advanced into the city. In some places they moved forward by punching holes in the interior walls of homes, while others fought pitched battles in the streets outside. Numerous civilians heeded Che's call to arms, making Molotov cocktails, providing refuge and food, and barricading their streets. As tanks fired shells and airplanes continued to bomb and rocket, however, both civilian and guerrilla casualties began to pile up in the hospitals.

Che was visiting one of the hospitals when a dying man touched his arm and said to him: "Do you remember me, Commander? In Remedios you sent me to find a weapon . . . and I earned it here." Che recognized him. It was a young fighter he had disarmed days earlier for accidentally firing his weapon. Che also recalled what he had told him at the time. "I [had] responded with my customary dryness," he wrote in his civil war memoirs a few years later. "'Go get yourself another rifle by going to the front line unarmed . . . if you're up to it.'" The man clearly had been, and with fatal consequences. "He died a few minutes later, and I think he was content for having proven his courage. Such was our Rebel Army."

The tide turned inexorably on the afternoon of December 29. After El Vaquerito's "suicide squad" took the train station, and other rebels stormed the Capiro Hills, the soldiers there fled for the protection of the armored train. Then, the train's twenty-two cars attempted an escape, moving out at speed. When it reached the missing track, the train's engine and first three cars derailed in a spectacular cataclysm of twisted metal and screaming men.

"A very interesting battle began," Che wrote, "in which the men were forced out of the train by our Molotov cocktails. . . . Cornered by men, who from nearby points and adjoining railroad cars, were throwing bottles with burning gasoline, the train became, thanks to the armored plating, a veritable oven for the soldiers. In a few hours, the whole complement surrendered with its twenty-two cars, its antiaircraft guns, its machine guns . . . its fabulous quantity of ammunition (fabulous, of course, compared with our meager supply)."

With battles still raging around the city, the international wires carried the false news that evening that Che had been killed. Early the next day, Radio Rebelde went on the air, trumpeting the news of the capture of the armored train and denying Che's death. *"For the tranquility of the relatives in South America and the Cuban population, we assure you that Ernesto Che Guevara is alive and on the firing line, and . . . very soon, he will take the city of Santa Clara."*

All too soon, however, Che had to go on the air himself, confirming the death of one of his most beloved men, Roberto Rodríguez, aka El Vaquerito. It lent a sad note to his broadcast, made to announce the imminent fall of the city. That afternoon, the diminutive leader of the Escuadra Suicída had been hit by a bullet in the head while attacking the police station. Vaquerito's loss was especially painful to Che, for the youth had been the living personification of what he sought in his fighters. The "Suicide Squad" had been Vaquerito's choice of names, but it was an elite attack squad made up of those fighters who strove to aspire to Che's highest measure.

"The Suicide Squad was an example of revolutionary morale," wrote Che, "and only selected volunteers joined it. But whenever a man died— and it happened in every battle—when the new candidate was named, those not chosen would be grief-stricken and even cry. How curious to see those seasoned and noble warriors showing their youth by their tears of despair, because they did not have the honor of being in the front line of combat and death."

Surrounded by death, it is a normal human reaction to reach out for life, and even Che was not immune to this instinct; so it happened that in the midst of the battle for Santa Clara, he realized he was in love with Aleida. As he told her privately later, the realization occurred when she left his side to dart across a street under fire. For the few instants she was out of sight, he was in agony, not knowing if she had made it across safely. As for Aleida, she had known what she felt since the sleepless night a few weeks before when his jeep had stopped for her, and she had climbed in.

On December 30, the Los Caballitos garrison surrendered to the Directorio, and some soldiers barricaded in a church also gave themselves up. Outside the city, Santo Domingo, lost to an army counteroffensive, was recaptured by Bordón's forces, effectively sealing the western approaches. To the south, the city of Trinidad fell to the forces led by Faure Chomón. Realizing he had not completely secured Las Villas in the east, Che had dispatched Ramiro Valdés to take the town of Jatibonico on the central highway, where an armored column of army reinforcements was attempting to break through.

With this deployment of forces and the capture of the armored train, Santa Clara was completely isolated, and an air of desperation now seized the soldiers and policemen holding out. The military high command in Havana ordered more air attacks on the city; resistance remained fierce at the garrisons and the police station; and a group of men had dug in on the tenth floor of the Gran Hotel and were directing sniper fire at the rebels.

But Che now had considerable extra firepower and fresh troops at his disposal. The bonanza of arms seized from the armored train had been truly staggering: six hundred rifles, a million bullets, scores of machine guns, a 20 mm cannon, and some precious mortars and bazookas. Throughout New Year's Eve day, one redoubt after the other fell to the rebels: first the police station, then the provincial government headquarters, followed by the courthouse and the jail, where escaping prisoners added to the confusion in the city. By the end of the day, only the No. 31 garrison, the Gran Hotel, and the main Leoncio Vidal garrison still held out.

In Oriente, in the meantime, Maffo had finally surrendered to Fidel's rebels after a ten-day siege, and Fidel had immediately set his sights on Santiago, Cuba's second-largest city. On December 28, he and General Cantillo met at the Oriente sugar mill near Palma Soriano and reached an agreement: Fidel would halt his offensive for three days, allowing Cantillo time to return to Havana and organize a military rebellion for December 31. That day, he was to arrest Batista and place the army at Fidel's disposal.

But as it turned out, Cantillo was playing a double cross. He returned to Havana, told Batista of the plot, and gave him until January 6 to leave the country. He then sent a message to Fidel, asking for a delay until January 6 before launching the revolt. Fidel was wary, but by then events had begun to move so fast, neither he nor Cantillo could foresee what would happen next.

VI

Che's seizure of the armored train had sent alarm bells ringing loudly at the military headquarters in Havana, Camp Columbia, and the subsequent rapid-fire succession of army surrenders around the nation had accelerated Batista's departure plans. By the afternoon of December 31, Batista's last hopes for buying time rested on the ability of Colonel Casillas to hold out in Santa Clara, but at nine o'clock that evening Casillas called the dictator to say he couldn't resist much longer without reinforcements. When, an hour later, Cantillo warned that Santiago was also about to fall, Batista knew it was time to go.

At a New Year's party for his top officers and their families at Camp Columbia, Batista led his generals into a room adjoining that where most of his guests were gathered, and revealed he would hand over the armed forces to Cantillo. Then, rejoining the party in the other room, he announced his decision to give up the presidency. He named Carlos Manuel Piedra, the oldest Supreme Court judge, as the new president; after formally swearing in Cantillo as the new armed forces chief, Batista and his wife and a coterie of handpicked officials and their families drove to the nearby military airstrip and boarded a waiting plane. By three o'clock in the predawn darkness of January 1, 1959, Batista was in the air, en route to the Dominican Republic with forty of his closest cronies, among them the "president-elect," Andrés Rivero Agüero. Before dawn broke, another plane had taken off carrying Batista's brother "Panchín," mayor of Havana, and several dozen more government and police officials. Separately, two other notorious characters also made their escape that day: paramilitary chieftain Rolando Masferrer and American mobster Meyer Lansky.

When, sometime that night, Colonel Casillas and his deputy, Colonel Fernández Suero, heard the news in Santa Clara, they made haste to save themselves. After concocting a flimsy excuse for their underling, the blissfully uninformed Colonel Cándido Hernández, they disguised themselves in civilian clothes and beat an escape.

As daylight broke in Santa Clara, the first rumors of Batista's flight were beginning to circulate. The No. 31 garrison surrendered, the final redoubts—the Gran Hotel and the Leoncio Vidal garrison—were surrounded, and by midmorning Colonel Hernández asked for a truce. Che told him he could accept nothing less than an unconditional surrender, and sent Nuñez Jiménez and Rodríguez de la Vega in to negotiate with him.

"The news reports were contradictory and extraordinary," Che wrote afterward. "Batista had fled that day, leaving the armed forces high command in a shambles. Our two delegates [meeting with Hernández] established radio contact with Cantillo, telling him of the surrender offer. But he refused to go along because this constituted an ultimatum, and [claimed] he had taken over command of the army in strict accordance with instructions from the leader Fidel Castro. We immediately contacted Fidel, telling him the news, but giving our opinion of Cantillo's treacherous attitude, an opinion he absolutely agreed with."

After the conversation with Cantillo, Hernández was understandably confused, but Che stood firm, insisting he surrender. At 11:30 in the morning their negotiations were interrupted by a broadcast address from Fidel over Radio Rebelde. Repudiating Cantillo's notion of a "military junta" or any understanding between them, he called for an immediate general strike, and a mobilization of rebel forces toward Santiago and Havana. He gave Santiago's defenders until six that evening to surrender or be attacked, and he ended with a slogan: *"Revolución Sí, Golpe Militar No!"*

The panorama was clearer now, and Che gave Hernández an hour to make up his mind; if he didn't surrender by 12:30, he would be attacked and be held responsible for the bloodshed that would follow. Hernández returned to the garrison, and the waiting began.

While Che had been negotiating with Hernández, his men had finally managed to dislodge the snipers from the Gran Hotel. The previous day, Enrique Acevedo had resorted to driving cars at high speed in front of the hotel to try to pinpoint the sniper fire, but abandoned the tactic after one of his men was shot in the leg. This morning, however, with their comrades surrendering all around them and their own ammunition almost exhausted, the snipers gave in. Acevedo watched them come out with their hands up.

They turned out to be a group of five *chivatos* and four policemen, some, in Acevedo's words, with "debts to pay to the revolutionary justice." Those debts were soon paid; at 2 P.M., after a brief summary trial, the five *chivatos* were executed by a revolutionary firing squad.

Nor had Casillas gotten very far in his new civilian disguise. Bordón's fighters, west of the city, had been ordered to halt any soldiers fleeing toward Havana, and Casillas, wearing a straw hat and a July 26 armband, soon fell into their hands. He immediately began trying to woo Bordón, praising him as "a great strategist," then told him that "the only thing he felt bad about was not being able to stay longer with me, because he had to carry on to the capital to participate in the military junta, which was going to 're-solve this business among Cubans.'"

Bordón cut him short. "I told him to stop flattering me, that we didn't need any junta, because it would be Fidel Castro who resolved life for the Cubans [from now on]. And that he was going with me to Santa Clara, so that Che could see him. That's where he changed color and asked me if I couldn't take him to another jefe. And I remember that when Che saw him, he told him: 'Ah! So you are the murderer of Jesús Menéndez.'"*

Casillas did not live out the day. The official revolutionary version is that he was shot dead trying to escape while en route to see Che, but this, quite obviously, doesn't mesh with Bordón's own account. Given Casillas's gruesome history of past atrocities and Che's record for applying revolutionary justice, it is possible that Casillas's failed "escape attempt" took place in front of a hastily assembled firing squad.

With ten minutes to go before Hernández's time was up, the officer agreed to surrender his garrison. His relieved troops droppped their weap-

*The Communist sugar-union leader murdered by Casillas in 1948.

ons and went out onto the streets, joining the rebels. A cheer went up around the city: Santa Clara had fallen. But Che was not celebrating yet. Order had to be restored in the city, there were henchmen and *chivatos* to be tried, and he needed to assemble his forces and give them their instructions.*

Cantillo's tenure as armed forces chief did not last long. Colonel Barquín, sprung that day from the Isle of Pines, was flown to Havana along with Armando Hart, and by early afternoon Barquín had arrived at Camp Columbia, where an outmaneuvered Cantillo promptly handed over his command. In Oriente, Santiago surrendered, and Fidel prepared to march into the city that night.

The next morning, January 2, Che and Camilo Cienfuegos were ordered to proceed to Havana. Camilo was to take over Camp Columbia, while Che was to occupy La Cabaña, the colonial-era fortress overlooking Havana at the mouth of the port. Camilo's column moved out first, for Che still had mopping-up duties to attend to, including executing some *chivatos* and appointing Calixto Morales, as the military governor of Las Villas. Afterward, Che addressed the people of Santa Clara, thanking them for their help in "the revolutionary cause." He and his men were leaving, he said, "with the feeling of leaving a beloved place. I ask you to maintain the same revolutionary spirit, so that in the gigantic task of reconstruction ahead, Las Villas may continue to be in the vanguard of the revolution."

At around three in the afternoon, with Aleida at his side, Che and his men began the drive to Havana. Most of his comrades were jubiliant at the prospect of liberating the Cuban capital, but to Che it was just the first step in the greater struggle that loomed ahead.

---

*One of those shot, according to historian Hugh Thomas, was Colonel Cornelio Rojas, the police commander. At the moment of his execution, Rojas asked to be allowed to give the firing order, which was granted.

Part Three
Making the New Man

The Supreme Prosecutor

*It is impossible for revolutionary laws to be executed unless the government
itself is truly revolutionary.*

LOUIS ANTOINE LEON DE SAINT-JUST,
1789, during the French Revolutionary "Terror"

*The executions by firing squads are not only a necessity for the people of Cuba,
but also an imposition by the people.*

CHE GUEVARA,
February 5, 1959, in a letter to Luis Paredes López of Buenos Aires

I

In Buenos Aires, the Guevara family was celebrating the New Year when
they heard the news flash of Batista's flight. Exactly two years since a mysterious hand had delivered "Teté's" letter with confirmation that he was
still alive, now the Guevaras once again had a reason to rejoice for Ernesto:
The international wires were reporting that the rebel columns led by Che
Guevara and Camilo Cienfuegos were advancing on Havana.

Their jubiliation was short-lived. As his father recalled, "In our house
we had not yet put down the drinks toasting the fall of Batista when some
terrible news came. Ernesto had been fatally wounded in the taking of the
Cuban capital." Once again, Guevara Lynch made desperate inquiries to find
out if the news was true, and two agonizing hours went by before the July 26
representative in Buenos Aires called to say the report was false. "We celebrated
the New Year that night with the happiness that Ernesto lived and that he
was in charge of the La Cabaña garrison in Havana," wrote his father.

Che's entourage arrived at the huge old Spanish colonial fortress in
the predawn darkness of January 3. Its regiment of three thousand troops,
which had already surrendered to July 26 militiamen, stood in formation
as Che arrived. He addressed them patronizingly as a "neocolonial army"
who could teach his rebel troops "how to march," while the guerrillas could
teach them "how to fight." Then he and Aleida installed themselves in the
comandante's house, built against the stone buttresses overlooking Havana.

The day before, Camilo had shown up at the military headquarters of
Camp Columbia across the city and taken over its command from Colonel

Ramón Barquín; General Cantillo had been arrested. Fidel had also made his triumphal entry into Santiago. Speaking before cheering crowds, he declared the city Cuba's provisional "capital," and proclaimed Manuel Urrutia, who had flown in from Venezuela, as the new president.

Carlos Franqui, who was with Fidel, couldn't understand why Che had been relegated to La Cabaña. "I remember pondering at length the reasons for this order of Fidel's: Camp Columbia was the heart and soul of the tyranny and of military power. . . . Che had taken the armored train and the city of Santa Clara, he was the second most important figure of the Revolution. What reasons did Fidel have for sending him to La Cabaña, a secondary position?"

Fidel had undoubtedly chosen the less visible position for Che because he wanted him out of the limelight. To the defeated regime, its adherents, and Washington, Che was the dreaded "international Communist," and it was only asking for trouble to give him a preeminent role so early on. By contrast the handsome, Stetson-wearing, baseball-playing, womanizing, humorous Camilo was Cuban, not known to be a Communist, and had already become a popular folk hero. *He* could take center stage.

Fidel needed Che for the indispensable job of purging the old army, to consolidate victory by exacting revolutionary justice against traitors, *chivatos,* and Batista's war criminals. Just as his brother Raúl, the other radical, was to be in Oriente—where Fidel had left him behind as military governor—Che was essential to the success of this task in Havana.

II

From the green rolling head of land where La Cabaña and its adjacent fortress El Morro sprawled, guarding Havana harbor, Che's view in January 1959 would have been much like that evoked in Graham Greene's latest novel, *Our Man in Havana,* published just months earlier.

"The long city lay spread along the open Atlantic; waves broke over the Avenida de Maceo and minted the windscreens of cars. The pink, grey, yellow pillars of what had once been the aristocratic quarter were eroded like rocks; an ancient coats of arms, smudged and featureless, was set over the doorway of a shabby hotel, and the shutters of a night-club were varnished in bright crude colours to protect them from the wet and salt of the sea. In the west the steel skyscrapers of the new town rose higher than lighthouses."

Closer up, Havana was a seamy, exciting city, booming with casinos, nightclubs, and whorehouses. There were even porno moviehouses, and the live sex show in Chinatown's Shanghai theater featured a performing stud called "Superman." Drugs such as marijuana and cocaine were available to those who wanted them. Havana's very seaminess had attracted Greene, who had made several recent visits to Cuba. "In Batista's day I liked the idea that one could obtain anything at will, whether drugs, women or goats." Through Greene's eyes, his fictional British vacuum cleaner salesman, Wormold, walked the streets of Old Havana, taking it all in. "At every corner there were men who called 'Taxi' at him as though he were a stranger, and all down the Paseo, at intervals of a few yards, the pimps accosted him automatically without any real hope. 'Can I be of service, sir?' 'I know all the pretty girls.' 'You desire a beautiful woman?' 'Postcards?' 'You want to see a dirty movie?'"

This was the raucous milieu into which Che and his men plunged after two largely abstinent years in the mountains, with fairly predictable results. Che kept his *escolta* (bodyguards) under strict control, but for Alberto Castellanos, the temptation was too much. "I was in wonderment. . . . I had never been in the capital before and I was in shock. . . . Because he kept me working with him until dawn, I didn't have time to see anything. [So], some nights I escaped to see the city, especially the cabarets. It fascinated me to see so many beautiful women."

Sex was heavy in the air. The guerrillas slipped out of La Cabaña's walls for trysts with girls in the bushes under the huge white statue of Christ that looms over the harbor. Aleida March raised her eyebrows in a suggestive expression of mock-scandal when recalling this period. It was a chaotic situation and had to be taken in hand. With an eye to the rebel army's public image and its own internal discipline, Che soon organized a mass wedding for all those fighters with lovers whose unions had not been made "official," inviting a judge to come and take their vows, and a priest for those wanting a religious ceremony. The wayward Castellanos, for instance, who had a fiancée back in Oriente, was one of those whose wings were clipped, in a La Cabaña ceremony presided over by Che himself.

Around the hemisphere, the celebratory mood brought about by Cuba's revolutionary triumph was less libidinous, but still widely shared. The war had captivated public interest, and hordes of foreign journalists descended on Havana to cover the installment of the new regime. "In Buenos Aires it was the only thing people talked about," wrote Che's father. "I felt as though I was suspended in the air. Our relatives and friends barraged us with questions and we responded with everything we knew. But the truth is that the greatest interest of our family was the life of Ernesto. And Ernesto was alive and the war had ended."

But even in Cuba, few people understood what it all meant. While still in Santiago, Fidel had taken pains to give the new regime a moderate front, but he had also set the pattern for his future relationship with "President" Urrutia by allowing him to name but one appointee, the justice minister, while *he* named the rest. Evidently feeling grateful to Fidel for making him president, Urrutia did not put up a fight. Even so, only a few July 26 men, mostly from the llano, were included in the initial cabinet roster.

From Santiago, Fidel began making his way slowly overland toward Havana, savoring his victory before adoring crowds. Reporters caught up with his caravan and followed its progress, filing dispatches to the outside world. To their interrogations, he repeated again and again that he had no political ambitions. He was at the orders of "President Urrutia," he said, and, as for its future policies, the revolution would obey the "will of the people." He had, however, "accepted" Urrutia's request that he serve as "Commander in Chief of the armed forces."

Wherever they appeared, throngs of civilians cheered the ragged guerrillas. A young rebel from Holguín, Reinaldo Arenas, recalled the atmosphere. "We came down from the hills and received a heroes' welcome. In my neighborhood in Holguín I was given a flag of the 26th of July Movement and for a whole block I walked holding that flag. I felt a little ridiculous, but there was a great euphoria, with hymns and anthems ringing out, and the whole town in the streets. The rebels kept coming, with crucifixes hanging from chains made of seeds; these were the heroes. Some, in fact, had joined the rebels only four or five months earlier, but most of the women, and also many of the men in the city, went wild over these hairy fellows; everybody wanted to take one of the bearded men home. I did not yet have a beard because I was only fifteen."*

In Havana, the atmosphere was a mix of festive anarchy and uncertainty. Hundreds of armed rebels were camped out in hotel lobbies, treating them as they would a guerrilla bivouac in the countryside. Most government troops had surrendered after Batista's flight and had remained in their barracks, but here and there a few snipers still held out, and manhunts were on for fugitive police agents, corrupt politicians, and war criminals. In a few places, mobs had attacked casinos, parking meters, and other symbols of Batista corruption, but quickly had been brought under control as the July 26 militias came out onto the streets. Even Boy Scouts were acting as ad hoc policemen. Meanwhile, the embassies were filling up with those military officers, police, and government officials left in the lurch by Batista's sudden flight.

---

*This quotation appears in Arenas's *Before Night Falls* (see Selected Bibliography). Arenas went on to become a well-known author, but suffered because of his homosexuality. Years later, he fled Cuba and settled in New York until his death.

On January 4, Carlos Franqui left Fidel's rolling caravan in Camagüey and flew ahead to Havana. He found the capital transformed. "The gloomy Camp Columbia, mother of the tyranny and of crime, which I had known as a prisoner, was now almost a picturesque theater, impossible to imagine. On the one hand, the bearded rebels with Camilo, no more than five hundred of them, and on the other hand, twenty thousand army soldiers intact—generals, colonels, majors, captains, corporals, sergeants, and privates. When they saw us walk by, they stood at attention. It was enough to make you burst out laughing. In the comandant's office was Camilo, with his romantic beard, looking like Christ on a spree, his boots thrown on the floor and his feet up on the table, as he received his excellency the ambassador of the United States."

Afterward, Che arrived. There were difficulties at the Presidential Palace. The Revolutionary Directory had installed themselves there and appeared to have no plans to give it up. Che had tried to talk with the leaders, but they had refused to see him. Wrote Franqui: "Camilo, half joking and half serious, said a couple of cannonballs should be fired off as a warning. . . . As I was not an admirer of the palace, I said it seemed like a good idea, but Che, with his sense of responsibility, told us it wasn't the right time to waste cannonballs, and he patiently returned to the palace, met Faure Chomón, and matters were straightened out. Camilo aways listened to Che."

By the time Fidel arrived on January 8, Urrutia was installed in the palace, and a semblance of governmental authority had been restored. The rebels had taken over public buildings, police stations, newspaper and trade union offices, while the Communist party had come out of the woodwork to call for mass demonstrations in support of the victorious rebels. Its exiled leaders began returning from exile, and its banned newspaper, *Hoy,* began publishing again. Even Carlos Prío, the former president, arrived back from Miami. Abroad, the major Cuban embassies had been occupied by July 26 representatives. Venezuela had recognized the new government, and so had the United States. The Soviet Union followed suit on January 10.

Cuba's civic and business institutions declared their support for the revolution with hyperbolic expressions of gratitude and fealty. The "nightmare" of Batista was over, the Fidelista honeymoon had begun. The business community bent over backward to pay tribute, volunteering to pay back taxes, and some major corporations announced new investments while declaring their optimism about Cuba's brave new future.

The media lionized Fidel and his heroic *barbudos.* The weekly magazine *Bohemia* became an unabashed revolutionary fanzine, printing obsequious homages to Fidel: One artist's depiction went so far as to render him with a Christlike countenance, complete with halo. Its pages were full of commercial advertisements tailored to suit the moment: The Polar beer brewery emblazoned a page with a graphic of a sturdy peasant cutting cane and the words, "Yes! IT IS TIME TO GET TO WORK. With the happiness of being free once more and feeling ourselves prouder than ever to be Cubans, we must blaze a trail of work: constructive and intense work to meet the demands of the Fatherland.... And after working, IT IS TIME FOR POLAR! There is nothing like a really cold Polar to complete the satisfaction of a duty fulfilled." The Cancha clothiers came out with a new men's shirt, the "Libertad," its ads showing a model sporting an appropriate revolutionary beard.

Carlos Franqui, who began bringing out the once-clandestine July 26 newspaper, *Revolución,* added to the flood of tributes by lauding Fidel as Cuba's "Hero-Guide." A theater debuted a play called *The General Fled at Dawn,* with a bearded, uniformed actor playing the role of Fidel Castro. After being hastily commissioned by some grateful citizens, a bronze bust of Fidel was erected on a marble plinth at an intersection near Havana's military complex, with an engraved inscription honoring the man who had "broken the chains of the dictatorship with the flame of liberty."

Che too came in for his share of lyrical tributes. Cuba's foremost living poet, the Communist Nicolás Guillén, was in exile in Buenos Aires when the triumph came, and at the request of a weekly newspaper editor there wrote a poem in honor of Guevara.

CHE GUEVARA

As if San Martín's pure hand,
Were extended to his brother, Martí,
And the plant-banked Plata streamed through the sea,
To join the Cauto's love-swept overture.

Thus, Guevara, strong-voiced gaucho, moved to assure
His guerrilla blood to Fidel
And his broad hand was most comradely
When our night was blackest, most obscure.

Death retreated. Of its shadows impure,
Of the dagger, poison, and of beasts,
Only savage memories endure.

Fused from two, a single soul shines,
As if San Martín's pure hand,
Were extended to his brother, Martí.

If Che was already a well-known figure to readers abroad, his literary consecration by Guillén—a peer of Federico García Lorca, Pablo Neruda, and Rafael Alberti—launched him into the pantheon of Latin America's most venerated historical heroes. Here he was, at the age of thirty, being compared with "The Liberator" José de San Martín.

The hyperbole had a resounding effect on Cuba's hero-hungry public. When, a few days after his arrival, Che sent for Juan Borroto, the sugar expert who had smuggled him economic intelligence reports while he was in the Escambray, Borroto felt overawed. "He was already a legend," Borroto recalled. "To actually see him for many Cubans was like a vision; you rubbed your eyes. He was physically imposing, too, with very white skin, chestnut-colored hair, and he was very attractive."

To the American embassy officials in Havana, however, Che was already being eyed as the fearsome Rasputin of the new regime. His ideological influence with Fidel and his uncertain new role behind the forbidding walls of La Cabaña was a topic of much worried speculation.

III

When he arrived, Fidel enacted his triumphal entry to Havana like a grand showman, riding into the city at the head of a noisy calvacade on top of a captured tank. After paying his respects to Urrutia in the palace, he hopped aboard the *Granma,* which had been brought to Havana and was now moored in the harbor. Then, accompanied by Camilo and Raúl—while Che stayed discreetly out of sight in La Cabaña—he proceeded to Camp Columbia through streets lined with thousands of ecstatic, flag-waving *habaneros.*

That night, Fidel gave a long speech broadcast live on television stressing the need for law and order and revolutionary unity. In the "new Cuba," there was only room for one revolutionary force; there could be no "private armies." His words were a warning to the Directorio, whose fighters had vacated the palace but still occupied the university's grounds, and were reported to be stockpiling arms. Adding to the ominous signs that a confrontation was in the offing, Directorio leader Chomón had publicly voiced the group's concerns about being shut out of power. But Fidel's speech and its implied threat of force brought about the appropriate response: Before Fidel had finished speaking, the Directorio relayed word that it would hand over its weapons. It was the end of the threat posed by the Directorio as a rival armed organization; Fidel's display of force majeure had won out.

Fidel also used his presence to reinforce the nationalistic nature of the new regime. Asked by a reporter what he thought of the rumored offer by the U.S. government to withdraw its military mission, he replied quickly:

"It *has* to withdraw it. In the first place, the Government of the United States has no right to have a permanent mission here. In other words, it's not a prerogative of the Department of State, but of the Revolutionary Government of Cuba." If Washington wanted good relations, Fidel was saying, it had some fence-mending to do, and the first step was to deal with Cuba as an equal.

Meanwhile, he told the nation, the army would be reorganized, made up of men "loyal to the Revolution," who would defend it if the occasion arose. He warned that the victory was not yet secure. With his stolen millions, Batista had fled to the Dominican Republic and sought the protection of that other reviled dictator, General Trujillo, and it was always possible the two of them might launch a counterrattack.

Fidel had deftly prepared Cubans for things to come, but what most people remembered from that night was the moment when several white doves flew out of the audience to alight on his shoulder. To many, it was a mystical epiphany that validated Fidel's standing as the charismatic *maximo lider* of the revolution; to others it was a masterful example of Fidel's ability to put forward an awe-inspiring public image at exactly the right moment.

In the blur of rapid-fire events that followed, contradictory signals about the direction of the revolution kept observers off balance and Cubans in a constant state of flux. By quickly recognizing the new regime, Washington had tried to appear conciliatory. In a second diplomatic gesture of appeasement, the Batista-tainted Earl Smith resigned as ambassador and left the country, leaving a chargé d'affaires in his place.

The Eisenhower administration could hardly complain about the makeup of the new regime. Urrutia's cabinet was stacked with politically "safe" Cuban political veterans and aspirants, virtually all solidly middle-class, probusiness anti-Communists, including many of Fidel's former rivals. By giving them posts with apparent authority in the new government, Fidel had swiftly placated the conservative political and business community and co-opted potential sources of opposition.

The biggest surprise was his appointment of Dr. José Miró Cardona, an eminent lawyer and secretary of the Civic Opposition Front, as the new prime minister. "Miró Cardona's designation was a bombshell," wrote Franqui later. "He was president of the Havana Bar Association, the representative of great capitalistic enterprises, and one of Cuba's most pro–North American politicians. Years before, he had defended the biggest thief among Cuban presidents, in the celebrated case of Grau San Martín, who had stolen 84 million pesos. He had defended Captain Casilla, the murderer of the black sugar workers' leader, Jesús Menéndez. We did not understand Fidel's choice but it was understood by those whom Fidel wanted to understand.

It was actually an intelligent move, which confused the Americans, the bourgeoisie, and the politicians."

Bouncing back from the ill-fated Miami Pact, the redoubtable Felipe Pazos was made president of the National Bank; Justo Carrillo became president of the Development Bank; and Harvard-educated economist Regino Boti returned from the United States to become minister of the economy. Rufo López Fresquet, an economist and analyst for the influential conservative newspaper, *Diario de la Marina,* was named minister of finance, while foreign affairs went to the Ortodoxo politician Roberto Agramonte.

Others, such as Faustino Pérez, appointed to head the newly created "Ministry for the Recovery of Illegally Acquired Property," came from the July 26 Movement's right wing. The Education Ministry went to Armando Hart; while Che's wartime nemesis Enrique Oltuski ("Sierra") became minister of communications. Fidel's old publisher friend, Luis Orlando Rodríguez, who had helped set up Radio Rebelde and *El Cubano Libre,* was made interior minister. Another new post, "minister for revolutionary laws," was given to Osvaldo Dorticós Torrado, a Cienfuegos lawyer with discreet PSP links. His appointment seemed innocuous enough at the time, but Torrado was to play a key role in Fidel's future plans.

The cabinet got to work, holding marathon sessions to reform the country's constitution, rebuild the country's damaged infrastructure, and clean up Cuba's debauched society; at the top of Urrutia's agenda was a bill to ban gambling and prostitution. At the same time, the new ministers began housecleaning, firing employees who had been receiving secret sinecures, or *botellas,* from the Batista regime. Their initial decrees were of a similar "purging" nature: All political parties were temporarily banned, while Batista's properties, as well as those of his ministers and of all politicians who had participated in the last two Batista-era elections, were confiscated.

Simultaneously, Fidel began speaking before large crowds in an ingenious exercise he dubbed "direct democracy." These were spontaneous referendums on revolutionary policy in which he took soundings of the crowd, similar to his first speech at Camp Columbia. Using his popular authority as the undisputed caudillo of the revolution, Fidel employed these forums to test, mold, and radicalize the public mood and, ultimately, to pressure the government. He repeated over and over that it was the duty of the new government to obey "the will of the people," because the revolution had been fought "by the people."

Fidel also began to reform the army, his true power base. The ranks of the "old" army and police forces were weeded out, their officers either sidelined or purged. Colonel Ramón Barquín was made chief of the military academies, while Major Quevedo, one of several career officers who had defected to the rebels after the failed summer offensive, became head of army logistics. Others were shipped off to "gilded exile" as military attachés in foreign countries. The new military elite was made up of loyal rebels. Camilo, already the military governor of Havana province, became the army chief of staff. Augusto Martínez Sánchez, a lawyer who had served as auditor with Raúl's Second Front, was named minister of defense. Efigenio Almeijeras, the head of Raúl's elite "Mau-Mau" guerrilla strike force, became chief of police. The pilot Pedro Díaz Lanz, Fidel's rebel "air force" commander in recent months, was now given that title officially. Perhaps most telling, loyal July 26 men had been installed as military governors in all of Cuba's provinces.

It was soon evident that the real seat of revolutionary power lay not in the ornate Presidential Palace in Old Havana, but wherever Fidel happened to be at the time—and for now, Fidel seemed to be everywhere. His base camp was a penthouse suite on the twenty-third floor of the new Havana Hilton in downtown Vedado, but he also slept and worked out of Celia Sánchez's apartment nearby—and in a villa in the fishing village of Cojímar, about thirty minutes east of Havana. It was in this villa, rather than at the Presidential Palace, where the future of Cuba was truly being decided. Over the coming months it became the setting for nightly meetings among Fidel, his closest comrades, and the Communist party leaders, aimed at forging a secret alliance to meld the PSP and the July 26 Movement into a single revolutionary party. Fidel, Che, Raúl, Ramiro, and Camilo represented the guerrillas, while Carlos Rafael Rodríguez, Aníbal Escalante, and Blas Roca, the party's secretary-general, led discussions for the Communists.

IV

On the surface, Che and Raúl were the odd men out in the distribution of plum appointments. Raúl was military governor of Oriente, while Che had the minor title of "commander of La Cabaña." But such job descriptions were misleading. As Fidel concentrated on presenting a moderate front for his revolution, hopefully avoiding a premature confrontation with the United States—vociferously denying accusations of "Communist influence"—Raúl and Che worked secretly to cement ties with the PSP and to shore up Fidel's power base in the armed forces.

Che kept up a formidable pace of activity. On January 13, he inaugurated the "Academia Militar-Cultural" in La Cabaña, to "raise the cultural level of the army." In addition to basic literacy and education, the academy was designed to impart "political awareness" to the troops. It included courses in civics, history, geography, the Cuban economy, "the economic and social characteristics of the Latin American republics," and current affairs. It also sought to reform his charges. After discovering that cockfighting had become popular among the troops, he banned it. As substitutes, he organized chess classes, an equestrian team, and sports events, and arranged for art exhibits, concerts, and theater productions to be held at La Cabaña. Movies were shown nightly in the fortresses' several cinemas. He founded a regimental newspaper, *La Cabaña Libre,* and soon helped kick off *Verde Olivo,* a newspaper for the Revolutionary Armed Forces.

Amid all this activity, Che quietly placed the school under the supervision of PSP men. Armando Acosta, his commissar in the Escambray, was already close by, commanding the small fortress of La Punta immediately across the harbor from La Cabaña, and before long Che named him the academy administrator.

By the end of January, Che had an additional title—"Chief of the Department of Training of the Revolutionary Armed Forces"—but it did not give a full picture of his activities, either. On Fidel's instructions, he was secretly meeting with Raúl—who shuttled back and forth between Havana and his Santiago post—and Camilo, Ramiro Valdés, and PSP man Víctor Pina to create a new state security and intelligence apparatus. The resulting agency, Seguridad del Estado, or G-2, was placed in the able hands of Ramiro Valdés, Che's wartime deputy. Osvaldo Sánchez, a PSP Politburo member and head of its "Military Committee," was his second in command.

Meanwhile, Cuban exiles were arriving home from all over the hemisphere. An airplane was sent to Buenos Aires to bring back the exiles living there, and the Guevara family was invited to board it. Che's parents, his sister Celia, her husband Luis Argañaraz, and Juan Martín, now a teenager of fourteen, accepted the offer. (Family and work obligations kept Roberto and Ana María at home, and it would be another two and a half years before they saw their famous brother.) They arrived in Havana on January 9, and an emotional Guevara Lynch kissed the tarmac at Havana's Rancho Boyeros airport. "We were immediately surrounded by bearded soldiers," Guevara Lynch wrote, "wearing really dirty uniforms and armed with rifles or machine guns. Then came the obligatory salutes and in a rush, they led us into the interior of terminal, where Ernesto awaited us. I understand that they had wanted to surprise him and he only knew of our arrival minutes before. My wife ran to his arms and could not contain her tears. A mountain of photographers and television cameras recorded the scene. Soon afterward I hugged my son. It had been six years since I had last seen him."

One of the photographs taken that day shows Che, in fatigues and beret and sparse beard, flanked by his mother and father, pressed in amid a tumult of curious onlookers. A submachine gun pokes up into view behind Che's

back. What is truly memorable, though, is the look of deep, passionate pride
on Celia's face, and on Che's. His conservatively dressed father stands to one
side like a bystander, smiling bemusedly.

The Guevara family was installed as guests of the revolution in a suite
of the Havana Hilton, just a few floors below Fidel's own rooms. As the de
facto seat of government, the hotel's swank lobby had become a rowdy
pandemonium of disheveled armed guerrillas, thrusting journalists, favor-
seekers, and perplexed-looking American tourists whose holidays had been
interrupted by the revolution. Finally alone with his son, Guevara Lynch
produced some bottles of Argentine wine that had been his son's favorite
brands back home.

"His eyes shone upon seeing those bottles. . . . Their sight surely brought
back to him pleasant memories of other happy times, when the whole family lived together in Buenos Aires." As they celebrated, Guevara Lynch
observed his son and thought he saw ". . . in his physique, in his expressions,
in his happiness . . . the same boy who had left Buenos Aires one cold July
afternoon more than six years before."

Guevara Lynch's estimation contained a fair degree of wishful thinking. His son Ernesto had become "Che," the man he wanted to be. And if
"Ernesto" was pleased to see his family, the truth was they couldn't have
arrived at a more inconvenient time. Even as his family settled into the
Hilton, Che had to rush back to La Cabaña; there were revolutionary tribunals to be carried out, and he was the man in charge.

Throughout January, suspected war criminals were being captured
and brought to La Cabaña daily. For the most part, these were not the top
henchmen of the ancien régime; most had escaped before the rebels assumed
control of the city and halted outgoing air and sea traffic, or remained holed
up in embassies. Most of those left behind were deputies, or rank-and-file
chivatos and police torturers. Still, Che, as supreme prosecutor, took to his
task with a singular determination, and the old walls of the fort rang out
nightly with the fusillades of the firing squads.

"There were over a thousand prisoners of war," explained Miguel
Ángel Duque de Estrada, whom Che had placed in charge of the Comisión
de Depuración, or "Cleansing Commission," "with more arriving all the
time, and many didn't have dossiers. We didn't even know all of their names.
But we had a job to do, which was to cleanse the defeated army. Che always
had a clear idea about the need to cleanse the army and exact justice on those
found to be war criminals."

The trials began at eight or nine in the evening, and, more often than
not, a verdict was reached by two or three in the morning. Duque de Estrada,
whose job was to gather evidence, take testimonies, and prepare the trials,

also sat with Che, the "supreme prosecutor," on the appellate bench, where Che made the final decision on men's fates.

"Che consulted with me," said Duque, "but he was in charge, and as military commander his word was final. We were in agreement on almost one hundred percent of the decisions. In about one hundred days we carried out about fifty-five executions by firing squad, and we got a lot of flak for it, but we gave each case due and fair consideration and we didn't come to our decisions lightly."

On top of his new job administering La Cabaña's finances, Che also made his twenty-one-year-old accountant Orlando Borrego a tribunal president. "It was very difficult because [most of us] had no judicial training," recalled Borrego. [Our] paramount concerns were [to ensure] that the sense of revolutionary morality and of justice prevailed, that no injustice was committed. In that, Che was very careful. Nobody was shot for hitting a prisoner, but if there was extreme torture and killings and deaths, then yes—they were condemned to death. . . . The whole case was analyzed, all the witnesses seen, and the relatives of the dead or tortured person came, or the tortured person himself, and in the tribunal, displaying his body, he would reveal all the tortures that he had received."

Each night, Che would go over the cases with his judges, but, detailing his role in the trials to some hostile Cuban television interviewers, he said that he never attended the trials or met with defendants himself. Instead, he explained, he examined their cases based on the evidence alone so as to reach his final verdicts coldly and neutrally. According to Borrego, Che also took great care in selecting judges and prosecutors; rebels who had been mistreated were not allowed to pass judgment on their former torturers, for instance. "The trial strategy was elaborated with great care," Borrego said, "because there were sometimes prosecutors who were on the extreme left, and . . . one had to moderate those who always asked for the death sentence."

When it came to the executions themselves, however, Che evidently overcame his earlier reservations about the American volunteer Herman Marks whom he had cashiered in Camagüey, because Marks reappeared at La Cabaña, where he took an active role in Che's firing squads.*

Over the next several months, several hundred people were officially tried and executed by firing squads across Cuba. Most were sentenced in conditions like those described by Borrego: above board, if summary affairs,

---

*Borrego, who got to know Marks at La Cabaña, described him as a strange, aloof man, who was "sadistic" and who liked to participate in the firing squads. He was about forty years old, spoke little Spanish, and was rumored to be on the run from U.S. justice. After several months, he disappeared from Cuba.

with defense lawers, witnesses, prosecutors, and an attending public. On a lesser scale, there were also a number of arbitrary executions. The most notorious incident occurred when, soon after occupying Santiago, Raúl Castro directed a mass execution of over 70 captured soldiers by bulldozing a trench, standing the condemned men in front of it, and mowing them down with machine guns. The action crystallized Raúl's reputation for ruthlessness and a proneness to violence, one that the years since have not mitigated.

In truth, though, there was little overt public opposition to the wave of revolutionary justice at the time. On the contrary: Batista's thugs had committed some sickening crimes, the Cuban public was in a lynching mood, and the media gloatingly chronicled the trials and executions of the condemned while dredging up the most sordid details of their crimes. In between exposés of Batista-era graft and corruption, Cuban papers were full of morbid revelations and gruesome photographs of the horrors and brutalities that had been committed by Batista's *esbirros,* or henchmen. *Bohemia* took its boosterism to unseemly lengths, publishing snide interviews with suspects awaiting trial, attending their executions with a ready camera, and providing sanctimonious captions.

An interview with a former Batista propaganda broadcaster appeared in its February 8 issue under the title "A Rat of the Tyranny Is Trapped." Under his photograph, the caption reads:

> This is the effigy of one of the most notorious henchmen of the dictatorship—Otto Meruelo—the mere mention of whose name besmirches the national atmosphere, one of the most repulsive spokesmen of the *batistato*. . . . The physical integrity of Meruelo—who never had moral integrity—is intact. What will the Revolution do about "this"? The question is on the lips of all Cubans.

Meruelo was, in the end, sentenced to a thirty-year prison sentence. In the same issue, *Bohemia* covered the trial of two of Rolando Masferrer's "Tigre" gunmen responsible for several murders in Manzanillo, the Nicolardes Rojas brothers, in an article entitled "The Accursed Brothers." Its author transcribed the culminating moment of the trial:

> The Prosecutor, Dr. Fernando Aragoneses Cruz: "Do the Nicolardes brothers deserve freedom?"
> Noooo! was the thundering shout of the enormous multitude.
> "Do they deserve prison with the hope that one day they can be useful to Society?"

Noooo!

"Should they be shot, as exemplary punishment to all future generations?"

Yeeees!

The Prosecutor . . . glanced over the infuriated multitude. And, in the face of their unanimous opinion, he expressed himself calmly, while directing a look that was part anger and part pity, to those who had been condemned by the People.

"That is, ladies and gentlemen, the petition of the citizenry, whom I represent in this session."

The Nicolardes brothers were immediately taken out and shot.

The *Bohemia* account seems to have been a fairly accurate depiction of the atmosphere prevailing in Cuba's revolutionary courtrooms. According to Orlando Borrego, he often felt under great pressure from his civilian audiences to be severe in his verdicts. "They [often] thought the sentencing was too benign. . . . Sometimes one asked for [a sentence of] ten years and the people wanted it to be twenty." Making Borrego's job doubly uncomfortable was the mounting criticism of the tribunals from abroad, with American congressmen decrying them as a bloodbath. Indignant over the accusations, in late January Fidel decided to hold some high-profile public trials—of Major Sosa Blanca and several other ranking officers accused of multiple acts of murder and torture—in Havana's sports stadium. Attending foreign reporters were repulsed, however, at the spectacle of jeering crowds and hysterical cries for blood, and Fidel's gambit backfired. A sympathetic Herbert Matthews tried to rationalize the trials from the "Cuban's perspective" in an editorial that the *New York Times* editor in chief refused to print.

Che was undeterred and pushed on. He warned his judges to be scrupulous about weighing the evidence in each case so as not to give the revolution's enemies any additional ammunition, but the trials had to continue if Cuba's revolution was to be secure. He never tired of telling his Cuban comrades that in Guatemala Arbenz had fallen because he had not purged his armed forces of disloyal elements, a mistake that permitted the CIA to penetrate and overthrow his regime. Cuba could not afford to repeat it.

In his memoirs, Guevara Lynch avoided the issue of Che's leading role in the tribunals, but did allude to his shock at discovering his son's transformation into a hard man. As he told it, one night he decided to go and visit his son at La Cabaña. Che wasn't there when he arrived, so he decided to wait. Before long, a jeep pulled up at the entrance and he saw a figure jump out. It was Che. "He confronted an armed youth who was on guard duty, grabbed his rifle away, and in a firm, dry voice, ordered his arrest. I saw the desperation on the boy's face, and I asked [Che] why he was arresting him. He answered me: 'Old man, nobody here can sleep on guard duty, because it puts the whole barracks in danger.'"

Until that moment, Guevara Lynch wrote, he had thought of his son as "the same boy who had said good-bye to us in 1953 in Buenos Aires." He now knew he was mistaken and began to see him in a new light.

Another day, Guevara Lynch asked Che what he planned to do about "his medicine." Smiling, Che replied that, since they both had the same name, his father could substitute for him if he wanted, hang up a doctor's shingle, "and begin killing people without any risk." Che laughed at his own joke, but his father insisted, until his son gave a more serious reply: "As for my medical career, I can tell you that I deserted it a long time ago. Now I am a fighter who is working in the consolidation of a government. What will become of me? I don't even know in which land I will leave my bones."

Guevara Lynch was baffled and didn't understand the significance of Che's last remark until much later. "It was hard for me to recognize the Ernesto of my home, the normal Ernesto. An enormous responsibility seemed to float above his figure. . . . Upon arriving in Havana, Ernesto already knew what his destiny was. He was aware of his personality and he was transforming into a man whose faith in the triumph of his ideals reached mystical proportions."

His father's befuddlement was shared by some of Che's old friends and acquaintances. Initially thrilled over his guerrilla war exploits, their delight had turned to horror with the news of his role in the summary executions, and they could not fathom what had happened to their friend to make him merciless.

Tatiana Quiroga and Chichina's cousin Jimmy Roca, Che's old Miami roommate, were now married and living in Los Angeles, and in early January they sent him a telegram offering their congratulations for the revolution's victory. "I sent a telegram to La Cabaña and it cost me five dollars," Tatiana recalled. "I still remember because, as a student, it was a lot of money for me, but I spent the five dollars to congratulate him. Then came the killings of La Cabaña, and I'll tell you I have never felt so horrible as to have spent five dollars on that telegram. I wanted to die."

Dr. David Mitrani, Che's old colleague at the General Hospital in Mexico City, was similarly revolted—and, when he arrived in Havana at Che's invitation eighteen months later, he told him so. Che gave an explanation that was as straightforward as it was unsatisfactory to Mitrani. "Look, in this thing either you kill first, or else you get killed."

V

Whatever the "necessity" of the revolutionary tribunals, they did much to polarize the political climate between Havana and Washington. Fidel lashed out: How could the country that had bombed Hiroshima brand what he was doing a bloodbath? Why hadn't his critics spoken out when Batista's murderers now on trial were committing their atrocities? Such criticism, he said, was tantamount to intervention, and he warned that if the "gringos" tried to invade Cuba, the price would be "200,000 dead Americans." Next, addressing the circulating rumors of an assassination threat against him, he warned that if *he* was killed, the revolution would survive: behind him stood other comrades who were prepared to lead it, men who were "more radical" than himself. If anyone had any doubts about whom he was alluding to, Fidel dispelled them in the next breath, announcing that his brother Raúl was his chosen "successor." On the heels of Raúl's mass execution in Santiago, Fidel's announcement bore an ominous note. In fact, although his official appointment as "minister of the revolutionary armed forces" did not come until October 1959, Raúl was already the Cuban military's de facto chief of staff. And where did that leave Che? The U.S. embassy was monitoring his activities and speeches closely, with a growing sense of disquiet.

On January 27, at a PSP-sponsored forum in Havana, Che gave a speech entitled "Social Projections of the Rebel Army." His speech left little doubt as to where *he* stood on things, and he hinted that the revolution had radical ambitions far beyond those so far acknowledged by Fidel. To anyone who grasped its significance, it was perhaps the most important speech delivered by any of the revolutionary leaders, including Fidel, since they had come to power. Quite simply, Che was outlining the future.

First of all, he said, one of the rebels' "projections"—"an armed democracy"—had already been achieved, but much more needed to be done. The revolutionary agrarian reform decree issued two months earlier in the Sierra Maestra was not going to be enough to right Cuba's wrongs. The revolution had a debt to repay to the campesinos, on whose backs the war had been fought, to carry out a true agrarian reform. The very landowning system had to be reformed—as contemplated in Cuba's constitution of 1940 —and in implementing it, he suggested, the revolution should defer to "the people."

"It will be the job of the organized peasant masses to impose the law that proscribes the *latifundio.*" What's more, constitutional requirement for prior recompense to owners of expropriated land needed to be waived. "If the Agrarian Reform proceeds in accordance with this precept it may become a little slow and onerous," an impediment to the goal of "a true and ample Agrarian Reform." Cuba also needed to create a strong domestic economy and to free itself from the sugar export economy by undergoing a process of rapid industrialization; only then could the country liberate itself from American capitalist domination. "We have to increase the industrialization of the country, without ignoring the many problems that this process brings with it. But a policy of industrial growth demands certain trade-tariff measures that protect the nascent industry and an internal market capable of absorbing the new products. We cannot expand this market unless we give access to the great peasant masses, the *guajiros,* who don't have acquisitive power today but do have needs to fulfill."

He warned that the United States was not going to take kindly to what he was proposing. "We must be prepared for the reaction of those who today dominate 75% of our commercial trade and our market. To confront this danger we must prepare ourselves with the application of countermeasures, among which stand out tariffs and the multiplication of external markets." To industrialize, Cuba must first rescue its natural resources, which had been given over to "foreign consortiums by the Batista dictatorship." The nation's mineral wealth and electricity should be in Cuban hands, and the state telephone company, an ITT subsidiary, should be nationalized.

"What resources do we have for a program like this to be carried out? We have the Rebel Army and this should be our primary instrument for the struggle, the most positive and vigorous weapon, and destroy all that remains of the Batista army. And understand well that this liquidation is not done out of vengeance or even merely a spirit of justice, but because of the need to ensure that all these peoples' conquests can be achieved in the least amount of time. . . . National recovery will have to destroy many privileges and because of that we have to be ready to defend the nation from its declared and its disguised enemies."

Alluding to the rumors of invasion plans being hatched in Trujillo's Domican Republic, Che again invoked the menacing specter of the United States. "We know that if we are attacked by a small island [Dominican Republic], it would be with the help of a power that is practically a continent; and we would have to withstand an aggression of immense proportions on our soil. And for this reason we must be forewarned and prepare our advance with a guerrilla spirit and strategy. . . . The entire Cuban nation should become a guerrilla army, because the Rebel Army is a growing body whose capacity is only limited by the number of six million Cubans of the republic. Each Cuban should learn how to use weapons and when to use them in his defense."

Most dramatic of all, Che bared his evolving vision of a continental revolution, not only challenging the conventional Communist theory of party-led mass struggle, but throwing down the gauntlet of violent confrontation throughout the hemisphere. "The example of our revolution and the lessons it implies for Latin America has destroyed all the coffeehouse theories: we have demonstrated that a small group of men supported by the people and without fear of dying were it necessary, can overcome a disciplined regular army and defeat it. This is the fundamental lesson. There is another for our brothers of America who are situated in the same agrarian category as us, and that is to make agrarian revolutions, to fight in the fields, in the mountains, and from there to the cities. . . . Our future is intimately linked to all the underdeveloped countries of Latin America. The Revolution is not limited to the Cuban nation because it has touched the conscience of America and seriously alerted the enemies of our peoples. . . . The Revolution has put the Latin American tyrants on guard because these are the enemies of popular regimes, as are the monopolistic foreign companies."

The revolution had its enemies, but it also had its friends, having "provoked enthusiasm in all of the Latin American and the oppressed countries." He ended with a call for a "spiritual union between all the people of the Americas, a union that goes beyond demagoguery and bureaucracy to an effective aid, lending our brothers the benefits of our experience. Today, all the people of Cuba are on a war footing and should remain so, so that the victory against the dictatorship is not a passing one but becomes the first step in the victory of America."

Che's speech was nothing less than a siren call to the hemisphere's would-be revolutionaries and an implicit declaration of war against the interests of the United States.

VI

On February 2, Daniel Braddock, the acting American chargé d' affaires in Havana, sent out a classified dispatch to the State Department, CIA, army, navy, air force, and the U.S. embassies in Ciudad Trujillo (Dominican Republic) and Managua, Nicaragua. It was headlined: "Cuba as a Base for Revolutionary Operations against Other Latin American Governments."

A number of leaders of the successful revolutionary movement in Cuba consider that efforts should now be undertaken to "free" the people of some other Latin American nations from their "dictatorial" governments. While Ernesto "Che" GUEVARA Serna is generally regarded as the principal force behind such thinking, and is indeed active in the planning, he is far from alone. Fidel CASTRO has reportedly made remarks along such lines, particularly during his recent visit to Venezuela.*

For once, the U.S. intelligence appraisal was on target. With Fidel's backing, Che had summoned prospective revolutionaries from around the hemisphere seeking Cuban sponsorship for their own *Granma*-style armed expeditions. One was the Nicaraguan Rodolfo Romero, who had shown Che how to use an automatic weapon during the Castillo Armas invasion of Guatemala. Now, four and a half years later, their roles were reversed. After the Guatemala debacle, Romero had returned to Nicaragua and become an advisor to the anti-Somoza student leader Carlos Fonseca, a Marxist intellectual, and during the war against Batista, Fonseca's group had supported the Cuban revolutionary cause in acts of homage and rhetoric. Now, Che offered the Nicaraguans help in organizing a Nicaraguan guerrilla army, and a revolutionary party to lead it. But the Nicaraguans were not the only revolutionaries being encouraged, as Braddock's cable noted:

> The countries most frequently mentioned [as candidates for Cuban-sponsored guerrilla invasions] are the Dominican Republic, Nicaragua, Paraguay and Haiti. Paraguay appears to be too far away for direct Cuban interference, but there is a great deal of preliminary talk and planning taking place about the other three countries. A number of Dominican exiles are in Cuba, including "General" Miguel Ángel RAMÍREZ. The revolutionary leaders, as distinct from the officers of the provisional Government, seem to feel that they have a piece of unfinished business to take care of in connection with the Dominican Republic, in the form of the abortive Cayo Confítes expedition of 1947, in which a number of the revolutionary leaders, including Fidel Castro, were involved.
>
> Louis DEJOIE is now in Habana, hoping to be able to organize and obtain support for a movement to overthrow the "fraudulent" [Haitian] government of DUVALIER. He is being assisted

---

*In late January, Fidel had gone to Venezuela to thank the outgoing Larrazábal regime, which had sent him arms during the war. While there, he made remarks that were interpreted as an implicit threat toward Nicaragua's dictator, Somoza. He also met with Venezuela's president-elect, Rómulo Betancourt—the politician Che had so distrusted upon meeting him in Costa Rica—and, as Betancourt would later reveal, asked if he could count on Venezuela to supply Cuba with oil, since he was planning a "game with the Americans." The solidly pro-American Betancourt told Fidel curtly that he could buy oil like any other customer, cash on the barrel.

by Pierre ARMAND, self-styled "President of the Haitian Revolutionary Front in Habana." It appears that the Cuban revolutionaries are mainly interested in the Haitian plans as a means of getting
a base from which to attack TRUJILLO. They would support
Dejoie, in return for his permitting an expedition against Trujillo
to be based in Haiti.

A number of Nicaraguan exiles are in town, including Manuel
GÓMEZ Flores. The Embassy has today received a report from a
fairly reliable source that the Nicaraguan group feels that they will
be the first to attack. . . . This report mentions Guevara specifically
as actively participating in the plotting, and as training some of the
participants. It was indicated that they hoped to be able to launch
an invasion within two months.

Braddock's cable ended with an uncannily prescient forecast. "The planning for these various adventures appears to be preliminary and unrealistic
at this stage, and the groups disunited. However, in view of the background
of many of the principal Cuban revolutionary leaders, and the support their
own movement received from abroad, it can be expected that Cuba will be
a center of revolutionary scheming and activities for some time, with consequent concern and difficulties for various governments including our
own."

Among his men at La Cabaña, it was no secret that Che was meeting
with revolutionaries from other countries, and rumored conspiracies of
the kind detected by the U.S. embassy were circulating throughout Cuba.
Schoolboys too young to have participated in the fight against Batista wrote
to Che, asking to be allowed to go fight against the dictator Rafael Trujillo.
On February 5, Che posted polite refusals to three young volunteers who
had offered their services.

To Juan Hehong Quintana, in Cárdenas, he wrote: "I appreciate your
gesture. It is always good when the youth are willing to sacrifice themselves
for a cause as noble as giving freedom to Santo Domingo, but I feel that in
these moments our combat post is here, in Cuba, where there are enormous
difficulties to overcome. For now, dedicate yourself to working enthusiastically for our revolution, which will be the best help we can offer to the
Dominican people, that is to say, the example of our complete triumph."

In spite of Che's epistolary discouragement, he was helping to lay the
foundations for a secret agency within Ramiro Valdés's State Security apparatus; this clandestine unit (which would eventually become known as
the "Liberation Department" within the DGI, or Dirección General de
Inteligencia), was to lead the way in organizing, training, and assisting for-

eign guerrilla ventures. Manuel Piñeiro Losada, one of Raúl's former "Second Front" aides, and the man who would eventually lead this agency, said that the "first guerrilla expeditions sponsored by Cuba were 'very artesianal,'" and in the case of the Nicaraguans and Guatemalans, were the result of "personal relationships" of Che's made in Central America and Mexico. As of early 1959, said Piñeiro, there was still no "structured policy" toward these missions on the part of the Cuban government. That would soon change, however. Osvaldo de Cárdenas, a mulatto high school student from Matanzas, was only sixteen years old in January 1959, but within a year he was recruited as an intelligence operative by Piñeiro, specializing in assisting foreign guerrillas. Cárdenas recalled how he and his young comrades felt in the early months of the Cuban revolution.

"We were convinced that the destiny of Cuba was to inspire revolutions. . . . We thought that the Cuban revolution was nothing more than a beginning for [similar] changes in Latin America, and that it would also happen very fast. And so, to work! We were all imbued with this spirit . . . everyone wanted to join a guerrilla army somewhere. There were plans to go to Paraguay; I don't know how we thought we were going to get there, but there were plans to go to Paraguay and overthrow Stroessner. There were plans to fight against Trujillo and some went, some with authorization and others without it. There were plans to topple Somoza. Yes, wherever there was a tyrant, a Latin American dictator, he was automatically our enemy."

Even Che's hardworking young protégé, Orlando Borrego, became infected by the liberation fever. In February or March of 1959, a rumor spread among La Cabaña's officers that an expeditionary force of Cuban revolutionaries was being organized to support the fledgling Nicaraguan guerrillas.

"Several of us tried to enlist to go to Nicaragua. There was an officer who seemed to be at the center of the organization, but as it turned out, it was, as they say, "freelance"; it wasn't authorized by Che or coordinated by him. And I remember that Che summoned this group and he chastised them sternly—because they were gathering weapons and planning this movement without permission—and it was [stopped]. But from that moment on it was pretty clear that such things . . . were being planned."

Indeed they were, although the more serious guerrilla conspiracies were kept under tighter wraps than the plot Borrego had tried to join. In late February, following a unimpressive initial meeting with a group of Nicaraguan leftists from the Partido Socialista Nicaragüense (PSN), Che sent word for his old acquaintance Rodolfo Romero to come to Havana. At their meeting, Che asked Romero to give him an appraisal of the Nicaraguan situation and what should be done to undermine the Somoza regime.

Explaining that the PSN was politically "prostrate," Romero replied that there was only one road left, "the road of Cuba." Che then revealed that a Nicaraguan guerrilla "column" was already being trained on the island, under the command of a former Nicaraguan National Guard officer named Rafael Somarriba. Romero could join if he wished.

Romero did so and became a member of the guerrilla expedition that set off for Central America in June to begin operations. It was to prove a disaster, but, over time, and with Che's continued support, Romero's comrades would form the Frente Sandinista de Liberación Nacional, or the FSLN; twenty years later, the Sandinistas would finally topple Anastasio Somoza and seize power.

VII

On February 7, Urrutia's government approved the new Cuban constitution. It contained a clause designed especially for Che, conferring Cuban citizenship on any foreigner who had fought in the war against Batista for two or more years, and who had held the rank of *comandante* for a year. A few days later, Che was officially made a Cuban citizen "by birth."

The bill coincided with the new Cuban government's first internal crisis. Fidel had been at loggerheads with Urrutia's cabinet over its moralizing decree banning the national lottery and its refusal to reopen the brothels and casinos, which had been ordered closed following the seizure of power. Now, the unemployed workers had demonstrated angrily, and the last thing Fidel wanted was to alienate *"los trabajadores"* whom he claimed as his constituency. The tawdry "entertainment sector" that was a visible part of Cuban life would have to be reformed, but gradually, with retraining and new jobs offered to those whose professions were to be purged. Fidel insisted that the cabinet reverse its decisions, and blusteringly threatened to find his "own" solution to the impasse if it didn't. Realizing Fidel was planning to run things his way whether the cabinet liked it or not, Prime Minister Miró Cardona resigned; taking his place would be none other than Fidel Castro.

To "accept" his post, Fidel insisted that Urrutia give him special powers to "direct governmental policy," a demand to which Urrutia obediently agreed. Next, a law was issued lowering the minimum age for holding high public office from thirty-five to thirty; now, both Che and Fidel, still only thirty and thirty-two, respectively, were eligible for ministerial posts. On February 16, Fidel was sworn in as Cuba's new prime minister, and in his acceptance speech promised Cubans "change." By the end of February, President Urrutia was, to all intents and purposes, a figurehead; Fidel was undisputably the *real* Cuban leader.

Che was more specific about what "change" meant. In an article in *Revolución* entitled "What is a Guerrilla?" published three days after Fidel's inauguration, he argued for the rebel army's right to determine Cuba's political future, and once again insinuated that it should include radical agrarian reform. He exalted the guerrilla as "the freedom fighter par excellence; the people's choice, the people's vanguard fighter in their struggle for liberation," as someone whose sense of discipline comes not out of blind obedience to a military hierarchy, but because of the "deep conviction of the individual" in his cause. Fidel's guerrilla force had created a "pure army" that had resisted the kinds of temptations "common to men," through each rebel's "rigid conscience of duty and discipline."

Besides being a disciplined soldier, the guerrilla was "mentally and physically agile." He was "nocturnal." In battle, "he needs only to show one face to the enemy. By retreating some, waiting, waging combat again and once again retreating, he has fulfilled his specific mission. Thus the army can be left bleeding for hours or days. The popular guerrilla, from his hiding places, will attack at the opportune moment."

Now, as during the civil war, Che was saying the guerrillas were waiting in the shadows, vigilant and ready to strike. And their mission was not over. "Why does the guerrilla fight? . . . The guerrilla is a social reformer. The guerrilla takes up arms in angry protest against the social system that keeps all his unarmed brothers in opprobrium and misery. He strikes against the special conditions of the established order at a given moment and dedicates himself to breaking the molds of that order, with all the vigor that the circumstances permit."

In the article, Che debuted his advocacy for rural guerrilla warfare, linking it to the revolution's essential future mission. To fight, he wrote, the guerrilla had certain tactical needs, places where he could maneuver, hide, escape, and also count on the people's support. This necessarily meant the countryside, where, coincidentally, the main social problem was land tenure. "The guerrilla is fundamentally and before anything else, an agrarian revolutionary. He interprets the desires of the great peasant masses to be owners of land, owners of their own means of production, of their livestock, of all that for which they have fought for years, for that which constitutes their life and will also be their cemetery."

It was for this reason, Che said, that the battle standard of the new Cuban army born in the Cuban backwoods was agrarian reform. This reform, which "began timidly in the Sierra Maestra," had then been transferred to the Escambray and, after recently being "forgotten in ministerial cabinets," would now go forward because of the "firm decision of Fidel Castro, who, and it is worthwhile repeating, will be the one who gives the

'July 26' its historic definition. This Movement didn't invent Agrarian Reform [but] it will carry it out. It will carry it out comprehensively until there is no peasant without land, nor land left untilled. At that moment, perhaps, the Movement itself may cease to have a reason to exist, but it will have accomplished its historic mission. Our task is to get to that point, and the future will tell if there is more work to do."

Che's closing comment was an early warning sign to the July 26 Movement that it might eventually be done away with, in favor of "unity" with other political tendencies: namely, the Communist party. "Unity" had become the watchword for the PSP–rebel army merger, which was already being implemented—primarily under the auspices of Che and Raúl in the revolutionary camp and under Carlos Rafael Rodríguez of the PSP. Still, all was not yet running smoothly between the two forces. Within the PSP, opinion about Fidel and his movement was divided; Carlos Rafael was an early and ardent enthusiast, but the party general secretary, Blas Roca, evidently was not. Party official Aníbal Escalante ultimately proved vital in the fence-mending process, but among the "old Communists," reservations about Fidel's leadership persisted for years.

And for all his overt sympathies, the freethinking Che Guevara, a nonparty member, also provoked some disquiet from the orthodox Moscow-line party men. His argument for a "vanguard role" for the rebel army—seemingly ignoring the role of urban workers and the traditional Communist party organization—was theoretical blasphemy, while his forceful advocacy of rural guerrilla warfare and agrarian revolution betrayed deviant Maoist influences. Yet, despite these troubling heretical symptoms, Che was obviously a friend and ally, and the PSP was indebted to him for providing it with a political opening to Fidel it might otherwise not have had. His ideological kinks would, no doubt, be ironed out over time.

In the meantime, the party remained politically ambitious and sectarian. At issue was political power and the Communist party's attempts to resist subjugation by Fidel. It was a problem that would come to a head in the future, but already existent toward the end of January 1959, in an incident that went almost unnoticed in Cuba at large, were the early symptoms of the underlying power struggle between the Communists and the July 26 Movement. In its February 8 issue, *Bohemia* ran a small article reporting the "first internal crisis" since "the Day of Liberty": the abrupt resignation of Calixto Morales, Che's appointee as military governor of Las Villas, who "had been displaying a close link with the communist factors."

At the root of the problem was a resurgence of the feud between Las Villas's conservative July 26 organization and the local Communist party organization. But racism reportedly played a part as well. Morales was a revolutionary radical who was offended by Santa Clara's racial caste system and, feeling his power, he had gone too far too fast. One of his first actions was to climb aboard a bulldozer and personally tear down the fencing around the city's whites-only central plaza, and before long he was openly feuding with the local and regional July 26 authorities. Finding an opening, Félix Torres, PSP chief in Las Villas, came to his aid, and according to Aleida's friend Lolita Rossell, Calixto soon fell under Torres's influence. Before the situation got any worse, Fidel removed Calixto from his post.

The affair highlighted one part of the turf war between the July 26 Movement and the PSP that had begun nationwide, but Morales's dismissal did not end the problem in Las Villas. Torres's aggressive politicking on behalf of the Communist party ultimately paid off when the PSP gained the upper hand in the province, only to alienate a great many *villaclareños* and fuel widespread antigovernment sentiment. Aleida herself, who still despised the Communists in Las Villas, privately blamed Che for having created the mess in the first place, beginning with Morales's appointment. Before long, disgruntled July 26 men would take up arms in the Escambray in a counterrevolutionary insurgency that would spread to other regions, receive CIA assistance and, in the Castro government's campaign to quell it, would become officially known as the "Lucha Contra Bandidos" (Struggle Against Bandits). It would persist until 1966, when Fidel's troops finally eradicated the last rebels and, emulating Stalin's successful counterinsurgency tactics, forcibly evacuated the Escambray's suspected civilian collaborators to several specially built "strategic hamlets" in distant Pinar del Río.

Meanwhile, on the personal front, Che's life was both complex and crowded. In addition to his relationship with Aleida, with whom he had little time to be alone, he had to make room for an old Guatemalan friend, Julio "Patojo" (The Kid) Cáceres, when he showed up in Havana. Patojo had worked with Che during his itinerant photographer period in Mexico City, and had lived with him and Hilda off and on. Sharing Che's dreams of revolution, Patojo had wanted to come along on the *Granma,* but Fidel had turned him down as one foreigner too many. Now, Patojo was in Cuba, and without a second thought Che moved him into his house.

In an inevitable encounter, Che also had to face Hilda, who arrived in late January from Peru with three-year-old Hildita in tow. The fearless Che of combat was somewhat less so in matters of matrimony; rather than go to the airport himself, he sent his friend Dr. Oscar Fernández Mell to greet his wife and child. Hoping for a reconciliation, Hilda was to be sadly disappointed. What transpired was a peculiar twist on the traditional "we've grown apart" breakup scene, one Hilda recorded in her memoir.

With the candor that always characterized him, Ernesto forth-rightly told me that he had another woman, whom he had met in the campaign of Santa Clara. The pain was deep in me, but, follow-ing our convictions, we agreed on a divorce.

I am still affected by the memory of the moment when, realizing my hurt, he said: "Better I had died in combat."

For an instant I looked at him without saying anything. Though I was losing so much at that time, I thought of the fact that there were so many more important tasks to be done, for which he was so vital: he *had* to have remained alive. He had to build a new society. He had to work hard to help Cuba avoid the errors of Guatemala; he had to give his whole effort to the struggle for the liberation of America. No, I was happy that he had not died in combat, sincerely happy, and I tried to explain it to him this way, ending with: "Because of all this, I want you always."

Moved, he said: "If that's how it is, then it's all right . . . friends, and comrades?"

"Yes," I said.

Whether Hilda did, in fact, let Che off the hook so easily might be debated, but the estranged couple did reach a quick and fairly amicable settlement. Hilda would stay on in Cuba and be given a useful job just as soon as things were organized. She and Che would get a divorce, and then he and Aleida would be married.

Che now made a special effort to establish a fatherly role with the little girl he knew only from photographs, and called upon Oscar Fernández Mell to help him in the task. Hildita had arrived in Cuba with an ingrown toe-nail, and Che asked him to extract it. "You do it," he told his friend. "If I do it after she's hardly ever seen me, she'll hate me." Fernández Mell did so, and many years later still laughed at the prescience of Che's words; when-ever Hildita saw "Oscarito" in later years, she reminded him of the painful moment when *he* had removed her nail.

Evidently trying to avoid direct contact with Hilda for Aleida's sake—the two women had despised one another at first sight—Che frequently sent for Hildita to be brought to him at La Cabaña. His men often saw them together, hand in hand, walking around the fortress, or saw the little dark-haired girl playing in his office as he went through papers.

On February 15, Che attended the little girl's third birthday party thrown by Hilda, and, in a photograph taken of the occasion, a smiling Hilda sits at the head of the table, holding Hildita close to her. On the other side of the table, separated from his daughter, Che sits hunched, wearing his beret, a leather jacket, and a sharp, self-contained look, as though he wished he were elsewhere.

At the same time, Che still had his family—who stayed in Havana for a month—to deal with. In the early days, their short visits and Che's hectic schedule had kept things pleasant enough, but between Che and his father tensions simmered. Quite apart from their divergent political views, Che had never forgiven his father over his treatment of his mother, Celia; as he confided to close friends, his father had "spent all the old lady's money and then ditched her."

Finally, an incident occurred that brought things to a head. It occurred after Guevara Lynch went to the home of a ham radio enthusiast to speak with friends in Buenos Aires. His "'Cuba support committee" in Argentina had acquired a shortwave radio transmitter, too late in the war to ever be used for its purpose—to communicate with Radio Rebelde—and he wanted to finally test it out, so he spent an afternoon on the air, speaking to Buenos Aires. That evening, he was reprimanded by his son. "Old man, you are very imprudent. You have been speaking by shortwave to Buenos Aires in the home of a radio *aficionado* who is a counterrevolutionary." Guevara Lynch made his excuses, insisting he had said nothing of political interest, and the matter was dropped, but later he reflected: "It was evident that the information services of the incipient revolutionary Government were [already] working."

After some time in the Hilton, the Guevaras were moved farther away, to the swank seaside Hotel Comodoro in Havana's exclusive western suburb of Miramar. Presumably, the greater distance made it harder for Guevara Lynch to drop in on his son at La Cabaña at inconvenient times, as he was in the habit of doing. From then on, Che visited them by helicopter, alighting on the hotel's lawns. "He descended," wrote Guevara Lynch, "chatted for a while with his mother, Celia, and left again." Celia herself, by all accounts, was enthralled by Cuba, caught up by her maternal pride and the euphoria of her son's triumph, and more or less uncritically tried to share the victory he had helped bring about.

Taking a brief break from his revolutionary duties, Che took his family on a sight-seeing trip, showing them Santa Clara and his old haunts in the Escambray, visiting Aleida's family house and the sites of battles he had led. At Pedrero, he left them to return to Havana, and two soldiers were delegated to guide them on horseback into the hills to see his old *comandancia*. There, Guevara Lynch provoked a new incident when, out of curiosity, he picked up the field telephone in the old general staff headquarters.

His rebel guides told him that it had been used to communicate with the nearby radio transmitter but was now disconnected, and Guevara Lynch got a shock when he heard a man's voice come on the line. "Who are you?" Guevara Lynch asked. "And who are *you*?" came the retort. "I am Che's father," he replied. The man on the other end sputtered in disbelief, insulted him threateningly, and hung up.

The escorting soldiers became alarmed. They tried to make contact on the radio themselves, but this time there was no reply, and they went off into the woods to investigate. In their absence, Che's father's vivid imagination got the best of him. "I began to get worried," he wrote. "Who were the people on the other side? If they were counterrevolutionaries, they could catch us easily, because we only had two soldiers as escorts and we were armed only with pistols. It would have been a magnificent blow for the counterrevolutionaries to take Che's father, mother, and brother and sister as prisoners."

Guevara Lynch ushered his wife, daughter, and youngest son into a fortified cave. "If any strangers approached, my son-in-law Luis and I resolved to defend the entrance together by shooting." But a short time later, their escorts returned, smiling. At the radio installation, they had found some militiamen who had been disassembling the transmitter at the very moment Guevara Lynch had called. At his voice, they too had become frightened, thinking counterrevolutionaries were about to attack them, and had taken up defensive positions. Afteward, Che guffawed with laughter when Celia told him the story, and soon the whole family joined in, laughing at Guevara Lynch's expense.

The visit from his family was a complication to Che in another way. Compared with many of his comrades, he felt an almost obsessive concern about the image he presented to the public, and took pains to avoid any impression that he was abusing his power, ruling out the dispensation of government favors to people because they were family or personal friends. If Camilo hadn't arranged the Guevaras' free flight, in a gesture intended to surprise him, Che probably would have forbade it. As it was, the Guevara family experienced Che's austerity measures firsthand during their visit. They were given a car and driver for their trips around Havana, but he gave firm orders that they pay for the gasoline themselves. When his father told him he wished to explore the battlefields of the Sierra Maestra, Che told him he would provide a jeep and a veteran soldier to guide him, but his father would have to pay for gasoline and meals out of his own pocket. Guevara Lynch had not brought enough money, and in the face of his son's unrelenting dictum he abandoned his plan.

The family's final departure was abrupt. As Guevara Lynch retold it: "My duties in Buenos Aires demanded my attention. Suddenly I decided to travel. I told Ernesto on the telephone that I was leaving that night. He went to say good-bye to me at the airport in the company of Raúl Castro."

As they chatted at the departure gate, a man came over and with a thick *porteño* accent addressed himself to Che. He was a fellow Argentine, he said, and wished to shake his hand. Che wordlessly assented, but when the man dug out a notebook and pen and asked for an autograph, Che turned his back. "I am not a movie star," he said.

Guevara Lynch was leaving Havana feeling estranged from his son, but, at the very last minute, they made a symbolic peace. When his flight was announced, Guevara Lynch removed from his wrist the old gold watch he wore, an heirloom that had belonged to Che's beloved grandmother, Ana Isabel Lynch, and gave it to his son. Che took it, and then slipped off the watch he was wearing and handed it to his father. It was, he told him, the watch Fidel had given him when he was promoted to *comandante*.

VIII

By the time his old comrade in arms Rodolfo Romero arrived from Nicaragua, Che was no longer living in the La Cabaña fortress. On March 4 he was diagnosed as suffering from a pulmonary infection, and he and Aleida were moved on doctor's orders to a requisitioned villa at the nearby beach community of Tarará.

Che had not been looking or feeling well for some time. Even in early January, sugar expert Juan Borroto had been struck by Che's wan appearance when he was summoned to La Cabaña. "He looked as though he was at death's door. He was gaunt, with a long mane and deep-set, sunken eyes." Ill health was one of the reasons Che hadn't accompanied Fidel to Venezuela, where he had been invited to speak by a medical society, but it wasn't until March 4 that he took a break in his schedule and allowed doctors to X-ray him. They immediately ordered a period of convalescence and they also ordered him to stop smoking cigars, but Che, who had became addicted to tobacco during the war, convinced them to allow him one *tabaco* a day.

The patient interpreted this rule liberally. Antonio Nuñez Jiménez, now a general factotum for Fidel, often went to and came from Che's villa in Tarara, and one morning "I found him smoking a cigar about a foot and a half long—with a naughty smile he explained: 'Don't worry about the doctors, I am being good to my word: one cigar a day, and not one more.'"

During his long convalescence, the Tarará house also allowed Che to conduct his revolutiuonary work with more secrecy. By now he was deeply involved in preparing Cuba's new agrarian reform law, and designing the agency that would implement it. It would be given the innocuous name of the Instituto Nacional de Reforma Agraria, or INRA, but in essence, it was to be the genesis of the *real* Cuban revolution. An amalgamation of the July 26 Movement's left wing, the former rebel army, and the Cuban Communist party, INRA was gradually to substitute for the functions of the regime headed by Manuel Urrutia until it could finally be dispensed with entirely.

Immediately after arriving at La Cabaña, Che had summoned his new group of unofficial advisors at the sugar institute, including Juan Borroto and PSP man Alfredo Menéndez, for talks. The 1959 *zafra,* or sugar harvest season, had begun, and Che suggested reducing the working day from eight to six hours to create more jobs. Menéndez disagreed, pointing out that while a reduced working day would create more jobs, it would probably also set off a wave of similar work-reduction demands throughout the Cuban labor market, increase the cost of sugar production, and affect Cuba's profits on the world market.

"You may be right," Che replied. "But look, the first mission of the revolution is to resolve the unemployment problem in Cuba. If we don't resolve it, we won't be able to stay in power."

He insisted that Menéndez give him a proposal on reducing the workday, but in the end Fidel quashed the idea. However popular the measure would be with the workers, it would set off too many other problems. Besides, the sugar industry was still in the hands of powerful private capital interests, both Cuban and American, and he couldn't afford to antagonize them just yet. "Fidel's vision was longer-range," observed Menéndez. "He was telling the workers that they shouldn't fight for crumbs, but for power. . . . He was already planning to nationalize the industry."

By February, the pace of consultations had increased, and Menéndez joined a high-level Communist party group that met in secret at a house in Cojímar, conveniently close to La Cabaña, rented in the name of Francisco García Vals. Although he hadn't participated in the war, Che had taken to the bright young man, a Communist party member who spoke both English and French, and named him a lieutenant and his executive assistant. García Vals's unearned military rank and new duties may have seemed inexplicable to outsiders, but for Che, "Pancho" García Vals served a vital function: Every night, the "Economic Commission" of the PSP met at his house to work on its draft proposal for the agrarian reform law.

Although he didn't attend the PSP's nocturnal meetings himself, Che was in the habit of dropping by García Vals's house in the afternoons. While García Vals and Menéndez worked away on economic affairs, Che dictated his thoughts on guerrilla warfare into a tape recorder. His new personal sec-

retary, José Manuel Manresa, a former Batista desk sergeant he had kept on
at La Cabaña, typed the outpourings. Occasionally Che would call Menéndez
over and ask him to read a section. The resulting book, *La Guerra de Guerrillas* (Guerrilla Warfare), was a how-to manual on guerrilla warfare based
on his own recent experiences. Just as he had been inspired by Mao's guerrilla writings, he now sought to adapt the lessons learned in Cuba to other
Latin American nations.

Paying a personal price for Che's prolixity, Manresa suffered swelling
in his legs from so much time spent sitting and typing. The book was not
published until 1960, but in the meantime Che made use of the material in
his public speeches. When the books arrived from the printers, Che gave
the very first copy to the diminutive Menéndez and inscribed it: "To the
little big sugar tsar. Che."

Once Che was in Tarará, the work to launch INRA intensified. Fidel,
who moved into a Cojímar villa himself around the same time, named
Nuñez Jiménez as chairman of an agrarian reform task force that included
Che, Fidel's old Communist friend Alfredo Guevara, Pedro Miret, Vílma
Espín—whom Raúl had married in January—and two senior PSP advisors.
The group met nightly at Che's Tarará house, discussing changes and adding new ideas to the proposals drafted by the PSP team at García Vals's
house. Alfredo Guevara told Tad Szulc, Fidel's biographer, that they usually worked until dawn, at which point "Fidel would come and change
everything." But gradually, the project began to take shape. All the while,
absolute secrecy was maintained from the ministers in Urrutia's government;
certainly, the putative agriculture minister, Humberto Sorí-Marín, was not
invited to attend. At the same time, Che was attending the long-range unity
talks between the rebel army and the PSP being held at Fidel's house.

The group's need to maintain a low profile helps explain Che's vehe-
ment reaction to a magazine article mentioning that Che was now living in a
luxurious confiscated Tarará villa. On March 10, teeth bared, he fired off a
self-righteous and obliquely threatening riposte for Carlos Franqui to publish in *Revolución*. The "apparently inoffensive" article, entitled "Comandante
Guevara Settles in Tarará," he wrote, had, "seemed to insinuate something
about my revolutionary posture."

> I won't analyze here who the gentleman journalist is, or divulge
> what I know about him from the files I have in my custody . . . [but]
> for the sake of public opinion and those who have put their trust in
> me as a revolutionary . . . I must clarify to the readers of *Revolución*
> that I am ill, that I did not contract my sickness in gambling dens or

staying up all night in cabarets, but working more than my body could withstand, for the revolution.

The doctors recommended a house in a quiet place away from daily visits. . . . I was forced to live in a house that belonged to representatives of the old regime because my salary of $125.00 as an officer of the Rebel Army does not permit me to rent one sufficiently large to house the people who accompany me.

The fact that it is the home of an old *batístiano* means that it is luxurious; I chose the simplest, but at any rate it is still an insult to popular sentiments. I promise Mr. Llano Montes [the author of the article] and above all the people of Cuba that I will leave it as soon as I am recovered. . . .

Che.

Two months later, when his health was better and the agrarian reform law had been completed, Che fulfilled his promise, leaving Tarará to live in a much humbler house in the countryside near the inland village of Santiago de las Vegas, on the other side of Havana.

The secret conclaves had coincided with the arrival of the new American ambassador, Philip Bonsal. After a pleasant first meeting with Fidel, Bonsal came away with the optimistic appraisal that Castro "could be handled," but the military-intelligence establishment thought otherwise; on March 10, the president's National Security Council discussed the possibility of "bringing another government to power in Cuba."

Whether or not Fidel was a Communist, most American political analysts now felt he was a loose cannon who had to be reined in before he could do real damage in Cuba and the region. Some politically moderate Latin leaders who had previously supported him lent their voices to this growing consensus; both Pepe Figueres and Rómulo Betancourt, for example, confided their suspicions to the Americans that "a firm Communist grip" had already been established "in most of the vital areas" in Cuba. All the while, however, Fidel continued his vigorous public denials of Communist inclinations.

It was all very confusing, but soon, the Americans learned, they would be able to take the young Cuban leader's measure for themselves. Fidel declared his intention to accept an invitation by the American Society of Newspaper Editors to be its keynote speaker at its annual convention, to be held in Washington in April. Already, hundreds of reporters were prowling around Havana, invited by Fidel in a lavish public relations campaign dubbed "Operation Truth," aimed at countering the negative publicity about his revolution. But it did not convince the skeptics.

By then, there was a lot of negative publicity to counter, for Fidel had gone ahead and "intervened" with the United States–owned Cuban branch of the International Telephone and Telegraph Company, in order to "investigate irregularities in its operations," an action that Che had urged in his January speech. He had publicly excoriated visiting Costa Rican president José "Pepe" Figueres, a wartime ally, for suggesting Cuba should side with the United States in the "Cold War confrontation," accusing him of "imperialistic tendencies." He had made wild-sounding predictions about the Cuban economy, going so far as to claim that within a few years, Cuba's standard of living would surpass that of the United States. His revolutionary tribunals had also continued unabated, and he had caused an international scandal by ordering the retrial of forty-four Batista airmen accused of bombing civilians after their courtroom acquittal for lack of evidence. Other fallout came from within the influential Catholic community. The clergy had been horrified by the revolutionary tribunals—it was the lot of the priests to administer last rites to the many condemned men—and Catholic militants who had been active supporters of the bid to oust Batista were becoming nervous about the revolution's leftward slide.

Fidel's latest speeches at Havana University, urging students to "purge it of corrupting influences," suggested little regard for the hallowed tradition of university autonomy either. A crackdown on press freedoms was yet to come, but Fidel expressed his willingness to do so when a satirical paper, *Zig Zag,* lampooned him.

To cast all this in a more favorable light and hopefully to win over skeptics abroad, plans were under way to create a "revolutionary" press. Jorge Ricardo Masetti, the Argentine journalist who had become so enamored of Cuba's revolution, was back in Havana, along with his Uruguayan counterpart, Carlos María Gutiérrez.* Both men held talks with Che over the creation of an "independent" international Cuban news agency, to be modeled after Perón's ill-fated Agencia Latina, which Che had briefly worked for in Mexico. Che's objective, as was Perón's, was to break free of such "Yankee capitalist" news monopolies as the AP and UPI. In a few months' time— with a hundred thousand dollars from unused July 26 bonds collected during the war—Cuba's own Prensa Latina was founded. Masetti became its first editor in chief, and it soon acquired an impressive roster of correspondents around the world. Within a few months, that other sierra convert, American journalist Robert Taber, was also helping out the revolution's propa-

---

*Upon his return to Buenos Aires, Masetti had published a short tract *Los Que Luchan y los Que Lloran* (Those Who Fight and Those Who Cry), about his time in the Sierra Maestra, lauding the Cuban revolution and its leaders.

ganda effort through the newly formed Fair Play for Cuba Committee, a pro-Castro U.S. lobbying group. It gained early support from liberal-left intellectuals such as Carleton Beals, C. Wright Mills, I. F. Stone, and Allen Ginsberg.

Along with his practical—and, at times, Machiavellian—approach to problem-solving, Fidel had begun to exhibit an unsettling penchant for embracing bizarre economic schemes that would "solve" Cuba's problems. He had dreamed up a project to drain the Ciénaga de Zapáta, a vast swamp delta on the southern coast, and open it up for rice farming. More important, his impolitic remarks about increasing Cuba's sugar harvest as a means to boost employment had already contributed to a fall in world sugar prices as futures investors bet on an impending market glut. In fact, the 1959 sugar *zafra* was larger than usual, with a harvest of 5.8 million tons.

Some of Fidel's more outlandish proposals may have been born of simple desperation, for economic problems loomed on all sides. Batista-era corruption, last-minute theft, and capital flight had stripped Cuba's treasury, leaving it with little more than a million dollars in reserves, a public debt of 1.2 billion dollars, and a budgetary deficit of 800 million dollars. The million-member-strong Cuban labor union, Confederación de Trabajadores Cubanos (CTC), a once-major Communist bastion before its co-option by Batista, was in the early stages of a Fidel-sponsored purge under its newly appointed leader, David Salvador. The constant reminders of an imminent agrarian reform were making landowners and agricultural investors nervous, and capital investment began grinding to a halt. In March, Fidel pushed through a bill, popular with the public, that lowered rents by 50 percent and expropriated vacant land, directly affecting the interests of landlords and land speculators. Tariffs were imposed on a range of imported luxury goods; laid-off workers began striking for job reinstatements, while other workers demanded pay raises. For the moment, Fidel temporized and begged for time to set things straight, but, increasingly uncertain about the future, a growing stream of affluent and middle-class Cubans began packing up to leave for new lives abroad. Most of them went to that venerable haven of Cuban exiles only ninety miles away, Miami.

On April 14, Daniel Braddock, the deputy chief of mission at the American embassy in Havana, sent to Washington a new confidential "action copy" dispatch entitled "Growth of Communism in Cuba." He warned that since the fall of Batista, the PSP had "emerged from hiding to achieve a semi-legal status which will probably become fully legal as soon as political parties register. The Party has increased its membership during these past three months by at least 3,000 and is still growing. Offices have been opened in every section of Habana and in most of the towns in the interior." The cable went on to warn that the Cuban armed forces were a primary target of the Communist infiltration.

> La Cabaña appears to be the main Communist center, and its Commander, Che GUEVARA, is the most important figure whose name is linked to Communism. Guevara is definitely a Marxist if not a Communist [*sic*]. Political indoctrination courses have been instituted among the soldiers under his command at La Cabaña. Material used in these courses, some of which the Embassy has seen, definitely follows the Communist line. Guevara enjoys great influence with Fidel CASTRO and even more with the Commander in chief of the Armed Forces, Commander Raúl CASTRO, who is believed to share the same political views as Che Guevara.

The American embassy was correct in its analysis, and its early appraisal of Che's program of Marxist indoctrination at La Cabaña provides an uncanny echo to the recollections of his lieutenants. Orlando Borrego, for instance, describes himself as typical of many of the men at La Cabaña at the time, young former rebels who had "no ideological formation whatsoever," but who shared a sense of revolutionary discipline and an "extraordinary respect for Che and for Fidel."

"From the political perspective, during those first months we were very confused. The rumors had begun that this [revolution] was going to be socialist. This was commented among the troops and I was one of those who said, 'No, it can't be.' And what *was* socialism, anyway? I didn't understand. Because of the [widespread] image that communism was bad, I shared that impression. . . . We wanted a revolution that was just, that was honorable, that would serve the interests of the nation and all of that, but would have nothing to do with Communism. We discussed this between ourselves. But we also said, 'Well, if Che and Fidel are Communists, then we are too,' but it was out of a sense of devotion to them, not because of any ideological position."

It was during his tenure as a revolutionary judge presiding over the trial of a former police chief, General Hernando Hernández, that Borrego began to wake up. During the trial, the defendant gave him a copy of Pasternak's book *Doctor Zhivago,* and dedicated it, "To Lieutenant Orlando Borrego, from General Hernando Hernández, respectfully." Borrego had no idea who Pasternak was, and afterward, in all innocence, he showed the book to Che. "Che looked at it and 'Ha!' he began to laugh. 'What an ignoramus you are,' Che said. . . . He explained to me who Pasternak, the Russian writer, was, and what he revealed about the Stalin era. That man had made me the gift intentionally, to see if I would comprehend all that was negative about the Soviet Union."

After that incident, Borrego's political "ignorance" gradually began to clear up. "Until that time Che had undertaken little direct political orientation—in the sense of the socialist idea—with us. Then came a moment, around February or March, when Che began to have meetings with us, the officers, in a little hall there in La Cabaña. He began to give political orientation talks. He didn't call them that, but that's what they were. He gave us conferences on what the role of the revolutionary fighters and the revolutionary army should be."

In his seminars, Che placed special emphasis on the idea that the seizure of power was not the most important revolutionary goal. Recalled Borrego: "Che told us that the most difficult and complex task was beginning at that moment. It was the stage where a distinct society would be built. He didn't speak of Communism, or of socialism, but in these conferences he began to introduce, from a historical perspective, the revolutionary ideas on an international scale, and one day he appeared there, explaining in front of a map, about the Soviet Union, the countries of the socialist bloc, what role Lenin had played, and he began to transmit to us Lenin's ideas, saying that there were valuable lessons to be learned."

Borrego said that he and his comrades left the seminar that day saying to one another: "This reeks of Communism." But by now, they were more intrigued than frightened by the new ideas. Most of the men remaining in La Cabaña were veterans of the Ejército Rebelde—Che had cashiered most of the government soldiers after their *depuración,* or purging—but it was still an uneasy period; the Revolutionary Armed Forces remained a hybrid and many continued to hold anti-Communist views.

Once Che had broken the ice among his junior officers, Armando Acosta, his regimental deputy, took over the job of indocrination. "He began to approach us, the officers, and give us political orientation," recalled Borrego. "It has to be acknowledged that he was very clever, very intelligent in the way he explained things to us. He clarified things in revolutionary terminology without talking about Communism, either, stressing above all the need for unity between revolutionaries, that there could be no political divisions."

For Borrego, Acosta's talks and his close daily working contact with Che soon gave him "an ideology." The real moment of truth for him came in April when a wealthy Cuban businessman, his last employer before he had joined the war, offered him a well-paying job in Guatemala. Tempted, Borrego went to tell Che about the offer and ask his opinion.

Che told Borrego to think seriously about his priorities because he was playing a vital role for the revolution. He told Borrego to mull it over for a

few days and to come back when he had made up his mind. Borrego did so
and finally returned to tell Che he would stay. "It was also out of a sense of
obligation with him. By now I had a very close affinity with Che. He had
established a great deal of influence over me very quickly."

Afterward, Borrego never looked back. His relationship with Che
became even closer, and Borrego eventually became one of Guevara's most
trusted personal friends and protégés. By the spring of 1959, it had become pretty obvious to most observers that Ernesto "Che" Guevara was a
highly unusual individual who confounded common stereotypes. He exercised an almost mystical influence on others and had begun to gather a
loyal coterie of disciples around him who, like Borrego, were followers of
"Che," rather than of any political credo. Yet, far from being sectarian,
he dealt respectfully with many of the defeated former army officers at
La Cabaña during the transition to rebel army control—even as he sent
others to die before the firing squad. To his new secretary, José Manuel
Manresa, had been the former army commander's personal typist, Che's
request that he stay on and work for him was an act of faith for which
Manresa was eternally grateful, and he remained at Che's side devotedly
throughout his time in Cuba.

Many years later, the tears stream down Manresa's face and he goes
mute with emotion when asked to speak about his beloved late jefe. Because
of bad blood circulation in his legs, he could not accompany him on his final
and fatal mission to Bolivia, and considers anything he might say a betrayal
of trust between himself and the man for whom he would have willingly
given his life.

For the Americans, an ideologically committed man so close to Fidel
and one who inspired such an unusual degree of loyalty among his soldiers
was a dangerous foe indeed. And, as the Havana embassy cables show, they
knew it, very early in 1959.

IX

The situation developing in Havana had not gone unnoticed in Moscow
either, and, for the Soviets as well, Che Guevara had emerged as a figure of
special attention.

In January 1959, in fact, the ruling Central Committee of the Communist Party of the USSR had decided to send an undercover agent to Havana to take soundings and explore the possibility of establishing relations
with the new regime. His first point of contact, it was agreed, should be with
Che Guevara.

The agent's name was Alexandr Alexiev. Tall, bespectacled, and gregarious, with a strong, angular face, Alexiev was a forty-five-year-old Soviet KGB agent working under diplomatic cover at the Soviet embassy in Buenos Aires when he was recalled to Moscow in August 1958. Early in his intelligence career he had served in the Spanish Civil War and in the Great Patriotic War of 1941–1945; ever since, he had specialized in Latin America.

Alexiev had begun hearing about Ernesto "Che" Guevara in 1957, when he was still in Argentina, from friends at Buenos Aires University. "They were revolutionaries," he recalled, "and were always talking about Che with pride . . . because their compatriot was fighting with Fidel." But, reflecting the official Soviet attitude at the time, Alexiev was suspicious about Fidel's true political inclinations, and, as he admitted later, had not given Cuba his full attention. "I didn't think much about the Cuban revolution. I thought it would be like any other [bourgeois] Latin American revolution . . . and I wasn't sure it was a very serious thing."

Once he was back in Moscow, Alexiev was named head of the Latin America Department of the Committee for Cultural Relations with Foreign Countries, attached directly to the Soviet leadership. He took up his new post in December 1958, and within weeks came the news of the Cuban revolutionary victory, then Moscow's prompt recognition of the new regime. Soon afterward, Alexiev's boss, Yuri Zhukov, who was in direct contact with Premier Nikita Khrushchev, came to tell him:

"Alexandr, I think you should travel and see what kind of revolution this is. It seems to be an anti-American revolution, and it seems worthwhile that one of you go there. You are the best candidate because you know Spanish, you were in Argentina, Che is Argentine, and there are ways to establish contacts."

Yuri Paporov, who was working in the same department as Alexiev since his own recall from Mexico a year earlier, recalled his colleague's reaction. "He didn't want to go, saying he 'didn't want to talk to those bourgeois revolutionaries.'" Paporov advised Alexiev to put aside his reservations and go because it would be "good for his career," an argument that Alexiev found more convincing.

Still there was a problem. Despite Moscow's recognition of Castro's government, no actual diplomatic links between the two nations had yet to be established. For appearance' sake, it was decided Alexiev would travel as a journalist, and the request for his visa was channeled through the Cuban embassy in Mexico City. The waiting began.

By late January, a still-skeptical Alexiev was preparing for his mission when some high-ranking Cuban PSP officials arrived in Moscow. The delegation, headed by Juan Marinello and Severo Aguirre, had officially come for a Communist party congress, but their journey had another purpose as well: to convince the Kremlin that Cuba's revolution was an opportunity not to be missed. They enthusiastically explained their party's decision to support Fidel Castro and their reasons for thinking he would embark upon a socialist form of government. They were, in fact, so hyperbolic in their praise that Alexiev was unmoved, attributing their euphoria to their party's newfound freedom after years of oppression under Batista.

As he waited for his visa, Alexiev spent his time monitoring Cuban news reports and, to bolster his false resume, making favorable broadcasts about Cuba's revolution over Radio Moscow's Spanish-language Latin America service. As time went on and he heard more about what was happening on the Caribbean island, Alexiev's cynicism began to evaporate, reviving the enthusiasm he had felt as an eighteen-year-old in the embattled Spanish Republic twenty years earlier. Still his Cuba visa didn't come. The months dragged by: spring rolled into summer, and Alexiev was still waiting.

Giorgi Kornienko, a high-ranking Soviet official working in the Central Committee's Information Department at the time, agrees with Alexiev's version that the Soviet ball started rolling only *after* Castro's rebel victory.

"I remember in January 1959, when Castro proclaimed a new regime, Khrushchev asked the department: 'What kind of guys are these? Who are they?' But nobody knew how to answer his question . . . not the Intelligence Services, not the Foreign Relations Ministry, not the International Department of the Central Committee. In reality, we didn't know who these guys in Havana were. We sent a telegram to our office abroad, later to Intelligence and others. A few days later, we received a telegram from one of the Latin American capitals—I think Mexico—with some information about Castro and his people. And there was information to the effect that, if not Fidel himself, maybe Raúl . . . very possibly Che . . . and some other people close to Fidel had Marxist points of view. I was present when this information was given to Khrushchev. 'If it's really like this,' he said, 'if these Cubans are Marxists and if they develop some sort of socialist movement there in Cuba, it would be fantastic! It would be the first place in the Western Hemisphere with a socialist or pro-socialist government. That would be very good, very good for the socialist cause!'"

But an accumulation of evidence indicates that the Kremlin did not suddenly "discover" Cuba by spinning a globe after reading the news reports of its revolution. A Soviet journalist and a trade union delegation had visited Havana in January. Contacts between the exiled PSP leadership and the Kremlin had persisted throughout the two-year civil war. Moscow's quick decision to recognize the new regime; the arrival of high-level PSP officials in Moscow so soon after Batista's downfall; the contacts between

Cuban Communist officials and Fidel, Raúl, and Che in the sierra—not to mention their prior contacts in Mexico with Soviet officials such as Yuri Paporov and Nikolai Leonov, both of whom would soon reemerge as Soviet emissaries to Cuba—all suggest a Soviet interest in Cuba's revolution *prior to* the rebel victory in January 1959. By all appearances, the Kremlin's policy gears on Cuba began ratcheting up sometime in mid-1958, after the defeat of the army offensive in the Sierra Maestra had increased the prospects of a rebel victory.

That said, there was certainly lingering skepticism about Castro's revolution in the Kremlin, for what had happened in Cuba was not in the Soviet playbook. The revolution was not the result of PSP strategy, the party was not in control, Fidel Castro was still an unknown quantity. Even if signs were promising—Fidel had allowed the party to play a role, and the men closest to him (Che and his brother Raúl) were Marxists—the jury was still out.

Meanwhile, there were good reasons for the foot-dragging over Alexiev's visa in Havana. It was not an opportune time to authorize an eyebrow-raising "journalist's" visa to a known Soviet intelligence official. More to the point, the Cuban chancellory was still (although not for much longer) in the hands of Roberto Agramonte, an anti-Communist *ortodoxo,* who would hardly have viewed such a request with equanimity. An abrupt loss of faith in Fidel's political allegiances by his allies, many of whom still believed he was merely biding his time before moving against the conniving, opportunistic Reds, might provoke a violent schism he could not contain.

Even more important, he needed breathing space from the potentially most dangerous quarter of all—the United States. Of necessity, Fidel's first foreign policy objective had to be to secure some sort of modus vivendi with Washington, if only to ensure that it didn't intervene to abort his revolution before it got going, and cozying up to the Soviets was not the way to accomplish it. By contrast, Che wanted nothing to do with the United States and had already begun to prepare for the showdown with Washington he saw as inevitable. In this he was seconded by Raúl. Both favored a sharp radicalization in revolutionary policy, a final consolidation of power, and a break with the West.

On April 15, Fidel flew off to Washington, accompanied by a large entourage that included his most conservative, pro-American government economic ministers and financial advisors. The radicals, Che and Raúl, were left behind. His traveling companions, certainly, were enthused, and, in spite of his repeated insistence that he was not going to ask Washington for economic aid in the time-honored tradition of new Latin heads of state, they believed it was one of the primary motives of his trip. "Let *them* bring it up," he told his advisors, "and then we'll see."

Dressed in his *guerrillero*'s fatigues, Fidel gave a well-received speech at the National Press Club in Washington and had an amicable lunch with acting Secretary of State Christian Herter. (Diagnosed as having cancer, John Foster Dulles had resigned the same day Fidel arrived in the American capital.) He spoke before the Senate Foreign Relations Committee, appeared on *Meet the Press*, and paid due homage to the Lincoln and Jefferson memorials.

Fidel was on his best behavior and bent over backward to dispel American fears about his revolution, reaffirming his commitment to foreign investment in Cuba and insisting that his agrarian reform law would affect only neglected or unused lands. He urged more American tourism and expressed his hope that the United States, Cuba's biggest sugar buyer, would increase Cuba's sugar quota. Cuba would, of course, honor its mutual defense treaty with the United States and continue to allow the U.S. Navy to use the Guantánamo base—and while it might come as a surprise to those in the know back in Havana, he was also opposed to Communism and in favor of a free press.

Everywhere he went, Fidel was followed by the press. With his beard and uniform, he was an exotic departure from the protocolar suit-and-tie norm for politicos of the day, and his habit of going on spontaneous "walkabouts" to meet with ordinary citizens only added to his charisma.

Fidel loved the public attention, but in his private meetings his ego took a bruising. The powerful figures he met with were patronizing, brimming with unwanted advice and stern warnings, as if he were an intemperate adolescent who, by dint of luck, had found himself in a position of power better suited to someone older and wiser. Repeatedly he found himself besieged by critical questions about his "purge trials" and executions, and probed about his timetable for elections. On both of these issues, he stood firm. The "people," he said, demanded the tribunals and punishment of war criminals. As for elections, he thought that more time, perhaps four years, would be needed before Cuba was ready.

Eisenhower arranged to be out of town during his stay, going off to Georgia for a golfing holiday and leaving Vice President Richard Nixon to stand in for him. They had a private talk in the Capitol building that lasted two and a half hours, and afterward, both men were polite in public, but it had not gone well; each emerged with a negative impression of the other. As Nixon later told Eisenhower, Castro was either a Communist himself or he was a dupe, "incredibly naive" about the Communist influence in his government, an appraisal that was to have serious consequences for U.S.-Cuban relations.

If Fidel had hoped for some sign of a more enlightened American policy toward Cuba, he was disappointed. If he had entertained genuine hopes of being offered some American economic aid, Nixon had dashed them by announcing that none would be forthcoming. Tactlessly, he had advised Fidel to emulate the policies of Puerto Rico's governor, who had encouraged private investment in his territory to improve economic conditions there. The notion that Cuba might benefit from the lessons of Puerto Rico, a small and heavily subsidized U.S. territory, was insulting, and Fidel had reacted by telling Nixon that the days of the Platt Amendment, when the United States had the right to intervene in Cuba, "were over." Fidel must have come away from the meeting convinced that the Americans would be satisfied only if he toed their line, at the expense of Cuba's sovereignty.

From Washington, Fidel moved on to New York. On April 21, after giving a talk at Princeton, Fidel agreed to a meeting with a CIA official who had asked López Fresquet to act as go-between. They spoke in private for over three hours. The CIA man, Garry Drecher, a German-American emigré who used the alias of "Frank Bender," told López Fresquet afterward that he was convinced Castro was an "anti-Communist" and that they had agreed to exchange information about Communist activities in Cuba. López Fresquet was to be their liaison.*

Most likely, Fidel used the meeting as a ruse to give the CIA *and* his own Cuban companions the impression that he was on their side, merely biding his time, until the Communists stuck their heads out far enough to be lopped off. Indeed, to one accompanying aide he spoke of the need to stop the executions and the Communist infiltration in the government, to another of his plans to send Che on a long trip abroad, a euphemism for a gilded exile.

In Boston, a few days after the meeting with "Mr. Bender," López Fresquet was present again when Fidel received a phone call from Raúl, who told his brother that there was talk back home that he was "selling out" to the Yankees. Fidel reacted indignantly, and, if one considers the battering he was taking in defending himself to a skeptical American audience, Raúl's words must have added insult to injury.

---

*While much has been made by historians of these pacifying remarks, carrying the suggestion that the Eisenhower administration "lost" Cuba through its insensitive treatment of Castro, subsequent events bolster the theory that Fidel was simply saying what his audience wanted to hear. Back in Havana a month after the U.S. visit, López Fresquet was contacted by an American official with a message from "Mr. Bender" for Fidel. "I gave Castro the intelligence," López Fresquet recalled. "He didn't answer me, and he never gave me any information to pass on to Mr. Bender . . ." In any event, within a year, the Urrutia government would be consigned to history, overtaken by Fidel and his radical comrades, and López Fresquet, the would-be liaison, would resign his post and go into exile.

Their exchange was followed by a strange encounter between the brothers in Houston a few days later. Fidel had decided to accept an invitation to visit with President Kubitschek of Brazil, and then attend an OAS-sponsored economic conference in Buenos Aires. On April 27, en route to Brazil, Fidel's plane made a refueling stop in Houston and Raúl and some aides flew in to meet him. After a brief closed-door meeting at the airport, Raúl flew back to Havana, while Fidel proceeded on his journey south.

A number of possible reasons for the meeting have been put forward. The historian Hugh Thomas wrote: "It has been said that the beardless commander of the army, Raúl, adjured his elder brother to maintain his revolutionary integrity. It seems equally probable that the main discussion was about the theme of the speeches that Raúl Castro and Guevara would make on May 1 in Cuba." Castro's biographer, Tad Szulc, on the other hand, linked their meeting to some recent embarrassing incidents that appeared to verify the American intelligence analysts' early warnings about official Cuban complicity in armed plots against several of its neighbors.

On April 18, the military commander of Pinar del Río, where most foreign revolutionaries were being trained, made a public display of rounding up over a hundred Nicaraguan guerrilla trainees and seizing their arms. He then made a public statement saying that Fidel had forbidden such expeditions from Cuban soil.

That same day in Havana, a Panamanian named Ruben Miro stated publicly that *his* group planned to invade Panama within a month. A few days later, while Fidel was in Boston, Panamanian authorities captured three armed rebels on the coast, two of whom were Cuban. According to Manuel Piñeiro this expedition was *"por la libre,"* a freelance venture that did not have prior government approval.

Approved or not, this series of events seriously threatened Fidel's efforts to construct a new public image in the United States and immediately after his Houston stop, while flying over Cuba's airspace, he made a radio broadcast condemning the Cubans involved as "irresponsible" and repeating that his government "did not export revolution."

Away from the island, Fidel could claim deniability for such actions and attribute the involvement of Cubans to the understandable "revolutionary euphoria" of the time. His government, he acknowledged, gave sanctuary and an opportunity to work to the exiles of tyranny—but, he insisted, it did not support the export of revolutions. In fact, the dragnet of the Nicaraguans seems more likely to have been an intentional decoy maneuver aimed at creating the impression that, far from supporting such activities, Cuba was taking steps to prevent them from happening.

Barely a month later, a Nicaraguan guerrilla group discreetly shipped out from Cuba to commence hostilities against Somoza. The expedition included Che's old comrade from the Guatemalan internationalist "Augusto César Sandino Brigade," Rodolfo Romero, who, along with the rest of his comrades, had received his training, arms, and funding from Cuba's new military. At the same time, an anti-Trujillo Dominican rebel group was undergoing training, as were Haitians and several other nationalities.

In order to tamp down the tempest, even Che rushed onto television to deliver a disclaimer. "The revolution must be honest at all costs," he said on the evening of April 28, "and I must regretfully admit that Cubans participated in it. What we have to say is that those Cubans left without our permission, without our authorization, without our auspices. . . . We are exporters of the revolutionary idea, but we do not try to be exporters of revolutions. The revolution will be fought by the people in the place where the [offending] government presides, with the people who must suffer that government. We are only the example, the rest is the work of the people."

As usual, Che's words were carefully scrutinized by the political officers at the American embassy. And, as usual, although he tried to be tactful, his honesty came through in the ways he dodged the tougher questions, most of which probed the intriguing issue of his political beliefs. To the first question—was he a Communist?—Che replied that he "didn't feel such a question had to be answered directly" by someone who was in public life.

"The facts speak for themselves. Our way of thinking is clear, our behavior is diaphanous. The fact that I am not a Communist affiliated with the Communist party, as I am not, has no importance. We are accused of being Communists for what we do, not for what we are or what we say. . . . If you believe that what we do is Communism, then we are Communists. If you ask me if I am affiliated with the Communist party or the Popular Socialist party, as it is called here, then I have to say that I am not."

Not surprisingly, the embassy's conclusions, sent to Washington in a confidential dispatch on May 5, were summarized by the following: "Statements by Ernesto 'Che' GUEVARA in Television Appearance Show Communist Orientation, anti-Americanism."

Immediately after his TV interview, Che rushed off for a meeting with Raúl, who had just returned from his Houston summit with Fidel. In view of what happened next, it seems clear that one of the main discussion points of the Castro brothers in Houston had been a decision by Fidel to halt the firing squads.

Since January, an estimated 550 executions had taken place in Cuba, and the issue, already becoming contentious within Cuba, had been a major source of irritation for Fidel during his U.S. trip. Fidel felt he needed to make a gesture of appeasement and earn some credit from the Americans for doing so. Che strongly opposed the decision but obeyed Fidel's order.

"Che wasn't in agreement," Orlando Borrego said, "but when Fidel explained the measure, demonstrating the advantages and disadvantages, that it was more favorable to the revolution to halt the process, Che accepted it. He accepted it, but it bothered him as much as it did the rest of us, because there were cases we were in the middle of processing."

Stopping the executions ultimately earned Fidel little credit in Washington. By now, the paramount American concerns were over the "Communist infiltration" in his government, the extent of his still-to-be announced agrarian reform bill, and the mounting evidence that the Cubans were trying to subvert their neighbors. To Whiting Willauer, the U.S. ambassador to Costa Rica, Cuba's disclaimers in the Panama affair were just smoke and mirrors.

A veteran Cold Warrior and, as ambassador to Honduras, a key player in the 1954 operation against Arbenz, Willauer cited the Panama incident as proof that the Cubans were up to no good. On April 30, while Fidel was still en route to Buenos Aires, he sent a seven-page, single-spaced typed letter labeled "SECRET" to Roy Rubottom, the assistant secretary of state for Latin American affairs. It was only the latest in an exchange of letters between them over Cuba, and Willauer made little effort to conceal his contempt for Rubottom's dovish position and argued the case for a preemptive strike—a la Guatemala—against Castro's Cuba.

"Unless there is some excellent explanation to the contrary I find it difficult to believe that this [Panamanian incident] could have happened without the connivance, to say the very least, of high officials in the Cuban Government, particularly in the army. This conclusion seems even more plausible in view of the fact that it is known that the army is riddled with Communists and that it is generally believed that "Che" Guevara, among others, holds a very strong position of control."

To Willauer, "the Castro visit to the United States was very probably one of the most blatant soft-soap jobs in recent Communist history." He would be prepared to believe Castro's denials of Communist links "when and only when 'Che' Guevarra [sic] and the other top Communists are given a one way ticket out of the country. . . . In short, while you state in your letter that "considerable progress is being made in calming down this phase of Caribbean tensions," I unfortunately find myself in complete disagreement. I feel that the situation in the Caribbean today is worse than it has ever been and that it is going to get much worse very rapidly unless the Communist beachhead in Cuba is liquidated."

"The guts of the situation," Willauer wrote, was the growing body of evidence that "the Communists have a very strong position of command and control in the army. This they never achieved in any effective manner in the Guatemalan situation."

Willauer was right. The lessons of "Guatemala 1954" had been a watershed experience for both victors and losers. Ernesto Guevara had watched and learned from the mistakes made by Guatemala's would-be socialist "revolution," and five years later, Che was in a position to apply preventive medicine before Washington could act.

Already, the Cuban revolution was one step ahead of the Americans. Che's many reminders to Fidel of the causes for Arbenz's failure had paid off: the old army was being thoroughly purged, and the "new army" was being staffed with trustworthy men whose loyalties and political orientation were beyond doubt. As for the rank and file, they were already being politically "reeducated." Arms and training would be given to "the people," and a nationwide citizens' militia would be organized to bolster the regular army. By the time Washington mustered its forces, as Che knew it must, Cuba would be armed, ready, and waiting.

X

Perhaps even more than Fidel himself, Che was well on his way to becoming Washington's number one nemesis in Latin America. On May 4, J. L. Topping, political affairs officer at the American embassy in Havana, sent out a new confidential cable to Washington, detailing his April 29 debriefing of Dr. Napoleón Padilla, a Cuban tobacco industry expert.

Padilla had recently been in meetings with Che as a member of "El Forum Tabacalera," a committee set up to explore the possibilities of increasing tobacco production and employment. Topping described Padilla as "liberal, nationalistic, Catholic," and a past supporter of the revolution against Batista, and also noted that "I felt that he was deeply worried, and sincere in his remarks."

Padilla says Guevara is a "stupid international Communist" —not even a bright one. (The word in Spanish is "vulgar".) He believes Raúl Castro is even worse. He says Guevara is violently and unreasoningly anti-American and bitterly opposed to the sale of American products, even if made in Cuba. He mentioned Coca-Cola and Keds, as well as American cigarettes. He feels that Guevara and Raúl Castro want to establish a "Soviet" system in Cuba, and that they will soon show their hands. Guevara talks frequently about how he controls Fidel Castro.

Guevara describes the new Army as a "people's Army," the "defender of the proletariat," as the "principal political arm" of the "people's Revolution." He also says that the new Army will be a principal source of "indoctrination" for the Cuban people, and that it will engage in "useful works"—apparently meaning construction, harvesting, and so on—but will always be ready to spring to arms in defense of the revolution, which will inevitably be attacked by the United States. . . .

Padilla said that Guevara talked frequently about the "Guatemalan incident." Guevara had said that freedom of the press was dangerous. He had pointed out that the freedom of the press in Guatemala under Arbenz had been one of the causes for the fall of the regime. He had said that freedom should be restricted in Cuba.

Che was not usually described as "vulgar," but most of Padilla's other observations have the ring of truth if we assume Che had spoken out intentionally to provoke Padilla; he had never lost his predilection for shocking people whom he sensed were shockable. Che's alleged bragging about "controlling Fidel," on the other hand, smacks of eager-to-please speculation by Padilla, for Che was never anything but respectful of Fidel outside conversations with his closest friends.

But evidently something *did* happen during Fidel's trip abroad to cause Che to lose his patience with the pace of events. According to one report, Che gathered his group of young bodyguards and told them: "*Yo sigo viaje*" ("I'm off"). Their assumption, in view of all the rumors circulating, was that he was planning to lead an imminent guerrilla expedition against Trujillo in the Dominican Republic. If this was a possibility being considered by Che, he had a change of heart. To judge from the events that followed, his decision to stay was due to a clear signal from Fidel that he was ready to accelerate his moves to build a socialist society in Cuba.

Fidel's days of temporizing were coming to an end. At the Buenos Aires economic conference, he had made new headlines and discomfited his Latin colleagues by calling on Washington to finance a "MacArthur-style Plan" to right Latin America's economic and social ills. The price tag he came up with for Washington was thirty billion dollars in economic development aid to Latin America over the next decade.

The Americans made clear they had no intention of supporting such a scheme, and the Latin American ministers quickly fell into line with Washington. Ironically, an American revision of Fidel's idea would be launched two years later by a new American president, John F. Kennedy: a twenty-billion-dollar program called "The Alliance for Progress." JFK's plan, of course, was intended not to appeal to the new Cuban leader but to prevent more Cuban-style revolutions from occurring in the hemisphere.

Within days of his return to Havana on May 7, Fidel signed the agrarian reform bill into law, and INRA became a reality. The agriculture minister, Humberto Sorí-Marín, who had been sidelined throughout the reform discussion, promptly resigned. Next, Fidel officially reconfirmed Che's status as a *comandante* of the Revolutionary Armed Forces before dispatching him on an extended "goodwill" tour abroad.

Officially, Che's mission was to increase diplomatic and commercial ties for Cuba with emerging industrial nations such as Japan and with the new nonaligned states of Africa, Asia, and Europe—most important, India, Egypt, and Yugoslavia. Unofficially, of course, Che's temporary removal from Havana also helped Fidel create the impression that he was, as he had hinted in the United States, "casting off" the Argentine Communist whom the Americans and his own July 26 aides found so troublesome.

In reality, Che's trip had been on the drawing board for some time. Alfredo Menéndez first learned of Che's interest in the so-called "third-position countries" or "Bandung Pact" states—the core of the future non-aligned movement—during their collaboration on the agrarian reform law at Cojímar, when Che had asked for an economic analysis of Egypt, India, Indonesia, and Japan. "He wanted to know what commercial relations existed between Cuba and these countries, what did we import, what we exported, and what possibilities we had to increase our trade with those countries."

Menéndez finished the study and gave it to Che, but he learned about the trip only when he was introduced to Fidel as "our sugar man" on the day of the signing of the agrarian reform law. With characteristic panache Fidel had made the entire cabinet travel to his old guerrilla base at La Plata for the ceremony, and, after asking Menéndez a few questions, Fidel suddenly said: "Get yourself ready—you're going on a trip with Che." Returning to Havana, Menéndez learned the purpose of their mission from Che. "Things had begun to chill [with the United States], the American pressure was getting greater and Cuba wanted to open up breathing space. The strategy of the revolution was to open relations with the greatest possible number of countries. That was the objective of the trip. It had a political and an economic objective, that is to say, to not let the revolution become isolated. This was a constant of Che's. . . . He always told me that Arbenz fell because he had allowed himself to become isolated, and that the [Cuban] revolution had to go out fighting in the international arena."

Before leaving, Che put his house in order. On May 22, he obtained his divorce from Hilda. On June 2, in a small civil ceremony he and Aleida were married and then threw a party at the La Cabaña home of his most rambunctious bodyguard, Alberto Castellanos. Efigenio Ameijeiras, the new police chief of Havana was there, and so were Harry Villegas, Celia Sánchez, and Raúl and his new wife, Vílma Espín. Camilo barged in with good-natured shouts, brandishing bottles of rum "to liven up" the party. Aleida looked pretty in a new white dress, while Che wore, as always, his olive-green uniform and black beret.

Two weeks earlier, he had written to his old friend Julio "El Gaucho" Castro in Buenos Aires, inviting him to come to Cuba:

Gaucho,

This experience of ours is really worth taking a couple of bullets for. [If you *do* come,] don't think of returning, the revolution won't wait. A strong hug from the one who is called and whom history will call. . . .

CHE.

21

"My Historic Duty"

I

On June 12, Che flew to Madrid, en route to Cairo. Fidel had urged Che to take his bride of ten days, Aleida, along and "make it a honeymoon" at the same time, but, according to Aleida, Che left her behind because of his insistence on the need for revolutionary leaders to show austerity in their personal lives. "That was how he was," she says simply.

Meanwhile, the news of Che's marching orders had been received by his men like a thunderbolt. Coming right after Fidel's order to halt the firing squads, Che's new assignment had all the hallmarks of a *tronazo,* or demotion, and in La Cabaña, the rumor spread among his men. "We were really upset when [we heard] he was going away," recalled Borrego. "We had the impression that they had stripped him as commander of the regiment. We interpreted it badly."

Their mood worsened when a "hard, uncultured" new commander, Filiberto Olivera, was named as Che's substitute. Borrego and some companions were so upset they went to see Camilo Cienfuegos to complain. Cienfuegos was unsympathetic and reprimanded them, telling them that they were soldiers and had to obey orders, and that Che would be upset if he learned of their behavior; chastised but unmollified, they returned to La Cabaña. Then, in a move that seemed to confirm their worst fears about Che's departure, they were told the La Cabaña regiment was to be demobilized and sent to Las Villas. "For me it was like the house falling down," said Borrego. "I had organized everything in La Cabaña, and it meant packing it all up in trucks and going back to Las Villas." But they did as they were told, and remained in Santa Clara until Che's return three months later.

II

Che's "delegation" was both tiny and eclectic. Traveling with him were his PSP aide "Pancho" García Vals, the sugar economist Alfredo Menéndez, a rebel army captain, Omar Fernández, and Che's adolescent bodyguard, Lieutenant José Argudín. The oldest member of the group was the fifty-year-old Dr. Salvador Vilaseca, a Havana University mathematics professor who was now on the executive board of Cuba's National Agricultural Development Bank (Banfaic), run by Javier Carrillo. A few weeks later, at Fidel's personal insistence, José Pardo Llada, the renowned political pundit and radio commentator, with a powerful audience in Cuba, joined the group in New Delhi.

Their main destinations were Egypt, India, Indonesia, Yugoslavia, and Ceylon, the key Bandung Pact states with which Cuba wanted to establish diplomatic relations and, most important, trade ties. The exception, but a high priority on the itinerary, was Japan, an important sugar importer and a heavily industrialized country. The agricultural reform bill would be issued soon, and Fidel and Che knew it was going to cause a heavy fallout with Cuba's landowners and the Americans; alternative markets had to be found for Cuba's sugar just in case.

Fidel's decision to add Pardo Llada to Che's traveling caravan was a curious one, since there was no love lost between Che and the right-wing journalist. They had met only once before, in January, when Pardo Llada had gone to La Cabaña to inquire about the fate of Ernesto De la Fé, a personal friend and Batista's former information minister. Che had told Pardo Llada flatly that there was nothing he could do for him; the case of De la Fé was in the hands of the revolutionary tribunals, and there was plenty of evidence against him. To end their meeting, Pardo Llada says Che told him: "To be frank, if it were up to me, I'd have him shot tomorrrow."

Since then, De la Fé's case had dragged on and become something of an issue in the Cuban media. Che had been questioned about it during his April 28 TV appearance, and had used the occasion to damn De la Fé further, pointing out that when arrested the ex-minister had in his possession copies of files compiled by BRAC, the notorious CIA-created anti-Communist police bureau. Indeed, Orlando Borrego said that Che's inability to "conclude" the De la Fé case was one of the things that had most frustrated Che when Fidel ordered an end to the revolutionary tribunals.

Pardo Llada himself told Fidel he saw little reason why he should go off on a trade mission—he was a journalist and he knew nothing about commerce—but Fidel told him: "Che doesn't know anything about it, either, but it's all a matter of common sense. What do you think I know about governing? In this we are all learning." With the precedent Fidel had already set on his U.S. trip, in which he had surrounded himself with his "bourgeois right-wing," Pardo Llada's inclusion in Che's entourage fit a pattern; it could do no harm to have an influential anti-Communist along with Che to calm his like-minded countrymen and convince them of the tameness of the mission. Fidel had another motive as well. Pardo Llado was bright, well respected both as a journalist and former opposition politician, and his daily radio program commanded a huge audience in Cuba; in other words, in the inevitable break that was coming, Pardo Llada was going to be a problem, and it behooved Fidel to find a place where he would not be a threat.

As it was, Pardo Llada went off to New Delhi suspecting that both he and Che were being put to pasture; he said as much to Che, who did little to disabuse him of the notion. But it was Pardo, not Che, whom Fidel hoped to tempt into exile. On his second day in Delhi, Che sounded out the journalist on the idea—proposed, he said, by Fidel—of Pardo staying on in India as ambassador. Pardo flatly refused to even consider the offer, and Che diplomatically dropped the subject.

He grudgingly stayed on with Che's mission for several weeks, through the visits to Indonesia and Japan, but as far as he could see, there were no benefits being gained from all their travel: No Cuban sugar had been sold, nothing had been purchased. In early August, as the delegation turned westward again, headed for Ceylon and on to Yugoslavia, Pardo Llada decided he'd had enough and told Che he was going home.

Che asked: "Might it not be that you don't want to compromise yourself by visiting a Communist country like Yugoslavia?" Pardo denied the suggestion and repeated his suspicion that Fidel had sent them both on a kind of exile's walking tour. Che was an army officer and had no choice but to follow orders, but *he* was a private citizen and free to make his own decisions, and his decision was to quit.

Pardo Llada left the group in Singapore, agreeing to hand-deliver letters Che had written to Aleida and Fidel. In Havana, Pardo dropped Aleida's letter off at the Guevara's new home in the countryside outside Havana, then went to Fidel's office in the new INRA building overlooking the huge civic square now named Plaza de la Revolución. Fidel asked a few questions about the trip and Che's health, then opened Che's two-page letter and read it slowly. When he had finished, he wordlessly handed Pardo one of the pages, pointing with his finger to a paragraph. Pardo Llada read it, and then reread it in order to memorize Che's words.

Fidel,

 . . . I'm talking advantage of the quick and unexpected return of your friend Pardito to send you this. Speaking of Pardo, as you'll see he didn't want to accept the Embassy [post] in India. And now it seems he isn't enthused about following us to Yugoslavia. He must have his motives. I have argued a lot during these two months with him, and I can assure you that Pardito isn't one of us. . . ."

Pardo thought that Fidel showed a "perverse satisfaction" by letting him read the passage, and when he handed back the letter, Fidel's only comment was, "So. It seems like Che isn't very fond of you."

Pardo Llada and Che were to meet up several more times and once again their dealings would concern a friend of Pardo's who was in trouble with the revolution. For now that problem—and Pardo Llada's own *via crucis*—still lay ahead, and the journalist resumed his activities as a radio commentator, increasingly worried about Cuba's political direction. Che's "commercial mission," meanwhile, continued its apparently fruitless perambulations across Asia and North Africa to Europe.

III

Significantly, the one member of Che's delegation whom Pardo Llada never met was the PSP sugar expert Alfredo Menéndez. There was probably a very good reason, for, despite its apparent aimlessness, Che's trip had an important ulterior motive. Fidel wanted to sell Cuban sugar to the Soviets, as a prelude to establishing trade relations with Moscow and the Communist bloc, and Alfredo Menéndez had gone along on the mission for this purpose.

In and of itself, such a trade deal shouldn't have raised eyebrows. The USSR had been a traditional, if minor, purchaser of Cuban sugar, averaging a half-million tons annually even after Batista had severed relations in 1952. But, according to Menéndez, the last sugar sale to Moscow, in 1956, had been permitted only after Washington gave the go-ahead. If true, the arrangement underscored the cruel realities that had ensured Cuba's role as a virtual economic vassal state to the Americans for generations. The absolute cornerstone of the Cuban economy was sugar. Since the United States was the world's largest sugar consumer, and the buyer of a huge portion of Cuba's annual crop, it meant it had enormous leverage over not just the Cuban economy but its politics and foreign policy as well. Given U.S. suspicions over the political direction of the Cuban revolution, therefore, it was important to keep any negotiations with the Soviets as discreet as possible.

For Menéndez, the mission was a dream come true. He was to be the point man in negotiations that he hoped would fulfill what he called "an old aspiration of the Popular Socialist party," to break free of Cuba's dependency on the United States once and for all.

"In 1959," Menéndez said, "Cuba had the objective capacity to produce seven million tons of sugar. [But] the U.S. only bought a little under three million tons, although it had the capacity to buy more. . . . And so we wanted to change the market. The first objective, that of selling sugar to the Soviet Union, was with a view to expanding our markets. . . . Not only with the Soviet Union, but with the rest of the socialist countries . . . It was a strategy."

To pursue that strategy, Fidel first covered his bases in clever fashion. On June 13, the day after Che's mission left Havana, Fidel publicly called on the United States to increase its Cuban sugar quota from three million to eight million tons. The offer to buy *all* of Cuba's sugar was immediately turned down, as Fidel no doubt anticipated, but it also put the rest of the world on notice that Cuba was looking for customers. (And indeed, a year later, when Nikita Khrushchev agreed to buy almost all of Cuba's sugar at above world prices, Fidel could maintain he had offered it *first* to the Yankees.)

Che's first contacts with the Soviets were made in Cairo, before Pardo Llada joined the group. Che was in charge of making the approach to sell the sugar, while Menéndez handled the details. Those details were hammered out in secret over the next month of travel, with Menéndez making two trips back to Havana to consult with Fidel. By late July, the Soviets had agreed to buy a half-million tons of Cuban sugar, to be negotiated in the neutral site of London, where the Soviets had a big trade mission and the deal could be done under the auspices of an international sugar brokerage firm.

By doing it in London, Menéndez explain, "it could go through without being noticed and we didn't give it any political connotation."

While the sugar sale itself later became publicly known, the complex prior negotiations between Che and the Soviets did not—nor have they ever appeared in the official chronology of Che's 1959 "goodwill mission." The reason for the omission is fairly obvious: The sugar negotiations were an important first step in the secret talks leading up to Cuba's alliance with the Soviet Union and are very much at odds with official Cuban history, which maintains that the Castro regime was pushed into the Soviet camp because of American hostility and aggression.

As for Alexandr Alexiev, the KGB man who had been cooling his heels in Moscow since January, awaiting permission to enter Cuba, his visa was now suddenly approved. "[The Cubans] had put in my passport—'TASS correspondent,'" said Alexiev. "They told me they had done it because they were still afraid to invite an official of the Soviet Union." Alexiev left for Cuba in September, taking a circuitous route via Italy and Venezuela, finally arriving in Havana on October 1. The delicate dance between the Cubans and Soviets would now pick up tempo.

IV

Che had arrived back in Cuba only three weeks earlier. His trip had lasted almost three months and taken him to fourteen countries. He had met and conversed with heads of state such as Egypt's Gamal Abdel Nasser, Indonesia's Sukarno, Yugoslavia's Josip Broz Tito, and India's Jawaharlal Nehru. He had been cheered by crowds in Gaza and Pakistan, toured factories and cooperative farms, and witnessed for himself the conditions of life in a part of the world where the old colonial empires were disintegrating. His mission, he told the press, had been a success, for he had seen for himself that the Cuban revolution was respected and admired by people around the world. Diplomatic and trade relations had been established with a number of countries, and he was confident that Cubans would soon see their benefits.

He followed up his public statements with a series of short, informative articles published in *Verde Olivo*. Occasional traces of irony and lyricism filtered through, but for the most part Che's travel accounts were dry. His traveling companions, however, came back with florid new tales to tell of their iconoclastic jefe, most of them featuring his infamous disrespect for protocol. Some of the most memorable vignettes were later written up by Pardo Llada.

In New Delhi, Che's meeting with his old hero Nehru took place over a sumptuous luncheon at the government palace. As Pardo retold it, Che was on his best behavior, wearing a dress uniform of gabardine cloth for the occasion instead of his usual olive-green fatigues, but as he entered the palace, he quipped irreverently to his companions: "I think I'm pretty elegant—enough, anyway, to dine with the gentleman Prime Minister of the most underdeveloped country on Earth."

Nehru, his daughter Indira, and her young sons, Sanjay and Rajiv, were all in attendance. The venerable Indian prime minister showed exquisite manners, explaining each exotic dish in turn to Guevara and his comrades, while Che, smiling politely, attempted to display some interest. The banquet went on in this fashion for over two hours, but the only words that came from Nehru's mouth were about the meal in front of them. Finally, Che could stand it no longer and asked: "Mr. Prime Minister: What is your opinion of Communist China?" Nehru listened with an absent expression, and answered, "Mr. Comandante, have you tasted one of these delicious apples?" "Mr. Prime Minister: Have you read Mao Tse-tung?" "Ah, Mr. Comandante, how pleased I am that you have liked the apples.'"

Afterward, Che wrote of his encounter with the architect of India's independence: "Nehru received us with the amiable familiarity of a patriarchal grandfather, but displayed a noble interest in the struggles and vicissitudes of the Cuban people."

In fact, Che came away from India feeling there was little to be learned from the founding fathers of modern India. While acknowledging the obstacles posed by the country's complex cultural and historic traditions, he was discomfited at the Nehru government's unwillingness to embark on a radical agrarian reform program, or to break the powers of the religious and feudal institutions that Che felt kept India's people mired in poverty.

In Djakarta, Che had fallen in with an amiable compatriot, the Argentine ambassador, and before they met Sukarno, his *paisano* had regaled him with stories about the Indonesian leader's sybaritic lifestyle: how he lived like a monarch and maintained a harem of women of different nationalities. His current favorite, he had told Che, was a Russian woman, a "gift" from Nikita Khrushchev.

When Che went to Sukarno's palace for a meeting, the Argentine envoy went along as his interpreter. Sukarno insisted on showing off his private collection of paintings. The tour went on and on, and Pardo could tell that Che was getting restless. Finally, he broke the silence: "Well, Mr. Sukarno, but in this entire tour we still haven't seen the little Russian girl, who they say is the best thing in your collection." Fortunately, Sukarno didn't understand Spanish. The Argentine ambassador nearly fainted with shock and disbelief, but recovered in time to invent a question about the Indonesian economy. Afterward, Che had a good laugh about it.

Menéndez recalled Che's reaction when he was told by the Cuban ambassador in Tokyo that he was expected to go the next day to lay a wreath at Japan's Tomb of the Unknown Soldier, commemorating the men lost in World War II. Che reacted violently. "No way I'll go! That was an imperialist army that killed millions of Asians. . . . And I won't go. Where *I will go* is to Hiroshima, where the Americans killed one hundred thousand Japanese." The diplomat spluttered and told him it was impossible, that it had already been arranged with the Japanese chancellor. Che was adamant, and told him: "It's your problem, not mine. You made the arrangements without my authorization, and now you can go and undo it!"

Japan, an emerging economic power, was one of the most important stops on Che's itinerary. He was excited about Japanese advances in the electronics field, and spent much of his time touring the highly mechanized factories of companies such as Mitsubishi and Toshiba. The Japanese bought a million tons of sugar on the world market in foreign exchange, a third of it from Cuba, and Che hoped to raise the Cuban share.

His idea was to propose that the Japanese could pay for anything over their present quota in yen; the money would then remain in Japan and be spent by Cuba on Japanese products. Che asked for a meeting to be arranged with the Japanese foreign trade minister. The signs were bad even before the meeting took place, however, when the official suggested they meet at the landmark Frank Lloyd Wright–designed Imperial Hotel, instead of in his office. Menéndez accompanied Che.

"Che made the proposal," recalled Menéndez, "but the man said he couldn't agree to it, that their economy was open and they couldn't make that kind of agreement; they would continue to buy sugar, but without any obligations. Che asked him: 'You're under pressure from the fair-haired Northerners, aren't you?' And the Japanese said: 'It's true,' at which Che told him there was no problem, that he understood the pressure they were under."

Throughout the journey, Che's personal security was a matter of concern to his companions. Before leaving Havana, PSP leader Carlos Rafael Rodríguez had told Menéndez he was worried because Che was not taking many bodyguards; the only military men going along were José Argudín and Omar Fernández, and they were traveling unarmed. "We don't have any intelligence that there are plans to shoot him, but you guys with him should take precautions, and don't leave him alone for a minute. And pick up some weapons in Europe on your way."

In Madrid, where the group stopped en route to Cairo, Menéndez heeded Carlos Rafael's instructions and bought two Colt pistols. Argudín, who never strayed from Che's side, carried the pistols throughout the trip—no difficulty in those prehijacking days—and as an additional security measure, one of the men (usually Pancho García Vals) always shared Che's bedroom. The arrangements worked well enough until Che and Dr. Vilaseca were invited to a Tokyo diplomatic reception that Argudín could not attend. Distressed, the bodyguard press-ganged the venerable professor into duty, sticking both pistols into his belt under his formal jacket and telling him to "take care" of his jefe.

Che, who turned thirty-one on the trip, showed a special deference to Dr. Vilaseca, a man nineteen years his senior. When the group's ration of Cuban cigars began to run out, Che ordered them confiscated. "The others protested," said Vilaseca, "but from then on, he said only he and I would be allowed to smoke them." Vilaseca appreciated the gesture.

As with the cigars, Che's austerity measures were sometimes stifling to his companions. In Osaka, Pardo recalled, they were invited by the Cuban consul to make a nocturnal visit to a famous cabaret, the Metropole, which, with six hundred women, was touted as the biggest in the world. Che said he was not interested and ordered the uniformed men to stay behind. Only the civilians—Pardo and Vilaseca—could go, if they wanted, and then risk "having a *Time* photographer take their picture and create a scandal, showing how the members of the Cuban delegation spend the people's money partying and getting drunk with whores."

Another evening, Che found that a couple of the entourage members had vanished. When asked where they were, Menéndez told Che he didn't know. "*I* know where they are," said Che. "They're out whoring, aren't they?" When Menéndez still insisted he didn't know, Che seemed to relent and, as if to show that he too could be "one of the boys," blurted out: "I know what it's like to *putear;* I whored round in my youth, too." As Menéndez recalled, Che then told him of the time he been at sea, and had "kept a whore in his cabin with him until he grew tired of her."

Occasionally, Che loosened up in a more public fashion. Once, in a traditional Japanese geisha house, where all the women in attendance were of a safe, advanced age, he enjoyed himself, drinking lots of sake and rising to mimic the geisha's dance steps. In the living room of the Chilean ambassador's residence in Delhi, he surprised his host by abruptly standing on his head, in order to demonstrate his knowledge of yoga.

But the pressure of having to maintain a rigid public posture gradually wore him down. Obviously feeling lonely, Che wrote to his mother from India and gave a bittersweet account of his frustration at the official straitjacket he had to wear on his travels.

Dear *vieja:*

My old dream to visit all these countries takes place now in a way that inhibits all my happiness. Speaking of political and economic problems, giving parties where the only thing missing is for me to put on a tuxedo, and putting aside my purest pleasures, which would be to go and dream in the shade of a pyramid or over Tutankhamen's sarcophagus. On top of that, I am without Aleida whom I couldn't bring because of one of those complicated mental complexes I have.

Egypt was a diplomatic success of the first magnitude; the embassies of all the countries of the world came to the farewell [reception] we gave and I saw firsthand how complicated diplomacy can be when the Papal Nuncio shook hands with the Russian attaché with a smile that was really beatific.

Now India, where new protocolar complications produce in me the same infantile panic [in deciding how to respond to greetings].

Then, as always with his mother, he became introspective.

Something which has really developed in me is the sense of the massive in counterposition to the personal; I am still the same loner that I used to be, looking for my path without personal help, but now I possess the sense of my historic duty. I have no home, no woman, no chil-

dren, nor parents, nor brothers and sisters, my friends are my friends
as long as they think politically like I do and yet I am content, I feel
something in life, not just a powerful internal strength, which I always
felt, but also the power to inject others, and an absolutely fatalistic sense
of my mission which strips me of all fear.

No one has ever defined the essence of what made Che Guevara unique
better than he did himself in this rare, private moment of truth. But then,
as usual, he defensively pulled back from his reverie.

I don't know why I am writing you this, maybe it is merely longing
for Aleida. Take it as it is, a letter written one stormy night in the skies
of India, far from my fatherland and loved ones.

A hug for everyone, Ernesto.

He may have longed for Aleida, but he resisted his urge to be with her.
Apparently both baffled and intrigued by this quirky self-denial streak in
his Argentine comrade, Fidel repeatedly tried to moderate it.

"Fidel was always trying to get us together," said Aleida. While Che was
in Japan, she recalled, Fidel summoned her to his office. He had arranged a
long-distance telephone call with Che, and Fidel took the opportunity to suggest again to Che that Aleida join him. Once more Che refused. Fidel tried
again when Che was in Morocco, but his lieutenant was unbudging.

One night in Tokyo, Che and the others gathered in a hotel room, to
talk, tell stories, and philosophize. According to Menéndez, Che veered the
conversation onto an odd topic, the significance of which Menéndez realized only much later. "Che started talking about his projects, but I never
associated it with a real plan. He said: 'There's an *altiplano* in South America,
there in Bolivia, in Paraguay, an area bordering Brazil, Uruguay, Peru, and
Argentina . . . where if we inserted a guerrilla force, we could spread the
revolution all over South America."

V

Three months is a long time in a revolution, and when Che returned to Cuba
in September 1959, a great many changes had occurred in his absence. Fidel
now had more political power, but the atmosphere was more tense and
polarized than ever.

The agrarian reform law had begun to cause heavy fallout. The first
seizures of land were made, and it was becoming clear that the reform was

not as straightforward as it had first seemed. The government was hedging on compensation, offering low-interest "bonds" to affected landowners instead of ready cash, but the United States was on the alert. It had issued a note of warning—so far left unanswered by Fidel—that it expected any expropriated American landowners to be recompensated promptly.

The affected wealthy cattlemen of Camagüey mounted a campaign against the land interventions, and the province's popular military commander, Huber Matos, had joined them by publicly denouncing the Communist encroachment in the armed forces and the INRA. Matos was emerging as the chief spokesman for the July 26 Movement's anti-Communist wing, as the dispute with the ascendant PSP became increasingly acrimonious.

Following the resignation of Agriculture Minister Sorí-Marín, Fidel had continued cleaning house. In the cabinet, the political moderates had begun getting the shove, and loyal Fidelístas were taking their places. Foreign Minister Roberto Agramonte was fired and replaced by Raúl Roa, the OAS ambassador and former dean of Havana University's Social Sciences Faculty. Despite his avowed anti-Communism after breaking with the party in his youth, the sphinxlike Roa now became both an unswerving Fidelísta and a brilliant diplomat, moving politically wherever Cuba's *jefe máximo* chose to go. Even Fidel's old friend Luis Orlando Rodríguez, who had helped found Radio Rebelde in the Sierra Maestra, was dropped as interior minister.

In mid-June, a Cuban-Dominican guerrilla expedition of some 200 fighters led by Delio Gómez Ochoa, Fidel's former July 26 commander, had landed in the Dominican Republic—only to be wiped out by Trujillo's forces, its members killed, imprisoned, or on the run. At the same time, an anti-Castro army calling itself the Anti-Communist Legion of the Caribbean was being trained at a Dominican air force base under Trujillo's auspices. Composed of 350-odd fighters, it included 150 Spaniards, 100 Cubans, and an array of right-wing foreign mercenaries, including Croatians, Germans, and Greeks, and they were sent to hunt down the rebel fugitives. Among the Cubans were Che's old nemesis Ángel Sánchez Mosquera, former police officials from Havana, and Batista's personal pilot. Their pursuit was assisted by Trujillo's offer to pay rural farmers a bounty of a thousand dollars *per head* for each rebel caught. Soon, peasants taking the generalissimo quite literally began appearing at Dominican army posts with burlap bags containing decapitated *bearded* heads to collect the reward. The legionnaires jokingly complained that the peasants, who eventually turned in more heads than there had been invaders, were not leaving them any Cubans to fight against.

As if the Dominican fiasco weren't bad enough, Cuba's air force chief, Pedro Luis Díaz Lanz defected, only to reappear before a Senate committee in Washington, where he denounced Communist infiltration in the armed forces. President Manuel Urrutia appeared on television to deny the charges and, in an obvious bid to get Fidel to declare himself, stated his own firm opposition to Communism.

Fidel dealt an unexpected counterblow, denouncing Urrutia for attempting to break "revolutionary unity" and insinuating that he was in league with the traitor Díaz Lanz. Then, at the same moment as thousands of Fidelistas were trucked into Havana to celebrate July 26, Fidel resigned as prime minister and let the crowds do their work. The popular clamor for his reinstatement grew. Belatedly realizing that he had created a trap for himself, Urrutia promptly resigned his office and sought asylum in an embassy. On July 26, Fidel reappeared in front of the crowds and assented to "the people's demand" that he resume his duties as prime minister. In place of the recalcitrant Urrutia, Fidel quickly named Osvaldo Dorticós, his docile revolutionary-laws minister, as the new Cuban president.

VI

"Counterrevolution" now became a catchphrase for the activities of those who, like Urrutia, had sought to "sabotage" revolutionary "unity." In fact, the first threats of counterrevolutionary activity *had* begun to appear. In addition to the force being trained in the Dominican Republic, there were exile groups openly organizing paramilitary forces in Miami. After several bombs exploded and an assassination plot was uncovered in Havana, Fidel pushed through a constitutional amendment to include the death penalty for the new crime of "counterrevolution."

In August, Trujillo's Anti-Communist Legion was finally mobilized for an invasion of Cuba, but Fidel had prepared a surprise for its fighters when they arrived, a clever ruse that Fidel had carried off with the complicity of former Segundo Frente commanders Eloy Gutiérrez Menoyo and the American William Morgan. Contacting Trujillo, Menoyo and Morgan had tricked the Dominican dictator into believing they were ready to lead an anti-Castro uprising (before too long, they would be doing precisely that, but for now they were cooperating with Fidel). At the crucial moment, they had radioed the Dominican Republic to say their forces had seized the Cuban city of Trinidad, the prearranged green light for the Anti-Communist Legion to lend their support. When their transport plane touched down in the countryside near Trinidad with its planeload of 100-odd Cuban fighters, flown by the same pilot who had flown Batista into exile, Fidel and his soldiers were ready and waiting. Quite a few of the legion's fighters had been left behind in the Dominican Republic, however, including one who would later have a profound effect on events in Latin America: an eighteen-year-old military cadet named Felix Rodríguez.

Rodríguez's uncle had been Batista's minister of public works, and when Castro seized power his whole family had fled into exile. Embittered at his family's misfortune, Rodríguez had left his military school at Perkiomen, Pennsylvania, and joined Trujillo's legion. By being left behind in the Dominican Republic, he had been saved from a long prison sentence, the fate of most of his captured comrades, but Rodríguez's sense of frustration would only be intensified by their defeat. Returning to Perkiomen to finish his studies, he resolved to dedicate himself to destroying the Cuban revolution. His future attempts were mostly to prove unsuccessful, but in the course of his career he was able to deal some heavy blows. Eight years after the Trinidad fiasco, his path would cross Che's, on the last day of Guevara's life.

VII

By the end of September 1959, Fidel faced a more immediate threat, a showdown between him and Huber Matos. The Camagüey military commander was making no secret of his disaffection with the radically leftward turn of the revolution, and had urged Fidel to convoke a meeting of the July 26 National Directorate to discuss the "Communist infiltration" in the army and INRA. Situated as he was in the wealthy and conservative Cuban heartland, Matos posed a real threat.

This was the volatile atmosphere in which the Soviet agent Alexandr Alexiev found himself when he arrived in Havana on October 1. Met by reporters from the Communist daily, *Hoy,* he was taken to the inexpensive, low-profile Hotel Sevilla in Old Havana. The next day, he met with PSP officials Carlos Rafael Rodríguez and Raúl Valdés Vivo, who briefed him on the current political situation. They offered to introduce him to Blas Roca and other Politburo members, but he declined; instead, Alexiev called Violeta Casals.

Casals was a well-known actress, a Communist, and a loyal Fidelista, having worked as one of Radio Rebelde's announcers in the Sierra Maestra. Alexiev had met her in Moscow during the summer, and he now asked for her help in contacting Che. Casals agreed to arrange the meeting. While he waited, Alexiev laid low, sending off a few TASS dispatches for appearance' sake.

Che had been back in Havana for only three weeks himself, and Fidel wanted him to immediately start up the "Industrialization Department" of

INRA. His new office was in an unfinished fourteen-story building that had been erected by Batista to house Havana's future municipal headquarters. It overlooked the large civic square dominated by a huge white obelisk and statue of of José Martí that had been renamed the Plaza de la Revolución.

Fidel was INRA's president, Nuñez Jiménez its executive director, and from its offices the *true* Cuban revolution was being launched. The official announcement of Che's new post would not come until October 8, but the rumors had already begun to spread and were duly picked up by the American embassy. In a September 16 dispatch to Washington, the embassy had reported: "Rumors are circulating that he [Che] is slated for an important position in the government. Most frequently mentioned are the directorship of an industrial development institute or the Minister of Commerce."

In late September, Che traveled to Santa Clara to see his old La Cabaña regiment. He gathered his officers at Víctor Bordón's home and told them of his new responsibilities; it was not what they had expected or hoped to hear. Orlando Borrego sat in the front row. "Che told us that Fidel and the revolutionary leadership had decided to create an Industrialization Department to develop the country. He explained to us the importance of this for the economy, and that he had been named to lead the industrial development of the country. This surprised us because we thought Che would once again take charge of the regiment. . . . To tell us he was going to the civil sector was a real blow."

It sounded to Borrego as if all the rumors he had been hearing for months about Che's demotion were true, and he was now merely trying to put a good face on a bad situation. "It seemed to us that Che, who had been commander of La Cabaña, the chief of a regiment, was more important than [this job] he was telling us about. . . . But he explained it to us with enthusiasm, he said it would be a really wonderful job that he wanted to do."

Suddenly, Che addressed him directly: "Borrego, do you want to come and work with me in this project?" Borrego replied that he was a soldier, and would do whatever Che asked of him. Looking pleased, Che told him: "Good, be at my house in Havana first thing in the morning."

The next morning, he and Che toured the INRA building's eighth floor. Nuñez Jiménez had already installed his offices on the fourth floor, and Fidel, as INRA's president, at the top, on the fourteenth floor. So far, the vaunted Industrialization Department was only Che, his twenty-one-year-old accountant, Orlando Borrego, and the bare concrete walls. "Well," said Che, looking around, "the first thing we have to do is finish the construction. . . . Then, I want you to take over the administration of the department."

In actuality, Fidel's choice of Che for the industry job was not so surprising. Ever since the days of the Sierra Maestra his Argentine lieutenant had been the leading proponent of creating self-sufficient industries, beginning with his modest bread ovens, shoe repair shops, and rustic bomb factories in El Hombrito and La Mesa. Now he wanted to extrapolate the lessons of the guerrilla experience to Cuba as a whole and, if possible, throughout Latin America. Since the rebel victory, he had been steadily advocating the industrialization of the country and, with it, the mass militarization of its society. He expected the Americans to invade, and if that happened, the entire Cuban population would have to leave the cities and fight as a guerrilla army. Even if that didn't happen, industrialization would end Cuba's dependency on agricultural exports that were controlled by the capitalist markets, and in particular by the meddlesome United States.

When Fidel made Che's INRA appointment official, he also announced that Che would be retaining his military rank and responsibilities. While Orlando Borrego said Che was excited about his new post, there are reports that Che had privately hoped Fidel would appoint him to the job that, on October 16, went to his brother Raúl: minister of the revolutionary armed forces. If Che was disappointed, he concealed his feelings.

Meanwhile, his hopes that Cuba's support for armed revolution elsewhere in the hemisphere would bring early results were taking a beating. Not only had the Dominican Republic expedition been crushed, but the Nicaraguan force he had sponsored had also failed the test miserably. This group, numbering fifty-four men, including Cubans and Nicaraguans, had been led by a man handpicked by Che, a former Nicaraguan National Guard officer named Rafael Somarriba, and had included Che's friend Rodolfo Romero and the intellectual Carlos Fonseca.

Beginning in early June, the group's members had begun leaving Cuba, traveling separately to Honduras, where they linked up on a farm near the Nicaraguan border; the night of June 12–13, Che's personal pilot, Eliseo de la Campa, had flown in a planeload of weapons for them. Three weeks later they struck out for the border, but there had evidently been a *chivatazo,* for they were ambushed in a ravine by a joint Honduran-Nicaraguan military force. Nine of the expeditionaries had been killed, including a Cuban, and Carlos Fonseca was badly wounded, with the survivors rounded up and put into a Honduran prison. Within a few weeks, however, they were released. According to Romero, the reason was that Honduran President Villeda Morales was "an admirer of Che," and his security chief, whose wife was Nicaraguan, was himself a fervent *antisomocista*. Romero returned to Havana. Shortly after returning from his long foreign mission, Che summoned Romero for a private meeting.

"He was really angry," recalled Romero. "Especially when I told him how they had fucked us." Romero blamed the fiasco on the "stupidity" of

Somarriba, who had led them into a ravine where they were easily ambushed. "Che's reaction was: 'The truth is all these career military guys are
shit.'" At Che's insistence, Romero drew Che diagrams of the ambush site
to show him exactly what had happened, and Che commented: "You're only
alive by a miracle."

Afterward, Romero's contacts with Che were more sporadic; it was
decided that the Nicaraguans needed more training and field experience
before they attempted a new guerrilla expedition. Soon, Romero and his
comrades were subsumed into the new military counterintelligence apparatus being run by Ramiro Valdés and his deputy "Barba Roja," the red-
bearded Manuel Piñeiro Losada, a onetime Columbia University student
and the son of Galician emigres who ran a wine-import firm and beer
distributorship in Matanzas. Given the early setbacks, it was clear that
Cuba's guerrilla-support program would have to be run in a more structured fashion.

For now, Che got on with the INRA job. First, his office was built,
with spaces for Aleida and for his private secretary, José Manresa. Then an
office was built for Borrego, who still didn't have a clue what he was to be
doing. Their ranks were bolstered by César Rodríguez, an engineeer, and
PSP official Pancho García Vals. The Industrialization Department became
a formal reality, but not even Che had a grasp of exactly how to proceed.
He was supposed to industrialize Cuba, but how?

Che hadn't been in his new office many days when Violeta Casals called
him. A TASS correspondent was in town, she explained, and wished to meet
him; Che agreed to receive the Soviet "journalist."

Alexiev was told to be at Che's office at two in the morning on October 13. Arriving at the appointed hour, he found the office dark except for
two lamps, one on Che's desk and one on a nearby desk where a pretty blond
woman worked in silence.

"We started to talk," recalled Alexiev. "He was very happy when he
heard I had been in Argentina just a few months before. We talked and . . .
since I knew he was Red I talked openly, because I could see *he* was very
open. . . . I had a carton of cigarettes that I had brought from Argentina,
and I gave him three or four packets of these, which were called Tejas [for
"Texas"]. I said: 'Che, I'd like to give you something that will bring back
memories to you.' Error! He was furious, and said: 'What are you giving
me? Tejas, do you know what that is? It's the half of Mexico that the Yankee bandits robbed!'" Che was so angry, Alexiev said, that he didn't know
what to do. "I said, 'Che, I'm sorry for giving you such a strange gift, but
I'm pleased that now I know how you feel about the common enemy.' And
we laughed together."

After that initial "delicate" moment had passed, recalled Alexiev, their conversation continued amiably, and quite soon they began using the informal *"tú"* to address one another. Che called him "Alejandro," and he no longer addressed his host as "Comandante," but called him "Che."

Finally, noticing the late hour and that the woman he assumed was Che's secretary was still working, Alexiev motioned to Aleida and joked: "'Che, you are such a fighter against exploitation, but I see that you exploit your secretary?' He said: 'Ah yes! It's true, but she's not just my secretary, she's my wife as well.'"

Their talk went until almost dawn, and toward the end Che told Alexiev: "Our revolution is truly progressive, anti-imperialistic and anti-American, made by the people. . . . But we cannot conquer and maintain it without the aid of the global revolutionary movement, and above all, from the socialist bloc and the Soviet Union." Che emphasized to Alexiev that this was *his own* personal viewpoint.

Alexiev understood the implication and explained that he was also eager to learn what the other revolutionary leaders thought; could Che arrange a meeting with Fidel? "Che said, 'The problem is that Fidel doesn't like to talk to *journalists*.'" Alexiev recalled, "So I told him, 'Well, my purpose is not to interview him—it's *not* for the press.' Che understood."

Three days later, on the afternoon of October 16, Alexiev received a telephone call at his room in the Hotel Sevilla. A voice asked him: "Mr. Alejandro Alexiev, what are you doing at this moment?" "Nothing," he replied. "Good. You asked for an interview with Comandante Fidel Castro. If you are available, he will see you right now; we are coming to pick you up."

Alexiev got ready as quickly as he could. "I put on a dark suit, black, white shirt, grey tie, to present a diplomatic image." He then took some Soviet vodka and caviar he had brought as gifts for the occasion, and went down to await his escorts. Two bearded boys with machine guns approached him in the foyer, and as they guided him away Alexiev thought mirthfully to himself: "Anyone who knows who I am must be thinking they are arresting the only Russian in Cuba."

His escorts took him to the same INRA building where he had met with Che, but this time he took the elevator to the top floor. When he stepped out, two more bearded men in uniform were waiting for him: Fidel Castro and Nuñez Jiménez. They ushered him into Fidel's office, where they sat around a large round wooden table and began to talk.

After a few minutes of polite chitchat, Fidel asked what was in the package he had brought. Alexiev pulled out the caviar and vodka and Fidel

immediately suggested they sample them. Moments later, as they sat drinking the vodka and eating the caviar with biscuits, Fidel, obviously enjoying
himself, turned to Nuñez Jiménez and, as if the idea had just occurred to
him, said, "Nuñez, the Soviet merchandise is great, isn't it? I never tried it
before. It seems to me it would be worthwhile reestablishing commercial
relations with the Soviet Union."

Alexiev immediately said: "Very well, Fidel—it is as good as done. But
I am also very interested in cultural relations and, even more importantly,
diplomatic relations." According to Alexiev, Fidel quickly responded:

"No, I don't think so, not *yet*. Formalities aren't important; I'm against
formalisms. You have arrived, you're an emissary of the Kremlin, and we
can say that we now have relations. But we can't tell this yet to the [Cuban]
people. The people aren't ready, they have been poisoned by the bourgeois
American propaganda to be against Communism."

Fidel then cited Lenin on the revolutionary strategy of "preparing the
masses"—telling Alexiev he was going to heed the dictum; he would eradicate the anti-Communist press campaign and, gradually, the people's prejudices, but he needed time. Until then, Alexiev had harbored a skeptical view
of Fidel, but the demonstration that he had read Lenin ("not too deep but
pretty good") impressed him. Still, he was a bit suspicious. He was staring
pointedly at the gold medallion of the Virgen del Cobre, Cuba's Catholic
patron saint, hanging prominently on Fidel's chest, when Fidel noticed his
gaze. "Alejandro," Fidel said. "Don't pay it any mind. My mother sent it to
me when I was in the sierra."

Alexiev understood that there was more to it than that. There was a
strong Catholic movement in Cuba, and it did Fidel little harm to keep up
appearances by wearing a medallion on his chest.

Despite himself, Alexiev found himself warming to Fidel and pointed
out that they had several things in common: His first name, in Spanish, was
the same as Fidel's second name—Alejandro. They were also joined by the
number thirteen. Fidel was born on August *13,* and Alexiev was *thirteen*
years older than him. In addition, Alexiev was born on August 1, which
meant their birthdays were *thirteen* days apart. Fidel, known for his fascination with numerology, was delighted by Alexiev's attempt to find their
symbological affinities.

All the while, Alexiev continued probing to ascertain how much Fidel's
conception of his revolution matched or differed from Che Guevara's. "It's
a true revolution," Fidel told him, "made by the people and for the people.
We want to build a just society without man exploiting his fellow man, and
an armed people to defend their victories. If Marx were to arise now he

would be pleased to see me giving arms to the people." Although Alexiev noted that Fidel avoided using the word "socialism," while Che *had,* Fidel "made it understood" that they shared the same philosophy.

By the time their meeting ended, Alexiev had been given a mission to fulfill. It came about in the same seemingly spontaneous fashion as Fidel's decision to renew Soviet-Cuban commercial relations while sipping Alexiev's vodka. As Alexiev tells it, after Fidel's explanation about the need to "go slow" with Cubans because of their rampant anti-Communist inculcation, Nuñez Jiménez had cut in, suggesting to Fidel that it might be a good idea to have Alexiev ask his government to bring the Soviet trade exposition, then in Mexico, to Havana. On a July trip to New York, Nuñez Jiménez had visited the exposition, which Soviet Deputy Premier Anastas Mikoyan had inaugurated, and had been impressed. "It's worthwhile, really!" Alexiev recalled Nuñez Jiménez saying to Fidel. "It would open the eyes of the Cuban people about the Soviet Union by showing that the American propaganda about its backwardness is untrue."

Fidel asked Alexiev his own opinion. Was it really good, this exposition? Alexiev said yes, he thought it was, but believed it would be hard to arrange. The itinerary for the Soviet exposition was already scheduled, Cuba was not on the list, and, in view of his country's grinding bureaucracy, it would be hard to alter the schedule.

But already, Fidel had made Nuñez's idea his own and refused to take no for an answer. "It *has* to come!" he told Alexiev emphatically. "And Mikoyan has to come and open it. Sure, it's all been planned but it *has* to come! We are revolutionaries! Go to Mexico and tell Mikoyan what kind of revolution this is—that it's worth him coming." Alexiev agreed to try but warned Fidel that he couldn't travel that freely on his Soviet passport. "Don't worry," Fidel told him. "Our ambassador in Mexico will fix everything."

Within days, Alexiev was on a plane to meet Mikoyan in Mexico City. So far, his mission to Havana was paying off. With Che's nudge, followed by Fidel's approval, the wheels of political destiny leading Cuba into the Soviet orbit had begun to turn.

22

"We Are the Future
and We Know It"

I

When Deputy Premier Anastas Mikoyan arrived in Havana on February 4, 1960, he brought along his thirty-year-old son, Sergo; the Soviet ambassador to Mexico; a personal assistant; and, as his bodyguard-interpreter, a young KGB officer, Nikolai Leonov. Mikoyan asked Leonov to deliver gifts to "the principal leaders of the revolution." The task gave Leonov the opportunity to see his old acquaintances from Mexico privately, and the first person he went to see was Che Guevara.

Che and Aleida had recently moved from their remote country house into the more secure confines of Ciudad Libertad, the sprawling former military headquarters on Havana's western edge. They now lived in one of the homes formerly housing Batista's officers, next to the military airstrip.

Only a little over three years had passed since their last meeting in Mexico, when Leonov had lent some Soviet books to the young Argentine doctor who had been so eager to learn about socialism, but already Leonov's intemperate early contacts with Castro's rebel group had been vindicated; here he was, in Cuba, escorting "the second–most important man" in the Soviet Union. As for Guevara and the Castro brothers, they were no longer importunate political exiles espousing a wild scheme, but the undisputed leaders of a new revolutionary Cuba, evidently prepared to "go socialist" and forge an alliance with his country at the risk of war with the United States.

This time, "on behalf of the Soviet people," Leonov carried a different kind of gift for Guevara: a Soviet-made precision marksman's pistol of the finest quality, sheathed in a beautiful holster, with a good supply of ammunition.

Following his peremptory recall to Moscow from Mexico in November 1956, Leonov had been discharged from the foreign service, and, deciding to pursue a career as a historian of Latin America, he had gone to work as a translator for the official Soviet Spanish-language publishing house, Editorial Progreso. In the late summer of 1958, he had been invited to join the KGB, and he accepted. On September 1, Leonov began a two-year intelligence training course that, he says, he didn't complete "because of the Cuban revolution."*

In October 1959, Leonov's KGB superiors ordered him to leave his studies and escort Mikoyan on his trip to Mexico. Because the deputy premier had been invited not by the Mexican government but by the Soviet ambassador, ostensibly to open the trade exhibit, he could not travel with the usual phalanx of aides; as someone who had previously lived in Mexico, Leonov would go along as his only companion, acting as his bodyguard, Spanish-Russian interpreter, and "advisor."

Leonov was with Mikoyan in Mexico when Alexandr Alexiev arrived on his secret mission from Cuba. As Alexiev retells it, he went straight to see Mikoyan. "I spoke of Fidel, of Che, of Raúl, of the revolution, and he listened with great interest. Since Mikoyan had been in the [Bolshevik] revolution in his youth, it reminded him of his youthful days, of the revolutionary romanticism of that time."

Alexiev told Mikoyan of Fidel's overture. "They don't want *just* the exhibition. *Fidel wants to talk*." After hearing him out, Mikoyan remarked that he too—like Fidel—was against "formalities," recalled Alexiev, but as the Soviet vice premier, he couldn't travel to a country with which Moscow had no diplomatic ties. He sent off a cable to the Kremlin and sent Alexiev on to Moscow to explain things.

"Moscow agreed to move the exhibition from Mexico to Cuba," said Alexiev, "because Khrushchev had by now also fallen in love with the Cuban revolution. I don't know exactly why, but [I think the reason was that] he was so happy to have another pawn against the Americans."

---

*A credible-sounding alternative version is offered by Anastas Mikoyan's son, Sergo, who accompanied his father and Leonov on the trip to Cuba. Mikoyan told the author in 1994 that he had known Leonov for years before the trip. They were about the same age and had gone to school together.

To Mikoyan's knowledge, Leonov was initially sent to Mexico by the KGB under the cover story of working for an official Soviet publishing house. He was sent there at the same time as another friend of his was sent in a similar capacity to the United States, and who, said Mikoyan, "was certainly KGB."

Leonov's first contact with Raúl Castro *was* casual, agreed Mikoyan, but his subsequent meetings in Mexico were intentional. "Ironically, he was told by the KGB to halt these contacts." Mikoyan's belief is that this order was due to pressure from the Cuban Communists, who still didn't approve of Fidel Castro, believing him and his movement to be "bourgeois and putschist."

After one lengthy delay, the Soviet exhibition opened in Havana in February 1960. (Its original opening date, November 28, 1959, had coincided with a Catholic congress being held in Havana, and Fidel saw little reason to rile conservatives.)

After arriving in Havana with Mikoyan, Leonov pulled up in a car in front of Che Guevara's house; it was almost noon, but Che was still asleep. "He was exhausted," Leonov said, "but he got up, and was really enthused to see me. '*Hombre!* What a miracle, it's like you dropped in from heaven!'" Over coffee, Leonov handed him the marksman's pistol, a gift that pleased Che immensely.

Leonov congratulated Che on the rebel victory, then, reminding him of their past conversations and the Soviet literature Che had been so avid to read in Mexico, asked, "So, it's true, you are really serious about building socialism?" "Yes," Che replied, "I'm going to devote my life to it. That's why first, I was reading, to build later."

II

If Leonov was curious to know why Che was still asleep so late in the day, he soon learned the answer. Along with his job at INRA, Che had also become president of Cuba's National Bank.

It was an extremely heavy workload, and by now his unusual working hours had become legendary. Stories abounded in Havana of foreign dignitaries who, after being granted interviews with Che at three o'clock, showed up at his offices at that hour of the afternoon, only to be informed by Manresa that their appointment was for 3:00 A.M. The after-midnight appointment Alexiev had with Che in October was now the rule, not the exception.

In a Christmas letter to his parents, Che had tried to give them a sense of his strange new life.

Dear *viejos:*

You know how hard it is for me to write. I am taking a pause at 6:30 in the morning, not at the beginning but at the end of the day, to wish you all that is wishable during these days. Cuba lives a moment that is decisive for America. At one time I wanted to be one of Pizarro's soldiers; but [to fulfill] my quest for adventures and my yearnings to overlook climactic moments, that isn't a necessity any longer; today it is all here, and with an ideal to fight for, together with the responsibility of leaving an example. We are not men, but working machines, fighting against time in the midst of difficult and luminous circumstances.

The Industrial Department was my own creation; I half-relinquished it, with the pain of a worn-out father, to plunge myself into my apparently God-given gift for finance. I also have the job of Chief of Training of the E. Rebelde and the direct command of a regiment in Oriente. We walk over pure history of the highest American category; we are the future and we know it, we build with happiness although we have forgotten individual affections. Receive an affectionate embrace from this machine dispensing calculating love to 160 million Americans, and sometimes, the prodigal son who returns in the memory.

Che.

Che's life with Aleida had also fallen into a circumscribed pattern. As his secretary, she saw him at work, but they had little privacy during his rare times at home. The Guatemalan, Patojo, had lived with them off and on since early 1959, and Oscar Fernández Mell moved into their spare bedroom at the front of the house in Ciudad Libertad; he worked nearby, in Batista's old naval headquarters, as chief of medical services of the new army.

Aleida took all of this in stride, but something *did* bother her, and that was the unflagging presence of Hilda Gadea on the scene. Che's ex-wife worked on another floor of INRA in an office set up to help peasant farmers whose homes had been destroyed during the war. In Aleida's estimation, Hilda had not given up hopes of winning Che back, and made her presence felt at every opportunity, dropping her daughter Hildita off to play in Che's office or taking her there to eat her lunch. Che didn't mind: his feelings for his only daughter were complex, paternal love mixed with guilt for having made her the innocent victim of a broken marriage and his long absence, and he tried to make up for it by having her with him as much as possible; when Hilda allowed, the little girl stayed at his home on the weekends.

Aleida put up with the little girl for Che's sake, but when the office visits became too frequent, with Hilda seeming to use them to dally and engage Che in conversation, she simmered with fury. Che seethed at Hilda's constant interruptions but kept his own temper in check to avoid making a scene. One day, however, he could take it no longer and, storming out of his office, shouted loud enough to be heard by a secretary: "I might as well not have gotten divorced."

Hilda often spoke to that same secretary, a young woman, to confide her feelings and to badmouth Aleida. Aleida, in turn, fulminated with the secretary about her talking to Hilda and demanded to know what they discussed. Finally, after a few months, the secretary could no longer stand feeling like a "pig in the middle," and asked to be transferred out of the department.

In the months since Che's return from his "goodwill" tour, an increasingly divisive mood had settled over Cuba. There had been a whirlwind of dramatic change as Fidel forced through more and more radical policies, extending revolutionary control to previously sacrosanct areas of Cuban society. Throughout, using cajolery in private and applause in public, Che had urged him along. Observers were beginning to take note of an intriguing pattern: What started out as "radical-sounding" proposals from Che were actually important early-warning signals, for almost invariably Fidel soon made them official revolutionary policy.

In January 1959, and again in April, Che had talked about Cuba's need to nationalize its oil and mineral wealth. In September 1959, Fidel had echoed him, saying it was an issue that needed to be "carefully studied." Nine months later, he would seize the refineries owned by the American-owned Texaco and Esso, and British Shell.

In November 1959, the U.S. embassy noted a recent Guevara interview published in *Revolución*, which made plain that, ". . . regardless of what the Agrarian Reform Law may say about making the peasants small property owners, as far as Guevara is concerned, reform will be aimed more in the direction of cooperatives or communies [*sic*]."

Three months later, in January 1960, Fidel issued his decree seizing all sugar plantations and large cattle ranches and making them state-run cooperatives. And, as for the issue that was becoming Washington's greatest grievance, the "nonpayment and illegal seizures" of American-owned properties in violation of Cuba's 1940 constitution and the 1959 agrarian reform law, few should have been surprised; in the very first weeks of the revolution's triumph, Che had given an early warning, publicly calling for the constitution's compensation clause to be waived.

October 1959 had been a particularly crucial month, for by its close the stage had been set for what Hugh Thomas has called "the eclipse of the liberals" and the final ascendancy of the anti-American, "radical" wing of the revolution. The course long advocated by Che was now being steered, more and more openly, by Fidel himself.

Employing the now heavily loaded argument for "revolutionary unity," Fidel had successfully orchestrated the takeover of Havana University's student union by Rolando Cubela, the former Directorio commander who had recently returned from a few months in Prague as Fidel's military attaché. Cubela's election victory was a de facto government takeover of the campus that had traditionally been both autonomous and a historic hotbed of anti-government plotting. Fidel knew this only too well, since that is where he had begun his own political career.

Che carried the same message to Cuba's second university, in Santiago, where he bluntly announced that university autonomy was over, and henceforth the state would design the curriculum. Central planning was necessary, Cuba was going to industrialize, and it needed qualified technicians—agronomists, agricultural teachers, and chemical engineers—not a new crop of more lawyers.

Che told them: "Who has the right to say that only 10 lawyers should graduate per year and that 100 industrial chemists should graduate? [Some would say that] that is dictatorship, and all right: it is dictatorship." Students should join the "great army of those who *do,* leaving by the wayside that small patrol of those who simply talk."

(And, in December, while accepting an honorary teacher's degree at the University of Las Villas, Che told the gathered faculty and students that the days when education was a privilege of the white middle class had ended. "The University," he said, "must *paint* itself black, mulatto, worker and peasant." If it didn't, he warned, the people would break down its doors ". . . and paint the University the colors they like.")

He spoke in Santiago amid a climate of tension caused by the first true outbreaks of counterrevolutionary activity: In Pinar del Río, a sugar mill was bombed by an unidentified plane, and a group of suspected rebels that included two Americans was captured; the long-simmering Huber Matos affair was finally about to blow up.

On October 20, following Raúl's official promotion as armed forces minister, Matos wrote to Fidel from Camagüey, tendering his resignation, urging him to alter his present course, and accusing him of "burying the revolution." Some fifteen of his officers planned to resign with him.

Fidel's reply came immediately. He repudiated Matos's claims and accused him of "disloyalty" and "ambition," among other offenses, then ordered Camilo to fly to Camagüey and arrest Matos and his fellow dissident officers. Camilo obeyed his orders, and Matos and his officers were arrested without incident. Fidel then flew to Camagüey himself to make a speech accusing Matos of planning an armed revolt, of "treason"; Matos and his officers were taken to Havana and imprisoned in La Cabaña.

For the Matos "plotters," the timing could not have been worse. As Fidel, back in Havana, prepared to address a convention of over two thousand American travel agents to encourage the expansion of U.S. tourism to Cuba, the defector Pedro Luis Díaz Lanz appeared overhead, piloting a B-26 bomber and dropping leaflets calling on Fidel to purge the Communists in his regime. Cuban air force planes scrambled to intercept him, and army personnel at La Cabaña opened fire with antiaircraft batteries, but Díaz Lanz flew away unscathed.

At the INRA building on Plaza de la Revolución, Che and his office-mates, Manresa and a secretary named Cristína, stood by a window watching Díaz Lanz loop down low and buzz the building, flying so close they could see him inside the pilot's cabin. Che said nothing, but he was icy with rage and frustration. Che's *escolta* asked for permission to go up to the roof and shoot down the plane, but Che told them no—they were bound to do more damage than the plane could. Then Díaz Lanz flew away, and inside Che's office the incident ended on a humorous twist. One of the secretaries, a plump and excessively nervous girl, had hidden under a desk when the plane appeared; others returning to work found her still there, stuck and unable to extricate herself. Everyone laughed as several of the *escolta* finally pulled her free.

But for Fidel, the affair was a public-relations disaster, his tourism-promotion scheme stillborn; the travel agents began leaving town in alarm as Fidel and the Cuban media denounced the "bombing attack" by an American plane that had left dead and injured civilians. Safely back in the United States, Díaz Lanz acknowledged making the flight but denied dropping anything except leaflets over Havana—if there were any casualties, they had probably been the result of the Cuban soldiers' random shooting—but the story that he had launched an aerial attack was officially adopted. The next day, large crowds demonstrated in front of the American embassy, and Fidel appeared on television, accusing Matos of plotting a military revolt in Camagüey, in complicity with Díaz Lanz. (The previous day, significantly, there had also been an attack by an unidentified plane that dropped bombs on a Camagüey sugar mill.) The United States, Fidel charged, harbored "war criminals" and had supplied Díaz Lanz with the warplane.

He followed up this appearance on October 26 with a mass rally in Revolution Plaza attended by an estimated half-million Cubans, repeating his charges and vowing that Cuba would defend itself from attack. The people would be trained and armed, and Cuba would get the planes and other weapons it needed. The next day, U.S. Ambassador Bonsal delivered an official note of protest to Foreign Minister Raúl Roa over Fidel's accusations; at the same time Fidel's cabinet voted to reinstate the revolutionary tribunals.

On October 28, after reorganizing the military command in Camagüey, Camilo Cienfuegos boarded his Cessna airplane for the return to Havana. He never arrived. Fidel and Che joined the three-day aerial search for the missing plane, conducted over a vast area, but no wreckage was found. What had happened? Camilo's pilot was experienced, and the weather that day had been fine. Many conspiracy theories sprang up: Fidel had done away with Camilo, either because he was in cahoots with Matos, or because he was becoming too popular. Another was that a Cuban air force fighter plane shot him down, mistaking his aircraft for a hostile intruder. Whatever the cause, Camilo was obviously dead, his plane having vanished forever beneath the blue Caribbean waters that lay under his flight path and the Revolution had lost one of its most charismatic and popular figures.*

In November, Fidel continued to consolidate his power base. He succeeded in cobbling together "unity" in the CTC labor confederation at the expense of the July 26 anti-Communists by imposing his own executive committee and ending the members' right to vote for delegates, paving the way for the CTC's gradual takeover by the Cuban Communist party. The creation of the "National Revolutionary Militias" was announced, the first step in the realization of Che's dream to convert Cuba into a "guerrilla society." Foreign Minister Roa denied an article by Carlos Franqui in *Revolución* that indicated Soviet Deputy Premier Mikoyan had been invited to Cuba.

It was just as well that Mikoyan's planned November visit had been postponed, for when the Catholic laymen's congress took place, it became an open demonstration of clerical opposition to Communism. Although its ecclesiastical hierarchy had so far maintained a public "wait and see" posture, the church was increasingly alarmed about the trend in the revolution, and its youthful militants had no such qualms about keeping quiet. Already, a few priests had begun to flee, reappearing amid great waves of publicity in Miami, where they echoed Díaz Lanz's claims that Cuba was going "Red." In Washington, meanwhile, the Central Intelligence Agency had quietly begun to study the ways and means of getting rid of Fidel Castro.

III

After Che's uncertain beginning at INRA, things began to move along. In late 1959, most of Cuba's industry, both small and large, was still in private hands, and his department's only possessions were a few small factories either

---

*The truth of what happened to Camilo Cienfuegos may never be known, but it is clear that Che never suspected Fidel in his disappearance. Che had a deep affection for Camilo; not only did he name his firstborn son after him, but when he left Cuba, the only picture hanging on the wall of his private study was a portrait of Camilo. If Che had ever suspected Fidel of complicity in Camilo's death, it seems highly improbable he would have remained loyally at Fidel's side for the next five years.

abandoned by their owners or confiscated for belonging to Batista and his associates. These fell under Che's new authority, and handpicked rebel army veterans were dispatched to administer them, just as they were being put in charge of the new agrarian cooperatives on the expropriated *latifundios*.

Using his contacts with the Chilean Communist party, Che now had a small team of economists from Chile and Ecuador working for him. More Cubans came in, some accountants were hired, and work began on a plan for the industrial development of Cuba. Since the early weeks, when Borrego had sweated over annual statistical reports to get a grasp of the Cuban industrial landscape, at least an agenda had gradually begun to evolve.

"Then very soon the first interventions of factories began," recalled Borrego. "These were interventions, *not* nationalizations. These were factories with labor conflicts, or because . . . the capitalists running them were doubtful about the revolutionary process and weren't investing . . . and so they were intervened."

The interventions were made *legal* through a resolution adopted by the Ministry of Labor—now in the safe hands of Augusto Martínez Sánchez, Raúl's former aide—allowing Che's department to intervene and administer factories for as long as necessary; nonetheless, Borrego said he never imagined the interventions would be permanent.

"Of course," he added, "to Che's way of thinking they [the takeovers] were definitive, but that wasn't legally declared yet." It was Borrego's job to operate these new properties, and his first headache was in finding people to run them. "We started naming some administrators. Basically we chose them from among those [men] of the rebel army whose schooling wasn't too low. When I talk about schooling, I mean men who had completed sixth grade or more. They had a very low cultural level, and [with such men] we began to administer the industries."

The previous April, Che had estimated that more than 80 percent of Fidel's rebels were illiterate. His literacy campaign at La Cabaña had been designed to eradicate the problem, but, for the most part, in late 1959 the military was still made up of semiliterate or very recently tutored *guajiros,* many of them little more than teenagers. When they were dispatched to run the factories, an inevitable series of disasters and chaos ensued. All the while, Che was cramming to overcome his own lack of economic knowledge. He studied economics with a Mexican economist, Juan Noyola. At his request, Dr. Vilaseca was teaching him advanced mathematics. Beginning in September, Vilaseca began coming over to the INRA office every Tuesday and Saturday morning at eight to give Che, García Vals, and Patojo an hour-long math class. For Vilaseca, the classes were the start of his day; for Che, they were a way to unwind before going home after working through the entire night. They began with algebra and trigonometry, and soon they went on to analytical geometry.

IV

Che loved retelling the joke of how he'd gotten the bank job. Supposedly, at the cabinet meeting held to decide on a replacement for Pazos—who had been ousted after protesting Matos's arrest—Fidel said that what he needed was a good *"economista."* Fidel was surprised when Che raised his hand. "But Che, I didn't know you were an economist!" Che replied, "Oh, I thought you said you needed a good *comunista*." Humor aside, Che's appointment sent a flurry of cold shivers throughout the financial and business community, and few believed Fidel's glib reassurances that Che would be "as conservative as" his predecessor.

When Che took over at the bank—a colonnaded stone building on a narrow street of Old Havana—he found a lot of empty desks; most of the senior staff had resigned along with Pazos.* Che called Dr. Vilaseca and asked him to become the bank's administrator, his deputy.

Vilaseca balked. Not only did he lack any experience in finance, but he was a personal friend of the man he was supposed to replace, "someone extraordinarily capable in banking." He tried to decline the post, but Che was adamant; in fact, he was not so much asking Vilaseca as ordering. "I don't know anything about banks, either, and I'm the president," Che told him. "But when the revolution names you to a post, you have to accept it, and then do it well." Vilaseca accepted the job.

One of the first people Che called in to the bank was Nicolás Quintana. He was a thirty-five-year-old Havana architect whose firm had been assigned funds by Pazos to build a new thirty-two-story National Bank building—an American-style skyscraper—on a site overlooking the seaside Malecón in central Havana. It was a huge project, the biggest construction scheme under way in Cuba, and was to cost an estimated sixteen million dollars. By late 1959, the bank's foundations had just been laid and the first phase of construction begun.

---

*The ministers who sided with Pazos in the Matos affair were unceremoniously fired. They were Justo Carrillo, Manuel Ray, and Che's old nemesis Faustino Pérez. Camilo's brother Osmany Cienfuegos, a longtime PSP member, replaced Ray, and a brother-in-law of Raúl's wife, Vílma Espín, took over Faustino's job. But while Pazos, Carrilo, and Ray eventually left Cuba, Pérez stayed on and soon regained Fidel's favor.

Following his firing and reassignment to an ambassadorship abroad, Pazos had urgently called Quintana. He'd confided that he was planning to seek asylum as soon as he got to Europe, and told Quintana why. "What they are doing to the country is a barbarity. You're going to inherit a new [National Bank] president, and his name is Che Guevara. He's not qualified for the post, and that's one of the reaons I'm going into exile. You're going to have to go, too; it's inevitable."

Quintana thought otherwise. He was young, involved in the biggest architectural project of his career, and believed that the help he had provided to the rebels during the war could help him with Che. In late 1958, he had given the July 26 Movement topographical maps of the Escambray area for use by Che, and surely this was a point in his favor.

After a summons, Quintana went to see Che at the bank and was shocked at the difference he saw. The once-pristine financial building was "dirty and disorganized," with papers lying all over the floor. "In fifteen days, everything had changed."

The first thing Che asked him was "Are you a petit bourgeois?" Quintana answered: "No, I'm not." "No? So, you're a revolutionary." "No, Comandante, I haven't said I'm a revolutionary. I am a *gran* bourgeois. My *shopkeeper* is a bourgeois." Che's eyes warmed, and, looking pleased, he said: "You're the only honest person of your class I've met since I got here." Quintana thought he'd won Guevara over, and replied in the same witty fashion, "No, there are many, the problem is that you don't give them a chance to talk." Che's expression froze, and he told Quintana to remember that he was speaking to "Comandante Guevara." Quintana realized that he had pushed his limits.

For a second meeting, Quintana and his senior partner returned with the building plans and specifications that required Guevara's approval; the funds, after all, were coming from the National Bank. Quintana showed Guevara the list of materials that had to be imported, and explained that the exposed seafront building would need hurricane-proof windows with rust-proof stainless steel frames; he recommended the elevators be bought from the American firm, Otis, which had offices in Havana.

Che listened to Quintana's suggestions and finally asked: "Why elevators?" Quintana explained that the building would be be thirty-two stories high. Che said he thought stairs would do; if *he* could climb them, with his asthma, why couldn't everyone else? At this, Quintana's partner got up and left the meeting in disgust, but the younger architect persisted.

They returned to the matter of the windows. Che asked Quintana why they had to come from the United States or Germany; why couldn't something cheaper be found, perhaps made from plastic, right in Havana? Next they talked about the number of lavatories proposed; Che looked at the figures and said: "Well, we can eliminate at least half of them."

"But in revolutions," Quintana pointed out, "people go to the bathroom just as much as before it." "Not the *new man*," Che countered, "he can sacrifice." When the architect tried to return once again to the matter of the hurricane-proof windows, Che finally cut him off: "Look, Quintana. For the shit we're going to be guarding here within three years, it's preferable that the wind takes the lot."

Quintana finally understood. This wasn't about windows or toilets; Che didn't want the new bank at all. "He was sending me a message, that the system was going to change so absolutely that everything we were talking about was unnecessary. They were not going to make that building."

Quintana was right. The new National Bank was never built. Instead, the work Quintana had begun was frozen, and, some years later, the Hermanos Ameijeiras Hospital was built in its place. Before long, new Cuban ten- and twenty-peso banknotes were issued. As president of Cuba's National Bank, it was Che's job to sign them—which he did, writing simply and dismissively, "Che." To Cuban businessmen, the symbolism of Guevara's gesture was quickly understood and bitterly resented. In the new Cuba, money was no longer a hallowed commodity but an onerous vestige of the soon-to-disappear era of capitalist private enterprise.

23

"Individualism Must Disappear"

I

The Matos "sedition" trial took place in December, and it quickly turned bitter and ugly, with both Raúl and Fidel intervening personally to accuse Matos. As he invariably did on such occasions, Raúl called for Matos's execution, and so did the prosecutor, Major Jorge "Papito" Serguera. Instead, the judges, all handpicked army officers and revolutionary veterans, sentenced Matos to twenty years in prison and gave his junior officers lesser sentences. That month, several other men were also tried, sentenced, and executed for counterrevolution. Rafael del Pino, Fidel's old friend and companion during the 1948 *"Bogotazo,"* was caught, charged with aiding *batístianos* fleeing the country, and given thirty years.

As he had promised Alexandr Alexiev over vodka and caviar, Fidel also began to wage battle against the "reactionary press" in Cuba. The conservative daily, *Avance,* was "intervened" after its editor fled the country; Fidel had accused him of siding with "the counterrevolution" for printing Díaz Lanz's accusations. Cuba's second television channel, 12, was intervened, too. *El Mundo* was taken over and put under the editorship of a Fidelísta journalist, Luis Wangüemert. The operation to close down the opposition mouthpiece, *Diario de la Marina,* and the rest of Cuba's independent press would come soon.

For now, the editors of *Bohemia* and *Revolución* remained publicly loyal, although they too were becoming unsettled about Fidel's accommodation with the Communists. Cuba's own international wire agency, Prensa Latina, was now up and running under the committed editorship of Jorge Ricardo Masetti, with bureaus opening around the hemisphere, doing battle to combat the reports put out by the AP and UPI, the two U.S. news agencies most galling to Che and Fidel.

The newspaper takeovers were aided by the printers' and journalists' unions, now in the hands of Fidelistas and functioning as pro-government strike forces in the surviving private media outlets. The CTC purge had continued over David Salvador's protestations, spearheaded by the Communists now on its executive committee. Even in the Union of Graphic Artists, there was purging to be done; the Communist actress Violeta Casals, Alexiev's initial contact for Che, became the new head of the union after her predecessor was accused of being a "counterrevolutionary" and fled the country.

Che's overseas mission of the previous summer had also begun showing some public dividends. Since the autumn, official diplomatic and trade delegations from Japan, Indonesia, and Egypt had begun visiting the island. A few trade agreements were signed, more significant for their symbolism than their commercial benefits. And since his return, Che had kept up a steady stream of articles about the countries he had visited, to be published in *Verde Olivo* and the magazine *Humanismo,* but his writings took on a more blatantly political hue.

In an article in the September-October issue of *Humanismo* called "America from the Afro-Asian Balcony," Che wrote that the common bond shared by Cuba with the newly independent former colonial states was the dream of freedom from economic exploitation. He argued that revolutionary Cuba, personified by Fidel Castro, was a model for change not only in Latin America but in Asia and Africa as well. He called for an international anti-imperialist alliance. Fidel, he seemed to be saying, could be its leader.

> . . . Might it not be that our fraternity can defy the breadth of the seas, the rigors of language and the lack of cultural ties, to lose ourselves in the embrace of a fellow struggler? . . .
>
> . . . Cuba has been invited to the new Afro-Asian People's Conference. [And Cuba will go] to say that it is true, that Cuba exists and that Fidel Castro is a man, a popular hero and not a mythological abstraction; but it will also go to explain that Cuba is not an isolated event, merely the first signal of America's awakening. . . .
>
> [And when they ask]: "Are you the members of the Guerrilla Army that is leading the struggle for the liberation of America? Are you, then, our allies on the other side of the sea?" I must say [to them] and to all the hundreds of millions of Afro-Asians that . . . I am one brother more, one more among the multitudes of brothers in this part of the world that awaits with infinite anxiety the moment [when we can] consolidate the bloc that will

destroy, once and for all, the anachronistic presence of colonial domination.

The notion of projecting himself onto the world stage made great sense to Fidel. With a climactic intensity, independence was sweeping Africa and Asia. Since 1957, a dozen new nations had won their independence from French, British, and Belgian colonial rule. Others, such as the Algerians, were having to wage war for it, but the trend was clear: The days of colonial rule were over, and the future was in the hands of men who had faced down the dying empires, men such as Nasser, Sukarno—why not Fidel himself? In January Foreign Minister Raúl Roa flew off to Asia and North Africa to extend Cuba's invitation to attend an international congress of developing nations, to be held in Havana.

The first anecdotal articles of Che's experiences in the guerrilla war, eventually compiled and published as *Episodes of the Cuban Revolutionary War,* had also begun appearing in print. In November, his tragic story "The Murdered Puppy" was published in *Humanismo*. Coinciding, as it did, with the intensifying pace of land expropriations and the resumption of the revolutionary firing squads, the story's real-life allegory—about the necessary sacrifice of innocents in a revolutionary cause—must have made disquieting reading for some Cubans.

II

By January, the architect Nicolás Quintana had come to the conclusion that the future looked bleak for him in Cuba. The revolution had moved sharply to the left, alienating him and most of his social class. His personal dream of building the National Bank had been dashed, while a close friend of his, a member of the *Juventud Católica,* had just been shot by a firing squad for distributing anti-Communist leaflets. Quintana went to see Che to complain. It was to be a shattering encounter.

As Quintana recalled: "Che told me: 'Look, revolutions are ugly but necessary, and part of that revolutionary process is in justice at the service of future justice.' I will never be able to forget that phrase. I replied that that was Thomas More's *Utopia.* I said that we [mankind] had been fucked by that tale for a long time, for believing that we would achieve something not *now,* but in the future. Che looked at me for a long time and said: 'So. You don't believe in the future of the revolution.' I told him I didn't believe in anything that was based upon an injustice."

Che then asked him, "Even if that injustice is sanitary?" To which Quintana replied: "For those who die I don't believe you can talk of sanitary injustice." Che's response was immediate: "You have to leave Cuba. You have three choices: You leave Cuba and there's no problem from me; or thirty years [in prison], in the near future; or the firing squad."

Dumbstruck and horrified, Quintana sat frozen in his chair, and Che added, "You are doing very strange things."

"I didn't say anything," Quintana said, "but knew what he was referring to. What surprised me is that he already *knew,* that really surprised me."

Quintana belonged to a group of professionals who had formed an organization they called Trabajo Voluntario (Voluntary Work), ostensibly dedicated to carrying out civic works, but its real purpose was to organize an anti-Castro opposition. "It was an excuse to meet at night and talk, well . . . you know . . . about what we were going to do about this [the revolution] . . ." After Che's warning, Quintana realized he was not going to be doing very much at all, and, within a few weeks, he fled the island.

Around the same time, José Pardo Llada, the television commentator who had had such a troublesome journey with Che the previous summer, called on the new National Bank president to take up the case of a friend, tobacco expert Napoleón Padilla.

After his INRA appointment, Che had asked Padilla to come and work for him at INRA, organizing tobacco cooperatives in Pinar del Río. Oddly, in light of his fear and dislike of Guevara's "Communism," which he had already denounced to the U.S. embassy, Padilla had agreed. Since then, he had worked at INRA, setting up the cooperatives, assisting in a large sale of export tobacco, and, at Che's behest, teaching a training course in "business administration."

But Padilla had become increasingly uncomfortable about what he saw at INRA, and argued with Nuñez Jiménez and the PSP's Oscar Pino Santos, now a top INRA official, over the way they were implementing the agrarian reform. Finally, he had exploded and accused Pino Santos of "practising Communism." From that day onward, Padilla had begun feeling frozen out of things. Then, on the evening of January 26, an anonymous phone caller had warned him: "Napoleon, hide yourself right away, they're going to arrest you." The caller had hung up, and, terrified, Padilla drove to the Honduran embassy to ask for political asylum. The ambassador had advised him to try to find out what his real status was before he took such an extreme step, and Padilla had called Pardo Llada to ask for his help.

At the National Bank offices, Pardo asked Guevara if Padilla had a problem with the authorities. Che showed him a piece of paper. It was a written affidavit signed by an army sergeant at the tobacco cooperative where

Padilla worked, accusing Padilla of being a "counterrevolutionary," and of "speaking ill" about Che's wife Aleida.

Pardo expressed his surprise that Che paid any attention to such petty gossip, to which Che revealed his hand. He also happened to know, he told Pardo, that Padilla met frequently with the U.S. embassy's agricultural attaché, and that he had also spoken negatively about the government in front of INRA officials. Pardo still insisted these weren't reasons to persecute Padilla. "All right," Che told him. "He can resign and leave INRA. And if he wants to leave the country, he can go join his gringo friends!" Che's word was good. Six months later—"with Che's express permission," acknowledged Pardo—Padilla was allowed to leave Cuba, taking his car and furniture with him, on the ferry boat to Miami.

III

Fidel had dubbed 1960 "The Year of Agrarian Reform," but a better label might have been "The Year of Confrontation." The month leading up to Mikoyan's visit saw a rapid deterioration in U.S.-Cuban relations and an open acceleration of Cuba's "socialization." A tit-for-tat war began in early January with a note of protest sent by Secretary of State Herter over the "illegal seizures" of American-owned property, for which no compensation had been paid. Cuba responded by seizing *all* large cattle ranches and *all* sugar plantations in the country, including those owned by Americans. More unidentified airplanes flew out of the United States, firebombing Cuban cane fields. The sabotage runs were being organized by the CIA, which was now planning to train a Cuban exile force for an eventual guerrilla campaign against Castro.

Reaction in Washington was being fueled by domestic politics as well. President Eisenhower was in the final year of his second term as president, and the early presidential campaign jockeying to succeed him had already begun. In opening his campaign, Vice President Richard Nixon used Cuba as a rallying cry, warning Castro that he could be punished for his actions, including having his sugar quota with the United States cut. Fidel responded with customary defiance; on January 19, INRA announced the immediate confiscation of "all *latifúndia,*" both Cuban and foreign-owned, in the country. The edict put every large remaining agrarian holding in the revolution's hands.

Next, a bizarre altercation between Spanish Ambassador Juan Pablo de Lojendio and Fidel occurred on live television, after Fidel insinuated during a speech that Spain's embassy was implicated in a covert U.S. program to smuggle anti-Castroites out of the island. The indignant ambassador stormed into the television studios while Fidel was still on the air to accuse Fidel of slander. A shouting match ensued until the apoplectic envoy was forcibly escorted out of the building. Fidel resumed his television speech by announcing that Lojendio had twenty-four hours to abandon Cuba, before veering off into a new rant against the United States. Secretary of State Herter reacted by going to Capitol Hill to request passage of a bill that would give Eisenhower the power to alter Cuba's sugar quota, then recalled Ambassador Bonsal "indefinitely" to Washington.

In the last week of January, there was one final attempt to find a way out of the spiraling crisis. On January 21, Eisenhower issued a statement calling for negotiations to halt further deterioration in the relations between the two nations. That same day in Havana, acting chargé d'affaires Daniel Braddock asked Argentine Ambassador Julio Amoeda to serve as intermediary between his government and Castro. Amoeda agreed and went to see Fidel with an American proposal: If Fidel stopped the anti-American attacks and met with Bonsal, Washington would consider extending economic aid to Cuba. After first refusing, Fidel relented, telling Amoeda he would halt the press campaign. Osvaldo Dorticós, the Cuban figurehead president, followed up the next day with a declaration that Cuba wished to keep and strengthen its "traditional friendship" with the United States.

The truce held: In Fidel's next speech on January 28, he did not mention the United States at all. The temporary back-down gave him breathing space before the next round, which he knew would be very soon in coming. On January 31, Cuba's government finally acknowledged the truth of the long-standing rumors and announced the imminent arrival of Soviet Deputy Premier Anastas Mikoyan.

IV

The Soviet trade fair turned out to be a great success. Over a hundred thousand Cubans visited during its three-week stay to view its *Sputnik* replica, the models of Soviet homes, factories, and sports facilities, its tractors and displays of farm and industrial equipment. These were the technological achievements of the nation that Nikita Khrushchev had told Americans would "bury" them in the not too distant future, and, to the average untraveled Cuban in early 1960, such claims were credible. After all, hadn't the Russians been the first country to put a satellite—even a live dog—into orbit?

Not all Cubans were impressed. Mikoyan's visit was attended by some angry demonstrations, and Cuba's independent media waged an unstinting campaign to attack him and expose the inequities and inefficiencies of the Soviet system. Throughout his stay, nocturnal incursions by small planes based in the United States, attacking Cuban sugar mills and cane fields, continued without letup.

When, in late February, one of the marauding planes crashed on Cuban soil, and the identity papers of one of the dead showed him to be an American citizen, Fidel cited it as evidence of U.S. complicity in the attacks. When the news broke, CIA Director Allen Dulles acknowledged to the blissfully uninformed Eisenhower that the dead man and those piloting the other sabotage missions were in fact CIA hirelings. In mid-February, Eisenhower had publicly ordered Customs to halt and prosecute any Cuba-bound illegal flights leaving from the United States. But now, he privately urged Dulles to come up with a more comprehensive plan to overthrow Castro.

Only five days earlier, on February 13, the Soviets and Cubans had made public the terms of their new "commercial agreement." The Soviets had agreed to buy almost half a million tons of sugar during 1960, and would buy a million tons per year for the next four years, in return for which Cuba would receive not cash, but Soviet products, including oil. In the fifth and final year of the agreement, Moscow would pay cash. Cuba was also to receive a hundred-million-dollar credit at a bargain-basement 2.5 percent interest rate over ten years for the purchase of machinery and factory buildings— to wit, financing Che's "industrialization" scheme. As for Fidel's dream of draining the Ciénaga de Zapáta swamp, which he promptly showed to Mikoyan by helicopter, Mikoyan promised Soviet technical assistance.

Fidel and Che crowed happily about the new deal, calling it a further step toward the "economic independence" of Cuba. Overshadowed by Mikoyan's presence, Polish and East German trade delegations arrived and signed their own trade deals with Cuba, and not far behind came the Czechs and the Chinese.

On February 20, fulfilling another of Che's recent public pronouncements, the era of Soviet-style "central planning" was ushered into being with the announced creation of JUCEPLAN, the Junta Central de Planificación. Fidel was its chairman, and Che, its main proponent, was on its Concejo de Dirección, or Management Council. In case anyone had missed the point in Che's recent speeches, Cuba was going to have a command economy.

The Soviet deputy premier's son, Sergo Mikoyan, accompanied his father on most of his peregrinations around the island and was able to observe Cuba's leaders closely; right away, he noticed the difference between Che and Fidel. After reading of the Argentine's past exploits, he had expected to meet "a manic guerrilla," a kind of fire-eating Latin American Bolshevik, but Che didn't fit the image. "I now saw a man who was very silent, with very tender eyes," Sergo recalled. "You feel a little distance when you talk with Fidel [because] . . . he almost doesn't listen to you, but with Che one didn't feel that. Although I had expected him to be the obstinate one, I realized he wasn't stubborn, but inclined to talk, to discuss, and to listen."

The high point of Mikoyan's tour was the obligatory visit to the city of Santiago and Fidel's old Sierra Maestra *comandancia* at La Plata. The whole entourage traveled to Oriente, but it was a select group that went up to La Plata: Mikoyan, Sergo, and Leonov; Fidel, Che, and their bodyguards. The press corps was left behind in Santiago.

Fidel had planned for them to spend the night at La Plata but found nothing had been prepared for their arrival. Some workers were there building huts, but they had not finished the job, and there were only a few tents. Fidel was embarrassed and angry, but Mikoyan told him not to worry, that he was not averse to sleeping in a tent. His son Sergo, however, decided to leave and take advantage of the opportunity to see Santiago. He later heard from his father what happened that night. After he had gone, Fidel and Che spoke openly with Mikoyan about their desire to create a socialist revolution, the problems they faced in doing so, and their need for Soviet aid to carry it off.

"It was a very strange chat," said Sergo Mikoyan. "They told [my father] that they could survive only with Soviet help, and they would have to hide the fact from the capitalists in Cuba. . . . [Then] Fidel said, 'We will have to withstand these conditions in Cuba for five or ten more years,' at which Che interrupted and told him: 'If you don't do it within two or three years, you're finished.' There was this difference [of conception] between them."

Fidel then launched into a soliloquy about how his rebel victory had proven Marx wrong. "Fidel said that according to Marx, the revolution could not have happened except along the paths proposed by his Communist party and 'our' [Cuban] Communist party . . . mass struggle, strikes, and so forth. 'But we did it, [Fidel said], not them! So we have overtaken Marx, we have proven him wrong.' My father contradicted him, he said: 'You think this way because your Communists are dogmatic; they think Marxism is just A, B,C, and D. But Marxism is a *way,* not a dogma. So I don't think you have proven Marx wrong, I think you have proven *your* Communists wrong.'"

They didn't talk directly about military aid, said Mikoyan, but they *did* ask for Soviet economic aid. "They explained that if they didn't receive it they were damned, due to two considerations. First, American imperialism. Second, the struggle with their own capitalists."

After this talk, everyone understood that the commercial agreement they announced a few days later was merely to be the first step in the reestablishment of full relations between Cuba and the Soviet Union. For now, it was all Fidel dared risk. Nonetheless, Alexiev, who hadn't gone to La Plata, was surprised to learn that Che and Fidel hadn't asked to buy Soviet arms. "They talked with Mikoyan about everything but arms . . . which was a little strange. In Mexico [even] Mikoyan said that he thought Fidel might request arms."

It was a logical presumption. Over the past year, Fidel had sent emissaries all over the world to buy airplanes and weapons, but had managed to buy only some of what he wanted in Belgium and Italy. His requests to Washington for airplanes had been predictably spurned, and the unwillingness of Great Britain and several other countries to sign arms deals was probably due to U.S. pressure, as well. Lately, in his speeches, defiant phrases such as "Cuba reserves the right to defend itself" and "Cuba will get the arms it needs wherever it has to buy them" had become a familar refrain.

Very soon, however, the subject was raised. On March 4, the French freighter *La Coubre,* which had just been towed into a dock in Havana harbor, exploded in a horrendous blast heard all over downtown. When the first explosion occurred, Jorge Enrique Mendoza, INRA's chief in Camagüey, was in a meeting with Fidel and the agency's other provincial bosses at the INRA building. Rushing to the port, they were starting down the wharf where *La Coubre* was docked when Mendoza saw Che hurry past him toward the burning ship.

Just as Che neared the ship, and with Mendoza, Fidel, and the others about a hundred meters back (300-odd feet), there was a terrific second explosion. Mendoza and some other men immediately threw themselves on top of Fidel, to protect him. Mendoza recalled, "Fidel began to kick and punch and yell: 'Damnit, you're suffocating me!' Then things began falling from the air." Mendoza turned to Raúl and urged him to take Fidel away for fear of another explosion; according to Mendoza, Raúl had to practically take Fidel prisoner to evacuate him. With Fidel safely out of the way, Mendoza turned his attention to Che, who was still trying to board the burning ship. "I walked quickly over to where he was. Someone, I don't remember who, was trying to stop him from getting on the ship, and I could hear Che say: 'Damnit, don't fuck with me! There's been two explosions; everything that was going to explode has exploded. Let me go on the ship!' And in he went."

It was a carnage. Up to a hundred people had been killed, mostly stevedores, sailors, and army soldiers, and several hundred others had been injured. *La Coubre* had been loaded with Belgian weapons bought by Fidel's arms-purchasers, and somehow the cargo had ignited. Fidel immediately accused the CIA of sabotage and invoked a new battle cry—*"Patria o Muerte!"*

The next day, Fidel and Che linked arms in martial fraternity at the head of the funeral cortege as it wended its way along the Malecón. Later, as Fidel spoke to the crowd from a balcony, flanked by the other revolutionary leaders, a young Cuban photographer named Alberto Korda found a good vantage point from which to take pictures. Finding Che in his lens, Korda focused and was stunned at the expression on Che's face. It was one of absolute implacability. He snapped, and the photo soon went around the world, eventually becoming the famous poster image that would adorn so many college dorm rooms. In it, Che appears as the ultimate revolutionary icon, his eyes seeming to stare boldly into the future, his very face symbolizing a virile embodiment of outrage at social injustice.

Not long afterward, Fidel called up Alexiev and asked to meet with him at Nuñez Jiménez's home in La Cabaña. "For the first time," said Alexiev, "Fidel spoke of arms. He said that after the explosion the [American] intervention might be inevitable, imminent. 'We have to arm the people,' [he said], and he wanted the Soviet Union to sell him some weapons he needed. He spoke of arms [such as] light machine guns, and said: 'You could bring these arms in a submarine. We have a lot of caves along the coast and we can hide them where nobody can know about them. Send a message to Khrushchev.'"

By then, a Soviet commercial mission had already established itself in Havana, and among its members was a cryptographer who handled communications with the Kremlin. After his meeting with Fidel, Alexiev went straight to the cryptographer. "I sent the message direct from Fidel to Khrushchev, and I thought that because of our bureaucracy it would take several weeks to get a reply. The very next day the reply came from Khrushchev, which said: 'Fidel, we share your worries about the defense of Cuba and the possibility of an attack, and we will supply you with the arms you need. But why do we have to hide them and take them in a submarine if Cuba is a sovereign nation and you can buy whatever arms you need without hiding the fact?' That was his reply. And the arms began to arrive."

V

On May 8, Fidel announced the reestablishment of diplomatic relations with Moscow. Former Directorio leader Faure Chomón, who had moved sharply to the left since the rebel victory, flew off to Moscow as Cuba's new ambassador. For its own envoy, Moscow named a veteran KGB man who worked under diplomatic cover, Sergei Kudriatzov. Alexiev, his TASS identity no longer necessary, was made his first secretary and cultural attaché, his traditional KGB cover.

Following the exchange of messages between Fidel and Khrushchev, a Soviet military delegation had quietly arrived in Havana. "We talked right away," said Alexiev. "Fidel, Raúl, Che—everyone participated. They outlined everything they needed. Above all they needed antiaircraft [guns] and planes, artillery, T-34 tanks, old ones that weren't of any use anymore in the Soviet Union. A[nother] delegation came and they talked of prices, although this wasn't really commerce."

By June or July, Soviet arms and military advisors were surreptitiously entering Cuba. According to Alexiev, Fidel was still nervous about the U.S. reaction—as were the Soviets—so some of the Soviet advisors came in on Czech passports.

The secret military agreement with the Soviets signed, Fidel felt strong enough to take on the Americans. In fact, immediately after the Soviet trade deal had been signed in February, he had begun pushing on the tentative detente initiated by Washington. In response to the State Department's overture of late January, which had been left in limbo during Mikoyan's visit, Foreign Minister Roa sent a note to Washington giving Cuba's "conditions" for talks. As long as Washington threatened cutting Cuba's sugar quota, there could be no negotiations. In its February 29 response, the State Department refused to back down, insisting the United States had the right to take any measures it felt necessary to protect American interests. When *La Coubre* exploded four days later, the exchange turned bitter again. Secretary of State Herter responded angrily to Fidel's charges of CIA complicity in the tragedy and questioned Cuba's "good faith" in continuing negotiations.

In the midst of all this activity, Washington made one final attempt to reach out to Fidel. In early March, Cuba's finance minister, Rufo López Fresquet, was approached by Mario Lazo, a U.S. embassy legal advisor, to tell him that the United States was willing to offer Cuba military planes and technical assistance. Fidel asked for two days to consider the offer. On March 17, President Dorticós told López Fresquet on behalf of Fidel that he had decided not to accept. Realizing what this rebuff signified, López Fresquet, the last of the old-style ministers, immediately resigned his office and left for the United States. He could not have known it, but his middleman's mission undoubtedly had coincided with—or had precipitated—Fidel's request for Soviet arms. If Fidel still had entertained any last-minute qualms about the course on which he was now embarked, Nikita Khrushchev's rapid response had dissolved them.

On the same day as Fidel's rebuff, Eisenhower approved the CIA plan to covertly recruit and train an armed force of several hundred Cuban exiles to lead a guerrilla war against Castro. CIA Director Dulles planned to model the operation after the aptly named Operation Success, the undermining of the Arbenz regime in Guatemala in 1954. He put his deputy director for planning, Richard Bissell, architect of the U-2 spyplane project, in command of the Cuba "task force." Other members of the team included Tracy Barnes, a covert operations veteran who had been instrumental in Operation Success; and Howard Hunt, the CIA's gung ho station chief in Montevideo. A skeptical member of the team was the Agency's Western Hemisphere division chief, J. C. King, who warned that "Cuba was not Guatemala"; King preferred a "dirty war" to destabilize the Cuban regime and advocated the assassinations of top figures such as Che, Raúl, and Fidel. But Dulles had overruled this option in favor of building up the anti-Castro forces and helping them "get a foothold" in Cuba.

Garry Drecher (aka Frank Bender), the CIA's Latin American Communist specialist, was sent to Miami to recruit Cuban fighters among the exile community. Drecher soon arranged for the fighters to be trained at a secret site in Guatemala, with the collusion of Guatemala's military president, General Ydigoras Fuentes.

A few days later, Che denounced the sugar quota as "economic slavery" for the Cuba people. By paying a higher-than-market-rate price for sugar, Castro argued, the United States obliged Cuba to maintain a single-crop economy instead of diversifying, a vicious cycle that in turn made Cuba dependent on U.S. imports. This attack on the sugar-quota system directly undercut one of Fidel's chief battle standards of the moment—after all, he was decrying the threatened cut of the U.S. sugar quota as an example of American "economic agression"—but, significantly, he did not counter Che's remark.

Meanwhile, Fidel kept moving against the media. The CMQ television station owners fled the country, and their station became government property. At the same time, the Ministry of Labor had begun to usurp most of the CTC's functions; the ministry, not the unions, now dictated working terms and conditions, while the CTC was rapidly becoming a mere supervisory agency.

VI

The face of Havana was changing dramatically. The days of privilege for Cuba's upper and middle classes were coming to an end, and increasing numbers of them were leaving on the ferries and shuttle flights to Miami. As many as sixty thousand had already fled by the late spring of 1960. The city that a year before had still been an American playground of exclusive yacht clubs, private beaches, casinos, and brothels—and whites-only neighborhoods —was disappearing. The roulette wheels were still spinning in the big hotels, but most of the prostitutes were off the streets. Instead, uniformed and armed blacks and *guajiros* chanting revolutionary slogans roamed the city.

A very different type of visitor was taking their place. Trade and cultural delegations were arriving from socialist-bloc nations, along with a growing stream of current and future Third World leaders; delegates to an international Communist youth congress filled hotels now emptied of weekending American tourists and businessmen. Left-wing European and Latin American intellectuals flocked to Havana to attend cultural congresses laid on by the revolution. Among the visitors were Jean-Paul Sartre and Simone de Beauvoir, who had been invited by Carlos Franqui.

Che's mystique had grown, and when the famous French couple went to see him, they talked for hours. For Che, it must have been a very gratifying experience, playing host to the renowned French philosopher whose works he had grown up reading. For his part, Sartre came away extremely impressed and after Guevara's death, gave him the highest possible tribute; to the Frenchman, Che was "not only an intellectual but also the most complete human being of our age."

Their visit had coincided with the *La Coubre* tragedy, and Sartre and de Beauvoir witnessed the funerals and Fidel's two-hour speech the next day. Afterward, they walked through the streets of Old Havana, where they saw the public fund-raising campaign already under way for a new consignment of arms. De Beauvoir was bewitched by the sensual, fervent mood.

"Young women stood selling fruit juice and snacks to raise money for the State," she wrote in her memoir. "Well-known performers danced or sang in the squares to swell the fund; pretty girls in their carnival fancy dresses, led by a band, went through the streets making collections. 'It's the honeymoon of the Revolution,' Sartre said to me. No machinery, no bureaucracy, but a direct contact between leaders and people, and a mass of seething and slightly confused hopes. It wouldn't last forever, but it was a comforting sight. For the first time in our lives, we were witnessing happiness that had been attained by violence."

On March 23, Che gave a televised speech called "Political Sovereignty and Economic Independence." Through the revolutionary seizure of power, he said, Cuba had attained its political independence but had not yet won its economic independence, without which it was not a truly *politically* sovereign nation. This was the revolution's current "strategic objective."

There had been some inroads made against the foreign, mostly U.S.-owned monopolies that had previously held sway over Cuba's economic freedom. The electricity and telephone rates had been cut, rents had been lowered, the large landholdings had been turned over to the people, but the island's oil, mineral, and chemical wealth were still in the Americans' hands.

> It is good to speak clearly. . . . In order to conquer something we have to take it away from somebody. . . . That something we must conquer—the country's sovereignty—has to be taken away from that somebody called monopoly. . . . It means that our road to liberation will be opened up with a victory over the monopolies, and concretely over the U.S. monopolies.

The revolution had to be "radical," and had to "destroy the roots of evil that afflicted Cuba" in order to "eliminate injustice." Those who opposed the revolution's measures, those who resisted losing their privileges, were counterrevolutionaries. The workers of the reigned-in CTC were contributing 4 percent of their wages to the "industrialization" program; it was time the rest of society shouldered its fair share of the revolutionary sacrifice.

Lately Che had been driving home the point that Cuba no longer was just Cuba but was the revolution, and the revolution was the people; going one step further, the people, Cuba, and the revolution were Fidel. It was time to get on board the new ship of state, or get off. Just as the men of the *Granma* had put aside their individual lives, ready to die if necessary in the war against Batista, so now did all Cubans have to sacrifice for the common aim of *total* independence. The enemy might well retaliate, he warned. And when the counterrevolutionary soldiers came—paid for perhaps by those same "monopolies" whose interests were being affected—Cuba's defense would be fought for not by a handful of men but by millions. All of Cuba was now "a Sierra Maestra," and together, Che said, quoting Fidel, "we will all be saved or we will sink."

The "individualistic" university students with their "middle class" mentalities seemed to especially provoke Che; perhaps in the students he saw his self-absorbed former self, and it rankled him. He had given up his self, his "vocation" for the revolution; why couldn't they? In early March he had gone back to Havana University to remind the students that they had a duty to perform in the economic development of Cuba, and there could be no duality of principles, with the students separated from the revolution. An individual's sense of "vocation" alone wasn't justification for deciding a career; a sense of revolutionary duty should and would take its place. He used himself as an example:

> I don't think that an individual example, statistically speaking, has any importance, but I began my career studying engineering, I finished as a doctor, later I have been a comandante and now you see me here as a speaker. . . . That is to say, within one's individual characteristics, vocation doesn't play a determinant role. . . . I think one has to constantly think on behalf of masses and not on behalf of individuals. . . . It's criminal to think of individuals because the needs of the individual become completely weakened in the face of the needs of the human conglomeration.

In practical terms, this meant certain faculties would be expanded, others would be collapsed. Humanities, for instance, was a field that would be reduced to the "minimum necessary for the cultural development of the country."

In April, Che's guerrilla warfare manual, *Guerra de Guerrillas,* was published by INRA's Department of Military Training. He had dedicated the book to Camilo Cienfuegos, and a photograph of Camilo graced the cover; his old comrade was seen astride a horse, holding aloft a rifle, his face beaming under a straw hat. "Camilo," wrote Che, "is the image of the people." Excerpts were widely published in the Cuban media and, before long, not only Cubans but U.S. and Latin American counterinsurgency specialists would be studying the manual with acute interest.

In his prologue, "Essence of the Guerrilla Struggle," Che outlined what he believed to be the cardinal lessons for other revolutionary movements seeking to emulate Cuba's successful guerrilla struggle:

1. Popular forces can win a war against the army.
2. It is not necessary to await for the conditions to be right to begin the revolution; the insurrectional *foco* (guerrilla group) can create them.
3. In underdeveloped Latin America, the armed struggle should be fought mostly in the countryside.

Within Cuba itself, opposition was hardening. An underground movement had begun forming under Manuel Ray, teaching at Havana University since his ouster from government, while another openly dissident quarter was the militant Juventud Católica, ever more vociferous since Mikoyan's visit. In the radicalized countryside, inflamed by uncompensated land seizures and general chaos, violence had broken out. Small counterrevolutionary groups were becoming active, many of them composed of former rebel army men. In Oriente, one of Che's old comrades, Manuel Beatón, had taken up arms against the state, having murdered another of Che's former fighters, evidently for personal reasons, and fled to the Sierra Maestra with twenty armed followers. In Raúl's old turf in the Sierra Cristal, one of *his* former fighters, Higinio Díaz, had gone back to war as well, allying himself with the disaffected July 26 veteran Jorge Sotús, who had led the first rebel reinforcements from Santiago into the mountains in March 1957. They had formed the MRR (Movimiento de Rescate de la Revolución), organizing themselves around Manuel Artime, a former naval academy professor living in exile in Miami. With Artime in Miami, Díaz in the sierra, and a network of underground supporters in Havana, the MRR had quickly come under the benevolent eye of the CIA.

It was not long before Fidel's "listeners" among Cuba's swollen exile community in Miami picked up rumors of the CIA's recruitment drive. In late April Fidel went to the podium to accuse the United States of trying to create an "international front" against him, and warned Washington that Cuba "was not another Guatemala." Guatemalan President Ydigoras Fuentes countered with a public accusation that Che was trying to organize a guerrilla invasion force against his country. On April 25, the two countries broke off relations.

Undeterred by the public fuss, the CIA program continued expanding, including broadcasting anti-Castro propaganda to Cuba from a radio transmitter installed on tiny Swan Island, near the Cayman Islands. The man running the station was David Atlee Phillips, who six years earlier in Guatemala had first brought the agency's attention to Ernesto Guevara.

One of the Cuban exiles to join the CIA's recruitment drive that summer was Felix Rodríguez. He was now nineteen years old and, in the aftermath of the Trinidad invasion fiasco of the year before, had returned to his military academy in Pennsylvania. After graduating in June 1960, he returned to his parents' home in Miami, then ran away to hire on with the CIA program. By September, he would join several hundred other Cuban exiles in Guatemala and begin receiving guerrilla training from a Filipino West Point graduate who had fought both the Japanese and the Communists in his country. Their force would eventually be called Brigade 2506.

On May Day, Fidel spoke to a Plaza de la Revolución packed with armed Cubans marching past his podium. He praised the new militias and, like Che, invoked the threat of an impending invasion; Cubans, like the Spartans, would stand, fight, and die without fear. He also took the opportunity to make two important points clear: If *he* died, Raúl would take his place as prime minister. What's more, there were not going to be any elections; since "the people" ruled Cuba already, there was no need to cast votes. The crowd cheered, repeating the catchphrase *"Revolución Sí, Elecciones No!"* and a new slogan, *"Cuba Sí, Yanqui No!"*

By that May Day, the United States estimated that Cuba's armed forces had doubled to fifty thousand since January 1959, with another fifty thousand civilians already incorporated into the new people's militias—and there was no end in sight. If the training and arming continued unchecked, Cuba would soon have the largest army in Latin America. Washington's private fears that Fidel may have already obtained Soviet military support gained credence on May 3, when the U.S. Senate heard testimony from two Batista-era officers, former Chief of Staff Tabernilla and Colonel Ugalde Carrillo; the latter accused Fidel of building Soviet missile bases in the Ciénaga de Zapata. Cuban Foreign Minister Roa quickly denounced the charge, and few gave it credit at the time, but, within a year, the fantastic notion would become a reality.

Fidel's militaristic May Day rally, and his decision to renew diplomatic relations with the Soviets a week later, sparked the final round between his government and Cuba's last surviving independent media. *Diario de la Marina*'s right-wing editorials compared Castro to "the Antichrist"; within days, its offices were attacked and occupied by "workers," and its presses closed down permanently. Its editor sought asylum and fled the country. By the end of the month, the two main remaining independent dailies, *Prensa Libre* and *El Crisol,* were also put out of circulation, soon to be followed by the English-language *Havana Post* and *La Calle.*

The first Soviet tankers were already crossing the Atlantic with oil for Cuba, fulfilling part of the barter agreement signed with Mikoyan. The U.S.-owned Esso and Texaco, and British-owned Shell, each of which had refineries in Cuba, had until now been supplying the island with oil from Venezuela. But Cuba had not paid for some time, and the outstanding bill amounted to some fifty million dollars. Che Guevara, as president of the National Bank, was the man to see about getting bills paid. But Esso's American manager got a cold reception and no clear answers when he asked Che about the debt.

Che now felt confident enough to take on the U.S. petroleum companies, and he told Alexiev his plan to offer them a deal he knew they would *have* to refuse, giving him the pretext he needed to seize their installations. Alexiev counseled caution, but Che went ahead anyway. On May 17, he informed the American oil firms that in order for him to pay off the debt owed them, they each had to buy three hundred thousand barrels of the Soviet oil that was arriving, and process it in their refineries. The companies did not reply right away but sought counsel in Washington, where the government advised them to reject Che's offer.

The opposition activities continued to grow, and so did the government's crackdown. The members of a rebel group in the Escambray, made up mostly of students from the University of Las Villas, were captured and shot. Former CTC leader David Salvador went underground and soon joined forces with Manuel Ray's creation, the MRP (Movimiento Revolucionario del Pueblo). The archbishop of Santiago, Enrique Pérez Serantes, a former Fidel supporter, issued a pastoral letter that both denounced Fidel's new Communist ties and seemed to bless the spreading antigovernment violence with the words: "Shedding blood is preferable to losing liberty." Still wishing to avoid a showdown with the church, Fidel remained mute. In Miami, the CIA hammered together "unity" among the anti-Castro exiles, merging Artime's and Justo Carrillo's MRR with a group led by Prío's former prime minister, Tony Varona. The result was the Frente Democrático Revolucionario (FDR), intended to provide a political front to the military force being trained in Guatemala.

But while the dissidents formed separate groups with different agendas to oppose him, Fidel's revolution had acquired an unstoppable momentum. In June he ordered the seizure of three of Havana's luxury hotels, justiying the action on the same grounds as Che's earlier "interventions" of factories: Their owners were intentionally underfinancing them, making them unprofitable, and therefore state takeover was necessary. Fidel also took up the gauntlet Che had thrown to the American oil companies. They would do as Cuba requested and process the Soviet oil, he declared, or face the confiscation of their properties. Days later, Cuba expelled two U.S. diplomats, accusing them of spying; in response, the Americans expelled three Cuban diplomats.

The war of wills quickly escalated. Fidel warned the United States that it ran the risk of losing all its property in Cuba; he would seize one sugar mill for every pound of sugar cut from Cuba's quota if Washington took that threatened step. On June 29, the same day that two Soviet oil tankers docked in Cuba, he ordered Texaco's Cuban installations seized; they waited for twenty-four hours before seizing Esso's and Shell's as well. In one fell swoop, Cuba had freed itself of a fifty-million-dollar debt and gained an oil-refining industry.

On July 3, the U.S. Congress authorized President Eisenhower to cut Cuba's sugar quota; Fidel responded with a legal amendment permitting the nationalization of all American properties in Cuba. On July 6, Eisenhower canceled the Cuban sugar quota for the rest of the year, some seven hundred thousand tons. Calling it an act of "economic aggression," Fidel now dropped broad hints of his Soviet arms deal, saying he would "soon" have the weapons he needed to arm his militias; ominously, he also ordered six hundred U.S.-owned companies to register all their assets in Cuba.

Khrushchev now entered the game openly. On July 9, he warned the United States, stressing that he was speaking "figuratively," that, "should the need arise, Soviet artillerymen can support the Cuban people by missile fire," pointing out that the United States was now within range of the Soviets' new generation of intercontinental ballistic missiles. Eisenhower denounced Khrushchev's threats and warned that the United States would not permit a regime "dominated by international communism" in the Western Hemisphere, something, he said, Khrushchev was obviously attempting in Cuba. The very next day, Khrushchev announced that the Soviet Union would buy the seven hundred thousand tons of sugar cut from the American sugar quota.

In Havana, Che shook a happy fist at Washington, saying that Cuba was now protected by "the greatest military power on earth; nuclear weapons now stand in the face of imperialism." Nikita Khrushchev insisted that he had been only speaking "figuratively," but before long, the world would discover that the threat was very real. And, as always, Che had been the first to say so.

VII

In spite of Che's endeavors to depersonalize his existence, he still had a personal life—at least the semblance of one. By July 1960, Aleida was nearly five months' pregnant with their first child, and a comparative peace and normality had been achieved in their married life. That had been aided by Che's move to the National Bank, since she and Hilda—who now worked at Prensa Latina—were no longer forced to see one another every day.

They had also moved again, their permanent house guest Fernández Mell in tow, to a pretty two-story neocolonial house with gardens in the residential neighborhood of Miramar, on Eighteenth Street and Seventh Avenue. Across the street lived the Harvard-trained economist Regino Boti, one of the few remaining moderates still at his job in the Ministry of the Economy. A block and a half away, located in a handsome neocolonial mansion on Fifth Avenue, was the headquarters for Cuban State Security.

To Che's delight, his old friend and traveling companion Alberto Granado showed up in time for the July 26 celebrations. It had been eight years since "Fuser" had said farewell to "Mial" in Caracas, promising to return after finishing his medical exams; while Ernesto had not returned, Alberto had continued his work at the Venezuelan leprosarium and married Delia, a Venezuelan girl. The birth of their first child had coincided with the headlines of the *Granma*'s landing and the false reports of Ernesto Guevara's death. Since then, Granado had followed the exploits of his old sidekick in the newspapers. He had been visiting his family in Argentina when the news of Batista's flight came and had celebrated the news of Che's arrival in Havana with the Guevara clan in Buenos Aires. When he heard that Che would be accompanying Fidel to Caracas in 1959, Granado had eagerly awaited his arrival, only to be crestfallen when he didn't come. They had corresponded, however, and now, finally, Granado and his family had made it to Cuba.

Granado spent as much time as possible with Che and went with him to greet the captain of one of the first Soviet tankers delivering Russian oil to Cuba. With Granado at his side, Che told the captain that he was grateful "for having friends who lend a hand at the necessary time." If Che's words were an oblique hint to Granado, they had effect; within a few months, Granado quit his faculty job in Venezuela, packed up his family, and moved to Cuba, where he too could lend a hand.

At Che's invitation, another friend flew in for the July 26 celebrations. Dr. David Mitrani, a friend and colleague from the General Hospital in Mexico, arrived eager to see Guevara. He also had a couple of missions to fulfill, one for the president of Mexico and one for the government of Israel.

Mitrani, born to European Jewish emigrés and a Zionist himself, had gone off to Israel to work on a kibbutz the month before Che boarded the *Granma*. Although they had argued over politics—Guevara had called Zionism "reactionary"—they were friends, and both considered themselves to be committed to the cause of socialism. After meeting Fidel in Mexico, Guevara had urged Mitrani to join the Cuban revolutionary venture, and ridiculed his plan to "go and pick potatoes" in Israel. Mitrani, put off by Fidel's arrogance, had told his friend at the time that he thought Fidel was "full of shit" and that their plan to invade Cuba was crazy. While their friendship had remained intact, they then lost contact after going off on their separate adventures. When Mitrani returned to Mexico from Israel on the eve of the rebel victory in Cuba, he had sent Che a telegram congratulating him and his comrades.

Since then, Mitrani had established in Mexico City a private medical practice that was beginning to do well. He had kept up with news from Cuba and been shocked to learn of his friend's role in the revolutionary executions, but when he received Che's invitation to come to Cuba in 1960, he accepted. Before going, he met with the Mexican president, Adolfo López Mateos, who asked Mitrani to bring him back a dedicated copy of Che's *Guerra de Guerrillas*. His other order came from the Israeli ambassador in Mexico, who asked him to use his contact with Che to see if relations with Cuba could be improved. A relative of Mitrani also happened to be the Israeli ambassador in Cuba.

In Havana, Mitrani was lodged in the elegant Hotel Nacional and summoned by Che for lunch in his private dining room at the National Bank. Che was in a sardonic mood and told him: "I know you're a bourgeois, so I've had a special meal prepared for you, with wine and everything."

Mitrani found Che far more acerbic than he remembered. He still had a sense of humor, but it was now cutting. They met several times, always at the bank, and in their first meetings there were always others present. It wasn't until his third or fourth visit that Mitrani felt he could talk openly.

Che asked if he wanted to go to Oriente, where Fidel was going to give his July 26 speech, and Mitrani told him no; he'd come here to see *him*, not Fidel, he explained, hiding none of his old antipathy for the Cuban leader. He told Che of Israel's desire for better relations and Che was supportive of the idea. (The days when Cuba would take the Soviet position in favor of the PLO were still years in the future.)

Eventually, Che spoke candidly with Mitrani about the revolution, telling him: "By the first days of August, we're going to transform this country into a socialist state." At least that was what he hoped and expected, Che said, explaining that Fidel himself was not yet totally convinced because he wasn't himself a socialist; Che was still trying to convince him.

Mitrani brought up the issue that had been troubling him the most: Che's role in the executions. Mitrani told him he couldn't understand his involvement, since he wasn't even Cuban and hadn't suffered himself at the hands of the *batistianos*. Where had this hatred, this desire for vengeance, come from? "Look," Che said, "in this thing you have to kill before they kill you." Mitrani let the matter drop but remained troubled by his friend's logic; it was something he would never learn to reconcile with the Ernesto Guevara he knew.

Before Mitrani left, Che gave him one of the new Cuban banknotes with his signature and three inscribed copies of *Guerra de Guerrillas:* for himself, for his old mentor in Mexico, Salazar Mallén, and for President López Mateos. His dedication to Mitrani read: "To David, in the desire that you return again to the right path."

VIII

In his triumphant July 26 speech in Oriente, Fidel took up what had until then been Che's own personal vision, warning his Latin American neighbors that unless they improved living conditions for their people, "Cuba's example would convert the Andean Cordillera into the hemisphere's Sierra Maestra." Fidel could claim that he was speaking only symbolically, but of course he wasn't.

The combination of Fidel's adoption of his "continental guerrilla" scheme and Khrushchev's veiled threat to Washington greatly excited Che. Two days later, speaking before the gathered delegates of the First Latin American Youth Congress, he was uncharacteristically emotional.

> This people [of Cuba] you see today tell you that even if they should disappear from the face of the earth because an atomic war is unleashed in their names . . . they would feel completely happy and fulfilled if each one of you, upon reaching your lands, can say:
> "Here we are. Our words come moist from the Cuban jungles. We have climbed the Sierra Maestra and we have known the dawn, and our minds and our hands are full with the seed of the dawn, and we are prepared to sow it in this land and to defend it so that it flourishes."
> And from all the other brother nations of America, and from our land, if it still survived as an example, the voice of the peoples will answer you, from that moment on and for ever: "It shall be so: may liberty be conquered in each corner of America!"

Once again, Che invoked the specter of death, now envisioned on a truly massive scale, to extol the beauty he felt in the collective sacrifice for liberation. He spoke with the heartfelt conviction of someone with no doubts about the purity of his cause. His words were a liturgy, used to convert. Che Guevara, aged thirty-two, had become the high priest of international revolution.

And present in the audience were plenty of eager listeners, left-wing youths from around the hemisphere, from Chile to Puerto Rico. He applauded Jacobo Arbenz, who was present, backhandedly thanking him for his "brave example" in Guatemala; the Cubans had learned from the "weaknesses" of his government, and been able to "go to the roots of the question and decapitate in one stroke, those in power and the thugs of those in power."

In Cuba, he said, they had done what *had* to be done: They had used the *paredón,* firing squad, and chased out the monopolies. They had done so against those who had preached moderation, most of whom, he said, had turned out to be traitors anyway. "'Moderation' is another one of the terms the colonial agents like to use. All those who are afraid, or who are considering some form of treason, are moderates. . . . [But] the people are by no means moderate."

In his next breath, Che took on Venezuela's anti-Communist President Rómulo Betancourt, whom he had despised in their 1953 meeting, and with whom Cuba's relations had openly soured, calling his government "prisoner to its own thugs." He also conveyed a warning, expressing his confidence that ". . . the [Venezuelan] people won't remain the prisoners of some bayonets or a few bullets for long, because the bullets and the bayonets can change hands, and the murderers can end up dead."

Che was alluding to Betancourt's heavy-handed use of his security forces to put down the mounting tide of demonstrations against his policies, and the recent upsurge of Marxist political opposition to his government. In May, the leftist youth wing of Betancourt's own party had split off to form the Movimiento de Izquierda Revolucionaria, MIR, inspired by Cuba's revolutionary example, and it would not be long before the *miristas* launched an insurrection against Betancourt with the collaboration of the Venezuelan Communist party. Che clearly knew what he was talking about when he delivered his warning to Betancourt in July.

Talking to a group of medical students, health workers, and militiamen on the topic of "revolutionary medicine" in late August, Che prepared them for the possibility that Cuba would soon be fighting a massive "people's" guerrilla war. Cuba's new generation of doctors should join the revolutionary militias—"the greatest expression of the people's solidarity"—and practice "social medicine," to give healthy bodies to the Cubans whom the revolution had liberated.

Drawing on his own life as an example, Che told the crowd that when he began to study medicine, he had dreamed of becoming "a famous researcher." "I dreamed of working tirelessly to aid humanity, but this was conceived as personal achievement." It was only upon graduating, he said, and traveling through a Latin America riven by "misery, hunger, disease" that his political conscience had begun to stir. In Guatemala, he recalled, he began studying the means through which he could become a revolutionary doctor, but then had come the overthrow of Guatemala's socialist experiment. "I became aware, then, of a fundamental fact: To be a revolutionary doctor or to be a revolutionary at all, there must first be a revolution. The isolated effort of one man, regardless of its purity of ideals, is worthless. To be useful it is essential to make a revolution as we have done in Cuba, where the whole population mobilizes and learns how to use arms and fight together. Cubans have learned how much value there is in a weapon and the unity of the people."

At the heart of the revolution, then, was the elimination of individualism. "Individualism as such, as the isolated action of a person alone in a social environment, must disappear in Cuba. Individualism tomorrow should be the proper utilization of the whole individual at the absolute benefit of the community." The revolution was not "a standardizer of the collective will"; rather, it was "a liberator of man's individal capacity," for it oriented that capacity to the service of the revolution.

In his talk, Che tried out a phrase that crystallized a concept he had been developing for some time, and which would soon become synonymous with him: the "New Man."

> How does one reconcile individual effort with the needs of society? We again have to recall what each of our lives was like, what each of us did and thought, as a doctor or in any other public health function, prior to the revolution. We have to do so with profound critical enthusiasm. And we will then conclude that almost everything we thought and felt in that past epoch should be filed away, and that a new type of human being should be created. And if each one of us is his own architect of that new human type, then creating that new type of human being—who will be the representative of the new Cuba—will be much easier.

Within a few days of that talk, Che met with René Dumont, a French Marxist economist who was trying to help Cuba in its difficult conversion to socialism. After extensive travels around the country, Dumont had concluded that one of the biggest problems of the newly established agricultural cooperatives was that their workers did not feel they were owners of anything and he urged Che to consider a scheme whereby the workers who did additional labor during the off-season to maintain the cooperatives would be paid, giving them a sense of co-ownership.

But Che "reacted violently" to the idea, according to Dumont. It was not a sense of ownership the Cuban workers needed, Che argued, but a sense of responsibility, and he spelled out to the French economist what that meant.

It was, wrote Dumont: "a sort of ideal vision of Socialist Man, who would become a stranger to the mercantile side of things, working for society and not for profit. He was very critical of the industrial success of the Soviet Union, where, he said, everybody works and strives and tries to go beyond his quota, but only to earn more money. He did not think the Soviet Man was really a new sort of man, for he did not find him any different, really, than a Yankee. He refused to consciously participate in the creation in Cuba 'of a second American society.'"

As far as Dumont could see, Che seemed to be advocating an attempt to "skip stages" in Cuba's socialist transformation of society, by going directly from capitalism to Communism, much as Mao had tried to do in China in 1956 with his radical "Great Leap Forward" campaign of forced collectivization. "In short, Che was far ahead of his time—in thought, he had already entered a communist stage."

For the first time, Che openly acknowledged the Communist influences in Cuba's revolution, while engaging in some heavy revisionism to prove they had come about of their own accord. It was only after he and his comrades had fought against the "encirclement and annihilation" tactics of Batista's army in the Sierra Maestra, he claimed, that "a pamphlet of Mao's fell into our hands" and the rebels discovered they had been fighting with much the same tactics Mao had used against a kindred foe. Similarly, it was only seeing the needs of the peasants of the Sierra Maestra that brought the rebel leaders to the threshold of political enlightenment. Was the revolution Communist? he asked rhetorically. "In the event that it were Marxist —and hear carefully that I say Marxist—it would be so because [the revolution] discovered the paths signaled by Marx through its own methods." As was their fashion, Che was going much further than Fidel; it would still be nine months before *el jefe máximo* publicly acknowledged that his revolution had a "socialist nature."

If there was growing disenchantment among some of Fidel's old allies —that summer several more of his former comrades in arms resigned their posts—the disenchantment was also spreading to the PSP.

For all the gains it had made since January 1959, it was clear that the Communist party was becoming increasingly subordinated to Fidel. By now, his preeminence over the party had been blessed by Khrushchev, who reportedly sent him a private note in May to the effect that the Kremlin "does not consider any party to be an intermediary" between Fidel and itself. Communist or not, what was being erected in Cuba was an old-fashioned personality cult.

Bohemia's owner-editor, Miguel Ángel Quevedo, experiencing a loss of faith since comparing Fidel to Christ the year before, now shut down his magazine and fled the country. Before he left, he accused Fidel of delivering Cuba into a shameful state of "Russian vassalage." Miró Cardona, former prime minister, also left for the United States, where he soon joined the ranks of the anti-Castro forces. A mass anti-Communist rally was held in Santiago by the Juventud Católica; a priest and some of the Catholic group's members were captured after a gun battle in which two policemen were killed. Cardinal Arteaga published a new pastoral letter that was harshly critical of the government. This time, Fidel responded, complaining of the church's "systematic provocations."

As the U.S. presidential election entered its final stretch, the fencing between Washington and Havana had accelerated; Cuba had become a central issue in the campaign with both candidates—Vice President Nixon and

Democratic Senator John F. Kennedy—promising to be tougher against Cuba than the other. Kennedy ridiculed the Eisenhower administration's "do-nothing" policies that had brought about the present crisis; *his* administration, he said, would take firm action to restore "democracy" in Cuba.

Kennedy's charges hit a nerve. The White House pushed through bills to impose sanctions against countries that bought Cuban sugar with American loans, and to cut off security assistance to nations that gave *any* aid to Cuba. A "who lost Cuba?" debate ensued at the State Department. Next, the United States took its case to the Organization of American States, and, dangling the promise of a new foreign aid handout at a conference of OAS foreign ministers in Costa Rica, pushed through a unanimous declaration condemning any intervention in the hemisphere by "an extra-continental power," a clear reference to Cuba's growing partnership with the Soviet Union

Fidel reacted to the "San José Declaration" with passionate indignation. On September 2, he made what became known as his "Havana Declaration," outlining Cuba's position in the hemisphere as a revolutionary example, and, without using the word socialist, proclaimed Cuba's determination to defend the rights of the oppressed by fighting against exploitation, capitalism, and imperialism; he added that if the United States dared attack his country, he would "welcome" Khrushchev's proffered missiles. Finally, he announced, his government would officially recognize Communist China.

Fidel followed up his Havana Declaration with a rowdy trip to New York for the opening session of the United Nations General Assembly. This time, he took pains to be as irritating as possible to Washington. He camped out in a Harlem hotel, the Theresa, on 125th Street, calling it a show of solidarity with oppressed black Americans. He played host to Khrushchev, who gave him a bear hug, and met with so-called "anti-imperialists" such as Kwame Nkrumah, Nasser, and Nehru. The Soviet-bloc presidents of Poland and Bulgaria also paid calls on him. In the General Assembly, Fidel and Khrushchev formed a mutual-admiration society, echoing one another's speeches that lauded the Cuban revolution, accused the United States of aggression, called for global nuclear disarmament, and argued for a revamped, more nonaligned United Nations.

At the same time, UN General Secretary Dag Hammarskjöld was dealing with the biggest Cold War crisis to involve the UN since the Korean War in the Congo, newly independent from Belgium. The nation was wracked by an internal power struggle, mutinous armed forces, and the secession of its copper-rich Katanga province. The Soviets, the Belgians, the Americans, and the UN all had intervened in support of various factions. With the air already thick with tension, Khrushchev made history when, during British Prime Minister Harold Macmillan's speech calling for improved relations between East and West, he angrily banged his shoe on the Soviet delegation's desk. If less dramatic, Fidel also inflicted some spite, giving the longest recorded speech in United Nations history, clocked at well over three hours. Eisenhower studiously ignored the bearded upstart from Cuba, but for the press Fidel and his bombastic entourage were the "Greatest Show on Earth."

Once he was back in Havana—on board a borrowed Soviet Ilyushin after the United States had impounded his own Cuban plane—Fidel began dismantling the last vestiges of American influence while simultaneously tightening the revolution's controls. On September 28, the Committees to Defend the Revolution (CDRs) were created. It was to be a nationwide network of civic organizations, with the inhabitants of each block in every town and city of Cuba forming a committee to ensure the implemention of revolutionary decrees and to provide a grassroots vigilante network for the State Security apparatus.

In Havana, the U.S. embassy began advising all American citizens to leave the island. Recruitment and arms-training for the national militia—according to Fidel already over two hundred thousand strong—had become the new national priority.

Ironically, the sheer number of Cuban exiles who now wanted to take up arms *against* Fidel was causing some headaches for the CIA in their ongoing recruitment drive. In Miami, Justo Carrillo resigned from the Americans' anti-Castro alliance, upset at the growing influx of ex-*batistianos*. There were now some six hundred men training in the Guatemala camps, with smaller groups receiving specialized guerrilla training in Panama and Louisiana. In Havana, Manuel Ray's group became active, carrying out a daring assault on La Cabaña and freeing some of the officers imprisoned with Huber Matos; afterward, Ray managed to escape to the United States. What was lacking in all these disparate efforts was any degree of cohesiveness or a leader strong enough to unite and bend the others to his will; in short, the anti-Fidelístas didn't have a Fidel.

In early October, a group of armed Cubans and an American were captured in Oriente after a gun battle with government troops, and a few days later Cuban soldiers captured a cache of weapons and ammunition dropped by a CIA plane in the Escambray mountains. There were now as many as one thousand rebels in the Escambray, sustained by CIA airdrops of arms and supplies, and they were being helped on the ground by the American expatriate mercenary William Morgan and one of his old comrades, the ex–Second Front warlord Jesús Carreras. Having learned well the lesson of his own ordeal in the Sierra Maestra, Fidel ordered the army and the militias to carry out a mass evacuation of the area's peasantry to isolate the rebels from sources of food and intelligence. Before long, most of the rebels had been either wiped out, or captured and shot by firing squad, among them Morgan and Carreras, although the Escambray would remain a focus of counterrevolutionary activity for several more years.

Against this backdrop, Che, Raúl, and Fidel attended the eleventh anniversary celebrations of the founding of the People's Republic of China with the head of China's new trade legation to Cuba. Trade deals were signed with Hungary and Bulgaria.

That same month Jean-Paul Sartre and Simone de Beauvoir returned to Cuba at Fidel's invitation. They were no longer so entranced. "Havana had changed; no more nightclubs, no more gambling, and no more American tourists; in the half-empty Nacional Hotel, some very young members of the militia, boys and girls, were holding a conference. On every side, in the streets, the militia was drilling."

The atmosphere was tense with invasion rumors, the revolution had "toughened up," and there was a notable air of repressive uniformity seeping into Cuban life. When they asked workers at a clothing mill how their lives had benefited from the revolution, a union leader had quickly stepped forward to speak on their behalf, parroting the government's dogma. In the cultural arena, Soviet-style "socialist realism" had arrived; writers told the French couple that they had begun to engage in self-censorship, and the poet Nicolás Guillén informed them that he considered "all research into technique and form counter-revolutionary."

They left after a few days, with de Beauvoir concluding: "[In Cuba there was] less gaiety, less freedom, but much progress on certain fronts." As an example of the latter, she cited a visit to an agricultural cooperative that had impressed her; still, "the 'honeymoon of the revolution' was over."

IX

On October 11, Che summoned Cuba's richest man, the sugar magnate Julio Lobo, to his office. As the owner of vast tracts of productive land—now expropriated—and thirteen sugar mills, Lobo was still a force to be reckoned with.

Yet Lobo, a cultured man, famed for his valuable private collection of art treasures and Napoleonica, was something of an enigma, having refused to leave Cuba or lend his voice to the flood of anti-Castro protest. Now, it was time to put him to the test. Fidel was going to seize the sugar mills in a few days, and Che wanted to convince Lobo to stay—and keep his expertise—in Cuba. Alfredo Menéndez, administering the state's sugar mills for INRA, was advised in advance of the offer Che was going to make Lobo: a monthly salary of two thousand dollars and the right to keep any one of his palatial homes. "We really didn't want him to leave," said Menéndez. "All that talent . . . was what Che wanted."

The very notion of offering such a wage to a man whose fortune was estimated to be in the hundreds of millions of dollars might appear absurd, but perhaps more than anything else, it reflected Che's singular devotion to his ideal, and his belief that others—even Julio Lobo—might share it. Beset by the brain drain of experienced technicians and administrators from Cuba, he had consistently tried to convince skilled personnel—men such as Napoleon Padilla—to stay, promising to honor their current capitalist-era salaries. In terms of the "new Cuba," in fact, the salary he was offering Lobo was high; he himself had refused the $1,000 monthly salary due him as National Bank president as a matter of principle, accepting only the $250 paid him in his capacity as a *comandante*.

Che informed Lobo that the time had come for him to make a decision: The revolution was Communist, and he, as a capitalist, could not remain as he was; either he could stay and be a part of it, or he had to go. Lobo gamely pointed out that Khrushchev believed in "peaceful coexistence" between the world's competing political and economic systems, to which Che replied that such a proposition "was possible between nations, but not *within* one."

Che then laid out his offer. Lobo was invited to become the administrator of Cuba's sugar industry. He would lose his properties but be allowed to keep the income from one of his mills. Lobo said he needed time to think about it, and Che agreed. Lobo had already made up his mind, however. He went home and, two days later, flew to Miami, before moving on to Spain, where he lived out the rest of his life in exile. The following day, the government nationalized all of Cuba's banks and large commercial, industrial, and transport businesses. All of Lobo's sugar mills and homes and their contents were seized, and his Napoleonica collection eventually becoming a state museum.

A second urban reform law banned Cubans from owning more than one home and took over all rented properties, making their inhabitants tenants of the state. On October 19, Washington responded to the latest mass seizures—which had affected many American companies—by imposing a trade embargo on Cuba, prohibiting all exports to the island except food and medicine. On October 25, Fidel nationalized 166 U.S.-owned companies, in effect signing the death certificate on all remaining American commercial interests in Cuba.

Fidel boasted that he now had both the people *and* the *arms* he needed to fight off an invasion. By now, Washington knew this claim was true. On October 28, the U.S. government filed a protest with the OAS charging Cuba with having received "substantial" arms shipments since the summer from the Soviet bloc. The next day Philip Bonsal was recalled to Washington for "extended consultations," never to return to Cuba. By then, Che was in Prague, en route to Moscow.

X

On November 7, Che stood in a place of honor next to Nikita Khrushchev in Moscow's wintry Red Square overlooking the annual military parade commemorating the forty-third anniversary of the October Revolution. Nikolai Leonov, his interpreter, watched from the stand where the diplomatic corps was assembled.

Moments earlier, Che had been at his side, shivering from the cold, when a messenger had come to inform Che that he was invited to go and join Khrushchev. "Che said no," Leonov recalled, "he didn't feel important enough to be in a place that was so sacred to him." The messenger had left but soon returned. The Soviet premier was insistent. Che turned to Leonov and asked what he should do; Leonov told him to go. To Leonov's knowledge, it was the first time a person who was not a head of state "or at least a party chief" had been invited to stand on the hallowed Supreme Soviet tribune above the red marble tomb where Lenin's embalmed body lies in state.

Che's old traveling partner José Pardo Llada was also in Red Square that day, as part of a Cuban press delegation invited by the Soviet Journalists' Union. Seeing Guevara on the exclusive terrace of the Presidium, Nikita Khrushchev next to him and surrounded by the luminaries of the Communist world, he noted that "Guevara, in the midst of the international paraphernalia of Communism, looked satisfied, radiant, happy."

Among the people Che was introduced to that day was a thin, dark-skinned Bolivian his own age named Mario Monje Molina, head of the Bolivian Communist party. Their meeting was brief and perfunctory—as Monje recalled later, Che had said little more than "I've been to your country" before he was ushered to the next introduction. Both went their separate ways, neither realizing just how intimately their destinies would become intertwined within a few years.

Che was on his first tour of the Communist bloc, a two-month trip that took him back and forth between Prague, Moscow, Leningrad, Stalingrad, Irkutsk, Peking, Shanghai, Pyongyang, and Berlin. Amid his travels, the hard-

486 Making the New Man

fought American presidential campaign wound to a close in a dead heat, with John F. Kennedy ultimately defeating Nixon by the narrowest of margins.

The main purpose of Che's trip was to secure the sale of that portion of Cuba's upcoming sugar crop not already committed to Moscow, a mission that had taken on some urgency following Eisenhower's decision to halt the purchase of all Cuban sugar for the rest of 1960. He knew that this was only a prelude to a total American ban on Cuban sugar imports, but he could hardly have been unhappy about that prospect; it was, after all, something he had worked hard to bring about ever since the rebel victory.

Che had left Havana on October 22, three days after the U.S. embargo had been announced. He was accompanied by Leonardo Tamayo, his eighteen-year-old bodyguard who had been with him since the Sierra Maestra; Héctor Rodríguez Llompart, his messenger for the talks with Mikoyan; and several Cuban, Chilean, and Ecuadorean economists who worked for him at INRA.

In their first stop, Prague, Che toured a tractor factory, gave interviews, and obtained a twenty-million-dollar credit to build an auto-assembly plant in Cuba. In Moscow, between talks with economic, military, and trade officials and tours of factories, he went sight-seeing. He visited the Lenin Museum and the Kremlin, laid a wreath at Lenin's tomb, attended a Tchaikovsky concert, and, with Mikoyan, watched a performance at the Bolshoi Theater. Leonov went with him everywhere.

"He was highly organized," recalled Leonov. "In that sense he was not at all Latin, rather more like a German. Punctual, precise, it was an amazement to all of us who knew Latin America. But the other members of his delegation were really undisciplined. One day, the [sugar] negotiations were programmed to start at ten in the morning. Che came down to where the cars were waiting, alone; none of the other members of the delegation had come down yet, they were all still half-sleep. I asked him: 'Che, shall we wait? Don't worry, I'll tell the minister to wait for us for fifteen or twenty minutes.' He said: 'No, let's go alone,' and he went off to the negotiations accompanied only by me. When we arrived the Soviets were amazed because they had the whole delegation sitting there, and on the other side was only Che."

The meeting began, and, after twenty minutes or so, the other members of the Cuban delegation started arriving, out of breath and without ties. "Che said nothing, not a single word of criticism, not even the slightest expression altered his face—nothing. But that night, he told me: 'Listen, Nicolás, organize a visit for us tomorrow to Lenin's Museum, and tell the guide to place special emphasis on the discipline Lenin demanded of the Politburo members of that time, tell him to talk about all that.'"

Leonov arranged everything, just as Che had requested, and the next day the whole group went off enthusiastically to the museum. "The young woman giving the explanations began to talk about Lenin's administrative discipline. She explained that when someone was late to a meeting of the Council of Ministers, the first punishment was a very serious warning. The second time they were late, it was a heavy fine and [their fault] was published in the Party newspaper. And the third time [such people were] fired from their job, without explanations." Che's comrades took the hint immediately. Leonov could see the impact on their faces and on Che's own, which was "grave . . . ironic." After that, Leonov said, there was no more lack of discipline in Che's entourage.

Llompart, however, was punished by Che for having done a sloppy job proofreading the text of a commercial treaty to be signed with the government of Rumania, one of the countries he intended to visit. Che spotted an error that Llompart had missed and upbraided him furiously.

"He told me horrible things. I felt crushed and I had no excuses, I simply hadn't done the things I was supposed to do," Llompart remembered. "At first he reacted violently, demanding explanations [but then] became aware of my humiliation and stopped talking. . . . He knew I understood my mistake and that I was ashamed of it."

That wasn't the end of it, however. A few days later, Llompart roused himself early to join the rest of the delegation who were off that day for a sightseeing tour of Leningrad. But when Che saw him, he asked: "Where are you going?" "Well, Comandante," Llompart said, "to Leningrad . . ."

"No," Che told him, "first you must learn to fulfill your duty." The group left without Llompart. A few days later, though, as they prepared to make another visit, Che came to tell Llompart personally that he should come along; the sanction had been lifted.

Che was always hardest on those he felt had the ability to become true revolutionaries, and obviously Llompart fell into that category. If they failed, he could be merciless; if they passed muster, he repaid them with his trust. A few weeks later, when they were in China, Che appointed Llompart as his representative to visit Vietnam. And when Che returned to Cuba, he named Llompart to head the delegation to the remaining Eastern-bloc states on his agenda: Poland, Hungary, Bulgaria, Rumania, and Albania.

Che was often blunt to the point of causing offense, as when Leonov decided to treat him to a private meal before leaving Moscow. Leonov's own apartment was too small for such an occasion, however, and he arranged with Alexiev's family, still in Moscow, to prepare a special dinner at their larger, more comfortable flat. They worked hard, preparing sturgeon and other Russian fish delicacies suitable for such an honored guest.

But, when Che arrived, he exclaimed: "*Madre mía!* I'm going to go hungry tonight!" before informing his crestfallen hosts that he couldn't eat fish because of his allergies; they hastily cooked him some eggs. Later, seated at the magnificently prepared table, Che began tapping on the plates and looking around pointedly at his dinner companions; the Alexievs, who had once lived in Paris, were showing off their best china. Lifting an eyebrow, Che remarked: "So, the *proletariat* here eats off of French porcelain, eh?"

Che never said so publicly, but those who knew him say he returned from his first trip to Russia privately dismayed by the elite lifestyles and evident predilection for bourgeois luxuries he saw among Kremlin officials, in contrast with the austere living conditions of the average Soviet citizen. Four and a half decades of socialism had obviously not created a new Socialist Man, at least not among the party elite, and this was not what he had expected to find in the *madre patria* of global socialism.

In a serious frame of mind, he talked about Guatemala with Leonov. It had obviously been a seminal experience for him, and although Che had only recently lauded Arbenz publicly in Cuba, he tore him apart in front of Leonov for having "given up the battle" without a fight. In Che's mind, leadership was a sacred duty granted to an individual "chosen" by the people on the basis of trust. It was a privilege that came with the obligation to honor that trust, if necessary, with one's life. It was obviously how he saw his own commitment to Cuba's revolution and, no doubt, his expectations of Fidel.

"I don't know if the Cuban revolution will survive or not," he told Leonov. "It's difficult to say. But [if it doesn't] . . . don't come looking for me among the refugees in the embassies. I've had that experience, and I'm not ever going to repeat it. I will go out with a machine gun in my hand, to the barricades. . . . I'll keep fighting to the end."

Leonov was present for Che's talks with Khrushchev. Among other things, Che wanted Cuba to have its own steel plant—the indispensable cornerstone to industrialization—with a capacity for a million tons of steel. He also wanted the Soviets to fund and build it.

"Khrushchev heard him out reservedly," Leonov recalled, "and said, 'Well, let's study it.' And for the several days that the ministerial experts were studying the project, according to Leonov, Che became more insistent. Every time he saw Khrushchev, Che asked, 'Well, Nikita, what about the factory?' [Finally] Nikita told him: 'Look, Che, if you want, we can build the plant, but in Cuba there is no coal, there is no iron, there isn't enough skilled labor, and there's not a consumer's market for a million tons with Cuba's incipient level of industry. Wouldn't it be better if you build a small plant to work from scrap metal, and not spend so much money?'

"But Che was intransigent. He said: 'If we build that factory we'll train the necessary cadres to [work it]. As for the iron ore, we'll get it from Mexico, or some other place nearby, and we'll find the coal somewhere else; we could bring it from here, on the ships going to pick up sugar from Cuba.'"

Later, when they were on their own, Leonov suggested to Che that perhaps Khrushchev was right, the Cubans might be better to build by stages, more gradually, and such a huge plant might be premature. But Che told him:

"Look, Nicolás, there are other factors at stake here—social and political ones. The Revolution must be something big, imposing. We must combat the single-crop economy of sugar, we must industrialize, and anyway, you, here in the Soviet Union, also began your industrialization program without a base."

"Well, in the end, that idea didn't prosper, and it seemed to me that Che's concept was a bit artificial, with more social and political foundations than economic ones," Leonov recalled. Later, Leonov said, after consulting with Cuba, Che lost some enthusiasm. He didn't push the idea anymore, and the Soviets didn't mention it, either.

Che took Leonov with him on his trip to North Korea, thinking he might be needed as an interpreter, but as soon as they arrived in Pyongyang, they were separated. The Sino-Soviet dispute was in full swing, and North Korea was an ally of Beijing.

"They didn't allow me to work with him," said Leonov, who was deposited at the Soviet embassy while Che was taken off to an official government guest house. He remained there through Che's trip to China, before they reunited for the return trip to Moscow.

According to Leonov, Che's motives for visiting North Korea and China were twofold: "In the first place, he wanted to see the examples of Asiatic socialism, and secondly . . . he wanted to secure some sales of sugar there. He resolved the two tasks, because he saw their socialism, a bit despotic, a bit Asian, in that style they have, and he made the sale, I believe, of two hundred thousand tons of sugar to China."

In fact, Che's trip to China had been extremely successful. He had secured the sale of one million tons of Cuba's 1961 sugar crop *and* obtained a sixty-million-dollar credit for the purchase of Chinese goods. He had met with the legendary leader of the Long March, Mao Tse-tung, and been feted by his deputy, Chou En-lai. Chou had praised the Cuban revolution, and in return Che had lauded China's revolution as an example for "the Americas." No doubt all of this irked the Soviets, and their discomfiture must have deepened when, upon leaving China, Che remarked that "in general there was not a single discrepancy" between himself and Beijing.

Che's fraternal remarks did not go unnoticed by the Americans either. In a secret U.S. intelligence report about his mission, his Chinese sojourn was mentioned with interest. "A noteworthy feature of Guevara's visit to Peiping [Beijing] was his apparent siding with the Chinese on several key points in the Sino-Soviet dispute.

"Speaking at a November 20 reception, Guevara praised Communist China's commune movement (which has come under Soviet attack) and two days earlier held up the Chinese Communist revolution as an "example" that has "revealed a new road for the Americas." Guevara made no such statement about the USSR's example while in Moscow."

While Che's statements may have betrayed his personal sympathies, he and Fidel were taking pains not to take sides openly in the festering quarrel between the two Communist giants. Back in Pyongyang, Che diplomatically expressed his hope to Leonov that "the differences could be settled" between the two nations, but both he and Fidel must have been aware that they were in a very good position to play Beijing and Moscow off one another. Indeed, after he returned to Moscow on December 19, the Soviets dramatically expanded their largesse, agreeing to buy 2.7 million tons of Cuba's forthcoming sugar crop, at a rate above world market prices. The joint Soviet-Cuban communiqué issued that day expressed Cuban gratitude for Soviet economic assistance and stressed the USSR's "full support" for Cuba's bid to maintain its independence "in the face of aggression." Echoing Guevara's plaudits for China, the Moscow communiqué extolled Cuba as "an example for other peoples of the American continent, and also Asia and Africa."

The very next day, Che left Moscow for Cuba, stopping briefly in Prague and Budapest. He had learned that an old childhood acquaintance, Spanish Republican refugee Fernando Barral, was living in Hungary. It had been ten years since they had last seen one another, before Barral's arrest for "Communist agitation" and his expulsion from Argentina. Since then, Barral had gone to medical school in Hungary, become a doctor, lived through the 1956 Hungarian uprising, and the Soviet invasion that had suppressed the revolt. Over the last couple of years, he had read the news about revolutionary Cuba with interest. As for this Argentine-born *comandante,* Ernesto Guevara, called "Che," he wondered: "Could it really be the same *loco* Guevara I knew?" During his brief stop in Budapest, Che had asked the Cuban embassy staff to find Barral, but they were unable to locate him. Che left the following note, which was later delivered.

Dear Fernando:

I know you had doubts about my identity but you thought that I was I. Indeed, although no, because a lot of water has gone under my bridge, and of the asthmatic, embittered and individualistic being you knew, only the asthma remains.

I learned that you had married, I too, and I have two children,* but I am still an adventurer. Only now, my adventures have a just purpose. Greetings to your family from this survivor of a past epoch and a fraternal embrace from Che.

[P.S.] What do you think of my new name [?]

As it had done for Granado, Barral's renewed contact with Guevara was to provide a new direction in his life. For the exile, Hungary's entrenched and bureaucratic socialist system no longer held any surprises, and the chance to be part of the "new" revolution in Cuba appealed to him greatly; he wrote back to Che, expressing his interest to come and work in Cuba. In February 1961, Che wrote again, welcoming him. "The salary will be decorous without permitting great luxuries but the experience of the Cuban Revolution is something that I think would be interesting for people like you, who must begin one day again in their countries of origin."

(Barral accepted Che's offer and emigrated to Cuba in November 1961. Almost immediately, Che sent him to see Ramiro Valdés, Cuba's security chief, who, as a test of Barral's revolutionary commitment, dispatched him to the Escambray to fight in the "Lucha contra Bandidos.")

A new face also entered Che's life on this trip. In Berlin, he met a twenty-two-year-old German-Argentine woman named Haydée Tamara Bunke, the interpreter for his meetings with German officials, and the daughter of Jewish Communists who in 1931 had fled Hitler's Germany for Argentina, where Tamara had been born two years later. She had spent her childhood there, returning with her family to the Communist-run German Democratic Republic when she was fourteen. Her parents had raised her to be a Communist, and she became a faithful child of the socialist state, joining the youth wing of the Communist party at eighteen. With her Spanish-language abilities, Tamara soon was made an official interpreter, but, according to a signed statement she made to the party in 1958, her true dream

---

*On November 24, while he was in Beijing, Aleida had given birth to a baby girl. She named her after herself, Aleida, but the little girl's dark hair and eyes were just like her father's.

was to return to Latin America—ideally to her birthplace of Argentina—
and "help the Party there."

By the time Che met her, the attractive, fair-haired Tamara was already
known to some of his comrades. Six months earlier, Che had dispatched
Orlando Borrego to Berlin as part of a Cuban trade delegation, and Tamara
had been their interpreter; later, both men recalled her avid interest in Cuba
and its revolution, and her wish to go and work there. Within five months
of meeting Che, her wish came true; in May 1961 she flew to Cuba, where
she would soon be given a role in Che's program of revolution for Latin
America.

As Che flew home, he must have felt pleased with himself. He had
met the leaders of the socialist world and obtained vital sales and credits for
Cuba. Over the last two years, he had been instrumental in welding the
Soviet-Cuban alliance; as Alexiev put it, "Che was practically the architect
of our relations with Cuba."

On New Year's Day 1961, Fidel called for a general military mobilization, and showed off Cuba's newly acquired Soviet tanks and other weaponry in a display of strength on Havana's streets. The next day, he ordered
Washington to cut its Havana embassy staff to eleven, the same number as
in Cuba's embassy in Washington. For the outgoing Eisenhower, it was the
final straw. All that remained for him to do was sign the divorce certificate
ending a tumultuous sixty-year relationship. The following day, January 3,
1961, in one of his last acts in office before handing the presidency over to
John F. Kennedy, diplomatic relations between the United States and Cuba
were severed.

24

These Atomic Times

I

On the morning of February 24, 1961, Che left his home on Eighteenth Street in Miramar. His car turned right, up to Seventh Avenue. Normally, he took a different route—turning left down his residential street to the tree-lined boulevard of Fifth Avenue, then right, driving past State Security headquarters into the tunnel beneath the Almendares River, then down the seaside Malecon to Old Havana and his office at the National Bank.

But today, Che headed for the Plaza de la Revolución. Fidel had turned his INRA department into a full-fledged ministry, and it was Che's first day as Cuba's new minister of industries. The unannounced change of route may have saved his life.

A few moments after he left home, a gun battle erupted just outside his home; Che's bodyguards entered the fray, shooting wildly. Inside, Aleida threw herself and the baby underneath the first-floor stairwell, where she was joined by the terrified latest addition to the Guevara household: Sofía Gato, a twenty-five-year-old girl from Camagüey, the nanny of three-month-old Aleidita.

Afterward Sofía was able to piece together most of what had taken place. Four or five armed men, *barbudos,* had lain in wait behind some bushes near the corner of Eighteenth Street and Fifth Avenue, and when one of their neighbors, an officer named Salinas, drove by in his car, they opened fire with automatic weapons. Believing it to be an attack on Che's house, his *guarnición* of bodyguards returned fire. A few minutes later, Salinas lay dead in his car, and one of the assailants, gut shot, writhed on the ground.

News of the shootout was quickly smothered, but plenty of people heard about it anyway. Che's and the government's unofficial version was that it had *not* been an assassination attempt against Che. According to

Oscarito Fernández Mell, who also lived at the house on Eighteenth Street, the dead man, Salinas, was indeed the attacker's intended target, the victim of an "affair of the heart" gone bad. As with so many things that have taken place in Cuba, the shooting became cloaked in official mystery, and so it has remained for decades.

Still, the notion that the incident on Eighteenth Street had been a botched attempt to assassinate Che is entirely credible, considering what was happening in Cuba at the time. All over the country, former *barbudos,* like those who fired on Salinas's cars that morning, had taken up arms against the revolution, against Communism. Among anti-Communists, Che was widely identified as the principal advocate of Cuba's "submission" to the Soviet Union, the "Red" flea in Fidel's ear.

At least one other plot to kill Che had already been foiled. One night in early 1960, back in the days before Mikoyan's visit—when Alexiev and Che had to meet clandestinely—the Soviet agent was talking with Che at his new office in the National Bank when Che suddenly said: "Look, Alejandro, let me show you the place where the counterrevolutionaries are planning to shoot me from." He pointed to a window right across the narrow street from where they sat. Alexiev was alarmed, but Che quickly reassured him that Cuba's intelligence services had already staked out the place and were about to move in.

Whatever the true cause of the shootout on Calle 18, Che took new precautions afterward. Visitors to the Ministry of Industries were frisked by guards, and Che began to carry a cigar box full of hand grenades on the seat next to him in the car, driving to work by a different route each day.

The Americans had also lost virtually all on-ground intelligence capability. The last American diplomats had vacated the embassy on January 20, a few days after prohibiting all American citizens from visiting Cuba. That same month, the Peruvian and Paraguayan governments broke off relations and pulled out their diplomats; more of Cuba's anti-Castro neighbors would follow their example in the coming months. At least one hundred thousand Cuban refugees had now fled into exile, most of them to Miami, and the U.S. government had set up a federally funded resettlement program to house them and give them jobs. Among those who had fled was Pardo Llada, Che's troublesome travel companion on his first international tour: After making indiscreet remarks about Communist party infiltration into the government, he too was eased out of Cuba. One who was not so lucky was Humberto Sorí-Marín, the former agriculture minister. Captured by Cuban troops and accused of CIA-sponsored counterrevolutionary activities, Sorí-Marín was shot by a firing squad. Beyond the human toll, the ongoing purge and mass exodus were serving Fidel's goal of "draining the swamp," removing potential fifth columnists and counterrevolutionary supporters from the scene.

In their wake, Soviet technicians, Russian-language teachers, economists, and military advisors had flowed in. The Mongolians, Albanians, Hungarians, Chinese, and North Vietnamese opened up embassies. Eastern-bloc trade and cultural delegations came and went. On January 17, Fidel had announced that one thousand Cuban youths would be sent to the USSR to study "agrarian collectives." The transformation had been so sudden and dramatic that even working-class Cubans were struck by the difference between the *rusos* and the Americans they had replaced.

The Americans had been rich and loud and had spoken terrible Spanish, but these newcomers looked and acted like peasants, rough-hewn and poorly dressed. The women were fat and wore long peasant dresses and headscarves, and the men, ill-fitting suits of poor-quality cloth. They sweated heavily in Cuba's heat, but used no deodorant, and to the finicky Cubans, the Russians smelled bad. They spoke no Spanish and stuck to themselves, and were trucked through the city to their new residential enclaves like so many cattle. They stared in wonder at the modern city, with its shiny American consumer products still in shop windows: televisions, refrigerators, and air conditioners; and at the swank architect designed homes with swimming pools and landscaped gardens. The huge American cars, luxuriant with chrome and fins, had them goggle-eyed.

On appearances, the Soviets did not inspire many as the representatives of the vaunted socialist "superpower." Che knew about the popular skepticism and addressed it while appearing on Cuban television on January 6 to talk about his recent trip to the USSR. After waxing poetic about all the nations he had visited, singling out North Korea and China for special praise, he turned to the subject on everyone's minds; the Soviets' evident backwardness in areas many Cubans had long taken for granted. Speaking of his USSR visit, Che said:

> We had to bring up some problems there that embarrassed us a little, really. . . . Because, for example, we brought up the problem that the Cuban people needed some raw materials to make deodorants with, and in those countries they don't understand that, because they are nations that are developing all their production for the general welfare of the people, and have still to overcome some enormous backwardnesses, and . . . they can't be bothered with these things. We too now have to occupy ourselves with more important things.

Che was speaking as diplomatically as he could in the circumstances. He *understood,* he was telling the finicky *habaneros,* but times had changed, there was a new national priority, and, just like the Russians, they were going to have to do without deodorant. He was also acknowledging that, yes, despite their technological advances, the Soviets were still a rustic people in many ways.

In the economy, the Soviet-bloc influence had also become more visible. The government's emphasis had already shifted away from the disorganized cooperative farms favored in the early days of land expropriations, to be replaced by Soviet-style state farms called *"granjas del pueblo."** Czech and Soviet advisors now worked at Che's ministry alongside the first-generation crew of South American economists. And Che organized a weekly Marxism study circle for himself and some of his aides, including Borrego, with Anastasio Mansilla, a Hispano-Soviet political economist, as their teacher.

Along with most other American influences—such as Santa Claus, who had been banned—the learning of English was now discouraged; Russian was now the second language to learn in the "new" Cuba. Che began taking twice-weekly Russian-language classes from Yuri Pevtsov, a philologist sent from Lermonstov University to be his interpreter and personal tutor. They had no Russian-Spanish manual to work from, so the two made do with a Russian-French primer.

Inevitably, in spite of the early popular ridicule about the *"bolos,"* a certain Soviet "style" began to seep inexorably into Cuban life in ways that were initially superficial. The government spearheaded the emblematic transformation. There was already the new central planning board, JUCEPLAN, an imitation of the USSR's GOSPLAN. Streets, theaters, and factories were rebaptized with the names of homegrown and foreign revolutionary heroes and martyrs such as Camilo Cienfuegos and Patrice Lumumba. The old Chaplin Cinema on First Avenue would become the Carlos Marx, and before long, there would be day-care centers named Heroes de Vietnam and Rosa Luxemburg.

Since the revolution there had been a spate of Cuban babies named Fidel, and Ernesto, after Che himself. Now, more and more Cubans began naming their children Alexei and Natasha. Before long, Che's own newest daughter had a Russian nickname—Aliusha.

---

*Despite the large expropriations, much of Cuba's cultivated land remained in the hands of small farmers, who continued to till their plots without hindrance from the state. In 1963, a new bill reduced the size of private landholdings still further, but the revolution never completely eradicated its fiercely independent *guajiro* farmers.

In the view of Washington's intelligence analysts, the island's dramatic embrace with the socialist bloc was largely attributable to the efforts of Che Guevara. In a secret March 23 assessment of his recently completed mission to the Sino-Soviet bloc, the State Department's Bureau of Intelligence and Research (INR) listed its considerable achievements.

"By the end of the visit, Cuba had trade and payments agreements and cultural ties with every country in the bloc, diplomatic relations with every country except East Germany, and scientific and technical assistance accords with all but Albania."

Whether or not Guevara had negotiated additional military assistance for Cuba on his mission wasn't known, but the report deemed it as a highly likely probability. "It may be assumed that the subject was discussed and delivery of new weapons agreed upon. According to one report, Guevara, early in his tour, asked Khrushchev for missiles and the Soviet Premier flatly refused, promising instead some automatic weapons from World War II."

II

The pros and cons of assassinating Che, Raúl, and Fidel had been discussed by the CIA for some time. In January 1960, Allen Dulles had initially rejected an assassination program in favor of the "exile army" scheme, but eventually the old-school Dulles would come around, for the sake of pragmatism, not blood lust, to whatever got the job done in the most efficient manner possible. If killing Cuba's top leaders helped ensure the success of the invasion plan, then it was an option that had to be pursued; in the intervening months, he had allowed his covert operations director, Richard Bissell, to explore assassination possibilities. Already some plots had been hatched, including an bizarre attempt to poison Fidel's favorite brand of cigars. Over the coming months and years, many more plots to kill Fidel and his top comrades would be planned or attempted, even including some in collusion with the American Mafia.*

Simultaneously, Allen Dulles was dealing with the burgeoning Congolese crisis. The former Belgian colony was a vital source of strategic minerals for the West, and Washington could not allow Moscow to establish a satellite government there; that, Dulles and his men feared, was exactly what Khrushchev was attempting to do. The African state's erratic-seeming prime minister, Patrice Lumumba, who had first called for UN troops

---

*By 1960, according to Evan Thomas, the author of a book about the CIA's early years (see "Selected Bibliography"), the CIA had come up with James Bondish code names for its intended targets: Fidel was "AMTHUG," while Che, a doctor, was "AMQUACK."

to halt the Belgian-backed secession of copper-rich Katanga province headed by a rival, Moise Tshombe, then asked the USSR for military support.

Back in August 1960, with Eisenhower's approval, Dulles had cabled the CIA station chief in the Congolese capital of Leopoldville, authorizing him to "remove" Lumumba "as an urgent and prime objective . . . of high priority." Lumumba had been ousted from office by his president, Joseph Kasavubu, and his army commander, Joseph Mobutu, but was still perceived as a threat. In September, Dulles had ordered that Lumumba be "eliminated from any possibility [of] resuming governmental position . . ."

A week later, the CIA station chief in Leopoldville received a visitor from Washington, Dr. Sidney Gottlieb of the CIA's "medical division." In his diplomatic valise, he had brought a syringe, rubber gloves, a mask, and a vial of untraceable biological poison; a practical solution had been found to help "remove" Lumumba. Before the CIA could get close to Lumumba, however, his own Congolese rivals did; he was captured by Congolese army troops and turned over to Tshombe's forces while under UN forces protection. While in captivity, Lumumba was murdered, on January 17, 1961, but the act was kept secret for nearly a month.

When Lumumba's death was finally announced in mid-February, it brought an angry denunciation by Khrushchev, who accused UN General Secretary Dag Hammarsjköld of being an "accomplice" to the murder. Cuba's foreign minister, Raúl Roa, echoed Khrushchev with an official note of protest to the UN. In Havana, Che lamented the murder of Lumumba, whom he looked to as a kindred revolutionary leader in Africa, and the Cuban government announced three days of official mourning. The men at the CIA were of course quietly pleased.

By March, the preparations for the CIA's Cuban invasion force were well under way, with its political front organization in place as well. After leaving behind a flourishing underground network in Cuba, Manuel Ray had been subsumed into the CIA-sponsored Cuban exile alliance, and former prime minister Míro Cardona had been named to head its vaunted "Cuban Revolutionary Council" as Cuba's future provisional president. All the anti-Castro activity, however, had caused major problems elsewhere.

The previous November, the six hundred–odd Cuban exile fighters of Brigade 2506 had completed a three-month guerrilla training course in Guatemala, but by then their presence—and the CIA's sponsorship—had been splashed all over the press. The scandal that ensued made life difficult for Guatemalan President Ydigoras Fuentes. Angered over the presence of foreign troops on their soil, a sizeable group of nationalistic Guatemalan military officers had staged a military uprising; on the night of November

13, troops had seized a military garrison in the capital, the Zacapa barracks in eastern Guatemala, and the Caribbean port of Puerto Barrios.

Despite their initial success, the rebel officers and their troops were unsure what to do next, turning away hundreds of peasants in Zacapa who tried to join up and asked for weapons with which to fight. The Eisenhower administration had been quicker off the mark. A U.S. naval flotilla was dispatched to stand off the coast and the CIA's Cuban guerrilla force deployed to help suppress the revolt, with CIA-supplied B-26 bombers piloted by exiled Cubans used to dislodge the rebels from their positions. The show of force worked, and the rebel troops quickly surrendered.

But what may have seemed to be a minor sideshow at the time was to have important consequences for the future. Two young U.S.-trained Guatemalan officers involved in the revolt, Marco Aurelio Yon Sosa, twenty-two, and Luis Turcios Lima, nineteen, did not return to their barracks. Instead, they went underground, determined to start a guerrilla war against the Guatemalan regime. Within fifteen months, they would be making their presence felt as the leaders of a left-wing guerrilla insurgency decried by Ydigoras Fuentes as "Cuba-directed," and, in time, Turcios Lima would become one of Che's favorite revolutionary protégés.

There had also been trouble in Venezuela that November, with the pro-Cuban *miristas* and Venezuelan Communists launching a violent insurrection in Caracas against Betancourt's regime. The left-of-center URD party of Venezuela's former president, Admiral Wolfgang Larrazábal, which had formed part of the ruling government coalition, deserted Betancourt to join a coalition with MIR and the Communists, forming a "National Liberation Council" to overthrow the government. Student demonstrations and street battles with police followed, but the revolt eventually was quashed. Betancourt reacted with increased repression, however, and, by year's end, constitutional guarantees would be suspended indefinitely; the universities closed, left-wing newpapers were banned, and the country's oil fields were occupied by troops. The Venezuelan stage was becoming propitious for an armed guerrilla struggle, and, with Cuban backing, it would come before too long.

Meanwhile, the "graduation" of the Guatemalan-based brigade of Cuban exiles coincided with a shift in CIA strategy regarding its future role in Cuba. The agency's original idea that the force could fight and survive as a guerrilla army looked increasingly doubtful, as they had learned through recent experience. While the main force was training in Guatemala, the CIA had run a parallel covert program, dispatching small teams of rebels and saboteurs to Cuba. Most had been quickly put out of action by Castro's forces. The CIA's airdrops had similarly failed to sustain the rebels in the mountains. What was required, therefore, was a rather more ambitious plan.

Switching tactics, Richard Bissell substituted conventional warfare instructors for the guerrilla trainers working with the Guatemalan-based brigade. Under the new plan, the brigade would make an amphibious landing on Cuba's coast. Supported by air strikes, they would establish a foothold and proclaim a provisional Cuban government, which would be instantly recognized by Washington and friendly Latin American governments; the United States could then theoretically intervene "to assist" Cuba's new "democratic government." While all of this was going on, it was hoped, Fidel, Che, and Raúl would already be dead. The CIA now had several schemes under consideration to assassinate the Cuban leadership on the eve of the landing.

Seven separate five-man infiltration groups called "Grey Teams" had been selected from the Guatemala brigade. They were to meet up with the underground resistance movement on the island and help coordinate the CIA's airdrops of weaponry. When the main invasion force landed, they were to act, hitting specific targets and leading armed uprisings throughout Cuba. The nineteen-year-old Felix Rodríguez was among those selected. He and the other Grey Team candidates were moved to a new jungle camp in Guatemala, where they were taught espionage "tradecraft" by war-hardened Eastern European anti-Communist exiles. A few days after Christmas, his Grey Team was ushered onto an American military transport plane with blacked-out windows and flown to Fort Clayton, one of the American military bases in the U.S. Panama Canal Zone. Their training had continued at Fort Clayton, but now they were being taught how to handle advanced weaponry of Soviet and Eastern European origin.

In early January, Rodríguez came up with a plan to assassinate Fidel and told his American handlers his idea. A few days later, they told him his plan had been given the agency's approval. He and a comrade were flown to Miami, where he was given a German-made sniper's rifle with a telescopic sight. The CIA had already selected the assassination site, a Havana house that Fidel was known to frequent. Three times Rodríguez was taken to the Cuban coast in fast boats traveling at night, and three times his rendezvous with the on-ground contacts failed. After the third failure, the rifle was taken away, and the CIA told Rodríguez they had "changed their minds" about the operation.

In the meantime, the other Grey Teams had been brought to a base camp on the outskirts of Miami. On February 14, the first infiltration team was smuggled into Cuba. A week later, four days after the ambush outside Che's home, Rodríguez and his four comrades, with a load of weapons, explosives, and ammunition, were dropped on Cuba's northern coast between the Varadero beach resort and Havana. They were picked up in cars driven by people belonging to the MRR underground.

Over the next month, Rodríguez and his friends met with the underground resistance in Havana and Camagüey, staying in safe houses and making preparations to receive a large airdrop of weaponry from the CIA. After getting the arms and distributing them, their mission was to largely replicate what Che and Camilo had done in the last phase of the anti-Batista war: to open up a guerrilla front in northern Las Villas and try to split the island in half, forcing the government to divert forces away from the south coast, where the invasion force was due to land.

At one point in mid-March, Rodríguez helped the Cuban underground transfer some weapons cached in a safe house located next door to the State Security headquarters on Fifth Avenue between Fourteenth and Sixteenth Streets. What he did not know was that the famed Che Guevara lived less than two blocks away; if he had, Rodríguez might well have devised a plan to kill *him*.

Certainly, none of this activity was likely to catch the Castro regime off guard, for it had quickly been disabused of any hopes that the new American president would accept a socialist Cuba as a *fait accompli*. Having so relentlessly used the soft-on-Castro theme against the Eisenhower-Nixon administration during the campaign, President Kennedy now seemed determined to show his mettle, and, in the two months since he had taken office, all the indications were that preparations were still under way for some kind of U.S.-backed military intervention.

In fact, Kennedy had been briefed about the planned "Cuban exile" invasion as soon as he had won the presidential election in November, and had given CIA Director Dulles his personal go-ahead. Since taking office, Kennedy had studied the CIA's beefed-up plans with a more tentative eye, expressing misgivings about the plan's viability—and some of his closest civilian advisors were vehemently opposed to it—but an effective combination of warnings and reassurances from the CIA men had won out in the end.

The exile force was well trained and itching to fight, Dulles's people told Kennedy; "D day" had to come soon. As matters now stood, the CIA could "take out" Cuba's small fleet of Sea Furies and B-26s before the invasion began, protecting the exile force from air attack. But that window was rapidly closing; Cuban pilots were being trained to fly Soviet MiGs in Czechoslovakia, and, although no MiGs had yet been delivered to Cuba, they probably would be before long.

The CIA had chosen a landing site, on Cuba's southern coast near Trinidad, in Las Villas province, but Kennedy thought it would be too "spectacular." He opted instead for a less visible spot farther west, at a remote beach called Playa Girón on the Bay of Pigs. Kennedy had been assured that if the rebels failed to hold their beachhead, they could make it to the "nearby" Escambray and, after meeting up with the rebels there, begin a guerrilla resistance movement.

The plan had many flaws. The "nearby" Escambray mountains were actually over one hundred miles away, and the very isolation that made Playa Girón seem ideal for a surprise landing made it a death trap if Castro's forces were able to get there quickly. If the rebels needed to escape, there were only two ways out: either along the narrow roads through the vast Zapata swamp or along the exposed strip of coastal beach. In either case, they could be easily ambushed, pinned down, and massacred. Evidently, none of this occurred to the CIA strategists.

Despite his misgivings, Kennedy gave his go-ahead, but ruled out direct U.S. troop involvement or any large-scale American air support once the assault was under way. The CIA men apparently believed that once the action had begun, the president would relent. In any event, this crucial bit of news was not imparted to the Cuban exiles involved; they thought they would be going in backed up by the full weight of America's military power.

Nor did the CIA have any clue about the extent to which their "covert" program had already been infiltrated by Castro's intelligence service. At least one of the thirty-five Grey Team members infiltrated into Cuba was a Castro government double agent, and there were undoubtedly others. In Miami, the general outline of the CIA's plans was widely known throughout the Cuban exile community, where Fidel had a flourishing spy network. What's more, Fidel now had plenty of armor at his disposal. As Alexiev gleefully confided years later, "We already had Soviet arms in Playa Girón. A lot of Soviet arms participated in Playa Girón."

III

Amid the heightened tension caused by the invasion rumors, the nocturnal air raids, and a spate of bombing attacks against expropriated stores in Havana, Che kept busy, giving speeches, writing articles, and receiving foreign delegations. When the Chinese, not to be outdone by the Soviets, held their own "Economic Edification Exposition" in the Hotel Habana Libre, he attended the opening and closing ceremonies. He cut the ribbon at one of the new Cuban acquisitions from the Soviet Union, a pencil factory, and visited the recently nationalized nickel mine of Nicaro, urging its workers to "work hard and sacrifice to produce more."

"Volunteer labor" had become Che's latest battle standard in his quest to create "a new socialist man" in Cuba. He had initiated the practice on a small scale shortly after Camilo's death, in the construction of a school built in his late comrade's memory, but, after seeing the volunteer work brigades in Mao's China, he had taken to the idea of replicating it en masse in Cuba with genuine conviction. Since his return, Che had begun devoting his Saturdays to the practice, lending a hand in factory assembly lines, cutting sugarcane, or lifting bricks at construction sites, and he urged his colleagues at the new Ministry of Industries to "set an example" by doing volunteer work during the sugar harvest. Before long, everyone at the Ministry of Industries who wanted to remain in Che's good graces began giving up their Saturdays at home to join him on these work sessions.

Che's program, which eventually came to be called *"emulación comunista,"* was based upon the principle that by volunteering one's labor on behalf of society, with no thought of remuneration, the individual takes an important step toward building a true Communist "consciousness." Che went out of his way to drive home the point among his comrades. One day, seeing Che was wearing no watch, his friend Oscarito Fernández Mell gave him his own, a fine watch with a gold wristband that he had bought for himself after graduating from medical school. Sometime later, Che came up to Oscarito and handed him a piece of paper; Oscarito noticed he was still wearing the watch, but it now had a leather wristband. The piece of paper was a receipt from the National Bank declaring that Oscar Fernández Mell had "donated" his gold wristband as a contribution to Cuba's gold reserves.

Everyone knew that Che had refused to collect the salary he was due as president of the National Bank, and he had continued the practice at the Ministry of Industries, steadfastly drawing only his minuscule *comandante*'s wages. Orlando Borrego, by now a vice minister, felt obliged to draw only an equivalent amount of his own salary, donating the rest to an agrarian reform fund; it would have been unseemly to be earning more money than his boss.

Not all of Che's comrades, including some of his ministerial-level peers, appreciated this revolutionary showmanship of his, acknowledged Borrego; he himself had been forced by Che to give up the car of his dreams. When Cuba's wealthy had fled the country, they had left behind a huge stockpile of cars, promptly nationalized, which the various government ministries allocated to their officials and certain employees. But Borrego had gone one better. During a visit to an "intervened" cigarette factory, a manager had pointed out a brand-new Jaguar sports car that had been abandoned by its owner and suggested that Borrego take it, since no one else knew how to run it. Borrego fell instantly in love with the car and sped around proudly in it for about a week, until the day he drove into the garage where he and Che parked their cars, and Che spotted him. He came toward him yelling: "You're a *chulo*—a pimp!"

Che pointed to the car and asked him what he thought he was doing, driving around in a car like that? It was a "pimp's car," ostentatious, not one a "representative of the people" should be seen driving. Borrego's heart fell, and he told Che he would return it. "Good," Che said, "I'll give you two hours."

Later, up in the office, Che told Borrego that he should be driving a car more like his, a much more modest, year-old green Chevy Impala. Before long, Borrego was given a car exactly like his jefe's, except that his was two-tone, and he would drive it for the next twelve years. "Che was superstrict," recalls Borrego, ". . . like Jesus Christ."

As Che busily made new enemies and allies, some of his older friends and acquaintances showed up in Havana. Granado had arrived with his whole family from Venezuela and was teaching biochemistry at the University of Havana. For entirely different reasons, Ricardo Rojo also showed up. Recently a diplomat stationed in Bonn for the Argentine government of Arturo Frondízi, which had tried unsuccessfully to intercede in the burgeoning U.S.-Cuba dispute, Rojo evidently hoped to use his relationship with Guevara to take soundings of Cuba's intentions. But Rojo could see that Cuba was already preparing for war. He observed militiamen jackhammering Havana's streets to lay explosive charges, and everywhere he looked, uniformed men and women wandered around with weapons. After passing through a gauntlet of bearded armed men in the foyer, he found his old friend Chancho Guevara in a half-furnished office. It had been six years since they had last seen one another, in Mexico. Guevara looked heavier, and Rojo told him so. Che denied that he was fat, attributing his "moon face" to cortisone treatments for his chronic asthma.

Probably cognizant that whatever he showed or said to the well-connected Rojo would filter back to Western policy-makers, Che took Rojo on a worker's tour of Cuba's countryside: to factories; to the cane fields; and to meet with peasant soldiers fighting in the Escambray against the counterrevolutionaries. He even press-ganged him into a day of volunteer labor cutting cane. Rojo came away certain of several things: that Cuba was definitely on the path to Communism; that the revolution was well armed and enjoyed widespread support among Cubans; and—judging from several inferences his old friend had made—that Che was interested in extending the revolution to South America.

Toward the end of March, Che accompanied Rojo to the airport. As they drove past numerous antiaircraft-gun emplacements, Che turned to Rojo. "They'll come," he said, referring to the Americans. "But we'll give them a reception. It's a pity you're leaving right now, when the party is about to begin."

On April 3, the White House released a "White Paper" on Cuba. Cuba, it said, posed "a clear and present danger" to the Americas. It was the Kennedy administration's call to arms for the military expedition that would soon be known as the Bay of Pigs invasion.

Five days later, with invasion jitters at a fever pitch, Che published an article in *Verde Olivo* entitled "Cuba: Historical Exception or Vanguard in the Anti-Colonialist Struggle?" Che answered his own question: Cuba was no exception, but merely the first Latin American nation to break the common mold of economic dependency and domination by imperialism. Its example was the path for its neighbors to follow to the goal of revolutionary freedom.

> What did we do to free ourselves from the vast imperialist system, with its entourage of puppet rulers in each country and mercenary armies to protect the puppets and the whole complex social system of the exploitation of man by man? We applied certain formulas, [the results] of discoveries of our empirical medicine for the great ailments of our beloved Latin America, empirical medicine that rapidly became part of scientific truth.

This was the "scientific" discovery that Ernesto Guevara had been destined for, the culmination of a process of searching that had begun with his work in medicine. But treating individuals' illnesses had never been his real interest; his motivation had always been that of the scientific researcher looking for a cure, a means to prevent; and, as it had been with medicine, so it had become with politics. Searching, crossing solutions off the list of possibilities as he went—"reformism, democracy, elections"—he had found Marx, then Guatemala, then Cuba, and in that baptism of fire, his discoveries of "empirical medicine" had led to "scientific truth." That truth, and the cure to man's ills, was Marxism-Leninism, and guerrilla warfare was the means to achieve it.

Before Cuba's revolution, he explained, "America lacked the subjective conditions, the most important of which is consciousness of the possibility of victory through violent struggle against the imperialist powers and their internal allies. These conditions were created through the armed struggle that clarified the need for change . . . and the defeat and subsequent annihilation of the army by the popular forces (an absolutely necessary condition for every genuine revolution). . . . The peasant class of America, basing itself on the ideology of the working class, whose great thinkers discovered the social laws governing us, will provide the great liberating army of the future, as it has already done in Cuba."

Che had created a "scientific truth," out of Cuba's experience, and scientific truth is not malleable to theories, but a natural law. In essence, Che was arguing that his formula for attaining socialism through armed struggle amounted to a scientific discovery, and through this discovery would come an end to injustice and the creation of a new form of man.

IV

Four days later, Havana's largest and most luxurious department store, El Encanto, was burned to the ground by one of the CIA-backed underground groups. Felix Rodríguez had been forewarned by his contacts that "something big" was about to happen and that he might want to leave town, because afterward, there would be "a lot of heat."

The next morning, in the predawn darkness of April 15, Sofía, the Guevara's nanny, awoke to the frightening noise of diving airplanes and exploding bombs. She ran out of her bedroom to the hall and called out to Che. Still shirtless, he instantly emerged from his bedroom. "The bastards have finally attacked us," he said.

From a window they watched the flashes and explosions; planes were bombing the airfield at nearby Campamento Libertad. Outside, Che's *escolta* had begun running around wildly, yelling and waving pistols, and Che shouted out the window: "I'll shoot the first man who fires!" The men calmed down, and within a few minutes he and his men had driven rapidly away. They went to Pinar del Río, his secretly prearranged battle station for the time when the invasion began. To have the end of the island closest to the United States well covered, Fidel had given Che command of Cuba's western army.

The next day, at the funeral for the victims of the bombing, which had destroyed the greater part of Cuba's minuscule air force, Fidel gave a fiery speech blaming the attack on the United States, which, he claimed, had done it because the nation could not forgive Cuba for having brought about "a socialist revolution" under its very nose. For the first time since seizing power, Fidel had uttered the dreaded word. Later, a bronze plaque would be secured on the spot consecrating the moment when Fidel "revealed the socialist nature of the Cuban Revolution."

Among the crowd listening to Fidel that historic afternoon were a young, prematurely balding artist from the Argentine mountain city of Mendoza named Ciro Roberto Bustos and his wife. They had just arrived in Cuba as volunteers to participate in the Cuban revolutionary experiment. As they walked Havana's streets soaking up the tropical atmosphere, everything was still new, strange, and exciting. The air was charged with por-tent. The future seemed promising and threatening at the same time—and indeed it was. Before long, Ciro Bustos's life would be completely absorbed, and irrevocably altered, by Che's vision of a continental revolution.

Just after midnight on April 17, the fifteen-hundred-man strong Cuban exile Liberation Army came ashore at Playa Girón on the Bay of Pigs. Days earlier, the units based in Guatemala had been transferred to Nicaragua's Caribbean port of Puerto Cabezas, where they had been seen off by Nicaragua's dictator, Luís Somoza, who cheered, telling them to bring him back "a hair from Castro's beard." They made the crossing to Cuba aboard ships lent them, as Che had forecast, probably jokingly, by the United Fruit Company, with U.S. naval destroyers as escorts. They were not told where they were going until they were out at sea.

Within hours of their landing, trumpeted loudly over the CIA's Radio Swan transmitter, Fidel had mobilized his forces for an attack on the invaders. Rather than push inland, the invaders dug into positions on the beach and awaited reinforcements. None came. By midmorning, the fighting had begun. But by dawn the next day, Dulles informed Kennedy that the exiles were bogged down; unless the United States intervened, they would be wiped out. Kennedy refused to give the order, authorizing only minimal air support.

In Havana, Felix Rodríguez heard about the invasion on the radio. He had had no advance warning. The CIA had not dared contact anyone in the underground resistance inside Cuba for fears of a leak. Cut off from the other members of his Grey Team, he tried to reach his Havana contacts on the telephone. In each case, there was either no reply or strange voices that told him to "come over right away." Realizing that many of the resistance people had probably already been arrested, and that the voices were those of security agents, he stayed where he was. Over the next three days he watched the events unfold on television and wept in frustration.

In Pinar del Río, Che's forces saw no action, but Che himself was nearly killed in a shooting accident. Aleida first learned of it when Fidel's all-purpose factotum, Celia Sánchez, called to inform her that Che had been lightly "wounded," grazed on the cheek and ear when his pistol fell out of its holster and a bullet went off. Celia sent a car to take Aleida to him, and another car to pick up Aliusha and her nanny, Sofía, so they could stay with her until the crisis was over.

Strictly speaking, Celia had told Aleida the truth. Che was out of mortal risk, but the bullet had come within a hairsbreadth of penetrating his brain. His greatest moment of danger, though, had come not from the bullet, but from the antitetanus injection his military medics had insisted on giving him, which had brought on a toxic shock reaction. As Che joked afterward to Alberto Granado, "My friends almost managed to do what my enemies couldn't: I nearly died!"

In Havana, Che's ex-wife, Hilda, also heard the rumors circulating of Che's wounding, initially relayed to her as an assassination attempt, but Che quickly dispatched a soldier to her house to tell her that he was out of danger and not to worry; it had been an accident.

For Sofía, the next forty-eight hours were a sleepless blur. Celia Sánchez's flat had become a communications nerve center for the revolutionary leadership, and Celia never put the phone down as an unending series of telephone calls gave her the latest battlefield reports, and she relayed the information on. At one point, a weary-looking Fidel came in, directly from the battleground, and collapsed on the same bed where Sofía lay with Che's daughter. As he slept, the baby played with his beard. Finally, exhausted herself, Sofía slept.

By the afternoon of April 20, it was all over. The exile force had bogged down, run out of supplies, and given up. One hundred and fourteen of the invaders were dead, nearly twelve hundred taken prisoner. At the happy news, Che returned to Havana from his post in Pinar del Río, picked up his friend Alberto Granado, and drove to Playa Girón. They arrived at the sugar mill of Central Australia, Fidel's command post during the battle. Now it was a chaos of military equipment, soldiers, and rounded-up POWs, with soldiers still combing the surrounding area for fugitives who had fled into the swamp. Jeeps roared off in all directions.

Che and Granado approached a group of prisoners. Upon recognizing Che, one of the POWs was so terrified that he defecated and urinated in his trousers. Che tried to question the man, but the prisoner was so afraid, he could not speak properly. Finally, Che turned away and told one of his bodyguards: "Get a bucket of water for that poor bastard."

Fidel, of course, was jubilant. He himself had directed the battle at Playa Girón, and he had personally fired a tank cannon at one of the American "mother ships"; his men swore afterward that he had scored a direct hit. All folklore aside, the battle had been a stunning victory for Cuba's revolution. The "people" had stood up to Washington, and they had won.

With the crisis over, Che went to see Hilda and Hildita. He seemed rather proud of his new gunshot wound, which had left a scar on his cheek, and as Hilda looked at it, he told her with studied dismissiveness: "It was an unimportant accident, but it was another close call. An inch closer and I wouldn't be here to tell it."

On the morning of April 26, Felix Rodríguez went from his Havana safe house in a chauffeur-driven green Mercedes belonging to the Spanish ambassador to the Venezuelan embassy compound. Four months later, he would be granted diplomatic safe-passage to leave the country, but he would soon be back in Cuba; neither he nor the CIA had given up the battle against Castro and his Communist government.

V

Four months later, in Punta del Este, Uruguay, Che delivered a message of gratitude to President Kennedy through Richard Goodwin, his young White House aide. "Thank you for Playa Girón," he told Goodwin. "Before the invasion, the revolution was shaky. Now, it is stronger than ever."

In recent months, the Cold War between East and West had intensified and become a personal test of wills between Kennedy and Khrushchev. Khrushchev seemed to revel in the competition, and pressed his advantage wherever he could, all the while thumbing his nose at the inexperienced young occupant of the White House.

For years, Washington and Moscow had fought to assert power in the vacuums left by the retreating European colonial governments in Africa, Asia, and the Middle East. So far, Moscow seemed to be winning. Since 1956 a series of international crises had pointed up the weaknesses and limitations of Western power abroad, as Washington or her allies took beatings in Suez, Lebanon, Indonesia, and Hungary.

The Soviets had raced ahead with their nuclear arms program, and the ensuing "missile gap" controversy in the United States had led Eisenhower to put U-2 spyplanes over Soviet Russia. This too had led to embarrassment, when American U-2 pilot Gary Powers was shot down in June 1960 and then reappeared on Soviet television, apologetically confessing he had been on a spying mission. (Before the end of 1961, U.S. intelligence would determine that the United States was far ahead of the Soviets in nuclear strike capability, but the missile-gap contretemps would continue to influence American policy for decades.)

In 1958, the USSR had become the first nation on earth to put a satellite into space and followed that in early April 1961 by launching cosmonaut Yuri Gagarin into orbit. On the eve of Kennedy's decision about whether to go ahead with the Bays of Pigs invasion, a triumphant Khrushchev had trumpeted his space victory, daring the West "to catch up." JFK grumbled that he didn't like having America come in second.

Simultaneously, new flash points had erupted around the world. Africa was in ferment. In the Congo, rival factions backed by East and West continued to struggle for power. Rwanda, Tanganyika, and Sierra Leone had all gained independence, but in the Portugese colony of Angola, an armed Angolan resistance movement began a struggle against Lisbon's steadfast colonial rule.

In Algeria, the seven-year-old independence war had already cost hundreds of thousands of lives and threatened civil war within France itself. In April, angered over de Gaulle's decision to negotiate Algerian independence with the Front de Libération National (FLN), top commanders of the French army revolted.

In Southeast Asia, Vietcong guerrillas backed by Ho Chi Minh's Communist North Vietnamese government in Hanoi were harassing the U.S.-backed government of South Vietnam. In neighboring Laos, Soviet and Chinese-backed Pathet Lao guerrillas launched a major offensive against the U.S.-backed Vientiane regime, forcing JFK to consider American military intervention there. In the end, a cease-fire was arranged, but Laos remained tense and unstable.

In the Caribbean, there was one less dictator to worry about after May 30, when Generalissimo Rafael Trujillo's life—and his thirty-year-long tyranny—were cut short in a fusillade of bullets. The assassination team's weapons had been supplied by the CIA; Washington had been under mounting pressure from the Latin American "reformist" governments to "do something about" Trujillo as a quid pro quo for their backing of Washington's anti-Castro policies.

But for Kennedy, Cuba remained an open sore, and Castro now had something Kennedy wanted: the twelve hundred POWs taken at the Bay of Pigs. Kennedy felt morally obliged to secure their release, and Fidel had been rubbing his face in his predicament. Fidel offered to free them for five hundred bulldozers; Kennedy was willing to give *tractors*. Fidel insisted on bulldozers, then asked for money. A haggling session ensued before talks broke down in June, and the POWs remained in Cuban prisons. (In December 1962 the prisoners were finally released in exchange for sixty-two-million-dollars' worth of medical supplies.)

Meanwhile, the Soviet-Cuban alliance looked cozier than ever. In May 1961, the Soviet Union awarded its annual "Lenin Peace Prize" to Fidel. The White House worried about the Soviets consolidating their foothold by installing missile bases on the island. Despite Khrushchev's reassurances to the contrary, Attorney General Robert Kennedy warned of this prospect in an April memo to his brother and urged prompt action. "The time has come for a showdown, for in a year or two years the situation will be vastly worse."

Kennedy spent summer weekends reading both Mao's and Che Guevara's writings on guerrilla warfare. Convinced that a new emphasis had to be put on counterinsurgency warfare to confront the growing threat of left-wing insurgencies, he instructed the army to beef up its antiguerrilla capability. By September, his initiative had resulted in the creation of a new elite counterinsurgency corps, the Green Berets.

In early June, Khrushchev and Kennedy met for the first time in Vienna for a two-day tough-talking session. They agreed on "neutrality" for Laos, but their talks on a nuclear test–ban treaty and disarmament were inconclusive. Khrushchev took the occasion to move another chess piece. Demanding that Berlin be "demilitarized," he threatened to deny the Western occupying powers—France, Great Britain, and the United States access to the city. These powers rejected the proposals and dispatched more troops to their sectors of the German city.

Invoking what he called "the worldwide Soviet threat," Kennedy called for a massive increase in the U.S. military budget and its troop levels. In August, East German and Soviet troops erected the Berlin Wall, sealing off East and West Berlin, and for some tense hours U.S. and Soviet tanks faced off against one another in the newly divided city.

The "loss" of Cuba to the Soviets had motivated Kennedy to take measures in Latin America to ensure continued American hegemony in the region. To thwart other Cuban-style revolutions from occurring in the hemisphere, Kennedy had drawn up a massive economic-development aid package for Latin America.

This was the tense international backdrop to the OAS economic conference held in August 1961 at Uruguay's Atlantic coast resort of Punta del Este. Kennedy sent his Treasury Secretary Douglas Dillon to unveil his vaunted "Alliance for Progress," the ambitious and unprecedented twenty-billion-dollar, ten-year aid-development package for Latin America. To represent Cuba at the forum, Fidel sent Che.

Punta del Este's staid atmosphere was electrified by the arrival of Guevara, who instantly stole the show from the other ministers; photographers and journalists eager for pictures and quotes followed him around everywhere. With Che, the conference had become high theater, a historic event. The Cold War had come to Uruguay.

Che lived up to his revolutionary reputation. His adolescent bodyguard, Leonardo Tamayo, went with him everywhere, lending an exotic touch to the proceedings. While all the other ministers attending the conference wore suits, Che wore his olive-drab military uniform. While the other ministers gave their own speeches sitting down, he delivered his speech on August 8 standing up. And, while Douglas Dillon ostentatiously looked to the ceiling and yawned, Che lambasted the American foreign policy proposal as an American plan to further isolate Cuba while extending its control over the rest of Latin America's nations through financial bribery, only increasing their subjugation to the great neighbor to the north.

On the other hand, Che argued, the Cuban example of asserting political and economic independence—by carrying out land and housing reform, by kicking out the monopolies and choosing its own trading partners and creditors—could provide a blueprint for the rest of Latin America. As for the U.S. estimates of spurring a 2.5 percent annual economic growth rate in Latin America through the Alliance for Progress, he declared, Cuba expected to best that by attaining an extraordinary *10 percent* growth rate within a few years.

Lest Cuba be seen only as a spoiler, Che suggested a series of conditions that should be set by the countries that joined the proposed alliance: freedom to export their raw materials wherever they chose; an end to the protectionist American subsidies of its own goods, which kept out competition; and aid to industrialize their economies, the real cornerstone to economic independence and prosperity.

Then, after a lengthy resume of the multiple acts of U.S. aggression against Cuba, culminating in the recent Bay of Pigs invasion, Che waved an olive branch to the Americans. Cuba wished no harm to its neighbors, he explained, and wished to be part of the American family of nations. It was willing to sit down and discuss differences with the United States at any time, so long as there were no preconditions. All Cuba asked for was a guarantee that she would not be attacked and would be granted her right to be *different* within her borders. "We cannot stop exporting an example, as the United States wishes, because an example is something that transcends borders. What we do give is a guarantee that we will not export revolutions, we guarantee that not a single rifle will leave Cuba, that not a single weapon will leave Cuba for battle in any other country of America."

But he warned that Cuba could not guarantee that her example would not be emulated. Unless her neighbors improved social conditions in their countries, the example of Cuba would inevitably "take fire"and, as Fidel had warned in his July 26 speech a year earlier, "the cordillera of the Andes would be the Sierra Maestra of the Americas."

As Che finished his two hour and fifteen minute speech, the hall was interupted by the loud cry of *"Asesino!"* and then, as security guards scuffled with the heckler and dragged him outside, two other strangers climbed onto the podium where Che stood and began insulting him. Ignoring them, Che calmly left the podium and conference room. Later, police informed the press that the hecklers were Cuban exiles who belonged to the Frente Democrático Revolucionario, the CIA-sponsored anti-Castro group.

Che's family had traveled to Uruguay, and for the first time since leaving Argentina, he saw his brother Roberto and sister Ana María again. His father, mother, brother Juan Martín, sister Celia, and aunt Beatriz were there as well. Quite a few friends also came: Julio "Gaucho" Castro, whom Che had tried to get to come to Cuba; Beto Ahumada; Pepe Aguilar; and his old business partner, "El Gordo" Carlos Figueroa, and that other *gordo,* Ricardo Rojo, who had resigned his post in Bonn since seeing Che in Cuba, and returned home.

Che and his brother Roberto could not have been more different. Roberto had married a woman from one of Argentina's aristocratic families, and, although publicly apolitical, he was a lawyer for the social welfare office of the Argentine navy, one of the most conservative political bastions in the country.

Roberto has never said if he and Che discussed their differences; in an interview, he would say about their Punta del Este encounter only that he found Che "radically different" from the brother he had last seen eight years before: austere, driven, and evidently lacking in humor. When he remarked about this transformation, Roberto recalled, Che told him curtly: "I'm no longer interested in witticisms, I have a different sense of humor now."

Che's bodyguard "Tamayito" said that there *was* an argument between the brothers, which he witnessed. "Che criticized Roberto for serving as an instrument of repression, and took the occasion to relate how *he* had evaded the military draft after graduating from medical school because he wasn't willing to serve in the armed forces of a corrupt regime that was an ally of American imperialism."

While Tamayito's recollection of what was said may not be accurate, Che's sermonizing must have rankled his brother. After all, Ernesto had been turned down by the draft because of his asthma, not because of any heightened political consciousness. A family photo taken at Punta del Este shows Che, looking scruffy and dressed in fatigues, surrounded by his family. Standing slightly behind him to one side, Roberto looks well groomed, conservatively dressed in slacks, a white shirt, cardigan, and tie. His hands are in his pockets, and he is staring intently at his brother.

Beto Ahumada, Ernesto's rugby-playing partner in the days of "Chang-Cho" and still close to the Guevara family, also found his old friend different. "He had always been a free man," Ahumada recalled, "and now here he was hooked into a process with responsibilities . . . a position that implied constant danger, and he always had people around covering him. He had changed. Changed completely. He was a more reserved man, more careful in the things he said."

After an initial and brusque meeting in public, Che arranged to spend a little time with his childhood friends in private. There, something of the old Ernesto returned. He handed out Cuban cigars, and they puffed away happily. All of them, said Ahumada, took the opportunity to offer Che their help if he felt they could be of service in Cuba.

"He joked with us, pulled our legs," recalled Ahumada. "He told Carlitos [Figueroa], who was selling real estate, that in Cuba they didn't need real estate specialists because the state owned the property, and nothing was for sale. And he ribbed me, telling me I wasn't needed as a lawyer, either, because in Cuba there were no lawsuits, so what could I possibly do there?"

Of all of them, Carlos Figueroa alone recalled Che as being the "same old Ernesto" who bantered and joked and tried to impress him with stories that sounded like adolescent tall tales. With a boyish relish, Che told Figueroa some of the more thrilling experiences he'd had. "You can believe it or not," he boasted, "but I went hunting on an elephant with Nehru." And he admitted that when the Russian cosmonaut Yuri Gagarin had recently come to Cuba, he had been so excited to meet the first man to go into space, he'd stayed "glued" to him for an entire day.

Another night, Che, his friends, and the whole family dined together. At one point, recalled Figueroa, his aunt Beatriz leaned over and asked Che about his new wife, Aleida. "She's a country girl," Che said, "a *guajira*." "And what is that?" Beatriz asked in bewilderment. "A *hacendada*?" At this description, Che laughed uproariously; his sheltered aunt obviously imagined he had married some aristocratic Cuban landowner's daughter.

Che paid special attention to his youngest brother, Juan Martín Guevara, who had just turned eighteen and was still living at home with Celia *madre*. Juan Martín was halfheartedly studying journalism at an institute in Buenos Aires and had begun going out with a fellow student, María Elena Duarte, four years older than himself. Juan Martín was at loose ends and chafed under his father's critical comparisons of his life with the achievements of his older brothers and sisters. At the same time, Juan Martín idolized Che and read Marxist texts avidly. Evidently aware of his youngest brother's predicament, Che sought to give him some direction during their time in Uruguay, inviting him to come to Cuba and go to university there. Juan Martín was enthusiastic, but the decision about exactly when he would go was left pending.

While Che was lodged in a nondescript hotel with the rest of his large official entourage, his family stayed in a nearby villa rented by a left-wing journalist, Julia Constenla de Giussani. Called "Chiquita" (Little One) by friends because of her petite size, Julia had become friends with Celia *madre* after interviewing her for a women's magazine that wanted a profile on "Che's mother."

Together with her journalist husband, Julia now edited a pro-Cuban political magazine called *Che* and worked closely with Alfredo Palacios, the venerable and eccentrically mustachioed leader of Argentina's socialist party. She had come to Punta del Este to cover the proceedings and interview Che, but her most vital mission was to meet with him privately. She was to make him a proposal on behalf of an Argentinian political coalition of socialists and left-wing *peronistas* that was preparing for upcoming elections. Specifically, they wanted to know if they proposed his name for a candidacy in the parliamentary elections, would Che be willing to return to his homeland?

When Julia finally met with Che alone, he quickly turned down the offer. Cuba still needed him, he explained, he had a destiny there to fulfill, and he didn't see himself as an Argentine politico. Then, looking directly at her, smiling ironically, he asked: "Madame, I am a minister. Do you see me as a parliamentary deputy in Argentina?"

But there was quite a bit more to the proposal Julia carried. She explained that they wanted him to lead a "symbolic" candidacy for the left. If a popular front gained power through elections, then he would have helped the effort; but if the elections were canceled and a peaceful solution was seen to be impossible, he could become the leader of a guerrilla movement, "the commander of Argentina's revolutionary transformation." It was up to him, she said; he could remain in Cuba, isolated, or he could help set in motion the process of change in Latin America.

"He asked me for precise details, explanations, descriptions of individuals in the various political groups, my analysis about union leaders and Argentine politics [in general]," recalled Julia. "It was like he was giving me an exam. I [think I] reminded him of his youth and how he had once been, and he wanted to find out how that world he had been a part of had changed."

Che went over Julia's proposal point by point, even discussing the relative merits of rural over urban guerrilla warfare, but at no moment did she feel that he wavered on his decision. He seemed to her to be completely pessimistic about the prospects for change through the electoral process in Argentina, and in the ability of its leftists to bring about true social transformation. He asked her how she thought the unions would react to an armed struggle, about the prospects for mobilizing the "urban masses," and which places she thought were best for the installation of a guerrilla force. He mentioned the recent spate of small-scale terrorist activities by the Argentine left and said he was against them. "Every action taken should be something that takes one closer to the seizure of power," Che told her, "and after the seizure of power [the goal should be] the conquest of the [national] territory."

Afterward, Julia said she realized there had been a logic to all his questioning. There were already Argentines in Cuba undergoing military training. She represented the viewpoints of those who had stayed behind; those who, as she put it, "were not within the bureaucratic structure of the export of the Cuban model."

Julia found Che to be a complex and fascinating man, but also one with a mean streak. One evening, dining with Che and his family, she reminded him of the dedication he had written in a copy of *Guerra de Guerrillas* and sent to the Argentinian Socialist party founder, Alfredo Palacios. Julia had seen what he had written: "To Dr. Palacios, who when I was a child, was already talking about revolution."

The subtlety had not been noticed by Palacios, who was thrilled and flattered by what he took to be Che's consideration of him, but Julia had caught the meaning of Che's inference immediately: Palacios had only *talked,* but never *done*. She thought it was cruel, and told him so at the dinner table. Che replied, simply: "That's all he ever did."

"With that he ended the discussion," said Julia. "It was an example of a part of his character; he could be really disrespectful to some people. . . . He could be really sharp and was capable of saying hurtful things. . . . It was as though the only people who merited his respect were the dispossessed, a hungry worker, a malnourished peasant. Even his parents didn't seem to merit the same respect."

Despite this "arrogant" side of him, Julia said that if she hadn't been so much in love with her own husband, she could easily have fallen head-long for Guevara. "As a person he had an incalculable enchantment that came completely naturally. If he entered a room, everything began revolving around him. . . . He was blessed with a unique appeal."

Julia also had opportunity to see Che's physical frailties. A few days after arriving at Punta del Este, he had such a severe attack of asthma that he had to spend a night in an oxygen tent; his bodyguard Tamayito stayed by his side the whole night. The next day, Che was able to walk around, but was still in great discomfort and breathing with difficulty. He didn't want to show his weakness in public, but the next day at the conference he made a discreet sign to Julia that he wanted to meet her in the lobby outside.

She went ahead and he appeared a couple of minutes later. He said nothing but leaned close to her, his back to the public, took out his inhaler, and sucked on it, then quickly slipped it back in his pocket. Afterward, Julia watched him for signs of distress, and whenever he gave his signal, she immediately walked out into the hall. "This happened seven or eight times during the conference. One time, he was in such a bad state that he leaned against the wall and he made a gesture with a limp hand because he didn't have the strength to get out his inhaler."

One day, Che disappeared from the conference for a couple of hours, his unexplained absence provoking rampant press speculation. One prominent journalist assured the others he had seen Guevara's car head toward where the American delegation was lodged. He had taken a gift box of Cuban cigars with him; the journalist even knew the brand.

In actuality, Che had escaped to go see his parents, but when he arrived at the rented villa, only Julia was there. Che came in anyway, and she served him tea and cakes, to which he observed acidly: "How nicely left-wing journalists live." But then he relaxed, taking off his boots, and sat in front of the fireplace, drinking his tea. He seemed exhausted and Julia let him be. They hardly spoke during the hour he stayed.

In a press conference the next day, Che was asked which of the myriad rumors circulating about his whereabouts the previous day was the correct one. "Some journalists are better informed than others . . . ," he replied enigmatically, before turning to Julia. "And you, madame, do you know anything?" "No, Comandante," she replied. "I'm not one of the better-informed journalists."

For another participant at the Punta del Este conference, the inveterate gadfly Ricardo Rojo, it had been only four months since he had last seen Guevara, on the eve of the Bay of Pigs invasion. Rojo had resigned his post in Bonn over his opposition to President Frondízi's policies, especially over his decision to grant U.S. companies oil-exploration rights in Argentina, a move seen by many Argentines as an affront to the country's national sovereignty. But Rojo was not the kind of man to burn his bridges entirely, and he now carried a message from Fidel: the Argentinian president wanted to meet with Che in secret.

Rojo had been stunned when approached by an intermediary to deliver the message. Frondízi was already deeply unpopular with the armed forces; there had been numerous coup plots and revolts against him, and such a meeting, if ever made public, could only aggravate his tenuous hold on power. But Che agreed to the encounter. In fact, he had already accepted a similar overture for a meeting from Brazil's president, Janio Quadros, through his representatives at Punta del Este. The two South American powerhouses were vital links in the Kennedy adminstration's new Latin policy proposal, and both had been involved in previous unsuccessful attempts to mediate between Cuba and their powerful northern neighbor. It was agreed that Che would travel to Buenos Aires after the conference ended, and from there go on to Brasilia.

On August 16, in his closing remarks to the conference, Che declared that Cuba could not ratify the resolution to support the Alliance for Progress.

Few of Cuba's suggestions had been discussed seriously, he pointed out, and few substantive changes had been made in what he considered a seriously flawed document. Finally, because it was, in the end, an initiative aimed at isolating Cuba, his government could not possibly approve it, but he took the occasion to reiterate Cuba's willingness to talk with the United States "on any issue, without preconditions."

The following night, at his behest, and with the connivance of some Argentine and Brazilian diplomats, Guevara was introduced to President Kennedy's twenty-nine-year-old personal assistant, Richard Goodwin, a key member of the U.S. delegation, at a birthday party for one of the Brazilian delegates. As Goodwin told President Kennedy afterward, the encounter came about after he had rejected several prior efforts by the Brazilians and Argentines to get the two of them together.

While having dinner with one of the Argentine delegates, a pair of Brazilian newspapermen, "and a couple of blondes," Goodwin had been invited to the birthday party. On the way there, Goodwin had "kiddingly" asked an Argentine: "You're sure Che won't be there?" to which his friend had protested vehemently that he "wouldn't do anything like that."

"There were about thirty people at the party," Goodwin recalled to Kennedy, "drinking and dancing to American music. I talked with several people and, after about an hour, I was told Che was coming. In a few minutes he arrived. I did not talk to him, but all the women in the party swarmed around him. [Then] one of the Brazilians said he (Che) had something important to say to me." They adjourned to an adjoining room, where they talked for the next "20–40 minutes," with interruptions from "waiters and autograph-seekers" until the American envoy took the initiative and broke off the conversation.

Face-to-face, Goodwin found Guevara quite different from the daunting public figure he had observed from a distance, as he told President Kennedy in an August 22 memorandum: "Che was wearing green fatigues, and his usual overgrown and scraggly beard. Behind the beard his features are quite soft, almost feminine, and his manner is intense. He has a good sense of humor, and there was considerable joking back and forth during the meeting. He seemed very ill at ease when we began to talk, but soon became relaxed and spoke freely. Although he left no doubt of his personal and intense devotion to communism, his conversation was free of propaganda and bombast. He spoke calmly, in a straightforward manner, and with the appearance of detachment and objectivity. He left no doubt, at any time, that he felt completely free to speak for his government and rarely distinguished between his personal observations and the official positions of the

Cuban government. I had the definite impression that he had thought out his remarks very carefully—they were extremely well organized."

Goodwin says he told Che that he possessed no authority to negotiate, but that he would report what he said to the "relevant officials" of the U.S. government. "He said 'good' and began.

"Guevara began by saying that I must understand the Cuban revolution. They intend to build a socialist state, and the revolution which they have begun is irreversible. They are also now out of the U.S. sphere of influence, and that too is irreversible. They will establish a single-party system with Fidel as Secretary-General of the party. Their ties with the East stem from natural sympathies, and common beliefs in the power structure of the social order. They feel that they have the support of the masses for their revolution, and that that support will grow as time passes."

Che warned Goodwin that if the United States thought Fidel could be overthrown from within, or believed he was actually a moderate surrounded by fanatics and could be won over by the West, these were false assumptions. The revolution was strong and could withstand such threats. He spoke of Cuba's appeal throughout the hemisphere, and warned that civil war would break out in many countries if Cuba were attacked. He brought up again the contradictions he saw inherent in the Alliance for Progress, which he thought might encourage the forces of social change, setting loose forces that would escape the Americans' ability to control, leading to Cuba-style revolution. "He spoke with great intensity of the impact of Cuba on the continent and the growing strength of its example."

Che spoke candidly of Cuba's problems: the armed counterrevolutionary attacks; disaffection on the part of the petite bourgeoisie and the Catholic Church; the damage caused by the U.S. embargo; the lack of spare parts or means to replace them; its inability to import consumer goods; and insufficient currency reserves. He told Goodwin that Cuba "didn't want an understanding with the U.S."—Cuba knew this would be impossible—but a "modus vivendi." In return, Guevara said, Cuba could agree not to make "any political alliance with the East." The expropriated American companies could not be returned, but compensation would be worked out in the form of trade. They would hold free elections once the revolution had been institutionalized. The U.S. naval base at Guantánamo "of course" would not be attacked, Che said, and "laughed as if at the absurdly self-evident nature of such a sentiment." He also hinted "obliquely" that Cuba would be willing to "discuss the activities of the Cuban revolution in other countries."

"He then went on to say," Goodwin wrote, "that he wanted to thank us very much for the invasion—that it had been a great political victory for them—enabled them to consolidate—and transformed them from an aggrieved little country to an equal."

Che couldn't pass up the opportunity for this jab, but he had not come to goad Washington, only to propose some form of negotiations. Before their meeting ended, he told Goodwin he would relay the substance of their conversation only to Fidel. Goodwin said he would not "publicize" it, either.

For all this easy repartee, Goodwin clearly saw Che's overture as a sign of weakness, and that is what he advised Kennedy in a follow-up memo on August 22. "I believe this conversation—coupled with other evidence that has been accumulating—indicates that Cuba is undergoing severe economic stress, that the Soviet Union is not prepared to undertake the large effort necessary to get them on their feet, and that Cuba desires an understanding with the U.S. It is worth remembering that Guevara undoubtedly represents the most dedicated communist views of the Cuban government—and if there is room for any spectrum of viewpoint in Cuba there may be other Cuban leaders even more anxious for an accommodation within the U.S."

Based on this premise, Goodwin outlined a series of actions for Kennedy to take. They included stepping up the economic pressure against Cuba and taking retaliatory measures against anyone doing business with the Castro regime, as well as intensifying anti-Cuban propaganda while simultaneously trying to find "some way of continuing the below ground dialogue which Che has begun. We can thus make it clear that we want to help Cuba and would help Cuba if it would sever communist ties and begin democratization. In this way we can begin to probe for the split in top leadership which might exist."

Was Che's offer a sincere one? Perhaps. He sought a means of stalling Washington from taking its policy of "regional containment" any further. But in fact his offer held little substance. The offer to decline membership in the Warsaw Pact was a formality Cuba could easily forswear. And if the United States accepted recompensation in the form of trade with Cuba, it could hardly enforce its trade embargo on other countries. As for elections, once the revolution was institutionalized and the remaining malcontents had left the island, this was a process that the revolution could easily control.

Significantly, Che had not said that he would end Cuban support for guerrilla insurgencies in the region. He had promised publicly that "not a single weapon" would leave Cuba for use in other countries, but he had not mentioned training guerrillas, or providing funds or fighters. As for weapons, they could be obtained anywhere, even in the United States.

The next day, August 19, Che was flown in a small plane to an airfield outside Buenos Aires. The military officer whom President Frondízi had sent to meet the plane was unaware of the identity of the person he was to pick up and take to the presidential residence; when he saw Che Guevara descend from the plane, he was dumbstruck.

Che met over a lunch with Frondízi, who plainly wanted to use their meeting to test the waters as to Cuba's future intentions. He outlined his hopes for peaceful coexistence with Cuba and that Cuba would not enter into a "formal alliance" with Moscow. Che assured Frondízi that Cuba had no intention of doing anything of the kind unless it was attacked by Washington.

After their luncheon, Che asked a favor from Frondízi. Could he visit his seriously ailing aunt, María Luisa, who lived in the suburb of San Isidro? Frondízi agreed, and Che went off to see his aunt for the last time. For the first time in eight years, Che saw the streets of Buenos Aires again, through the windows of a presidential car, a clandestine visitor to his own country. He was then driven back to the airfield and flown across the Río de la Plata to Uruguay. He did not leave the airport there, but got on board the Cubana plane where his entourage awaited and flew off to Brasilia.

The news of Che's "secret" visit spread rapidly, however, causing real consternation in military circles. That same night a bomb exploded in Buenos Aires, blowing out the front door of the apartment building on Calle Arenales where Che's uncle, Fernando Guevara Lynch, lived. When the press questioned him, Che's uncle said he had not seen his nephew, and learned about his lightning visit only afterward. "It was 1953 when he left the country. It would have given me great pleasure to have seen him." Then he excused himself and, with true Guevara aplomb, told the reporters that he was going out for dinner with friends, and hoped to make it "if a bomb hasn't been placed under the hood of my car."

The bombing was not the only fallout from his visit. Over succeeding days, Argentina's newspapers ran stories about the "concern" felt by the armed forces over Che's unorthodox visit, along with photographs of grave-faced generals coming and going from tense meetings with the president. Argentina's foreign minister was forced to resign, and seven months later, when Frondízi himself was overthrown in a military coup, most political observers agreed that his encounter with Guevara had hastened his fall.

Indeed, wherever Che alighted, calamities followed. During a speech he had given at the University of Montevideo, there were protests and a shot was fired, killing a Uruguayan professor in the crowd. Tamayito was convinced it had been a plot to kill Che, carried out by anti-Castro exiles flown in by the CIA. At his meeting with Janio Quadros, the president of Brazil, Che was decorated with the prestigious Orden Cruzeiro do Sol. Five days later, besieged by criticisms over the controversial ceremony, Quadros resigned. Apparently Quadros expected his gesture to be rejected by Congress, but instead it was accepted, and his political career was suddenly over.

VI

Within a few weeks of Punta del Este, Washington had sent a clear message it was not interested in Che's overture: Congress passed a bill banning U.S. assistance to any nations dealing with Cuba. That same month, Costa Rica broke off relations with Havana, and in November Romulo Betancourt's government in Venezuela followed suit.

By now, Latin America's armies were on the alert for any signs of Cuban "subversion," and U.S. military aid and specialized training was on offer to deal with the threat. In October 1961, the first "Inter-American Counterrevolutionary War Course" began at Argentina's Escuela Superior de Guerra. At the inaugural ceremony, echoing the language used by Che Guevara to unite Latin Americans for the common struggle against "imperialism," Brigadier General Carlos Turolo invoked the spirit of "international solidarity with the people of the Americas . . . [faced with the] . . . imperative necessity to coordinate action, prevent and combat the common enemy, communism."

The counterinsurgency era had arrived in Latin America. Faced with the threat posed by people such as Che Guevara and their power to inject others with the demon seed of subversion, Washington had decided to use preventive medicine to "inoculate" the hemisphere. The vaccine was a potent one: counterinsurgency training; coordinated action by the region's military, police, and intelligence agencies; a stepped-up role for the CIA; economic and social development programs through the Alliance for Progress; and military "civic action" projects in backward areas to win the guerrilla-targeted civilians' "hearts and minds."

CIA Director Allen Dulles had been fired after the Bay of Pigs disaster, but under the new director, John McCone, the agency had more strength to deal with Cuba. In November 1961, JFK gave Langley a fifty-million-dollar annual budget for a new covert action program against Cuba, code-named "Operation Mongoose." Coordinated out of Washington and the CIA's Miami station, the ambitious program aimed to destabilize the Cuban regime through espionage, sabotage, military attacks, and selective assassinations. In time, it would become the CIA's largest covert operation in the world.

As the planning for Operation Mongoose got under way, the CIA was actively trying to rebuild its underground resistance network in Cuba, devastated in the massive roundup of suspected dissidents by Cuba's security forces after the Bay of Pigs. In October, only weeks after he had left his Venezuelan embassy asylum, the agency's contract employee Felix Rodríguez was on his way back to the island. His mission: to rebuild the CIA's infiltration routes for future paramilitary actions.

By year's end, Kennedy's policy of "containment" was enjoying some success. In December, an OAS resolution by Cuba's neighbors condemning its Soviet-bloc alignment was virtually unanimous; only Mexico sided with Cuba in voting against it. That same month, Colombia, Panama, Nicaragua, and El Salvador severed relations. In Havana, Fidel made a speech that definitively sealed Cuba's break with the West. "I am a Marxist-Leninist," he declared, "and will be until I die."

At the end of January 1962, the OAS voted to suspend Cuba's membership in the organization and ban arms sales to the island by member states, and agreed on measures for joint defense against Cuban actions in the region. In February, Kennedy tightened the already stringent trade embargo against Cuba, banning all exports except medical supplies.

Operation Mongoose director Edward Lansdale came up with a rip-roaring schedule for a package of actions, including "attacks on key leaders," to culminate in Castro's overthrow by October. (This plan was then scaled down, but the final guidelines for Mongoose, while calling for the CIA to make "maximum use of indigenous resources" to bring about Castro's overthrow, also concluded that, to achieve its aims, U.S. military intervention would be "required.")

In February, in Buenos Aires, a bomb was discovered and defused by police outside Celia's house on Calle Araoz. A week later, Argentina severed its diplomatic links with Cuba. In March, with agricultural production sharply down in Cuba and consumer shortages in all the shops, mandatory government rationing for foodstuffs and other basic goods was imposed. From now on, Cubans would have to line up to buy food with ration booklets used to record their weekly allowances. It had been only seven months since Che had confidently predicted that Cuba would soon be virtually "self-sufficent" in food.

Who was to blame for the shortages? Was it caused by the U.S. trade embargo? In part, yes. Was it the revolution's radicalization that had caused the crippling exodus of technicians, managers, and traders from the island? Yes. Was it the incompetence of the revolution's leaders in attempting to convert a capitalist economy to a socialist one? Yes, all of these were contributing factors.

Although neither Che nor Fidel would acknowledge the fact, the advent of food rationing heralded the end of their illusion of making Cuba a self-sufficient socialist state, free of external dependencies. As for Che's illusion that a global fraternity of socialist nations could bring about the demise of capitalism, it was about to be dashed to pieces.

VII

In late April 1962, Alexandr Alexiev was urgently summoned back to Moscow by Nikita Khrushchev. No explanations were given, and Alexiev was alarmed. A child of Stalinism, Alexiev says he immediately began thinking the worst and preparing himself for some kind of punishment while racking his brain to figure out what he could have possibly done wrong.

He stalled for time, asking to remain for the May Day festivities in Havana. A million people were expected in the Plaza de la Revolución, and the "International" was to be sung for the first time in the now openly socialist state of Cuba. He was given permission to stay for the event, but told to come to Moscow immediately afterward.

On the third of May, Alexiev flew to Mexico, where the Soviet ambassador told him he had orders to lodge him at the embassy, not in a hotel. It was the same story at his next stop, London. Quite obviously, the Kremlin wanted to keep a close eye on Alexiev, and he arrived in Moscow extremely worried. A department chief of the Soviet Foreign Ministry was waiting for him at the airport, not a normal assignment for such a high-ranking official. Alexiev was by now truly mystified and was left none the wiser by the official, who would tell him only that he would learn "tomorrow" why he had been called home.

The next morning, Alexiev was escorted into the Kremlin and taken to the office of Mikhail Suslov, Khrushchev's deputy. Suslov wasn't there, but two high-ranking Central Committee secretaries were: Yuri Andropov and the KGB chief, Alexander Shelepin.

Shelepin took Alexiev into his office and explained that he was to be the new Soviet ambassador to Cuba; that Nikita Khrushchev himself had made the decision. While they talked, Khrushchev called and asked Alexiev to come quickly to his office.

Khrushchev was alone, and the two of them talked for about an hour. The premier confirmed Alexiev's ambassadorship, which Alexiev tried to decline with humility; what Cuba needed with all her current problems, he said, was an ambassador who knew about economics, and he was an "illiterate" in that field.

"That's not important," Khrushchev told him. "What is important is that you are friendly with Fidel, with the leadership. . . . And they believe in you, which is the most important thing." As for economists, he would give Fidel however many experts he needed. Right there and then, Khrushchev made a call and ordered a team of twenty top-level ministerial advisors from every field of the economy to be assembled, to accompany Alexiev back to Cuba. He then turned to Alexiev and told him they were through for now, but he wanted to see him again in a couple of weeks to talk more "concretely."

Toward the end of May, Khrushchev sent for Alexiev again. This time, he found the Soviet leader with six other officials: his aide Frol Koslov, Deputy Premier Mikoyan, Foreign Minister Andrei Gromyko, Defense

Minister Rodion Malinovski, and the Politburo alternate member, Sharif Rashidov. Alexiev was invited to sit down.

"It was a very strange conversation," said Alexiev. "Khrushchev asked me again about Cuba, the Cuban comrades, and I talked about each one, and then, when I was least expecting it, he [Khrushchev] told me: 'Comrade Alexiev, to help Cuba, to save the Cuban revolution, we have reached a decision to place [nuclear] rockets in Cuba. What do you think? How will Fidel react? Will he accept or not?'"

Alexiev was astounded. He told Khrushchev that he thought Fidel wouldn't accept the offer because his long-held public stance was that his revolution had been carried out to restore Cuba's independence. They had thrown out the American military advisors, and if they accepted Soviet rockets on their soil, it would seem to violate their own principles. It would also be viewed through the eyes of international public opinion, and especially by Cuba's Latin American neighbors, as a serious breach of trust. "For these reasons," Alexiev concluded, "I don't think they will accept."

Malinovski reacted angrily. "Malinovski attacked me," Alexiev recalled. "What kind of revolution is this that you say won't accept? I fought in *bourgeois* Republican Spain, which accepted [our help] . . . and socialist Cuba has even more reason to!" Alexiev was intimidated and kept quiet as another official rallied to his defense, but Khrushchev said nothing, and the argument fizzled. They began talking about other subjects and finally adjourned for lunch in the adjoining dining room.

Over lunch, Khrushchev announced that while Fidel might not accept the offer, he was at least going to send a couple of high-ranking commanders—Sharif Rashidov, the Politburo official, and Marshal Sergei Biryusov, commander of the Strategic Rocket Forces—back to Havana with Alexiev to talk with Fidel. "There's no other way for us to defend him," Khrushchev said. "The Americans only understand force. We can give them back the same medicine they gave us in Turkey [where the United States had installed nuclear missiles pointing at the USSR]. Kennedy is pragmatic, he is an intellectual, he'll comprehend and won't go to war, because war is war. Our gesture is intended [precisely] to avoid war, because any idiot can start one . . . but we're not doing that, it's just to frighten them a bit. . . . They should be made to feel the same way we do. . . . They have to swallow the pill like we swallowed the Turkish one."

Khrushchev was referring to the threatening U.S. deployment of nuclear-tipped Jupiter missiles taking place in neighboring Turkey that same month—the culmination of a 1959 agreement negotiated by the Eisenhower administration with its NATO partner and reluctantly followed through by Kennedy.

Khrushchev warned that the operation to install the missiles in Cuba
would have to be carried out in the utmost secrecy, so that the Americans
"wouldn't suspect anything" until *after* their upcoming congressional elections in November. It could not be allowed to become a campaign issue. If
it was done right, he said, he was convinced the Americans would be too
busy with their campaigning to notice anything, and by then the missiles
would be in place.

A day or two before he was to leave for Cuba, Alexiev was tracked
down by Kremlin officials; Nikita Khrushchev wanted to see him again.
They took him to Khrushchev's dacha at Peredelkino in the forested countryside outside Moscow, where he found the premier and the entire Politburo gathered. Khrushchev presented him to the assembled officials, and
then announced: "Alexiev here says Fidel won't accept our proposal."
Khrushchev had thought up an approach that might work, however, and
he tried it out on the others.

He would tell Fidel that the missiles would be placed only as a last
resort; first, the Soviet Union would attempt all other means of persuasion
to dissuade the Americans from attacking Cuba, but he would offer his
strong personal opinion that only the missiles would do the job. He hoped
that would convince Fidel, he said, and told Alexiev to relay the proposal.

A few days later, still convinced that the overture would be rebuffed,
Alexiev returned to Cuba with his "agricultural delegation," which included Rashidov and a disguised Marshal Biryusov in tow, with Biryusov
traveling as a simple engineer named "Petrov." As soon as they arrived,
Alexiev went to see Raúl Castro, and told him his group was on a mission
for Khrushchev and needed to meet with Fidel immediately. "Engineer
Petrov is not engineer Petrov," he told Raúl. "He is a marshal [in charge]
of the Soviet missile [program]."

Raúl understood Alexiev's insinuation and went into Fidel's office; he
didn't come out again for two or three hours. Then, they met with Fidel in
Dorticós's office. "I saw that Raúl," Alexiev recalled, "for the first time ever,
was writing things down in a notebook."

When the Soviets had finished explaining Khrushchev's missile proposal, Fidel was noncommittal but made favorable noises; he told the Soviets to give him until the next day. The way Alexiev understood it, Fidel
wanted to consult with Che.

The next day Alexiev was summoned by Fidel. Once again they met
in Dorticós's office, but this time, several others were present, including Che,
Dorticós, Carlos Rafael Rodríguez, and Blas Roca. They had considered the
proposal and, agreeing that the missiles could stop the Americans from
invading Cuba, were willing to go ahead with the missile program. The con-

versation then turned to the likelihood of a U.S. invasion, and Alexiev recalled that Che was the "most active" in the discussion that followed, making his opinion on the missile issue clear. "Anything that can stop the Americans," Che said, "is worthwhile."

The Soviets and their Cuban counterparts proceeded immediately with the job of selecting missile sites, and then Fidel told Alexiev he wanted a "military pact" to formalize the affair, and would send Raúl to Moscow to sign the agreement. According to Vitali Korionov, a Central Committee advisor, Fidel outlined for inclusion in the pact a list of Cuban objectives he wanted the Soviets to negotiate with the Americans once the presence of the missiles was made public. In addition to securing a noninvasion commitment from Washington, he wanted "the dismantling" of the U.S. naval base at Guantámano Bay. The Soviets agreed to the demands, and over the next week Alexiev and Raúl worked closely to produce a Spanish-language version of the agreement. Then, said Alexiev, Raúl and Marshal Malinovski signed each page of the document.

By July 2, 1962, Raúl was in Moscow carrying the treaty draft. Over the next week, according to Alexiev, he met with Khrushchev twice. But Vitali Korionov recalled things differently. He said that when Raúl and his wife, Vílma Espín, arrived, he was called by Prime Minister Alexei Kosygin to go with him to receive them at the airport. Then they were taken to a protocol house. There Korionov, Kosygin, and Raúl went into the dining room, where there was a grand piano. It was just the three of them. "Raúl put the document on the piano, with Fidel's points, now translated into Russian, and there, without sitting down, Kosygin and Raúl signed the document. Afterward, Kosygin said he was leaving, and told Korionov to stay and "calm down" Raúl, who was extremely nervous.

"He was in a state of tense expectancy," said Korionov. "[As if thinking] 'What is going to happen now?' Because the Cuban comrades understood how this could end." As requested, Korionov stayed with Raúl, and they sat up all night, talking and drinking Armenian cognac.

Fidel had also told Raúl he wanted Khrushchev to answer one question: What would happen if the Americans discovered the operation while it was still in progress? Alexiev said that Khrushchev's reply was short and breezy: "Don't worry, nothing will happen. If the Americans start getting nervous, we'll send out the Baltic Fleet as a show of support." Raúl accepted Khrushchev's answer as a firm commitment of support. Alexiev recalls Raúl remarking to him: "This is great, just great! Fidel will accept everything; he may correct a few things but that's all. In principle he'll accept."

It was a fearsome and hefty military package indeed: twenty-four medium-range and sixteen intermediate-range ballistic missile launchers,

each equipped with two missiles and a nuclear warhead; twenty-four advanced SAM-2 surface-to-air missile batteries; forty-two MiG interceptors;
forty-two IL-28 bombers; twelve *Komar*-class missile boats, and coastal defense cruise missiles. The arsenal would be accompanied by four elite Soviet combat regiments totalling forty-two thousand troops. The agreement
was renewable every five years, and stipulated that the missiles would be
completely under the command of the Soviet military.

Around July 15, even before Raúl had left Moscow or Fidel had seen
the agreement, the first missiles were surreptitiously shipped out from the
Soviet Union's Black Sea ports concealed aboard cargo ships. Military men
and troops also began to leave for Cuba secretly. On July 17, Raúl flew back
to Havana, followed in three weeks by Alexiev, now the new Soviet ambassador. With him, he brought the agreement that had been ratified by Raúl.

Before leaving Moscow, Khrushchev had informed Alexiev that there
were "already" Soviet missiles in Cuba, and stressed again the necessity to
maintain total secrecy about the operation until November or later. Not one
cable should be sent from Havana; if he had something important to discuss, Alexiev should come to Moscow himself or send an emissary.

As yet, Khrushchev had not signed the agreement, pending Fidel's
final approval. His plan was to travel to Cuba himself for the January anniversary of the Cuban revolution triumph and there, after he and Fidel had
signed the agreement, sensationally divulge it to the world. By then, everything would be in place, and the fait accompli would give Khrushchev tremendous strategic bargaining power with Washington.

As it turned out, of course, things did not go as planned. First, Fidel
did not like the draft agreement; it was "too technical" with not enough
of a "political framework." In particular, says Alexiev, Fidel took issue
with the preamble that originally read: "In the interests of ensuring her
sovereignty and to maintain her freedom, Cuba requests that the Sovet
Union considers and accepts the possibility of installing missiles [on her
territory]. . . ."

As Alexiev explained it, Fidel's changes shifted the onus of the decision to install the missiles from appearing to be a Cuban request to a responsibility shared equally between the two nations. In essence, he wanted to
formalize what Khrushchev had already promised rhetorically—that an
attack against Cuba would be considered an attack on the USSR. Accord-
ingly, the new preamble read: "It is necessary and has been decided to take
the necessary steps for the joint defense of the legitimate rights of the people
of Cuba and the Soviet Union, taking into account the urgent need to adopt
measures to guarantee mutual security, in view of the possibility of an imminent attack against the Republic of Cuba and the Soviet Union."

Che Guevara and Fidel Castro, 1964. Although Fidel named his brother Raúl as his successor, many observers considered the influential Che Guevara to be his right-hand man. *Salas.*

Castro's victorious rebel army drives through Santa Clara toward Havana, early January 1959. *Photo by Burt Glinn, Magnum Photos Inc.*

Havana, New Year's Day 1959. After hearing the news of Batista's flight, underground rebels and their sympathizers took to the streets to hunt down government informers and police agents. *Photo by Burt Glinn, Magnum Photos Inc.*

La Cabaña, the Spanish colonial-era fortress and army garrison that overlooks the harbor and city of Havana. Che assumed command of the bastion on January 3, 1959, and quickly turned it into the headquarters for the roundup of suspected *batistiano* war criminals. Over the next three months, some fifty-five prisoners were executed here by firing squads after revolutionary tribunals in which Che served as "Supreme Prosecutor." *Salas*

In January 1959, Che's first wife, Hilda Gadea, and their daughter, Hilda Beatriz, arrived in Havana. Che told his wife that he had fallen in love with Aleida March and asked her for a divorce. She assented, but decided to stay on in Cuba. On February 15, Che attended his daughter's third birthday party. From left (foreground): Che, Hilda, and "Hildita." *Cuban Council of State Office of Historical Affairs*

Following the rebel victory, Che's parents, sister Ana María and brother Juan Martín arrived for a visit. Amid a milling crowd of curious onlookers, Che met them at Havana airport. From left: Ana María, Celia Guevara, Che, and Ernesto Guevara Lynch. *Cuban Council of State Office of Historical Affairs*

Che and his daughter Hildita with Antonio Nuñez Jiménez, the geographer who joined Che in Santa Clara and came with him to Havana. To make up for their long separation, Che often sent for his daughter to visit him in La Cabaña. *Salas*

Che, shirtless, with his mother, Celia, during the first annual Ernest Hemingway Marlin Fishing Tournament, in 1960. His mother made several trips to Cuba to see her beloved son, but Che's father never returned while his son was alive. At far right, Fidel's secretary-confidante, Celia Sánchez. *Cuban Council of State Office of Historical Affairs*

On June 2, Che and Aleida were married at the La Cabaña home of his bodyguard Alberto Castellanos. Ten days later, Che left for a long trip abroad. From left, front row: Raúl Castro, Vílma Espín, Che, Aleida, and Alberto Castellanos. *Cuban Council of State Office of Historical Affairs*

Working on Havana's docks, 1961. Che was rarely at home. He normally worked eighteen- to twenty-hour days, six days a week, and on Sunday mornings, he went off to do "volunteer labor," a practice he introduced to set a personal example of Communist dedication and sacrifice. *Liborio Noval*

During the six years Che remained in Cuba, Aleida bore him four children. This final family portrait was taken in March 1965, shortly before he left for the Congo. From left: Che with his newborn son, Ernesto, Camilo, Aliusha, and Aleida with daughter Celia on her lap. *Cuban Council of State Office of Historical Affairs*

Che and his young aide, Orlando Borrego, doing volunteer labor on a construction site in 1960. When he departed from Cuba, Che left Borrego his "heretical" unpublished critique of the Soviet political economy. *Salas*

In late 1960, on his first trip to the USSR, Che met with Soviet leader Nikita Khrushchev, who had "fallen in love" with the Cuban revolution. The man with them is Nikolai Leonov, the KGB "translator" whom Che knew from his days in Mexico City. *TASS/Prensa Latina*

Che and Mao Tse-tung, November 1960. Che thought the Chinese showed a "higher socialist morality" than the Soviets. Because of his efforts to spread Chinese-style "rural guerrilla warfare" throughout the Western hemisphere, the Kremlin would later accuse him of being a radical "Maoist." *Prensa Latina*

Che is met at Havana airport by his wife, Aleida, and the white-shirted Soviet ambassador, Alexander Alexiev. When Alexiev, a KGB official, was sent to Cuba in 1959, his first port of call was Guevara, and he later said that "Che was practically the architect of the Soviet-Cuban relationship." *Prensa Latina*

In 1959, Egyptian president Gamal Abdel Nasser was a foremost "anti-imperialist" leader of the world's newly independent nations, and Che established fraternal relations with him. But Nasser saw Che's later plans to fight in the Congo as unwise and warned he would become a "Tarzan" figure, doomed to failure. Behind Nasser is Anwar Sadat. *UPI/Corbis-Bettmann*

Che and Algerian leader Ben Bella, 1964. The two enjoyed close ties, coordinating actions to assist guerrilla movements in Africa and Latin America. *AP/Wide World Photos*

A stream of international leftist luminaries came to "Free Cuba" and called upon Che Guevara. Among them were Simone de Beauvoir and Jean-Paul Sartre, seen here with Che and Antonio Nuñez Jiménez (far left), in 1960. After Che's death, Sartre would exalt Guevara as "the most complete human being of our age." *Cuban Council of State Office of Historical Affairs*

In December 1964, Che addressed the United Nations General Assembly, decrying "racist" intervention in the Congo by white Western powers. Within months, Che would vanish from public view, leading a Cuban guerrilla force to assist the Congolese revolutionaries. *UPI/Corbis-Bettmann*

John F. Kennedy and his wife, Jackie, addressing Cuban exiles at Miami Stadium on December 29, 1962. Kennedy's short-lived presidency was overshadowed by the confrontation with Cuba. *Photo No. ST-C75-2-62 in the John F. Kennedy Library*

Che Guevara, during a lull in the August 1961 economic summit held by the Organization of American States in Punta del Este, Uruguay. Sipping *mate*, he holds forth to Uruguayan president Víctor Haedo (at right, in white hat) and a rapt audience. At the summit, the U.S. delegation unveiled the "Alliance for Progress" aid package for Latin America, a cornerstone of Kennedy's policy to "contain" Communist Cuba. *AP/ Wide World Photos*

Havana: May Day parade, 1963. The "Big Three" of the Cuban revolution: Che, Raúl, and Fidel Castro. *Salas*

Havana airport, March 15, 1965. Returning to Cuba after making a controversial speech in Algiers criticizing Moscow's tepid support for socialist revolution in poor countries, Che was met by Fidel, his wife, Aleida, the goateed *"viejo comunista"* Carlos Rafael Rodríguez (center), and President Osvaldo Dorticós. Immediately afterward, Fidel proposed to Che that he lead a Cuban expeditionary force to the Congo. Two weeks later, Che left Cuba in disguise, never to be seen again in public. *Prensa Latina*

Top: As president of Cuba's National Bank, Che oversaw over the demise of the capitalist era in Cuba. By casually signing the new Cuban banknotes "Che," he sent worried flurries throughout the business community. Bottom: Cuban banknotes issued after Che's death honored the man described officially as "The Heroic Guerrilla." Left: Cuban postage stamps were also issued bearing Che's visage. *Collection of the author*

Left: Che's manual on guerrilla warfare, *La Guerra de Guerrillas*, published in 1960. Right: Che's March 1964 article in *Cuba Socialista*, "Banks, Credit and Socialism," was part of an ongoing series he wrote outlining his theories on the correct path forward for Cuba's socialist economy. *Collection of the author*

In an unusually lighthearted moment, Che, Aleida, and Che's bodyguard Harry Villegas Tamayo (or "Pombo") and (background) his wife, Cristina. Pombo was one of Che's most trusted protégés, accompanying him to fight in the Congo and Bolivia. *Agenzia Contrasto*

The Congo, 1965. From left: Che, as "Tato"; José Ramón Machado Ventura, the Cuban Minister of Health; Emilio Aragonés (aka "Tembo," or Elephant, for his sizeable girth), organization secretary of Cuba's ruling Partido Unificado de la Revolución Socialista; and Che's friend Oscar Fernández Mell ("Siki," or Vinegar). *Cuban Council of State Office of Historical Affairs*

Che, as Comandante "Tato" in the "liberated zone" of the former Belgian Congo, 1965. Che gave daily classes in general culture and French language to the Cuban fighters in his guerrilla camp. *Cuban Council of State Office of Historical Affairs*

A rarely seen self-portrait taken by the disguised Che — as the middle-aged Uruguayan economist Adolfo Mena González — in his suite at the Hotel Copacabana in La Paz, Bolivia, shortly after arriving to begin his guerrilla adventure. November 1966. *Courtesy of Richard Dindo*

Before he left for Bolivia, Fidel invited the newly disguised Che to attend a meeting of some of their closest comrades, who didn't recognize him until Fidel revealed his true identity. *Cuban Council of State Office of Historical Affairs*

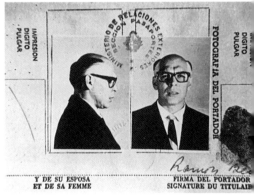

Che's false passport photographs as "Ramón Benítez." *Courtesy of Richard Dindo*

Wearing a Cuban military uniform, the East German–Argentine Haydée Tamara Bunke, or "Tania" as she would become known, speaking with a Cuban soldier in 1961. In 1964, Cuba's secret services sent her to Bolivia as a deep cover agent, but after Che arrived in Bolivia, she joined his group and was killed in an ambush on August 31, 1967. *Courtesy of Thomas Billhardt*

In Che's Bolivian guerrilla base, Ñancahuazú, in the spring of 1967. From left: Che's Argentine emissary, Ciro "El Pelao" Roberto Bustos; the Peruvian Juan Pablo "Chino" Chang; Che Guevara as "Ramon"; and the Frenchman Régis Debray, code-named "Dantón." *Che Guevara's confiscated film, courtesy of Gen. Luis Reque Terán*

Che and some of his fighters in the Ñancahuazú camp. Seated to his right, wearing a hat and smoking a pipe, his bodyguard Carlos Coello ("Tuma") dressed up in imitation of his *comandante*. From left: Alejandro, Pombo, Urbano, Rolando, Che, Tuma, Arturo, and Moro, or "Mogorogoro." *Courtesy of Richard Dindo*

For much of the Bolivian guerrilla campaign, Che was so ill he was unable to walk. He rode mules or horses whenever possible, but he and his men were often so hungry they had to slaughter and eat their mounts. *Courtesy of Richard Dindo*

Che pushing a primitive *trapíche*, or sugarcane mill, somewhere in the Bolivian backwoods. This is one of several previously unpublished photographs obtained by the author from the estate of the late Bolivian officer Andrés Selich. *Che Guevara's confiscated film, courtesy of Socorro Selich*

Bolivia's peasantry, as viewed through Guevara's eyes. This photograph, taken by Che in the hamlet of Moroco, was among those on a roll of film in Che's possession confiscated by Lt. Col. Andrés Selich. *Courtesy of Socorro Selich*

Bolivia. Bolivian Diary, *Pathfinder Press*

Detail of Che's 1966–67 guerrilla odyssey. Bolivian Diary, *Pathfinder Press*

The Bolivian Campaign
MARCH–OCTOBER 1967

POPULATION (1967)	
ABAPÓ	965
ALTO SECO	420
CAMIRI	12,871
FLORIDA	280
LAGUNILLAS	932
LA HIGUERA	296
MUYUPAMPA	876
SAMAIPATA	1,696
SANTA CRUZ	137,406

A Bolivian army propaganda leaflet distributed by the Bolivian military during its campaign against Che's guerrilla band. In this flyer, Che is depicted as a terrified Don Quixote figure being relentlessly chased to ground by a pursuing government bayonet. *Courtesy of Gen. Luis Reque Terán*

Bolivia's swashbuckling military president, General René Barrientos (center), in Vallegrande, Bolivia. To the right, wearing sunglasses and a peaked officer's cap (head visible), is Lt. Col. Andrés Selich. He spoke with Guevara before his execution and was in charge of the secret burials of Che and his comrades in and around Vallegrande. *Courtesy of Socorro Selich*

One of the pages of Che's notes on Régis Debray's polemical monograph *Revolution in the Revolution?*, which Che lost during a skirmish with the army. The author obtained this and other papers from the widow of Lt. Col. Andrés Selich. *Courtesy of Socorro Selich*

October 9, 1967. Che, hours away from death. Standing next to him is the Cuban-American CIA agent Félix Rodríguez. Soon after this picture was taken, Rodríguez informed Che he was going to be executed. *Courtesy of Félix Rodríguez*

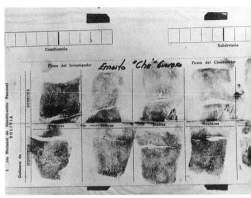

From the camera of the late Lt. Col. Andrés Selich: the La Higuera schoolhouse where Che was held for twenty-four hours and then executed. *Courtesy of Socorro Selich*

The fingerprints taken from the dead Che Guevara. On the night of October 10, prior to the "disappearing" of his body, Che's hands were amputated and preserved in jars of formaldehyde; his fingerprints were taken and handed over to Argentine forensic experts to match with those on file in Buenos Aires. *Courtesy of Socorro Selich*

Che's body lying on public display, inspected by his uniformed enemies in the laundry house of the Vallegrande hospital, Nuestro Señor de Malta, on October 10, 1967. *Freddy Alborta*

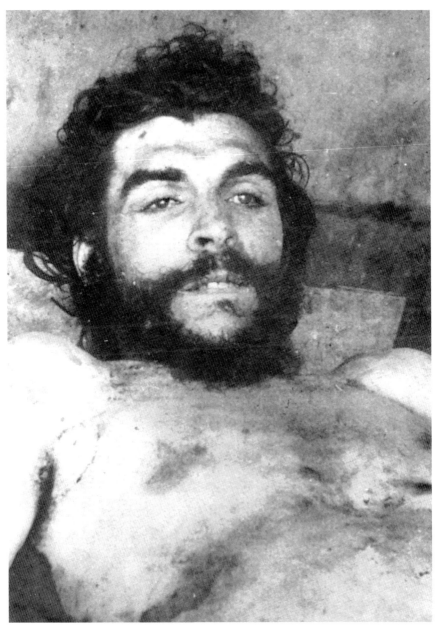

Hundreds of curious civilians, soldiers, and journalists filed past Che's body. The nuns at Vallegrande's hospital thought he resembled Jesus Christ, and local women clipped locks of his hair as keepsakes. To this day, they keep them as good-luck talismans and pray for Che's soul on the Day of the Dead. *Courtesy of Richard Dindo*

Che's funeral wake, in Havana's Plaza de la Revolución in October 1967. In death, Che Guevara quickly acquired international status as a folk hero of mythical proportions. His image has been reproduced on posters, scarves, baseball hats, and key rings, even "Che" brand cigars and beer. Worldwide fascination with Guevara, whether as a commercial product or a historical figure, endures three decades after his death, and it seems there is truth in the old sixties slogan "Che vive!" (Che lives!) *Salas*

When the revised draft was ready in late August, Fidel did not send Raúl back to the Soviet Union. Instead, he sent Che, and with him Emilio Aragonés, an old July 26 associate and now one of his close advisors. On August 30, they met Khrushchev at his summer dacha in the Crimea. Khrushchev agreed to the amended language of the accord, entitled: "Agreement between the Government of the Republic of Cuba and the Government of the USSR on Military Cooperation for the Defense of the National Territory of Cuba in the Event of Agression," but stalled on signing it, saying he would do so when he came to Cuba in a few months.

Probably concerned that the Soviets were carrying out a double cross, Che argued for the agreement to be made public, but Khrushchev refused, insisting that it should remain secret for now. Che and Aragonés then repeated Fidel's nagging worry—one shared by several senior Soviet officials, including Foreign Minister Andrei Gromyko—about a premature discovery of the operation by the Americans. As Aragonés later retold it, Khrushchev was as dismissive about this concern as he had been with Raúl. "[He] said to Che and me, with Malinovski in the room, 'You don't have to worry; there will be no problem from the U.S. And if there is a problem, we will send the Baltic Fleet.'"

Aragonés recalled that when they heard this, "Che and I looked at each other with raised eyebrows." Clearly, neither man was convinced by Khrushchev, through they had little choice at this point but to take him at his word.

Meanwhile, U.S. intelligence had learned to keep an acute watch on Che's movements, and it was scrutinizing his activities in Russia with a wary eye. On August 31, a CIA cable went out noting that the "composition" of Che Guevara's delegation to the USSR "indicates the delegation may have a broader mission than is [sic] announced agenda, which pertains to industrial matters. Guevara is accompanied by Emilio Aragonés, apparently not trained or experienced in economics or industrial matters. The Guevara mission was met at the airport by Soviet economic officials and by First Deputy Premier Kosygin, a member of the Soviet Party Presidum."

By September 6, when Che arrived back in Havana, the Soviet military buildup in Cuba had already been detected. In recent days, American U-2 reconnaissance planes had discovered the new SAM-2 missile sites and coastal-defense cruise missile installations. Kennedy had been assured by his experts that the weapons were not a threat to U.S. national security, but their presence was a danger sign that could not be disregarded. On September 4, Kennedy had sent his younger brother Robert, the attorney general, to discuss the buildup with the Soviet ambassador to the United States, Anatoli Dobrynin. Dobrynin had relayed Khrushchev's reassurances that no "offensive" weaponry had been deployed in Cuba, the new weapons were purely intended for Cuba's "defense."

But the White House remained suspicious. New reconnaissance photos indicated that a Soviet submarine base might be under construction. Kennedy issued a public statement announcing that the United States had detected not only the SAMs but an increased number of Soviet military personnel in Cuba. He admitted that the United States had no evidence of the presence of either Soviet-bloc *combat* troops or offensive ground-to-ground missiles, but warned that if they existed there, it would give rise to the "gravest issues."

The next day, Kennedy asked Congress for approval to call up 150,000 military reservists. The United States announced plans to hold a military exercise in the Caribbean in mid-October, which Cuba denounced as proof of Washington's intention to invade. Once again, Dobrynin insisted that Moscow was supplying "only" defensive weapons to Cuba.

Each day brought the tension levels higher, as new details of the Soviet buildup filtered in, and U.S., Soviet, and Cuban accusations and denials flew back and forth. Then, on September 9, U.S. intelligence monitors recorded some unsettling remarks made by Che at a reception at the Brazilian embassy in Havana. Speaking to a reporter, Che had called the latest Soviet military aid deal to Cuba "a historic event" that heralded a reversal in East-West power relations; in his opinion, it had shifted the scales in favor of the Soviet Union. As one classified cable paraphrased him, Guevara had said: "The United States cannot do anything but yield." It concluded: "He seems to feel that the Soviet military aid to Cuba is a gesture of great importance."

As the United States and the rest of the world was about to learn, indeed it was. In a few short weeks the deal concluded by Che would bring the world to the brink of nuclear war.

25

Guerrilla Watershed

The blood of the people is our most sacred treasure, but it must be used in order to save the blood of more people in the future.

CHE GUEVARA,
late 1962, in "Tactics and Strategy of the Latin American Revolution"

One day I reached the summit of a mountain with a rifle in my hand and I felt something I had never felt before—I felt so strong! I had a beautiful feeling of freedom and I said to myself: "We can do it!"

HÉCTOR JOUVE,
one of Che's guerrillas in Argentina in 1963–1964

I

In December 1961, Julio Roberto Cáceres (El Patojo), Che's young Guatemalan friend and protégé, secretly left Cuba for his homeland, determined to help launch a Marxist guerrilla struggle there. Che had always been especially brotherly with the introverted Patojo and had tried to help nurture his revolutionary aspirations. Che had kept him with him at La Cabaña, INRA, and the Ministry of Industries, and for most of the last three years Patojo had lived with him and Aleida.

A few months earlier, Che had asked the economist Regino Boti, who ran the Central Planning Board, JUCEPLAN, to find a job there for his Guatemalan friend. Boti did so, and when Patojo disappeared soon afterward, Boti understood that Che had used the office as a means of disappearing Cáceres from his usual habitués and "laundering" his exit from the country.

Patojo's return to Guatemala coincided with a propitious climate for revolution there. Congressional elections had just taken place amid widespread allegations of fraud. Then, in late January 1962, Ydigoras Fuentes's secret police chief had been assassinated, and two weeks later the first hit-and-run attacks against military posts were launched near Puerto Barrios by the guerrillas led by Yon Sosa and Turcios Lima. Calling their group the "Alejandro de León November 13 Guerrilla Movement," in commemoration of the date of their earlier failed uprising and in honor of a late comrade, the rebels made their aims public in a February communiqué calling

for a rebellion against Guatemala's "tyranny" to restore the country to democratic rule. Patojo's own mission, backed by Guatemala's Communist party,
the PGT, was launched independently at around the same time.

In March 1962, only four months after Patojo had left, Che received
word that his friend had been killed in action. When, a few months later,
Myrna Torres visited Havana, she brought Che a notebook Patojo had left
with her in Mexico en route to the battlefield. It included a poem to his girlfriend back in Cuba. Che wrote a eulogy to Patojo that was published in
Verde Olivo that August, a bittersweet parable of redemption aimed at Cuba's
Revolutionary Armed Forces. After giving a brief account of Patojo's life
and their own relationship—how they had lived and worked together as
itinerant photographers in Mexico; how Patojo had also wanted to join the
Granma expedition but had been left behind; how he had then come to help
in Cuba's triumphant revolution—Che wrote:

> After he came to Cuba we almost always lived in the same
> house, as was fitting for two old friends. But we no longer main-
> tained the early intimacy in this new life, and I suspected El Patojo's
> intentions only when I occasionally saw him studying one of the
> native Indian languages of his country. One day he told me he was
> leaving, that the time for him had come to do his duty. . . . He was
> going to his country to fight, arms in hand, to reproduce some-
> how our guerrilla struggle. It was then that we had one of our long
> talks. I limited myself to recommending strongly three things:
> constant movement, constant wariness and constant vigilance. . . .
>
> This was the synthesis of our guerrilla experience; it was the
> only thing—along with a warm handshake—that I could give to
> my friend. Could I advise him not to do it? With what right? . . .
>
> El Patojo left, and with time the news of his death came. . . .
> And not only he, but a group of comrades with him, all of them as
> brave, as selfless, as intelligent perhaps as he, but not known to me
> personally. Once more there is the bitter taste of defeat. . . .
>
> Once again, youthful blood has fertilized the fields of the
> Americas to make freedom possible. Another battle has been lost;
> we must make time to weep for our fallen comrades while we
> sharpen our machetes. From the valuable and unfortunate expe-
> rience of the cherished dead, we must firmly resolve not to repeat
> their errors, to avenge the death of each one of them with many
> victorious battles, and to achieve definitive liberation.
>
> When El Patojo left Cuba . . . he had few clothes or personal
> belongings to worry about. Old mutual friends in Mexico, how-

ever, brought me some poems he had written and left there in a
notebook. They are the last verses of a revolutionary; they are, in
addition, a love song to the revolution, to the homeland, and to a
woman. To that woman whom El Patojo knew and loved in Cuba,
are addressed these final verses, this injunction:

> Take this, it is only my heart
> Hold it in your hand
> And when the dawn arrives,
> Open your hand
> And let the sun warm it . . .

El Patojo's heart has remained among us, in the hands of his beloved and in the grateful hands of an entire people, waiting to be
warmed beneath the sun of a new day that will surely dawn for
Guatemala and for all America.

Patojo's commemorated death signaled only the beginning of a new
wave of Cuban-backed guerrilla activity in Latin America, for through Che's
efforts Cuba became a fully operational "Guerrilla Central" in 1962, activating manpower and material resources to fuel the far-flung substations
of armed revolution throughout the hemisphere. In the face of Washington's
continued hostility, Cuba's hemispheric isolation, and the unflagging threat
of an American military invasion, Che's dream of a "continental revolution"
now made strategic sense: The spreading guerrilla threat helped divert
American pressure away from Cuba and simultaneously made Washington pay a high price for its regional containment policy.

What's more, Fidel had made it government policy. Responding to
the January 1962 expulsion of Cuba from the OAS, Fidel had rallied back
on February 4 with what he called his "Second Declaration of Havana"
proclaiming the "inevitability" of revolution in Latin America, in what jittery Latin American governments took to be a tacit declaration of war by
Cuba against their countries.

Juan Carreterro, alias "Ariel," a high-ranking Cuban intelligence officer
at the time, says he began working with Che in 1962 to create a transcontinen-
tal, anti-imperialist, "revolutionary theater in Latin America." Ariel worked
directly under Manuel Piñeiro Losada, alias "Barba Roja" (Red Beard), Ramiro
Valdés's deputy at State Security, who oversaw the guerrilla programs.*

---

*See the appendix for elaboration.

By the spring of 1962, Che was overseeing a campaign to recruit and organize guerrilla trainees from among the hundreds of Latin American students invited to Cuba on revolutionary scholarships; among them was Ricardo, the younger brother of his ex-wife, Hilda. He had finished high school in Peru and, in 1958, gone to study journalism at Argentina's renowned University of La Plata, a magnet for students from all over Latin America. There he had joined the Peruvian *Aprista* youth movement, and like many of his student friends, Ricardo quickly became imbued with the Cuban revolutionary cause, seeing it as a model for political change in Latin America. With Che Guevara as his brother-in-law, there was also a personal incentive. In his spare time he helped out at the July 26 support committee's offices in Buenos Aires, working with Che's father.

In 1960, he decided to go to Cuba himself to finish his studies and to participate in the revolution he sympathized with so strongly. With Hilda there, it made things easier for him; she was no longer Che's wife, but had stayed on in Cuba and could help set him up. When Ricardo arrived, he learned that he wouldn't be able to pursue his journalism career. The official university-reform process was under way, and the journalism school at Havana University—not a priority profession in the new Cuba—was, as he put it, somewhat "disorganized." Instead, he began studying economics. The dean of his faculty was none other than the venerable "old Communist" Carlos Rafael Rodríguez. When the CIA-backed invasion came at Playa Girón, Ricardo and many of his fellow Latin American students volunteered for the revolutionary militias, hoping to be sent to the front, but instead he and his expatriate comrades were left behind in Havana to guard public buildings. For Ricardo, it was a disappointment, but undeterred, he remained in the university's militia forces.

By early 1962, hundreds of new Latin American students had arrived in the country as part of a general invitation made by Cuba to the hemisphere's Communist and left-of-center opposition parties. There were Bolivians, Venezuelans, Argentines, Uruguayans, Nicaraguans, Guatemalans, Colombians. About eighty came from Peru, and Ricardo immediately fell in with his compatriots. Before long, however, a schism opened between those students who "only wanted to study" and those who, as Roberto described it, "wanted to take advantage of Cuba's revolutionary experience to learn from it, and return to our own country to carry out our own revolution." It was a moment of definition for Ricardo, and he opted for the latter group.

His decision coincided with the March 1962 military coup in Peru that annulled the election results, suspended congress, and placed the whole Peruvian political system in doubt. For Peruvians seeking to apply the Cuban model to their nation, it was the time to strike.

By mid-1962, Ricardo Gadea and his Peruvian comrades had left the university for guerrilla training in the Sierra Maestra. Their instructors were veterans of the Cuban struggle; Fidel himself spoke to them and gave them advice; but it was Che, said Gadea, who was their undisputed revolutionary mentor. "Of all the leaders," said Ricardo, "Che was the most charismatic, sensitive, and involved, as a Latin American. He understood us, knew our difficulties, and helped us overcome many of our problems."

Another country whose "liberation" was a goal close to Che's heart was Nicaragua. Since their early debacle on the Honduran-Nicaraguan border in the summer of 1959, the Nicaraguan rebels battling the Somoza dynasty had been coming to and going from Cuba. Carlos Fonseca, the group's ideologue, had recovered from the wounds he suffered in that experience in Cuba, then returned to Central America to seek a political alliance between his university-based group, other exiles, and *antisomocistas* within Nicaragua itself.

While Fonseca was traveling around, one of his closest disciples, a short, squat, and full-lipped former law student named Tomas Borge, traveled to Havana seeking help for their recently formed Juventud Revolucionaria Nicaragüense (Nicaraguan Revolutionary Youth) group. He and another comrade named Noel Guerrero joined Che's friend Rodolfo Romero on a visit to Che at the National Bank.

As Borge recalled it, he launched into a flowery greeting "on behalf of Nicaragua's youth," which Che cut short, telling him curtly: "Let's forget the greetings and get down to business." But at Borge's insistence that his intended speech was "not demagogic," Che agreed to hear him out. When Borge had finished his heartfelt discourse, he said Che embraced him, told him he "accepted" the greeting, and gave him and his comrades twenty thousand dollars to organize themselves.

Rodolfo Romero was designated the military chief of the group, and with Che's funding Borge and the others began bringing Nicaraguans to Cuba from all over the region. Eventually numbering about thirty, they were inducted into Cuba's revolutionary militias and sent off for firsthand combat experience in the counterinsurgency war taking place in the Escambray. In 1961, Romero went into the Cuban counterintelligence school for training in espionage and tradecraft—"the only Nicaraguan there," as he proudly recalled—then joined Borge, Fonseca, and others at an artillery-training course given by Czech advisors at a remote Cuban military base.

By July 1961 Carlos Fonseca was back in Nicaragua, and by the following summer his organization was developing. Fonseca oversaw the anti-Somoza urban underground effort in Nicaragua's cities, pulling off bank robberies and carrying out propaganda and sabotage actions, while Tomas

Borge and about sixty other guerrillas under Noel Guerrero's leadership slipped into Nicaragua's northern jungle from Honduras. The group that would eventually call itself the Frente Sandinista de Liberacíon Nacional (FSLN) was ready for action.

While generous with the future cadres of the Latin American revolution, Che was considerably less so with his own family, refusing his parents any financial help that would allow them to visit him. After their first visit in 1959, Celia *madre* had come back to Cuba for a visit in 1960, and the following year Guevara Lynch had written to Hilda to say he was trying to save up enough money for a return visit with Celia. They wanted to meet their newest granddaughter, Aleidita, and to see Hildita again. Very soon, they knew, they would have another grandchild, for Aleida was pregnant a second time and due to give birth in May 1962.

When Hilda took it upon herself to ask Che why he didn't assist his parents, the query earned her a sharp retort. "So," Che said, "you're one of those who don't believe I'm on a fixed salary, and can use the public funds as I like." Stung, Hilda denied she meant anything of the kind. "I only suggested you pay your father's passage because he wants to come," she said. "You can pay it back in installments." Che then calmed down, and said: "All right. But let's leave it for later on. Now's not the time."*

In Venezuela, meanwhile, an insurrectionary climate had taken hold in the country following the political ruptures in Betancourt's ruling coalition. Here and there, guerrilla forces had begun operating; in May 1962, troops at a naval base near Caracas revolted against the government. The Communist party openly backed the uprising, and in retaliation Betancourt banned both the Communist party and the MIR.

In June, a second naval uprising was put down after two days of bloody fighting with loyalist army troops. Dissident officers and troops fled into the hills, where many of them joined the fledgling guerrilla forces. In December the outlawed Communist party officially endorsed the "armed struggle," and two months later a guerrilla coalition group, Fuerzas Armadas de Liberación Nacional (FALN) announced its creation and intention to wage war against Betancourt's regime. Calling itself a "Democratic and Nationalist"

---

*Some months later, however, when Argentina broke off relations with Cuba, and Havana's diplomats and a group of Argentine Communists were preparing to leave aboard a charter flight, Che saw the opportunity to get his brother Juan Martín to Cuba. According to María Elena, his wife at the time, Juan Martín was prepared to go, but some last-minute difficulties prevented him from making the flight. In the end, as his personal life became complicated with a wife, children, and the need to earn a living, Juan Martín never did return to Cuba while his brother was alive, nor did Guevara Lynch or anyone else in the family, except Celia *madre*.

movement, the FALN also had a Communist-dominated political front, the FLN, or Frente de Liberación Nacional. Reminiscent of Fidel Castro's wartime communiqués, those of the FLN denied government accusations that it was "Communist" or "anti-American" and called for Venezuelans of all creeds to join its "united front" to make Venezuela "master of her own destiny and her own riches."

Just as he was helping the guerrilla movements of Nicaragua, Peru, and Guatemala, Che also assisted the new Venezuelan revolutionary organization. With each new rifle raised aloft, his vision of a continental guerrilla struggle against American imperialism was coming one step closer to reality.

II

By now, Che was also planning to launch an insurgency in his native Argentina. He had been cultivating the idea for some time, but it had taken on new vigor after the Argentine military toppled President Frondízi. He had chosen the far northern jungle of Argentina, near Salta, not far from the rugged Bolivian border, as an exploratory theater of war. Interestingly, it was the same area he had journeyed through in 1950 on his motorbike trip, during which he had paused to reflect about the meaning of life, death, and his own destiny.

Che's plan was for the Argentine journalist Jorge Ricardo Masetti to lead his advance patrol; his mission was to become acquainted with the terrain and quietly establish a guerrilla base of operations. Before engaging the enemy, he was to build up a base of support among rural peasants and a civilian-support infrastructure in Argentina's cities. Later on, when the conditions were right, Che would come and lead the force himself.

Che asked Alberto Granado for help in recruiting Argentines for the guerrilla venture. In October 1961 Alberto had moved with his family from Havana to Santiago to start up a biomedical research school at its university, and during 1962 he used his job and nationality to assess the potential of his fellow expatriates for Che's Argentine revolution scheme. In Santiago, he became friendly with the Argentine painter Ciro Roberto Bustos, who had arrived in Cuba as a revolutionary "volunteer" about the same time as he had. Bustos had set up a small ceramics factory in the Oriente countryside and was also giving twice-weekly painting classes at Santiago University; Granado invited him to stay at his house when he was in town. Their conversations soon broached the topic of "armed struggle," and when Granado learned that Bustos supported the idea of a Cuban-style revolution in their homeland, he passed along his positive appraisal of the painter to Che. Before long, Granado arranged for them to meet.

That year, Granado made a trip to Argentina. He journeyed around the country, working through the Argentine Communist party to recruit "technicians and other skilled people" to work in Cuba—a plausible cover story for his recruitment of guerrilla cadres. However, as Granado acknowledged years later, the Argentine security services were already suspicious and had evidently monitored his movements, for several of the people he met with were "temporarily detained" after his visit. Even so, he was able to recruit a couple of men who soon arrived in Cuba for guerrilla training.

Masetti was no longer at Prensa Latina. After the Bay of Pigs invasion, he had conducted a televised interrogation of the prisoners, then dropped from view. Officially, he had been forced to resign his job; it was well known that Masetti was no Communist, and, after a long-running standoff with the doctrinaire Communist party faction at the agency, he had been removed. Afterward, he was said to be employed by the propaganda department of Cuba's armed forces, but in reality he was working for Che.

After leaving Prensa Latina, Masetti went through an officer's training course to gain military experience, graduating with a captain's rank, and traveled on secret missions for Che to Prague—a new way station for Cuba's overseas espionage activities—and to Algeria, where he smuggled a huge quantity of American weapons seized at Playa Girón to the FLN insurgents, via Tunisia. One of Granado's recruits, an Argentine mechanic in his early twenties named Federico Méndez, who had military experience, accompanied Masetti. For several months, they stayed at the FLN's general staff headquarters, where Méndez gave the Algerians training courses in the use of the American arms. By the time they returned to Cuba, they had established close links with the grateful Algerian revolutionary leadership and its top military officers.

Che was casting his net wide to take soundings of Argentina's political situation. When Cuba's diplomats were expelled from Argentina in March 1962 and flew home on a plane from Uruguay, he sent a telegram to his old Dean Funes high school friend, the *radicalista* youth militant Oscar Stemmelin, inviting him to take advantage of the evacuation flight to come and visit him. Stemmelin and another old Dean Funes classmate of Che's took up the invitation and stayed in Havana about a month. Later, Stemmelin couldn't be certain exactly why Guevara had invited him to Cuba—apart from the fact that they were old friends and he was one of the few *cordobéses* Che knew personally who was politically active. During Stemmelin's stay, he and Che met eight or ten times to talk about old times, Cuba's revolution, and Argentine politics.

On May 25, the Argentine Day of Independence, the 380 members of Cuba's Argentine community in Havana gathered to celebrate with a traditional outdoor *asado,* complete with folk music, traditional dances, and typical Argentine costumes. When Che was invited to attend as the guest of honor, he suggested to its organizers that they invite the young German-Argentine woman Haydée Tamara Bunke. Since her arrival from Berlin, "Tamara," as everyone knew her, had been working as a German-Spanish translator at the Ministry of Education, and she was enthusiastic about everything going on. She joined in volunteer labor sessions, worked as a literacy instructor, signed up for the militias and her local CDR watch committee—activities that had quickly earned her a reputation for revolutionary zeal. She had become a regular fixture at the social gatherings of Latin American guerrillas in Havana and espoused great sympathy with their causes.

She and Che's deputy, Orlando Borrego, had also renewed their friendship begun in Berlin. To him, Tamara made no secret of her desire to become a revolutionary fighter in one of Latin America's guerrilla wars, and was constantly asking Borrego to introduce her to Che. But Borrego stalled her; he knew that there were always people trying to see Che, and he didn't want to waste his jefe's precious time. Tamara finally got her way by arranging to participate in a day's volunteer work alongside him at a school being built near his house. "I underestimated her," observed Borrego wryly.

At the Independence Day *asado,* Che gave his usual speech on the revolutionary struggle in Latin America, putting special emphasis on Argentina. He spoke of the need for Argentina's "anti-imperialist forces" to overcome their ideological differences, specifically including the *peronistas* in this appeal. According to a Cuban who was present, at one point during their meal, Che scribbled something on a matchbox and wordlessly handed it to an Argentine sitting near him. It bore the word *"unidad"* (unity). As the matchbox circulated, Che's message was clear. No more sectarian infighting.

It was a significant moment to the group of *peronista* exiles who were present, and their leader John William Cooke stood up to echo Che's appeal for revolutionary unity and laud Cuba for leading "the Second Emancipation" of Latin America. Cooke, a former Peronist Youth leader and personal representative of Perón, had been living in Cuba for several years, but he continued to correspond regularly with the exiled caudillo living in Madrid. Cooke had been won over by Cuba's revolution and evoked it for Perón in flattering terms, extending Fidel's invitation for Perón to visit, promising a reception "with the honors of a head of state." (Perón never took up the invitation but sent flattering responses back, much as he continued to play

kingmaker from exile with all the various *peronista* factions that competed
for his approval.)*

Stealthily, Che was setting up the chessboard for his game of continental guerrilla war, the ultimate prize being his homeland. He was actually training several different Argentine action groups, distinct in their ideologies but
united by a common desire to take to the field. At the right time each group
would be mobilized to take its place in a united army in the Argentine campaign under Che's command. Masetti's forward patrol was Che's first move
on that chessboard; the others would follow at the right time.**

Beyond all of this behind-the-scenes activity, a number of events that
were to have a direct bearing on Che's future had occurred. The previous
September, UN General Secretary Dag Hammarskjöld had been killed in
a suspicious plane crash while visiting the Congo, after UN troops had intervened against Belgian and South African mercenary-backed secessionist
rebel forces in the copper-rich Katanga province. The new UN secretary,
Burmese diplomat U Thant, had inherited the job of resolving the seemingly insoluble crisis in the Congo, where the Western-supported central
government in the capital of Leopoldville continued to fence for power with
the standard-bearers for the late prime minister, Patrice Lumumba, based
in the distant northern city of Stanleyville.†

The long-simmering Sino-Soviet dispute had finally become public
in October 1961 when Chinese premier Chou En-lai walked out of a Communist party congress held in Moscow; both powers now increased their
jockeying for global influence, pressuring Cuba and Latin America's Communist parties to choose a side.

---

*Cooke dreamed of bringing about Perón's triumphal return to his homeland at the head of
a reconstituted, Cuban-backed revolutionary alliance. According to Cooke's former comrades,
after a tepid beginning, due to Che's lingering skepticism about Perón, he became friends
with Cooke and his wife, Alicia Ereguren; in the course of their many conversations, Cooke's
arguments gave Che a broader view of *peronismo*'s potential as a revolutionary force, while
Che in turn was influential in Cooke's assimilation of Marxist-Leninist concepts. This helped
to galvanize the revolutionary "current" Cooke founded, Acción Revolucionaria Peronista
(ARP). With Che's approval, that same summer of 1962, Cooke's men also began receiving
guerrilla training to prepare themselves for a future revolutionary war in Argentina.

**Ironically, neither Che, Masetti, nor Cooke would live to see the day, but the forces they
helped set in motion eventually brought about a period of revolutionary violence and vicious
counterrepression by the military that would drastically alter the political landscape of modern Argentina in the years to come.

†The Congo was later renamed Zaire; its capital, Leopoldville, became Kinshasa, while
Stanleyville became Kisangani.

In Cuba, the "sectarianism" waged by the PSP's "old Communists" through its attempt to control the Organizaciónes Revolucionarias Integradas, or ORI (the new official party, headed by Fidel, which had subsumed the July 26 Movement along with the PSP and Directorio Revolucionario), was publicly denounced by Fidel in March 1962. Accused of favoring party comrades for a wide variety of government posts, ORI's organization secretary, the former PSP eminence Aníbal Escalante, was the leading victim of the purge. Publicly castigated, he was sent into exile in Moscow. Afterward, Fidel announced a new name for the reformed party: PURS, the Partido Unificado de la Revolución Socialista, the next stage in the creation of a new Cuban Communist party.

Che was immensely gratified by Fidel's purge. He loathed the holier-than-thou party apparatchiks who sought to impose themselves and their own ideological guidelines throughout Cuba, and he had defended a number of people whose careers had been damaged, giving them posts—and protection—at his ministry. In May, he issued strict guidelines forbidding the practice of "ideological investigations" at his ministry.

The "sectarianism," as the period of Communist party dogmatism was called, had affected even non-Cubans such as Ciro Bustos. Taking its cue from the chauvinistic PSP, the Argentine Communist party had tried to wield its control over all the Argentines living and working in Cuba. While he was in Holguín, Bustos had been summoned by the party's representative in Cuba and questioned about his political background and party affiliations. When he explained that he didn't have an official Communist party membership, he was warned that if he didn't "regularize" his situation, he would have to leave the country. The "antisectarian" purge had come just in time for him, however, and he was once again breathing freely when, in the summer of 1962, Granado arranged for him to meet with Che.

Their midnight encounter, which took place in Che's Havana office late in July, was peremptory. Che explained to Bustos that there was "a group" being prepared for Argentina, and asked him if he wanted to participate. The painter said yes. That was all. Bustos was told not to leave his hotel; some people would be coming by to pick him up. In the next stage of his revolutionary metamorphosis, Bustos was first taken to a house in Havana's Miramar neighborhood, where he was greeted by a man he recognized from news photographs to be Jorge Ricardo Masetti; in fact Masetti's 1959 book about the Cuban war, *Los Que Luchan y los Que Lloran* (Those Who Fight and Those Who Cry), had helped spark Bustos's interest in Cuba.

Masetti explained to Bustos that this was "Che's project," but since the *comandante* couldn't leave Cuba just yet, Masetti was to lead the guerrilla force in its start-up phase; then Che would come, and the war would begin.

He asked Bustos if he was prepared to leave everything to join the project, and once again Bustos said yes. For appearance' sake, he would return to Holguín until he was called, and then a Ministry of Industries "scholarship" for him to study in Czechoslovakia would be arranged to explain his subsequent disappearance. His wife would have to stay behind and keep the secret. Later, once the guerrillas had secured a liberated territory, she could undergo training and join him.

By September, Bustos was ensconced in a safe house with three other Argentines: Leonardo, and doctor, and Granado's recruits Federico and Miguel. Their new home was an elegant villa in the exclusive "Country Club" neighborhood on Havana's eastern edges. Deserted by the exodus of Cuba's wealthy, the leafy, tree-lined enclave of walled compounds was now guarded by Cuban security forces, offering maximum discretion to the group. The Argentines settled down to life, camping in one room of the mansion they occupied, getting to know one another and preparing for the life ahead of them. Their training consisted of hikes and practice at a firing range. For something to do at night, they went out on patrol, trying—with little luck—to catch the gangs of thieves they discovered were breaking into the empty villas and carrying off whatever they could find. "But they were always smarter than we were," recalled Bustos. "We made too much noise."

Masetti, Che, and intelligence officials such as Ariel and Piñeiro came and went. Che's men—Orlando "Olo" Tamayo Pantoja, who was one of Che's officers during the sierra war, and Hermes Peña, one of Che's bodyguards—took active part in their training sessions, and they soon found out that "Capitan Hermes" would be going with them as Masetti's deputy commander.

In that same month, August 1962, Hermes Peña's disappearance from Che's security detail was noted by his fellow bodyguards, Alberto Castellanos and Harry Villegas. In response to Che's insistence that they better themselves, they had been away at a training course for future Ministry of Industries administrators and knew nothing beforehand about the guerrilla project, but with Hermes gone upon their return, they realized something was up. Castellanos went to see Che, told him that he knew something was being planned, and said: "I just want to tell you that if you are going off anywhere, I am ready to go with you, and Villegas wants you to know he feels the same." Che wouldn't confirm or deny anything, but merely told Castellanos that he would keep him and Villegas "in mind."

Another personality who showed up regularly at the safe house was Abelardo Colomé Ibarra, alias "Furry," none other than Havana's police chief. He too would be joining the Argentines as their future rearguard base commander and liaison for communications with Cuba. Their chief trainer was neither Cuban nor Argentine, however, but a Hispano-Soviet general, a man they knew only as "Angelito." Ciro Bustos and the others understood that they were not to ask too many questions of him; at this point the presence of Russian military men in Cuba remained a highly sensitive subject. Actually a Spanish-born Catalán, Angelito, also know as "Ángel Martínez," was nonetheless an active general in the Red Army, a Spanish Civil War hero whose real name was Francisco Ciutat, one of a half-dozen Spanish Republican exiles dispatched to Cuba by the Moscow-based Spanish Communist party to help train Cuba's militias in the "Struggle against Bandits." "He was a real personality," recalled Ciro. "Tiny, with quite a few years on him, but like a gymnast, he could do flips in the air."

As Angelito's deputy, Hermes Peña worked as their hands-on instructor, reconstructing sierra war battles for them to study and emulate in their training exercises. Before long, each of the men in the safe house was assigned specific duties for which he showed a special aptitude. Leonardo was to be the expedition medic, Miguel to handle logistics, and Federico, whom Bustos described as a no-nonsense tough guy of few words, was put in charge of armaments. Bustos himself was given specialized training in security and intelligence.

Che himself always arrived at the safe house extremely late, at two or three in the morning. Ciro Bustos recalled his impression of the first meeting he and his companions had as a group with Che. "Practically the first thing he told us was 'Well, here you are: you've all agreed to join, and now we must prepare things, but from this moment on, consider yourselves dead. Death is the only certainty in this; some of you may survive, but all of you should consider what remains of your lives as borrowed time.'"

Che was throwing down the gauntlet for his future guerrillas, just as he had done during the Cuban struggle with his "invasion column" before marching for the Escambray. It was important that each man prepare himself psychologically for what was to come, and Ciro understood the message. "We were going to go and get our balls shot off, without knowing if any of us were going to see it through, or how long it would take." Che let them know he was not sending them off alone to an uncertain fate, however, telling them he planned to join them as soon as he could.

III

The October missile crisis forced Che to accelerate plans for his Argentine guerrilla force. As had been his duty during the Bay of Pigs invasion, Che commanded Cuba's western army based in Pinar del Río during the crisis.

His command post was situated in some mountain caves near one of the Soviet missile installations.

When the crisis erupted, Che took his Argentine guerrilla trainees with him and placed them in a battalion under the command of Cuban officers. If there was fighting, they were to join in.

At the moment of maximum tension—after a Russian SAM (surface-to-air) missile brought down an American U-2 spyplane, killing its pilot—Fidel cabled Khrushchev, telling him he expected Moscow to launch its missiles *first* in the event of an American ground invasion; he and the Cuban people, he assured him, were ready to die fighting. Only a day later, Fidel learned that Khrushchev had made a deal with JFK behind his back—offering to pull out the missiles in exchange for a promise not to invade Cuba and a withdrawal of U.S. Jupiter missiles from Turkey. Fidel was incredulous and furious, and reportedly smashed a mirror with his fist when he was told. When he heard the news, Che tersely ordered his troops to sever his command post's communications line with the adjacent Soviet missile base, and rushed off to Havana to see Fidel.

Over the coming days, Fidel recriminated bitterly with Khrushchev, and the hapless Mikoyan was dispatched to Havana to patch things up. Mikoyan did what he could, but Fidel and Che were convinced Khrushchev had sold them out for his own strategic interests. Their talks went on for several weeks and at times were exceedingly tense. One day, a mistranslation by the Russian interpreter even sparked a shouting match. When the misunderstanding was cleared up, Che calmly removed his Makarov pistol from its holster, handed it to the interpreter, and said: "If I were in your place, for instance, the only thing left to do . . ." According to Alexiev, everyone laughed, including Mikoyan; Che's dark humor had cleared the air.

In public, relations between Moscow and Havana remained "fraternal," but under the surface the climate was extremely tense, and it stayed that way for some time. In the streets of Havana, indignant Cubans chanted: *"Nikita, mariquita, lo que se da no se quita!"* (Nikita, you little queer, what you give, you don't take away!)

In his memoirs, Khrushchev later acknowledged that the "Soviet position" had been the foremost concern in his decision to install the missiles. "The fate of Cuba and the maintenance of Soviet prestige in that part of the world preoccupied me. . . . One thought kept hammering away in my brain: what will happen if we lose Cuba? I knew it would have been a terrible blow to Marxism-Leninism. It would gravely diminish our stature throughout the world, but especially in Latin America. If Cuba fell, other countries would reject us, claiming that for all our might the Soviet Union hadn't been able to do anything for Cuba except to make empty protests to the United Nations."

In an interview with Che a few weeks after the crisis, Sam Russell, a British correspondent for the socialist *Daily Worker,* found Guevara still fuming over the Soviet betrayal. Alternately puffing a cigar and taking blasts on his asthma inhaler, Guevara told Russell that if the missiles had been under Cuban control, they would have fired them off. Russell came away with mixed feelings about Che, calling him "a warm character whom I took to immediately . . . clearly a man of great intelligence, though I thought he was crackers from the way he went on about the missiles."

They also discussed another subject close to Guevara's heart—global Communist strategy. Russell found Guevara to be extremely critical of the Western Communist parties for adopting "a peaceful parliamentary strategy for power." "He said this would deliver the working class bound hand and foot over to the ruling class."

Che was, of course, determined to do something about it. As Ciro Bustos recalled: "When the [missile crisis] tension relaxed, we were brought back to Havana and Che told us: 'You're leaving. I want you out of here.' Those were special days. They were still afraid there might be a [U.S.] invasion. There was a very heavy war atmosphere. . . . There was also bad blood with the Soviets. . . . He was very cold, and very angry with the Soviets."

The men in the safe house were told to leave the house as they had found it, to remove all traces of their presence. Federico Mendez was sent off for a field-radio training course, and Bustos underwent a weeklong intensive course to learn the art of secret codes and cryptology. He was taught a Soviet code system based on ten never-repeated numbers. "It was James Bond–style," recalled Bustos. "You burned the papers after using the codes."

Then Piñeiro's "passport experts" began to arrive. They gave each man in the group a different nationality, and Bustos became an Uruguayan, but he was unhappy when he saw his passport. "It was unbelievable," he said. "They gave me a really young age and blond hair. I was pretty bald even then, and what hair I did have left was black." When he complained, the expert reassured him that it was to be used only as far as Czechoslovakia, a friendly country where no questions would be asked.

By now the men knew they were to continue their training until Cuba's security apparatus could prepare a safe rearguard base of operations for them on Bolivia's southern border with Argentina. They knew few more details than that, except that the Cubans had made arrangements with "Bolivian friends" to help make the arrangements. They also knew that they were to be called the *Ejército Guerrillero del Pueblo* (People's Guerrilla Army).

All were given noms de guerre: Bustos was now "Laureano"; Masetti was "Comandante Segundo." The *comandante primero,* of course, was Che, who for the moment would remain their invisible guiding hand, dubbed "Martín Fierro." Their operation itself was called "Operacion Sombra" (Operation Shadow). All were literary double entendres: Their names and that of the operation corresponded to the Argentine gaucho archetypes, Martín Fierro and Don Segundo Sombra.

In Prague, the group of five was met by Major Rafael "Papito" (Little Daddy) Serguera, whom they had briefly met during their training in Havana and who was now operating out of the Cuban embassy in Prague. He drove them to Lake Slapie in the countryside about an hour outside the capital, where they were booked into an exclusive lakeside hotel. It was the dead of winter, and there were no other guests; it was just them and the hotel staff. By agreement with the Czech intelligence services, however, they were given a simple cover story to explain their presence. "We were a group of Cuban scholarship students," said Bustos, "who were going to stay awhile."

Papito Serguera visited them once or twice, but apart from that, the five prospective guerrillas were on their own. They had nothing to do, so, to keep fit, they began making cross-country treks through the snow—"20 to 25 kilometers [12 to 15 miles] in every direction." Finally, growing ever more frustrated as the weeks dragged by, they contacted Serguera at the embassy in Prague to complain, and he told them to be patient: The Bolivian farm that was to be their base had not yet been purchased, and more details had to be settled before they could travel. Meanwhile, he told them they were to stop their hiking around. The Czech military had relayed its irritation to him about these treks, for they had apparently been seen wandering into an unauthorized military zone.

Masetti and his men spent another month incommunicado at the Lake Slapie hotel before Serguera finally allowed them to come to Prague. The Czechs, they were told, were not pleased by this security breakdown, so they were split up; Ciro Bustos and the others lodged in one hotel, while Masetti stayed in another. "Masetti was really restless," said Ciro. "There were meetings with Papito. He asked us for more patience, [telling us] things were almost resolved."

But by now it was December, and the Czechs were becoming increasingly upset over the Cubans' prolonged presence. Finally Masetti could stand it no longer and announced he was flying to Algeria to arrange for the group to go there to complete its training; the Algerian revolutionaries owed him a favor, and now they were in a position to repay it. In July, Algeria's freedom from French colonial rule had finally been secured through the peace talks with de Gaulle, and the Front de Libération National was now the government of an independent Algeria. Ben Bella, the new Algerian leader, had been in Havana on the eve of the missile crisis, had met with Che and Fidel, and, before leaving, had signed a declaration of revolutionary fraternity with Cuba.

"Masetti flew off to Algiers and came back two days later," said Bustos. "He told us Ben Bella and [Houari] Boumedienne [the Algerian minister of defense] had welcomed him at the airport and agreed to help us. We left immediately." But to fly to Algiers the band had to lay over in Paris for several days, and for Bustos, still traveling on his "blond" passport, this posed a problem. He solved it by dying his scarce hair with peroxide. "Suddenly my hair was yellow," he recalled, laughing ruefully. "I looked like a cabaret transvestite."

It was New Year's Day 1963 when they arrived in Paris. For three or four days, they stayed in the old Palais de Orsai hotel above the Orsai train station. Imbued with the need to maintain absolute secrecy about their mission, they took precautionary measures, with Bustos in charge of the group's security, having the final say on what they could and couldn't do. He found humor in the incongruity of having Furry, Havana's chief of police now under his orders. So as not to arouse suspicions, Bustos decided, they would pretend to be tourists. "We went to the Louvre," he recalled, "and we walked around a lot."

On January 4 they arrived by airplane in the whitewashed Mediterranean city of Algiers, where the sweeping dockside French corniche and stone colonial edifices of the city center gives way to the walled maze of the ancient Muslim Quarter blanketing the hillside like a great Cubist beehive. While bullet-pocked buildings and the uncleared rubble of blown-up dwellings provided untidy evidence of the recent human ferocity that had taken place, the city's prolonged bloodletting had not destroyed its arresting beauty.

While coming to grips with their transition from resistance army to national government, the Algerians were still engaged in the "cleansing" process that revolutionary Cuba had applied four years earlier to its *chivatos* and war criminals. A palpable war psychosis endured as FLN gunmen roamed the city hunting down suspected wartime collaborators or extorturers, and suspicious Arab civilians looked upon Europeans or foreigners with open hostility. Conscious of the risks faced by Che's guerrillas in the uncertain climate, Algeria's revolutionary leaders sent two generals and an entire security retinue to meet them at the airport. They were immediately driven to an isolated seaside villa on the city's outskirts, and left under armed guard for their own protection.

After some time, they were moved to a villa with a walled garden in Algiers itself, but because of the danger of being misidentified as French, they rarely went out. Whenever they did, they were surrounded by armed Algerian security men.

For the next few months, with a permanent retinue of Algerian revolutionary veterans, the Argentine team practiced their marksmanship, did calisthenics, and took military courses in their assigned specialities. The Algerians took them to see their former front lines, the ingenious cave-and-tunnel system they had used to hide their fighters and cache weapons during the war, and showed them the former French lines as well. Conveniently appointed as the new Cuban ambassador, Papito Serguera soon arrived and, in addition to his other duties, served as the group's relay for communications with Che. Retaining his role as the group's "security man," Bustos alone was allowed out of their safe house to visit the embassy in order to pick up messages. Bustos still hadn't been able to get rid of the peroxide in his hair, however, and Serguera jokingly began calling him *"El Soviético."*

During their stay, the Argentines established close affinities with their Algerian liaisons. They were feted by their hosts with a banquet, and they had reciprocated with a traditional Argentine *asado* at their seafront villa attended by Houari Boumedienne. But time was dragging on, and Masetti was anxious to get moving. In answer to his incessant queries, Papito Serguera relayed what Bustos called "strange and contradictory" messages from Havana, supposedly sent by Che. Furry flew back to Havana to find out what was going on and returned with some disquieting news: Together he and Che had gone over the messages the group had received, and Che had identified several that had not originated with him. Since all their communications were channeled through Barba Roja Piñeiro, whom they also called "El Colorado" (The Red Man), they speculated about a "malfunction" in his security apparatus. Some, including Bustos, came to suspect there was more to it than that—perhaps even an intentional "sabotage" of Che's plans. It would remain a mystery that Bustos, at least, was never able to unravel.*

In Cuba, Che's bodyguards, Alberto Castellanos and Harry Villegas, had awaited their own marching orders from their *comandante,* but many months had gone by and Che had not sent for them. Castellanos had finished his administrator's classes, reentered the armed forces, and begun a military training course. Arriving home in Havana on a weekend pass in late February 1963, he had almost forgotten about his August conversation with Che, but then his jefe suddenly sent for him. Because of the peremptory nature of his summons, the happy-go-lucky Castellanos assumed he was going to be punished for something. "Every time Che sent for you it was to

---

*While leaving some of the complaints against him unanswered, Piñeiro refuted Bustos's version of events, indicating that Masetti's movements were all coordinated out of Havana. "If Masetti went off to Algeria, it was with prior approval from Che and if not, Ben Bella would have asked us for our approval."

pull your ear about something or other," he said. "I said to myself: 'Well, what a coincidence! This weekend I didn't do anything—didn't even get drunk,' so I couldn't imagine what Che wanted to see me about."

In a worried state, Castellanos presented himself at Che's office and asked the secretary, José Manresa, what was going on. The sphinxlike Manresa told him: "Nothing, everything is normal."

When he walked into Che's office, Che asked him: "Do you remember something?" Castellanos drew a blank, but then Che shot him a meaningful look, and it struck him. "What, you mean about us going? When do we go?" he asked, excitedly. Che told him to hold on a minute, to listen to what he had to say. Reminding Castellanos that he had a wife to consider, he warned him that the mission was not to be taken lightly: "This mission is either twenty years fighting, or else you don't come back at all."

Che told him to think about it seriously before making up his mind; Castellanos says he stood there and "thought" for a moment or two before asking again: "When do I go?" "OK," Che told him. "But don't go getting dressed up as Indian because you're not one, and tell Villegas he can't go with you because he's black, and where you're going there's no blacks."

Che didn't spell it out any clearer than that, except to tell Castellanos that where he was headed, he would find some people he knew personally. He added: "You're going to wait for me with a group of comrades I'm sending; you are going to be the boss until I arrive." He said he intended to join them by the end of the year. Afterward, Castellanos went off to see Piñeiro for his debriefing, his new *leyenda* (clandestine identity), and his travel itinerary.

IV

At about the same time, the young German-Argentine woman Tamara Bunke began receiving training in tradecraft and espionage by Piñeiro's department, after being subjected to what her official Cuban biographers described as "months of security clearance."

"She approached us and asked to be taken into consideration for a mission," said Piñeiro's deputy, Ariel, adding that Cuba's secret services had "checked her out" and cleared her for training. At the time, Ariel said, they considered her a prime candidate as a future espionage asset in Argentina, "to be activated when the need arose."

Ariel's pointed mention of Tamara Bunke's security clearance is noteworthy because of the enduring mystery surrounding "Tania," as she later became known. According to former East German State Security files, Tamara Bunke was an "IM" (informal informant) for the Stasi, or secret police, before she went to Cuba in 1961. At the time, she was also under consideration by its overseas espionage division, the HVA, as a deep-cover agent for insertion first in Argentina, and eventually the United States.

Considering the tightly controlled internal security system of the German Democratic Republic and Tamara's own Marxist-Leninist upbringing, the fact that she became an informant for East Germany's secret services is hardly surprising. To "inform" on her fellow citizens or foreign visitors on behalf of the Communist state she so fervently believed in was a patriotic duty she would have performed—and evidently did perform—without compunction. But who was Tania working for when she was in Cuba: the Cubans, East German intelligence, or both? Speaking with the habitual opacity of a lifelong revolutionary *cuadro* still living in Cuba, Tania's friend Orlando Borrego has offered that he has "no doubt that she worked for the German services," but neither did he have any doubts about her loyalties to the Cuban revolution. Speaking in a vastly altered Moscow nearly three decades after Tania's death, the veteran KGB official Alexandr Alexiev indicated that she had been a German agent seconded to the Cubans for their own use. "The Germans wanted to help," he explained. "They tried to have a friendship with revolutionary Cuba that was as good as ours, and they wanted to do even more, and for that reason they fulfilled any desire or whim of the [Cuban] leaders—even more than we did."

Pressed for additional details, Alexiev insinuated that when it came to assisting Che in his foreign revolutionary ventures, German and Soviet intelligence had an agreement to "divide up the work." "The Germans considered themselves to be more . . . revolutionarily aggressive than us. They were younger; we were older, had more experience and maturity. And if we [the KGB] had gotten involved, there would surely have been even more risk of failure. Our services were a big bureaucracy, but the Germans were technically [more equipped], the case of Tania being probably the most important."

As for Tania, Alexiev agreed with Borrego, saying he had no doubt her loyalties were "with the Cubans, with Fidel and with Che." He surmised that Che had "conquered her with his ideas; he was such a convincing and attractive personality."

Another man, an Argentine who worked closely with Che and who also knew Tania personally, offered his view. "My impression was that Tania worked for the German services and transferred to work for Che's intelligence service, that she asked for license to do it. Neither Che nor the Germans would have liked her to be sending reports to two places at the same time. Che wasn't stupid; he wasn't going to permit a double loyalty."

According to recently released former East German Stasi files, Tamara Bunke, as she was still known, had been recruited as an informant by a East German counterintelligence official named Gunter Mannel, in charge of the United States department of the Stasi's HVA.

A month after Tamara's departure for Cuba in 1961, Mannel slipped into West Berlin, defected, and before long was working for the CIA. He soon betrayed the identities of some of his agents, who were arrested in the West, and it might be presumed that he also informed the CIA about Tamara, the gifted and fiercely committed young Communist agent who had just gone to Cuba.

Evidently, the HVA made this presumption. Immediately after Mannel's defection, according to an internal HVA report dated July 23, 1962, Bunke had been sent a letter in Cuba warning her of the danger and requesting that she not attempt to "go to South or North America and that in any case she should consult with us beforehand."

Since then, there had been no further contacts with her, according to the report, but it was "known" that Tamara appeared to be "progressively asserting herself" in Cuba, working with a whole series of government institutions, and was always "importuning" visiting GDR delegations to be their interpreter. It added that she had "apparently given up her resolve to go on to Argentina [and] intends to stay in Cuba and also to assume Cuban citizenship. She also has close ties to Cuban security . . . [and] permission to wear a military uniform, and she makes use of it constantly."

The Stasi files suggest that the East German counterespionage agency had an agreement with Tamara Bunke but that she severed contact after she arrived in Cuba. The Stasi files, however, give rise to other questions. When Tamara was accepted for service by Cuban intelligence, did she tell her handlers about her prior links with German intelligence or the fact that her recruiter had defected a month after her arrival? If she did tell them, why did Cuba eventually use her in the same region—Bolivia and Argentina—as that in which the HVA had originally planned to use her? It surely had to be assumed that both Tamara's identity and her intended future espionage role were known to the CIA and its allied intelligence agencies after Mannel's defection.

In response to these questions, Barba Roja Piñeiro said: "I handled Tania directly. And I asked her if she had been recruited by the German [intelligence] services. She said 'no.'" Piñeiro added that if he had known about Mannel and the letter she had been sent, he would have approved her anyway, both because she displayed "excellent qualities" as an agent, and because he trusted his organization's ability to build her an undetectable new false identity.

V

As Tania began her Cuban training and Masetti's men continued theirs in Algeria, Che analyzed the political developments in his native Argentina, determined to have all the information possible to help him decide when to strike. One of the ways he did this was to send for Argentine friends and acquaintances—as he had done with Oscar Stemmelin the year before—and engage them in long discussions over several weeks, pumping them for information, trying out his theories, and debating them point by point. In February he sent for Ricardo Rojo. "I want to talk," he told Rojo when he arrived. They didn't see eye to eye politically—Rojo was liberal, an "anti-imperialist," though not a socialist—but the two of them went back a long way, and Che knew him to be both well connected and an acute political analyst. It was Rojo, after all, who had introduced him and Hilda, who had first sent Masetti to Cuba, and who, most recently, had become a close friend of Che's mother.

Che put Rojo up in a top-flight government protocol house in the former "Country Club" section of Miramar, not far from the Masetti group's former safe house. He remained there for two months, and Che called for him frequently to talk. Rojo later wrote that he found Guevara depressed about Cuba's growing regional isolation, and still upset over the Soviets' "paternalistic" treatment of Cuba in the missile crisis. In their conversations, Che made clear his belief that Cuba could not break out of its regional strait-jacket until socialist revolutions had taken power in the other Latin American countries, and made no secret of the fact that he was actively studying how to bring that process about. Rojo recalls that together they discussed each Latin American country until one day Che asked him to discuss Argentina with him "systematically."

As they talked, Che took notes. Rojo noticed that Che showed special interest in the Argentine labor and university movements, and was anxious to update his knowledge about "who was who" in Argentina's opposition politics. They also discussed Perón's enduring popularity with the Argentine working class, and Che showed Rojo a letter he had received from the deposed caudillo expressing his admiration for the Cuban revolution. It seemed to Rojo that Che was weighing the pros and cons of an alliance with the *peronistas* as a means of sparking revolt. There was an unpopular military government in Argentina, and increased labor strife; Che wondered aloud what "the reaction of the masses" would be if Perón were to come to Cuba to live—something Perón's leftist disciple John William Cooke had been trying to convince Che to arrange for some time.

In early April 1963, just before Rojo left Cuba, there was a brief but bloody naval uprising in Buenos Aires. It was rapidly suppressed by the army, but to Che, the incident revealed the existence of serious disunity in military ranks, and he told Rojo that he thought the "objective conditions for struggle" were beginning to appear in Argentina. It was time to follow up with "subjective conditions" to show the people that they could overthrow their rulers by violent means. Rojo argued that the revolution had worked in Cuba because the Americans had been caught off guard, but that day had passed, and the United States and its regional allies were now on the alert. Che conceded the point but, as always, refused to accept that Cuba's success was "an exception" that could not be repeated elsewhere.

Che never told Rojo explicitly that he was preparing a guerrilla *foco* in Argentina, but there were enough hints for his friend to draw his own conclusions. For instance, he had shared his flight to Havana with a left-wing *peronista* guerrilla, a leader of a short-lived December 1959 uprising in Tucumán province. He too had come to see Che. And then there were Che's last words to Rojo, as he prepared to leave Cuba. "You'll see," Che said, "Argentina's ruling class will never learn anything. Only a revolutionary war will change things."*

Back in Algeria, Masetti learned that Piñeiro's people had finally purchased a farm for their use in Bolivia, but there was still no sign that he and his men were about to be moved. Masetti decided he could not wait any longer, and asked the Algerians to assist them in getting to Bolivia, to which they immediately agreed.

"The Algerians gave us everything," recalled Bustos. "They would have given us arms, but we couldn't take them, since we were going to have to go through the border controls of several different countries—but they gave us all kinds of military equipment, passports, everything."

In May 1963, seven months after leaving Havana, Masetti's group was finally on its way to South America. But they were minus one man. Miguel, one of Alberto Granado's recruits, had been left behind in rather chilling fashion.**

Miguel had become increasingly argumentative and disobedient during their long wait. One of the strict rules they had all observed since entering clandestine life—and which Ciro Bustos was supposed to enforce—was

---

*In his book *My Friend Che* Rojo claimed that Masetti was present in some of the sessions with Che, while Ciro Bustos insists that Masetti never left his group except for his short visit to Algeria from Prague.

**The real name of "Miguel" has apparently been forgotten by his surviving former comrades, but they remember him as a well-educated Argentine Jew, a significant detail in light of what happened within the group when they reached Argentina.

that nobody wrote letters home, "not even to their mothers," and Miguel had violated that rule; Bustos had caught him trying to mail some letters when they were in Paris. That was only the start of the downward spiral: In Algeria, Miguel had become steadily more critical of Masetti, openly questioning his leadership and causing bad blood. The two argued constantly and became fiercely competitive with one another; one day, trying to best Miguel in their physical training exercises, Masetti had strained his back quite badly, an injury that was to cause him great pain in the months ahead.

Matters reached a head as they were preparing to leave Algeria, when Miguel announced he didn't want to go if Masetti was the leader, predicting that the two of them would end up shooting each other. As Bustos recalled: "Masetti, who had been in the Argentine navy, and who always tried to be 'the macho of the movie,' did not take it lying down." There and then the two men squared off for a fistfight. The other men intervened, but Masetti still wanted vengeance. He insisted that a "summary trial" be held to decide whether Miguel should stay in the group. Bustos was appointed prosecutor, and Federico as Miguel's defense "lawyer."

At this point, Bustos believed the problem was that Miguel had gotten cold feet and provoked the fight with Masetti in order to stay behind. As prosecutor, Bustos argued that Miguel's negative attitude posed a security risk, and since they were about to undertake a delicate trip across several foreign borders, the reasonable solution was that he be left behind. Even Miguel's defender, Federíco, did not oppose this solution.

But it was not enough for Masetti. He argued that Miguel's wish to withdraw from the group was tantamount to a "defection," a crime punishable by death, so Miguel should be condemned to stand before a firing squad. What's more, he said, he could arrange for the execution to be carried out by his Algerian military friends. Masetti's argument won the day, and the group unanimously voted for Miguel to die. Masetti, Papito Serguera, and Furry talked with the Algerians, and a military unit came and took the condemned man away.

Afterward, Bustos remained convinced that the decision had been the right one, but felt badly nonetheless. "One of the things that affected us the most," he recalled, "because we were sure they took him away to shoot him, was that the guy had behaved really well, he wasn't offensive or anything. He prepared his things and he left . . . like a man, correctly, without any lamentations or begging for clemency."

From that moment forward, Bustos and the others referred to Miguel not by his name, but as "El Fusilado" (He Who Was Shot), their first sacrifice in the cause for the Argentine revolution. It would be much later when they learned they had been wrong to speak of him in the past tense.

Traveling in separate groups under false identities, with Algerian diplomatic passports, and accompanied by the two Algerian agents who had been their constant companions of late, Masetti and his men flew to Rome. There they reconvened, and while Masetti and Furry took a different itinerary, Bustos, Federico, Leonardo, Hermes, and the two Algerians flew on to Sao Paolo, Brazil, with the Algerians carrying the rebels' gear in their sealed diplomatic luggage. From Sao Paolo, they traveled overland by train to the city of Santa Cruz de la Sierra, in Bolivia's tropical eastern lowlands. There, for discretionary reasons, the Algerians parted from them and traveled on to La Paz, where they left their equipment at a drop-site before continuing on their "diplomatic mission" to Bolivia's neighbors on behalf of the new Algerian regime. A few days later, Bustos and his comrades arrived in La Paz and got in touch with their contacts, all young members of the Bolivian Communist party, soon to be joined by Furry.

After linking up with Furry, they headed to their base of operations and met Masetti near the old colonial mountain capital of Sucre. The group's cover story was that they were the Argentine and Bolivian partners of a new joint venture, traveling together to set up a farming and cattle ranching operation on a tract of land they had recently bought. They reached their "farm," in a remote area where the Río Bermejo forms Bolivia's border with Argentina and makes a sharp dip south; their land was strategically set in the middle of this mountainous and forested triangle, with Argentina on either side. There was only one dirt road leading in or out, and they were miles from the nearest neighbors.

They already had a "caretaker," actually a Bolivian Communist party member, on site; an older man, he spent his days doing little else but making peanut soup. Furry, the "administrator," came and went in his jeep, bringing them supplies and arms, but when they saw the gear that had been locally bought for them by Piñeiro's people and the Bolivians working with them, they were stunned. "There were thin uniforms made out of shiny nylon," said Bustos. "Ordinary nylon shirts, and Tom Mix–style holsters with little stars on them . . . It really seemed like a joke."

Their backpacks and boots were poor quality, as well, but fortunately the Algerians had provided them with some good Yugoslav military uniforms, cartridge belts, and field binoculars. Their arsenal, somehow smuggled in from Cuba, was plentiful and in good condition: Chinese bazookas, pistols, a Thompson submachine gun, automatic rifles, and lots of ammunition. Ciro Bustos acquired a gun with a silencer.

After exploring some access routes into Argentina, Masetti decided they were ready to go. On June 21, the five-man vanguard of the Ejército Guerrillero del Pueblo crossed the border into Argentina.

VI

Masetti's mission nearly coincided with the rout of another Cuban-trained guerrilla force in Peru a month earlier. In May, Héctor Béjar's Cuban-trained Ejército de Liberación Nacional (ELN), consisting of a column of forty guerrillas, had been detected and turned back in its attempt to cross from Bolivia into Peru. Béjar's mission had been to reach the Valle de la Convención in Peru's southern Andes, where the military were trying to corral a small rebel band led by Trotskyist peasant leader Hugo Blanco. Blanco's band had attacked a Guardia Civil post the previous November and been on the run ever since, and the Cubans saw the fracas as a good opportunity for the ELN to go into action.

Just as for Masetti's guerrillas, the large, mostly undeveloped country of Bolivia, situated at the heart of the South American continent—with its porous and ill-protected borders shared with Peru, Chile, Argentina, Paraguay, and Brazil—was the most logical point of entry for Béjar's guerrillas. Another factor in Bolivia's favor was the good relationship between Cuba and the center-left MNR (Movimiento Nacionalista Revolucionario) government of Víctor Paz Estenssoro, one of the few remaining Latin American governments that still retained diplomatic ties with Havana. As its envoy, Cuba had dispatched a man close to Che—Ramón Aja Castro, who had accompanied Che to the Punta del Este conference—and placed Piñeiro's man Ariel on his staff. Not least, the Communist party was legal in Bolivia and could help Cuba with contacts, safe houses, and transport for guerrillas. Cuba had asked for the help of the Bolivian party in getting Béjar's column as far as the Peruvian border, and Masetti's to the Argentine frontier. The party had agreed and assigned some of its cadres to help both groups, but its decision to support these operations was a tactical one, and taken reluctantly.

The Bolivian Communist Party, or PCB, operated legally, but like most of the kindred parties in neighboring countries, its leaders had eschewed the kind of armed struggle espoused by Cuba—and Che in particular—in favor of gaining further ground through electoral politics. The Bolivian party had established amicable relations with Paz Estenssoro's government, and hoped to keep things that way.

In essence, the Bolivian Communists agreed to help Havana in its guerrilla plans for Argentina and Peru in hopes of discouraging Cuba from starting an insurgency in their own country. Within the party's youth wing was a faction of pro-Cuban militants who could well provide the nucleus to such a group, but allowing them to help the Argentines and Peruvians would perhaps channel their revolutionary fervor elsewhere, preventing an internal schism like the one that had riven the Peruvian party. As Mario Monje, Bolivia's former Communist party chief, tells it, he was first approached on the subject by Cuba's diplomats in La Paz.

"They told me that they needed help for some young Peruvian Communists who had been trained and wanted to return to their country. They thought the best country to enter from was Bolivia, in the altiplano [Andean plateau] region." Monje says he told the Cubans he didn't agree with the strategy, that the Cuban experience was unique and couldn't be repeated elsewhere. He also told them he could not do anything behind the backs of his comrades in Peru's Communist party, and would have to inform them and ask their opinion. When Monje told the Peruvian party about the Cuban proposal at meetings in Chile and Uruguay, he found them adamantly opposed. "They did not want to have anything to do with guerrillas," he said.

Despite his agreement with them, Monje says he tried to convince the Peruvians not to precipitate an open break with Havana, urging them to "be flexible and try to control the situation." Otherwise, he warned, "this thing [Cuba's export of armed struggle] will hit the fan everywhere and do damage to the Peruvians and everyone else."

By now, however, Monje and his comrades had already begun hearing "rumors" that Havana wanted to get a guerrilla war going in Bolivia as well. The Bolivian Politburo held a meeting and voted unanimously against the notion of an armed struggle in their country, and afterward Monje traveled to Havana with fellow Politburo member Hilario Claure. Their mission, according to Monje, was to express the Bolivian party's official policy opposing Cuban "interventionism" in the region generally, while also trying to "mediate" between Havana and the indignant Peruvians.

Meeting with the éminence grise of Cuba's guerrilla-support agency, Manuel Piñeiro, Monje reminded him that in the 1930s, under Stalin, the Soviets had backed guerrillas in Latin America and it hadn't worked. "They pushed armed struggle over here, guerrillas over there," he told Piñeiro. "They tried it in different countries and failed, and now you are trying to repeat what they did."

Piñeiro suggested they speak directly with Fidel, and arranged a meeting where, Monje says, he once again outlined his and the Peruvian party's opposition to the scheme. Calling Cuba's revolutionary experience a genuine alternative to the traditional Communist party approach, Fidel said that he could not and would not deny that alternative to other young guerrillas who wanted to emulate Cuba's struggle. "We are going to help them," Fidel told Monje. "I understand your position, but I think we have to help those who are going to be arriving in your country now. I'm not asking for the help of the Peruvian party, I'm asking for *your* help."

Evidently believing that they had bought Fidel's gratitude and that he would not authorize any guerrilla activity in Bolivia behind his party's back, Monje says that he and Claure acceded to Fidel's request; without informing the Peruvian Communist party, they would assist in getting Béjar's group into Peru. Afterward, they met with Che, but their meeting with him was less friendly. Che expounded his defense of the guerrilla project "aggressively and firmly," recalled Monje, and the air between them was one of tension, not trust.

Claure offered a subtly different account of the Havana talks. He agrees that he and Monje made clear their opposition to a Cuban-sponsored guerrilla war in Bolivia, but found Fidel noncommittally "diplomatic," while Che was "arrogant," dismissing their argument by retorting: "That's what the Communists here told us when we wanted to make the Cuban revolution. If we'd listened to them, there wouldn't have been one."

Afterward, Claure says he and Monje returned to La Paz with the suspicion that the Cubans were going to go ahead with whatever they had already planned in spite of the Bolivian Communist party, and thereafter they remained watchful of the Cubans' moves. Before long, they sensed their worries were well founded. On a subsequent visit to Havana, says Monje, he and Che were relaxing outside one day, lying on some grass and talking, when Che turned to him and said: "Hey, Monje, why don't you get a guerrilla war going in Bolivia?" "And why should I?" Monje retorted. "What will it get us?" Che challenged him: "It's because you're afraid, isn't it?" Monje says he shot back: "No, it's that you have a machine gun stuck in your brain, and you can't imagine any other way to develop an anti-imperialist struggle." Monje says Che laughed at his retort, and let the matter rest.

Quite apart from their conceptual differences over revolutionary theory with Cuba, Monje and his Bolivian party comrades suspected Cuba's guerrilla push was not for their own benefit so much as to further its own interests. Not long after his exchange with Che, Monje said a "top Cuban official" told him that "it would be great" if his party began an armed struggle in Bolivia "because it would distract the imperialists and release pressure on us."

For the time being, Monje kept his relations with the Cubans as fraternal as possible. Anxious to appear conciliatory and to keep abreast of the Cubans' intentions at the same time, he even requested Cuban permission to send some young party cadres to Havana on the grounds that his party was keen "to learn from Cuba's revolutionary experience." Meanwhile, his people began helping Béjar's and Masetti's groups, assigning some young party members to work with them, providing them with safe houses, food, supplies, and transport. While Masetti and his men were still in Algeria, the Bolivians had located and purchased the Argentines' future rearguard base of operations on the Río Bermejo. And, after some delays and changes of itinerary, they had moved Béjar's column out of La Paz and on a long river journey through Bolivia's eastern jungle toward the Peruvian border.

Béjar's group had reached the Peruvian border in May, by which time their intentions had evidently become well known to the Peruvian authorities. Béjar sent an advance party across the border, but it was discovered almost immediately by police in the Peruvian town of Puerto Maldonado. One of the fighters, a talented young poet named Javier Heraud, was killed in the resulting shootout. Most of the others managed to escape back into Bolivia, whereupon a dozen or so of Béjar's men were captured by local authorities, but then released in an apparent goodwill gesture to Cuba by Paz Estenssoro's government. By late May, Hugo Blanco had also been captured and imprisoned in Peru. In early June, Peru's military junta held the elections they had promised after seizing power the year before, and the winner was the center-right candidate Fernando Belaunde Terry, a U.S.-educated engineer. The first Peruvian guerrilla venture had failed miserably, but Béjar and his comrades began reorganizing, and before long they would try again.*

Posthumous suspicions about the quick detection of Béjar's group soon focused more on the local Communist parties; Béjar himself later accused Monje's party of acceding to Peruvian Communist party demands to thwart his effort, pointing out that the Bolivians had delayed their entry by rerouting his force to a point hundreds of miles from where Blanco was operating. To their critics, however, Bolivia's party leaders could say they had complied with Cuba's wishes: Its cadres had escorted the ELN to the Peruvian border and even helped them after their debacle by lending refuge and other assistance. Still, the suspicions of internal treachery persisted over the years. As Humberto Vázquez-Viaña, a PCB youth militant at the time,

---

*In the face of persistent and proven inadequacies of the Cuban security apparatus to successfully implement Che's guerrilla programs, a number of former guerrillas, including Ciro Bustos and several of his comrades, have singled out Piñeiro for blame. Piñeiro's task was a thankless one, however. In addition to Béjar's and Masetti's groups, his department was simultaneously assisting the Guatemalan, Colombian, and Venezuelan guerrillas, among others. And there were problems arising on every front, ranging from logistical and communications difficulties to factional splits, and military and political setbacks.

later quipped acidly, his former organization had striven to be "good with both God and the Devil."

As for Che's ex-brother-in-law, Ricardo Gadea, he had missed the Béjar fiasco. After a factional split, he and other would-be guerrillas formed the MIR, which opted for a different approach from the Cuban-ELN model: They believed they should build up a social and organizational base in Peru before beginning a war. The Cubans did not approve, and Gadea said that he and his comrades were "kept on ice" in Cuba. Piñeiro confirmed Gadea's version, explaining that the "difference in treatment had to do with their different conceptions." Béjar was willing to go into action immediately, which is what Cuba thought was the best plan, while Gadea's group had a looser, longer-term, and therefore less attractive agenda. So, while Béjar and his followers were shipped out to Bolivia, Gadea's group was dispatched to the Escambray mountains to fight the counterrevolutionary *"bandidos"* operating there. Their requests to return to Peru were rebuffed or not answered at all, and after several months they realized they were being kept against their will. It wasn't until after Béjar's fiasco, and after a special trip was made to Havana by their group's leader, Luis de la Puente Uceda, that they were finally allowed to depart. Before he left, Gadea saw Che one last time.

"It was an important conversation for me," Gadea recalled, "because it was the first time Che saw me not just as a student or out of a family obligation, but because of the decision I had made regarding the revolution in Peru." Che made it clear that there was no bad blood and gave him his blessing. "He told me: 'Well, go have your experience. Everyone has to test himself, and you must learn and gain knowledge through your own experiences.'"

Gadea described his feelings upon leaving Cuba as akin to those of an adolescent who leaves home to his parents' disapproval and nagged by self-doubts, but nonetheless determined to prove himself. More than thirty years later, he is still proud of the fact that all the members of his group made it to Peru without being arrested, began their work of underground organization, and within two years were ready for war.

Thinking of his own future plans, meanwhile, Che anxiously awaited the outcome of Masetti's effort to establish an Argentine guerrilla *foco*.

VII

Aleida did not want Che to leave, but she knew she couldn't stop him, either. He had been a revolutionary fighter when she met him, and he had never stopped being one. From the beginning, he had made clear to her that one day he would leave, to carry the revolution to his homeland.

Until 1962 his departure had seemed like an abstraction, but once Masetti's group had been formed and their training was under way, she could no longer ignore the prospect.

Their second child, Camilo, had been born in May 1962. Just as their daughter Aliusha had inherited Che's darker coloring, the new baby had Aleida's fairness. He would grow up to have her blond hair, but his father's massive forehead and intense stare. During the missile crisis, Aleida had become pregnant again, and they had moved to a new, larger house on Calle 47, in a residential neighborhood in Nuevo Vedado, a few blocks from the zoo and close to the government complex around Plaza de la Revolución. On June 14, 1963—Che's thirty-fifth birthday—Aleida gave birth to a second daughter, whom they named Celia, after Che's mother.

Their name choice for the new baby was a particularly poignant homage to Che's mother, for at that moment, Celia *madre* was in prison. She had arrived in Cuba in January 1963, stayed with them for three months, and on her return to Argentina in April been arrested and imprisoned on charges of possessing subversive Cuban propaganda, and of being an agent for her infamous son.

On June 9, Celia wrote to Che from the Women's Correctional of Buenos Aires. "My dear," she began. "You had asked me to write you, and a lot of time has gone by since then. The correctional isn't such a nice place to write a letter from. . . .

"I share my present kingdom with 15 people, almost all communists." They were fine companions, Celia noted, apart from their enforcement of an "overly iron discipline and an irredentist dogmatism" that she found trying. Aside from that, she spent her time enjoyably enough. She didn't know when she'd be freed, "but you know that if there is someone who is well constituted to withstand prison in good humor, that's me. It will also serve me as an exercise in humility. . . .

"The only thing I find uncomfortable is not having a single minute of intimacy in the entire day. We eat, sleep, read and work in our cell of 14 by 6 [meters] and [exercise] in a gallery where you can see the sky through the bars and from which they throw us out when a common prisoner arrives. It seems we might infect them with a terrible contagious disease. . . .

"I eat breakfast at eight, [do] exercises; from three to four we play volleyball in the patio. I am practically the oldest [on the team], apart from Consuelo, a detainee of seventy, and there's a group of six very young girls, all students. By unanimity I've been proclaimed the best player and the team I belong to is the [prison] champion." She had also learned some prison crafts, such as making papier-mâché dolls. "They're horrible, but a good way to kill time."

She had a good bed, a warm blanket, the food was acceptable, and the guards didn't mete out any "unnecessary cruelties." Apart from the lack of privacy, her biggest complaint were the body searches she was subjected to before and after each visit, and the reading of all her letters, which she found especially humiliating. "The searches include doubtful caresses: almost all the prisoners here are lesbians and I suspect that the guards have elected this wonderful work because they have the same inclinations. . . .

"I don't know, or rather yes I do know why the government has wanted to put me in this place. . . . I'll tell you as a point of curiosity that one of the questions they asked me in the DIPA [Argentine secret police] was 'what is your role in Fidel Castro's government?'"

She reassured Che that she hadn't been mistreated. The police who had interrogated her hadn't even "raised their voices" to her, but that hadn't stopped her from thinking of them as "sons of whores." As for the military junta running the country, she hoped they got "a good kick in the ass" in the elections they had agreed to call in July.

"As you can see they always provoke elevated thoughts. [Prison] is a marvelous deformatory, as much for the common prisoners as for the political ones: if you are lukewarm, you become active; if you're active, you become aggressive; and if you're aggressive, you become implacable."

In fact, ever since her son Ernesto had become "Che," Celia had undergone a significant political radicalization. In recent years she had actively supported Ismael Viñas, a former *radicalista* politician who had formed his own leftist party after breaking with Frondízi. She claimed now to believe in "socialism," but she was not a Communist, and she didn't really like or trust Fidel, according to people who knew her well. Most of all, she didn't like what she saw as his hold over her son, and Che's subservience to him, but in spite of her private qualms about Cuba's disorganization and incompetence, she vigorously defended Cuba's right to determine its own political destiny on grounds of principle. Above all, she defended the revolution because of her son's role in it.

Whatever the Argentine security forces suspected, there was a bitter irony to Celia's imprisonment along with members of the Argentine Communist party. Although she downplayed it in her letter, Celia's life was made extremely difficult by her doctrinaire cellmates. According to her daughter-in-law, María Elena Duarte, they made her life "impossible," to the extent that Celia broke down and cried about it when she visited her.

"They imposed rules even the jailers didn't impose. For instance, she liked to read, and as if to persecute her, they turned out the lights. The lights had to be turned out at such and such an hour. If she wanted to play a certain sport in the patio, [they told her] no, that was not the correct hour for that sport. It was so cruel . . . and so obviously directed against her! Celia used to say they were worse than the jailers."

The leader of the Communist women, and the person María Elena Duarte holds chiefly responsible for Celia's ill-treatment, was Fanie Edelman, a veteran party activist and founder of the Communist-front Argentine Women's Union. Many years later, Edelman acknowledged that she and her comrades had "organized life in the prison" and imposed "very rigorous norms of conduct." But she reacted with indignation at the notion that Che's mother had been in any way singled out for persecution. "We were a harmonious group. On the contrary, we respected her a great deal, precisely because she was Che's mama."*

Not long after she wrote to Che, Celia was released from prison, but life was not the same; she had been cut from her moorings, her children had grown up and moved on, and she no longer had a real home of her own.

After the bomb incident the previous year, she and her youngest son, nineteen-year-old Juan Martín, had left the house on Calle Araoz in the care of their Indian maid, Sabina Portugal, and moved into a small, rented apartment, soon to be joined by Juan Martín's new bride, María Elena. While Celia was in prison, María Elena had given birth to a baby boy; rather than inconvenience them, upon her release, Celia let them have the apartment and went to live with her daughter Celia in a dark old house on Calle Negro.

María Elena and Juan Martín felt badly for Celia, and they had asked her to stay with them. "No," she had said. "We have an excellent relationship and I don't want to ruin it by living together." They saw each other frequently, meeting up most weekends at Roberto's home, but Celia lived an immensely solitary life, aspects of which not even her children knew about. They knew she loved going to the cinemas, for instance, but it was only after her death that they found ticket stubs in her coat pockets and discovered she had almost always gone on her own.

---

*At the same time, Edelman admitted that her party at the time was "dogmatic" and "reformist," out of touch with the revolutionary impulse, and rejected outright the "armed struggle" as a means of gaining power. "It was a historical period in the life of our party in which all guerrillas, all armed groups, were taboo."

Indeed, for all its official trumpetings of revolutionary solidarity with socialist Cuba, at home the Argentine Communist party was a monolithic, well-entrenched bureaucracy that sought political respectability above all else. Like its kindred parties in Bolivia, Peru, and Chile, it was vehemently opposed to the Cuban-inspired calls for armed struggle that had begun issuing from the ranks of its younger militants. Che was aware of this, and for that very reason not only was his bid to install a guerrilla *foco* being conducted behind the party's back, but he was counting upon party dissidents to join up and become its fighters.

"Celia had her circle of friends, her political activities, but she had compartmentalized her life in a very private, solitary kind of way," said María Elena, "and I think in some way she enjoyed the solitude. She read and thought a great deal, and was undergoing a period of reflection, a reevaluation of her political points of view."

Of course, being Che's mother had turned Celia's life upside down, just as it had altered the lives of all of the family members in one way or another. Friends describe the effect on the Guevaras of Ernesto's transformation into Che the revolutionary as "an explosion," forcing them to come to terms with their own political attitudes, and, involuntarily, to suffer persecution merely for being related to the famous *comandante comunista.*" For Celia *madre,* the consequences were the most immediately dramatic. As revolution and war had become features of Che's life, bombs, imprisonment, and political persecution had entered her's. The unique mother-son symbiosis that Ernesto had severed during his soul-searching years on the road had been strangely restored.

Celia had come into confrontation with her own society, and Che likewise was finding himself at a new kind of watershed in his adopted Cuban homeland. In her letter from prison, Celia had wished him a happy birthday, saying that she imagined he would spend it "submerged in the Ministry and its problems," and added: "I almost forget, can you tell me about the progress of Cuba's economy?"

As Celia undoubtedly knew, it wasn't really a matter of progress. Ricardo Rojo's latest trip to the island had coincided with her own visit, and he had instantly noted the marked decline since his earlier stay. The neon signs that had once lit up Havana had been switched off; American cigarettes, no longer available, had been replaced by Cuban brands such as Criollos and Dorados; Cuba's cars and buses now looked shabby from lack of spare parts and maintenance, while hundreds of neglected U.S.-built tractors were rusting in the fields for the same reasons.

Cuba's revolutionaries clearly had not thought through the consequences of going for a complete break with the United States. The old system had been brought to a screeching halt, and the new one had not caught up with Cuba's present needs—much less its ambitious future plans. Soviet petroleum was highly sulfuric and corroded the piping in the U.S.-built refineries, while the Eastern-bloc technicians had proven ill equipped to take over the modern American-built technology left behind in Cuba. Even the simplest logistical detail caused enormous difficulties: For example, the Soviets' tools were metric and didn't fit the American-manufactured machinery in Cuba.

And there were other disappointments: Much of the industrial equipment bought from the Soviet bloc by Cuba had turned out to be shoddy and outdated. Oscar Fernández Mell recalled Che's outrage over the crude file-lathing equipment he had purchased from Russia. "Che used to say: 'Look at the shit they've sold us!'" claiming all it consisted of was a system to turn out rough, elongated pieces of metal that were then dipped in silver-colored paint.

Beset by a multitude of practical problems, Che told Rojo that to get Cuba's industrialization under way, he needed to produce construction materials, but he had two large kilns standing idle because they didn't have firebricks. "We even have to improvise screws," he explained. Textile plants had shut down because the quality of thread they were producing was "too uneven." And so on.

"Were I to draw a conclusion about Guevara's state of mind during those months," wrote Rojo, "I would say that the struggle was undermining his optimism. His ingenuity seemed blunted, his spirit smothered under the mountains of statistics and production methods."

To Alberto Granado, Che's malaise was also due to his loss of faith in the imperfect Soviet model he had originally embraced with such innocent fervor. He now chafed at the slipshod efforts to transplant it in Cuba, complete with its concomitant inefficiency, bureaucracy, and triumphalist rhetoric. Granado recalled how Che had described his conversion to Marxism when he was in Guatemala and Mexico. Che had remained a "skeptic," he had told Granado, until his "discovery of Stalin" in books, and he had been bowled over by what he had read. "That was when he began to find a world that was not all slogans and manifestos—an important world—and I think that intoxicated him and made him feel that in the Soviet Union lay the solution to life, believing that what had been applied there was what he had read about. But, in 1963 and 1964, when he realized they had been tricking him—you know Che couldn't stand being lied to—then came the violent reaction."

As Sartre had remarked, the revolutionary "honeymoon" was over by late 1960, and that, in revolutionary terms, was a very long time ago. Che was now, at the threshold of middle age, the father of four children, and a government minister at the pinnacle of his career in revolutionary Cuba. He carried a grave air about his person, he seemed less lighthearted. And he looked his age. He had shorn the long locks of hair that he had grown in the mountains and worn during the first year of "free Cuba." He still wore the beret, but his face appeared puffy and swollen; despite what he had once told Ricardo Rojo about "cortisone" giving him a heavier appearance, he *had* gained weight. So had Aleida, who had grown plump from her string of pregnancies.

Ever the iconoclast, Che steadfastly wore the shirt-jacket of his olive-green uniform outside his trousers, with his belt on top—the only Cuban *comandante* who refused to conform to the military dress code. More often that not, he wore his trousers hanging loose, outside his boots, instead of tucking them in. No one dared reproach him, of course. *"Che es como es,"* his colleagues would say, with a shrug of their shoulders, "Che is the way he is."

When he was home, Che spent hours closeted away in the austere little rooftop office full of books he had outfitted there, reading, writing, and studying. Its only adornments were a bronze bas-relief of Lenin, a small bronze statue of Simón Bolívar, and a large framed photograph of Camilo Cienfuegos. When people asked him why he didn't take a break, he gave a work-related excuse. There was never very much time to be with Aleida and the children. More often than not, duty called, and his trips away were invariably long ones; he never took Aleida with him. In Cuba he inspected factories, military units, cooperatives, and schools; gave speeches; received foreign dignitaries; attended diplomatic receptions. To such functions, when-ever possible, he brought Aleida along. But his workweek lasted from Mon-day through Saturday, including nights, and on Sunday mornings he went off to do volunteer labor. Sunday afternoons were all he spared for his family.

At such times, he threw himself down on the living room floor and played with his children and his dog, a German shepherd named Muralla (Wall), who also escorted him to the office. His eldest child, Hildita, now almost eight, was usually there on weekends, and they watched boxing matches and soccer games together on television, pretending to place bets on who would win. Occasionally he stopped by to see Hilda. She noted his extreme tiredness, and later recalled how he used to take their daughter in his arms and tell her he wanted to take her on a trip with him someday—but he never did.

At other times, Che's disciplinarian streak showed up. Once, when Aliusha had a tantrum, Che walked over and smacked her bottom. Her wails increased. When her nanny, Sofía, tried to pick her up and comfort her, Che told her to leave her, so she would remember why she had been punished. He was especially severe with his bodyguards, who lived in an annex of the house. One of their fiancées recalled the time Che made Harry Villegas, his favorite, strip off his clothes, locking him in a closet as punish-ment for some misdemeanor. It occurred when Celia *madre* was visiting and she yelled at Che, telling him to be more lenient. He had told his mother to keep out of it, that he knew what he was doing.

This was "Che the Implacable," Cuba's revolutionary avenging angel and ultimate political commissar, demanding the impossible of those around him but above reproach himself because he lived up to his own severe dictates. He was respected and admired, despised and feared, but nobody was indifferent to him. Summing up the unusual personality of his late comrade, Manuel Piñeiro said: "Che had something of the missionary in him."

Perhaps his most controversial disciplinary innovation was Guanacahabibes. Like his volunteer labor scheme, Guanacahabibes was part of Che's scheme to create a new revolutionary morale. It was a rehabilitation camp at the remote, rocky, and devilishly hot westernmost tip of Cuba, where he dispatched transgressors from the Ministry of Industries to undergo periods of self-effacing physical labor to redeem themselves before returning to their jobs. The sanctions were "voluntary," and could last from a month to a year depending on the offense, generally of the ethical variety. If someone had practiced nepotism, intentionally covered up a mistake, or had an affair with a comrade's wife, he was called before Che. He gave offenders an opportunity to "accept" their punishment with a stint at Guanacahabibes, or else they could leave the ministry. If they did their time and showed that they had learned the errors of their ways, they could return to the ministry with no black mark on their record. If they refused, they were out of a job. (In time, due to the excesses of the camp's *comandante,* Guanacahabibes acquired a sinister reputation, a Cuban equivalent of a Siberian gulag. Despite his dismissal, however, Guanacahabibes remained controversial, and around the time Che left Cuba, it was closed down.)

Another pet project of Che's was the Ciro Redondo Experimental Farm in Matanzas province. The Ciro Redondo was an agricultural cooperative farm where mostly illiterate *guajiros* from his old sierra column lived and worked communally according to his doctrine of moral incentives. He insisted they better themselves through schoolwork as well and had assigned them a teacher. He often flew there to check up on their progress in the little Cessna airplane he had learned to fly with his private pilot, Eliseo de la Campa.

Once, he took the economist Regino Boti with him to the farm and tested some of the men on their reading comprehension. One man did so badly that Che insulted him, saying: "Well, if you keep studying, maybe you'll get to be as smart as an ox in twenty years," and turned on his heel. The poor *guajiro* was so humiliated that he began crying. Boti went and talked to Che, telling him that he had been wrong to be so harsh, to go back and talk to the man, to lift his spirits again.

Such episodes were commonplace. Che's tendency to be harsh often had to be tempered by a more diplomatic companion or friend. He seemed to have little sense of the intimidating effects his words could have on others. There were also some comic incidents that served to remind him of his public celebrity, however.

One such instance occurred right on the seafront Malecón in Havana, when Che, a notoriously bad driver, rear-ended another man's car. The man's reaction was typical: He emerged cursing the mother and father of whoever it was who had hit him. But when he saw it was Che, he became cravenly apologetic, and his expression of bug-eyed choler turned to one that was beatific. "Che, Comandante," the man reportedly sighed. "What an honor for me to have my car struck by you!" Then, caressing his new dent, he announced that he would never have it repaired, but would keep it as proud reminder of his personal encounter with Che Guevara.

Such tales remain enduring folklore in Havana. Most have to do with his famous working hours, his hatred of *adulónes,* or "brownnosers," and his personal austerity. Evidently, he was as strict with Aleida as he was with his underlings at the Ministry of Industries. People speak of the time Celia Sánchez, Fidel's great dispenser of favors, sent Aleida a new pair of Italian shoes and of how, when Che found out, he made her return them. Did the average Cuban wear imported Italian shoes? No. Then she couldn't, either.

When they moved from their house on Calle 18 in Miramar to their new home in Nuevo Vedado, Che discovered Aleida fixing decorative lamps on the walls of the new house. When she explained that she had taken them from their last home, he blew up and ordered her to take them back. Another time, one of the children was sick, and Aleida asked to be allowed to take the child to the hospital in his car. He refused, telling her to "take the bus like everybody else"; the petrol she would use was "the people's," intended for use in his public duties, not for "personal" reasons.

When food rationing began, and one of his colleagues complained, Che criticized him for the remark, telling the man that his own family was eating fine on what the government allowed them. When the colleague pointed out that Che was eating well thanks to a special food supplement, Che had the claim investigated. Finding out that it was true, he had the benefit eliminated; his family would receive no special favors.

Rumors circulated about how the Guevaras often didn't have enough to eat, and that Aleida had to borrow money secretly from the bodyguards to make ends meet. Timur Gaidar, a former *Pravda* correspondent in Cuba, recalled the time a sympathetic Soviet embassy official furtively slipped some hors d'ouevres into Aleida's purse at a diplomatic reception when he was sure Che wasn't looking. Whether or not Che was as severe as these stories suggest, his widow will not say; she feels a duty to protect the image of the man who has become an international myth, and insists he was "a man without defects."

Che's relationship with Aleida was a source of curiosity to many, for they were a true study in contrasts. He was an intellectual, a scholar, and an assiduous reader of books. Aleida preferred movies and social gatherings. He was austere and shunned the good things in life. Aleida, like most people, appreciated them, and aspired to possess some of the comforts enjoyed by most *comandantes'* wives—even in revolutionary Cuba. It was a constant bone of contention between them and evidently produced frequent arguments.

Some Cubans close to them have drawn comparisons between their relationship and that of Karl Marx with his unintellectual wife, Jenny Westphalen. While Che had his head in the clouds with his work, his philosophizing, and revolutionary theory, Aleida kept the house running, the bills paid, and the children fed. She was fiercely devoted to him. And, despite their differences, they enjoyed each other's company, had a strong physical attraction for one another, and, by all accounts, were faithful. Both enjoyed an open, earthy repartee; at times it was shared with others. Once, while he was visiting his mother-in-law's house in Santa Clara, the old woman asked him if he wanted a bath, and he quipped wickedly: "Not if Aleida's not in it."

Both of them were also romantics at heart, although Che rarely showed this side of himself in public. At night, in the privacy of their bedroom, he used to recite poetry to Aleida, a habit that thrilled her. His favorite, as always, was Pablo Neruda.

Another thing they shared was their bluntness of speech. If anything, Aleida was less tactful and even more brutally honest than Che. If she didn't like someone, she would say so to his face. It was, Che used to say, one of the things he liked about her the most.

But the main reason Che loved Aleida, say their closest friends, was that she provided him with a "home," something he'd never really had in the conventional sense. Che regarded his father warmly for the parenting he had given him, said Aleida, but because of his father's *"locuras"* he sometimes thought of him as immature, even younger than himself. (Aleida herself never had much time for Guevara Lynch and acknowledged that, after Che's death, they had a public falling out when, at a gathering of people, she heard the old man say he had been responsible for inculcating Che's early socialist leanings. She challenged him, telling him it was a lie, and the old man never forgave her for that.)

With Celia *madre* it was something different. She and Che were like "splinters off the same tree," as the Latin American saying goes. When Celia came to Havana, she and Che would spend hours talking and were always "fighting," said Aleida. They would argue about everything from Latin America to their opinion of world figures; Celia still defended her old "imperialist" World War II hero, Charles de Gaulle, for instance. "Celia was very political and opinionated, and sometimes if you heard them, you'd think they were finishing off the world, but it was just the way they discussed things."

But as much as Che loved his mother, she had never been a physically demonstrative woman, and it was something he had always craved. Just as in his adolescence Che had gone to his aunt Beatriz for some maternal attention, he now sought it as a grown man from Aleida. She recognized this need of his and responded as best she knew how by mothering him, dressing him, and even bathing him.

Aleida said that before Che left for the office each morning, she used to make sure he had "everything in order" because he was notoriously careless about his appearance. The reason he wore his uniform shirt outside of his trousers, with the web belt over it, Cossack-fashion, with the top button undone, she said, was that he suffered from the high level of humidity in Cuba, which exacerbated his asthma. They never had carpets at their homes or in his office. The heat was also why he often sat on the floor—as numerous visitors to his office recall finding him—because it was cooler there. Since Che disliked air conditioning, the solution they came up with for his office was to seal the windows tightly so that no air came in or out. It was the only way, said Aleida, that they could control his asthma. (Che's asthma was a legacy that endures: Two of their four children "inherited" their father's asthma, and now, another generation along, some of their children are asthmatic as well.)

Such eccentricities added to the popular myth being woven around Che's figure in Cuba. He was aware of it, and, if there were those who saw him as a *"bicho raro,"* he seemed not to care. As one Cuban woman who knew him remarked: "Che was a really strange man to find in Cuba. Here was a man whose favorite form of relaxation was mathematics and whose favorite sport was chess."

Indeed, for all his posthumous mythification in Cuba, throughout his years there, Che stood out in contrast to almost everyone around him. Some Cubans saw this as a disdain for their national culture. He didn't like parties—a Cuban national pastime—and rarely invited people to his home, or went to theirs, for that matter. Borrego, one of his closest friends, says Che dropped by his house only once in all his time in Cuba, although they lived just two blocks from each other. In a country where the people loved to dance, and sensual Afro-Caribbean rhythmic music was the heart blood of the culture, Che liked to listen to tangos, but was tone-deaf and didn't dance. On a Caribbean island with beautiful beaches, to which Cubans traditionally escape during the hot summers, Che didn't swim.

In a country where the native rum is the time-honored means of relaxing and passing the time with friends, Che didn't drink. He allowed himself red wine when it was available. Even in this habit, he stood out, for most Cubans do not like wine. In a nation of coffee drinkers, where the average Cuban punctuates his or her day with little cups of hot, sweet espresso coffee, Che vastly preferred his native home-brewed *yerba mate,* which is a peculiarly Southern Cone predilection. Above all else, Cubans love to eat roast pork, while Che preferred a good grilled beefsteak. Cubans have a sense of humor that is straightforwardly bawdy or scatological; Che's was ironic, witty, and acid.

Despite his honorary Cuban citizenship and the passage of time, Che was culturally still very much an Argentine. He liked to say, pointedly, that he considered himself a "Latin American." This fit into his scheme to unite the nations of the hemisphere into a socialist fraternity. But he was an Argentine, really, and even in Cuba, his best friends, the people he talked most freely to, were those of a similar heritage, such as Alberto Granado, one of his dearest friends.

Granado was one of the few people who could criticize Che to his face and get away with it. Granado challenged him on many things he saw as *"irreflexivo,"* or overly rigid, in Che's personality, such as his vociferous contempt for "cowards," liars, and brownnosers. And, although he had helped him recruit people for the Masetti expedition and evidently also served as his liaison with some of the Venezuelan guerrillas, Granado actually disagreed with Che's belief in "jump-starting" the revolutionary climate in Latin America through guerrilla warfare. It was an issue they argued over frequently, and which they never resolved.

Granado recalled one conversation with Che where he pointed out what he believed was the fundamental difference between them. Che could look through a sniperscope at a soldier and pull the trigger, knowing that by killing him he was helping reduce repression—"saving 30,000 future children from lives of hunger"—whereas when *he* looked through the scope, Granado saw a man with a wife and children.

With his own penchant for dance, drink, and good times, Granado fit right into Cuban society. But Che never really did, and even Granado, desperately loyal to Che, conceded that his friend's caustic nature rubbed some Cubans the wrong way. To many, he seemed altogether too serious about revolution, unrelentingly moralistic, and holier-than-thou.

The one intrinsically Cuban habit Che *did* indulge was to smoke Havana cigars—disastrous, of course, for his asthma condition. But even this he did with singular determinism, smoking the *tabacos* right down to the nub in order not to "waste" anything that human labor had helped produce.

His asthma affliction was itself another paradox of Che's presence in Cuba. Very humid, Cuba has an extremely high incidence of asthma, making it one of the worst places on earth for him to have lived.

While many of his subordinates tried to emulate him—unsuccessfully, it must be said—his *"austeridad"* was a constant reproof to many of his high-living and philandering fellow revolutionaries. In a country where many of the men had second and even third "wives" simultaneously with their marriages, sired children with several women, and had affairs quite openly, Che was, by all accounts, steadfastly monogamous in Cuba, despite the fact that woman flocked to him like groupies to a pop star.

Given the noticeable effect Che had on females, Borrego once asked him with characteristic Cuban bluntness why he had ever married a woman as "ugly" as Hilda Gadea. Che reproved him for the remark, though admitted that she was not physically beautiful. But, he said, she had been a great *"compañera"* to him and, in her defense, added that a person didn't have to be beautiful to be good in bed.

One of his aides was with him at a social gathering where a pretty young woman blatantly flirted with Che. Instead of being flatttered and responding with gallantry or banter, Che primly scolded the woman, telling her to "behave herself." But such severity was not constant; even Che recognized a good-looking woman when he saw one. At a dinner in a foreign embassy, another of Che's friends was with him. They had been seated with the ambassador's gorgeous daughter. There was an obvious implication that the young woman was "on offer" by their host, who clearly wanted to "get close" to Che. The daughter, said Che's friend, was "so beautiful" that any man would have forgotten any marriage or revolutionary vows he had ever made just to sleep with her. Che clearly was finding it difficult to resist as well, for he finally turned to his companion and whispered: "Find an excuse to get me out of here before I succumb. *Ya no puedo más.* [I can't bear any more.]"

Che was suspicious of anyone doing him an unsolicited favor, seeing it as a sign of craven pandering, or worse, a symptom of moral corruption. The stories begin from his time in the sierra and continue throughout his life in Cuba. A classic example was the time a new bodyguard brought Che his boots, freshly shined. Che gave him a kick in the rear and called him a *guataca* (brownnoser). Then, when the humiliated soldier reacted by hurling the boots into the street, Che punished him by docking his pay for a week.

Yet Che's devotion to those who earned his trust was reciprocated by a fanatical loyalty. Known to everyone as *"los hombres del Che,"* they included bodyguards, accountants, economists, and revolutionary fighters. For them, Che personified "the revolution," which was why, despite everything, men such as Hermes Peña, Alberto Castellanos, and Jorge Ricardo Masetti had willingly volunteered to leave their jobs, wives, and children to go off and fight in his wars.

VIII

For two weeks, Masetti and his small band hacked their way through the northern Argentine wilderness, trying to reach their target area south of the town of Orán. Their chosen path brought them up against great jungle cliffs, however, and finally they gave up and returned to the farm to recuperate before trying a different route.

When they got back, they discovered that a political sea change had occurred in Argentina. The Argentine military had allowed elections to be held on July 7, and since the military had prevented the country's biggest voting bloc—the *Peronistas*—from participating, Masetti and most other Argentines expected the armed forces candidate, the right-wing General Aramburu, to win. Instead, the centrist Radical Party of the People's candidate, a respected sixty-three-year-old doctor from Córdoba, Dr. Arturo Illia, had won by a slender majority of votes.

The revelation caused a major crisis in the fledgling EGP. All of them realized that it was one thing to declare war on a military regime that had illegally seized power; but quite another to wage war against a democratically elected civilian president. The news from Argentina was all about the imminent "democratic aperture." "Our project disintegrated just like that," recalled Bustos. "And we spent a couple of days doing nothing, with everything on hold."

Masetti decided to call the whole thing off. Furry drove off to La Paz to advise Havana through the embassy there, and he sent Federico "El Flaco" (The Thin Man) Mendez into Argentina, to catch up with Jorge "El Loro" (The Parrot) Vázquez-Viaña, a young Bolivian Communist acting as one of their liaisons. Loro had been sent there to coordinate activities with a Trotskyite splinter group whose militants wanted to join the armed struggle, and now Masetti wanted him to suspend everything.

While Masetti and his men pondered what to do next, Che was in Algeria to attend the first anniversary celebrations of the triumphant Algerian revolution. As his Argentine subordinates had recently done, he toured the country's wartime battlefield sites, and no doubt he also thanked the Algerian president for the help his government had provided Masetti and his companions. He returned to Havana in time for the July 26 celebrations, bringing with him Algeria's minister of defense, Houari Boumedienne, a public display that Algeria and Cuba were strong revolutionary allies, two important links in the Afro–Asian–Latin American "anti-imperialist struggle."

By the time Che returned to Cuba, Masetti had changed his mind again. In fact, only two days after sending Furry and Federico off with orders to suspend operations, he had reanalyzed the Argentine elections and decided to go ahead. He sat down and wrote what he called a "Letter from the Rebels" to President-elect Illia.

After praising him for his past reputation as a civic-minded man worthy of respect, Masetti castigated Illia's decision to "lower himself" and play the military's game by seeking office "in the most scandalous electoral fraud in the history of the country." He urged him to resign to restore his reputation and to ally himself with the Argentines who wanted to be free of the military, those "blackmailing gunmen, and bodyguards for imperialism and the oligarchy." The People's Guerrilla Army (EGP), he announced, armed and organized, had gone into the mountains. "We are the only free men in this oppressed republic . . . and we won't come down unless it is to do battle." He signed the letter: "Segundo Comandante, Ejército Guerrillero del Pueblo, July 9, 1963, Campamento Augusto César Sandino . . . *Revolución o Muerte*."

As soon as it was ready, he ordered Ciro Bustos to go after Federíco and rescind the suspension order. Bustos was also to take the open letter to Illia and see that it was published, then travel to Argentina's cities where he knew people and lay the groundwork for an urban support network for their rebel force.

For the next several weeks, Bustos was on the move, all over Argentina, between Córdoba and Buenos Aires and his home city of Mendoza. He managed to have Masetti's letter published, but only in *Compañero,* a leftist *peronista* fringe publication, and it made little public impression. He was more successful in establishing a support network. In Córdoba he approached a leftist academic he knew from childhood, Oscar del Barco, a cofounder and editor of the intellectual Marxist journal *Pasado y Presente,* revealed his mission, and asked for help. Within a day, del Barco had assembled a group of people, mostly intellectuals and Communist party dissidents like himself working at Córdoba University's Faculty of Philosophy and Letters. As they listened, Bustos outlined the EGP's plan of action with frank candor: He told them that the project had Che's backing, that the core group had trained in Cuba and Algeria, and that funds were not a problem. What they needed was recruits to swell their ranks in the mountains, safe houses, urban contacts, and suppliers—in short, a clandestine national urban infrastructure.

It was what these intellectuals had been arguing for—"revolutionary action"—a position that had earned them their expulsion from the mainstream Argentine Communist party. Within days, they had enthusiastically begun to organize, and before long a small but well-coordinated network was being set up in a half-dozen cities and towns across the country, from Buenos Aires to Salta, with Córdoba as its epicenter.

By now an important new personality had also arrived at the guerrilla base. José María "Papi" Martínez Tamayo was a Cuban army captain and one of the most valuable assets in Piñeiro's intelligence apparatus, seconded to Che for his own use. After serving with Raúl during the war, Papi had stayed in the military, and since late 1962 had been Piñeiro's roving envoy to various Latin American guerrilla groups. He had joined Turcios Lima in Guatemala, served as an instructor in Cuba for Tania's ongoing clandestine training, and helped train the Argentine Trotskyite group of Vasco Bengochea.

Good-looking, strong, and energetic—"an impassioned conspirator," Bustos remarked, "and a stupendous guy"—Papi had come to see the *foco* through its initial stages and help prepare the way for Che's arrival.

Papi also came to take some of the load off the hard-pressed Furry, who was acting not only as the group's permanent base commander but also as its liaison with Cuba's embassy in La Paz, handling communications, logistics, and arms supplies. With Papi around to do some of these tasks, Furry could safeguard his cover as a pioneering rural *"finquero."* Over the coming months, Papi came and went constantly, between Bolivia, Argentina, and Cuba.

By September, the signs were that the time to get moving was now. Curious Bolivian police had already paid the farm a visit, no doubt having heard rumors from locals about the unusual amount of traffic at the newly purchased *finca*. Fortunately, there was only one road to the farm, and a car engine could be heard long before it arrived; the police came, poked around, and left, having seen nothing overtly suspicious. In case they returned, a camp was built for the fighters in the forest a short distance away, where they could be concealed from nosy outsiders.

But when Papi brought Alberto Castellanos to the farm "in late September or early October," Masetti and his men were still there. Segundo had been into Argentina exploring, and had returned to base. The scouts had to be extremely careful and usually traveled by night, for the Argentine police of the Gendarmería Nacional, with posts throughout the border area, patrolled constantly, on the lookout for smugglers of contraband. Also, the rural north was very sparsely settled, and strangers, especially armed, bearded, and uniformed ones, were soon noticed.

Castellanos's orders had been to wait for Che, but seeing that one of Masetti's men was sick, and anxious to get into action himself, Castellanos asked Masetti to take him on as a fighter. He wrote a note to Che explaining his decision, and sent it back with Papi. The group was still tiny. Besides the flap-eared, jovial Castellanos, who became known to everyone as "El Mono" (The Monkey), there were only one or two newcomers so far. In light of his initial success at organizing the urban network, Masetti now asked Bustos to assume the duty of liaison with the outside and to begin enlisting volunteers.

Among Bustos's first recruits were the Jouve brothers from a small town in Córdoba province. Emilio and Héctor were the sons of a French-Basque emigré builder of anarchist leanings. Both in their early twenties and former members of the Communist Youth, they had grown disenchanted with the party's inactivity and had begun forming a small "action group" of their own in Córdoba—collecting a few guns, painting wall graffiti, and not much else. They had jumped at the chance to go to *"la montaña"* when El Pelao Bustos showed up asking for volunteers.

By then the group had bought a truck in which a Cordobés doctor friend of Bustos, "El Petiso" [Shorty] Canelo, drove the recruits north. A "bookstore" was opened in the city of Salta as a cover for the storage and transport of supplies to the guerrillas. From Buenos Aires, three more volunteers arrived.

By October Masetti and his men had moved across the border and installed themselves in a camp in the forest above the Río Pescado, some fifteen kilometers from the Argentine border town of Aguas Blancas. It lay in the mountains just off the road from Salta, south of Orán. While Bustos came and went from the city, the little force began to grow, and hiked deeper into the hills looking for peasants to engage in "armed propaganda." This consisted of impromptu consciousness-raising talks where they explained they had come to liberate the peasants from poverty and injustice. But their first efforts were discouraging.

"It was shocking," recalled Bustos. "You couldn't even call these people *campesinos.* These were people who lived in little bush clearings, full of fleas and dogs . . . and snot-nosed kids, with no links to the real world, nothing. They didn't even live in the conditions of the Indians who at least have their food, their tribes and things. These people were really lost, marginalized. They could hardly be called a social base for what we were trying to do. They were experiencing problems that were real, but their misery was such that they were completely ruined."

The zone they had selected was too sparsely populated, and to reach the isolated settlers they had to hike for hours up and down steep jungle hills, fording rivers in between. It was the rainy season and the rivers were swollen, so they spent much of the time soaked to the skin. Their muscles ached, their feet were blistered, and they were flea-bitten. Swarms of mosquitos plagued them. With so few farmers around, food was a problem, and they depended entirely on provisions brought to them by truck from the city. It was a task that had to be done carefully, so as not to raise suspicion.

So far, the EGP could hardly be called an indigenous force. Without the help of a peasant strongman such as Crescencio Pérez, who had provided Fidel's tiny rebel force with his first local guides, couriers, and fighters, Masetti and his men were alien transplants on foreign soil. Most of his volunteers were city boys, young middle-class university students impelled by visions of becoming heroic guerrillas and creating a new utopian society. A few had been through obligatory military service, were physically fit, and could handle weapons, while others adapted, but most were ill-equipped to deal with the rugged terrain, the exhausting marches, the lack of food, and the rigid military discipline demanded by Masetti.

The darker side in Masetti's personality began to appear more and more frequently. His frustration over the slow beginning, exacerbated by the political transformation in Argentina, turned to a kind of simmering rage as he led his greenhorn guerrillas fitfully around the sodden jungle. He channeled it mostly against the newcomers who found it tough going, contemptuously calling them "Pan Blanco" (White Bread), and meting out strict punishments for petty errors—extra guard duty, "mule" work carrying supplies, and in some cases "hunger diets" for two or three days. Hermes, the tough *guajiro* from Cuba's Oriente and already a veteran of war and Che's strict disciplines, backed him up.

Masetti had his favorites, such as Héctor "El Cordobés" Jouve, whom he made his political commissar at the same time that he assigned El Pelao to continue his role as the coordinator between the *foco* and the city. Jouve was tall, physically fit, and had been in the military; he took to the guerrilla life with ease. Those who didn't, however, soon found themselves under Masetti's brutal scrutiny. Just as he had focused on the unlucky Miguel as the object of his hostility in Algeria, Masetti now cast his gaze among the youths who had joined him, watching for a new "potential deserter." He soon found him.

Adolfo Rotblat was a Jewish boy of twenty from Buenos Aires whom they called "Pupi." He suffered from asthma and began lagging behind on the marches, complaining about the harshness of the guerrilla life. It was obvious he wasn't cut out for it, but instead of letting him leave, Masetti dragged him along. With every day that passed, Pupi's physical and mental state deteriorated. Soon he was completely broken.

When he rejoined the guerrillas in October for a few weeks, Bustos found Pupi in a pathetic condition. He lived in a state of terror, wept, fell behind in the marches, and slowed everyone down. Men had to be sent back to drag him forward. The others felt disgusted by him. "A process of degradation began," recalled Bustos.

One day he went out with Pupi on a reconnaissance hike and they became lost. Finally Bustos found his bearings at a river, but Pupi refused

to cross it. "He wanted me to kill him right there. So, arguments, things . . .
finally I pulled out the pistol and put it against his head and I made him
walk like that, more or less by force . . . kicking him in the ass. I made him
walk until night fell."

Unable to see well enough to continue, they slept in the forest that
night. Bustos tried to console Pupi, who was deeply depressed. The next
morning they set out again. Halfway to camp they found Hermes, who had
been sent out to look for them. Once again, because of Pupi, the group had
been held up.

A few days later, Masetti told Bustos, "'Look, this situation is becoming unbearable. He's psychologically ruining the guerrillas and no one can
stand it anymore. Nobody wants to carry him, and so a measure has to be
taken that sanitizes the group's psychology, that liberates it from this thing
that is corroding it.' That was more or less the general consensus. Segundo
had decided to shoot him."

Segundo decided to kill Pupi the same night three new volunteers
arrived in camp and he selected one of them, "Pirincho," a student from a
wealthy and aristocratic Buenos Aires family, to carry out the task. The way
Bustos understood it, Masetti wanted to harden Pirincho, whose gentle,
diplomatic personality "bothered him." "He wanted hard fighters, guys of
steel who responded to him."

Pupi had been unwittingly "prepared" for his execution—given tran-
quilizers and tied into his hammock, hung a short distance from the camp.
The others gathered. Masetti explained what had to be done and ordered
Pirincho to do it. Pirincho's face told it all—he was terrified—but he complied.

"Pirincho went . . . and we heard the shot," Bustos said. "Then Pirincho
came desperately, saying 'He won't die' . . . and so I was sent . . . I go there
and see he's got a bullet [in the head] and he was a dead guy but convulsing
and so I decided to end it."

Bustos pulled out his pistol, fired a bullet into Pupi's brain, then returned to his comrades. Pirincho's face showed that he was devastated by
his experience, but everyone else broke into high spirits. "Suddenly there
was euphoria. . . . It was curious, it reminded me of when someone dies and
then everyone feels the necessity to have a lunch and everyone drinks toasts.
. . . Segundo handed out promotions and began making plans about moving to another zone."

It was November 5, 1963. The raison d'être of the EGP had been consecrated by bloodshed. Comandante Segundo was temporarily restored to
good spirits and exhibited a renewed determination to forge ahead.

But it was already too late. The gendarmería had picked up the rumors
spreading among locals about a group of armed strangers in the forests

around Oran. Discreet inquiries were made among local cattle ranchers and rural storekeepers who had sighted them, and a suspicious profile had begun to emerge; by year's end, there seemed little doubt that the men in the forest were the same "rebels" who had sent the communiqué to Illia. The security forces began making plans to infiltrate the area.

Papi told Masetti that he thought they were staying too long in one area, that the zone they were in was not appropriate for building a guerrilla *foco*. He endorsed opening up a second front in the Chaco region, east of the Andean precordillera region they were installed in; "El Flaco" Méndez had lived there for years and was well connected. For fighters, Papi proposed activating Vasco Bengochea's Trotskyite group in Tucumán province, which he had trained in Cuba; Papi could be the military chief, and he would take Héctor Jouve with him as the "responsible politico."

Masetti angrily rejected the idea and accused both men of trying to undermine his authority. "You've always wanted to be *comandante*," he told Jouve. "But I'm not going to let you—you're staying here."

Papi came and went. In November, he had brought one of Che's *hombres de confianza* to the Bolivian base camp. It was Miguel Ángel Duque de Estrada, Che's former *auditór* in the Escambray, summary tribunal judge in La Cabaña, and "Special Operations" man at INRA. Duque's job was to wait at the farm until Che arrived, and then go into the battle zone with him.

Meanwhile, Castellanos had acquired a bad throat infection, and by December it became obvious that he needed an operation. Their courier, Doctor Canelo, took him to Córdoba, where he arranged an operation with an unsuspecting doctor. For public purposes, Castellanos was "Raúl Dávila," a Peruvian. He spent Christmas and New Year's in Córdoba, had his operation, and stayed on in the city through the month of January, convalescing.

That month, Papi showed up to inform Castellanos that Che wasn't coming just yet, and that Duque had been withdrawn from the farm and returned to Havana. Che's orders were for the group to "keep exploring . . . not to recruit peasants until we were ready to fight."

IX

Back in Havana, the ground beneath Che was shifting. He had new enemies, at home and abroad. The Kremlin's ideological section was concerned about the growing body of evidence that Che Guevara's affinities lay not in Moscow, but Beijing, and a senior Kremlin apparatchik had been dispatched to Havana to take his political pulse.

The Sino-Soviet split was now fiercer than ever. Both Beijing and Moscow were vying for the loyalties of the world's Communist parties, and in Latin America the race for influence had caused open ruptures as *"pro-chino"* factions broke away to form their own parties. As did Cuba herself, most of the Latin American Communist parties depended on subsidies from Moscow for their survival and had quickly aligned themselves with the Soviet Union. Put to the squeeze, the Cuban government had finally abandoned its officially neutralist posture in the feud, with Fidel himself implicitly supporting the Soviet position during his trip to the Soviet Union in the spring of 1963. Khrushchev had treated him like a conquering hero and Fidel had reveled in the acclaim. There had been a joint Soviet-Cuban declaration in which Cuba was lauded by Moscow as a fully recognized member of the socialist community; Moscow formally pledged its commitment to defend Cuba's "independence and liberty," while in turn Fidel had reaffirmed Cuba's support for "socialist unity" and for Moscow's policy of "peaceful coexistence" with the capitalist West. It was a rhetorical vote of support, more tepid than Khrushchev would have liked but just enough to make the Chinese nervous without alienating them completely. Fidel probably thought it was a fair trade, and he came home laden with new Soviet economic commitments for Cuba. Just in time, for Cuba's economy was in dire straits: The 1963 sugar harvest, at under four million tons, was the lowest in years, and the rest of the economy was crumbling.

Che may have been the original architect of the Soviet-Cuban relationship, but now he was a figure of concern. In direct contradiction to the policy of "peaceful coexistence," his ceaseless call to armed struggle, his emphasis on *rural* guerrilla warfare, and his stubborn determination to train, arm, and fund Communist party dissidents—even Trotskyites—over the protests of their national organizations had led to the growing suspicion in Moscow that he was playing Mao's game.

Ever since late 1962, in fact, the Kremlin had placed a KGB agent close to Che. His name was Oleg Darushenkov, and although his official cover duty in Havana was to be the Soviet embassy's cultural attaché, he had a special task to perform as Che's new Russian-language interpreter; his sunstroke-prone predecessor, Yuri Pevtstov, had been withdrawn for health reasons after only a year in Cuba, just before the missile crisis. Che's own feelings about Darushenkov aren't recorded, but several people who were part of his innermost circle at the time expressed their beliefs in off-the-record interviews that Darushenkov was a "provocateur" whose real mission was to spy on Che.

Especially after the missile crisis, there were many in the Kremlin who feared that Cuba's escalating support for guerrilla "adventures," which everyone knew was being spearheaded by Che Guevara, might drag the Soviet Union into a new confrontation with the United States. "After the crisis, there was Soviet concern over what the Cubans might do," said Giorgi Kornienko, Ambassador Anatoli Dobrynin's deputy at the Washington embassy during the crisis. "We didn't want our relations with the U.S. [further] complicated because of those activities."

Feder Burlatsky, a former Khrushchev advisor, says that in the senior circles of the Soviet Central Committee, opinion was divided between those officials who supported Che and a more predominant group of those who distrusted him. Burlatsky counted himself among the latter group. "We disliked Che's position. He became an example for adventurers, which could have provoked a confrontation between the USSR and the U.S."

Burlatsky said the opinion that Che was a "dangerous character" took on added weight because of his remarks after the missile crisis, when he told the Soviets "they should have used their missiles." It was a sentiment that Fidel had also expressed privately, but Che had said so publicly—and if Fidel had soon modified his rhetoric, few doubted that Che meant what he said. Che's position echoed the sentiments of many Cubans, but his words were infinitely more embarrassing coming from such a high-level revolutionary figure; more pointedly, they echoed Beijing's accusations that the Soviets had "capitulated" to Washington.

"That's why Che was seen as dangerous, as against our own strategy," said Burlatsky. But he acknowledged, "Even though Che was against our interests, there was still some sympathy for him. . . . There was a romantic aura around him; he reminded people of the Russian Revolution. . . . Opinion was divided. . . . Some compared him to Trotsky, or to some of the Bolshevik terrorists. Advisors of Khrushchev like [Mikhail] Suslov, who described themselves as revolutionaries, had sympathy for Che."

The opposition to Che took on real vigor with his "interventionist" guerrilla expeditions in Peru and Argentina, and was spearheaded by Victorio Codovilla's powerful Argentine Communist party. Kiva Maidanek, an eminent Soviet Communist party analyst of Latin American affairs at the time, was well aware of the Argentine lobby in Moscow against Che, and its repercussions.

"The [Argentines party's] accusations against Che were that he was an adventurer, pro-Chinese, and a Trotskyite. This offended Che a great deal. But this view took on weight here too, especially in the Latin America section of the Central Committee. Anything to the left of the Soviet line was considered pro-Chinese and pro-Trotskyite. The USSR began to incline toward the [Latin American] Communist parties. Beginning in 1964, the Latin American area began to be seen less as a battleground between the U.S. and the USSR and more as a war of influence between China and the USSR."

Seeming to play into the charges of heresy, Che had continued to test the limits of Soviet tolerance. In September 1963, emboldened by practice and by Fidel's "Second Havana Declaration" (decreeing the inevitability of revolution in Latin America), which he had begun to cite as the guiding philosophy of the Cuban revolution, Che had outlined his call for continental guerrilla war in an ideologically refined sequel to his *Guerra de Guerrillas* how-to manual, the sequel called *Guerrilla Warfare: A Method*.

In a rebuke to the Latin American Communist party's claims to leadership roles in the struggle of their countries, Che wrote: "To be the vanguard of the party means to be at the forefront of the working class through the struggle for achieving power. It means to know how to guide this fight through shortcuts to victory."

Bolstering his argument with a quote from Fidel, Che wrote: "The subjective conditions in each country, the factors of revolutionary consciousness, of organization, of leadership, can accelerate or delay revolution, depending on the state of their development. Sooner or later, in each historic epoch, as objective conditions ripen, consciousness is acquired, organization is achieved, leadership arises, and revolution is produced."

And, something palpably new had emerged in his call to arms—less reliance on the old Communist euphemism "armed struggle," in favor of the far more candid "violence." "Violence is not the monopoly of the exploiters and as such the exploited can use it, too, and, what is more, ought to use it when the moment arrives. . . . We should not fear violence, the midwife of new societies; but violence should be unleashed at that precise moment in which the leaders have found the most favorable circumstances. . . . Guerrilla warfare is not passive self-defense; it is defense with attack. . . . It has as its final goal the conquest of political power . . . The equilibrium between oligarchic dictatorship and the popular pressure must be changed. The dictatorship tries to function without resorting to force. Thus we must try to oblige the dictatorship to resort to violence, thereby unmasking its true nature as the dictatorship of the reactionary social classes."

And finally: The revolution in Latin America must be of a continental nature, in order to outwit the Yankees, who would do all they could to divide, conquer, and repress the rebelling peoples. "The unity of the repressive forces must be met with the unity of the popular forces. In all countries where oppression reaches intolerable proportions, the banner of rebellion must be raised; and this banner of historical necessity will have a continental character. As Fidel stated, the cordilleras of the Andes will be the Sierra Maestra of Latin America; and the immense territories which this continent encompasses will become the scene of a life or death struggle against imperialism. . . . This means that it will be a protracted war; it will have many fronts; and it will cost much blood and countless lives for a long period of time. . . . This is a prediction. We make it with the conviction that history will prove us right."

The rich nation of Argentina had long been coveted by the Kremlin, its Communist party leaders receiving preferential treatment in Moscow and wielding an unusual degree of influence over Soviet policy in Latin America. With few exceptions, the other regional parties lent their voices to the Argentine position, and by late 1963 their message was the same: Che was intervening in their countries and had to be reined in.

Initially, Khrushchev's enthusiastic desire to have an "informal" relationship with revolutionary Cuba had won out over the Kremlin's skeptical conservatives; they would have preferred a straightforward party-to-party relationship with Cuba that they could dominate, like those they enjoyed with the Eastern European satellite states. In their eyes, Cuba was still an unproven arriviste to the socialist bloc, and despite Fidel's declared commitment to socialism and intention to build a Soviet-style Communist party in Cuba, they remained discomfited by their lack of control over the process.

Nikolai Metutsov, Party Secretary Yuri Andropov's deputy in charge of relations with the non-European socialist states, acknowledged the Soviet effort to exercise a firmer control over Cuba. "There was a whole group of comrades who were of the opinion that we had to teach the Cuban comrades . . . that we had to help them become Marxists, true Marxists, because they weren't sufficiently prepared theoretically. Among some leaders in the Central Committee department where I worked there was this opinion that we had to embrace our Cuban friends as strongly as possible, to squeeze them so they would not be able to breathe."

It was this Soviet lobby that had led to the efforts made by the "old" Cuban Communists and their Argentine comrades to secure greater party control over the reins of the Cuban state, and that had culminated in Fidel's 1962 purge. Khrushchev's position had been weakened internally after his missile crisis backing-down, and this had strengthened the Cuba skeptics. Angered over Cuba's foot-dragging neutrality in the Sino-Soviet dispute, the escalation of Cuban-sponsored guerrilla activity in Latin America, and the divisions in the Latin American Communist parties, the ideologues demanded Cuba's unequivocal allegiance. Che was seen as the fly in the ointment.

Metutsov, whose last foreign post had been Beijing, was the man dispatched by the Kremlin to ascertain Che's ideological loyalties. "For me, as deputy of the department . . . the ideological position of the Cuban leaders was an affair of the foremost importance," said Metutsov. "For me, for Andropov, for Khrushchev, of course, and other members of the Politburo, the first thing was to clarify the theoretical and ideological positions of the Cuban leaders." In particular, he said, it was imperative to determine their positions on what he called "the theoretical problems of the global revolutionary process," a euphemism for the Beijing-Moscow rivalry.

Metutsov traveled to Cuba at the end of 1963 in a Soviet delegation led by Nikolai Podgorny, president of the Presidium of the Supreme Soviet. When he spoke about his mission many years later, he made clear that neither Fidel nor Raúl was really the issue. "We knew about the process by which they had come to Marxism, how sincere their comprehension of Marxism was. . . . We knew that in his essence Fidel was a liberal bourgeois democrat, and we knew that his brother Raúl was closer to the Communists and was in the party. Now, about Che Guevara: He seemed to me to be the most prepared theoretically of all the political leadership."

That, of course, was the problem. Che had been the guiding hand in moving Fidel toward socialism, to his relationship with the Soviet Union, and now he had become the revolution's foremost revolutionary heretic, an enfant terrible with international aspirations.

During his visit, Metutsov had many conversations with Che, but it was one all-night talk they had together, early in January of 1964, that Metustov recalled in special detail. That night they sat talking until dawn in the library of the Soviet ambassador's residence and, when they had finished, took a swim together in the pool.

"The conversation began . . . with a reproach by him," recalled Metutsov. "He said he had heard the news that in the Soviet Union, in the party Central Committee, Che Guevara was considered to be pro-Chinese, that is, that he was the person proposing Maoist tendencies within the leadership. And of course, this was the most acute question."

Metutsov said that Che then began explaining "why" he wasn't a Maoist. "I said, 'Che, believe me . . . such evaluations . . . of this Maoist aura you have . . . I tell you someone is weaving a spiderweb. . . . In our party no such attitude toward you exists; someone is trying to sow discord between us.'"

As he spoke, trying to reassure the younger man, Metutsov said he began to experience a strange sensation. A jowly, beetle-browed man with huge ears and pale blue eyes, Metutsov found himself "falling in love" with Che.

"I told him: 'You know, I'm a little older than you, but I like you, I like above all your looks' . . . and I confessed, I confessed my love for him because he was a very attractive young man. . . . I knew his defects, from all the papers, all the information [we had], but when I was talking to him, when we dealt with one another, we joked, we laughed, and we talked about less than serious things, and I forgot about his defects. . . . I felt attracted to him, do you understand? It was as if I wanted to get away, to separate myself, but he attracted me, you see. . . . He had very beautiful eyes. Magnificent eyes, so deep, so generous, so honest, a stare that was so honest that somehow, one could not help but feel it . . . and he spoke very well, he became inwardly excited, and his speech was like that, with all of this impetus, as if his words were squeezing you."

Snapping back from his romantic reverie, Metutsov said that as Che spoke, he became convinced that Che was sincere. "[He said that] according to his ideological and theoretical convictions as a Marxist he was closer to us than to the Chinese . . . and he asked me to keep this in mind, to [let my comrades] know that he was a true friend of the Soviet Union and the Leninist party."

Still, Metutsov went away with an appraisal of Che Guevara that escaped easy definition. "Externally one could truly say that, yes, Che Guevara was contaminated by Maoism because of his Maoist slogan that the rifle can create the power. And certainly he can be considered a Trotskyite because he went to Latin America to stimulate the revolutionary movement . . . but in any case I think these are external signs, superficial ones, and that deep down, what was most profound in him was his aspiration to help man on the basis of Marxism-Leninism."

Che's "peculiarity," noted Metutsov, was his personal commitment to the revolutionary cause. "He understood that his nickname, 'Che,' had become the expression of his personality. In our conversations I had the impression that he knew that his portrait already hung on history's walls, the history of the national liberation movement. He was sufficiently intelligent to understand this, without arrogance, and meanwhile he remained a normal person, looking for ways with his comrades to build socialism in Cuba and to make that historical portrait of his more relevant, more permanent."

The issue of Che's support for the "armed struggle" may have been a source of worry for some of his Central Committee comrades, but Metutsov denied that it was perceived as one by the Kremlin leadership or by Khrushchev personally. "Was the Soviet Union interested in developing the global revolutionary movement? Yes. So what was wrong if Cuba helped and lent its portion of support? It all went into the same piggy bank."

Even as Metutsov and Che had their nocturnal conversation, Fidel was preparing to make a return visit to the Soviet Union. On January 2, 1964, on the fifth anniversary of the revolution and the eve of his trip, he gave a lengthy address to the Cuban people.

Fidel was evidently expecting a great deal out of his upcoming mission, and was already preparing to jettison Cuba's neutrality in the Sino-Soviet dispute and align himself openly with Moscow's foreign policy. He spoke with hyperbolic enthusiasm about the future of Cuba's economy and lauded Cuba's partnership with the Soviet Union. He reiterated Cuba's support for the policy of peaceful coexistence and its desire to live "in peace" with any country, whatever its political system, including the United States.

His speech was also clearly intended for American ears. Only two months earlier, he and President Kennedy had been edging toward a behind-the-scenes detente, sending exploratory messages back and forth with a view to "normalizing" relations, when Kennedy was assassinated in Dallas.* With his national address, Fidel was sending a clear signal that he hoped the new American president, Lyndon Johnson, would resume the abruptly severed initiative.

Fidel came back from Moscow laden with a generous new six-year, twenty-four-million-ton sugar agreement in one hand, and a joint Soviet-Cuban communiqué in the other. This time, he had gone all the way; Cuba and the Soviet Union rejected "factional and sectarian activity" in the world Communist movement, they agreed on Moscow's terms for unity, and, pointedly, Cuba was "ready to do whatever is necessary to establish good neighborly relations with the United States of America, based upon the principles of peaceful coexistence." Khrushchev praised this new Cuban "orientation," which would help "consolidate peace and relax international tensions."

To Maurice Halperin, an American political scientist and economist who was then teaching in Cuba at Che's invitation, the document Fidel had signed in Moscow was unequivocal. "The endorsement of the Soviet 'line' vis-à-vis China was enormously strengthened by Fidel's signature on a document enjoying the status of a joint communiqué." At the same time, "The message to the United States—and to Latin America, for that matter—was clear: Castro offered to negotiate an accommodation with Washington, Khrushchev approved, and the unavoidable inference for Latin America was that Castro was prepared to abandon the Latin American revolution for the sake of an accommodation."

Of course, like most of Fidel's passionately stated "positions," it was a public posture, one he would revise before long, and then continue to revise in future years. As for his affirmation of support for "peaceful coexistence," it was largely intended as a statement of intent to use as a bargaining chip in

---

*Che Guevara remained a suspect for almost any kind of international skullduggery, evidently, for his name popped up in a number of reports filed during the Warren Commission's investigation into the JFK assassination, including some quite bizarre ones from J. Edgar Hoover's FBI field agents. One, in particular, reported an alleged sighting of Che Guevara and Jack Ruby—Lee Harvey Oswald's assassin—together in Panama.

hoped-for negotiations with Washington. At that very moment, Cuban arms and personnel were directly involved in a number of conflicts in Latin America and at least one in Africa. As he spoke, Masetti's men were prowling the Oran jungle, Héctor Béjar's ELN guerrilla column was busily reinfiltrating Peru, and it had been only two months since Venezuelan authorities had captured a shipment of three hundred tons of weapons sent from Cuba for the guerrillas there. Cuba's former revolutionary police chief, Efigenio Ameijeiras, and other Cuban military men were in Algeria, secretly helping command an armored battalion in the border war that had broken out with neighboring Morocco.

To Che, the term "peaceful coexistence" was anathema, mere appeasement of the imperialist system dressed up in diplomatic language. For the moment, he kept his mouth shut, but there was no longer any doubt that his and Fidel's paths had begun to diverge. Fidel's goal was to consolidate Cuba's economic well-being and his own political survival, and for that he was willing to compromise. Che's mission was to spread the socialist revolution. The time for him to leave Cuba was drawing near. He put great store in Jorge Ricardo Masetti's abilities to give him the opportunity to do just that.

X

In February, the Cuban guerrilla Alberto Castellanos returned to the "war zone" from Córdoba. He was overweight and out of shape after an inactive month in the city, drinking beer and eating well. On the six-hour hike up to the guerrilla camp he fainted three times. When he arrived, he learned that Masetti had decided the EGP was going to become active. The guerrillas were going to *"dar un pingazo"* [stick the dick in hard], timed with the second anniversary of the military coup that had toppled Frondízi: March 18.

But, as the months had rolled by in the sodden green forests of Oran, Masetti's authoritarian streak had become frightening, his paranoia about potential deserters now pathological. He had begun persecuting Henry Lerner, a young medical student from Córdoba who had arrived in camp the same night as the execution of Adolfo "Pupi" Rotblat.

Lerner, like Rotblat, was a Jew, but at the time he didn't think there was a connection. The son of a veteran Communist, and a doctrinaire self-described "Stalinist" at the time, Lerner was proud of his own fortitude and conviction, and expected military discipline. But as Masetti's remarks toward him became increasingly hostile, and the commander singled him out for especially punishing assignments, Lerner began to realize that Masetti thought he was inadequate as a guerrilla and was trying to break him.

Lerner despaired. Conditioned to obey orders and respect his jefe, he tried to overcompensate and win Masetti's approval by performing all his duties well. But nothing seemed good enough; it was obvious Masetti thought he was "Pan Blanco."

At Christmas, the urban network had sent up a whole pile of delicacies for the guerrillas, and after their dinner Lerner sat against a tree, smoking a cigarette and feeling nostalgic. His thoughts had turned to his family and the wife he had left back in the city, when Masetti crept up behind him. "Hey, what are you thinking about?" demanded Masetti. When Lerner told him, Masetti said: "So, you're planning to desert, aren't you?"

After that, Lerner understood that his situation was serious. By now he had heard about El Fusilado, and of course Pupi had been executed the night he had arrived. In Masetti's view, to be suspected of even thinking about desertion was punishable by death. Bustos also noticed the tensions on his trips back to camp and became alarmed; he could see another "Pupi situation" developing.

Lerner talked to Bustos privately and asked for his help. Bustos interceded, telling Masetti he was wrong; Lerner was a good *cuadro,* committed to the cause, and definitely not a potential deserter. He urged Masetti to give Lerner a chance to "prove himself," and Masetti finally agreed. He gave Lerner a task: to monitor the behavior of two other fighters he had singled out for punishment.

One, Nardo, was a new arrival whose real name was Bernardo Groswald, a nineteen-year-old Jewish bank clerk from Córdoba. He had almost immediately fallen apart in the harsh jungle and was exhibiting the same symptoms of distress that had finished off Pupi. Lerner had guided Nardo on his first hike up to the camp, and recalled that the young man clearly had no idea what he was getting into.

"Nardo asked if we gave talks, if we had meetings . . . as if he was coming to some kind of flower show. He was done for after two days. He had flat feet, was frightened of going down slopes, and he began animalizing. It was truly repellent, and as the days went by he began physically to look more like an animal. To go down a hill he went down on his ass, walked on all fours; a pathetic image for a guerrilla . . . He was dirty, unclean, and finally he was punished, given the hardest jobs, that kind of thing."

The other detainee was "Grillo" Frontíni, a photographer and the son of a well-known and affluent *porteño* lawyer. Grillo had been in charge of coordinating things for the EGP in Buenos Aires but had been profligate and careless with the organization's money. Masetti had ordered Bustos to arrest him and bring him to the mountains to be tried.

He placed both young men under "arrest" and, as a test for Lerner, gave him the job of guarding them at a bivouac in the forest for a week. He was to watch them, talk to them, and determine whether or not they were trustworthy; depending on what he reported back, there would be a summary trial to decide their fates.

There was a kind of madness floating in the air. Masetti saw enemies all around him. He had become emotionally unpredictable. One moment he was euphoric, and the next he would plunge into a deep depression that could last for days. The sciatic nerve in his spinal column, injured in Algeria in his competitions with El Fusilado, hurt him terribly.

Bustos was especially concerned for the fate of Nardo, and Bustos says he begged Masetti not to "do anything" until he could make arrangements for Nardo to be evacuated. He would find some people who could be trusted on a farm where Nardo could be kept in custody until it was safe enough to release him. Masetti promised he would wait.

Meanwhile, Pirincho had left on a special mission. He hadn't been the same since killing Pupi but had managed effectively to conceal his anguish. Having won Masetti's complete trust, he had convinced him to let him return to Buenos Aires. A Cuban agent was supposed to arrive in Uruguay with a shipment of arms, and Pirincho was to meet him and smuggle the arms across the Río de la Plata in his family's yacht.

Masetti wanted the arms for his new plan of action. The CGT, Argentina's huge *peronista*-dominated workers' confederation, was planning a general strike against the Illia government, which had given organized labor the cold shoulder. Masetti's idea was to get arms to Bengochea's group and launch a series of coordinated lightning attacks against rural military targets in the area where the Salta and Tucumán provinces joined. With the attacks coinciding with the CGT strike, the EGP could advertise its presence and show its support for Argentina's workers at the same time. The guerrillas would then escape, moving over the Andean cordillera to a new base of operations a couple of hundred kilometers to the south; Masetti had already carried out some initial exploration of the mountains for their escape route. Their disappearance would throw off the security forces by creating the impression they were a much bigger force than they really were. It was a tactic Fidel and Che had employed with success in the early days of the sierra war, and Masetti wanted to emulate it.

He was also anxious to get things organized. In February, he asked Bustos to make contact with Pirincho in the city and find out how the arms-transfer preparations were going. Bustos went to Buenos Aires and arranged a meeting with Pirincho. Pirincho didn't show. They arranged another encounter; another no-show. Finally, Pirincho agreed to meet Bustos in the Belgrano train station. When Bustos arrived, he saw that Pirincho had taken precautions, clearly afraid he had been marked for an "extreme measure." Not only had he selected a public place to meet, he had several watchful friends stationed nearby, staking out the exits.

"Pirincho told me he had agreed to meet to give me explanations," Bustos recalled, "but not to Segundo. He wanted to explain why he wasn't going back because he knew I would understand. Then he told me the whole story, his breakdown, how he had lost faith because of the murder [of Pupi], and how he knew the [guerrilla] thing went beyond the personality of Segundo, and that was what he respected and he would maintain loyalty to it. [He said] 'I want to get out of here. I'm going to Europe. . . . I give my word I won't say anything to anyone.'"

While Bustos was away, Masetti broke his promise about Nardo. After spending his week with Nardo and Grillo, Lerner had returned with them to camp and reported to Masetti on their behavior. Grillo was "recuperable," but there was "nothing to be said" about Nardo, whose behavior had worsened.

Recalled Lerner, "Totally broken, he didn't talk. He got down on all fours, he dragged himself, poor thing, he wept, he masturbated. That was how he cleaned himself, like a primitive form of hygiene."

Masetti ordered a trial for Nardo. Federíco was the prosecutor, Héctor the defense lawyer, and Hermes played the role of tribunal president. Lerner recalls that they all sat around, "like a chorus." Lerner's memory blocked out much of the trial, which lasted ten or fifteen minutes, but he recalled feeling that Nardo had "decided to inculpate himself" because he said nothing to refute the charge that if they freed him and he was caught by the police, he would tell all he knew.

It was, of course, a foregone conclusion and the verdict was quickly delivered. "He was condemned to death," Lerner said, "told that he would be shot by firing squad, for not complying with the revolutionary laws."

But Nardo's agony was not over yet; he had to spend a final night alive, under guard. Masetti decided that he would be shot at dawn the next day, February 19, and that the newest volunteers would form the *"pelotón de fusilamiento,"* to toughen them up.

At dawn the grave was dug, and at the side of the grave he was shot. Lerner stood to one side watching. At the last minute, when the order to fire came, he saw Nardo swell out his chest. "He looked straight ahead, he didn't tremble, he didn't fall on his knees, he didn't ask for anything."

Afterward, nobody said a word. "We all tried to hide from ourselves," recalled Lerner. Masetti acted as if nothing had happened. "[He ordered] the task to be completed. Nardo was buried, his grave covered over, life went on. . . . It was part of guerrilla life."

The EGP was once again "free of contagion" by the debilitating presence of "White Breads" in its midst. Masetti's treatment of Henry Lerner improved afterward, the veil of suspicion that had hung over him now lifted. It was only many years later that Lerner came to grips with the fact that he himself had come very close to becoming one of Masetti's victims. He reflected on the fact that he, Miguel, Pupi, and Nardo were all Jews, and wondered on Masetti's political origins in the ultra-nationalist and anti-Semitic Alianza Libertadora Nacionalista.

Bustos arrived back. He was upset about Nardo, but there was little to be done about it now; they had bigger problems. When he told Masetti about Pirincho's desertion, Masetti refused to believe it. Pirincho was one of his golden boys, he wouldn't desert him. He knew Pirincho had a problem with his girlfriend, surely that was all it was, and Bustos had misunderstood him. He ordered Bustos to return to Buenos Aires and bring Pirincho back with him.

But it was too late. Not only for Pirincho, who had, as promised, left for Europe and vanished. It was also too late for the Ejercito Guerrillero del Pueblo. A few days after Bustos left again for the city, five new volunteers arrived, forwarded by a dissident Communist party cell in Buenos Aires. Two of them were undercover agents for the Argentine DIPA, the secret police. Their orders were to infiltrate the EGP, find their base, and return with information.

The DIPA agents' infiltration coincided with the *gendarmerías'* detection of the guerrillas' location. The group's supplier and courier in Salta, the young and cultured Enrique Bolini-Roca, had simply not been a believable provincial bookstore owner; he made too many unexplained trips out of town in his *camioneta,* and he was also too handsome for his own good. The local women chased him: he attracted attention. The gendarmes soon had the remote spot he drove to on the Salta-Orán road staked out. Now it sent its first reconnaissance patrol into the forest.

Almost immediately, the soldiers stumbled into a group of guerrillas at the small supply camp where provisions were stored before being dispatched up to the main group in the mountains; among them were Castellanos, Lerner, Grillo Frontini, and another guerrilla known as "El Marqués." They claimed they were hunters, looking for "wild turkeys" in the bush. Nobody believed that story. The two DIPA agents were also captured, but soon told the gendarmes their identity and what they had learned. More patrols were sent in, and gradually the EGP began to fall.

By April 18, Che's advance patrol had been liquidated. Hermes was dead, ambushed by a patrol at a peasant's house. With him died Jorge, a philosophy student, their peasant host, and one of the ambushing soldiers. Led by Masetti, the rest of the guerrillas split up and tried to find a way across the mountains.

They climbed and climbed. Before long they were in the sodden cloud forest high in the mountains, at an altitude of some three or four thousand meters (over 10,000 feet). They had no food. They could barely see because of the fog. Three of the newcomers died in their sleep of starvation.

Masetti, barely able to walk because of his injured back, was with a separate group—Atilio, Héctor, and Antonio Paul. He sent Héctor and Antonio back to find the others. As they climbed down the mountain, Antonio fell off a high cliff above a river; Héctor tried to catch him and fell, too. Antonio hit the rocks and broke his neck, while Héctor hit the water. He crawled over to where Antonio lay, gave him an injection of morphine, and stayed with him until he died.

Within a few days the remaining survivors were captured. Bolini-Roca and other members of the urban underground were caught and arrested in Jujuy, Orán, and Buenos Aires. Bustos and the members of the Córdoba network went into hiding, fleeing into Uruguay. Furry made it back to Cuba undetected.

Nothing more was heard of Masetti and Atilio. Gendarmes combed the forest for them but came back empty-handed. By the end of April, there were eighteen men in Oran's prison, among them Castellanos, Lerner, Frontíni, Federico and Héctor Jouve. The group was hermetic and unrepentant. They acknowledged and defended their revolutionary goals, but kept silent about their Cuban links and even managed to keep the true identity of Che's bodyguard, Alberto Castellanos, a secret.

The Cuban connection was soon uncovered, however. Hermes's diary was found, and, from the slang terms he used, police were able to determine that the dead man had been a Cuban. The Argentine security forces checked the origin of the arms seized and learned that their Belgian FAL automatic rifles were from a shipment sold by Fabrique Nationale to Cuba. Some dollars found on the guerrillas were also traced back to Cuba. As for their Soviet-issue weapons, Cuba was the only country in the hemisphere that they could have come from.

The press speculated out loud. Was Che Guevara the driving force behind the EGP? When the late Hermes Peña was revealed to be one of his former bodyguards, the connections were easily made. When the missing Comandante Segundo was identified as Jorge Ricardo Masetti and Che paid public homage to him as a "heroic revolutionary," the question became a moot point.

But neither Che nor anyone else involved in the adventure confirmed anything more specific than that. The whole episode of the "guerrillas of Salta" remained something of an enigma, a small incident that was quickly overtaken by larger, more dramatic events. Only a handful of people knew how important the episode had been to Che, or that Masetti's failure had altered the course of his life and of history.

Masetti was never found, and his surviving companions believe there are only three possible explanations regarding his fate. One theory is that when Masetti realized it was all over, he and Atilio committed suicide. The second is that they starved to death. And third, that the gendarmes did find them, stole the estimated twenty thousand dollars Masetti had in his possession, and then murdered both men to keep the secret.

Before long, the guerrillas were brought to trial. They had a good team of lawyers, including Grillo's father, Norberto Frontíni; a left-wing Córdoba lawyer named Horacio Lonatti, Ricardo Rojo, and Gustavo Roca—but all received prison sentences ranging from four to fourteen years. Federico "El Flaco" Méndez was given the highest sentence for his role as the prosecutor in Nardo's execution; Héctor Jouve was given a dozen years for his part in the same trial. Castellanos and Lerner each were given sentences of five years. Their sentences would be appealed, but little could be done for them immediately.*

Che was devastated and bewildered by the news of his *foco*'s nightmarish collapse. He learned about it while traveling in Europe, where he had gone to speak at the founding conference for UNCTAD, the UN Conference on Trade and Development, being held in Geneva at the end of March 1964. Afterward, he had traveled to Paris, where Gustavo Roca met him and informed him of the unraveling disaster. After stopping briefly in Algiers and Prague, he returned to Cuba, arriving on April 18, the same day Hermes was killed. As the weeks passed and Masetti wasn't found, Che knew he was probably dead. It was a personal tragedy as well as a major setback to his carefully laid plans to launch the armed struggle in Argentina.

---

*Gustavo Roca was a Marxist, the enfant terrible of the eminent conservative Córdoba clan, a cousin of Che's old love, Chichina Ferreyra, and a friend of Che's since adolescence. Over the coming months and years, Roca did what he could to denounce the "human rights abuses" and anomalies in the sentences of the imprisoned guerrillas, but his most important role was as a personal courier among Che, the prisoners, and the surviving guerrilla underground network in Argentina.

Not only had Che lost two of his closest disciples—Hermes and Masetti—but it was obvious that they hadn't heeded his warnings, and had committed a number of errors that had led to their discovery.

Few people realized the depth of Che's longing for his homeland. An Argentine journalist named Rosa María Oliver thought she had caught a glimpse of his feelings during a conversation they had in February 1963. They had been sipping mate together and talking nostalgically about their country when suddenly Che struck his knee with his hand and exclaimed, almost imploringly: "Enough: Let's not talk about Argentina anymore."

"Why, if you love it so?" Oliver asked.

"For that very reason . . ."

Not long after the news of Masetti's disappearance, Alberto Granado went to see Che at his office. He looked depressed. Trying to cheer him up, Granado quipped: "Che, what's the matter, you've got the face of a dead dog." Che answered: "Petiso, here you see me, behind a desk, fucked, while my people die during missions I've sent them on."

Che continued talking, wondering out loud why Hermes, an experienced guerrilla, hadn't followed his instructions to keep on the move. The group's downfall had been to stay in one place long enough for the Argentine gendarmes to find them. Constant movement was a cardinal rule of guerrilla warfare, and Hermes should have known better, even if Masetti didn't. That was why Che had sent him along, to lend a guerrilla veteran's instincts and expertise to the mission, and it hadn't helped.

The failure of the guerrillas of Salta was a crucial watershed for Che. Once again, "good" but inexperienced men had failed trying to test his theories for guerrilla warfare. It was plain that he would have to demonstrate personally that his ideas could work. Just as the Cuban revolution had been able to count upon Fidel as a figure to rally around and unite disparate revolutionary forces into an effective fighting machine, the success of the continental revolution depended upon the physical presence of a recognized leader, and he was it.

26

The Long Good-Bye

I

By the summer of 1964, Che had resolved to leave Cuba and return to the revolutionary battlefield. The question was, where? The conditions had to be prepared for him, somewhere. From now on, this goal became Che's greatest single obsession.

In Cuba, he was no longer indispensable. The revolution was probably as secure as it would ever be. Although there was still plenty of CIA-sponsored counterrevolutionary activity and continuing U-2 spyplane overflights of Cuba's airspace, it seemed unlikely that the Americans would invade anytime soon; Kennedy had, after all, promised not to in return for the withdrawal of the Soviet nuclear missiles. A promise could always be broken, but Kennedy's successor, Lyndon Johnson, had his hands full with the acrimonious black civil rights issue, the upcoming presidential race, and the escalating conflict in Vietnam, where American troops had intervened directly to shore up an unstable South Vietnam against the Communist North.

Khrushchev now extolled Cuba as "the daughter"of the USSR, and in Havana nobody chanted *"Nikita mariquita"* in public anymore. Soviet aid flowed more generously than ever to the island, but with it there was a clear trend towards Cuba' dependency on Moscow. The situation displeased Che, but, at least for now, Fidel appeared to have fewer qualms, and, in any case, no ready alternatives.

Che remained convinced that in the long term, Cuba's independence depended not on Soviet subsidies but on the success of the Latin American revolution. Sharing their collective resources, a fraternal community of revolutionary Latin American states could reduce their countries' traditional dependencies on external forces, including Moscow, and usher in a new socialist era in the developing world.

There were other factors influencing Che's decision to leave. They had existed in 1962, when the Salta *foco* was still in the planning stages, but by 1964 they were much more acute. Cuba's political atmosphere was becoming claustrophobic; he had new enemies at home and abroad.

Latin America's mainline Communist parties were furious with his export of the armed struggle to their countries. The Salta episode had outraged Victorio Codovilla, the Argentine Communist party's venerable strongman, and his party had vigorously condemned the Masetti *foco,* pointing out that the Communists involved were radicals who had been "expelled" from the party. Needless to say, Peru's Communist party, and Monje and his Bolivian comrades shared Codovilla's feelings and, like him, had made their feelings known in Moscow.

Despite Che's reassurances, the enduring consensus in the Kremlin was that he was a Maoist, a dangerous extremist, a "Trotskyite." The Chinese were well aware of the rumors and had begun doggedly pursuing Che. When he was in Geneva for the UN Conference on Trade and Development, Chinese agents had tailed him everywhere, staking out the lobby of his hotel, watching who went up and down the elevator to his floor.

Sergo Mikoyan had been in Geneva at the time and, hoping to dispel the rumors, tried to arrange an informal get-acquainted meeting between Che and the Soviet foreign trade minister, Nikolai Patolichev.

When Mikoyan went to Che's hotel, he noticed the Chinese in the lobby. In his hotel room, Che was happy to see him and immediately agreed to the meeting with Patolichev, then asked: "Did you see any Chinese downstairs?" When Mikoyan said he had, Che nodded. "In Moscow you think I'm China's agent or connected to them, but [I'm not]. The truth is they follow me around all the time."

But Che's protestations of innocence sounded disingenuous to most of the Soviet leadership. In Cuba, his preference for the Chinese's more "disinterested" display of revolutionary solidarity was well known among his aides. Orlando Borrego pointed out that the only Chinese technicians working in Cuba were attached to Che's ministry and worked for free, while the Soviets required salaries and housing, paid for out of the credits Moscow provided to Fidel's government. Che made no secret of his opinion that the Chinese showed a "truer" socialist "morality." In these ideological times, when any deviation from the Kremlin's policy was seen as heretical, even treasonous, Che had allied himself time and again with the Chinese policy on socialist revolution. Any attention he received from Beijing could be seen only as having been bidden.

The suspicion had cast a pall over his work in Cuba and his dealings with even some of his closest comrades such as Raúl Castro, who had developed strong links with the Soviet military and its party leadership. Since the days in Mexico and the sierra when Raúl had been Che's chief ally and shown deference to him, their relationship had steadily deteriorated to the point of becoming adversarial. In Cuba, some say, the turning point was the Soviet missile negotiations in the summer of 1962, when Che had been called in to do "clean-up duty" after Raúl. As Che's own relations with Moscow soured, Raúl had become increasingly pro-Soviet and was reportedly given to cracking jokes about Che's being "China's man" in Cuba.

On another front, Che's industrial policies were now being openly challenged and he was engaged in a fierce, if fraternal, ideological debate over the direction and control of Cuba's economy. Che's advocacy of the so-called "budgetary finance system," whereby state-owned enterprises shared assets and resources communally instead of competing among themselves in the system of "state capitalism" practiced and advocated by the USSR, had run into fierce opposition. His main opponents were Carlos Rafael Rodríguez, whom Fidel had put in charge of agriculture as the INRA chief, and Marcelo Fernández, his old July 26 sparring partner, now at the Ministry for Foreign Trade.

At the core of the ideological dispute was Che's insistence upon the application of "moral incentives" in addition to "material incentives" as a means of developing a Communist consciousness among Cuba's workforce. The system employed in the Soviet Union had grown out of the New Economic Policy (NEP) adopted by Lenin in 1924 as a way of jump-starting the stagnant post–civil war Soviet economy. It allowed for capitalist forms of competition between factories and individual workers as a means of increasing production. Che believed that this system prevented workers from achieving a true socialist regard for their labor, a regard that only moral incentives could achieve. That was the impetus behind his volunteer labor scheme, his effort to demonstrate a "willingness to sacrifice" for the common good.

Also at issue was the future direction of Cuba's economy. Che's dream to bring about Cuba's rapid industrialization had quickly bogged down. He accepted part of the blame himself for having moved "too fast," with an unprepared workforce and insufficient resources to cope, but there were other factors beyond his control: incompetence, lack of technical expertise, and often the poor quality of the Soviet-bloc equipment and materials imported— which angered him, and which he was not averse to pointing out. The other option was for Cuba to return to "King Sugar." By mid-1964, with the new Soviet-Cuban sugar deal, and Khrushchev's offer to help invent a cane-cutting machine to mechanize Cuba's sugar harvests, it was fairly clear that agriculture, not industry, was what the future held for Cuba—and to some extent this undercut Che's dream of creating the New Socialist Man.

Finally, Che was not a Cuban, but an Argentine, and although he never said so publicly, there must have been a sense in him that it was "their" country, after all. He had trained loyal cadres who believed in his methods and they could carry on the battle in his absence, but it was time for him to leave the scene.

Perhaps Che was also becoming aware of his age. He was now almost thirty-six; he could still march and fight and lead men, but if he waited much longer, it would be too late.

II

His first task was to rebuild and expand the clandestine guerrilla infrastructure in South America, shaken but not shattered by the Salta fiasco. With the exception of Alberto Castellanos, the Bolivians and Cubans involved had come out unscathed, as had the urban underground in Córdoba, Buenos Aires, and other Argentine cities. Most of the damage had been limited to the guerrillas themselves and to their immediate support network in Salta. Even as Masetti's column collapsed, Che had deployed an important new asset in South America; Tania was on her way.

Tania had finished her espionage training in March 1964, and Che had summoned her to his office at the Ministry of Industries; Renán Montero, the pseudonym of one of Piñeiro's top agents, was with him. Among other missions, Renán had participated in the ill-fated 1959 Nicaraguan guerrilla expedition with Rodolfo Romero. Che informed Tania that he wanted her to go to Bolivia, to be his deep-cover agent there, to establish a legal profile and become acquainted with as many of the country's leaders as she could. She would remain indefinitely, to be activated when the right moment came. According to Piñeiro, Tania had been selected for Bolivia because, among other talents, she spoke German, useful for penetrating Bolivia's influential German emigré community. He said she was not informed that Che eventually planned to join her there.

Tania left the meeting with a feeling of pride; Che had recognized her merits, and assigned her a vital role to play in the continental revolution. Shortly afterward, she left Cuba in disguise to travel around Western Europe and test out her false identity, her *leyenda,* and to acquaint herself with the places in her false personal biography.

Following the meeting with Tania, Che summoned Ciro Bustos to Havana for a debriefing and to issue him new instructions. Since the Masetti debacle, Bustos had been engaged in mopping-up duties while waiting for his marching orders from *"la isla"* (the island), as Cuba was called in underground circles. With the help of the academics in Córdoba, he had put together the prisoners' legal defense team, and had smuggled Furry and two other conspirators, "Petíso" Bellomo and Héctor Jouve's brother Emilio, out to Montevideo, Uruguay, where he rented a safe house.

Most significantly, Bustos had also orchestrated the transferring of arms to two independent groups from the weapons caches intended for the Salta *foco*. One was the Trotskyite splinter faction of "El Vasco" Bengochea, which intended to open a new *foco* in Tucumán, and the other was a nascent group led by Raúl Sendíc, the leader of the Uruguayan *"cañeros,"* a leftist sugar cane-cutters' movement. Bustos's meeting with the latter was cloaked in clandestine drama.

"Sendíc asked for a meeting with me through some contacts of Petiso Bellomo," recalled Bustos. "The meeting took place one Sunday afternoon on a beach of El Cerro, on the industrial outskirts of Montevideo. He was disguised as an old, poor fisherman and I as a solitary stroller. Beyond, not far away, some youths—his guys—played soccer on the beach. A little closer, was *el gordo* Emilio, Héctor's brother, serving as my backup 'fisherman.' Sendíc questioned me extensively on the reasons for the [Salta] failure and asked me for two things: a training course in security and some 'irons' [arms]."

Bustos agreed to train one of Sendíc's men in the basics of security and tradecraft. (Three decades later, Bustos observed with a little irony, his old "student" had become a well-known and respected economist working for the Uruguayan government.) He also authorized Emilio to transfer part of the EGP's arms cache in Uruguay to Sendíc's group. Bustos's decision to aid the Uruguayans was much more historic than he realized at the time. From this humble beginning, Sendíc's organization soon became renowned as the sophisticated Tupamaro urban guerrilla movement, whose actions would shake Uruguayan society to the core.

For his meeting in Havana with Che, Bustos traveled with "Pancho" Aricó, editor of *Pasado y Presente* and the ideological mentor of the Córdoba support group. He was the only one of the support group who had gone up to the mountains to see Masetti before his demise, and since then had become convinced—as had his colleagues, Oscar del Barco and Héctor "Toto" Schmucler—that Che's *foco* theory wouldn't work in Argentina.

"Pancho went to Cuba to see Che, carrying our critical views, that we thought the [rural guerrilla] thing wouldn't work tactically," said Toto Schmucler. "But when he got there, he couldn't open his mouth. Che talked for two or three hours, and Pancho didn't say anything." Afterward, Pancho told his friends that once he was sitting in front of Che, he felt overcome by the force of his presence and his arguments, and felt too intimidated to contradict him. "It was *Che,*" Pancho Aricó explained simply.

It was the same for Bustos, who met with Che several times to go over what had happened in Salta and to decide on a new plan of action. Che said he could not fathom why some of the men had starved to death. Bustos tried to explain the conditions of the jungle around Orán, an area with virtually no peasants and no food; the difficulties of hunting, how at one point the guerrillas had shot a tapir but found it impossible to eat because the meat simply decomposed. "When I told him that, Che said no, they should have boiled it longer, so that the acids converted or something, and then it would have been fine."

Che's viewpoint was obvious. A rural guerrilla *foco* could be done, but it had to be done right. Bustos had his doubts, but unlike Aricó he had not lost all hope. Any new attempt, he felt, should concentrate on building up its infrastructure, spread out over several zones for survival's sake. The guerrillas couldn't expect to live off the land by hunting, nor could they rely, as Masetti's group had, on a flow of canned goods from the city, with pickup trucks coming and going suspiciously in a pattern that ultimately alerted police to its movements. They needed to blend into an area and be as self-sufficent as possible, without raising suspicions.

Bustos says that Che agreed with him. "He told me: 'Tie things up well here, then go back and put your plan in action. Start working with the people. Make use of the [Communist and Peronist] splinter groups, and let's see what develops.'"

Bustos understood that he was to work with whichever group was willing to embark on the armed struggle, and simultaneously try to forge a coordinated national guerrilla front. There was to be no politico-military commander named for now, no imminent call-up to the mountains; his was to be preparatory work of indefinite duration.

One very big obstacle to all this was going to be money: Bustos says Che didn't give him a budget as such to work on, but did provide him with "some help." They discussed fund-raising, and Bustos mentioned an "expropriations" strategy advocated by some of his action-minded comrades: robbing banks to obtain cash. It was the same proposal Che had made when he arrived to take command of the revolutionary forces in Las Villas in late 1958, but this was a different situation; Cuba had been in a full-fledged state of civil war, and Che had been in command personally. Conditions weren't the same in Argentina, and he didn't want things there to get out of hand before the insurrection had taken root. Che ruled out the bank robbery scheme. "Not at this stage," he told Bustos. "If you start out by robbing banks you end up as a bank robber."

Before leaving, Bustos saw Furry, Ariel, and Papi, and they worked out entry lines and contact points for receiving and sending messages, people, money, and logistics to and from Havana. Uruguay, one of the last countries in Latin America to maintain diplomatic relations with Cuba, would remain their relay station for the time being.

On May 20, while he was still in Cuba, Bustos received a cable informing him of an explosion on Calle Posadas in downtown Buenos Aires. "Vasco" Bengochea and four of his men had been making bombs on the sixth floor of an apartment building and blown themselves to pieces. That was the end of the "Tucumán" group. It was another setback, but as Bustos recalled, Che seemed fairly "unperturbed" about the incident. "He assumed these things with great calm."

After Bustos's departure, Che and Fidel had a temporary falling-out over strategy. In the midst of sharpening language from the Johnson administration, which tightened trade sanctions and renewed U.S.-sponsored measures to isolate Cuba by the OAS, Fidel embarked on an appeasement offensive.

In a series of July interviews he gave a *New York Times* correspondent, Richard Eder, Fidel obliquely offered to end Cuba's support for Latin America's revolutionary movements if the hostilities against Cuba ceased. For Fidel, it was a matter of realpolitik. He had learned his lesson in the art of quid pro quo the hard way by watching Khrushchev during and after the missile crisis—Khrushchev had followed up the missile crisis by pursuing talks with Washington and signing a nuclear test–ban treaty in August 1963—but he now saw how he could apply it to Cuba's benefit. Fidel hinted strongly to Eder that his gesture was being made on Soviet advice, and made clear his hope that Johnson would win the upcoming November presidential election over his arch-conservative rival, Republican Senator Barry Goldwater, and resume the exploratory talks toward detente with Cuba that had begun with John Kennedy.

The day after Fidel's remarks were published, the State Department released a statement flatly rejecting his olive branch; there could be no negotiations with Cuba while she remained tied to the USSR and continued to "promote subversion in Latin America." In an indication of his own seriousness, Fidel maintained an unusually diplomatic silence, despite the rebuff.

He even managed to avoid provocation when, on July 19, a Cuban soldier was killed by a gunshot fired by an American from within the Guantánamo base. Raúl spoke at the massive funeral that was held for the dead man and made clear that he was following his brother's cue. The shot fired, he said, was aimed at Cuba and at President Johnson and against the cause of peace. If Goldwater was elected, there would be war.

Within a few days, however, Che made his own uncompromising views public. On July 24, speaking at a factory in Santa Clara, he reminded his listeners that it was their common duty to fight imperialism "whenever it appears and with all the weapons at our disposal." It didn't matter, he said, who the Americans elected as their president, the enemy was the same. It was the closest Che had ever come to a public rebuttal of the doctrine espoused by *el jefe máximo,* and if Fidel took him to task, he did so behind closed doors. As it turned out, Che—not Fidel—was more the realist this time around.

Two days later, the OAS voted to impose mandatory sanctions on Cuba by all member states and ordered all those who had not severed ties with Cuba to do so. One holdout, Brazil, had already broken off relations in May, and now the stragglers followed suit; in August, Bolivia and Chile broke off ties, followed in September by Uruguay. Mexico was the only nation that refused to go along with the ruling.

As Washington crowed victory, Fidel reiterated his offers of detente. In return for a normalization of relations with its neighbors, he declared on July 26, Cuba was willing to live within accepted "norms of international law." If attaining peace meant giving up Cuba's "material aid to other revolutionaries," so be it, as long as the gesture was reciprocated. Leaving no doubt that his overture was couched within the framework of the existing Soviet foreign policy of "peaceful coexistence," he concluded: "Our position is that we are disposed to live in peace with all the countries, all the states, of this continent, irrespective of social systems. We are disposed to live under a system of international norms to be complied with on an equal basis by all countries."

That was Fidel's carrot to the Americans, and then came the face-saving stick: "The people of Cuba warn that if the pirate attacks proceeding from North American territory and other countries of the Caribbean basin do not cease, . . . as well as the dispatch of agents, arms and explosives to Cuban territory, the people of Cuba will consider that they have an equal right to aid with all the resources at their command the revolutionary movements in all those countries that engage in similar intervention in the internal affairs of our Fatherland."

There was no question that Fidel was gingerly offering terms for peace, but, as with Che's 1961 overture at Punta del Este, this new gesture was perceived by U.S. policy-makers as a sign of weakness, and once again they spurned it. Coinciding with the OAS ruling, Fidel's placating speech put the Americans in a triumphalist mood: The pressure on Cuba was showing results, and by keeping it up they could finally finish Castro off. They were, of course, quite wrong. With the failure of his Kremlin-backed peacemaking bid, Fidel returned to the path of confrontation advocated so unstintingly by Che.

Outside events greatly aided his turnaround. On August 5, American planes began bombing North Vietnam in retaliation for alleged attacks by Hanoi's gunboats against American naval forces in the Gulf of Tonkin. Two days later, Congress passed the Gulf of Tonkin Resolution, giving Johnson the green light to escalate U.S. military involvement in Vietnam. The Vietnam War, as it would become known to the Americans, had begun in earnest. Cuba issued a ringing denunciation of the American bombing, calling for "unity" in the global socialist camp to defend Vietnam against "Yankee imperialist aggression." For Cuba, the crisis in Vietnam afforded a grand opportunity to repair the lauded socialist fraternity so damaged by the two feuding Communist giants.

Che stepped into the breach. At an August 15 Havana awards ceremony for outstanding Communist workers who had set records for volunteer labor, he reassured Cubans that for all their increased isolation, they were now part of an expanding international community of revolutionary states. And in those Latin American nations that had aligned themselves with Washington's policy of "containment," revolutionary armed struggles would triumph and extend the socialist alliance still further.

"It does not matter if these are the times when the bad winds blow," Che explained, "when the threats increase from day to day, when the pirate attacks are unleashed against us and against other countries of the world. It does not matter if we are threatened with Johnson or Goldwater . . . it does not matter that every day imperialism is more aggressive. The people have decided to fight for their liberty and to keep the liberty they have won. They will not be intimidated by anything. And together we shall build a new life, together—because we are together—we here in Cuba, in the Soviet Union, or over there in the People's Republic of China, or in Vietnam fighting in southern Asia."

He reminded his audience that in Latin America, there were two revolutionary struggles—in Guatemala and Venezuela—which were making progress, "inflicting defeat after defeat on imperialism." Throughout Africa, national liberation movements were ascendant. In the former Belgian Congo, the inheritors of Patrice Lumumba's revolutionary example were still fighting and would inevitably win. In the Portuguese colony of Guinea, the liberation army led by Amilcar Cabral already controlled half the national territory—soon, it too would be free, as would Angola. Zanzibar had recently won its independence, and Che unrepentantly acknowledged that Cuba had played a part in that happy outcome. "Zanzibar is our friend and we gave them our small bit of assistance, our fraternal assistance, our revolutionary assistance at the moment when it was necessary."

But Che was now ready to go further than he ever had before publicly, in defending the nature of the war ahead, even invoking the specter of atomic apocalypse. He called it a prospect that was real, given the inevitability of confrontation between the "liberation movements" and the "forces of imperialism," which could unleash a nuclear war through an "error" of calculation.

"Thousands of people will die everywhere, but the responsibility will be theirs [the imperialists], and their peoples will also suffer. . . . But that should not worry us. . . . We as a nation know we can depend upon the great strength of all the countries of the world that make up the socialist bloc and of the peoples who fight for their liberation, and on the strength and cohesion of our people, on the decision to fight to the last man, to the last woman, to the last human being capable of holding a gun."

If anyone had missed his point, reiterated and refined over time, Che had said it again, only now in starker terms. The global battle against imperialism was a struggle for world power between two diametrically opposed historical forces, and there was no sense in protracting the people's agony through doomed attempts to forge tactical short-term alliances with the enemy, or appeasement strategies such as "peaceful coexistence." The root causes of the problems would remain and inevitably lead to conflict, and moderation ran the risk of giving the enemy an opening where he could seize an advantage. History, science, and justice were on the side of socialism; therefore, it must wage the necessary war to win, whatever the consequences—including nuclear war. Che did not shrink from that outcome, and he was telling others they should not, either. Many would die in the revolutionary process, but the survivors would emerge from the ashes of destruction to create a new, just world order based upon the principles of scientific socialism.

For all this to take place, the emergence of the New Socialist Man was essential. A true revolutionary consciousness was the crucial ingredient to bring about a new society. And this, in the end, was the crux of his August speech entitled "Creating a New Attitude." He had begun by quoting from a poem by the Spaniard León Felipe, describing the tragedy of human toil. "No one has been able to dig the rhythm of the sun, . . . no one has yet cut an ear of corn with love and grace."

> I quote these words because today we could tell that great desperate poet to come to Cuba to see how man, after passing through all the stages of capitalist alienation, and after being considered a beast of burden harnessed to the yoke of the exploiter, has rediscovered his way and has found his way back to play. Today

in our Cuba, everyday work takes on new meaning. It is done with new happiness.

And we could invite him to our cane fields so that he might see our women cut the cane with love and grace, so that he might see the virile strength of our workers, cutting the cane with love, so that he might see a new attitude toward work, so that he might see that what enslaves man is not work but rather his failure to possess the means of production.

When society arrives at a certain stage of development and is capable of initiating the harsh struggle, of destroying the oppressive power, of destroying its strong arm—the army—and of taking power, then man once again regains the old sense of happiness in work, the happiness of fulfilling a duty, of feeling himself important within the social mechanism.

He becomes happy to feel himself a cog in the wheel, a cog that has its own characteristics and is necessary though not indispensable, to the production process, a conscious cog, a cog that has its own motor, and that consciously tries to push itself harder and harder to carry to a happy conclusion one of the premises of the construction of socialism—creating a sufficient quantity of consumer goods for the entire population.

Che's habit of referring to the people, the workers, as bits of machinery, as the worker ants in a vast revolutionary agro-industrial collective, affords a glimpse of his emotional distance from individual reality. With the coldly analytical mind of the medical researcher and chess player, the terms he employs for individual humans are reductive and dehumanizing, while the value of their labor in the social context is idealized, rendered in lyrical and sympathetic description. But in his rendering of the Cuban peasant or worker as a "happy cog in a wheel" (and for that matter the anonymous guerrillas fighting around the world, whom he had likened to participants in a "beehive" in his article "Guerrilla Warfare: A Method"), he was also speaking for himself.

Che had found meaning, a form of happiness, for his own life in his identity as a revolutionary within the large family of socialism. There is a discernable parallel between his own experience—the craving for camaraderie of his own youthful quest, culminating in his adoption of Marxism as his creed, and his discovery of true comradeship in the vortex of guerrilla war—and the methodology for attaining the revolutionary consciousness he now preached. The fraternal nature of guerrilla life, in which men are bound by common cause, irrespective of their different pasts, bound together by the conscious willingness to sacrifice oneself while facing the dual prospect of imminent death or ultimate victory, was the crucible of Che's own transformation, the experience that had crystallized him as a man. That experience Che was now extrapolating to the larger world. To achieve a Communist state, that unique consciousness had to be extended, made a permanent part of man's nature. Since society required both workers and fighters, both had to perceive their roles in the same hallowed light of significance.

And so, to the volunteer workers assembled before him, Che said: "You comrades, who are the vanguard of the vanguard, who have demonstrated your spirit of sacrifice toward work, your Communist spirit, your new attitude toward life, ought always to be worthy of Fidel's words . . . 'What we were at a time of mortal danger, may we also learn to be in production; may we learn to be workers of Liberty and Death!'"

Reality, however, was at variance with Che's philosophy. The Communist consciousness he had attained was still an elusive, abstract, and even unwanted state of being for many people, even those who believed themselves to be socialists and happily echoed his shout of "Freedom or Death." The willingness to sacrifice material comforts and even life itself for the cause was a state of mind Che might have achieved, but most other men and women had not, and they probably had little interest in trying. Finally, the happy global socialist fraternity of which he spoke was in fact a house bitterly divided; already, the Sino-Soviet quarrel had caused some of the Latin American Communist parties to be split apart as pro-Chinese militants broke away to form their own groups.

Che put his own views forth in some public remarks he made in August, calling the Sino-Soviet quarrel "one of the saddest developments for us," but stressing that Cuba had not taken sides. "Our party's position is not to say who is right and who is wrong. We choose our position, and, as they say in American films, 'any resemblance is purely coincidental.'"

In socialist Cuba itself, the ill feeling caused by the purging of "sectarianism" had been put to rest officially since Fidel's rapprochement with Moscow, but it had not gone away. Aníbal Escalante was moldering away in his Moscow exile, but some of his comrades had retained influence with Fidel. Only the previous March, while Che was in Geneva, a bizarre trial had been held to determine the guilt of a former PSP man named Marcos Rodríguez. He was accused by ex-Directorio leader Faure Chomón of having betrayed some of his comrades to Batista's police after the 1957 palace assault. Because of Rodríguez's links to senior "old Communist" eminences, the event at first took on the appearance of a purge trial. But then, evidently in an effort to stop the airing of more dirty laundry, Fidel intervened. A new trial was held in which the honor of the Communists was restored, and Marcos Rodríguez—now portrayed as a twisted and resentful "loner"—was executed by firing squad.

Che, away in Geneva, had managed to avoid any association with the distasteful proceedings. His repulsion for the Communist party's sectarianism was well known. Beginning with his selection of José Manresa, former Batista army sergeant, as his personal secretary, he had set forth a precedent, and thereafter stood up for anyone he felt was sincere and willing to work for the revolution despite their past jobs or affiliations. He had consistently made a home at the Ministry of Industries for purged or disgraced revolutionaries, whether the victims of the old Communists' chauvinism or the casualties of Fidel's own sometimes fickle purges of valuable cadres.

He had done so with Enrique Oltuski, his old July 26 rival, after the latter was ousted as communications minister under Communist pressure in 1961. He had removed Jorge Masetti from harm's way after he alienated the PSP faction in Prensa Latina. And Alberto Mora, the son of one of the martyrs of the Directorio's palace assault, was another. When he was ousted by Fidel as the minister of foreign commerce in mid-1964, Che brought him over to his ministry as an advisor, even though Mora was one of his most outspoken economic critics.

Another was the poet and writer Heberto Padilla, an old friend of Mora's. Since the beginning of the revolution, Padilla had worked in the New York and London offices of Prensa Latina; in Havana for *Revolución* under Carlos Franqui and for its now-defunct literary supplement, *Lunes de Revolución,* edited by the novelist Guillermo Cabrera Infante. Perceived as troublesome nonconformists in Cuba's increasingly repressive intellectual climate, Franqui and Cabrera Infante had been sent into diplomatic exile in Europe, from which neither man would return.

Padilla had just finished a stint working at the Spanish-language edition of the Soviet magazine *Moscow News,* and was well aware of the intrigues and authoritarianism that had begun to stifle cultural freedoms in Cuba. In spite of his own doubts and Franqui's warnings, Padilla decided to go back home.

Back in Havana, Mora arranged for Padilla to meet with Che, an admirer of his poetry. Mora was still minister of foreign commerce and was then engaged in a collegial polemic with Guevara over the economy, at odds with Che's insistence on a centralized Soviet-style economy, favoring one that was more market-oriented. Since Padilla had returned with a jaundiced view of what he had seen in the Soviet Union, Mora wanted him to tell Che his views.

Padilla and Mora found Che in the midst of a bout of asthma; he was shirtless and prostrate on the floor of his office, trying to regulate his breathing, and he remained there as his visitors began talking. He cut off Padilla's critical appraisal of the USSR straight away, saying: "I must tell you I don't need to listen to what you have to say because I already know all of that is a pigsty, I saw it myself."

Che went on to tell him that China, not Russia, was the model to be studied, for they were making a genuine effort toward the realization of Communism. "Many people criticize me because they say I put too much emphasis on sacrifice, but sacrifice is fundamental to a Communist education. The Chinese understand that very well, much better than the Russians do."

By the end of their talk, which ranged over into Padilla's poetry, Che had urged Mora to give him a job in the ministry of foreign commerce, remarking laconically: "These are not good times for journalism." Padilla became the director general of a department that dealt with cultural items. When Mora was fired and arranged to leave Cuba on a grant to study political economy with the French Marxist economist Charles Bettleheim (with whom Che had also been debating economic theory), Padilla also arranged to leave, obtaining a post as a roving emissary for the ministry, based in Prague.

Before they left, he and Mora went to see Che for the last time. Mora was unhappy and couldn't conceal it from Che; he explained that he felt depressed when he woke up in the morning. "Che walked up to Alberto slowly," recalled Padilla, "put his hands on his shoulders, and shook him, looking straight into his eyes. 'I live like someone torn in two, twenty-four hours a day, completely torn in two, and I haven't got anybody to tell it to. Even if I did, they would never believe me.'"*

It was a poignant moment of personal revelation coming from Che, one of the few ever recorded that hint at the incredible stresses he put himself through to maintain his persona of the exemplary Communist revolutionary. He had told Mora and Padilla that "sacrifice is fundamental to a Communist education," and he had insisted on being his own guinea pig, but the resulting concoction had come with a heavy price. His father, usually so myopic about his son, had nonetheless perceived this when he wrote that "Ernesto had brutalized his own sensitivities" to become a revolutionary. His mother once told the Uruguayan journalist Eduardo Galeano that from

*After Che's departure from Cuba, both Padilla and Mora suffered unhappy fates. Mora never recovered from his fall from grace, and committed suicide by shooting himself in the head in 1972. That same year, after his arrest by State Security, Padilla was put through the humiliating ritual of a public "confession" by the officialist Cuban Writer's Union for his alleged crimes as a "counterrevolutionary author," enduring imprisonment, house arrest, and years of official harassment and ostracism before finally being allowed to emigrate from Cuba.

the time of his asthmatic childhood, her son ". . . had always lived trying to prove to himself that he could do everything he couldn't do, and in that way he had polished his amazing willpower."

Celia told Galeano that she teased Che for being "intolerant and fanatical," and explained that his actions were "motivated by a tremendous necessity for totality and purity." "Thus," wrote Galeano, "he had become the most puritanical of the Western revolutionary leaders. In Cuba, he was the Jacobin of the revolution: 'Watch out, here comes Che,' warned the Cubans, joking but serious at the same time. All or nothing: this refined intellectual must have waged exhausting battles against his own doubt-nagged conscience."

Supplied with Celia de la Serna's insights, Galeano met with Che in August of 1964 and thought she noted the symptoms of impatience in the famous revolutionary. "Che was not a desk-man: he was a creator of revolutions, and it was apparent; he was not, or was in spite of himself, an administrator. Somehow, that tension of a caged lion that his apparent calm betrayed had to explode. He needed the sierra." Galeano may have written this appraisal with the benefit of hindsight, but it was accurate nonetheless. As they spoke, Che was searching for a way back to the battlefield, even as he worked himself to exhaustion on Cuba's industrial economy.

Several possibilities loomed. Besides the insurgent groups in Guatemala, Venezuela, and Nicaragua, there was now a Cuban-backed guerrilla organization in Colombia, the Ejercito de Liberación Nacional (ELN), formed in July. In Peru, Héctor Béjar's guerrilla force and Luis de la Puente Uceda's MIR were both preparing to launch their own revolutionary bids. But Che had his heart set on the Southern Cone and his Argentine homeland.

That posed a problem, for Ciro Bustos and his comrades had a lot of work to do before conditions would be ready for a new insurrectional attempt in the region, and Tania was still traveling in Europe, en route to her future post in Bolivia.

Probably the most "promising" of potential battlegrounds for the immediate future lay in Africa. All over the continent, rebel movements had formed to do battle with the last colonial holdouts: in the Portuguese colonies of Angola and Mozambique, in white-ruled South Africa, and in the former Belgian Congo, that vast nation comprising the geographic heart of Africa.

In October 1963, an antigovernment coalition calling itself the National Liberation Council had been formed by a potpourri of former Lumumbist government officials and disaffected regional, often tribally based, strongmen. The council had offices across the Congo River from Leopoldville in the city of Brazzaville, capital of the People's Republic of the Congo, formerly French Equitorial Africa. These rebels had managed to attract Chinese and some Soviet aid, as both superpowers vied for their favors. Since then the various allied rebel leaders had sparked revolts in southern, eastern, central, and northern Congo, seizing provincial towns and huge portions of the ill-defended national territory. One Chinese-backed rebel column had seized the distant northern city of Stanleyville in August 1964 and declared a "People's Republic of the Congo." By September, the stage was set for a renewed escalation of the Congolese crisis as the government struggled to respond to the rebellion.

That response would not be long in coming. And, with sensationalist reports trickling out about atrocities being committed against white people by the so-called "Simba" rebels in Stanleyville, the West would lend a hand. An ambitious trio—former leader Moise Tshombe, President Joseph Kasavubu, and Joseph Mobutu, the armed forces commander in chief—ruled the Congo and, faced with the renewed rebel threat, took quick action to bolster their threadbare army's fighting strength, calling in the South African mercenary commander Mike Hoare and asking him to recruit a thousand white fighters from South Africa and Rhodesia.

The African resistance struggles, and particularly the Congolese conflict, had begun featuring more and more prominently in the Cuban press and in Che's speeches. In fact, he had begun to seriously consider temporarily transplanting his program for continental revolution to the African continent. To that end, Fidel had given Red Beard Piñeiro's agency the task of preparing the way. Although Che had reserved his ultimate decision about the best base for a pan-African guerrilla struggle until he could tour the area and meet with the various guerrilla leaders himself, the huge Congo, located in the midst of the continent, seemed to offer the perfect setting and conditions for a rurally based guerrilla war that could "radiate" out to its neighbors.

There were other advantages to fighting in Africa: The Soviets were less concerned about direct involvement there than in Washington's "backyard" in Latin America, and the nature of the wars, against foreign, white colonial regimes—or in the Congo's case, against a Western-backed dictator with little political legitimacy—were sustained by widespread popular support. Finally, the continent was already inflamed with conflict; it was not a situation that had to be "created," as had been the case with the ill-fated Masetti mission to Argentina. The Soviets, the Chinese, the Americans and their Western allies were all involved in Africa, providing money, arms, and advisors to their chosen factions. There were also a number of anti-imperialist national leaders friendly to Cuba whose strategically placed territories could provide invaluable rearguard bases, trans-shipment points, and means of access to the zones of conflict. In addition to the regimes holding power in Mali and the "Brazzaville" People's Republic, they included Ben Bella in Algeria, Sekou Touré in Guinea, Kwame Nkrumah in Ghana, Julius Nyerere in Tanzania, and Gamal Abdel Nasser in Egypt. In particular, these "radical" states were outraged at the specter of white mercenaries and "neocolonial" Western powers intervening on behalf of the Leopoldville regime, and openly supported the Stanleyville rebel government.

In Africa, Che saw the opportunity to finally pursue the implementation of his long-held dream: building a new, Cuban-led international anti-imperialist alliance to replace the ineffectual, Cairo-based Afro-Asian People's Solidarity Organization. It would give a truly global dimension to his scheme for the upcoming continental revolution in Latin America by forging a coordinating council for kindred struggles in Asia and Africa. In an ideal world, the alliance would come under Fidel's political direction, and be bankrolled and armed by the two socialist superpowers, China and the USSR. In short, what Che invisioned was a repairing of the Sino-Soviet split through the shared burden of waging war.

Throughout the autumn of 1964, Che honed this idea, and obtained Fidel's approval to travel abroad and take soundings. The notion of projecting himself internationally had always appealed to Fidel, and after his rebuff by the Americans, he had become newly receptive to Che's position. While trying not to appear to take Beijing's side, he once again questioned the value of toeing the Kremlin line on "peaceful coexistence"; so far, it had brought him precious little.

In September the OAS had pushed through yet another resolution, further tightening commercial sanctions on Cuba. The attacks by the CIA-backed Cuban exiles had also stepped up in intensity: Hijackings, sabotage attacks, and armed commando raids against Cuban shipping were now taking place with alarming frequency. On September 24, a seaborne CIA action team based in Nicaragua attacked the Spanish freighter *Sierra de Aranzazu* as it sailed toward Cuba with a cargo of industrial equipment. In the raid, the Spanish captain and two crew members were killed, the ship set ablaze and disabled. The incident caused an international outcry and recriminations within the CIA, especially when it learned the raiders had attacked the freighter by mistake, believing it was the Cuban merchant marine ship *Sierra Maestra*. The agent back at base who had authorized the attack was Felix Rodríguez.

Since late 1963, Rodríguez had been in charge of communications for a brigade of anti-Castro commandos based in Nicaragua, led by Manuel Artime and bankrolled by the CIA. The group had over three hundred active members scattered across Nicaragua, Miami, and Costa Rica. It was a well-supplied operation: The exiles had at their disposal two 250-foot "mother ships," two 50-foot fast boats, and other craft for their military raids as well as a C-47 transport plane, several Cessnas, and a Beaver floatplane. They had a refueling and resupply facility in the Dominican Republic, and for weaponry they could take what they needed from their 200–ton arms cache in Costa Rica, which included 20 mm antiaircraft cannon, 50 and 75 mm recoilless rifles, and .50-caliber machine guns. In two years, Rodríguez claimed, the commandos expended about six million dollars in CIA funds and carried out fourteen raids against Cuban targets, one of the most successful strikes being a commando raid against the Cabo Cruz sugar refinery—not far from where the *Granma* had landed—inflicting serious damage.

By late 1964, however, the operation's budget had been cut back as the Johnson administration's priorities shifted from Cuba to Vietnam, and the death knell came after the embarrassing attack on the *Sierra de Aranzazu*. "We subsequently discovered that the ship was carrying a boiler for a Cuban sugarcane facility as well as some Christmas foodstuffs," wrote Rodríguez. "We felt terrible. Soon after the incident, our operations were rolled up. Our fast boats were taken by the agency and sent to Africa, where they saw service in the Congo. Some of the people who served with me in Nicaragua volunteered to fight in Africa too."

Felix Rodríguez returned to Miami, where he resumed his work for the CIA's Miami "station." It would be nearly three years before he received the telephone call that would lead to the most important assignment of his life, the mission to hunt down Che Guevara.

III

When Che flew from Havana on November 4, 1964, Raúl Castro, Foreign Minister Raúl Roa, and Emilio Aragonés were there at the airport to see him off. The joint presence of Cuba's armed forces chief, foreign minister, and the "organization secretary" of its official ruling party, the Partido Unificado de la Revolución Socialista (PURS),* respectively, carried great symbolic significance. Once again, Che was to be the revolution's anointed emissary to the *"madre patria"* of world socialism, heading a Cuban delegation to attend the forty-seventh anniversary celebration of the Bolshevik revolu-

---

*In 1962, after Fidel's ouster of Aníbal Escalante from his influential post in Organizaciones Revolucionarias Integradas and the purge of the "old Communists'" sectarianism, he announced the replacement of ORI with the PURS as Cuba's new official ruling party, in the latest stage of the gradual transformation of Cuba into a single-party state. That process, which did away with the July 26 Movement, the Popular Socialist Party, and the Revolutionary Directorate, would end in October 1965 with the formal launching of the new Cuban Communist party.

tion in Moscow and the opening of the new "Soviet-Cuban Friendship House." Aleida was also there to say good-bye, along with two of their children. She was visibly swollen, six months into the fourth and final pregnancy of her union with Che Guevara.

Che's final visit to Moscow came exactly three years after his first. Once again, he stood in Red Square in the wintry month of November, but things were different this time. He was not the same uncritical Che of 1961, full of hopes about the rosy future of Soviet-Cuban relations; too much contaminated water had gone under the bridge. A great deal had changed within the Soviet Union as well. Nikita Khrushchev, discredited by his economic failures at home and his perceived reckless adventurism abroad—most notably the Cuban missile crisis—had been ousted from power a few weeks earlier, and Leonid Brezhnev was the new Soviet premier.

There was another reason for the timing of Che's visit. Reportedly at the behest of the Argentine Communist party chief, Victorio Codovilla, who was still incensed over the Cuban-sponsored Masetti incursion, the Kremlin had pushed for a first-ever Latin American Communist party conference to be held later that month in Havana. The Soviet decision had a double significance: On the one hand, it deferred to Fidel, indicating the Kremlin's recognition of his regional stature; on the other hand, the gesture came with an implicit expectation that Fidel would hammer together a pro-Soviet alliance of regional parties and further isolate Beijing. Lately the Chinese had taken their dispute with Moscow to new levels, aggressively pursuing adherents to the Maoist line. In January 1964, Peru's Communist party had been severely weakened after pro-Beijing members broke away to form a rival party; in Bolivia and Colombia similar factional splits were looming; and in Guatemala, a Trotskyite faction was emerging that would soon split the Cuban-backed FAR coalition.

It was a good time for Che to test the intentions of the new Soviet leadership, now that he and Fidel were both in a challenging mood. In October, Fidel's spokesman, President Dorticós, had already given vent to the Cuban jefe's new mood at a leadership conference of the new nonaligned countries' association held in Cairo. While still maintaining that Cuba supported the USSR's policy of peaceful coexistence in its relations with the West, as a means of reducing the risks of a nuclear "world conflagration," Dorticós argued that peaceful coexistence could not exist at the same time as "imperialist aggression against small countries" was taking place. Given the new world situation, with escalating intervention by the United States and its Western allies in Southeast Asia, in the Congo, and in the counterinsurgency campaigns in Latin America, a show of greater solidarity toward its Third World partners was needed from the Kremlin.

In Moscow, Che went through with the pro forma appearance in Red Square and cohosted the inauguration of the new "Friendship House" with the cosmonaut Yuri Gagarin. Behind the scenes, he also conducted a series of secret meetings with Kremlin officials, anxious for their views so he could attempt a mediation in the Sino-Soviet quarrel, and for their attitudes toward Cuba's revolutionary proposals for Latin America. This time, however, Che did not have his old acquaintance Nikolai Leonov as his interpreter. Since Che's last Russian visit, the KGB had reassigned Leonov to Mexico, where he was involved in aiding the Guatemalan guerrillas, among his other duties.*

Instead, Che was assisted by his Kremlin-provided translator in Cuba, Oleg Darushenkov, and another Soviet intelligence official, Rudolf Petrovich Shlyapnikov, the two alternating as his interpreters during his stay. Shlyapnikov worked under Yuri Andropov, in the Cuba section of the Central Committee's International Department, and was a specialist in Latin American Communist Youth groups; he had been to Cuba on several missions and had met Che previously. During Che's stay in Moscow, said Shlyapnikov, the two of them developed the habit of sitting up on the stairs of the house at night, playing chess until the wee hours. As they played and talked, Che drank milk, and Shlyapnikov drank cognac.**

Among the high Soviet officials Che saw during his visit, according to Shlyapnikov, were his boss Yuri Andropov, and Vitali Korionov, the sexagenarian deputy chief of the Soviet Central Committee's Americas Department. Korionov's brief was to handle relations with the Communist parties in capitalist countries, which included all Latin American parties except Cuba, and Korionov says Che asked especially to see him to discuss "the attitudes" of the Latin American Communist parties.

Korionov had already received bitter complaints from some leading Latin Communists—specifically the Bolivian Mario Monje and the Venezuelan Jesús Faria—about the pressure the Cuban regime was putting on their parties to enlist in the Cuban "continental revolution" scheme of guerrilla warfare. The Bolivians had formally voted against such an idea, while the Venezuelan Communist party was reconsidering its involvement in the Cuban-backed FALN guerrilla coalition.†

---

*See the appendix for elaboration.

**See the appendix for elaboration.

†Within a few months, in April 1965, the Venezuelan party plenum voted in favor of giving "priority" to legal forms of political change, leading eventually to a bitter split between the party and the Cuban-backed guerrillas led by Douglas Bravo.

From his meeting with Che, Korionov said he understood Che and Fidel to be proposing nothing less than a modern-day repetition of the epic liberation war strategy waged by San Martín and Bolívar more than a century before: a joint effort made by Marxist armies of the northern countries of Venezuela, Colombia, and Ecuador, sweeping south like Bolívar's troops, while those of the south—Chile, Peru, Uruguay, and Argentina—marched north a la San Martín's. The meeting-ground would be the nation named after "El Libertador"—Bolivia.

Korionov said that he and Che drank "a lot of good Armenian cognac" during their session, and that Che wanted to find out the Kremlin's view on the policies of the Latin parties, many of whose leaders had come to Moscow for meetings with the new Soviet leadership.

Korionov bluntly told Che what he had come to find out, so that by the time he left Moscow, "Che could see for himself what was going on, that the Fidel and Guevara line on armed struggle did not meet with their [Latin American Communist] support." Since the Kremlin's official position was to "respect" the policies of the regional Communist parties, it left no room for doubt. Moscow was against the Cuban initiative. Korionov also concluded several things about Che Guevara: The Argentine was determined to push ahead with the armed struggle in Latin America, he distrusted the Kremlin's policy of peaceful coexistence, and in the Sino-Soviet schism, he was on the Chinese side.

Upon his return from Moscow, Che's response to the Communist Party Congress convened in Havana could hardly have been heartening, either to the Latin American parties or to the Soviet leadership. He made himself conspiciously absent from the weeklong forum, traveling instead to Oriente. But he did not remain silent. On November 30, he gave a speech in Santiago castigating Latin America's Communist parties for their reluctance in pursuing the path to power.

The Congo also featured prominently in Che's speech; just days earlier the Lumumbist revolutionaries had been ousted from their Stanleyville stronghold by Belgian paratroopers flown in on American planes. Che emotionally characterized the "massacres" committed in Stanleyville as an example of "imperialist bestiality . . . a bestiality which knows no frontiers nor belongs to a certain country. Just as the Hitlerian hordes were beasts, so are the Americans and Belgian paratroopers beasts today, as were yesterday the French imperialists beasts in Algeria, because it is the very nature of imperialism which bestializes man, which converts them into bloodthirsty wild animals willing to slit throats, commit murder and destroy even the last image of a revolutionary or the ally of a regime which has fallen under its boot or struggles for his liberty."

Afterward, Che took Aleida to see Alberto Granado and his wife, Delia, and they all went out together to eat pizza at the Fontana de Trevi restaurant. It was the last time the two old friends Mial and Fuser would see one another. Granado later realized the visit had been his "silent good-bye." Indeed, although few people in Cuba realized it at the time, Che's no-show at the Havana conference was the first visible sign that something fundamental had shifted. For anyone who cared to notice, Che was already in the process of extracting himself from his normal routine and would soon vanish from their midst.*

At the Havana conference, meanwhile, a compromise resolution had been ratified, with Fidel's approval. It tilted heavily in favor of Moscow's foreign policy, but approved the backing of guerrilla movements in nations where neither the parties nor Moscow saw opportunities for open, "legal" political involvement. Other decisions were to send a mixed delegation from the conference to both Moscow and Beijing to seek ratification of the agreements, and to attempt a mediation in the Sino-Soviet dispute.

A week after returning to Havana from Oriente, Che was gone again, flying this time to New York, the city he had once told his aunt Beatriz he wished to see for himself in spite of his visceral aversion to the United States. But this time he was going as the official spokesman for revolutionary Cuba, and his selection as Cuba's representative before the United Nations General Assembly was eloquent testimony to the fact that, in spite of Fidel's own diplomatic temporizing with the Soviets, he continued to have Fidel's support for a more aggressive "anti-imperialist" strategy. It was cold when Che arrived in New York on December 9, and the photographs of his arrival show him dressed in a winter greatcoat, wearing his beret and the aloof, unsmiling expression of one who knows he has just stepped onto enemy territory. It was to be his second and final incursion into the land of the Yankee, and, this time, unlike his 1952 Miami sojourn, his presence did not pass unnoticed.

---

*According to the author's sources in Cuba, Che had by now told Fidel he no longer wanted to remain in Cuba's revolutionary government. He made his decision after his Moscow trip, having determined that the Soviet pressure on Fidel to accept the Kremlin's socialist model in Cuba was overwhelming. A small circle of comrades were privy to Che's decision and begged him to stay on for at least two more years to give time to "prove" that his "budgetary finance" economic model was better for Cuba than the one the Soviets were persuading Fidel to adopt. Che refused, replying that two more years were not necessary: his ministry was up and running according to his theories and had already proven itself.

      Having already tendered his resignation—and having it accepted by Fidel—Che's trip abroad that began in December 1964 was undertaken with an eye to deciding where he should go next.

IV

When he appeared before the Nineteenth UN General Assembly on December 11, Che took pains to groom himself for the occasion: His boots were polished, his olive-green uniform pressed, and his hair and beard were neatly combed. Nevertheless, he presented a striking contrast to the conservatively attired diplomats who filled the hall to hear him speak, and his defiant speech did not disappoint those who had anticipated a harangue worthy of the famous apostle of revolutionary socialism.

Che had come to sound the death knell for colonialism, to decry American interventionism, and to applaud, on Cuba's behalf, the "liberation wars" taking place in Latin America, Africa, and Asia. In a bitter reference to the Congolese conflict, he took the United Nations to task for having allowing itself to be drawn in and used there as an instrument of Western imperialism—"a carnivorous animal feeding on the helpless." As for the latest Belgian-U.S. operation in Stanleyville, which had given the city back to Tshombe's troops at a cost of hundreds of dead, Che declared: "All free men throughout the world must make ready to avenge the Congo crime." He then proceeded to link the "white imperialist" action in the Congo with Western indifference to the apartheid regime in South Africa and the racial inequalities in the United States. "How can the country that murders its own children and discriminates between them daily because of the color of their skins, a country that allows the murderers of Negroes to go free, actually protects them and punishes the Negroes for demanding respect for their lawful rights as free human beings, claim to be a guardian of liberty?"

Addressing one of the main themes of the assembly—a debate on global nuclear disarmament—Che expressed Cuba's support for the concept but stressed its refusal to ratify any such agreement until the United States had dismantled its military bases in Puerto Rico and Panama. Che's speech also reiterated Cuba's determination to follow an independent course in global affairs. While reaffirming that Cuba was "building socialism," Cuba considered itself a "nonaligned country" because it identified with those in that new community of states in Africa, Asia, and the Middle East that were "fighting against imperialism." Under the circumstances, this could be taken as an implicit dig at Soviet inaction on behalf of those struggles. In separate references to the feuding socialist superpowers, Che said Cuba strongly supported the Soviet stance over the Congo—while on behalf of China, he argued for its inclusion in the United Nations and the ouster of the U.S.-supported Nationalist Chinese government of Chiang Kai-shek.

Not surprisingly, Che's words provoked vigorous denunciations by U.S. Ambassador Adlai Stevenson and some of the Latin envoys present, while outside the UN building Cuban exiles angrily protested his appearance. Some

went considerably further. Several *"gusanos"* were arrested after firing bazookas at the UN building from across the East River. Elsewhere, a woman was
prevented from trying to stab Che with a knife as he entered. Throughout
the ruckus, Che maintained his composure and seemed delighted at the anger
he had aroused. To the shouted insults of the *gusano* protestors, he raised his
hand in that universally understood gesture meaning "Fuck you."

Not everyone was displeased with Che's presence. The renowned black
American activist Malcolm X had just returned from travels in Africa and
the Middle East and had been making speeches about what he had seen and
learned there. Like Che, Malcolm X was inflamed over the Congolese conflict, and he similarly equated white intervention in Africa with racism in
the United States. They had found a common cause: During his stop in Ghana,
Malcolm X had reportedly discussed with Cuba's ambassador in Accra the
idea of recruiting black Americans to help fight in Africa's wars.

On December 13, in a rally at the Audubon Ballroom in Harlem,
Malcolm X introduced the crowd to a special guest from the East African
island of Zanzibar. Less than a year earlier, Abdul Rahman Muhammad
Babu's Cuban-trained political movement had helped seize power in the
former sultanate, then fused with Tanganyika on the nearby African mainland to form the new nation of Tanzania. Just before Babu appeared onstage,
Malcolm X read out a message from Che Guevara.

"I love a revolutionary," Malcolm X told his audience. "And one of
the most revolutionary men in this country right now was going to come
out here with our friend Sheikh Babu, but he thought better of it. But he
did send this message. It says:

"'Dear brothers and sisters of Harlem. I would have liked to have been
with you and Brother Babu, but the actual conditions are not good for this
meeting. Receive the warm salutations of the Cuban people and especially
those of Fidel, who remembers enthusiastically his visit to Harlem a few
years ago. United we will win.'

"This is from Che Guevara," Malcolm X explained. "I'm happy to hear
your warm round of applause in return because it lets the [white] man know
that he's just not in a position to tell us who we should applaud for and who
we shouldn't applaud for. And you don't see any anti-Castro Cubans around
here—we eat them up."*

According to Pedro Álvarez Tabío, Fidel Castro's official historian,
who accompanied Che's entourage on the UN trip, the reason Che didn't
show up was to avoid an appearance that the U.S. government could claim
was an "intromission" in its internal affairs.

---

* Only two months later, on February 21, 1965, Malcolm X himself was gunned down by
rival Nation of Islam assassins while giving a speech in New York. He was thirty-nine.

Che did not return to Cuba from New York. Instead, on December 17, after giving some colorfully defiant interviews to the American media, he flew to Algiers. It was the start of a three-month odyssey throughout Africa, to China, and back to Africa again, with stops in Paris, Ireland, and Prague. Outwardly, Che was acting as Fidel's roving goodwill ambassador to the emerging nations of Africa, but his trip also had an important ulterior motive: acquainting himself with the continent that was to be the scene of his next adventure. Africa, Che had decided, would be the proving ground for his dream of a "tricontinental" alliance against the West.

Between Christmas 1964 and early February 1965, Che moved around the African continent, from Algeria to Mali, to Congo-Brazzaville, Guinea and Ghana, to Dahomey, then back to Ghana and Algeria. He met with Algeria's Ben Bella, with Ghana's Kwame Nkrumah, with the Congolese-Brazzaville leader Alphonse Massamba-Débat, and with the leader of the anti-Portuguese Angolan independence movement, Agostinho Neto—to whom he promised Cuban military instructors for his MPLA guerrillas operating out of the adjacent Angolan enclave of Cabinda.*

Everywhere he went, Che's public message was the same: Cuba identified with Africa's liberation struggles; there should be unity among all of the world's anticolonial and anti-imperialist movements, and there should be common cause between them and the socialist community. The fighting in the Congo featured heavily in his press pronouncements, as did far-off Vietnam, that other former colonial dominion whose people were now fighting American troops.

To Josie Fanon, widow of the late Martiniquean revolutionary Frantz Fanon, author of the fiery anticolonialist manifesto *The Wretched of the Earth,* Che gave an interview for the magazine *Révolution Africaine.* For Cuba, he told her, Africa represented one of "the more important fields of struggle against all forms of exploitation existing in the world—against imperialism, colonialism and neocolonialism." There were, he felt, "great possibilities for success due to the existing unrest" but also many dangers, including the divisions among the Africans that colonialism had left. The positive, he said, seeming to paraphrase her deceased husband's language, was "the hate which colonialism has left in the minds of the people."

When Fanon asked him about the prospects for revolution in Latin America, Che acknowledged that she had touched on a subject "very close" to his heart, in fact, his "major interest." He thought the struggle there would be "long and hard" because of the stepped-up counterinsurgency activities of the United States.

---

*Those instructors soon arrived, marking the beginning of more than two decades of Cuban military involvement in Angola.

"That is why," Che said, "we foresee the establishment of a continental front of struggle against imperialism and its internal allies. This front will take some time to organize, but when it is formed it will be a very hard blow against imperialism. I don't know if it will be a definitive blow, but it will be a severe blow."

In early February, Che flew to China. He was accompanied by Cuba's construction minister, Osmany Cienfuegos—his late friend Camilo's older brother—and the influential PURS "organization secretary," Emílio Aragonés, Che's companion to the Soviet Union during the secret 1962 nuclear missile negotiations. Both of these men would be heavily involved in the secret Cuban operation in Africa, and their presence with Che at this juncture suggests they were also involved in its planning stages.

By now, in fact, Fidel had already approved a secret Cuban military mission in the Congo; it remained for Che to determine only where Cuba's services could be best directed, and with which of the rebel factions the mission should be carried out. The month before, in January 1965, a group of handpicked black Cubans had been offered the honor of volunteering for an unspecified "internationalist mission," and they were now training at three separate camps in Cuba. Another sign of the impending operation was the recent appointment of Pablo Ribalta—Che's old PSP friend from the Sierra Maestra—as Cuba's envoy to Tanzania, a nation bordering the Congo.

What transpired behind closed doors during Che's trip to China has never been made public by Cuba's government, but according to Humberto Vázquez-Viaña, a well-informed former Bolivian Communist party member, Che's party met with Chou En-lai and other top People's Republic officials, but not with Mao himself.*

In his Congo plans, Che must have seen the potential for turning around the disfavor into which Cuba had fallen with China. Richard Gott, the British historian of Latin American revolutionary movements—who as a journalist covered Che's subsequent guerrilla campaign in Bolivia, and worked in Tanzania in the early 1970s—believes that the motive of Guevara's Chinese mission was to talk to the principal backers of the Congolese revolu-

---

* According to one Chinese official, the snubbing was not directed at Che, who was said to have "behaved correctly," but at Osmany Cienfuegos, who had offended the Chinese by "shouting" and "talking too much," and led them to fear he would provoke an embarrassing incident in Mao's hallowed presence. In fact, it seems probable that, coming on the heels of the disastrous visit by the Latin American Communist delegation, an effort with which Che was identified by dint of his position in Cuba, Mao's no-show was a gambit to force Che into a stand more clearly identifiable as pro-Chinese.

tionaries. "The Chinese were certainly interested in Africa," Gott reasons. "Chou En-lai was to make two visits that year—and they were also at that stage supporting the strategic notions of Lin Pao, the Chinese defense minister. He had made a famous speech advocating the encirclement of degenerate cities by radical revolutionary peasants. This was of course music to the ears of Guevara."

After leaving China, Che stopped in Paris, where he took a few hours off from plans of revolution to tour the Louvre. Then he returned to Africa. Over the next month, in Algeria, Tanzania, and Egypt, he met again with Gamal Abdel Nasser, Ben Bella, and Julius Nyerere, and began to take soundings for his ambitious plan for pan-African revolution.

Dar-Es-Salaam was the crucial stop on his itinerary, a place where white colonial rule was a very fresh memory. The port city, built on a lagoon bordering the Indian Ocean in the 1860s as the site for the Arab sultan of Zanzibar's summer palace, had been the capital of the colony of German East Africa until the First World War. Then the British had taken over and ruled it as the colony of Tanganyika until granting independence in 1961. Since then, under leftist president Julius Nyerere, "Dar" had become the headquarters for numerous African guerrilla movements. It was a promising revolutionary outpost: The U.S. embassy had been shut after the two countries had severed relations the previous year, and the Cubans had opened one of their own.

But Che's first encounters with African revolutionaries were disappointing. In what he titled "The First Act" of an unpublished book— "Pasajes de la Guerra Revolucionaria (Congo)"*—he wrote on his Congolese experience later that year, Che recalled his initial meetings with the men he derisively called, in English, "Freedom Fighters." These men, he noted, had a common "leitmotif": Almost all were living comfortably in Dar-Es-Salaam's hotels and all invariably wanted the same things from him, "military training in Cuba and monetary help."

The first thing that struck Che about the Congolese rebel leaders was their "extraordinary number of tendencies and diverse opinions." These included Gaston Soumaliot, the self-styled "President of northeastern Congo," whose forces had liberated a swathe of territory in eastern Congo, to which they had access from Tanzanian territory across Lake Tanganyika. Che found Soumaliot vague and inscrutable—"little developed politically"—and cer-

*This 153-page manuscript, of which there were reportedly only five copies made, was kept under lock and key at the highest levels of Cuba's revolutionary government for nearly three decades until a few leaked copies began circulating to a number of researchers, including the author.

tainly not a "leader of nations." He also discerned Soumaliot's rivalry with
some of his council comrades, especially Christophe Gbenye, whose fighters
had seized Stanleyville.

One rebel leader who did impress Che was Laurent Kabila, a French-
schooled Congolese in his mid-twenties who was the overall military commander of Gaston Soumaliot's eastern front. In contrast to Soumaliot, Che
found Kabila's exposition about his struggle to be "clear, concrete and firm,"
although he too spoke ill of fellow Liberation Council leaders such as Gbenye
and even Soumaliot himself.

Later, Che also noted that Kabila had lied to him in their first meeting. Kabila had announced that he had just arrived "from the interior" of
the Congo, but, as Che later learned, Kabila had merely been to the seedy
bar-and-brothel port of Kigoma on the Tanzanian shore of Lake Tanganyika, used by the rebels as a rearguard base for "rest and recuperation."
Che chose to ignore Kabila's bluster, however, in light of his avowedly leftist worldview. "Kabila understood perfectly that the principal enemy was
North American imperialism," Che wrote, "and he said he was ready to fight
consequently to the end against it; his declarations and his self-assuredness
gave me . . . a very good impression." Finding a receptive ear to the concept
upon which his entire African plan hinged, Che told Kabila of his distress
at the shortsighted resistance to outside involvement in the Congolese rebellion by many of the African states, and said, "Our viewpoint is that the
problem of the Congo is a problem of the world." When Kabila agreed with
him, recorded Che, he offered him Cuba's support on the spot. "In the name
of the [Cuban] Government I offered some 30 instructors and whatever arms
we might have and he accepted with pleasure; he recommended speed in
the delivery of both things, which Soumaliot had also done in another conversation, the latter recommending that the instructors be blacks."

Next, Che decided to take the pulse of the other "Freedom Fighters"
in town. He had planned to meet them in separate groups for informal talks,
but "by mistake," he wrote, the Cuban embassy assembled a "tumultuous
gathering . . . of fifty or more people, representatives of the movements of
10 or more countries, each one divided into two or more tendencies."

Che found himself faced with a roomful of guerrillas who "almost unanimously" requested Cuba's financial support and the training of their fighters
in Cuba. To the exasperation of his audience, Che begged off, arguing that to
train their men in Cuba would be costly and wasteful, that true guerrilla fighters were forged on the battlefield, not in military "academies." "Therefore, I
proposed that the training should be carried out not in our faraway Cuba, but
in the nearby Congo, where the struggle was not merely against a common
puppet like Tshombe, but against North American imperialism."

The Congolese struggle, insisted Che, was extremely important. Its victory would have "continental repercussions," as would its defeat. What Che envisioned was a Cuban-led "grand *foco*" in the eastern Congo where the guerrillas of surrounding countries could come and, by helping in the war to "liberate" the Congo, gain fighting and organizational experience to do battle in their own countries.

"The reaction," Che acknowledged in his Congolese "Pasajes," "was more than cold. Although the majority abstained from any kinds of commentary, there were those who asked to speak to reproach me violently for my advice. They said their people, mistreated and brutalized by imperialism, would demand an accounting if their men died . . . in wars to liberate another State. I tried to make them see that what we were dealing with was not a war waged within national boundaries, but a continental war against the common master, as omnipresent in Mozambique as in Malawi, Rhodesia or South Africa, the Congo or Angola."*

But, Che wrote, nobody in the room agreed with him. "Coldly and courteously they said good-bye." Che was left with the clear impression that Africa faced a long road ahead before it would acquire "a true revolutionary direction." What he was left with, then, was "the task of selecting a group of black Cubans, voluntarily of course, to reinforce the Congolese struggle."

V

In Cairo, Che revealed his Congolese plans to Nasser, according to the Egyptian leader's personal advisor, Muhammad Heikal, but when he mentioned that he was thinking of personally leading the Cuban military expedition, Nasser was alarmed. He told Che it would be a mistake for him to become directly involved in the conflict, that if he thought he could be like "Tarzan, a white man among blacks, leading and protecting them," he was wrong. Nasser felt it was a proposition that could only end badly.

Despite such warnings, the poor reception his strategies had received in Dar-Es-Salaam, his own doubts about the Congolese rebel leaders he had met, and his lack of hard information about the real situation inside the Congo, Che resolved to push ahead with his plans.

Che's last speech on the African continent was also his swan song as a public figure or, as it is sometimes discreetly referred to in Cuba, "*su último cartucho* [his last bullet]." On February 25, in Algiers, speaking before the "Second Economic Seminar of Afro-Asian Solidarity," Che discarded all

---

*See the appendix for elaboration.

ambiguity and called upon the socialist superpowers to disinterestedly support "Third World" liberation movements, and to underwrite the costs of
transforming their underdeveloped nations into socialist societies.

He addressed the forty-odd African and Asian delegations—
representing a colorful array of Third World states, newly independent
nations, and active guerrilla movements—as "brothers." Then "on behalf
of the peoples of America," Che defined the cause that united his part of
the world with theirs as "the common aspiration to defeat imperialism."
Many of those present were from nations either struggling against or
recently freed from old-style colonialism, he noted, while Cuba had triumphed over the other form of imperialism that dominated the Americas—
neocolonialism—the co-option and exploitation of underdeveloped countries
through "monopolistic capital." To prevent this from happening in the new
societies being forged, he declared, it was "imperative to obtain political
power and liquidate the oppressing classes."

"There are no frontiers in this struggle to the death. We cannot remain
indifferent in the face of what occurs in any part of the world. A victory for
any country against imperialism is our victory, just as any country's defeat
is a defeat for us all. The practice of proletarian internationalism is not only
a duty for the peoples who struggle for a better future, it is also an inescapable necessity. . . . If there were no other basis for unity, the common enemy should constitute one."

Therefore, he argued, it was not only in their "vital interest" but a
"duty" of the developed socialist countries to help make the separation between the new underdeveloped nations and the capitalist world effective.
"From all of this," Che said, "a conclusion must be drawn: The development of the countries that now begin the road to liberation must be under-
written by the socialist countries. We say it in this manner without the least
desire to blackmail anyone or to be spectacular. . . . It is a profound conviction. There can be socialism only if there is change in man's consciousness
that will provoke a new fraternal attitude toward humanity on the individual
level in the society that builds or has built socialism and also on a world level
in relation to all the peoples who suffer imperialist oppression."

Having laid the foundation for his argument, Che then launched into
a shocking rebuke of the developed socialist states, for their talk of "mutually beneficial" trade agreements with the poorer ones. "How can 'mutual
benefit' mean selling at world market prices raw materials that cost unlimited sweat and suffering to the backward countries and buying at world
market prices the machines produced in the large automated factories of
today? If we establish that type of relationship between the two groups of
nations, we must agree that the socialist countries are, to a certain extent,

accomplices to imperialist exploitation. It can be argued that the amount of trade with the underdeveloped countries constitutes an insignificant part of the foreign trade of the socialist countries. It is a great truth, but it does not do away with the immoral nature of the exchange. The socialist countries have the moral duty of liquidating their tacit complicity with the West."

To all who were listening, it was clear that Che was directing his attack directly at Moscow, which, along with China, had sent observers to the forum. While he took care to credit both nations for giving Cuba advantageous trade agreements for its sugar exports, he stressed it was only a first step. Prices had to be fixed to permit real development in the poor nations, and this new fraternal concept of foreign trade should be extended by the socialist powers to all underdeveloped nations on the road toward socialism.

It was not the first time Che had criticized what he saw to be the Soviets' capitalist-style "profiteering" in its trade with Cuba or its relationships with other developing nations—his views were widely known among the revolutionary elite in Havana—but it was the first time he had been critical in an international forum. By doing so, he was consciously and willfully pushing the limits, evidently hoping to "shame" Moscow into action—and he wasn't done yet.

He called for a "large compact bloc" of nations to help others liberate themselves from imperialism and from the economic structures it had imposed on them. This meant that weapons from the arms-producing socialist countries should be given "without any cost whatsoever and in quantities determined by their need and availability to those people who ask for them."

Again Che paused to credit the USSR and China for having followed this principle in giving military aid to Cuba, before turning to chastise them once more. "We are socialists, and this constitutes the guarantee of the proper utilization of those arms; but we are not the only one, and all must receive the same treatment." He singled out the beleaguered North Vietnamese— whose country had come under systematic American bombardment just two weeks earlier—and the Congolese as worthy recipients of the "unconditional solidarity" he was demanding.

Not surprisingly, the Soviets were outraged by Che's speech. Calling the Kremlin "an accomplice with imperialism" was an astounding breach of protocol within the socialist bloc, and, considering the degree to which Moscow was already bankrolling Cuba, Che's speech was nothing less than an ungrateful slap in the face.

As Che wound up his long peregrination—from Algiers back to Egypt again before flying on to Prague on March 12—new developments in the Congo seemed to bear out requests by Soumaliot and Kabila for speed in delivering his promised Cuban instructors and arms. The white mercenar-

ies assembled by Mike Hoare had gone into action against the rebels, leading government troops in ground assaults and carrying out aerial bombing
raids. They seized several key outposts and quickly threatened the "liberated territory" along the eastern shore of Lake Tanganyika. If Cuba was
going to throw itself into the Congolese conflict, the time to act would be
very soon.

VI

Just as Kremlinologists looking for signs of power shifts once carefully observed the placement of the Politburo members during Red Square celebrations, Che's reception in Havana following his provocative Algiers speech
was long scrutinized for evidence of either cameraderie or conflict between
him and Fidel.

When Che arrived at Rancho Boyeros airport on March 15, Aleida was
waiting for him, together with Fidel, President Dorticós, and, perhaps most
significantly, Carlos Rafael Rodríguez. Aleida will not speak about what
transpired next, nor has Fidel Castro so spoken, but reports are that Che
went directly from the airport to a closed-door meeting with Fidel that lasted
for many hours. Given the absence of any public disclosure about their dialogue and Che's subsequent disappearance, some skeptical observers have
traditionally interpreted the meeting as the fateful climax to the tensions
that had supposedly built up between the two men. Questioned about this
still-delicate topic, a knowledgeable Cuban government source said elliptically that there were "probably" some "strong words" from Fidel, but that
they would have been less over fundamental differences of opinion than
Che's "tactlessness" in his Algiers speech. In this context, the presence of
Carlos Rafael Rodríguez can probably be interpreted as providing representation on behalf of the ruffled Kremlin.

Historian Maurice Halperin saw it rather differently. "I was astonished
when I read the speech a few days later," wrote Halperin. "When I asked a
high official in the ministry of foreign trade what the meaning was of Che's
blast, he answered with a broad grin: 'It represents the Cuban point of view.'"
Halperin concluded that this was quite likely, considering some of Fidel's
recent remarks and what he knew to be Fidel's "growing annoyances with
Soviet trading methods in the ministry." In the end, Halperin decided that
Fidel's appearance at the airport to welcome Che back to Cuba personally
was his way of showing his approval. Indeed, Che's Algiers speech was later
printed in *Política Internacional,* the official government quarterly, which
would seem to erase any lingering doubts about Fidel's own position.

Indeed, most evidence suggests that Che and Fidel were working in tandem, even coordinating their public remarks. In his January 2 speech for the sixth anniversary of the revolution, Fidel had delivered a strong critique of the Soviet socialist model—though without mentioning it by name—and, for the first time ever to the Cuban people, spoke of "problems" existing within the socialist fraternity of nations. Cuba's people had the right to speak with their own voice, he said, and to interpret the ideas of Marx, Engels, and Lenin according to their own perceptions and conditions, and they should be prepared to survive on their own if the current aid received from abroad were to be abruptly halted. It was an unequivocal message to Moscow that Fidel would not accept Soviet efforts to impose its political model in Cuba.

And on March 13, two days before Che's return to Havana, Fidel had spoken again, this time allusively blasting China and the USSR for their rivalry and demagoguery about supporting "people's liberation," while doing nothing to help the Vietnamese in the face of escalating American military involvement there. "We propose that Vietnam [should] be given all the aid which may be necessary! Aid in weapons and men! Our position is that the socialist camp run whatever risks may be necessary!"

There was, he reminded his audience at Havana University, a recent precedent for the kind of solidarity he was referring to: Cuba itself. During the missile crisis, Cuba had volunteered to face the threat of "thermonuclear war" over its acceptance of Soviet missiles on its soil for the purpose of strengthening the socialist camp. For its part, Fidel proclaimed, Cuba continued to believe its historic duty was to fight against Yankee imperialism and felt a common bond with kindred efforts being made elsewhere in the world.*

As usual, though, Che had gone even further in Algiers than Fidel, saying everything he felt and believed—and damn the consequences. He had issued his challenge, and there was no stepping back from the brink. On a more direct level, he would now show personally how "proletarian internationalism" worked, and let others take his lead. Those remarks, however, made it harder than ever for Fidel to continue defending his "Maoist"

---

*Fidel also alluded to the irritation he felt over the fact that the Chinese and Soviets had brought their rivalries to his island. Again, without naming a nation—but he was referring to China—he decried the efforts being made to circulate unauthorized political propaganda on Cuban soil. Only Cuba's ruling party had the right to issue propaganda, he said, and he warned that he would not tolerate it any longer. Despite his warning, however, this problem had yet to reach its climax. (See the appendix for elaboration.)

friend to the Soviets. The result was that Fidel "suggested" to Che that he leave Cuba immediately and return to Africa, to lead the Cuban guerrilla contingent already in training for the Congo mission. It was not where Che's heart lay, which was in South America, but the conditions there were not yet ready, while the present moment in Africa seemed to offer real revolutionary possibilities. He agreed to go.

According to the Cuban intelligence official Juan Carreterro ("Ariel"), he, his boss Piñeiro, and Fidel himself had all "urged" Che to accept the mission after his return. It would be for only a couple of years, and in the meantime, they promised him, Piñeiro's people would continue building the guerrilla infrastructure in Latin America until conditions were right for him to transfer there. The Congo war would be an invaluable toughening-up exercise for Che's fighters and would provide a useful screening process for those who would go with him afterward to South America. As Piñeiro recalled it, Che didn't need much convincing. "Che came back really enthused by his contacts with the Africans, so Fidel told him: 'Why don't you go to Africa?' He was really restless with the passing of time, and his inability to fulfill [what he saw as] his historic mission."

Events now moved swiftly. On March 22, Che gave a speech in the Ministry of Industries, briefing his colleagues about his African trip but making no announcement that he was leaving. A week later, he visited the *guajiro* veterans from his old sierra column who worked on his Ciro Redondo experimental farm in Matanzas, and told them he would be going off to "cut cane" for a while.

Back in Havana, he assembled some of his closest comrades at the ministry and told them the same story. Very few people knew that Che was making ready to leave Cuba for good, but that was his intention. His return to Havana amounted to a fifteen-day-long disappearing act in which he gradually withdrew from sight, avoiding public contact and saying good-bye to only a selected handful who could be trusted to keep the secret. For the Cuban people at large, Che's well-publicized March 15 airport arrival back from Africa was the last time they would ever see him.

It would also be the last time his children would see him as their father, and the youngest of them would retain no memory of him at all. Once again, Che had been away for the birth of one of his children; on February 24, as he was flying toward Algiers from Cairo, Aleida had given birth to their last child, a boy she had named Ernesto.

Aleida was upset. She asked Che not to go, but his decision was final. However, he promised her that when the revolution was in a more "advanced stage," she could join him.

One day, just before Che left, as he, Aleida, and their nanny Sofía were eating lunch, he asked Sofía what had happened to the widows of the Cubans who had died in the revolution. Had they remarried? Yes, Sofía told him, a lot of them had. Che then turned to Aleida and, pointing to his coffee cup, said: "In that case, this coffee you serve me, may you serve it to another." Forever shaken by her memory of that moment, Sofía understood that Che was giving Aleida his blessing to remarry if he were to die.

At dawn on April 1, he left his home of the past eight years not as Che Guevara, but as a staid-looking, clean-shaven man wearing glasses named Ramón Benítez.

27

The Story of a Failure

I

"One fine day, I appeared in Dar-Es-Salaam," Che wrote. "Nobody knew me; not even the very ambassador [Pablo Ribalta], an old comrade-in-arms . . . could identify me upon my arrival."

Still in disguise, Che had arrived in Dar-Es-Salaam on April 19 after a circuitous journey via Moscow and Cairo. He was accompanied by Papi Tamayo, his roving guerrilla emissary, and Víctor Dreke, the Cuban officer who had been selected as the "official"—and acceptably black—commander of the Cuban internationalist brigade.

Che himself remained anonymous, but he was full of high expectations as he stepped back onto the continent that he had once dreamed of visiting at the end of a ten-year world tour: "Africa for adventuring, and then that's it for the world," he had written his mother a decade earlier. Since then, paradoxically, Che had seen more of the world than he had ever imagined, but too often within the restrictive persona imposed by his role as a government minister and an international personality. Now, as a new chapter in his life opened, Che, in his clandestine disguise, was free once again to be himself—although not without feelings for the life and loved ones he had once again left. As he would later write in his Congo "Pasajes":

"I had left behind almost eleven years of work for the Cuban Revolution at Fidel's side, a happy home—to the extent one can call the house where a revolutionary dedicated to his work lives—and a bunch of kids who barely knew of my love. The cycle was beginning again."

One cycle had begun by breaking away from his family and his roots in Argentina to forge himself as a revolutionary, and had ended with him leaving Hilda and his newborn daughter behind to fulfill his transformation into "Che." He would leave behind even more with the conclusion of his Cuban cycle—his wife Aleida, their children, his Cuban citizenship, his *comandante*'s rank and ministerial position, not to mention friends and comrades, and the shared experiences of a decade of intense life.

II

While they awaited the arrival of more members of the Cuban brigade, who were traveling in various groups using different itineraries, Ribalta housed Che and his two comrades on a little farm he had rented on the outskirts of Dar-Es-Salaam. Pulling out a Swahili dictionary, Che chose new names for the three of them. Dreke was henceforth "Moja" (One); Papi was "Mbili" (Two), and Che himself "Tato" (Three).

In the unexpected absence of Laurent Kabila and the other Congolese rebel leaders, who were away in Cairo for a revolutionary summit meeting, a mid-level Congolese political representative in Dar-Es-Salaam, a young man named Godefroi Chamaleso, was contacted and introduced to the group, told only that they were advance men for the promised Cubans. To explain the unexpected presence of white men in the group, Chamaleso was informed that the man calling himself Tato had been brought along because he was a doctor, spoke French, and was a guerrilla veteran, while Mbili, also white, had come because of his vast and invaluable guerrilla experience.

But this was all a temporary subterfuge, of course, and the decision of when to reveal the group leader's true identity, and to whom, loomed as a genuine dilemma. Che told Chamaleso that the number of Cuban men coming would be greater than that originally planned—130; to his relief, the representative seemed unperturbed. Che then told him that they wanted to enter Congolese territory as soon as possible. While Chamaleso went off to Cairo to inform Kabila of their arrival, still unaware that the man he had met was Che, the trio waited, sending an advance man to arrange for their crossing of Lake Tanganyika as another purchased the supplies they would need—backpacks, blankets, knives, and plastic sheeting—in the city's bazaars.

"I hadn't told any of the Congolese my decision to fight here," Che wrote afterward. "In my first conversation with Kabila I hadn't been able to do so because there had been nothing yet decided, and after the plan was approved [by Fidel] it would have been dangerous for my project to be known before I arrived at my destination; there was a lot of hostile territory to cross. I decided, therefore, to present a fait accompli and act according to however they reacted to my presence. I was not unaware of the fact that a negative would place me in a difficult position, because now I couldn't go back, but I calculated that it would be difficult for them to refuse me. [In essence] I was carrying out a blackmail with my physical presence."

Che was unable to return to Cuba not because of any falling out between himself and Fidel, but because he had made his decision to leave, and it was an irrevocable one. Until now, he had built his reputation by keeping scrupulously to his own word, and nothing conceivable could change that. He had undertaken the same oath of commitment that he had demanded of Masetti's followers as they prepared to leave for Argentina: They should consider themselves dead from that moment on; if they survived, which was doubtful for the majority, they would probably spend the next ten or twenty years of their lives fighting. This was the obligation Che had now assumed for himself.

Indeed, Che had not just "left Cuba," but truly burned his bridges, scribbling a note that Fidel was to make public at what he deemed to be the most opportune moment. It was at once a résumé of their life together, a farewell letter, a deed absolving Cuba's government of any responsibility for his future actions, and a last will and testament:

"Fidel," he began.

> At this moment I remember many things—when I met you in the [Mexico City] house of María Antonia, when you proposed I come along, all the tensions involved in the preparations. One day they came by and asked me who should be notified in case of death, and the real possibility of that fact struck us all. Later we knew it was true, that in revolution one wins or dies (if it is a real one).
>
> Today everything has a less dramatic tone, because we are more mature. But the event repeats itself. I feel that I have fulfilled the part of my duty that tied me to the Cuban revolution in its territory, and I say good-bye to you, to the comrades, to your people, who are now mine.
>
> I formally resign my positions in the leadership of the party, my post as minister, my rank of commander, and my Cuban citizenship. Nothing legal binds me to Cuba. . . .
>
> Recalling my past life, I believe I have worked with sufficient integrity and dedication to consolidate the revolutionary triumph. My only serious failing was not having had more confidence in you from the first moments in the Sierra Maestra, and not having understood quickly enough your qualities as a leader and a revolutionary.*

---

*Che was evidently referring to his brief loss of faith in Fidel in the aftermath of the Miami Pact during the revolutionary war.

I have lived magnificent days, and at your side I felt the pride of belonging to our people in the brilliant yet sad days of the Caribbean [missile] crisis. Seldom has a statesman been more brilliant that you in those days. . . .

Other nations of the world call for my modest efforts. I can do that which is denied you because of your responsibility at the head of Cuba, and the time has come for us to part.

I want it known that I do so with a mixture of joy and sorrow. I leave here the purest of my hopes as a builder and the dearest of my loved ones. And I leave a people who received me as a son. That wounds a part of my spirit. I carry to new battlefronts the faith that you taught me, the revolutionary spirit of my people, the feeling of fulfilling the most sacred of duties: to fight against imperialism wherever one may be. This comforts and more than heals the deepest wounds.

I state once more that I free Cuba from any responsibility except that which stems from its example. If my final hour finds me under other skies, my last thought will be of the people and especially of you. . . . I am not sorry that I leave nothing material to my wife and children. I am happy it is that way. I ask nothing for them, as the state will provide them with enough to live on and to have an education. . . .

Hasta la victoria siempre! Patria o muerte! I embrace you with all my revolutionary fervor.

Che.

Che had also left a letter to be forwarded to his parents:

Dear *viejos:*

Once again I feel under my heels the ribs of Rocinante.* I return to the trail with my shield on my arm. Nothing essential has changed, except that I am more conscious, my Marxism is deeper and more crystallized. I believe in the armed struggle as the only solution for the peoples who fight to free themselves and I am consequent with my beliefs. Many will call me an adventurer, and I am, but of a different type, of those who put their lives on the line to demonstrate their truths.

It could be that this will be the definitive one. I don't go looking for it but it is within the logical calculations of probabilities. If it is to be, then this is my final embrace.

*Rocinante was Don Quixote's horse.

I have loved you very much, only I have not known how to show my love. I am extremely rigid in my actions and I believe that at times you did not understand me. On the other hand, it was not easy to understand me. . . . Now, the willpower that I have polished with an artist's delectation will carry forth my flaccid legs and tired lungs. I will do it.

Remember once in a while this little *condottiere* of the 20th century. . . . A great hug from a prodigal son, recalcitrant for you.

Ernesto.

For Aleida, he left behind a tape recording of his own voice, reciting his favorite love poems to her, including several by Neruda. And to his five children, in a letter to be read to them only after his death, he wrote:

If one day you must read this letter, it will be because I am no longer among you. You will almost not remember me and the littlest ones will remember nothing at all. Your father has been a man who acted according to his beliefs and certainly has been faithful to his convictions.

Grow up as good revolutionaries. Study hard to be able to dominate the techniques that permit the domination of nature. Remember that the Revolution is what is important and that each one of us, on our own, is worthless.

Above all, try always to be able to feel deeply any injustice committed against any person in any part of the world. It is the most beautiful quality of a revolutionary.

Until always, little children. I still hope to see you again. A really big kiss and a hug from Papa.*

As for Hilda *madre,* she may have once been Che's wife, but in recent years their personal contacts had become more formal, mostly limited to Che's visits to see his daughter. Hilda last spoke to him in person on the eve of his trip to address the United Nations in November 1964, when he came to say good-bye to her and Hildita. When Hilda showed Che a letter she had received from his father, saying he was planning to come to Havana soon, Che seemed surprised and concerned and, according to Hilda, blurted out: "Why didn't he come . . . ! What a pity! *Now there's no more time.*"

*See the appendix for elaboration.

She didn't understand what Che was referring to until later, when she realized he must have had his African guerrilla project already in mind. When, months later, he had returned from Algiers, on March 15, his daughter Hildita was at the airport to greet him, and he had brought her home before continuing on immediately with Fidel to Havana. There had been no time to talk with Hilda, but he had told his daughter that he would come back later. "Two or three days later he called and told me he would come to talk to me," Hilda wrote, "but at the last minute he called me again to say that he had to leave for the countryside to cut sugar cane, and that when he came back from the volunteer work, he would visit me." Of course, Hilda never saw him again, and neither did Hildita.*

For a handful of his closest friends, Che had selected books from his office library and written personal dedications inside each of them; he left them on the shelf to be discovered, without saying anything. For his old friend Alberto Granado, he left a book on the history of Cuban sugar, *El Ingenio.* In it, he wrote:

"I don't know what to leave you as a memento. I oblige you, then, to immerse yourself in sugar cane. My house on wheels will have two feet once again and my dreams no frontiers, at least until the bullets have their say. I await you, sedentary gypsy, when the smell of gunpowder dissipates."

To Orlando Borrego, who had asked to go with Che but been refused—his young protégé now had an important job as the minister of sugar, and Che told him his services were too invaluable for him to leave it—he left his three-volume set of *Das Kapital,* and wrote:

"Borrego: This is the wellspring, here we all learned together by trial and error looking for what is still just an intuition. Now that I leave to fulfill my duty and my desire, and you remain behind to fulfill your duty against your desire, I leave you evidence of my friendship, which I rarely expressed in words. Thank you for your constancy and your loyalty. May nothing separate you from the path. A hug, Che."

(Unbeknownst to Che, after he left, Borrego undertook a special mission to honor his mentor: to publish a special edition of Che's collected works, a compendium of his essays, articles, speeches, and letters. It was to be Che's oeuvre, his literary legacy to Cuba, and a means to ensure that the revolutionary principles he stood for survived on the island.)

*Che could not tell Hilda of his secret agenda for a good reason. According to one of his closest friends who was privy to his plans, Hilda had become something of a security risk because of her penchant for playing "fairy godmother" to any Latin American guerrilla who showed up in Havana. Some were genuine, others wannabes, and at least one, a Mexican, was later arrested and unmasked by Cuba's security services as a CIA agent.

For now, Che's farewell letters were secret, but in addition to the Algiers speech that had been his last international public appearance, Che had also left behind one final manifesto that can be described only as his opus. It was a long essay he had written during his three-month journey in Africa and sent off in the form of a letter to the editor of *Marcha,* the Uruguayan weekly, before returning home. "Socialismo y El Hombre Nuevo en Cuba" had appeared in March and, even before Che had vanished, had begun to cause a stir in left-wing circles around the hemisphere. In Cuba, it was published in *Verde Olívo* on April 11 as Che was en route back to Tanzania.

"Socialism and the New Man" was at once the crystallization of Che's doctrinal message and an immensely revealing self-portrait. In it, he reasserted Cuba's right to the "vanguard" role at the helm of Latin American revolution and issued a stinging disquisition challenging the docile application of Soviet dogmas by fellow socialists. In a further critique of the Soviet model, Che reiterated his argument in favor of "moral" as opposed to material incentives.

Che denied that the building of socialism meant the "abolition of the individual." Rather, the individual was the essence of the revolution: the Cuban struggle had depended on those individuals who fought and offered their lives for it. A new notion of self, however, had emerged in the vortex of that struggle—"the heroic stage" that had been attained when those same individuals "vied to achieve a place of greater responsibility, of greater danger, and without any other satisfaction than that of fulfilling their duty . . . In the attitude of our fighters, we could glimpse the man of the future."

When one reads these lines, it is difficult not to feel that Che was rendering his own truth, including others but above all else the account of his *own* revolutionary transformation. And this, really, was the essence of Che's philosophy: believing himself to have achieved the sublimation of his former self, the individual, he had reached a mental state through which he could consciously sacrifice himself for society and its ideals. If he could do it, then so could others.

And finally, Che wrote:

> It must be said with all sincerity that in a true revolution, to which one gives oneself completely, from which one expects no material compensation, the task of the vanguard revolutionary is both magnificent and anguishing.
> Let me say, with the risk of appearing ridiculous, that the true revolutionary is guided by strong feelings of love. It is impossible to think of an authentic revolutionary without this quality. This is perhaps one of the greatest dramas of a leader; he must

combine an impassioned spirit with a cold mind and make painful decisions without flinching one muscle. Our vanguard revolutionaries must idealize their love for the people, for the most sacred causes, and make it one and indivisible. They cannot descend, with small doses of daily affection, to the places where ordinary men put their love into practice.

The leaders of the Revolution have children who do not learn to call their father with their first faltering words; they have wives who must be part of the general sacrifice of their lives to carry the Revolution to its destiny; their friends are strictly limited to their comrades in revolution. There is no life outside it.

In these conditions, one must have a large dose of humanity, a large dose of a sense of justice and truth, to avoid falling into extremes, into cold scholasticism, into isolation from the masses. Every day we must struggle so that this love of living humanity is transformed into concrete facts, into acts that will serve as an example, as a mobilizing factor.

We know that we have sacrifices ahead of us and that we must pay a price for the heroic act of constituting a vanguard as a nation. We, the leaders, know that we must pay a price for having the right to say that we are at the head of the people of America.

Each and every one of us punctually pays his quota of sacrifice, aware of receiving our reward in the satisfaction of fulfilling our duty, conscious of advancing with everyone toward the new man who is glimpsed on the horizon.

III

On April 20, amid mounting rumors that something had "happened" to Che, Fidel broke silence to announce mysteriously that Che was fine, that he was where he would be of "most use to the revolution." It was all he would say.

That same day, Hildita received a letter signed by him. He told her that he was "a little far away," doing some work for which he had been commended, and it would be "a little while" before he could return. He told her to look after her "other" brothers and sisters, and to make sure they did their homework, that he was "always thinking" of her.

At around the same time, Che also had dispatched a clue to his father that he was fine, hinting strongly which part of the world he was in. It was a postcard, mailed after he had left Cuba, which said simply:

"*Viejo:* from the Saharan sun to your [Argentine] fogs. Ernesto renews himself and goes for the third [round]. A hug from your son."

Despite Fidel's reassurances, the rumors as to Che's fate continued to fly. Some of the earliest reports held that Che was in the neighboring country of the Dominican Republic, where a major crisis had erupted within days of his disappearance. U.S. President Lyndon Johnson (who had won the November 1964 election, defeating Republican Barry Goldwater) had dispatched marines to quash an armed leftist uprising there, in the first American military invasion in the Western Hemisphere in decades, and the streets of Santo Domingo had become a battleground between the rebel loyalists of deposed leftist civilian President Juan Bosch and the Dominican military.*

As members of Cuba's secret services have hinted, the "Che in Santo Domingo" rumor may have been one of those generated in Havana; as long as he was en route to the Congo and vulnerable to detection or capture, it was of paramount importance to keep his whereabouts a secret. As time dragged on, new reports would emerge to suggest his presence in Vietnam and an exotic array of other locations, some of them leaked disinformation planted by Cuban intelligence, others probably disseminated by the CIA to cast doubt on the Castro regime. One of the more lurid reports that soon began doing the rounds, however, had a Soviet aroma. It was a supposedly secret memorandum reporting that Che had suffered a psychiatric breakdown and been interned in a mental clinic, where he spent his time reading Trotsky and writing constant letters to Fidel promoting his ideas for creating a "permanent revolution." (The "R Memorandum," as it was known, pointed with alarming proximity toward Che's true location, saying that among the places Che mentioned in his letters was Zanzibar, where it was possible to "work with the Chinese.")

Indeed, as Sergo Mikoyan recalled, the initial reports trickling through Moscow held that there had been a confrontation between Fidel and Che, and the rumor was that Che had been exiled or punished. "The general opinion among the apparatchiks was that there had been a fight between Fidel and Che. Or maybe not a fight, but that Fidel didn't want Che in Cuba—that he wanted to be the only leader, and that Che was in competition with him." Mikoyan stressed that he, for one, had never given credence to this scenario. "I knew them both and I knew that Che was absolutely unambitious. . . . He would not even imagine competing with Fidel [for leadership].

---

*The fighting was soon ended, and the U.S. and allied Latin American troops that had intervened were eventually withdrawn after a OAS-mediated cease-fire agreement and the scheduling of new elections, which were held in 1966. Bosch lost to his rightist rival, Joaquín Balaguer, who dominated his country's politics as on-and-off again president for the next thirty years.

That version seemed ridiculous and I didn't believe it. But our people thought of Stalin and Trotsky, then Khrushchev and Brezhnev, who were always fighting—and they thought it was the same thing [in Cuba]."

Soviet Ambassador Alexandr Alexiev had also heard the rumors, but by now he knew better. In March, Fidel had invited him to a special event: He planned to lead a volunteer labor brigade composed of the revolutionaries to cut sugarcane in Camagüey. When, after Che's return from Algiers, Alexiev learned that Che would not be part of the Camagüey ceremony, Alexiev began wondering himself if the rumors of a split were true.

Then Che had vanished, and the rumor mill picked up momentum. At Camagüey, Fidel had taken Alexiev for a walk out of earshot of their camp. "Alejandro," Fidel told him, "you have probably noted Che's absence. He is in Africa, he went to stay there, to organize a [revolutionary] movement. But I am telling you just for yourself. By no means should you communicate this [with the Kremlin] by cable."

Alexiev interpreted Fidel's warning to mean that he should put nothing in *writing* that might be witnessed by third parties and somehow leak out, but Alexiev was duty-bound to inform his government, and he did. Thirty years after the fact, he found it difficult to recall exactly how he had passed the information along—he believed it was with "someone of great trust" who had come to Havana in a Soviet delegation—but he stressed that he had put nothing "in writing." Then, during a return visit to Moscow, Alexiev followed up by informing Leonid Brezhnev in person.*

In light of the recent deterioration in relations between Havana and Moscow, Fidel's whispered confidence to Alexiev about Che's mission was a discreet hint to Moscow that Fidel remained privately loyal despite his public bearbaiting; Che might be off assisting a predominantly Chinese-backed revolutionary faction in the Congo, but that should not affect the relations between the Kremlin and Havana. Indeed, Fidel may have been hoping that with his overture, and by presenting the Soviets with a fait accompli, he might elicit an appropriate response from the new Kremlin Politburo—already giving some aid to the Congolese rebels—in the form of direct support for Cuba's own African guerrilla program. At about the same time that Fidel revealed the secret to Alexiev, the advance column of that initiative, led by Che, was preparing to go into action.

*Alexiev said that Brezhnev "did not seem very interested" in what he told him, and gave few additional details of their meeting. But Alexiev hinted that Brezhnev would not have let the matter become an issue affecting relations with Cuba, saying: "[Brezhnev] was *with* Fidel; he was trying to capitalize on Fidel's [past] friendship with Khrushchev and have the same [kind of relationship]."

IV

At dawn on the morning of April 24, Che and thirteen Cubans set foot on the Congolese shore of Lake Tanganyika. Behind them lay an expanse of fifty kilometers (thirty miles) of water, separating them from the safety of Tanzania and its vast open savannah extending to the Indian Ocean, land they had traversed in two days and nights by car from Dar-Es-Salaam. Above them loomed the western edge of the Great Rift Valley, a green jungle escarpment rising steeply from the lakeshore. Beyond lay the vast "liberated" territory held by the rebels. Its northern "front line" began 170 kilometers to the north, at the town of Uvira on Lake Tanganyika's northern shore, bordering Burundi, their fallback position since losing the town of Bukavu farther up the Rift Valley, where the frontiers of the Congo, Rwanda, and Burundi meet. From there, the rebels' writ ran south for a hundred kilometers to the place where Che and his men now stood in the lakeside village of Kibamba. Inland, the territory extended through the forest for two hundred kilometers as far as Kasongo on the Lualaba River, on the northern edge of Katanga province. Altogether, it was a domain that mercenary leader Mike Hoare likened in size to Wales, a region of open plains and jungle mountains bisected by untamed rivers, where herds of elephants still roamed, and a complex mosaic of tribal peoples lived off the land as subsistence farmers and hunter-gatherers. It contained few roads or towns, and the handful of inhabited dots on the map consisted of native villages, isolated former Belgian colonial garrisons, missions, and trading posts.

Godefroi Chamaleso, the political commissar from Dar-Es-Salaam, had come to help smooth the way for the Cubans; so far, he was Che's only official link to the revolutionaries he had come to whip into shape. Kabila had not appeared but stayed on in Cairo, sending word that he would return in a fortnight, and in his absence Che had been forced to remain "incognito." "To be honest," he acknowledged later, "I wasn't too upset [about it] because I was very interested in the war in the Congo and I was afraid that my appearance would provoke overly sharp reactions, and that some of the Congolese, or even the friendly [Tanzanian] government, would ask me to abstain from joining in the fray."

So far, so good. But already, in Kigoma, the Tanzanian port on the eastern shore of the lake, Che had seen the first evidence that the Congolese rebels he was joining were undisciplined and badly led. A local Tanzanian official had complained to him about the rebels, who regularly crossed the lake to hang out and disport themselves in its bars and whorehouses. Also, he had had to wait for a day and a night while a boat was made ready for their crossing—nothing had been prepared for him despite his advance man's efforts. Then, after crossing the lake to Kibamba on the opposite side, he found that the rebels' general staff headquarters was a mere stone's throw up the mountainside from the lake, too conveniently close to the village and the "safety valve" of Tanzania for his liking.

In Kabila's absence, Che found himself dealing with a group of "field commanders," the men calling the shots in the various "army brigades" stationed around the rebel zone. Fortunately, some of them spoke French, which allowed Che to discern immediately that serious divisions existed among them. In their first meeting with the rebel commanders, Chamaleso enthusiastically tried to help establish a rapport between his compatriots and the newcomers by proposing that the Cubans' "leader," Víctor Dreke, along with another Cuban of his choosing, be allowed to join in all the meetings and decisions of the general staff. But the Congolese officers were eloquently noncommittal. "I observed the faces of the participants," Che noted dryly, "and I could not see approval for the proposal; it seemed that [Chamaleso] did not enjoy the sympathies of the chiefs."

The commanders' displeasure with Chamaleso derived from the fact that he visited the front from Dar-Es-Salaam only occasionally, and the military men felt neglected by the head office. There was additional ill feeling between those commanders who stayed in the field and those constantly leaving on endless errands to Kigoma and its sundry fleshpots. The rank-and-file fighters, for the most part, were simple peasants who spoke only their own tribal languages, or, in some cases, Swahili, and who seemed to Che to inhabit a world completely apart from their officers.

Still another unpleasant surprise for Che was to discover the rebels' widespread faith in witchcraft. Called *dawa,* it consisted of a "magic" potion that they believed protected them from harm. Che learned about this magic in his very first meeting with the Congolese command from a pleasant-seeming officer who introduced himself as "Lieutenant Colonel Lambert." Che wrote: "With a festive air, [Lambert] explained to me that for them, the [enemy] airplanes were not very important because they possessed the 'DAWA,' a medicine which makes them invulnerable to bullets."

Lambert went on to assure Che that he had been hit by bullets several times, but because of the *dawa,* they had fallen harmlessly to the ground. "He explained it between smiles," wrote Che, "and I felt obliged to go along with the joke, which I believed was his attempt to demonstrate the little importance he conceded to the enemy's armaments. After a little while, I realized the thing was serious, and that the magical protector was one of the great victory weapons of the Congolese Army." Che evidently absorbed Lambert's revelation with diplomatic aplomb, but very soon he would have cause to worry, for *dawa* was to be one of the most bedeviling obstacles he faced in carrying out his mission to create a revolutionary New Man in Africa.

After the inconclusive initial meeting with the commanders, Che took Chamaleso aside and revealed his true identity. "I explained who I was," Che wrote. "The reaction was devastating. He repeated the phrases 'international scandal' and 'no one must know, please, no one must know'; it had fallen like a lightning bolt in a serene day and I feared for the consequences, but my identity could not continue hidden much longer if we wanted to take advantage of the influence that my activity here could have."

After the shaken Chamaleso left, heading back to Dar and once again to Cairo, this time to inform Kabila of Che's presence, Tato attempted to get his training program under way. He tried to convince the Congolese jefes to let him and his men set up a permanent base more adequate for their mission on the Lualaborg ridge, five kilometers above them, but the commanders stalled, telling him that the base commander was away in Kigoma and nothing could be done until he returned. In lieu of that, they suggested he begin an ad hoc training program there at the Kabimba headquarters. Che countered with a proposal to train a hundred-man column divided into groups of twenty men over a five- or six-week period, then send them out with Mbili (Papi) on patrol to carry out some military actions; while they were gone, he could train a second column, which would enter the field when the first group returned. After each expedition he could select the truly worthwhile guerrilla cadres to build up an effective guerrilla force. This proposal too was met with evasions.

The days began rolling by. Boats came and went across the lake, carrying rebels to and from furloughs in Kigoma, but the base commander didn't return. For wont of anything better to do, Che began helping out in the rebels' clinic, where one of the Cubans, a doctor rebaptized as "Kumi," had begun working. Che was stunned by the number of cases of venereal disease among the rebels, which he attributed to their Kigoma visits. A few wounded men were brought in from the various fronts, but they were accidents, not battle-casualties. "Almost nobody had the least idea of what a firearm was," Che recalled. "They shot themselves by playing with them, or by carelessness." The rebels also drank a local corn- and yucca-based brew called *pombe,* and the spectacle of reeling men having fights or disobeying orders was distressingly commonplace.

Hearing of the presence of "doctors" in the area, local peasants began showing up in droves at the dispensary. Their depleting stocks got a boost with the arrival of a cargo of Soviet medicines, unceremoniously dumped on the beach along with a great pile of ammunition and weaponry, but when Che asked for permission to organize the rebels' logistics depot, that request also fell on deaf ears. Meanwhile, the beach acquired the appearance of a "gypsy market," Che wrote, as rebel commanders began arriving and demanding quantities of the newly arrived medicines for "fabulous sums of men." One officer claimed he had four thousand troops, another said two thousand, and so on, but they were "all invented numbers."

By early May, Che had received word that the rebel council's Cairo summit had been a success, but that Kabila wouldn't be returning just yet; he needed to have an operation on a cyst, and it would be several more weeks before he was back. Che and his men were beginning to feel the first symptoms of malaise brought on by their inactivity, and to keep them occupied, Che began daily classes in French, Swahili, and "general culture." "Our morale was still high," Che recalled, "but already the murmurs were beginning among the comrades about how the days were fruitlessly slipping by."

The next afflictions to hit them were malaria and tropical infections. Che handed out antimalarial tablets regularly, but observed that their side effects included symptoms of weakness, apathy, and lack of appetite, and he later blamed the medication for exacerbating the feelings of "incipient pessimism" felt by the Cubans, including, although he was loathe to admit it, himself.

In the meantime, Che was getting an ongoing private debriefing about the situation inside the rebel movement from an informant called Kiwe. Kiwe was one of the more voluble general staff officers, "an inexhaustible talker who spoke French at almost supersonic speed" and who had plenty to confide. As was his longtime habit, Che wrote pithy little profiles laced with his own remarks based on Kiwe's information.

Of "General" Nicholas Olenga, the military "liberator" of Stanleyville, Kiwe claimed he had been just a soldier whom he had personally dispatched to make some explorations in the north; Olenga had then begun launching attacks, giving himself a new military rank with each town he seized.

The current president of the rebel council, Christophe Gbenye, was the political leader for whom "General" Olenga had "liberated" Stanleyville, but to Kiwe, Gbenye was a dangerous, immoral figure; he held him responsible for an assassination attempt against Laurent Mitoudidi, the currrent council military chief of staff. As for Antoine Gizenga, one of the early revolutionary figures to emerge in the wake of Lumumba's death, Kiwe declared him a left-wing opportunist who was interested more than anything else in using the rebel effort to build his own political party. As Che wrote afterward, the chats with Kiwe had been enlightening, giving him an idea of the complex internal rivalries within the not so very revolutionary Congolese Liberation Council.

On May 8, Laurent Mitoudidi, the rebel chief of staff, finally arrived, bringing eighteen new Cubans with him, and word from Kabila that for the time being, Che's identity should remain a secret. Mitoudidi left almost immediately, but for the first time since meeting Kabila, Che was favorably impressed with a Congolese officer, finding him "assured, serious and possessing an organizational spirit." Even better, Mitoudidi approved Che's transfer to the "upper base" on Lualaborg mountain.

Che took his men up the mountain to the huge grassy plateau that began at the top of the escarpment. It was four hard hours of steep hiking and took them up to a chilly and damp altitude two thousand seven hundred meters (over 8,000 feet) above sea level, but as Che looked around and surveyed the scene, he felt the spark of renewed optimism. Herds of cattle and the tiny hamlets of ethnic Tutsi Rwandan herdsmen dotted the plain; good Argentine that he was, Che wrote that during his stay there, the availability of "wonderful beef was almost a cure for nostalgia."

Che quickly began getting organized, overseeing the building of huts to house his fighters, together with about twenty bored and lonely Congolese. Once again he began daily classes to cut through the mounting apathy and listlessness that threatened to consume them, but very soon Che became aware of still more problems he would have to deal with. In addition to the civilian herdsmen living around Lualaborg, he learned, there were several thousand more Tutsis living in the area who were armed and had allied themselves with the Congolese rebels. They had fled their country following Rwanda's independence from France a few years earlier, when their traditional rivals, the Hutus, had begun massacring them. By helping the Congolese to victory, they hoped next to carry the revolution to Rwanda, but despite their marriage of convenience, the Rwandans and Congolese didn't get along at all, and this emnity, like *dawa,* was to cause serious problems in the months ahead.

After only a few days, Che succumbed to an extremely high fever and became delirious. It was a month before he regained his strength or his appetite. He was not the only man affected; ten of the thirty Cubans were ill with one fever or another. "During the first month, at least a dozen comrades paid for their initiation into hostile territory with these violent fevers," Che wrote, "the aftereffects of which were so bothersome."

Coinciding with Che's return to health, Laurent Mitoudidi arrived back with ambitious orders for him to lead an attacking force of two rebel columns against the enemy bastion at Albertville. "The order is absurd," wrote Che at the time. "There's only 30 of us, of whom 10 are sick or convalescing." But despite his strong misgivings, Che didn't want to start out on the wrong foot, and so he told his men to prepare themselves for battle.

On May 22, as they were thus engaged, a Congolese runner arrived in camp announcing excitedly that "a Cuban minister" had arrived. By now,

Che was accustomed to hearing all sorts of wild rumors, the Congolese having a "Radio Bemba" bush telegraph every bit as florid as Cuba's own, but shortly afterward he was stunned to see none other than Osmany Cienfuegos appear before him at the head of a fresh contingent of seventeen new Cubans. A further seventeen had remained behind in Kigoma, awaiting transport to cross the lake. It brought the number of Cuban guerrillas on hand to more than sixty.

"In general, the news [Osmany] brought was very good," wrote Che afterward. "But he brought for me personally the saddest news of the war: through telephone conversations from Buenos Aires, they informed me that my mother was very sick, with a tone that indicated that this was just a preparatory announcement. . . . I had to wait for a month in that sad uncertainty, awaiting the results of something I could guess but with the hope that the report had been a mistake, until the confirmation of my mother's demise arrived. . . . She never saw the farewell letter that I had left in Havana for my parents."*

The fact that Che even included something so personal in his account is an indication of how deeply the episode had affected him, but "sad uncertainty" was an understatement. Among Che's personal belongings that later came into Aleida's possession were three pieces of writing, rather like short stories, all very dark and anguished, written in that same tortured symbolism of some of his youthful literary efforts, expressing his grief over the loss of Celia *madre*.**

In fact, Celia had died on May 19, three days before Osmany arrived in Che's base camp. At the age of fifty-eight she had succumbed to cancer, as many of her siblings already had and would do later. Toward the end, she had been living alone in her little apartment adjoining her daughter Celia's, meeting with her small circle of friends during the week, and seeing her children and grandchildren on the weekends. Few people around her realized she was ill, and according to her daughter-in-law María Elena Duarte, she had intentionally concealed it until the very end, when she collapsed and nothing remained but the deathwatch.

On May 10 Celia was taken to the exclusive Stapler Clinic of Buenos Aires, where she was placed in a private room with a large picture window. When María Elena visited her, she would find her mother-in-law staring

---

*Che noted that the letter to his parents was released only in October 1965, when Fidel finally broke silence and publicly divulged Che's farewell letter to him.

**Despite repeated requests by the author to review these stories, Aleida refused, arguing that they were "too intimate" to show anyone.

out the window with a look of rapturous longing: "All I ask for," Celia said, "is one more day."

Friends such as Ricardo Rojo and Julia "Chiquita" Constenla rallied around, visiting with Celia and taking turns at her bedside. Desperate to help despite their long estrangement, her ex-husband, Ernesto *padre,* rushed around to find some way to save her, even going to the Russian embassy after hearing the Soviets had discovered a cancer cure. His presence must have comforted Celia during these final days because, as she confided to María Elena, he had been the first and only man in her life, and despite everything, she still felt love for him.

But the specter of Che interrupted even now. When the clinic's management made evident their displeasure over having the mother of a prominent "Communist" in their facility, the family moved her to another clinic.

Celia's final thoughts were for her son Ernesto. She begged Ricardo and Julia to call Havana and ask Aleida where he was. Back in March, Che's childhood friend Gustavo Roca had been in Havana and carried a letter from him to Celia in which he had told her he was about to resign his jobs, go cut cane for a month, and then work in one of the Ministry of Industries factories in order to study things from the ground level. But Celia had not received the letter until April 13, by which time Che had vanished and all kinds of rumors had begun to circulate; Celia was unsettled, and even more upset by the letter. The next day, she wrote a reply to Che, which Ricardo Rojo agreed to send to Havana with a trusted friend.

A few days later, Rojo found out that the friend who was to carry Celia's letter to Havana had been refused a Cuban visa. Celia asked him to hold onto the letter until he could find a new courier to convey it.

On May 16, with Celia's death imminent and her anxiety about Che unresolved, Rojo called Havana to talk to Aleida and find out what he could, but Aleida could say nothing except that Che wasn't there and wasn't in a place where she could contact him quickly. On April 18 Aleida called back and spoke to Celia. Rojo was present, and he wrote: "Celia was in a near-coma, but she sat up in bed as if an electric shock had run through her. It was a frustrating conversation, with a great deal of shouting and a sense of hopelessness."

Celia learned nothing new from the conversation, and so, in a final, futile effort, Rojo sent off a cable addressed to "Major Ernesto Guevara, Ministry of Industries, Havana." "Your mother very ill wants to see you. Your friend embraces you. Ricardo Rojo." No reply came, and the next day Celia passed away.

Celia's last letter to her son was finally made public in Rojo's book, *My Friend Che,* released three years later. In it, Celia expressed her disquiet over her son's fate, obviously assuming that there was truth, after all, to the rumors that he and Fidel had had a falling-out.

My dear one:

Do my letters sound strange to you? I don't know if we have lost the naturalness with which we used to speak to each other, or if we never had it and have always spoken with that slightly ironic tone used by those of us from the shores of the [Río de la] Plata, exaggerated by our own private family code. . . .

Since we have adopted this diplomatic tone in our correspondence, I . . . have to find hidden meanings between the lines and try to interpret them. I've read your last letter the way I read the news . . . , solving, or trying to, the real meanings and full implication of every phrase. The result has been a sea of confusion, and even greater anxiety and alarm.

I'm not going to use diplomatic language. I'm going straight to the point. It seems to me true madness that, with so few heads in Cuba with ability to organize, you should all go cut cane for a month . . . when there are so many and such good cane cutters among the people. . . . A month is a long time. There must be reasons I don't know. Speaking now of your own case, if, after that month, you're going to dedicate yourself to the management of a factory, a job successfully performed by [Alberto] Castellanos and [Harry] Villegas, it seems to me that the madness has turned to absurdity. . . .

And this is not a mother speaking. It's an old woman who hopes to see the whole world converted to socialism. I believe that if you go through with this, you will not be giving your best service to the cause of world socialism.

If all roads in Cuba have been closed to you, for whatever reason, in Algiers there's a Mr. Ben Bella who would appreciate your organizing his economy, or advising him on it; or a Mr. Nkrumah in Ghana who would welcome the same help. Yes, you'll always be a foreigner. That seems to be your permanent fate.

At her funeral service, Che's framed photograph sat prominently upon her coffin, and María Elena recalled how badly she felt for Celia's other children: "It was as if they weren't there, that Celia had only one child—Che." And in a way, as painful as it must have been for the others, the perception was true. That special bond that had always linked, Celia and her firstborn son, Ernesto, to some degree had excluded the others and endured, obvious to everyone, right through to the end.

V

Still recovering from Osmany's ill tidings, Che sat down with Laurent Mitoudidi to discuss their military plans. He managed to convince Mitoudidi that an attack on Albertville was premature, that they first needed to find out the real situation existing in the different sectors of the front. He didn't know the true picture, and neither did the general staff, depending as it did upon the reports of its far-flung field commanders, who, as Che was learning, were often unreliable. Mitoudidi finally agreed with Che's proposal to send out four groups of guerrillas to the various front lines.

Che immediately dispatched some of his men and within days began getting the first reports back. At a couple of the fronts, the men seemed well armed and disposed to fight, but everywhere there was inaction and general chaos. The jefes were often found drinking themselves to the point of stupefaction, passing out in full view of their troops as if it were a normal pastime. Enjoying control of the roads, the rebels raced back and forth in jeeps, but did little to further the war effort. They occupied fixed positions, did no training, did not patrol or gather intelligence, and forced the intimidated local peasants to supply them with food. The peasants were often afraid of the rebels, for, as Che noted, they frequently suffered "outrages and mistreatment" at their hands. "The characteristic of the Popular Liberation Army," Che concluded, "was that of a parasitic army."

Che was also finding the Congolese to be lazy. During marches, they carried nothing except their personal weapons, cartridges, and blankets, and if asked to help carry an extra load, whether food or some other item, they would refuse, saying: *"Mimi hapana Motocar"* (I am not a truck). As time wore on, they began saying: *"Mimi hapana Cuban"* (I am not a Cuban). The majority of the Cubans quickly developed an extremely low opinion of their Congolese comrades.

On the Lulimba front, Víctor Dreke found that the rebels were holding a hilltop position seven kilometers (about four miles) from the enemy post and had not descended from it in months. Instead of launching raids, they spent their days firing off a huge 75 mm recoilless rifle in the general direction of the enemy, far out of range. The chief of this front, the self-proclaimed "General Mayo," had manifested open hostility to both Kabila and Mitoudidi, seeing them as "foreigners." Mitoudidi had ordered Mayo to come and see him, but the man had refused.

Meanwhile, at Lualaborg, Mitoudidi did his best to whip his men into shape, punishing the *pombe* drinkers by burying them in the earth up to their necks, suspending the distribution of arms, and giving stern lectures. At Che's mention that he felt isolated from the Congolese rank and file because of the language barrier, Mitoudidi lent him one of his own aides, a teenaged boy named Ernesto Ilanga, to give him daily Swahili classes.

By early June Che was getting increasingly claustrophobic, and described the tedium he felt and the unending view from the camp, framed by two peaks that allowed him to see only a small piece of the lake below, as "hateful." He sent out more exploration groups, but without the approval of Mitoudidi's superior officer, Laurent Kabila, they could undertake no action on their own. There was an erratic flow of notes from Kabila, saying that he was about to come, that he was delayed, that he would arrive tomorrow without fail, or the day after. "And boats kept arriving with good quantities of arms of great quality," wrote Che. "It was really pathetic to observe how they wasted the resources of the friendly countries, fundamentally China and the Soviet Union, the efforts of Tanzania, the lives of some fighters and civilians, to do so little with it."

On June 7, Che saw Mitoudidi off down at the Kibamba base; the general staff camp was being moved to a new spot a short distance down the lake shore, and Mitoudidi was going to inspect it. Before they parted, Che asked Mitoudidi what the truth was behind Kabila's nonappearance; Mitoudidi confessed that the commander probably wouldn't be visiting just yet, since the Chinese premier Chou En-lai was coming to Dar, and Kabila had to meet him to discuss aid requests he had made.

Che headed back up the mountain, but even before he had reached the top, a messenger caught up with him to report Mitoudidi's death by drowning. It was a major blow, for Che had come to see Mitoudidi as his best hope for achieving anything at all in the Congo. In "Pasajes," Che titled the chapter in which he wrote of this death as "A Hope Dies," and indeed, the murky circumstances of Laurent Mitoudidi's demise seemed to sum up everything that was wrong about this "revolution" Che had come to assist.

According to a couple of Cubans who had been out in the boat with Mitoudidi, the lake had been choppy with a strong wind blowing, and Mitoudidi had apparently fallen into the water "by accident." But what he heard made Che suspicious. "From that moment on a series of strange events occurred, which I don't know whether to attribute to imbecility, to the extraordinary degree of superstition—since the lake is populated by all kinds of spirits—or something more serious." Mitoudidi had remained afloat and calling for help for ten or fifteen minutes, but two other men who dove in to save him had drowned. Meanwhile, the men in the boat had cut the engine, and when they restarted it, "it seemed that some magical force did not permit them to go to where Mitoudidi was; in the end, as he was still crying for help, the boat was steered to the shore and the comrades watched him disappear a little while later."

Tragic as it was, the setback of Mitoudi's death had to be overcome. In late June, after two months of doing "absolutely nothing," the Cubans' war in the Congo finally began. Mudandi, a Chinese-trained Rwandan Tutsi rebel commander, arrived from Dar, and he had brought battle orders from Kabila: The plan to attack Albertville had been scrapped, and Che was now to launch an assault on the military garrison and hydroelectric plant at Fort Bendera instead. Kabila wanted the Rwandans and Cubans to lead the raiding party, which should take place in a week's time. Che was not enthusiastic about the plan. He had heard from Mudandi's Tutsis that the Bendera garrison was well entrenched, with as many as 300 defending soldiers and 100 white mercenaries. It seemed too large a target for his ill-prepared force, much less the Congolese. He proposed a smaller target, but in the end decided to go ahead with Kabila's plan, reasoning that any action at all was better than none. But after sending repeated requests to Kabila to be allowed to accompany the attack force himself as a mere "political commissar" and receiving no reply, Che was forced to stay behind; in late June the column of 40 Cubans and 160 Congolese and Rwandan Tutsis set out for Bendera.

The June 29 attack they launched was a catastrophe. The assault leader, Víctor Dreke, reported that at the first outbreak of combat, many of the Tutsis had fled, abandoning their weapons, while many of the Congolese had simply refused to fight at all. Over a third had deserted before the fighting had even begun. What's more, four Cubans were killed, and one of the men's diaries had fallen into enemy hands. This meant that the mercenaries and the American CIA—which had sent anti-Castro Cuban exiles to fly bombing and reconnaissance missions for the government forces—now knew that Cubans were directly assisting the rebels. Indeed, as the mercenary commander Mike Hoare wrote later, the unusually audacious rebel attack had led him to suspect the rebels were getting outside help; the captured diary, which among other things mentioned a Havana-Prague-Peking travel itinerary, was his first conclusive proof of a Cuban guerrilla presence in the region.

As Che took stock of the fiasco, he found himself confronting the pernicious *dawa* in all its vigor. The Africans were attributing their defeat to "bad *dawa*," and said that their own witch doctor, or *muganga,* who had applied it to the fighters beforehand, had been "inadequate." Wrote Che: "[The witch doctor] tried to defend himself blaming it on women and on fear, but there were no women there . . . and not all the men were prepared to confess their weaknesses. It didn't look good for the witch doctor and he was demoted."

After the Bendera debacle, the Congolese and Rwandans were humilated and demoralized, but the Cubans who had participated were furious; if the Congolese wouldn't fight for themselves, why should they? The spirit of "proletarian internationalism" was something Che had taken to heart with profound personal conviction, but under these adverse circumstances it was evident that not all his Cuban comrades had the same level of commitment, and a number were overheard saying they wanted to return home.

"The symptoms of decomposition among our troops were palpable," admitted Che. "Maintaining the morale [of the Cubans] was one of my main worries." Hoping for some action, he fired off a letter to the general staff officers in Kibamba, expressing his irritation over the Bendera performance and demanding to know what he was supposed to do with the new Cubans who were arriving. He also wrote to Kabila, arguing that he needed to be allowed to join personally in future military operations.

Summing up the month of June, Che wrote in his diary: "The balance [of the month] is the poorest yet. Just when everything seemed to indicate we were beginning a new era, the death of Mitoudidi occurred, and the uncertainties have grown. The exodus [of fighters] toward Kigoma continues, Kabila has announced his entry on repeated occasions and has never done so; the disorganization is total."

While a steady stream of wounded men were carried back from the battle zone, a fourth group of Cubans arrived at the lakeside Kibamba base. Among the thirty-nine men was Harry Villegas, Che's young former bodyguard, who had been with him since the Sierra Maestra and who had been left out of Masetti's mission because he was black. Fidel had handpicked Villegas to provide personal security for Che, and to make sure he came to no harm in the Congo. Villegas had recently married one of Che's secretaries, a pretty Chinese-mulatta girl named Cristina Campuzano, but had left her and their newborn son to be with his jefe and teacher. Harry was now renamed "Pombo," a pseudonym that in time would become more famous than his own real name.

Che took advantage of the newcomers' arrival to give a pep talk and a warning at the same time, appealing to the Cubans' spirit of *"combatividad"* to try to quash the growing dissension. "I emphasized the need to maintain a rigid discipline," he wrote. He went on to publicly criticize one of the Cubans for making "defeatist remarks." "I was very explicit about what we faced; not just hunger, bullets, suffering of all kinds, but, also, in some opportunities, the possibility of death from our own [African] comrades who didn't have a clue how to shoot properly. The struggle would be long and difficult; I made this warning because at that moment I was prepared to accept that any of the newcomers air their doubts and return [to Cuba] if they so desired; afterward it would not be possible."

None of the newcomers showed "signs of weakness," but to his dismay, three of the men who had been in the Bendera attack did. "I recriminated with them for their attitude and warned them that I would request the strongest sanctions against them."

Che's sense of indignation turned into one of personal betrayal when "Sitaini," one of his bodyguards for the past six years, and a man who had been with him since the sierra, asked to leave as well. Wrote Che: "What made it even more painful was that he used phoney arguments about not having heard what I had warned everyone, that the war would last at best three years and with bad luck five. The duration and harshness of the war had been one of my constant litanies and Sitaini knew it better than anyone because he was always with me. I told him that he couldn't leave because it would be a discredit to both of us; he was obliged to stay."

From that moment on, wrote Che, Sitaini was like a "dead man." A couple of months later, Che allowed him to leave, but evidently he didn't speak to him again, and people in Cuba who know him say Sitaini has never recovered from his precipitous and humiliating fall from grace.

More bad news had come from farther afield. On June 19, a coup had toppled his friend, Algerian president Ben Bella, and the coup leader had been none other than Ben Bella's own defense minister, Houari Boumedienne. It boded ill for the Cuban operations in Africa; Algeria was an essential partner in the multilateral effort to support the Congolese rebels against the Western-backed regime in Leopoldville. With Fidel's angry early reaction, condemning the coup and its new leadership, the hard-won "unity" between the two revolutionary states appeared to have come apart in one fell swoop.

Before Che had even had a chance to organize an effective fighting force, everything seemed to break down. With Mitoudidi dead, he was forced to deal with men who had little political schooling or sense of mission, and even less fighting spirit. And, after three months in the field, Kabila still hadn't shown up. Lately the Congolese commander had taken to sending barbed little notes urging Che to buck up, to "have courage and patience," patronizingly reminding him that he was "a revolutionary and had to withstand such difficulties," and of course repeating the message that he would soon be coming.

Che must have been furious, but he was exquisitely diplomatic in his responses, reiterating his respect and loyalty, both to the Congolese cause and to Kabila as "his" commander, merely stressing that he needed to talk to him and offering him an apology over his covert manner of showing up. Che included this mollifier because he now strongly suspected Kabila of resenting his presence, and feared this might be the reason the commander had not come to the front. "There are serious indications that my presence doesn't give him the least pleasure," observed Che. "It is yet to be known whether this is due to fear, jealousy, or wounded feelings over the method [I employed in coming]."

Meanwhile, the mercenary-led government troops had begun to probe deeper into rebel territory, sending spotter planes over the lake and launching strafing runs against boat traffic and the lakeshore base at Kibamba. It caused alarm at the general staff headquarters, and in response to their plea for help, Che begrudgingly dispatched some of his Cubans to man the heavy machine guns in order to provide some antiaircraft defense.

"My state of mind was very pessimistic in those days," Che acknowledged, "but I climbed down with a certain happiness on July 7 when it was announced that Kabila had arrived. At last the Jefe was in the field of operations!"

Kabila had indeed come, and brought with him a commander to replace Mitoudidi, Ildefonse Masengo. But, in a further sign that all was not well within the rebel leadership, Kabila had even worse things to say this time about Gaston Soumaliot, his political leader, calling him a demagogue, among other things. He returned to Tanzania after only five days, however, explaining that it was important he meet with Soumaliot to work out their problems. For a few days Kabila's presence had galvanized his troops. Enthused by his presence, the Congolese had set to work digging antiaircraft trenches and building a new clinic, but when he left—some jaundiced Cubans had taken bets on how long he would stay—everything fell apart again; the Congolese put down their shovels and refused to work.

In fact, an internal power struggle was taking place between the political leaders who made up the Liberation Council, each of whom drew strength from alleged power on the military battlefield via a series of shifting alliances with various regional guerrilla commanders. These men were the visible faces of the Congolese rebellion to the outside world—holding summits, meeting with heads of state such as Nasser, Nyerere, and Chou En-lai—and they had also become the privileged recipients of huge amounts of foreign aid. The Chinese were still the primary supplier of the rebels' arms and, in some areas, even of military advisors, but the Soviets and Bulgarians were also competing, funneling in aid such as the Soviet medicines Che had seen dumped on the lakeshore, and all three nations were providing military and political training courses in their countries to Congolese fighters.

There were new problems at the front as well, with relations between the Rwandan Tutsis and the Congolese falling to an all-time low. Mudandi, the Tutsi commander whom Che held responsible for his fighters' pathetic performance at Bendera, had begun airing his own grievances. His men had not fought, he said, because the Congolese didn't fight, and it was *their* country and *their* war after all. Over the succeeding weeks, Mudandi's rancor deepened and extended to open hostility against Kabila and the council leadership, whom he accused of willfully neglecting the men at the front.

Things went from bad to worse. Soon, word arrived that Mudandi had shot his own deputy commander to death, apparently on charges that he was responsible for the "bad *dawa*" at Bendera. A Congolese rebel officer went to Mudandi's camp to investigate and was unceremoniously expelled; now this officer threatened to leave the Congo unless Mudandi was shot. Mudandi remained defiant and from his zone made it clear he was in a state of virtual rebellion against Kabila and the Liberation Council, declaring that his men would no longer fight unless the Congolese did.

Matters were certainly not helped by the fact that, in addition to their mistreatment of the peasants and one another, both the Tutsis and the Congolese showed an extraordinary degree of cruelty toward their prisoners. At one point, Che heard that a French mercenary had been captured on the lake and brought to a rebel camp where, by local custom, he had been buried up to his neck in the dirt. When Che sent men to seek the prisoner's release in order to obtain information, they got an evasive reply from the commander, and a day later were told that the prisoner had died.

The dissension in the Cubans' ranks continued to grow. Four more men, including two doctors, asked Che for permission to leave. "I was much less violent but much more hurtful with the doctors than with the simple soldiers, who reacted to things in a more or less primitive way," he recorded. But the growing specter of mass desertion by his own comrades drew him to deeper reflection.

"The reality is that at the first serious reverse . . . several comrades lost heart and decided to retire from a struggle that they had [sworn to] come and die for, if it were necessary: what's more, voluntarily; surrounded by a halo of bravura, spirit of sacrifice, enthusiasm—in a word, of invincibility. What meaning does the phrase 'If necessary, unto death' have? In the answer to this lies the solution to the serious problems we face in the creation of our new men of tomorrow."

As for the military situation, Che had arrived at a crossroads. So far, he had doggedly clung to hopes that he could somehow get the Congolese rebels moving and turn the deteriorating situation around, but after Bendera he knew that unless something dramatic was done soon to improve the rebels' fighting ability, they were doomed. By the end of July, Che realized that his original time frame for seeing the "Congolese Revolution" to victory was unrealistic, and he mused that "five years [now seemed] a very optimistic goal . . ."

All the while, Che had been trying to keep up the pressure on the enemy by sending out Cuban-led patrols to lay road ambushes and, since he now knew that the rebels' own information network was worthless to gather intelligence on the enemy's positions. These efforts produced some tragicomic results. One group, led by a Cuban named "Aly," attacked a police unit, but, as Che recorded gloomily: "Of the 20 Congolese who went with him . . . 16 ran away." In another, more successful attack, Papi Martínez Tamayo led a combined force of Cubans and Congolese to lay siege to the road between the enemy-held forts at Albertville and Bendera, and was able to score a respectable blow, destroying two armored cars and a jeep driven in convoy by a crew of white mercenaries, killing seven. But in another joint Cuban-Rwandan ambush against an army truck, the Rwandans had run away, firing their weapons wildly, and one of the Cubans had lost a finger from this "friendly fire." To make amends, the Rwandan commander had pulled out a knife and proposed cutting off the fingers of the culprit, but Papi successfully prevailed upon him not to do so. Then the commander and his men proceeded to drink the bottles of whisky and beer they found in the ambushed truck and got hopelessly drunk before shooting dead a peasant who happened by, claiming he was a "spy."

On August 12, Che issued a candid message to his Cuban fighters, acknowledging that their situation was bad and giving a fairly honest appraisal of the weaknesses of the rebel organization they had come to help. Its leaders, he said, did not come to the front, the fighters themselves did not fight and had no sense of discipline or sacrifice. "To win a war with such troops," he confessed, "is out of the question." As for his original plan of bringing guerrillas from other countries to be trained in the Congolese "school" of guerrilla warfare, such a notion was now unthinkable. (When, a few days later, Pablo Ribalta sent him word that he was dispatching a group of Cubans to assume the task of organizing a training base for Mozambican and other African guerrillas, Che wrote him back to advise against it, citing the "indiscipline, disorganization and total demoralization" they would find.)

Ever since the defeat at Fort Bendera, Che had redoubled his efforts to convince the Congolese to adopt his proposals. He outlined a plan for a new unified central military command, a rigorous training program, and a streamlined and disciplined food-supply system and communications network. He proposed that a rebel posse be formed to go after the armed deserters who were now marauding all over the region and disarm them, both to restore order and to recapture valuable weapons. He had kept up a barrage of petitions to Kabila, which typically received oblique or evasive responses, and pursued his objectives in frequent conclaves with Masengo. On the surface, the new Congolese chief of staff seemed receptive, but he lacked authority to make decisions, and the situation dragged on without resolution.

Che again asked to be allowed to go into the field himself, but this request, made to Masengo, was met with alarm, ostensibly out of concern for Che's "personal security." Che refused to accept his explanation and demanded to know if the real problem was a "lack of trust." Masengo strenuously denied this, and he relented, agreeing to take Che on a visit to some of the regional commands. Writing about this later, Che concluded that both Masengo and Kabila were well aware of the ill feeling their absences had spawned among their fighters, and feared being "shown up" if he were to visit the fronts where they had never even appeared.

As promised, Masengo took Che on a short inspection trip to nearby bases, but then a message came from Kabila asking his chief of staff to come to Kigoma. The power struggle within the rebel leadership had finally climaxed. In early August, Gaston Soumaliot ousted Christophe Gbenye as the leader of the "Congolese National Revolutionary Council" on the grounds that Gbenye had betrayed his comrades by secretly negotiating with the Congo regime. Masengo promised Che he would be back in a day. When, a week later, he still hadn't returned, Che took off for the rebel front line near Fort Bendera, determined to see the conditions firsthand. It was August 18.

VI

Meanwhile, with the enthusiasm of a chess master who senses victory, Fidel had continued dispatching a regular stream of Cuban fighters to Tanzania. In early September 1965, a fifth group arrived. Among them were the corpulent PURS secretary, Emilio Aragonés—immediately dubbed "Tembo" (elephant)—and Che's old sierra war sidekick and housemate, now chief of staff of Cuba's western army, Dr. Oscar Fernández Mell, renamed "Siki" (Vinegar) for his allegedly sour personality.

Fernández Mell had been on vacation at the Varadero beach resort when he got the surprise call from Havana. Although he had been privy to Che's disappearance—he had even taken Che's dental impression so that false dentures could be made for him as part of his disguise for leaving Cuba—"Oscarito" had not known, nor asked Che his destination, and had assumed it to be South America.

"It was something he had talked to me about, and that he had proposed as far back as the Sierra Maestra," said Mell. "He had said that after liberating Cuba he was going to liberate his country [Argentina]. It was his final objective—that's the great truth. . . . When they called me, I thought it was for *that,* but when [I was told] it was for Africa, I didn't even think about it, I said 'Well, if he's there, that's where we go.'"

Fernández Mell said that in Cuba the general feeling toward Che's African mission was one of euphoria. "They said that everything was all right, that everything was marching along and they had had some victorious battles, etcetera. And that our mission was to lend Che a hand and help in everything and to serve as a kind of backup." He and Aragonés had gone off feeling optimistic and enthused, even though Fidel had expressed concern that Che seemed "overly pessimistic" about the prospects. It hadn't taken them long to realize things on the ground were not as had been painted for them.

In Dar-Es-Salaam, they had met Kabila, who was driving around in a Mercedes Benz, an image Mell didn't like at all. Then, in Kigoma, Kabila's men refused to let them cross the lake in what they called "Kabila's launch," a new fast motorboat that the Cubans and Soviets had provided; instead they had to cross in a larger, slower boat. Then, upon reaching Kibamba, Kumi, the Cuban doctor at the base dispensary, told them: "You'll see what this is: a piece of shit." Che's bodyguard Pombo came down the hill to meet them as they struggled on the climb up, and from him they heard more details of just how bad things really were, and that Che, fed up with being "retained" at the base, had taken off. Knowing Che as he did, Mell was not surprised.

"Underneath that calm demeanor he had, always writing, reading and thinking, Che was a man of enormous activity. . . . He was an erupting volcano who wanted to do things, and in the Congo, he wanted it to be like it was in the Sierra Maestra, he wanted to fight, he wanted to go to where the mercenaries were."

Che headed back to base when he heard of the arrival of Fernández Mell and Aragonés, but privately he was worried they had orders to bring him back to Cuba. He was relieved and gratified to learn he was mistaken: They had both volunteered to come out of a desire to be a part of his mission.

The brief trip had also revived Che's spirits. For the first time, he had entered into friendly contact with the peasants, and had reveled in it. "Like the peasants anywhere in the world, they were receptive to any human interest taken in them," he wrote. He had carried out a little "social action," handing out vegetable seeds for planting and promising to send doctors on regular medical visits to the area. He briefly even returned to his old profession of doctoring, giving injections of penicillin against the most "traditional" disease he found, gonorrhea, and dispensing antimalaria pills. In one place, the villagers dressed up as "bush devils" and put on a ritual dance for him, dancing around a stone idol and sacrificing a sheep. "The ritual seems complicated, but it boils down to something very simple: a sacrifice is made to the god, the stone idol, and afterward the sacrificed animal is eaten, and everyone eats and drinks profusely."

Wherever he went, Che had tried hard to get the commanders to agree to send their men to his base for training but invariably found that they wanted the Cuban instructors to be sent to *them*; their presence was seen as a sign of prestige. He had even set up some ambushes in which, for the first time, some of the Rwandans hadn't run but actively participated. These were slim grounds for optimism, but after so many months of gloom and inaction Che felt some headway had been made, and held out new hope for the future.

September brought him back to reality, however. The Tanzanian government was now throwing obstacles in the way of the Congolese, and it was becoming difficult for them to move men and supplies out of Kigoma. In the Congo itself, a pro-Gbenye faction had begun causing problems in some of the outlying rebel areas, and there were a few armed standoffs between pro- and anti-council factions. Masengo was shot at in a couple of pro-Gbenye villages and had to beat a retreat. The situation was becoming dangerous for the Cubans, who no longer knew who was friend or foe. Still, Che was anxious to pull together some coordinated actions against the mercenaries before they took the initiative. After sending units out to reinforce rebel defences, he went to the town of Fizi, domain of the rebel strongman and self-styled "General" Moulana, where he found the general's antiaircraft defenses to consist of a single machine gun manned by a Greek mercenary prisoner. Che tried to convince Moulana to bring his men for training to the lake, but the general refused; the trip wasn't a total waste, however, as Moulana provided Che with one of the more colorful spectacles of his time in the Congo. Taking his distinguished visitor to his home village of Baraka, Moulana dressed himself up for the occasion. "It consisted of a motorcycle helmet with a leopard skin on top, which gave him a really ridiculous appearance," observed Che, while his quick-tongued bodyguard, Carlos Coello—now "Tumaini"—dubbed Moulana "the Cosmonaut." In Baraka, the Cubans had to endure a "Chaplinesque" parade ceremony. The saddest thing about it, Che noted later, was that the Congolese fighters seemed to enjoy parading around more than actually learning how to fight properly.

Next Che moved on to the house of "General Lambert," a rival of Moulana's and the man who had first introduced him to *dawa*. Lambert promptly got smashed on *pombe,* and was such a funny drunk that Che did not even bother to lecture him. He left after securing only with Lambert's promise of "350 men" for an operation against the Lulimba garrison. (Inevitably, however, Lambert never produced such a force.)

By early October, Che realized that it was going to be impossible to organize a successful attack unless he altered his approach radically—and when Masengo finally returned, he had come up with a plan. To avoid having to deal with the existing—and to Che's mind, completely incorrigible—rebels, he wanted to recruit fighters from among the local peasantry, for an independent fighting column, which he would command. "We would create a kind of fighting school," Che explained later. "Also, we would organize a new and more rational General Staff that would direct operations on all fronts."

While Che was in the midst of his meeting with Masengo, "trying to raise the Liberation Army from the ruins," as he described it, one of the Cubans in camp dropped a burning lighter, and in a flash a fire began. One after the other, their straw huts burst into flames. Pombo managed to save Che's diary and a few other things from their hut, but then everyone fled as grenades left in the huts began exploding. Che punished the unlucky culprit, an otherwise good cadre, by ordering him to go three days without food.

"In the midst of this party of bullets and exploding grenades," he wrote, "Machadito, our minister of Public Health arrived, with some letters and a message from Fidel."

José Ramón Machado Ventura, or "Machadito," the same doctor who had extracted the M-1 bullet out of Che's foot in the sierra, had come to inspect the health needs in the rebel territory as the result of a remarkable request made by Gaston Soumaliot for fifty Cuban doctors. When, a few weeks earlier, Che had learned that Fidel was planning to host Soumaliot on a visit to Havana, he had fired off a message advising him not to receive the rebel leader, and not to give him any material assistance. Che's missive either arrived too late or was ignored, for Fidel had feted Soumaliot, who had "painted an idyllic picture for him" of the Congolese revolution; when asked for "fifty Cuban doctors," Fidel had quickly agreed. After hearing Che's adamant objections and seeing the situation for himself, Machadito promised to relay Che's feelings to Fidel.

"I had already learned through 'Tembo' [Aragonés] that the feeling in Cuba was that my attitude was very pessimistic," wrote Che. "This was now reinforced by a personal message from Fidel in which he counseled me not to despair, reminded me of the first stage of the [Cuba] struggle, and to remember that these inconveniences always happen."

Taking advantage of Machadito's prompt departure, Che wrote a long letter to the jefe. "Dear Fidel: I received your letter, which provoked contradictory feelings in me, since in the name of international proletarianism we commit errors which can be very costly. Also, it worries me personally that, whether for my lack of seriousness in writing, or because you don't comprehend me totally, it could be thought that I suffer from the terrible sickness of undue pessimism. . . . I'll just tell you that here, according to those around me, I have already lost my reputation as an objective observer, as the result of maintaining an entirely unwarranted optimism in the face of the existing situation. I can assure you that if I was not here, this beautiful dream would have dissolved long ago in the general chaos."

Che went on to give Fidel a brutally realistic picture of the way the foreign aid was being wasted by the Congolese : "Three brand-new Soviet launches arrived little more than a month ago and two are now useless and the third, in which your emissary crossed, leaks all over the place." All he wanted was one hundred more Cubans—"they don't all have to be black"— and some bazookas, fuses for their mines, and R-4 explosive.

As for the requested doctors, Che told him: "With 50 doctors the liberated zone of the Congo would have an enviable proportion of one for every 1000 inhabitants, a level that surpasses the USSR, the US and the two or three other most advanced nations of the world. . . .

"Have a little faith in my criteria and don't judge by appearances," Che finished, adding that Fidel should "shake up" the people supplying him with information, who he said, "present utopic images which don't have anything to do with the truth. I've tried to be explicit and objective, concise and truthful. Do you believe me?"

Indeed, the efforts of Cuba and the other nations helping the Congolese rebels were being squandered. A group of Congolese fighters had recently arrived at the lake, fresh from six months of training in Bulgaria and China, but Che noted with sarcasm that their first concern was to ask for fifteen days of vacation to visit their families. "Later they would stretch it because it had been too short. In any case, they were trained revolutionary cadres, they couldn't risk themselves in the fighting, it would have been irresponsible; they had come to inundate their comrades with the mountain of theoretical knowledge they had accumulated in six months, but the revolution should not commit the crime of making them fight."

Che turned to the task at hand: creating his envisioned "fighting academy," which in its latest genesis would be made up of 210 men, including peasants and rebels from the three main fronts. After what he had seen there, he was also doubtful about General Moulana's ability or willingness to defend the strategic Fizi plain, a certain attack route in the event of a government offensive. He sent Mell with some men to try to "talk sense" to the "Cosmonaut-General," with orders to do what he could to organize Fizi's defenses.

Once again Che had to lecture his grumbling Cuban troops. "I told them that the situation was difficult," he wrote. "The Liberation Army was falling apart and we had to fight to save it from ruin. Our work would be very hard and unpleasant and I could not ask them to have faith in the triumph; personally I believed that things could be fixed although with a lot of work and a multitude of partial failures. Nor could I ask them to have confidence in my leadership ability, but, as a revolutionary, I could demand that they showed respect for my honesty. Fidel was aware of the fundamentals, and the incidents that had occurred had not been concealed from him; I had not come to the Congo to win personal glory, nor would I sacrifice anyone for my personal honor." The important thing now was for the men to obey him, but Che realized that his words were not convincing. "Gone were the romantic days when I threatened to send the undisciplined ones back to Cuba; if I had done that now, I would have been lucky to keep half [the troops]."

On top of everything else, malarial fever as well as gastroenteritis continued to plague the Cubans. Che also succumbed, as he wrote with black humor: "In my field diary I had recorded the statistics, in my case, of more than 30 depositions [defecations] in 24 hours, until the rigors of my runs vanquished my scientific spirit. How many more there were, only the bush knows."

Meanwhile, it did not appear he was making any headway in getting through to the Congolese fighters. One day, when they refused to do some work he had ordered, Che blew up.

"Infuriated, I talked to them in French, I told them the most terrible things I could find in my poor vocabulary, and in the heights of my fury, I told them that I would put dresses on them and make them carry yucca in a basket (a female occupation) because they were worthless, and worse than women; I preferred to form an army with women rather than have individuals of their category. As the translator interpreted my outburst to Swahili, all the men looked at me and cackled with laughter with a disconcerting ingenuousness."

There were some other cultural barriers that simply never came down. One of them was the *dawa,* and Che finally opted for a pragmatic approach, hiring a witch doctor, or *muganga,* for his Congolese troops. "He occupied his place in the camp and took charge of the situation immediately," noted Che.

By mid-October, the onset of the rainy season, the long-awaited government offensive began. Che and his men were still unprepared. Backed up by a fleet of gunboats, fast launches, and a small air force of bombers, helicopters, and spotter aircraft, Mike Hoare's mercenaries began moving in on the rebel domain in a three-pronged encirclement manuever. They took General Moulana's front at Baraka and Fizi with ease, then Lubonja. General Lambert's defenses collapsed, and his men and the Cubans with them escaped in headlong flight toward the lake. Che sent Mell and Aragonés with Masengo to the lake to take charge there, while he dug in at a new camp at the edge of the foothills.

VII

The noose was being drawn tightly around Che, and then it was given another tug—not by Hoare's mercenaries, but by a political settlement reached between the Congolese government in Leopoldville and the Congolese Liberation Army's backers in the Organization of African Unity (OAU), including Tanzania.

The OAU had blacklisted the Congo regime of Prime Minister Moise Tshombe over his unholy alliance with the Belgian and white mercenary forces. On October 13, President Kasavubu ousted Tshombe and, in a meeting of African presidents in Ghana ten days later, announced that the white mercenaries would be sent home. It was to be a quid pro quo, however. If the mercenaries went, those states aiding the rebels would have to end their support as well. All foreign intervention in the Congo was to cease—and that meant the Cubans too.

Mike Hoare was not pleased when he heard the news and, in a meeting with Joseph Mobutu, the Congolese army chief, insisted his men's contracts be honored. Mobutu successfully prevailed upon Kasavubu to let the mercenaries stay until the rebellion had been completely crushed.

Che had been forewarned about the mounting external pressures for a negotiated settlement, and knew from Masengo and others that the Tanzanians had become increasingly uncooperative. But in the field, events now took place in rapid-fire succession, too quickly for Che to react effectively, much less to concentrate on the political machinations taking place. On the morning of October 24, the six-month anniversary of his arrival in the Congo, his base camp was overrun by government troops. Che had time to order that the huts be torched, but in the confusion of the retreat they left behind large stocks of weapons and ammunition, communications equipment, food stores, papers, and two pet monkeys Che had kept at the camp.

As they withdrew, Che castigated himself for having been caught unaware. He had not posted sentries on the route the enemy had taken to approach, not believing they would come that way. He was even more bitter when he discovered that the initial panicked reports of the approaching enemy vanguard had been mistaken: they had actually been peasants fleeing the advancing government troops. If he had waited and found out the truth, Che could have mounted a good ambush and struck an important blow against the enemy. Now, it was too late.

"Personally, my morale was terribly depressed; I felt responsible for that disaster through weakness and lack of foresight," he wrote later. As Che and his Cubans retreated, the Congolese fled past them, finding their own escape, and when Che reached a hilltop where he had ordered some Cubans who had gone ahead to wait for him, he found they had carried on. Che looked around at the little band of men who were still with him: it included Víctor Dreke, Papi, and his bodyguards Pombo and Tumaini—and Chamaleso, his original Congolese contact. "I made the bitter reflection that we were thirteen [in number]," Che wrote. "One more than Fidel had at a certain moment [after the *Granma* landing], but I was not the same leader."

Che and his men marched on through a desolate landscape of abandoned hamlets, their peasant inhabitants having joined the rebels' flight toward the lake. They hiked on through the night and at dawn reached a village where they found one of the Cubans, Bahaza, gravely wounded with a bullet in the lung.

After doing what he could to alleviate Bahaza's condition, Che ordered the column forward, leaving the valley to find safer refuge in the hills. Under a heavy rainfall, and up a steep mountain trail slippery with mud, with the men taking turns carrying Bahaza, everyone experienced the next six hours as a grinding ordeal. From the heights, they observed a terrible spectacle: On adjacent hills were fleeing peasants, while in the valley below columns of smoke rose from burning huts as the advancing government troops burned everything in their path. Reaching a small village filled with hungry refugees, Che was berated by angry peasants who said the soldiers had carried off their wives, but they had been helpless to save them because they only had spears; the rebels had not given them guns to defend themselves.

Bahaza died at dawn the next day. "Bahaza was the sixth man we lost and the first whose body we were able to honor," Che wrote. "And that body was a mute and virile accusation, as was his conduct from the moment of his wounding, against my . . . stupidity." Che gathered his men around and launched into what he described as a "soliloquy loaded with self-reproach."

"I recognized the errors I had committed and I said, which was a great truth, that of all the deaths that had occurred in the Congo, Bahaza's was the most painful for me, because he had been the comrade I had seriously reprimanded* for his weakness and because he had responded like a true

---

*Che had censured Bahaza only days before for abandoning a weapon in the exodus from Lambert's front.

communist [by acknowledging it] . . . , but that I hadn't been up to my responsibilities, and I was guilty of his death. For my part, I would try to do everything I could to erase that error, through more work and more enthusiasm than ever."

But it was not to be. As Che dug in at his new site, the recriminations began, coming now from the Congolese rebels. Word came that commanders such as Lambert were saying the defeat was Che's fault, that the Cubans were cowardly and had betrayed the Congolese. Fernández Mell and Aragonés kept up a flow of messages to Che from the lakeside base at Kibamba, urging him to abandon his position; an enemy attack could be expected at any moment, and he could easily be cut off from escape to the lake.

Along with the near-total collapse of the military front, the Congolese government was now trying to press its advantage by forging alliances with some of the rebel leaders. Masengo had informed Aragonés and Fernández Mell that President Kasavubu had sent him a secret message, offering him a government ministry if he abandoned the struggle. "If they've approached Masengo," Aragonés and Mell warned Che, "they must also be 'working' on Soumaliot and Kabila."

On October 30, they sent Che a new urgent note, begging him to join them on the lake. Planes had begun firebombing positions around Kibamba, and they feared it was just the prelude to a final assault. The base was becoming chaotic, a refuge for all kinds of "deserters, criminals and traitors," and there was no control. "The thing is really alarming," they stressed. "We think we've been writing you quite enough and have kept you abreast of the international situation as well as the one here. We almost seem like two gossipy old ladies. We beg you to do the same as us since we are always anxious for news (then we can be three gossips)."

Che finally decided to heed their advice. Leaving Papi with a group of Congolese at his new village base with orders to continue the military training sessions, he headed down to Kibamba. Although virtually everyone around him believed the so-called Congolese Revolution to be in its death throes, Che refused to give up hope, and even now was trying to shore up the outlying fronts that had not yet been overrun. In his habitual end-of-month summary, he concluded that October had been a "month of disaster without qualifiers . . . In summary, we enter a month [November] which may be definitive."

But even as Che was writing, the rug was being pulled out from under him. On November 1, Ambassador Ribalta was called in by the Tanzanian government and informed that, because of the agreements reached at Accra, Tanzania had decided to end "the nature of its assistance" to the Congolese

National Liberation Movement. An urgent message was sent to Che, telling him the news.

"It was the coup de grace for a moribund revolution," wrote Che. Given the delicate nature of the information, he decided not to tell Masengo, and to base any decision he made on how matters developed over the next few days. Then on November 4, Che received a telegram from the embassy giving him an advance summary of a letter from Fidel, the full text of which was being brought to him by courier. It was Fidel's response to the letter Che had sent with Machadito a month earlier. The summary of Fidel's points was as follows:

"1. We must do all we can short of the point of absurdity. 2. If in Tatu's [Che's] judgment our presence is becoming unjustifiable and useless, we should think about retiring. You should act according to the objective situation and the spirit of our men. 3. If you think you should stay, we will try to send as many human and material resources as you deem necessary. 4. We are worried that you erroneously fear that your attitude has been considered defeatist or pessimistic. 5. If you decide to stay, [you] can remain present status quo returning here or remaining in another place. 6. We support any decision you take. 7. Avoid annihilation."

Using the field radio, Che dictated a message to Dar-Es-Salaam to be relayed to Fidel, briefing him on the current situation. A few days earlier, he told Fidel, when rumors were spreading of a mass escape by the Congolese rebel leaders to Tanzania, he had resolved to stay behind with twenty handpicked men. They would have continued to try to assemble a guerrilla force; if they failed, he would go overland to "another front" or seek political asylum in Tanzania. That option had ended, however, with the Tanzanian decision to suspend its support.

Che proposed that a high-level Cuban delegation be sent to Tanzania to speak with Nyerere and outline the Cuban position, which was that "Cuba [had] offered its aid subject to Tanzania's approval. It was accepted and the aid became effective. We comprehend Tanzania's present difficulties but we are not in agreement with its proposals. Cuba does not retreat from its promises, nor will it accept a shameful escape leaving its [Congolese] brother in disgrace at the mercy of the mercenaries. We will only abandon the struggle if for well-founded reasons or force majeure, the Congolese themselves ask us to, but we will continue fighting so that this does not come to pass."

Che also asked Fidel to solicit a minimum of continued support from Tanzania: to allow them to keep open their communication with Dar-Es-Salaam, and permission to continue using the lake for food and arms supply runs. Finally, he advised Fidel to pass a copy of his letter along to the Chinese and the Soviets "to forestall any discrediting maneuver."*

By November 10, the situation was continuing to unravel on the perimeters of the reduced rebel territory. One of the Rwandan Tutsi positions was overrun and the enemy was advancing steadily toward the lake. With food and medical supplies running low at Kibamba, Che fired off a telegram to the Cuban stations in Kigoma and Dar-Es-Salaam. "Enemy pressure increases and the [Tanzanian] lake blockade still in place. Substantial quantities of Congolese currency are urgently needed in event of isolation. You have to move quickly. We are preparing to defend the base."

On November 14, Che's Cuban launch captain, "Changa," crossed the lake from Kigoma carrying food and a Cuban intelligence official from Dar with a new message from Fidel. He advised Che that the Tanzanian government was showing no sign of moderating its position. The emissary from Dar asked if he should begin preparing a "clandestine base" for Che in Tanzania, given the current official posture, and Che told him he should.

In a ludicrous sideshow, the boat captain had also brought over forty new Congolese rebel "graduates," fresh from a training course in the Soviet Union. Like their Bulgarian- and Chinese-trained predecessors, they immediately requested two weeks of vacation, while also complaining that they had nowhere to put their luggage. "It would be a little comic if it weren't so sad," Che wrote, "to see the disposition of these boys in whom the revolution had deposited its faith."

Despite the efforts of Cuban commanders in the field, the rebel defenses continued to crumble. On November 16, Che sent an SOS to the Cuban embassy in Dar-Es-Salaam requesting arms supplies from their cache in Kigoma. He accused the Tanzanian authorities of intentionally blockading his logistics pipeline, and asked the embassy to demand a clear-cut response as to what their intentions were. Enemy gunboats were patrolling the lake, and he needed action now.

*A Cuban intelligence official who was directly involved in the Cuban operation in the Congo at the administrative level told the author that Soviet rivalry with the Chinese exerted a direct influence in the Congolese denouement, saying: "I think the Soviets wanted to be rid of Che," and indicating that the Soviets, while cooperating with the Cuban- and African-backed rebel alliance, had done so primarily in order to compete in an area staked out by the Chinese; that when the winds shifted, Moscow had thrown its weight behind the negotiated settlement, thus dooming the Congolese revolutionary cause—and Che's personal effort. Bolstering this analysis, a senior Cuban official acknowledged seeing something in Che's notes (presumably his original, unpublished Congo diary) alluding to his suspicion that the Soviets had "pressured" Tanzanian president Nyerere into calling for a Cuban withdrawal.

That same day, Papi, still in the mountains, sent word that he needed reinforcements urgently. The Rwandans with him had silently deserted en masse that morning, taking their weapons with them, and now the Congolese were leaving, as well. It was devastating news: without sufficient men at the front there was no way to hold back the enemy advance.

Che held a conclave to discuss strategy with the Congolese leaders at hand: Masengo, Chamaleso, and a couple of others (despite repeated entreaties, Kabila had still not crossed the lake). As they saw it, there were only two alternatives: a fight to the end in their present position or a breakout attempt, cutting through enemy lines and escaping either north or south. The first option was discarded because of the unreliability of their fighters, and they tentatively decided to make a break for the south, through an area called Bondo. Che ordered Dreke and another of his officers, Aly, to make a quick reconnaissance trip there to see what the possibilities were.

As Che recorded it, Aly exploded, saying it was time to stop "running over hills without having these people's cooperation." "I answered him cuttingly that we would organize the evacuation from Bondo and he could leave with the group that left the struggle; he replied immediately that he would stay with it to the end."*

Deciding that it was unfair to keep the secret any longer, Che now told Masengo of Tanzania's decision to end its support, telling him to draw his own conclusions. Evidently, the news was definitive for Masengo and his comrades; that night, Chamaleso came to tell Che that all the rebel officers in camp had decided to end the campaign. Che took the news badly, telling Chamaleso that if that was the case, he wanted their decision in writing. "I told him that there was something called history, which is made up of much fragmentary data and which can be twisted." Che wanted documentation in case the Congolese later said that it had been a Cuban decision to withdraw. Chamaleso said he didn't think Masengo would agree to signing such a letter, but went off to confer.

As he did, a field telephone call informed Che that his upper base had just fallen. His men had retreated without a fight, and the enemy was advancing in large numbers. Che reacted swiftly, proposing an immediate retreat, which Masengo immediately accepted. Chamaleso took the occasion to inform Che that he had talked again with the officers and they were still unanimous in their desire to withdraw "definitively" from the battlefield. That was a moot point now, as Che noted: "Within five minutes, the telephone operators had disappeared, all the military police had run away and chaos took over the base."

*See the appendix for elaboration.

VIII

It was November 18, and night was already upon them. Che radioed Kigoma to say he was withdrawing, and to prepare the boats for an evacuation. After ordering his men to burn the huts and conceal what equipment they could in their secret deposits, Che ordered them to bring the heavy weapons, in case they had to make a last stand. At dawn they began slowly walking toward the lakeshore, straining under their loads, abandoning some by the side of the trail. Che noted that his men's faces showed "a centuries-old weariness," and he tried to hurry them along. Behind them, explosions shot fire and smoke up into the sky: someone had set fire to their ammunition stores. The Congolese had mostly fled, and Che let them go, knowing that when they reached the lake, there would not be enough boats to transport everyone.

They had decided on a rendezvous point on the lakeshore ten kilometers south of Kibamba, and during their march, Che sent new radio messages to Kigoma, asking for the launches to meet them that night. By that afternooon they had reached the evacuation point; Che radioed again, saying he and his men were in place, the war was over, and it was urgent they be withdrawn. His calls finally got a response: "Copied." Wrote Che: "When they heard the 'copied' from the lake, the expression of all the comrades present changed as if a magic wand had touched their faces."

But the boats did not arrive that night, or the next day. While they waited with increasing anxiety, Che set up ambushes to protect their perimeter, and sent men back to look for missing men. One appeared the next morning, hobbled by a sprained ankle, but two other Cubans were still unaccounted for. That afternoon, November 20, Che radioed his launch captain, Changa, in Kigoma, telling him he had two hundred men to evacuate. Changa radioed back to explain that he had been detained by the Tanzanian authorities but would cross that night.

At this news, wrote Che, "the people were euphoric." He had already talked with Masengo and his general staff, and they had agreed that one of the Congolese commanders would stay behind with his men; Masengo and the others would be evacuated with the Cubans. But for the plan to work, those escaping had to deceive the Congolese fighters, and Che and Masengo decided to use various "pretexts" to embark the stranded fighters on a boat that would take them to a nearby village. When they were out of sight, the "real" evacuation would take place.

But things did not turn out so smoothly. While they managed to coax a good portion of the Congolese onto the first boat that arrived, those who remained "smelled something," recalled Che, and announced they wanted to stay where they were. On the spot, Che ordered his men to carry out a selection of those Congolese who had shown the "best behavior" to be taken with them "as Cubans."

As he stood on the lakeshore, overseeing the final evacuation of the Cuban mission in the Congo, Che continued to mull over the possibility of staying behind to carry on the struggle. "For me the situation was definitive; two men who I had sent out on a mission . . . would be abandoned unless they arrived in a few hours. As soon as we left all the weight of calumnies would fall upon us, inside and out of the Congo. . . . I could extract, according to my research, up to twenty men who would follow me, [although at this point] with knit brows. And afterward, what would I do? The chiefs were all retreating, the peasants were displaying more and more hostility toward us. But the idea of evacuating completely and . . . leaving behind defenseless peasants and [practically defenseless] armed men . . . in defeat, and with the sensation of having been betrayed, I found deeply painful."

One of the options Che had been toying with in the last few days was the possibility of crossing the Congo to try to join up with the rebel force led by Pierre Mulele, but Mulele's territory was located hundreds of miles away through the jungle, and it would be a feat just to survive the odyssey, much less organize an effective guerrilla force.

As they waited for the boats, Che continued to weigh his options, none of them good. "In reality," he acknowledged later, "the idea of staying behind continued to circle around in my head until the wee hours of the night." One of the things most disturbing to him was the demeaningly fugitive manner of his retreat and the deception being used to leave the Congolese fighters behind. He was tormented with thoughts of how he and his comrades would be remembered by these men.

"This is how I passed the last hours," he wrote, "solitary and perplexed, until, at two in the morning, the boats arrived."

First the sick and wounded were boarded, then Masengo, his general staff, and about forty Congolese men they had selected to go with them. Finally, Che and the Cubans climbed aboard.

"A desolate, sobering and inglorious spectacle took place. I had to reject men who pleaded to be taken along. There was not a trace of grandeur in this retreat, nor a gesture of rebellion. The machine guns were prepared, and I had the men ready just in case, according to custom, the [abandoned fighters] tried to intimidate us with an attack from land, but nothing like this happened, just some sobbing, as [I], the leader of the escapees, told the man with the mooring rope to let go."

28

No Turning Back

I

Within a couple of days of the Congo disaster, Che was safely concealed inside a small two-room apartment in the Cuban embassy residence on the outskirts of Dar-Es-Salaam. Ambassador Ribalta cleared out all the employees except for his cryptographer-telegraphist, a male secretary, and a cook, who never knew that there was a stranger living upstairs.

The other Cubans on the ill-fated expedition had all been ferried by truck to Dar-Es-Salaam, from where, at the Cubans' request, the Soviets had them flown out to Moscow and on to Havana aboard their own aircraft. Fernández Mell had been left behind in Kigoma to organize a search and rescue mission for the two missing Cubans, and to evacuate the Congolese who had been left behind; it would be four months before he found them, in an odyssey that was to take him almost all the way to Rwanda.

Che and his men had crossed Lake Tanganyika safely, in spite of a very close encounter with an armed Congolese government cutter. In a bold bluff, Che had ordered his men to mount their 75 mm recoilless rifles on the prows of their boats to give the appearance that they were well armed and prepared for battle. It was an audacious move: If fired, the weapons' afterblast alone would have killed many of those on board. Whether due to this warlike display, or because of higher orders to let the fugitives escape, the gunboat did not approach.

A small motorboat piloted by Cubans was waiting for Che when they neared the Kigoma shore. Taking Papi and bodyguards Pombo and Tumaini —or "Tuma"—with him, Che boarded the small boat and said good-bye to the others, telling them that he hoped to see them again, probably in "another country," and that he hoped some of them would go on to fight in other lands. It was an awkward and emotionally laden farewell for the Cuban fighters who, overjoyed to be going home to their homes and families, were also leaving with mixed emotions about their experience and the man they had followed to Africa.

Once Che was ashore he turned to his three young followers and, according to Pombo, said: "Well, we carry on. Are you ready to continue?" They understood: Che was not going back to Cuba. "Where?" asked Pombo. "'Wherever.' He didn't have a firm idea at that moment which place we were going to go."

Harry "Pombo" Villegas was twenty-five, Carlos "Tuma" Coello just a year older, and both had been close to Che since 1957, when they were mere teenagers and had joined him in the Sierra Maestra. José María "Papi" Martínez was twenty-nine and had been Piñeiro's point man in Che's guerrilla programs since 1962, first in Guatemala, then with Masetti's mission, and had also assisted in Tania's clandestine training. These were three of the half-dozen or so men Che believed he could call upon to follow him "without knit brows," and he was not disappointed; in reply to his question on the Tanzanian shore, all said "yes."*

"He could not return to Cuba without . . . having achieved a success," explained Pombo. "He thought that the best thing was to continue. Through his own efforts, with whatever possibilities, he had to continue the struggle."

Indeed, Che had crossed much more than just a lake, and he had left much more than a collapsing revolution behind in the Congo. He had planned to be fighting for five years, but only after six months it was all over. A month earlier, at the inaugural ceremony of the Cuban Communist party, Fidel had made public Che's farewell letter. Now, for reasons of pride alone, Che felt he could not reappear in public. He had committed himself before the world to lend his hand in "new battlefronts." What's more, the news of Cuba's supposedly covert presence in the Congo had been known since the capture of the Cuban guerrilla's diary at Bendera in June. If the CIA did not already know Che was there, it was safe to assume that it had put the Congo on the shortlist of possibilities, and Che had to assume they would be looking out for him.

As of late November 1965, Che was probably the world's best-known Marxist revolutionary, a man for whom the goal of "proletarian internationalism" knew no frontiers. But for now, Che had nowhere to go, and had truly become a man without a country.

*See the appendix for elaboration.

II

On November 25, three days after Che and his men left the Congo, Congolese armed forces chief Joseph Mobutu overthrew President Kasavubu. It marked the beginning of a despotic, Western-backed dictatorship that would endure for the next three decades and bleed the nation dry; the Congolese "revolution" was truly over.

After a few days in Dar-Es-Salaam, Tuma and Pombo had flown on to Paris, then to Moscow and Prague. There, they were installed in a safe house provided by the Czech intelligence service to wait for Che. Holed up in his little room in the Tanzanian capital, visited only by Pablo Ribalta and the Cuban telegraphist, who took dictation, Che set to work on his Congolese memoirs.

Just as he had measured his final actions in the Congo with an eye to history, Che set about writing his account with the intention of its eventual publication—"at the convenient time"—as his contribution to the annals of global socialist revolution. By titling it "Pasajes de la Guerra Revolucionaria (Congo)," the same title he had chosen for his book on the Cuban revolutionary war, Che was making the point that for him the Congo was just one more stage in a historic struggle that had as its final goal the "liberation" of the world's oppressed.

There was a marked difference between his two accounts, however. Although the first contained many blunt reminders of the mistakes and sacrifices made, it was above all a paean to the heroism of the Cuban guerrillas; an exaltation of Fidel's unerring leadership that had taken them to victory; and a moral tale for others to emulate. This second memoir was a starkly negative reflection of the first, as Che made clear in his opening pages when he wrote, "This is the story of a failure."

By dedicating it, "To Bahaza and his comrades, looking for a meaning to the sacrifice," Che was showing his determination to expunge his sins in a classic Marxist *autocrítica,* or self-criticism. At the end of the book, after a retelling of the entire experience and a lengthy critique of the errors and inadequacies he had found in the Congolese movement and among the Cuban fighters, he listed his own faults. "For a long time I maintained an attitude that could be described as excessively complacent, and at other times, perhaps due to an innate characteristic of mine, I exploded in ways that were very cutting and very hurtful [to others]."

Che wrote that he felt the only group with whom he had maintained a good rapport had been "the peasants," but he chastised himelf for his lack of willpower in learning Swahili well. By relying on his French, he had been able to speak to the officers, but not with the rank-and-file soldiers.

In my contact with my men, I believe I showed enough commitment to prevent anyone from impugning me in the personal and physical aspects. . . . The discomfort of having a pair of broken boots or only one change of dirty clothes, or to eat the same slop as the troops and live in the same conditions, for me is not a sacrifice. But my habit of retiring to read, escaping the daily problems, did tend to distance me from contact with the men, without mentioning that there are aspects of my character that don't make intimate contact easy.

I was hard, but I don't believe excessively so, nor unjust; I utilized methods that a regular army doesn't apply, like making men go without food; it is the only effective [punishment] method I know of in times of guerrilla warfare. At the beginning I tried to use moral coercion, and failed. I sought to make my troops have the same point of view as I did regarding the situation and I failed; they were not prepared to look optimistically into a future that had to be viewed through a gloomy present.

Finally, another thing that weighed in my relations with the others . . . was the farewell letter to Fidel. This caused my comrades to view me, as they did many years ago, when I began in the Sierra, as a foreigner [merely] in contact with Cubans. . . . There were certain things in common that we no longer shared, certain common longings that I had tacitly or explicitly renounced and which are the most sacred things for each man individually: his family, his nation, his habitat. The letter that provoked so many eulogistic comments inside and out of Cuba separated me from the combatants.

Perhaps these psychological musings seem out of place in the analysis of a struggle that has an almost continental scale. I continue faithful to my conception of the nucleus; I was the leader of a group of Cubans, a company no more, and my function was to be their true leader, their guide to a victory that would impulse the development of an authentic popular army. But at the same time my peculiar status turned me into a soldier, the representative of a foreign power, an instructor of Cubans and Congolese, strategist, a high flying politician on an unknown stage, and a Caton-censor, repetitive and tiresome. . . . With so so many strands to deal with, a Gordian knot formed which I didn't know how to untie. . . .

I have learned in the Congo; there are errors I won't commit again. Maybe there are others I will repeat, and new ones I will

commit. I have come out with more faith that ever in the guerrilla struggle, but we have failed. My responsibility is great; I will
not forget the defeat, nor its most precious lessons.

III

From the moment he left the Congo, Che became totally dependent on
Cuba's secret services for his protection and survival. For the first time in
his adult life, he was no longer the master of his own destiny.

The intelligence and guerrilla-support network run by Barba Roja
Piñeiro now operated throughout Africa just as it did in Latin America and
other parts of the world, often under the cloak of diplomatic cover. The Cuban
chargé d'affaires in Cairo, José Antonio Arbesú, was one of Piñeiro's operatives, as was Ulíses Estrada, chief of his Africa and Asia Section. Ulíses was
the tall, thin black man who had been Tania's lover in Cuba and had also been
Masetti's controller before he left for Argentina. Throughout Che's time in
the Congo, Ulíses had been a primary liaison, constantly traveling between
Cuba and Tanzania to coordinate the flow of arms, men, and intelligence. Since
the debacle, Ulíses was responsible for getting the Cuban fighters back to
Havana and for coordinating Che's future movements. For the moment, Che's
future remained an open question. Fidel wanted Che to come back to Cuba,
but Che had refused, saying he wanted to go "directly" to South America. But
where? Piñeiro's chief deputy, Juan Carretero, or Ariel, who had helped implement the Béjar and Masetti expeditions in Peru and Argentina, was drawn
into the dilemma, and found that Che was not an easy man to deal with.

"He was very hard to argue with," Ariel said. "He had a very ascetic
mentality. He didn't want to come back to Cuba publicly after the [fare-
well] letter because of his obligation to the revolutionary cause. It simply
was not a possibility."

The weeks began to drag by; Christmas and New Year's came and
went, and Che remained in seclusion. In early January 1966, following a
request by Che to see his wife, Ariel brought Aleida to Tanzania. Years later,
Aleida showed two different photographs of her clandestine travel identity,
one of a fleshy-faced, mature-looking woman with wavy black hair, the
other of a slim woman with straight black hair cropped in a fashionable
above-the-shoulder sixties style.

After their arrival in Dar, Ariel took Aleida straight to the embassy
residence where Che was lodged. All she registered was that it was a two-
story building because she was rushed straight from the car into the building and, once inside, quickly upstairs. There, she and Che shared a two-room
flat. One was a tiny photographic darkroom with a bed, where they slept,

and a small living room where they spent their days. For the next six weeks, neither she nor Che left those rooms, and the curtains on the windows were permanently drawn. Just once, Aleida dared to peek out: She saw a nearby grove of trees, and no other houses in sight. Their only visitor was Pablo Ribalta, who brought their meals upstairs. In a communications room on the same floor was the cryptographer and Che's typist, a Cuban named Coleman Ferrer. Nobody else knew their identities or even saw them.

Che didn't seem bothered by the confinement, said Aleida, because he had plenty to do. He had already finished his Congo memoirs by the time she arrived, and had begun two other projects simultaneously: "Apuntes Filosóficas," (Philosophical Notes)* and "Notas Económicas" (Economic Notes), a book outline based on his critical review of the Soviet *Manual of Political Economy,* the standard socialist bible since Stalin's day. When he wasn't writing, Che spent his time reading books, including poetry and fiction for mere enjoyment. When Aleida arrived, he also set her a "curriculum" of books to read, like homework, which they discussed at the end of each day.

Although the question of Che's future hung like a perpetual cloud over them, Aleida recalled their shared interlude with special fondness, pointing out that "it was the first time we had ever been alone together," and was the closest thing she ever had to a "honeymoon." In a giggling allusion to their "bed" in the darkroom, Aleida hinted that they had made up for lost time. She added that in the past they had often talked about one day visiting Mexico and Argentina together, but she concluded: "There was no time, and there was not to be any."

When she returned to Cuba at the end of February, Aleida left in the same way she had come: down the stairs, out the front door, into a waiting car, and straight to the airport. She rued the fact that she had been to East Africa and seen nothing, especially the fabled game parks. "Later I saw what I had missed," she said, "in a movie starring Yves Montand and Candice Bergen."

IV

By the time Aleida left, Ariel had finally dissuaded Che from his plan to go straight to South America in favor of Prague. There, he would be safer and could "wait things out" until Cuba found somewhere for him to go.**

---

*Che eventually bequeathed this as-yet unpublished outline for a manual on philosophy to Armando Hart, who had moved sharply to the left politically since the rebel victory. Hart is currently the Cuban Minister for Culture, a job he has held for years.

**See the appendix for elaboration.

Before Che left Tanzania, sometime in March, Fernández Mell came to see him. He had finally rounded up the missing Cubans, rescued the abandoned Congolese fighters across the lake, and helped wind up the Cuban operation in Kigoma. Che showed his friend the passages in his Congo memoirs where he referred to him critically, and said: "See how I dump on you?" Fernández Mell retorted that anything Che criticized him for was a direct reflection on him, since he had only followed Che's orders.

The Congo experience had distanced them. They were still friends, but they no longer believed in the same things. "Oscarito" had done a lot of thinking about Che's notions on "continental guerrilla war" and had begun to doubt the wisdom of the strategy, at least for Africa. And he also thought that in his stubbornness to see it succeed, Che had deluded himself.

"[In the Congo] Che had said things to us that I am convinced he knew weren't realistic," Fernández Mell explained, "although he wasn't a man who said things he didn't feel. . . . But in reality Che *did* believe that [the Congo] could triumph. . . . He had it stuck deeply in his head that he had found the path to liberate the people and that it would be successful, and he expounded it as an absolute truth. And so he could not accept that the attempt in the Congo ruined that strategy he had thought out so well."

Fernández Mell knew that Che was probably going on to South America, and ultimately—as he had always planned—to his Argentine homeland. Before the Congo, it had always been implicitly understood that he would join him there, but now the subject didn't come up. Mell didn't inquire about Che's plans or volunteer himself to be a part of them. Their mutual silence said it all: It was a parting of ways between two friends. A few days later, Fernández Mell returned to Havana, taking Che's latest "Pasajes de la Guerra Revolucionaria" with him to deliver to Fidel. He would never see Che again.

V

When Che arrived in Prague, accompanied by Papi, Pombo and Tuma were waiting at their safe house, a large, stately villa on the outskirts of Prague, discreetly screened by a row of tall juniper trees.

The Cuban and Czech intelligence services had an arrangement that had been established soon after Fidel's triumph in 1959, whereby the Czechs had turned over a number of safe houses in Prague for Cuba to use as it saw fit. These safehouses were "hermetic," according to Ariel, and run by the Cubans independently of the Czechs. "Che was brought in as just another

Latin American revolutionary under a false identity. The Czechs never knew he was there."

After Che arrived, Pombo recalled, they lived quietly in the villa, "killing time" and keeping their guerrilla skills honed with shooting practice. Winter ended and spring began. Aleida rejoined Che for a few weeks, this time in a new disguise. Piñeiro's agent Ulíses Estrada came and went from Havana bearing messages between Fidel, Piñeiro, and Che. (Eventually, according to another of Piñeiro's officers, Ulíses was replaced by Ariel at Che's request; as a black, Ulíses attracted "too much attention" in Prague.)

Initially, according to both Ariel and Pombo, Fidel continued trying to persuade Che to return to Cuba, but Che wouldn't budge. "Che didn't want to return under any circumstances," said Pombo. Those who were close to Che suggest that, in addition to his own pride, a decisive factor was his recognition that he had become a political liability for Fidel with the Soviets who, after all, were now bankrolling the Cuban ship of state. Che was more useful to Fidel abroad, where he could carry forward Cuba's revolutionary foreign policy, with Fidel discreetly backing him on the grounds that he was aiding an "old comrade."

Che's departure from Cuba had coincided with Fidel's swing back to an aggressively "internationalist" stance. It had become explicit in his May Day 1965 speech, when he blasted the concept of "peaceful coexistence," and his bellicose posture had continued ever since. In January 1966, at the "First Tricontinental Conference," a Cuban-promoted outgrowth of the Cairo-based Afro-Asian People's Solidarity Organization—attended by hundreds of delegates from over eighty different Latin, Asian, and African states, sundry armed "national liberation movements" as well as the Soviets and Chinese—Fidel had once again played the feuding socialist superpowers off against one another. He had discomfited Moscow by pushing through a resolution lauding the guerrilla movements fighting in Venezuela, Guatemala, Colombia, and Peru, while simultaneously tweaking the Chinese by mentioning the "misunderstandings" between Havana and Beijing over China's decision to reduce Cuba's badly needed rice imports. (In February, Fidel would abandon his diplomatic language and come out publicly with his list of grievances against China, accusing them of trying to meddle in Cuba's politics and seeking to use rice as a bludgeon to secure its political obeisance.)

But Fidel also had other items on his agenda at the Tricontinental: both dampening the continuing rumors of a rift between him and Che, and creating an opening for his Argentine comrade to enter a new battlefield. At the conference, Fidel proclaimed 1966 the "Year of Solidarity," and pledged common cause with the guerrilla struggles taking place against imperialism around the globe. If there was ever a crack in time for Che to seize the moment, this was it. Indeed, finally bowing to Che's emphatic insistence on carrying on with the "armed struggle," Fidel instructed Piñeiro to find a place for Che to go.

It was not an easy choice to make. In early 1966, the Latin American revolutionary panorama was vibrant, but in a bewildering and violent state of flux. There were now pro-Chinese Communist party factions in Bolivia, Peru, and Colombia, and a myriad of guerrilla groups were popping up all over the place. There were some senior Cuban agents in place with the guerrillas in Venezuela and Colombia, but the situation in those countries was tenuous; along with the guerrilla upsurge had come an increased American military and CIA presence.

In Guatemala, the Cuban-backed rebel coalition was in the process of being riven in two by a Trotskyite breakaway movement. In spite of their internal splits, the guerrillas had pulled off some spectacular attacks recently, including the assassination of the head of the U.S. military mission, and, a few months later, that of the Guatemalan deputy defense minister.

In June 1965, after two years of underground organizing, the Peruvian MIR guerrillas led by Luis de la Puente Uceda and Guillermo Lobatón had finally gone into action. In September, the Cuban-backed ELN led by Héctor Béjar began fighting as well, having recovered from its 1963 rout. Peru's government had suspended constitutional guarantees, and U.S.-assisted Peruvian troops had launched a fierce counterinsurgency war. By October 1965, they had killed Luis de la Puente Uceda, then Lobatón only three months later, leaving the MIR leaderless and its combatants on the run. By December, the ELN was in a similar situation; before long, Béjar himself was captured and imprisoned.

In Colombia, the picture was similar. There had been an official state of siege imposed in May 1965 following the appearance of the new Cuban-backed ELN guerrillas at the beginning of the year. By December, an outspoken revolutionary Catholic priest, Camilo Torres, had joined the ELN, lending its effort a charismatic blend of social vision and potentially broader appeal. By February 1966, Torres was dead, but the Colombian insurgency would continue, with the appearance of new offshoots and mutations, for years to come.

Inside Venezuela's Cuban-supported FALN guerrilla organzation, problems were brewing. The Communist party, which had initially supported the "armed struggle" in 1962, was now stepping back in the wake of the imprisonment of many of its leaders. In April 1965, in a move openly criticized by Fidel, its party plenum had voted to alter course in favor of "legal struggle." By March 1966, the Communist party was rewarded by the Venezuelan government for its new policy of moderation with the release of its leaders from prison. Repudiating the Communists, however, the Cuban-backed guerrillas continued the fight.

Bolivia was engulfed in crisis. A military junta had overthrown Víctor Paz Estenssoro, the civilian president, in November 1964, and the charismatic president of the powerful Bolivian workers' union, Juan Lechín, had led a campaign of vociferous opposition to the military regime. In May 1965, Lechín had been exiled, a general strike called in protest, and a state of siege declared by the ruling generals. Still, the pro-Moscow Bolivian Communist party led by Mario Monje was reticent about launching the "armed struggle." A pro-Chinese breakaway faction, formed in April 1965 in a movement spearheaded by student leader Oscar Zamora, had previously sought Che's backing to launch a guerrilla war and been given the go-ahead, but in Che's time away in the Congo, Cuban-Chinese relations had soured, and little had been done to push this option by either Piñeiro's agency or Zamora.

By March 1966, with Che still waiting in Prague, his options narrowed further. That month, Guatemalan security forces swooped down on a secret meeting of the Guatemalan Communist party leadership, murdering the twenty-six top officials it captured; combined with the widening schism in the Guatemalan guerrilla movement, their deaths temporarily decapitated the Cuban- and Soviet-backed guerrilla leadership.

According to Pombo, the first possibility proposed by Che as his next destination was Peru, but to go there he would need the help of the Bolivians, strategically located next door. To be his advance scout, Che sent Papi off to Bolivia in April, planning to follow if he gave the "all clear." "The first thing," explained Pombo, "was to establish contact with the Peruvians, see what state their movement was really in, and [get] the support of the Bolivian Communist party. The Bolivian party had helped us with the Masetti thing, in the Puerto Maldonado thing [with Héctor Béjar's ELN group]; there were people who had shown they were loyal to the ideas of the revolution, who had worked with us before with these [other] movements and, what's more, had been trained in Cuba."

The "loyal" Bolivian cadres Pombo was speaking about were a group of young Bolivian Communist party members who had aligned themselves with the Cuban policy of armed struggle. Among them were the Peredo brothers, Roberto, or "Coco," and Guido, or "Inti," who came from a large and prominent family in Bolivia's northeastern Beni province and were veteran Communist party militants. A younger brother, Osvaldo, or "Chato," was studying in Moscow. Also, there were the Vázquez-Viaña brothers, Humberto and Jorge, the European-educated sons of a well-known Bolivian historian; Jorge, or "Loro" (the Parrot), had worked closely with Furry and Masetti in the 1963–1964 Salta campaign. Another was Rodolfo Saldaña, a former miner and unionist, who had helped hide Ciro Bustos and his companions in his La Paz home after their arrival from Algeria. Loyola Guzmán, a young woman of predominantly Quechua Indian blood, was the daughter of a Communist teacher in Bolivia's mining communities, and a graduate of the elite Communist party political cadres' training school in Moscow; she too had helped with the logistics for the Argentine and Peruvian guerrillas. These, and a handful of other Bolivians, some of whom were already training in Cuba, were the hard core of activists that the Cubans could count upon to support a war in Peru or to get a war going in Bolivia itself.

There is enduring controversy over the true target of Che's next—and last—war making effort. Pombo said that it wasn't until after he and Tuma arrived in Bolivia that the Peruvian plans changed, and Bolivia itself came under consideration. Ariel has a different story: that it was with Bolivia already in mind that he, Piñeiro, and Fidel had managed to lure Che out of his confinement in Tanzania.*

"One of the ways we convinced him to come to Prague was by getting him enthusiastic about the possibilities in Bolivia, where some agreements had been made and conditions were being prepared. Previously under consideration were Venezuela and Guatemala, but Bolivia offered many advantages. First, because of its proximity to Argentina, which was very important to Che. Next, because of the agreements, the prior experience there, the human assets, and the party's militant traditions. And finally, because of its geographic location, which offered good possibilities for the later 'irradiation' of guerrillas trained in the Bolivian guerrilla front to the neighboring countries of Argentina, Peru, Brazil, and Chile. He became enthusiastic over this possibility and agreed to go to Prague."

This is perhaps the most crucial single question about the life of Ernesto Che Guevara to remain unanswered: *Who* decided he should go to Bolivia; when and why was that decision made? Fidel has said that Che made the selection of Bolivia himself, and that he tried to stall him, urging him to wait until conditions were more advanced. Manuel Piñeiro concurs. He says that Fidel persuaded Che to come back to Cuba after they learned from Papi that

---

*Pombo told the author that it was with Peru in mind that Papi was sent ahead to Bolivia from Prague, to talk with Monje about facilitating their entry into Peru, and to set things in motion for Che's arrival; that he and Tuma were then dispatched to Peru to assist Papi. He said that it was only after they were in Bolivia that the Peruvian guerrillas began falling apart and were suspected of being "penetrated," at which point the idea of beginning a war in Bolivia itself was discussed. One problem with this version—in addition to its being contradicted by Ariel—is that Pombo didn't arrive in Bolivia until July 1966, while the disintegration of the Peruvian guerrillas had begun months earlier with the deaths of MIR leaders Luis de la Puente Uceda and Guillermo Lobatón, followed by the arrest of Ricardo Gadea. And the Havana-aligned ELN's leader Héctor Béjar, had been arrested back in March.

Che was ready to head straight to Bolivia from Prague without anything prepared for his arrival there. Hoping to prevent his headstrong Argentine lieutenant from marching into danger, Fidel offered him Cuban help in selecting and training his men, as well as laying the groundwork for a Bolivian guerrilla *foco*. Fidel's and Piñeiro's explanations do not exactly mesh with the accounts given by Ariel and Pombo, but then, *their* versions don't match up, either. How to explain the contradictions between the versions of Ariel and Pombo—one a senior Cuban intelligence official and diplomat, the other a high-ranking military general and officially recognized "Hero of the Revolution"—let alone between them and the version offered by Piñeiro and the *jefe máximo?* The true answer might lie in this never-before-published preamble to Pombo's diary, begun in Prague and written up later based on his notes.

> Seven months following the termination of the guerrilla operations in African territory and in the midst of an intense period of preparation and organization for our next adventure, conceived to take place in Peruvian territory . . . Ramón [Che]* gathered Pacho, Tuma and myself and read us a letter he'd recently received, in which Fidel analyzed [the situation] and urged him to coldly reconsider his decision, and as a consequence of that analysis he proposed:
>
> [Che's] return to Cuba for a short period of time, and at the same time he pointed out the perspectives for fighting in Bolivia, the agreements reached with Estanislao (Mario Monje) to launch the armed struggle.
>
> [Che] told us that, faced with the correctness of these proposals, he had decided to send Francisco** to La Paz, to explore the possibilities of the struggle. . . . We anxiously awaited the return of Francisco. This took place in the first days of June. His report is that the results are positive. Papi affirmed that the conditions were propitious, even for our arrival there [in Bolivia]. Notwithstanding that, Francisco told Ramón he wanted to abandon ship, asking him not to tell us because he felt ashamed; as a reason he cited his feelings about dying far from Cuba.†

*Che's name had changed again, from "Tato" in Africa, to "Ramón" in Prague—one of several, including "Mongo" and "Fernando," he would use in Bolivia.

**The identity of "Francísco" has never been disclosed; he is referred to in the published version of Pombo's diary as "a Cuban liaison" who had decided not to continue in the venture. Piñeiro says Francisco was a brave man, seasoned in urban combat, but that unexplained "psychological reasons" were behind his desire to withdraw.

†During his stay in Cuba, the author obtained a partial copy of Pombo's original handwritten diary, the typewritten manuscript that he wrote later, and a copy of the editing corrections he made. The above excerpt is taken from the original typed document. In 1996, after

So, it would appear that it was Fidel himself who persuaded Che to go start the struggle in Bolivia, sometime in the spring of 1966—and that the plan was set into motion soon after Francisco's return from La Paz and his and Papi's positive assessments of the situation.

Che sent Pombo and Tuma ahead to La Paz, while he and Pacho made their way back to Cuba, arriving there around July 21. Che had been away for more than a year, but he was not returning "home." Instead, he was lodged in a safe house on the rural fringe of eastern Havana, his presence there known to only a handful.

VI

One aspect of the secret planning for Che's Bolivian mission that most parties involved agree upon is that, at a certain point, an "agreement" had been forged between Cuba and Bolivian Communist leader Mario Monje. Most everyone, that is, except Mario Monje. Speaking at length from his self-imposed exile home in wintry Moscow nearly three decades later, Monje offered up a lengthy and candid explanation of his own tangled and often-duplicitous dealings with Piñeiro, Fidel, and Che.

Monje's relationship with the Cuban revolution extended back to its early days and, as he told it, he had approved his party's help for Béjar's and Masetti's guerrilla groups in hopes that Cuba would not try to start a guerrilla war in his own country. Even after the Masetti and Béjar episodes, however, Monje remained suspicious of Cuban intentions, keeping a watchful eye on their activities and, most especially, on Che Guevara.

When Che disappeared from Cuba in 1965 and rumors began circulating as to his whereabouts, Monje took notice. He never believed the stories of a rift between Fidel and Che; he knew that they shared the goal of revolutionary expansion, and suspected Che was probably somewhere in Africa.

So matters stood until September 1965, when his party received an invitation from the Cuban government for three of its members to attend the Tricontinental Conference convening in Havana in January 1966. Monje soon learned, however, that Oscar Zamora, leader of the rival Maoist Communist party of Bolivia, had also been invited to attend and was being al-

---

being suppressed for three decades, the *edited* version of Pombo's diary was published in Cuba and Argentina with Cuban government approval, less this key passage. (Pombo, whose real name is Harry Villegas, is an active general in Cuba's Revolutionary Armed Forces, and a loyal Fidelísta.) In 1966, a Bolivian newspaper reprinted Pombo's entire original diary after being granted access to the vault of Bolivia's Central Bank, where it is safeguarded along with Che's original diaries.

lowed to head a larger delegation. To Monje and his Politburo comrades, it appeared clear that, for whatever reasons, the Cubans were favoring the pro-Chinese party. In November, Monje's comrades urged him to travel to Havana ahead of time and get to the bottom of the mystery.

More than just a protocol snub, the Cuban overture to Zamora's group raised the disquieting possibility in Monje's mind that the Cubans were still plotting an insurrection in Bolivia. Zamora was known to have offered his forces to the Cubans for this option, and, significantly, Zamora was friendly with Che. At this point, said Monje, he began wondering: "Where is Che? What is his role in this?"

From then on, recalled Monje, he began to study news reports closely, looking for clues as to Che's whereabouts. Meanwhile, he told his comrades that when he went to Havana, he would be as conciliatory as possible, to ingratiate himself with the Cubans in order to learn what they were up to. His idea was to tell the Cubans that his party wasn't opposed to "preparing themselves" for an eventual armed struggle with Cuba's help, and would even offer himself and other party members to personally receive Cuban military training.

Feeling "somewhat cautious," Monje left for Prague in December 1965, where many of the foreign delegations heading to the Tricontinental Conference were assembling for the flight to Havana. On the plane to Havana he recognized Régis Debray, a young French Marxist theoretician whom he knew to be closely linked to Fidel and Cuba's security apparatus, and who had visited Bolivia the year before. By now, Debray was known—largely on the strength of a series of articles he had written—to be an active proponent of the Cuban revolutionary model in Latin America.*

When he arrived in Havana, Monje told the Cuban security service that he was there not only for the Tricontinental Conference but to discuss "another matter." He was quickly transferred from his hotel to a safe house run by Cuban intelligence. There he was joined by two Bolivian party comrades previously selected as escorts, and would later be joined by the other two Tricontinental delegation members still on their way.

Monje quickly got in touch with the circle of young Bolivian "students" in Havana, all of them Bolivian Communist Youth members, and discovered that many had been receiving military training without party approval. Instead of confronting them, he "joined" them, as it were. Meeting with the Cuban Interior Ministry officials—Piñeiro's people—Monje told them of his interest in undergoing military training along with some other comrades. "They were very happy," Monje recalled.

*See the appendix for elaboration.

So happy, in fact, that Monje's scheme enabled him to thoroughly outmaneuver Zamora's group. In what he proudly described as a game of brinksmanship, Monje boldly demanded that the Cubans choose between granting official status at the conference to his group—now disposed to take up arms—or Zamora's. His delegation was accepted as the official one, while, as Monje put it, Zamora's group was sent on "a tour" of the Cuban countryside.

At the conference, Monje quickly realized that it was not the speeches being given that were important, but what was happening behind the scenes. "The Cubans began seeking out contacts with this group and that," he recalled, "but always with the same intention of seeing about creating new guerrilla focos in Latin America. They gave most attention to the more radical groups, the more defiant groups, those who to a certain degree were in contradiction with the more traditional Communists."

Meanwhile, said Monje, he knew that the Soviets were also uncomfortable with this Cuban guerrilla recruitment campaign, and when the Tricontinental was over he decided to make a quick trip to Moscow to "take soundings." To his surprise, he was ushered straight through to Boris Ponomoriov, the supreme boss of the Central Committee's International Department.

"We began talking about Bolivia . . . and he asked me about the Tricontinental, and what the thinking of the [Bolivian] Communist party was about what [Cuba] was preparing. I gave him my criteria, more or less, and told him what we were planning to do, and then he asked me if I knew where Che was. I told him that I knew that he had been in Africa, but that he had already left." Monje got the distinct impression that this was fresh news to Ponomoriov.*

It also became clear to Monje that the Kremlin was "disturbed" by what had transpired at the Tricontinental, where the Cubans had encouraged "the most radical groups." "This could create problems and so they wanted to find out what [Che's] role was, where the figure [behind it all] was." The Soviets had come to the same conclusion Monje had: The driving force behind the Tricontinental Conference had also been its most conspicuous absentee—Che Guevara.

After his Kremlin briefing, Monje returned to Cuba to begin his military training with the Bolivians he had left behind. He had also come up with a plan to stall the return to Bolivia of those students who had already

---

*Monje was giving himself a little more credit than was due. The Kremlin, of course, already knew where Che had been, ever since Alexiev had informed Brezhnev, and had only recently helped evacuate the Cuban fighters from Tanzania.

been trained; he would ask them to stay until he and the other newcomers had finished their own military training, at which point he would try to ship them all off to Moscow for "theoretical training." This ruse, he reasoned, would forestall any surreptitious Cuban plan to put these youths in the field behind his party's back, as he suspected the Cubans were anxious to do. Monje knew that his own training would take three or four months to complete, giving him time to alert his party comrades back in Bolivia about what was happening.

As he was about to begin his training in late January 1966, Monje was summoned by Fidel. At the meeting were several others, including Piñeiro and some of his agents. According to Monje, Fidel asked him what his intentions were regarding his Bolivian cadres in Cuba.

Monje gave Fidel a less than sincere answer, but one that sounded credible. Reminding him that Bolivia had a history of popular uprisings, he told Fidel that the current situation, with the nation again under military dictatorship, indicated the possibility of another insurrection. "If there is one," he told Fidel, "we'll be able to take control of the situation." With the active backup of his Cuban-trained cadres, he explained, he could push for elections, in which the Communists would emerge in a strengthened position.

It was not the answer Fidel wanted to hear. What about the possibilities for a guerrilla struggle? Monje explained that he didn't see that as a realistic possibility in Bolivia. At this, several of Piñeiro's agents leapt in to offer their own opinions; from what they said, Monje knew they already had been to Bolivia and had been studying it closely.

After the meeting, says Monje, Piñeiro buttonholed him and told him, "Fidel didn't like the interview. He doesn't like your plan because you're not thinking of the guerrilla struggle, and these people in training are [destined] for the guerrilla struggle. You have two or three months. Revise your points of view, and then start a guerrilla war."

Using the excuse that he hadn't realized he would be away so long, and that he had left unattended problems back in Bolivia, Monje asked Piñeiro to send for Ramiro Otero, the Bolivian Communist party representative in Prague. "I played that game," explained Monje, "because I knew they couldn't let me leave."

When Otero arrived in February, Monje took him into the garden of his safe house and gave him explicit instructions: "Go to Bolivia, ask for a meeting with the Politburo, and tell them the Cubans are preparing for a guerrilla war in Bolivia."

With Otero hurrying back to La Paz, Monje's training began. At thirtyfive, he was the oldest in the group—most of the others were in their mid- to late twenties—but he tried to keep up in the exercises. Otero returned with bad news. He hadn't been able to talk to the Central Committee, only to members of the lesser Secretariat, and they hadn't believed Monje's story. They also sent word that the military training should end and Monje should return immediately, for serious doubts had been cast on his activities during his absence, and he was in danger of losing his post to his substitute.

Monje felt caught between a rock and hard place. According to his own slightly tortured explanation, he had gone along with the Cuban plan for war in Bolivia only as a means to forestall that war, but now his party compatriots were thoroughly alarmed. He needed to return to Bolivia to explain what was going on to the right people in his party and clear up the misunderstandings, but the Cubans would be highly suspicious if he did so. It was also too late for his original plan—to keep the cadres away from Bolivia by sending them all to the Soviet Union—because his own training had almost ended and the cadres were now itching to go home. In desperation, Monje arranged to meet with Fidel, along with a visiting Bolivian Politburo member, Humberto Ramírez, to define the situation. In May, they flew to Santiago, to talk with Fidel in his car during his drive back to Havana.

Along the way, said Monje, Fidel talked about everything other than Bolivia. "He would stop the car and explain to us how he had carried out ambushes. . . . [It seems] he was interested in having us see how the guerrilla struggle is waged. We even stopped to shoot along the way, doing marksmanship, testing out weapons."

Their car journey ended in Camagüey, where they stayed overnight. They still hadn't spoken about Bolivia. The next day they boarded a plane for Havana. Monje, seated with Ramírez, began to fear his mission had failed. Then Papi walked down the aisle to tell Monje that Fidel wanted to speak to him alone.

He sat down next to Fidel, who asked him how he "saw things." Before Monje could answer, however, Fidel started talking again: "You know, you've been a good friend of ours. You have developed an internationalist policy with us. Frankly I want to thank you for all the help you've given us, and now it turns out that a mutual friend wants to return to his country, someone whose revolutionary caliber nobody can question. And nobody can deny him the right to return to his country. And he thinks the best place to pass through [to get there] is Bolivia. I ask you to help him pass through your country."

Monje didn't need to ask who "the mutal friend" was, and immediately agreed to help. At that, Fidel added: "Look, as for your own plans, just keep developing them as you see fit. If you want us to help in training more people, send us more. . . . We are not going to intervene in your affairs." Monje says he thanked him and repeated his willingness to help in the "transit" of their mutual friend.

Then, using his trademark combination of flattery and enigmatic language, Fidel said: "You've always been good at selecting people; I'd like you to choose the people that will receive [Che], accompany him in the country, and escort him to the border. If you and your party agree, they could accompany him within the country to gather experiences, or just go to the border and that will be the end of it."

He then asked Monje to give him some names. Monje named the four cadres he had authorized for training in Cuba: Coco Peredo, Loro Vázquez-Viaña, Julio "Ñato" Mendez, and Rodolfo Saldaña. Papi, who was listening, commented "Excellent." Fidel noted down the names and told Monje: "That's it." Their business was finished.

Monje felt greatly relieved and told Humberto Ramírez that they needn't worry, the Cubans' plans were different from what they had suspected, but they still needed to inform the party.

By June, Monje was done with his training. He sent his four hand-picked comrades back to Bolivia but told the original group of students to stay and "continue their studies" in Cuba until the party decided what was to be done with them. He wrote a letter to Jorge Kolle Cueto, his substitute in La Paz, explaining his promise to Fidel that the party would assist their "mutual friend" in passing through Bolivia. Before returning to Bolivia himself, Monje decided to take a short trip to Moscow.

Before he left, said Monje, the Cubans suggested he stop over in Prague en route, so that "someone" there might look him up. But Monje decided to avoid Prague, suspecting the Cubans might lay a "trap" for him. "They waited for me in Prague. What for?" Monje surmised the Cubans were planning to present him with a fait accompli, telling him that by undergoing training he had in effect approved the armed struggle option for his country, and that he had no choice but to go forward with it.

Monje revealed neither why he went to Moscow on this trip nor whom he met with there, but, to judge from his earlier admissions, one can reasonably assume he spoke in the Kremlin about Fidel's request and revealed Che's next destination. And in view of the Kremlin's increasing impatience with the "fire-starters" in Cuba, their reaction can also be surmised. Undoubtedly, Monje was advised to stand up for his rights as the Bolivian party chief, and told not to let Che or Fidel push him around. As things turned out, that is exactly what Monje would try to do.

VII

With Fidel's help, Che was putting his chess pieces in motion, laying the board for the scene of his next "adventure with a cause." He was hoping to eventually go to Argentina, but Argentina was not ready just yet; the conditions for it would have to be prepared from Bolivia. There, Che envisioned, guerrillas from the neighboring countries would come and join in the fighting, then fan out to form allied guerrilla armies in their own countries. When the Argentine rebellion was finally up and running, he would leave Bolivia and take command.

It was with this ultimate goal in mind, say the Cubans, that Che had placed Tania in La Paz. For the time being, she could provide them with valuable intelligence about the regime and the political situation in Bolivia, but she was also to be used as a liaison with the evolving insurgencies in the neighboring countries, especially Argentina.

So far, her selection as an agent seemed to be paying off handsomely. As "Laura Gutiérrez Bauer," an attractive single white woman, an Argentine ethnologist of independent means, Tania was able to make quick headway in penetrating the small and racially stratified social environment of La Paz. Within two months of arriving, she had established a circle of valuable contacts within the political and diplomatic community, obtained her Bolivian residency and work permit, and even found a volunteer job in the Ministry of Education's Folklore Research Committee. On the side, she taught German to a small group of students.

One of her best contacts was Gonzalo López Muñoz, President Barriento's press secretary, who gave her documents with his office's letterhead and a credential as a sales representative for a weekly magazine he edited.* By late 1965, she had found a suitable "husband," a young Bolivian engineering student, and married him. The move would gain her Bolivian citizenship, and her husband could be gotten rid of by being sent abroad on a study scholarship, an idea she had already implanted in her guileless groom's mind.

In January 1966 she was visited by one of Piñeiro's men, posing as a businessman. The agent, code-named "Mercy," brought her mail carried inside a false shoe heel, and the news that she had been honored with membership in the new Cuban Communist party. Explaining to her acquaintances

---

*Later on, after the guerrillas were discovered, López Muñoz was arrested and charged with aiding them. He claimed he had been innocently duped and was later released, but he was in fact a willing partner in the guerrilla plan, recruited by Inti Peredo, whose wife was his wife's cousin.

that she had been offered some interpreting work, she slipped out of La Paz to meet up again with the agent in Brazil, where he gave her a counterintelligence refresher course. In April, she traveled to Mexico, where another Cuban agent gave her a new Argentine passport, and she debriefed him on the "politico-military" situation in Bolivia. She returned to La Paz in early May with instructions to lay low until she was contacted again.

Meanwhile, "Mercy" wrote an extensive and detailed report of the time he had spent with Tania. He found her deeply committed to the cause and the work she was doing, but under extreme nervous tension and emotional strain, throwing fits on several occasions. He decided that her behavior was caused by the stress of being so long alone in a "capitalist country," but concluded on a bright and sloganeering note, saying: "I believe she is aware of the honor of being a link in a chain that in the not-too-distant future will strangle imperialism, and she is proud of having been chosen for special work to aid the Latin American Revolution."*

But, as a poem she wrote in April showed, Tania was in a sentimental and melancholic frame of mind, seemingly questioning the cost of her clandestine existence and the effacement of her real identity. Calling it "To Leave a Memory," she wrote:

So I must leave, like flowers that wilt?
Will my name one day be forgotten
And nothing of me remain on the earth?
At least, flowers and song.
How then, must my heart behave?
Is it in vain that we live, that we appear on the earth?

To protect Tania's false identity, Che had passed along orders for Papi to minimize his contact with her; he didn't want Papi to blow her cover by spending too much time around her. He also sent orders that Tania not be used in the set-up phase of the guerrilla war. She was too valuable as a deep-cover asset to risk losing; in addition, Che needed her as a courier who could come and go without detection to Argentina, Peru, and the other countries where he planned to recruit fighters.

---

*"Mercy's" identity remains undisclosed, but Manuel Piñeiro revealed that he was not a Cuban, but some other nationality, an older, experienced agent he had dispatched to monitor Tania's progress.

By the time Pombo and Tuma arrived carrying Che's orders in late July, however, Papi had been in regular contact with Tania since May. He had not only briefed her on the guerrilla plans but introduced her to the man dispatched to be the mission's permanent liaison with Havana, Renán Montero, also known as "Iván." Tania recognized him from the meeting in Havana two years before, when Che had told her of her mission.

As always, Argentina loomed large in Che's mind, and with his arrival in Bolivia only a matter of months away, he tried getting things moving on that front as well. In May 1966, while Che was still in Prague, his Argentine lieutenant Ciro Bustos was summoned to Havana by Piñeiro. The last time Bustos had seen Che was in the summer of 1964, six months before Che went off on his last world tour and then vanished from sight. In that meeting, Che had ordered Bustos to return to Argentina and keep up his organizing work, to "lean on the schisms," as he put it—that is, to avoid the Argentine Communist party and recruit cadres from disaffected factions. Bustos had spent the intervening two years doing just that, with the hopes of launching a future guerrilla group. With no firm timetable for action in hand from Che with which to draw potential recruits, it was not an easy job, but Bustos had had some success. When Che disappeared in April 1965, Bustos was unperturbed, knowing he was involved in revolutionary work somewhere, and would one day reappear to assume control of the guerrilla network he was building for him.

When Bustos arrived in Cuba, he assumed he would be meeting with Che, but instead he was placed alone in a security safe house, a mansion in the Marianao district of Havana. A special provisions truck came by regularly and left him food and cases of beer. He spent several weeks there waiting, with no explanations offered about how long he was to wait or exactly why he was there. Finally, boiling with impatience and hearing that his friend Furry was now the army commander in Oriente, Bustos flew to Santiago. He found Furry at a military base in Mayarí.

Bustos gave Furry his litany of complaints, and Furry immediately got on a radio-telephone in his office and had a long cursing conversation with someone—Bustos believes it was El Colorado Piñeiro—demanding that he attend to Bustos "properly" and to fix up his meeting with "the man," presumably Che. It was a strange scene that Bustos can still recall vividly. As Furry made his call, "Soviet officers passed back and forth nervously outside in the fog at five in the morning."

Once back at the safe house in Havana, Bustos said, "everything changed." Bustos was told that Che wanted a report from him and needed it quickly; a secretary was brought in to take shorthand. "I dictated a report about our work and the national [Argentina] political situation, predicting a military coup, which did in fact take place before I returned to the country." Finally, Bustos was informed he would not be seeing Che on this visit; he should await a "contact" in Córdoba, but he wasn't told when it would take place or who it would be.*

Back in Córdoba, Bustos put on a wig to disguise himself and went into the Salta prison, where he and his imprisoned comrades held a whispered "general staff council." Their cases were all on appeal, but it would be some time yet before they had a resolution, and under the new military regime that had seized power while Bustos was away, their prospects looked bleak. In Cuba, Bustos had explored the possibility of organizing a breakout to free them, and Ariel, Piñeiro's deputy, had promised to look into it.** For now, all Bustos could do was go home to his family, resume the routine of "normal life," and await the promised "contact" that would lead him to Che.

VIII

By the end of summer, the troops for Che's Bolivian mission had been selected and were assembled at a secret training camp in the eastern Cuban province of Pinar del Río. It was in an area called Viñales, distinguished by a peculiar geological formation, called *"mogotes,"* a series of large bulbous jungle-covered hills that rise steeply like great green puffballs from the red-earthed tobacco fields and river valleys. Their base camp was an ironic choice. Nestled on top of one of the *mogotes* was a luxurious country villa with a stream-fed swimming pool, which had formerly belonged

---

*Before returning to Argentina, Bustos would be involved in a very strange and intriguing odyssey. On an invitation from Mao's government, he flew to China, where he spent three weeks being grandly feted as Che's chief Argentine guerrilla lieutenant. Over the course of a series of meetings, Chinese government officials offered to give military training to "Che's men" and to provide them with unspecified material and financial support. The tantalizing offer came with a catch, however, as Bustos discovered during a meeting with the vice president of the National People's Congress in Beijing, when he was asked to publicly denounce Fidel Castro for having "allied with imperialism." A stunned Bustos quickly refused, and his "goodwill tour" ended shortly afterward. When they later met up in Bolivia, Bustos told Che about his uncomfortable encounter, at which Che laughed, saying: "You were lucky. It was the beginning of the Cultural Revolution; it could have cost you your balls." Che never clarified for Bustos if *he* had engineered the trip, or what his own dealings with the Chinese had been; because of the rapid-fire sequence of events that followed their talk, this was to be the only time they discussed it.

**Ariel told the author he did speak to several left-wing Argentine underground groups, including the leaders of a small "rather terrorist group," about the breakout idea. In the end, it was deemed too difficult to pull off, and Cuba fell back on the "legal option," supporting the efforts of Gustavo Roca and the other lawyers to get the prisoners' sentences reduced.

to an American accused of being a CIA agent. It had been expropiated, and now it was serving as the launching pad for Che's next anti-Yankee expedition.

Che had chosen an eclectic group for his latest venture. It included a few men who had been with him in the Congo, others who had been with him in the sierra war and members of his bodyguard corps. From different parts of Cuba, they had been put on planes to Havana, where they were taken to Raúl Castro's office. There they recognized other men, old friends they hadn't seen for some time. None of them knew why they were there. Finally, Raúl told them they had been honored by their selection for an "internationalist mission." For most of them, it was a dream come true—to be an internationalist revolutionary had become one of the highest aspirations for Cubans serving in the armed forces.

There were a dozen men. One of them was Dariel Alarcón Ramírez, "Benigno," a tough, lean *guajiro* in his late twenties who had proven his mettle as a hardy fighter in the sierra and as a member of Camilo's invasion column; most recently he had been in the Congo with Che and proven his mettle as a hardy fighter. Another was Eliseo Reyes, or "Rolando," twenty-six, another sierra veteran who had been on Che's long march to the Escambray. Smart and loyal, he had served for a time as the head of police intelligence, then fought against counterrevolutionaries in Pinar del Río.

Thirty-three-year-old "Olo" Pantoja, or "Antonio," had been one of Che's rebel officers in the sierra and one of the instructors of Masetti's group. Papi Martínez Tamayo's younger brother, René, or "Arturo," was a veteran of clandestine work for State Security and the military. Twenty-nine-year-old Gustavo Machín de Hoed—"Alejandro"—had come out of the Directorio Revolucionario and joined Che in the Escambray; later he had been one of Che's vice ministers of industry. "Manuel" or Miguel Hernández Osorio, was thirty-five and had led Che's vanguard squad during the march to the Escambray.

Che's traveling companion from Prague, and his personal courier with La Paz, was thirty-one-year-old Alberto Fernández Montes de Oca. Also called "Pacho" and "Pachungo," Montes de Oca had been a teacher before joining the July 26 urban underground during the war. Besides "Pombo," there were three more black men. Octavio de la Concepción de la Pedraja, "Morogoro" in the Congo, was a thirty-one-year-old doctor, an anti-Batista veteran and a career officer in Cuba's armed forces. One of Raúl's veterans, thirty-three-year-old Israel Reyes Zayas, "Braulio," another military careerist, had been with Che in the Congo as "Azi." And Leonardo "Tamayito" Tamayo, or "Urbano," as he was now called, had been with Che since 1957 as a member of his bodyguard corps.

Juan "Joaquín" Vitalio Acuña, heavyset and the oldest of them all at forty-one, had been in Che's column in the war and become a *comandante* himself during the final push to power. Another Central Committee man and career officer, Antonio Sánchez Díaz, also called "Marcos" or "Pinares," had been one of Camilo Cienfuegos's officers and had been promoted to *comandante* after the rebel victory. And finally, there was the thirty-year-old and extroverted Jesús Suárez Gayol, or "Rubio," Orlando Borrego's friend since the Escambray, and currently his deputy as Cuba's vice minister of sugar.

Nobody knew where they were going to fight or who their commander would be until the day a stranger in civilian clothes, balding and middle-aged, showed up at their camp. "Ramón" began walking up and down before the assembled men, caustically insulting them. It was only when he had taken the joke quite far with Eliseo Reyes, who grew offended, that Ramón revealed his true identity: Che. From then on, Che lived with his men, overseeing their physical training and target practice, and, as always, imparting daily classes, this time in "cultural education," French, and a new language—Quechua. They were going to Bolivia.

By August, a base of operations had been located in Bolivia, a remote 1,500-hectare (3,700-acre) tract of wilderness land in the country's backward southeastern region, with a seasonal river, the Ñancahuasu, running through it. It lay in a hilly, forested area abutting the eastern foothills of the Andean cordillera and at the edge of the vast tropical desert of the *chaco* that spreads eastward to Paraguay, the nearest border. It was situated 250 kilometers (about 150 miles) south of Santa Cruz along a dirt road, and a similar distance from the Argentine border, while the nearest town, an old Spanish colonial outpost called Lagunillas, was about 20 kilometers (12 miles) away. A few hours drive farther south lay the oil-drilling and army garrison town of Camiri.

Since his return from Cuba, Monje had complied with his promise to Fidel, assigning his Cuban-trained party cadres to help make the arrangements for Che's arrival, buying equipment and weapons, renting safe houses, and lining up transport. Papi, who had gone to Bolivia with no clear directives about where he should establish a base, had agreed to the Ñancahuasu purchase based on Monje's recommendation.

Years later, Monje admitted that it was an almost arbitrary choice and certainly not a "strategic" one. He sent Coco, Loro, and Saldoña off to look for a good base "near" the Argentine border—assuming that was where Che was headed—and two weeks later, Loro returned, having located Ñancahuasu; Monje says he looked at a map, decided that it seemed "close" enough to Argentina, and gave the go-ahead. On August 26, Loro and Coco, posing as prospective pig-breeders, bought the land.

When Pombo and Tuma arrived in late July and told Monje that their "plans had changed," that the "continental" guerrilla operations would now have to begin in Bolivia rather than Peru, Monje told them he was in agreement. When the Cubans sounded him out on the possibility that Che might be personally involved, Monje expressed his willingness to go to the field himself and agreed to give them more men to set up a rural guerrilla front, while still stating his preference for a "popular uprising."

But a few days later, Monje had changed his tune again, saying he did not remember promising the Cubans more men, and reminding them threateningly that he could withdraw the party's help altogether. He had to be in control of what was happening in his country, he said, and resented the way the Cubans were trying to dictate terms to the Bolivians. In an attempt to pull rank, he alluded to conversations he had had in Moscow detailing *his* plans, and said he would request Soviet aid at the appropriate moment. He had, he said, agreed to lend his party's help in getting Che to Argentina and to assist the guerrilla efforts in Brazil and Peru, but Bolivia itself had never been under discussion. The Cuban advance team remonstrated with him and Monje backed off, but from that time forward the air was full of mutual distrust.

One of the reasons for Monje's latest demurral was the outcome of Bolivia's general elections that had been held at the end of July. With the Communist party given permission to field candidates, Monje and his fellow Politburo apparatchiks had opted to participate while simultaneously telling Cuban-trained Young Turks such as Coco Peredo that they were only delaying, not abandoning, the "armed struggle" option. In the elections, the party had picked up some votes, a mere fraction of the total, but still the biggest number it had ever obtained. For the party moderates, it was an argument to continue working within the system.

In early September, while Monje continued to vacillate and send mixed signals, Che dispatched Pacho to La Paz to assess the situation. The Cubans began taking soundings among the party Bolivian cadres to determine their affinities; would they join them if a guerrilla war was launched independent of the party? Coco Peredo, for one, told them he would fight with them to the death, but some of the others, loyal to the party hierarchy, clearly could not be counted on. Meanwhile, Che sent word that he wanted the guerrilla base to be in the Alto Beni, a tropical farming region in the upper Amazonian watershed, northeast of La Paz and at the other end of the country from Ñancahuasu. He told his men to make a land purchase there, and to then transfer the weapons they had stored in Santa Cruz.

Meanwhile, Monje learned from party informants that Régis Debray had been sighted moving around the Bolivian countryside—in Cochabamba, in the Chapare and in the Alto Beni—all regions that had been under discussion by the Cubans as possible guerrilla sites. He also heard that Debray had met with Moisés Guevara, an action-minded, dissident miners' leader, who had broken off from Oscar Zamora's pro-Chinese Communist party faction. Monje accused the Cubans of operating behind his back, and demanded to know if they were having any dealings with the *fraccionalista* Guevara. The Cuban advance team denied any knowledge of Debray's presence, and assured Monje that there had been no contact with Moisés Guevara. Both assertions were, of course, untrue. In fact, Che had sent the Cubans a message explaining Debray's mission: to recruit Moisés Guevara's force, and to make an assessment of the Alto Beni area he had chosen as the war's launching ground.

Pombo, Papi, and Tuma were caught in the middle. They already had a guerrilla base, but it was in the southeast. They had a semblance of Bolivian Communist party support and a whole network established. All of it had come about through their dealings with Monje, they told Che, and as difficult as the party leader was to read, he was really all they had at the moment. As for Moisés Guevara, he had promised to join the armed struggle, but so far had produced no men and was demanding money of them. They urged Che to reconsider his choices.

To complicate things further, they were also dealing with the Peruvian guerrillas who had expected to be the primary focus of Cuba's guerrilla assistance efforts in the area. The Peruvians were led by a Peruvian-Chinese Mao look-alike named Juan Pablo Chang, an old friend of Hilda Gadea's, who was now trying to rebuild the clandestine infrastucture shattered after the deaths of Lobatón and Uceda and the imprisonment of Ricardo Gadea and Héctor Béjar. Chang had a man with the Cubans in La Paz, Julio Danigno Pacheco—alias "Sánchez"—but he and his comrades were upset about the Cubans' change of focus to Bolivia. The Cubans were diplomatic, holding a meeting with Sánchez to placate him and explain the new strategy.

Finally, despite Che's orders to find a place in the Alto Beni, his lieutenants were finding it difficult to oblige. They sent him a long report lobbying in favor of the Ñancahuasu property already purchased, and pointed out that the Beni was heavily populated; the large amount of land they would need was not available, and if they set up camp on a smaller farm, they ran the risk of early detection. At last, Che relented, sending word that the present farm would do for the moment.

It was now October, but many things still hung inconclusively in the air. In a new twist, Monje announced that his Central Committee had voted in favor of the armed struggle but, as usual, emphasized that it would have to be Bolivian-led. He intended to go to Havana to make this policy understood. Despite the obvious need for urgency, however, Monje first made a visit to Bulgaria; he would not arrive in Havana until late November. There he would discover that the man who was becoming his nemesis was nowhere to be found. In fact, Che had already left for Bolivia, having decided to arrive unannounced except to his closest circle of Cuban comrades.

In his meeting with Fidel, Monje recalled, the Cuban leader would not confirm or deny that there had been a change of plans. He let Monje make his point that in Bolivia the revolution had to be directed by Bolivians, but deferred the issue, suggesting that he and Che "get together and talk." Where was Monje going to be around Christmas? Fidel asked. In Bolivia, Monje replied. Fidel announced that a meeting would be arranged around that time, somewhere "outside" Bolivia, but near the border.

By now, Monje said, he knew where that place was—not outside Bolivia at all, but in Ñancahuasu. He returned to Bolivia in mid-December, more certain than ever that the Cubans had deceived him.*

IX

Che had lain low until the final days of his stay in Cuba. Aside from Fidel, the men in his training camp, and a handful of high-ranking revolutionary leaders, Orlando Borrego was one of the few people who knew of his presence. Still only in his late twenties, Borrego was now the Cuban minister of sugar but was keen to accompany Che to the battlefront. When Che sent word that he had selected Jesús Suárez Gayol, Borrego's deputy, to go to Bolivia with him, Borrego asked to go, too. Che refused, but promised he could join at a future stage, when the revolution was more secured.

There was another reason why Che wanted his protégé to stay. After one of Aleida's recent clandestine reunions with Che abroad, she had returned with a special present for Borrego. It was Che's own heavily marked-up copy of *Economía Política,* the official, Stalin-era Soviet manual for the "correct" interpretation and application of the teachings of Marx, Engels, and Lenin in the construction of a socialist economy. With it came a ream of accompanying notations and comments, many of them highly critical, in which he openly questioned some of the basic tenets of "scientific socialism" as codified by the USSR. He also sent an outline on his theory for the "Budgetary Finance System" he favored against the established Moscow-line theories. What Che had had in mind was a new manual on political economy, better applied to modern times, for use by the developing nations and revolutionary societies in the Third World. As for his economic theory, he wanted it expanded into book form. He knew he was not going to have

---

*Although Monje would not say he had done so, it is believed in Cuba that he traveled to Moscow as part of his return trip to Bolivia for the express purpose of complaining to his Kremlin handlers about the Cuban plans for his country.

time to finish either project and was now entrusting Borrego with completing the tasks for him.

With Che's package came a personal letter, addressing Borrego by his pet name "Vinagreta" (Sourpuss). Referring to the material he had sent him via "Tormenta" (Storm, a teasing reference to Aleida), Che urged Borrego to "do his best" with it. He also told him to "be patient" about Bolivia, but to "be ready for the second phase."

In Che's critique of the Stalinist manual, he pointed out that since Lenin's writings, little had been added to update the evaluations of Marxism except for a few things written by Stalin and Mao. He indicted Lenin—who had introduced some capitalist forms of competition into the Soviet Union as a means of kick-starting its economy in the twenties—as the culprit for many of the Soviet Union's mistakes, and, while reiterating his "admiration and respect toward that culprit," he warned, in block letters, that the USSR and Soviet bloc were doomed to "return to capitalism."

When Borrego read this, he was stunned, and thought to himself: "Che is really audacious; this writing is heretical!" At the time, he admitted, he thought Che had gone too far, and wasn't convinced of his dire prognosis. With the passage of time, of course, Che would be proven right.*

As Borrego understood it, Che was hoping to have his writings come to light in one fashion or another. "Even if he realized that the new path he was proposing could not be implanted here, for a variety of reasons, he probably hoped he could get something going and try it out for himself if he were able to take Bolivia or one of those countries." In the increasingly Sovietized Cuba of the subsequent years, Borrego never found "the right time" to push for the publication of Che's writings. Reportedly, Fidel considers them highly sensitive even today and has yet to authorize their publication.

While Che had been in the Congo and Prague, Borrego and Enrique Oltuski had worked around the clock for months on his "collected works"; in the end, they had produced a seven-volume set entitled *El Che en la Revolucion Cubana,* compiling everything from *Guerra de Guerrillas* and *Pasajes de la Guerra Revolucionaria* to Che's speeches and a sampling of letters and articles, including some that were previously unpublished. Che was both surprised and pleased when Borrego showed him the final result, but with characteristic dryness, he looked through the books and cracked: "You've made a real potpourri."

Borrego had two hundred editions printed and gave the first set off the press to Fidel, but the Cuban public never saw them. The books went to the revolutionary *dirigentes* and to individuals on a special list that Che com-

*See the appendix for elaboration.

posed, one of the last things he did before leaving Cuba. In the end, only some 100 sets were sent out; the remainder were stored in a warehouse.*

X

For Borrego, Che's impending departure was very hard, and he tried to spend as much time as possible with him in the last days. He made frequent trips to the house in Pinar del Río, as did Aleida, who stayed for the weekends and cooked up meals for everyone.

Borrego also accompanied Che during his last physical transmogrification. Along with the usual prosthesis in his mouth to give him a puffier look, for his latest disguise, Che was going to have much of his hair plucked out to give him the severely receding hairline of a man in his mid-fifties. As the Cuban intelligence "physiognomy specialist" in charge of the operation plucked Che's hairs one by one, Borrego sat beside him. When Che was unable to bear the pain any longer and yelped, Borrego growled at the barber to "take it easy," only to have Che bark at him to "keep out of it!" The hair had to come out at the roots for it to look naturally bald, and the pain was something he had to bear alone.

One day in October, not long before Che was due to leave, Borrego took four gallons of his favorite strawberry ice cream to take to the men in training. A special feast had been prepared, and everyone sat at a long picnic table. When everyone had eaten and served themselves ice cream, Borrego got up, intending to get a second helping. Che called after him in a loud voice: "Hey, Borrego! You're not going to Bolivia, so why should you have seconds? Why don't you let the men who *are* going eat it?"

Che's criticism, heard by everyone, lacerated Borrego; involuntarily, tears began running down his cheeks. Without saying a word, he got up and walked away, burning with shame and indignation. While sitting on a log, he heard the rough-and-ready guerrillas titter and break into guffaws behind his back, and he knew they were laughing at him. A few moments later, he heard steps behind him. A hand was placed softly on his head and tousled his hair. "I'm sorry for what I said," Che whispered. "Come on, it's not such a big thing. Come back." Without looking up, Borrego said, "Fuck off," and stayed where he was for a long time. "It was the worst thing Che ever did to me," said Borrego.

---

*In 1997, in commemoration of the thirtieth anniversary of Che's death, an "abridged" version of Borrego's special edition of Che's works was finally approved by Cuba's government for public consumption.

In a suit and hat, Che now looked something like the Mexican actor Cantinflas, a resemblance first perceived by the late Jorge Ricardo Masetti. That is how Che, as a visiting foreign "friend" of Fidel's, was introduced to a handful of the highest-ranking ministers of Cuba by a complicit Fidel a day or two before Che was to leave. Nobody, according to Fidel, recognized the man in the suit. "It was really perfect," Fidel recalled years later. "Nobody recognized him, not even his closest comrades, who were talking with him the way they would talk with a guest. So we went so far as to play jokes such as this on the day before he left."

Fidel described his good-bye with Che as a hug, a manly *abrazo* as befitted two old comrades in arms. Since both were reserved men when it came to public displays of emotion, their hug, he recalled, had "not been very effusive." But Benigno, one of the guerrillas present, recalled it as a deeply charged emotional moment at the end of Che's farewell banquet.

The time had finally come: the operation to "liberate" South America was beginning, and all the men present felt the momentousness of the occasion. Special food had been prepared—a cow cooked *asado* style, red wine, and a roast pig and beer—for Che had wanted it to be an "Argentine-Cuban" meal. But as Fidel talked and talked, Benigno recalled, giving advice and encouragement to Che, reminding him of past times and moments shared in the sierra, everyone forgot the food and sat listening raptly. Hours passed. Finally, realizing it was nearly dawn and time to go to the airport, Che leapt up.

Che and Fidel met in a quick and short embrace, then stood back looking at one another intently, their arms outstretched on each other's shoulders, for a long moment. Then Che got into the vehicle, told the driver: "Drive, damnit!" and was gone. Afterward, said Benigno, a melancholy silence fell over the camp. Fidel didn't leave, but walked away from the men and sat by himself. He was seen to droop his head and stay that way for a long time. The men wondered if he was weeping, but no one dared approach him. At dawn, they heard him call out and saw Fidel pointing to the sky. There went Che's plane, heading to Europe.

The last few days had been emotional for everyone, but the most poignant were Che's final encounters with Aleida and his children, who were brought out to the *finca* to see him. But Che did not reveal himself as their father. Instead he was "Uncle Ramón." He told them he brought news of their father who had been away for such a long time, that he had recently seen him and was there to pass on his love, along with little pieces of advice for each of them. They ate lunch together, with *tío* Ramón sitting at the head of the table, just like "Papá" Che used to do.

For Borrego, Che's final visit with his three-year-old daughter, Celia, brought separately to see him, was one of the most wrenching experiences he had ever witnessed. There was Che, with his child, but unable to tell her who he was or to touch her and hold her as a father would, for she could not be trusted to keep the secret. And of course, it was also the ultimate test of his disguise: If his own children could not recognize him, nobody would.*

The most Che could do was ask his children to give him a kiss so that he could pass it on to their father. During another visit, five-year-old Aliusha came up to give him a peck on the cheek and then ran back to Aleida's side to exclaim in a loud whisper: "Mama, I think that old man's in love with me." Che overheard the comment, and at that instant tears welled up in Che's eyes. Aleida was devastated but managed to contain her own tears until she was out of sight of the children.

On their final visit, *tío* Ramón waved good-bye to his wife and children. It was to be their last sight of one another, and, as he had once predicted in his farewell letter, the youngest of them would retain no memory of him at all.

---

*Hildita was the only one of his children Che did not see. She was ten years of age, old enough to see through his disguise.

29

Necessary Sacrifice

Bolivia must be sacrificed so that the revolutions in the neighboring countries may begin.

CHE,
December 1966, speaking to his guerrillas in Bolivia

Wherever death may surprise us, let it be welcome.

CHE,
April 1967, in his "Message to the Tricontinental"

I

In his postmortem on the Congo fiasco, Che had acknowledged that one of his greatest mistakes was to attempt a *"chantaje de cuerpo presente,"* or blackmail by physical presence, foisting himself unannounced on the Congolese rebels. This had caused animosity and suspicion among the rebel leadership, he noted in "Pasajes de la Guerra Revolucionaria (Congo)," and it was one of the mistakes he had vowed to learn from. Yet, when he flew to Bolivia in early November 1966, he neatly replicated his Congo *chantaje,* once again appearing on alien turf without an invitation, convinced that the Bolivian Communist party leadership wouldn't back out of the impending guerrilla war once he presented it with the fait accompli of his presence. This time, his mistake would prove fatal.*

Things began well enough. When Che—or rather Adolfo Mena González, a middle-aged Uruguayan businessman on a economic fact-finding mission for the Organization of American States—arrived with Pacho in La Paz on November 3, he was met by his closest aides: Papi, Pombo, Tuma, and Renán. He checked into a third-floor suite of the comfortable Hotel Copacabana, on the graceful, tree-lined Prado boulevard of central La Paz, overlooked by his favourite old mountain, Illimani, snowcapped and blue.

He took a photograph of himself in the mirror of his wardrobe door. Sitting on his hotel room bed, the pudgy-looking man with a balding pate stares back at the viewer with an intense, inscrutable expression.

*See the appendix for elaboration.

The reflective interlude was brief, for Che was not in a mood to waste any time. Two days later, be had descended the bright chill of the altiplano into the dry season dust and swelter of the *chaco*. Accompanied by Pombo, Tuma, Papi, Pacho, and the Bolivian Loro Vázquez-Viaña, he set out on a three-day drive to Ñancahuasu.

During one roadside pit stop to eat lunch, Che finally revealed his true identity to Loro, asking him not to reveal his presence to the party until he had spoken with Monje. According to Pombo, "He told [Loro] his decision to come to Bolivia was because it was the country with the best conditions for a guerrilla base in the Continent." He then added: "I've come to stay, and the only way that I will leave here is dead, or crossing a border, shooting bullets as I go."

II

By New Year's Eve, Che's hair had begun to grow back and he once more had a sparse beard. His Cuban comrades and a Peruvian guerrilla, "Eustaquio," had arrived at Ñancahuasu, joining the Bolivians who had been in training there. He had an army of twenty-four men, but only nine were Bolivians, among them, Coco Peredo's older brother Inti and Freddy Maymura, a Japanese-Bolivian former medical student. Both had just undergone training in Cuba.

His men had built a proper base camp and a secondary bivouac concealed in the forest above a steep red-stoned canyon several hours' hike upriver from the place they called the "Casa de Calamina"—a tin-roofed brick house, their legal "front" for the future Ñancahuasu "pig and timber farm."

They had a mud oven for baking bread, a meat-drying hut, and a rustic medical dispensary, even crude log tables and benches for eating. They had dug a latrine, and tunnels and cave deposits for their food, ammunition, and most compromising documents. In one cave they had set up their radio transmitter for sending and receiving coded communications from Havana, or "Manila," as it was now referred to. The urban underground in La Paz was taking shape, while Bolivians such as Rodolfo Saldaña, Coco Peredo, and Loro Vázquez-Viaña—the "owner" of the farm—came and went to buy supplies, courier messages, bring newcomers, and transport weapons.

But already Che was worried about the preponderance of foreigners in his "Bolivian army."* What's more, the signs of competitive discord be-

---

*In the end, the breakdown of nationalities in Che's guerrilla force—excluding the members of his urban network—would be as follows: one Argentine (Che), one German (Tania), three Peruvians, sixteen Cubans, and a total of twenty-nine Bolivians.

tween the Cubans and Bolivians were already showing, which Che tried to remedy with lectures about discipline and by announcing that the Cubans would temporarily be the officers of the little troop, until the Bolivians had gained more experience. This measure, obviously, was not popular with the Bolivians. When Juan Pablo Chang communicated that he wanted to send him twenty Peruvian fighters, Che stalled him, concerned about "internationalizing" the struggle before Monje was involved. What Che needed was a solid base of Bolivian support, and he wanted to have at least twenty Bolivians with him before beginning operations. To do that, he needed Monje.

Despite precautions, the presence of newcomers soon provoked the interest of their few neighbors in this backwoods region—just as it had done at Masetti's base near the Río Bermejo farther south. Even before Che had arrived, in fact, his advance men had learned that Ciro Algarañaz, their only immediate neighbor, was spreading the word that he suspected the newcomers to be cocaine traffickers, already a budding profession in this coca-producing nation. Algarañaz's house and pig farm lay at the roadside on the approach to their own *finca*, and they had to pass it to get to their Casa de Calamina; though Algarañaz lived in Camiri during the week, his caretaker lived on the property permanently. Already, on one of their first scouting trips into the bush, Pombo and Pacho had been spotted by the man they called "Algarañaz's driver."

By late December, Che was expecting Monje, and before their guest showed up at camp Che talked to his men about the proposals he would make to the Communist party secretary. First, he would insist that he should be military commander, and in charge of finances; he had no interest in being the political chief, however. For outside support, he proposed asking both the Soviet Union and China for aid, and suggested that Moisés Guevara could go to Beijing with a letter from him to Chou En-lai to ask for help with "no strings attached," while Monje could go to Moscow "together with a comrade who could at least say how much [money] he was given."

Che's proposal shows that even at this late date, he could hammer out the differences between the pro-Chinese and pro-Soviet Communists in Bolivia, and use that unity to engage both socialist giants in a common cause. If he could forge a local peace on the ground in South America, then perhaps there was still hope for socialist unity on a larger scale. Finally, he said: "Bolivia will be sacrificed for the cause of creating the conditions for revolution in the neighboring countries. We have to create another Vietnam in the Americas with its center in Bolivia."

From his crude camp in the Bolivian outback, Che foresaw an astonishing, even fantastic sequence of events—and starting the war and spreading it to the neighboring nations were only the first two stages. In the third stage, wars in South America would draw in the Americans. This intervention would benefit the guerrillas by giving their campaigns a nationalistic hue; as in Vietnam, they would be fighting against a foreign invader. And by deploying forces in Latin America, the United States would be more dispersed and, ultimately, weaker on all fronts, in Bolivia as well as Vietnam. Finally, the spreading conflagrations would lead China and Russia to stop their feuding and align forces with the revolutionaries everywhere to bring down U.S. imperialism once and for all. To Che, what happened in Bolivia was to be no less than the opening shot in a new world war that would ultimately determine whether the planet was to be socialist or capitalist. First, though, he had to deal with Mario Monje.

On December 31, Monje was brought to Ñancahuasu, and at long last the two rivals had their showdown. Che and Monje went together and sat in the forest to talk. Two very poor photographs have survived as visual evidence of that encounter. In one, Che lies on the ground, looking archly toward the seated Monje, who is talking with his legs drawn up defensively.

Monje demanded overall leadership of the armed struggle in Bolivia for himself. He also demanded that no alliance be formed with the *"pro-chinos."* Che told him he could forswear an alliance with the pro-Chinese Communists, but on the question of command he was unbudging. He would be the military commander because he was better qualified. And he also thought he could handle political decisions better than Monje. But he offered to make Monje the "nominal chief" of the guerrilla operation if that would help him "save face."

Afterward, Monje told the men in camp that he would resign his post as party chief and come and proudly fight with Che—not as party secretary, but as "Estanislao," a simple combatant. He would now return to La Paz and inform the party about the imminent guerrilla war so its members could take precautionary measures, while he himself would resign and return to join the band within ten days.

Either this was a bluff intended to provoke Che into offering him an additional face-saving gesture, or Monje was simply lying. Before leaving the next morning, he assembled the Bolivians and told them the party did not support the armed struggle, they would be expelled if they stayed on, and the stipends to their families would be suspended. Only four men— Coco, Saldaña, Ñato, and Loro—had the party's permission to be there, and that would be honored, but for the rest the choice now was between party and war. They chose the latter; Monje left and did not return.

Rafael Segarra, a Communist party official in Santa Cruz, said that Monje stopped to see him on his return trip from Ñancahuasu and warned: "The shit's going to hit the fan. This thing is going ahead and either we bury it or it'll bury all of us." He urged Segarra to lay low or to disappear, and in the coming days, Monje gave the same advice to party people everywhere.

Monje's actions remain dubious, cloaked in the web of intrigue and suspicion that he helped create. Pombo insists that what Monje perpetrated was an act of "conscious treason"; thirty years after the event, Che's widow Aleida still considers Monje—"*ese índio feo*" (that ugly Indian)—as the man who betrayed her husband.

The meeting between Che and Monje had culminated in disaster, and Che's tactlessness had played as great a part in the unhappy ending as had Monje's duplicity and indecision. The die was cast. As of January 1, 1967, Che and his two dozen fighters were, to all intents and purposes, on their own.

III

Content that a number of young Bolivian Communists had remained loyal to him, and trusting in Fidel's superior powers of persuasion to sort things out with the party hierarchy, Che refused to allow the rupture with Monje to affect his vision of the future. In a coded message to Fidel, or "Leche" (Milk), as he was now referred to, Che told him what had happened in unalarmed tones.*

Indeed, it seemed things were progressing fairly smoothly for Che. Tania had come to Ñancahuasu at the same time as Monje, and Che had dispatched her to Buenos Aires to summon Ciro Bustos and Eduardo Jozami, a young journalist, law student, and the leader of a dissident faction of the Argentine Communist Party—with an eye to getting the Argentine guerrilla movement up and running. Meanwhile, his people were busy organizing his underground network throughout Bolivia.

At his summons, Moisés Guevara came calling. Che told him that he would have to dissolve his group and join up as a simple soldier, that there could be no more factional activity. At first taken aback, the Bolivian Guevara agreed, and announced he would return to the highlands and recruit some men before returning himself.

At Ñancahuasu, Che's men were now patrolling the vicinity, and a semblance of military discipline had been obtained. The fighters did sentry duty, fetched water and firewood, took turns cooking and washing, while regular porters' missions, or *gondolas,* were organized to carry supplies into

---

*A short while later, Fidel wrote him back that Bolivian Communist Simón Reyes was already there, and Jorge Kolle Cueto was on his way for talks to amend the crisis.

the camp. Some men hunted, bringing in turkeys and armadillos for the cooking pot, and Quechua classes began again. There were, of course, the usual discomforts of life in the bush—pernicious insects, cuts and scrapes, men falling ill with malaria fever—but Che took it all with aplomb. "Boron day," he wrote on January 11. "Larvae of flies removed from Marcos, Carlos, Pombo, Antonio, Moro and Joaquín."

In the meantime, there were the usual behavior problems, and Che returned to his old strict self in laying down the law. Loro was operating a little too freely, finding time to *"enamorar"* (seduce) women on his supply-buying trips, while Papi was moping around, feeling he had fallen in Che's disfavor. After scolding Papi for what he had called his "many mistakes" in the Bolivian advance work—including making unwanted advances on Tania—Che had ordered Papi to stay with him in the field. Marcos—the man he had designated his deputy, which Tania had complained about in Cuba—had been abusive with the Bolivians, and in his Sierra Maestra style, Che publicly upbraided and demoted him, naming the oldest man, Joaquín, in his place.

At the same time, their neighbor, Ciro Algarañaz, was continuing to be an irritation. He and another man had been snooping around, until one day Algarañaz finally approached Loro. He was "a friend," Algarañaz told him, he could be trusted and wanted to know what Loro and his friends were up to. Loro brushed him off, but a few days later some soldiers arrived at the forward camp, questioned Loro, and took away his pistol, warning that he and his friends were under observation and hinting that if they were "up to anything," *they* would have to be taken into consideration. Clearly, the locals believed the guerrillas were contrabandists and wanted a piece of the action. After this incident, Che mounted lookouts to keep an eye on Algarañaz's house.

Then, on February 1, Che left a few men in camp and took most of the others off for what he intended to be a fortnight's conditioning trek into the surrounding *chaco*. The fortnight, however, turned into a grueling forty-eight-day ordeal as the band became lost and endured torrential rain, hunger, thirst, and exhausting marathon hikes. They were reduced to eating palm hearts, monkeys, hawks, and parrots, and with the men worn-out and demoralized, there had been several quarrels. There was also tragedy. Two of the young Bolivians drowned in the swollen rivers, a coincidence Pombo noted as eerily reminiscent of how their stay in the Congo had begun, with the drowning death of Laurent Mitoudidi. For his part, Che lamented the deaths, but also the loss of six good weapons in the second drowning incident.

Even before returning to camp on March 20, Che knew something had gone awry in his absence: A small plane was persistently circling the vicinity of Ñancahuasu. He soon learned why from an advance party that had come out to meet him.

While he had been gone, some of Moisés Guevara's "volunteers" had arrived, but became rapidly disenchanted with camp life and their relegation to menial chores by the Cubans left in charge. Two had deserted, been captured by the army, and confessed to everything they knew, including stories about "Cubans" and a *comandante* named "Ramón." A few days earlier, Bolivian security forces had raided the Casa de Calamina below the camp; fortunately, nobody had been there at the time, but the army was rumored to be on the move in the area. The aircraft Che had seen circling overhead was obviously a spotter plane; his men told him it had been up there for the past three days.

Walking on, Che was met by runners with more bad news. The army had just returned to their "farm," confiscating one of their mules and their jeep, and capturing a rebel courier—one of Moisés Guevara's men—on his way to the camp. Che sped up his pace to reach the camp. When he arrived, he observed "a mood of defeat," some more new arrivals, and "complete chaos" and indecision among his men.

On top of everything else, he had to attend to visitors: Régis Debray, Ciro Bustos, Tania, and Juan Pablo Chang were all there to see him. After bringing Monje to the camp on New Year's Eve, Tania had been busy: after traveling to Argentina on Che's orders, she had ferried Chang and two Peruvian comrades to Ñancahuasu, and had now returned again with Debray and Bustos.

Che dealt first with "Chino" Chang, who had been to Cuba and asked Fidel for help in setting up a new Peruvian guerrilla column; Fidel had told him to get Che's approval. "He wants $5,000 a month for ten months," wrote Che. ". . . I told him I agreed on the basis that they would go to the mountains within six months." Chang's plan was to lead a band of fifteen men and begin operations in the Ayacucho region of Peru's southeastern Andes. Che also agreed to send him some Cubans and weapons, and they discussed plans for maintaining radio contact with one another.

As they spoke, Loro arrived. He had been doing forward sentry duty downriver from the camp and killed a soldier he had caught by surprise. Clearly, the war was about to begin, whether Che wanted it to or not.

He hastened to deal with his other visitors, polishing up details with Chang, then conferring with Debray. The Frenchman, slight and pale, said he wanted to stay and fight, but Che told him that it would be better if he worked on the outside, promoting his cause with a European solidarity campaign. Che would send him out with news for *"la isla"* and write a letter for Bertrand Russell, the champion of international peace, asking for help in organizing an international fund in support of "the Bolivian Liberation Movement."

Then it was Ciro Bustos's turn. Bustos had been awaiting his "contact" in Argentina since his return from Cuba and China the summer before,
and after five months it had come in the form of Tania. She had told Bustos
to go to La Paz, which gave him the first inkling that Che was in Bolivia.
At the same time, he had begun to have doubts about the wisdom of Che's
rurally based guerrilla war theory. Bustos sought out the advice of his most
trusted comrades in Córdoba, who urged him to express his doubts, which
they shared, when he saw Che.

Using a hastily prepared false passport, he had flown off to La Paz in
late February. There he was instructed to board a particular bus leaving for
the city of Sucre. He spotted another European-looking man on the bus—
Régis Debray, he would soon learn—but as the bus was leaving the city, a
taxi raced up, and out of it and into the bus came Tania. Bustos thought her
actions and their form of transport a reckless public display that could only
attract notice. "There we were, the only three foreigners on the bus, like three
flies [in the midst of everyone else], looking around, but not talking to one
another, and I wasn't very pleased about things."

According to Bustos, the rest of the journey was characterized by
amateurish behavior on Tania's part, whom he feared drew undue attention by speaking too loudly, using Cuban slang in the roadside restaurants
they stopped in, and driving too fast. (For the final leg, from Camiri, Tania
drove them in her jeep, which she had stashed there after her last trip with
the Peruvians.)

At the camp, they found quite a few Bolivian recruits, but Che and
most of the Cubans were gone, still out on their trek. Almost immediately,
said Bustos, Tania pulled out some packets of photographs she'd taken on
her earlier trip and had brought to show everyone. There they were, virtually all of them, posing with their rifles, hamming it up, cooking, reading, or
standing around and talking. Incredulous, Bustos spoke to Olo Pantoja, the
Cuban left in charge of the camp, and Olo quickly ordered the photos gathered up.

In Che's prolonged absence, discipline had fallen apart, and Bustos
found Olo embarrassed about how matters had slipped out of his grasp. The
next day, two of Moisés Guevara's "volunteers" went out with their guns to
hunt but did not return. Alarm bells rang; the two had seen all the photographs and heard everyone talking openly about "Cuba" and other delicate
topics. After sending out a search party in vain, Olo ordered the camp evacuated, and they went to a hiding place farther into the hills. Within a couple
of days, when the plane began buzzing the area of the camp, it was clear
their worst fears had come true: the deserters had been picked up by the army.
It was then that the first men from Che's expedition began returning.

Bustos was stunned when he saw Che. "He was torn apart, practically didn't have clothing; his shirt was in shreds, his knee poked out of his trousers, and he looked really skinny. But imperturbable, he gave me an *abrazo,* which was really emotional for me; there were no words or anything."

Bustos hung back, watching as Che ate and simultaneously took charge of the situation. He harangued Olo and the other men he had left in charge, using a degree of verbal "violence" that surprised Bustos, and which he had never witnessed before. Later, he would see that it was a pattern in Che's behavior. "Afterward, [Che] would become calm, he would go read, serenely, while the guys he'd punished went around hangdog, turned into shit."

When it came time for Che and Bustos to talk, the first thing Che wanted to find out was why Bustos hadn't come earlier. Bustos told him Tania had not given him a specific time frame. Once again, he observed Che's severity. Calling Tania over, Che tongue-lashed her for having misrepresented his instructions. "Damnit, Tania, what did I tell you to tell El Pelao [Bustos]?" he demanded. "What the fuck do I tell you things for!"

"I can't remember exactly what he told her," said Bustos, "but they were strong and violent things, which weren't funny at all, and she started to shake . . . and went away crying." Later, feeling sorry, Che told Bustos to try to comfort her. (He was already unhappy with Tania for having risked exposure by coming to the camp again. After her first visit, he had told her not to return.* What's more, his second Argentine guest, Eduardo Jozami, had come to Bolivia and gone home again when she hadn't shown up for the prearranged rendezvous with him.)

Turning back to his business with Bustos, Che told him: "My strategic objective is the seizure of political power in Argentina. For this I want to form a group of Argentines, to prepare a couple of columns, season them in war for a year or two over here, and then enter. I want this to be your mission. And I want you to hang on as long as possible until you have to join up [in the mountains]. I want you to be the coordinator sending me people."

Che added that the work had to be done well, "not like this shit here, where everyone does what they want." He told him he should work together with Papi on the means of transporting the people, and with Pombo on the question of provisions, and reeled off names of others he should liaise with for specific issues. Che said his idea was to form a central command divided

---

*Loyola Guzmán, Che's new "national finance secretary" and a member of his urban network in La Paz, has explained that Tania's initial return trip was really the fault of her group, who had decided to send her along with the Peruvians because they were all busy.

into two columns totaling about five hundred men, including Bolivians, Argentines, and Peruvians, who would later split off and take the war to other zones.

As Che talked, Bustos wondered privately how he was going to arrange a food-supply line between Ñancahuasu and Argentina. And how was he supposed to liaise with Pombo, when Pombo was in the bush with Che? For the moment, these details weren't discussed, but already it didn't sound realistic to Bustos. "It was like something magical," he said. "Out of this world . . ."

Che then told Bustos that his first priority was to see him out safely so he could get to work in Argentina, but a dense air of tension and uncertainty hung over everything. The guerrillas' presence had been detected. A soldier had been killed. It was only a matter of time before an army patrol came in looking for them.

IV

It came two days later, on March 23, a day Che recorded in his diary as one "of warlike events." Che had sent ambushes out, creating a defensive perimeter, and at 8:00 A.M. Coco came running in to report that they had ambushed an army unit, killing seven soldiers, and taking twenty-one prisoners, four of them wounded. They had also seized a nice booty of weapons, including three mortars, sixteen carbines, two bazookas, and three Uzi submachine guns. They also captured a document that showed the army's operational plans. Seeing that it called for a two-pronged advance, Che quickly dispatched some men to the other end of the river canyon to lay an ambush. In the meantime, he sent Inti Peredo—whom he was impressed by and was beginning to groom as a leader for the Bolivians—to interrogate the two captured officers, a major and a captain. Che reported later: "They talked like parrots."

Che recorded the victory tersely: he was worried about food supplies now that the approaches to Ñancahuasu were cut off, and they had been forced to leave their camp with their stores behind. Another problem, and a serious one, was that their radio transmitter was malfunctioning: They could receive broadcasts and "Manila's" messages, but they could not send.

The next day brought no new ground troops, but a plane flew over and bombed around the Casa de Calamina. Che sent Inti back to interrogate the officers again, then ordered the prisoners to be set free; the soldiers were ordered to strip and leave their uniforms behind, while the officers were allowed to keep theirs. The major was told he had until noon on March 27 to return and collect his dead.

After the prisoners had gone, Che turned his attention to his men. Marcos had been repeatedly insubordinate, his mistreatment of some of the Bolivians had led to bad blood and open complaints, and Che had already warned him that if his behavior continued, he would be expelled from the guerrillas. Now he stripped him of his role as chief of the vanguard, naming Miguel in his place.

Che's guerrilla "family" had not been very happy to start with, but since the desertions the tensions between the new Bolivians and their Cuban comrades had increased. The *"firmeza,"* or revolutionary fortitude, of the four remaining Bolivians Moisés Guevara had recruited—Paco, Pepe, Chingolo, and Eusebio—was openly questioned, and these men soon found themselves treated with contempt and suspicion and referred to dismissively as the *"resaca,"* or the dregs. On March 25, Che demoted them and told them that if they didn't work, they wouldn't eat. He suspended their tobacco rations and gave their personal belongings away to "other, needier comrades." Another Bolivian, Walter, he criticized for being "weak" on their trek, and for the "fear" he had shown during the previous day's aerial bombardment. To another couple of men, he gave words of encouragement; they had performed well in the last few days. Finally, Che chose that day to name his little army: the "Ejército de Liberación Nacional" (ELN), or National Liberation Army.

Over the next few days, the guerrillas concentrated on looking for food. Scouts came back having sighted groups of soldiers not far away, while others observed a group of about sixty and a helicopter stationed at Algarañaz's house. On March 27, Che wrote "The news exploded, monopolizing all the space on the radio and producing a multitude of communiqués including the [President] Barrientos press conference." He noted that the army was making wild claims of having killed fifteen guerrillas and taken four prisoners, including two "foreigners." He resolved to write up the first guerrilla communiqué to refute the army claims and announce the guerrillas' presence at the same time.

"Obviously the deserters or the prisoners talked," wrote Che. "But we do not know exactly how much they told and how they told it. Everything appears to indicate that Tania is spotted, whereby two years of good and patient work are lost. . . . We will see what happens."

V

What happened was a whirlwind of bellicose activity that threw all of Che's plans out the window and forced him to pursue the war he had begun, almost inadvertently, through a cumulative series of errors and and mishaps.

He had no choice now but to fight, stay on the move, and try to survive. This imperative would dominate what remained of his life.

The eruption of guerrilla warfare hit Bolivia like a bombshell. Within a few days of the ambush the news reports became more and more exaggerated as the government mobilized its available troops. After first deriding the existence of guerrillas, Barrientos had seized upon evidence found at their camp, including photographs, to decry the foreign invaders as agents of "Castro-Communism," and to call upon the patriotism of his fellow citizens in resisting the outsiders. In this intensely nationalistic nation, the appeal to xenophobia was an effective tool with which to isolate the civilians from the guerrillas; the "foreign" nature of the "Reds" was something Barrientos would now propound ceaselessly, with his army taking up the theme as well.

Right now, there was little Che could do to combat the propaganda except write communiqués. More immediately, he and his men needed to avoid being wiped out. Che surmised from the radio reports that the army knew exactly where his band was located. He ordered men to dig new caves to store their weapons in at a smaller camp they had called "El Oso," since an anteater, or *"oso hormiguero,"* was shot there.

In Cuba, the two dozen-plus guerrillas who were preparing for the "second phase" did not include Borrego, but he and his brother-in-law, Enrique Acevedo, begged Fidel to be allowed to go to Bolivia as well. They were refused. The guerrillas had been prematurely discovered, Fidel said, and the situation was too volatile: what's more, direct contact with Che had been lost, so there was no way to insert new fighters safely into the field. As the months passed, Borrego and his comrades read the reports from Bolivia with increasing anxiety as the situation of Che and his band seemed to slide irrevocably toward disaster.

In his end-of-the-month summary for March, Che wrote laconically: "This month was full of events. . . ." After analyzing his troops and the current situation, he wrote: "Evidently we will have to get going before I had thought. . . . The situation is not good but today begins a [new] phase to test the guerrillas, which should do them much good once they get over it."

Their days now were spent on the move, alternately looking for or hiding from the army, which seemed to be everywhere in large numbers around them. On April 10 they struck again, firing upon an approaching platoon of soldiers as they came down the river. "Soon the first news arrived, and it was unpleasant," wrote Che, who had stayed at his command post. "Rubio, Jesús Suárez Gayol, was mortally wounded; he was dead on arrival at our camp, a bullet in his head."

Che had lost his first man in action, a Cuban, but three soldiers had been killed, and several others wounded and taken prisoner. After interrogating the prisoners and determining that more enemy forces were on their way, Che decided to leave his ambush in place. By the afternoon, more soldiers appeared and they too fell into the trap. "This time," he wrote, "there were seven dead, five wounded and 22 prisoners."

That night, Bustos recalled, Che did something he found very strange. Rubio's body was placed on the ground in the middle of the camp and remained there all night. It was, Bustos said, like a kind of wake. Nobody referred to the body, but it was right there, unavoidable, a grim reminder of what could await each of them. The next day, after Che made some remarks about Suárez Gayol's bravery—and his carelessness—Rubio was buried in a shallow grave and the prisoners were set free, the captured enemy officer sent off with Che's "Communiqué No. 1," announcing the commencement of hostilities by the ELN. Che noted the motley composition of the men sent in against him. "There are Rangers, paratroopers, and local soldiers, almost children."

Reluctantly, Che was forced to concede that there might be truth to what the news media were reporting: that the army had found their original camp and uncovered photographs and other evidence of their presence. A group of newsmen had been taken there, and on April 11 Che listened to one reporter on the radio describe a photo he had seen in the camp of a man "beardless and with a pipe." It sounded like a photo of Che, but it seemed his identity had not yet been discovered. Two days later came the news that the United States was sending military advisors to Bolivia in a move that it said had nothing to do with "the guerrillas," but was only part of a long-standing military assistance program between the two countries. Che didn't believe it for a second and made a hopeful note: "We may be witnessing the first episode of a new Vietnam." Che was partly right. The United States *was,* of course, sending advisors to help the Bolivians quell the guerrilla threat, but if he thought it would spark off a campaign of national resistance as in "Vietnam," he was wrong. On April 20, his cause suffered a new blow when Debray and Bustos were captured by the army as they tried to exit the *"frente"* by walking into the little village of Muyupampa.

Ever since the shooting had begun a month before, the question of what to do with the two emissaries had remained unresolved as Che's band reacted to the emergency at hand. It had already been decided that Che's other visitor, Chino Chang, would stay on for the time being, as would Tania, whose cover had been blown since the discovery of her jeep, left in Camiri, along with her identity papers as "Laura Gutiérrez Bauer." Debray, meanwhile, had become increasingly nervous and, as Che, obviously viewing him as *"Pan Blanco"* (White Bread), observed on March 28: "The Frenchman stated too vehemently how useful he could be on the outside." A few days later, as Che tried to move his band out of the dragnet, he spoke to Bustos and Debray, outlining their options: to stay with them, to try to leave on their own, or else to stay on until the guerrillas reached a town where they could be left safely. They settled on the final option.

Three dramatic weeks had passed since then, with more clashes and constant movement. The government had outlawed the Communist party and declared a state of emergency in the southeastern region.

Emulating the tactics he and Fidel had used in the first days of the sierra war, Che had decided to surprise the enemy by operating in a new area, around the village of Muyupampa; if it were possible, Bustos and Debray would leave from there. Then he and his men would move north to the eastern Andean foothills.

He prepared his "Communiqué No. 2" for Debray to take out with him, as well as a coded message to Fidel informing him of his present situation. According to Bustos, Che also stressed to him the importance of getting news of the guerrillas' actual circumstances to the island. He needed a new radio urgently, and Fidel should dispatch the men in training in Cuba to open a new front, farther north, to distract attention from his group.*

As they approached Muyupampa, Che had joined the vanguard column and left Joaquín behind at a river crossing to wait for him. In order to make faster progress, Che had decided to split the column in two, leaving Joaquín in charge of the rearguard column, made up of those who were sick—both Tania and Alejandro had high fevers—or malingering, such as the Bolivian *resacas.* Joaquín was ordered to make his presence felt but avoid frontal combat, and to expect Che's return in three days. Che, Bustos, Debray, and the rest moved on, through an area inhabited by peasants who were clearly terrified by their arrival. And when they approached Muyupampa, they found that the army had taken up positions there, and civilian spies had been sent out to look for them. Che's advance men captured the civilians, who confessed

---

*Fidel had sent him word that he was doing what he could to help. He'd met with the union leader Juan Lechín. Lechín had promised his help and men for the cause. He would be returning secretly to Bolivia in a few weeks. But Lechín ran into problems of his own and, as with so many of the Bolivians who at one time or another had promised him their support, did little to help in the end. Previously, Fidel had sent Che a message telling him that his meetings with Kolle Cueto and Simón Reyes from the Bolivian party had gone well; they were "understanding," he said, and had promised their help. Kolle was supposedly going to visit Che; now, of course, that was out of the question. The army had flooded the area, picking up any civilian suspected of dealings with them, and, since Barrientos's ban on their activities, the party leaders had had to go underground.

their mission. With them was a suspicious character, an Anglo-Chilean reporter named George Andrew Roth who had come, he said, for an interview with the rebel leader.

After Inti Peredo gave Roth an "interview," Bustos and Debray agreed on a plan. Using Roth as their cover, they would try to outsmart the soldiers by separating from the guerrillas and walking into the village posing as journalists. But the ruse failed; they were immediately arrested. When Che learned what had happened, he calmly noted the odds of their survival; both Bustos and Debray had been carrying false documents. Che thought it "looked bad" for Bustos, but speculated that Debray "should come out all right."*

Che now concentrated his efforts on rejoining Joaquín and the rearguard column, and exploring the route they would have to take to reach the Río Grande, beyond which lay the mountains of central Bolivia, their gateway to the Andes and, hopefully, escape from the army dragnet. Over the next few days, however, they ran into more enemy patrols and took more losses. In one clash, Loro disappeared. In another ambush, Eliseo Reyes ("Rolando"), a comrade since his days as an adolescent courier for Che's sierra column, was mortally wounded. He died as Che tried to save him, and for the first time since his arrival in Bolivia Che's diary reflected a real sense of loss. "We have lost the best man in the guerrilla band," he wrote. "Of his unknown and unheralded death for a hypothetical future that may materialize, one can only say: 'Your valiant little body, captain, has extended into immensity its metallic form.'"

The scouts Che had sent out to search for Joaquín's group returned with more bad news. They had run into the army, losing their rucksacks in a firefight, and still had no idea where the rearguard column was. Judging from where the skirmish had taken place, near the Ñancahuasu, Che concluded that their only two river exits toward the Río Grande were now blocked. They would have to go over the mountains.

Still desperate to find Joaquín's group, Che and his band began moving north, cutting their way with machetes through the dense brush of the mountains. At the end of April, his summary presented an overwhelmingly bleak outlook. After describing the deaths of Rubio and Rolando and Loro's

*When, the next day, the radio reported ominously that "three foreign mercenaries" had been "killed in battle," Che made a note in his diary to launch a revenge mission if it turned out they had been murdered by the army. Luckily for the three men, however, a local newspaper photographer had taken pictures of them alive in custody. The publication of that photograph may have saved their lives, for by the end of the month they were reported to be in prison in Camiri.

still-unexplained disappearance,* he concluded: "[Our] isolation appears to be complete, sicknesses have undermined the health of some comrades, forcing us to divide forces, which has greatly diminished our effectiveness. As yet we have been unable to establish contact with Joaquín. The peasant base has not yet been developed although it appears through planned terror we can neutralize some of them; support will come later. Not one [Bolivian] enlistment has been obtained. . . ."

The hard-nosed use of force to gain a civilian constituency had always been a part of guerrilla warfare, and he and Fidel had employed it in the sierra. In Che's own public writings about the Cuban struggle he had never used the word "terror," of course, but rendered the guerrilla-peasant alliance as a kind of idyllic mass wedding, an organic symbiosis. But this was now bare-bones survival, and there was no time to wax poetic; Che would have to use whatever tactics seemed necessary in order to survive.

On the bright side, he noted that the public "clamor" about the guerrillas' activity was being matched by propaganda efforts in Cuba. Che had left behind a call to arms entitled "Message to the Tricontinental," which had been published that same month in Cuba. "After the publication of my article in Havana there must not be any doubt about my presence here." He also noted that while the army was performing better in the field against them, it had not so far mobilized the peasants, only some spies, who were "bothersome" but could be "neutralized."

For Che, the capture of Debray and Bustos was a heavy blow. They had been his only chance to get word to the outside world and he now had no means of contact with La Paz or Cuba. "Dantón [Debray] and Carlos [Bustos] fell victim to their own haste, their near desperation to leave," he wrote. "And to my own lack of energy to stop them, so the communication with Cuba (Danton) has been cut and the plan of action in Argentina (Carlos) is lost."

Che and his men were truly on their own now. The enemy was alerted, his forces were cut in half and on the run; he had no backup from Cuba or Bolivia's cities, and no peasant support. Things could not be much worse. And yet, faced with this harsh reality, Che ended his April summary with a strangely optimistic conclusion. "In short: a month in which everything resolved itself in the normal manner, considering the necessary hazards of guerrilla warfare. The morale is good among all the combatants who have passed their preliminary test as guerrillas."

*Jorge Vázquez-Viaña was reported captured and wounded, but later the army said he had "escaped." In fact, he had been removed from his hospital bed and executed, his body taken up in a helicopter and hurled into the forested mountains near Lagunillas.

VI

According to his former interrogators, it was Régis Debray who provided the final confirmation of Che Guevara's presence in Bolivia.* At first, Debray claimed he was a French journalist, having nothing to do with the guerrillas, but after his interrogation became tougher he succumbed, confirming that the guerrilla *comandante* known as "Ramón" was in fact Che Guevara.

In truth, Debray could not have held out for long, for his links to Cuba were already well known. Just months earlier, Cuba had published a book he had written, *Revolution in the Revolution?* which had begun circulating around Latin America, causing a storm of controversy in leftist circles. Based on his notes from dialogues with Fidel, culling Che's writings and speeches, and including his own observations from the guerrilla battlefields of the region, Debray's monograph sought primarily to give a theoretical foundation to Cuba's argument for the "guerrilla option" over the Communist parties in Latin America. His argument, more explicit than Che's or Fidel's, was that the rural guerrilla *foco*, or nucleus, should be the elite vanguard of the revolutionary struggle, from which the future party leadership would be born. (Debray had brought Che a copy of the book, which Che had read from cover to cover in one sitting, condensing it in his own notes, and which he used to give a few classes to his fighters.)

To his interrogators, Bustos, meanwhile, was pretending to be a "traveling salesman" of leftist leanings who somehow got mixed up in things, but who knew very little about what was going on. His true identity was secured after several weeks, however, when Argentine police forensic experts arrived to take his fingerprints and match those on file in Buenos Aires. When the results came back and Bustos was confronted with his lie, he says he told the truth. Learning he was an artist by profession, his interrogators asked him to draw profiles of the members of the guerrilla band. He did so, and also maps of the Ñancahuasu camps and cave complexes. Fortunately, however, his identity as Che's Argentine guerrilla liaison was never revealed, so the people in his underground Argentine network remained safe from arrest.

The Americans were now directly involved in Bolivia. The interior minister, Antonio Arguedas, was already on the CIA payroll.** Working

*At the end of June, General Ovando Candia confirmed publicly that Che was in Bolivia. Writing in his diary June 30, Che observed: "Ovando's declaration is based on the statements made by Debray. It appears the latter said more than was necessary, although we cannot know the implications this may have, nor the circumstances in which he said what he did."

**The enigmatic Arguedas was not only working for the CIA, but he was also an ex-Communist party member and a friend of Mario Monje's. Over the next several years, Arguedas functioned as a triple agent, working for the CIA, the Bolivian Communist party, and eventually the Cubans. Thirty years later, none of his former colleagues in these various services can say with certainty where his true loyalties lay at any given time. (See the epilogue and appendix for elaboration.)

closely with him was a Cuban-American agent who operated under the name of "Gabriel García García," and who was present during some of the Debray and Bustos interrogations. When the news of Che's presence in Bolivia broke, things swung into action. A group of American Special Forces "Green Berets" quickly arrived in Bolivia to create a counterinsurgency Rangers Battalion, and the CIA began interviewing men on its payroll for a new mission: to find Che and stop him from getting a foothold in Bolivia.

One of those candidates was Felix Rodríguez, the young Cuban-American CIA paramilitary operative who had been with the agency's covert anti-Castro program since the beginning. He had been working for the CIA's Miami station since his withdrawal from Nicaragua in 1964, and until the summer of 1967 one of the questions that had been bedeviling the agency concerned Che's whereabouts.

"As I remember it," Rodríguez said, "there were some high-ups in the agency who had reported that Che had been killed in Africa, and so . . . when people started saying he was in Bolivia, well . . . [there were those] who said 'no, he's not there.' So when the evidence was confirmed by Debray that he *was* there, that's when they really decided to move forward and put out a maximum effort in Bolivia." (According to Rodríguez, the agency would have moved more quickly if it hadn't been for the "Congo" theory, and he attributed this to the fact that the man who defended it was a senior CIA official who had staked his reputation on the story.)

It was in June 1967 when Rodríguez got a telephone call from his CIA control officer. When Rodríguez arrived at the office, he was introduced to a CIA division chief who explained a new project to him. It was believed Che Guevara was in Bolivia, and the agency was interviewing men for the purpose of "capturing" him; would Rodríguez be willing to go on the mission? Rodríguez immediately said yes.

It was the mission of his life, and Rodríguez knew it, and he also knew the agency had given it a high priority. "It feared [what might happen if] Che grabbed Bolivia," he recalled. ". . . With a secure Cuban base there, they could easily expand the revolution to important countries like Brazil, Argentina . . ." Adding to those anxieties, he said, was the clear impression that Che's operation was being directed out of Havana, and the language coming from there was all about creating "various Vietnams" in Latin America.

Indeed, Che's "Message to the Tricontinental," written on the eve of his departure from Cuba, had caused a sensation when it had been published in April. In it he appealed to revolutionaries everywhere to create "two, three, many Vietnams" as part of an international war against imperialism. Opening with a quote from José Martí: "Now is the time of the furnaces, and only light should be seen," Che questioned the validity of the so-called "peace" of the unjust postwar world, and demanded a "long and cruel" global confrontation to bring about the "destruction" of imperialism in order to bring about a "Socialist revolution" as the new world order.

And in a litany of the qualities that would be required for this battle, he cited: "Hatred as an element of the struggle; a relentless hatred of the enemy, impelling us above and beyond the natural limitations that man is heir to, and transforming him into an effective, violent, seductive and cold killing machine. Our soldiers must be thus; a people without hatred cannot vanquish a brutal enemy."

It would be a "total war," to be carried out against the Yankees first in their imperial outposts and eventually in their own territory. The war had to be waged in "his home," his "centers of entertainment"; he should be made to feel like a "cornered beast," until his "moral fiber begins to decline," and that would be the first symptom of his "decadence," and of victory for the popular forces. He urged men everywhere to take up their brothers' just causes, as part of the global war against the United States. "Each spilled drop of blood, in any country under whose flag one has not been born, is an experience passed on to those who survive, to be added later to the liberation struggle of his own country. . . ."

> We cannot elude the call of the hour. Vietnam is pointing it out with its endless lesson of heroism, its tragic and everyday lesson of struggle and death for the attainment of final victory. . . . How close we could look into a bright future should two, three, many Vietnams flourish throughout the worlds with their share of death and their immense tragedies, their everyday heroism and their repeated blows against imperialism, impelled to disperse its forces under the sudden attack and the increasing hatred of all the peoples of the world!
>
> If we, at a small point on the world map, are able to fulfill our duty and place at the disposal of this struggle, whatever little of ourselves we are permitted to give; our lives, our sacrifice, and if some day we have to breathe our last breath on any land, already ours, sprinkled with our blood, let it be known we have measured the scope of our actions. . . . Our every action is a battle cry against imperialism, and a battle hymn for the peoples' unity against the great enemy of mankind: the United States of America. Wherever death may surprise us, let it be welcome, provided that this, our battle cry, may have reached some receptive ears and another hand may be extended to wield our weapon and other men may be ready to intone the funeral dirge with the staccato singing of the machine guns and new battle cries of war and victory.

Che's apocalyptic language had been present in past manifestos, but this one, which synthesized his true convictions in unabashed implacability, made all the more chilling and dramatic for the fact that now everyone knew Che was somewhere in the battlefield, trying to do exactly what he proposed: in essence, to spark another—and he hoped, definitive—world war.

As part of its effort to thwart him, the CIA summoned Felix Rodríguez to Washington for a briefing. There, he was shown the mounting pile of evidence pointing to Che Guevara's presence in Bolivia, including the "confessions" made by Debray and Bustos, as well as Bustos's drawings. Afterward, traveling undercover in his new identity as the "businessman Felix Ramos," Rodríguez arrived in La Paz on August 1. There, he joined fellow Cuban-American agent Gustavo Villoldo Sampera (aka "Eduardo González")—a veteran of the CIA's recent Congolese antiguerrilla operation who had been in Bolivia since March—in the latest hunt for Che Guevara.*

VII

By August, Che was sick and exhausted, and so were many of the two dozen men still with him. On August 7, the nine-month anniversary of the guerrilla army's birth, he noted: "Of the [original] six men, two are dead, one has disappeared, two are wounded, and I with a case of asthma that I am unable to control."

Since the captures of Debray and Bustos three months earlier, Che and his men had hacked their way with machetes through the brutal spiny bush of the southeast, alternately enduring searing cold winds, rain, and blistering heat, vainly trying to make contact with the rearguard column led by Joaquín, and constantly foraging for food and water. They often got lost, occasionally skirmished with army patrols, and listening to Radio Havana was their sole outlet to the outside world.

When they were bivouacked, Che spent much of his time reading, writing in his diary, and filling his notebooks with thoughts about socialist economy, as if divorced from the reality around him. A new fatalism laced with dark humor now peppered many of his daily diary entries. He observed the continuous bickering and petty thievery of food among his men from a curious distance; occasionally, he took charge and issued warnings and lectures. Much of the time, however, he was simply too weak to be stern anymore. Once, in early June, he had even let an army truck carrying "two little soldiers wrapped in blankets" go by without opening fire on it. "I did not feel up to shooting them, and my brain didn't work fast enough to take them prisoner." Another time, after capturing a policeman posing as a merchant who had been sent out to spy on them, Che considered killing him but in-

*See the appendix.

stead let him go with a "severe warning." On June 14, his thirty-ninth birth-day, Che reflected: "I am inevitable approaching the age when my future as a guerrilla must be considered. For now, I'm still in one piece."

An attempt to send a friendly peasant youth out from the mountains as a courier with messages to fetch help ended in failure. In a skirmish, Che's tape recorder was lost, meaning he could no longer decode the messages received via Radio Havana. With it, he also lost his notes on Debray's book and a volume by Trotsky he had been reading, and he rued having given the army another propaganda tool to use against him.

What remained of Che's support network had crumbled. In March, Renán had been evacuated by Piñeiro because his passport had expired, and a replacement for him had not been sent.* Cut off both from Che and from Havana, the urban cadres such as Loyola Guzmán, Rodolfo Saldaña, and Humberto Vázquez-Viaña were uncertain what they should do, and had resorted to listening to commercial radio in the vain hope of hearing a message from Che. They had even considered, then abandoned, an idea to pose as itinerant merchants and travel into the war zone, hoping to bump into the guerrillas. Under Fidel's pressure, Monje's comrades in the Communist party had adopted a more conciliatory attitude toward those cadres who had joined Che's efforts, but their aid went little beyond rhetorical expressions of solidarity and offers to help the urban cell in printing propaganda leaflets.

In Cuba itself, Che's friends and comrades monitored the news reports from Bolivia with growing concern. A second group of several dozen guerrillas was in training, but with Che out of contact, there was no point in dispatching them. Said Piñeiro: "After we lost contact with Che, we felt a tremendous uncertainty, but we were also confident he would pull through."

Whenever possible, a much-weakened Che traveled on mules or horses, which the guerrillas took from the army or bought from peasants, but the campesinos for the most part remained frightened of them. Already sick and emaciated, Che had begun succumbing to asthma in late June, with no medicine to treat it. Once, he became so ill with vomiting and diarrhea that he lost consciousness and had to be carried in a hammock for a day; when he awoke, he found he had defecated all over himself. "They lent me a pair of trousers but without much water my stench extends for a league." Despite his stench, Che had reverted to his nonbathing Chancho days. On Sep-

---

*According to Piñeiro, it was important to bring Renán back to Cuba to provide him with new documentation and to debrief him in order to assess whether or not he had been "detected." Ariel says Renán was withdrawn because he was extremely ill with "acute parasites." Whichever the case, Piñeiro did not allow Renán to return to Bolivia out of fear for his security. Piñeiro concedes that the decision did not make him popular. To this day, he says, "Renán blames me for denying him his chance to have been part of a historic mission."

tember 10, he recorded a historic moment. "I almost forgot to mention that I took a bath today, the first in six months. It is a record that many others are attaining."

Fatigue, hunger, and vitamin deficiencies had weakened all of them, and the pressing concerns of food and health gradually began to dominate the men's thoughts and Che's diary entries. Once, after they had eaten some pork bought from a peasant, he wrote: "We remained completely immobilized, trying to digest the pork. We have two cans of water. I was very sick until I vomited, and then I felt better." The next day, he called an assembly to discuss the "food situation." "I criticized Benigno for having eaten a can of food and then denying it; Urbano for having eaten a *charqui* [jerky] on the sly."

For periods they lived off their own steeds, slaughtering and eating their horses and mules. At one point, the men were so hungry, they began coveting Che's mount, a jack-mule, but he refused to kill it. Their hopes were given an unexpected boost one day when the mule took a spectacular head-over-heels tumble down a steep incline. The men held their breaths, hoping it would break its neck in the fall, but to their disappointment, and Che's relief, it survived.

The strain of command and Che's own disabilities showed up in dramatic form one day when he stabbed the mare he was riding because she was moving too slowly. It made a big gash in her side, and afterward Che assembled the men and spoke about the incident. "We are in a difficult situation," he told them. ". . . I am in a mess and the incident of the mare shows that there are moments in which I lose control of myself; that will change, but we must all share alike the burden of the situation, and whoever feels he cannot stand it should say so. This is one of those moments in which great decisions must be made, because a struggle of this type gives us the opportunity to become revolutionaries, the highest step in the human ladder, and also allows us to test ourselves as men." While some of the men remained silent, most announced their willingness to continue.

No rapport had been established with the locals, and by the end of June Che had called the "lack of enlistment" among the scarce peasantry "a vicious circle." To expand, they needed to make their presence felt in a more populated area, but to do that, they needed more men. At the moment, he barely had enough manpower to get through each day, much less engage in political tasks of consciousness-raising and recruitment. Fear and panic from civilians often greeted their arrival, and to obtain food and information they frequently had to resort to coercion, adopting the practice of holding people hostage while a relative or friend was sent off on errands for them. A couple of times, they hijacked pickup trucks belonging to the state petroleum company based in Camiri and were able to exult in the unaccustomed luxury of covering distances quickly, until either the gas or engines gave out.

On July 6, six of Che's men had hijacked a truck on the main road between Santa Cruz and Cochabamba and driven into the town of Samaipata. The site of an ancient Incan temple, Samaipata was a roadside way station for travelers, large enough to have its own hospital and small army detachment. Paradoxically, their most daring mission to date did not have a military objective: It was to secure badly needed medicines for Che's asthma, remedies for the other sick men, some food and other supplies. They took over the garrison after a brief cross fire, in which one soldier died and then, before the stunned civilian onlookers, went to a pharmacy to buy medicines. They left town with ten soldiers as hostages and, after stripping them of their clothes, left them at the roadside.

The Samaipata action represented a propaganda victory for the Ejército de Liberación Nacional, but it had been a failure from Che's point of view; the guerrillas had not found any asthma medicine. A few days later, he recorded that he had given himself "various injections in order to continue," but worried that they might have to return to Ñancahuasu to retrieve his asthma medicine hidden there. Even this possibility was dashed in mid-August when the radio carried news of the army's discovery of their remaining Ñancahuasu supply caches. "Now I am doomed to suffer asthma for an indefinite time," he wrote. "They also took all types of documents and photographs of every type. It is the hardest blow they have ever given us. Somebody talked. Who? That is what we don't know."*

Inevitably, more men had died. On June 26, Carlos "Tuma" Coello, caught in cross fire, had been shot in the stomach. Che tried desperately to save him, but it was too late; Tuma's liver had been destroyed, his intestines punctured, and Tuma expired in his arms. Afterward, Che wrote: "I lost an inseparable companion of many years' standing, whose loyalty survived every test, and whose absence I already feel almost like that of a son." Che took Tuma's watch and slipped it on his own wrist, planning to give it to the newborn son back in Cuba whom Tuma had never seen.

On July 30, José María Martínez Tamayo, "Papi," was killed when an army patrol took them by surprise, practically walking into their camp before dawn. In the firefight that followed, one of Moisés Guevara's men, Raúl, was also killed, with a bullet in the mouth. Pacho had escaped with a graze across his testicles. In his diary Che remembered Papi as "the most undisciplined" of his Cubans, but "an extraordinary fighter and old comrade in

---

*Two Bolivian deserters from Joaquín's column, Eusebio and Chingolo, had led the army there on August 8.

adventure." As for the Bolivian, he wrote: "Raúl hardly needs to be counted. He was an introvert, not much of a worker or fighter."

By the end of July the new losses had reduced Che's force to twenty-two, two of whom were wounded, he noted, "and I with my asthma going full speed." Meanwhile, Che observed with satisfaction that he had successfully internationalized the Bolivian conflict. Argentina's military president, General Juan Carlos Onganía, had closed the border with Bolivia as a security precaution, and Peru was reported to be taking measures along its border as well. In his end-of-the month summary for July, Che noted these developments and wrote: "The legend of the guerrillas is acquiring continental dimensions." On the other side of the coin, Che observed that some things hadn't changed. Radio Havana carried news of a Czech condemnation of his "Tricontinental" message. "The friends [Czechs] call me a new Bakunin and deplore the blood that has been shed and that will be shed if there are 3 or 4 Vietnams."

Ever alert to news of Joaquín, Che listened closely for reports of skirmishes or rebel activity elsewhere. He had been searching for the lost column north of the Río Grande, assuming it had headed in that direction, but Joaquín had actually remained south of the river. Finally, in mid-August, the radio reported a clash near Muyupampa in which a guerrilla had been killed, and his name was divulged: It was a man from Joaquín's group. A few days later, two Bolivians who had deserted from Joaquín's column—Eusebio and Chingolo—were produced in public by their government captors, and Che realized Joaquín had remained in the south. He began heading in that direction to find him. Coincidentally, Joaquín began heading north to search for Che.

Their paths nearly crossed. At dusk on the evening of August 31, after reaching the home of one of their few peasant collaborators. Honorato Rojas, Joaquín's group of ten, including an ailing Tania, waded into the Río Grande not far from its confluence with the Masicurí River. What Joaquín did not know was that Honorato Rojas had been arrested, pressured, and "turned" by the army, and the man who now commanded his loyalties was Captain Mario Vargas Salinas of the Santa Cruz–based Eighth Army Division. As Rojas led the unsuspecting guerrillas downriver toward him, Vargas Salinas waited until they were within close range, then signaled his men to open fire.

It was a massacre. At the cost of one soldier dead, Joaquín's column was wiped out. The dead included Tania, Che's former vice minister of industries, Gustavo Machín, Moisés Guevara, and Joaquín himself. The bodies were recovered and taken to the army's field headquarters in the town of Vallegrande for public display, except for Tania's, which would be found downstream, blackened and disfigured, some days later. The only visible survivors were a Bolivian, José Castillo Chávez, or "Paco," and Freddy Maymura, the Japanese-Bolivian medical student trained in Cuba, but within a few hours Maymura was murdered by the soldiers.* A third surviver, the Peruvian doctor José "El Negro" Cabrera, was caught and killed four days later.

When Che heard the news that an entire guerrilla column had been "liquidated" nearby, he refused to believe it, suspecting it to be army disinformation. Over the coming days, however, as the names and descriptions of the members of Joaquín's group began to filter out, he knew it was true. Remarkably, the two groups had come within a day of meeting. On September 1, Che's group had crossed the river, reached the house of traitor Honorato Rojas, and moved on after finding signs of a recent army presence, and Honorato and his family gone.

For Che, the ambush had meant the loss of a third of his fighting force. At the same time, he was now released from the moral obligation of searching for Joaquín; he could now concentrate on saving himself and his remaining men by escaping to a more populated area and making contact with his support network in La Paz and with Cuba. For the Bolivian military, meanwhile, the so-called "Vado del Yeso" massacre was a morale-boosting triumph, celebrated with parades and a visit by President Barrientos and his top generals and their wives to Vallegrande. Barrientos promoted Captain Vargas Salinas, the hero of the day, to major, and publicly congratulated the "civilian hero" of the episode, Honorato Rojas—an unwise move that the peasant would pay dearly for later on.

After lying on gruesome display in the laundry house of the church-run Nuestro Señor de Malta Hospital, the guerrillas' bloated and ravaged bodies were secretly buried at night on the outskirts of town under the direction of Lieutenant Colonel Andrés Selich. A tall, thin mustachioed man of Yugoslavian ancestry and a dedicated anti-Communist, Selich was the deputy commander of the Vallegrande-based "Pando" Regiment of military engineers.

When Tania's unrecognizable body was brought in on September 8, however, President Barrientos personally ordered that as a woman she be honored with religious rites and given a "Christian" burial. For the devout Communist Tamara Bunke, Barrientos's "honor" was ironic in the extreme.

---

*According to Vargas Salinas, he assented to the "execution" when his soldiers demanded to take the life of one of the two prisoners in revenge for the death of their fellow soldier. As he tells it, Maymura was "defiant," while Paco was terrified, and as he pondered he could feel Paco, who had been sitting next to him, squirm underneath his legs for protection. At that moment, said Vargas Salinas, he made a motion with his head toward Maymura, who was immediately shot to death by his men. Paco's life was spared.

Her body was placed in a coffin and a small service was held, officiated by an army chaplain, at the army post across from the graveyard. But Tania was not buried there. At 11:00 P.M. that night, Selich took charge of the operation to bury her secretly, as he had done with the others, carrying out the curious official decision to "disappear" the dead guerrillas, a morbid policy that would endure to the end of the antiguerrilla campaign.

Another habit of the military's was to take keepsakes from the dead guerrillas as personal talismans. While most captured documents, address books, and letters were forwarded to Army Intelligence, and to Interior Minister Arguedas and his CIA advisor, García, many other items remained in the hands of individual military officers. Among those that found their way into Lieutenant Colonel Selich's possession—along with gruesome snapshots of the bullet-riddled bodies of the guerrillas and photos of himself posing with prisoners—was a piece of paper with the handwritten lyrics to a melancholic Argentine ballad called "Guitarrero" (Guitar-player).

> *Don't leave,* guitarrero
> *for the light in my soul goes out*
> *I want to see another dawn*
> *To die in the* cacharpayas *

Bedraggled, filthy, and with a long tangled beard, Paco had been taken to Vallegrande along with the bodies of his comrades. There he was paraded like a trophy. Officers had pictures of themselves taken with the young Bolivian, who looked like a wild man from the forest. Terrified and completely broken psychologically, Paco began to talk.

The Cuban-American CIA agents Felix Rodríguez and Gustavo Villoldo were now intimately involved with the antiguerrilla operation at the field level. (In fact, according to Villoldo, he and Rodríguez had themselves participated in the ambush of Joaquín's column with Vargas Salinas's troops, camouflaged in Bolivian army uniforms.) Felix Rodríguez said he had immediately perceived Paco's usefulness. Over the opposition of Paco's initial interrogator, Lieutenant Colonel Selich, who wanted to execute him, said Rodríguez, he was given custody of the prisoner. Over the next few weeks, Rodríguez worked on Paco daily, gradually obtaining a clearer picture of life inside the guerrilla ranks. From his information, Rodríguez said, he was gradually able to learn who had died and who was still likely to be alive in the field, as well as their relative strengths, weaknesses, and relationships with Che.

---

*An Andean farewell party, with singing, dancing and drinking. This poem was confiscated by Lieutenant Colonel Selich, whose widow showed it to the author.

After a few days of trying to sort out what had happened to Joaquín's column, Che and his men decided to head back north. On September 6, they left the Río Grande and began climbing into the mountains, out of the region that had been their home, and their graveyard, for the last ten months.

VIII

North of the Río Grande, the forested land rises massively toward the sky, climbing away in blue mountain eddies toward the brown lunar scree of the Andean highlands in the far distance. Above the tree line, the great denuded hills and chilly plateaus give way to swooping ravines, dotted sparsely with rustic hamlets linked to one another by footpaths and the occasional dirt road. The inhabitants, mostly Indians and mestizos, live by tending pigs or cows, their corn patches and vegetable gardens forming geometric patterns on hillsides around their adobe houses. There is little foliage, and the natives can spot a stranger coming from miles away.

For two weeks, Che's band climbed steadily upward, fording rivers, climbing cliffs, running once or twice into army patrols with tracker dogs. By now, the men were all showing the symptoms of breakdown of one sort or another. They squabbled over things such as who had eaten more food, accused one another of making insults, and, like children, came to tell Che their grievances and accusations. The most alarming symptom of all was displayed by "Antonio"—Olo Pantoja—who one day claimed to see five soldiers approaching; it turned out to be a hallucination. That night, Che made a worried note about the risk this troubling apparition of war "psychosis" might have on the morale of his men.

Che continued to listen attentively to the radio. Barrientos had now put a price on his head—a mere forty-two hundred dollars—while at the same time announcing his belief that Che was dead. Debray's pending trial, which was attracting international media attention, had been suspended until September 17. Another day, he recorded: "A Budapest daily criticizes Che Guevara, a pathetic and apparently irresponsible figure, and hails the Marxist attitude of the Chilean Party for adopting practical stands. How I would like to take power just to unmask cowards and lackeys of every sort and to rub their snouts in their own filth."

Perhaps because of his powerlessness to alter the course of events, his acid humor returned. Radio Havana reported that "a message of support had been received from the ELN" at the recently convened Organización Latinoamericana de Solidaridad conference in Havana, a message, Che noted, that must have been received through "a miracle of telepathy." At the conference, Che's emblematic visage had dominated the proceedings in huge posters and banners, and he was heralded as a hero by Fidel and the attending revolutionary conferees.

In mid-September, news came of the arrest and attempted suicide in La Paz of Loyola Guzmán, the young woman Che had made his Bolivian "national finance secretary" back in the days when everything was just beginning and still held promise. During a lapse in her interrogation session on the third floor of the Interior Ministry, Loyola had hurled herself out of the window to avoid being forced to betray her comrades. She was badly hurt but survived.

On September 21, the group reached an elevation of two thousand meters, or over 6,000 feet, the highest altitude they had yet experienced. Walking along a dirt road under bright moonlight, they headed toward Alto Seco, an isolated hamlet of fifty houses perched on a great rocky dome of mountain. As they marched toward it the next day, Che noticed that "the people are afraid and try to get out of our way." They reached Alto Seco that afternoon, received with a "mixture of fear and curiosity," and discovered that the local mayor, or *corregidor,* had gone off the day before to tell the army they were approaching. In reprisal, Che seized the food supplies in the man's little grocery store and was deaf to his weeping wife's entreaties that she be paid something in return.

Instead of leaving immediately, Che and his men stayed in Alto Seco that night, organizing an assembly in the little schoolhouse, where Inti gave a speech explaining their "revolution" to a "group of 15 downtrodden and silent peasants." Only one man spoke up, the schoolteacher, who asked provocative questions about socialism, and whom Che profiled as "a mixture of fox and peasant, illiterate and guileless as a child."

To such isolated people, the bearded, dirty, and armed guerrillas who appeared in their midst were bewildering. Some even thought they were supernatural creatures. After a visit by the guerrillas, who were looking for food, a peasant woman who lived near Honorato Rojas told the army that she believed they were *"brujos,"* sorcerors, because they seemed to know everything about everyone in the area. When they paid her with paper money for her food, she thought their money was enchanted and would turn worthless in her hands.

At the same time, the government had been doing a good job of psychological warfare. In addition to its large-scale military "civic action" program —consisting of road-building, distributing antiguerrilla propaganda, granting land titles to peasants, and handing out school supplies in rural areas— the army and police had been actively ferreting out intelligence from the peasant communities for months. Even before the guerrillas began moving away from Ñancahuasu and operating north of the river, the town of Vallegrande, with its civilian population of six thousand and military garrison, had been put on a war footing. In April, had the military declared the entire province an "emergency zone," imposing martial law and advising the population that "groups of Castro-Communist tendency, mostly foreigners, have infiltrated our country, with the sole objective of sowing chaos and halting the Progress of the Nation, carrying out acts of *bandolerismo*, pillage and assault against private property, especially among the peasantry. . . . The Armed Forces, conscious of its specific obligations, has been mobilized to detain and destroy the foreign invasion, as malicious as it is vandalous."

Since late summer, Vallegrande had become the main base for the army's counterinsurgency operations, and an atmosphere of war hysteria had taken over. A public megaphone blared out antiguerrilla information in the public square, the handful of local leftist students were arrested, foreign-looking strangers detained and questioned. On August 23, according to Lieutenant Colonel Selich's daily log, the entire population of Vallegrande had been "mobilized in the face of a possible Red attack."

On September 1, when the army command in Vallegrande had made radio contact with Captain Vargas Salinas after his ambush of Joaquín's column the night before, there was euphoria—and confusion—at his initial list of *"exterminados,"* for it included the name "Guevara." As the assembled armed forces chiefs of staff listened in from La Paz, there was palpable excitement in the voice of army chief General David La Fuente as he pressed Vallegrande for clarification: "Does he mean *Che* Guevara?" They soon discovered that the dead man in question was Moisés Guevara, not the legendary *comandante guerrillero,* but were satisfied the action had been a great success.

What's more, the military now knew that Che Guevara was hungry and sick, with a greatly reduced force of men. A soldier, Anselmo Mejía Cuellar, one of three taken prisoner by the guerrillas for a five-day period in August, told Selich that they walked little and moved slowly, gradually cutting their own path through the bush with machetes—and were "very dirty." He described their weapons and each of the guerrillas' duties, and made some interesting observations about Che. "The jefe travels by horse . . . [and] the others serve him like a God, they made his bed and brought him *yerba mate.* He smokes a pipe, of silver . . . and travels in the center [of the column] with the wounded man [Pombo, recovering from a leg injury]; he has green trousers and a camouflaged shirt with a coffee-colored beret . . . and wears two watches, one a very large one." Cuellar's fellow ex-prisoner, Valerio Gutiérrez Padilla, said that although Che "never complained," he was obviously "bad off" because his men had to dismount him from his horse.

By the time the guerrillas reached Alto Seco, the army already knew they were coming and had began mobilizing to go after them. On September 24, the garrison in Vallegrande dispatched a regiment of soldiers to establish a forward base of operations at the village of Pucará, some fifteen kilometers (about ten miles) northwest of the advancing guerrillas.

From Alto Seco, the guerrillas moved on, meandering for the next two days through the open landscape at a leisurely pace. Che, sick with what he called "a liver attack," seemed almost in a reverie as he observed "a beautiful orange grove" where they stopped to rest. Approaching the next village, Pujío, he casually noted that he had bought a pig to eat "from the only peasant who stayed home. . . . The rest flee at the sight of us."

Reading these passages, one can't help but conclude that Che had become strangely detached from his own plight, an interested witness to his own inexorable march toward death. For he was breaking every rule sacred to guerrilla warfare: moving in the open without precise intelligence about what lay ahead, without the support of the peasants, and knowing that the army was aware of his approach.*

Something Che wrote during his odyssey suggests he knew his time was running out. It was a poem he had evidently written for Aleida in the form of a last will and testament, and he entitled it "Against Wind and Tide."

> *This poem (against wind and tide) will carry my signature.*
> *I give to you six sonorous syllables,*
> *a look which always bears (like a wounded bird) tenderness,*
>
> *An anxiety of lukewarm deep water,*
> *a dark office where the only light is these verses of mine*
> *a very used thimble for your bored nights,*
> *a photograph of our sons.*
>
> *The most beautiful bullet in this pistol that always accompanies me,*
> *the unerasable memory (always latent and deep) of the children*
> *who, one day, you and I conceived,*
> *and the piece of life that remains for me,*
>
> *This I give (convinced and happy) to the Revolution.*
> *Nothing that can unite us will have greater power.*

As peasants spread the news of their slow approach, the *corregidores* of the villages went ahead to alert the army. On September 26, reaching the

---

*See the appendix for elaboration.

miserable little hamlet of La Higuera, located in a bowl of land between two ridges, they found only women and children; all the men had left, including the *corregidor* and the telegraph operator. Che sent his vanguard ahead to scout the way to the next village of Jagüey, but when they reached the first rise of land leading out of La Higuera, they walked straight into an army ambush. Killed instantly were two Bolivians, Roberto "Coco" Peredo and Mario "Julio" Gutiérrez, and the Cuban Manuel "Miguel" Hernández. Camba and Léon, both Bolivians, seized the opportunity to desert. Benigno, Pablo, and Aniceto survived and returned to La Higuera, but Benigno was wounded and Pablo had a badly hurt foot.

It had been Vallegrande soldiers who had struck the devastating blow. From his base there, Lieutenant Colonel Selich listed the three dead guerrillas and then crowed proudly that his soldiers "had not suffered a single death, or injury, or even a scratch. A crowning victory won by the Third Tactical Group for the Bolivian Army."

With the smell of victory approaching, the different army units now began to compete to see which would claim the ultimate prize: the final defeat of Che Guevara. Colonel Joaquín Zenteno Anaya, commander of the Eighth Army Division; Colonel Arnaldo Saucedo, his intelligence chief, and CIA advisor Felix Rodríguez had arrived in Vallegrande. Various army units patrolled out of bases both in front of and behind the guerrilla band, in Alto Seco and Pucará. Fresh from their weeks of training, the new U.S.-trained Bolivian Army Rangers now entered the field, reinforcing the soldiers at Pucará.

After the ambush outside La Higuera, Che and the survivors exchanged fire with the army positioned on the heights above them, then withdrew, escaping into a canyon. The next day they tried to find a way out of their predicament, climbing up to a higher elevation, where they found a small patch of woods to hide in. For the next three days, they remained there, anxiously watching the army pass back and forth on a road that cut across the hill just in front of them. Other soldiers were posted at a nearby house. When there were no soldiers in sight, Che sent out scouts to fetch water, gain a sense of the enemy's movements, and find an escape route back down to the Río Grande. For the moment, though, they were surrounded.

In Vallegrande, the three new dead guerrillas had been brought in by mule and jeep and laid out in bloody rows in the Nuestro Señor de Malta Hospital. On September 27, Selich noted that "the astonished people of Vallegrande dared to look at them only from a distance." The next night, the troops who had carried out the ambush returned to base and were "rendered tribute" at a special party thrown by Colonel Zenteno Anaya. After a government commission arrived from La Paz to identify the bodies, Selich once more performed burial duty. At 11:00 P.M. on the night of September 29, he noted: "In absolute secrecy and in some place, the remains of the Red mercenaries killed in the action at [La] Higuera were buried."

On September 30, bringing with him a large retinue of officials and press, President Barrientos returned to Vallegrande to share in the latest triumph. That same night, only fifty kilometers (about thirty miles) away, an exhausted Che and his men stole from cover and began making their way cautiously into the canyon below, careful to avoid contact with any of the peasants whose little farms dotted the area. The radio carried news of the large military mobilization under way; one report said eighteen hundred soldiers were in the zone; another said that "Che Guevara was surrounded in a canyon"; still another gave the news that when Che was caught he would be "brought to trial in Santa Cruz." Then the captures of Camba and León were reported. Both men had obviously "talked," even telling their captors that Che Guevara was sick. "So ends the tale of two heroic guerrillas," Che remarked disgustedly in his diary.

By October 7, the guerrillas were in a steep ravine near La Higuera, where a narrow natural passage leads down toward the Río Grande. Their progress had been slow because Chino Chang, whose glasses were broken, was almost blind at night, he held them back considerably. Still, Che was in a reasonably upbeat mood, beginning his diary entry that day by writing: "We completed the 11th month of our guerrilla operation without complications, in a bucolic mood."

At midday, they spotted an old woman grazing goats and seized her as a precaution. She said she knew nothing about soldiers—or anything else, for that matter. Che was skeptical and sent Inti, Aniceto, and Pablo with her to her squalid little farmhouse, where they saw she had a young dwarf daughter. They gave the woman fifty pesos and told her not to speak to anyone about their presence, although they did so, Che noted, "with little hope that she will keep her word."

There were seventeen of them left now. That night they set off downhill again, under "a very small moon," walking through a narrow stream gulley whose banks were sown with potato patches. At two in the morning they stopped because of Chang, who could not see well enough to walk farther. That night, Che listened to "an unusual" army report on the radio that said that army troops had encircled the guerrillas at a place between the "Acero" and "Oro" rivers. "The news seems diversionary," he observed. He wrote down their present altitude: "2,000 meters [about 6,500 feet]." It was the final entry in his diary.

IX

Early the next morning, October 8, a company of freshly trained Bolivian Army Rangers led by a tall young army captain, Gary Prado Salmon, took up positions along the ridgeline above them. They had been alerted to the guerrillas' presence by a local peasant.

As daylight broke, the guerrillas spotted the soldiers on the bare ridges hemming them in on either side. They were trapped in a brushy gulley called the Quebrada del Churo, about three hundred meters long and not more than fifty wide, in places much narrower than that. Their only possible escape was to fight their way out. Che ordered his men to take up positions, splitting them into three groups. Several tense hours passed. The battle began at 1:10 in the afternoon, when a couple of the guerrillas were detected by the soldiers as they moved around. As the soldiers opened up on the men below with mortar and machine-gun fire, the Bolivian Aniceto Reinaga was killed.

In the the prolonged firefight that ensued, Arturo and Antonio were both killed and the guerrillas lost track of one another. Partially concealed behind a large rock in the middle of a potato patch, Che fired his M-2 carbine, but it was soon hit in the barrel by a bullet, rendering it useless. The magazine of his pistol had apparently already been lost; he was now unarmed. A second bullet hit him in the calf of his left leg; a third penetrated his beret. Helped by the Bolivian Simón Cuba, "Willy," he tried to climb up the bank of the gulley in an attempt to escape. Some concealed soldiers watched them approach. When they were a few feet away, a short, sturdy highland Indian named Sergeant Bernardino Huanca broke through the brush and pointed his gun at them. He claimed later that Che told him: "Don't shoot. I am Che Guevara. I am worth more to you alive than dead."

A moment later, alerted by Huanca's yells that he had captured two guerrillas, Captain Prado arrived. Without preamble, Prado asked Che to identify himself. Just as bluntly, Che told him. Next, pulling out one of Ciro Bustos's sketches, Prado positively identified Che from his pronounced brow and the bullet scar near his ear, from the accident that had nearly killed him during the Bay of Pigs invasion. Then he tied Che's hands with his own belt. After sending out a radio message to Vallegrande, he told his men to guard Che and Willy closely, and returned to the combat.

At 3:15 P.M., Lieutenant Colonel Selich was informed by radio of the "bloody combat" the Rangers were fighting with "the group of Reds commanded by CHE GUEVARA!" Hearing that Guevara himself was a casualty, Selich excitedly boarded a helicopter and flew to La Higuera. When he arrived, he headed immediately for the battlefield.

Taking La Higuera's helpful *corregidor* with him, Selich climbed down into the canyon where Che was being held, even as the fighting continued in different parts of the *quebrada* between the soldiers and the rest of Che's men. As they descended, they met soldiers bringing up a mortally wounded comrade, and Selich was told there were two more army dead still below. Finally reaching the place where Che was being held, Selich had a short dialogue with him, which he would later record in a confidential report.

"I told him that our army wasn't like he imagined, and he replied that he had been wounded and that a bullet had destroyed the barrel of his carbine, and in those circumstances he had no other alternative than to surrender himself. . . ."

With night approaching and the combat continuing in the *quebrada,* Selich led his two prisoners, Che and Willy, toward La Higuera. By now, he had been rejoined by Captain Prado and his commanding officer, Major Miguel Ayoroa. For the steep hike out of the ravine, Che had to be helped by two soldiers because he could bear down only on his unhurt right leg. Bringing up the rear, some peasants carried the bodies of the Cubans René "Arturo" Martínez Tamayo and Orlando "Olo" Pantoja ("Antonio").

Later that evening, Che lay bound hand and foot on the dirt floor in a room of the mud-walled schoolhouse in La Higuera. Next to him lay the bodies of Antonio and Arturo. In the other room, still alive and unhurt, Willy had been imprisoned.

Because of the darkness, the army pursuit of the fugitive guerrillas was suspended until 4:00 A.M., but Selich took precautionary measures in La Higuera, posting guards in case Che's comrades tried to rescue him. At 7:30 P.M. Selich radioed Vallegrande asking what to do with Che and was told to "keep him in custody until new orders." Then he, Prado, and Ayoroa went into the schoolhouse to talk with Che. Selich recorded their forty-five-minute dialogue in some abbreviated private notes.

"Comandante, I find you somewhat depressed," Selich said to Che, according to his notes. "Can you explain the reasons why I get this impression?"

"I've failed," Che replied. "It's all over, and that's the reason why you see me in this state."

Selich then asked why Che had chosen to fight in Bolivia instead of his "own country." Che evaded the question but acknowledged that "maybe it would have been better." When he proceeded to praise socialism as the best form of government for Latin American countries, Selich cut him off.

"I would prefer not to refer to that topic," said the officer, claiming that in any event Bolivia was "vaccinated against communism." He accused Che of having "invaded" Bolivia and pointed out that the majority of his guerrillas were "foreigners." According to Selich, Che then looked over at the bodies of Antonio and Arturo.

"Colonel, look at them. These boys had everything they could want in Cuba, and yet [they came here] to die like dogs."

Selich tried to elicit some information from Che about the guerrillas still on the run. "I understand Benigno is gravely wounded since the [September 26] La Higuera battle, where Coco and the others died. Can you tell me, Comandante, if he is still alive?"

"Colonel, I have a very bad memory, I don't remember [and] don't even know how to respond to your question."

"Are you Cuban or Argentine?" asked Selich.

"I am Cuban, Argentine, Bolivian, Peruvian, Ecuadorian, etc. . . . You understand."

"What made you decide to operate in our country?"

"Can't you see the state in which the peasants live?" asked Che. "They are almost like savages, living in a state of poverty that depresses the heart, having only one room in which to sleep and cook and no clothing to wear, abandoned like animals . . ."

"But the same thing happens in Cuba," retorted Selich.

"No, that's not true," Che fired back. "I don't deny that in Cuba poverty still exists, but [at least] the peasants there have an illusion of progress, whereas the Bolivian lives without hope. Just as he is born, he dies, without ever seeing improvements in his human condition."*

The officers began going through the documents captured from Che and, finding the two volumes of his Bolivian campaign diaries, stayed up until dawn reading them.

At 6:15 A.M. on October 9, a helicopter flew into La Higuera carrying Colonel Joaquín Zenteno Anaya and "Captain Ramos," the CIA agent Felix Rodríguez.

No doubt due to their earlier clash over the custody of the prisoner Paco, Selich was not pleased to see the CIA man arrive and scrutinized him closely, observing that Rodríguez had come with a powerful portable field radio and a camera with a special for photographing documents. The group went into the schoolhouse, where Selich noted that Zenteno Anaya "chatted with the *Jefe Guerrillero* for approximately 30 minutes."

---

*After maintaining a hermetic silence for twenty-nine years, Selich's widow, Soccoro, allowed the author to review and copy her late husband's documents in 1996. They include photographs, cables, and internal army memoranda, Selich's daily log of military activities for 1967, the uncompleted notes of his talk with Che Guevara, and a secret report he filed to General La Fuente about the events and circumstances of Che Guevara's execution. See the appendix for elaboration.

Rodríguez recorded in detail the gruesome encounter with his arch-enemy. Che was lying on his side in the dirt, his arms still tied behind his back and his feet bound together, next to the bodies of his friends. His own leg wound oozed blood, and to Rodríguez he looked "like a piece of trash."

"He was a mess," wrote Rodríguez. "Hair matted, clothes ragged and torn." He no longer even had boots; instead, his mud-caked feet were encased in crude leather sheaths, like those a medieval peasant might have worn. As Rodríguez stood silently observing, "absorbed in the moment," the Bolivian colonel asked Che why he had brought war to his country. He received no reply. "The only sound was Che's breathing."

Immediately afterward, as Selich watched suspiciously, "Mister Felix Ramos [Rodríguez] . . . set up his portable radio set and transmitted a coded message . . . to an unknown place." Then Rodríguez began photographing Che's diary and the other captured documents on a table set outside. Taking Ayoroa with him, Zenteno Anaya then headed off for the *quebrada* where the military operations had resumed, leaving Selich in charge of La Higuera. When they returned, at around 10:00 A.M., Felix Rodríguez was still taking photographs. By eleven o'clock, he had finished his task and asked Zenteno Anaya permission to speak to "Señor Guevara." Selich was distrustful and, "considering my presence necessary in this talk," went into the schoolhouse with Rodríguez. Selich's notes reveal only that the talk dealt with "diverse themes of the Bolivian Revolution as well as the Cuban Revolution."

In his own memoirs of the encounter, Rodríguez does not mention Selich's presence in the room with him but, like Selich, noted Che's proud defiance. When he first entered, Che warned Rodríguez that he would not be interrogated, and only relented when the CIA man said he merely wished to exchange views. According to Rodríguez, Che acknowledged his defeat, blaming it on the "provincial" mind-sets of the Bolivian Communists who had cut him off. Whenever Rodríguez tried to glean from him information about specific operations, however, Che refused to answer. He especially refused to "speak badly about Fidel," although Rodríguez tried to coax him.

Finally, Che asked Rodríguez a question. Rodríguez was clearly not Bolivian, he observed, and to judge from his knowledge of Cuba, Che guessed that he was either a Cuban or a Puerto Rican working for U.S. intelligence. Rodríguez confirmed that he was born in Cuba and had been a member of the CIA-trained anti-Castro 2506 Brigade. Che's only response was "Ha."

At 12:30 a radio message for Colonel Zenteno Anaya came from the Bolivian high command in La Paz, and he relayed the order to Selich. According to Selich's notes, it was to "proceed with the elimination of Señor Guevara." He pointed out Zenteno that it was Major Ayoroa's duty to take charge of the executions, since he was the commanding officer of the unit that had captured Guevara. In Selich's words: "Ayoroa then ordered the fulfillment of the order."

Immediately afterward, leaving Ayoroa and Rodríguez behind, Selich and Zenteno Anaya boarded a helicopter to fly back to Vallegrande with their booty of captured documents and weaponry. Upon their arrival at about 1:30 P.M., they were advised from La Higuera that the execution of Che Guevara had been carried out.*

In his version, Felix Rodríguez claimed it was he, not Zenteno Anaya, who had received the coded message ordering Che's death, and that he had taken Zenteno Anaya aside to dissuade him. The U.S. government, he claimed, wanted to "keep the guerrilla leader alive under any circumstances," and U.S. aircraft were on standby to evacuate Che to Panama for interrogation. According to Rodríguez, Zenteno Anaya told him that he could not disobey the order, which had come directly from President Barrientos and his joint chiefs of staff. He said he would send a chopper back at 2:00 P.M., and wanted his word of honor that Che would be dead by then, and that he would personally bring back his body to Vallegrande.

After Zenteno and Selich left, Rodríguez pondered his options. He had relayed word to the CIA that morning after positively identifying Guevara, asking for instructions, but no reply had come, and now it was too late. He could disobey Zenteno and spirit away Che, but realized that if he did, he might be making a historical mistake of huge proportions; at one time Fidel Castro had been imprisoned by Batista, and that obviously hadn't put a stop to him. In the end, he wrote, "It was my call. And my call was to leave it in the hands of the Bolivians." While still debating, Rodríguez heard a shot coming from the schoolhouse. He rushed first into Che's room. Che was alive and looked up at him from his place on the floor. He went into the next room, to see a soldier, his gun smoking, and beyond, Willy "collapsing over a small table." "I could literally hear the life escape from him." The soldier told Rodríguez that Willy had "tried to escape."

According to his chronology of events, Rodríguez then went outside to talk with Che again and at one point took his picture. Those photos, kept secretly by the CIA for years, have survived. In one, a youthful-looking and

---

* According to Selich's report, none of the officers in La Higuera—including himself and Felix Rodríguez—agreed with the decision to execute Guevara. "We believed it would be better to keep Sr. Guevara alive because in our judgment it would be more advantageous to present him before the world opinion in defeat, wounded and sick, and to then obtain compensation [from Cuba] to offset the expenses incurred by fighting the guerrillas, and to compensate the families of the soldiers murdered by the Guerrilla Band."

plump-faced Rodríguez stands with his arm around Che, who resembles a wild beast brought to heel, his emaciated face grimly turned downward, his long hair tangled, his arms bound in front of him.

After the photo session they went back inside the schoolhouse and resumed their talk, only to be interrupted this time by more gunfire. This time the executed man was reportedly Chino Chang,* who had been captured, wounded, and brought in alive that morning; by now the bodies of Aniceto and the Cuban Alberto Fernández ("Pacho,") who had been killed in the ravine, also were there. "Che stopped talking," Rodríguez recalled. "He did not say anything about the shooting, but his face reflected sadness and he shook his head slowly from left to right several times. Perhaps it was at that instant that he realized that he, too, was doomed, even though I did not tell him until just before one P.M."

According to his chronology of events, Rodríguez then went outside, shuffling documents and "postponing the inevitable" when the village schoolteacher came up to ask when he was going to shoot Guevara. He asked her why she wanted to know, and she explained that the radio was broadcasting the news that Che had died of combat wounds.**

Rodríguez realized he could stall no longer and went back into the schoolhouse. He entered Che's room and announced that he was "sorry," he had done everything in his power, but orders had come from the Bolivian high command. He didn't finish his sentence, but Che understood. According to Rodríguez, Che's face turned momentarily white, and he said: "It is better like this. . . . I never should have been captured alive."

Rodríguez asked if he had any messages for his family, and Che told him to "tell Fidel that he will soon see a triumphant revolution in America. . . . And tell my wife to remarry and to try to be happy."

*Rodríguez's account contains certain claims that are contradicted by the Bolivian officers who were also present in La Higuera—just as there are numerous discrepancies between their own. According to the now-retired officer Miguel Ayoroa, for instance, Willy and Juan Pablo Chang were held together in the second room of the schoolhouse and executed at the same time. This testimony coincides with the most widely believed version of events, which is that Che's photo session with Rodríguez came *before* Willy's execution, and that afterward, he and Willy and Juan Pablo Chang were executed almost simultaneously, by Bolivian army "volunteers."

**While her story has been impugned by military officers who were present, the twenty-two-year-old woman, Julia Cortéz, claims that she had been allowed in to see Che that morning, after he had asked to see her. She had been nervous, and when she entered Che fixed her with a penetrating stare that she found impossible to meet. He motioned to the blackboard and pointed out a grammatical error in what she had written, then told her that the squalidness of the school was shameful and that in Cuba it would be called a prison. After a short talk, she left, but according to her, Che called to see her again shortly before his execution, but she had felt too afraid to go.

At that, Rodríguez says, he stepped forward to embrace Che. "It was a tremendously emotional moment for me. I no longer hated him. His moment of truth had come, and he was conducting himself like a man. He was facing his death with courage and grace."

Rodríguez then left the room. At Major Ayoroa's request for volunteers, a man had already offered himself for the job, a tough-looking little sergeant named Mario Terán, and he waited expectantly outside. Rodríguez looked at him and saw that his face shone as if he had been drinking. Terán had been in the firefight with Che's band the day before and was eager to avenge the deaths of his three comrades who had died in the battle.

"I told him not to shoot Che in the face, but from the neck down," said Rodríguez, for Che's wounds had to appear as though that they had been inflicted in battle. "I walked up the hill and began making notes. When I heard the shots I checked my watch. It was 1:10 P.M."

There are different versions, but according to legend, Che's last words, when Terán came through the door to shoot him, were: "I know you've come to kill me. Shoot, coward, you are only going to kill a man." Terán hesitated, then pointed his semiautomatic rifle and pulled the trigger, hitting Che in the arms and legs. Then, as Che writhed on the ground, apparently biting one of his wrists in an effort to avoid crying out, Terán fired another burst. The fatal bullet entered Che's thorax, filling his lungs with blood.

On October 9, 1967, at the age of thirty-nine, Che Guevara was dead.

Epilogue: Dreams and Curses

I

On the night of October 8–9, as Che lay trussed on the floor of the school-house in La Higuera, Aleida had awoken suddenly from her sleep with an inexplicable feeling that her husband was in grave danger. The premonition was so strong that when the men sent by Fidel from Havana appeared at her doorstep the following afternoon, she was already expecting them.

For several months the news reports from Bolivia had made her increasingly anxious; Fidel had come by regularly to give her updates, and she knew that Che's situation was bad. Aleida was back in the Escambray mountains where she and Che had first met, doing field research; after Che's departure, she had gone back to school, attending Havana University to obtain a history degree. It was something Che had urged her to do, to "keep herself occupied."

In Havana, Fidel had been reviewing the news reports coming out of Bolivia with both suspicion and mounting concern. On October 9, Che was reported captured, then "dead of his wounds." When the first photograph of the body said to be his came over the wires, there was some resemblance, but it was hard for Fidel to imagine that the emaciated corpse was that of the same man who had left Cuba eleven month before.

After Aleida arrived in Havana, she and Fidel pored over the reports and new photographs coming in. At first, neither wanted to believe the worst, but when Aleida identified Che's handwriting from the first photographed pages of his captured diary, there was no longer any doubt.

With Cuba awash in rumors, Fidel addressed the nation on television on October 15. He confirmed that the reports of Che's death were "painfully true," decreed three days of national mourning, and announced that henceforth October 8, the day of Che's last battle, would be officially known as "The Day of the Heroic Guerrilla."

Aleida suffered an emotional breakdown. Fidel took her and the children to his house and, over the next week, comforted her. Then he moved her to another house, where she and children lived incommunicado, out of public view. As Aleida recovered, Fidel came by every day to see her.

Orlando Borrego went through an emotional crisis lasting several months. Che's death affected him, he said, more than his own father's had. His grief had been suspended at first as he rallied to comfort Aleida and the children, but it finally hit him. "It was as if my equilibrium had been thrown off," he recalled. "I couldn't come to terms with the idea that Che was dead, and I had recurrent dreams in which he appeared to me, alive."

On the night of October 18, in Havana's Plaza de la Revolución, Fidel spoke to one of his largest-ever audiences. Nearly a million people had gathered in a national wake for Che. His voice raspy with emotion, Fidel rendered an impassioned tribute to his old comrade, extolling him as the incarnation of revolutionary virtue. "If we want the . . . model of a human being who does not belong to our time but to the future, I say from the depths of my heart that such a model, without a single stain on his conduct, without a single stain on his behavior, is Che! If we wish to express what we want our children to be, we must say from our very hearts as ardent revolutionaries: we want them to be like Che!"

II

On the afternoon of October 9, Che's blood-drenched body had been placed on a stretcher, tied to the landing skids of a helicopter, and flown over the bleak hills to Vallegrande. Wearing his Bolivian army captain's uniform, Felix Rodríguez accompanied it; after touching down he melted into the waiting crowds and disappeared.

Within a few days, Rodríguez was back in the United States for debriefings with his CIA bosses. He had brought back some personal relics from his trip, among them one of several Rolex watches found in Che's possession, and Che's last pouch of pipe tobacco, half-smoked, which he had wrapped in paper; later, he would put the tobacco inside a glass bubble set into the butt of his favorite revolver. The strangest legacy of all, though, was the shortness of breath he developed soon after arriving in Vallegrande. "As I walked in the cool mountain air I realized that I was wheezing, and that it was becoming hard to breathe," Rodríguez wrote twenty-five years later. "Che may have been dead, but somehow his asthma—a condition I had never had in my life—had attached itself to me. To this day, my chronic shortness of breath is a constant reminder of Che and his last hours alive in the tiny town of La Higuera."

Slung onto the concrete washbasin of the laundry house in the rear garden of Vallegrande's Nuestro Señor de Malta Hospital, Che's body lay on view that evening and throughout the next day with his head propped up, his brown eyes remaining open. To prevent his decomposition, a doctor slit his throat and injected him with formaldehyde. As a procession of people including soldiers, curious locals, photographers, and reporters filed around the body, Che looked eerily alive. Among the hospital's nuns, the nurse who washed his body, and a number of Vallegrande women, the impression that Che Guevara bore an extraordinary resemblance to Jesus Christ quickly spread; they surreptitiously clipped off clumps of his hair and kept them for good luck.

Lieutenant Colonel Andrés Selich and Major Mario Vargas Salinas posed for photographs next to the body. Selich kept Che's leather portfolio and one of the several Rolex watches Che had been wearing, as did Captain Gary Prado. The executioner, Mario Terán, kept his pipe. Colonel Zenteno Anaya kept Che's damaged M-2 carbine as his personal trophy, and allowed Prado to distribute the money found in Che's possession—several thousand American dollars and a large quantity of Bolivian pesos—among his junior officers and soldiers.

By now the decision to deny Che a burial site had been made; his body, like those of his comrades who had died previously, would be "disappeared." To counter the initial reactions of disbelief coming out of Havana, General Alfredo Ovando Candía wanted to decapitate Che and preserve his head as evidence. Felix Rodríguez, who was still in Vallegrande when this was proposed, claims to have argued that this solution was "too barbaric," and suggested that they just sever a finger. Ovando Candía compromised: they would amputate Che's hands. On the night of October 10, two wax death masks were made of Che's face, and his fingerprints taken; his hands were sawn off and placed in jars of formaldehyde. Soon, a pair of Argentine police forensic experts arrived to compare the fingerprints with those on file for "Ernesto Guevara de la Serna" in Buenos Aires; the identification was positive.

In the early morning hours of October 11, Che's body was disposed of, as usual, by Lieutenant Colonel Andrés Selich, with a couple of other officers acting as witnesses, including—according to him—Major Mario Vargas Salinas. It was dumped, according to Selich's widow, in a secret grave dug by a bulldozer somewhere in the brushy land near the Vallegrande airstrip, while another mass grave was dug nearby to bury six of his comrades.*

Che's brother Roberto arrived in town later that morning, hoping to

---

*Selich's widow, Socorro, told the author in 1996 that several years later, her husband—who had never before confided the details of his role in Che's burial—showed her the map coordinates marking the secret gravesites for Che and the other guerrillas. Those coordinates have since vanished, but she says her husband told her that Che was buried separately; Vargas Salinas, on the other hand, says Che and his comrades were buried together, in a single mass grave. Interestingly, the logbook in which Selich normally recorded his burial duties is blank from

identify his brother and retrieve his remains, but it was too late. General Ovando Candía told him he was sorry, Che's body had been "cremated." It was only one of several versions of the story of his remains that would circulate in coming days as the Bolivian generals contradicted one another, and the whereabouts of Che's body would remain an unsolved mystery for the next twenty-eight years.

For Roberto, grim-faced, wearing a dark suit—looking very much like his famous brother, and yet so different—there was nothing to do but return home to Buenos Aires, where his father, brothers, and sisters waited. Now they too accepted the sad news, but Aunt Beatriz refused to ever acknowledge her favorite nephew's death or even discuss the matter.

III

Over the succeeding days, in Bolivia four more of the fugitive guerrillas—Moro, Pablo, Eustaquio, and Chapaco—were tracked down and killed; their bodies too were buried in secret mass graves around Vallegrande.*

Incredibly, however, three Cubans (Pombo, Benigno, and Urbano) together with three Bolivians comrades (Inti Peredo, Darío and Ñato) had managed to escape the ravine. But the army continued to track them, and on November 15 they were caught in a firefight with army troops. Julio Méndez ("Ñato") was gravely wounded and asked his comrades to kill him. Benigno has said it was he who delivered the coup de grâce, and afterward the remaining five fled their encirclement. Eventually, and with the help of members of the Bolivian Communist party who belatedly mustered their courage in order to save the survivors of Che's insurgency, they emerged three months later in the snow-covered Andes. There, under the protection of the Chilean socialist and Communist parties, the Cubans were rescued; socialist Senator Salvador Allende flew with them to Easter Island, and they flew home from there via Tahiti, Ethiopia, Paris, and Moscow.

Harry "Pombo" Villegas stayed in the military and went on to become a commander of Cuba's expeditionary military forces in Angola. Promoted

---

3:45 P.M. on the afternoon of October 9, until 9:00 A.M. on the morning of October 11, omitting all mention of Che Guevara or what was done with his remains.

Meanwhile, to add to the contradictions, the Cuban-American CIA agent Gustavo Villoldo claims to have personally presided over Che's burial with several of Selich's men, but denies that either Selich or Vargas Salinas was present.

*"Moro," or "Morogoro," were the noms de guerre of the Cuban doctor Octavio de la Concepcíon; the real names of the Bolivians "Pablo" and "Chapaco" were Francisco Huanca and Jaime Arana, respectively. Lucio Edilberto Galván was the true name of "Eustaquio," a Peruvian citizen.

to general, he was made a living "Hero of the Revolution" and continues to live in a modest apartment not far from Che's old house in Havana. Leonardo "Urbano" Tamayo remains in the Cuban military with a colonel's rank; he apparently suffered a nervous breakdown after return-ing to Cuba, but recovered and today lives a low-profile life in Havana. Dariel Alarcón Ramírez—"Benigno," Che's able *machetero* in Bolivia— went on to work in Cuba's prison system, and to train guerrillas from more than a dozen Latin American countries, into the late 1980s. In recent years, however, he became disenchanted with the regime he had helped install in power as a youth. While in France in 1996, he published a harshly critical book on Fidel's regime, blaming him for numerous crimes, including his alleged "abandonment" of Che and his guerrillas in Bolivia. Benigno is now considered a traitor in Cuba and lives in exile in Paris.

Despite Benigno's charges and some enduring questions about the extent of Cuba's efforts to support Che in Bolivia, most of the evidence suggests that Havana did what it could within the realms of its possibili-ties. After Che's discovery and the arrival of the Americans, the maneuvering room for Cuba's agents in Bolivia became extremely difficult. With Bolivia's borders either sealed or under heavy surveillance, and the Communist party outlawed, any new guerrillas arriving to bolster Che's effort would have been easily detected. As it was, the Bolivian military were detaining any suspicious foreigners they spotted. According to Ariel, Cuba tried to keep abreast of the events by a variety of means. In the spring of 1967, Régis Debray smuggled out word about Che's situation to Cuba's secret services via his Venezuelan girlfriend, Elizabeth Burgos, who was allowed to visit him in his Camiri jail. Ciro Bustos also asked his wife, Ana María, to get word to Havana that Che desperately needed new radio equipment and added his recommendation that a second guerrilla *foco* be started to distract attention away from Che. Ana María wrote a letter, but, due to a number of problems, it did not reach Havana until the eve of Che's capture. In September 1967, Bustos's friend Héctor "Toto" Schmucler was asked by Cuban intelligence agents in Paris to travel to Argentina, and then to Bolivia, to find out what he could about Che's situation. Schmucler said he got the impression the Cubans were "very worried." He agreed to go, but by the time he arrived in Argentina in early October, it was already too late.

Cuba's support for guerrilla war in Bolivia did not end with Che's death. Inti Peredo and Darío also made it to Cuba and, with a new contin-

---

In 1995–96, following General Mario Vargas Salinas's revelations, four skeletons, believed to be those of these four men, were uncovered in shallow graves outside Vallegrande. As of early 1997, however, only Eustaquio's had been positively identified. Elsewhere in Bolivia, the remains of Carlos Coello, or "Tuma," were also found, identified and returned to Cuba for burial.

gent of Bolivians, returned home to resume the guerrilla war in 1969. But before it even got going, Inti was gunned down in a La Paz safe house that same year; Darío (David Adriazola) was caught and murdered a few months later. Inti's younger brother, Chato, became the new leader, taking seventy-odd mostly untrained young Bolivian students to launch a guerrilla war near the mining outpost of Teoponte, north of La Paz on the headwaters of the Río Beni.* After a few months in the field, disorganized, hungry, and surrounded by the army, the ELN's second attempt to build a guerrilla *foco* expired in a miasma of blood and wasted lives. Today, Chato, who survived, is a successful psychotherapist in the Bolivian city of Santa Cruz; his specialty is taking his patients "back to the womb."

After impassively observing the fatal denouement to Che's guerrilla attempt, Bolivian Interior Minister Antonio Arguedas inexplicably refound his Marxist leanings in 1968 and, employing Bolivian Communist friends, smuggled a microfilmed copy of Che's diary, then Che's amputated hands, out to Cuba. Finally under suspicion himself, Arguedas fled Bolivia, reappearing eventually in Cuba as a kind of "secret hero" of the whole episode. In a mystifying series of about-faces, he later left Cuba, reinitiated contact with the CIA, and returned to Bolivia, where he narrowly escaped an assassination attempt. After a number of years of obscurity, he reemerged publicly in 1996 in La Paz, where he still lives.

Mario Monje lost his leadership of the Bolivian Communist party and went into exile in Moscow, where he has remained ever since. Upon his arrival Soviet intelligence officials, he says, told him "not to talk"—which he didn't do until the 1990s. For several decades he was subsidized by the Latin America Institute, a party-run policy research office. Since the collapse of the Soviet Union, however, Monje remains a man without a country or a "big brother" to look after him.

Most of the survivors of Masetti's guerrillas in the Salta prison were released in 1968 through the efforts of their lawyer, Gustavo Roca. During their time in prison, some of them got the shock of their lives, when "El Fusilado," the man Masetti condemned to death in Bolivia, showed up one day as a "visitor." According to him, the Algerians had spared his life, and instead of shooting him, had locked him up in a prison cell. He had remained there, cut off from the outside world, for a year or two, until one day he was inexplicably freed and sent to Cuba. He believed that his predicament may have been brought to the attention of Che, during his visits there in 1965, and that Che

---

*In the summer of 1967, at a time when Che and his brothers, Coco and Inti, were still alive and in the field, Chato, then studying in Moscow, says he asked the Soviets to give him and other Bolivian students military training so they could go to Bolivia and help in the struggle. He was turned down, with the Soviets telling him that such a request could only be channeled—or approved—through the Bolivian Communist party.

had ordered his release. Back in Cuba, he was sent off to fight counterrevolutionaries in the Escambray, and then, deemed "rehabilitated," he had been dispatched to explore the possibilities of organizing a breakout attempt to rescue his former comrades. He told them he bore no grudges against them for what had happened; he was thankful merely to be alive. According to Henry Lerner, who met him for the first time, "El Fusilado" was a fellow Jew.

After three years and eight months in prison, Che's bodyguard Alberto Castellanos was spirited out of the country and made it back to Cuba. The appeals for Héctor Jouve and Federico Méndez were denied; their fourteen- and sixteen-year sentences were extended to life imprisonment. After Juan Perón's return to Argentina in 1973, they were amnestied, but they fled the country after the regime of Perón's second wife, Isabela, was overthrown by the military, who immediately initiated a wave of anti-Communist repression. With the restoration of civilian rule in the early 1980s Méndez and Jouve returned home. Méndez died a few years ago; Jouve lives with his family in Córdoba. A deeply reflective man, he is now a psychotherapist.

Henry Lerner, who nearly died at Masetti's hands, was captured by the Argentine military and spent three years officially "disappeared," slated for execution. He was ultimately saved in an unusual deal arranged by the Catholic Church, whereby a group of one hundred–odd people in government detention were spared but expelled from Argentina. As a Jew, Lerner was accepted for asylum by Israel. Later, he emigrated to Madrid, where, like his old comrade Héctor Jouve, he became a psychotherapist.

In what became known as Argentina's "dirty war" against the left, which began with vigor in 1976, the Guevara family soon found themselves targets. Guevara Lynch fled his homeland for Cuba with his new bride, Ana María Erra, a painter some thirty years his junior. They raised a new family and named one of their boys Ramón, Che's Bolivian nom de guerre. After his brother's death, Roberto's politics radicalized, and he and Juan Martín became active in a "Guevarist" Argentine guerrilla movement. Roberto moved between Cuba and Europe, but Juan Martín made the mistake of returning from Cuba to fight in his homeland; within a month he had been arrested, and he spent the next nine years in prison. His sister Celia spent much of the 1970s and early '80s in London, working through Amnesty International to secure his release.

With the end of the dirty war, Che's siblings gradually returned to Argentina. Roberto works as a lawyer for leftist labor unions, while Juan Martín runs a bookshop in Buenos Aires. Che's youngest sister, Ana María, died from an illness a few years ago; Celia Guevara lives a quiet life in Buenos Aires. Their father, however, did not return. *"El viejo"* Guevara died in Havana in 1987, at the age of eighty-seven. He spent his final years producing books about his late son, after mining his letters and diaries. His wife and children—Che's half-brothers and -sisters—remain in Cuba.

In 1970, nearly three years into the thirty-year prison sentences they had been given at their trials, Ciro Bustos and Régis Debray were released from prison on the orders of Bolivia's new military ruler, a reformist named General Juan José Torres; they were flown to Chile, where the socialist Salvador Allende was then president. Debray, a famous figure for the celebrity he gained during his public trial in Bolivia, remained an active voice in the leftist intellectual circles of Europe, becoming an advisor on Latin American policy to French President François Mitterand in the 1980s. Gradually, however, his infatuation with Cuba's revolution soured. In 1996 he published a memoir highly critical of Fidel Castro, whom he called a "megalomaniac," and of Che Guevara, whom he described as "more admirable" but less "likeable" than Castro, accusing him of being harsh and unfeeling to his men in Bolivia.

Of those who survived the Bolivian affair, perhaps none suffered more than Che's loyal protégé, painter Ciro Bustos. Despite the fact that Debray's former captors say he cooperated with them, it was Bustos, for the portraits he drew, who took the brunt of the blame for "betraying" Che's presence in Bolivia. Vilified by Debray and frozen out by Cuba, Bustos worked for a time in Chile before fleeing during the CIA-backed coup of General Augusto Pinochet in 1973. He returned to his native Argentina and resumed painting, only to flee once more when the dirty war began. He now lives quietly in Sweden, where he paints beautiful portraits of people without faces.

Loyola Guzmán, Che's Bolivian "national finance secretary," was freed from prison in 1970 after her ELN comrades took two German engineers hostage to force her release. Afterward, she made her way to Cuba. There, she met Che's widow, Aleida, who took her under her wing, for Loyola found that nobody in Cuba's secret services wanted to see her or offer her explanations for what had gone wrong in 1967, and that in his adoptive homeland Che had become an unmentionable subject. The Soviets had finally clasped Fidel in a bear hug. That hug would last for the next seventeen years, and Che-style "adventurism" was discredited, at least for now.

Loyola Guzmán and some comrades returned unaided to Bolivia, intending to continue with the guerrilla effort. But in 1972, she, her husband, and a few other guerrillas were surrounded by the military in a La Paz safe house. Her husband and the others escaped, only to be killed and disappeared later. Pregnant, Loyola was caught and spent the next two years in prison, where she gave birth to her first son; she named him Ernesto in honor of Che. In future years, as the region's U.S.-backed armies became ever more brutal in their efforts to quell the spreading Marxist insurgencies Che had helped inspire, Loyola became the spokesperson for Latin America's "Families of the Disappeared." Today, she lives in La Paz, a tireless champion of the efforts to locate the bodies of Che and his comrades killed in 1967, as well as the 150-odd others who were disappeared under the Bolivian military regimes of the 1970s and early '80s.

The tense and tight-lipped reception Loyola found in the Cuba of 1970 was indicative of the many shifts the island would go through under Fidel's long tenure as *jefe máximo*. Indeed, Cuba's overt vassalage to the Soviet line marked a stunning turnaround in less than three years, for in the immediate aftermath of Che's death, Cuba's relations with the Soviet Union had gone into a deep freeze. Angered over Moscow's implicit backing of the Bolivian Communist party line, and for harshly critical articles on Che and the "export" of revolution published in *Pravda,* Fidel shunned the Kremlin. Seen as too close to Fidel, Ambassador Alexandr Alexiev was withdrawn from his post in 1968 and dispatched to, of all places, Madagascar.

As an expression of his displeasure, Fidel sent only his health minister to attend the annual November festivities in Red Square in 1967. And in early 1968 he launched a new purge of the pro-Soviet "old Communists" after allegedly uncovering a dissident faction engaged in a talking conspiracy against him with members of the Soviet embassy staff. As with the 1962 purge of "sectarianism," this plot featured the redoubtable Aníbal Escalante; this time, he was not sent to Moscow, but given a fifteen-year prison sentence. Among his and his fellow conspirators' tape-recorded crimes: to have criticized Che.

Next, invoking Che's spirit, Fidel tried to launch a desperate attempt for Cuba's economic self-sufficiency. Proclaiming that the nation would produce an unprecedented ten million tons of sugar in 1970, he poured all of Cuba's hard-stretched resources toward the goal. When Orlando Borrego, the minister of sugar, warned Fidel that it could not be done, he was fired. It was *not* done, and the Cuban economy was left in a state of near-total collapse. For all intents and purposes, it represented the end of any hope for Cuban autonomy, and the Soviets—already buoyed by Fidel's declaration of support for their invasion of Czechoslovakia—swiftly asserted themselves. Che's Ministry of Industries was divided up into many smaller ones, gutted of his loyalists, and many of the foreigners who had come to work for him left Cuba. The rehabilitation camp, Guanacahabibes, and his Ciro Redondo experimental farm were shut down, while his "department of control," with over forty thousand archives on individuals cataloguing their revolutionary aptitudes and work records, was destroyed. Despite his dismissal in 1968, Orlando Borrego remains loyal to Fidel and the revolution, and today, at the age of sixty-one, works as an advisor to the Ministry of Transportation and a state-owned chain of tourist hotels.

In spite of his officially induced "hibernation"—a decade and a half long—Che reemerged as a revolutionary touchstone in Cuba. When the USSR itself began to change in the late 1980s under Mikhail Gorbachev, Fidel opposed the liberal reforms of glasnost and perestroika with what he called the "rectification" process, reinstituting Che Guevara's ideas as the correct ones for Cuba's Communists to follow. That process, however, never truly began, for it coincided with the collapse of the Soviet bloc and the end of the thirty-one-year-long flow of Moscow's subsidies to Cuba. Forced to allow limited foreign investment and other "market reforms" to rescue Cuba's battered economy, Fidel has nonetheless maintained Che's resurrection as the spiritual validation for what little remains of "revolutionary" Cuba. In keeping with the revolutionary tradition of giving each year an official title, 1997 was consecrated as "The Year of the Thirtieth Anniversary of the Death in Combat of the Heroic Guerrilla and His Comrades."

IV

Many of the men who were associated with Che's death in Bolivia went on to die violently, leading some to believe in a so-called "curse of Che." The first to die was Bolivia's military president, General René Barrientos, whose helicopter fell out of the sky in unexplained circumstances in April 1969. Honorato Rojas, the peasant collaborator who had betrayed Joaquín's column, was executed by the "second" ELN in late 1969. In 1971, Colonel Roberto Quintanilla, Arguedas's intelligence chief at the Ministry of Interior, the man who had made Che's fingerprints, was murdered in Germany.

The populist president General Juan José Torres—who as a member of Barrientos's joint chiefs of staff had cast his vote in favor of Che's execution in 1967—was murdered by the Argentine death squads in 1976, after his overthrow and flight into exile. Only two weeks earlier, General Joaquín Zenteno Anaya had been gunned down in Paris in an action claimed by the obscure "Che Guevara International Brigade."

After his acclaimed role in the "defeat of Che," however, Captain Gary Prado rose rapidly within the armed forces, eventually becoming a colonel. But, during an operation to suppress an armed revolt in Santa Cruz in 1981, he was shot and left paralyzed from the waist down. After retiring from the army as a general, he went into politics, aligning himself with the center-left, and for a period served as Bolivia's ambassador to London. Captain Mario Vargas Salinas also became a general, and a government minister for dictator General Hugo Banzer Suárez in the 1970s.

Lieutenant Colonel Andrés Selich fared the least well of those who were directly involved in the capture and execution of Che Guevara. In 1971, Selich led a military revolt that ousted President Juan José Torres and brought the right-wing General Hugo Banzer Suárez to power. After serving as Banzer's interior minister for only six months, however, Selich was sidelined and sent into diplomatic exile as ambassador to Paraguay.

He soon began conspiring against the dictator, and after secretly reentering Bolivia in 1973, preparing to launch a new revolt, he was caught and beaten to death by army thugs on Banzer's orders. Since retiring from the military with a colonel's rank, Miguel Ayoroa lives discreetly in Santa Cruz and denies having anything to do with Che's death, laying the blame for the act squarely on the late Andrés Selich's shoulders.

The executioner, Mario Terán, is a pathetic figure, a man who continues to live in hiding—at times wearing wigs and other disguises—out of fear for his life, convinced he has long been targeted for assassination by Cuba or its allies. Given a series of menial jobs by the army to keep him going, including that of bartender in the officers' club of Santa Cruz Eighth Army Division headquarters, Terán is a deeply bitter man, seeing himself as a scapegoat for his superior officers who have written books and gained glory and titles through their participation in Che's defeat. He offers to speak about the events that took place in La Higuera on October 9, 1967, but only for money.

Stout, rumpled, and with a face marred by a curving scar that cuts over his upper lip, Terán explodes with rage when asked if he regrets what he did. "What do you think?" he says. "You imagine that I was just walked into that room and pulled the trigger? I was down in the *quebrada* the day before, I was there! I saw three of my friends die that day."

Felix Rodríguez believes he was targeted by Cuba for assassination, as well, and speaks of one incident in the 1970s when he was warned by American intelligence of a plot to hijack a plane he was planning to travel on. His career in the CIA continued in Vietnam, El Salvador, and other war-torn countries, but his cover was finally blown in the late 1980s when he had to appear before the Senate committee investigating the Iran-contra affair, after Rodríguez worked as Oliver North's point man in providing illegal aid to the Nicaraguan contras, and in operations against the Salvadoran Farabundo Martí guerrillas. Today, Rodríguez is a heavyset man, the den of his suburban Miami house filled with the necromantic ornaments of his long career as a CIA hireling: framed in glass, the brassiere he confiscated from a Salvadoran female guerrilla *comandante* he once captured, grenades, rifles, honorary plaques and diplomas from a myriad of counterinsurgency forces, a "thank-you-for-services-rendered" letter from George Bush. The largest space of all on Rodríguez's crowded wall, however, is occupied by the framed portrait of him standing next to the wounded, doomed Che Guevara.

Whether they fought with him or against him, a curious symbiosis unites those who knew Che: Not only are they joined by feelings of respect for him, but since his passing many live on with the awareness that if their own obituaries were to be written, it would be because of their relationships to Che.

Ricardo Rojo, Che's occasional companion and political sparring partner, wrote an internationally best-selling book, *My Friend Che,* in the immediate aftermath of Che's death. It earned him fame and some wealth on the one hand, but bitter condemnation by Cuba and Che's comrades on the other, for Rojo perpetuated the story that Che had had a falling-out with Fidel. Rojo also fled Argentina in the 1970s, returning home after the restoration of civilian rule in 1983 to practice law. He remained active in political and media circles, a social rancõnteur as charming and sharp-tongued as ever, and died of cancer in Buenos Aires in 1996.

Che's friend Alberto Granado remains in Cuba. Now in his mid-seventies, he is a sprightly grandfatherly figure who retains a taste for rum and good tangos. Venerated as Che's "friend," he has published a few books about his relationship with Che and travels the world giving talks about their experiences together.

Che's children were raised in Cuba, growing up under the protective eye of *"tío"* Fidel and *"tío"* Ramiro Valdés. His sons, Ernesto and Camilo, both went through five years of study at a KGB training academy in Moscow. Today, Camilo works in the Ministry of Fisheries under Che's old friend Enrique Oltuski and Ernesto with Ramiro Valdés in a state-owned electronics firm. Like her father, Aliusha became a doctor with a specialty in allergies. Against her mother's wishes, she volunteered for internationalist duty in Nicaragua and Angola in the 1980s, at the height of Cuban military involvement in those countries. For a time, she was married to a son of Gustavo Machín de Hoed, one of the men who died with Che in Bolivia. Daughter Celia became a marine biologist and works with dolphins and sea lions at Havana's Seaquarium.

Bearing a striking resemblance to her father—his same penetrating eyes and sharp tongue, if not his acid sense of humor—Aliusha has emerged as the family's spokesperson and foremost defender of her father's legacy in Cuba, a role hastened, perhaps, by her mother's gradual withdrawal from public life.

Aleida herself remarried, as Che wished, and moved out of the house on Calle 47 to a new one in Miramar down the street from Alberto Granado and directly across from the widow of *"el viejo"* Guevara. For years she was active in Cuba's Communist Party Congress as a deputy, and in the Cuban Women's Federation. Now a matronly grandmother of sixty, but still attractive, with tastefully dyed blond hair and a girlish laugh, Aleida has given up those public duties to dedicate herself to her family and the perpetuation of her husband's legacy, opening a research center in their old home.

"La Casa del Che," as it is called, is painted marine-blue, its roof-garden and entryway overgrown with red and purple bougainvillea. Some neighbors recently cut down a huge fir tree Aleida had planted out front, a mere seedling when Che was alive. In the foyer, paintings of Che adorn the walls but are threatened by water damage from the leaking roof. Upstairs, Che's little office remains as it was when he left, with his small white Formica-covered desktop built into varnished plywood, his vinyl-backed office chair on wheels, and the double windows at either end of the room looking out to the same view.

His books are there: the works of Marx, Engels, and Lenin, their margins messy with his jottings; biographies of Fouchet and Marie Antoinette by Stefan Zweig. In a little alcove under his desk are the books he was reading last: several about Bolivia, Africa, and Algeria's revolution, many of them in French, and one, by "T. Buchanan," about the assassination of John F. Kennedy.

The portrait of Camilo still hangs behind his desk, and on top of the bookcase that stretches across the front sit Simón Bolívar's bust and a bronze bas-relief of Lenin. A carved ornamental *yerba mate* gourd and silver sipping straw is on a side shelf, and on the floor, a bronze statue symbolizing "New Soviet Man" gathers dust. On the shelf of a narrow closet are some of the belongings Che left behind: an olive-green army backpack, a web-belt, and other military apparel, all now beginning to disintegrate in the Cuban humidity.

When Che's first wife, Hilda, died of cancer in 1974, their daughter, Hildita, went to Europe. She lived life the hard way, working at odd jobs and hitchhiking, participating in the "hippy" experience of the period in Italy and other countries. She later lived in Mexico and married a Mexican guerrilla named Alberto. They came to live in Cuba, but Alberto's conspiratorial activities against Cuba's staunchest ally discomfited Fidel's regime and he was asked to leave; Hildita went with him, but they eventually divorced. Returning to Cuba in the mid-eighties with two young sons, she worked at Cuba's foremost house of culture, La Casa de las Americas, as an archivist and researcher, and began to compile a bibliography of her revered father's writings.

Loyal to Cuba's revolution but outspoken about what she saw as its defects, Hildita earned the quiet disapproval of the regime for her views and personal conduct. When her teenaged son, Canek, a heavy-metal rock and roller, made remarks to the foreign press that were critical of Fidel's government, the mantle of opprobrium fell more heavily over her little clan. In 1995, Hildita died of cancer at the age of thirty-nine, the same age her father was when he was killed. Neither Fidel nor Raúl appeared at her wake, but sent large wreaths. At the funeral in the vast Cementerio Colón, where she was interred in the Pantheon of the Revolutionary Armed Forces, no one spoke.

V

Che's unshakable faith in his beliefs was made even more powerful by his unusual combination of romantic passion and coldly analytical thought. This paradoxical blend was probably the secret to the near-mystical stature he acquired, but seems also to have been the source of his inherent weaknesses—

hubris and naïveté. Gifted at perceiving and calculating strategy on a grand scale, yet at a remove, he seemed incapable of seeing the small, human elements that made up the larger picture, as evidenced by his disastrous choice of Masetti to lead the Argentine *foco*. There, and in Cuba, the Congo, and Bolivia, the men he believed in consistently failed him, and he consistently failed to understand how to alter the fundamental nature of others and get them to become "selfless Communists." But along with his mistakes, what is most remembered about Che is his personal example, embodying faith, willpower, and sacrifice.

As the veteran Cuban intelligence official "Santiago" observed recently: "Toward the end, Che knew what was coming, and he prepared himself for an exemplary death. He knew his death would become an example in the cause of Latin American revolution, and he was right. We would have preferred him to remain alive, with us here in Cuba, but the truth is that his death helped us tremendously. It's unlikely we would have had all the revolutionary solidarity we have had over the years if it weren't for Che dying the way he did."

Today, Che is once again as controversial and as universally recognized as he was back in the days when he was an icon for student revolt. After lapsing into obscurity in the 1970s and '80s, he has made a popular resurgence in the '90s, an enduring symbol of passionate defiance to an entrenched status quo.

Those who believed that Che, or guerrilla warfare, had passed from "fashion" with the eclipse of Marxist insurgency and the end of the Cold War have been proven wrong, as the three-year-old indigenous "Zapatista" uprising led by the balaclava-clad "Subcomandante Marcos" in southern Mexico has shown. The Zapatistas' less than aggressive military tactics and avowed political goals—to win autonomy for Chiapas's indigenous peoples —are far more modest than were Che's, but his legacy is apparent in the guerrillas' repudiation of Mexico's subservience to U.S. capital interests and their appeals for sweeping social, political, and economic reforms. And the charismatic figure of Marcos himself—gun-wielding, pipe-smoking, reflective, ironic, and lyrical—has caught the popular imagination as Che once did. Indeed, it is hard not to see Marcos as a reborn Che Guevara, adapted to modern times—less Utopian still idealistic, but still willing to fight for his beliefs—perhaps having learned from his predecessor's mistakes but modeled on him nonetheless.

Elsewhere, Che's ghost continues to reappear as a specter in the unreconciled conflicts persisting since his time. In December 1996, the seizure of hostages in the Japanese embassy in Lima, Peru, by a "Guevarist" guerrilla group, the Movimiento Revolucionario Tupác Amaru, focused world attention on a previously obscure cause and rattled the confidence of a regime that had thought itself secure. And, only a few weeks earlier, in Africa, with regional tensions rising from the presence of several million Rwandan Hutu refugees and the armed militias hiding in their midst in eastern Zaire, a previously unknown Zairean rebel movement made a spectacular appearance, forcing the refugees back into Rwanda, seizing Zairean towns, and putting the Hutu militias on the run.

The man leading the rebellion soon made his appearance. It was Laurent Kabila, the rebel leader Che had tried to assist in the Congo three decades earlier; Kabila had reemerged from obscurity to raise the battle standard once again.

By May 1997, after a stunningly rapid-fire military campaign, Kabila had ousted Mobutu's thirty-one-year-old dictatorship, assumed power himself, and renamed Zaire as "The People's Democratic Republic of the Congo." Whether Kabila has assimilated his past mistakes, or recalls how he squandered the assistance of Che Guevara to "liberate" the Congo over three decades ago, remains unknown. It also remains to be seen whether or not he will prove to be a better leader than his corrupt predecessor, but at the very least, Kabila's return is another reminder that some of the battles waged by Che in the sixties still await their denouement.

In the little town of Vallegrande, Bolivia, the efforts to find and exhume Che's body finally paid off. In July 1997, his skeleton, minus his hands, was discovered by a Cuban-Argentine forensic team. It lay together with six others at the bottom of a two-meter pit dug under the town's dirt airstrip. After their exhumation, the guerrillas' remains were placed in coffins and flown to Cuba, where they were received in a discreet and emotional ceremony presided over by Fidel and Raul Castro, and Che's widow and children. In October 1997, his body was publicly reinterred in a specially built mausoleum on the outskirts of the city of Santa Clara. After thirty years, Che Guevara had finally returned to his adoptive homeland.

Left behind, in Vallegrande, is a graffiti scrawl in Spanish on the adobe wall of the public telephone office: *"Che—Alive as they never wanted you to be."* Perhaps more than any other, the statement best describes Che's true legacy. Somehow, he has retained a powerful hold on the popular imagination, seeming to transcend time and place. Forever youthful, brave, implacable, and defiant, perpetually staring out with those eyes full of purpose and indignation, Che has defied death. As even his closest friends and comrades wilt with age or succumb to the comforts of a life where *"la revolución"* no longer has a place, Che remains unalterable. He is immortal because others want him to be, as the solitary example of the New Man who once lived and dared others to follow.

Appendix

p. 105: In 1968, Rojo wrote a book, *My Friend Che,* in which he gave his account of Guevara's life and their friendship. Perhaps because it was written in a rush to publish following Guevara's highly publicized death, the book is riddled with factual inaccuracies.

Rojo apparently tried to make more of their relationship than actually was there, but he is not alone in seeking a vicarious limelight among the posthumous horde of former Guevara friends and acquaintances. The fact is, they did know one another, were friendly, and therefore Rojo's book has some historically salvageable aspects.

In his book Rojo claimed that from La Paz, he traveled with Calíca and Ernesto for most of their journey northward. This is untrue. They met again in Lima, in Guayaquil, Costa Rica, Guatemala, and Mexico, but always traveled separately. He later visited "Che" a couple of times in Cuba.

p. 125: "Note on the Margin" was published as part of *Notas de Viaje* by Guevara's Cuban widow, Aleida March, although he had instructed her to burn this and other early writings after his death. Fortunately, she decided not to. She believes that the enigmatic person he described may be a fictional composite of several people encountered along his journey or a literary device that he employed to evoke the scene of self-revelation.

Alberto Granado cannot recall anyone of this person's description met during their journey, and is still mystified at the notion that his friend "Fuser" was thinking such thoughts so long before his adoption of Marxism became known to his friends and family.

p. 147: Out of the "Operation Success" bandwagon emerged a number of men whose careers were to become symbiotic with Ernesto Guevara's. Among them was Daniel James. As the editor and chief Latin American correspondent of the anti-Communist weekly *New Leader,* James was involved in the U.S. media campaign against Arbenz. In mid-1954 he wrote *Red Design for the Americas,* a book that lobbied for the overthrow of the Arbenz government. According to the authors of the definitive book on the overthrow, *Bitter Fruit: The Untold Story of the American Coup in Guatemala,* James's forceful arguments that Communists were in control of Guatemala were "so convincing" that the CIA bought hundreds of copies and distributed them to American journalists and other "opinion moulders."

In 1968, James was given exclusive access to publish the CIA-captured documents belonging to Che's guerrillas in Bolivia, including Guevara's own diary. He followed this book up a year later with a highly caustic biography of Guevara.

p. 213: There are supposedly only two copies in existence of Che's 1957–1959 sierra diary, according to Aleida March—hers and Fidel's. At the time the author was in Cuba, this diary was undergoing the process of "sanitization" in order to remove names of present-day Cuban government officials who were mentioned critically or antagonistically by Che, with a view toward its eventual publication in Cuba.

p. 235: Che examined a document brought by the visitors outlining the July 26 Movement's ideological platform, and was guardedly impressed. "In it, a series of quite advanced revolutionary decrees were proposed, although some were very lyrical such as the announcement that no diplomatic relations would be established with the [Latin] American dictatorships."

Che was probably referring to the latest issue of *Revolución,* the movement's new clandestine organ published by Carlos Franqui, a former Communist who worked as a journalist in Havana and secretly handled underground propaganda for the July 26 Movement. The February 1957 issue of *Revolución* carried an article called "Necessity for Revolution," extracted from a draft pamphlet entitled *Nuestra Razón.* Franqui had commissioned the manuscript from Mario Llerena, a political writer, intending it to become "The Manifesto-Program" of the July 26 Movement.

In the article, the "Revolution" was described as: "A continuous historic process. . . . The Revolution is struggling for the complete transformation of Cuban life, for profound modifications in the system of property and for a change in institutions. . . . In accordance with its goals, and as a consequence of the historic, geographic and sociological reality of Cuba, the Revolution is democratic, nationalist and socialist."

When *Nuestra Razón* was published a few months later, however, Fidel distanced himself from it, evidently anxious to avoid any ideological pronouncements that might alienate potential July 26 adherents.

p. 295: In his letter to Daniel (published in Carlos Franqui's *Diary of the Cuban Revolution*), Che wrote: "Because of my ideological background, I belong to those who believe that the solution of the world's problems lies behind the so-called iron curtain, and I see this Movement as one of the many inspired by the bourgeoisie's desire to free themselves from the economic chains of imperialism. I always thought of Fidel as an authentic leader of the leftist bourgeoisie, although this image is enhanced by personal qualities of extraordinary brilliance that set him above his class. I began the struggle with that spirit: honestly without any hope of going further than the liberation of the country; and fully prepared to leave when the conditions of the later struggle veered all the action of the Movement toward the right (toward what all of you represent). What I never counted on was the radical change in his basic ideas in order to accept the Miami Pact. It had seemed impossible, and I later found out that it was. . . . Fortunately, Fidel's letter arrived during the intervening period . . . and it explained how what we can call a betrayal came about."

As to the issue of supplies, he said, neither he nor Fidel was getting what was needed quickly enough, and so he would continue to make his own arrangements. His main supplier might be "a shady character," but he considered himself capable of dealing with him without risk. *He* did not compromise his values, he told Daniel pointedly, unlike those who had gone along with the Miami Pact, where "all that happened was that an ass was yielded up in what was probably the most detestable act of 'buggery' in Cuban history. My name in history (which I mean to earn by my conduct) cannot be linked with that crime, and I hereby put that on record. . . . If this letter pains you because you consider it unfair or because you consider yourself innocent of the crime and you want to tell me so, terrific. And if it hurts you so much that you cut off relations with this part of the revolutionary forces, so much the worse."

Four days later, Daniel responded in an eloquent rebuttal of his own; he too was writing to leave "proof of his revolutionary integrity." As for keeping Che's letter private, as Che had requested, Daniel informed him that he had shared it with the rest of the Directorate; Che could therefore consider his reply as coming from all of them. "I am not the slightest bit interested in where you situate me, nor will I even try to make you change your personal opinion of us. . . . Now is not the time to be discussing 'where the salvation of the world lies'. . . . Our fundamental differences are that we are concerned about bringing the oppressed peoples of 'our America' governments that respond to their longing for Liberty and Progress. . . . We want a strong America, master of its own fate, an America that can stand up proudly to the United States, Russia, China, or any other power that tries to undermine its economic and political independence. On the other hand, those with your ideological background think the solution to our evils is to free ourselves from the noxious 'Yankee' domination by means of a no less noxious 'Soviet' domination."

p. 319: By divulging details of the sierra-llano dispute in his article, published just before he left Cuba, Che broke silence on a topic that had been officially taboo since the revolutionary triumph. In it, Che chose to skip over Faustino Pérez's disagreement with the decisions reached at the May summit, and to give the impression that the rift had been definitively settled.

It must be remembered that at the time Che wrote his article, not only was Faustino on the "same side" as himself, he was also a prominent member of Cuba's revolutionary leadership, and their past differences had become as irrelevant as they were inconvenient to rehash extensively in public.

Faustino Pérez's later career showed that in addition to his other virtues enumerated by Che, he was an inveterate survivor. The former opponent of Fidel's caudillismo became one of the grand viziers of *fidelismo;* the former anti-Communist became a member of the Central Committee of the reconstituted Cuban Communist party when it was officially inaugurated by Fidel in 1965, and remained a leading apparatchik until his death in 1993.

p. 330: In his letter, Fidel warned Raúl: "We must consider the possibility that elements of the dictatorship, exploiting this incident, are hatching a plan for physical aggression against North American citizens; given Batista's hopeless situation, this would turn international public opinion against us, as it would react with indignation to the news, for example, that several of those North Americans had been murdered by the rebels. It is essential to declare categorically that we do not utilize the system of hostages, however justified our indignation may be against the political attitudes of any government. . . . You must keep in mind that in matters that can have weighty consequences for the Movement, you cannot act on your own initiative, or go beyond certain limits without any consultation, Besides, that would give the false impression of complete anarchy in the inner circles of our army." (From Franqui's *Diary of the Cuban Revolution.*)

p. 340: By the end of 1958, Che had already recruited or was acquainted with most of his future guerrilla comrades. Eliseo Reyes, later "Rolando," Carlos Coello, aka "Tuma," Orlando "Olo" Pantoja, later "Antonio," and Manuel Hernández Osorio, aka "Miguel," were all with him on the march to Las Villas. Also, Harry Villegas, "Pombo," one of his bodyguards, and Leonardo Tamayo, "Urbano," in El Vaquerito's "Suicide Squad." The third Cuban survivor of Bolivia, Dariel "Benigno" Alarcón Ramírez, was with Camilo's invasion column, as was Antonio "Pinares" Sánchez. José María "Papi" Martínez and Octavio de la Concepción Pedraja, "El Moro," were with Raúl in Oriente. Juan Vitalio Acuña, aka "Joaquín" in Bolivia, had stayed behind in the Sierra Maestra and been made a *comandante* by Fidel. Three more future fighters would soon join Che in the Escambray: Alberto Fernández Montes de Oca, "Pachungo," Gustavo "Alejandro" Machín de Hoed, and Jesús "Rubin" Suárez Gayol.

p. 533: The Latin American guerrilla program had Fidel's early support, and the secret agency known as the "Liberation Department" was set up under Manuel "Barba Roja" Piñeiro as a vice ministry named the Viceministerio Téchnica within the newly formed Interior Ministry run by Ramíro Valdés. As Piñeiro explains: "I was responsible for the intelligence organizations and the Dirección Nacional de Liberación Nacional, which handled Latin America and Africa." In that capacity, he says, he sustained "an active and intense relationship with Che," joining in his many predawn conclaves with revolutionaries from around the world. Valdés is said to have concentrated more on "counterespionage" directed against the United States, while he also had "some involvement" in implementing the guerrilla programs. The role of Raúl was evidently less direct; in a pattern established early on by Fidel, he was deferred to by being allowed to select his own cadres from within the army for the operations. But Che was the true overseer. "From Day One, Che was in charge of the armed liberation movement supported by Cuba," explained a Cuban government source with access to the relevant classified files.

p. 614, top: In November 1963, with his habitual knack of meeting historic personalities on the eve of momentous events, Leonov came face-to-face with Lee Harvey Oswald. Oswald had arrived at the Soviet embassy in Mexico City and asked to speak to an official. According to Leonov, he was called out to deal with him. But when he saw that Oswald was both armed and agitated, Leonov decided he was "psychotic and dangerous," and says he quickly called other embassy personnel to help remove him from the premises. Leonov says he was stunned when, soon afterward, he recognized him as the man who had been arrested in Dallas, accused of murdering the American president. In a conversation about the various JFK assassination theories, Leonov dismissed the notion that Oswald might have acted on KGB orders, citing the "psychotic" behavior he had witnessed firsthand, and said that, theoretically speaking—even if the KGB *had* wanted to kill JFK— it would never have used someone so unbalanced and difficult to control.

In the course of the author's three separate conversations with Leonov in Moscow during 1993, Leonov expanded on different aspects of his life, his intelligence career, and his relationship to Che Guevara and other figures. During one session, he spoke passionately of the Guatemalan revolutionary cause, in particular, of the murders of Guatemalan Communist party "friends" of his by that country's military death squads. He did not go into details about what kind of relationship they had had, other than to say he had supported their cause. But in his 1995 book *El Oro de Moscú,* the well-informed Argentine Isidoro Gilbert, a former TASS correspondent, says that Leonov actively assisted the Guatemalan revolutionary cause, and suggests that he did so as part of an officially approved, if covert KGB program. More elliptically, Manuel Piñeiro told the author that Leonov "always showed solidarity toward Latin America's revolutionary fighters and the Cuban revolution."

To judge from a recently declassified memorandum that KGB Chief Alexander Shelepin sent to Khrushchev on July 29, 1961, the Soviets did not have a problem with guerrilla wars in the countries where the local Communist party was outlawed and sometimes gave their support to such action.

According to extracts published in *Inside the Kremlin's Cold War: From Stalin to Khrushchev,* by Zubok and Pleshakov, Shelepin's memo proposed a series of covert activities around the world to distract the United States from the confrontation in Berlin. "Shelepin advocated measures 'to activate by the means available to the KGB armed uprisings against pro-Western reactionary governments.' The subversive activities began in Nicaragua, where the KGB plotted an armed mutiny through an 'internal front of resistance,' in coordination with Castro's Cubans and with the 'Revolutionary Front Sandino.' Shelepin proposed making 'appropriations from KGB funds in addition to the previous assistance of 10,000 American dollars for the purchase of arms.' The plan also envisaged the instigation of an armed uprising in El Salvador, and a rebellion in Guatemala, where guerrilla forces would be given $15,000 to buy weapons." (Khrushchev approved this plan, and it was passed by the Soviet Central Committee on August 1, 1961.)

p. 614, middle: Shortly after Che's Moscow visit, Rudolf Shlyapnikov traveled to Cuba to take up a post at the Soviet Embassy, as the official in charge of the thousands of Soviet Komsomol "volunteers" working in Cuba. In February 1968, accused of colluding with the unrepentant Aníbal Escalante and other disgruntled "old Communists" in a plot to undermine Fidel's revolutionary authority, Shlyapnikov and several other Soviet agents were expelled from Cuba; Escalante was sentenced to fifteen years in prison. From his own embassy post in Havana, Oleg Darushenkov rose rapidly in party ranks to become head of the Central Committee's "Cuba" department. In the 1980s, he became Soviet ambassador to Mexico, and, after the fall of Communism in the USSR, he resigned his post and remained in Mexico, working as an executive for the Mexican television conglomerate Televisa. (Shlyapnikov's last diplomatic post, as Soviet consul in Veracruz, Mexico, also coincided with Darushenkov's tenure as ambassador to Mexico.)

These men are considered to have represented the anti-Guevarist Soviet line. Che's widow, Aleida March, believes that Oleg Darushenkov was "a provocateur," and is still rankled by the fact that after Che's death, when he came to her house and offered his condolences, he undiplomatically asked her: "Why did Che go to Bolivia, when he was a foreigner?" She took offense, and says that she cited the precedent of the Dominican general Máximo Gómez, who helped in Cuba's war of independence against Spain. Finally, she asked him how he dared to pose such a question in "this house," meaning Che's.

Borrego agreed with Aleida's assessment of Darushenkov, whom he knew well, and described him as extremely bright, capable, and highly ambitous, but also "wicked," given to badmouthing people and making provocative comments in a pattern that seemed to indicate an ulterior motive.

p. 623: Among those in the room, according to Che's widow, Aleida March, was the young Angolan resistance leader Jonas Savimbi. Savimbi would go on to obtain Chinese aid and found the UNITA guerrilla movement. Later, with Cuba supporting the rival MPLA guerrillas, he turned for patronage to the West. But in the multisided battle against the Portuguese, which finally culminated in the country's independence in 1974, Savimbi's forces lost out to the MPLA, which seized power and installed a Marxist regime. He continued to wage war, however, with CIA and South African military support. During the the 1980s, Savimbi's UNITA had lavish offices in Washington, D.C., and the strongman himself was lauded by President Ronald Reagan as an anti-Communist "freedom fighter" in the best Western tradition. But after participating in and losing national elections following a internationally brokered cease-fire agreement in 1992, Savimbi returned to war; hundreds of thousands of Angolans died in the renewed fighting, which left much of Angola destroyed. In 1996 he was once again involved in power-sharing negotiations with the regime.

p. 627: Fidel had other problems with the Chinese as well. While Che was away, in late 1964—with Cuba's rice crop drastically reduced by revolutionary incompetence, the country facing a severe shortfall for consumer needs in the 1964 harvest—China had dramatically increased its rice exports to the island at Fidel's personal request, but only after he offered a sugar-for-rice barter agreement that was highly advantageous to the Chinese. The fact that he had had to go personally to the Chinese embassy to strike the deal had obviously been galling to Fidel, and he remained rankled. Combined with the rather scurrilous Chinese propaganda campaign in Havana, the tensions began to mount. In a March 1965 speech he issued an implicit public warning to China's embassy about the "proselytizing," and, when the leaflet campaign continued, he followed with a visit to the ambassador in September 1965, to complain and demand an explanation for the activity. No answer apparently came, but in December the Chinese suspended the rice exports to Cuba. In February 1966 Fidel went public with the whole affair and denounced the "insolence" of the Chinese. A month later, he followed with a ringing indictment of China's Communist government, calling it "monarchical" and insinuating that its "leadership"—Mao—was senile. Afterward, the two countries maintained their embassies, but for years relations were almost nonexistent, and did not improve when Cuba entered a phase of unabashed Soviet alignment in the early 1970s. This whole episode is dealt with comprehensively by Maurice Halperin in *The Taming of Fidel Castro.*

p. 634: In addition to the tape-recorded poems Che left her, says Aleida, he also wrote her a special poem. "It's mine," she says, explaining why she has never made it public. "The world can read it after I'm dead." Aleida has always guarded the details of her life with Che with an almost obsessive zeal. Her eldest daughter, Aliusha, says it wasn't until she was in her twenties, prepared to follow in her father's footsteps by going off to Nicaragua for internationalist duty as a doctor, that fear of losing her made her mother open up. At that point, Aleida read to her a love letter Che had written to her, kept under lock and key in a special desk at their home. And, while Aliusha was in Nicaragua, Aleida sent her a copy of the tape-recorded love poems he had left her.

In addition to his "public" farewell letter to his children, Che also sent his children some postcards from Africa, and a tape recording of his voice telling them how he felt to be their father. "Che was a *'machista'* like most Latins," said Aleida, in an affectionately chiding tone, explaining that in a letter to his two sons, Camilo and Ernesto, excluding the girls, he told them that at the end of the century—if he was still alive and if imperialism "still existed"— they would have to fight it together, and if not, they would "go together to the Moon on a spaceship." In a letter to his daughters, he told them to look after their brothers, especially Camilo, to get him to stop using bad words.

p. 667: In unpublished notes dated November 21, 1965, from Pombo's diary, sections of which were obtained by the author in Cuba, Pombo wrote about problems that Che omitted in his own account.

"After making the decision to retreat from that place and return to the neighboring country of Tanzania, open discrepancies began to appear between Tatu and the other high-ranking leaders of the Party who had been designated to collaborate with him in the exercise of such a difficult duty (Tembo, Siki, Uta, Karim).

"The fundamental root of the aforementioned divergences lies in the attitude of the *compañeros* toward the reality in which we found ourselves, their poor comprehension of the attitude taken by Tatu [Che] in the face of the situation on the ground, due to the fact that [they] . . . didn't trust in him as a national leader of our revolution and as a leader of our detachment designated to fight in those distant lands.

"They felt that Tatu was being willful in his determination to stay there, and that he hadn't been able to appreciate the fact that the subjective conditions didn't exist to carry out the revolution; that even if the insurrection were to win, the [Congolese] revolution did not have leaders to take it forward because they were all pseudo-revolutionaries, without principles, and it could even be said that they had few morals.

"But the reality is that Tatu was aware of this, aware about the impossibility of carrying out a social revolution; it was something he had told all of us, except for Siki [Fernández Mell] and Tembo [Aragonés] who weren't present because they were at the base, where it wasn't sent." (Pombo was referring to Che's August 12 "Message to the Combatants.")

"I personally said that his position of sacrifice was due to his conviction that the withdrawal of the Cubans should be a decision that should come from the Cuban government . . . [and] that we should never [beg or] shout asking to be authorized to withdraw. . . . "

p. 671: When he went off to join Che in the Congo, Pombo had left behind a bride of less than three years; they had an infant son, Harry Jr. His wife, Cristina Campuzano, had been a secretary of Che's in the early period of "Industrialización," and a friend of both Hilda Gadea and Aleida. The families of Che's men were extremely close in those days: Tuma had been the best man at the wedding of Pombo and Cristina.

It was "terribly hard" for the wives, Cristina acknowledges, because they rarely saw their husbands. "When they were in Cuba they were up at all hours with Che, then they went to the Congo, then Bolivia." Understandably, these families formed a tight-knit group, and when their husbands went off with Che, they were "withdrawn" from circulation for security reasons. A group of them lived in a semicommunal block of flats in Miramar.

At one point, like Aleida, Cristina was to have joined Pombo during his underground European period, and was given a *leyenda* to study so she could join him there. At the time, she says, Pombo was living in concealment in the Cuban embassy in Paris.

After Pombo's departure to Bolivia, Cristina, again like Aleida, was told that she could go when "the conditions were right." She hadn't gone as far as military training, however; Pombo had argued that their son, Harry, was too young to be left, and that she should not come until the "ground was secured."

Papi also left behind a wife and young son. Only Tuma was childless, but after returning to Cuba from Prague, he impregnated his wife; their son, whom he would never know, was born after he left for Bolivia.

p. 675: Since there has been no extensive on-the-record Cuban clarification of Che's exact movements, meetings, and whereabouts between the time he left the Congo and reappeared in Cuba, the author based his account on the most credible sources available to him: his widow, Aleida March; General Harry Villegas, alias "Pombo"; Manuel "Barba Roja" Piñeiro; Juan Carreterro, the senior Cuban intelligence official and diplomat, alias "Ariel"; and Oscar de Cárdenas, who was Ulíses Estrada's deputy in charge of the African department of Cuban intelligence at the time Che exited the Congo. All of them say that Che went to Prague from Tanzania, and from there back to Havana.

But there are other versions. Mario Monje, the former Bolivian Communist party secretary, told the author that he had learned, without naming his sources of information, that Che, after leaving Tanzania, went to the German Democratic Republic, where he lived "under the protection of the German intelligence services."

Another knowledgeable Cuban source indicated the possibility that Che did spend "some time" in the GDR during his underground period, but that this followed his secret return trip to Cuba, while he was en route to Bolivia in the fall of 1967. This source also added that Aleida "may" have visited him there. If true, neither Aleida nor the Cuban government is thus far prepared to acknowledge it. (Bolstering the possibility of Che's presence in the GDR is the circumstantial evidence that Che himself provided upon his capture. The first of his two Bolivian diaries, which he began writing in during November 1966, was manufactured in East Germany.)

His widow, Aleida March, told the author she had joined Che abroad, clandestinely, on three separate occasions. The first, in January–February 1966, in Tanzania; the second time, in Prague, before his return to Cuba in mid-1966; and a third time that she did not specify.

Added to the rather complex mosaic of chronologies is the account provided by Che's "official" Cuban biographers, former Ministry of Interior agent Froilán González and his wife, Adys Cupull, who were given access by Cuba's Interior Ministry to false passports that were allegedly used by Che to travel following his disappearance from public view in April 1965.

According to them, Che left Tanzania on December 28, 1965, for an unspecified country in Eastern Europe and stayed there until July 14, 1966, whereupon he traveled to Prague; between July 19–20 he traveled from Prague to Vienna, Geneva, Zurich, and Moscow, where he immediately left for Havana.

But Ariel, Manuel Piñeiro's deputy, told the author: "The various passports held by Cuban intelligence with different stamps on them showing different countries don't mean anything. Various *leyendas* [clandestine identities and itineraries] would have been prepared for him, and the stamps applied by us, here in Cuba."

Ariel also offered that at the time Che left for Prague from Tanzania, he was personally involved in spreading "disinformation" about Che so as to confuse Western intelligence agencies and help throw them off his scent.

Manuel Piñeiro confirmed that Che did not stay rooted in Prague. At one point, he acknowledged, Che took a trip to Paris, to put his latest *leyenda,* or false identity, through a test.

p. 683: According to the author's sources in Cuba, Régis Debray, like "Tania," was part of the intelligence network run by Manuel "Barba Roja" Piñeiro. He was handled directly by Ulíses Estrada and by Juan Carretero, or "Ariel," who implemented Cuba's guerrilla programs. These sources say that Debray's involvement in the program derived from the period when he came to Havana as a philosophy graduate student in 1961. His public "cover" for his trip to Bolivia, as a French journalist, was both genuine and useful, for he did write about Latin America for the French publisher Maspéro. But he was also an underground courier for "Barba Roja." It is said that it was in this latter capacity—as a propagandist and courier for the cause—rather than as a theorist and ally at the command level, that Debray was regarded as useful by the Cubans.

p. 697: In these unpublished notes, Che softened his criticisms of Lenin by pointing out that his errors did not make him "an enemy," and that his own criticisms were "intended within the spirit of Marxist revolutionary criticism," in order to "modernize Marxism" and to correct its "mistaken paths" to help underdeveloped countries that were "struggling for freedom." Che anticipated attacks against him from fellow socialists if his work was published, saying: "Some will take this writing as counterrevolutionary or reformist," and he stressed that for this reason the arguments posed needed to be well elaborated and based on airtight scholarship.

Some of the remarks he scribbled on the margin of the Soviet manual, however, were no less irreverent than his observation of Lenin. Signaling a passage that boldly declared: "Socialism need not come about through violence, as proven by the socialist states of Eastern Europe, where change came through peaceful means," Che quipped in humorous disbelief: "What was the Soviet army doing, scratching its balls?"

p. 701: Speaking of his Bolivian expedition, a Cuban government source acknowledged: "Che was not in *command* of the situation into which he was inserted. It was the "Department of the Americas" [the name later chosen for Piñeiro's restructured "Liberation Department"] that studied the conditions for revolution in other countries and made the recommendations to Fidel."

Piñeiro's people seem to have overplayed their hand in assuring Fidel that the conditions were right for Che to come to Bolivia. People close to Che in Cuba still privately blame Piñeiro and his men for "fucking things up" in Bolivia. Few suggest that there was any betrayal, but rather shoddy work and *guaperia*—a Cuban term meaning bully-boy arrogance—brought about the chain of multiple errors that characterized the Bolivian operation.

Most of the survivors agree that one of those "errors" was the decision to withdraw "Renán," or "Iván"—the agent Renán Montero—from La Paz after the group's premature discovery in March 1967. It left the tiny urban cell that included Loyola Guzmán, Humberto Vázquez-Viaña, and Rodolfo Saldaña without a means of communicating with Havana—or with the guerrillas in the field. Indeed, by the summer of 1967, Che's Bolivian guerrilla operation was fragmented into four groups, each incommunicado from the other: Che's group, isolated and on the run, out of contact with Havana and the city; Joaquín's group, wandering separately from Che's column and equally cut off from the outside; the urban group, which had no idea what was happening anywhere; and finally, Cuba itself, where the security apparatus was evidently reduced to monitoring events in Bolivia through news reports.

Why was Renán pulled out at such a crucial moment? As the author has written elsewhere, Piñeiro says it was to renew his documentation, and run a check on his cover identity. But Loyola Guzmán, who met with Renán several times in 1967, got the distinct impression in her last rendezvous with him that he was "running scared," Ariel, meanwhile, says Renán was "extremely ill." They were preparing another man to replace him, he says, but events in Bolivia disrupted that plan. By the time the other agent was ready to go, it was too late. But Loyola remains puzzled. She sent two letters via couriers to Havana stressing the urgent need for a substitute for Renán and later, after Che's diary was captured and published, she found out the messages had arrived, because in August he wrote down the fact that he had received a coded message from Havana essentially retransmitting her remarks, and advising him that a replacement was on his way. She asked: "How is it possible that they could get my letter, retransmit it to Che, and still take no action?"

By late August, Loyola Guzmán and her companions in the city had resolved that she would go to Havana to explain the urgency of their dilemma. First, she followed up a message that the party was reconsidering its position and was willing to meet her in the city of Cochabamba. Before setting out, she began to feel that she was being followed. She told Humberto Vázquez-Viaña, who ran a test to see if her suspicions were true. She spent a day moving around the city, getting on and off buses, with Humberto following from a discreet distance, watching. At the end of the day, he confirmed it. She was being followed.

A couple of days later, she was arrested.

To the accusations thrown in the direction of him and his agents, Piñeiro is adamant that Che's survival and ultimate success was their main concern and rejects as "repugnant" any suggestions to the contrary.

p. 717: Arguedas' name came up in a meeting between Pombo, Papi, and Mario Monje on the night of August 8, 1966, in La Paz. In Pombo's original diary, he recorded the meeting and Monje's boast of having key allies placed inside Bolivia's government, but omitted their names for security reasons. But in some unpublished notes obtained by the author, Pombo scribbled: "He spoke to us of Arguedas who had been named minister [of Interior]. . . . He explained that, as a member, he [Arguedas] had been authorized to occupy said post by the [Bolivian Communist] Party, that he was situated in a key post, [to which] we expressed our worries over the method applied and our belief that it was a double-edged sword[.] He stressed that [Arguedas] was a colleague who was easy to dominate (but he was very wrong)."

p. 720: In June 1997, Villoldo—who had previously not come forth in public—told the author that the CIA had additional intelligence sources in Bolivia, most importantly an informant who was an active member of the Bolivian Communist party. Villoldo would not disclose the traitor's identity, whom he described as "someone close to the Peredo brothers," who was still alive today. Villoldo also alleged that the Bolivian Communist party chief Mario Monje was a regular informant of Antonio Arguedas' intelligence chief at the Interior Ministry, Colonel Roberto Quintanilla, who in turn passed Monje's information along to the CIA.

As for Bustos and Debray, Villoldo said both men broke down during their first days in captivity, and "told what they knew." But he added that "anyone" would have done the same in their situation, because they were being threatened with death, and were in fact going to be killed by the Bolivian military, but that he and his CIA colleagues "saved them" in order to obtain their information.

p. 730: Among some of his friends and associates in Cuba, it is acknowledged off the record that Che's Bolivian operation was a total catastrophe from beginning to end. They cite the fact that Che never had the support of the peasants in Bolivia, that the Cuban and Bolivian guerrillas never established a good rapport, and that Che, older and weaker than his tougher former sierra self, was loath to act against the slackers in his ranks. Said one Cuban official: "This humanity cost him in the end, because a lesser man would have carried out some executions, but Che didn't; he didn't want to scare people off, he wanted to get people to join him, and he knew he was, after all, a foreigner."

Manuel Piñeiro, meanwhile, defends Che's efforts in Bolivia and the Congo, calling them "heroic exploits" and quoting Fidel on the issue of whether or not Che's final battles were failures: "I always say that triumph or failure does not determine the correctness of a policy."

p. 735: In his rendition of their encounter, the author used extracts from Selich's notes from his talk with Che. The following exchange was not included:

SELICH: What do you believe is the reason for your failure? I think it was the lack of support of the peasants.

CHE: There maybe something of truth [in that], but the truth is that it is due to the effective organization of Barrientos's political party, that is to say, his *corregidores* and political mayors, who took charge of warning the army about our movements.

Selich's notes end, inexplicably, with an unanswered question he posed to Guevara: "Why didn't you manage to recruit more national [Bolivian] elements, such as the peasants of the zone?"

Notes on Sources*

Part One: Unquiet Youth

Field Research and Interviews

To research Che's childhood and family history, I spent three months in Argentina in 1994, much of the time traveling in the company of his friend Alberto Granado. Roberto and Celia Guevara were extremely helpful with clarification of the family history, as well as in their reflections on their brother "Che" himself. Celia Guevara de la Serna's friend Julia Constenla de Giussani provided me with the account of Che's "true" birthdate. Ana María Erra, Ernesto Guevara Lynch's second wife, also helped with details of Guevara family history.

Alberto Granado and I traveled together to Misiones and found the Guevaras' old Puerto Caraguataí homestead. We interviewed a number of people who remembered Che's parents, including Gertrudis Kraft and Johann Fahraven; others who helped with local history were Emiliano Rejala, Dr. Oscar Darú, and Leonor and Epifanio Acosta.

With Alberto Granado and "Calica" Ferrer, I traveled to Alta Gracia and Córdoba; Carlos Figueroa let us stay in his old family house on Calle Avellaneda in Alta Gracia, just down the street from the Guevaras' old homes, Villa Chichita and Villa Nydia.

With these men, I was able to gain a privileged glimpse into the past as they reminisced together and took me to meet Guevara's other childhood friends and acquaintances. These included Rodolfo Ruarte, Sarah Muñoz, Enrique Martín, Paco Fernández, Carlos Barceló, Mario and Chicho Salduna, Blanca de Alboñoroz, Juan and Nelly Bustos, José Manuel Peña, Alberto

*For a more complete list of source materials, see the Selected Bibliography.

Ferrer, and Ofelia Moyano. Also, Rosario López, the Guevaras' former housekeeper, and Elba Rossi, Ernesto's third-grade schoolteacher at the Escuela Liniers.

In Córdoba and Buenos Aires, I interviewed a number of his Dean Funes schoolmates, among them Raúl Melivosky, Oscar Stemmelin, Roberto "Beto" Ahumada, Osvaldo Bidinost, Carlos López Villagra, Jorge Iskaro, José María Roque. Among his teenaged acquaintances, Miriam Urrutia, Nora Feigin, Betty Feigin (the widow of Gustavo Roca), Tatiana Quiroga de Roca, Jaime "Jimmy" Roca, Carlos Lino, and "Chacho" Ferrer. In Spain, I interviewed Carmen González-Aguilar and her brother "Pepe." In Cuba, Fernando Barral gave me his own reminiscences.

In Rosario, Alberto Granado and I were assisted by the *Pagina 12* journalist Reynaldo Sietecaser, a Che aficionado, and together we explored the place where Che spent his first month of life. Granado's cousin, Naty López, recalled for us the day long ago when, as "Míal" and "Fuser," Alberto and Che roared through town on "La Poderosa," on their "escape to the north."

For Guevara's Buenos Aires and on-the-road years, I talked with Ricardo Rojo, Carlos Infante, Dr. Emilio Levine, Fernando Chávez, Adalberto Ben-Golea, Nelly Benbibre de Castro, Andro Herrero, Anita García, Gualo García's widow, and Mario Saravia. Alberto Granado and Calica Ferrer both shared with me their memories of the trips they took with Ernesto.

For Che's Guatemalan and Mexican period, I was assisted greatly by the journalist Phil Gunson, who arranged all of my interviews and conducted a number himself on my behalf. Those interviewed included Ricardo Romero, Edelberto Torres Jr., Antonio del Conde ("El Cuate"), Yuri Paporov, Alfonso Bauer Paiz, Fernando Gutiérrez Barrios, Dr. David Mitrani, Dr. José Montes Montes, Dr. Baltazar Rodríquez, and others. I interviewed Nikolai Leonov in Moscow on three separate occasions in 1994.

Material Sources

For Che's childhood and youth I referred to *Mi Hijo el Che,* the memoir written by Che's father, Ernesto Guevara Lynch. The extracts of Che's first trip around Argentina, in 1951, are taken from this book. The short story "Angustia" he wrote while at sea in 1950 was published in the Argentine newspaper *Primer Plano* in 1992. For his 1951–1952 travels with Alberto Granado, I referred to Granado's book, *En Viaje con el Che por Sudamerica,* and Che's own *Notas de Viaje,* published in English as *The Motorcycle Diaries.* I made extensive use of *Ernestito, Vivo y Presente,* the book of oral testimony encompassing Che's life from 1928 to 1953, compiled by the Cuban Guevara historians Froilán González and Adys Cupull. Their published chronology of Che's life, *Un Hombre Bravo,* was a useful reference for this and subsequent periods. Also, *El Che y los Argentinos,* by Claudia Korol, and *Testimonios Sobre el Che,* edited by Mírta Rodríguez. Quotations by Dolores Moyano are taken from a *New York Times* article she wrote in 1968.

Che's widow, Aleida March, shared with me the full collection of Che's "Diccionario Filosófico," reflecting his reading of philosophy, religion, mythology, and psychology between the ages of seventeen and twenty-eight, and his "Indice Literario," his reading list covering the same period.

For Che's life from mid-1953, when he left Argentina, through to his meeting in Mexico with Fidel Castro, I based much of my narrative on his unpublished diary "Otra Vez," provided by Che's widow, Aleida March. Also, *Aquí Va un Soldado de las Americas,* Che's letters home compiled by his father in book form. Fernando Barral gave me an original manuscript of the same book, containing letters not included in the published version.

Calica Ferrer gave me copies of his letters written home while traveling with Che in 1953. Anita de García also shared her late husband "Gualo" García's letters, and Andro Herrero gave me excerpts from his own diary, as well as letters he received from Ernesto Guevara, Gualo García, Oscar Valdovinos, and Ricardo Rojo after they left him in Guayaquil and traveled north to Guatemala.

I was able to review original materials covering Che's life from his infancy to his Mexico City period—including some previously unpublished family letters and early writings—at Cuba's Council of State Historical Archives, with permission from its director, Pedro Álvarez Tabío. Heberto Norman Acosta, a specialist in the pre-*Granma* "exile" period of the July 26 Movement, allowed me to review Che's censored Mexican police interrogation testimony and other materials. Lionel Martin lent me the late Harold White's copy of the Marxist anthology that the young Ernesto Guevara helped him translate in Guatemala.

I employed Hilda Gadea's book, *Ernesto: A Memoir of Che Guevara* for her rendition of their relationship, which includes a number of short memoirs by others, including Myrna Torres, Harold White, Lucila Velásquez, Juan Juarbe y Juarbe and Laura Meneses de Albizu Campos.

Che's own *Reminiscences of the Cuban Revolutionary War* refers to his time on the road in Mexico and Guatemala as well. On October 17, 1967, Cuba's official Communist party newspaper, *Granma,* dedicated a special edition to Che following his death, and I drew a number of quotations from this publication, including the recollections of Mario Dalmau and others. The Cuban house of culture, Casa de las Americas, also published a number of special editions devoted to Che; the quotations from Alfonso Bauer Paiz, referring to the Guatemala-Mexico period, are taken from them. Phil Gunson obtained articles published in 1956–1957 on the Cuban revolutionaries from Mexican press archives of that period.

Tad Szulc's biography, *Fidel: A Critical Portrait,* and Hugh Thomas's *Cuba: The Pursuit of Freedom* were invaluable resources for this historical period. Lionel Martin provided me with a treasure trove of index cards from his personal archive including quotations from many primary interviews he conducted in the 1960s, when he was planning to write a Che Guevara biography.

Part Two: Becoming Che

Field Research and Interviews

In Cuba I interviewed a number of people who fought with Che in the Sierra Maestra, among them Harry Villegas ("Pombo"), Ricardo Martínez, Jorge Enrique Mendoza, Dariel Alarcón Ramírez ("Benigno"), and Oscar Fernández Mell.

Aleida March, Lolita Rossell, Miguel Ángel Duque de Estrada, and Orlando Borrego also gave details of Che's Escambray period, the battle for Santa Clara, and the drive on Havana.

Material Sources

I based most of my narrative for part 2 on Che's unpublished "Diario de un Combatiente," provided to me by his widow. I also used his published account of the war, *Episodes of the Cuban Revolutionary War,* in both the English and Spanish-language editions.

Hugh Thomas's *Cuba,* Tad Szulc's *Fidel: A Critical Portrait,* Lionel Martin's *The Early Fidel,* Carlos Franqui's *Diary of the Cuban Revolution,* and Robert Quirk's *Fidel Castro* were all invaluable reference tools that I used extensively. Also, Jorge Ricardo Masetti's *Los Que Luchan y Los que Lloran,* Robert Taber's *M-26: Biography of Revolution,* Herbert Matthews's *The Cuba Story,* and Heinz Dieterich's *Diarios Inéditos de la Guerrilla Cubana.* For internal rebel correspondence and Che's letters written in this period, I relied upon Franqui's *Diary,* Guevara Lynch's *Mi Hijo el Che,* and the Casa de las Americas commemorative compilation of Cuban army and July 26 reports, memos, and cables. I also made use of *Descamisado* by Erique Acevedo and Cuban *comandante* Juan Almeida's own series of autobiographical books on the sierra war.

The Cuban historian Andrés Castillo Bernal provided me with his own extensively researched unpublished manuscript on the war, and I also drew from the Cuban oral histories *Ellos Lucharon con el Che, Los Doce, Testimonios Sobre el Che,* and *Entre Nostoros.*

Part Three: Making the New Man

Field Research and Interviews

I conducted interviews with Orlando Borrego, Alfredo Menéndez, and Oscar Fernández Mell for the posttriumph La Cabaña period and early revolutionary period. Aleida March, Alberto Castellanos, Enrique Viltres, Colonel Ricardo Martínez, and Nicolás Quintana also shed light on this time.

Dr. Salvador Vilaseca and Alfredo Menéndez both shared their accounts of Che's 1959 world trip to the nonaligned countries. For Che's work at the National Bank, the Ministry of Industries, and the Central Planning Board, I was helped by Aleida March, Orlando Borrego, Dr. Salvador Vilaseca, Regino Boti, Nicolás Quintana, Nestor Laverne, Tirso Saenz, Juan Gravalosa, and Cristina Campuzano Ángel Arcos Vergnes and others gave me their insiders' accounts. For Che's 1961 trip to Punta del Este, Julia Constenla, Ricardo Rojo, Roberto Guevara, and Carlos Figueroa shared their recollections.

In three visits to Moscow, I also interviewed a number of former Soviet officials who spoke about the Cuba-Soviet relationship and Che's dealings with Moscow. Che's pivotal role in forging Cuba's links with the Soviet Union was explained to me in depth by Alexandr Alexiev, Giorgi Kornienko, Sergo Mikoyan, Nikolai Leonov, and Yuri Paporov, among others.

I conducted other interviews with Yuri Pevtsov, Vladimir Bondarchuk, Timur Gaidar, Feder Burlatksy, Nikolai Metutsov, Kiva Maidanek, Yuri Krasin, Yvgeny Kosarev, Marat Muknachov, Vitali Korionov, Rudolf Shlyapnikov, and former Soviet generals Gribkov and Garbus.

My most comprehensive accounts of Che's life in all its facets, both public and private, during his time in Cuba, came from his widow, Aleida March, and his friend Orlando Borrego. Other details came from Lolita Rossell Sofia Gato, Che's late daughter Hilda Guevara, and Aliusha Guevara; also, Alberto Granado, Fernando Barral, Pepe Aguilar, Harry Villegas, and Alberto Castellanos. For his relationship with his family in Argentina, Aleida March, Ana María Erra, and María Elena Duarte were especially valuable sources.

To document Che's guerrilla activities I interviewed people in Moscow, Havana, Argentina, Paraguay, Bolivia, Spain, and Sweden. They included Aleida March, Orlando Borrego, Manuel Piñeiro, Juan Carreterro ("Ariel"), Osvaldo de Cárdenas, Regino Boti, General Harry Villegas ("Pombo"), Dariel Alarcón Ramírez ("Benigno"), Alberto Castellanos, Ricardo Gadea, Rodolfo Saldaña, Ciro Roberto Bustos, Héctor Jouve, Henry Lerner, Alberto Granado, Oscar del Barco, Toto Schmücler, Alberto Coría, Alberto Korn, Nestor Laverne, Loyola Guzmán, Marlene Lorjiovaca, Humberto Vázquez-Viaña, Ana Urquieta, Chato Peredo, Antonio Peredo, José Castillo ("Paco"), Oscar

Zalas, Jorge Kolle Cueto, Simón Reyes, Juan Lechín, Gustavo Sánchez, and others. I interviewed Mario Monje on two separate occasions in Moscow.

Among Che's list of enemies, I met with former CIA agent Felix Rodríguez; former Bolivian generals Reque Terán, Gary Prado Salmon, and Mario Vargas Salinas; ex-sergeant Mario Terán, and former Bolivian army majors Rubén Sánchez and Miguel Ayoroa. The former CIA station chief in La Paz, John Tilton, spoke to me over the telephone from his home in Georgia. In Asunción, Paraguay, the widow of Colonel Andrés Selich, Socorro Selich, provided me with her account of her late husband's activities in the campaign against Che.

Material Sources

A great many books have been written on the Cuban revolution, and I have had access to most of them. Among those I found useful were Hugh Thomas's *Cuba,* Tad Szulc's *Fidel: A Critical Portrait,* Richard Gott's *Rural Guerrillas in Latin America,* Carlos Franqui's *Diary of the Cuban Revolution* and his *Family Portrait of Fidel,* Robert Quirk's *Fidel Castro,* K. S. Karol's *Guerrillas in Power,* and Maurice Halperin's *The Taming of Fidel Castro.* Also, Hilda Gadea's *Ernesto: A Memoir of Che Guevara,* Ricardo Rojo's *My Friend Che,* and Ernesto Guevara Lynch's *Mi Hijo el Che.*

Other resources were Regis Debray's *Revolution in the Revolution?, Castroism: The Long March in Latin America,* and *La Guerrilla del Che en Bolivia.* Also, *El Che y los Argentinos* by Claudia Korol; *Tania: Misión Guerrillera en Bolivia* by Marta Rojas and Mírta Rodríguez; Simone de Beauvoir's memoir *All Said and Done; A Thousand Days* by Arthur Schlesinger Jr.; Che's own *Diario del Che en Bolivia;* the seven-volume set of Che's collected works edited by Orlando Borrego, *El Che en La Revolución Cubana;* Casa de las Americas two-volume selected works, *El Che Guevara: Obras 1957–1967;* Gianni Miná's *An Encounter with Fidel;* Harry Villegas's memoir, *Un Hombre de la Guerrilla del Che,* and Humberto Vásquez-Viaña's monograph, *Antecedentes de la Guerrilla del Che en Bolivia;* the five-volume collection of documents and interviews entitled *El Che en Bolivia,* edited by Carlos Soria Galvarro. Paco Ignacio Taibo II, Felix Guerra, and Froilan Escobar's book, *El Año Que Estuvimos en Ninguna Parte,* is the first to be written on Che's time in the Congo; Gary Prado's *La Guerrilla Immolada,* General Arnaldo Saucedo Parada's *No Disparen Soy el Che,* and General Reque Terán's *La Campaña de Ñancahuazú* were insightful accounts of the Bolivian military's view of Che's campaign in Bolivia, as was filmmaker Richard Dindo's extensively researched feature documentary *The Diary of Che in Bolivia.*

In addition to these interviews and published sources, I had access to a good deal of previously unpublished documentation, including a review of Che's critique of the Soviet Manuel on Political Economy, his "Notas Económicas"; unexpurgated sections of Pombo's 1966–1967 Prague-Bolivia diary; Inti Peredo's original draft manuscript for his book *Mi Campaña Junto al Che,* written in Cuba following his escape from Bolivia; interrogation transcripts, photographs, and army propaganda from the archives of General Reque Terán; assorted documents and photographs from the personal archive of the late Colonel Andrés Selich, including his field log during the 1967 antiguerrilla campaign, his question-and-answer session with the captured Che Guevara, and his private report on the capture and execution of Che Guevara to Bolivian General David La Fuente.

Selected Bibliography

By and About Ernesto Che Guevara

Adams, Jerome R. *Latin American Heroes.* New York: Ballantine Books, 1991.

Alexandre, Marianne, ed. *Viva Che.* London: Lorrimer, Third World Series, 1968.

Álvarez Batista, Gerónimo. *Che: Una Nueva Batalla.* La Habana: Pablo de la Torriente, 1994.

Ariet, María del Carmen. *Che: Pensamiento Político.* La Habana: Editora Política, 1993.

————. *El Pensamiento del Che.* La Habana: Editorial Capitán San Luis, 1992.

"Bones Now Seem to Prove That Che Is Dead," by Jon Lee Anderson, *The New York Times* (July 5, 1997).

Bourne, Richard. *Political Leaders of Latin America.* London: Pelican Books, 1969.

Bruschtein, Luis. *Che Guevara: Los Hombres de la Historia.* (Magazine supplement.) Buenos Aires: Pagina 12, Centro Editor de America Latina, 1994.

Candía, Gen. Alfredo G. *La Muerte del Che Guevara.* La Paz, Bolivia: La Liga Anticomunista de los Pueblos Asiaticos, Republica de China, 1971.

Castro, Fidel. *Che: A Memoir by Fidel Castro.* Melbourne, Australia: Ocean Press, 1994.

Centro de Estudios Sobre America. *Pensar al Che,* Tomo I and 2. La Habana: Editorial José Martí, 1989.

"Che." La Habana: Casa de Las Americas No. 43 (Jan.-Feb. 1968).

"Che": Edición Especial de *Moncada.* La Habana: Ministerio del Interior, October 6, 1987.

778   Selected Bibliography

Cupull, Adys, and Froilán González. *Cálida Presencia: Su Amistad con Tita Infante.* Santiago de Cuba: Editorial Oriente, 1995.
———. *De Ñancahuasu a La Higuera.* La Habana: Editora Política, 1989.
———. *El Diario del Che en Bolivia.* La Habana: Editora Política, 1988.
———. *Entre Nosotros.* La Habana: Ediciones Abril, 1992.
———. *Ernestito: Vivo y Presente.* La Habana: Editora Política, 1989.
———. *La CIA contra El Che.* La Habana: Editora Política, 1992.
———. *Un Hombre Bravo.* La Habana: Editorial Capitán San Luis, 1995.
Debray, Regis. *La Guerrilla de Che.* Barcelona: Siglo Veintiun Editores, 1975 (orig. Paris: Maspéro, 1974).
Escobar, Froilán, and Félix Guerra. *Che: Sierra Adentro.* La Habana: Editora Política, 1988.
Espinosa Goitizolo, Reinaldo, and Guillermo Grau Guardarrama. *Atlas Ernesto Che Guevara: Histórico Biográfico y Militar* La Habana: Editorial Pueblo y Educación, Ministerio de las Fuerzas Armadas Revolucionarias, 1991.
Gadea, Hilda. *Ernesto: A Memoir of Che Guevara: An Intimate Account of the Making of a Revolutionary by His First Wife, Hilda Gadea.* London and New York: W. H. Allen, 1973.
Galvarro, Carlos Soria. *El Che en Bolivia: Documentos y Testimonios,* vols. 1–5. La Paz, Bolivia: CEDOIN Coleccion Historia y Documento, 1994–1996.
Gambini, Hugo. *El Che Guevara: La Biografía.* Buenos Aires: Grupo Planeta, 1968, rev. ed., 1996.
Garcés, María. *Materiales sobre la Guerrilla de Ñancáhuasu: La Campaña del Che en Bolivia (1967) Atravéz della Prensa.* Quito, Ecuador: Editorial La Mañana, 1987.
García Carranza, Araceli, and Joseph García Carranza, eds. *Bibliografía Cubana del Comandante Ernesto Che Guevara.* La Habana: Ministerio de Cultura Biblioteca Nacional José Martí. Dept. de Investigaciones Bibliográficas, 1987.
González, Luis J., and Gustavo A. Sánchez Salazár. *The Great Rebel: Che Guevara in Bolivia.* New York: Grove Press, 1969.
Granado, Alberto. *Con el Che Guevara de Córdoba a la Habana.* Córdoba, Argentina: Opoloop Ediciones, 1995.
———. *Con el Che por Sudamerica.* La Habana: Editorial Letras Cubanas, 1980.
Granma: Edición Especial. *"Dolorosamente Cierta La Muerte del Comandante Ernesto Guevara."* La Habana: Comité Central del Partido Comunista de Cuba, October 17, 1967.
Guevara, Ernesto Che. Trans. Carlos P. Hansen and Andrew Sinclair. *Bolivian Diary.* London: Jonathan Cape/Lorrimer, 1968.

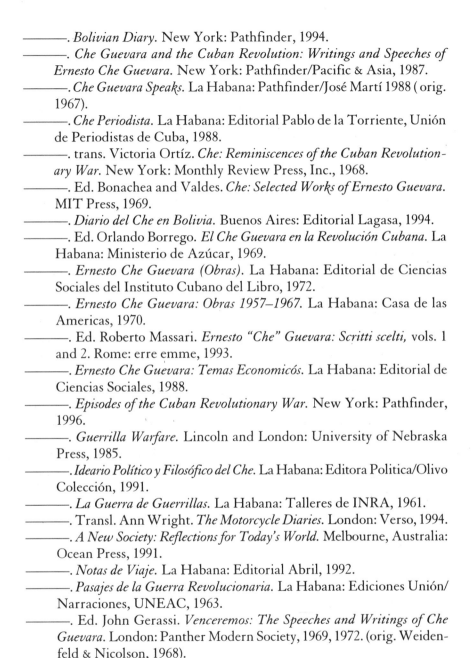

————. *Bolivian Diary*. New York: Pathfinder, 1994.

————. *Che Guevara and the Cuban Revolution: Writings and Speeches of Ernesto Che Guevara*. New York: Pathfinder/Pacific & Asia, 1987.

————. *Che Guevara Speaks*. La Habana: Pathfinder/José Martí 1988 (orig. 1967).

————. *Che Periodista*. La Habana: Editorial Pablo de la Torriente, Unión de Periodistas de Cuba, 1988.

————. trans. Victoria Ortíz. *Che: Reminiscences of the Cuban Revolutionary War*. New York: Monthly Review Press, Inc., 1968.

————. Ed. Bonachea and Valdes. *Che: Selected Works of Ernesto Guevara*. MIT Press, 1969.

————. *Diario del Che en Bolivia*. Buenos Aires: Editorial Lagasa, 1994.

————. Ed. Orlando Borrego. *El Che Guevara en la Revolución Cubana*. La Habana: Ministerio de Azúcar, 1969.

————. *Ernesto Che Guevara (Obras)*. La Habana: Editorial de Ciencias Sociales del Instituto Cubano del Libro, 1972.

————. *Ernesto Che Guevara: Obras 1957–1967*. La Habana: Casa de las Americas, 1970.

————. Ed. Roberto Massari. *Ernesto "Che" Guevara: Scritti scelti,* vols. 1 and 2. Rome: erre emme, 1993.

————. *Ernesto Che Guevara: Temas Economicós*. La Habana: Editorial de Ciencias Sociales, 1988.

————. *Episodes of the Cuban Revolutionary War*. New York: Pathfinder, 1996.

————. *Guerrilla Warfare*. Lincoln and London: University of Nebraska Press, 1985.

————. *Ideario Político y Filosófico del Che*. La Habana: Editora Politica/Olivo Colección, 1991.

————. *La Guerra de Guerrillas*. La Habana: Talleres de INRA, 1961.

————. Transl. Ann Wright. *The Motorcycle Diaries*. London: Verso, 1994.

————. *A New Society: Reflections for Today's World*. Melbourne, Australia: Ocean Press, 1991.

————. *Notas de Viaje*. La Habana: Editorial Abril, 1992.

————. *Pasajes de la Guerra Revolucionaria*. La Habana: Ediciones Unión/ Narraciones, UNEAC, 1963.

————. Ed. John Gerassi. *Venceremos: The Speeches and Writings of Che Guevara*. London: Panther Modern Society, 1969, 1972. (orig. Weidenfeld & Nicolson, 1968).

Guevara, Ernesto Che, and Raúl Castró Ed. Heinz Dieterich and Paco Ignacio Taibo II. *Diarios Inéditos de la Guerrilla Cubana*. Mexico: Editorial Joaquín Mortiz. Grupo Editorial Planeta, 1995.

Guevara Lynch, Ernesto. *Aquí Va un Soldado de las Americas.* Sudamericana Planeta, 1987.

———. *Mí Hijo el Che.* La Habana: Editorial Arte, 1988.

Harris, Richard L. *Death of a Revolutionary: Che Guevara's Last Mission.* W. W. Norton & Co., Inc., 1970.

Hodges, Donald C. *The Legacy of Che Guevara: A Documentary Study.* London: Thames & Hudson, 1977.

"In Cold Blood: How the CIA Executed Che Guevara," by Michele Ray. *Ramparts* (February 5, 1968).

James, Daniel. *Che Guevara: A Biography.* New York: Stein and Day, 1969.

———. *The Complete Bolivian Diaries of the Che Guevara and Other Captured Documents.* New York: Stein and Day Publishers, 1968.

Korol, Claudia. *El Che y los Argentinos.* Buenos Aires: Ediciones Dialéctica, Colección Testimonial, 1988.

Larteguy, Jean. *Los Guerrilleros.* Mexico: Editorial Diana, Mexico. 1979.

Lavretsky, I. *Ernesto Che Guevara.* Moscow: Progress Publishers, 1977.

Maestre Alfonso, Juan. *Ernesto Che Guevara: Antología del Pensamiento Político, Social y Económico de America Latina.* Madrid: Ediciones de Cultura Hispánica, 1988.

"The Making of a Revolutionary: A Memoir of Young Guevara," by Dolores Moyano Martin. *The New York Times Magazine* (August 18, 1968).

Martínez Estévez, Diego. *Ñancahuasu: Apuntes para la Historia Militar de Bolivia.* La Paz, Bolivia: Transcripción e Impresión Laser "Computacion y Proyectos," 1989.

Martínez Heredia, Francisco. *Che, el Socialismo y el Comunismo.* La Habana: Ediciones Casa de las Americas, 1989.

Massari, Roberto, Fernando Martínez, et al. *Che Guevara: Grandeza y Riesgo de la Utopia.* City TK: Txalaparta, 1993.

———. *Che Guevara: pensiero e politica dell'utopia.* Roma: erre emme, 1993.

———. *Guevara para Hoy.* La Habana: Centro de Estudios Sobre America/ La Universidad de Camilo Cienfuegos, Matanzas/erre emme edizioni, 1994.

———. *Otros Documentos del Che en Bolivia.* La Paz, Bolivia: Ediciones Katari (undated).

Peredo, Inti. *Mi Campaña con el Che.* Mexico: Editorial Diogenes S.A., 1972.

Pérez, Galdos, Víctor. *Un Hombre Que Actua Como Piensa.* La Habana: Editora Política, 1988.

Prado Salmon, Gen. Gary. *La Guerrilla Inmolada: Testimonio y Análisis de un Protagonista.* Santa Cruz, Bolivia: Co-Edición Grupo Editorial Punto y Coma, 1987. (Published in English as *The Defeat of the Che Guevara.* Westport, Conn.: Greenwood Press, 1990.)

Rodriguez Herrera, Mariano. *Con la Adarga al Brazo*. La Habana: Lectura para Jovenes, Editorial Política, 1988.

————, *Ellos Lucharon con el Che*. La Habana: Ediciones Políticas, Editorial de Ciencias Sociales, 1989.

Rojas, Marta. *Testimonios sobre el Che, Autores Varios*. La Habana: Colección Pablo de la Torriente, 1990.

Rojo, Ricardo. *My Friend Che*. New York: Grove Press, 1969 (orig. Dial Press, 1968).

Saucedo Parada, Gen. Arnaldo. *No Disparen Soy El Che*. Santa Cruz, Bolivia: Talleres Gráficos de Editorial Oriente, 1988.

Sinclair, Andrew. *Guevara*. London: Fontana/Collins, 1970.

"The Spirit of Che." *Evergreen Review* No. 51 (February 1968).

Tablada, Carlos, Jack Barnes, Steve Clark, and Mary-Alice Waters. *Che Guevara: Cuba and the Road to Socialism (Che Guevara, Carlos Rafael Rodríguez)*. New York: New International, 1991.

Tablada Pérez, Carlos. *El Pensamiento Economico de Ernesto Che Guevara*. La Habana: Ediciones Casa de las Americas, 1987.

Taibo, Paco Ignacio II. *Ernesto Guevara: También Conocido Como El Che*. Mexico: Editorial Joaquín Mortiz, Grupo Editorial Planeta, 1996.

Terán, Gen. Reque. *La Campaña de Ñancahuasu: La Guerrilla del "Che" Visto por el Comandante de la IV Division del Ejercito Boliviano*. La Paz, Bolivia: 1987.

"Tras Las Huellas del Che en Bolivia," by Carlos Soria Galvarro. *La Razon* (October 9, 1996).

Vargas Salinas, Gen. Mario. *El Che: Mito y Realidad*. La Paz/Cochabamba: Los Amigos del Libro, 1988.

Vásquez-Viaña, Humberto. *Antecedentes de la Guerrilla del Che en Bolivia*. Research Paper Series, No. 46. Stockholm: Institute of Latin American Studies, September 1987.

Vásquez-Viaña, Humberto, and Ramiro Aliaga Saravia. *Bolivia: Ensayo de Revolucion Continental*. Bolivia (privately published, undated).

Villegas, Harry (Pombo). *Un Hombre de la Guerrilla del Che*. Buenos Aires and La Habana: Ediciones Colihüe. Editora Política, 1996.

"Where Is Che Guevara Buried? A Bolivian Tells," by Jon Lee Anderson. *The New York Times*, November 21, 1995.

About Cuba, Fidel Castro, and Che

Acevedo, Enrique. *Descamisado*. La Habana: Editorial Cultura Popular, International Network Group, 1993.

Almeida Bosque, Juan. *Atención, Recuento!* La Habana: Editora Política, 1988.

————. *La Sierra.* La Habana: Editora Política, 1989.

————. *La Sierra Maestra y Mas Allá.* La Habana: Editora Política, 1995.

————. *Por las Faldas del Turquino.* La Habana: Editora Política, 1992.

Arenas, Reinaldo. *Before Night Falls: A Memoir.* New York: Viking Penguin, 1993.

Beschloss, Michael R. *The Crisis Years: Kennedy and Khrushchev, 1960–1963.* New York: HarperCollins, 1991.

Borge, Tomas. *Fidel Castro: Un Grano de Maíz. Conversacion con Tomas Borge.* La Habana: Oficina de Publicaciones del Consejo de Estado, 1992.

Blight, James G., Bruce J. Allyn, and David A. Welch. *Cuba on the Brink.* New York: Pantheon. 1993.

Brugioni, Dino A. *Eyeball to Eyeball: The Inside Story of the Cuban Missile Crisis.* New York: Random House, 1991.

Cabrera Infante, Guillermo. *Mea Cuba.* New York: Farrar, Straus & Giroux, 1994.

————. *Vista del Amanecer en el Trópico.* Barcelona: Seix Barral, 1974.

Castro, Fidel. *La Historia Me Absolverá.* La Habana: Oficina de Publicaciones del Consejo de Estado, 1993.

Castro, Fidel, and Che Guevara. *To Speak the Truth.* New York: Pathfinder, 1992.

Chang, Lawrence, and Pete Kornbluh, eds. *The Cuban Missile Crisis 1962.* New York: New Press, 1992.

Chaviano, Julio O. *La Lucha en las Villas.* La Habana: Editorial de Ciencias Sociales, 1990.

Cuervo Cerulia, Georgina, ed. *Granma—Rumbo a la Libertad.* La Habana: Editorial Gente Nueva, 1983.

Darushenkov, Oleg. *Cuba, El Camino de la Revolución.* Moscow: Editorial Progreso, 1979.

Debray, Regis. *Prison Writings.* London: Pelican Latin America Library, Penguin Books, 1973.

————. *Revolution in the Revolution?* London: Pelican Latin America Library, Penguin Books, 1968 (orig. Paris: Maspéro, 1967).

————. *Strategy for Revolution.* London: Pelican Latin America Library, Penguin Books, 1973.

Draper, Theodore. *Castroism: Theory and Practice.* New York: Frederick Praeger, 1965.

Dumont, René. *Cuba: Socialism and Development.* New York: Grove Press, 1970.

Ediciones Políticas. *Cinco Documentos.* La Habana: Editorial de Ciencias Sociales, Instituto Cubano del Libro, 1971.

Edwards, Jorge. *Persona Non Grata: An Envoy in Castro's Cuba.* London: The Bodley Head, 1977.

Franqui, Carlos. *Diary of the Cuban Revolution.* New York: A Seaver Book, Viking Press, 1980.

————. *Family Portrait with Fidel.* New York: Vintage, 1985.

————. *The Twelve.* New York: Lyle Stuart, Inc., 1968.

Galeano, Eduardo. *El Tigre Azul y Otros Relatos.* La Habana: Editorial de Ciencias Sociales, Editora Política, 1991.

Geyer, Georgie Anne. *Prince: The Untold Story of Fidel Castro.* New York: Little, Brown & Co, 1991.

Gosse, Van. *Where the Boys Are: Cuba, Cold War America and the Making of a New Left.* London and New York: Verso, 1993.

Habel, Janette. *Cuba: The Revolution in Peril.* London: Verso, 1991.

Halperin, Maurice. *The Taming of Fidel Castro.* Berkeley: University of California Press, 1979.

Hinckle, Warren, and William Turner. *The Fish Is Red: The Story of the Secret War against Castro.* New York: Harper & Row, 1981.

Iglesias, Joel. *De la Sierra Maestra al Escambray.* La Habana: Letras Cubanas, 1979.

Jenks, L. H. *Nuestra Colonia de Cuba.* La Habana: La Empresa Consolidada de Artes Gráficas (orig. published 1928).

Karol, K. S. *Guerrillas in Power.* New York: Hill & Wang, 1970.

Kennedy, Robert. F. *Thirteen Days: A Memoir of the Cuban Missile Crisis.* New York: A Mentor Book, Penguin, 1969.

Lara, Jesús. *Guerrillero Inti Peredo.* Cochabamba, Bolivia: Edición del Autor, 1980.

Lazo, Mario. *Dagger in the Heart: American Policy Failures in Cuba.* New York: Funk and Wagnall, 1968.

Llovio-Menéndez, José Luis. *Insider: My Life as a Hidden Revolutionary in Cuba.* New York: Bantam, 1988.

Lockwood, Lee. *Castro's Cuba, Cuba's Fidel.* New York: Westview Press, 1990.

Mallin, Jay. *Covering Castro: The Rise and Decline of Cuba's Communist Dictator.* New Brunswick, New Jersey: U.S.-Cuba Institute, Transaction Publishers, 1994.

Martin, Lionel. *The Early Fidel: Roots of Castro's Communism.* New York: Lyle Stuart, Inc., 1977.

Martínez Víctores, Ricardo. *RR: La Historia de Radio Rebelde.* La Habana: Editorial de Ciencias Sociales, 1978.

Masetti, Jorge Ricardo. *Los Que Luchan y Los Que Lloran.* Buenos Aires: Puntosur, 1987.

Matthews, Herbert L. *The Cuban Story.* New York: George Braziller, 1961.

————. *Castro: A Political Biography.* London: Pelican Books, 1970.

Minà, Gianni. *An Encounter with Fidel.* Australia: Ocean Press, 1991.

Nuñez Jiménez, Antonio. *En Marcha con Fidel.* La Habana: Editorial Letras Cubanas, 1982.

—————. *Patria o Muerte.* La Habana: INRA, 1961.

Padilla, Heberto. *Self-Portrait of the Other: A Memoir.* New York: Farrar, Straus & Giroux, 1990.

Pérez, Louis A. *Cuba: Between Reform and Revolution.* New York: Oxford University Press, 1988.

Quirk, Robert E. *Fidel Castro.* New York: Norton, 1993.

Robbins, Carla Anne. *The Cuban Threat.* New York: ISCHI Publications, 1985.

Rojas, Marta, and Mírta Rodríguez. *Tania la Guerrillera Inolvidable.* La Habana: Instituto del Libro, 1970. (Published in English as *Tania: The Unforgettable Guerrilla.* New York: Random House, 1971.)

Rodríguez, Felix I., and John Weisman. *Shadow Warrior: The CIA Hero of a Hundred Unknown Battles.* New York: Simon & Schuster, 1989.

Salkey, Andrew. *Havana Journal.* London: Penguin Books, 1971.

Sarabia, Nydia. *Médicos de la Revolución.* Apuntes Biográficos. La Habana: Editorial Gente Nueva, 1983.

Stubbs, Jean. *Cuba: The Test of Time.* London: Latin America Books, 1989.

Szulc, Tad. *Fidel: A Critical Portrait.* New York: William Morrow Co., 1986.

Taber, Robert. *M-26: The Biography of a Revolution.* New York: Lyle Stuart, 1961.

Thomas, Hugh. *Cuba or The Pursuit of Freedom.* London: Eyre & Spottiswoode, 1971.

Timmerman, Jacobo. *Cuba.* New York: Vintage Books. 1992.

"Una Leyenda llamada Tania," by Mario Rueda and Luis Antezana Ergueta. *La Razón* "Ventana" (October 15, 1995).

Welch, Richard E., Jr., *Response to Revolution: The United States and the Cuban Revolution, 1959–61.* Chapel Hill: The University of North Carolina Press, 1985.

Wyden, Peter. *Bay of Pigs.* New York: Simon & Schuster, 1979.

About Argentina

Barnes, John. *Evita: First Lady—A Biography of Evita Perón.* New York: Grove Press, 1978.

Baschetti, Roberto, ed. *Documentos 1970–1973: De la Guerrilla Peronista al Gobierno Popular.* Buenos Aires: Editorial de la Campana, Colección Campana de Palo, 1995.

Crasweller, Robert. *Perón and the Enigmas of Argentina.* New York: W. W. Norton, 1987.

Gilbert, Isidoro. *El Oro de Moscú: La Historia Secreta de las Relaciones Argentino-Soviéticos.* Buenos Aires: Planeta/Espejo de la Argentina, 1994.

Luna, Felix. *La Argentina: De Perón a Lanusse, 1943–1973.* Buenos Aires: Planeta, Espejo de la Argentina, 1993.

Main, Mary. *Evita: The Woman with the Whip.* London: Corgi Books, 1977, 1978.

Rock, David. *Authoritarian Argentina: The Nationalist Movement, Its History and Its Impact.* Berkeley: University of California Press, 1993.

Scobie, James R. *Argentina: A City and a Nation.* New York: Oxford University Press, 1971.

Tulchin, Joseph S. *Argentina and the United States: A Conflicted Relationship.* New York: Macmillan, 1990.

About Latin America

Aguilar, Luis E., ed. *Marxism in Latin America: A Borzoi Book on Latin America.* New York: Alfred A. Knopf, 1968.

Borge, Tomas. *The Patient Impatience.* New York: Curbstone, 1992.

Brown, Michael F., and Eduardo Fernández. *War of Shadows: The Struggle for Utopia in the Peruvian Amazon.* Berkeley: University of California Press, 1991.

Cajías, Lupe de. *Juan Lechín, Historia de una Leyenda.* La Paz, Bolivia: Los Amigos del Libro, 1994.

Castañeda Jorge G. *Utopia Unarmed: The Latin American Left After the Cold War.* New York: Alfred A. Knopf, 1994.

Dunkerley, James. *Rebellion in the Veins: Political Struggle in Bolivia 1952–1982.* London: Verso Editions, 1984.

Gerassi, John. *The Great Fear in Latin America.* New York: Collier, 1963.

Gott, Richard. *Guerrilla Movements in Latin America.* London: Thomas Nelson and Sons Ltd., 1970. (Reissued as *Rural Guerrillas in Latin America.* London: Pelican Latin America Library, Penguin Books, 1973.)

————. *Land without Evil: Utopian Journeys across the South American Watershed.* London: Verso, 1993.

Gunson, Chamberlain, Thompson. *The Dictionary of Contemporary Politics of Central America and the Caribbean.* New York: Simon & Schuster, 1991.

Herrera, Hayden. *Frida: A Biography of Frida Kahlo.* New York: HarperCollins, 1984.

Lindqvvist, Sven. *The Shadow: Latin America Faces the Seventies.* London: Pelican Latin America Library, Penguin Books, 1969.

Miná, Gianni. *Un Continente Desaparecido.* Barcelona: Ediciones Península, 1996.

Pendle, George. *History of Latin America.* London: Penguin, 1963, 1990.

Schlesinger, Stephen, and Stephen Kinzer. *Bitter Fruit: The Untold Story of the American Coup in Guatemala.* New York: Anchor Press/Doubleday, 1983.

Szulc, Tad. *Twilight of the Tyrants.* New York: Henry Holt & Co., 1959.

Ydigoras Fuentes, Miguel. *My War with Communism*. New York: Prentice-Hall, Inc., 1963.

About Cuba and Africa

Bridgland, Fred. *Jonas Savimbi: A Key to Africa*. New York: Paragon House Publishers, 1987.

"Che's Missing Year: Che Guevara and the Congo," by Richard Gott. *New Left Review* No. 220 (1996).

"Comrade Tato," by José Barreto. Prensa Latina (June 1993).

García Márquez, Gabriel and Jorge Risquét, Fidel Castro. *Changing the History of Africa, Angola and Namibia*. Australia: Ocean Press, 1989.

Heikal, Mohammed Hassanein. *The Cairo Documents*. New York: Doubleday, 1971.

Jiménez Rodríguez, Limbania. *Heroínas de Angola*. La Habana: Editorial de Ciencias Sociales, 1985.

Moore, Juan Carlos. *Castro, the Blacks and Africa*. Berkeley: Center for Afro-American Studies, University of California Press, 1988.

Taibo, Paco Ignacio II, Froilán Escobar, and Felix Guerra. *El Año Que Estuvimos en Ninguna Parte*. Mexico: Editorial Joaquín Mortiz, Grupo Planeta, 1994.

"Tatu: Un Guerrillero Africano," by Juana Carrasco. *Verde Olivo* (June 1988).

About the Cold War

Andrew, Christopher, and Oleg Gordievsky. *KGB: The Inside Story*. London: HarperCollins, 1990.

Frankland, Mark. *Khrushchev*. Lanham, Maryland: Madison Books, UPA, 1969.

Goodwin, Richard. *Remembering America: A Voice from the Sixties*. Boston: Little Brown & Co., 1988.

Grose, Peter. *Gentleman Spy: The Life of Allen Dulles*. New York: Houghton Mifflin, 1994.

Kwitny, Jonathon. *Endless Enemies: The Making of an Unfriendly World*. New York: Viking Penguin, 1986.

Schlesinger, Arthur Jr. *A Thousand Days: John F. Kennedy in the White House*. New York: Houghton Mifflin, 1965.

Steele, Jonathon. *World Power: Soviet Foreign Policy under Brezhnev and Andropov*. London: Michael Joseph, 1983.

Ranelagh, John. *The Agency: The Rise and Decline of the CIA*. London: Weidenfeld & Nicolson, 1986.

Thomas, Evan. *The Very Best Men: Four Who Dared—The Early Years of the CIA*. New York: Touchstone, Simon & Schuster, 1995.

Zubok, Vladislav, and Constantine Pleshakov. *Inside the Kremlin's Cold War: From Stalin to Khrushchev.* Cambridge, Mass.: Harvard University Press, 1996.

Miscellaneous

Allaine, Marie-Françoise. *Conversations with Graham Greene.* London: Penguin, 1991.

Anderson, Benedict. *Imagined Communites.* London: Verso, 1991 (orig. 1983).

Armiño, Mauro, ed. *Lucha de Guerrillas: Según los Clásicos de Marxismo-Leninismo.* Madrid: Biblioteca Jucar: 1980.

Bottomore, Tom, ed. *A Dictionary of Marxist Thought.* Oxford: Blackwell's, 1991.

Cantor, Jay. *The Death of Che Guevara.* (Fiction.) New York: Alfred A. Knopf, 1983.

De Beauvoir, Simone. *All Said and Done.* London: Penguin Books, 1977 (orig. Paris: Gallimard, 1972).

———. *The Force of Circumstance.* London: Penguin Books, 1968 (orig. Paris: Gallimard, 1963).

Debray, Regis. *Loues Soient Nos Seigneurs: Une Education Politique.* Paris: Gallimard, 1996.

Desmond, Adrian and James Moore. *Darwin.* New York: Warner Books, 1992.

Fanon, Frantz. *The Wretched of the Earth.* New York: Grove Press, 1982 (orig. Paris: Maspéro, 1963.)

Greene, Graham. *Fragments of Autobiography.* London: Penguin, 1991.

———. *Our Man in Havana.* London: Heinemann, 1958.

Harris, Nigel. *National Liberation.* London: Penguin, 1990.

Malcom X. Ed. George Breitman. *Malcolm X Speaks.* New York: Grove Weidenfeld, 1990 (orig. 1965).

Nehru, Jawaharlal. *The Discovery of India.* Oxford University Press, 1985 (orig. Calcutta: Signet Press, 1946.)

Neruda, Pablo. Ed. and trans. Ben Bellit. *Five Decades: A Selection (Poems 1925–1970).* New York: Grove Press, 1974.

Payne, Robert. *The Life and Death of Lenin.* New York: Simon & Schuster, 1964.

Salisbury, Harrison. *The New Emperors: China in the Era of Mao and Deng.* New York: Avon Books, 1992.

Schama, Simon. *Citizens: A Chronicle of the French Revolution.* London: Penguin, 1989.

Snow, Edgar. *Red Star over China.* New York: Grove Weidenfeld, 1973 (orig. Random House, 1938).

Westoby, Adam. *The Evolution of Communism.* New York: The Free Press, Macmillan, Inc., 1989.

Index